America
and the
American
Record
Business

A History

Don Cusic

Published by
Brackish Publishing
P.O. Box 120751
Nashville, TN 37212

ISBN 978-0-9990537-3-7

Production Coordinator
Jim Sharp
Sharp Management

Cover design and interior layout by PricelessDigitalMedia.com

TABLE OF CONTENTS

INTRODUCTION

The recording industry is the music, the business and the technology all rolled together. They are equally important at any given time, although the music remains after business structures and technology have been left behind. The recording industry is also an important and vital part of American culture.

The recording industry began in 1877 when Thomas Edison invented the phonograph. The industry was led by technology, which had to be invented, developed and refined. Next, a business structure had to be assembled to allow recordings to reach consumers and generate a profit. Without a profit, there is no business. Finally, genres of music had to be discovered, recorded and exposed to the world. Today, we look back on those early recordings of popular songs, musicals, blues, country, jazz, and gospel performed by legendary singers and musicians and find cultural treasures. We don't usually stop and think about the early technology or the formation of business models that recorded and preserved that music for us today.

Those who read this book will undoubtedly say "but you left out..." That is undeniably true; I have left out a number of important recording artists, musicians, songs, executives and those who developed, refined and pioneered the technology. However, I hope that I have presented enough to give a fairly accurate view of how the recording industry began and how it evolved to become the recording industry as it is today. I also hope to show how it is connected to American culture and American history. The record business does not exist in isolation; it is the soundtrack to American life. The diversity of music shows the diversity of America; the story of America is embedded in its music.

The American record business is not just about American music; since the British Invasion during the 1960s, the American record business has embraced recordings made in the U.K., Australia and Canada as well as non-English speaking countries. The American record business is international but rooted in American culture. We influence the music, business and technology of other cultures, making the American sound a global sound.

When there are cataclysmic events in the world, the music business steps up to help. Music makes a difference. We have witnessed that countless times.

In the midst of the day-day world of the contemporary music business, it feels like there is constant change and change constantly; each day is different and each artist or recording is "fresh" and "new." That is true. Those involved in the music business live in a fast paced world that sometimes seems like things move at Mach speed. For those actively and intimately involved in the music business, it is not a job, it is a lifestyle. An important part of that lifestyle is keeping up with what is new as well as keeping up with the news.

Although the music business feels like it is in the midst of a constant whirlwind of change, there is also a more timeless, long range perspective that reminds us that the music business has not fundamentally changed in 150 years. The core purpose of the music business is to get a song in front of the public so people will buy it, then, link the song to the singer so people will purchase other recordings by that artist and pay to see them perform live in a venue.

Great music will raise the spirit, touch the heart and move the soul. That is a timeless truth about music. The recording industry is the vehicle that allows us to hear great music from the past and exposes us to the great music of today.

This book is an attempt to tell the story of how the recording industry began, how it arrived at where it is today and how it is an integral part of American history.

Don Cusic

SECTION I:
1800 TO 1929

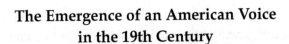

The Emergence of an American Voice
in the 19th Century

The nineteenth century produced a new America, a nation that extended from Coast to Coast and emerged as a new world power. That century also altered the texture of American culture and democracy through political and social changes. Those nineteenth century changes began when a fiddle player became President.

Shortly before Thomas Jefferson (who enjoyed playing the violin) was elected President in 1803, the Capital of the United States was moved to Washington, D.C. At that time, the United States boundary was from the Atlantic seaboard to the Mississippi River, but that changed when Jefferson engineered the Louisiana Purchase in 1803, which gave the United States the territory in what is now the middle of the country--from the Mississippi River to the Rocky Mountains and northward to the Canadian border--and doubled the size of the United States. Jefferson sent Meriwether Lewis and William Clark to map the West and that, in essence, opened up the land west of the Mississippi to exploration, first by trappers, then by settlers.

During James Madison's tenure as President, the United States fought Great Britain in the War of 1812. The American victory in that war led to a strong nationalism and a burst of self-confidence and unity. Prior to that time, Americans were fearful of Great Britain, as well as France, because many felt the young nation would not be able to defend itself against those strong powers. The War of 1812 proved the young United States could defend itself successfully and, after that time, Americans never felt threatened by Great Britain, or any other European power, like they had in the past.

The War of 1812 also gave Americans a war hero in Andrew Jackson, who became President 1829-1837 after gaining fame in that war. Prior to Jackson, the Presidents of this country were a wealthy elite, usually landowners who were products of the European tradition of the elite serving in government and ruling the country. Jackson's Presidency served as a break from the past; his background was anonymous poverty rather than genteel raising and his Presidency ushered in Jacksonian Democracy, or the era of the "common man." Here, Americans found a leader who exemplified the "average" person pulling himself up by the bootstraps to become President. It sent the message that there was wisdom in the masses, that wisdom and greatness were not born to a certain class but could be obtained from hard work and determination. This was the era that led to a flowering of the arts as an American voice emerged.

The nineteenth century produced a distinctive American voice in literature, painting, architecture and music. Prior to that time, Americans saw themselves--at least in terms of the arts--as an extension of Europe. All of the great painters, authors and musicians were Europeans and the general notion was that if you wanted great culture--the arts, fashion, etc.-- you looked to Europe.

There were practical reasons for this. First, Americans were widely caricatured by Europeans as being loud, rude, and crude--stump jumpers with no sense of refinement or appreciation of the arts or beauty. Americans were builders and had land to clear and territory to explore as the population pushed westward. When the United States was the Eastern seaboard, and ships regularly arrived from Europe, the influence of European culture was strong. However, as the population pushed further inward, there was less European influence. By and large, early nineteenth century Americans were preoccupied with the challenges of building a nation, creating prosperity, developing politics, fighting battles, establishing folk religions, and expanding west. For those reasons, Americans had little time for relaxation; the frontier experience was rough and crude; it took all your wits to survive.

An American voice in literature came from writers like James Fennimore Cooper with his Natty Bumpo or Leatherstocking tales, providing the first "westerns" with books like *Drums Along The Mohawk* and *The Deerslayer.* Washington Irving used folk tales like "The Legend of Sleepy Hollow" and "Rip Van Winkle" in his *Sketches.* Perhaps the greatest American voice at that time was Ralph Waldo Emerson and his *Essays.* Emerson, along with Henry David Thoreau, gave America a philosophy to call its own, a transcendental optimism that honored nature and viewed man as a deity himself. Thus, the American voice articulated what the American felt: he was a superior creature because he could tame and control nature, could alter the work of God; indeed, God resided within each individual American.

In painting, nature was celebrated in the Hudson Valley School with painters like Thomas Cole, Thomas Doughty, Asher B. Durand and, later, Albert Bierstadt, Frederick Church, Jasper Cropsey, John Kennsett and Thomas Moran, who painted landscapes that captured the splendor of untamed nature as opposed to the peaceful country sides of tamed nature in Europe.

The roots of American popular music are in the broadside ballad and the ballad opera. The broadside was the precursor to popular sheet music; the ballad opera the precursor to musical comedy. Broadsides were topical verses using everyday vocabulary, often written about current events or using satire, wit and ribald stories. They were printed on small sheets of paper without a musical score and sung to popular tunes or folk melodies. Those broadsides achieved wide circulation because they were printed on a single folio sheet and sold cheaply.

The first ballad opera was "The Beggar's Opera," written by John Gay and J.C. Pepusch, which premiered in 1728. That opera--and others that followed--used the folk tradition in an opera context, lampooning society, politics and other events with singers singing in the Italian opera tradition. However, folk tunes and folk songs were incorporated in the productions.

Like most other art forms in early America, the idea of popular music went back to Europe, particularly the troubadour tradition in France. Robert S. Briffault, in his book, *The Troubadours*, states that troubadour songs were "largely descanted and delivered by strolling singers, common crowders who had been wont to collect their audiences at fairs and junketings of yokels, before a boon of fortune sent them basking in memorial halls and princely courts...Their highest design did not aim above providing pleasant entertainment." In other words, those troubadours performed for "ordinary" people, or what later became known as the "working class."

The "art" songs (or classical pieces) and parlor songs co-existed in Europe throughout the eighteenth and nineteenth centuries. The art song dominated concert halls while the parlor songs were sung in homes, with people gathered around a piano. Early American songwriters attempted to compose both "art" songs and parlor songs, transplanting the European culture to American soil, but they had no real success. Neither was the English garden, a park where people came to stroll and be entertained, successfully transplanted, although attempts were made.

The essential problem with classical music as popular music is that it is a European heritage; Americans have tended towards populist and

11

folk traditions with their entertainments. Too, classical was elitist but Americans have always wanted a democratic entertainment to match their democratic temperament.

A problem with parlor songs during the early part of the nineteenth century was that pianos had to be imported from Europe, which made them prohibitively expensive for any but the most wealthy. That was solved during the 1820s when the first domestically manufactured upright pianos were produced in the United States.

The Piano in America

By the 1830s pianos were selling for $300 each and piano makers stepped up their production as the instrument became "a symbol of social status" and "an indication of the rising middle class's wish to hear music of its own choice."

In 1822 Robert Stodard joined William Dubois, a music store owner and music publisher in New York. Stodard was a grandson of a British piano maker who developed the "English grand action" in 1777 and made British pianos the preeminent brands. Dubois manufactured less expensive instruments and added Stodard's name to the firm, which then became Dubois and Stodard. Dubois bought out his partner in 1834 and, after several other business partners, left the music publishing business after 1839 to confine his activities to piano manufacturing.

John Firth and William Hall were also in the piano manufacturing business; they were joined by Sylvanus B. Pond in 1827 in New York City. William Hall withdrew from the partnership in 1847 but continued to make pianos with his son James while Firth Pond & Co. expanded into a music publishing firm.

Firth, Pond & Co. was a major music publisher with annual income from sheet music and music books totaling about $70,000. Their top songwriter was Stephen Foster and his most commercial song, "Old Folks at Home," sold an astounding 150,000 copies. Firth, Pond & Co. became a giant firm that manufactured violins, flutes, and guitars, but their major instrument was the piano. In 1855, the company received $50,000 from the sales of pianos, built in their Connecticut plant.

The Bradbury piano, which became one of the most popular of its time, was created in 1854 from a partnership between William B. Bradbury, his brother E. G. Bradbury, and F. G. Light in New York. Bradbury began publishing religious songs before the Civil War and eventually sold over two million copies of songbooks, Sunday School compilations and hymn books. He was also the leading publisher of children's religious songs, giving the world "Jesus Loves Me" in the 1862 book, *Golden Showers*.

When the nation suffered an economic depression in 1857, William Wallace Kimball left Iowa and moved to Chicago. Kimball swapped land he owned for four pianos, after a chance encounter with a piano salesman. Renting space in a storehouse, Kimball began a rental piano business, then began to manufacture his own, which in time became one of the leading names of piano manufacturing.

After the Civil War the production of pianos and player pianos continued to climb as families looked at the purchase of a piano, after buying a house, as their major financial purchase. Piano sales climbed steadily throughout the late nineteenth century--there were 800,000 manufactured between 1857 and 1887--and reached an all-time high in 1899 when more than 365,000 were manufactured. Piano sales continued to average 300,000 annually until after World War I.

William Knabe & Co., formed in 1837 in Baltimore, opened a New York office. Cabinetmaker Jonas Chickering began making pianos in 1843 in Boston after he opened his shop; by 1851 the Chickering piano accounted for 15 percent of all pianos sold in America, and in 1853 the firm produced 2,000 pianos. That same year the Steinwegs opened their piano manufacturing firm in New York, three years after leaving their home in Germany. They changed their name to *Steinway* and put that name on their pianos.

By 1890 the three major piano manufacturing firms were Knabe, Chickering and Steinway. The Steinway pianos quickly became known for their high quality and by 1880, seventy percent of American made pianos sold in Europe and just under seventy percent sold in the United States were Steinways.

The popularity of the piano created the music publishing business because, after someone bought a piano, they needed sheet music. It is not surprising that several early music publishers evolved from piano manufacturing firms. That was the first step in the creation of a music "business" in the United States.

Minstrel Shows

The impersonation of blacks by whites is one of the most unique forms of entertainment developed in America. One of the reasons America as a nation was unique was the presence of a black culture. In entertainment and music it gave Americans a diverse heritage, a cultural mix, which influenced the entertainment and music industries.

The use of burnt cork to blacken the face was used by George Washington Dixon, an American actor, to establish his reputation as a blackface entertainer. Dixon performed in the North during the 1830s. Another actor, Thomas Dartmouth Rice, established the character of "Jim Crow." According to legend, the actor overheard an African-American man in Cincinnati singing "Turn about an' wheel about an' do jis so, An' eb'ry time I turn about I jump Jim Crow.'" Rice took this refrain and began to work it into his act. At a show in Pittsburgh, he reportedly found an old African-American working at a hotel. The Negro was poor and made money opening his mouth for boys to pitch pennies into and by carrying trunks for passengers from the steamboats to the hotels.

Rice enticed the man to accompany him to a theater and take off his clothes, then Rice put the clothes on and, with a wig of matted moss, waddled into view. The effect was instantaneous and audiences roared with laughter and thundered with applause. From that came "Jim Crow," an American popular song that became an international hit. From Pittsburgh, Rice traveled to Louisville, Cincinnati, Philadelphia, Washington, D.C, Baltimore and New York in 1832, performing to enthusiastic audiences at each stop. The audience laughed at Jim Crow--they did not laugh with him--they laughed at his dialect, his shabby clothes, and his shufflin' walk.

The characterizations of blacks by whites was the way most Northerners knew about blacks during that time. Note that the actors were Northern, the venues were in Northern cities in front of audiences who were Northerners and, when this was reported in the press, was done so by Northern writers. The initial result was to characterize African--Americans--who most Northerners had never met--as simpletons, innocent, child-like, lazy, shiftless and unable to care for themselves. To that end, it justified slavery. It was obvious from those characterizations that blacks could not take care of themselves because they were inferior creatures. Therefore, according to this logic, the white slave owner was doing a favor by looking after the black race, giving them something to do and a place to live. For many Americans, that stereotype remained valid even after the Civil War and the Emancipation Proclamation.

The development of minstrel shows--whites in blackface imitating blacks--became popular before the Civil War. Minstrel songs were composed that achieved their effect primarily through lyrics, which were in dialect. Musically, the songs were an extension of theater songs and British folk melodies.

The essential element of minstrel songs is the dialect, which differentiated "black talk" from "white talk." African-Americans *did* talk differently than whites, and author James Weldon Johnson cited the reason for the evolution of black dialect in his book on *Negro Spirituals*. He wrote: "Negro dialect in America is the result of the effort of the slave to establish a medium of communication between himself and his master. This he did by dropping his original language, and formulating a phonologically and grammatically simplified English; that is, an English in which the harsh and difficult sounds were elided, and the secondary moods and tenses were eliminated. This dialect served not only as a means of communication between slave and master but also between slave and slave; so the original African languages became absolutely lost."

Those first minstrel songs reinforced stereotypes of African-Americans: they were lazy, loved to eat watermelon, could not speak proper English, were inferior creatures but had a "knack" for singing, dancing and entertainment. And, of course, they were very entertaining for white folks.

The first full-time minstrel group was the Virginia Minstrels, formed in early 1843 in New York. This "Ethiopian band" consisted of banjo, fiddle, bone castanets and tambourine. It was led by Daniel Decatur Emmett, who was born in Mount Vernon, Ohio and began his musical career as a drummer and fifer in the Army. Later, he became a banjo player and blackface singer in travelling circuses before coming to New York in 1842. He is credited with writing the song "Dixie."

The Virginia Minstrels performed primarily between acts in plays or circuses. They performed a number of songs throughout the evening, but never as a whole show; rather their songs were inserted into other shows.

The most significant minstrel group was E.P. Christy's Minstrels. Christy was born in Philadelphia and the original Christy Minstrels consisted of E. P. on banjo and singing, George Christy, dancing, actor and bones player, Tom Vaughn on banjo, and "jig dancer" Lansing Durant. The company eventually totaled seven members and provided a whole evening's entertainment, generally in three parts. The full band performed songs, did skits, dances, and sang, performing a dozen or more songs. In addition to being the first to present a full evening's program, the Christie Minstrels introduced the songs of Stephen Foster to the American public.

Stephen Foster

Stephen Foster was born near Pittsburgh, Pennsylvania around noon on July 4, 1826. Later that day two of the nation's founders, Thomas Jefferson and John Adams, died.

As a boy, Foster "was among the first white boys to do what white boys (and the occasional girl) have been doing ever since--mimicking black music, or what they think is black music and black style." There were no songwriters making a living writing songs in America before Stephen Foster; Foster was influenced by Thomas Moore, whose song "Tis The Last Rose of Summer" was perhaps the first song ever to sell more than a million copies in the United States, and Henry Russell, an Englishman who wrote the music to "Woodman! Spare That Tree" (the lyrics were by George P. Morris) and who often put music to other people's lyrics.

At the age of nine, Foster became the "star" of a local musical group, comprised of boys from his neighborhood. They often performed "crude comic songs written in blackface dialect." Foster grew up in a region of the country that nurtured blackface entertainment. According to Ken Emerson, author of *Doo Dah*, a biography of Stephen Foster, "Blackface expressed an urban nostalgia for an agricultural economy, for a preindustrial, pastoral state of affairs, at the same time it drew parallels between bondage on the Southern farm and the Northern factory." Emerson states that blackface was also "an expression...of racial anxiety, economic insecurity, and class resentment...also a rejection of the femininity, the foreignness, and the effete affectations of parlor ballads" as well as "a veil and a vehicle for discussion of sex and violence, money and class--all the dirty stuff of life that many white Americans preferred to sweep under the parlor rug. Behind the mask of burnt cork, they felt freer to speak their minds and express their urges."

That helps explain why blackface entertainment thrived in a region that knew little if anything about plantations or the lives of real African-Americans in the South but it does not fully explain why Foster or any others living during that time sang or enjoyed blackface. According to biographer Ken Emerson, "Stephen Foster and his friends sang blackface because it was popular, because it was 'cool,' and because it offered a freedom that white middle-class culture couldn't furnish. But they seldom wondered what it meant or implied.".

At the age of 14 Foster wrote his first song, "The Tioga Waltz" and, in 1844, at the age of 18, he first copyrighted a song, "Open Thy Lattice Love." Those were essentially parlor ballads. The audience for parlor ballads was primarily women, especially young upper class women, who used those songs as a way to become refined and for courtship. Women remained the primary audience and consumers for parlor ballads and the target of publishing companies who marketed those ballads in sheet music throughout the nineteenth and early twentieth century.

When he was 20, Foster, after attending Jefferson College for about a week, dropped out and moved to Cincinnati and became a bookkeeper for his brother, Dunning, in the firm Irwin & Foster, commission merchants who arranged the shipment of cotton and other goods. That same year Foster's song "There's a Good Time Coming" was published by W. C. Peters in Cincinnati.

In August, 1847, the Eagle Ice Cream Saloon advertised a "Musical Entertainment Extraordinary" and Stephen's brother, Morrison Foster, obtained a copy of Stephen's song, "Away Down Souf" and submitted it; it was performed by Nelson Kneass and was an immediate success. An even bigger success originated from the Kneass performance of "Oh! Susanna!" on September 11, 1847; that same year those two songs, along with "Wake Up Jake," were published by W. C. Peters as *Songs of the Sable Harmonists*." A minstrel group that included Kneass, as well as William Roark, distributed copies of Stephen Foster's music. Foster's songs caught the public's fancy although, as biographer Emerson notes, "Foster's early music moved in mysterious, roundabout ways, and Foster himself played a passive, elusive role in its circulation."

"Oh! Susanna" was soon performed on New York concert stages as well as in California gold mining camps, where it became an unofficial theme song. Between 1848 and 1850 at least sixteen different music publishers came out with different arrangements of "Oh! Susanna" but Foster probably didn't make a cent from any of them. Publishers were businessmen who took the risk of publishing songs and reaped the rewards--or took the loss. The publisher may have paid for the right to be the *first* to publish a song; the money paid to the songwriter was necessary to get the jump on other publishers, but once the song was out, anyone could publish it if they had money and access to a printing press.

There was a lack of copyright protection for songs. United States copyright law did not include musical compositions until 1831, which encouraged Americans to publish British (and European) songs as their own. That discouraged American songwriters because publishers could publish "hit" songs without cultivating new writers and had a ready source of existing songs available to them for the printing costs. An international copyright agreement protecting European songs from being exploited did not became effective until 1891.

No American had ever made a living as a songwriter before Stephen Foster; there were no performance rights organizations to collect money for songwriters and publishers regularly bought the rights to a song outright to avoid paying royalties on sheet music sales. Not that there was a wealth in royalties from sheet music; most "hits" sold less than 50,000 copies and publishers were lucky to break even on most of the songs they published.

Although it is impossible to deny this grave injustice to Stephen Foster's songs, he was more fortunate than most songwriters. On September 12, 1849, he signed a contract with Firth, Pond for first rights to publish his songs. The contract stated it "would allow you two cents upon every copy of your future publications issued by our house, after the expenses of publication are paid," adding that "it is advisable to compose only such pieces as are likely both in the sentiment and melody to take the public tastes." During the next seven years Foster earned $10,168.81 from his songs, an average of about $1,400 a year, while the entire country sang his songs for free.

In 1850 Foster moved back to Pittsburgh from Cincinnati and rented an office where he set up business as a full-time songwriter. He made a living that way until his death, 14 years later. During those fifteen years as America's first professional songwriter--or at least the first to make a living solely from songwriting--Foster made a good amount of money, although not as much as he had hoped and certainly not as much as he would have made 100 years later. In the period 1850-1860 he made over $15,000--a good sum in those days--but died broke. The reason he did not become wealthy was because the business structures were not in place to allow a songwriter to become rich.

Foster achieved most of his fame, and his money, from his early minstrel songs like "Oh! Susanna," "Old Uncle Ned" and "The Lou'siana Belle." Later he wrote "Old Folks at Home," "Nelly Was a Lady" and "My Old Kentucky Home." In June, 1851 he wrote to E. P. Christy and offered him new songs that had not been published. Foster received $10 for each song under this agreement, which is how Christy's name was on "Old Folks at Home" when it was first released. Since the success of a song depended on a popular performer doing the song at live shows, that was a good agreement for Foster. However, the lack of copyright protection meant that the income he received was limited to the initial copies sold by Firth, Pond; any other publisher could also print the song and sell it without paying Foster.

Foster's songs were popular with minstrel groups, especially E.P. Christy's, as well as the general public, but his songs received even greater exposure when they were included in the play *Uncle Tom's Cabin* during the 1850s. *Uncle Tom's Cabin*, written by Harriet Beecher Stowe, was originally published as a series of stories in an abolitionist magazine, *The National Era*. On March 20, 1852 it was published as a book and swept the nation. Since copyright law did not protect the printed page going to the stage until 1856, anyone could adapt Stowe's story for the stage without her permission. Stowe had no control over those productions--and received no money from them. Neither did Stephen Foster, whose songs were in a number of theatrical adaptations of that book.

Foster and his wife separated in Spring, 1853; according to biographer Emerson, Jane Foster "did not care for music and hoped that Stephen would give up songwriting," and she "nagged Stephen constantly so that he became increasingly moody." Stephen Foster took his songwriting seriously; he "could not bear the slightest noise or interruption in his work" and was a perfectionist who was "so persnickety about his music that he lectured even E.P. Christy about following it precisely, note for note."

During the 1860s Foster lived in New York where he began to churn out songs simply to obtain money from publishers in order to survive. During that time "he no longer cared enough to labor over the songs he was cranking out, and he seldom wrote his own lyrics anymore...His factory was a bar in the backroom of a shabby German grocery store in the Bowery, on the corner of Christy and Hester streets." There, Foster "drank constantly but was never intoxicated. He was indifferent to food, often making a meal of apples or turnips from the grocery shop, peeling them with a large pocket-knife."

On January 9, 1864--a Saturday night a year before the Civil War ended--Foster went to his room in the Bowery. The next morning, Foster spoke briefly to the chambermaid, then fell "as if he had been shot." He was taken to Bellevue Hospital where, on Wednesday, January 13, 1864, he died. At the time of his death he had no debts and his rent was paid; his possessions were "a worn brown leather purse containing a piece of paper where he had written the words 'dear friends and gentle hearts'" and 38 cents in pennies.

Foster lived during a time when "any career in music was by definition disreputable in a society that venerated the Protestant work ethic, the virtues of practicality and profitability. Music was for women and children; men outgrew it. As anything other than a hobby, music was not just ungentlemanly, it was unmanly." Foster longed for acceptance and respectability; although his blackface songs were his most popular works, he did not write very many: of the almost 200 songs he wrote, less than twenty-five are in blackface dialect. Among these songs are American classics; even today, most Americans know songs like "Oh! Susannah."

> I come from Alabama wid my banjo on my knee;
> I'se gwan to Lou'siana, my true lub for to see.
> It rain'd all night de day I left, de wedder it was dry;
> The sun so hot I froze to def, Susanna, don't you cry.

> Oh! Susanna, do no cry for me;
> I come from Alabama, wid my banjo on my knee

What was appealing about Foster's songs was that his were the first to have full choruses with three and four part harmony, in the tradition of the family singers who toured the country during Foster's time. Other minstrel songs generally had refrain lines, or a line at the end of each verse the whole troupe sang in unison. A few others might have a brief chorus sung in unison. Foster--who had never actually heard a minstrel troupe--was basically unaware of that. Because of his musical training, Foster naturally thought in terms of harmony and when he applied himself to writing minstrel songs, he included harmony in the choruses. Although that was a perfectly natural move for Foster, it was a radical change from then-current minstrel numbers and brought a breath of fresh air into the Minstrel repertoire.

The first "darkey" songs were derogatory, presenting African-Americans in an unfavorable, albeit amusing, light. Gradually, however, more people became aware of the inhumanity of slavery and the humanity of African-Americans. Fueled by the abolitionist movement, and religious groups like the Quakers, Americans were forced to take a new look at slavery. The abolitionists were viewed as extremists by most and the Quakers were decidedly not mainstream either; however the book *Uncle Tom's Cabin* and the plantation songs that evolved *were* mainstream and showed African-Americans in a new light.

The plantation songs presented African-Americans as having feelings like whites; for example, feeling sorrow and loss when children and families were pulled apart. Songs like Foster's "Nelly Was a Lady" portray deep, human feelings of blacks towards one another.

> Down on de Mississippi floating
> Long time I trabble on de way,
> All night de cottonwood a toting,
> Sing for my true lub all de day

CHORUS: Nelly was a lady
Last night she died,
Toll de bell for lubly Nell
My dark Virginny bride

Now I'm unhappy and I'm weeping,
Can't tote de cottonwood no more;
Last night, while Nelly was a sleeping,
Death came a knockin' at de door,
Chorus

When I saw my Nelly in de morning,
Smile till she open'd up her eyes,
Seem'd like de light ob day a dawning,
Jist 'fore de sun begin to rise
Chorus

Close by de margin ob de water,
Whar de lone weeping willow grows,
Dar lib'd Virginny's lubly daughter;
Dar she in death may find repose
Chorus

Down in de meadow mong de clober,
Walk wid my Nelly by my side;
Now all dem happy days am ober,
Farewell my dark Virginny bride.
Chorus

Foster's most popular song, "Old Folks at Home" presents a lament for loneliness and the feelings of loss towards home, friends and youth.

'Way down upon de Swanee ribber,
Far, far away,
Dere's wha my heart is turning ebber,
Dere's wha de old folks stay.
All up and down de whole creation,
Sadly I roam,
Still longing for de old plantation,
And for de old folks at home.

All de world am sad and drary
Eb'ry-where I roam;
Oh! darkeys, how my heart grows weary,
Far from de old folks at home

Foster was uncomfortable with slavery but even more uncomfortable with his minstrel songs, like "Camptown Races," "Hard Times Come Again No More" or "Massa's in de Cold Cold Ground." He wanted to write successful, popular parlor songs, which is why he wrote songs such as "I Dream of Jeannie with the Light Brown Hair" and "Beautiful Dreamer," but Foster is chiefly remembered now as he was then, for those old minstrel songs.

When Stephen Foster died, the Civil War was still raging--it would not end until the surrender at Appomattox in April, 1865--and the brutal bloody battles of Cold Harbor, Richmond, and Petersburg were still ahead. Foster's songs lived long past that War and that period of time; when Thomas Edison demonstrated the phonograph for President Rutherford B. Hayes in 1878, one of the songs played was "Old Uncle Ned." During the early twentieth century, Foster's songs were among the earliest recorded by music entertainers. Al Jolson performed a number of Foster songs throughout his concert career as well as in the 1939 movie about E.P. Christy, *Swanee River*. When the score for *Gone With The Wind* was composed for its 1939 release, ten Foster songs were used. Minstrelsy did not die at the end of the Civil War either; the success of "The Amos 'n Andy" show on radio throughout the 1930s and 1940s, then on television in the 1950s proves that. So do the early Mickey Mouse cartoon movies by Walt Disney where Mickey looks amazingly like a minstrel show performer.

Although people like Stephen Foster, E. P. Christy and Thomas Dartmouth Rice are immortal in the history of American entertainment, they had a rough time when they were alive. Rice, who created "Jim Crow," a term that would later become synonymous with Southern segregation practices, appeared in a stage adaptation of *Uncle Tom's Cabin*. Rice died in a New Orleans charity ward in 1861. Christy--who never met Foster--committed suicide during the Civil War when he jumped out a window. Stephen Foster, who only traveled south once, in 1852 to New Orleans to visit Mardi Gras, died broke and unappreciated.

In *The Round Table*, a New York paper, the editorial on Stephen Foster's death said this:

"Foster possessed a fund of plaintive melody which, had it coursed through more respected channels in art, might have given him a proud position as a composer. As it was, he can hardly be said to have been more than an amateur writer. We believe that he was only tolerably acquainted with the rules of composition, and in putting his ideas upon paper did so rather as a recreation, for he was engaged in some active mercantile calling until within a short period before his death."

The Music Business During the Civil War

The American Civil War has been called "The Singin'est War ever." Twenty-two years after the War ended, in 1887, a 640-page collection called *Our War Songs, North and South* was published by Brainard of Chicago. It contained 438 songs sung by troops. That was only a portion of the songs written during the Civil War; over 10,000 were published during the conflict, mostly in the North where there was unrestricted access to paper, ink, type and plates as well as good distribution. In the South, songs were published under the control of the Board of Music Trade, which existed until the end of the nineteenth century.

The North had a decided advantage in music publishing during the Civil War, reflected in the very nature in the two parts of the country, essential differences which led to the conflict. The South was a rural area while the North was full of manufacturing; consequently, the North controlled the manufacture of pianos, printing presses and 95 percent of the paper mills.

In the South there were music publishing firms in Nashville, Macon, Mobile and New Orleans which continued to operate. The Confederate States of America enacted a copyright law and, by the end of the War, over 1,000 pieces of music had been copyrighted and published. The oldest publishing company in the South belonged to the Seigling family in Charleston, South Carolina, although the largest wartime Southern music publisher was the Blackmar brothers, Armand and Henry Clay, who published about half the songs issued during that time. The third major publishing firm in the Confederacy was owned by a German immigrant, Hermann Schreiner, who came to the United States with his father in 1849 and settled in Macon, Georgia.

Other music publishers were located in Nashville, where John McClure's firm published the well known comic song, "Here's Your Mule," and Mobile, Alabama. Although Richmond was the center of book publishing, it published relatively little music. All in all, there were less than 50 Southern publishers in the Confederacy operating during the Civil War; they issued the almost 1,000 musical works that emanated from the region.

It is interesting to note that a number of ships who made it through the blockade established by Union ships to stop goods and supplies coming into Southern ports during the Civil War, often contained sheet music of European songs. The South was plagued by shortages of materials and sharply rising costs as well as inflation. In the North there were no shortages of materials but inflation caused paper to rise 300 percent in price, which affected the quality of sheet music paper and a lack of covers on published songs.

It is estimated that an average of 8,000 titles were copyrighted during the 1860s, a rise from 3,000 during the previous decade. Some of the reasons may have been that Congress required a copy of each published work to be sent to the Library of Congress and, if the copyright owners failed to do so within a year after publication, they lost all rights to exclusive ownership.

The Northern printing and distribution networks dominated the music publishing business during the Civil War: one was headed by Oliver Ditson of Boston and included Firth, Pond; Lee and Walker of Philadelphia; Lyon & Healy, in Chicago; and John C. Church in Cincinnati. The other network included William Hall & Son in New York; W. C. Peters in Cincinnati; S. Brainard's Sons in Cleveland; Henry Tolman of Boston; D.P. Faulds of Louisville; Henry Hempsted in Milwaukee; and Root & Cady in Chicago.

When the Civil War ended, the music publishing industry continued to thrive and sheet music was printed with the hope that each newly composed song would become a hit and sell thousands of copies, but there was a shift in the tastes of the public. Minstrel shows became less popular, although a number of traveling minstrel shows continued to be developed; however, by 1880 the original sixty major publishing firms had been reduced to 12. Blackface and minstrelsy was still an important and integral part of stage shows, although audiences increasingly wanted it as part of a variety of entertainment, rather than just an entire evening of minstrelsy.

Americans of that period tended to like loud, coarse and broad entertainment. The theory (and practice) for entertainers was that anything that made an audience laugh was good and should be kept and used over and over again. The blackface performer--who was not so much an imitation of a Negro as a separate character--provided those laughs. In doing so, blackface performers stereotyped blacks: the three most prevalent characters were Jim Crow, the shuffling inadvertently comedic Negro by virtue of his simplicity and ignorance; the citified dandy Zip Coon, who put on airs; and the preacher Sambo, who misused words and terms.

Although minstrel shows eventually opened the stage for African-Americans--and created demand for genuine black entertainment--it saddled African-Americans with stereotypes that would long haunt them. They gave Americans rollicking entertainment and plenty of laughs but, in the end, blackface entertainers reinforced a racism that caused many Americans to look at African-Americans as not quite human, or at least not developed as highly on the human scale as whites.

By the end of the Civil War, audiences increasingly wanted variety shows with more than just minstrelsy; they also wanted comics, acrobats, jugglers, dancers, skits, tragicomic plays, animals, freaks, singers, and anyone else who could entertain a crowd.

Post-Civil War Entertainment

Americans have an insatiable appetite for entertainment and during the latter half of the nineteenth century, entrepreneurs filled audience's appetites with an assortment of acts. Those "varieties," as they were called, were aimed for men in taverns or theaters; only women of ill repute or questionable morals were found in those places. Usually, booze was served in plentiful quantities (often the theaters were part of a barroom or saloon) and the humor was loud, brash, and coarse. Actors had to make themselves heard over dins of talking, arguments, and fights, and only the broadest or most slapstick humor worked.

Actors traveled from city to city or place to place to perform. They wore heavy, crude make-up, with bright red on their cheeks and noses and solid black for wrinkles, eye shadow and other expressive marks. Whiskers were mounted with wires and clothes were seldom clean. None of that mattered much in the dark saloons, but when electric lighting came along, those actors looked like frights.

Lighting in those saloons and theaters was provided by "bunch" lights, which were gas burners grouped together with bright new dishpans used for reflectors. Floods and spotlights were created by flames blowing in jets from two pressure gas tanks against two pieces of lime, inserted vertically into a lamp, one above the other. The flames were directed towards the stage and, as the whole apparatus belched forth hisses, sputters and cracks while dropping sparks and chunks of burning lime, the actors on the stage basked in the glow of the "limelight," which was a milky white aura.

In the "varieties" of the latter 1800s, the banjo was an important instrument, accompanying dances of jigs, clogs and solo numbers, as well as serving as a prop for comics and to fill in any gaps during the show. In the better theaters in the larger towns, there was often an orchestra, usually consisting of three pieces--piano, cornet, and drums--for the show. A drum was used for percussive sounds--drum rolls, cymbal crashes, and rim shots--to accompany falls of comics, the flight of an aerialist and jumps through rings of fire. In seven-piece orchestras, the group generally consisted of violin, cornet, piano, clarinet, trombone, string bass and drums.

A typical or "standard" show, described by Douglas Gilbert in *American Vaudeville: Its Life and Times*, "opened with a sketch." After that came a "single--a song and dance man or woman or instrumentalist--any act that could be done in one to give the stagehands opportunity to reset." The full stage was taken by the next act, "usually an alley oop" before a single (perhaps a comic who did some drama as well) was followed by a blackface comedy using the full stage. The evening would be rounded out with "a female song and dance single in one; a double specialty, usually a musical, in full stage; a pedestal or straight clog, or sand jig in one; a blackface song and dance team, full stage; a protean man or women or costume change act in one; a juggler, full stage; then an afterpiece, musical extravaganza, or drama, with full company." Those final dramas were often plays which could be either tragedy or comedy and lasted over an hour. At first, only men performed on stage but stage managers began adding women to the cast as the nineteenth century progressed in order to appeal to the all-male audiences.

The music performed was generally minstrel show numbers and comedy songs. The comedy of the varieties and vaudeville depended heavily on stereotypes, with the Irish being buffooned the most, followed closely by blacks. In this contemporary era of sensitivity, where the prevailing consensus seems to be that no group should be offended, it is difficult to imagine an open season on all groups--ethnic, racial, cultural, and women--could be construed as acceptable comedy, yet it was. Audiences generally enjoyed themselves, saying they meant no harm, they just wanted to let off some steam and have a good laugh to replace the burdens and cares of the day with some rousing evening fun.

The varieties continued throughout the nineteenth century but were changed by Tony Pastor, who had a theater in New York during the 1880s. Antonio Pastor was born in Greenwich Village c. 1837 and was a noted singer and master of ceremonies in minstrel and variety shows. In New York, he opened a club connected to a wine room and then organized a touring company that offered singing, dancing, comedy and sketches.

Like a number of other impresarios and performers, he struggled to find an audience to fill his theaters. In 1881 he came up with the novel idea of a "clean" variety show that would appealed to all people. Previously, blue humor dominated the stages, which suited the generally all-male audiences, but Pastor elected to clean up the show so that women and children could come and feel welcome. The reason was simple: if he could attract women as well as men, Pastor could double his audiences.

Pastor's shows were immensely successful, attracting numerous women to his afternoon matinees. Although the lure of entertainment was certainly an essential element to his success, perhaps equally important was Pastor's inducement of door prizes for the women who came.

Vaudeville

During the latter part of the nineteenth century the term "vaudeville" was increasingly used to describe "varieties," although Pastor refused to use the term for his shows, claiming it was too "sissy" and "unmanly." The term "vaudeville" was derived from the French "Vau de Vire," which means "from the area of Vire, France." The Valley of the Vire River was the location of a mill of Olivier Basselin, who received fame from composing drinking songs. In the fifteenth and sixteenth centuries, the popular art of composing ballads was established as entertainment and by the end of the seventeenth century ballads accompanied by spoken dialogue came to be known as "vaudeville." That evolved into all kinds of popular entertainment presented at fairs and in saloons.

The person most responsible for popularizing the term "vaudeville" in America was B. F. Keith. Born in New Hampshire in 1847, Benjamin Franklin Keith ran away with the circus when he was 14. He landed a job selling a "blood tester" for a dollar--or more if he could get it--that consisted of a small round glass bowl partially filled with red dye and water. There was a closed spout at the top and when someone held the glass ball in his hand, the heat from the hand made the water rise up into the spout. Keith informed his audiences that this proved the person had high blood pressure and that "if he owned a tester he could check up on his blood pressure every day, saving endless doctor's fees." The machine cost Keith ten cents each.

In 1883 Keith and a partner opened "Keith's Museum" in Boston. He began with a single exhibit, "Baby Alice," a real, live prematurely born two-week old Negro baby who weighed only a pound and a half. Soon, however, Baby Alice grew into a normal sized baby and could no longer be used. At this time, Keith's first partner left and he acquired a second partner and the duo organized exhibits of monkeys, exotic birds, and relics from an Arctic expedition. There was also a dancing chicken act, created by putting chickens on a heated metal plate.

A number of impresarios attempted to gain a degree of respectability by calling their shows "museums" and featured various human oddities (bearded women, a man covered with tattoos, two headed babies, etc.), some exotic animals and a few fakes. P. T. Barnum entered show business in 1835 with a "museum" like this, calling his place "an educational exhibit." Barnum founded "P. T. Barnum's Grand Traveling Museum, Menagerie, Caravan & Hippodrome" which billed itself as "The Greatest Show on Earth." That circus evolved into the Ringling Brothers and Barnum and Bailey Circus and Barnum became the first show business millionaire.

It was difficult for "varieties," "museums" and "circuses" to receive any sort of respect because the humor was so coarse, the performers were travelers--and hence unknown to the local folk--and the crowds that traveled with those entertainments were often suspect. In 1867, Reverend Frederic Denison warned his followers: "Various wandering companies, bands, troupes, mostly comic and vulgarly theatrical, are often flaunting their handbills on the streets and inducing vulgar crowds to attend on their mimicries. Usually the characters of the acts comport with the scenes. Such coarse buffoonery, set off by stale songs and monkey dances, only degrades and corrupts the spectators."

In a number of towns, boardinghouse keepers--forerunners to modern motels and hotels--often had signs in their windows, "No dogs or actors allowed."

The circuses were the worst offenders because a regular group of con men, pickpockets, professional burglars and card sharps traveled with circuses, usually paying the circus for the season's privileges. When the circus came to town, local houses were burglarized and clothes lines were stripped while the circus played. Pickpockets roamed the crowds, relieving patrons of their wallets. A favorite ruse was for a barker to stand in front of the crowd and warn them about pickpockets and to watch out for their valuables; individuals in the crowd would immediately check their wallets and jewelry, letting the professional pickpockets watching know exactly where to strike.

Ticket sellers in the circus did not receive wages; they made their money shortchanging customers. Ticket sellers generally had to pay the circus to work, with prime ticket booth locations costing the most.

Keith and Albee

Edward Franklin Albee, born in 1857 in Maine, joined the circus as a laborer when he was 17 and soon became cashier at the outside ticket booth, which was the biggest money maker for ticket sellers. Those booths charged ten cents extra per ticket because buyers could go immediately into the tent and obtain the best seats instead of waiting in line.

Albee was an expert at palming coins and folding dollar bills over so the customer would count one bill twice when checking his change. The customers were hustled along by someone outside the booth so there was little time to check change. If someone did discover their shortfall and went back to the booth, Albee's "regal bearing and bored manner often discouraged him." However, if the customer looked like trouble, Albee would secretly shift the required amount into a corner of his booth, then disdainfully point to it and say, "It was waiting for you all the time, my friend."

Albee saw Keith's museum in Boston and was immediately attracted to the place, going to work for Keith without being hired; soon, he was hired and made manager. Keith then moved to the Bijou in Boston, which became the first "vaudeville" house. The Catholic church--through Mrs. Keith's connections--financed the organization in the early years and because the Catholic church was involved in the financing, and since Mrs. Keith's senses were offended by traditional varieties, there was a sign posted for performers backstage at Keith's theaters: "Don't say 'slob' or 'son-of-a-gun' or 'hully gee' on this stage unless you want to be cancelled premptorily. Do not address anyone in the audience in any manner...If you have not the ability to entertain Mr. Keith's audience without risk of offending them, do the best you can. Lack of talent will be less censured than would be an insult to a patron...If you are guilty of uttering anything sacrilegious or even suggestive, you will be immediately closed and will never again be allowed to appear in a theater where Mr. Keith is in authority."

The shows staged by Keith and Albee began at 11 a.m. and ended at 10 p.m. They charged a dime for each seat (later raised to a quarter) and did not pay their acts much. In 1887 they opened a theater in Providence, Rhode Island, then constructed a million dollar theater in Philadelphia. In 1893 they opened a theater in New York.

The early vaudeville impresarios made their money by establishing a chain of theaters. Eventually, Keith and Albee dominated the world of vaudeville, owning or controlling theaters all over the country. Other vaudeville pioneers include Frederick Proctor who, with partner, Henry Jacobs, established theaters in Providence and New York before Keith; and Marcus Loew, whose small theaters led to his entrance into Hollywood as the owner of movie "palaces," as the early theaters were called.

The Phonograph

In early July, 1877, 30-year-old Thomas Alva Edison drew a design in his notebook for a device that would record a voice and play it back. He had been working with the telephone and was trying to solve four problems: (1) develop a speaker for the telephone; (2) produce a copying machine based on the electromotographic principle; (3) develop the technology and devices for the autographic telegraph, to be used for transmitting facsimiles of drawings and of handwriting; and (4) figuring out how to use the telephone in Western Union's telegraph operations.

The common element in all of those experiments was a cylinder, or roller. In early July, Edison and his assistants, Charles Batchelor and James Adams, were experimenting with diaphragms and cylinders in attempts to send messages over the telegraph wires that would be received by an embossing autographic telegraph. Those experiments led to Edison placing a sheet of paraffined paper around the electromotographic cylinder and speaking through the telephone speaker. Nothing really came of that; however, the men noticed that when they continued to turn the cylinder some of the sound waves left impressions that emitted a humming type sound when the point of the diaphragm passed over them. (About twenty years previously, a European, Leon Scott, had shown that sound produced a distinctive shape.)

Edison thought about those experiments for the next several days and on July 18 returned to the machine. Edison shouted toward the diaphragm as the strip was run through. When he pulled the paper strip back through, Edison could faintly hear a muffled, murmuring sound. Next, he shouted "halloo" loudly into the diaphragm as the paper strip ran through. When Edison and Batchelor listened, they could hear "Halloo" buried beneath the noise. In his notebook Edison wrote "Just tried an experiment with a diaphragm having an embossing point and held against paraffin paper moving rapidly. The spg [speaking] vibrations are indented nicely and there is no doubt that I shall be able to store up and reproduce at any future time the human voice perfectly."

On August 12 Edison named the machine the phonograph (phono=sound; graph=write or "sound-writing" machine). On that day he made a sketch of the first cylinder machine and gave it to John Kruesi, an assistant who had a genius for building mechanical machines from Edison's sketches. However, the two men were occupied with other inventions, so the machine was not built at that time.

In early September, Edison, ever mindful of publicity, prepared a press release announcing his new invention which played back sound, even though he hadn't actually invented it yet and really had not even recorded the human voice; it was still sound waves. First he had to return to the telephone to solve the essential problem of that machine: a speaker.

The problem with the telephone speaker was resolved on November 9 when Edison collected carbon deposits from kerosene lamps and molded them into a button, then incorporated it into the speaker. On December 1, the carbon button became part of the telephone and this was incorporated by Western Union investors.

In early November, Edison read in *Scientific American* about the work of two French scientists, Professor Etienne Marey and Dr. Rosapelly, recording graphically different sound vibrations. This piqued Edison's curiosity and he returned to the phonograph. Although Edison had essentially figured out how to *record* sound, he had not figured out how to get the sound to play back. By the final week in November, Edison had decided that tin foil was the best material to record and play back and was experimenting with various thicknesses.

On November 29, 1877, Edison drew a sketch of what would become the first phonograph; it was "a spiral-grooved, solid brass cylinder three and one-half inches in diameter...mounted on a feed-screw operated with a hand crank...the cylinder turned and moved laterally from right to left, wrapped in a sheet of thin tinfoil...Riding on the surface of the foil was a stylus connected to the center of a diaphragm, activated by the human voice spoken (actually, yelled) into a funnel-like mouthpiece made from a telephone transmitter."

Edison handed his assistant, John Kreusi a drawing of the phonograph and told him to build it. The next machine had a cylinder about half as long as the one in July but twice the diameter; there was a speaker mounted on one side and a reproducer on the other. Kreusi built the machine during the day and that evening delivered it to Edison. The inventor put a piece of tin foil over the cylinder and, as he was doing this, Kreusi bet him two dollars the invention wouldn't work. Two other assistants, James Adams and William Carman each bet a box of cigars it wouldn't work. Edison shouted "Mary had a little lamb" into the machine with his lips almost directly against the speaker. After he finished, Edison disengaged the speaker and moved the reproducer against the cylinder, turning the handle again. When nothing was heard, Edison said, "I guess you've won the cigars." Then, suddenly, a faint but distinct voice was heard reciting the rhyme. After a moment of suspended silence, everyone erupted "in elation."

On Friday morning, December 7, "after which everyone stayed up all night playing with the thing," Edison took the phonograph to the New York office of Alfred Beach, editor of the *Scientific American*. The machine amazed the crowd gathered in the editorial offices. Two days later Edison filed a patent application for the "phonograph or speaking machine."

The rest of December was spent experimenting with different versions of this invention. The difficulties with tin foil caused Edison to consider using a disk, although that was never actually built. The first commercial venture attempted for the phonograph was in early January when Edison and Batchelor made several trips to the Ansonia Brass and Clock factory in Connecticut where they tried to adapt the phonograph to clocks so the time would be announced and messages advertised.

The Edison Speaking Phonograph Company was formed on January 24, 1878. One of the major investors was Gardiner Hubbard and he and the other backers agreed to raise $50,000, with Edison to receive $10,000 directly to perfect the machine and a 20 percent royalty on all machines sold. Everyone knew the invention needed a lot of work but all could see it had enormous potential as a business machine, especially in the government offices located in Washington, D.C., where Hubbard and the other investors lived. Although this company was organized to control the manufacture as well as exhibition of those machines--not the sale of recordings--this could be called the first recording company. It was certainly the first company established to exploit the new phonograph which led, ultimately, to the contemporary recording industry.

On April 18, 1878, Edison received his greatest publicity for the phonograph when he traveled to Washington, D. C. for a meeting of the National Academy of Sciences. Edison and Batchelor demonstrated the device--Batchelor singing, whistling and crowing like a rooster into the diaphragm and then Edison playing back the sounds. During the demonstration, two girls fainted and one onlooker remarked "It sounds more like the devil every time."

Edison demonstrated his phonograph to a group of newsmen that evening and, just before midnight, was driven to the White House where he demonstrated the machine for President Rutherford B. Hayes. Edison and his group stayed at the White House until 3:30 a.m. entertaining the President and his wife with the new contraption.

In the June, 1878, issue of the *North American Review*, Edison published ten uses for the phonograph. They were:

(1) Letter writing and all kinds of dictation

(2) Phonographic books that will speak to the blind. (Talking books for the blind first appeared in 1934.)

(3) The teaching of elocution.

(4) Music. (The first musical recording was made in mid-1878 when Jules Levy, cornet, performed "Yankee Doodle" at a public demonstration of the phonograph in New York.)

(5) The family record; preserving the sayings, voices, and last words of the dying members of the family and of great men.

(6) Music boxes and toys so that a doll may speak, sing, cry or laugh. (The first talking dolls were developed in 1878.)

(7) Clocks to announce the hour of the day, call you to lunch.

(8) Preservation of language by reproduction of our Washingtons, our Lincolns, our Gladstones. (The first politician to make a recording was President Hayes in April, 1878.)

(9) Education purposes, like preserving instructions of teachers so the student can refer to them later or at other times.

(10) Perfection or advancement of the telephone's art. (In short, telephone answering machines.)

The Industrial Revolution

During the Industrial Revolution, the time was ripe for experimentation and research, for mechanics, inventors and tinkerers.

Prior to the Civil War there were three major technological developments that changed the country: the creation of the steam engine and its use on steamboats to transport goods and people up and down waterways; the development of the telegraph that linked the country and allowed distant regions to communicate with each other; and the development of the network of railroads, which facilitated distribution of goods as well as passenger service. Bankers, seeing new markets open, made money available for businessmen and inventors. It was the era of the machine and people increasingly believed that machines were the key to making a better world for business as well as consumers.

The changes in technology meant a change in the market as well as a population shift. Business activity centered in cities so people moved to cities in record numbers. In addition to Americans moving from rural areas to cities, there was a large number of immigrants--over 25 million--who entered the country between 1870 and 1916. Those immigrants by and large settled in cities and caused the population of the country to double, adding workers as well as consumers to the economy.

The North was the major area for industrial growth--the South was still agrarian as well as in the grips of Reconstruction. The result was an economic boon that saw the value of goods produced by American industry increase almost ten fold from 1870 to 1910. In addition to actual goods produced, there were also advanced production methods introduced. During the 1870s the telephone and typewriter were invented and oil was discovered in Pennsylvania in 1859. Breakthroughs in refining oil led to the use of kerosene as the major fuel for light, lubricating oil to help machines run smoothly, and gasoline, which powered the internal combustion engine. In the early 1900s, Henry Ford and Eli Olds used mass production to produce automobiles while Charles Goodyear and Harvey Firestone developed new ways to use rubber. The creation of the oil industry led to the first "trust" whereby one company, Standard Oil, headed by John D. Rockefeller, controlled about 85 percent of the market for this valuable commodity.

Government did little if anything to regulate business during the 1800s, the idea being that a "free market" was the best way to insure economic growth. However, although there was large economic growth, there was also the development of trusts and monopolies--John D. Rockefeller and Standard Oil inspired other capitalists to control the market for a product--and an abuse of labor. The capitalists chief concern was making money; they had little if any concern for social responsibility. That led to a reform movement which began with the formation of labor unions like the American Federation of Labor in 1886, and farmer's groups, like the National Grange in 1867 and Farmers Alliances during the 1870s and 80s. The abuse of labor, and the rise of "robber barons" who treated the American public as well as their own workers ruthlessly, led eventually to the "muckrakers," journalists who exposed the corruption of society and the enactment of business and labor laws that abolished trusts and ended child labor. That led to the reform Presidency of Teddy Roosevelt, under whose leadership agencies like the Food and Drug Administration were initially developed while he sought to rein in the "robber barons" whose heyday was the 1890s.

The Industrial Revolution created a climate for technological inventions, which led to changes in how people worked, where they lived, and what they did. Ultimately, this Industrial Revolution produced an Industrial-based economy to replace the Agrarian-based economy and the resulting shifts in population, values, wealth, and society affected American popular culture--and popular music--for the next century.

Thomas Edison

Thomas Edison was a well-known inventor before he invented the phonograph. Born on the snowy night of February 11, 1847 in Milan, Ohio, he moved with his family to Port Huron, Michigan in 1854 when he was seven. Edison was the youngest of seven children and had only three months of formal schooling. According to biographers, Edison probably had what is known today as Attention Deficit Disorder (ADD) so he "was most decidedly not a natural student" and "did not respond well to rigidly systematic teaching methods." "Little Al," as he was called, overheard a teacher say he was "addled and it would not be worthwhile keeping me in school any longer." He went home crying to his mother, who pulled him out of school and taught him at home. Learning at home, Edison became "a voracious, even omnivorous, life-long reader" who, in later years, "would request every available book and periodical" on a subject that aroused his interest.

At nine or ten, Edison read a book on physical science and chemistry that excited him so he established a chemistry laboratory in his basement and began doing the experiments in the book. He spent the next five years studying and reading about chemistry and doing experiments.

During the time Edison was growing up, boys around the ages of 10-12 years old were expected to begin manhood and work--usually on the family farm. At the age of twelve, Edison obtained a job aboard a commuter train that ran between Port Huron and Detroit as a "news butcher," selling newspapers, magazines, and sandwiches to passengers. He set up a chemistry laboratory in the baggage car and established his own newspaper, condensing the news of the day. This came to an abrupt end one day when the train lurched, the chemicals in his make-shift laboratory and print shop fell on the floor and a fire started; the conductor immediately expelled Edison and his chemicals from the train.

According to a story told by Edison, in the fall of 1862 he saved the life of three-year-old Jimmie MacKenzie, son of railroad station master J.U. MacKenzie. Young Jimmie had wandered onto the train tracks as a freight train approached; young Tom Edison ran to the tracks and shoved him to safety. J.U. MacKenzie then taught young Edison telegraphy in gratitude and three months later Edison obtained his first job as a telegraph operator.

Thomas Edison came along at a fortunate time because the telegraph was linking the eastern half of the country, allowing communication between distant places. During the Civil War (1861-1865) Edison was too young to serve (he was 14 when the war began) and benefited from so many telegraph operators leaving to join the Army. That led to a number of job openings and allowed young Edison numerous job opportunities, especially with railroads.

Thomas Edison had long suffered from hearing loss due to numerous ear infections when he was a boy. According to legend, he suffered further hearing loss when he was pulled aboard a train leaving a station by a conductor. The conductor grabbed him by his ears and Edison reportedly heard something "pop" as he was hauled aboard; after that his hearing continually declined. That event may or may not have contributed to his hearing loss; however, the hearing loss actually served as an advantage for several reasons. First, it allowed Edison to concentrate totally on the task at hand, eliminating most outside distractions. Next, Edison's thought processes were believed to be highly visual, so there was less need for hearing as he developed his thoughts. It is ironic that the father of the recording industry was nearly deaf.

The first patented invention by Edison was the electric vote counter, which he presented to Congress as a fast, efficient way of counting votes. Congress turned him down, preferring the old system where names were called and votes were counted one by one and Congressmen talked amongst themselves and traded votes, compromised, stalled or negotiated during the process. The turn-down came as a surprise to Edison, but he was determined to make inventing a way of life. He loved tinkering and inventing--at his lab he set goals of inventing something every 10 days and something really big every six months--so he set about to build his own world and attract financial investors. In his failures he always saw opportunities; he was never defeated when one of his inventions did not work out, he simply learned lessons and applied them to future projects.

Edison's big break came when he moved to New York, penniless after one of his inventions had failed. That invention involved sending two different telegraph messages over the same wire; however, the person he enlisted to help had problems at one end and didn't know how to solve them; the result was that, with investors and other onlookers watching, the experiment was a grand failure.

Edison went to work for General Marshall Lefferts, president of the Gold and Stock Telegraph Company, who commissioned him to design a new stock ticker. Here Edison, at the age of 23, developed his work methods. He worked round-the-clock, and "reminded his financial supporters that they were paying just as much for the experiments themselves as they were for the successful results" because "no experiments are useless."

Edison was a fascinating man and biographer Robert Conot, in *A Streak of Luck* states "When Edison's imagination latched on to a concept, ideas tumbled through his head and he was unable to sleep. He emptied his mind as if it were a barrel of apples." He was eccentric and less concerned with people than with his work. Conot states, "Although Edison habitually stood people up and failed to keep promises, he did not deliberately intend to slight them. His intentions were usually good. But he had trouble turning anyone down, and kept committing himself to far more than he could accomplish. Human relationships meant little to him, clocks and schedules were nuisances, and he never compromised his egocentricity to accommodate himself to anyone. His overriding desire was to be left alone to do what he wanted. And though he did not object to intruders, and in fact made them welcome, he did not feel they had reason to expect anything from him."

Edison was also volatile, and Conot states, the inventor "had little tolerance for frustration, and if events and men seemed to conspire to thwart him he could explode into cyclonic cursing and tantrums. He was open-minded about everything until he came to a conclusion, and then his dogmatism bordered on the fanatic. Once he decided on a goal, he pursued it with dogged simplemindedness and stubborn belief in his own vision." Conot goes on to state that Edison's laboratory was his "work, play and companionship combined." The inventor's only diversion was the theater and his "principle recreation continued to be reading two, three, and more newspapers a day."

Biographer Neil Baldwin in his book *Edison: Inventing the Century* notes that Edison "was a compulsive worker...His tenacity when faced with a problem...blurred into utter possession and an aching urge to have issues resolved, and was further compounded by his addiction to working on several matters simultaneously...The twenty-four-hour clock meant nothing to him, and conventional sleep, in his middle years at least, was irrelevant

Edison loved attention and sent out numerous press releases trumpeting his inventions. He eventually hired a clipping service and, though he often did not read his mail for weeks or months, he always read the clippings on himself.

In early 1876 Edison built his laboratory and home in Menlo Park, New Jersey, about twenty-five miles from New York City and twelve miles south of Newark. There he established a six-day, ten-hours-a-day work week and set up his "office" in a corner of a large room, with his desk "facing the wall, isolated from the main flow of communal work yet in plain sight."

The Telephone

On February 14, 1876, Alexander Graham Bell patented a device that transmitted the human voice electrically over a distance. The device had a strip of iron connected to a membrane. The sound waves of a voice agitated this membrane and vibrated before a battery-activated electromagnet. This sent an electric current along a wire. At the other end of the wire was a similar device constructed in reverse which allowed the voice to be reproduced. That became the telephone. Later, in 1876, the American Telephone & Telegraph Company (AT&T) was formed to market this and other inventions by Bell.

The announcement of Bell's invention came on March 10, 1876 and this inspired Edison, already working with sound, to use Bell's invention to help solve the problem of sound amplification. Underwritten by Western Union, who needed to improve their telegraph operations, Edison began work on the "speaking telegraph."

In England, David Hughes discovered the same thing about the same time and announced a new invention: the microphone. Hughes took all the credit for himself and Edison was furious, although Edison probably did not appreciate the fact that the device could also be used as a sound amplifier or used for things other than the telephone, like Hughes did.

Bell's telephone was marketed by licensing companies in other "territories" to market the telephone--each state was a "territory" and one company was assigned the rights--with the parent company controlling the manufacture of the telephone. That worked well for establishing the telephone network nationally and the organizational structure was appealing to other companies. When the early phonograph companies were beginning, they established the same basic organizational pattern, licensing other companies--many formed just for that purpose--in different territories. The central office manufactured the machines and rented them to the field offices, who in turn rented them to customers. The original idea was that those companies would convince businesses to use the phonograph as a dictating machine in their offices. However, the machines were too bulky and difficult for that to occur. Also, the stenographers--who the machines were marketed to replace—did all they could to discredit the machines and their entry into the work place.

First Customers for the Phonograph

The initial customers for phonograph machines proved to be owners of saloons, in order to attract customers and keep them entertained, and drugstores, which were forerunners to the dime store or, later mass merchandisers such as Wal-Mart. In order to drum up interest and sell those phonograph machines there were a number of showmen booked by a lyceum company headed by James Redpath in Boston to demonstrate the phonograph. They were provided with an instrument and a number of tin foil "blanks" and sent out to gather a crowd in their territory. They kept a percentage of the gate receipts and sent the rest back to the home office. It was a profitable venture; a single phonograph could earn up to $1,800 a week.

Edison was engaged in the promotion of his phonograph during the first half of 1878.

There were several basic problems with the early tin foil machines. First, it was operated by a hand crank, so there was no regular speed and tones could change. Next, the tin foil was used over and over, so that a number of sounds--whistling, the cornet, speaking--could all be on one cylinder. The end result of a session like this was cacophony. Finally, the tin foil didn't last very long; after a few playings, it could not be used any more.

Edison worked with the phonograph during 1878 but on July 29 he went to Wyoming to witness an eclipse of the sun. During his journey there, some investors encouraged him to work on the electric light, promising him any amount of money he needed for the venture. Edison finally agreed and, when he returned to Menlo Park, laid aside all other experiments and inventions--including the phonograph--to work on the electric light. From the end of 1878 until 1886--almost eight years--Edison did nothing with the phonograph and the early phonograph companies folded or went into retirement. During that time he perfected the electric light and created the Edison Electric Light Company. Edison also worked on the electric generator, which cities in the United States and Europe purchased and put into place, ushering in a world of electric lights and electricity which changed the world from one governed by nature's schedule of light and dark, hot and cold, into one where humans controlled the rhythms of life.

The Graphophone

In 1880, Alexander Graham Bell received $20,000 for the French Volta prize, awarded for his invention of the telephone. With this money, Bell established Volta Laboratory Associates in Washington, D.C. The company consisted of Bell, his cousin Chichester Bell and Charles Tainter. Edison told his assistant, Samuel Insull, that no one "will try to steal the phonograph. It is not of any commercial value" but Tainter, who began as an apprentice in Boston in Charles Williams's shop in 1870 (he was sixteen at the time) was curious and worked on the machine.

Like others, Tainter knew that tin foil was not an adequate recording material so he began using wax, a material which had also been suggested by Edison. Tainter and Chichester Bell experimented for months and developed a cardboard-backed wax cylinder that produced recordings by cutting into the wax, rather than indenting the tin foil. The machine used was almost identical to Edison's; however, to make it different they reversed the terms and called it a "graphophone" instead of a "phonograph."

The Bells lost interest in the machine because they could not manufacture it without infringing on Edison's patents. However, Tainter continued to work on the machine and in early 1882 achieved a breakthrough by developing a moveable, or floating, reproducer which adjusted itself to the groove. That was the situation until 1885 when Thomas Edison did not renew his British patent on the phonograph. The lapse of the foreign patent meant the end of American patent protection as well, according to then prevalent court decisions, and so on June 27 the Bells and Tainter filed patent applications for their machine. By October, they had six graphophones made. In May, 1886, the patents were granted and the Bells and Tinker incorporated the Volta Graphophone Company.

In October Edison began working again on the phonograph. He assigned an assistant, Ezra Gilliland, the task of developing a small phonograph for use in offices. It had to be driven by a motor (preferably electric) and the cylinders had to be interchangeable with shellac, gum or wax to comprise the recording surface. Edison recruited a number of singers to test those recordings. However, during the last week of December on a bitter, damp, cold night, Edison developed a fever and cold which turned into pneumonia and pleurisy. When 1887 dawned, he was quite sick in bed. As he lay near death, he decided to build a new laboratory. On February 19, Edison, his wife Mina and a male nurse went to Fort Myers, Florida for three months so the inventor could recuperate and there he built his new laboratory.

Back in New York, Bell and Tainter put a treadle-powered graphophone on exhibit at a New York hotel. In May, 1887, just after Edison returned from Florida, Chichester Bell and Tainter visited Edison and offered a joint business arrangement: they would let the graphophone go and provide money for future development and marketing of the phonograph. Edison would receive all credit and honors for the invention. In exchange, Bell and Tainter would receive half interest in the venture. Edison countered with an offer of a fourth interest; Tainter turned that down and he and Edison parted as bitter competitors.

The Bells and Tainter formed The American Graphophone Company in June, 1887 in Washington, D.C. to market their machine. Edison responded by developing a new phonograph, which looked amazingly like the

Graphophone; it had a "floating stylus" and used wax as a recording material. The major difference was in their "phonograms," which was Edison's name for recordings. The graphophone's recordings were wax on cardboard while Edison's was solid wax, which meant that Edison could "shave" his cylinders and use them over again for another recording.

The 1878 patent of Edison's specified a process of "embossing or indenting" for the recording process while Bell and Tainter used the term "engraving" to describe their process. Those terms--"embossing or indenting" vs. "engraving" could almost be interchangeable, although Edison used the first for tin foil while Bell and Tainter used the latter for wax, but it was the matter of the "floating stylus," which Edison adapted to his new machine, which caused Bell and Tainter to contact attorneys for litigation against Edison. In late summer, 1887, Edison formed a new corporation, the Edison Phonograph Company, capitalized at $1.2 million, to market his phonograph. Attorneys began to line up for litigation.

The North American Phonograph Company

Jesse Lippincott, a Civil War veteran who began his career in Pittsburgh as the owner of a grocery store, became cash rich, receiving one million dollars when he sold his Rochester Tumbler Company of Pittsburgh, a glass manufacturing firm, and decided to establish a recording monopoly. In the spring of 1888 he agreed to pay half a million dollars to the Graphophone group for the rights to market their machine, then Lippincott offered to buy the Edison Speaking Phonograph Company for the same amount. In addition to the half million dollar purchase price, Edison would receive a five percent royalty for every machine sold for the next fifteen years. Edison himself did not know of the negotiations; they were concluded with Ezra Gilliland, who owned part of the company, and John Tomlinson, Edison's personal attorney. Tomlinson then convinced Edison to consummate the deal without informing him of Gilliland's or the Bell's involvement. With those two companies, Lippincott formed the North American Phonograph Company.

Lippincott made a horrible deal, paying too much money for the Graphophone Company and too much money for the Edison Company. Edison was kept in the dark about the involvement of Tainter and Bell and, when the inventor finally found out, he exploded.

In addition to incurring the wrath of Edison, Lippincott organized the North American Phonograph Company along the same lines as American Telephone and Telegraph, giving companies "territories" to market their machines, with the central office in New York holding all the patents and responsible for manufacturing the machines. This was the heyday of the trusts--John D. Rockefeller controlled the American oil industry with Standard Oil, owning processing plants as well as distributorships. Lippincott wanted to be a robber baron as well, controlling the phonograph industry in America. By autumn, 1888, it looked like he might succeed, having consolidated the two major competing firms under one roof and ending litigation over patents.

The phonograph did not sell like Lippincott envisioned. Part of the reason was that Lippincott, like Edison, saw the phonograph primarily as a business machine instead of home entertainment. He would not sell the instruments, leasing them for an annual fee of $40 to be split between the parent company and the subsidiary.

There were 30 subsidiary companies organized but in 1889 only one company made any money: the Columbia Phonograph Company. That company covered Maryland, Delaware and the District of Columbia and the major reason it showed a profit while the others didn't is because it inherited the business of servicing the existing Graphophones in government offices in Washington.

Lippincott could not meet all of his financial obligations and, in 1890 after two years of losing money, began to lose his health. That fall he was stricken with paralysis and a little later lost control of the company to Edison, who was his principal creditor.

Edison was besieged by major problems with Lippincott's organization. First, the subsidiaries weren't making any money and, further, were invading each other's territories and engaging in unethical business practices. Next, the machines needed to be sold instead of rented; it was obvious that the current system was just not working.

Edison let the company flounder until 1894; during that year, Lippincott died and Edison put the North American Phonograph Company into bankruptcy. The phonograph wasn't ready for mass marketing; Edison kept pushing the idea of a battery-driven phonograph and diverted his energies towards developing a talking doll, but the mechanical device could not hold up under the problems and pressures of shipping, so the operation shut down in 1890.

One bright spot emerged in 1890. J. Walter Fewkes took the phonograph to the Maine woods and, on thirty-six cylinders, recorded the Passamaquoddy Indians singing and speaking. This was the first "field recording" on the 100 pound machine; about thirty-five years later field recordings were used to record early hillbilly and blues music.

First Commercial Recordings

The first commercial music recording for Edison was made in 1888 when 12-year old pianist Josef Hofmann visited Edison's laboratory and recorded some two minute cylinders. This was followed by the real beginning of the recording industry, which was Edison's first commercial recordings 1889-1892. Commercial cylinders officially began from May 24, 1889.

Recordings at that time were made by violinist Alf Armhein, who made 50 cylinders of 11 pieces, cornetist John Mittauer, who produced 84 cylinders, all confined within a playing time of two minutes, and a small group of three musicians--clarinetist Henry Giese, flautist C. August Joepl, and bassoonist John Helleberg--who produced 141 cylinders of 16 titled recordings. Recordings by a pianist and flute and clarinet duets were also made.

The first multiple recordings were made by Frank Goede on June 3, 1889, when he played simultaneously into seven machines. That became a regular practice after August, 1890, when artists, who had previously made recordings one at a time, now faced a battery of as many as ten machines to record.

Although the human voice was considered the easiest sound to record (along with the cornet, banjo and xylophone), during the first two months of recording, the entire repertoire consisted of instrumental music. Clarinetists Henry Giese and Max Franklin were the two most regular visitors to the studio. Although cornet solos abound, there are no recordings of the banjo until September, 1889 and the first singer was not recorded by Edison until July 9, 1891. On that date, a Miss Stewart recorded "My Love and I," "Pattison's Waltz Song," and "Le Pre aux Cleres." On July 15, a Mrs. Lankow, made two recordings.

The first male soloist was a Mr. Handel, who recorded on January 10, 1890, while the next was George W. Johnson, a black laughing comedian, who performed a variety of singing and whistling tunes for two and a half hours. He was accompanied on piano by Edward Issler on June 1, 1891.

George J. Gaskin, the "boy tenor" (who was actually approaching 30) first recorded for Edison on August 3, 1890, and made 20 recordings of popular songs like "Drill, Ye Tarriers, Drill," and "Picture Turned To The Wall." Joseph Natus was another early singer; he made 15 recordings accompanied by pianist Edward Issler. Edison also marketed a line of "darkey" records, which came about when Edison met a black man on the ferry from New York who could whistle. Edison labeled him "The Whistling Coon."

On March 18, 1892, the first duplicated recordings were made by a system in which a master cylinder was recorded and as many as 150 copies could be obtained from this original. The first cylinders produced for private use were done by the North American Phonograph Company on April 1, 1892, although they were purchased mainly by shopkeepers and fairground stall holders who displayed them as a gimmick to attract customers. The market for the earliest recordings seems to have been shops, saloon keepers and other merchants who used the machine to entice people into their establishments.

The first recordings were made by people in and around New York simply because Edison was in that area. Since Edison was attracted to the theater, he naturally sought out those musicians he or his friends knew about. Although there was a wide variety of music around--ragtime, blues, hillbilly--none of that was recorded because of geographical location (they were not in the city where the recording technology was developing) or because neither Edison nor any of the other pioneers came into contact with those musics.

The music first recorded was music that appealed to the white, middle class (or upper middle class). It defined "popular" music and while vaudeville tunes were recorded, the prevailing thought at the time was that the wealthy, the powerful, and those in authority should present to the mass audiences things they *ought* to do, know, or hear. Too, the first machines were relatively expensive and so only the upper middle class white audience could afford them.

Ironically, in the first 100 years of the music industry, that trend remained: new technology would be introduced with "high brow" or classical music because those consumers were more affluent and could afford the machines and were reached more easily through the print media.

Although music was recorded and sold those first few years of the commercial recording industry, it is difficult to draw any conclusions. The music was secondary or even third in consideration. The first consideration was the technology: at that point (1888 to 1895 or so) the industry was dominated by inventors, tinkerers and mechanics. They spent considerable time and effort to perfect an early recording device, without really knowing what the long-term effects or market would be.

The next consideration was with business; specifically, how to attract investors so that further work could be done to perfect the technology. That meant developing a purpose and market for the machine. The first business ventures were, by and large, disasters and numerous people lost money in the early recording industry. Edison himself was a bad businessman and his recording companies consistently lost money and left investors hanging. It was not until 1900 when the Victor Record Company was established that the recording industry was on sound financial footing selling recordings.

The Columbia Phonograph Company

When Edison threw the North American Phonograph Company into bankruptcy, he was restrained by law from selling phonographs until the bankruptcy case was settled and a receivership was negotiated. That brought the phonograph industry to a virtual halt, since most of the subsidiary companies began to flounder and then fold. The exception was the Columbia Phonograph Company, headed by Edward Easton, based in Washington, D.C.

Edward Easton was born in Gloucester, Massachusetts in 1855 and became a prominent stenographer in Washington, D.C. before he earned a law degree from Georgetown University. He became a stockholder in the Volta Graphophone Company, established by Bell and Tainter, and then the American Graphophone Company, which was organized in June, 1887. In February, 1888, Easton and some partners bought sales rights from the American Graphophone Company to market the graphopone as a business machine. The new company was named Columbia Phonograph and the sales territory was Virginia, Delaware and Washington, D.C. Soon after their incorporation, in January, 1889, Columbia began recording music.

When the American Graphophone Company made their agreement with Jesse Lippincott, one sales territory was not available-the Washington, Virginia and Delaware territory that was franchised to Easton and his partners. Easton and his lawyers "manipulated some stock and, with a little Wall Street razzle-dazzle, soon had control of both Columbia and American Graphophone." When the legal machinations were complete, the legal restraints placed upon Edison did not apply to them so the American Graphophone Company and Columbia's relationship was combined under Easton in 1889 and they set about marketing their machines and recordings.

Although Edison and Lippincott had envisioned the phonograph as a business machine, those leasing the machines soon discovered that most "business" was for entertainment. Each subsidiary could record cylinders to sell with their machines, and many did.

In 1889, Leon Glass of San Francisco invented a device that, when attached to the phonograph, allowed the phonograph to be coin-operated.

Listeners heard the recording on a set of earphones that looked like a stethoscope.

In order for businessmen leasing the machine to make money, the "coin-in-the-slot" was instituted where a customer dropped a nickel into a slot to play a selection. That was the earliest form of the jukebox and this nickelodeon quickly proved profitable; soon the machine was in a number of public places. That was the only way phonographs could have been profitable. In hindsight, it seems obvious that those machines were not compatible with offices, but they were not really conducive for home entertainment either. Their batteries were heavy, acid storage affairs, too troublesome for the average home, while the machine itself was too expensive for the average wage earner.

Edison fought the idea of the phonograph being used for entertainment, feeling it demeaned it. In January, 1891 in his in-house publication, *The Phonogram*, he wrote "The coin-in-the-slot" device is calculated to inure the phonograph in the opinion of those seeing it only in that form, as it has the appearance of being nothing more than a mere toy, and no one would comprehend its value or appreciate its utility as an aid to businessmen and others for dictation purposes when seeing it only in that form."

The most profitable phonograph company in 1891 was in New Orleans, which collected enough nickels to average $500 a month in receipts.

John Philip Sousa

In 1891 Columbia issued its first catalogue of recordings available to customers. It was 10 pages long and contained 27 marches, 13 polkas, 10 waltzes and 34 items listed as "miscellaneous." Their most popular act was the Marine Corps Band, headed by John Philip Sousa; they were the first act to sign an exclusive recording contract when they agreed to record only for Columbia.

John Philip Sousa was America's first musical superstar. He was born in Washington, D.C. on November 6, 1854, son of a member of the Marine Corps band. Sousa learned violin and trombone and joined the Marine Corps band in 1867; in 1872 Sousa left the band and played in theater orchestras, then rejoined the Marine Band in 1880 as musical director, a position he kept until 1892. In 1890 the band recorded Sousa's composition "Semper Fidelis" for Columbia and in 1891 "The Washington Post March" was recorded; both sold well and were early recording "hits."

Sousa formed his own band in 1892 and toured the United States and Europe; from 1895 on the band recorded a number of marches, including

"Stars and Stripes Forever" in 1897, as well as dance tunes like "In the Good Old Summertime" (1903).

Sousa and his band toured constantly, playing amusement parks, schools and anywhere he could attract a crowd. Their success was made possible by the railroad; by that time, railroads criss-crossed the country and Sousa's group could travel by rail to anywhere in the country. Only a relatively few years before, the kind of touring that Sousa did, covering the breadth of the country, was impossible, which is how Sousa pioneered the big road tour.

Known as "The March King," Sousa's marches were hit songs; people danced to them as well as marched. His biggest hit during his lifetime was "The Washington Post March," which was popular in Europe as well as the United States. Sousa was the first American composer who was taken seriously by Europeans. The first sustained national attention Sousa received came in 1893 at the Columbia Exposition in Chicago, where people from all over the world came to enjoy the wonders of a World's Fair.

Sousa's concerts featured selections from composers like Beethoven, Verdi and Wagner and he arranged Gilbert and Sullivan songs for his concert band in addition to his march tunes. In addition to his performances, Sousa worked hard cultivating the press and received extensive press coverage all over the country when he and his group performed.

Although Sousa benefited from the recordings of his marches by his band, he was rather indifferent to the actual recording process, preferring to let his concert master Arthur Pryor, supervise the sessions with Sousa collecting money for the use of his name. Sousa is credited with first using the term "canned music," a derisive term about recordings and, in 1906, referred to "the menace of mechanical music." Sousa signed an exclusive contract with Victor in 1902 but put Pryor in charge of the sessions; in 1904 Pryor formed his own band, which soon became nearly as popular as Sousa's.

John Philip Sousa never retired; he once said "My religion lies in my compositions." He had a family--a wife, a son and two daughters--but was usually on the road performing. After one performance, in Reading, Pennsylvania on March 6, 1932, Sousa went back to his room, laid on his bed, and passed away. He was 77 years old.

Columbia Recordings

Next to Sousa and the Marine Corps Band, the most popular act on Columbia was John Y. Atlee, a whistler, who had 36 selections in their first catalogue. Atlee was a government clerk by day; his piano accompanist was a young teenager named Fred Gaisberg. There were 13 selections for clarinet and piano, nine for cornet and piano, and 32 songs for voice and orchestra. The vocal recordings were divided into categories such as "Sentimental," "Topical," "Comic" "Negro," and "Irish." There were also 20 "speaking" records.

Columbia sold its cylinders primarily by mail, generally to coin-in-the-slot phonograph operators. They sold 300-500 cylinders daily, although the recording process was so primitive that a singer could only record three cylinders at a time and a band could only record ten. An early recording session where a brass band was recorded illustrates the problems of recording cylinders during the early 1890s. First, the brass band sat surrounded by ten phonographs in a circle, with a giant metal horn protruding from each. According to Gelatt, "An attendant has checked all the batteries and has inserted a fresh wax cylinder in each machine. Now the recording engineer steps before the horn of the first phonograph, starts up the motor, and announces in stentorian tones: "My Country 'Tis of Thee,' played by Cappas' Seventh Regiment Band, record taken by Charles Marshall, New York City." He stops the motor, steps over to the second phonograph, and repeats the same announcement--and so on, through the group of ten. When every cylinder has been inscribed with an announcement, all ten motors are started up simultaneously. Music pours into the big horns until each cylinder has received as many sound impressions as it can hold, whereupon Mr. Marshall holds up his finger, and the band comes to a full stop at the end of the next musical phrase. If "My Country 'Tis of Thee" has not run its full appointed course, no one seems to worry much. The recorded cylinders are taken off the instruments and put aside in pasteboard boxes, and fresh ones are inserted."

That recording session lasted three hours, at the end of which--if all went well--the company had 300 cylinders ready for sale the next day for one dollar each; however, the recording industry was beset by problems with its distribution, organization, and litigation (or threatened litigation). The quality of recordings was poor and only played for two minutes (or less) and there was no way to duplicate cylinders; each cylinder sold was custom made.

Emile Berliner

Emile Berliner was another inventor working with sound in the late nineteenth century and whose inventions furthered the phonograph. Born in Hanover, Germany in 1851, Berliner emigrated to the United States in 1870 and worked at a haberdashers in Washington, D.C., building a small research laboratory in his apartment where he studied the sciences of acoustics and electricity. Berliner's first patent was a carbon button transmitter to improve Bells' telephone. That was patented in March, 1877, and sold it to American Telephone and Telegraph in 1878 for a sum large enough--with a monthly retainer fee--to allow him to continue his research.

Berliner returned to Hanover, Germany in 1881 and, with his brother Joseph, established Telephon-Fabrik to provide telephones for the German market. The success of the telephone in Germany made Berliner a rich man and he returned to the United States in 1883 determined to work on the phonograph and sound waves. In May, 1888, a patent by Berliner was approved for a talking machine, called a "Gramophone" which created lateral cut discs, instead of the "Phonograph," which created vertically-cut cylinders. The invention of the "disc," which would replace the cylinder, was Berliner's most important invention for the recording industry.

In March, 1888, a number of musicians came to Berliner's home in Washington, D.C. to record selections. In May, 1888, Berliner first publicly demonstrated his disc recording at the Franklin Institute in Philadelphia. Unlike Edison, Berliner believed his invention would be used primarily in the home, not the office, and in his talk before the group of scientists at the Institute, presented that idea for the future of the gramophone, never mentioning it as a business machine or for uses in dictation. Also in his talk before the Franklin Institute, Berliner discussed the concept of artists receiving royalties from their recordings and multiple pressings from a single disc.

The United States Gramophone Company was formed in Washington, D.C. in the fall of 1893 by Berliner with friends and relatives. The first gramophone records, called "plates," appeared on the market toward the end of 1894, pressed in hard rubber; the first discs sold for 50 cents each or $5 for a dozen. Berliner hired 21-year old Fred Gaisberg to be an accompanist on record and as a talent scout. Previously, Gaisberg had worked for Columbia, the subsidiary of the American Graphophone Company. A number of musicians continued to make recordings, so Berliner began to release new recordings every month.

The earliest gramophones were manual machines, and needles to play the recordings were the size of darning needles (in fact Berliner recommended a broken darning needle for the stylus). The gramophones were simpler and sturdier than the phonograph and the recordings had far greater volume than the cylinders.

In the autumn of 1895, a group of investors from Philadelphia bought into the Gramophone company for $25,000 and, on October 8, 1895, the Berliner Gramophone Company Inc. was established in Philadelphia. The idea of producing recordings for home entertainment was taking hold; it was certainly Berliner's vision and, at this point, the only advantage the gramophone had over the phonograph or graphophone. Previously, Berliner had taken his invention to the Bell Telephone Company and F.A.O. Schwartz in New York. Both the Bell company and Schwartz suggested using the technology for a talking doll but Berliner, like Edison, resented his invention being viewed as a "toy."

By 1896 Columbia was the leading recording company and major player, using the two years when Edison could not legally market his machines because of the Lippincott litigation to aggressively market their machines and recordings. They had emerged with a strong catalogue of recorded material and in the winter of 1895-1896 began advertising a phonograph starting at $450 in *McClure's*, *Cosmopolitan*, *Munsey's* and *Harper's*--all large circulation American magazines.

The name "Edison" was still magic for most Americans and of great value when marketing. In January, 1896, Edison formed the National Phonograph Company and sold phonographs with spring driven motors with prices beginning at $40. By 1898 the Edison Standard Phonograph sold for $20 and by the end of the century was a close second behind Columbia. Profits were beginning to increase and the recording industry showed indications of becoming big business because of the reduced costs of the machines, the improvement of the recordings, and the improvement of the sound amplifying horns on the machines, which made the recordings both louder and clearer.

Into this fray stepped Emile Berliner and the Gramophone Company. He was far behind the other two companies when he began and did not have a "name" to promote. His gramophones used discs instead of cylinders, which meant that buyers could not record their own cylinders; the disc making process was far too complicated and messy to do at home or in an office but the discs played louder than cylinders and were more convenient, easier to store and less bulky than the cylinders. Berliner was convinced that his machine would be used in the home so he made no attempt to market it as an office machine. Those essential differences allowed Berliner and the gramophone to emerge as a major player in the recording industry by the turn of the century.

By the end of the 19th Century, there were three major firms in the recording industry: Edison, Columbia and Berliner's company and they were selling 500,000 units annually. Those companies were already reaching out to the international market, with Edison's cylinder machines successful in Paris, Berliner's company opening an office in London, then spreading throughout Europe, and Columbia opening offices in Paris, London and South America. One of the top recordings as the 19th century came to a close was "My Wild Irish Rose," sung by tenor George Gaskin.

Eldridge Johnson and Victor Records

In Camden, New Jersey, across the river from the Philadelphia offices of the Berliner Gramophone Company, Eldridge Johnson had a small machine shop. The gramophone was operated manually and Berliner knew the machine needed a motor to succeed. Johnson was sent a design for a clockwork motor for the gramophone but the design proved impractical; however, Johnson continued working on ideas for a motor because the gramophone fascinated him. Finally, the twenty-nine year old machinest designed a motor that worked and satisfied the Berliner directors. In the summer of 1896, the directors gave Johnson a contract to manufacture 200 motors.

The technical problem solved, the Berliner directors set about solving the next problem: how to promote and market their gramophone. For that they hired New York promoter and advertising man Frank Seaman, who suggested the Berliner company give him the exclusive rights to sell the gramophone. In exchange, he established a company to promote, advertise and distribute gramophones and recordings. The Berliner Gramophone Company signed a fifteen-year contract with Seaman in 1896 and three companies were created: the National Gramophone Company, owned by Seaman in New York, advertised and sold the machines; the Berliner Gramophone Company in Philadelphia manufactured the machine and recordings; and the United States Gramophone Company, Berliner's original company in Washington, D.C. owned and controled the gramophone patents.

The gramophone, with Johnson's spring driven motor, cost $25 (and included two records) and soon Seaman had more business than he could handle. The Berliner group began ordering thousands of motors from Johnson; meanwhile, the machinist had come up with two new inventions. First there was an improved sound box (developed with Alfred Clark) and the other was an improved motor. That machine was marketed as the Improved Gramophone and became famous because the dog, Nipper, peered into it in the painting, "His Master's Voice."

With more machines selling, Seaman pressed for more and better recordings. In Philadelphia, a recording studio was established by Fred Gaisberg, then a second studio was established by Calvin Child in New York. At that time a recording studio consisted of a piano, a recording machine, and four walls.

The big advantage of disks over cylinders was that a number of copies could be made from a single recording after it was placed on rubber and "stamped" onto the record. In late 1897, Berliner switched to shellac for his records.

Those who recorded on those early gramophone records include Dan Quinn, Len Spencer, George J. Gaskin, Will F. Denny, Vess Ossman, Cal Stewart, and Russell Hunting. Most of the operatic arias were sung by tenor Ferruccio Giannini. Evangelist Dwight L. Moody was recorded, as was railroad entrepreneur Chauncey Depew, actor Joseph Jefferson, orator Robert Ingersoll, comedienne Ada Rehan, music hall entertainer Marucie Farkoa, and bandleader John Philip Sousa.

In 1898 the National Gramophone company claimed sales over $1 million and Johnson's machine shop showed a $40,000 profit. Johnson was now manufacturing whole machines instead of just the motor. Columbia and the Graphophone company, which manufactured only cylinders at that time, attacked the Gramophone in public with vitriolic ads; Seaman responded in kind.

Litigation

The American Graphophone Company had an attorney in Washington, Philip Mauro, who began scrutinizing Berliner's patents, even though the cylinder and disk machines were world's apart. Mauro, watching the gramophone play with the needle propelled by the grooves of a record, decided this could be construed as "floating," which was the primary component of the Bell and Tainter patent: a "floating stylus." However, instead of suing the patent holding United States Gramophone Company, Mauro sued Frank Seaman and the National Gramophone Company.

Mauro won his suit, with Judge Lacombe of the Circuit Court in New York ruling that the "gramophone infringed a fundamental patent of the American Graphophone Company" effective January 25, 1899. Seaman appealed and the restraining order was lifted for two months until the entire case could be heard in detail.

In March, 1899, Seaman transformed the National Gramophone Company of New York into the National Gramophone Corporation of Yonkers, then created a subsidiary, the Universal Talking Machine Company, which established a factory in New York to manufacture gramophones. Seaman continued doing business with Berliner and opened branch offices in Boston, Chicago, Cincinnati, Cleveland, Philadelphia and Providence. Then, in October 1899, all orders from Berliner by Seaman stopped. The Improved Gramophone was dead in the water; Seaman then began advertising his new machine, the Zonophone. There were some minor changes from the gramophone but the major difference was in name. Seaman went to court against Berliner and in May, 1900, testified the gramophone patents were an infringement on the "floating stylus." Two weeks later it was announced that an alliance had been formed between Seaman's companies, the National Gramophone Corporation and Universal Talking Machine Company, with the American Graphophone Company and Columbia Phonograph Company and the Zonophone would be "manufactured and sold under the protection of the joint patents of all parties to the agreement." By June 25, Seaman convinced the court to issue an injunction against the Berliner Gramophone Company because "no disc talking machine could be legally marketed in the United States" other than those protected under the joint patent agreements."

It became impossible for the Berliner company to manufacture their own machine and merchandise while Frank Seaman was doing a booming business. Berliner, fuming mad, instituted lawsuits against Seaman and his companies for "infringements of patents, damages, and an accounting."

The Victor Company

When Frank Seaman pulled his coupe de grace with the Berliner Company, making Berliner's patents and the Improved Gramophone worthless, Eldridge Johnson looked around the new four-story building he was constructing and found himself with $50,000 worth of unpaid merchandise ordered by the Berliner Company. Unless Johnson could sell those gramophones, Johnson would be bankrupt.

Since 1897 Johnson had been experimenting with the recording process, combining the wax engraving method of Bell-Tainter for a disc. The sound of the wax pressings convinced him that this was the best way to improve the sound of the recordings.

Johnson formed the Consolidated Talking Machine Company and hired Leon Douglass to promote and sell the machines. Douglass and Johnson began with a novel offer: a free wax record made from Johnson's new process for anyone who owned a gramophone if they wrote in. Soon, the company was selling their stock.

Frank Seaman reacted immediately, going to court to charge that Johnson's business "was a thinly disguised subsidiary of the Berliner Gramophone Company" and asked for an injunction to stop Johnson manufacturing the machines and to stop the use of the word "gramophone" by Johnson. Johnson argued his case in the Philadelphia court and won against Seaman except for one matter: he could not use the word "gramophone." Although that decision was reversed two months later, Johnson decided the term actually belonged to Berliner and created a new name for his company: the Victor Talking Machine Company. From that moment--March 1, 1901--Victor Records and Victor Talking Machines entered the recording industry. The term "gramophone" soon became obsolete in the United States, although it remained popular in England.

Johnson had to resolve the issue of patent ownership with Berliner. Berliner owned the original patent but Johnson had made a number of substantial improvements--a motor and improved sound box as well as the process of recording on wax disks--and, further, had a factory and sales organization that were doing well. Johnson did not like big business and offered to sell his entire business to the Berliner group, but they could not raise the money to buy it. Finally, a new corporation was formed with Berliner owning 40 percent, Johnson the remainder, with management under Johnson. The Victor Talking Machine Company was incorporated on October 3, 1901.

More patent problems were on the way. Joseph Jones had worked in Berliner's Washington laboratory during his summer vacation during the 1890s and perceived that wax was the best material for gramophone recordings. He filled out a patent claim for recording on wax and filed it November 19, 1897. Johnson had never filed a patent on his wax process because his attorney had informed him that Bell-Tainter's patent on the wax cylinder made another patent on the wax process impossible. The Patent Office surprisingly awarded a patent to Joseph Jones for this process, over four years after he had originally filed it.

Meanwhile, attorney Philip Mauro contacted Jones and purchased the patent rights for $25,000. By 1902 there was another legal battle looming, engineered again by attorney Mauro. Columbia Disc Graphophone was obviously in violation of the Berliner-Victor gramophone patent but Victor was now infringing on the wax recording process patent. Finally, Victor and the Graphophone Company reached a settlement before going to court: they would pool their patents and thus the two companies "controlled every important patent bearing on the manufacture of disc machines and records."

By the end of 1902, Columbia and Victor were both producing discs and making large profits: Victor's profit that year was almost $1 million. Too, Johnson had brought to the market an improvement on the phonograph: a tone arm. That allowed the "sound box to be coupled with the metal horn without having to support its weight" which "made for easier handling and reduced record wear."

By 1906, Johnson had named his device a "Victrola" and inserted the speaker horn in a cabinet, which also featured internal storage space for discs. The Victrola was designed and marketed as furniture and was sold in furniture store for $200. The discs were seven inches in diameter and held two minutes of music.

Early Recordings

The first Victor catalogue was released in 1902 and featured a number of recordings by Emilio de Gogorza under several different aliases (Signor Carlos Francisco, Herbert Goddard, M. Fernand) singing Italian opera arias, English songs and French opera arias. There were also recordings by Rosalia Chalia, a Cuban singer and Ferruccio Giannini. The opera recordings did not sell as well as popular recordings of "The Holy City" and "Lead Kindly Light" by Harry MacDonough, Dan Quinn, the Haydn Male Quartet and John Philip Sousa's band.

On Columbia, a series of Grand Opera Records featured Edouard de Reszke, Marcella Sembrich, Ernestine Schumann-Heinke, Suzanne Adams, Charles Gilbert, Giuseppe Campanari, and Antonio Scott. Those celebrity recordings from the Metropolitan Opera cost Columbia dearly--they paid Marcella Sembrich $3,000 for three discs and Edouard de Reszke $1,000 for three discs--but the fees did not guarantee a high quality recording.

Meanwhile, Victor created their own celebrity recordings, putting their opera and classical stars on discs with a red seal. The first Victor Red Seal session was held in Carnegie Hall on April 30, 1903; the first artists recorded during the ensuing months were Ada Crossley, Zelie de Lussan, Louise Homer, Johanna Gadski, and Antonio Scotti, but Victor soon came to dominate this field because of an artist first recorded in Europe.

Enrico Caruso

Enrico Caruso made his first recordings in Milan, Italy, for the London-based Gramophone & Typewriter Ltd. on March 18, 1902. He had recorded earlier--in 1898 for Pathes--but Fred Gaisberg decided to record him for the British company. He was to record ten arias in one afternoon for 100 pounds sterling, which translated into approximately $50 a side. Just before the session the London office cabled Gaisberg "Fee exorbitant. Forbid you to record" but the engineer decided to ignore the message and recorded Caruso anyway. When those recordings were released in London, at the same time of Caruso's debut there, the sales were phenomenal.

Caruso's greatest hit, "Vesti la giubba," from Act I in "Leoncavallo" by Pagliacci, was first recorded in 1902. That, and subsequent recordings of this song by Caruso, sold over one million copies during Caruso's lifetime.

During the period between 1902 and 1921, Enrico Caruso became the first serious music artist to fully appreciate the value of the gramophone. In part, this was because his voice recorded so well, due to its quality, power and tone. During the time he recorded he received approximately $2 million in royalties from The Gramophone and Telegraph Company, which later became HMV in the United Kingdom, and with his releases on Victor in the United States.

Victor signed Caruso on January 28, 1904, just after his debut with the Metropolitan Opera in New York. His first American recordings were made February 1-10 at Carnegie Hall; for those recordings Caruso was paid $4,000 and guaranteed $2,000 a year for the next five years. In return, he could not record for any other recording company except the Gramophone and Typewriter Company in London.

His Master's Voice

Victor developed one of the most famous trademarks of the twentieth century. "His Master's Voice" was the picture of a dog looking quizzically into a phonograph horn. The dog's name, Nipper, became part of the Victor family.

Nipper was a bull-terrier cross born in the early 1880s in England. His first owner was scenery painter Mark Henry Barraud, who died in 1887. The dog was taken by the painter's brother, Francis Barraud, who lived in Liverpool and was an artist. Francis owned a cylinder playing phonograph and occasionally recorded his own voice. When hearing his master's voice, Nipper stared at the black horn with quizzical attention. That prompted Barraud to create a watercolor which was exhibited in London.

Barraud attempted to interest the London agent of Edison in his painting but to no avail. Meanwhile, William Barry Owen, head of the Gramophone Company, Victor's affiliate in London, saw the picture, liked it and agreed in September, 1899, to purchase it. However, Owen insisted on two changes. First, he wanted the black enamel horn changed to the more visually attractive brass horn and, second, he wanted the Edison cylinder machine to become a Gramophone disc player. Those changes made the picture incorrect and, some would say, ridiculous. First, if a dog heard his master's voice on a disk playing machine, that would mean the master was a recording artist--a fact which gave rise to the rumor at one time that this was Caruso's dog. Next, the machine's design was out of date--the supposedly prominent artist couldn't even afford a modern gramophone! However, most never noticed those discrepancies.

In October, 1899, Barraud delivered the revised painting to William Barry Owen, who paid Barraud 100 pounds sterling: 50 pounds for the painting and 50 pounds for the copyright. Although Owen liked the painting, he did not think of it for a trademark; the Gramophone Company already owned a famous trademark of an angel writing with a quill on a gramophone disc. The "recording angel" had become famous as the logo for Gramophone recordings.

Owen hung "His Master's Voice" on his wall, where it was seen by Emile Berliner, who took out an American copyright on it in July, 1900. Eldridge Johnson immediately adopted the logo and Nipper first appeared on a record supplement sheet in January, 1900, and was first used in an advertisement later that year by Eldridge Johnson's Consolidated Talking Machine Company. The Victor Talking Machine Company, which was registered in March, 1901, first used the picture on its disc labels in 1902.

London and Europe

William Barry Owen, head of the Gramophone company in London, was concerned the gramophone was a fad and wanted to broaden his investment. He decided to invest in the Lambert Typewriter, which used a rotating disc instead of a keyboard. At the end of 1900, the London company was re-named "The Gramophone & Typewriter Company Ltd." Unfortunately, the typewriter proved to be a dud. Although it cost much less than most other typewriters, it took a typist much longer to twist the dial than to push down the keys on the machine, so the commercial business world ignored it. That led to Owen's resignation from the company and he returned to the United States in 1905. He moved to Martha's Vineyard where he raised chickens and died a poor man.

Fred Gaisberg, however, was busy with profitable ventures, traveling all through Europe to record artists. As soon as those recordings were made they were shipped to Hanover, Germany, where they were stamped and shipped to the appropriate market. By 1900 there were 5,000 recordings advertised in the Gramophone catalogue.

The European operation was a major source of profits for Eldridge Johnson, especially the branch in Russia. There was a gramophone shop in St. Petersburg run by a gentleman named Rappaport which featured an elaborate, plush setting for people to listen to gramophones. It was Rappaport who suggested to Fred Gaisberg that recordings of singers from the Imperial Opera be marketed on red seals to differentiate them from the black label issues of music hall singers, comedians, and brass bands. In 1901 the company offered the first of its Red Seal label recordings; they were 10 inches in diameter and sold for $5 each. Soon, the Russian Red Seal idea was accepted by the London office so Gaisberg and Owen set out to record European opera singers to market there and in the United States. In 1902 they headed to Milan to record Enrico Caruso.

Segregation is Formalized

The end of the nineteenth century gave rise to a New America. By the end of the century, there were 45 states in the United States, with a population of about 50 million. That contrasts with 22 million in the 1860s census. More people were moving to the cities, with 45.7 percent in urban areas and 54.3 percent in rural areas by 1910. This contrasts with 15.3 percent living in urban areas in 1850 while 84.7 percent lived in rural areas.

The fabric of the country was changing, with numerous immigrants arriving from Europe. The potato famine in Ireland during the 1845-49 period led to the arrival of large numbers of Irish to America; during the period 1840-1860, 400,000 immigrants came to the United States, with 39.3 percent from Ireland and 32.2 percent from Germany. In 1880, of the 800,000 immigrants admitted to the United States, 21.9 percent were German while 11.7 percent were Irish. In the entertainment industry, this meant that Irish and Germans--as well as other immigrants--were stereotyped in variety and vaudeville routines.

The Irish, especially, were lampooned as mentally slow, hard drinking, manual laborers, or as country bumpkins; the Germans had thick accents and butchered the language. During the 1890s, vaudeville stereotyped the Irish more than any other ethic group, with blacks coming in a close second.

African-Americans had an increasingly difficult time during the 1890s as racism became intellectually fashionable. The "coon songs" reflected a growing movement from intellectual circles that promoted the idea that African-Americans belonged to an inferior race. Most African-Americans still lived in the South (90 percent) and southern politicians increasingly erected social and economic barriers against them. There were numerous lynchings of African-Americans--in 1900 there were 107--and the Tuskogee Institute published an annual report on the number of blacks lynched.

Southern states increasingly enacted "Black codes" which separated African-Americans from whites and excluded them from the mainstream of life. That movement was promoted by racial bigots as well as people with good intentions who firmly held the belief that blacks were inherently inferior to whites and the two races could never co-exist as social equals. It reached its zenith in 1896 when the Supreme Court handed down its decision of Plessey vs. Ferguson, which stated the "separate but equal" doctrine for blacks and whites. The result was a Federally sanctioned separation of the races that caused black and white cultures to exist apart at the same time they were together in the same country. The groups shared an area--although there were black and white sections--and a common language. The mass media reached the general population while black-owned newspapers were written for the African-American community. There were African-American churches, schools, restaurants, and separate rest rooms in public facilities. In the areas where both African-Americans and whites were allowed--such as a Court House or, later movie theatres--there were separate bathroom facilities and water fountains or sections for blacks only.

Those "Jim Crow" laws isolated black citizens. The music that developed within the black culture increasingly spoke to that culture and was foreign to whites. Many whites were upset by the black influence on music, considering it savage and morally repugnant to middle-class sensibilities. Since many African-American musicians performed in brothels or "sporting houses" in the red light districts of town, or in honky tonks and dives, the music acquired a reputation (even within the black community) as being the "devil's music."

The conflict of "devil's music" vs. "God's music" was an important part of the black culture for years to come. It affected the rhythmic composition of the music because sporting houses and honky tonks were places to relieve tensions, and thus the music was heavily rhythmical and conducive to losing inhibitions. The lyrics often dealt with sexual themes and wild living and were believed to be dangerous and immoral according to the prevailing opinions of the majority of white Christians.

However, the music was infectious and many whites heard it and liked it, thus a number of whites incorporated black rhythms into their own music, giving it more rhythm while blacks heard and adopted white music as part of the normal interchange of the creative process--synthesizing various influences from musicians, songs, and instruments.

Many African-Americans saw music as a way to achieve success and respectability--as well as money--so they often consciously adopted their music to the white culture. Black composers sought to have their pieces published and disseminated to white audiences while white composers tried to capture the infectious rhythms from the African-American musical culture.

Black Entertainers in Late Nineteenth Century

Negro singing groups like The Fisk Jubilee Singers had done concert tours since the 1870s. In 1890, *The Creole Show*, which featured attractive young African-American women, was organized by Sam T. Jack.

The Black Patti Troubadours was formed in 1896 by Sissieretta Jones, an African-American concert singer who was barred from performing on many concert stages. Her managers, Voelckel and Nolan, organized and promoted the show, which featured popular songs and vaudeville numbers. A short concert of operatic airs was performed by Jones at the end of each show. Sissieretta Jones was known as the "Black Patti" because of her comparison to the leading Italian opera singer, Andelina Patti.

Bert Williams and George Walker, the comedy team known as Williams and Walker, arrived in New York in 1896 and were an immediate hit on the vaudeville stage. During the next ten years, Bert Williams became the top African-American comedian.

A Trip to Coontown, starring Bob Cole and Billy Johnson, opened in New York in April, 1898, and is generally considered to be the first critically acknowledged black musical comedy. *Clorindy, or The Origin of the Cakewalk*, considered to be the first black show staged in a Broadway theater, premiered in New York in July, 1898. The music for *Clorindy* was composed by Will Marion Cook while Paul Laurence Dunbar wrote the libretto and lyrics; however, the star of the show, Ernest Hogan, re-wrote much of the libretto and lyrics. *Jes' Lak White Folks* by Cook and Dunbar premiered in 1899.

Williams and Walker

During his career Bert Williams was described as "not just a star: he was the sun" [who] "drew every major black composer, lyricist, and librettist of his time into his orbit. All wrote for him, some wrote with him, and many of them flourished in his light as they never would again."

Egbert Austin "Bert" Williams was born on November 12, 1875, in Nassau, the Bahamas, but moved with his family to Florida, then to Riverside, California. He moved to San Francisco after high school, and joined Martin and Selig's Mastodon Minstrels in 1893 where he teamed with George Walker for skits and the two soon became partners.

George Walker, a year older than Williams, was a dancer from Lawrence, Kansas. Williams and Walker toured as "The Two Real Coons" with Williams playing the "Jim Crow" character while George Walker played "Zip Coon."

In 1896 Williams and Walker went to New York and auditioned for *The Gold Bug*, an operetta by Victor Herbert. One of the producers turned them down but *The Gold Bug* was a flop when it opened on Broadway so Williams and Walker were contacted; they joined and did their regular vaudeville routine during the performance. The high point of their act was a comic version of "The Cakewalk," a new dance fad.

Williams and Walker performed as members of the Dahomey Village during the Chicago World's Fair in 1893. Dahomey was a village in Africa that sought to gain its independence from France but failed. In Chicago, Williams and Walker appeared in The Octoroons, an all-black production in Chicago that was based on the traditional minstrel show format.

Bert Williams used black face during his entire career. According to Williams' biographer Camille Forbes, "instead of being trapped inside the mask, he viewed it as 'a great protection...I shuffle onto the stage, not as myself, but as a lazy, slow-going negro...[that] hid the real Williams...Burnt cork became part of what enabled him to step into that onstage self, the buffer between the audience and the inner Williams."

Bob Cole

In 1899, James Weldon Johnson and his brother, Rosamond, traveled to New York to audition a musical they had written.

James Weldon Johnson, was born June 17, 1871 in Jacksonville, Florida where his mother, a public school teacher and accomplished musician, taught him and his brother, John Rosamond Johnson (born August 11, 1873) to play piano, although James preferred the guitar. In 1894 Johnson graduated from Atlanta University and became Principal of Stanton, a school for African-American students. In 1897, Johnson passed the bar exam and became the first African-American admitted to the Florida bar. His brother, Rosamond, studied music at the New England Conservatory of Music in Boston and taught music in Jacksonville.

The brothers wrote a comic opera, *Tolsa*, that they wanted to see produced in New York so, during the summer of 1899—when school was out—they went to New York. On that trip to New York the Johnson brothers met Bob Cole, "one of the most talented and versatile Negroes ever connected with the stage," wrote James Weldon Johnson. "He could write a play, stage it, and play a part. Although he was not a trained musician, he was the originator of a long list of catchy songs."

Born July 1, 1868 in Athens, Georgia, Robert Allen Cole was the son of a carpenter who was a local political figure. During his teens, Robert lived in Jacksonville, before he moved with his family to Atlanta where he attended Atlanta University, but did not graduate. During the 1890s Cole began his show business career in vaudeville with partner Lew Henry. By 1890 he was a member of the original Creole Show Company in Chicago where he met singer-dancer Stella Wiley, who he later married. In the Creole Company, Cole served as a singer, dancer and monologist as well as director; he also began writing songs during that time.

In 1894, at the age of 26, Cole and Wiley moved to New York where he founded his All Star Stock Company, which conducted workshops and classes for black performers. Billy Johnson was one of Cole's students; he was from Charleston, South Carolina and a veteran of minstrel shows. Cole and Johnson joined the Black Patti Troubadours in 1896, where they served as comedians and writers. Their one-act sketch, "At Jolly Coon-ey Island" was successful.

In 1897, Cole asked owners Voelckel and Nolen, owners of The Black Patti Troubadours, for a raise; they refused so Cole took his score of songs written for the show and left. Although he was arrested for theft, Cole established legal ownership of his music in court and was paid for its use as the Troubadours continued to use his score.

Ernest Hogan, who performed in a re-written version of "At Jolly Coon-ey Island," joined the show after Cole left.

Bob Cole and Billy Johnson wrote a two-act musical in 1897, *A Trip to Coontown*, that was first performed in September, 1897. *A Trip to Coontown* was modeled on *In Gay New York* and *In Gayest Manhattan* which was a "sightseeing show." It opened in New York in 1898 and stayed on the road for most of 1900 but the Cole-Johnson partnership was coming apart; Bob Cole was looking to write with someone other than Billy Johnson when he met James Weldon and J. Rosamond Johnson.

After that first summer in New York, James and Rosamond Johnson returned to Jacksonville and resumed their teaching careers. James wrote several poems, including "Lift Every Voice and Sing," which Rosamond set to music for a special program on the anniversary of President Lincoln's birthday on February 12, 1900. The song was performed by a children's chorus and spread rapidly; it was later adopted by the National Association for the Advancement of Colored People and is known as "The Negro National Anthem."

When the school year ended in late Spring, 1900, the Johnson brothers made their second trip to New York and re-united with Bob Cole. The three formed a partnership to write songs and plays.

During that period in American theater, songs were often "interpolated" into musicals. Since a musical needed hit songs, a singer was always on the look-out for catchy material; if the song drew good audience response (and sold sheet music) then it was added to the score. A musical at that time generally had a story line but the songs were not integral to the plot. Cole and the Johnson Brothers were soon in demand to write songs that were a hit with white audiences.

Paul Laurence Dunbar

One of the first African-American writers to become nationally known was Paul Laurence Dunbar. Born in Dayton, Ohio (June 27, 1872), Dunbar was the only African-American at Central High School in Dayton where he was editor of the school newspaper and class president. He began writing poetry when he was six and gave his first public recitation when he was nine.

Dunbar became friends with Wilbur and Orville Wright and edited a newspaper they owned, *The Tattler*. His first collection of poetry, *Oak and Ivy*, was published in 1893; his second, *Majors and Minors*, received a strong, positive review from critic William Dean Howells in 1896, which led to Dunbar's work receiving national attention.

Dunbar wrote in Negro dialect, which was popular with both white and Negro audiences.

Ernest Hogan

"All Coons Look Alike To Me," written by Ernest Hogan in 1896, originated the craze in "coon songs." "Coon songs" were songs whose lyrics stereotyped African-Americans as being laughable, comic, lazy, shiftless creatures given to excesses and vices. Songwriters—black and white-- took ragtime rhythms and added lyrics in black dialect. In addition to the lyrics, sheet music covers further perpetuated stereotypes of blacks.

The covers pictured blacks with full or large lips, rolling eyes, or dandified dress indicating they were socially out of place.

Ernest Hogan was born Reuben Crowders in Bowling Green, Kentucky, shortly after the Civil War. During his teen years, he performed in tent shows and minstrel shows and took the stage name "Ernest Hogan." He was living in Chicago by 1891, where he was a performer and co-owner of Eden and Hogan's Minstrels. Hogan was living in New York when he wrote "All Coons Look Alike to Me," which was published in August after arranger Max Hoffman added an extra syncopated chorus. After that song, "an explosion of coonery in pop songs" occurred. Over a million copies of the sheet music were sold during the next several years and the song became popular with vaudeville singers."

All Coons Look Alike to Me

Talk about a coon a having trouble
I think I have enough of ma own
It's alla bout ma Lucy Jane Stubbles
And she has caused my heart to mourn
Thar's another coon barber from Virginia
In soci'ty he's the leader of the day
And now ma honey gal is gwine to quit me
Yes she's gone and drove this coon away
She'd no excuse to turn me loose
I've been abused, I'm all confused
Cause these words she did say

Chorus:
All coons look alike to me
I've got another beau, you see
And he's just as good to me as you, nig!
Ever tried to be
He spends his money free,
I know we can't agree
So I don't like you no how
All coons look alike to me

Never said a word to hurt her feelings
I always bou't her presents by the score
And now my brain with sorrow am a reeling
Cause she won't accept them any more

If I treated her wrong she may have loved me
Like all the rest she's gone and let me down
If I'm lucky I'm a gwine to catch my policy
And win my sweet thing way from town
For I'm worried, yes, I'm desp'rate
I've been Jonahed, and I'll get dang'rous
If these words she says to me
Repeat Chorus

Coon Songs

It is not popular now to discuss—or even acknowledge—the popularity of "coon songs" during the late nineteenth and early twentieth centuries. We look back at those songs and say they denigrated blacks and many in the African-American community during that time felt the same way. W.E.B. DuBois, one of the founders of the NAACP and part of the Harlem Renaissance, was an outspoken opponent of "coon songs" because they portrayed an image of blacks that was false, misleading and detrimental to any attempts for better civil rights during that critical period in history. But for the white audience, "coon songs" were viewed as simply entertainment, good time songs that were fun and funny, and a generally acceptable way of viewing blacks.

"Coon songs" took ragtime rhythms and added lyrics in black dialect, stereotyping African-Americans into several broad categories. In time "ragtime" denoted any song with a snappy, up tempo melody, especially if it was connected to some new fad or dance, and since ragtime supposedly came from the black culture, it was natural the lyrics talked about that culture. Tin Pan Alley songwriters--predominately white--took those basic premises to present a body of work that was overwhelmingly biased in presenting African-Americans as uncultured, unlettered, and unfit for equality with the white race.

The American white culture basically saw nothing wrong with coon songs during the time they were popular. The "black peril" was the subject of a number of books and articles with best-selling books like *The Negro is a Beast* by Charles Carroll (1900) and *The Leopard's Spots* by Thomas Dixon (1902) pontificating on this treatise. Enlightened academics presented theories to "prove" the inferiority of the black race and scientists chimed in with their scientific proof that African-Americans were inferior to whites. No wonder that music publishers asserted "Seems hard--but people will have coon songs--we must supply their demands and needs."

The white culture further justified coon songs and other stereotyping of blacks in theater and entertainment by saying the "cullud bruder" loved and laughed at all this fun, enjoying it just was much as the "white fo'ks." Even those who felt a bit uneasy on moral grounds put it all behind them when it came to the economics of the situation: if you can make a lot of money with something--in this case coon songs--then you can justify writing them and there was money to be made by music publishers with coon songs.

The black male in coon songs was generally pictured to be "lazy, cowardly, faithless, given to excesses and vices" and, like all blacks, according to those songwriters, "wanted to be white." That desire to be white generally expressed itself "as a sort of covetousness of white values or standards" which, because it conflicted with the stereotype of the black, made blacks foolish, comic figures hopelessly out of place in the white world of culture and refinement."

Unlike the white man, who worked hard and earned his money, the black man was pictured as having money because "of good fortune in gambling or success at cheating; it was hardly ever the result of having worked honestly for it." According to historian and musicologist Sam Denison in *Scandalize My Name*, "white dogma held that only fortuitous circumstance could bring wealth to the shiftless, ignorant black, excepting in dreams."

Author Sam Denison has noted that "Destruction--or at least the severe crippling--of the black male's ego appeared to be a primary goal of the coon song. Human weaknesses were distorted, amplified, and presented as racial traits peculiar to the black." Denison goes on to point out that, according to those stereotypes, blacks could not stop gambling and were hopelessly addicted to chicken, which had replaced the raccoon (hence "coon" song) that blacks had previously feasted on uncontrollably in a number of minstrel songs. To satisfy this insatiable craving for chicken, the African-American had to steal and a number of songs featured blacks eating chicken or stealing a chicken with comic effects coming when the simpleton is caught stealing a chicken to satisfy his gastronomic craving.

Thus "stupidity, and a crudely drawn, loutish logic, were important elements of the black male image in the coon song," according to Denison. Those songs, he continued, "stamp the black male as weak-brained. In the songs, incapacity for rational thought and the erratic behavior resulting from this defect were seen as racial characteristics," adding that "The comic possibilities of such views were endless."

There was a huge fear that society had to face: black men with designs on white women. That was a major threat because the black man's sexual prowess was widely circulated in songs. At the same time, those same stereotyped black men--who were often belligerent with a mean, jealous streak--were often being cuckolded by their own women.

"All Coons Look Alike To Me" presented a black woman as fickle and mean--another common stereotype--and the black man as a victim of this flighty woman.

Another stereotype was the black preacher, which was exploited by Bert Williams in a series of "deacon" songs. Here, black religious figures were often shysters, sex-crazed, simple-minded and more given to African voodoo than "true" white Christianity. According to Sam Denison, "The figure of the black preacher was thus undermined by constant references to fraudulence, cowardice, superstition, phylogeny, and intemperance. Religion itself was hardly ever recognized as a matter of real importance."

African-American children, called "pickaninnies," could only be loved by their "Mammy" who somehow wished they were all white. As such, the "pickaninnies" were harmless, comic creatures whose naive innocence further proved the inferiority of blacks. Sam Denison stated that in the late nineteenth century "the black was still a largely unknown person in the United States, despite three centuries of life here. Even the efforts of black composers to portray their black brother in song left the character essentially unchanged."

Coon songs reflected American attitudes at the end of the nineteenth and beginning of the twentieth centuries. The Federal government's indifference to the racial question, and subsequent lack of action in enforcing laws to insure civic and political equality for blacks, led to State laws that made integration a crime. Those black codes, or "Jim Crow laws" kept blacks and white segregated and further stripped blacks of opportunity, legal protection, and dignity. Perhaps the attitude adapted by blacks in the wake of white America's intent to "keep them in their place" is summed up best in the song "Stay In Your Own Back Yard," where a black mother talks to her child.

Now honey, yo' stay in yo' own back yard,
Doan min' what dem white chiles do;
What show yo' suppose dey's a gwine to gib
A black little coon like yo'?
So stay on dis side of de high boahd fence,
An honey, doan cry so hard;
Go out an' a play, jes' as much as yo' please,
But stay in yo' own back yard.

The End of the First Era of Black Music Theatre

The 1908-1909 theatre season was, in many ways, a very good one for black musical theater. *The Red Moon* by Cole and Johnson had a successful year, although they were plagued by financial problems. Williams and Walker closed the second year of their well-received production *Bandanna Land"* (book and lyrics by Frogs Jesse Shipp and Alex Rogers, music by Will Marion Cook) after playing Broadway. However, George Walker became too ill to continue in February; those were Walker's last stage appearances. In May, Ernest Hogan died; on January 8, 1911, Walker died.

Bob Cole collapsed on stage from a nervous breakdown. He was recuperating at a boarding house in the Catskills where, after several quiet days he went swimming with friends and, during the swim suddenly went still and disappeared under the water. His death by drowning, on August 2, 1911, was probably a suicide."

The loss of Ernest Hogan, George Walker and Bob Cole within a two year period was devastating to black theatre; it was the end to the first black Broadway era.

Ragtime

Ragtime began with "ragging" existing songs, adding rhythm and syncopation to known songs until new songs developed with distinctive rhythms and syncopation. As time moved on, "ragtime" became the term generally used for popular songs.

Blacks were the main developers of ragtime, and the music was primarily developed by piano players in brothels and sporting houses, but as the music was published and caught on with audiences, a large number of white songwriters adapted the rhythms and incorporated them into their own work. There are two early major black ragtime composers--Scott Joplin and James Scott--but the greatest number of ragtime songs came from white Tin Pan Alley songwriters in New York. That led to a changing definition of it the music as it went from being a new way to play old songs to a distinctive genre of syncopated music, then to any song with a snappy rhythm.

Ragtime has been defined as a "dance based American vernacular music, featuring a syncopated melody against an even accompaniment." It is a piano-based music with four major types: (1) instrumental rags, (2) ragtime songs, (3) ragtime or syncopated waltzes, and (4) "ragging" of classical and other preexisting pieces."

Although the most direct antecedent for ragtime is "coon songs" the roots actually extend back for several decades. The term derives from "ragged time" or "broken time," a way of describing new rhythms to known songs or syncopated rhythms to existing pieces. It is generally agreed that the music came from the Midwest, particularly St. Louis and Indianapolis.

Ragtime is significant because it led directly to the development of jazz. It brought Afro-American rhythms into the music culture, creating a truly American musical genre and provided a way for African-American musicians to be accepted into American culture during a particularly difficult time. On the other side, it showed the piano to be a much more versatile instrument than the parlor organ and ultimately expanded the repertoire of the piano, introducing new songs and rhythms while providing a strong, lasting body of work.

Ragtime achieved its greatest fame from 1910 to 1920. Probably the single most important song for ragtime was "Alexander's Ragtime Band," which was really not a ragtime song, but it had "ragtime" in the title and became a major hit in 1911, providing the first major hit for Irving Berlin.

After the heyday of ragtime, the music faded away until a ragtime revival occurred in the 1970s, based on two major events: (1) the New York Public Library issued a two-volume LP of the *Collected Works of Scott Joplin* edited by historian and concert pianist Vera Brodsky Lawrence in 1971 and (2) the adoption of some Scott Joplin rags into the successful movie *The Sting* in 1974.

Scott Joplin

Although no one person single-handedly creates a whole genre of music, and no one place is the singular birthplace for a genre of music, there is usually a person and place where a music coalesces and the various elements of the music are brought together and defined. Often, a person defines a music simply by being the premier player or composer of that music, or a city is linked with a music because a player or several major players emerge from there. Thus, Scott Joplin and St. Louis are linked with ragtime.

Scott Joplin was born on November 24, 1868 on the northeastern border of Texas, an area that later became known as Texarkana. Joplin's father, a violinist, left the family early and his mother, Florence, had to raise a family of seven. Joplin's mother played the banjo and the combination of her singing and playing plantation songs and his father playing waltzes, schottisches, polkas and quadrilles, meant Joplin heard a variety of music in his home.

Since his mother was the caretaker at a Negro church, he "learned firsthand the Negro method of superimposing syncopated patterns on the melodies and changing the words of the hymns sung in church." As a member of the church, Joplin became aware of "folk melodies, the syncopated rhythms, and the repeated choruses, all of which were characteristic of Negro music in the nineteenth century."

Joplin studied piano at home and later entered George R. Smith College for Negroes in Sedalia, Missouri, where he studied harmony and advanced composition. He was also exposed to music in clubs and honky tonks and heard musicians "ragging" songs, or taking existing marches and piano numbers and "jazzing them up," adding syncopated rhythms to alter the tempo, rhythm and timing of a piece.

Joplin played professionally from his early teens and began composing songs for an early group, the Texas Medley Quartette, for which he played piano. Sometime around 1885 he left Texarkana and went to St. Louis, Missouri where he settled in the Chestnut Valley area, known for its cafes, saloons and sporting houses; there Joplin played at the Silver Dollar Saloon. African-American men had three basic choices for an occupation other than manual labor: preacher, teacher, or musician. If you were a professional musician, you most likely played brothels and honky tonks. Of all those occupations, playing music in the red-light district was the most financially lucrative.

Joplin lived in St. Louis for about eight years, although he frequently traveled to other cities, including Louisville and Cincinnati. In 1893, he traveled to Chicago for the World's Fair. Joplin spent two years in Chicago and those were the most formative years for him and his "ragtime" compositions. He played on the outskirts of the Columbian Exposition in the red-light district and met other pianists, including "Plunk" Henry and Johnny Seymour, both from Chicago, who were adept at "ragged time" numbers. Joplin organized his first bands there, probably comprised of clarinet, cornet, tuba and baritone horn.

Joplin formed a lasting friendship with Otis Saunders at that time. Saunders, a rag pianist, became aware of Joplin's genius when he heard him play and encouraged him to write down the compositions he was improvising. Saunders and Joplin left Chicago for St. Louis in 1894 and began playing at the saloon of "Honest" John Turpin, who also encouraged Joplin with his compositions. Joplin and Saunders then went west to Sedalia, Missouri. Sedalia was the home of the George R. Smith College for Negroes, which had a music department, and the publishing firms of John

Stark and A.W. Perry. Joplin entered the College in 1897 where he learned how to "notate the syncopations of rag, something which previously had eluded him."

Sedalia had one of the largest red-light districts in Missouri, a major reason Joplin and Saunders moved there, and Joplin began performing at the Maple Leaf Club. Joplin soon became the most sought-after pianist in the district. Joplin's first important composition, and his first published rag, "The Maple Leaf Rag," is named after this club. It was published in 1898 after publisher John Stark heard him perform it there.

Joplin also published a number of songs during his lifetime that were not ragtime pieces, including marches, waltzes, "coon" songs and songs from the genteel tradition of parlor songs.

Joplin's first two rags, "Original Rag" and "Maple Leaf Rag" were submitted to publisher Carl Hoffman in Kansas City in 1898 but only "Original Rags" was accepted; later Joplin took "Maple Leaf Rag" to A.W. Perry of Sedalia, but it was rejected again. However, in the summer of 1899 John Stark heard "Maple Leaf Rag" at the club and invited Joplin to his music store. They signed a contract on August 10, 1899 for the publication of "Maple Leaf Rag." That was the beginning of a five-year relationship between Joplin and Stark which "catapulted the composer to eventual worldwide fame."

Joplin was not the only composer of ragtime, and was not the first to publish a ragtime piece. That honor belongs to William H. Krell, a white songwriter-bandleader, who published "Mississippi Rag" in January, 1897, and "Harlem Rag," published by African-American composer Tom Turpin, which was published in December, 1897. However, Joplin's "Maple Leaf Rag" was the first ragtime song to become a "hit," eventually gaining recognition nationally as well as in Europe.

Music Publishing and Tin Pan Alley

After the Civil War the music publishing industry continued to grow and there were publishing companies in most major cities. However, at that point (1865) there were only nine cities with a population large enough to be considered "major." They were New York, Philadelphia, Boston, Baltimore, Brooklyn, New Orleans, Cincinnati, St. Louis and Chicago and they were major cities because they had over 100,000 people. Music publishing continued to grow, a direct result of the popularity of American made pianos, which dramatically increased from 25,000 sold in 1866, the year after the Civil War. Chicago was an important city for publishing, dominated by

George Root and the Root & Cady firm, but New York increasingly became the most important city due to its large number of theaters, large number of vaudeville and playhouses, and large number of immigrants.

In the mid-1890s there were 5,000 theaters in 3,500 cities in the United States and they looked to New York for new theater productions. The lure of Broadway was popular enough to lure bookings so New York theater producers obliged by mounting a show in New York and opening on Broadway at a loss, then touring on the road for their profit. Early giants in the field, like George M. Cohan and Victor Herbert, received large incomes from shows they wrote that toured. That was also the best way to popularize a song nationally as performers created a demand for sheet music by singing songs before audiences, then selling the sheet music in the lobby.

Several business trends emerged. First, a theatric trust was formed by six major booking agents in 1896, called the Klew & Erlanger Syndicate, so that individual theater owners relied on those New Yorkers to determine which shows would become popular. That syndicate lasted until 1916, although it received its major competition beginning in 1907 from the Shuberts, who formed a competing trust. The Syndicate booked shows into 700 playhouses around the country. As cities grew after the Civil War (approximately 10 million people lived in cities by 1900) this proved to be a lucrative and growing market.

As publishing companies began to centralize in New York, beginning with T. B. Harms' move there in 1878, they congregated in the theater and variety house district around Union Square at East 14th Street. M. Witmark & Sons began in 1885 and moved to 49-51 West 28th Street between Broadway and Fifth in 1893; other firms soon joined them. That area became known as "Tin Pan Alley," a term originally coined by journalist Monroe H. Rosefeld (who was also a part-time songwriter) after his visit to the Harry Von Tilzer Music Co. when he noted the cacophony of sounds coming from the open windows of the publishing companies with their tinny upright pianos sounded like a "tin pan alley." The term caught on during the 1903-1910 period and came to mean manufactured songs.

In an era where mass production and mass marketing were increasingly important, it is no surprise the music industry was affected. The growth in sheet music and music book sales indicated a heavy demand for new songs, spurred by the popularity of the piano. Too, the importance of vaudeville and musical theater meant songs were constantly needed so publishing companies were set up and songs were generally purchased from songwriters. The songs were then printed and taken to singers and actors by "song pluggers" whose job consisted of persuading singers to sing the songs, thus generating exposure and sales of sheet music.

Song Pluggers

The idea of song promotion, or "song plugging," developed in New York. In 1884 music publisher Willis Woodward offered singers free lead sheets and orchestrations if they agreed to sing his songs in shows or vaudeville performances. Later, he began to pay "advances" to artists in return for exclusive rights to a song. The singer guaranteed performances of the material and then sold sheet music of the song in the theater lobbies afterward. Long songs with many verses were preferred because the audience needed the sheet music in order to learn the lyrics and melody.

By 1900 the song plugging business had developed to an art form. Clever promotions, like hiring someone to sit in the audience and applaud loudly or even singing the song on the street were used but as the 1900s progressed a pattern emerged. First, singers received free copies for lead sheets and orchestrations, their picture on the sheet music, and a royalty for selling the music. They often received writing credit for the songs. This was the first type of "payola" in the music industry--song pluggers offering singers money, goods, or a financial interest in a song in order to promote it. The reason was simple: without a singer performing the song in a major venue, it had little, if any, chance to become popular. Soon, the practice got out of hand, with singers increasing their demands while publishers, feeling they were forced to pay, saw their resources and profits drained. That led to several efforts by the Music Publishers Protection Association to stop this "payola"; however, those efforts failed because everyone would not abide by the rules. Publishers felt they had to have an "edge" so they continued to supply singers with money in order to have their songs performed.

Woolworth's

The retail outlet where most consumers bought printed music was the "five and dime cent store." The "Five and Dime" had its origins in five-cent counters set up in retail stores where a traveling salesmen left surplus stock and hoped he would not have to come back and pick it up. In 1877, Frank. W. Woolworth began clerking at a dry-goods store in Watertown, New York. Impressed by the amount of business the five cent counter did, he opened his own five-cent store in 1879 in Lancaster, Pennsylvania. Success followed and he developed a small chain which eventually by-passed the middleman and bought directly from manufacturers in such large quantities that he received huge discounts, thus keeping his own prices low.

Woolworth merged his stores with some competitors in 1911 and created a chain of 600 five-and-ten cent stores in the United States, Canada and Europe. Woolworth had known of the power of music to bring people into stores so he began selling sheet music at a special counter. By getting the wholesale price reduced to six cents, Woolworth was selling 150 million pieces of sheet music a year by 1913, retailing them for a dime, which soon became the standard price for all popular sheet music, except for those of Irving Berlin, whose popularity and power was so strong that his music always sold for 30 cents.

Success bred problems; by 1906 performers were asking for more money and the amount of free copies demanded had cut into profits. Prices for sheet music were down, a result of the success of the "five and dime" format pioneered by F.W. Woolworth, and a number of new companies were formed in New York, increasing competition from established firms. Still, publishing overall continued to grow: in 1900 there was $2.2 million in sheet music sales, in 1904 there was $4.1 million and in 1906 there was $6 million. In 1906, the theater was responsible for contributing about $200 million to the national economy. Most of that money originated in Tin Pan Alley where the songs were produced and a good amount ended up there as publishing companies reaped profits from the song business.

Irving Berlin

The songwriter who is most representative of Tin Pan Alley is Irving Berlin. Composer George Gershwin once stated "Irving Berlin IS American music," biographer Lawrence Bergreen called him "Tin Pan Alley incarnate" while Alex Wilder, author of *American Popular Song* stated. "He is the best all-around, over-all song writer America has ever had" and concluded that "only one composer as the master of the entire range of popular song-- Irving Berlin."

Not since Stephen Foster had a songwriter had such an impact on American culture and, fittingly, Foster was Berlin's musical hero and he kept a picture of Foster in his office throughout his career.

Irving Berlin was born Israel Baline on May 11, 1888, in Mohilev, Russia, about 25 miles east of Minsk. He claimed to have only one memory of his homeland: laying on a blanket by the side of a road and watching his house burn down. That was a period of Russian persecution of Jews, who had to flee in order to survive. That was the story of the Balines, who came to the United States in September, 1893. Moses and Lena Baline brought their six children and eight pieces of luggage and when they disembarked from the ship at Ellis Island they were met by relatives, who took them to the Lower East Side in New York. New York City's population had swelled with recently arrived immigrants until the city was three-fourths immigrants at the time the Balines arrived. In addition to Russian Jews there were also Irish and German immigrants.

Moses Baline was a cantor, or song leader for Jewish services, who survived in the new world by menial jobs. The parents never learned to speak English and Moses died in 1901 when young Israel, the youngest of the six children, was thirteen.

The family lived in poverty on Cherry Street in a largely Jewish immigrant neighborhood but Israel, or Izzy as he was called, was determined to assimilate into the American mainstream. He left home and began singing as a "busker," a singer who sang on the streets or in saloons while patrons tossed coins. He went from saloon to saloon in the Bowery and for several years "music was his sole source of income and independence, and he learned to gauge the kind of songs that would appeal to his disparate and indifferent audiences, for his survival depended on their approval."

In 1902 he landed a role in the chorus of a musical, *The Show Girl*. He continued as a busker but soon applied for a job as song plugger at Harry Von Tilzer's firm. Von Tilzer's office was at 42 West 28th Avenue in the heart of "Tin Pan Alley" and the publisher hired Baline to go to Tony Pastor's music hall and applaud loudly when songs by the publisher were sung. That was Baline's first exposure to vaudeville.

Izzy Baline continued to scrape by and landed a job as a singing waiter at the Pelham Cafe on Pell Street, called "Nigger Mike's" after owner Mike Salter. There he wrote his first song, "Marie From Sunny Italy" in order to attract publicity to the Cafe; another cafe had produced a modest hit so Salter encouraged Baline to try his hand. Baline wrote the lyrics while the piano player, Mike Nicholson, wrote the music. Baline was singing parodies of hit songs at the Pelham and had become more of a strolling singer than a waiter by this time. The song was published by Joseph W. Stern and became the first song published for the young singer, who gave his name as "I. Berlin" for the lyrics.

In 1908 Berlin landed a job as a singing waiter at Jimmy Kelly's at 14th St. and Union Square and continued to write songs. He was described as someone who "radiated nervous energy; he was as high strung as a whippet, teeming with plans, schemes, hunches, and notions--all related to the music business. And he was eager to ingratiate himself with whomever he thought might help him achieve his goals. He was willing to talk with anyone, consider any idea, but he made up his mind in a flash, and once he did, could rarely be dissuaded."

Berlin wrote the lyrics for "She Was a Dear Little Girl" which appeared in the show *The Boys and Bett*. The song was "interpolated," which meant it was not in the original score; however, singers regularly added songs to a show in order to beef up their parts or pick up slow sections in a show. A number of songwriters got their start with those "interpolations" and publishers put money and energy into getting one of their songs into a successful show. Berlin continued to write songs and with his composition, "Dorando," managed to write both words and music. Composing music was a problem because Berlin could neither read nor write music and could only play on the black keys (the key of F#) on the piano. The first problem was solved by musical secretaries, who wrote down the songs as Berlin sung them; he employed a musical secretary his entire life. The second problem was solved with a mechanical device popular on Tin Pan Alley pianos. The device was a lever beneath the piano keys which allowed the song to be heard in any key while the songwriter played in a different key.

Berlin's next hit, "Sadie Salome, Go Home" became a hit for the publishing company of Waterson and Snyder and led to Berlin receiving a contract as staff lyricist. A dedicated, hard worker, Berlin worked at night, generally between 8 p.m. and 3 or 4 in the morning, and set himself a goal of writing four to five songs each night. Later, after he was successful, his business partner noted that Berlin regularly wrote a song a day. He also scrutinized his songs and rendered harsh judgments on them.

Berlin wrote many songs that were not published but always kept those "trunk" songs in mind and returned to them to re-write or obtain ideas for new songs or use later when an opportunity presented itself. Berlin also "haunted the vaudeville and burlesque theaters in search of singers he thought could benefit from his material, and he would approach them backstage after their acts to discuss business or, if necessary buy them a drink."

Irving Berlin continued his string of successes as a songwriter in the rough and tumble world of Tin Pan Alley: in 1909 he wrote lyrics for over 24 published songs and in 1910 had over 30 titles published, mostly as a lyricist. He began to write music as well as lyrics and in 1911 had over 40 songs published, mostly as composer and lyricist. In 1911 the Ziegfeld Follies used four of his songs and that same year Berlin became a partner in his publishing firm, which was renamed Waterson, Berlin & Snyder.

The year 1911 would be known as the year of Irving Berlin's first huge hit, "Alexander's Ragtime Band." That song defied the rule of popular music with its 32 bar chorus, the change in key between the verse and chorus (from C to F) and its success was equally astounding; by the end of the year it had sold over one million copies of sheet music and was on its way towards becoming a major hit in Europe.

Prior to "Alexander's Ragtime Band," the general way for hits to emerge from Tin Pan Alley was for them to succeed in a Broadway revue or in the cafes, slowly spread to the streets and bars of New York, then receive national exposure with a touring company. "Alexander's Ragtime Band" altered this trend; it first appeared in the revue *The Merry Whirl*, which opened on May 30, 1910, and was the hit of the show. The following summer, it became a national phenomena almost overnight through sheet music sales.

The song was actually a coon song; the name "Alexander" connoted a Zip Coon like character who assumed a grand name bigger than himself. The term "ragtime" was a misnomer; it was not a ragtime song by any stretch of the imagination, but used the term, which had come to mean any up tempo or syncopated song, especially those connected with African-American music. The song overcame all of those limitations and established the word "ragtime" as an acceptable, middle-class term while the coon song elements were soon lost or buried.

That song established Berlin as the quintessential Tin Pan Alley composer in the public mind, although it colored his view of the music industry for the rest of his career because, "To Irving, it would always be the summer of 1911 on Tin Pan Alley and 'Alexander's Ragtime Band' was just beginning to take the country by storm."

Irving Berlin was a small man, standing five foot six inches and weighing less than 125 pounds; he developed a schedule of working all night, sleeping in the mornings, then spending the afternoons selling and promoting his songs. His life was marred by personal tragedy when his wife contacted typhoid fever on their honeymoon in Cuba and died less than five months after their wedding day. Berlin remained single twelve years before he married again. The only song the songwriter ever admitted was autobiographical, "When I Lost You" was written during that period; it was his first ballad and sold a million copies of sheet music.

Berlin was heavily involved with Tin Pan Alley as a publisher as well as a songwriter and often edited songs from other writers, not taking any credit. Publishers at that time wholesaled their sheet music at six and a half cents a copy and paid a one cent royalty each to the composer and lyricist.

One of the reasons Berlin insisted his songs be composed solely by himself was that he could collect twice as much money.

Publishers made three to five cents per copy of sheet music sold but had huge overheads. Large publishing companies had offices in a half dozen cities to promote their songs, a staff of two to three in each branch office, and a staff of eight or nine piano players in their home office as well as a number of song pluggers and song boosters. Publishers had to pay singers to perform their songs; the singer received his own sheet music free, had his picture on the sheet music, and took a royalty percentage from sales. If a singer was especially popular he or she also received songwriting credit, even though they had written nothing. By the beginning of World War I, a publisher had to sell 500,000-600,000 copies of a song in order to break even.

Publishers earned the majority of their money from sheet music sales and some from piano rolls but hardly anything from the sale of recordings until after 1910.

The Castles and James Reese Europe

At the beginning of the twentieth century the idea of European dances still dominated. Those dances, such as the waltz, had strict and intricate steps, moved from the feet upwards and music was specifically written for those dances. The dances themselves were cultured, refined and difficult; lessons were necessary and even then few could master them, but in the first ten years of the twentieth century a new kind of dance emerged. Rooted in black culture, those dances came as a reaction to music and the movement of the dancers began with the hips. Those new dances scandalized most Americans.

With names like "Funky Butt," "Turkey Trot," "Bunny Hug," "Kangaroo Dip," "Monkey Glide" and "Grizzly Bear" they have often been called "animal" dances because they aroused animal passions. Those dances were an extension of the "Cakewalk" on plantations and in minstrel shows and were more spontaneous and less rigid than European dances and appealed to the informality and improvisation of Americans.

From 1911 until World War I a dancing craze swept the nation, led by Irene and Vernon Castle, a handsome, athletic couple, whose style was a combination of the "animal" dances with European elegance. Vernon Castle was an elegant, graceful man and his ability to subdue the raw emotions of the African-American dances made him a star. Castle used a number of black dances as the basis for his steps and black bandleader James Reese Europe coached Castle on those steps.

The Castles danced to Europe's band, the Syncopated Dance Orchestra, a group of black and Puerto Rican musicians, and created a dance mania in America. The dance craze led to a new kind of band--a large dance band that was an extension of the military band and included stringed instruments in addition to horns. Europe's band had eighteen pieces, although most bands had ten players. The line-up was usually cornet, trombone, two saxophones, a piano, two banjos, drums, a violin and double bass. Smaller bands had two brass instruments, two saxophones and a rhythm section comprised of a piano, banjo and drums.

During the dance craze of 1912-14, led by Vernon and Irene Castle, Berlin wrote "Everybody's Doin' It Now," which became the standard dance song of the era. He put Tin Pan Alley on Broadway with the musical *Watch Your Step*, which starred the Castles, with the book written by Harry B. Smith. The show opened in December, 1914 and was a huge success. Berlin composed a score that included "Minstrel Parade," "I'm a Dancing Teacher Now," "Show Us How to Do the Fox Trot," "Let's Settle Down in a One-Horse Town" and "Ragtime Opera Melody." That same year he opened his own publishing company, Irving Berlin, Inc. at 1571 Broadway.

The Castles operated dancing schools, wrote a popular book about dancing, and were signed as recording artists for Victor Records, backed by the Syncopated Society Orchestra, led by James Reese Europe.

James Reese Europe moved to New York from Alabama in 1906 and directed several all-black stage shows. He also produced concerts of Negro Music, including a Carnegie Hall concert in 1912 that featured 145 black musicians in an orchestra. The Castles and Europe began working together after the dancing couple returned from Paris in 1912. The Syncopated Orchestra became the first black band to be signed to a recording company (Victor) and they enjoyed success with the Castles until 1917.

Al Jolson

The greatest entertainer of that period, Al Jolson, came out of vaudeville and his image remained linked with vaudeville even after he became a star in movies and on records.

Al Jolson came to the United States from Lithuania when he was seven years old. A Russian Jew, he arrived at Ellis Island on April 9, 1894, and the family was greeted by his father, Rabbi Mosche Reuben Yoelson, who was a cantor at the Talmud Torah Congregation in Washington D.C. Born Asa Yoelson on May 26, 1886, the fifth child in the family, young Asa was his mother, Naomi's "favorite" and was devastated by her death on February

6, 1895 when he was eight, less than a year after they arrived. He never got over her death. Jolson's biographer states that "audience was a replacement for Naomi."

In Washington, D.C., young Asa and his brother, Hirsch, discovered the theater and watched entranced as vaudeville performers weaved their magic. Asa and Hirsch Americanized their names to Al and Harry Joelson and became street entertainers in 1896, singing songs such as "Sweet Marie," "The Sidewalks of New York," "When You and I Were Young, Maggie," "Oh Dem Golden Slippers," "Listen to the Mocking Bird" and Stephen Foster songs. In 1900 the brothers went to New York to attempt to break into show business where Jolson finally landed a job as a "stooge" for Agnes Behler in the Victoria Burlesquers. Jolson sat in the audience until Miss Behler sang "My Jersey Lillie," then he stood and joined her on the chorus to generate excitement from the audience.

Joelson teamed with Frederick Ernest Moore to create an "illustrated singing act" in 1901. Those acts sang songs while slides were projected to illustrate the song (a forerunner to videos years later) and the two performed in a burlesque show which toured the country, beginning in Chicago and then working back east to New York. Here, Jolson "learned all the fundamentals needed to become a 'pro'--the proper way to come onstage; the proper way to exit; how to take applause; how to end a song so that the audience applauded."

In New York Jolson struggled, busking in East Side restaurants, working with his brother Harry to sell song books from the Charles K. Harris Company, and renting a rehearsal room at the Harry von Tilzer Music Company where they could "run into" bookers, agents, and others who might help them get started. With Joe Harris, the two brothers developed an act based on a comedy sketch written by Ren Shields. Previously, Al had been a straight man, but in this sketch he was cast as a comedian, which provided an essential change for him. The act appeared with a blackface monologist named James Francis Dooley, who suggested to Al that he perform his role in blackface. He told the young Jolson that wearing burnt cork "was like wearing a mask. You looked, and *felt*, like a performer." Al Jolson remained a blackface performer his entire life.

That experience provided a critical change for the Joelson brothers. They appeared as "Joelson, Palmer and Joelson" and went to have cards printed but their names would not fit on the cards with the chosen design. The printer suggested the brothers drop the "e" and become "Jolson," which they did. Out of Joelson, Palmer and Joelson came "Al Jolson" the blackface entertainer who was a stage comedian. Jolson was known more as a comedian than a singer until his appearance in the movie *The Jazz Singer*.

A disagreement between the brothers resulted in Harry leaving the act, which Al and Palmer revamped to become "The Hebrew and the Coon."

Vaudeville was controlled by the United Booking Office, formed by 25 men under the direction of B. F. Keith and E. A. Albee in 1906. William Morris opposed the trust and tried to form an opposition circuit; Jolson signed with Morris and when the Morris circuit folded, Jolson was blacklisted by the UBO affiliates, which controlled big time vaudeville. Jolson then left New York for the west coast where he performed on the Sullivan and Considine circuit. There he began performing as a single act and on October 1, 1906 opened at the National Theater in San Francisco and worked around California the following four months.

In 1908, Jolson was twenty-one years old and the "golden boy" of the Sullivan and Considine Circuit. He wanted to play the Keith and Orpheum Circuits, the really big time vaudeville circuits, but because of the blacklist imposed as a strong arm tactic by Keith, Albee and other members of the UBO, he could not break in. Jolson decided to gamble and gave up his lucrative single act and signed with Lew Dockstader's Minstrels, who were not blacklisted. On their opening performance in August, 1908, reviewer Sime Silverman singled out Jolson in his review in *Variety* and Jolson finally appeared before a New York audience in February, 1909, when Dockstader's Minstrels appeared there. Jolson impressed both crowds and reviewers and was approached by Arthur Klein, the booking agent of vaudeville theater owner Percy G. Williams, one of the major powers in the UBO. Klein offered Jolson a deal: he would book the entertainer in the biggest theaters in New York if he became his manager and received ten percent of Jolson's income. Jolson agreed and the two signed a contract. Klein secured a four week booking which, in effect, ended the blacklist.

Jolson opened a solo booking on July 19, 1909, but had to return to Dockstader, who had acquired new booking agents, the Shubert brothers. The Shuberts, Lee and Jake (or "J. J." as he was listed) were ruthless, driven entrepreneurs who signed Dockstader with an eye on Jolson. The Shuberts were carving out their empire and had established a rival (and hostile) organization from the Theater Syndicate, originally organized in 1896, which controlled the bookings of musical theater shows outside New York.

In December, 1909, Dockstader was persuaded to give Jolson his release from the show and in January, 1910, Jolson debuted at the Hammerstein's Victoria in New York singing a Harry Van Tilzer song, "Hip Hip Hypnotize Me." He performed in eastern vaudeville for the next five months and in March, 1911, opened at the Winter Garden, the theater owned by the Shuberts at Seventh Avenue and Fiftieth Street that Jolson would always be identified with. Jolson first appeared in *The Musical Review of 1911* which featured about 100 performers in a mammoth show. There he sang "That Lovin' Traumerei" and, despite a show that was too long with numerous other distractions, managed to become the star of the evening; he was now twenty-five years old.

During his period at the Winter Garden, another key element in the Jolson legend emerged when a runway was constructed down the center aisle of the theater which Jolson used to advance into the audience. He also recorded a number of sides for Victor during the 1911-1914 period.

In 1913 Jolson split from Arthur Klein after a power play engineered by the Shuberts. After the split, Jolson signed with the Shuberts for a $10,000 signing bonus, $1,000 a week for 35 weeks a year, and ten percent of the profits for each show he appeared in. He became nationally famous when the Shuberts sent him on a national tour with the musical, *The Honeymoon Express*. He was twenty-seven, the king of the Winter Garden, and had begun another trademark, dropping to one knee while he sang, which he adapted after watching Blossom Seeley do it in her performance. He became "the most popular musical comedy performer in the country" through songs such as "Tennessee, I Hear You Calling Me," "I'm Seeking for Siegfried," "When I Leave the World Behind," "Sister Susie's Sewing Shirts for Soldiers," and "Bring Along Your Dancing Shoes."

When Jolson returned to New York he began rehearsals for *Robinson Crusoe, Jr.*, which marked the first of a series of starring vehicles for Jolson that included *Sinbad*, *Bombo*, and *Big Boy*. In *Robinson Crusoe, Jr.* Jolson's hit songs were "Yaaka Hula Hickey Dula" and "Where Did Robinson Crusoe Go With Friday on Saturday Night." That led to a 15 month tour which began in August, 1916, and featured his name billed above the title of the show for the first time.

Jolson loved to tour and perform in front of audiences and biographer Herbert Goldman noted he "would tour more often, and more willingly, than any other star in the American musical theater. The more one-night stands he played, the better Jolson liked it." Beginning in January, 1917, in Chicago he was billed as "The World's Greatest Entertainer."

George M. Cohan

The most successful composer of Broadway musicals before World War I was George M. Cohan, who's importance to Broadway is acknowledged today by the statue of him in Times Square in New York.

Cohan was born July 3, 1878 in Providence, Rhode Island. He wrote 22 musicals, including *Little Johnny Jones* (1903); *Forty-Five Minutes from Broadway* (1906); *George Washington, Jr.* (1906); *Fifty Miles from Boston* (1908); *Little Nelly Kelly* (1922); and *Ah! Wilderness* (1933). Later, he was the subject of the 1942 movie *Yankee Doodle Dandy*.

Cohan's hit songs include standards such as "Give My Regards to Broadway" (1905), "Harrigan" (1907), "If I'm Gonna Die, I'm Goin' to Have Some Fun" (1907), "Over There" (1917), and "You're a Grand Old Flag" (1906).

The 1909 Copyright Law

Two events in the early 20th century affected the music industry for the rest of the century: the 1909 Copyright Act and the formation of the American Society of Composers, Authors, and Publishers (ASCAP), the first performing rights organization, organized to collect monies for publishers and songwriters from public performances of their works.

The United States had instituted its first Copyright Act in 1790, basing its statute on British copyright law. In the late nineteenth century there was a movement by music publishers to revise and upgrade the Copyright Act and in 1889 a statue was passed guaranteeing performance rights.

The late nineteenth and early twentieth century was a period of reform and "trust-busting" in America and the 1909 Revised Copyright Act reflected that movement. It was an attempt to break a publisher's trust that controlled most of the popular sheet music sales and licensing to a single piano roll manufacturer. The idea that one firm controlled so many piano rolls brought cries of "monopoly" to the ears of President Theodore Roosevelt and in his attempts to reform business in America, he signed the 1909 Copyright Act to bust that trust. That act fixed a fee of two cents per "reproduction," the first time "musical reproductions" were addressed in a Copyright Law. However, it wasn't the reproduction of music on recordings that Congress was addressing--although that would be the primary means of musical reproduction throughout the 20th century--but the musical reproduction created by pianola manufacturers when they put songs on piano rolls to play in player pianos.

Mechanicals

The "player piano" was created by Edwin Votey in 1902. The piano "played" by inserting interchangeable rolls of paper—piano rolls--that had small holes. Powered by suction, the piano played a song as the paper was pulled through. The first devices stood in front of a piano but later versions saw the device enclosed within the piano. In 1898 the Wurlitzer Company of Cincinnati developed a coin-operated player piano.

The major problem with piano roll production was brought on by the music publishers themselves. James F. Bowers, president of the Music Publishers Association since its inception in 1895, had persuaded eighty-seven publishers to sign exclusive agreements with Aeloian for the exclusive rights to cut piano roles in exchange for a guaranteed royalty of 10 percent of retail price.

The Copyright Act was the last statute signed by Roosevelt as President--he signed it on the morning of the inauguration of William Howard Taft--and ended up benefiting Aeolian by reducing the amount they had to pay publishers. That meant that Aeolian continued to dominate the piano roll business, which grew from 45,414 piano-roll playing pianos in 1909 to 208,541 in its peak year of 1919.

Pianos had become a part of middle class homes, as well as being popular in saloons and other places of entertainment. After 1910 coin-operated automatic pianos were established in penny arcades, billiard parlors and other public places of entertainment; they soon replaced the nickel-in-the-slot phonographs and peep-shows. In 1916, Aeolian introduced a "word roll" for its player piano where lyrics of popular songs were printed on the margins.

Sales of Pianolas reached their peak in 1920 and throughout the 1920s annual sales averaged 200,000 units, or more than half of all pianos manufactured and sold. The money collected from piano rolls was called "mechanicals" because it was a mechanical device. As the market for the sales of records developed, the money collected by publishers from those sales (two cents a copy) was called "mechanicals," a term still in use today to define the money earned by songwriters and publishers from the sales of recordings.

The Formation of ASCAP

Publishers banded together to form the Music Publishers Association as an offshoot of the Board of Music Trade, a trust formed in 1855 to impose a standard uniform price for sheet music. There were problems within the organization, to a large extent because it was more intent on publishing European songs than promoting American copyrights. The reason was simple: European songs did not have international copyright protection so American publishers could publish them without paying royalties; throughout the nineteenth century 70 percent of sheet music business came from European songs.

Music publishers wanted more protection and more money. A number of publishers wanted to stop payments to singers for sales of sheet music and wanted to raise the wholesale price of sheet music to ten cents. In October, 1913, a number of songwriters--including Victor Herbert, Glen McDonaugh, Gustave Kerker, Louis Hirsch, Silvio Hein, and Raymond Hubbell--and their publisher, Isidore Witmark, met to discuss forming an organization.

A performance rights organization was first organized in France in 1911. The French Societe des Auteurs, Compositeurs et Editeurs de Musique opened a New York office to collect money from theatrical producers and concert managers on all French songs performed in the United States. Some American songwriters, including Irving Berlin, joined the organization but were dissatisfied with the distribution of monies.

In January, 1914, the American Society of Composers, Authors and Publishers was formed, with George Maxwell elected the first president. They announced they would collect monies for songwriters and publishers from theater orchestras, cabarets and phonograph records for distribution to their members. In July, 1914, a new Music Publishers' Board of Trade was formed with one of its central tenants the stopping of payments to singers.

ASCAP had a difficult time during its early days. Although their fees were relatively modest ($5-15 monthly). A number of cabarets and hotels refused to sign agreements and some even pushed the head of the musician's union to not allow any of their members to play ASCAP songs. A number of old melodies were then adapted for new dances.

An early court case assured the success of ASCAP and future performing rights organizations. In the spring of 1915, attorney Nathan Burkan, counsel to the Music Publishers' Board of Trade, filed suit against Shanely's Broadway restaurant claiming the show *Sweethearts* featured the performance of a song, "Sweethearts," which was published by G. Shirmer and for which the cabaret did not pay to use. A lower court ruled for the cabaret but the Supreme Court reversed that decision and, in a monumental opinion, Justice Oliver Wendall Holmes wrote "If music did not pay, it would be given up. If it pays, it pays out of the public's pocket. Whether it pays or not, the purpose of employing it is for profit, and that is enough." It was then assured that users of music would have to pay for its use.

Tin Pan Alley songwriters and publishers at first were wary of ASCAP, perceiving it as a union and therefore restrictive. They had been used to fighting it out, every man for himself, and did not trust an organization that wanted to collect money for them and distribute it. Irving Berlin did not like ASCAP during the early years and only converted when it began to collect large sums from radio airplay for him. Berlin resisted innovation in general; he learned the old rules of Tin Pan Alley and became good at playing them; he spoke out against ASCAP, recordings and radio as each appeared. He would accept each only when it was proven that he could make money in the new medium, although he was never truly comfortable with anything outside his Tin Pan Alley world.

From the latter half of the nineteenth to the first part of the twentieth century, music publishing dominated the music industry, but things were changing. Technology played a large part in changing the industry; the invention of the movie camera, the development of the disc and then electrical recording, and the development of radio all occurred. The business was also changing: the development of two major labels--Victor and Columbia—took advantage of the increased demand for phonographs and recordings. The development of radio networks, the creation and development of the movie industry, and the decline of vaudeville all caused music publishers to lose much of the power they held between 1900 and 1920, but for this period, publishers and songwriters reigned as kings in the music industry.

In 1909 the phonograph industry emerged as a major power, selling over 27 million records and cylinders with a wholesale value of about $12 million. The phonograph industry achieved much of its sales success from furniture stores because people viewed the early phonograph as a piece of furniture. Just before World War I, most of the original talking machine patents began to expire, allowing a number of new companies to enter the recording industry.

The Movies

The movie industry began with the invention of Thomas Edison's Vitascope. The machine was actually the product of the efforts of William K. L. Dickson, a laboratory assistant for Edison, who took Edison's ideas and early efforts and refined them. Using the technology of flexible film developed by George Eastman for his Kodak camera, Dickson developed the moving picture camera.

The Vitascope, as it was called, had its patent filed in August, 1891. Sound was supplied by a phonograph cylinder, which was synchronized with the film.

Edison did not take out a foreign patent on his new invention--he felt the $150 was too much--and so entrepreneurs in England and the Continent developed the movie camera further. In 1893 Edison built the first movie studio in West Orange, New Jersey. It consisted of a fully covered stage and was called the "Black Maria."

The first ten machines from Edison's factory were installed in a Kinetoscope Parlor in New York in 1894 where, for a penny, people could view a short reel. Soon there were penny arcades established in other cities; they consisted of a row of kinetoscopes along with other coin-in-the-slot machines for listening. The first movies were rather simple: a man sneezing, some dancing girls, Buffalo Bill shooting, a tooth being extracted, a kissing couple, and slapstick comedy.

Edison did not see the commercial potential of movies. He felt the novelty would soon wear off, so he did not develop it further. Again, it was Edison's predilection to look to the business world as the major market and denigrated the idea of entertainment for his patents.

Like the telephone, Edison thought the movie industry would be organized with a single company controlling the hardware with the software licensed or locally produced. He did not sell his early cameras but sold the movies outright. By the summer of 1896, two Keith vaudeville theaters were showing movies as part of their vaudeville shows, in between dancers, singers, and other acts.

The first movie with a story was *The Great Train Robbery*, produced in 1903 in New Jersey and, essentially a cowboy movie. The first theater for movies was opened by the Warner brothers in McKeesport, Pennsylvania in 1905. Called a "Nickelodeon," it thrived and within two years there were 5,000 such establishments in the country.

Early Warner Brothers Studio

In 1887, the Warner family sailed from Poland to Baltimore, Maryland, then moved on to Youngstown, Ohio. There were a dozen children, but four of them--Harry, Abe, Sam and Jack-- became the "Warner Brothers" who created the company named after them.

In 1904 they bought a "Kinetoscope," or movie projector, and rented the Dome Picture Palace. Harry, the eldest, was the business head while Abe sold tickets (at a nickel each) and Sam ran the projector. Jack, the youngest brother, sang at the end of the screening, serving as a "chaser," or an act that signaled the end of the show and thus "chase" the sitting audience out so the next audience could come in.

The Warner Feature Film Company began making movies and by 1918, Sam and Jack were in Los Angeles. Harry Warner, in New York, incorporated Warner Brothers Pictures in 1923 and sold 40 percent of the stock to the public, keeping 60 percent for the brothers. Warner Brothers began cranking out silent movies; their first hit was *My Four Years in Germany*, which grossed $1.5 million.

The first star for Warner Brothers was a dog, "Rin Tin Tin," who starred in a number of pictures. The company began to expand in 1925 when Harry Warner bought Vitagraph, a movie company based in Brooklyn . The acquisition of Vitagraph meant the company now had a library of films and 50 distributors.

The fledgling movie industry sought to unite and in 1908 the Motion Picture Patents Company was formed with membership consisting of Edison, American Biograph, Kalem, Lubin, Selig, the Essanay Company and Pathe Freres and George Melies et Cie of Paris. Soon independents like William Fox, Harry and Jack Warner and Adolph Zuker began making their own movies.

The early movies appealed to the large immigrant population because they were silent and many immigrants could not speak English. Their success was helped by the fact that many American were moving out of rural areas into cities at the beginning of the century.

The earliest movies were only 15-20 minutes long, and were often supplemented by lectures or song slides--a series of slides shown while music played, usually in vaudeville theaters as another act. However, by the middle and late teens, feature length pictures were produced and cinemas built for movies began to replace the nickelodeons. Some of those new cinemas, like the Capitol Theater in New York, seated 5,300 and had carpeted floors, upholstered seats and uniformed ushers.

Southern California appealed to independent movie makers because it was a long way from New York, home of the Motion Picture Patents Company, that wanted to enforce its monopoly on the various film-making patents. A number of Trust members, including Selig, Biograph and Vitagraph, were all attracted to Southern California because of the climate and variety of settings nearby--deserts, mountains, villages, and seaside. The cost of labor was much lower in Los Angeles than in New York and the area was underdeveloped, with cheap land to build on.

Hollywood

What became "Hollywood" started as a 120-acre ranch by that name, registered in 1887 by Harvey Henderson Wilcox; in 1903 it was incorporated as a municipality and the Hollywood Hotel was built. In 1907 director Francis Boggs filmed scenes for *The Count of Monte Cristo* for the Selig Company and the next year Colonel Selig constructed a studio in Edendale. The New York Motion Picture Company built a studio in Edendale in 1909, that was occupied by Mack Sennett's Keystone Comedies beginning in 1912 and, later, by Mascot Pictures. In January, 1910 the Biograph Company came to Southern California for filming during the winter; they would do that again the next two winters. At that point, the population of Hollywood was around 5,000.

In 1911 the New York Motion Picture Company built a large studio for filming westerns on an area at the entrance of the Santa Ynez Canyon, four miles north of Santa Monica. This was "The Miller 100 Bison Ranch," which later became known as "Inceville" because producer-director Thomas Ince worked there.

The first major commercially successful film produced in Hollywood was *The Squaw Man*, a western, filmed by the Jesse L. Lasky Feature Play Company in its studio at the corner of Selma and Vine; filming began in December, 1913. In 1916 the studio was enlarged after Lasky merged with Famous Players. Griffith Fine Arts Studio is where D.W. Griffith worked and where he filmed his two successful early features, *The Birth of the Nation* in 1915 and *Intolerance* in 1916.

Universal Studios was opened in 1915 by Carl Laemmle in Universal City in the San Fernando Valley while Thomas Ince built a new studio at Culver City that same year. Also in Culver City, Harold Lloyd and Hal Roach opened the Rolin Film Company in 1916. That same year William Fox purchased the Selig studio in Edendale, Metro rented its first Hollywood studio, and Mutual opened its "Lone Star" studio at 1025 Lillian Way for Charlie Chaplin's films.

In 1917 the Fox Film Corporation moved into a studio at Sunset and Western Avenue, Metro took over Mutual's "Lone Star" studio, and Charlie Chaplin built a new studio at the corner of Sunset and La Charles. In 1918, Producer Louis B. Meyer moved to California, used the Selig studio, then built his own studio. The following year, Thomas Ince built a studio in Culver City while Douglas Fairbanks became the first movie star to move into a home in Beverly Hills in a house called Greyhall, where the plans for

United Artists were made. By that time, the population of Hollywood had grown to 35,000.

The first movie blockbuster was *The Birth of a Nation*, which cost $2 to see. It opened in New York on March 3, 1915, and eventually reaped a profit of $50 million. Based on a novel, *The Clansman* by Thomas Dixon about the South after the Civil War and directed by D. W. Griffith, that movie is what brought the movie industry from a group of fledgling entrepreneurs to maturity. After this, the movie business was a major player in the entertainment world.

In 1914 over 16 million people went to see a movie each day. The movie industry responded by building new movie theaters; there were 30,000 by 1914. By the time the movie makers had produced *The Birth of a Nation* the movie industry had its basic infrastructure of movie theaters and an audience willing to watch movies to take its place as an entertainment medium for middle Americans. After 1916, 35 million Americans went to movie theaters at least once a week. The movie industry was now set to challenge E.F. Albee's vaudeville monopoly for the hearts, minds and money of middle Americans who wanted to be entertained.

The Electrification of America Before World War I

The electrification of the United States began in the 1880s and by World War I all the major cities had been "electrified." New York was the first to have a "Great White Way" when Broadway was lit by electric signs during the 1890s; those "Great White Ways" were soon an integral part of every American city. In 1905 the Times Building in New York was lit by a giant ball that dropped on New Year's Eve to symbolize the beginning of the new year, a tradition that was first witnessed by those present, then heard on radio by the nation and finally witnessed by TV viewers all over the world. New York was a leader in American electrification, and the entertainment industry--particularly the theaters, playhouses and clubs along Broadway-- benefited from those lights and gave value to New York, which became the recognized center for entertainment while the "Broadway show" became a symbol of glamour and cultural sophistication.

The first stage of electrification, roughly 1885 to 1910, lit wealthy homes, theaters, hotels, department stores and clubs and presented an image of glamour, prestige and power. Many of those places had to have their own private generating power. Private, middle-class homes did not become electrified to any great extent until after 1910 and the large growth in the number of electrically wired homes did not occur until after World War

I, but the entertainment industry used electricity from the beginning until lights became a symbol of the glamour of show biz.

This electrification of America led to cities becoming centers for culture and entertainment. Electricity made possible street trolleys, which allowed people to live outside a city, in the suburbs, while still remaining linked to the city. The trolley companies built tracks outside a city which led to an amusement park in order to entice riders during non-rush hours of the day and on weekends, and thus increased their ridership and profits. Those amusement parks became centers for entertainment with their brass bands and vaudeville shows but began to change the central American ethic from production to consumerism. In *Electrifying America* author David E. Nyes states that the amusement parks "temporarily overturned and wrote the social order. It inverted central values of American society--thrift, sobriety, restraint, order, and work--and exploited technology for pleasure. It temporarily overcame the separation between social classes, ethnic tensions, the differences between country and city, and the segmentation of the city itself into suburbs. It transformed the public into a crowd to be manipulated into spending money for momentary pleasures and gaudy visions of self-transformation. It was among the first institutions to make a sustained use of advertising and publicity as an integral part of success."

In New York, Coney Island became the first nationally famous amusement park, fully established by the turn of the century.

In 1910 over half the population in the United States lived in rural areas but the change from being a rural nation to an urban nation was under way; the 1890-1902 period saw a huge expansion of cities, made possible partly by the electric trolley because it made distances easier to travel, allowed a city to expand beyond walking distance and still remain a central city while creating the modern day suburb. While this expanded in all cities, New York saw huge growth as the Bronx received a large influx of new inhabitants.

Electrical transportation into and out of a city cleaned up the city from the smells of animals and imposed an order on city streets. With horses, there were no street lights and chaos generally reigned. Electric streetcars brought in cleanliness and orderliness to transportation as traffic lights and other rules developed to insure an orderly flow of large numbers of people and vehicles.

Shopping was also changed by electricity. Stores were not limited to daylight hours, electric signs attracted customers and advertised wares, and the department store, located in a city with its numerous "departments," the forerunner to the contemporary shopping mall with its numerous shops all under one roof, allowed customers a large choice of goods. That began the heyday for stores like Macy's, Marshall Field, and Jordan Marsh. Mail order firms such as Sears, Roebuck also benefited from the electric streetcars because goods could be shipped to the suburbs on those trolleys.

In 1910 less than five percent of all American homes had electricity, although by this point there were a number of homes with running water and indoor toilets. The first services added were electric lights, followed by irons and vacuum cleaners. Conspicuous consumption through lighted Christmas trees, outdoor Christmas displays, electric toys and novelties were part of this early electrification. As electricity became available to urban dwellers and businesses and factories of the United States began to use electrification in their production, the country changed in a dramatic way, but World War I called a brief halt to progress in this area as the country directed its efforts towards winning "the war to end all wars."

The entertainment industries in the United States could not have developed into our contemporary entertainment industries without the electrification of America.

The Development of Radio

During the summer of 1890 a concert comprised of dance music, and the recitation of a poem, delivered by telephone wire, was broadcast from Madison Square Garden to about 800 people at the Grand Union Hotel in Saratoga, New York. The concert came in on the telephone, where a large funnel-shaped resonator was hooked up to magnify the sound. The term "broadcast" was not used; that term was an agricultural one, used to denote scattering seeds.

In essence, that concert was a telephone call from the concert hall to the hotel ballroom, but the idea of wireless transmission was already taking shape. In the period 1886-1889 in Germany, Heinrich Hertz had conducted experiments that showed the existence of radio waves, called "Hertzian waves." In Italy, during the summer of 1894, a young man, Guglielmo Marconi, read an article about "Hertzian waves" and began a series of experiments on his own. In his experiments, Marconi added an antenna to his set to help send and receive waves; that was a major step towards wireless broadcasting.

Marconi worked with the telegraph, sending wireless messages in Morse Code in the area where he lived. He took his invention to the Italian Minister of Post and Telegraph, who was not interested. Marconi and his mother then went to England (his mother was Irish), where customs officials destroyed his black box because the French President had been killed by an Italian anarchist two years previously, and that contraption looked suspicious. Marconi built another "black box" that contained his wireless telegraph, and demonstrated it to Sir William Preece, chief engineer of telegraphs for the British Post Office system and someone who had conducted his own wireless experiments. Preece was immediately interested and on July 2, 1897 Marconi, backed by a group of British investors, founded the Wireless Telegraph and Signal Company, Ltd, which was later renamed Marconi's Wireless Telegraph Company, Ltd. Guglielmo Marconi was twenty-three years old.

In October, 1899, Marconi came to the United States to demonstrate his wireless telegraph by reporting the America's Cup Races in New York. The British navy was interested in the wireless telegraph because of the problems of ship-to-shore and ship-to-ship communication; the American navy was interested for the same reason.

Marconi arrived in New York City on September 11, 1899; on November 22 the Marconi Wireless Company of America was incorporated, with the controlling interest held in England. The company was established to sell *communication*--not equipment. It installed its equipment on a ship and provided a man to work it and constructed stations on shore so that ships could communicate with land based stations.

The world had grown smaller for the United States by 1899. In 1896 it had won the Spanish-American War, called a "splendid little war" by Secretary of State John Hay, that lasted 111 days. As a result of that war, the United States acquired the territories of Puerto Rico, Guam, and the Philippines and became an imperial power. The war provided two heroes: Theodore Roosevelt, who led his Rough Riders up San Juan Hill and liberated Cuba, and Commodore George Dewey, who defeated the Spanish fleet in Manila Bay. Communicating with such distant areas was a problem; it took three days before the American public knew of Dewey's victory.

Several other inventors were at work on wireless communication. A Canadian, Reginald Aubrey Fessenden, professor of electrical engineering at Western University (later renamed the University of Pittsburgh), was a former employee of Thomas Edison as well as the Westinghouse company. He had experimented with wireless voice transmission and concluded that radio waves should be continuous, rather than a series of bursts, like Marconi's. He contracted with the General Electric plant in Schenectady for an alternating-current generator. Since the regular engineers at General Electric thought the project absurd, they assigned it to Ernst F. W. Alexanderson, a recent immigrant from Sweden. Alexanderson invented an "alternator," the key component in this generator, which allowed it to perform the way Fessenden required.

On Christmas Eve, 1906, the first wireless broadcast of music and the human voice was sent over the waves from Fessenden in Brant Rock, Massachusetts. A violin solo of "O, Holy Night" by Fessenden, a phonograph recording of Handel's "Largo," along with spoken Christmas greetings from Fessenden, were heard by ships as far away as the West Indies. That broadcast led directly to the United Fruit Company purchasing wireless equipment so it could communicate to its ships carrying perishable cargoes into ports as well as provide communication between plantations scattered throughout Latin America.

In 1899 Lee de Forest received his Ph.D. from the Sheffield Scientific School of Yale University; his dissertation was a study of Hertzian waves. De Forest was born in 1873 in Iowa, but grew up in Alabama where his minister father headed Talladega College, a school founded by missionaries after the Civil War to educate freedmen. In 1893 de Forest entered Yale to study science against the wishes of his father, who wanted him to follow in his footsteps and become a minister.

In 1901 De Forest took his wireless machine to New York to demonstrate it; there he met Abraham White, a Wall Street promoter of questionable ethics, and in 1902 the De Forest Wireless Telegraph Company was incorporated and capitalized with a public stock offering. De Forest was an inventor, not a businessman, and he agreed to a salary of $20 a week and some stock in the company. White bought a mansion in Long Island and drove the company into bankruptcy.

De Forest made an important invention during his time with White; in 1905 he added a "grid" to the vacuum tube developed by a British Professor, John Ambrose Fleming. De Forest's grid, or "Audion," as he called it, was patented in 1906 and increased the vacuum tube's effectiveness as a detector and amplifier. That became "one of the key elements on which radio, and the whole electronics industry, were to grow."

Early in 1907 De Forest formed the De Forest Radio Telephone Company and broadcast music on Columbia phonograph records from his laboratory in New York. On January 13, 1910, De Forest engineered the broadcast of a concert by Enrico Caruso, direct from the stage of the Metropolitan Opera. Amateur radio operators and ships heard the broadcast.

Radio excited amateurs all across the country, who built small sets and set about broadcasting and receiving messages. Those amateurs set up in bedrooms, attics and in science laboratories at Universities. The unregulated airwaves created problems for the armed forces, whose messages and communications were "jammed" or, in some cases, the victims of pranks who issued fake orders to naval vessels. Like the computer programmers of the late 20th and early 21st centuries, those amateur radio operators were exploring a new field and making important discoveries; also, like the computer hackers in that future era, they caused problems with the government. That led to the first radio licensing law by Congress, signed by President William Howard Taft in 1912; that remained the law of the land for radio until 1927.

The law required a station license, available upon application from the Secretary of Commerce, for transmission of radio signals, and also required that those transmitting have an operator's license, given on the basis of an examination. Although a number of amateurs obtained licenses (almost 1,000 were issued and by 1917 there were 8,562 licenses), a number of others either ignored the law or were blissfully ignorant of it, and amateur radio experimentation continued.

In 1912 a major event occurred that brought publicity to wireless communication. On Sunday, April 14, at 10:25 p.m., a wireless was received stating that the luxury passenger liner, The Titanic, was sinking in the Atlantic. The messages from the Titanic's wireless alerted the Carpathia, a ship about 58 miles away, to travel three and a half hours to rescue the survivors. However, two other ships nearby (even closer to the Titanic) either ignored or did not receive the wireless message. Marconi was in New York City at the time, holding a ticket for the return trip of the Titanic, and quickly became a center of attention as people wanted news of the disaster, but news was scarce.

According to Tom Lewis in his book *Empire of the Air*, "Evidence suggests that Marconi himself colluded with some of his operators to limit news of the Titanic's demise, even the list of survivors. The longer the public remained in suspense, the more his Company benefited, as the delay underscored the importance of making wireless mandatory on all ships. For a time, the stock of American Marconi rose to new heights."

Another person who benefited from the Titanic disaster was a young wireless operator, David Sarnoff, who collected information about the survivors from his position as a Marconi telegraph employee, and gave it to William Randolph Hearst's newspaper, *The American*.

David Sarnoff

David Sarnoff was born in Minsk, Russia, on February 27, 1891. In 1896 his father emigrated to New York City; four years later he sent for his family to join him. David was nine years old when he arrived in New York in 1900 in the steerage section of a large steamship. He arrived on July 2 in the largest city in the United States and settled in a three-room apartment with his parents and two brothers on the Lower East Side. Sarnoff's father, an unskilled worker who took whatever jobs he could, was ill when the family arrived; young David soon obtained a job selling a Yiddish newspaper, then took English classes at the Educational Alliance, a community home that helped European immigrants become acclimated to the new country.

Sarnoff's formal education stopped in the eighth grade, but his hunger for learning drove him to self-education, especially in the field of radio. He obtained a job with the Commercial Cable Company as a messenger boy, where he learned Morse code from telegraph operators. On September 30, 1906, he started work for the American Marconi Wireless Telegraph Company as an office boy.

In December, 1906 Marconi visited the American office and fifteen-year old David introduced himself and the two hit it off. According to Tom Lewis, "By the time Sarnoff left that evening, he had established himself as Marconi's personal messenger boy. In subsequent visits, the inventor came to rely on him to deliver flowers, gifts, and messages to his numerous female liaisons about the city."

David's father died when the son was sixteen; by that time he was the major breadwinner in his family. Sarnoff became a telegraph operator and rose through the ranks of the company. He served on a ship, managed some of Marconi's land stations, and studied hard on his own, learning algebra, geometry and trigonometry from correspondence courses and reading voraciously in technical journals and books. He also took an intensive course in electrical engineering at the Pratt Institute. That was how he came to be manager of the Marconi station located atop the Wanamaker Building at Ninth and Broadway, which is where he was in April, 1912, when the Titanic disaster occurred.

Sarnoff, who possessed a canny opportunism and self-confidence, took advantage of the Titanic story to help his own career. Years later, when he was president of the Radio Corporation of America (RCA), he authorized this biography of himself and the Titanic story: "On April 14, 1912, he was sitting at his instrument in the Wanamaker Store in New York. Leaning forward suddenly, he pressed the earphones more closely to his head. Through the sputtering and static...he was hearing a message: 'S.S. Titanic ran into iceberg. Sinking fast.' For the next seventy-two hours Sarnoff sat at his post, straining to catch every signal that might come through the air. That demanded a good operator in those days of undeveloped radio. By order of the President of the United States every other wireless station in the country was closed to stop interference...Not until he had given the world the name of the last survivor, three days and three nights after that first message, did Sarnoff call his job done."

Some of this is fact and some of it is fancy; Sarnoff was probably *not* at his post when the first messages arrived. However, "Of all the wireless operators...Sarnoff alone had the prescience to embellish his role as the sole wireless link between the *Titanic* and the mainland. In that single incident he saw better than anyone else the power of the new medium."

The Senate's Committee on Commerce held hearings on the Titanic disaster within a week; this led to Congress requiring wireless equipment and operators in all ships.

Radio Rivals

On October 29, 1913, Edwin Howard Armstrong applied for a patent for "an audion wireless receiving system." His second patent application came on December 18 that year "for a circuit that used the vacuum tube as a generator of continuously oscillating electromagnetic waves--the basic circuit of a radio transmitter." Those inventions "changed forever the way radio waves are created."

Armstrong was an amateur radio operator who enrolled in Columbia University's school of engineering where he studied under Michael Pupin, one of the leading physicists of that time and a pioneer in wireless research. In June, 1913, Armstrong graduated and embarked on a life working with radio. Unfortunately, his genius as an inventor did not match his skills as a businessman. His troubles began early; in the October patent he failed to disclose the fact that his circuit transmitted as well as received. That left the door open to litigation, which eventually caused him to lose control of his patent.

The man he lost it to was Lee De Forest, who claimed in 1915 that he, not Armstrong, should receive the patent for the "oscillating audion." Armstrong knew what he had invented and De Forest did not. Armstrong received the first benefits of the invention when he licensed his circuit to the Telefunken Company in Germany, which needed wireless communication after the British cut the telegraph cables linking Germany and the United States at the outbreak of World War I in Germany. The agreement lasted until the United States entered the War.

World War I helped radio in several ways. First, it put an end to the litigation over patents--inventors such as Edison, Armstrong, De Forest and others spent a good part of their lives in litigation defending their patents which had broad, commercial appeal--and it standardized the industry, moving it away from competing technologies which were incompatible. The government--particularly the Navy--was involved with wireless communication early, considering it essential for ship-to-ship and ship-to-shore communication, and hence essential for national defense.

The American Marconi Company, American Telephone and Telegraph (AT&T) and the United States Navy were the chief rivals. AT&T depended on telephone wires for a large portion of its income by charging telegraph and radio operators to use its wires. It also made a great deal of money linking the world with transatlantic cables under the oceans and charging people to send messages. The idea of wireless communication, bypassing AT&T's telephone wires, was perceived as a threat to the company.

After the Titanic disaster, Congress enacted legislation requiring the Navy to develop radio communication. In March, 1913, Josephus Daniels was sworn in as Secretary of the Navy under the new President, Woodrow Wilson. His Assistant Secretary was Franklin D. Roosevelt. Daniels believed the Navy should control the airwaves, or "ether" as it was called. Working with AT&T, the Navy developed wireless stations to send signals around the world.

When the United States declared war on Germany on April 6, 1917, the Navy took over all amateur and commercial radio stations--in essence, the entire wireless industry in the United States. That included the Marconi interests. The government declared a moratorium on radio patent litigation and used all the inventions connected with radio for the duration of the War. It also set up schools for radio operators and trained young men in the use of radio.

The government then gave contracts for the production of radio equipment to various manufacturers. That "forced manufacturers to think on a larger and more uniform scale than ever before...they had to produce components in enormous numbers to particular specifications...[and] applied principles of mass production to the manufacture of components--especially vacuum tubes."

For most manufacturers of radio equipment, the government became the only customer during World War I. The Navy had 10,000 radio sets installed in ships; the Army developed radio communications for their ground forces. The government created standards for radio equipment "so that operators would not be forced to master a new system each time they were transferred to a new vessel or outfit." The government's actions "brought about an institutionalization of radio development that signaled the end of the lone inventor...Increasingly, individuals who possessed great talents would have to submit them to the whims of a large corporation like Marconi or American Telephone and Telegraph, or to the government. The war had transformed radio from a novelty into a necessity whose worth was greater and more important than any single inventor's reputation."

During the War, Edwin Howard Armstrong served in Paris, in the division of research and inspection where he invented "the superheterodyne, the circuit that makes possible the precise tuning of virtually every one of today's radio and televisions."

David Sarnoff, now Commercial Manager for the Marconi Company, was denied a commission in the Navy, then a position with the Army, primarily because of anti-Semitism. However, Sarnoff "negotiated all the wireless service contracts for Marconi in the United States; supervised the sales of millions of dollars of equipment to the U.S. government and other private concerns" and led the way in American Marconi receiving $5 million in sales--mostly to the government--in 1917.

By the time the Armistice was signed on November 11, 1918, the radio industry had changed a great deal. The War "made possible a vast coordinated development of radio technology during World War I... financed by government, coordinated largely by the navy." Because of the demand for vacuum tubes, manufactured by lamp-bulb manufacturers General Electric and Westinghouse, two more major corporations entered the field of radio.

By the end of World War I, radio was prepared to move forward, but first the role of radio in American business had to be determined. This produced a conflict between the government and private business and influenced the direction radio took in the United States, making it different from the rest of the world.

Joe Hill and Songs in the Labor Movement

Music can make a difference in this world. During the Civil War, abolitionists used songs and music to voice their opposition to slavery.

Harriet Beecher Stowe's anti-slavery novel, *Uncle Tom's Cabin*, was presented as a musical using Stephen Foster's songs and the Hutchinson Family Singers began performing in 1839 and expressed their abolitionist views to Presidents John Tyler and Abraham Lincoln. The Hutchinson Family did not limit their songs to abolition; they also sang songs about temperance, politics, women's suffrage and war. Many of the Spirituals, such as "Go Down Moses," "Oh, Freedom" and "Follow the Drinking Gourd," expressed anti-slavery sentiments.

During the early years of the 20th century, the Labor Movement provided a number of songs advocating better working conditions through workers joining a Union.

Joe Hill was the best known composer of labor songs during those early years. Born Joel Hagglund in Sweden (October 7, 1879), Hagglund immigrated to the United States in 1902, first to New York and then to a number of places before he landed in San Pedro, California, where he joined the Industrial Workers of the World (IWW), better known as "The Wobblies."

The IWW was formed in Chicago in 1905 and was organized because "eastern radicals...wished to influence the American Federation of Labor and the Knights of Labor toward their socialist ideas, and the militant philosophy of the Western Federation of Miners." The Wobblies were characterized by their "plunging into areas of maximum danger; the impatience with compromises and gradualist solutions; the deep suspicion of politics...the emphasis on direct, militant, mass action...the migrant, shabby existence of the organizer...the songs and humor; the dream of a new brotherhood."

Prior to the formation of the Wobblies, the unions were based somewhat on the old European Guilds, which consisted of skilled workers. As the Industrial Revolution increasingly dominated the economic landscape, unskilled workers laboring on docks and in factories comprised a large workforce who were often treated shabbily by their employers, who used child labor and demanded long days with no breaks and had no concern for the safety of their workers. The Wobblies sought to unionize those unskilled, mostly immigrant workers.

The educational publication of the IWW was their *Little Red Song Book*, which contained songs that expressed the Wobblie's views and "were sung on picket lines, in hobo jungles, at mass meetings, during free speech demonstrations—wherever members gathered to agitate for a new world built 'from the ashes of the old.'" That book, originally published in January,

1909 was officially titled *Songs of the Workers* but became widely known as the *Little Red Song Book*.

In 1912, 25,000 textile workers in Lawrence, Massachusetts went on strike for ten weeks to publicize "the plight of poorly-paid, foreign-born factory workers, dramatizing the problems of child labor in the mills and disseminating the organization's philosophy of radical unionism." Gibbs Smith, in his biography of Joe Hill, quotes a reporter who wrote of the strikers, "They are always marching and singing."

Joel Hagglund Americanized his name to Joe Hill by the time he arrived in San Pedro, California, and began writing songs for the labor movement. Hill primarily wrote lyrics and used the tunes of popular songs; often his lyrics were parodies of the original songs. Hill's songs left a legacy of someone who "was translator and scribe for the migrant workers and hobos of America, turning into lyrical expression their everyday experience of disillusionment, hardship, bitterness and injustice. His lyrics, for the most part, are tough, hard bitten, and scornful of what seemed to him the futility of trying to improve the worker's lot within the existing framework of American society."

Some union organizers felt that workers should be educated about the class struggle and the advantages of socialism over capitalism and the best way to do that was through pamphlets and other publications. Joe Hill argued that "A pamphlet, no matter how good, is never read more than once, but a song is learned by heart and repeated over and over; and I maintain that if a person can put a few cold, common sense facts into a song, and dress them up in a cloak of humor to take the dryness off of them, he will succeed in reaching a great number of workers who are too unintelligent or too indifferent to read a pamphlet or an editorial on economic science."

The first song by Joe Hill published in *The Little Red Book* was "The Preacher and the Slave" in 1911. Here is the first verse and chorus:

"The Preacher and the Slave"
(To the tune of "Sweet Bye and Bye")

Long-haired preachers come out every night,
Try to tell you what's wrong and what's right;
But when asked how 'bout something to eat
They will answer with voices so sweet:

CHORUS:
You will eat, bye and bye
In that glorious land above the sky;

Work and pray, live on hay,
You'll get pie in the sky when you die.

In that song he coined the term "pie in the sky."

Another well-known song from Joe Hill was "Casey Jones—The Union Scab," which was written for strike breakers when workers went on strike against the Union Pacific Railroad.

"Casey Jones—The Union Scab" (to the tune of "Casey Jones")

The Workers on the S.P. line to strike sent out a call;
But Casey Jones, the engineer, he wouldn't strike at all;
His boiler it was leaking, and its drivers on the bum,
And his engine and its bearings, they were all out of plumb.

CHORUS:
Casey Jones kept his junk pile running;
Casey Jones was working double time;
Casey Jones got a wooden medal,
For being good and faithful on the S.P. line.

Those involved in the labor movement during the early 1900s judged a song on how directly it expressed their political, social and economic philosophy. Songs were not judged on their poetic language or "originality"—most were parodies of other songs or at least used the melody of a well known song—but how much they were sung to unite and inspire the union members. What made Joe Hill unique was that although he, too, wrote parodies and used known melodies, his songs were more poetic and, although his motivation was to write for the movement, his songs transcended the labor movement during the early 1900s.

The song that sums up Joe Hill's—and the Wobblies—political and economic beliefs is contained in "Workers of the World Awaken."

"Workers of the World Awaken"

Workers of the world, Awaken!
Break your chains, demand your rights.
All the wealth you make is taken
By exploiting parasites.
Shall you kneel in deep submission
From your cradles to your graves?
Is the height of your ambition
To be good and willing slaves?

Workers of the world, awaken!
Rise in all your splendid might;
Take the wealth that you are making,
It belongs to you by right.
No one will for bread be crying,
We'll have freedom, love and health,
When the grand red flag is flying
In the Workers' Commonwealth.

In 1914 Joe Hill was arrested for the murder of a Salt Lake City butcher, John G. Morrison, and his son, Arling, at their butcher shop. The killing took place on January 10 and that evening Joe Hill went to a local doctor with a bullet wound. During the robbery Arling Morrison had wounded one of the two men involved in that shooting.

Hill denied he was involved in the robbery and murder but claimed he was shot in an argument over a woman but refused to name the woman or say where he was when the robbery occurred. (Hill was probably in bed with a married woman and, if he had named her, would have ruined her reputation and destroyed her life.)

Joe Hill was a well-known figure in the labor movement and local leaders in the political and business community had no love for the IWW, which led to the belief that he was judged guilty because of his affiliation with the Wobblies. There was some evidence to substantiate that claim; four others had bullet wounds that evening and several prominent people, including President Woodrow Wilson, lobbied for clemency. The Utah authorities would not allow that; on November 19, 1915, Joe Hill sat in a chair in front of a firing squad.

Prior to his execution, Hill wrote a letter to IWW leader Bill Haywood, saying "I die like a true blue rebel. Don't waste any time in mourning. Organize." That phrase, shortened to "Don't mourn: Organize" became a rallying cry for labor organizers in the years ahead and Joe Hill became a legendary figure in the history of the labor movement.

In 1930 Alfred Hayes wrote a poem, "I Dreamed I Saw Joe Hill Last Night" and in 1936 Earl Robinson put music to the song, usually titled simply "Joe Hill." A number of versions have been recorded but the most famous is probably Joan Baez's performance of the song during the Woodstock Festival in 1969.

The Music Business in World War I

By 1914, the phonograph was spreading Tin Pan Alley recordings across the country. The movies were even more popular; about ten million people a day went to the movies. The music business was still dominated by music publishers and the sheet music business.

In that world, Irving Berlin stood tall and learned how to court the media and play the role of the popular songwriter as an American hero. He changed his name officially from Israel Baline to Irving Berlin in 1912 and became an American citizen in 1918, just before his thirtieth birthday. America had declared war on Germany in April, 1917, and Berlin was shocked to discover that he'd been drafted soon after he became a citizen. Assigned to Camp Upton in nearby Long Island, Berlin detested the Army routine and devised a way to get out of it by writing a musical for the Army to be staged on Broadway with all the money raised going to the Army. The Army agreed and Berlin was allowed to return to his schedule of working all night and sleeping all day. The experience provided a song for the musical, *Yip, Yip, Yaphank* and furthered Berlin's career when he performed in it. The song "Oh, How I Hate to Get Up In The Morning" made Berlin a Broadway star while he was in the Army and the show was successful, although the war ended in November, 1918, before it went on tour.

Several important developments came out of that musical. First, it gave Berlin the basic vehicle to present the Army with an idea during World War II to stage a show and carry it all over the world entertaining troops. That show, *This is the Army*, also featured Berlin singing "Oh, How I Hate To Get Up In The Morning." Berlin wrote "God Bless America" for *Yip Yip Yaphank*, although he cut it out of the score before the production. He pulled it out of his trunk just before World War II and gave it to Kate Smith when she needed a song for her network radio show to honor Armistice Day. That song would become a second national anthem for the country, beginning just before the second World War.

World War I provided James Reese Europe an opportunity to tour in France as a bandleader, performing for troops. Vernon Castle joined the Air Force and flew planes; however, after he returned to the United States his plane crashed and he was killed during a training mission. Europe was killed in 1919 after an altercation with his drummer over a woman. His death occurred just before he was to begin a national tour and his funeral became the first public funeral for an African-American in New York.

America in World War I

In 1914 the old world order collapsed when an Austrian Archduke was assassinated in Sarajevo, setting off a chain of events which led to World War I. The United States was isolationist at that point and citizens were primarily concerned with staying out of Europe's problems, preferring to see it as "their" problem and not "ours." For the next three years the United States managed to stay out of the confrontation, even though there were increasing provocations from Germany, including the sinking of the passenger ship, the Lusitania in May, 1915. Woodrow Wilson had campaigned on a platform of peace and was elected for his second term in November, 1916, although no one was sure how long he could keep his campaign promise to avoid war.

America gained a great deal during World War I in terms of economic investment from the War as well as research and development of radio technology, chemicals, aviation, and mechanical engineering. Those developments paved the way for commercial radio, commercial and military airplanes, and the building of roads between cities.

America lost its innocence from its involvement during World War I. During the War the draft was instituted, the federal government was inflated, and a system of spying and surveillance of American citizens was established. The War exacerbated ethnic hatreds--especially against German-Americans--and there were fears of Communism and Bolshevism after the Russian Revolution, which occurred during the War.

The greatest loss of innocence came from the disillusionment with the war and resultant peace. About five million men served during World War I; 75,658 died and many were buried in Europe. After the initial wave of exuberant patriotism, soldiers discovered the brutality of war, living through a frigid winter in 1917-1918, fighting in muddy trenches, facing machine guns and gas attacks, and the blitzkreig tactics of the German army.

If the War itself was not brutal enough, when the veterans came home many discovered their jobs were gone. President Woodrow Wilson's peace initiatives, aimed at restoring Germany as a nation and the establishment of a League of Nations, did not sit well with many Americans, who wanted revenge and the destruction of the German state.

Although the assassination of an Austrian Prince in Serbia triggered a chain reaction of alliances that caused Germany to fight England and France, in truth, Germany was armed and waiting for something to trigger a war. They had built a powerful military and were looking for a fight.

The War saw the introduction of the German U-Boat, or submarine, that sank British and French vessels, the airplane in war, and the machine gun. It was a War fought in trenches, a series of deep ditches where opposing armies faced each other with barbed wire across a "no man's land" in between. Soldiers lived underground and during rainy periods had to cope with mud and filth.

The United States stayed out of the War 1914-1917, although German boats sank American vessels. Woodrow Wilson had been elected President in 1912, then reelected in 1916 with the theme "he kept us out of war," but in January, 1917, the German ambassador in Washington informed the American government that American ships, which had been sending supplies to England and France, would be sunk by the German Navy. On April 2, President Wilson spoke before Congress, requesting that War be declared on Germany; on April 6, he signed the Declaration of War at the White House. For the next nineteen months, the United States took an active part in World War I.

Prior to the War, the United States was changing from an agrarian nation to an industrial one; that led to a growth in cities, development of new technologies, and a large influx of immigrants. From 1871 until 1920, 26.3 million immigrants arrived; 8.8 million came between 1900-1910. By 1914 the total population of the United States was 100 million and one third was either foreign-born or had a foreign born parent. The newest group of immigrants came primarily from Russia, Middle Europe and the Mediterranean and few spoke English. Predominantly Catholics and Jews (many Orthodox), the immigrants did not easily assimilate into American culture, and that caused concern and problems with Americans already in the United States. In 1914, America's population included nine million who spoke German, with an additional 15 million who were of Germanic stock. Americans tended to fear and distrust the new immigrants and were suspicious that the United States was losing its "Americaness." They were especially fearful of German-Americans, wondering where their true loyalty lay as the War in Europe raged on.

Henry Ford was an American hero by 1914; there were five million automobiles on the road by that time, and 20 percent were made by Ford. Henry Ford promoted the idea of "100 percent American" and set up classes at his Ford plants to help teach immigrants English and the American way.

At the end of June, 1916, the regular Army had 107,641 men in uniform, ranking it 17th in the world with an Army smaller than at any time since the beginning of the Civil War. In order to join in the War in Europe, the United

States had to create an Army of five million and convince the population that the War was worth fighting with American soldiers.

President Wilson was an idealist who sought to cast the war as a moral crusade, an effort to "make the world safe for democracy." In order to do this, he needed to dominate the peace negotiations after the war was finished, and in order to accomplish that task, he needed for a large American Army to provide a decisive force in winning the War.

On May 13, 1917, the Selective Service Act became law, providing the Army with draftees for the first time since the Civil War. Wilson appointed General John Joseph Pershing to head the American Expeditionary Force (AEF) in Europe and set in motion the process whereby young men were conscripted and trained to fight as soldiers.

Wilson also set about mobilizing the population to accept the war as necessary and view the enemy as a hated evil. That led to Americans looking at foreigners with suspicion, fear, hatred and intolerance; those feelings were also directed to American minorities (such as African-Americans and religious minorities) and those who opposed the war. In June, 1917, the Espionage Act became law and "any statement that might interfere with the success of the armed forces, incite disloyalty, or obstruct recruiting to the Army became a punishable offense."

By the summer of 1918, "America was no longer a place of tolerance, openness, and democracy; it was divided, intolerant, vindictive, and submissive to the demands of a central authority that attempted to control people's lives down to the details of the food they ate, the newspapers they read, and the conversations they were permitted to hold in public." In that atmosphere, "The nation surrendered itself to the draft, to censorship, to repression. Dissent was forbidden, and even honest criticism was outlawed. Worse, ordinary Americans volunteered to police the system, to spy on their neighbors, to condone violence and the abuse of civil rights, to participate in a shameful travesty of their former lives."

Once in Europe, the Army found the two sides facing each other in trenches that stretched from the English Channel to Switzerland. The winter of 1917-1918 was one of the worst in Europe's history and American soldiers did not have adequate overcoats, gloves or blankets for the subzero temperatures.

In September, 1918, the Americans launched an offensive in the Meuse-Argonne area in France, west of Paris near the German-French line. The German Army ran out of steam and by the end of October Pershing demanded an unconditional surrender of German forces; the armistice went into effect on the eleventh day of the eleventh month at the eleventh hour; November 11 at 11 a.m.

Wilson proposed a 14-point plan for the surrender, with the central point being the creation of a League of Nations where democratic countries united for arbitration and protection, but in the November election the Republicans won a majority in the House and Senate, and they opposed Wilson's plan.

On December 4 Wilson left for Europe where he took an active part in the negotiations at Versailles. The British and French were determined to exact revenge on Germany and insisted Germany pay the cost of the war, hand over the Kaiser (who had escaped to Holland) and place over 400 leaders on trial. They took possession of Germany's overseas colonies as well as parts of what had been Germany, adding Alsace and Lorraine to France and tracts of Prussia to Poland. The treaty was harsh and nakedly vengeful and laid the groundwork for Hitler's rise to power during the 1930s. Part of Hitler's appeal to the German people was the idea that justice and fairness would have to be won by the German military in order to right the wrongs Germany suffered from that Treaty.

Wilson lost on most of his 14 points, although the European nations approved the League of Nations; however, in November, 1919 the Senate refused to ratify the treaty and the League. The month before, President Wilson suffered a crippling stroke and spent his last months in office nearly invalid.

American soldiers returned to the United States disillusioned by the horrors of war; further, many of the five million had no jobs after the victory parades. The American people were relieved and triumphant after the war, but filled with grief, rage and hatred as well. In their book, *The Last Days of Innocence: America at War, 1917-1918*, authors Meirion and Susie Harries state, "America went to fight in 1917 with an innocent determination to remake the world; the nation emerged in November 1918 with its sense of purpose shattered, with its certainties shaken, and with a new and unwelcome self-knowledge. Many Americans wanted to turn their backs on the war almost from the moment it ended."

The soldiers returned more worldly wise and a popular song of the day expressed a common feeling: "How you gonna keep 'em down on the farm after they've seen Paree?"

The 1920s

The era known as "The Roaring 20s," and "The Jazz Age," was a time for the Lost Generation, flagpole sitting, zoot suits, flappers dancing the

Charleston, women's liberation, a sexual revolution, speakeasies, bathtub gin, feverish frivolity, an orgy of self-indulgence, an obsession with get-rich-quick schemes, and a faith in prosperity. In short, it was the end of the era of Victorian restraint. It was also the end to the progressive era that had attempted the rein in the excesses of big business and create an activist government that protected consumers.

The progressive era had given Americans the Meat Inspection Act, the Pure Food and Drug Act, the Hepburn Act which regulated railroads, the Clayton Antitrust Act (which replaced the ineffective Sherman Antitrust Act), the Federal Reserve Act, which regulated banking, and the 16th Amendment, which provided for an income tax. It also provided the 1909 Copyright Law, which helped songwriters and publishers, and the formation of the American Society of Composers, Authors and Publishers, which allowed songwriters and publishers to collect money for the public performance of their songs.

In 1919 and 1920 two Constitutional Amendments passed which were a precursor of the roaring 20s. In January, 1919, the 18th Amendment granted women the right to vote. For many, this was pulling women into the nasty arena of politics and away from their chief responsibilities at home and child-raising. For women, it represented a step towards equality--a step that was not welcomed by those with traditional Victorian values. Americans saw women wearing short, tight dresses, rolling their stockings down to their knees, putting on lipstick and make-up, cutting their hair in a "bob," dancing cheek-to-check with their partners or kicking up their heels to the latest dance crazes and felt the country was coming apart.

In January, 1920, the Volstead Act, prohibiting the manufacture and sale of alcoholic beverages brought in Prohibition. That brought Federal law into millions of everyday lives; it was viewed as an attempt by a well-organized minority to legislate morality on the hapless majority. Prohibition was viewed as a way to help clean up communities, assure political and social righteousness, help women and children whose husbands/fathers lost their paychecks to demon alcohol and thus strengthen the family. Evangelical Christians welcomed prohibition because they felt it would lead to a sober, Christian America.

Many politicians and community activists welcomed Prohibition because it eliminated the neighborhood saloon, which was viewed as a center for vice as well as a key part of urban political corruption because many ward bosses used the saloons as a central location to organize voters. The working class and immigrants generally opposed Prohibition. The working class saw the saloon as a cheap source of entertainment while immigrants saw it as an affirmation of their culture, especially Germans and Irish, whose social life revolved around the neighborhood saloon.

After having endured the loss of liberties and the sacrifices they made during World War I, most Americans saw Prohibition as one more problem created by a large, intrusive Federal government which was taking away their individualism and regulating their lives. Obviously, outlawing liquor did not eliminate people's taste for booze; it merely handed over a $2 billion industry to a criminal element which used guns and bloodshed to enforce its business. That led to a rise of lawlessness as even law abiding citizens--and law enforcement personnel--flaunted their disapproval of this law. That breakdown of law and order gave rise to powerful organized crime families in major cities like New York and Chicago.

In November, 1920, the American public elected Warren G. Harding as president with his campaign theme "A return to normalcy." Harding believed there should be "less government in business, more business in government." The idealism of Woodrow Wilson and his League of Nations had been repudiated. Americans tend to grow tired of periods of reform, many turning their backs on social problems to pursue personal interests. The ideas of reformers became dated, their programs were enacted but problems still existed, and people who favor liberal reform when they are young find themselves growing more conservative as they grow older. Then, a new generation comes of age who seek a personal redemption as well as societal change, upset with themselves and others after a period of ignoring others and pursuing hedonism. The 1920s generation fell into the first category: they rejected the progressive era and pursued a selfish individualism.

The moniker "Jazz Age" did not fit everyone during the 1920s. In the 1920 census, over half of the 105 million Americans lived in an "urban" area--although urban was defined as any town with over 2,500 inhabitants. There was a move to cities and modernity; however, farmers and rural citizens felt their values were mocked during the roaring 20s. The notions of hard work, thrift, sobriety, and strict adherence to a moral code were being challenged. Farmers and other rural dwellers who had once seen themselves as the backbone of America, embodying "true" American values, were derided as hicks, hayseeds, hillbillies and yokels. The new generation was hip and played fast and loose with the old values. Religious fundamentalists suffered shame and humiliation with the Scopes Trial in 1926 in Dayton, Tennessee. Even though Scopes was found guilty and fined

$100, the trial, led by religious conservative William Jennings Bryan and evolutionist Clarence Darrow, put the national spotlight on a set of beliefs that seemed outdated and behind the times in an age when scientific inquiry took precedence over religious beliefs.

Actually, religious beliefs were incorporated into business during the 1920s as religious leaders tried to emulate businessmen and "market" Christianity. One of the most popular books of the 1920s was *The Man Nobody Knows* (1926) by Bruce Barton, an advertising man who presented Jesus as the ultimate businessman.

The prosperity of the 1920s came primarily from mechanized production, especially the automobile. Henry Ford had pioneered a method of mass producing automobiles on an assembly line in 1914; during the 1920s the automobile became a "necessity" and spurred road construction as well as growth in related businesses of steel, glass, oil and gasoline. During the 1920s, Henry Ford was the model American, a hero for modernizing American life with his Ford Model T, then Model A. Ford declared that "Machinery is the new Messiah" and by the end of October, 1925, a new car came off his Detroit assembly line every ten seconds or 9,575 each day. By 1929, 20 percent of Americans owned cars; there were 23 million cars on the road, up from seven million in 1919.

Farmers suffered throughout the 1920s. After being encouraged to overproduce during World War I, they found an economy that could not consume all they produced, leading to a precipitous drop in farm products as supply outstripped demand. In 1922 farm families constituted 22 percent of Americans, but they received only 15 percent of the national income. In 1928 farmers accounted for only nine percent of national income and by 1929 the annual per capita income of farm persons was $273 while the average for all Americans was $750.

The Republican administrations of the 1920s were more interested in helping big business than they were in helping farmers. Harding died in 1923 and was succeeded by his vice-president, Calvin Coolidge, who was then elected in 1924. Coolidge believed the government that governed best governed least, and wanted to be the "least" President the country ever had. In 1928, Herbert Hoover was elected President and took office in March, 1929.

Hoover was an excellent administrator who headed up the post-World War I efforts to transport food to Europe to help alleviate starvation. He served as Secretary of Commerce under Harding and Coolidge and had only run for office once--as treasurer of his class at Stanford--before the 1928

Presidential election. Six months after taking office, Hoover watched the beginning of the end of the Roaring 20s.

The stock market crash actually occurred over several months. The bull market hit its peak on September 3, 1929, then began to go down. On Black Thursday and Black Tuesday, October 24 and 29, there were huge drops, but the stock market recovered a little after each until it finally bottomed out on November 13. But, for most people, October 29 is when people knew that the roaring 20s were over.

The Creation of RCA

The United States government intervened in an agreement General Electric made to sell American Marconi $5 million worth of essential equipment; word of that came to Edward J. Nally, vice-president of American Marconi from Owen D. Young, vice-president of General Electric, at a lunch in New York on May 12, 1919. The reason: the government (particularly the Navy) did not want such essential communications equipment in the hands of "foreigners."

The idea that the navy would take over the radio industry seemed unlikely because of opposition in Congress; however, the sale of important equipment for such a large sum might tip the scales towards the navy if Congress saw this issue in a protectionist light, preserving national security. Also, a number of key patents in radio were held by the navy, and further use of those patents depended on navy cooperation; it was extremely doubtful they would cooperate with a foreign-owned firm.

Young and other executives at General Electric thought they could start a new company doing what Marconi was doing. Negotiations began and a tentative agreement between the two companies was signed at the end of July, 1919. British Marconi had to agree, and they did--or else lose their American arm.

The new company was named the Radio Corporation of America (RCA) and was incorporated on October 17, 1919. General Electric purchased all Marconi stock not owned by private investors and it was agreed that "the new corporation would always remain under American control. No more than 20 percent of its stock could be owned by foreigners; its executives had to be United States citizens; a representative from the navy was invited to attend meetings of its board of directors." Edward Nally became president of the new company, David Sarnoff was commercial manager, and Owen Young was named chairman of the board of directors.

During the Fall of 1916, David Sarnoff wrote a memo to Edward Nally laying out the future of radio. In that memo he stated he had "a plan of development which would make radio a 'household utility' in the same sense as the piano or phonograph" by bringing music into homes by wireless. He called the proposed new idea a "Radio Music Box." Nally ignored the memo.

With the formation of RCA, Sarnoff sent a twenty-eight page memo to Owen Young on January 31, 1920, discussing the future of radio; in that memo he included, word-for-word, the proposal he had given Nally four years earlier. Sarnoff predicted that the new company would benefit from manufacturing the new radio box to the tune of $75 million. He arrived at that figure by setting $75 as the price of a new Radio Music Box and projected 100,000 would be sold the first year, 300,000 the second year, and 600,000 the third year--adding up to one million radio music boxes. That memo by Sarnoff "stood as a blueprint for making RCA into the dominant radio company in the world."

In June, Sarnoff was given $2,500 to develop the idea. Sarnoff produced a "radiola," developed by Dr. Alfred Goldsmith, a professor at City College in New York. The company decided to move forward, but needed access to key patents from AT&T and its subsidiary, Western Electric. Young negotiated to give AT&T a million shares, or about 10.3 percent ownership in the company, to get a cross-licensing agreement for the patents. Negotiations with Westinghouse at the end of 1920 meant that firm also received one million shares of RCA stock, as well as shore transmitting stations. RCA agreed that forty percent of manufacturing orders would go to Westinghouse, while the remaining orders would be processed by General Electric. Westinghouse agreed on March 25, 1921, and became owner of 20.6 percent of RCA's stock. RCA also gave the United Fruit company 200,000 shares of RCA stock, or 4.1 percent of the company, for patents it controlled.

During the negotiations, Westinghouse and its radio station, KDKA in Pittsburgh, eclipsed RCA for the honor of having the first commercial radio broadcast. Actually, the honor was shared with a Detroit station--but that is not how history has presented it.

The Detroit station, 8MK, was owned by the *Detroit News*, published by William E. Scripps and began broadcasting in early 1920. The "station" was originally in a file room at the *News*, then in the conference room. On August 31 the *News* began advertising that it would broadcast election returns for the November Presidential election; in the meantime, it broadcast music.

On November 2, 1920, using returns received over the telegraph wire at the *News*, it broadcast the Harding-Cox presidential returns.

Meanwhile, down in Pittsburgh, the Westinghouse Electric and Manufacturing Company had a problem: after World War I, government contracts had stopped and business was down. The company acquired the patents of Reginald Fessenden as well as Edwin H. Armstrong's patents for his "superheterodyne" circuit--completing the purchase on October 5. That gave the company two key radio patents.

The Department of Commerce was contacted for a license on October 16--a commercial license for a broadcasting service. The station was first assigned the call letters 8ZZ for an amateur station, then given the letters KDKA (commercial shore-station call letters) and assigned a frequency away from amateurs. Prior to the election, the station broadcast recordings from a hand-wound phonograph then, on the evening of November 2, broadcast the election victory of Warren G. Harding and received a great deal of publicity for it.

In analyzing why Westinghouse received all the credit for broadcasting that election return, historian Erik Barnouw stated, "Although no sets were yet on the market, Westinghouse focused from the start on the aim of developing a demand for them. For this reason its publicity emphasis was quite different from that of the *Detroit News*; this may help to account for the vast difference in impact...The *Detroit News*, which had no special interest in selling equipment, depicted its radio listeners as technical prodigies, referring to them as 'radio operators,' who could be expected to report back by wireless on the quality of the 8MK transmission...Westinghouse, on the contrary, presented the activity as something for everyone, a social delight for home or country club...*The Detroit News*, intent on publicizing itself, could perhaps not expect extensive publicity in rival papers. The Westinghouse bulletins, on the other hand, came to newspapers not from a rival but from a large-scale advertiser, launching a nation-wide merchandising campaign. It readily won wide publicity."

The election returns represented a turning point in the history of radio in another way as well: both Warren Harding and James Cox had come to power as newspaper publishers. Their election was a symbolic beginning to an era when radio, not newspapers, became the dominant media in the United States.

Radio grew rapidly during the 1921-1925 period; at the end of 1922 there were 670 stations licensed. Americans spent $60 million that year on receiving equipment; RCA received $11 million of this. During the spring of

1922 the Department of Commerce began issuing four-letter combinations of call letters because it had run out of three-letter combinations while the performance licensing organization, ASCAP, demanded royalties for songs used on the air, as well as copyright permission from broadcasters. Broadcasters were incredulous and adamant; after all, they felt they should not have to pay for music in this developing technology--another expense could hurt growth--and, after all, the broadcasts popularized the songs, so songwriters and publishers could make their money from the sale of sheet music. In 1923, WEAF agreed to a one-year license fee of $500 for the use of ASCAP music. As a backlash, broadcasters founded the National Association of Broadcasters in Chicago that year; they attempted to convince songwriters to allow free broadcast of their songs while the NAB received the mechanical royalties from phonograph records and piano roll music. The songwriters and publishers received their income from sheet music sales of the songs radio had popularized.

Networks

The first "network" began in 1922, a result of AT&T linking thirty-eight stations through its phone lines. The flagship station was WEAF in New York; the venture was financed through "toll broadcasting." This "toll" was a fee charged to businesses to advertise, but over a month went by before the first customer was found. That customer was the Queensboro Corporation, which wanted to advertise the sale of apartments in New York; their ten-minute advertisement promoting the apartments was broadcast on August 28, 1922. Two other companies soon followed: Tidewater Oil and the American Express Company. Each advertisement was a ten-minute spot and featured a long-winded explanation of their business without every really "advertising" it.

In 1923, Americans purchased $136 million worth of radios and in 1924 that figure climbed to $358 million. Listeners heard a lot of music on radio, although not much from recordings. In 1923 the Department of Commerce decided to assign radio stations different frequencies--at first, all radio stations broadcast on the same frequency, creating a cacophony of sounds--but those assigned the highest power were not allowed to use recordings. The result was a lot of live music performed, but it was mainly "conservatory music," with vocal and instrumental music generally alternating. One program director called it "potted palm" music and a writer described it as "the music played at tea time by hotel orchestras." That was the kind of music that dominated on radio throughout the 1920s. Even though the low-powered stations played phonograph recordings and player pianos, "parlor music" also dominated. Ironically, those on-the-air recitals led to a tremendous growth in American music.

The Recording Companies in the 1920s

The disc had proven to be the preferred format for music. In 1913 Edison began producing phonograms that played discs and Columbia discontinued cylinders the year before.

There were 18 recording companies in 1914 and they sold $27 million worth of products; four years later there were 166 companies that produced $158 million worth of products. .

In 1921 the recording industry had a banner year: sales totaled $121 million. That would be the high water mark for the recording industry for over 25 years; after that time sales of recordings dropped until they hit an all-time low in the Depression in 1931 ($6.5 million). It would not be until after World War II that the recording industry surpassed the 1921 sales figures.

Radio was blamed as the major culprit for the drop of record sales, but it wasn't the only thing to blame. Sheet music sales also dropped--and records as well as radio were both blamed. Why take the trouble of learning to play an instrument when music could be heard on the radio and phonograph? That was the explanation many publishers gave for the drop in sheet music sales. Vaudeville also suffered; vaudeville houses began closing--over 550 closed in 1920--or were changed to movie houses. Still, in 1921 vaudeville made over $10 million and the Orpheum circuit showed net profits in 1920 of $4 million, but the end was in sight, a direct result of the popularity of silent movies.

At the end of World War I the recording industry was dominated by three majors: Victor, Columbia and Edison, but a number of patents ran out, resulting in about 200 companies manufacturing machines and recordings during the 1920s. Discs dominated the industry, but cylinders were still being manufactured. Edison had reluctantly agreed to disc production in 1914 but his company continued to manufacture cylinders until 1928. Although sales of recordings decreased, there were still profits to be made; recordings sold an average of about 150 million a year during the 1920s.

Recording companies begun during that period include Polygram, Bell, Arto, Black Swan, Brunswick, Emerson, Gennett, Grey Gull, Harmony, Hit of the Week, Imperial, Nordskog, American Odeon, Okeh, Oriole, Paramount, Parlophone, Rex, Silvertone, and Vocalion. It was those small, start-up companies that recorded what became American popular music, which was originally known as jass, race and hillbilly music.

Independent Labels

In 1915 the Starr Piano Company of Richmond, Indiana, began manufacturing phonographs, then created a record-making division, named Gennett. By 1920 Starr manufactured 15,000 pianos, three million records and 3,000 phonographs a year. Gennett then opened a recording studio in the midst of their manufacturing plant and began making recordings. The man in charge of recordings was Fred Wiggins and he enticed a number of musicians from Chicago to make the five-hour train ride to Richmond, Indiana, for recording sessions.

In addition to Gennett, the company developed the labels Champion, which was a low budget line, Buddy, Superior and Supertone. The first records were issued in October, 1917. They were sued for patent infringement by Victor, but won the suit, opening the door for a number of new, start-up labels to form during the 1920s. In addition to the recording studio in Indiana, the company also had a studio in New York at East 37th Street. The records by Gennett sold for 65 cents, 75 cents or $1 each and featured some of the first recordings by a number of jazz acts, including King Oliver, Louis Armstrong, Johnny Dodds, Bix Beiderbecke, the New Orleans Rhythm Kings, Hoagy Carmichael, Jelly Roll Morton, and the Mills Brothers.

Brunswick became a major recording company during the 1920s and remnants of that company survive today. It was begun by the Brunswick-Balke-Collender Company of Dubuque, Iowa in 1916. The parent company was a piano manufacturer formed in 1845 and the first records were released in January, 1920. Brunswick's early recordings were done in Chicago. They later launched the Panatrope, a machine which could play electrically recorded records. Al Jolson had a major hit for Brunswick with "Sonny Boy."

Okeh Records was started in 1916 by Otto Heinemann as the American branch of the German-based Carl Lindstrom empire. The term "Okeh," pronounced "Okay," had an Indian origin and meant "It is so" or "So be it." After World War I, Heinemann renamed the firm the General Phonograph Corporation. Okeh was a pioneer in race and hillbilly recordings, recording Mamie Smith's "Crazy Blues" in 1920, then beginning a "Race" series in the summer of 1921. Heading the "Artists Department" was Ralph Peer, who is credited with discovering the race and hillbilly markets. He conducted field recordings in Atlanta, New Orleans, San Antonio, Detroit, St. Louis and Kansas City. Among the artists who recorded were jazz acts Louis

Armstrong, King Oliver's Jazz Band and Clarence Williams, country acts Frank and James McCravy, Earl Johnson and his Clodhoppers, Fiddlin' John Carson, Henry Whitter, Aiken County String Band, the Carolina Mandolin Orchestra, Salem Highballers, Smith Ballew and Vernon Dalhart. Parlophone was division of Okeh Records, although it was devised for West Coast recordings. In October, 1926, Okeh was acquired by Columbia.

Grey Gull was based in Boston and produced recordings which were released to a number of other labels. Their subsidiaries included Madison, Radiex, Supreme and Van Dyke. They recorded from 1922-1926 and used a number of studio bands for pop songs.

Emerson Records was formed by Victor H. Emerson, who was General Manager of the Record Department at Columbia for 17 years. He began his label in 1916 with studios on West 23rd St. in New York and in May, 1916 opened studios in Los Angeles. The company was unprofitable and went into receivership in December, 1920. Then, in June 1922, Benjamin Abrams and Rudolph Kamaret formed a syndicate for Emerson and Regal labels and issued recordings. In January 1924 they formed the Emerson Radio Corporation but the label was then sold to Scranton Button Company in November, 1924.

Black Swan was the first black-owned label. Begun by W. C. Handy and Harry Pace, the label was headquartered in Harlem and featured Fletcher Henderson as the group leader and resident accompanist. The label never really succeeded and in April, 1924, merged with Paramount. The biggest successes for the label were "Oh Daddy" and "Down Home Blues" by Ethel Waters.

The Bell label was begun by the Standard Music Roll Company of Orange, New Jersey, which also began the Arto label. Bell issued recordings from 1920 to 1928.

Autograph Records is perhaps the most interesting story because it was this label that issued the first electrical recordings. Created by Orlando Marsh and the Marsh Recording Laboratories in Chicago, the label lasted from 1924 to 1926 (it issued the first electrical recordings in 1925) and recorded top jazz acts, including King Oliver and Jelly Roll Morton. The Marsh recording facilities were excellent and a number of other labels did their sessions there.

Vocalion was originally the Aeolian Vocalion label, a subsidiary of the piano manufacturer Aeolian Company. In 1916 the company produced its first machines in recordings; in the summer of 1925 it was taken over by Brunswick-Balke-Collender.

Paramount began in 1916 and had their studios in New York, although they recorded much of their product in Chicago. Their recording manager was Arthur E. Satherley. Their biggest star was Ma Rainey and they recorded a number of race records; in April, 1924 they obtained the Black Swan catalog and in August, 1926, they were acquired by Columbia.

In 1928 Sears, Roebuck and Company, the Chicago based mail-order retail firm, established Conqueror Records, to sell through is catalogue. However, Sears did not want to get into the business of record production, so they worked out an agreement with Plaza to lease masters from that company to market under the Conqueror name. Sears also had a leasing agreement with Gennett Records, which recorded masters that were sold through their catalogue.

Silvertone was also a label made by Sears. Those record labels lasted from 1920 to 1930.

In July, 1929, the American Record Company was formed by consolidating several small labels, including the Regal and Cameo Recording complexes.

Electrical Recordings

In recording technology, the advent of electrical recording changed everything. Specifically, the introduction of the microphone to the recording process, which replaced the old horns which people sang or spoke into, made it possible to regulate and control the sound better, as well as enhance it. For singers that meant an end to the vaudeville type singer who belted out a tune so that folks in the last row could hear and the beginning of the era of the "crooner." The first to successfully make this transition was Gene Austin, whose 1927 hit "My Blue Heaven" ushered in this new era. The ultimate crooner would be Bing Crosby, whose major fame came during the 1930s.

AT&T, through their work with the telephone, provided the technological breakthroughs for electrical recordings. Bell Laboratories had originally approached Victor with this new technology in 1924 but Victor turned them down. Lagging sales of acoustic discs caused them to re-consider something new to revitalize their recording sales, but it was the interest of a competitor which spurred them to make the decision quickly.

Louis Sterling, head of Columbia in the United Kingdom, quickly grasped the new technology and saw its potential. He had been sent a copy of a new electrical master by Frank Kapps, in the Pathe lab in Brooklyn. Kapps was a friend of Sterling and wanted him to be aware of the new technology. Sterling quickly contacted Western Electric, the licensing division of AT&T,

and discussed the possibility of obtaining the technology. AT&T had wanted to share the technology with Victor in exchange for royalties--causing Victor to balk. AT&T was going to offer the technology on an exclusive basis to Victor, thus assuring a monopoly of the new technology, and would not make the new technology available to the international market unless licensed by an American company--a nod to Victor's strong international organization. Sterling convinced Western Electric to share the patent with him and Victor, then purchased American Columbia Co. so he could obtain that license and have an American firm to distribute his recordings as well.

Columbia had fallen on hard times during the 1920s and was bankrupt at the time Sterling purchased it. The firm had been purchased by Wall Street investors during the early 1920s after they saw large profits, but those investors did not know anything about running a record label and did not care to spend any money on the label, so when profits ran out they dumped the company and it went into bankruptcy and receivership.

The recording industry entered a new era in 1925 when Victor and Columbia released their first electrically recorded discs. Label executives were fearful at first of a consumer backlash when they realized that the new recordings required new machines to obtain the full effect, but people bought the new machines and the new process revitalized the industry. From that time on recording would be different--with microphones--and the industry would increasingly be dominated by a few major corporations.

Broadway and American Popular Music

The center for American popular music during the 1920s was on Broadway in New York. There, Tin Pan Alley writers cranked out songs for vaudeville performers, music revues and musical theater. Great American composers like Irving Berlin, Jerome Kern, Cole Porter, Rodgers and Hammerstein, and George and Ira Gershwin all wrote songs for audiences who attended vaudeville or theater shows. Those songs were recorded as the recording industry increasingly became the dominant means to preserve a performance. Sheet music was still important during the 1920s, but increasingly a hit song was measured by how many records it sold.

During the 1920s Tin Pan Alley, where the songwriters, music publishers and song pluggers centralized, moved up to the West 40s--there were major publishing firms on West 45th, 46th, and 47th Streets. M. Whitmark, who had been the first publishing company to move to West 28th, where the term "Tin Pan Alley" was coined, moved to 1582 Broadway while Irving Berlin was at 1587 Broadway, on the corner of 47th Street. Those moves came after a number of new theaters were built along West 44th, 45th and 46th Streets, along with new hotels, restaurants and the radio networks. There were approximately 80 theaters in the Broadway area during the 1920s and 40-50 musicals were produced each year. It was during this period that the pop song reached a standard form: 32 bars consisting of four segments of eight bars each.

Irving Berlin: Songwriter

After World War I, Irving Berlin continued his string of hit songs, writing seven songs for the Ziegfeld Follies of 1919, including the song "A Pretty Girl Is Like A Melody." He also opened his own theater, The Music Box, where he staged revues with his own songs, and had his song "You'd Be Surprised" become his first hit record when the song was recorded and released by Eddie Cantor in 1919.

As Berlin became successful as a songwriter, turning out songs for vaudeville performers, revues and musicals, several things became obvious about his work habits. First, "he was willing and able to deliver whatever would sell" and relentlessly plugged his own songs. He looked at music as a business and once stated "writing songs is a matter of having to pay bills and sitting down to make the money to pay them with." He worked constantly at songwriting, staying up until three or four in the morning composing. Berlin "avoided parties and the temptations offered by ever-present chorus girls, preferring to comport himself with the dignity and reserve of a sober businessman rather than a Tin Pan Alley tunesmith...in a field noted for careers cut short by alcohol, neglect, and personal excess, Berlin's ability to stay above the fray counted as much as his talent and determination."

Berlin "was more concerned...with song writing as a business than as an art form," stated Alec Wilder. He did not hide his primary motive in writing songs and once said "This is a business, and I'm in it to make money." Berlin could never understand "what was wrong with the idea of doing something just for the money; with few exceptions, that was what popular music was all about." His whole life was writing songs, then selling them to others to sing. The world of ideas, of theories and philosophies held no allure for him. Berlin's thoughts were deep and narrow: how to write songs and sell them.

If there was a secret to his songwriting it was that "though he wrote for the moment, he lavished extraordinary care on his creations; a large part of his genius consisted of his willingness to take infinite pains in fashioning them. They were built to last." Alec Wilder notes that Berlin "always had an uncanny ability to adjust to the demand or needs of the moment, the singer, or the shift in popular mood. And so phenomenal has been this ability that he is as difficult to define as the color of a chameleon. One searches for stylistic characteristics and is baffled. For the sea of his talent is always in motion. It's mercurial and elusive."

Irving Berlin was a man who loved success and the American dream and worked hard for it. He obtained wealth, honors and prestige but, according to biographer Laurence Bergreen "beneath the preening and the custom tailoring and the Bermuda tan, he remained an insecure and naive as Izzy Baline had been in his days as a singing waiter." He "found it impossible to relax, to assume anything less than total control over his business, his finances, himself." He constantly checked sales figures for his songs and "no matter how many copies were sold, Berlin was never satisfied."

In short, Berlin was totally dedicated and self-absorbed in the business of songwriting or, as one associate put it, "Irving was interested only in Irving."

Songs written by Irving Berlin include "God Bless America," "White Christmas," "Easter Parade," "Blue Skies," "A Pretty Girl is Like a Melody," "All By Myself," "Always," "Anything You Can Do (I Can Do Better)," "Always," "Cheek to Cheek," "Count Your Blessings (Instead of Sheep)," "Puttin' On The Ritz," "The Girl That I Marry," "There's No Business Like Show Business" and the songs from the musical, *Annie Get Your Gun*," which includes "You Can't Get a Man With a Gun."

The Golden Age of Songwriters

During the "golden age of song," roughly 1920-1955, the songwriters wore suits and ties when they wrote their songs. Their songs expressed a yearning for culture and sophistication and an acceptance of middle class values. Those songwriters wanted to be respected; they worked in a field that was "feminine" and was not considered "respectable," so they dressed as respectable businessmen.

(People during the first half of the twentieth century tended to have work clothes and "dress" clothes. For a factory worker or manual laborer, that was their wardrobe. It is only in the second half of the twentieth century that people had a wardrobe full of leisure clothes.)

The great early songwriters were a mixed group; George M. Cohan and Walter Donaldson were Irish-Americans; Fats Waller, Eubie Blake, James P. Johnson, Sheldon Brooks, and Duke Ellington were African-Americans, while the Gershwins, Irving Berlin, Harold Arlen, Arthur Schwartz, Howard Dietz, and E.Y. Harburg were Russian Jews; Hoagy Carmichael and Johnny Mercer were considered "outsiders," having been born in Indiana and Georgia, respectively.

Many of those songwriters were Jewish and many were immigrants who were born poor. They came along at a time when the Broadway musical was in its heyday and the ultimate for a songwriter was to write a hit Broadway musical. Because they wrote for musicals, they had to write "outside" themselves, composing songs for characters and situations; the purpose of their writing was to fit a story--not to express their own deep emotions or as self-expression. They wrote on demand and with deadlines--they could not wait for inspiration.

The songwriters were usually divided between lyricists and composers with only a few writing both melodies and lyrics. Broadway was the anchor--and aspiration--for those writers. During the 1920s, those "Tin Pan Alley" songwriters directed their energies towards Broadway; however, after the Wall Street Crash in 1929, and the ensuing Depression, the lights of Broadway grew dimmer. That diminution of Broadway coincided with the rise of talking pictures in Hollywood, so the songwriters shifted from New York to California, where they wrote for movies.

Those songwriters viewed themselves as professionals; when asked "which comes first, the words of the music?" Sammy Cahn answered "First comes the phone call" while Richard Rodgers answered "First comes the advance."

Jerome Kern

Jerome Kern (b. January 27, 1885 in New York City) was influenced and inspired by European musical drama. He began writing songs during his teenage years, after learning the piano at an early age. He studied at the New York School of Music, then became a song-plugger and rehearsal pianist before he achieved success writing for Broadway. Starting before World War I, Kern wrote over 100 songs for 37 Broadway shows during his lifetime.

P.G. Wodehouse, the British writer who worked as a lyricist with Kern, said of the composer, "his well of melody was inexhaustible, and he loved work. You could not give him too much of it...It was this habit of always working and seldom sleeping that eventually undermined his health. He hated to go to bed. His idea of a quiet home evening was to sit at the piano composing till about five in the morning."

Kern's best work was *Show Boat*, written with Oscar Hammerstein, which premiered in December, 1927 and introduced songs such as "Ol' Man River" and "Can't Help Lovin' That Man." During the 1930s, Kern moved to Hollywood and wrote for the movies. He died in 1945 in New York City after collapsing on the street. Among the hit songs he composed (in addition to the previously mentioned), were "All the Things You Are," "All Through the Day," "Babes in the Wood," "Bill," "Bojangles of Harlem," "Can I Forget You," "Dearly Beloved," "A Fine Romance," "The Folks Who Live on the Hill," "How'd You Like to Spoon with Me?," "I Dream Too Much" "I Won't Dance," "I'm Old Fashioned," "I've Told Ev'ry Little Star," "In Love in Vain," "The Last Time I Saw Paris," "Long Ago (And Far Away)," "Look for the Silver Lining," "Lovely to Look At," "Make Believe," "Once in a Blue Moon," "Smoke Gets in Your Eyes," "Come Dance With Me", "They Didn't Believe Me," "Till the Clouds Roll By," and "The Way You Look Tonight."

The Gershwins

George Gershwin was a songwriter who wrote and played for the love of music. He also loved life and during his short life was the bachelor man-about-town who personified the Jazz Age in New York--elegant, dapper and charismatic.

Born Jacob Gershvin on September 26, 1898, in Brooklyn, Gershwin took piano lessons for two years. He dropped out of school to become a song plugger when he was 16 and wrote "Swanee" (the lyrics were by Irving Caesar) which became a hit for Al Jolson when Gershwin was only 19. Heavily influenced by jazz and ragtime, with classical piano lessons in his background, Gershwin composed songs for the theater and movies as well as symphonic suites like "Rhapsody in Blue" (1924) and "Concerto in F" (1925). His opera, *Porgy and Bess* is a highlight in the history of musical theater.

Gershwin composed songs for the annual *George White's Scandals* 1920-1924, then composed his first musical, *Lady, Be Good* in 1924. That was followed by *Tip-Toes* (1925), *Oh, Kay!* (1926), *Funny Face* (1927), *Rosalie* (1928), *Show Girl* (1929), *Strike Up the Band* and *Girl Crazy* (1930) and *Of Thee I Sing* (1931). Film scores were composed for *A Damsel in Distress*, and *Shall We Dance* (both in 1937) and *The Goldwyn Follies* (1938).

Gershwin composed and performed "Rhapsody in Blue" when he was 26 years old; the work premiered at Paul Whiteman's Aeoleon Hall Concert on February 24, 1924. The title came from George's brother, Ira, who borrowed it from a Whistler painting.

Beginning in 1924, George's brother, Ira, wrote lyrics for their songs and the team wrote numerous classics. In 1936, they moved to Hollywood to write songs for Fred Astaire movies. For Astaire they wrote "They Can't Take That Away From Me," "They All Laughed," "Let's Call the Whole Thing Off," and "I've Got Beginner's Luck."

George Gershwin died in Beverly Hills, California on July 11, 1937 at the age of 38. He is the composer of the songs "Embraceable You," "Fascinating Rhythm," "I Got Plenty O'Nuttin," "I Got Rhythm," "It Ain't Necessarily So," "Let Call the Whole Thing Off," "The Man I Love," "Nice Work if You Can Get It," "Oh, Lady Be Good," "S'Wonderful," "Someone To Watch Over Me," and "Summertime."

Richard Rodgers and Lorenz Hart

Rodgers and Hart were a magic team of songwriters during the 1920s, 1930s and early 1940s who wrote the Broadway musicals *A Lonely Romeo* (1919), *The Garrick Gaieties* (1925), *Dearest Enemy* (1926), *The Girl Friend* (1926), *A Connecticut Yankee* (1927), *Present Arms* (1928), *Spring Is Here* (1929) *Simple Simon* and *Evergreen* (1930), *Jumbo* (1935), *On Your Toes* (1936), *Babes in Arms* (1937), *The Boys from Syracuse* (1938), *Too Many Girls* (1939), *Pal Joey* (1940) and *By Jupiter* (1942).

The duo also scored the films *Love Me Tonight* (1932), *Hallelujah I'm a Bum* (1933), and *Hollywood Party* (1934).

Hit songs from Rodgers and Hart include "Blue Moon," "Bewitched," "Falling in Love with Love," "I Could Write a Book," "I Didn't Know What Time It Was," "I've Got Five Dollars," "The Lady Is a Tramp," "My Funny Valentine," "Slaughter on 10th Avenue," "You Took Advantage of Me," and "Where or When?"

Richard Rodgers (born June 28, 1902 in Long Island, New York) was the composer while Lorenz Hart wrote the lyrics. Rodgers, the son of a Manhattan doctor, was educated at Columbia University and his mother was a pianist. He began composing songs with Lorenz Hart in 1918 for amateur musicals at Columbia University. New York publishers handed Rogers and Hart five years of rejections, turning down their musicals, after their initial hit of *A Lonely Romeo* in 1919.

Hart (born May 2, 1895) has been described as "witty, intellectual and decidedly urbane." Before he collaborated with Rodgers, Hart adapted and translated European operettas. Richard Rodgers was a methodical man but Lorenz Hart was an alcoholic who was not as disciplined or methodical as Rodgers. He held within him a genius for lyrics that could be humorous and poignant. The Rodgers-Hart team wrote together until 1942, when Rodgers began his collaboration with Oscar Hammerstein II.

When writing with Lorenz Hart, Rodgers tended to write the melody first, or at least part of the melody, before Hart began working on a lyric. That method of writing songs changed when Rodgers teamed with Oscar Hammerstein, who wrote the lyrics first, then Rogers worked on a melody to go with the words.

Hammerstein said of Rodgers, "All composers have a reservoir of melodies which come to them at different times and which they write down in a sketchbook. When they start work on a new musical, they play over these melodies for their collaborator, and it is decided which ones can be used. Dick Rodgers, however, does not work in this way. He writes music only for a specific purpose. Ideas for tunes seldom come to him while he is walking down the street or riding in taxicabs, and he doesn't rush to his piano very often to write a tune just for the sake of writing a tune...We can write words and music best when they are required by a situation or a characterization in a story."

Cole Porter

Cole Porter was the epitome of the witty, urbane, debonair cosmopolitan. Born June 8, 1891, in Peru, Indiana, to a family of wealth, Porter entered Yale, where he wrote musicals, then studied law at Harvard. Porter was not really interested in law, but studied it so he could receive an inheritance from his grandfather, millionaire financier J.O. Cole.

Porter wrote the Broadway musicals *See America First* (1916), *Fifty Million Frenchmen* (1929), *Wake Up and Dream* (1929), *The New Yorkers* (1930); *The Gay Divorcee* (1932); *Anything Goes* (1934); *Jubilee* (1935); *Red, Hot and Blue* (1936); *You Never Know* (1938); *Leave It to Me* (1938); *Dubarry Was a Lady* (1939); *Panama Hattie* (1940); *Let's Face It* (1941); *Something for the Boys* (1943); *Mexican Hayride* (1944) *Seven Lively Arts* (1944); *Around the World in Eighty Days* (1946); *The Pirate* (1947); *Kiss Me Kate* (1948); *Out of This World* (1950); *Can-Can* (1954) and *Silk Stockings* (1955).

He wrote music for the movies *Born to Dance* (1936); *Rosalie* (1937); *Broadway Melody of 1940* (1940); *Something to Shout About* (1943); *High Society* (1956); and *Les Girls* (1957).

Among Porter's best-known songs are "Anything Goes," "Begin the Beguine," "Don't Fence Me In," "I Get a Kick Out of You," "I've Got You Under My Skin," "Let's Do It (Let's Fall in Love)," "Love for Sale," "My

Heart Belongs to Daddy," "Night and Day," "True Love," "You'd Be So Nice to Come Home To" and "You're the Top."

In a horseback riding incident in 1937, Porter lost the use of both of his legs, and lived in constant pain for the rest of his life. That did not stop him from writing songs, or attending a constant round of parties given by the upper crust.

Porter married a wealthy divorcee who disliked sex, which allowed him to pursue his homosexual lifestyle. Porter was a dandy who "was constantly preoccupied with his physical appearance, studying himself in the looking-glass, nurturing his suntan with comic meticulousness...He became notorious for inflicting countless discourtesies on those unable to defend themselves, and often walked out of a room in mid-conversation, sometimes even in mid-sentence" and, as he grew older he "grew envious of the success of his musical contemporaries."

Writing songs, Porter stated that "I like to begin with an idea and then fit it to a title. I then write the words and music. Often I begin near the end of a refrain, so that the song has a strong finish, and then work backwards. I also like to use the title phrase at the beginning of a refrain and repeat it at the end for a climax," adding that, for him, "Writing lyrics is like doing a crossword puzzle."

Porter lived the life he wrote about in his musicals and his songs, an elegant man in cultured surroundings with sophisticated tastes whose wit and innate snobbery provided a comfortable distance to observe all that was going on. He toured Europe, spent time in Paris and on the Riviera, and attended a virtual non-stop round of glittering parties,

Cole Porter died on October 15, 1964 in Santa Monica, California.

Vaudeville and Al Jolson

The 1920s began with vaudeville still king of entertainment, although dying. Over 70 vaudeville houses closed in 1921 as houses switched to movies while the film companies, which owned the theaters as well as the films, hastened that move. However, vaudeville was still the training ground for performers; it was there that recording companies looked for singers and Broadway theaters looked for talent.

During World War I vaudeville suffered a major setback because touring became nearly impossible, a direct result of the government taking over the railroads. Vaudeville owners, who already used movies, began to use more and this hastened the death of that show business tradition.

Al Jolson performed in New York during World War I as the biggest star on Broadway. In February, 1918 he opened in *Sinbad*, which featured songs such as "Rock-a-Bye Your Baby with a Dixie Melody," "Why Do They All Take the Night Boat to Albany,?" "Cleopatra," "I Wonder Why She Kept On Saying, 'Si, Si, Si Si, Senor,'" and "N'Everything." His new manager, Louis Epstein, made sure Jolson's name was listed as co-writer on "N'Everything" and five other songs in the show. That would be a standard policy for Jolson, which angered songwriters; whenever he sang a song in a show, he usually had his name listed as co-writer and took co-writer money. Jolson had a five-year contract with the Shuberts guaranteeing him $2,500 a week and 15-25 percent of the gross receipts for all the shows he was in.

During the 1919-20 season Jolson appeared in *Bombo* and popularized "Swanee," which became George Gershwin's first and biggest commercial song hit. He began recording for the Columbia Graphophone Company and found the song "My Mammy" from Saul Bornstein at Irving Berlin's publishing company. "Mammy" was first performed in the show *Sinbad* as an interpolation. "My Mammy" became Al Jolson's signature song for the rest of his life. Performed in blackface, Jolson dropped to one knee and adlibbed bits and parts to his departed "Mammy." According to biographer Herbert G. Goldman, Jolson's mother, Naomi, was his "mammy" and the song was actually directed to her.

In 1921 Jolson was scheduled to open the show *Bombo* at the Imperial Theater on Fifty-ninth Street across from Central Park, because the Winter Garden was booked with another performance. He balked. The Shuberts then renamed the venue "Jolson's Fifty-ninth Street Theater" making this the first theater named after a living performer. In *Bombo*, which premiered in October, Jolson sang "April Showers."

Al Jolson has been described as "an ego who walked and talked like a man." Biographer Herbert Goldman notes that "On the stage or off it, Jolson mugged almost incessantly."

He was described as "a mean man," "frequently obnoxious," "very bossy" and "rarely laughed at any joke except to be polite." Jolson was "noted for his inexhaustible energy," but was also "a hypochondriac who exacerbated his physical ailments." Goldman noted "There was a deep well of anger in him that released itself as arrogance when he felt threatened, and as hatred when he was provoked."

Jolson did well in the world of vaudeville and show business because he "was a businessman...he was at home in the hard-nosed theatrical world of his times. He dealt with the Shuberts on their own terms, and he usually beat them...Al had no stomach for the Never-Never Land that ne'er-do-well performers like to live in." In show business, where so many spend more than they make and getting ripped off is an ongoing story, Jolson lived and died a rich man. He started penniless and ended up a multi-millionaire, a result of his cold eye for the business side of his profession. Few other performers have that eye.

Goldman notes that Jolson was "one of the most disliked men in the theatrical profession" and "lived only for applause" Jolson has been described as "a self-assured braggart who was terrified of being alone, a sentimentalist with a heart of gold who made life miserable for most of those around him, and a lothario who chased, conquered, and, in turn, ignored young women."

Once on stage, no one could touch Al Jolson. It has been said that "Jolson in a theater was electricity personified--thrilling, immediate, memorable, and unfortunately, unrecordable." During Jolson's time, a critic noted that during a performance "He sings ragtime with voice, shoulders, arms, and legs; he dances with no thought for the morrow; he tells stories such as the man who started to commit suicide by lying on the Erie railroad tracks and starved to death."

Jolson's most famous line, which he proclaimed to numerous audiences, was "Folks, you ain't heard nothin' yet" before he launched into a performance. Biographer Goldman states that "Jolson's talent...was basically his genius for communicating with an audience--establishing a unique 'oneness' by which every thought, joke, utterance, or lyric became a private moment between Al and anyone who occupied a seat."

Unfortunately, Al Jolson never did well in any mechanical medium except for his performance in *The Jazz Singer*. His recordings are difficult to listen to by audiences more comfortable with studio singers. His radio appearances never achieved that intimacy that great radio performers have. And, since the mid-1960s Jolson's use of blackface has been viewed as "racist" (a word that hadn't even been invented during Jolson's time) and "as an insulting caricature of black people rather than as a theatricalization with overtones of harlequins and ancient rites." In an age that measures performers by how well they perform in the electronic medium, Jolson is seen as an outdated failure. The true essence of Al Jolson--his live performances--excited audiences and created the Jolson legend. They were never really captured so contemporary audiences cannot appreciate his performing genius. Still, even if they had been captured, Jolson would not be acceptable to contemporary audiences because of his use of burnt cork and his broad stereotypical ethnic humor, which is now viewed as insulting, degrading and demeaning rather than humorous. It is impossible to defend or justify Al Jolson to today's audiences, but in his time he was "The World's Greatest Entertainer."

The Songs and Musicals

The dominant themes for popular songs during the 1920s were escapism and a pseudo-sophistication. The era of piano players playing live was about to be left behind in favor of an era of listeners to radio and records.

George Gershwin's first major song, "Swanee," was recorded by Al Jolson on January 9, 1920 for Columbia and soon became a national hit. Gershwin and other composers dominated that era with their songs and their publishing firms formed the power base for the industry. The insiders were going to Harlem and listening to black artists for inspiration.

The musical *Dardanella* appeared in 1920 and the song "Dardanella," recorded by Ben Selvin and his Novelty Orchestra, became the first pop dance record to sell over a million copies; it sold 6.5 million records and over 2 million copies of sheet music without appearing in a film or on radio. In 1921 *Shuffle Along*, a black musical, revolutionized musical theater by putting black singers, dancers, actors, and composers in mid-town Manhattan.

In 1921 The Jolson theater opened at 59th and Seventh in New York and debuted with Jolson in *Bombo* while that same year The Music Box at 239 W. 45th, a theater built by Irving Berlin for his songs, also opened. The first production was *Music Box Revue*. The "Revue" was the major form of musical theater at the beginning of the 1920s. Consisting of a series of "skits" or "scenes," the revue was flexible because it was not tied closely to a book or storyline, which meant a song or segment could be jettisoned if it wasn't working and another could be inserted. Revues were topical, urbane, witty, and sophisticated with elegant costumes and lavish sets and lots of seemingly naked girls.

The premier presenter of lavish shows with gorgeous young women appearing in the illusion of nudity was Florenz Ziegfeld whose "Follies" began in 1907 but reached their zenith during the jazz age. Here was the essence of the Jazz Age: pseudo sophistication and sexual liberation, naughtiness wrapped in sophistication with the look of elegant indulgence covering all. One of the best "Follies" was the 1919 version which featured Irving Berlin's song, "A Pretty Girl is Like a Melody." Ziegfeld mounted the shows in New York, then took them on a road tour and finished in time to vacation in Paris before he began work assembling the next year's version. The show at various times featured the black comedian Bert Williams, singing star Eddie Cantor, bandleader Paul Whiteman, made a star of Fannie Brice, and presented cowboy philosopher Will Rogers. The indulgence lasted past its peak as Ziegfeld spent increasingly large amounts of money on each new show (and squandered large amounts of money in his private life) until the last "Follies" appeared in 1931.

"Yes! We Have No Bananas" became one of the biggest novelty songs of the era when it was recorded by Eddie Cantor for Victor in 1923. In October of that year, the black musical *Runnin' Wild* opened and featured dancer Elizabeth Welch doing the "Charleston." That song, written by piano player James P. Johnson and Richard D. McPherson (under the pseudonym Cecil Mack) became the dance that defined the era. Although this was by far the most popular dance of the time, there were other popular dances, including the Varsity Drag, Shimmy, Black Bottom and others. Eddie Cantor had another novelty hit with "Barney Google."

At the Music Box Theater, Irving Berlin presented his last *Music Box Revue* in 1924. The song "All Alone" was a hit and "What'll I Do?" continued Berlin's domination of hit songs. Berlin was in the news more from courting a socialite, Ellin Mackay, a Catholic, whose father vehemently disapproved of the Russian Jew from the Lower East Side. It was a tabloid scandal that lasted for several years, until January, 1926, when the couple eloped. Mackay's father immediately wrote her out of his will (she was to receive $10 million) and dictated to all that no Berlin song was to be played at any social gathering he attended.

Hit musicals in 1924 included *Lady Be Good* and operettas *Rose Marie* and *The Student Prince* in 1924. The dancing team of Fred and Adelle Astaire appeared in *Lady Be Good* with the song "Fascinating Rhythm." The song "My Blue Heaven" was introduced in vaudeville in 1924 while the singer who made that a hit recording three years later, Gene Austin, was a vaudevillian who wrote two hits in 1924: "How Come You Do Me Like You Do?" and "When My Sugar Walks Down the Street, All the Little Birdies Go Tweet Tweet Tweet."

Perhaps the most significant development in the musical theater occurred in 1924 when composers, supported by ASCAP, finally received the right to control their scores. Prior to that time, songs could be interpolated into musicals by singers or producers--and other songs dropped--regardless of the composer's work on the original score. This meant that after 1924 shows increasingly had a set score, there were no interpolations, and the old "extravaganzas" which were a hodge podge of scenes and songs were a thing of the past. In an era dominated by composers such as George Gershwin, Jerome Kern, Richard Rogers, Irving Berlin, Cole Porter, Howard Arlen, Vincent Youmans and others, that strengthened the role of the composer and, ultimately, strengthened the musicals themselves, which increasingly had scores related to a plot rather than shows dominated by individual songs and performers.

The musical comedy *No, No Nanette* opened on Broadway on Thursday, September 16, 1925 after a year on the road, and featured a flapper as the central character. Out of *Nanette* came the hit songs "Tea for Two" and "I Want to Be Happy." That same week, *The Vagabond King* and *Sunny* also opened in New York.

In 1925 Al Jolson was popular in the musical *Big Boy* with hit songs "Keep Smilin' at Trouble" and "It All Depends on You" while Irish tenor John McCormack sang popular songs, including Berlin's "All Alone" which created huge sales when he performed it on network radio. Other flapper songs appeared, including "Five Foot Two, Eyes of Blue" and "If You Knew Susie."

In 1926 there were two million selling disks: "Who?" by George Olsen and his Band and "Some of These Days" by Sophie Tucker, a song she began performing in 1910 in vaudeville. Stardom came to Clara Bow, who became the "It" girl, and the largest dance hall in the world opened in Harlem in 1926. The Savoy occupied the entire second floor of a building that covered a block in Harlem; "The World's Most Beautiful Ballroom" opened with a performance by The Fletcher Henderson Band.

The year 1926 was a year for live music to accompany movies; movie companies announced that after this there would be recordings to accompany silent movies. Large orchestras were at the top movie houses while in small cities with local movie houses there was a pianist, sometimes accompanied by a violinist. The idea of sound or "talking" pictures was still considered impractical.

In 1925, Paul Robeson presented a concert of Negro spirituals. The spiritual "Deep River" brought him his first fame. Negro spirituals became popular and respected that year when Henry T. Burleigh arranged them for voice and piano in the style of art songs. The two-volume *Book of American Negro Spirituals* was edited by brothers John Rosamond and James Weldon Johnson in 1925-6 and presented songs like "Go Down Moses," "Nobody Knows de Trouble I've Seen" and "Swing Low, Sweet Chariot" in a serious, studious light. The interest in spirituals came from the Harlem Renaissance, which popularized the history and culture of the Negro.

Showboat

The most important musical of the 1920s was *Show Boat*, which opened at the National Theater in Washington on December 16, 1927; it's New York opening was at the Ziegfeld Theater on December 27. The musical score was composed by Jerome Kern with lyrics by Oscar Hammerstein II and included songs like "Can't Help Lovin' Dat Man," "Make Believe," "Why Do I Love You," "Bill," "You Are Love" and "Ol Man River." That musical pointed the way for the future of musicals with its songs supporting a tight story line, although it would not be until *Oklahoma* appeared in 1942 that Broadway composers regularly required the songs to support the story rather than having the story somehow loosely relate to the songs.

Show Boat was a musical with comedy but it was also a serious story, in contrast to the light-hearted entertainment that musicals had provided with their emphasis on pretty girls and trivial plots.

The role of the stevedore, Joe, was expanded from the character in the novel, written by Edna Ferber, for Paul Robeson but, because of the delays getting the musical on the stage, the role of Joe was played by Jules Bledsoe in the original production. Paul Robeson played the role of "Joe" in the London premier in 1927 and his performance virtually defined that role for future actors. His version of "Old Man River" set the standard for singers who sang that song.

Paul Robeson performed the role of Joe in the Broadway revival in 1932, in the first film version in 1936 and in the stage revival in Los Angeles in 1940.

Paul Robeson

Paul Robeson excelled in theater, singing, sports and academics but his career was thwarted by racism, which spurred his political activism. He was born on April 9, 1898, the fifth child of Reverend William Drew Robeson, minister of the Witherspoon Street Presbyterian Church in Princeton, New Jersey, and Maria Louisa Bustill. Problems between Reverend Robeson, pastor of the all-black congregation, and its white supporters led to his resignation in 1901. Hard times hit the Robeson family as Reverend Robeson took menial jobs to support his family. In 1904, when Paul Robeson was six, his mother died in a house fire.

In 1910 Reverend Robeson became pastor of the St. Thomas A.M.E. Zion church in Summerfield, New Jersey. At Summerfield High School, Paul became involved in theater, performing in *Julius Caesar* and *Othello*, sang in the school chorus and starred in football, basketball, baseball and track. When he graduated, he had a scholarship to Rutgers University after winning a statewide academic contest.

Paul Robeson was the only African-American at Rutgers in late 1915 and only the third to attend at that time. Despite racial taunts and physical roughhousing from his teammates that left him with a broken nose and dislocated shoulder, Robeson, through his determination, won a place on Rutgers's Scarlet Knights football team.

Robeson excelled on the football field but had to sit on the sideline and watch when a southern football team refused to take the field because Rutgers had a Negro player. An exceptionally talented singer, Robeson earned money by singing at off-campus events. He was an unofficial member of the Glee Club because he was not allowed at all white mixers. During his junior year in college, his father became ill and Robeson cared for him before he died.

During World War I, Robeson openly criticized the involvement of blacks in the military, fighting for a country that would not give them full rights at home. His outspokenness for Civil Rights led to further conflicts; however, he graduated from Rutgers with varsity letters in several sports and was named first team All-American in football as an end and tackle.

During the fall of 1919, Robeson entered the New York University School of Law and became an assistant football coach at Lincoln College; however, in early 1920 he transferred to the Columbia School of Law and moved to Harlem. His theatrical debut in New York came in 1920 with a role in *Simon of Cyrene*, written by Ridgely Torrance. He met Eslanda "Essie" Goode and they were married in August, 1921.

Paul Robeson met Fritz Pollard, the first African-American coach in the National Football League (NFL) during the summer after his high school graduation when he worked as a waiter in Rhode Island. Pollard recruited Robeson to play in the early NFL while Robeson was in law school. During the off season—and still in law school—Robeson starred in the play, *Taboo*, written by Mary Hoyt Wiborg; he also performed in the chorus of *Shuffle Along*. Robeson joined the cast of *Taboo* in England and then returned to the United States and continued law school at Columbia while playing for the Milwaukee Badgers in the NFL. In 1922 he ended his career in the NFL and graduated from law school

Robeson worked as a lawyer for a short time but his career was limited by racism; frustrated with the limitations, he was supported by his wife and then, at the end of 1924, obtained the lead role in *All God's Chillun Got Wings* by playwright Eugene O'Neill. The play dealt with the issue of a black man married to a white woman and was so controversial that its opening had to be postponed because a national debate was caused by the plot.

During the delay of *All God's Chillun Got Wings*, Robeson starred in the play *The Emperor Jones*. Robeson became a star in the theatre, which led to his entrée in top social circles. His wife Essie played a major role in Robeson's career, encouraging him and becoming his agent. She negotiated his first film role, a silent film titled *Body and Soul*.

Robeson became friends with Lawrence Brown, a classically trained pianist during his time with *Taboo*; to support a charity for unwed mothers, Robeson and Brown performed a concert of spirituals, which led to Victor Records signing Robeson to a recording contract. During 1926 and 1927 Robeson and Brown performed a number of concerts featuring spirituals.

Paul Robeson became a prominent member of the Harlem Renaissance because of his success in athletics and the theater. However, he paid a price during the years ahead because of his political activism. Paul Robeson was a victim of racism, not just because of the limitation put upon his race, but because of his out-spoken criticism of racism and the fact that the United States not only tolerated it, but endorsed and encouraged it.

The Harlem Renaissance

The Harlem Renaissance was a turning point in the history of African-Americans. Here, blacks found an intellectual center, an artistic environment, a freedom to write, think, paint, and create which they had not known before. Here is where the "Old Negro," who was docile and deferential to whites, was thrown off and the "New Negro" took his place. The "New Negro" was self-confident, self-assertive, self-respecting, intellectual, capable of great works of art, music and literature. The Old Negro was a problem; the New Negro was a people and the self-confidence led to a new freedom in the arts that flowered in Harlem.

The move to Harlem by blacks began before World War I when large numbers of blacks fled to New York and other cities from the south and small towns, trying to find work and escape racism and restrictions. The attraction of Harlem came because of a depressed real estate market at the time which allowed blacks to settle in large numbers. Harlem is located between 125th and 135th Streets on the east and west and bordered by Lennox Avenue on the south. J. Rosamond Johnson was one of the first blacks to buy a house in the area and his brother, James Weldon Johnson joined him in Harlem in 1917. James Weldon Johnson was a Tin Pan Alley songwriter ("Under the Bamboo Tree," "The Congo Love Song") a novelist (*The Autobiography of an Ex-Coloured Man*), and the first black executive secretary of the NAACP. Later he served as Adam K. Spence Chair of Creative Literature at Fisk University. Johnson was a powerful leader and intellectual force for Negro thought who also wrote journalism, poetry, and edited a collection of Negro spirituals (with his brother, J. Rosamund).

Another intellectual leader was W. E. B. DuBois, who had degrees from Fisk and Harvard (including a doctorate) and had studied in Europe. The NAACP was formed by DuBois and others in 1910 and Dubois was appointed editor of their monthly publication, *Crisis*, which was the reason he moved from Atlanta to New York that same year. He had written an influential book, *Souls of Black Folk*, which challenged the philosophy of Booker T. Washington, head of the Tuskogee Institute in Alabama and a leader in Negro education. Washington saw the future of the Negro's improvement in terms of job training (industrial and agricultural) to improve economic skills while DuBois saw it in terms of intellectualism, aspiring to a higher culture; thus there emerged two different and competing philosophies about Negro progress. In one sense, the two philosophies reflected an America changing from a rural society to an urban one with Washington reflecting the former while DuBois reflected the latter. It also indicated a deeper drive within many blacks towards militancy and against appeasement and "getting along" as they created a new era and shook off the past.

By the time the poet Langston Hughes arrived in 1921, Harlem was well-established as a thriving black community and the intellectual center for black life. The mass media was the printed word--there was no radio or TV--so the emphasis in Harlem was on writing. Harlem intellectuals saw themselves as leaders and creators of a new society. They generally felt that if whites saw them at their best as thinkers and doers then racism and inequality would disappear. They knew that culture defined civilization so they actively encouraged the arts: literature, painting and music. Their emphasis was on "high culture" and the intellectual leaders (except Hughes) disparaged jazz. Further, the idea of blacks performing on stage in musicals singing and dancing was viewed as entertainment, not culture. The folk culture of spirituals, blues, dancing and jazz was to be thrown off and replaced by European symphonies, operas and ballets written and performed by blacks.

Ironically, it was the "folk" music of blacks which survived the Harlem Renaissance and proved most influential in American culture. There were plenty of outlets for black musicians in Harlem, numerous clubs, theaters and ballrooms, including the Alhambra, Apollo, Crescent, Lincoln, Odeon, Oriental, Lafayette, Harlem Opera House and the famous Savoy Ballroom on Lenox Avenue, which covered a block between 140th and 141st. Musicians such as Louis Jordan and his Tympani Five, Art Tatum, Eubie Blake, Fats Waller, Louis Armstrong, Ethel Waters, Mamie Smith, Perry Bradford, Bessie Smith, Ma Rainey, Lovie Austin, James P. Johnson, Jelly Roll Morton, Luckey Roberts, Zez Confrey, Ernest Hogan, and Bob Cole were all in Harlem performing and writing.

The most famous club, the Cotton Club, was actually a club for an all-white clientele with black performers controlled by the Mob. Duke Ellington found national fame when he performed at the premier on December 4, 1927 and stayed five years, broadcasting nightly on network radio coast to coast. The Mafia controlled a number of clubs in Harlem (as well as in the black sections of other cities) because during Prohibition police were less likely to patrol the black sections of a city, preferring to let the clubs alone while the upper class white areas were off limits for crime. Blacks benefitted because black performers played before large audiences every night, the establishments employed blacks, and it allowed whites to hear and see black performers. Business was brisk, although there was another side. Black musicians were preferable because they were more easily controlled by the Mob, less likely to go to police if trouble erupted, and the speakeasies led the black sections of town to be centers for gambling, prostitution and other vices.

During the 1920s Harlem became the in place to go for well-heeled whites from mid-town Manhattan out on the town. Black music, black performers and black culture was the rage. The rage for black entertainment in New York began with *Shuffle Along*, which premiered in 1921. That was not the first all-black theater offering in New York--the first commercial show organized, written, produced and managed by Negroes was *A Trip to Coontown* in 1898 and *Clorindy: or the Origin of the Cakewalk* written by black composer Will Marion Cook and lyricist Paul Laurence Dunbar.

Shuffle Along opened at a theater on West 63rd Street on May 23, 1921. The score was written by Eubie Blake and Noble Sissle and the book was written by vaudeville comics Flournoy Miller and Aubrey Lyles, who had been writing plays since they were at Fisk University in Nashville. *Shuffle Along* starred Josephine Baker, Florence Mills, and Hall Johnson, had hit songs ("I'm Just Wild About Harry," "Love Will Find a Way," and "Bandana Days") and featured wild, exciting dancing. The dances covered a variety of styles--soft shoe, buck and wing, tap--and the music was jazz.

The success of *Shuffle Along* created a demand for more black musicals and during the 1920s there were sometimes as many as twenty different all-black shows on Broadway. It was followed by *Strut Miss Lizzie* and *Seven-Eleven* in 1922; *Elsie* in 1923, whose score was also written by Blake and Sissle; *Dixie to Broadway* and *Runnin' Wild* in 1924; *Chocolate Dandies* in 1925; *Blackbirds* in 1926; *Africana* in 1927 (starring Ethel Waters); *Blackbirds in 1928* (which starred Bill "Bojangles" Robinson); and *Keep Shuffling* in 1928 (also by Miller and Lyles).

All of the shows were not as successful as *Shuffle Along* but they all provided an opportunity for black performers, composers and writers to appear on Broadway. The next big success came from *Runnin' Wild* in 1923 with the book written by Miller and Lyles which featured the hit song and dance "Charleston" by Cecil Mack and James P. Johnson. That song captured the Jazz Age; no other musical performance encapsulated the wild, crazy, uninhibited spirit of the time more than that dance.

The final hit black show in the 1920s, *Hot Chocolates* premiered in June, 1929, with the score written by Andy Razaf and Fats Waller. The song "Ain't Misbehavin'" came from that musical and Louis Armstrong tasted stardom when he came out from the pit orchestra during the performance and played a solo.

The Harlem Renaissance was responsible for the blues craze of the early 20s and for Tin Pan Alley songwriters writing blues and ragtime songs. Pianist James P. Johnson developed his "stride piano" style and songwriters Fats Waller, Duke Ellington, Eubie Blake and Jelly Roll Morton all pushed the limits of jazz and ragtime. This movement was also responsible for the first black "stars" of entertainment.

The Harlem Renaissance ended like the Jazz Age ended, with the stock market crash in 1929 and the Great Depression. Whites stopped going uptown and money was scarce for everybody; the repeal of Prohibition in 1932 drove the final nail in the coffin because it shut down the speakeasies and the network that supported black entertainers. The final black musical hit was *Green Pastures*, a gospel musical that opened in 1930, but the Harlem Renaissance was over by then because people could no longer afford the pursuit of art and the heady air of intellectualism shaping ideas and thought. Instead, people had to figure out how to survive and contend with the day to day struggles of getting by after an entire economy collapsed.

Although the Harlem Renaissance succeeded in fostering an environment when black musicians, writers and singers succeeded to the point where they had a major influence on American popular music, there was criticism that the music and dances in New York "mainly continued to exploit a corrupt tradition." Black historian Nathan Irvin Huggins writes in his book, *Harlem Renaissance*, that Harlem was "a stage; the performers played for all they were worth to a white world. Dance as no one can; sing with the humor or pathos no one else has; make jokes about oneself (make oneself into a joke), anything, everything but with style; then turn to the audience and bow deeply and smile broadly and live in that rare luxury of applause, approval, love. If the figure of theater is appropriate, then the Negro was the performer in a strange, almost macabre, act of black collusion in his own emasculation. For that white world, itself unfulfilled, was compelled to approve only that view of the Negro which served its image."

Few can doubt that American music benefited from the Harlem Renaissance. The continued success of the blues after World War II, the merging of rhythm and blues into rock'n'roll in the 1950s, and the rise of black superstars during the 1960s and 70s all have a direct connection to that period and that movement. The wide acceptance of creative black talent in the recording industry began when Mamie Smith recorded "Crazy Blues" for Okeh Records in 1921 and the success of that record proved to recording executives that there was an African-American audience ready and able to buy recordings of Negro music by Negro talent. Although that market shrank during the 1930s, it emerged after World War II to create an entire industry of African-American music that had a dominant influence on mainstream American music throughout the rest of the twentieth century.

1927

The entertainment industry made 1927 a landmark year in a number of ways. During that year, when the nation's attention was captured by Charles Lindburgh flying nonstop from New York to Paris in his small "Spirit of St. Louis" plane in May, and Babe Ruth hitting 60 home runs as the Yankees dominated baseball, the hit recording of "My Blue Heaven" by Gene Austin set a record in sales in the post-electric recording era that would not be matched until Bing Crosby hit with "White Christmas" in 1942.

Music publisher Irving Mills became the manager of Duke Ellington and landed him the job of playing at the Cotton Club in Harlem. Those shows, which began on December 4, 1927, enabled Ellington to become nationally famous because of the network radio hookup that broadcast his show. Mills, the former publisher of numerous coon songs, had his name appear as co-writer on numerous Ellington songs and regularly took some of Ellington's songwriting income for his management services. However, he opened doors that only a white manager could open, which made Duke Ellington a star.

The Ziegfeld Follies of 1927 featured the songs of Irving Berlin sung by Eddie Cantor in blackface. Also in 1927 Red Nichols's disk "Ida, Sweet as Apple Cider" sold over a million copies.

Jazz

The first jazz recording was made in February, 1917, by the Original Dixieland Jazz Band for Victor. "The Livery Stable Blues," b/w "Original Dixie Land One-Step" soon became a million seller. Although a follow-up "jazz" hit would not occur for a number of years, this marks the beginning of the history of recorded jazz.

The city most closely linked with jazz is New Orleans; and a number of people refer to New Orleans as the birth place of jazz. That is both true and a bit misleading; in some ways it may be asserted that jazz was born in a thousand different places, all over America; however, the long tap root of jazz certainly goes to New Orleans. Two of the earliest, most influential jazz musicians came from New Orleans. King Oliver and Louis Armstrong, and the history of a section of New Orleans known as "Storyville," is key to understanding how those musicians came to prominence in Chicago and New York.

Storyville

The Storyville section of New Orleans was created by city alderman Sidney Story in 1897, who proposed that a 38 block section of the French Quarter be identified as the "official" red-light district of the city in order to control and limit the spread of prostitution. During the early 1900s there were at least 100 night clubs, tonks, brothels and sporting houses where musicians performed. Sometimes it was only a piano player while in other venues it might be a small dance orchestra or primitive jazz bands that featured fiddles, harmonicas, brass instruments, penny whistles and various homemade instruments.

In August, 1917, Newton D. Baker, the Secretary of War under President Woodrow Wilson, ordered that prostitution would not be conducted within five miles of an army base. The Secretary of the Navy, Josephus Daniels, issued a similar order for the Navy, which caused New Orleans Mayor Martin Behrman to shut down Storyville. The ordinance was issued on October 17 and on November 12, 1917 prostitution was officially declared illegal in Storyville, essentially abolishing this red-light district.

The musicians who made their living playing in Storyville had to find new places to play, which caused many to leave New Orleans. Some moved to Los Angeles, Chicago, New York and other cities while others obtained jobs on riverboats that featured gambling and ran up and down the Mississippi River.

It was because of the closing of Storyville that the music which had been played in New Orleans was forced to expand beyond the borders of New Orleans. That music, which came to be called "jazz," made New Orleans famous as the birthplace of jazz and brought the city renown as this vibrant music made its way onto the national stage through recordings and performances of musicians from New Orleans.

The Roots of Jazz

Jazz is a direct descendent of ragtime, which descended from brass band music. Although jazz is a child of ragtime, it's ancestors also include the rhythms of West Africa, classical music from Europe (with its harmonic structure), American folk music, gospel or religious music, work songs, blues, and minstrel show music.

Jazz is a social music in several ways. First, it is a public music, played for social occasions; specifically for dancing and socializing (listening clubs came much later). Second, it came from the American Black culture. The segregated culture forced African-Americans to be separate from whites, yet part of the general culture at the same time. That dichotomy, where blacks were Americans but not entitled to the freedoms and privileges of white Americans--part of this country but separate from it--isolated musicians in a myriad of ways at the same time they were part of the cultural mainstream.

In "Sixty Years of Jazz, An Historical Survey," Leonard Feather states, "During the Civil War and postwar years the Negro was fashioning his own music on plantations and in chain gangs, in levee camps and on railroads, poverty confining his expression to the human voice or to crude homemade fiddles, guitars and banjos; that at the same time he was developing spirituals that owed more to white sources than his secular melodies...it was not until the white and Negro, secular and religious influences spread through the country during the 1890s that a form of music directly linked with jazz developed. This was the era of the cakewalk, and it was probably because of the national popularity of that dance that ragtime began to evolve as a distinct musical style."

The term "jass" was originally used as a verb to describe the sex act and so the term became "jass music" which became a popular fad in Chicago,

New York and New Orleans, replacing the term "ragtime." Musically, there was not much difference between ragtime and jazz at that time, except the music got a new name. Ironically, as jazz developed and moved further from ragtime, the term "ragtime" was lost--and so was the music--for a number of years.

In the 19-teens, several jazz groups played in New York. Tom Brown's Five Rubes was a white group and That Creole Band was a black group, both from New Orleans. The Tennessee Ten was another group playing in New York theaters and vaudeville houses while The Tempo Club Orchestra appeared in Ziegfeld's Midnight Follies. The Original Dixieland Jazz Band was a group of five white men who performed at a New York restaurant during that time.

In 1917, when a federal order closed the Storyville area of New Orleans, the Lincoln Gardens in Chicago offered trumpet player King Oliver a job. Oliver had been playing in a band with trombonist Kid Ory; when Oliver left New Orleans, Louis Armstrong took his place in the Ory band. Fate Marable, a pianist on the Mississippi riverboats, began a band leading career in 1917; his bands carried a number of jazz musicians north. Jelly Roll Morton moved to California, taking his barrelhouse piano style West; in 1919, Kid Ory also went to California. In London, the British received their first taste of jazz when the Original Dixieland Band played there, and jazz became a fashionable fad in London society.

In 1921 the New Orleans Rhythm Kings opened at the Friars' Inn in Chicago. Two soloists, clarinetist Leon Rappolo and trombonist George Brunies outshone leader Paul Mares (trumpet) during their solos. Brunies was also one of the first to use humor extensively with jazz, which helped put the music across to the public.

Meanwhile, in Los Angeles, Kid Ory and his band had their first recording session for an independent label while James P. Johnson recorded the first jazz piano solo record for Okeh.

As labels increasingly began to target the "race" market in 1922 and 1923, jazz benefited. King Oliver's group in Chicago, which included Louis Armstrong and clarinetist Johnny Dodds, recorded for the Gennett Company at a session in Richmond, Indiana. The Richmond studio also saw Jelly Roll Morton record some sides. Back in New York, Fletcher Henderson, leader of the first black group to specialize in orchestrations, made recordings with his group. He also accompanied singers like Bessie Smith and Ma Rainey on their sessions.

In 1924 Louis Armstrong joined Fletcher Henderson's band in New York and Thomas "Fats" Waller recorded "Birmingham Blues" on his first session. That was also the year Ethel Waters combined blues and jazz to sing "Dinah" and cornetist Bix Beiderbecke came to New York to join a band, the Wolverines, who played at a Times Square dance hall.

Duke Ellington moved to New York from Washington in 1923 and by 1926 was gaining recognition at the Kentucky Club on Broadway. Red Nichols became the central figure of a group of white jazz musicians who played in commercial bands and recorded under names like the Red Heads, and Red Nichols and his Five Pennies. Nichols' musicians included Jimmy Dorsey on clarinet, Joe Venuti on violin, Miff Mole on trombone, and Eddie Lang on guitar.

New York was the major town for the music business because that was where the major recording companies were located. It was not until 1926 that they did extensive field recordings, due to the technological jump to electrical from acoustic recording.

In Chicago at the Plantation was King Oliver's Dixie Syncopators; at the Apex were Jimmy Noone's band with Earl Hines; and in Detroit there were two important groups: McKinney's Cotton Pickers and the Jean Goldkette band, which included Bix Beiderbecke, Frank Trumbauer and Pee Wee Russell in 1926-7. In 1927 Goldette's band dissolved and Beiderbecke joined Paul Whiteman.

The golden years of jazz recording are considered to be 1926-1929. The American economy was doing well, the recording companies were making money, and the music was growing and developing at an enormous pace. It was the prime time for small units like Louis Armstrong's Hot Five and Hot Seven, Jelly Roll Morton and his Red Hot Peppers, Red Nichols and his Pennies, Bix Beiderbecke, Trumbauer, Venuti and Lang. Key studio session players included trombonists Floyd O'Brien and Jack Teagarden, saxophonists Mezz Mezzrow and Fud Livingston, and drummers Gene Krupa and Dave Tough.

Duke Ellington appeared at the Cotton Club in Harlem, Jimmie Lunceford's group was in Memphis, Andy Kirk's "Twelve Clouds of Joy" was in Kansas City, and Earl Hines' first big band was in Chicago.

At that time a "big" band was anything with two cornets, a trombone and three saxophones. Among the "big" bands for black musicians were those of Fletcher Henderson, King Oliver, and Louis Armstrong. For white bands, there was Ben Pollack on the West Coast who, in 1926, had a sixteen-year-old clarinetist named Benny Goodman.

Jazz and Prohibition

During the era of Prohibition, the country turned the liquor, gambling and prostitution industries over to organized crime. The United States was a segregated country; there was a black section of town and a white section of town. Police regularly patrolled the white section of town but did not usually venture into the black section; in fact, most police forces did not have an black policemen. Therefore, "Speakeasies" where liquor, gambling and prostitution could be found were generally found in the "black" section of town.

The "speakeasies" or "black and tan clubs" featured black musicians. In most of those clubs, if you were black you could wait on tables or be on the bandstand but you could not be in the audience.

The owners of speakeasies—generally connected to organized crime—preferred to hire black musicians instead of white ones because the black musicians could be more easily controlled. White musicians had access to police, so if a shooting or some other "happening" occurred inside a club controlled by organized crime, they had access to police. Black musicians did not have that easy access.

That was a real boon for black jazz musicians because they were in demand by organized crime to play in those establishments and their talent flourished. Jazz historians may attribute the opportunities offered to black musicians to perform in those clubs as due to their superior playing and performances; that will not be contested. However, the fact that black musicians had the opportunities to perform in clubs controlled by organized crime is directly related to the fact that organized crime did not want white musicians playing in their clubs.

Paul Whiteman

Paul "Pops" Whiteman had a great talent as a band leader, but his greatest talent was as a promoter; he promoted himself, his group and the music he played. That should not obscure the fact that Whiteman had a tremendous talent for making jazz commercial and fashionable and his band was a forerunner to the Big Band era.

Whiteman pioneered a symphonic approach to dance music and, in doing so, featured in his group great soloists and future stars such as Jimmy and Tommy Dorsey, Jack and Charlie Teagarden, Bix Beiderbecke, Frankie Trumbauer, Joe Venuti, Eddie Lang, Henry Busse, Mike Pingatore and Roy Bargy. Additionally, singers Bing Crosby, Mildred Bailey, Johnny Mercer, Morton Downey, Red McKenzie, Jack Fulton and Joan Edwards were also featured in his group at one time or another. Indeed, Whiteman was probably the major farm club to the Big Band era of the mid-1930s.

Paul Whiteman was a great salesman who talked, thought and acted big and was never afraid to spotlight new talent. He was born March 28, 1890, in Denver, Colorado, where his father, Wilberforce J. Whiteman, taught music in the public schools and was musical director at Trinity Methodist Church. In 1894 Wilberforce became superintendent of music education for the Denver school system, a post he held for 30 years. Wilberforce was an influential music teacher and among his students were jazz greats Jimmie Lunceford and Andy Kirk. However, Wilberforce himself preferred classical music and disliked ragtime and jazz.

Young Paul Whiteman joined the San Francisco Symphony in 1915, playing viola. In addition to the Symphony, Whiteman performed in hotel orchestras and salon ensembles. In 1918 he resigned from the Symphony and joined the orchestra at Tait's Cafe, playing "jazz." That same year he enlisted in the Navy and served on a submarine chaser.

Back in San Francisco after his short stint in the Navy, Whiteman put together an orchestra consisting of violin, saxophone, banjo, accordion, drums and piano and performed at Neptune's Palace. In 1919 he took over the dance orchestra at the Fairmont Hotel, then the Belvedere where he played for dinner dances, society hops, tea dances and Sunday evening concerts.

In major cities after World War I there were a number of large hotels and ballrooms where people gathered to dance. Brass bands played for the "society" crowd, although a number of young people also showed up to party. Paul Whiteman's group was one of many who played in those hotels, ballrooms, and resorts, but Whiteman was an ambitious man and his musical tastes increasingly leaned towards jazz.

In late 1919, Whiteman moved to Los Angeles where he performed at the Alexandria Hotel. His band in L.A., known later as the "original Whiteman" group, consisted of pianist Charles Caldwell, drummer Harold McDonald, trombonist Buster Johnson, bass player J.K. Wallace, trumpeter Henry Busse, saxophonists Leslie Canfield and Charles Dornberger and banjoist Mike Pingitore. Busse was a composer as well as trumpeter and helped compose two songs that became Whiteman hits, "Wang Wang Blues" and "Hot Lips."

Ferde Grofe joined Whiteman's group as an arranger and the group soon attracted the attention of the Hollywood crowd. In late Spring, 1920, Whiteman and his group moved to Atlantic City, where they performed at the Ambassador Hotel. Business was scarce until the Victor Phonograph Company held its annual convention in that city. Impressed by Whiteman's group, the Victor talent scouts offered Whiteman a recording contract and on August 9 the group entered the studio and recorded four songs. The group returned to the studio on August 19 and 23 and in September the Victor company shipped a two-sided single, "Whispering" b/w "Japanese Sandman" and supported it with a promotional and sales campaign. That first record sold a million copies.

Starting in 1921, Victor scheduled a Whiteman disk to be released each month--and some months there were two released.

Paul Whiteman and his group moved to New York, where they began a four year run at the Palais Royal Restaurant. In New York there were the orchestras of Ben Selvin at the Moulin Rouge, Sam Lanin at Roseland, Arnold Johnson at Reisenweber's, Bill Munro at Cafe de Paris and Joseph C. Smith at the Hotel Plaza. Whiteman, with agent Harry Fitzgerald, soon organized a series of bands to play at other hotels and clubs; by October, 1922 there were 19 groups.

In 1923 Whiteman and his group toured England. By that time "Whispering" and "Three O'Clock in the Morning" (recorded in 1922) were both hits (both sold over a million copies) and the Whiteman group was going into the Victor studios three or four times a month to record.

Whiteman was a pioneer in adding vocal choruses to his dance numbers. In 1921 vocalist Morton Downey, an Irish tenor, joined the group but it was not until 1923 that he made regular appearances; at that time, the singer was just another instrument who sat around when he wasn't singing, which was most of the time because the emphasis was on the orchestra and instrumentals. That caused Downey to hold a reedless saxophone when he wasn't singing so it would look like he was a part of the group.

In 1923 Billy Murray recorded "Mr. Gallagher and Mr. Shean," a comedy number with Whiteman. That same year the American Quartet, featuring Murray and Frank Croxton, sang "Last Night on the Back Porch." Other vocalists who sang with Whiteman include Ed Smalle, Franklyn Baur, Lewis James, and Billy Murray.

Whiteman's most famous contribution to the history of jazz occurred in 1924 with his concert at Aeolian Hall in New York. The idea for the concert, which mixed symphonic and jazz music and featured "Rhapsody in Blue," a work by George Gershwin that was commissioned by Whiteman, came from a concert Whiteman attended in 1923. At that concert, Eva Gautier included jazz in a performance that included works from Bellini, Purcell and

Hindemith. George Gershwin provided piano accompaniment to Gautier, performing "Alexander's Ragtime Band," "Swanee," "I'll Build a Stairway to Paradise," "Carolina in the Morning" and "Innocent Ingenue Baby."

On February 12, 1924, Paul Whiteman spent four hours on the podium, conducting 23 musicians in a concert that "changed his life and the direction of his orchestra virtually overnight." According to biographer Thomas DeLong, "Within days Paul's office telephone rang incessantly with offers of concert tours, promotional schemes, private party bids, and proposals for personal appearances. The size of his orchestra and the number of people on his staff started to grow. 'Rhapsody in Blue' became his signature tune and his theme song."

Although Whiteman was in demand for personal appearances, and his income soared to over $400,000 a year, his father did not approve, stating of his favorite son, "He can't conduct. Besides, it's not real music, just some honkytonk outpourings that don't mean a thing in the long run."

The Aeolian Hall concert, and the ensuing personal appearances, made Whiteman the "King of Jazz," the spokesman for popular music and the leading authority on jazz. As the public symbol of jazz, he made the music more respectable to the middle class because, although his orchestra included a number of jazz musicians, they played a "soft jazz" that featured a symphonic approach to the music.

Jazz critics and historians have often dismissed Whiteman's role in the evolution of the music, but during that time only a white man could have brought jazz to a society crowd and only a white man could proclaim himself as "King of Jazz" and promote the music like Whiteman did. It's not all about the music; the marketing and other business aspects of recordings are as important as the music itself during its time.

Paul Whiteman lived lavishly and treated his musicians well; by mid-1925 the orchestra had 28 pieces (six violins, two violas, two cellos, one string bass, three trombones, three trumpets, four saxophones, one banjo, one guitar, one bass, one set of drums and two pianos) performing songs arranged by Ferde Grofe. The musicians received double what other bandleaders paid, which meant that Whiteman's musicians earned about ten times what the average American worker earned.

During 1925, Whiteman's group appeared in about 300 cities and towns, released over 25 records, and spent about eight months on the road, earning approximately $800,000. At the end of the year, the group performed a concert at Carnegie Hall. That was another high point of Whiteman's career as a big band leader.

Jazz was the subject of scorn for most of the cultural elite. Quotes like "The jazz band of life is wrecking the American home," "The jazz spirit of the times is causing many suicides," "Jazz music causes drunkeness," "Jazz is cheating the home, since folks are spending on dances and cafes the money they might otherwise spend on home appliances and improvements," and "Jazz has doubled insanity in the United States," attributed to doctors, preachers and other "authorities" were printed in leading periodicals and newspapers.

Leading music critics didn't care for the music either. *London Sunday Times* music critic Ernest Newman stated, "Your typical jazz composer or jazz enthusiast is merely a musical illiterate who is absurdly pleased with little things because he does not know how little they are. Jazz has no composers in the full sense of the term. The brains of the whole lot of them put together would not fill the lining of Johann Strauss's hat. At present jazz is not an art, but an industry: the whirring of a standardized machine endlessly turning out a standardized article. The thing is dead from the neck up."

Whiteman came to the defense of jazz with a three part series on the music that ran in the *Saturday Evening Post* in 1926. Those articles, written by Whiteman with Mary Margaret McBride, were collected into a book titled *Jazz*.

Whiteman was open minded about black jazz musicians, recognizing their talent, but pragmatic about having them in his group. He knew that a racially mixed band would not be accepted in the South or other parts of the country and he would lose bookings. Since few hotels allowed blacks to come through their front door, traveling arrangements would be incredibly complicated and audiences all over the country simply wouldn't pay to see black musicians perform at a "respectable" hotel or club.

Whiteman incorporated the sound of black musicians in his group by hiring black arrangers and songwriters, like Don Redman and William Grant Still.

Louis Armstrong

During the 1920s Louis Armstrong developed his talents to the point where he became one of the most influential musicians in the history of recorded music. Armstrong took the music he learned and performed in New Orleans and expanded, refined and carried it to Chicago, New York, Los Angeles and, then, all over the world as he pioneered the music that would be defined as the essence of jazz.

Widely known as "Satcho," an abbreviation of "Satchelmouth," a nickname he had acquired in New Orleans, Armstrong viewed music as "a heightened form of existence, and he sang and he played as if it could never be loud enough, or last long enough, or go deep enough, or reach high enough. He believed there could never be enough music in the world, and he did his damnedest to fill the silence with all the stomping, roaring, screeching, sighing polyphony he could muster."

Louis Armstrong was born August 4, 1901, although he believed during his lifetime that he was born July 4, 1900 (a birth certificate uncovered after his death revealed his true birth date). Armstrong's parents split shortly after he was born and his mother became a prostitute. Armstrong's father later returned briefly, then married someone else. Louis was raised primarily by his maternal grandmother, Josephine, who lived in the Storyville section of New Orleans. Armstrong also spent part of his childhood with his mother, Mayann and sister, Beatrice (called "Mama Lucy").

Armstrong learned to read and write at the Fisk School of Boys but dropped out in the middle of the fifth grade. His early musical influences included Buddy Bolden, a New Orleans musician who never recorded, and Joe Oliver, who led the top jazz band in New Orleans during Armstrong's early years.

As a youngster, Armstrong worked for the Karnoffskys, a Jewish family who were junk dealers. The Karnoffskys took the young Armstrong under their wing, virtually adopting him, and helped him purchase his first cornet from a pawn shop. Armstrong played his horn to attract people to the wagon the Karnoffskys drove through the streets, collecting junk to sell.

When Armstrong was 11, he was arrested on New Year's Eve for firing a gun in public. He was sentenced to a reform school, the Colored Waif's Home, just outside New Orleans. There, Armstrong received his first formal music training. Armstrong stayed at the Waif's home for a year and a half.

During Armstrong's early teen years he hauled coal on a horse drawn wagon. He began to sit in with Kid Ory's band and by February, 1915, was playing in a tonk each night, then driving the coal cart each day. Fourteen year old Armstrong supported his mother, sister and a young boy, Clarence, who was the son of his cousin.

In June, 1918, a little over six months after the closing of Storyville, Joe Oliver moved to Chicago, where he began performing in clubs with his group. After Oliver left, young Louis Armstrong took his place in a group managed by Kid Ory.

During 1918, Louis Armstrong played cornet in the band organized by Ory and second trumpet in the Tuxedo Brass Band. The Ory band members did not read music and there was a pride felt by groups who did not read music because they held the belief that "reading got in the way of feeling the music...it got in the way of improvisation by confining musicians to a rigid set of choices with given keys, and it got in the way of listening and responding to the complicated rhythms and harmonies of other musicians... reading music stifled the music inside the music, the notes that only musicians heard, or thought they heard."

Louis Armstrong knew that not reading music held him back from playing in the top bands and before wider audiences. In the Spring of 1919, Armstrong had the opportunity to learn how to read music from Fate Marable, a band leader who performed on Mississippi riverboats. Armstrong joined Marable's 12 member band--a reading group--on the Dixie Belle and during intermissions and breaks, learned from Marable the rudiments of reading music.

The performances on the riverboat allowed Armstrong to hone his skills on cornet and gave him experience performing before white audiences. The Marable group played a wide variety of songs--from pop tunes to folk songs to hits of the day--and Armstrong developed the ability to play a wide repertoire as well as establish a platform to become a showman.

During the Fall and Winter months, the riverboats did not travel the Mississippi so Armstrong performed in clubs and honky-tonks throughout New Orleans. Armstrong stated of that time, "I could read music very well by now and was getting hotter and hotter on my trumpet. My chest had filled out deeper and my lips and jaws had got stronger, so I could blow much harder and longer than before without getting tired. I had made a special point of the high register, and was beginning to make my high-C notes more and more often.

As Armstrong continued to perform with the Marable Orchestra throughout 1920 and 1921, biographer Laurence Bergreen noted that "Louis became the only instrumentalist to take solos, a practice that had crucial consequences both for his own musical development and the future of jazz, for it was here, on the riverboats, that the idea of the jazz soloist was born."

Bergreen continued that, until this time, "jazz performers, black and white, generally played together, occasionally taking turns, each man having his brief moment in the spotlight to show off the sound of his instrument and to introduce himself with a nod toward the audience. But Louis had something different in mind; he was beginning to work toward the idea of his cornet leading the entire orchestra...[he] began to assert himself onstage."

On August 8, 1922, Armstrong received a telegram from Joe Oliver in Chicago, inviting him to join the New Orleans Creole Jazz Band, which performed at the Lincoln Gardens Cafe. Armstrong caught a train and arrived at the club that evening, joining a band that consisted of Oliver, Baby Dodds and his brother Johnny, Honore Dutrey and Bill Johnson, a group considered one of the pioneers in jazz.

Prohibition was in force in Chicago, which meant the Mafia took over the liquor trade and bribed the police department to stay away--or at least tip them off about raids--from the speakeasies. Many clubs were established in the black sections of a city--this was an era when segregation dictated that there was a "black" section of a city and a "white" section of a city--and "black and tan" clubs were established. Those "black and tans" generally featured black musicians playing for white customers or, in some cases, audiences where there were both blacks and whites. For the jazz musicians playing those clubs, it meant that their bosses were generally gangsters, hoodlums or those with connections to the underworld.

The addition of Louis Armstrong to King Oliver and His Creole Jazz Band juiced up the band musically. The other musicians "soon realized he was doing a hell of a lot more up there on the bandstand than showing off. He was in the process of developing the vocabulary of modern jazz, taking it out of sleepy New Orleans and sticking it right into the fast-beating heart of Chicago. He was showing them a new way to be a jazz musician, inventing the idea of the modern jazz soloist right before their astonished eyes and ears. He was giving them a new musical language."

While playing in Chicago, Armstrong was introduced (by Oliver) to Lil Hardin, who later became his wife and an integral part of Armstrong's developing career. Hardin was performing at the Dreamland Cafe but joined Oliver's band as pianist.

Armstrong also met the great African-American performer Bill Robinson, known as "Mr. Bojangles," in Chicago and "Robinson's persona had a liberating effect. This was the way he wanted to appear on stage--sharp, aggressive, compelling. Within weeks of his arrival in Chicago, Louis set his sights on becoming more than a jazz musician; he wanted to be an all-round performer who could play, sing, dance, joke, and beguile audiences into a trance-like state. Bojangles showed him how to be a star."

Louis Armstrong made his first recordings with Oliver's group on April 5 and 6, 1923, in Richmond, Indiana, for the Gennett Company. During that first session the group recorded "Just Gone," "Canal Street," "Mandy Lee Blues," "I'm Going to Wear You Off My Mind," and "Chimes Blues." The next day they recorded "Snake Rag" and "Dippermouth Blues."

The problem with recordings was that they all had to be less than three minutes in length, because early discs could only hold that much, so they did not accurately capture the "authentic" sound of a jazz group, who usually played songs longer than three minutes. Joe Oliver never grasped the importance of recordings, feeling, as many musicians did, that he would lose his audiences if they could hear him on record instead of live. Armstrong embraced the technology and, over the years, amassed a huge collection of recordings, often studying other performers and becoming a student, as well as performer, of jazz.

In February, 1924, Armstrong married Lil Hardin, after he received a divorce from his first wife. At the beginning of 1925, Louis left Oliver's group and joined Ollie Powers group, then received an offer from Fletcher Henderson to join Henderson's group, which performed at the Roseland in New York. The Fletcher Henderson Orchestra was the top group in New York so when Armstrong joined in October, 1924, he became not only part of the top musical group but also part of the Harlem Renaissance.

Fletcher Henderson was a graduate of the University of Atlanta and had come to New York to obtain an advanced degree in Chemistry from Columbia University; however, once in New York, Henderson, a classically trained pianist, became immersed in jazz and formed a dance band.

Armstrong recorded sides with Henderson soon after he arrived, playing "Manda," "Go 'Long, Mule," "Tell Me, Dreamy Eyes," "My Rose Marie," "Don't Forget You'll Regret Day by Day" and "Shanghai Shuffle." Armstrong always wanted to sing because it appealed to him as a showman and allowed him to rest his lips. His first vocal recording, "Everybody Loves My Baby" was done with Henderson's group in November.

During the winter of 1924-1925 Armstrong kept a busy schedule, performing and recording with Henderson and playing in the studio behind top blues singers such as Bessie Smith, Ma Rainey, Alberta Hunter, Margaret Johnson and Clara Smith. During the summer of 1925, the Henderson group played a series of bookings in New England, then returned to Roseland in October.

Biographer Laurence Bergeen noted that "For Henderson, jazz was light, polite music for dancing and socializing. It was, above all, elegant, and not intended as a means of self-expression or, God forbid, experimentation." That limited Armstrong's musical adventurism.

Back in Chicago, Armstrong's wife, Lil (who had not accompanied him to New York) obtained a slot at Dreamland and sent for Louis to join her group. When he arrived, he discovered she had billed him "The World's Greatest Trumpet Player."

On November 12, 1925, Armstrong and four other musicians went into the studio for a recording session. Labeled the "Hot Five," because there were five of them, the group consisted of Kid Ory on trombone, Johnny Dodds on clarinet, Johnny St. Cyr on banjo, Lil on piano and Louis on trumpet. On that first session they recorded "My Heart," "Yes! I'm in the Barrel," and "Gut Bucket Blues." In February, 1926, they returned to the studio and recorded "Georgia Grind," "The Muskrat Ramble," and "Cornet Chop Suey" as well as "Heebie Jeebies," a song Armstrong had been performing at the Vendome Theater with Erskine Tate's group.

The success of "Heebie Jeebies," where Armstrong did "scat" singing, gave the group national recognition and, even though the group had never performed live together, they quickly became recognized as the most famous jazz band in America.

In April, 1926, Armstrong joined the Carrol Dickerson Orchestra, that performed at the Sunset Cafe, managed by promoter Joe Glaser. Glaser later became Armstrong's manager and guided his career to stardom in the music world. Glaser billed Armstrong as "The World's Greatest Trumpet Player" and then renamed the group "Louis Armstrong and His Stompers" after he fired Dickerson. Armstrong was never a good bandleader; he did not have the temperament for it, but he was always the star of any band he played in. In that group, Earl Hines was the musical director while Percy Venable managed the show, which consisted of singers, dancers, showgirls and dance contests.

In November, 1926, the Hot Five recorded "Big Butter and Egg Man" and in May, 1927, the Hot Five became the Hot Seven when they added a tuba player and Baby Dodds on drums. That group recorded for several days, laying down "Wild Man Blues," "Willie the Weeper," "Alligator Crawl," "Potato Head Blues," "Weary Blues," "Twelfth Street Rag," "Keyhole Blues," "That's When I'll Come Back to You" and "Gully Low Blues."

In November, 1927, Armstrong's gig at the Sunset ended and he decided to open his own club in Chicago, The Warwick, which failed miserably. Armstrong was a great musician, but not a great businessman. He could not manage a club and he could not be a bandleader, who's major skill is managing people and finances. Although Louis was a great front man, he always had to depend on others to actually run the band.

Armstrong stayed in Chicago throughout 1928, then went to New York where he appeared in the Broadway revue *Hot Chocolates* and performed at Connie's Inn. In 1930 he moved to Los Angeles where he performed at the New Cotton Club, which broadcast his performances on the radio while celebrities like Bing Crosby dropped by to listen.

Duke Ellington and Irving Mills

At the beginning of the 1920s, the Fletcher Henderson Orchestra was the most popular group in Harlem; by the end of the 1920s, it was Duke Ellington who held that claim. Ellington was a pianist who aspired to be a bandleader and emerged as a major composer, generally considered a genius, as his career unfolded throughout the twentieth century.

Edward Kennedy Ellington was born April 29, 1899 in Washington, D.C., the son of James Edward (J.E.) Ellington, who worked as a butler for Dr. M.F. Cuthburt. J.E. Ellington catered at some of the great houses in and around Washington and knew how the upper class lived, talked and acted, and instilled that model of behavior in his son.

Ellington had a comfortable childhood, taking piano lessons as a child and attending school until he dropped out of high school. He grew up in Washington, a city with a large black elite class, an historic black university, Howard, and government jobs available for African-Americans.

Ellington acquired the nickname "Duke" early in life and the moniker fit him; his insistence in always going first class, his sense of style and elegance and his regal bearing all created the image for a man called "Duke."

Ellington began playing for parties and dances and from musician Oliver Perry learned "a system for recognizing chords from a piece of sheet music. This meant that, even if Duke could not actually play the notes on the sheet music as written, he could pick out the melody with his right hand and fit an approximately correct set of chords to it with his left."

Biographer James Lincoln Collier states that Ellington was "exceedingly resistant to formal study. He did not like the self-discipline it involved, and he liked even less having anyone tell him what to do." Although Ellington had piano lessons, the greater part of his piano playing was self-taught and by ear. Collier noted that Ellington "was unwilling to do the hard work needed to acquire a sound piano technique. The lack of skill then forced him to invent, improvise, find ingenious solutions to problems, and it drove him early into a creativity a trained pianist.was not forced into."

Ellington loved the good life and good times and saw his piano playing as a way to attract women. In July, 1918, he married Edna Thomas and his son, Mercer, was born the following March.

Ellington played in dance bands in Washington, performing everything from ragtime to the hits of the day. In the winter of 1922 he went to Harlem and joined a band led by clarinetist Wilbur Sweatman, but the band had trouble finding work and Ellington returned to Washington in March, 1923. Later that year he went back to Harlem where he landed a gig at Barron's Exclusive Club, performing popular songs and background music.

In 1924 Ellington and his band, The Washingtonians, began performing at The Hollywood, a basement club in New York, where they performed from 7 p.m. until 7 a.m. Those four years were integral to the development of Ellington and his group and by the time that job ended, in 1927, the group was performing Ellington's music.

Ellington emerged as a bandleader because "he was always in control of his situation" and had a "need to dominate everywhere." According to biographer James Lincoln Collins, "The others probably settled on Ellington because they admired his manner and respected his authoritative bearing and because he was more reliable than most of the rest and could be counted on to tend to such business as needed to be done."

In 1924 the Washingtonians had their shows broadcast a number of times over WHN in New York. The Hollywood club had burned, then been rebuilt and became The Kentucky Club, where Ellington's shows continued to be broadcast in New York. Ellington began to write songs at The Hollywood, after developing the talent of arranging popular tunes to fit his own style, and with lyricist Joe Trent, wrote a show, *Chocolate Kiddies*, that was staged in Germany.

Blacks and Jews formed alliances in show business because both groups were excluded from mainstream American life during the early 20th century. Like blacks, Jews could not live in a number of areas and certain careers were off limits to them. They were ostracized by white non-Jews, shunned as friends or guests in homes. However, Jews could be intermediaries between show business heads (many of whom were also Jews) and black entertainers. Black entertainers needed white managers to succeed beyond the level of clubs and cabarets and Jews needed blacks because those entertainers provided opportunities for success unavailable to them in other fields. Many great black entertainers, such as Jelly Roll Morton and King Oliver, never had white managers, but Louis Armstrong had Joe Glaser and Duke Ellington had Irving Mills.

Irving Mills (b. 1894) began as a singer, demonstrating songs at five and ten-cent stores to entice customers to purchase sheet music. He graduated to song plugger for Lew Leslie, a producer of Broadway shows, then, in 1919, started a publishing company, Mills Music, with his brother, Jack. They were blessed with luck; the second song they published, "Mr. Gallagher and Mr. Shean," sold two million copies of sheet music.

Mills signed a number of bandleaders as songwriters to his publishing company because bandleaders pushed their own songs. Will Vodery, Tim Bymn, Lovie Austin and James P. Johnson were all bandleaders signed by Mills, as well as black songwriters Shelton Brooks ("Darktown Strutters' Ball"), Henry Creamer ("Way Down Yonder in New Orleans") and Spencer Williams ("I Ain't Got Nobody").

Record companies allowed Mills to record anything he wished as long as he paid for the session, although they did not release everything he recorded. It was an arrangement that was beneficial to both Mills and the record companies, allowing them to acquire a catalog of recordings with a minimum of financial risk.

When Mills saw and heard Ellington's group, he quickly grasped that Ellington was a man he could work with and the group was perfect for recording and promoting songs he published. Irving Mills has been criticized for his relationship with Ellington, with critics accusing him of exploiting Ellington and his group and for Mills adding his name as co-writer to Ellington's creations, but one thing remains certain: Irving Mills made Duke Ellington a star.

During the first half of the 20th century, it was not unusual for a singer or publisher or even someone connected to promoting a song to have their name listed as co-writer. Later in the century, this was viewed as "stealing" from a songwriter, not giving the writer his or her due for their creation. But creating is often a collaborative effort and, in the case with Ellington, Mills often suggested changes in the songs, titles, or created situations where Ellington was forced to create when otherwise he would not have bothered.

Ellington himself noted that "Without a deadline I can't finish nothing." Biographer Collier notes that he "was not a man of great self-discipline... he would always do what was required, but not until it was required." Irving Mills was the man who forced Ellington to continuously create songs during the bandleader's early career.

Biographer Collins stated that Mills played an important role in Ellington's compositions. "He often suggested to Duke the sorts of tunes he thought would sell...He arranged for words to be put to Duke's songs, sometimes suggesting titles and themes. And he even made changes in the music itself." Collier quotes Mills, who said that Ellington "followed instructions. He did what I wanted...I want this kind of a tune or that kind of a tune," adding that "Whatever they did, I thinned out. His music was always too heavy...He over-arranged...I simplified most all the tunes." The Ellington band was, for Mills, "primarily a machine for making hits."

Mills obtained recording and radio contracts and jobs in clubs for Ellington and demanded that Ellington be treated as well as major white acts. Mills understood Duke Ellington, knew his need for respect and his insistence on a lifestyle that embraced elegance and the best of everything, from travel arrangements to band outfits to stage sets, and Irving Mills made sure Ellington was provided with those things. In early 1926, Mills and Ellington established a corporation with each owning 45 percent (attorney Sam Buzzell owned 10 percent) that benefitted them both. Ellington was president and Mills was treasurer of the corporation.

During 1926, Ellington's status as bandleader was assured; on the recordings made in March, the group was listed as "The Washingtonians," those made in April saw the group listed as "Duke Ellington and His Washingtonians" and by November the group was known as "Duke Ellington and His Kentucky Club Orchestra." The following year they became "Duke Ellington and His Orchestra" and that's the way it remained.

Musically, the group evolved from a Dixieland band, heavily influenced by the Original Dixieland Jazz Band and King Oliver's Creole Jazz Band into a smoother, more sophisticated, symphonic sound. The major influence on this latter sound was Paul Whiteman's group, although Ellington received the credit for this sound. Whiteman's group showed the way for future bands, pioneering a music that was complex and dominated by arrangers; Ellington's star was hitched to that sound.

Ellington also benefited from Prohibition and segregation because there was a demand for black musicians in the tenderloin areas of American cities where drinks, drugs and erotic entertainment were in vogue. In New York, Harlem was not only a center for black culture and intellectual pursuits, but also the black and tan clubs where white audiences came to be entertained, shielded from police by gangsters who ran the clubs, supplied the liquor, and kept the police away. Those clubs, where blacks were the entertainers and waiters, were created to attract money from white folks who wanted a less inhibited atmosphere than what was found in speakeasies in the white parts of town. Prohibition created that situation; segregation nurtured it.

The Cotton Club, located at 142nd Street and Lenox Avenue in Harlem, was taken over by a syndicate of gangsters, led by Owney Madden, in 1923. The club seated 400-500 people and the false palm trees and other accoutrements provided a "jungle" atmosphere. The idea that the black section of town was a "jungle" and that blacks were primitive with their sexually suggestive songs, featuring double-entendres and dancers featuring bump-and grind moves, was a trendy idea. Mills and Ellington took advantage of that fact.

On December 4, 1927, Duke Ellington began performing at the Cotton Club with a ten-piece band. The band performed at the club during the Fall and Winter, then in the summer usually toured New England. There, Ellington built his band into a premier jazz unit.

Mills and Ellington took advantage of the gimmick of "jungle music" and the Cotton Club used a number of "jungle" skits where barely dressed ladies performed erotic dances. Ellington had to create a number of songs that suggested savages dancing, blues, hot up tempo numbers and soft songs in minor keys; many of those songs--and scenes--were suggested by Irving Mills.

According to biographer James Lincoln Collins, Ellington was not driven by an "inner flame" to compose, but rather because "he wanted his band to succeed." Ellington often had his name on melodies created by members of his band. The songs Ellington created came not by "composing" in the traditional sense of someone sitting alone (or with a co-writer) at the piano, working out phrases, but usually came in the studio through a collaborative effort with his band members.

"He would begin by bringing into the recording studio or rehearsal hall a few musical ideas--scraps of melodies, harmonies, and chord sequences usually clothed in the sound of particular instrumentalists in the band," states Collier. "On the spot he would sit down at the piano and quickly rough out a section--four, eight, sixteen bars. The band would play it; Duke would repeat it; the band would play it again until everybody got it...Here's a section, here's a section and here's another and, in between, he begins putting the connecting links." Ellington worked quickly, creating those songs.

Collier stated that "Everyone in the band would pitch in and help write songs, everything that, almost, Duke did in those days...it would frequently be up to the men in the sections to work out the harmonies, usually from chords Duke would supply." The different sections of the band rehearsed their parts while Ellington "controlled the process. He would make changes as he saw fit, moving a solo from one man to another, changing the harmonies, switching sections around. A piece was never really finished but went on changing for as long as the band played it."

In the songs composed during his days at the Cotton Club, Ellington created music for people sitting at tables in the club or listening on the radio. The hour-long broadcasts came over the CBS network and were key to the Cotton Club becoming one of the most famous nightclubs in America and Duke Ellington and his band becoming established stars.

Key members of Ellington's band were Barney Bigard on clarinet, Johnny Hodges, a premier soloist who played soprano sax, Cootie Williams on trumpet, Juan Tizol on trombone, Harry Carney on saxophone, Bubber Miley and Joe "Tricky Sam" Nanton on trumpets, drummer William "Sonny" Greer, Wellman Braud on bass and tuba, and Freddie Guy on banjo.

During their stay at the Cotton Club, the Ellington group began wearing tuxedos, solidifying Ellington's image of elegance and sophistication. Although Ellington always had a need to appear aristocratic, he did not demand that of his band members, believing that "'instinctive' players would produce a freer, more 'natural' music" and tolerating a good deal of irresponsible behavior on the part of his men."

During the 1929-1931 period, Duke Ellington and his group recorded extensively, although not always under their own name. Because Victor had exclusive rights to "Duke Ellington," the group recorded for a number of labels under the names the Harlem Footwarmers, the Ten Blackberries, the Jungle Band, and the Harlem Hot Chocolates because Mills wanted the songs he published to be recorded.

Musically, the band progressed into a jazz swing group, with the recording of *Black and Tan Fantasy*, recorded in April, 1927, the recording that established Ellington as a major composer. Duke was inspired by Fletcher Henderson's group, "His was the band I always wanted mine to sound like when I got ready to have a big band," he said. The musicians were inspired by one of Henderson's band members, Louis Armstrong, who showed the musicians how to "swing" and whose playing pioneered the sound that became widely known as "jazz" during the 1920s.

In 1930, Duke Ellington appeared in two movies, *Black and Tan Fantasy*, a 19 minute short, and the Amos 'n' Andy film, *Check and Double Check*. In 1931, he ended his stay at the Cotton Club.

"Pops" and Bing

The biggest jazz act during the 1920s, in terms of recognition, record sales, and income was Paul Whiteman's group. Whiteman attracted fledgling musicians and singers, including one who would become the biggest pop music star in American during the first half of the 20th century, Bing Crosby.

During a tour in 1926, Crosby and his musical partner, Al Rinker, stood at Union Station in Los Angeles and watched the Whiteman band arrive. Crosby and Rinker were appearing at the Metropolitan Theater when one of Whiteman's band members, Jimmy Gillespie, caught their act and told Whiteman he needed to see them. Whiteman reportedly said, "Oh boy, I need them like I need another chin" but then told Gillespie, "If you think they're the bees' knees, bring 'em to me."

Whiteman hired the duo, who joined the group in Chicago in mid-December. In Chicago, Whiteman made some recordings, including Crosby and Rinker's version of "Wistful and Blue." In February, 1927, Whiteman opened at the Cinderella Ballroom in New York. Whiteman's father, Wilberforce, had urged one of his popular vocal students, Harry Barris, to audition for his son. The audition was fortuitous; Crosby and Rinker hadn't been going over with audiences as a duet, so Whiteman teamed them with Barris to form "The Rhythm Boys." Barris wrote a tune, "Mississippi Mud," launched the act. By June, 1927, the trio was a hit.

In an effort to incorporate more jazz into his group, Whiteman hired musicians "Red" Nichols on trumpet, drummer Vic Berton, and reedman Jimmy Dorsey, who were with Nichols' group Red Nichols and the Five Pennies. Jimmy's brother, Tommy Dorsey, who was with the Jean Goldkette group, soon followed. In 1927, Whiteman hired Frankie Trumbauer and one of the most influential cornet players in the history of jazz, Bix Beiderbecke.

In 1928, Whiteman left Victor and joined Columbia, whose roster of big bands included those led by Paul Ash, Cass Hagen, Fred Rich, Harry Reser, Don Voorhees, Jan Garber, and Ted Lewis. Big bands on Victor included those led by Irving Aaronson, Coon-Sanders, George Olsen, Jelly Roll Morton, Ben Pollack, and Nathanial Shilkret.

The Rhythm Boys--Bing Crosby, Al Rinker and Harry Barris--were popular on records and with Whiteman but the bandleader dropped them from his tour schedule in 1927 and booked them on the vaudeville circuit. The problem was a lack of discipline in the group; they didn't like to practice and spent too much time at parties and not enough time rehearsing their music. The year-long vaudeville tour forced them to shape up.

Whiteman's first major radio exposure came in 1928 on a 47 station hook-up sponsored by the Dodge Motor Company. In 1929 he debuted with "The Old Gold-Paul Whiteman Hour," sponsored by Old Gold cigarettes. The show became a tour, "The Old Gold Special" and arrived in Los Angeles in June, 1929 where Whiteman was scheduled to star in his first movie *The King of Jazz*. Unfortunately, there wasn't a script written and the group hung around the studio for two months before returning East. During their stay in Los Angeles, Whiteman signed Mildred Bailey to sing with his group--the first female solo vocalist with a major orchestra.

In 1929 Whiteman made $640,000. The movie, *The King of Jazz* was completed in early 1930 at a cost of $2 million and featured the big screen debut of Whiteman and his star singer, Bing Crosby who, because of a run-in with the law, had to leave the movie set and return to a jail cell each evening.

W. C. Handy

W. C. Handy is known as the "Father of the Blues," which was the name of his memoir, published in 1941. However, according to biographer David Robertson, Handy "was not properly the Father of the Blues, as he was later acclaimed, but he was certainly the maker of the blues in the early twentieth century. He made the blues as a consciously composed art...and he also made them in that word's sense of guaranteeing their success and of commercially promoting this music." Robertson stated in his biography of Handy that "The genius of Handy over the years between 1904 and 1920 was his realizing the commercial potential of the Mississippi Delta blues music to reach beyond a regional and racial folk song and become part of mainstream American music. Handy 'polished' the folk blues into a new, sophisticated popular music that delighted hundreds of listeners."

William Christopher Handy was born in Florence, Alabama on November 16, 1873. Handy's father and grandfather were preachers in the African Methodist Episcopal Church; Handy's father did not approve of his son's interest and career in music and told him "I'd rather see you in a hearse. I'd rather follow you to the graveyard than to hear that you had become a musician." Handy's teacher warned him "What can music do but bring you to the gutter?"

W.C. Handy learned to play the cornet, the most popular instrument for young musicians in the 1880s, because of its role in brass bands. The cornet to young musicians of the 1880s was like the electric guitar to young musicians in the latter half of the twentieth century, leading bands and playing the most popular music of the day. The most popular musician at that time was John Phillip Sousa and the most popular music was marching band music. Handy's earliest ambition was to be "the colored Sousa."

Handy performed at the Chicago World's Fair in 1892 and then as a traveling musician in minstrel shows during the 1890s. In the early 1900s he returned to Florence and taught music at the State Agricultural and

Mechanical College for Negroes in addition to performing locally. Handy left college after less than two years and toured with the Mahara Company in a minstrel show 1902-1903. In 1903 Handy took a job as band director for a school in Clarksdale, Mississippi.

Clarksdale is located in the Mississippi Delta, about eighty miles south of Memphis. In addition to teaching, Handy continued to tour with a band and one night, in late 1903 or early 1904, he was waiting at the station in Tutwiler for the train back to Clarksdale. Half-asleep, he was "startled by hearing a strange music." According to Handy, in his autobiography, "A lean, loose-jointed Negro had commenced plunking a guitar beside me while I slept. His clothes were rags; his feet peeked out of his shoes. His face had on it some of the sadness of the ages. As he played, he pressed a knife on the strings of the guitar in a manner popularized by Hawaiian guitarists who used steel bars. The effect was unforgettable. His song, too, struck me instantly. 'Goin' where the Southern cross' the Dog.' The singer repeated the line three times, accompanying himself on the guitar with the weirdest music I had ever heard."

Later, during a performance by Handy and his group in Cleveland, Mississippi, the musicians took a break to smoke cigarettes and "a rustic-looking black string band consisting of players of a battered bass, mandolin, and guitar, led 'by a long-legged chocolate boy,' in Handy's description, took the stage and began to play the new music later known as the blues." The song was "'one of those over-and-over trains' that 'seem[s] to have no very clear beginning and certainly no ending at all' and therefore was open to improvisation in both its playing and its shouted lyrics. It was the 'kind of stuff that has long been associated with cane rows and levee camps'… certainly not the sophisticated ragtime, quick-step marches, genteel dance music, or even ragged coon songs that Handy had made his living playing since 1896."

Handy related that "'A rain of silver dollars began to fall around the outlandish, stomping feet' of the three countrified musicians,…'My idea of what constitutes music was changed by the sight of that silver money cascading around the splay[ed] feet of a Mississippi string band."

"That night a composer was born, an American composer." Handy wrote in his memoir and his biographer states "Thus was born, if not the Father of the Blues, at least the Father of the Commercialization of the Blues." After that encounter with those Delta blues musicians, Handy went back to Clarksdale and began to work on this kind of music and the popularity of his orchestra "increased by leaps and bounds."

In 1905 W.C. Handy moved to Memphis to further his career as a musician and composer. He landed in a city that had a vibrant musical scene and large Negro population. By 1910 Memphis had more African Americans than any other city except New Orleans and Beale Avenue was known as "the Main Street of Negro America." The social center of the black section of town was Beale Avenue (the street was renamed "Beale Street" after Handy's "Beale Street Blues" made the street nationally famous) which was "owned largely by Jews, policed by the whites, and enjoyed by the Negroes."

There were vaudeville theaters on Beale—the Lincoln, the Grand, the Daisy, and the Savoy--operated by Anselmo Barrasso and his extended family, who managed black performers and booked them on a national circuit through their booking agency, Theater Owners Booking Association, or TOBA, known by performers as "Tough On Black Asses." The major vaudeville booking companies allowed "no more than one black performer—or 'unbleached American,' as sometimes advertised—to appear at local performances, usually singing a minstrelsy song from the last century." However, on the black vaudeville circuit, an all black revue performed for African-American audiences, generally booked by TOBA, headquartered on Beale Avenue in Memphis.

In 1909 Edward H. Crump—later known as "Boss" Crump—ran for Mayor of Memphis and, because there were so many African-Americans in Memphis who were registered to vote, he courted the black vote. W. C. Handy wrote a song, "Mr. Crump" for the campaign—although Crump was probably not aware of it at the time—and that song became known "as among the first of the written blues" after the title was changed to "Memphis Blues."

W.C. Handy had to write out a sheet music manuscript every time someone wanted to perform "Boss Crump Blues" so in 1912 he decided to go to a print shop and "publish" the work; however, in order to broaden the appeal of the song, he retitled it "Memphis Blues (or Mr. Crump.)." Handy lived in Memphis but sought to have his song published by a music publisher in New York that had national distribution. In order for a song to be popular, it usually had to be performed in the theater and sheet music had to be available for piano in retailers.

Handy had no success with New York publishers so, at the suggestion of L.Z. Phillips, a Memphis sheet music salesman, financed the printing of the sheet music himself, using the Otto Zimmerman & Son music printing firm in Newport, Kentucky to print a thousand copies. Handy hoped to attract the attention of New York publishers with sales of sheet music but immediately ran into a problem: retailers in the white sections of town would not stock sheet music written or published by a person of color. Ironically, stores in the "white" sections of town regularly displayed and sold sheet music advertised by Bert Williams and George Walker, the popular African-American minstrel and vaudeville team.

Because of that setback, Handy sold his claim to the copyright of "The Memphis Blues (or "(Mr. Crump)" for fifty dollars to a white music publisher, Theron Catlin Bennett, who had New York connections. Bennett and L.Z. Phillips knew each other. Bennett managed to get Handy's sheet music displayed at Bry's Department Store, one of the finest retail stores in Memphis. Handy took copies to sell but the bulk of the copies were sent to Bennett and, after Handy was unsuccessful selling his copies, went to Bry's store and saw a thousand unsold copies. That led Handy to sell the copyright for $50; however, what Handy did not know was that Bennett and Phillips had sold the first thousand within three days and ordered a second printing—so Handy saw the second batch of sheet music awaiting sale. Further, the song had proven itself so popular that Bennett and Phillips had taken orders from other retailers and, after the purchase of the copyright, ordered 10,000 more copies of the sheet music printed. On the new cover was a white fiddler. A year later, in 1913, "Memphis Blues" had another press run of 50,000 but Handy did not receive a single cent from the sales. On the cover of the sheet music, he was credited as composer, which gave him valuable publicity and new lyrics by George A. Norton—Handy's song was originally published with no lyrics—mentioned Handy ("I went out dancing with a Tennessee dear,/They had a fellow there named Handy with a band you should hear").

"Memphis Blues" was recorded by Arthur Collins and Byron Harlan, white comedians who performed as a "coon duo" and released on Columbia Records. In 1914 it became the signature tune of Vernon and Irene Castle and was recorded for Victor by the James Europe Society Orchestra. The song was used to demonstrate a new dance, the "fox trot."

In 1914 Handy wrote "St. Louis Blues," which became the most famous published blues song of the twentieth century. That led of a five-year period in Memphis when Handy wrote "Yellow Dog Blues," "Beale Street Blues" and "St. Louis Blues." Mindful that he needed to keep his copyrights and needed a business partner, Handy joined forces with Harry H. Pace, who moved to Memphis in 1905 to become editor of W.E.B. Du Bois' newspaper, the *Moon Illustrated Weekly*. The newspaper failed in 1906 and Pace left Memphis for his hometown of Atlanta but returned to work for Robert

Church at the black-owned Solvent Savings Bank on Beale Avenue. Pace, a bank cashier, met Handy in 1907 and wrote the lyrics to "In the Cotton Fields of Dixie" to a score by Handy. That song failed but the two started a publishing company, Pace & Handy Music Company, with offices at 392 Beale Avenue, and the first song they published was Handy's "St. Louis Blues."

The young firm struggled. In 1913, Pace moved back to Atlanta and took a job with the Standard Life Insurance Company. The following year "Yellow Dog Blues" (originally titled "Yellow Dog Rag") had strong regional sales and in 1915 Pace and Handy formalized their partnership. In 1917, Pace went to New York on a business trip and arranged for Handy and his orchestra to make their first recordings for Columbia Records. Handy's "orchestra" was actually comprised of only four of Handy's Memphis musicians, seven Chicago musicians (three had once played for him in Memphis) and a New York clarinetist. The group, led by Handy on cornet or trumpet, recorded fifteen songs; two were released the next year by Columbia.

W.C. Handy was fortunate to live in Memphis and work on Beale Street because a number of black vaudevillians, booked by the Barrassos, sang blues and, specifically Handy's blues, during their performances. To achieve national success for his songs, Handy had to move to either Chicago or New York. At first, he looked to Chicago but, in 1918, moved to New York. He was 45 years old when he settled in Harlem. He set up shop at 1547 Broadway, inside the Gaiety Theater. He wrote and published "A Good Man Is Hard to Find," which was sung by Sophie Tucker; the sheet music sales on that song were 500,000.

In 1920 Henry Pace joined Handy in New York and that year Miss Marion Harris, known as the "Jazz Vampire," recorded "St. Louis Blues" for Columbia Records. Harris also sang the song on stage and her version "is how most people now recognize its melody and regard it as a masterpiece." After that recording, "St Louis Blues" "became one of the most frequently performed and recorded songs of the twentieth century.".

In 1921 Pace left the partnership and began a recording company, first called the Pace Phonographic Company and then Black Swan Records. Handy continued to compose and publish music but his greatest songs had been written. He had succeeded in making the blues popular, but the singers were white and the audiences for those songs were white. The term "blues" became part of the Tin Pan Alley vocabulary, and a number of songwriters were African-American. At that point, the blues was a way to market black culture to a white audience.

Blues

In 1920 the country was in a major recession, a direct result of the problems of returning World War I veterans trying to find work and the reduction in government spending for the war effort, which had spurred the economy through the War years. The record companies had nearly exhausted their initial markets and were looking for ways to broaden their consumer base. They recorded a number of ethnic acts and songs to appeal to the large number of immigrants, particularly in New York. That search for new markets ultimately led them to record blues and country music as they reached toward new fields to obtain profits.

The first company to do this was Okeh Records, a small label begun in 1916 by Otto Heinemann. The label was financed by the German company, Carl Lindstrom.

Ralph Peer and Okeh Records

Ralph Peer was born May 22, 1892 in Independence, Missouri; his father owned Peer Supply in Kansas City. One of his clients was the Columbia Phonograph Company, who needed parts to repair their phonographs. When he was 11, Ralph Peer began working, often delivering records, machines and parts from the Peer Supply Company to Columbia, which led to him meeting men who worked there which, in turn, led to Peer working there, filling in for whatever jobs needed doing. In 1909, after high school graduation, Peer worked full time for Columbia as a clerk.

Peer was ambitious and moved up the ranks at Columbia; he worked as credit manager, then retail manager and then traveling salesman. He was promoted to assistant manager in 1915, when he was 23, and moved to Chicago, where he learned about record company sales, marketing and promotion. W. C. Fuhri was Peer's boss and mentor; when Fuhri joined the Otto Heineman Supply Company in New York, Peer joined him as assistant manager. The company at first supplied parts for phonographs. Heineman purchased the Rex Talking Machine label, which brought the company into the recording business. Rex's technical director and recording engineer, Charles Hibbard, joined Heineman. General Phonograph was the name of the new company and the new label was named "Okeh," based on Heineman's initials. Ralph Peer was a traveling salesman, working with General Phonograph's distributors and record dealers.

The Music Director for Rex was Fred Hager and he, too, joined Heineman's company. At Rex, Hager used studio groups to make recordings and gave them various names; popular music was dance driven so most of the recordings were "dance" music; for classical recordings, Heineman leased recordings from European labels.

A small company like Okeh could not compete with majors like Victor and Columbia by recording popular music, so they depended on finding undeveloped markets for music. This is the background for Okeh recording the first commercially successful blues record.

Mamie Smith and "Crazy Blues"

In August, 1920, a record was released on Okey that changed the music business.

"Crazy Blues," recorded by Mamie Smith in New York, proved to be an astounding commercial success and led recording companies to look to African-American musicians and consumers for future releases. That recording, by an African-American singer released nationally, let white music industry executives realize there was a large market for "race" music and that the Negro population could and would buy recordings of blues singers and blues songs. It was a giant revelation to white executives, who generally did not understand black music or black culture, but sought to capitalize on it because there was money to be made.

The copyright to the song "Crazy Blues" was held by Perry "Mule" Bradford, an African-American composer, manager and entrepreneur. Bradford was born in Montgomery, Alabama in 1895 but moved with his family to Atlanta in 1902, where he grew up in a home next to the Fulton Street Jail. From the jail, young Bradford heard inmates singing; that is how he first heard blues.

Bradford entered vaudeville as a singer, dancer and piano player in Atlanta. He went on the road with Allen's New Orleans Minstrels in 1907 and arrived in New York, where he was involved in staging the musical revue, *Made in Harlem*, which featured one of his compositions, "Harlem Blues." The song came from a number he learned in 1912, "Nervous Blues," but he had revised the original.

(Early blues and country songs were generally versions of songs that had been heard by the singer who may have forgotten some of the words, or changed them or altered the melody. To say someone "wrote" an early blues or country song is misleading when compared to contemporary songwriting. Early songwriters often put pieces of different songs together and a number of artists, who needed to come up with an original song, often purchased a song outright from a songwriter.)

Bradford and "Crazy Blues" had been turned down by Columbia and Victor. Mamie Smith sang the song regularly in *Made in Harlem*, a New York musical revue at the Lincoln Theater. Bradford argued that "fourteen million Negroes...will buy records if recorded by one of their own."

Fred Hager, manager of Okeh, a small label belonging to the General Phonograph Company, agreed to part of that argument; some of Bradford's songs would be recorded, but only if sung by Sophie Tucker. Tucker was a powerful vocalist, a Russian born immigrant who broke into show business during the early 1900s in New York. Since she was a big, heavy-set woman, the vaudeville theater owners--knowing she could never be a sex symbol--had her wear blackface and perform "coon songs," fitting her into the "Mammy" stereotype. Later, she did away with the blackface but continued to record and popularize African-American songs, including "St. Louis Blues" by W.C. Handy, which became the first million selling blues song in 1917.

During that period, several white women—usually with a buxom figure--performed African-American songs in a style mimicking African-American performers; they were known as "coon shouters" (later as "blues shouters") and among those were May Irwin, Marie Cahill, Elizabeth Murray, Stella Mayhew, Artie Hall, and Clarice Vance. African-American performers such as Bessie Smith, Ma Rainey, Carrie Hall, Bessie Gillam and Rosa Scott were also known as "coon shouters" before they were called "blues" singers.

Sophie Tucker could not do the session because of contract commitments so Mamie Smith, Bradford's original choice, was allowed to record the song. In recording the song, Bradford changed the name from "Harlem Blues" to "Crazy Blues" to avoid any possible copyright litigation by the musical revue backers.

The song's melody had been used before. Pianist Willie Smith recalled that James P. Johnson once used it in his "Mama and Papa Blues" (composed in 1916) and other pianists remembered part of the melody coming from "Baby Get That Towel Wet," an old bawdy song played in sporting houses.. The Mamie Smith release sold 75,000 copies during the first month of its release and during the first year sold over one million copies. Perry Bradford reportedly received almost $20,000 in royalty fees, less than half of what he was legally entitled to receive. It was extremely difficult to get record labels to pay accurate royalty fees because the record companies were the only ones who documented how many records were manufactured and sold.

Bradford owned his own publishing company, "Perry Bradford Music Company," and engaged in some questionable business practices, was accused of publishing other's songs under his name and spent time in jail as a result of a copyright suit brought against him. Okeh Records pressured Bradford to waive his royalty rights to "Crazy Blues" when it became a commercial success, but Bradford responded, "Please be advised that the only thing Bradford waves is the American Flag."

Early Recordings by Black Artists

Although "Crazy Blues' marks the beginning of African-American performers successfully recording blues numbers, and record companies successfully marketing them to the African-American population, this was not the first time the American public had heard blues or black performers who had been recorded.

Thomas Edison's company recorded George W. Johnson, the only African-American to record on cylinder; Johnson recorded his "Whistling Coon" minstrel number for the company. The Victor Talking Machine Company recorded comic Bert Williams, believing he would be popular with white audiences as well as gain sales in the African-American community. Williams recorded 15 titles for Victor, mostly show tunes or comedy routines from his stage repertoire; "Elder Eatmore's Sermon" sold over half a million units.

The Dinwiddie Colored Quartet, who played authentic African-American folk music, was recorded by Victor in 1902. The six songs recorded by the group were all slow spirituals sung acapella. The Fisk Jubilee Quartet recorded in 1909, 1910 and 1911. The next major breakthrough for black recording artists did not occur until 1914 when James Reese Europe's Society Orchestra recorded for Victor as part of the series endorsed by the white dance team, the Castles.

Although the major white owned recording companies did not record African-American artists, they did record songs that were blues-influenced. (Columbia Record Company excluded black performers from recording until 1920; they turned down Bert Williams before the great Negro performer recorded for Victor.) Those songs were all done by white performers and were advertised as "negro novelty," "Up to date comic songs in negro dialect," "plantation airs," "Ethiopian airs" and, most often, "coon songs."

Tin Pan Alley songwriters also wrote a number of songs derived from blues and African-American folk songs, particularly after W.C. Handy moved from Memphis to New York in 1915. African-Americans who came to New York and opened publishing companies included Sheldon Brooks from Mobile, Alabama, Clarence Williams, from New Orleans, Perry Bradford from Atlanta and Bert Williams.

Before 1920, Handy had published his most famous blues compositions, including "Memphis Blues" in 1912, "Jogo Blues" in 1915, "Saint Louis Blues" in 1914, "Yellow Dog Blues" in 1914, "Joe Turner Blues" in 1916 and "Beale Street Blues" in 1917. The success of Handy showed Tin Pan Alley the commercial potential for blues songs and a number of derivative tunes came from the songwriting assembly line to satisfy the demand of vaudeville theaters, dance halls and cabarets. By 1920, a form of the blues had entered mainstream popular music. That form was generally referred to as "vaudeville blues," which was based on commercial, rather than folk tradition. Those songs used cliché song formulas in the standardized twelve bar, A-A-B stanza format. They became popular standards when performed by authentic African-American vocalists or transformed by African-American composers. Among the vocalists who popularized vaudeville blues were Ma Rainey, Ida Cox, Sara Martin, Alberta Hunter, Sippie Wallace and Bessie Smith. Composers included W.C. Handy, Perry Bradford, James and Rosamond Johnson, Spencer Williams, Porter Grainger, Clarence Williams and Thomas Dorsey. Most of the composers and performers were connected to the South and traditional black folk music.

The success of "Crazy Blues" led a number of small labels to record and release blues recordings. "The Jazz Me Blues" and "Everybody's Blues" by Lucille Hegamin was released on the Arto label in 1921; Lillian Brown released blues songs on Emerson and Daisy Martin released sides on Gennett, all in 1921. Recording companies Perfect, Pathe, Ajax, Vocalion and Paramount also recorded and released blues recordings.

African-Americans started record labels during the 1920s but success was difficult to achieve. Black Swan was started by W.C. Handy and Harry Pace in January 1921. They recorded Ethel Waters and Alberta Hunter and had an excellent year in 1921; however, in 1924 they were deep in debt and had to sell their assets to Paramount. The Sunshine label was formed in Los Angeles by two African-American record store owners in 1922 and released songs by Roberta Dudley, Ruth Less and an instrumental by Kid Ory's jazz band. That label also folded.

Meritt Records, formed by Winston Holmes in 1925 in Kansas City lasted three years. Black Patti, begun by "Ink" Williams, the premier black talent scout in Chicago during the 1920s, was formed in 1927 but lasted less than a year. The major problem with Williams' label was that, although he had access to the best African-American singers and musicians in the business, he could not get his product distributed effectively outside Chicago.

It was difficult for any new label to get a foothold in the industry; even more so for a black-owned label. However, the small labels did show the majors that there was a market for blues recordings to African-American consumers and the major labels began recording traditional blues in earnest around 1926.

History of Blues

Slavery in America began in 1619 when a Dutch ship with Africans arrived in Jamestown, Virginia; the Negroes were soon purchased by colonial planters. After 1808, the importation of slaves from Africa into the United States was illegal; however, government officials tended to look the other way. In 1859, there were more slaves imported into the United States than at any time during the years when the slave trade was legal. Before the Civil War there were slaves who had just arrived from Africa as well as slaves whose ancestors had been in America for several generations; this meant that African influence on music varied a great deal throughout the slave population.

In work songs done with a group, a leader generally set the tempo of the labor by singing while fellow workers sang an answer in unison. That form of singing--the leader-and-chorus or call and response--had direct links to African traditions. Drums and horns were banned by slave owners in the south because it was felt those instruments could be used to send messages which could lead to slave revolts, a constant fear amongst southern whites before the Civil War.

The only instrument imported directly from Africa during the pre-Civil War years was the banjo, or "banjer" as it was called. The instrument developed from lute-like instruments that migrated from Middle Europe to West Africa, then to the United States during the slave trade. In addition to the banjo, blacks learned to play the fiddle and the fiddle and banjo became the nucleus for string bands on plantations. The songs played were most likely jigs and reels from Scots and Irish traditions.

The major crop for plantations in the pre-Civil War South was cotton and that crop needed a large, slave work force to make it economically profitable. Since cotton fields were large, the types of singing included an individual singing to himself (or herself), which were generally "moans," or the call and response where a leader sang out a line and the others answered. There were "hollers" or "hoolies" where a singer sang or perhaps gave a shout or a long, loud melody that rose and fell and perhaps broke into falsetto. That melody would be picked up by another worker and reverberated like an echo around the field or, perhaps, several joined in a chorus. That "holler" or "hoolie" replaced the group work song since there was no need for cotton field workers to work together in unison. If the hoolie was done in a cornfield, it was called an "arhoolie." In both cases, there were notes bent or struck slightly off key or slurred. The "blues slur" comes when the third note in a chord is flatted to a seventh and emotion was communicated by singing around a note.

The work song and field hollers were of African origin and became an extension of the African tradition. However, it was not until blacks came to the United States that they had a common culture. It was here they had one language--English--rather than a number of tribal languages--and here they were influenced by British folk songs with their harmonic patterns. Thus the blues came from African influences blending with European folk songs, melodies, and harmonic structures, in the American culture.

According to African-American historian and ethnomusicologist James Weldon Johnson, "Generally speaking, the European concept of music is melody and the African concept is rhythm. Melody has, relatively, small place in African music, and harmony still less; but in rhythms African music is beyond comparison with any other music in the world." Gradually, blues singers emerged and Johnson noted, "In the old days there was a definitely recognized order of bards, and to some degree it still persists. These bards gained their recognition by achievement. They were makers of songs and leaders of singing. They had to possess certain qualifications: a gift of melody, a talent for poetry, a strong voice, and a good memory."

Although slavery was abolished after the Civil War, and plantations broken into small farms, the South kept gang labor through penitentiaries. Large gangs of prisoners sang work songs while they split rocks, built roads and other public works as they rebuilt the South. In work songs, the value of singing came from it being a comfort and solace as well as a way to combine strength for more effective working in rhythm and unison. It also provided safety.

In addition to work songs the blues had another source as well, rooted in the leisure activities of Saturday night. The work songs and field songs served a function; they helped men and women get through their work days. At night, particularly Saturday night, the ballads with the eight and twelve-bar forms and conventional harmonic progression created another aspect of the blues, but that was not the blues of people working; that was the blues of people at leisure.

Recordings vs. Performances

Listening to the recordings of blues and country artists gives us a distorted view of what musicians actually played. Many assume that blues musicians just played blues or that country musicians just played country music; however, those musicians played a wide variety of music, from pop tunes to fiddle tunes to folk songs. If a musician made a living, it was because they could play a wide variety of music. For example, a "blues" musician might be hired to play a wedding reception for whites; that musician probably entertained that crowd with the pop tunes of the day. From a Saturday night in a juke joint or honky tonk to a Sunday afternoon ice cream social, musicians performed for a wide variety of audiences and played a wide variety of music. They were proud of being a "musicianeer," the term used for a professional musician.

There was no honor in only playing one kind of music because that meant the musician was limited and therefore could not gain regular paying work. When the recording companies came, they did not want to record musicians playing current popular tunes or a wide variety of music; instead, they needed to fill a marketing niche so they wanted blues musicians to play blues and country musicians to play country. Further, they wanted to record what had not been recorded before so they could gain copyrights. There was no reason to record a wide variety of music already recorded and released so recording companies insisted on music that filled their marketing needs.

The problem is that when we listen to those recordings now, we come to the conclusion that blues and country musicians were locked into one kind of music. That was definitely not the case. Most of the great blues and country artists were capable of playing a wide variety of music.

Field Recordings of the Blues

After the initial recordings by vaudeville blues singers Mamie Smith, Sippie Wallace, Sara Martin, Victoria Spivey, Ma Rainey, Ida Cox and Alberta Hunter--a field dominated by women--in New York, recording companies hit the road. Paramount recorded more blues than any other label; other labels recording blues in the mid-1920s included Okeh, Columbia and Victor. In 1926 Vocalion, owned by the Brunswick-Balke-Collender Company of Chicago emerged as another major "race" label with Jack Kapp head of the "race" division.

The heyday for traditional blues recording was 1926-1929 because that was when the major labels did their first extensive field recordings. Those labels generally recorded in Dallas, Memphis, Atlanta and Chicago.

The first major blues artist to emerge from those recordings was Blind Lemon Jefferson, who recorded 75 songs for Paramount from 1926 to 1930. He was the best selling rural bluesman during the 1920s. The songs he recorded usually list him as a writer (31 list him as composer) and the remaining list no composer. In reality, a number of those songs came from the folk and oral tradition and the singer's contribution was one of interpretation, altering existing songs and adding verses instead of creating something new. The singer either received royalties as a writer or, more likely, signed over his writer's royalties to someone who collected and kept them.

The success of Blind Lemon Jefferson and other rural blues artists encouraged labels to head south to conduct field recordings of African-American artists. Perhaps the most successful of those field recorders was Ralph Peer, who's first field recording was in Atlanta in 1923, when he recorded "Fiddlin'" John Carson, which began the hillbilly industry. Peer visited Atlanta in the early twenties for the Okeh label and recorded blues singer Lucille Bogan. Peer then moved over to Victor and continued his field recordings.

Ralph Peer gave both "hillbilly" and "race" recordings their labels. He named the music "Race" because that was the term the influential black-owned newspaper, The *Chicago Defender* used, after a debate about whether the terms "Negros," "colored," "African," "blacks" or something else should be used. African-Americans who referred to themselves as "the race" during that time did so proudly.

Ralph Peer eventually recorded a number of well-known blues musicians, including Tommy Johnson, Blind Willie McTell, Furry Lewis, Gus Cannon, and His Jug Stompers and the Memphis Jug Band.

The major labels doing field recordings during the 1920s were Victor, Gennett, Columbia, Okeh and Vocalion. The major cities for Victor were Nashville, Bristol and Memphis, Tennessee; Louisville, Kentucky; Cincinnati Ohio; Charlotte, North Carolina; Dallas Texas; Savannah, and Atlanta, Georgia; and New Orleans, Louisiana. All of those field recordings for Victor were done under Peer's supervision.

Columbia Records held field sessions in Atlanta, Memphis, New Orleans and Dallas while Okeh did recordings in San Antonio, Texas; Memphis, St. Louis and Kansas City, Missouri; Louisville, Shreveport, Louisiana; Atlanta, Richmond, Virginia and Jackson, Mississippi. Vocalion held field recording sessions in San Antonio, Dallas, Memphis, Atlanta, New Orleans, Birmingham, Alabama; Knoxville, Tennessee; and Columbia, South Carolina while Gennett held a field recording in Birmingham, Alabama.

Blind Lemon Jefferson

There were a number of blind blues singers recorded during the 1920s and 1930s. The reason so many blues singers were blind is because there was no social safety net so someone had to work in order to earn a living. If someone was blind, their options were limited; however, if they could play and sing, there was the possibility of earning money by playing and singing.

The image of a blues singer as a single performer playing the guitar was popularized by Blind Lemon Jefferson, often referred to as the "Father of the Texas Blues."

Lemon Henry Jefferson was born near Coutchman, Texas on September 24, 1893, in a family with six or seven other children; he was the youngest and born blind (or possibly partially blind). His family were sharecroppers.

Jefferson began playing the guitar during his teen years and performed at parties and picnics as well as on the street. Jefferson met and performed with Leadbelly in Dallas; he also showed T-Bone Walker the basics of blues guitar.

Blind Lemon Jefferson's first session was either December 1925 or January, 1926 in Chicago; the first songs he recorded were gospel numbers, "I Want to Be Like Jesus in My Heart" and "All I Want Is That Pure Religion" which were released as by "Deacon L.J. Bates."

In March, 1926 Jefferson recorded "Booster Blues" and "Dry Southern Blues"; they were released under his name and sold well. Two other songs from that session, "Got the Blues" and "Long Lonesome Blues" were also released with sales reported to be over 100,000 units. During the period 1926-1929 Jefferson recorded around 100 tracks with 43 records released.

During the 1920s, Paramount became the most successful company recording blues; in addition to Jefferson, artists Blind Blake and Ma Rainey were on the label. The label was based in Grafton, Wisconsin.

In 1927, Mayo Williams, who had worked with Paramount, joined Okeh Records and recorded Jefferson singing "Matchbox Blues" and "Black Snake Moan" for Okeh. That was Jefferson's only recording for Okeh and his only release not on Paramount, whose releases were of inferior quality to Okeh's.

"Matchbox Blues" was so successful that he re-recorded it for Paramount as well as "See That My Grave Is Kept Clean," which was released under the name Deacon L.J. Bates. Jefferson's "Matchbox Blues" was the basis for the Carl Perkins song "Matchbox," later recorded by the Beatles.

Blind Lemon Jefferson died on December 19, 1929 in Chicago; he is buried in Wortham, Texas

Charlie Patton

One of the most influential blues performers from the 1920s was Charlie (also spelled Charley) Patton, who is often considered to be the "Father of the Delta Blues." His date of birth and heritage are questionable; he was probably born in April, 1891 and was of mixed blood with suggestions of black, white, Mexican and Cherokee ancestors.

Patton played the guitar on his lap—Hawaiian style—and his voice was deep and gravely.

Charlie Patton lived most of his life in Sunflower County, Mississippi, in the Delta. In 1897, Patton's family moved to the Dockery Plantation near Ruleville, Mississippi; during his early years Patton developed his guitar style, influenced by Henry Sloan.

Patton was a showman, playing his guitar behind his back and between his legs, which excited crowds but drew the ire of other bluesmen who were not "showy." He had a wide repertoire of blues, country songs and nineteenth century popular ballads as well as country dance music. (Patton often played for white dances).

Patton's first recording session was in June, 1929, in Richmond, Indiana, for Paramount; on that session, Patton recorded 14 songs; the first recorded was "Pony Blues" which became his most well-known song. Patton made further recordings in November, 1929, in Grafton, Wisconsin (11 songs), in December, 1929, also in Grafton (12 songs), and in May, 1930, in Grafton (four songs).

In January, 1934 Patton recorded ten songs for Vocalion in New York City.

Charlie Patton died on April 28, 1934 in Holly Ridge, Mississippi.

Leroy Carr

In 1928 Leroy Carr became famous for his "How Long, How Long Blues." Carr, born in Nashville in 1905 and raised in Indianapolis, became one of the most influential blues singers with his piano-guitar backing (Carr was a pianist and his guitar accompanist was Scrapper Blackwell) and his smooth, pop sounding vocals, which were a step away from the raw vocal sound of most early blues singers in the South.

According to Arnold Shaw in his book *Honkers and Shouters*, "Carr moved blues singing into a sophisticated, urban direction, formulating a style that was widely imitated by bluesmen into the early '40s, so his collaboration with Scrapper helped establish piano-guitar as the new distinctive accompaniment for the blues."

Arnold continued, "His diction was crystal clear, and he accompanied himself at the piano--he was possibly the first impressive blues pianist--aided and abetted by the jazzy guitar work of Scrapper Blackwell...Carr was not an involved vocalist. Singing in a thin, high-pitched, Hoosier-inflected voice, with a slight rubato but few sustained notes, he talked rather than shouted, mused rather than worried, complained rather than cried...his great forte was in creating a mood, especially of longing and loneliness." Arnold concluded, "in a brief seven-year career, [Carr] was...influential in moving the blues in an urban and urbane direction."

Carr was so popular and influential that when he died in 1935 there were two songs about his death. Bumble Bee Slim (real name Amos Easton) recorded "The Death of Leroy Carr" for Decca and Bill Gaither recorded "The Life of Leroy Carr" on Okeh.

Tampa Red and Georgia Tom

Another early influential artist was Tampa Red (real name Hudson Woodbridge) who, with Georgia Tom, recorded "It's Tight Like That" in 1929. Georgia Tom was Thomas Dorsey, who later became known as the father of black gospel. "Tight Like That" was definitely not a gospel song; the double entendre song reportedly sold 750,000 copies and provided Dorsey with his first professional success.

Tampa Red continued to record after Georgia Tom split and had hits with "Somebody's Been Using That Thing" and "It's All Worn Out." Another important blues act before the Depression was Memphis Minnie (Minnie Douglas) who had a hit in 1931 with "Bumble Bee" on Columbia.

After 1930 as the Great Depression grew and spread, the recording labels limited blues recordings. The major reason was that the market dried up--blacks could hardly afford the basics of food, clothing and shelter, much less a record.

A History of the Guitar

The history of the guitar goes back thousands of years. The first stringed instruments had one string and were played with a bow; the "body" was usually a gourd, although tortoise shells and skulls were also used as sound chambers. The earliest strings were animal tendons or plant fibers. Some of the earliest instruments that developed into guitars came from Asia and when Marco Polo returned to Italy from his travels, he brought with him a number of guitars and lutes from China and India.

The ancestors to the contemporary guitar include instruments that look like the modern mandolin, with eight strings in four pairs, as well as the lute, which looks similar to a guitar but has a shorter neck, an oval body shape, and a deep, round back.

The guitar developed further in Spain and France as people stopped using a bow and began plucking the strings with their fingers; a guitar with four strings was most popular. During the 1600s, the guitars in France and Italy began to be indented in the middle, a forerunner to the curves in the body of the contemporary guitar.

Sometime around American independence in 1776, a sixth string was added to these early instruments and the six strings were tuned like the modern guitar: E A D G B E. Another important development was making the fretboard slimmer--to about two inches--which made fingering the guitar easier.

The Hawaiian Influence

The popularity of the contemporary guitar can be traced back to the late 19th and early 20th centuries with mail order catalogues and Hawaiian music. The guitar had come to Hawaii from South American cowboys during the 19th century and by the late 1860s there were advertisements for guitars and guitar lessons in Honolulu newspapers.

Native Hawaiians, known as Kanaka Maoli, saw a number of sailors, missionaries and traders from other countries visit Hawaii, which became a crossroads for merchants and travelers on the Pacific Ocean. In 1893, the Hawaiian monarchy was overthrown by American and British capitalists and in 1898 Hawaii became an American territory. In an effort to preserve their culture (American missionaries wanted to ban the "hula") the Kanaka Maoli began developing their own music.

Sometime before the overthrow in 1893, Joseph Kekuku began laying the guitar across his lap to play it. He tuned his guitar to open chords and slid a piece of metal along the strings. During a seven year period, Kekuku developed that style of guitar playing; along the way he developed finger picks, steel bars and a nut that raised the strings higher above the fret board. Those changes "increased the instruments volume" and "he created shimmering glissando sounds on the strings, mimicking, perhaps better than any other instrument on the islands, the human voice."

Other guitarists copied Kekuku's style and it became popular in Hawaii, which led to Hawaiian musicians touring the United States. In 1904 Kekuku traveled to California and performed; his tour preceded the Lewis and Clark Exposition held in Portland, Oregon, which featured Hawaiian music and musicians. An "Exposition," which was a "World's Fair," was a way to introduce the public to new inventions and technologies. The Alaska Yukon Pacific Exposition was held in Seattle in 1909 and that event was visited by over 31 million people. Hawaiian music was a main attraction at that fair. In 1914, to celebrate the completion of the Panama Canal, the Panama Pacific International Exposition (PPIE), was held in San Francisco. Over 13 million people attended the exposition in San Francisco which featured, among its many attractions, a special exhibit on Hawaii.

In 1909, July Paka made the first commercial Hawaiian guitar recording. A number of Hawaiian musicians, including July Paka, Pale K. Lua, David Kaili and Palakiko "Frank" Ferera, toured the United States; Kekuku spent thirty years touring the United States and Europe.

The Hawaiians had Polynesian roots, which meant they were dark-skinned people. When they toured in the South—and there were extensive tours of Hawaiian musicians during the first twenty years of the twentieth century--they were barred from white only hotels, restaurants and other establishments. That led to them staying with African American families and performing on vaudeville shows as novelty acts as well as on shows that featured black performers. That is how African Americans became exposed to the Hawaiian slide guitar style.

In 1923 the first blues recordings with a slide guitar were made by Sylvester Weaver on November 2 when he recorded "Guitar Blues" and "Guitar Rag." That song later became known as "Steel Guitar Rag" by Leon McAuliff, who is credited as the writer; McAuliff was a member of Bob Wills' western swing group and is credited with popularizing the steel guitar after he recorded the song in 1935.

African American performers developed their own style of playing "Hawaiian guitar" "by placing a metal or glass cylinder on a finger rather than holding a piece of steel, and by positioning the instrument upright rather than on their lap." One of the most influential blues guitarists, Lonnie Johnson, recorded "Blue Hawaii" and "Hawaiian Harmony Blues" using the slide guitar with Henry Johnson and His Boys.

The introduction of Hawaiian music to the United States led to the slide guitar for blues musicians and the steel guitar in country music. It also led to a demand for ukuleles and guitars from Sears after the Panama Exhibition so Sears turned to Harmony, it's supplier of guitars, for those instruments.

Harmony and Sears

The Harmony Company was started in 1892 by Wilhelm J.F. Schultz, a German immigrant in Chicago. The first building for the company was at Washington and Market Streets in Chicago. Harmony was known for making inexpensive guitars and their major account was the Sears, Roebuck Company. Their chief competitor in making guitars was Oscar Schmidt of New Jersey; Schmidt also made guitars for Sears as well as their chief competitor, Montgomery Ward.

During the 1892-1915 period, Harmony was an independent company whose location in Chicago was fortuitous because the major retailers-- Montgomery Ward and Sears--were both located there. The mail order houses were primarily responsible for the early success of the guitar. Montgomery Ward began its catalog sales in 1872 and by 1890 was the largest retailer in the world. Sears, Roebuck began in Minnesota as a watch business in 1885 and became a mail order catalog business late in 1893. In 1895 Sears moved to Chicago and by 1900 Sears was the world's largest store, surpassing Montgomery Ward.

The Montgomery Ward catalogue was the first to offer guitars for sale, although the exact year is unknown (it was after 1875 and before 1894). The first guitars that Ward sold were imported, probably from Germany, and the passage across the Atlantic caused problems with the wood. Those early guitars were all gut string and warnings were issued from Ward and Sears that the guitars would not hold up with steel strings.

At first, Sears sold the same guitars and mandolins as Ward but in their 1897 catalogue offered "original" guitars and mandolins. Those guitars came from the Harmony Company. The most popular early guitars were small, often called "parlor guitars," and used in mandolin and banjo orchestras as well as a solo instrument. The "concert" guitars were larger than the "parlor" guitars and by 1905 there were "grand concert guitars," which were even larger, but not the size of the contemporary guitar.

Sears expanded its line of guitars in its 1899 catalogue, featuring guitars from Harmony as well as Oscar Schmidt. Generally, the Harmony guitars were budget or lower end models while Schmidt's guitars were more expensive or higher end models. Prices range from $2.95 for the "Troubadour" model to $8.25 for the "Magnolia."

In 1904 the Harmony Company moved to a new factory at 1738-1754 Lawndale in Chicago and expanded again in 1906. In 1910 Sears offered guitars that could use either gut or steel strings and Sears promoted the fact that steel strings could be used, an answer to the requests for guitars that were "louder" and could compete with other instruments in sound volume. Harmony continued to manufacture the lower end models offered by Sears while Oscar Schmidt built the higher end models.

During World War I, the Harmony Company began to manufacture violins, since the major sources of violins--Germany and Northern Italy--were at war..

In 1916, just before the United States entered World War I, Sears purchased the Harmony Company. The following year there was a full line of Hawaiian instruments in the Sears catalogue. The popularity of the Hawaiian guitar and the ukulele led to an interest in the guitar through the mail order catalogues--Sears and Montgomery Ward--which offered both. The other impetus for interest in the guitar came from country music, both on the radio and on recordings during the 1920s.

The Martin and Gibson Companies

The guitar became popular with the mass of Americans through the mass produced guitars sold in mail order catalogues. However, the history of quality, hand-made acoustic guitars--those played by professional musicians--centers on two brands: Martin and Gibson.

Martin Guitars

Martin Guitars was started by C.F. Martin in 1833 in New York City; prior to that time, the Martin Family made guitars in Germany as early as 1807. In 1839 C.F. Martin moved to Nazareth, Pennsylvania. Martin had a music store that sold a variety of instruments and built violins, cellos and bass violas in addition to guitars. Most of Martin's early guitars were small and inexpensive; the headstock had all six tuning keys on one side, much like the Fender electrics developed during the 1940s and 1950s. Those early guitars were known as "parlor guitars" and were played primarily by women, since playing music was not considered "manly."

C.F. Martin's company was successful and was soon known for building quality guitars. C.F. Martin, Sr. died in 1873; by that time, he had gone into partnership with his son, C.F. Martin, Jr., who became sole owner of the Martin Guitar Company around 1885. In 1888, C.F. Martin, Jr. died and the company passed into the hands of his son, Frank Henry Martin, who led the company through its greatest growth.

The factories of the Martin Guitar Company began building mandolins by 1895 and in 1898 published its first catalog.

At the beginning of the 20th Century, Martin produced the Size 0 guitar and the Size 00, which was slightly larger. The size 000 was even larger, answering requests for a "louder" guitar. For a while, Martin produced more mandolins--which had a bowl back--than guitars and in 1914 began producing flat-back mandolins.

When the craze for Hawaiian music swept the country during the early 1900s, Martin began producing ukuleles around 1915, which became a major financial success for the struggling company. During that period, they made instruments for other companies; for example the Ditson guitars were made by Martin but sold by the retailing firm, The Oliver Ditson Company.

During the 1920s, Martin continued to grow, adding and expanding their factory. The earliest Martin guitars were gut string but in 1922 Martin produced a line of guitars with steel strings, although they had manufactured steel-string guitars earlier..

Martins were endorsed by country music's first superstar when Jimmie Rodgers received an 000-45 Martin from C.F. Martin III in 1928.

Gibson Guitars

The Gibson Company was founded by Orville Gibson, who began making mandolins in Kalamazoo, Michigan, where he was living by 1881. Gibson was born in 1856 in upstate New York and moved to Kalamazoo around the time he was 25. He began his business making stringed instruments--guitars, mandolins, violins, lutes and others--by 1896 and on October 10, 1902 the Gibson Mandolin-Guitar Mfg. Co., Ltd was formalized as a partnership with five men from Kalamazoo. Orville Gibson, who built the instruments, was paid $2,500 for the company he had started but lacked the capital to expand and grow.

Gibson was to serve as a mentor, tutor and consultant for those building instruments but about seven months after the company was formed he was virtually dismissed from an active role; instead, he collected royalties from the sales of the Gibson Company's instruments and then received a monthly stipend until his death. Around 1909, Gibson left Kalamazoo and returned to upstate New York, where he died on August 21, 1918.

Gibson issued its first catalog in 1903 and it featured four instruments: mandolins, mandalas, guitars and harp guitars. In 1918, Gibson began manufacturing banjos.

A key figure in the growth of Gibson was Lloyd Loar, who joined the company in June, 1919, working as a design consultant to develop new models. Loar created the L-5 during the early 1920s, an archtop guitar with a f-hole. Eddie Lang popularized the L-5 while he performed with Bing Crosby; in country music, Maybelle Carter performed on an L-5, using the famous "Carter Lick."

Under the leadership of Guy Hart, who ran Gibson from 1924 to 1948, the guitar became the centerpiece for Gibson. The Super 400 and SJ-200 were developed under Hart, as well as the ES-150. In the late 1920s, the guitar gained popularity, helped by country performers playing through a microphone on radio and recordings. The guitar became the best multi-purpose instrument as singers used it as an accompaniment.

The Harmonica

A German, Christian Buschmann, patented an instrument called the "aura" with steel reeds in small channels in 1821; in 1825 a mouth organ was developed by Richter and that became the basis of the harmonica. Later, a German, Matthias Hohner adopted mass production to harmonicas which were imported into the United States. The accordion was perfected by Charles Wheatstone in England in 1844.

By the end of the nineteenth century, the most popular folk instruments were the fiddle and banjo; the guitar and harmonica were available but their great popularity occurred during the 1930s with the Singing Cowboy movies from Hollywood.

Musicians Union

The business structure for musicians was established in the late nineteenth and early twentieth century. On November 11, 1896 the American Federation of Musicians was established in New York City with Owen Miller as President; on March 15, 1897 a local AFM was chartered in Los Angeles and a Chicago local was formed on September 17, 1901. In 1902 the Nashville AFM, local 257, was established.

The Roots of Folk Music

The term "folk music" may be defined as music of the "common" folk--black and white--who later became known as the "working class." It is the music from those who are generally musically illiterate, but who have musical talent and are musically accomplished. This music is developed outside the circles of the musical elite and represents the basis of popular culture, where music comes from the grass roots, or the bottom up to the mainstream.

In American popular music, mainstream music often has folk roots, and the most popular music of the twentieth century originated first with the "folk," then gained acceptance in the mainstream. That "folk" music was usually played on stringed instruments and the musicians were, by and large, self-taught while the songs were passed down through the oral tradition.

Robert Burns

Robert Burns, the Scottish poet and songwriter, should be considered the Godfather of Pop Music Songwriters because his writing and collecting folk songs is reminiscent of many early country, blues and rock songs and songwriters. He was born on January 25, 1759 in the Scottish lowlands, or south Scotland. His father, William Burness, was a tenant farmer and his mother, the daughter of a tenant farmer, knew a number of old folk songs and sang them at home. His father was sternly religious, and young Burns studied the Bible at school--reminiscent of the deep religious roots of many country songwriters.

Robert Burns, too, was a farmer and, like his father, never did well farming. In school he was an unremarkable student, his talents lying outside the notice of teachers, who generally favor bright, studious students who learn well and quickly. However, Burns possessed a lively, fertile imagination, which became apparent in his poetry and songs.

The first collection of Burns' poetry, *Poems, Chiefly in the Scottish Dialect*, was published on July 31, 1786, paid for by Burns. The book came to the attention of literary critic Thomas Blacklock in Edinburgh, who praised it, and soon the twenty-seven year old poet was well-known in southern Scotland. In 1789 the second edition of this work was published by William Creech, who paid Burns 100 guineas for the copyright, and that edition "advanced him rapidly to the rank of one of the world's poets." That edition was published in London and the new United States. Although the first work contained several songs, the second edition contained a number of Burns's songs, which established him as a songwriter.

Burns heard folk-songs from his mother when he was a child; as he grew older he heard them when he traveled. In Edinburgh, James Johnson collected folk songs and published them in his book, *Scots Musical Museum*, which was "the first systematically documented collection of its kind to appear in print." Burns began collecting songs for this work and Johnson's book soon contained a number of Burns's songs. Generally, Burns heard an old folk song and either put new lyrics to it or rewrote the old lyrics. This was similar to the method used by the Carter Family when they began recording country music for Victor in 1927; A. P. Carter collected old folk songs, re-wrote them or added lyrics to make them commercial. The same process occurred with early blues and rock songwriters (particularly the rockabillies). That is how a number of old folk songs, such as "Wildwood Flower," originally titled "I'll Twine With the Ringlets Round My Bosom," came into popular music.

In Johnson's first book, two of Burns's songs were included; after Burns met Johnson in April, 1787, the second volume contained forty of Burns' works, as well as an "Introduction" by him. The third volume, in 1790, had over fifty songs by Burns. Ian Gimble, a Burns biographer, notes that "It is not merely that Burns rescued and improved, where so many 'improvers' of folk material have destroyed the essential quality of it, if not worse. Burns also possessed an unerring gift for matching words to melodies, which he would catch out of the air and sing over and over to himself, sometimes altering their speed to match them perfectly to the words with which he joined them in a lasting marriage." In other words, Burns also wrote original songs with new melodies and words.

George Thompson replaced James Johnson as publisher of *Scots Museum* and invited Burns to re-write his lyrics and improve them for a number of folk songs. Burns did that and the fourth volume of this work, published in 1792, had about half the songs in it written by Burns. In February, 1793, Creech published a new edition of Burns's poems, which included "Tam o' Shanter," which further increased Burns' fame.

Burns never accepted payment for the songs he wrote, although Thompson offered payment. The income from his poetry came from "subscriptions," or people who purchased his work. However, most of that money went directly to George Creech, the publisher, and Burns only received money for the books he sold directly.

Robert Burns fit the image of the careless, carefree songwriter, fathering several illegitimate children before marrying; after he was married, his wife and mistress gave birth to a child within days of each other. He failed as a farmer and finally earned his living as a tax collector in several cities.

A biographer compared Burns with the poet Lord Byron, who "never met anyone as interesting as themselves." The son of a tenant farmer, he was extremely class-conscious and, although he often socialized with aristocracy, suffered an "inverted snobbery" his entire life. Burns preferred male company "with whom he shared a taste for bawdy conversation and sexual adventures." He held "advanced liberal opinions" and intensely disliked Calvinist fundamentalism. Burns was "ever forthright to the point of tactlessness in his expressions of opinion." Although he received a good, basic education in his youth, and was an inveterate reader, he presented an image of himself to the world as an "unlettered peasant." Burns described himself as "a man who had little art in making money, and still less in keeping it."

Writing about his songwriting, Burns stated "I am delighted with many little melodies, which the learned musician despises as silly and insipid," emphasizing his affinity for the simple, folk tunes rather than high-minded fare. One of his most famous songs, "Flow Gently, Sweet Afton," was originally published in 1789 as "Afton Water." Perhaps his most famous song is "Auld Lang Syne," written in 1789, which is still sung each New Year's Eve.

Should auld acquaintance be forgot
And never brought to mind?
Should auld acquaintance be forgot
And days of auld lang syne
(Days of "auld lang synce" is "days of old long since")

In November, 1791, Burns and his family moved to Dumfries, where he continued his work collecting Excise taxes. He had a heart condition that was degenerative and, like Hank Williams, died an early, tragic death on July 21, 1796 at the age of thirty-seven. During the funeral, his wife gave birth to their ninth child.

Robert Burns left a legacy of songs that show the roots of popular music. He wrote some solely by himself, while for others he used old folk songs and re-wrote the lyrics. Biographer Ian Gimble noted, "Countless songs and airs might have been lost if he had not rescued them, or would not have survived in the beautiful form in which he presented them." Many of those songs found their way to America, which became the United States during Burns's lifetime, and became part of the catalog of country songs when that music was first recorded during the 1920s.

The history of American folk music begins with the early folk songs from Scotland, Ireland, and England, like those of Robert Burns. But the roots are not "pure" folk music, songs anonymously composed and handed down through oral tradition. Rather, from the beginning, folk music was a mixture of songs from anonymous sources as well as songs that a singer re-wrote or changed, as well as songs composed by songwriters who knew the songs that went before them and composed new songs from this old tradition.

Country Music

Country music has often been linked to "hillbilly culture" and a definition of a "hillbilly" was printed by the *New York Journal* in 1900; it stated "A Hill-Billie is a free and untrammeled white citizen of Alabama, who lives in the hills, has no means to speak of, dresses as he can, talks as he pleases, drinks whiskey when he gets it, and fires off his revolver as the fancy takes him." The first movie version of a "hillbilly" came in 1904 with *The Moonshiner*. and between 1910 and 1916 about 300 movies about moonshining and feuding were produced, including the movie *Billie--the Hill Billy*, which appeared in 1915. In 1913 the vaudeville group Cicero and Elviry with Abner (later known as the Weaver Brothers and Elviry) performed as hillbillies on the RKO circuit, playing mandolin, guitar, fiddle, banjo and musical handsaw.

The fact that early country music was called "hillbilly," and the performers "hillbillies," indicates that most Americans looked down their noses at them. The fight for respect country musicians and country audiences endured for their music was an ongoing battle throughout most of the twentieth century.

"Country music" before World War I was fiddling contests, home entertainment, and local dances in rural areas. The basic instruments had been developed; the violin had been developed in the 1600s and the first known fiddle contest was held in 1736 near Richmond, Virginia. Famous early "fiddlers" include Thomas Jefferson and Davy Crockett. The banjo was developed in West Africa and brought to the United States by slaves; those early instruments were refined and popularized in minstrel shows.

Fiddlin' John Carson

In 1923, Polk Brockman was a regional representative (salesman) for Okeh Records in Atlanta. Ralph Peer had recently been promoted to General Recording Manager, overseeing the label's "race" records. Brockman's grandfather, James K. Polk, owned a local furniture store that sold phonographs and records (most phonographs and records were sold in furniture stores during that time) and Polk Brockman had been successful getting records from Okeh stocked in his grandfather's store.

Brockman encouraged Ralph Peer to record an Atlanta act, Warner's Seven Aces, a white dance band on WGM and plans were made to bring them to New York to record before the decision was made for Peer and Okeh to come to Atlanta to record them. That decision came because Peer thought he could find "race" acts in Atlanta to record.

During the week of June 12, Peer arrived in Atlanta where a warehouse on Nassau Street had been set up by an Okeh engineer to record. The Seven Aces were recorded, then Lucille Bogan recorded "The Pawn Shop Blues" (the first blues record recorded in the South). After recordings by a Morehouse College quartet and some vaudeville blues by Fanny Goosby, Peer ran out of talent he wanted to record; he could not find blues artists in Atlanta that he felt were commercial.

Fiddlin' John Carson had appeared on WSB and had a local reputation as a popular fiddler so Polk Brockman suggested that Peer record him, since, like the Seven Acts, the radio performances would promote record sales. Brockman felt that he could sell 500 records by the fiddler in and around Atlanta.

On June 19, 1923, Fiddlin' John came to Okeh's makeshift studio and recorded a former minstrel number written by Will Shakespeare Hays, "The Little Old Log Cabin in the Lane" and an old fiddle tune, "The Old Hen Cackled and the Rooster's Going to Crow." Like the first record by Elvis that clearly showed the roots of rock'n'roll—one side was a blues song and the other was a country song—Fiddlin' John's first record clearly showed the roots of country music—one side was a song written for the stage and the other was an old folk tune that had been handed down, fiddler to fiddler, through the years.

The wax pressings were sent back to New York and the consensus was that they were "terrible" (they were referred to later as "pluperfect awful" but, encouraged by Brockman, Peer sent a thousand copies to Brockman after he "took the precaution of eliminating the catalogue number from the label, as I could not believe that such a bad recording could be used." (Peer was also referring to the sound quality of the record.)

On a Thursday morning, the thousand records arrived in Atlanta; the next morning by 10 o'clock Polk Brockman called requesting ten thousand more be sent immediately.

There was an established market for blues recordings but there was no proven market for country music. The sales of that record established the fact that there was a market for recordings of white, southern music—the last genre to be exploited by the early recording industry.

The success of Fiddlin' John set off a demand for hillbilly music. Okeh brought Fiddlin' John to New York for more recordings and Peer also recorded Henry Whitter in New York. The two singers were marketed together as singers of "Old Time" and "Hill Country Music." In the Okeh catalogue published in 1925, the recordings by Carson and Whitter were listed as "Old Familiar Tunes."

Fiddlers and Fiddlin'

It is appropriate that country music began with fiddlers because country fiddling had a long, rich history by the time Fiddlin' John Carson recorded his two songs. Davy Crockett was a country fiddler who played his fiddle at the Alamo before it was overrun by Santa Anna's troops in 1836 and country fiddlers played for house dances, in minstrel shows, in vaudeville and at fiddlers conventions throughout the nineteenth and early twentieth centuries.

In 1913, the Georgia State Fiddlers Convention was first held in Atlanta. Fiddlers were spotlighted because they were "true" musicians; they played the melody, breakdowns, began the tune and were the lead instrumentalist in a string band. Throughout the nineteenth century the major accompanist was the banjo but in the early twentieth century the guitar became more popular. Banjo and guitar players played supporting roles, keeping a rhythm for the fiddler or singer. It was the fiddle that was the most difficult to play; guitarists and banjoists generally played chords and rhythm.

Rural fiddlers had to endure those cultured souls who preferred the violin to the fiddle. In his book *Pickin' On Peachtree: A History of Country Music in Atlanta*, Georgia author Wayne Daniel quoted Atlanta attorney Eb T. Williams, who stated, "A fiddle is an old, common instrument, clumsily and roughly finished with wire strings, the bridge a thick piece of wood set in the wrong place, the sound post sometimes in front instead of behind the bridge, and not infrequently a mouse hole gnawed in the 'F' holes as big as a goose egg, where several generations of mice were born and raised. A violin is, on the other hand, a thing of beauty, the most dainty and exquisitely finished instrument in the world, made of the most beautiful grained maple and spruce pine, with old Cremona varnish that has foiled the centuries; beautiful, fresh and oily...and it has a divine voice that appeals to you like the voice of an angel, and in the hands of a master wails with sorrow or laughs with joy, having concealed in its body a human soul sounding every depth of the human heart."

The fiddle and violin were the same instrument when laying in their cases, but the musicians who played them and the songs they played divided them into two different camps. Rural fiddlers were proud of their instrument and their tradition and Daniel quoted fiddler, Judge Tump Jackson, who stated, "The difference between a fiddler and one of these here violinists is that a violinist plays by note and a fiddler by plain natural disposition and elbow grease. You might go on to say that a violinist draws down about a thousand a night, a week, a month or whatever it is, if it's so, and a fiddler is lucky to get the neck of a chicken and what's left in the bottle after it's been done around the room."

Most old time fiddlers were proud of the fact that they played by ear--a more "natural" talent--and could not read music. Daniel quoted another fiddler who stated, "Fiddlers are never taught; they do their own learning. We figure that music comes from a person's soul. If you have it in you, you can play; and if you haven't there is no use trying to learn. If a person taught you how to play a tune, you would simply be playing his music, and not your own."

The notion that the fiddles played by rural fiddlers were crude instruments was discounted by Charles Wolfe in his book, *The Devil's Box: Masters of Southern Fiddling*, where he notes that many of the rural fiddlers preferred 19th century European instruments such as the Stainer, Guarnerius and Hoff models.

Although Fiddlin' John Carson was the first recorded fiddler to achieve commercial success, he was not the first fiddler ever recorded. Uncle Eck Robertson was a Texas fiddler who attended an Old Confederate Soldiers reunion in Richmond, Virginia in June, 1922. Robertson, born in 1887, was the son of a Confederate veteran; at the reunion he met Henry C. Gilliland, a 74-year old Confederate veteran, and the two traveled to New York after the reunion to visit a friend of Gilliland's, attorney Martin W. Littleton, who occasionally did legal work for Victor Records. While in New York Robertson, Gilliland and Littleton stopped by the Victor Records offices and received an audition. On Friday, June 30, Robertson and Gilliland recorded four tunes, "Arkansas Traveler," "Turkey in the Straw," "Forked Deer" and "Apple Blossom." The next day Robertson returned alone and recorded six more tunes, including "Sallie Gooden," which was released, along with one of the duet tunes, on September 1. Although Robertson's record was available to the public before Carson's, it did not achieve the sales success of Carson's recording.

Another fiddler, Kentucky native William B. Houchens, first recorded fiddle tunes on September 18, 1922, for the Gennett label, owned by the

Starr Piano Company in Richmond, Indiana, but those did not receive wide circulation or commercial success.

The heyday of old time fiddling occurred during the 1925-1926 period when Henry Ford, concerned about the erosion of "American values," held a number of fiddling contests at his Ford dealerships throughout the South and Midwest in order to promote traditional, old-time values. Those fiddling contests received wide publicity. The recording companies took notice and during the 1922-1942 period about 300 different Southern fiddlers had recordings released. As Charles Wolfe noted in his book *The Devil's Box*, "A lot of the recording executives couldn't tell one fiddle tune from another, and the fiddlers soon figured this out. When some studio boss rejected a tune title because he already had out a version on that label, a lot of fiddlers just changed the name of the tune and went on and recorded what they like."

Folk Song Collectors

The first recordings of country music were by fiddlers and small record companies were among the most adventurous. However, early country music was not just fiddle music, there were singers and songs too, so it is natural that early recording companies discovered those songs as they recorded in that field.

That was first revealed when Harvard Professor Francis James Child published the last volume of his five-volume study, *The English and Scottish Popular Ballads*, in 1898. Those who studied the collection soon discovered that a number of those songs were still sung in America, particularly in the South. Some of the songs had been rewritten or changed to reflect local language, but the original songs formed the core of the new ones. Scholars and folk song collectors began collecting American versions of those old songs, encouraged by the American Folklore Society, which was formed in 1888. The "Child ballads" were often found in mountainous regions in the South that contained pockets of people who were more isolated than their urban counterparts. That is why many of those songs had been preserved through the years.

An Englishman, Cecil Sharp, traveled into the Appalachian region 1916-1918 and listened to folk songs, which he transcribed into his notebooks. Sharp was fifty-seven when he began collecting British folk songs in America. Previously, he achieved fame collecting folk songs in England and Scotland. In 1914, with war on the horizon in England, Sharp came to the United States and gave a series of lectures. In Lincoln, Massachusetts, Sharp was confined by lumbago when Olive Campbell appeared.

Olive Campbell's husband, John, worked for the Russell Sage Foundation, researching Appalachian schools. That was part of the crusading spirit of reform that began after the Civil War and extended to the early 1920s with the work of muckrakers, trust busting and business regulation, and ultimately Prohibition. For the Appalachian region, that meant a number of missionaries and teachers came to the area.

John Campbell took long trips into the mountains and Olive went with him. She loved the old mountain ballads and began writing them down. There were other song collectors around but when she heard that Mr. Sharp, the international authority on English ballads, was in the North lecturing, she packed her bags and manuscripts and headed for Boston.

Sharp was constantly approached by amateur collectors but few gave him anything worthwhile; however, Mrs. Campbell's songs intrigued him. She had old English songs, like "Lord Randall," that had been changed to "Jimmy Randal" and "my mules and wagons" bequeathed instead of "lands and houses." There were also changes in the melodies he knew.

Sharp decided to go South to collect ballads and in July, 1916, was in Asheville, North Carolina. After an 11 hour car and buggy trip covering 40 miles, Sharp and his assistant, Maud Karpeles came to White Rock, North Carolina.

Collecting folk songs wasn't easy because the native mountain folk were suspicious of Sharp. A number thought he was a surveyor trying to steal their land--minerals had been discovered in the mountains and an influx of businessmen invaded the area--and some even thought he was a German spy. Sharp persisted with his dogged manner, singing to a recalcitrant native a song with a few wrong words until the native felt compelled to correct him. He also spent time chatting away on a porch until a family was relaxed.

Sharp recorded the songs in his notebook. Unlike previous folk song collectors, he wrote both melody and words (other folk song collectors had only recorded words). His assistant, usually Maud Karpeles, took down the words in shorthand.

Sharp toyed briefly with the idea of hauling a cylinder phonograph into the region but decided it was too awkward and bulky; besides, it inhibited the singers. Instead, he wrote down the musical notes, which looked like magic to the natives when he sight-read the melody back to them.

(NOTE: The earliest field recordings by a folk song collector were done in 1890 when anthropologist J.W. Fewkes recorded Passamaquoddy Indian music on Edison cylinders. Later, in the 1920s, Robert Winslow Gordon made over 1,000 field recordings of North American Indians. Those are in the Archive of Folk Culture in the Library of Congress.)

Sharp collected 387 tunes in nine weeks in 1916 in the western North Carolina region. Then, for 37 weeks in 1917 and 1918, he went back to the mountains, criss-crossing the region and collected more folk songs. The areas that were the richest in songs for Sharp were western North Carolina, southwestern Virginia, and eastern Kentucky. Those were all isolated pockets where songs had been sung for generations and where singing was as natural as talking for those mountain folk.

Sharp noted that the songs generally had a five-or six note scale, rather than the standard eight note scale, and that a number of the notes were "worried" or slurred. The singers often changed the melody slightly when singing the song over again, an intriguing bit of creativity, with some notes being drawn out a bit longer or perhaps slurred a little more.

Sharp collected songs like "Barbara Allen," "The Swapping Song," "Gypsy Davey," "Lord Randal" and "The Riddle Song" ("I gave my love a cherry"). The result was *English Folk Songs from the Southern Appalachians* which "introduced the world to the mountains' treasure of music." Sharp and other folk song collectors discovered interesting facts about folks singers and mountain musicians. The primary instrument was the fiddle, generally held in the crook of the arm instead of off their shoulder. In playing the fiddle, the musicians "usually moved their instrument as much as their bow."

Playing the fiddle was often considered "sinful" because it was connected to laziness and hence "fiddlin' around" was a derogatory term, indicating someone who was "playing" instead of working at a job. Thus the fiddle was popularly known as "the Devil's box."

A number of folk singers were women, who sang while doing chores at the house or in the evening for entertainment. The women often passed old folk songs down to their children. It was unusual for a woman to play an instrument--the fiddlers were primarily men--and singing in general was usually unaccompanied. The guitar was virtually unheard of, although the banjo was a popular instrument. The banjo and fiddle played instrumental tunes while the singers sang unaccompanied, telling stories with the songs unencumbered by instruments. Slides and slurs were introduced into lyrics and the meter might be changed to fit the mood of the singer.

In addition to singing while working, or home entertainment, music played an important part in the social life of most mountain communities. There was singing at churches--which were often the social centers in a community--school houses and at house parties. Those were often scenes of "frolics," "hops" or "dances" where families gathered to sing and dance all evening, putting the children to sleep in another room or in a corner while the festivities continued. A fiddler was a valuable prize for a community, and the best community fiddler knew a lot of tunes. It was better that a fiddler could play a lot of songs during an evening rather than playing a few extremely well; a fiddler's technical skill took a back seat to his ability to entertain a crowd for an entire evening.

Folk Songs

There are two deep tap roots in American popular music. The first is folk songs which were passed down from generation to generation. Nobody knows who wrote those songs and each singer or fiddler altered the song, played it a little different or adapted new words to the old tunes. The second tap root is songs written for the stage. That root began during the minstrel era and continued through vaudeville and the early recording industry. The notions of melody and harmony can be traced back to the folk songs from the British Isles while the roots to rhythm and dance are generally from African influences.

By the beginning of World War I, a number of folk song collectors were busy writing down songs they found. The publication of *The English and Scottish Popular Ballads*, by Francis James Child in 1898, a collection of 305 ballads found in England and Scotland, inspired American collectors to look for and find those ballads, or variations, in rural areas of the United States. A "ballad" was a British narrative song that told a story; immigrants from England, Scotland, Ireland and Wales brought them over and some, like "Barbara Allen," were sung by early recording artists.

A number of songs that became part of early popular music repertoire were written in the nineteenth century, including the fiddle tune "Zip Coon," which later became known as "Turkey in the Straw." Although Stephen Foster died in 1864, his songs remained popular throughout the nineteenth and early twentieth century. Another popular songwriter was Will Shakespeare Hays, born in 1837 in Louisville, who worked as a riverboat captain, then as a newspaperman in that city and wrote songs in his spare time. By the time he died, in 1907, Hays had written "Write Me a Letter From Home," "We Part By the River Side," "I'll Remember You, Love, in My Prayers," "Nobody's Darling," "Mollie Darling" (later popularized by Eddy Arnold), "Jimmy Brown the Newsboy" (later popularized by the Carter Family and Flatt and Scruggs) and "The Little Old Log Cabin By the

Lane," which was recorded by Fiddlin' John Carson in 1923 and became the first commercially successful country recording. In all, Hays wrote over 300 songs, which may have sold 20 million copies of sheet music.

Other important early songs were "The Letter Edged in Black" written in 1897, "The Drummer Boy of Shiloh," a Civil War song that became the basis for the Christmas song, "The Little Drummer Boy," and "Down By the Old Mill Stream," published in 1910.

Vernon Dalhart

Since there was a market for old folk songs, proven by early country record sales, executives began to hire New York singers to sing them for recordings when they found one they felt had commercial appeal. The use of New York singers meant they were readily available for recording sessions, mostly done in New York, who sang in a more pure, clear voice than the nasal, tight-throated style of rural singers. Record label executives generally felt this "pure" singing style was more appealing to a mass audience.

One singer, Marion Slaughter, was a hopeful opera or pop singer who made his living doing studio sessions. He went from label to label, recording whatever songs were presented to him. Since he came from Texas, executives recruited him to record country songs. Slaughter recorded under about 150 different pseudonyms; the one he used for his most successful hillbilly recording was Vernon Dalhart.

Slaughter, born April 6, 1883 in Jefferson, Texas, was a member of the Century Opera Company in New York. The tenor had moved to New York to pursue a career in light opera and began making records in 1916, recording under a variety of pseudonyms. He heard Henry Whitter sing "The Wreck of the Old '97" and copied Whitter's version. On the other side of the record he recorded "The Prisoner's Song" for Victor in 1924. "The Prisoner's Song" b/w "Wreck of the Old '97" by Vernon Dalhart became a huge success--country music's first million seller--outselling recordings of pop and jazz artists.

Field Recordings of Early Country Music

The success of Vernon Dalhart's recording of "The Prisoner's Song" and "Wreck of the Old '97" created a demand for more country recordings by the labels, who by the mid-1920s had saturated their original market of opera, vaudeville and pop songs so they needed new audiences. The rural southern audiences were a good target. The development of the electrical recording process made it possible to have portable recording equipment and recording engineers began to travel to various cities doing field recordings. That is what led the period 1926-1929 to become the heyday for early country and rural blues field recordings. It also led record company talent scouts to tour the south and record hillbilly and race performers. The most popular cities were Atlanta and Dallas, followed by Charlotte, North Carolina, New Orleans, and Cincinnati.

Three rival companies dominated: Columbia, headed by A&R man Frank Walker; the Aeolean Company, which had Vocalion Records, and the Starr Piano Company of Richmond, Virginia, which had the Gennett and Champion labels and leased their product to the Sears, Roebuck and Company mail order firm to release under the Sears imprints of Silvertone, Challenge and Supertone.

The recording companies sent scouts into the South to audition performers for upcoming sessions and determined which performers should be recorded; those who were well known, or had recorded successfully before, received a letter from the company informing them of the upcoming session dates. Local music store owners and record dealers were major sources of information about musicians.

During the 1920s Atlanta was the most important site for field recordings and the acts recorded there, Fiddlin' John Carson, Gid Tanner and the Skillet Lickers with Riley Puckett and Clayton McMichen are among the most important early country artists. OKeh had field recording studios in Asheville, North Carolina, Bristol and Johnson City, Tennessee, St. Louis and Dallas. Companies also recorded in New Orleans and Memphis. In 1925 Columbia introduced a series of records for white country music; among the artists featured were Gid Tanner's Skillet Lickers (with Riley Puckett), Charlie Poole and the North Carolina Ramblers, Smith's Sacred Singers, Vernon Dalhart, and Darby & Tarlton. Best selling songs from that series included "The Death of Floyd Collins," "Little Mary Phagan," "The Scopes Trial" and "The Santa Barbara Earthquake."

In 1925 "the band that named the music" first recorded for Ralph Peer on OKeh. After a session by a group led by Al Hopkins, Peer asked the quartet for their name and Hopkins replied, "We're nothing but a bunch of hillbillies from North Carolina and Virginia. Call us anything." Peer called them "The Hill Billies" and named the music "hillbilly" music--a name it continued to have in the music business until the 1940s.

The following year, 1926, Columbia purchased OKeh Records, which allowed OKeh to use the electrical recording process (Columbia and Victor shared the patent) while it gave Columbia access to a number of field recordings done by OKeh.

Ralph Peer

In 1926 Ralph Peer left OKeh Records and joined Victor. Peer stated that "I had what they wanted. They couldn't get into the hillbilly business and I knew how to do it." Peer accepted his job at Victor Records for no salary; in exchange, he kept the publishing to the original songs he recorded. Victor agreed; the accountant liked the idea of not having to pay someone for working.

Victor dominated the recording industry throughout the 19-teens and early 1920s. At the end of 1926, founder Eldridge Johnson sold the label to two Wall Street investment houses, Speyer and J & W Seligman, for $40 million. David Sarnoff, head of Radio Corporation of America (RCA), wanted to purchase Victor but was thwarted at that time; RCA organized the National Broadcasting Company (NBC) network the same year Victor was sold to the investment companies.

When he was at Okeh, Peer paid hillbilly artists a "performance" fee of $25 per side with no royalties. At Victor, Nathaniel Shilkret, musical director for Victor, told him that $25 sounded too cheap; Victor artists should receive more so Peer raised the amount to $50 as well as a royalty. Peer had pioneered a royalty contract at Okeh whereby the artist assigned the copyright of the song to the recording label, who served as the publisher. Then, a royalty of 25 percent of two cents or a half a cent a record ($.005) was paid to the songwriter for each record sold. That figure came from the "standard" composer royalties during the 1920s and 1930s, known as "mechanicals" because the two cents figure was set by the 1909 Copyright Law (originally written for the player piano rolls).

Peer learned the value of copyrights from Polk Brockman, who set himself up as publisher for all the material recorded by Fiddlin' John Carson. In the music business, the publisher--not the songwriter—controls the copyright, including other recordings of a song, sheet music sales, and renewals--as long as the copyright is protected (Until 1978, the copyright was for twenty-six years, with the owner able to renew for another twenty-eight or a total of fifty-six years).

Peer, by drawing up contracts with artists and paying a royalty on each record sold instead of paying a flat performance fee and then collecting all the composer royalties, established a legal, binding contract that set the precedent for publishers and songwriters in the music business.

By the end of 1928, Peer was earning so much money from publishing (he made almost $250,000 in the second quarter of 1928 alone) that Victor executives became upset and demanded he sell his publishing interests to Victor.

Peer sold his firm to the label and handed over control of his publishing to Victor in 1928, primarily because he wanted to be respected as a major, popular publisher and RCA Victor agreed to send it's pop material into the Southern Music catalog. However, the conflict between A & R head Eli Oberstein and Ralph Peer resulted in Victor ignoring the Southern Music catalog.

Ralph Peer learned how to do field recordings when he was with Okeh Records. First, he traveled to various cities or towns to "scout" local talent, aided by recommendations from native citizens, usually the owner or manager of a store which sold records. During the 1920s it was usually a furniture store that sold Victrolas as part of "furniture," thereby creating a demand for records to play on their Victrolas. Peer auditioned talent and determined who had commercial potential. He looked for songs that had not been recorded or copyrighted as well as good singers.

By 1927, a host of fiddlers and fiddling tunes had already been recorded, so Peer was not particularly interested in fiddle tunes. The success of Vernon Dalhart and other singers showed the commercial appeal of songs that were sung, so finding good singers was a priority for Peer. Because he was interested in copyrighting a song, he wanted one with lyrics so other singers might record it as well, increasing his income as a publisher.

The Bristol Sessions

Victor budgeted $60,000 for Peer's southern recording trip in 1927, which included sessions in Bristol, Tennessee, Charlotte, North Carolina, and Savannah, Georgia. The Bristol sessions were the first held by any company in the Appalachian region except for a session Peer did for Okeh in Asheville, North Carolina during the summer of 1925. Bristol, located on the Tennessee-Virginia border (the main street is the state line), was part of "the Tri-Cities," consisting of that city, Kingsport and Johnson City and that area had a population of 32,000 in the 1920s--the largest "city" in Appalachia. It was within driving distance of Kentucky, North Carolina and West Virginia, allowing Peer to draw talent from five different states.

Ralph Peer arrived in Bristol on Friday, July 22, 1927, accompanied by his wife and two engineers, Eckhart and Lynch, who operated the new electrical recording equipment. This was Peer's first field session using microphones; previously he recorded using the acoustic process which did not give a clean, clear sound like the electric microphone or allow him to "balance" the vocal with the musical accompaniment.

Bristol was a fertile area for recording artists and a number of acts in the area had recorded previously. Peer had contacted the Victor dealer there, Cecil McLister and asked him to help find talent; Peer also contacted Ernest Stoneman to help set up auditions for talent.

Peer recorded nineteen different groups performing seventy-six songs in Bristol; seven were instrumentals and thirty-one were gospel songs. Before the session Peer had the artists sign three different contracts; the first was a recording contract with Victor which guaranteed $50 per side and a royalty; a publishing contract with Southern Music; and a personal management contract with Peer. Peer did not "manage" the artists in terms of career development but instead used the contract to keep the artist tied to him and Victor.

On Monday, July 25, Peer spent the entire day with Ernest Stoneman, recording ten songs. The next day he recorded Ernest Phipps and His Holiness Quartet doing six songs. On Wednesday, July 27 he invited the editor from the *Bristol News-Bulletin* to the morning session, which featured Uncle Eck Dunford and Ernest Stoneman (and resulted in the first recording of the song "Skip To Ma, Lou, My Darling") and gave him an interview. The story appeared in the afternoon paper and concluded with a paragraph that the session allowed Stoneman to receive $100 and "each of his assistants $25" and that Stoneman had earned "$3,600 last year as his share of the proceeds on his records." After that story, a number of acts contacted Peer by long distance telephone, requesting auditions, and Peer auditioned a number of those acts.

The Carter Family

On Monday, August 1, 1927, the Carter Family--A. P. Carter, his wife Sara, and Sara's cousin and A.P.'s sister-in-law, Maybelle, drove to Bristol from Maces Springs, Virginia, auditioned for Peer and recorded four songs for him that evening. The songs were "Bury Me Under The Weeping Willow," "Little Log Cabin By The Sea," "The Poor Orphan Child" and "The Storms Are On The Ocean." The next morning Sara and Maybelle recorded two more songs, "Single Girl, Married Girl" and "The Wandering Boy."

Alvin Pleasant Delaney (A.P.) Carter was born on December 15, 1891 in Maces Spring, Virginia; Sara Dougherty was born on July 21, 1899, in nearby Flat Woods, Virginia; they were married on June 18, 1915. A.P. was the son of a banjo playing father and a mother who sang old folk songs; he learned shape note singing from churches and played the fiddle; Sara played the autoharp. The couple played, often at churches, in the area and in early 1927 auditioned for the Brunswick Record Company but did not record. Maybelle Addington, born May 10, 1909, in Nickelsville, Virginia, learned to play the guitar, developing a method of plucking the melody with her thumb on the bass string while brushing the chord with her fingers, which became known as the "Carter lick." Her guitar technique became influential for country pickers in the years ahead. She married Ezra Carter, A.P.'s brother, in March, 1926 and soon joined Sara and A.P. when they performed locally.

Sara was the lead singer in the group, often joined by Maybelle with A.P. occasionally singing harmony. A.P. was the one who found songs, collecting them from old songbooks, other folk singers, or remembering them from his childhood. Ralph Peer listed the songs that had not been copyrighted in A.P.'s name.

That rich repertoire of songs, as well as Maybelle's unique guitar playing, established the Carter's as one of the most influential groups in country music. Among the more than 300 songs they recorded for Victor were "Keep On the Sunny Side," "Wildwood Flower," "I'm Thinking Tonight of My Blue Eyes," "Wabash Cannonball," "Worried Man Blues," "Anchored in Love," "John Hardy Was a Desperate Little Man." "You Are My Flower," and "Hello, Stranger."

Jimmie Rodgers

On Thursday, August 4, Ralph Peer recorded two songs by Jimmie Rodgers, "The Soldier's Sweetheart" and "Sleep, Baby, Sleep." Rodgers had arrived in Bristol with his group, the Jimmie Rodgers Entertainers, consisting of himself, Jack Pierce and the Grant Brothers, on the evening before and auditioned for Peer, who was not impressed by the dance songs they did. However, Rodgers assured him they would rehearse that night and Peer agreed to record them the next day. During the rehearsal the group argued with the result that Pierce and the Grants recorded Thursday morning as The Tenneva Ramblers while Rodgers recorded solo that evening.

Rodgers was born September 8, 1897 in Meridian, Mississippi, son of a railroad foreman. Rodgers wanted to be an entertainer but worked for the railroad for a number of years. In 1924 he developed tuberculosis and turned to music full time. During the summer of 1927 he was working at WWNC in Asheville, North Carolina with the Tenneva Ramblers at a resort in the Blue Ridge Mountains. His first Victor recording was released in October, 1927, and achieved modest success; the ambitious Rodgers traveled to New York, met with Peer, and persuaded him to record more selections.

During the following years Rodgers had a string of hits, including "T for Texas," "Waiting for a Train," "Daddy and Home," "In the Jailhouse Now," "Miss the Mississippi and You," "Mother the Queen of My Heart" and "Peach Pickin' Time in Georgia." Many of those were co-written with his sister-in-law, Elsie McWilliams. He recorded 110 songs for Victor.

Jimmie Rodgers made the "blue yodel" famous. That "yodel," or slipping into falsetto during a song, gave Rodgers a distinctive sound on his recordings and influenced country singers for years. Known as the "blue yodels," they were in standard blues format, with the first line repeated before a "tag" line (AAB) sums up the verse. According to Nolan Porterfield, in his biography of Rodgers, it is "impossible to exaggerate the popularity of Jimmie Rodgers during the late '20s and early '30s when he was alive and recording...it spread across all age brackets.".

"Blue Yodel #1 (T for Texas)" was released in February, 1928. That same month he went to Camden, New Jersey, for two days of recording sessions; on those sessions he recorded "In the Jailhouse Now" as well as "Blue Yodel #2" ("If you ever had the blues...") and "Blue Yodel #3." ("She's long, she's tall...") In June he recorded "My Old Pal," "Mississippi Moon," "Daddy and Home" and "I'm Lonely and Blue" in Camden.

In October, 1928, he recorded in Atlanta, doing "My Carolina Sunshine Girl," "Blue Yodel #4" ("I'm going to California...") and "Waiting for a Train." In February, 1929, Rodgers recorded "Any Old Time," "Blue Yodel #5" ("It's raining here, stormin' on the deep blue sea...") and "High Powered Mama." In October, at a session in Dallas, he recorded "Yodeling Cowboy," "My Rough and Rowdy Ways," "I've Ranged, I've Roamed, I've Travelled" and "Blue Yodel #6" ("She left me this morning, midnight was turning day..."). In November he recorded "Hobo Bill's Last Ride" in Atlanta.

Dressed in the latest uptown style, with a spiffy modern box back coat, bow tie, and straw boater hat, Rodgers traveled, singing Tin Pan Alley hits as well as his own. He was an original; there was nobody like him before he came, so there was no one to copy. During the 1930-1933 period he recorded "Pistol Packin' Papa," "Jimmie's Mean Mama Blues," "T.B. Blues," "Jimmie the Kid," "My Good Gal's Gone Blues," "Hobo's Meditation," "My Time Ain't Long," "Mother, the Queen of My Heart," "Peach Pickin' Time in Georgia," "No Hard Times" "Miss the Mississippi and You," and six more blue yodels (for a total of 12). The rural audience loved him and bought his recordings and wore them out on their phonographs.

Jimmie Rodgers is considered the father of contemporary country music and was the most influential early country recording artist. Rodgers' "blue yodels," a series of songs that featured him breaking into a falsetto yodel, inspired almost every country artist before World War II. Gene Autry, Ernest Tubb, Roy Rogers, Eddy Arnold and numerous others looked at Rodgers as their first inspiration in the country field; they sang his songs, and their early works reflected the influence of Rodgers.

Jimmie Rodgers was considered a hillbilly or "folk" artist because he came from the South and his recordings sold to rural audiences but Rodgers was no hillbilly. He dressed like a dandy and his most famous recording, "Waitin' For a Train" was recorded with a Dixieland jazz band, featuring Louis Armstrong. Jimmie Rodgers was a Southern country artist who sang pop music, and this combination of a rural Southerner reaching beyond his origins and roots into the pop world is the story of country music's first major success.

The financial success of Jimmie Rodgers for a major recording label did not go unnoticed in the label's northern headquarters. Rodgers' ability to be sophisticated and yet relate to country audiences opened doors for other country artists; after Jimmie Rodgers country artists found employment on radio stations and northern publishers and record men saw the commercial potential of country music. Booking agents booked country talent into major theaters and other venues in major cities, and young southern boys bought guitars as country music switched from a music dominated by the fiddle to one dominated by the sound of a singer with a guitar.

Jimmie Rodgers was as smooth vocally as Gene Austin, Bing Crosby or any other crooner during the 1930s. The major difference between artists like Jimmie Rodgers and his counterparts in the popular music field was the accident of birth and early musical influences; if someone was born in a northern city and raised on vaudeville and Tin Pan Alley songs, they were a pop performer, but if they were born in the South (particularly the rural south) and grew up with folk or hillbilly music, then they were a hillbilly performer.

Jimmie Rodgers had a foot in both worlds and his success came as a result of that fact. Further, because he had a foot in both worlds, he advanced country music, which saw increased acceptance by those in popular music, from businessmen who saw profits, to urban audiences who found a voice they enjoyed in someone like Jimmie Rodgers. That was a lesson the record business--and country music establishment--learned again and again.

The recording sessions in Bristol during the summer of 1927 became known as the "Big Bang" of country music. They are considered the beginning of the commercial country music industry because Jimmie Rodgers and the Carter Family were both rooted in the Southern folk tradition, sold large numbers of records that made Victor profitable throughout the 1930s and dominant in the country field.

Other Country Recordings

Vocalion's country series of recordings, "Songs From Dixie," was initiated in April, 1927 by Brunswick. In their August, 1927 catalogue, Columbia listed "Old Familiar Tunes" for their country selections; by that point Charlie Poole and the North Carolina Ramblers had sold 250,000 records during the past two years. In November, 1927, one of the most influential country recordings was made when Tom Darby and Jimmy Tarlton did "Columbus Stockade Blues" and "Birmingham Jail" with a slide guitar in Atlanta for Columbia. That sound would be the basis of the dobro and steel guitar sound in the years ahead.

The period 1924 to 1935 is when "old-time" music dominated what was later to become known as country music. The early country acts who recorded 1923 to 1926 were primarily folk musicians who learned their songs orally and a number of songs from the nineteenth century were recorded. Examples include "Barbara Allen" by Bradley Kincaid, "Pretty Polly" by Dock Boggs, "When the Work's All Done This Fall" by Carl Sprague, "Knoxville Girl" by Mac & Bob and fiddle tunes such as "Devil's Dream," "Leather Breeches," and "Soldier's Joy." The term "old" had positive connotations, indicating a time more simple and wholesome than the loose morals perceived in the contemporary sounds of jazz. The Skillet Lickers were perhaps the best of the string bands and are the basis for what later became known as bluegrass while the harmony singing of the Carter Family was a pioneer sound. The brother duets of the Delmore Brothers was an influential sound that echoed through later recordings of the Louvin Brothers, Everly Brothers and even the Beatles. Solo artists such as Uncle Dave Macon, Bradley Kincaid and Jimmy Rodgers pointed the way to the future, when country music became dominated by vocalists, and the sound of Jimmie Rodgers blue yodels and his use of white blues influenced later artists such as Gene Autry, Ernest Tubb, Lefty Frizzell and Eddy Arnold. Rodgers and Vernon Dalhart transcended country music, pulling it towards the pop market, and that too was a harbinger of things to come.

Black Gospel Quartets

The black gospel quartet has its roots at Fisk University in Nashville. In 1905 Fisk made a decision to feature a male quartet instead of a mixed choir of Jubilee Singers. The decision came because if female members traveled, they were required to have a chaperone. The school had led the way for mixed choirs with the Fisk Jubilee Singers; they were followed by "Jubilee singers" from Hampton, Tuskegee, Utica, Mississippi and Wilberforce Universities.

The first quartets were formed at black universities and generally operated as clubs, electing officers, paying dues, wearing uniforms and singing formal arrangements at concerts. Those quartets were primarily Baptists, who generally ridiculed the Holiness singers and their improvisation, emotionalism and untrained singing; the Baptists preferred trained voices, singing the melody in a "concert demeanor"--standing erect, with proper enunciation, in a formal, reserved style. This, they felt, elevated the music and themselves. The Holiness singers, on the other hand, sang spontaneously and emotionally during a church service.

The "Jubilee quartets" often found themselves in front of audiences who responded with shouts of "Amen," "Hallelujah" and "Praise the Lord" during their songs. Gradually, the quartets began borrowing from the emotional style of singing by the Holiness singers. The quartets became so popular that members of a community or church, not a university, formed four-man groups. A major difference between the university quartets and the quartets formed in communities and churches was the untrained voice. Rhythmically more free, the quartets moved on stage and used gestures with their hands, such as patting their thighs and swaying back and forth.

Although quartets were influenced by the Holiness movement, they did not use instruments but sang acapella. The Baptist and Methodist congregations grew as large numbers of blacks left the South and moved North during the World War I era and joined established churches. The Holiness movement expanded by "planting" churches--finding a community and setting up a "store-front" church. Music was an important part of the Holiness churches, which appealed to the less-educated and those who wanted to feel a connection to their Southern roots.

The holiness singers had a pianist accompany their singing. The first-known gospel pianist was Arizona Dranes, a blind woman, from

Dallas, Texas. Dranes introduced the "gospel beat" to the piano--adding a syncopated rhythm akin to ragtime, with a heavy left hand driving the rhythm. She sang in a high, nasal voice and was an effective song leader. Richard M. Jones, a talent scout for Okeh Records, heard Dranes play at one of Reverend Samuel Crouch's services and arranged for her to go to Chicago, where she recorded "My Soul is a Witness for My Lord." Between 1926 and 1928 she recorded over thirty songs for Okeh, including "I Shall Wear a Crown."

In 1921 the National Baptist Convention published *Gospel Pearls*, edited by Willa A. Townsend, who worked at Roger Williams University in Nashville. Although the 163 songs in the book contained many standard Protestant hymns, such as "Battle Hymn of the Republic," the book also included newer songs, such as "Stand By Me," "We'll Understand It Better By and By," "Leave It There," "I'm Happy With Jesus Alone," "Shine for Jesus" and "If I Don't Get There," the first gospel song published by Thomas Andrew Dorsey. When The National Baptist Convention put their stamp of approval on those songs, they became widely accepted in black congregations across the country.

Gospel Pearls broadened the style of music available to Baptists and led to the formation of several important groups. The Tindley Gospel Singers, organized in 1927 at the Tindley Temple Methodist Episcopal Church in Philadelphia, was the first male group to be accompanied by a piano. The Golden Gate Quartet was organized in Norfolk, Virginia during the late 1920s by students attending Booker T. Washington High School. In 1925 the Golden Gate Quartet was heard live on radio over WBT in Charlotte, North Carolina.

The worlds of blues and gospel were, literally, worlds apart. Gospel music was for the church while blues was for the honky tonks and dives; blues appealed to man's carnal nature while gospel sought to purify and elevate the soul. Blues was aligned with the "the Devil" while those who sang gospel did "God's work." Still, the popularity and commercial success of blues recordings during the 1920s helped black gospel because the recording companies saw both as music for the African-American audience.

Thomas Dorsey

The key figure in black gospel songwriting and publishing is Thomas Dorsey, who became known as a great personality, composer, publisher, performer, teacher, choir director and organizer as well as minister of music for the Pilgrim Baptist Church in Chicago. More than any other individual,

Thomas Dorsey defined contemporary black gospel music, even though he was not the first African American to have his songs published. It was Dorsey himself as well as his songs that unified the movement which became black gospel, giving a definition to the music that has survived.

Thomas Dorsey was able to capture the spirit and essence of "soul-singing" and compose in the unique black idiom. His influence and popularity is also attributed to his practice of reproducing his words and music on single sheets for sale, selling them directly to churches and singers. The alternative was to purchase large collections of songs in books.

Dorsey was a gigantic figure in gospel music outside his publishing. He trained and accompanied countless singers and fought for recognition with ministries and church musicians who were opposed to adding his songs to church services. Finally, the National Baptist Convention (Negro), which convened in Chicago in 1930, allowed the performance of two Dorsey songs, "How About You" and "Did You See My Savior." The positive reaction from delegates charted the direction for black gospel.

Thomas Andrew Dorsey was born in Villa Rica, Georgia in 1891, son of a Baptist minister, Reverend T.M. Dorsey and his wife, Etta. He moved with his family to Atlanta in 1906, where he was influenced by early blues and jazz as well as Isaac Watts hymns. Although his parents disapproved of show business, Dorsey was attracted to it and mastered several instruments in his youth. During his teens he played blues and ragtime in Atlanta. In 1916 his family moved to Chicago, but Dorsey often went back to Atlanta to play piano in clubs. During the latter half of 1919, Dorsey moved permanently to Chicago.

In Chicago, Dorsey enrolled in the Chicago School of Composition and Arranging and learned musical notation; with that knowledge he obtained work with publishing companies as a composer/arranger. That led to him copyrighting his first composition, "If You Don't Believe I'm Leaving, You Can Count the Days I'm Gone," in October, 1920.

Dorsey worked for the Chicago Music Publishing Company, which was aligned with Paramount Records, which led him to organize a band and play for Paramount recording artist Ma Rainey from 1924 to 1926.

Throughout the 1920s Dorsey was a prolific composer of blues songs. He was initially "saved" through a song, "I Do, Don't You" at a Baptist convention in 1921. During the following years, he kept a foot in both worlds--gospel and blues--and performed a variety of music. He always returned to the church after recovering from a grave illness, but the demands to support his wife led to his continued involvement in the blues field.

Dorsey made a name for himself in blues music under the name "Georgia Tom," writing "Tight Like That" with Hudson Whitaker, known as Tampa Red. The success of "Tight Like That" led to Georgia Tom and Tampa Red writing more double entendre blues, including "Pat That Bread," "You Got That Stuff," "Where Did You Stay Last Night," "It's All Worn Out" and "Somebody's Been Using That Thing." During the late 1920s and early 1930s, Georgia Tom and Tampa Red made over 60 recordings.

In gospel, Thomas Dorsey found his calling and his genius took root and flourished. As director of the gospel choir at Pilgrim Baptist Church in Chicago, Dorsey helped a number of singers and had a forum for writing and experimenting with new songs he composed. He was heavily influenced by preachers, and composed for those who used his songs as a mini-sermon, singing a line, then expounding while the audience shouted. The choir joined in on the chorus while Dorsey played the accompaniment on the piano.

Dorsey's songs ushered in a new era for black gospel at the same time that great gospel singers emerged, most of whom came out of choirs (often Dorsey's) as soloists. As black gospel was recorded and released, those singers established national reputations and influenced others who would never have seen or heard them otherwise. That served to unify black gospel and increasingly brought it to the attention of white churches and singers, who were influenced by the style and rhythms and often copied some of the songs and bought the records.

Dorsey's first gospel song was "If You See My Savior, Tell Him That You Saw Me." Initially, Dorsey mailed copies of the sheet music to churches around the country, but the first order did not come until two years later. The breakthrough for Dorsey and his gospel songs, as noted earlier, occurred in 1930 at the National Baptist Convention for blacks in Chicago. The musical directors there, Lucie Campbell and E.W. Isaac, invited him to sell his music and that launched Thomas Dorsey as a gospel songwriter.

As his music became more accepted in churches, Dorsey's stature as a songwriter grew until he was, in the words of Mahalia Jackson, "our Irving Berlin."

The Beginnings of Southern Gospel

The roots of Southern Gospel can be traced to the singing schools and shaped note song books, as well as to revivals in rural areas of America during the nineteenth century. The singing school movement began in New England during the 1720s in order to increase musical literacy in churches so that congregations could sing from songbooks. In 1798 William Little and William Smith created "character notes" or "shaped notes" and published *The Easy Instructor.* That new method caught on quickly. (The shape of the written note corresponded to the actual note.)

Although shaped note books were popular, particularly in southern rural areas, there was a backlash against them from trained musicians who insisted the traditional "round notes" were the only way to learn music. Part of this was rooted in class conflict--with shaped notes, the educated elite no longer had control of musical literacy. Further, the rural "unlettered" Southerners were more likely to embrace folk tunes instead of music from the European classical tradition. The urban areas shunned shape notes while rural areas embraced them; that set the pattern for the future of what eventually became known as Southern Gospel music.

In 1885 A.J. Showalter began a singing school, the Southern Normal Institute, which later became the Southern Normal Conservatory of Music. One of his students at this school was Jesse Randall (J.R.) Baxter, who later became a major publisher of shaped-note songbooks. In 1890 Showalter married and moved to Cisco, Texas.

James D. Vaughan taught his first singing school in 1882 and, to publicize the school, created a family quartet that became the forerunner of all Southern Gospel quartets. That quartet demonstrated songs and showed how a trained quartet could effectively promote the selling of songbooks.

In 1902 Vaughan moved to Lawrenceburg, Tennessee and built his James D. Vaughan Music Company. In May, 1910, Vaughan sponsored the first Vaughan Quartet to advertise and sell his songbooks; by this time he published a new songbook every year. During the first appearance by the Vaughan Quartet the group sold 5,000 songbooks; that convinced James D. Vaughan that the best way to sell songbooks was to hire quartets to sing the songs, which began the shift in gospel publishing away from congregation singing to that of an audience watching a trained quartet performing the songs.

Most singing schools, called "Normals," held classes over a ten-day period with classes usually conducted at night. The students were drilled in sight-reading shaped notes, harmony and pitch. At the end of ten days, the graduating class generally put on a "concert" in which they demonstrated their ability to sing from shaped-note songbooks. For a rural youngster raised on a farm who had a talent for singing, this was a mark of prestige and honor. Watching the singing school teacher, many saw a way out of southern farm life and a chance to make a living doing what they loved--singing.

Singing conventions, usually held annually, were social as well as musical events and it didn't take song publishers long to realize this was fertile ground for songbook sales. There was resistance to singing conventions from traditional churches, who felt the theology was shallow and the "acrobatics" of the singers distasteful and "ungodly." The Holiness and Pentecostals were individualists who loved spirited, emotional singing, were not biased against non-traditional church music, and generally ignored--even disdained--the views of so-called "experts" in church music. Shaped-note songbooks, singing conventions and trained quartets who performed new songs became widely accepted in the rural South. Those Southern Pentecostals were usually open to instrumental accompaniment, particularly from "folk" instruments like the guitar.

In 1914, V.O. Stamps attended the Vaughan Music School in Lawrenceburg and the following year returned to his home in Texas as a traveling representative of the Vaughan Music School. Stamps, born near Gilmer, Texas in 1892, attended his first singing school in that area in 1907. After he joined Vaughan, he worked selling songbooks and recruiting students for Vaughan's school in Lawrenceburg.

V.O. Stamps was the best salesman James D. Vaughan had. He joined the Vaughan Quartet in 1917; in 1918 Stamps transferred to Timpson, in east Texas; the following year he moved to Jacksonville in that state and remained there for five years, building the most successful branch of the Vaughan Music Company.

The technologies of radio and recordings had an effect on Southern Gospel, beginning in the 1920s. In 1921 Vaughan Phonograph Records started in Lawrenceburg; the initial quartet recordings included "Couldn't Hear Nobody Pray," "Steal Away," "Magnify Jesus," "Look for Me," "Someday" and "Waiting at the Gate." The phonograph company led to the formation of a new group, the Vaughan Recording Quartet. The quartet did not record exclusively for Vaughan but also recorded for Homer Rodeheaver's Rainbow Records as well as for the Gennett label.

Early in 1924 V.O. Stamps broke away from the Vaughan Company and formed his own firm, the Virgil O. Stamps Music Company; his brother, Frank, formed a traveling quartet to promote their songbooks. By 1926 Stamps's company was struggling, which led him to acquire a partner, Jesse Randall (J.R.) Baxter, Jr. Baxter, a singing school teacher who had worked for the A.J. Showalter Company, decided to merge with Stamps in March 1926 and moved to Chattanooga while Stamps remained in Texas.

In 1926 a young songwriter, Albert E. Brumley, born in 1905 in Spiro, Oklahoma (it was Indian Territory at the time) joined the Hartford Music Company. In 1927 Brumley published his first song, "I Can Hear Them Singing Over There"; during the coming years he became the most popular Southern Gospel writer, penning classics such as "I'll Fly Away," "I'll Meet You in the Morning," and "Turn Your Radio On."

In 1927, V.O. Stamps' company was renamed The Stamps-Baxter Music Company. Stamps continued to operate out of the home office in Jacksonville, Texas while J.R. Baxter operated the branch office in Chattanooga. That same year the Frank Stamps Quartet made recordings for Victor Records; Frank hired pianist Dwight Brock as an accompanist. Prior to this, a quartet usually sang acapella, although sometimes a member played piano. The addition of the "fifth man" was a revolution in the quartet line-up. Another revolution was Brock's piano playing; he introduced the idea of what became known as the "turnaround," playing a short improvised solo between verses that added a "lift" to a song and gave the singers time to catch their breath for the next verse while keeping the audience entertained.

The most successful quartet on recordings was the Smith Sacred Singers, who were not aligned to any publishing firm. Frank Smith was a barber from Braselton, Georgia who formed a quartet that performed on WSB in Atlanta on Sunday afternoons. In April, 1926, Smith's Sacred Singers had their first recording sessions for Columbia; during the next four years they recorded 66 songs for the label.

Gospel accounted for about 20 percent of the releases from Columbia during that time, with the material consisting of sacred harp material, quartet material, convention songs, and solos or duets of sacred material. An "average" sale was 15,600 per record, with 15 records selling over 100,000 units each. The material included both pre-war and post-war material, some traditional songs as well as songs from the widely circulated paperback convention books.

By the end of the 1920s two major firms, the James D. Vaughan Music Company and Stamps-Baxter, stood at the forefront of shaped-note publishing, though there were numerous other companies vying for business.

The Creation of NBC and CBS

From the earliest days of radio, music was broadcast. The music was not "popular" music at first; rather, it was what programmers thought audiences ought to hear. That was in line with the idea of radio as a public service, which is also why they did not have advertisements on the air. Singers were not paid although, as the 1920s progressed, there was a growing resentment among musicians and singers towards free performances. Radio programmers responded that performances were free publicity, which resulted in increased bookings. Radio did not pay for the use of recordings, arguing that free publicity created a demand for sheet music sales.

A large number of people were infatuated with radio, but nobody was making any money except AT&T, which rented its telephone lines to stations for their broadcasts. At end of the summer of 1923, AT&T began to link stations together in a "network" which sold broadcasting time, called "toll" broadcasting, like a "toll" road where access is given for a payment.

The flagship station was WEAF in New York. A deal was worked out whereby WEAF had the right to sell time over WJAR in Providence, Rhode Island. In compensation, WEAF provided WJAR two hours of free programming. Soon, a network of six stations was linked and by the end of 1924 there were 26 stations linked from coast to coast.

The first major "event" broadcast was the 1924 Democratic National Convention, held in Chicago in June. Prior to this, political conventions featured politicians who wheeled and dealed, gave fiery speeches and threw insults at each other. The Republican convention, held earlier that month, was rather dull; Warren Harding had died in 1923 and was succeeded by his vice-president, Calvin Coolidge; during the Republican convention, the ticket was quickly confirmed. The Democrats, who had been out of office since Woodrow Wilson left in 1921, were a different matter. Radio audiences heard violence erupt and tension fill the air as the issue of the Ku Klux Klan (which was rumored to control a large number of votes) was denounced or subtly courted. Finally, a Catholic, Al Smith, was chosen as a candidate with Franklin D. Roosevelt the vice-presidential candidate.

Radio audiences were drawn to the convention drama. AT&T put together an 18 station network for the event; General Electric and RCA managed to put together stations over telegraph lines to compete with AT&T, but the telegraph lines contained a "hum" which created an inferior service. General Electric and RCA were upset that AT&T, using their cable technology, dominated radio because of their control of telephone wires.

The first result of the 1924 convention was a surge in the number of radio sets purchased by Americans; by the end of the year Americans had spend $358 million on radio--up from $136 million the previous year. The next result would be a major change in how radio was financed.

The first beneficiaries of radio were equipment manufacturers, who reaped profits because Americans purchased radio sets. But how would radio programming be financed? What about the stations who broadcast--how could they earn income?

A number of ideas were presented, mostly connected to city or state financing or "public" broadcasting whereby listeners sent in money which would be allocated by a board. A tax on radio receivers was also discussed; that idea was promoted by David Sarnoff, who saw broadcasting as a national service. That last idea was adopted in England by the British Broadcasting Company, that charged a fee for every radio owned. Initially, advertising was never discussed because the idea of hawking ware on the air was considered too "vulgar" and an affront to the tastes of radio listeners.

The first advertisers were "sponsors" who paid for a program in order to have their brand name on the air. There was the "Lucky Strike Orchestra" sponsored by Lucky Strike cigarettes and the "Ipana Troubadours" sponsored by Ipana toothpaste. Stations began to negotiate with sponsors through advertising agencies and WEAF insisted the agency sign contracts with the sponsor; radio collected money from the agency and broadcast the program. In exchange, the radio station paid the agency a 15 percent commission; this established the way advertising agencies were paid by broadcasting stations from that time forward.

One of the first successful programs was the "Eveready Hour," sponsored by Eveready batteries. That was a variety program that sometimes offered a drama, sometimes concert music, and sometimes popular music. The N. W. Ayer advertising agency brokered the deal and controlled the content. The performers and announcers were anonymous at first, but audiences demanded to know who the popular performers and announcers were. Radio management fought that idea; they felt that if the announcers became celebrities they would be difficult to control.

Radio stations were proliferating because, until 1925, anyone who asked for a broadcasting license from the Department of Commerce received one. However, after 1925 Secretary of Commerce Herbert Hoover announced that no more licenses would be issued because all the wave lengths were taken. That led to a consolidation of stations or the purchase of stations and broadcast licenses from those who wanted to enter the radio field. That led directly to the idea that a radio station was private property rather than a public trust; a station was "owned" by a company or investors and not "the public," which made radio a business concerned with generating income for the owners instead of a public service provided by a business.

The conflict between RCA and AT&T came to a head when AT&T tried to market radio sets and tubes after it had reaped profits from its "toll" broadcasting through the use of its telephone cables. The conflict came to a head at the beginning of 1926 when the RCA Board of Directors agreed to start a new company to be owned by RCA (50%), General Electric (30%) and Westinghouse (20%) which leased AT&T's wires under a long term contract worth millions of dollars. AT&T agreed to sell WEAF for $1 million and withdrew from active broadcasting; instead it received income from leasing its wires. In August, 1926, the new company was given the name the National Broadcasting Company and on September 9 it was incorporated. The new company linked the entire country; by that time five million homes had radios while 21 million did not. Named to head the new broadcasting company was Merlin H. Aylesworth, managing director of the National Electric Light Association who, at that time, did not even own a radio. George McClelland was named General Manager of NBC while Bertha Brainard was Program Manager. The debut for the network was set for November 15, 1926.

The premier was a lavish one, with a host of stars broadcasting from the Grand Ballroom at the Waldorf-Astoria hotel, as well as acts from Chicago, Kansas City, and other cities. It was agreed that after the initial premier, which cost NBC $50,000, the sponsors, through advertising agencies, would pay for programs.

By January, 1927, NBC had two networks; the "red" network originated at WEAF in New York and the "blue" network originated from WJZ in New York. Although radio was a national phenomena, with stations and talent all across the country, New York became the major city for national entertainment. During 1927, programs such as "The Maxwell House Hour," the "Palmolive House," "The General Motors Family Party," the "Wrigley Review," the "Ipana Troubadours" and the "Eveready Hour" were presented.

During 1926 Arthur Judson met with David Sarnoff while Sarnoff was organizing NBC to discuss musical talent for the new network. Judson was a former violinist who had gone into artist management and managed the New York Philharmonic, the Cincinnati Orchestra and the Philadelphia Orchestra before forming Concert Management. Judson was concerned about the impact broadcasting was having on the concert world and wanted an outlet for concert music; in September he formed the Judson Radio Program Corporation. Sarnoff was interested in Judson's ideas and requested a plan; Judson submitted one but did not hear from Sarnoff. After the premier of NBC, Judson and Sarnoff met again; Sarnoff informed him that NBC would not use Judson or his plan. Judson replied, "Then we will organize our own chain." Sarnoff replied, "You can't do that" because there would be no lines available from AT&T with the NBC agreement.

In January, 1927, Judson and his associate, concert promoter George A. Coats, formed the United Independent Broadcasters. They were joined by J. Andrew White, editor of the magazine *Wireless Age*, begun in 1913 by Marconi. Twelve stations were organized, with WOR in New York the flagship station. The group guaranteed $500 to each station in exchange for ten hours of its broadcast time. They approached AT&T, who turned them down, then went to Washington D.C. before the Interstate Commerce Commission, which regulated the telephone industry.

During 1927 Congress passed The Radio Act, signed on February 3 by President Coolidge. The Act had been debated throughout 1926; one of the amendments that was defeated exempted radio from complying with the Copyright Law, which barred ASCAP from collecting money for broadcasting songs. Broadcasters were almost universally against ASCAP, seeing the payments for music as an intrusion into profits and private business. However, the Radio Act did free up telephone lines for the new network.

Unfortunately, the new network still faced a steep uphill battle. First, they had no start up money; that was initially provided by Mrs. Christian Holmes, a wealthy patron of the New York Philharmonic, who contributed $29,500. The other problem was that Judson wanted to be a talent agent for concert music; he had no desire or ambition to run a network. The group searched for someone to take over the new network and found Adolph Zukor of Paramount, but talks fell through. The Victor Talking Machine Company was also interested but talks fell through again because RCA was negotiating to buy the cash rich company. Finally, the Columbia Phonograph Company came through; for $163,000 the network was renamed the Columbia Phonograph Broadcasting System and the Judson Radio Program Corporation agreed to supply ten hours of programming for $10,000 a week. The talent included soloists, a dance orchestra, a singing group and a concert orchestra. The debut program was broadcast on September 18, 1927.

Troubles continued to arise because sponsors consistently chose the NBC network; next the Columbia Phonograph Record Company pulled out of the agreement. Mrs. Christian Holmes came to the rescue again, sending a check for $45,000 to keep the new network afloat, then a group of investors from Philadelphia, Isaac and Leon Levy, who owned WCAU, and Jerome H. Louchheim, a subway builder, purchased the new network for $135,000 and renamed it the Columbia Broadcasting System.

A few sponsors were found but the company continued losing money. One of the sponsors was La Palina cigars, a brand of the Congress Cigar Company. That company was owned by the Paley family in Philadelphia. Twenty-six year old William S. Paley was an executive with the company, which had seen sales double from radio. Young Paley was ambitious and restless; in September, 1928, he agreed to become President of the new network. Soon, he negotiated with Adolph Zukor and Paramount to become a partner, with Paramount owning 49 percent of the stock. By the end of 1928, CBS was on its way to becoming the second major network.

Meanwhile, the financing of radio programming was changing, a result of the business environment of the late 1920s. President Coolidge openly proclaimed "The business of America is business" and it was a pro-business era. Companies were merged and unified their advertising campaigns; that led to the tremendous growth of advertising agencies as well as big business. By the end of the 1920s the two hundred largest corporations (excluding banks) controlled about half the corporate wealth in the United States.

There had long been opposition to advertising on radio; the early pioneers saw it as a public service providing news, information and culture. In 1928 the National Association of Broadcasters created a code of ethics that stated "Commercial announcements, as the term is generally understood, should not be broadcast between seven and eleven p.m." However, during 1927 six hundred commercial sponsors had brought NBC a large amount of money that provided notable programs and time for a number of music-appreciation broadcasts, farm programs and religious programs that were not commercially successful. The evening "prime time" hours appealed to sponsors because they could reach the largest audience and those sponsors were attracted to a network which could reach the entire country. In March, 1927, there were 732 broadcasting stations in the United States; over 600 operated independently and about 90 were operated by educational institutions--most not selling time. The less than 100 network affiliated stations received the most attention and made the most money.

The purchase of radio sets by Americans continued to grow, from $430 million spent in 1925 to $650.5 million in 1928. By 1927 sets were running on house current; that same year Philco became a leader in providing radios for cars.

Amos 'n' Andy

For audiences, the major appeal of radio was entertainment, especially "Amos'n'Andy," the most popular radio show created. The show was blackface comedy, set in the South Side of Chicago. The lead characters were two white men, Freeman Fisher Gosden (Amos) and Charles J. Correll (Andy). The two performed Negro dialect routines in blackface before they began weekly over WEBH in Chicago at the Edgewater Beach Hotel. They moved to WGN, where the show was originally called "Sam 'n' Henry" and ran for two years. WGN was owned by the *Chicago Tribune* Company; when their contract ran out, Gosden and Correll could not locate anyone with the authority to deal with them, so they moved to WMAQ, owned by the *Chicago Daily News*, where they renamed the show "Amos 'n' Andy" because the *Tribune* owned the name "Sam 'n' Henry." At WMAQ, Gosden and Correll recorded their program and sold it to other stations, which was a pioneer effort in radio syndication. Early in 1928 they were on 30 stations and by 1929 they were nationally known.

The show was broadcast 7-7:15 Eastern time and was so popular that movie houses postponed movies until after the show was over, broadcasting the show live to the waiting audience. Department stores broadcast the show as well. The popularity of the show was so great that sales of radio sets and parts went from $650.5 million in 1928 to $842.5 million in 1929.

The show later became an example of blatant racism, but that view was seldom considered during its time. The creators saw it as an honest depiction of Negro life, white audiences listened in huge numbers and radio stations saw the show as a way to entertain their audience and provide sponsors with an in-demand product. It was the market economy at its best and worst; it was the will of the majority and the tyranny of the minority; it was hilariously funny and demeaningly stereotypical. It was also the most popular radio program of its era that ushered in the idea of popular culture in the electronic media and laid the groundwork for what the electronic media would become from that time forward. It also marked the beginning of the Golden Age of Radio.

This "Golden Age of Radio" created a national audience and a national standard for musicianship. Audiences heard the best musicians and the best bands, which raised the bar for musicians and orchestras. Listeners heard the best performers and demanded that other performers and musicians meet that level.

The Harry Fox Agency

In 1927, the National Music Publishers Association formed the Harry Fox Agency to collect and distribute mechanical royalties, collected from the sales of recordings. It became the major mechanical rights organization for the music industry with money collected by record labels sent to the Harry Fox Agency, which sent those monies to publishers.

The Movies

For the movie industry, 1927 was a landmark year because of the introduction of "talkies" with *The Jazz Singer*, starring Al Jolson.

Sam and Jack Warner went to Bell Labs/Western Electric where they saw a demonstration of a movie with sound. Sam Warner, the driving force behind the purchase of their first "kinetescope," saw a future in "talkies," although is brother, Harry, did not. Sam began producing movies with the new system, filming music stars in short films, akin to later music videos. On October 6, 1927, *The Jazz Singer* opened in New York; unfortunately, the day before, Sam Warner died from a cerebral hemorrhage. Within three years, 83 percent of the 20,000 movie theaters in America were wired for sound.

Jack Warner replaced Sam in making movies. Harry arranged the purchase of a studio in Burbank, First National, and the purchase of the Stanley Corporation, which owned 250 theaters. Abe Warner ran the theaters.

The Jazz Singer was based on a story that originally appeared in *Everybody's Magazine* as "Day of Atonement." It concerned a Jewish boy who ran away from home to find a place in show business but came back home on the evening of Yom Kippur, the sacred Day of Atonement, to take his dying father's place as cantor. Much of the story was autobiographical for Jolson and the singer expressed initial interest in the project. Warner Brothers (and other movie studios) had been pursuing Jolson, the top stage entertainer of the time, to do movies but he had not done so because of contract restrictions with the Shuberts.

The story was first developed as a Broadway show, which premiered in July, 1926, starring George Jessel and then toured the country in 1926-27.

When Jolson became available for the film, Warner Brothers offered him $75,000 for the role and he accepted; filming began on July 11, 1927 and the premier was held in New York on October 6. That marked the beginning of the "talkies." It took about five years for the film industry to iron out the problems of making talking films and for movie theatres to install new equipment but it marked the beginning of the end of silent movies. Ironically, *The Jazz Singer* was not really a full-fledged "talkie" because only the singing was heard, a result of the Vitaphone process developed by Western Electric for Warner Brothers. The rest of the movie was a "silent" with dialogue written on the screen.

Silent movies had become universally accepted and many openly wondered if "talkies" would have the same appeal. For immigrants who did not speak English--and New York had large numbers of those immigrants--a silent movie was easily understood. However, with the restrictions placed on immigration by 1924, the number of immigrants dramatically decreased. By 1927, the movie audience was comprised of people who could understand English. The audiences for live performances in theaters was also hurt; between radio and the talkies at the end of the 1920s and then the Depression in the 1930s, the live theaters very existence was in peril. Broadway and the American Theater would never die, but it would never claim its place as the apex of entertainment after talkies came in.

Movie Studios

The movie industry was changing, consolidating into a small group of major studios.

The movie companies built air-conditioned palaces around the country and produced movies to be shown in them. Thus began the era of the Hollywood Moguls. It was also the beginning of the Hollywood Musical. In 1928 Jolson's follow-up to *The Jazz Singer*, *The Singing Fool*, was released by Warner Brothers and was a major hit; songs in the movie included "Sonny Boy," "There's a Rainbow Round My Shoulder" and "It All Depends on You."

In 1929, Hollywood "discovered" musicals and filled the movie screens with singing and dancing. Because the sound revolution in movies allowed songs to be heard, a new source of income was opened for songwriters and the movie industry had an incentive to work with the recording industry.

Metro-Goldwyn-Mayer filmed *The Hollywood Revue of 1929*, hosted by Jack Benny and Conrad Nagle, that featured the song "Singin' in the Rain" performed by Cliff "Ukulele Ike" Edwards. Also in 1929 were *Glorifying the American Girl*, featuring Rudy Vallee singing Irving Berlin's "Blue Skies"; *Lady of the Pavements*, and *Coquette*, with songs composed by Irving Berlin, *Makers of Melody* from Paramount with songs composed by Richard Rogers and Lorenz Hart, *Lucky Boy*, a spin-off of *The Jazz Singer* starring George Jessel, *Rio Rita*, and *The Gold Diggers of Broadway*, which featured the songs "Tip Toe Thru' the Tulips" and "Painting the Clouds with Sunshine."

Hallelujah, the first all-black sound feature, was released by MGM in 1929 with songs "Swing Low, Sweet Chariot," "Going Home" and "Swanee River" as well as some Irving Berlin songs ("At the End of the Road" and

"The Swanee Shuffle"). The classic Broadway musical, *Show Boat*, was filmed that same year.

Two of the earliest movie musical singing stars were Jeanette MacDonald and Maurice Chevalier; their debut was *The Love Parade* with songs "Nobody's Using It Now," "Anything To Please the Queen," "Dream Lover," "Paris, Stay the Same" and "Champagne."

Most of the movie musicals were adaptations of Broadway musicals; however, *Sunny Side Up*, starring Janet Gaynor with songs written by G.B. DeSylva, Lew Britton and Ray Henderson, was one of the first musicals created for the screen; songs included "I'm a Dreamer (Aren't We All?)" and "If I Had a Talking Picture of You."

The first sound film to win the Academy Award for "Best Picture" was a 1929 musical, *The Broadway Melody* produced by MGM which featured the songs "The Wedding of the Painted Doll," "You Were Meant For Me," "Harmony Babies from Melody Lane" and "The Boy Friend."

Talent Agencies: William Morris and MCA

During the 1920s, two booking agencies that would have a major impact on the music business came into prominence. The William Morris Agency was begun in 1898 by a German-Jewish immigrant, William Morris, on Fourteenth Street in New York. Prior to World War I, the Morris Agency represented European singer Harry Lauder and humorist Will Rogers, taking them both to stardom. During the 1920s, the Agency represented Al Jolson, Eddie Cantor, Maurice Chevalier and the Marx Brothers. In 1912 Abe Lastfogel joined the agency as a personal secretary to William Morris; he later headed the Agency.

In 1900, the Keith-Albee organization tried to seize control of vaudeville by creating the Vaudeville Managers' Association, a central office to book acts into theaters, bypassing and eliminating independent agents like William Morris. Albee blacklisted performers signed to Morris in an attempt to put the Agency out of business. Keith and Albee wanted to keep performers salaries low--and eliminate competitors--by providing security with longer bookings. The blacklisted performers fought back by forming a union, the Exalted Order of the White Rats.

In 1922, the Keith-Albee circuit in the East and the Orpheum circuit (connected to Keith-Albee) in the West controlled 12,000 performers playing before 1.6 million people each day. In 1927 Albee merged his Keith-Albee empire with the Orpheum circuit, bringing big time vaudeville under his dominion. However, the next year Joseph Kennedy seized control of the

Keith-Albee-Orpheum chain and merged it into his Film Booking Office to form Radio-Keith-Opheum. RCA and David Sarnoff wanted a guaranteed market for the movie theater sound process that they controlled. Kennedy made a deal with RCA so the corporation could have a motion picture division, which is what R-K-O became.

By that point, vaudeville was dying, being replaced by the movies.

One of William Morris's clients, Al Jolson, took advantage of the synchronization process by starring in *The Jazz Singer* for Warner Brothers but vaudeville performers found it easier to enter radio and, since Morris represented so many vaudeville performers, acts like Amos'n'Andy, Jack Benny and Eddie Cantor moved to radio.

In Chicago, a band booking agency was started by Julius Caesar Stein, the son of Lithuanian Jews, who was born in 1896. Young Stein learned the saxophone at the age of 15 and performed in a neighborhood band for birthday parties. In 1915 he graduated from the University of Chicago, then entered the University of Chicago's medical school in 1917; after graduating with a medical degree, he studied in Vienna for a year.

While in college and medical school, Stein played violin and saxophone in bands for extra money. His band was popular and he had more offers than he could fill, so he began booking other bands. As he entered the band booking business he discovered he could make a lot more money booking a number of bands than by playing in one band.

After he returned from Vienna, Stein began work at the Cook County Hospital in Chicago, but still booked bands. Leading this double life, he soon discovered he could make more money booking bands than he could as an ophthalmologist so, with $5,000 and partners Fred Hamm and Ernie Young, they began The Music Corporation; the first band they sent on the road was King Joe Oliver's Creole Jazz band that featured Louis Armstrong on the cornet.

Stein discovered that by getting a 50 percent down payment for a band's booking, he could pay the band before they played. He craved dignity and respect, and dressed stylishly in a suit, white shirt, and black tie, emulating a young businessman in the seedy world of band booking.

On May 24, 1924, the Music Corporation of America was incorporated, after Stein gave Ernie Young and Fred Hamm $10,000 for the rights to the name. On the first Board of Directors was Stein, his brother Bill, and Stein's employer, Dr. Harry S. Gradle; shares were valued at $5.

Chicago was a hot town for bands and Stein signed a number of them. He established a method whereby hotels were guaranteed a series of bands, which provided hotels with fresh entertainment. Bands liked it because they were employed for good money while MCA took care of publicity, travel, food and lodging.

Stein also pioneered the exclusive contract with bands which guaranteed bands steady work; however, a band had to provide $1 million in Agency fees (or $10 million in bookings) before they could be released from their contract. Only five bands ever did so: Benny Goodman, Tommy Dorsey, Guy Lombardo, Tid Fiorito and Horace Heidt. (That contract was eventually banned by the musician's union.)

The Kansas City Night Hawks were booked by MCA into the Blackhawk Restaurant in Chicago, a club controlled by gangster Al Capone; Stein supplied Capone's clubs with a number of bands in Chicago throughout the 1920s. Stein arranged for the band, renamed the Coon Sanders Orchestra, to play over WGN, owned by Colonel Robert McCormick's *Chicago Tribune*, for a network feed. In a pattern that was repeated a number of times over the years, Stein managed to get a commission on the advertising revenue as well as hook-up charges.

MCA's first star act was Guy Lombardo and his Royal Canadians, who arrived in Chicago in 1927, then moved to Cleveland the next year. In 1928 MCA opened an office in New York and signed most of the best bands and the best ballrooms to contracts where the bands were guaranteed work and the ballrooms were guaranteed music. Lombardo's band was booked into Manhattan's Roosevelt Hotel and signed to the CBS network.

Stein and MCA benefited from their connection to the Mob in Chicago, who controlled many of the top night spots where bands played. James Caeser Petrillo, head of the Chicago Musicians Union and backed by the Mob, was an ally; Petrillo allowed Chicago bands with MCA to play in New York if a New York band was booked into Chicago. No other booking agency was allowed that favor.

MCA played tough and hard with a take-it-or-leave it policy; there would be no bands available if the hotel owner, radio programmer or advertiser did not accept the band that was offered. William Morris represented vaudeville acts while MCA represented Big Bands. Both benefited from the emergence of radio which, by 1929, was established as a major commercial venture. In terms of the music business, MCA had a closer connection through its representation of bands, but both ultimately made their mark in Hollywood, where movies were quickly becoming a major force in entertainment.

The End of the Twenties

In 1928, there were marathon dances, flagpole sittings and Times Square was lit by a headline sign at the intersection of Broadway, 42nd Avenue and Seventh Avenue that operated until 1977. Helen Kane achieved stardom as the "boop-a-doop girl" with her song "I Wanna Be Loved by You" in the musical *Good Boy*. Rudy Valley made his debut on radio that year while the Rhythm Boys, the singing group comprised of Bing Crosby, Al Rinker and Harry Barris who performed with Paul Whiteman's band, had their first hit record, "Mississippi Mud." This is the year that songwriter Johnny Mercer came to New York from Savannah, Georgia while *Yamekraw (Negro Rhapsody)* was presented at Carnegie Hall. The show was conducted by W. C. Handy and featured Fats Waller as the piano soloist in a work originally done on solo piano by James P. Johnson.

At the end of the 1920s Cole Porter has his first success with a musical, *Paris* which featured the songs "Let's Do It" and "Let's Misbehave" while playwright Noel Coward debuted with *This Year of Grace*. There were problems looming in the music industry at the end of the 1920s as payola was getting out of hand. Publishers had regularly paid vaudeville and revue performers a weekly payment for singing their songs during shows; now publishers found they had to also pay band directors, masters of ceremonies and radio stars as well for performing songs and money was running thin, cutting deeply into profits.

In 1929 came the Teapot Dome Scandal, which indicted President Hoover's Secretary of the Interior Albert B. Fall, the destruction of New York's monument to elegance, the Waldorf-Astoria Hotel, and the St. Valentine's Day Massacre in Chicago. In Gastonia, North Carolina, textile workers on strike were shot to death while the world of literature saw the publication of the novels *Look Homeward Angel* by Thomas Wolfe, *A Farewell to Arms* by Ernest Hemingway, *The Sound and the Fury* by William Faulkner and *Dodsworth* by Sinclair Lewis. Charles Lindburgh married Anne Spencer Morrow, daughter of the Ambassador to Mexico. In February of that year a riot broke out at the New York Theater when radio star Rudy Vallee appeared, presaging the riots that were later created by singing stars Frank Sinatra, Elvis Presley, and the Beatles. The song "Stardust" by Hoagy Carmichael came out in 1929 as well as *Hallelujah*, the first all-black film musical produced by MGM, and *The Broadway Melody* which became the first 100 percent all talking, all singing and all dancing movie. Guy Lombardo opened at the Roosevelt Grill in New York and began to build one of the most successful dance bands ever as well as a New Year's Eve tradition of bringing in the New Year with music and dancing.

The year 1929 witnessed the first steps in the shift of the center of American popular music from Broadway in New York to the movie studios in Hollywood. During that year Warner Brothers purchased the song catalogues of Harms & Chappell-Harms, Famous, T.B. Harms, DeSylva, Brown & Henderson, Remick, and obtained executive board control of ASCAP. Another movie studio, MGM, purchased Robbins, Leo Feist, and Miller Music and other New York publishing companies.

With those purchases, the movie industry could build a publishing empire by developing hit songs for movies, which were replacing Broadway shows as the major outlet for new hit songs. They could also control fees which had to be paid for the use of songs, thus avoiding hindrances and negotiations to increase profits. Because of the introduction of "talkies" and solving the technical problems of sound on film, Hollywood increasingly became the place and movies became the medium where American images were created and presented. Hollywood took the musical off the stage and put it on film and increased the exposure of a song. Instead of having to rely on traveling road productions and sheet music sales over a period of eighteen months in order to make a song a hit, audiences all over the United States could see a new musical and hear new songs at the same time.

The Broadway musical was not only replaced by movies as the route for hit songs to take, it was also replaced by radio with its network shows, bands which performed on radio, and recording labels. By the end of the 1920s Tin Pan Alley was moving to Hollywood; during the 1930s Hollywood replaced New York's Broadway as the creative center for entertainment.

RCA Buys Victor and the
American Record Company Formed

In July, 1929, RCA purchased Victor Records from two New York banking houses, Speyer & Co., and J. & W. Seligman and Company for $22.3 million. RCA also purchased two music publishing companies, Leo Feist, Inc. and Carl Fischer, Inc., as they expanded into the music business.

The American Record Company (ARC) was formed in August, 1929 after purchasing Cameo, the Pathe Phonograph and Radio Corporation and the Plaza Music Company. Labels in the merge included Cameo, Lincoln, Romeo, Muse, Tremont, Variety, Actuelle, Pathe, Perfect, Banner, Domino, Jewel, Oriole and Regal. Herbert Yates, owner of a film processing company, purchased the American Record Company.

Happy Days Are Here Again

A song that was used by Franklin Delano Roosevelt as his campaign theme song in 1932. "Happy Days are Here Again" was introduced to the public on Black Thursday, the day of the Stock Market Crash that caused investors to lose $18 billion in 24 hours and precipitated the Great Depression.

The song had been written for the movie *Chasing Rainbows* but the movie's release had been delayed. The publishers Ager, Yellen and Bornstein had a contractual obligation to have the song out to the public by October 29 and so they had arranged for it to be performed by George Olson and his band at the Hotel Pennsylvania in New York. On the darkest day in America's economic history, as a few souls gathered to share their grief, the band struck up this seemingly inappropriate number. It took three years for the song to redeem itself but its time came when the song that was introduced at the beginning of the Depression became the anthem which signaled the beginning of the Presidency which guided the nation to the end of The Great Depression.

SECTION II:
1929 TO 1953

The Great Depression

The United States had suffered a number of economic depressions before the one that occurred during the 1930s, but never one quite as devastating, or quite as deep or long lasting. Prior to the stock market crash in October, 1929, there were signs the nation was not in good economic health. In spite of the much ballyhooed publicity about the affluence of Wall Street, about 78 percent of the population made less than $3,000 a year. Although stock market speculators were reaping huge fortunes, the nation's farmers were in dire economic straits, and had been for several years.

President Herbert Hoover continued to argue for the free market during that time, feeling unrestricted business would bring the country back. On New Year's Eve, 1929, Hoover stated that "Any lack of confidence in the... basic strength of business in the United States is foolish" and announced a $160 million tax cut. However, it was only the extensive government intervention by Franklin Roosevelt, which included welfare, unemployment insurance, work programs for the unemployed, bank regulation, social security and a host of other programs, that the country was able to rebound. The recovery came slowly. Although statistics show that by 1937 the United States was coming out of the Depression, people did not feel they were out of the Depression until after World War II, when the economy enjoyed a post-war expansion boom.

In 1930 the population of the United States was 122.7 million, an increase of 30 million over the 1920 census. New York was still the largest city but Los Angeles had a tremendous population growth and by 1930 was the fifth largest city in the U.S. Life expectancy for Americans was 61 years; there were over 25 million cars on the road. At the Massachusetts Institute of Technology, Vannevar Bush invented a "differential analyzer," which was an analog computing device with a "mechanical brain" that could do quick calculations. That huge device was the forerunner to the modern hand calculator.

In 1931 political humorist Will Rogers observed "We are the first nation... to go to the poorhouse in an automobile." Unemployment was between four and five million and 800 banks had failed after "runs" from the public withdrawing their funds. Movie theaters showed double features with gangster and horror films such as *Public Enemy* starring James Cagney, *Dracula* starring Bela Lugosi, and *Frankenstein* starring Boris Karloff, all box office hits. William Fox had been wiped out by the Wall Street crash and had to sell his share of Fox studio for $18 million. Studies showed that crime was rampant, a direct result of Prohibition. The first modern supermarket, King Kullen Grocery, was opened in Queens, New York.

In March the "Star Spangled Banner" was declared the National Anthem and in May the Empire State Building, the world's tallest building with 86 floors, was opened on the spot previously occupied by the Waldorf-Astoria Hotel and, before that, the mansion of John Jacob Astor, who died when the Titanic sank.

On October 18, 1931, Thomas Edison died and the lights of the nation were turned off for one minute in his honor. In December, President Hoover announced an injection of $500 million to aid businesses in general and the railroads in particular, but opposed any direct or indirect payments to individuals, saying it would only create more unemployment.

In 1932 the first highway stretching coast to coast, Route 66, was opened. The two-a-day vaudeville shows on Broadway in New York closed and in July Federal troops under General Douglas MacArthur and his aid, Major Dwight D. Eisenhower, forced the dispersion of 9,000 former World War I veterans from Washington. The veterans came to Washington to lobby for veterans payments, scheduled for 1945, to be paid immediately because of their dire financial situation. The Federal troops burned the temporary settlement the veterans erected; two died during the evacuation.

On November 8, 1932, Franklin D. Roosevelt was elected President, receiving 23 million votes to Hoover's 15 million, and promised a "new deal for the American people." At the end of the year, Radio City Music Hall, the world's largest theater, opened in Rockefeller Center.

In 1933 dust storms began in Texas and Oklahoma, where there had been a drought for several years. The storms filled the air with dust so thick that people could not see or leave their homes. A number of residents packed up and moved West to California in search of jobs and hope. Those migrants were known by the derisive term "Okies."

In his inaugural address in March, 1933, Roosevelt told the American people that "The only thing to fear is fear itself." By that time, 5,000 banks had collapsed, wiping out nine million savings accounts and the national income was less than half of what it had been in 1930. During Roosevelt's first One Hundred Days he sent 15 major pieces of legislation to Congress. On the day of his inauguration, he closed all the nation's banks; on March 31 he created the Civilian Conservation Corps that put young men to work on public projects; on May 12 he set up a national relief program and established a policy where farmers could refinance their farms. He introduced the National Industrial Recovery Act, which provided business codes for fair labor practices and established Federal guarantees for bank deposits. Each week, he spoke to the nation over the radio on "Fireside Chats" explaining what he was doing and why.

In 1934 the drought in the midwest had grown catastrophic; there had been nine months without rain and farm prices had fallen by over half in four years. The Securities and Exchange Commission was formed to prevent another stock market collapse; it required that businesses on the stock exchange provide full disclosure of their financial situation to the investing public. The Federal Communications Commission was created, replacing the Federal Radio Commission, in order to help develop and oversee the radio industry as well as help the public obtain efficient telephone and telegraph services at reasonable rates.

In 1935 the Works Progress Administration (WPA) paid 6,000 writers to collect oral histories and write research guides to states while artists were paid to paint murals for schools and post offices. Oklahoma and Texas were known as the "Dust Bowl" because the biggest dust storm hit in May, obscuring the sun as far east as the Appalachian Mountains.

In Hollywood, the Fox Company merged with Twentieth Century while MGM produced the first Technicolor movie. In real life, gangsters were being hunted by J. Edgar Hoover's FBI; in 1931 Al Capone was sentenced to eleven years for tax evasion, in 1934 Bonnie Parker and Clyde Barrow were killed in Ruston, Louisiana after a murder spree, and John Dillinger, "Public Enemy Number 1," was shot down in Chicago while Charles Arthur "Pretty Boy" Floyd and George Baby Face" Nelson were shot down in Ohio and Illinois, respectively. Dillinger, Floyd and Nelson had robbed a number of banks. In 1935 Kate "Ma" Barker was killed in a gun battle with the FBI;

she was the reputed brains behind the bank robberies of the Barker gang. The Mafia dispensed their own form of justice; Dutch Schultz was gunned down in a gangland killing under orders from Charles "Lucky" Luciano.

In 1935 the Rural Electrification Administration was passed, providing low cost loans to companies to provide electricity to rural areas; nine out of ten farms did not have electricity. That same year the Social Security Act was signed by President Roosevelt; business owners, required to match employee funding, were upset because it would cut into profits while conservatives complained that pensions, scheduled to begin in 1942, would "Sovietize America."

In Hollywood the biggest movie star was eight-year old Shirley Temple; at the Olympic Games in Berlin, Fuhrer Adolph Hitler proclaimed that Negroes were an "alien race," then watched Jesse Owens, an African-American, win four Gold Medals. Two influential books were published that year; *How to Win Friends and Influence People* by Dale Carnegie and *Gone With the Wind* by Margaret Mitchell. The Carnegie book became a bible for business people wanting to get ahead while Mitchell's book fostered pride in the South, the most economically disadvantaged region of America.

In October, 1936, the Hoover Dam, located on the Arizona-Nevada border, opened. The dam cost $120 million and took three years to construct; it held over ten trillion gallons of water and provided hydroelectric energy for much of the southwest. Without the Hoover Dam, the growth of California, Arizona, Colorado, Nevada and Utah would have been curtailed.

In November, 1936, Franklin Roosevelt won his second term in a landslide; at his inaugural he said "In this nation...I see millions denied education, recreation, and the opportunity to better their lot and the lot of their children...I see one-third of the nation ill-housed, ill-clad, ill-nourished." There was an ideological chasm between those for and against Roosevelt; 77 percent of those on relief were for him while 69 percent of the richest, most prominent people were against him. Republicans labeled New Dealers "fanatics, fascists, theorists and impractical experimenters."

In 1937 trans-Atlantic air service between Germany and the United States was inaugurated with the blimp Hindenberg flying the maiden voyage. It made it across the Atlantic in 60 hours, but exploded just before it landed, killing 35 of the 97 aboard and one on the ground as it went down in a fiery wreck.

That same year John D. Rockefeller died, King Edward of England abdicated his throne in order to marry American divorcee Wallis Warfield

Simpson, and Amelia Earhart vanished while trying to fly around the world. In Chicago there was a massive taxi driver strike while violence erupted at a Ford plant when labor tried to organize a union. That year Ford Motors made its 25 millionth automobile.

At a strike at U.S. Steel on Memorial Day, eighteen were killed. In Austria, Nazi troops marched in and took over that country while in Yaphank, Long Island, 20,000 American Nazis gathered to celebrate "German Day."

The Great Depression and the Entertainment Industry

The entertainment industry benefitted in several ways from the Depression. Since people could not afford to spend money for entertainment, the radio became the dominant entertainment medium. Families huddled around the radio and listened to the networks present musical variety shows, dramas, comedies and other fare. Big Bands dominated the music on radio, and those performers lived well. The movie industry also did well during the Depression; people managed to watch movies and many of those in the movie industry hardly knew a Depression was going on.

It is said that Americans react two ways to adversity: on one hand they face it head on and deal with it realistically; on the other hand, they seek escapism. It is significant that two major books came out of the Great Depression that affect our view of that time. *The Grapes of Wrath* by John Steinbeck was a harsh, unrelenting portrayal of the poverty and despair of the Depression as it applied to the "Okies" who migrated to California. *Gone With the Wind* by Margaret Mitchell provided a romantic escapism back to the time of the Civil War and the "Lost Cause." Both were released as movies within months of each other; *Gone With the Wind* in 1939 and *The Grapes of Wrath* in 1940.

Experiments in television were done by Ernst F. W. Alexanderson at General Electric in 1928 (he broadcast over W2XAD in New York) and Vladimir Zworykin of Westinghouse. Paramount acquired CBS stock in 1929 because Adolph Zukor felt television would soon be on the market. The premier of the movie *The Jazz Singer* on October 6, 1927 led to an upheaval in Hollywood which led to a change-over in theaters and studios to accommodate sound. In 1928 RCA, along with General Electric and Westinghouse, formed RCA Photophone after buying the Film Booking Office owned by Joseph P. Kennedy and the Keith-Albee-Orpheum chain of theaters to create Radio-Keith-Orpheum, or RKO. With those purchases, RCA entered the movie business.

Despite plummeting record sales, Victor remained strong throughout the 1930s because of the financial backing of the RCA corporation. A number of small labels folded during that period, or were bought by a major company.

The American Record Company (ARC), which had been formed in August, 1929 after purchasing a number of small labels, was purchased by Consolidated Film Industry, owned by Herbert Yates, in October, 1930.

Warner Brothers attempted to get into the record business by purchasing the Brunswick, Vocalion and Melotone labels in 1930 for $8 million. Brunswick had Al Jolson, Duke Ellington, Furry Lewis, Uncle Dave Macon, LeRoy Carr, Scrapper Blackwell, Tampa Red, Georgia Tom, Memphis Minnie and Kansas Joe on its artist roster. Herman Starr, who joined Warner Brothers as an accountant, was on the Board as a director and assistant treasurer and headed the music division for the studio. Starr named Jack Kapp to head the recording label and Kapp signed Gloria Swanson, Noah Berry, Harry Richman, and Bing Crosby.

It was the wrong time to enter the music business. In 1930, Warner's stock was worth over $200 million; it owned 93 film distributorships, 525 theaters in 188 cities, had 51 subsidiary companies and 18,500 employees; in 1931, the studio lost $8 million. The brothers were in legal trouble, guilty of insider trading. In December, 1931, Harry Warner sold the Brunswick and Vocalion labels, plus their pressing plants to the American Record Company; they had lost a great deal of money and Herman Starr swore he would never again have anything to do with the record business.

Sales Drop

In 1932 RCA Victor sold Southern Publishing back to Ralph Peer for the same amount they had purchased it; RCA was forced to divest itself of some of its companies because of government investigations related to monopolies. The Society for European Stage Authors and Composers (SESAC) was formed by a German immigrant, Paul Heincke, in 1930. The firm was founded to collect royalties for European songwriters, which weren't represented by ASCAP. Heinecke owned and ran SESAC until his death in 1972.

In 1933 income from sales of recordings was only seven percent of what it had been in 1928. That same year Montgomery Ward Records was established; Ward leased recordings primarily from RCA Victor, later Bluebird, for catalogue sales. The major trade magazine, *Variety*, acknowledged the popularity of country music, but usually did it with a showbiz sneer with headlines like "Curse of a Sour Hillbilly Note" or "Hollywood Goes Hillbilly."

At RCA Victor, A&R head Frank Walker created a budget line, Bluebird Records, to be sold for 35 cents each instead of the standard 75 cents. The first Bluebird releases were in April, 1933; all their race and hillbilly product was released on this label. Heading the race and hillbilly division was Eli Oberstein.

In 1934 the American Record Corporation purchased the Columbia Phonograph Company from Grigsby-Grunow; also included in the purchase was Brunswick, which had the Vocalion and Melotone labels. ARC did not use the Columbia or Okeh names; instead they marketed records on Melotone, Perfect, Banner (sold by W.T. Grant stores), Oriole (McCrory's) and Romeo (S.H. Kress). Sears Roebuck also leased ARC/BRC-derived product for its Conqueror label from early to the late 1930s. Among the artists on those labels were Roy Acuff, Gene Autry, Big Bill Broonzy, Bill & Cliff Carlisle, the Chuck Wagon Gang, Al Dexter, Red Foley, Blind Boy Fuller, Robert Johnson, the Light Crust Doughboys, Patsy Montana, the Prairie Ramblers and Bob Wills.

Decca

The Decca Gramophone Company was formed in London on July 1, 1929, by Edward Lewis, a stockbroker who purchased the company. The Decca company was originally established in 1914 to market portable gramophones, which became popular with soldiers in the trenches during World War I. In 1933 the company acquired the American Edison Bell Company and the following year, 1934, the American Decca Company was formed, headed by Jack Kapp.

Jack Kapp, the son of a Russian immigrant father who became a distributor in Chicago for Columbia Records, was born in Chicago on July 15, 1901. In 1905 the father of Jack and David Kapp worked as a door-to-door salesman for the Columbia Phonograph Record Company. Mr. Kapp was known as a "canvasser" in Chicago; he moved up to become a franchised dealer and covered an assigned territory with a horse and buggy. Customers often brought phonographs on credit and Mr. Kapp made the rounds each month to collect the payments and sell a few records.

Kapp's father opened the Imperial Talking Machine Shop and Jack, the eldest of four children, worked for him. As soon as he finished high school, Kapp went to work for his father, where he showed a flair for sales.

In 1921 teenagers Jack (19) and David (16) opened a Kapp's record store in Chicago at the edge of the Negro section of town. By that time record stores no longer carried only one company's products but instead stocked records from a variety of labels. The Kapps began stocking what was known as folk, jazz and race records and attracted a black as well as white clientele of young people anxious to hear and purchase those new sounds. The cultural elite hated jazz, calling it "unhealthy" and "immoral," and an "abomination" that should be "absolutely eliminated."

In 1926 Jack Kapp joined Brunswick-Balke-Collender, which operated the record labels Brunswick and Vocalion. Jack was placed in charge of Vocalion, where he hired black recording director J. Mayo Williams, who signed and produced King Oliver, Jimmy Noone, Jelly Roll Morton, Earl Hines, Andy Kirk and Louis Armstrong. Kapp also worked with established Brunswick stars Al Jolson, Fletcher Henderson and Ted Lewis.

When Warner Brothers decided to enter the record business in 1930, and bought Brunswick for $5 million, it sent Kapp to New York as General Manager of Recording. Kapp hired Victor Young as his house conductor and signed Bing Crosby, Mildred Bailey, the Mills Brothers, the Boswell Sisters, Glen Gray and Cab Calloway. That was the wrong time for Warner Brothers to enter the record business so the company made a deal with the American Record Company to take over its operations. ARC sent Kapp to London in 1932 to negotiate with Edward R. Lewis for the sale of Brunswick's British arm to Lewis's company, Decca.

In April 1934, Kapp, with several other Brunswick executives, convinced Edward Lewis to finance a 50 percent option to purchase Columbia Records for $75,000, with another option to purchase Brunswick from the American Record Company. Kapp was maneuvering to combine Columbia and Brunswick into one company, which would be purchased by Lewis's firm, Decca. However, the American Record Company (ARC) purchased Columbia for $70,500 and decided against pursuing the Brunswick option.

Edward Wallerstein, who had been president of Brunswick, joined Victor, which led Kapp to believe that he was going to be appointed president of Brunswick. Kapp informed Lewis that if he were not named president of Brunswick, he would resign and take Bing Crosby with him. That was possible because Crosby had a "key man" clause in his contract, which meant that if Kapp left Brunswick, the contract the label had with Crosby was no longer valid. Jack Kapp had originally signed Bing Crosby in 1931 to a six month contract; the first session yielded "Out of Nowhere," the first record released under Bing's name as a solo artist and that record became a top seller.

After the sale of Columbia to ARC, Kapp resigned (on July 16) and contacted Crosby, who agreed to remain with the executive. Kapp then announced the formation of Decca Records with himself as president, an agreement Lewis allowed because, as Chairman and chief stockholder, Lewis felt he held the ultimate power in the company.

British Decca issued 25,000 shares of common stock, holding on to 18,000 and gave Warner Brothers 5,000 shares, Kapp 1,250 shares and another executive 750 shares. The rest were put on the market to raise an operating fund of $250,000. The company then bought a pressing plant and office from Warner Brothers. American Decca was incorporated on August 4, 1934; their first session was on August 8, with Bing Crosby recording "Just a-Wearyin' for You" and "I Love You Truly."

Jack Kapp cultivated the loyalty of the acts on Brunswick, who followed him to Decca. Those included Crosby, Glen Gray's Casa Loma band, the Mills Brothers, the Boswell Sisters and Jimmy and Tommy Dorsey, which meant that the fledgling Decca label started with a roster of top recording artists. Kapp hired Victor Young as music director and band leaders Guy Lombardo, Isham Jones, Ted Lewis and Earl Hines soon followed. Artists Chick Webb, Ethel Waters, Art Tatum, Noble Sissle, Johnny Mercer, Jimmie Lunceford and Bob Crosby were then added. Within a year, Kapp signed Louis Armstrong.

Brunswick's production team of producers and engineers, including J. Mayo Williams and Joe Perry, also joined Decca. The company then built a studio at 5505 Melrose Avenue in Los Angeles. Kapp named his younger brother, Dave, as the talent rep in Chicago.

Lewis and Kapp agreed that the key to selling records during the Great Depression was to offer top artists at bargain prices, in effect cutting the price on their top of the line artists. While other labels sold their top acts for 75 cents a record, Decca sold theirs for 35 cents or three for a dollar. They reduced payments to songwriters and advances to artists, invested heavily in advertising and pursued the jukebox industry, which became the largest buyer of records.

Dropping the price of something—in this case records—is welcomed by consumers but, for the label, the perceived value goes down. It is easy to drop prices; it is difficult to raise them. When prices drop, the perceived value drops and that hurts income and profits. The only way to make that up was through volume; a company had to sell over twice as many records at 35 cents to reach the income of half as many 75 cent records. Decca gambled that the price of records was higher than the perceived value and that stopped people from buying records. Fortunately, Kapp's gamble paid off and the drop in price encouraged consumers to purchase more records.

The first problems for Decca occurred at their manufacturing plant, which produced records slightly too large for jukeboxes, so distributors returned them. Correcting that problem required British Decca to put more cash into the company, which was struggling to stay afloat.

Kapp was determined to create a large catalog of recordings as quickly as possible, so he scheduled four or five sessions a week, producing over 200 recordings with a few months. Their first hit was "The Music Goes 'Round and Around" by Mike Riley and Eddie Farley in Autumn, 1935.

In 1934 there were 25,000 jukeboxes; in 1938 there were 250,000 jukeboxes, which bought 13 million records. In 1939, Decca sold 36 percent of the total records sold in the nation, or 18 million discs out of a total 50 million sold. By 1937 the company was showing a profit and led Victor and Columbia to issue a line of recordings for 35 cents.

In 1934 Dave Kapp joined Decca as head of the Race and Hillbilly division; also Paul Cohen, a Chicago friend of the Kapps, joined Decca and moved to Cincinnati and became Decca's midwestern branch manager, where he was responsible for scouting and signing new talent in addition to marketing records

The Record Industry in the United Kingdom

Electric and Musical Industries, Ltd, or EMI, was formed in London in 1931 when two companies merged. The Gramophone Company Ltd and The Columbia Graphophone Co. Ltd had both formed in the nineteenth century; up to the time of their merger, they were competitors.

The story began in the United States in 1889 when the The Columbia Phonograph Company was created; it was then purchased by Jesse Lippincott to form the North American Phonograph Company. When that company went bankrupt, Edward Easton reconstructed the Columbia Phonograph Company with the American Graphophone Company to create the Columbia Phonograph Company General.

Frank Dorian established The Columbia Phonograph Company General, a foreign branch of the American company, in August 1897. In 1917, The Columbia Graphophone Company Ltd was formed in Paris and operated as a wholly owned sub-company of its American parent. The company moved its European headquarter to London in May, 1900.

The American Columbia was nearly bankrupt at the end of 1908, causing the British branch to almost close. Frank Dorian, head of the company, returned to the United States to help Edward Easton, head of the American firm, attempt to rescue the company. Dorian was replaced by John A.B. Cromelin, who hired Louis Sterling as British sales manager. Sterling had founded The Rena Manufacturing Company in 1908 to sell phonographs and recordings; British Columbia pressed his recordings and sold him Columbia catalog recordings. In 1909, Cromelin purchased Rena Records and persuaded Sterling to join Columbia.

Louis Sterling was born in New York in 1879, the son of an accountant, who had been hired for The Gramophone Company in 1904 by William Barry Owen. In Great Britain, Sterling decided to go into business on his own, forming The Rena Manufacturing Company.

Sterling received no salary from Columbia; instead he was paid by commission on the records sold. By 1911, British Columbia was on its feet and by 1914 Sterling had re-established Columbia as a major British recording company; the previous year it had changed its name to The Columbia Graphophone Company.

In 1922, the American Columbia company went into receivership and the British firm purchased shares in the company; by 1927, the British firm owned practically all of the shares in the American firm. Under the leadership of Louis Sterling, Columbia began to show a profit and acquired several other companies, including OKeh, the German firm Carl Lindstrom, and the French Pathe company.

Alfred Clark, born in 1873 into an affluent New York family, began his career with the North American Phonograph Company in 1889; during the 1890s he worked for Thomas Edison's kinetoscope company, producing the movie *Mary Queen of Scots*. In 1895 Clark became sales manager for Emile Berliner's store in Philadelphia that sold records made by the The Berliner Gramophone Company. In 1899 he was sent to Paris to establish the French Gramophone Company. Clark ran the company until 1908, although he sold his holdings in the firm in 1904. After a brief retirement, which lasted less than a year, Clark became The Gramophone Company's managing director, or head of the daily operations of the firm, in London.

Frank Seaman secured the rights to sell Berliner's products; Seaman hired William Barry Owen as General Manager and Owen moved to London to establish a European venture in 1887. Owen, born in 1860 in Vineyard Haven, Massachusetts, was the son of a whaling captain; he studied law at Amherst. In July, 1897, Owen moved to London.

In 1899, The Gramophone Company Ltd was incorporated in London, with Trevor Williams as Company Chairman and William Barry Owen as managing director. The Gramophone Company purchased the British and European gramophone patents from Emile Berliner and Eldridge Johnson and opened offices throughout Europe.

In December 1900, the Gramophone and Typewriter Ltd was formed to acquire The Gramophone Company Ltd; however, the typewriter the company invested in was not successful so, in 1907, the company changed its name back to The Gramophone Company Ltd.

The American firm, Victor, had a close relationship with the British company. In the early 1900s the two companies divided the world into two non-competing trading areas; Victor had the Americas and the Far East while the Gramophone Company had the rest of the world. Victor manufactured and supplied the gramophone machines while a licensing agreement allowed each company the rights to the other's recordings.

In 1904 William Barry Owen returned to the United States and was succeeded by Theodore Birnbaum as managing director; in 1909 Birnbaum resigned and was succeeded by Alfred Clark, who shared the post with Sydney Dixon during the first three years in that office.

The most prominent artist on The Gramophone label was Sir Edward Elgar, Britain's leading composer, who was born in 1857. Elgar began his recordings for the Gramophone Company in 1914; his most popular work was "Pomp and Circumstances March No. 1," perhaps best known as the march played at graduations.

World War I interrupted the British recording industry; Russia and Germany seized the branch offices of The Gramophone Company in their countries, reducing the assets of the Gramophone Company by a third. However, in 1919 the gramophone industry resumed full time operations, although the country faced the problem of a recession. That led The Gramophone Company to join in a partnership with the American Victor Company in order to raise capital. In 1921, the Gramophone Company opened their flagship store, HMV (for His Master's Voice) on Oxford Street.

Electric and Musical Industries, Ltd. (EMI)

The shareholders of The Columbia Graphophone Company and the Gramophone Company met in June, 1931 and approved proposals to merge and form a new venture, Electric and Musical Industries Ltd (EMI). At its creation, EMI became the largest international recording company in the world with 50 factories in 19 countries.

A new Board was formed, comprised of Alfred Clark, chairman; Louis Sterling, managing director; and non-executive directors David Sarnoff, president of RCA Victor and Trevor Williams, both from The Gramophone Company; Lord Marks, Michael Herbert and Edward de Stein from the Columbia Graphophone Company.

The group originally saw the new venture as a holding company that would oversee two existing competitors, managing their assets. However, it soon became obvious that this type of arrangement would not work. Between 1931 and 1934, sales of records fell and the company lost over one million pounds sterling, causing the company to carry out a massive reorganization.

EMI acquired a large house at 3 Abbey Road, St. John's Wood, London and renovated the building, converting it into recording studios. The Abbey Road Studios were opened in November, 1931, with a recording by Sir Edward Elgar, EMI's most prestigious recording artist. Sir Elgar conducted the London Symphony Orchestra in his "symphonic study" of "Falstaff" for that first recording in the new studio in front of an invited audience.

By the end of the 1930s, there were only two major labels in Great Britain, Decca and EMI. Sales had been declining throughout the decade for three reasons: (1) the world-wide Depression; (2) the increase in the number of people owning radios and preferring to listen to music on the radio instead of purchasing it; and (3) the increase in the number of people attending "talking" movies.

Electricity Between the Wars

During the 1920s most American homes in urban areas were wired for electricity. By 1930, 70 percent of homes had electricity, compared with 10 percent in 1910. The first difference electrical wiring made was in lights, which was the first benefit Americans received from electricity. Electric lights replaced gas lamps which emitted much less light and gave off smoke and acidic fumes that were harmful to fabrics, fogged up windows, dampened interiors and covered rooms with a film. Each gas light had to be cleaned regularly to eliminate the possibility of home fires as well as receive the maximum light and each gas light had to be lit and extinguished individually. The electric light, on the other hand, was turned on and off with a flick of a switch and gave off no odors or fumes. Further, a whole house or street could be lit or darkened by flipping a few switches.

After the electric light, American consumers bought appliances such as irons, fans and vacuum cleaners. Before electric irons, women ironed with heavy irons that had to be heated on a stove. There was a wooden handle that was removable and poor women could afford only one handle. Even those who could afford several often got blisters from those irons burning their hands. The bottom of the iron had to be clean or else dirt would be ironed into a shirt; for a white shirt this meant the shirt had to be washed again and washing meant doing it by hand with water boiled on a stove with a tub and scrub board. During the 1920s, 90 percent of wired households had electric irons. Ironically, lighted Christmas trees were also among the first things a family bought when they received electric current.

As Thomas Edison developed the idea of electrical homes, he predicted that "electrification of the home would eliminate the distinction between night and day and speed up women's mental development, making them the intellectual equals of men" and that "Constant light might lead to the elimination of sleep." It certainly changed the lives of women, who began to be viewed as "domestic engineers" with their new electrical homes. It made a major difference in "women's work" and made it physically easier in some respects, but much more difficult in others as it changed expectations for women in the home. Author David Nye noted that "Long work hours in the home persisted as a result of rising expectations for middle-class women, who were exhorted to prepare more varied meals, vacuum the house more often, maintain a larger wardrobe, do laundry more frequently, and spend more time with the children. Electrical conveniences made individual household tasks easier, but their number, frequency, and complexity increased. At the same time, some tasks were displaced from men and children to women. Vacuuming a rug may be easier than beating it, but men and boys had much of the responsibility for dragging a rug outdoors and cleaning it, which they did only a few times a year. The housewife was expected to vacuum at least once a week."

During the 1920s "Home Economics" became a required course for female students.

The role of the home changed with electricity. Prior to electricity, the home was a place of production; afterwards, it became a place of consumption. Before electricity, a whole economic system was based on serving the home; after electricity, the home became a place to leave in order to obtain goods and services. Author David Nye stated, "A whole set of trades began to disappear. The iceman, who often sold more than ice, would no longer be needed once the electric refrigerator came. Laundry service, milkmen, knife sharpeners, fruit and vegetable dealers, fish peddlers, and other door-to-door salesmen gradually disappeared. Not only had these vanishing tradesmen once eliminated many of the housewives chores, such as making bread and washing, but they also came to the house, rather than requiring her to go out and shop. Electrification was part of the general process in which the home became more isolated from the rest of society."

Another casualty of electrification was the electric streetcar, which had virtually disappeared by 1931.

Electricity affected language, and terms such as "energetic," "a human dynamo," "electrifying," "blow a fuse" "plugged in," "juiced up," "short circuit," "shocked" "turned off and turned on," "attracted to her," "animal magnetism," "switched on," "overloaded," "burned out," "out like a light," "live wire," "blown circuit," "get their wires crossed," and "power houses" to give a few examples, all came directly from America being electrified. It also affected insurance rates; insurance companies realized by the 1890s that electricity was safer and cleaner and home rates reflected that.

By 1934, 96 percent of homes in towns and cities had electricity, although less than half had central heating. Over half (55 percent) used stoves and 37 percent had no bathtubs, 18 percent only outdoor toilets, 13 percent had no running water inside the home, and 34 percent had only cold water in their house. Virtually all of the homes had light and during the darkest days of the Depression, people struggled to pay their electric bill; if they had to give up a home service, they gave up the telephone. In 1945, at the end of World War II, less than half of all homes had a telephone.

Despite the hard times the country faced during the 1930s, electrical consumption continued to surge. Americans bought primarily small appliances and stoves and did not invest in refrigerators in large numbers until after World War II. In 1935, 69 percent of people in towns still cooled their food with ice while only 20 percent had an electric or gas refrigerator. On the other hand, about 60 percent had a gas or electric range. It was not until the 1940s that it was economically advantageous to own a refrigerator instead of an ice box. Until that time, refrigerators were priced too high to be affordable and ice was still relatively cheap. When the refrigerator entered American homes it made a significant change in habits. Here was a place of consumption and people became used to opening the door just to gaze inside to decide if they were hungry. The idea of snack foods and munching became popular and people began to store items other than food there (such as money and film). The refrigerator allowed food to be preserved and made it last longer. It eliminated the daily shopping trip and the problems of obtaining fresh fruit and vegetables in the winter as well as foods such as milk spoiling quickly. On the other hand, it became a major reason so many Americans suffer from weight problems.

Electricity did not just affect physical lives, changing behavior; electricity also changed the way we think and the image of ourselves. At first electricity represented progress and modernity. It caused the nation to regulate time; for most of the nineteenth century each local area kept its own time and there could be a variance of 15-30 minutes from town to town. Railroads and the telegraph standardized time for their schedules and during the 1870s the railroads imposed a single time zone on the United States. The introduction of electricity blurred distinctions in time because the rhythms of night and day were altered. No longer were people forced to be up in the day if they wanted light; it was now available at night. Conversely, people were not forced to go to bed when it was dark because with electric light they could work round-the-clock. Family life was disrupted as factories began round-the-clock shifts and being "on time" became important when time was not governed by daylight.

Electricity changed ideas about social status. Advertisers soon discovered that appliances were sold if buyers believed they were "moving up" when they bought one.

Men and women became increasingly separated with electricity and the industrial revolution. Men left the home to work; women stayed behind and the work inside the home with electrical appliances no longer required men. Houses changed, too. In the past, homes were either small, with just a few rooms, or large, divided into several large rooms, but with electricity there could be more rooms given to special purposes. Since electric light could light any room, and electrical outlets were available anywhere in the house, each person could have their "own" room and rooms were not set up according to function (kitchen, parlor) but instead according to self-image and convenience (a recreation room, a separate room for each child).

Electricity transformed the workplace as well as the home. At first, factories put in lights, which allowed them to work round-the-clock and increase production. Later, they added electric motors until by 1930 80 percent of all motor power was electrical, compared with less than ten percent in 1905. In Detroit, Ford's factories perfected the assembly line using electric lights and electric motors. That use of electricity made cars available to all Americans, rather than divide them by class into the upper class, who owned a car, and the rest, who didn't. In 1913 it took over 12 hours of labor to build a Model T; in 1914 it took an hour and thirty-three minutes. The assembly line made work dull and labor interchangeable, often stripping workers of dignity and self-worth. In early factories the average laborer stayed less than four months and it was not until labor unions demanded benefit packages and high wages that the labor force was stabilized. F. W. Taylor, who revolutionized management theory before World War II, looked at people as machines and provided flow charts and timetables to explain jobs and functions. There is no denying that electricity made the United States a more productive nation; between 1890 and 1940 productivity in the United States increased by 300 percent, mostly a direct result of electricity.

By 1935 most of the cities and towns in the United States had electricity, but most rural areas did not. Electrical companies refused to run lines to rural areas, saying it was unprofitable and insisted that farmers could not afford electricity and would not pay their bills. It was not until 1935, when President Franklin D. Roosevelt required electric utilities to provide electricity to rural areas through the Rural Electrification Act, that those rural areas began to receive electricity. Even that law could not alter the fact that it would not be until after World War II when virtually the entire country had access to electricity.

Electricity played a major role in America becoming a consumer nation and the entertainment industry benefited from that. Radio became a common household item in the 1920s and during the 1930s became the center of home entertainment. As Americans accepted the idea of consumerism, the idea that entertainment was a necessity followed, which helped movies, radio and phonographs. Electricity made home entertainment possible and dramatically altered the old ideas of live entertainment. With the advent of electricity, it was possible for more people to see and hear an entertainer sing or act, but less likely to see them in person. For entertainers, it became more important to have a great voice for records and a great face for movies (and later TV) but not as important to have a great act before a live audience.

Radio in the 1930s

Many local radio stations suffered during the early years of the Great Depression because businesses could not afford to buy advertising. Hotels had low occupancy during that time and that led a number of hotels to offer radio stations a "home" in exchange for announcements promoting the hotel. That was part of the "barter" economy which evolved when money was scarce; that also led to products being offered to station managers in exchange for free ads.

At the networks, programming was increasingly dependent on advertising agencies who wrote the shows, arranged for sponsors and then delivered them to the radio station. Since a number of vaudeville performers, like Jack Benny or George Burns and Gracie Allen, moved over to radio, advertising agencies signed them and found sponsors. The networks bought stations around the country and had others as "affiliates." That led to the situation where the network controlled radio programming on local stations because it provided the shows. In return, the network provided "sustaining" programs free to the local station and the local station could sell advertising revenue to local businesses.

Under pressure from music publishers and the musicians union, both NBC and CBS banned the playing of records in 1930. Sales of record players and records had plummeted; there were almost no record players manufactured by 1930 and sale of records totaled six million in 1932, down from 110 million ten years earlier.

At the beginning of 1932, CBS bought out its investor, Paramount, and gained complete control; by this time it had 79 stations coast to coast on its network while NBC had 61 stations. Each network also started its own booking and management agency and signed artists to those companies.

In 1930 David Sarnoff became President of RCA but soon after that the Department of Justice brought an anti-trust suit against RCA, GE, Westinghouse and AT&T. In late 1932 the companies came to an agreement where RCA kept the radio manufacturing facilities while GE and Westinghouse could compete with RCA after a period of two and a half years. NBC became a wholly owned subsidiary of RCA while GE and Westinghouse kept their own broadcasting stations.

In 1930 the first ratings service was instituted for radio, formed by Archibald Crossley for the Association of National Advertisers. Officially known as the Cooperative Analysis of Broadcasting, those ratings became known as "Crossley ratings" and were based on telephone interviews. That let advertisers know which programs were most popular and thus affected demand for air time as well as advertising rates.

Beginning in 1933, network radio was filled with comedy, drama and music programs. The leading programs had a sponsor and a star; the sponsor paid for the production of the program and generally had its name in the title of the program. Because local radio stations relinquished their role in providing programming, the advertising agencies stepped in and, in exchange for purchasing time on the station, became the power brokers in the entertainment industry. The programs were not created just to entertain an audience; they were created to sell a product. That growth in advertising led some to view commercial broadcasting as "venal, boorish, corrupt, tiresome" while others saw it a "varied, educational, cultural, magnanimous." It led to radio programming being aimed at the popular taste or, as some noted, "the lowest common denominator."

Commercial programming provided the networks with large profits during the Great Depression and allowed the public to hear popular entertainment nightly. Radio provided President Franklin D. Roosevelt with a forum for his "Fireside Chats" where he talked to the American public about the Great Depression and the programs he was introducing to help them. By speaking to an audience like he was speaking to a single person, Roosevelt connected with the American public via radio. Entertainers also began to visualize a single listener rather than an auditorium full of faces as an intimacy was established between performers and audiences.

Dance Bands

The Golden Age of Radio produced the Big Band era. Big Band music was at first an extension of "potted plant" music that radio was comfortable with. It merged with jazz because audiences wanted that sound, and radio stations needed audiences for their sponsors.

Author James Lincoln Collier credits three people with the creation of the modern dance orchestra: Art Hickman, Ferde Grofe, and Paul Whiteman. Hickman was born in Oakland and developed a dance band in San Francisco around 1913; he hired Ferde Grofe to write arrangements and provide scores for the jazz band. Grofe divided Hickman's band into saxophone and brass sections, "playing contrapuntal lines which at points merged into straight-forward harmony and then separated again. Solos were frequent." In 1919 Grofe left and the Hickman band went to New York, where they worked for Florenz Ziegfeld at the New Amsterdam Theater. Among the innovations that Grofe made with the Hickman band was to make the saxophone the key instrument of jazz; prior to that time the saxophone was considered a novelty instrument. The introduction of the saxophone to jazz resulted in over 100,000 saxophones being sold between 1919 and 1925.

Grofe then went to work for Paul Whiteman, who popularized and commercialized the dance/jazz band like no one had before. Whiteman was the first "star" bandleader and his 1920 recordings of "Whispering" b/w "Japanese Sandman" sold millions. Working for Hickman and Whiteman, Grofe established the basic format of the dance band. According to Collier, "The principles for the modern dance arrangement were: (1) the division of the orchestra into sections, at first brass, reed and rhythm, and later with brass sometimes further split into trumpet and trombone sections; (2) the playing off of the sections contrapuntally or in call-and-answer fashion; (3) the intermixing throughout of shorter or longer solos, mostly improvised jazz, but occasionally straight renditions of a melody; and (4) the playing of ensemble passages with the jazz-like feel of an improvised solo."

Bands had to become bigger for a simple reason: as they played larger and larger dance halls and hotel ballrooms, they needed to be heard, since there were no sound systems or microphones used. Thus Big Band jazz had to have more instruments in order to be heard by a large crowd of dancers.

The development of radio throughout the 1930s helped because musicians were unable to find employment in dance halls--crowds declined during the Great Depression. Meanwhile, radio had a large audience and a large budget to accommodate those musicians. Sponsors realized that audiences liked music on the radio, so advertisers sought out dance bands for shows to promote their products. As the bands developed musically, they were influenced by jazz--the popular music of the day--and by dancers, who wanted music with a lively beat. The soft, sentimental sound was needed for the radio audience, so that was what the big band era first produced, with lush arrangements for the "older" audience. But the young audience wanted fast, beat-driven music, and the bands soon adapted to this, which created the "swing" craze at the end of the 1930s.

Bing Crosby

The pop music singer who best personifies the 1930s is Bing Crosby, whose relaxed, easy-going persona and singing style was a soothing influence for those faced with the wrenching hard times of the Great Depression. His recording of "Brother, Can You Spare a Dime" served as an anthem for that era.

With the development of electrical recording and the microphone, a new style of singing evolved where the singer used the microphone as an instrument. This "crooning" style allowed a singer to sing softer and develop vocal inflections and an intimacy with the audience. Prior to the microphone a singer had to project his or her voice to an audience; after the microphone a singer could sing in a softer tone, transforming the audience from a large group to a single listener. Nobody did this better than Bing Crosby, who dominated the recording industry during the 1935-1954 period like no other singer. He was the most commercially successful recording artist, the most influential, and the public found him to be one of the most likeable stars.

Crosby was not a natty dresser; he was usually seen with a pipe in his mouth, wearing mis-matched sox, worn sweaters, beat-up hats with his shirt tails out of his pants. He always appeared calm and collected, as if nothing could ruffle him.

On radio, Bing Crosby appeared on the "Kraft Music Hall" from 1935 to 1946, broadcast over the CBS network. Crosby's show came on every Thursday evening, and approximately 50 million people across America tuned in to listen to him. Crosby was always marketed to the broad American populace--young, old and in-between, no matter what color or ethnic origin.

Harry Lillis Crosby was born May 3, 1903, although early show biz biographies generally listed his birthday as May 2, 1904. He became "Bing" when he was six years old, after a teenaged neighbor began calling him "Bingo From Bingville" from a popular newspaper comic strip; later, the nickname was shortened to "Bing."

Crosby grew up in Tacoma, Washington; he excelled as an athlete (swimming and baseball), although he was often in trouble from being a member of a local gang that committed petty crimes. At Gonzaga University in Spokane, Crosby enrolled in a combination college and law course that awarded a bachelor's and law degree in six years. However, Crosby dropped out before finishing his law degree.

Crosby's biggest influence as a performer was Al Jolson, who performed in Spokane in the summer after Crosby's freshman year in college. Crosby stated about Jolson's performance, "I hung on every word and watched every move he made. To me, he was the greatest entertainer who ever lived." Crosby stated further, "I got an awful lot of mannerisms and I guess you could say idiosyncrasies [from Jolson]--singing traits and characteristics and delivery," noting that, unlike Jolson, "I'm not an electrifying performer at all."

Bing Crosby bought his first musical instrument--a set of drums-- during his fourth year in college. They were purchased from a mail-order catalog and news about the drum set traveled quickly throughout the small community. At North Central High School, 16-year old Alton Rinker played piano in a small band that played arrangements Rinker learned from jazz records. The drummer in Rinker's band was not very good, so when he heard that a 21-year old college student at Gonzaga had a drum set, he gave him a call.

Crosby was not embarrassed to be playing with high schoolers, even though he was a college guy. The band wasn't particularly good; no one could read music and they could only play songs in A flat or E flat. Bing wasn't much of a drummer, but he kept time.

Al Rinker, and later Rinker's sister, Mildred Bailey, had a profound influence on Bing Crosby's life. An energetic leader, Rinker spurred the easy-going, laid back Crosby along.

Crosby and Rinker played together until 1925, when the band broke up. Bing and Al had to come up with a duo act and did so in the Spring of 1925. Spurred by Rinker's ambition, the duo decided to try to make a career in show business and headed to Los Angeles; the two had relatives already there, Rinker's sister and Crosby's brother. It was a tough drive from Spokane; it took two days to reach Seattle and three weeks to get to L.A. The two young men drove 1,200 miles, averaging 200 miles a day, and arrived at Rinker's sister's home on November 7, 1925.

Rinker's sister, Mildred Bailey, had already established herself as a singer. Bailey introduced the two to key people and arranged auditions; she informed them of auditions for Fanchon and Marco, who produced traveling vaudeville units for Loew's California circuit and Crosby and Rinker were hired for $75 each per week for a 13-week tour in a revue, "The Syncopation Idea." On a bill with jugglers, dancers, a dog act and an all-girl chorus line. They opened on December 7, 1927--exactly a month after their arrival.

Bing loved the showbiz life, especially the drinking, gambling and chorus girls. He had a tendency to get drunk after each show.

After the revue closed, Crosby and Rinker joined Will Morrissey's Music Hall Revue, where they sang between acts and developed a comedy routine. Bing Crosby was 23 and Al Rinker was 17.

In 1926 Crosby and Rinker caught the attention of Paul Whiteman, who signed them for $150 a week each. Crosby had made his first recording in October for Columbia, doing "I've Got the Girl!" and "Don't Somebody Need Somebody," singing the chorus in those two songs. In Chicago, where the duo joined Whiteman, Crosby and Rinker recorded "Wistful and Blue" in late December; the duo eventually recorded about 100 titles with Whiteman.

Whiteman thought the duo of Crosby and Rinker needed help, so 21-year old Harry Barris, a former vocal student of Whiteman's father, was hired and, with Crosby and Rinker, formed a trio known as "The Rhythm Boys."

Barris was a pianist, songwriter, singer and jokester who had played local dances in Denver since he was 15. The act developed into a trio where Crosby took most of the solos while Barris and Rinker filled in the background or "answered" Crosby's lines. Some of their earliest popular songs were "Mississippi Mud" (which Barris wrote with lyrics by Jimmy Cavanaugh), "Ain't She Sweet," and "I'm Coming, Virginia." Soon after forming, Whiteman arranged for them to receive a recording contract from Victor.

In December, 1927, Whiteman debuted on NBC with his own show. Crosby was featured on some songs but the most important aspect of this phase of Crosby's life was the impact that jazz musicians had on him. Mildred Bailey introduced Bing to Louis Armstrong's recordings, and Crosby admired the New Orleans talent for the rest of his life. Bix Beiderbecke, Whiteman's trumpet player, who became one of the all-time greats in the history of jazz, roomed with Crosby at the Belvedere Hotel in New York. Crosby became personally close to Beiderbecke and memorized some of his cornet solos, scat singing them. He also continued to be influenced by Al Jolson, who appeared regularly on New York stages.

The Rhythm Boys days were numbered. Bing and Barris both drank heavily and Bing became unreliable. Rinker was the steadiest, but fought a losing battle. The fun side of showbiz took precedence over the side of hard work and dedication and the group lost their edge. Whiteman took them out of his group and put them on the vaudeville circuit for six months. During that period, they worked out a comedy routine and honed their 15-minute act.

Bing's singing talent caught the attention of other bandleaders, who hired him to provide "vocal refrains" in their recordings. In 1929, Sam Lanin had 25-year old Bing record "If I Had You," along with guitarist Eddie Lang. Crosby's first recording under his own name came in March, 1929 when Columbia recorded "My Kinda Love."

According to biographer Gary Giddens, "Bing imparted a near regal nonchalance. His innate propriety deflected the kind of vanity that curdles into narcissism. The distinct warmth that defined his singing and later his acting made him seem cool yet approachable...His working class man's man insouciance was found no less fascinating by men. He had none of the brilliantined conceit and manicured irony rife in Hollywood. He came across as an extraordinary ordinary guy."

Bing Crosby entered the music industry at the right time. In 1925 the industry was converting from acoustic to electrical recordings, which introduced the microphone to studio singers. Crosby used the microphone like an instrument and popularized a new singing style, called "crooning."

Bing in the Movies

Bing's big break in the movies was set of happen when Universal made a film of Paul Whiteman, *King of Jazz*. But in November, 1929, Crosby was arrested in Los Angeles for drunk driving; he almost drove through the lobby of the Roosevelt Hotel. Crosby was scheduled to sing "Song of the Dawn" in that movie but was sentenced to 60 days in jail. Through the intervention of Universal Studios owner Carl Laemmle and Whiteman, Crosby arranged to be transferred to a jail in Hollywood and came to the movie set, accompanied by two detectives, each day. He lost the opportunity to sing the big vocal number in the movie; that song went to John Boles, although Crosby sang over the credits as the picture began.

Filming for the movie finished in March, 1930, and premiered in Hollywood in April and in New York in May. In 1930, Crosby toured with the band until they got back to New York, where he quit, wanting to return to California with the trio.

In Los Angeles, Crosby and his group sang at the Cocoanut Grove nightclub, located in the Ambassador Hotel. Crosby established himself as a solo singer of ballads during that time, while Barris increasingly tailored his songwriting to Crosby's voice. Here is where Crosby learned to use a microphone as an instrument.

Early in 1931 Crosby recorded "I Surrender, Dear," which became a hit at the club and on radio.

On September 29, 1930, Bing Crosby married Dixie Lee Wyatt. The two went through an early period of trying to adjust to each other--and to married life--until Dixie left Bing and demanded a divorce. Crosby was a life-long Catholic, so divorce was out of the question. In an attempt to win her back and save his marriage, Crosby agreed to quit drinking and take control of his life; the decision to quit the booze marked a turning point in Crosby's career because the major factor holding him back was now gone.

Although Crosby backslid a few times, during the next several years he imposed a self-discipline on his personal life and career that allowed him to become a superstar and remain one for the rest of his life.

Crosby, Jack Kapp and Decca Records

Jack Kapp was known as a man whose taste was "corn," which is another way of saying he believed in making records that sold instead of appealing to the tastes of critics or highbrows. He was unabashedly commercial and possessed a businessman's drive and ambition or, as Kapp himself noted, "I know how to keep my pulse on the multitude."

In Bing Crosby, Kapp saw an artist who could appeal to the masses and he oversaw Crosby's recordings (the later term would be "produced") from 1934 until Kapp died in 1949. Kapp could not play or sing a note but he became the most important musical collaborator with Bing Crosby for 15 years. Kapp had a simple rule: sing the melody. It was what he felt the public wanted and he was right. He never appealed to the musical elite, but Kapp's tastes were perfect for middle America.

Jack Kapp believed in covering all the musical bases. He had Crosby sing pop tunes, Hawaiian numbers, western songs and a wide variety of material to cover the spectrum of tastes shared by Americans. Crosby noted that Kapp "had me on a recording program that embraced every type of music--sextets, choral music, light opera, liederspiel, jazz, ballads, comic songs, plays, recitations...And that kind of diversified record program, I believe, was the most important thing in the advancement of my career. I thought he was crazy, but I did what he told me...I wasn't doing it. He was doing it. He'd say, 'You ought to do this' and I'd say, 'Oh, Jack, this is silly.' And he'd say, 'You come on down and do it' and I'd do it because I thought he was a nice guy and he had good taste. I know I didn't have any. I just did it because he wanted me to."

Bing Crosby trusted Jack Kapp without reservation, and Kapp guided him to become "the voice of America." The two shared four things in common, outsized ears (Crosby was once described as looking like a taxi cab with both doors open), a love of Al Jolson, an incredible memory and a bedrock belief that in terms of taste, the public was right. Bing Crosby and Jack Kapp set out to make records that would sell millions to Americans of both sexes, all ages, and in every part of the country. They succeeded and because they did, Decca succeeded. Crosby was loyal to Kapp and turned down lucrative offers from other labels; that allegiance helped make Decca a major label.

Bing Crosby's recording sessions, "became known as the easiest in the business," according to biographer Giddens. "He would arrive early, chew gum and smoke his pipe, read the racing form or newspaper, run down the material if it was new to him, and stick a pencil behind his ear. When he and the band were ready, he stepped over to the microphone, on which he habitually parked his gum, and, on average, completed five songs in two hours." The two developed their own lingo: "a Kappastrophe was an arrangement Jack disliked; those Jack approved were Kapphappy."

Although he was never a model of piety, Crosby faithfully stuck with his Catholic upbringing his whole life and attended mass every single Sunday. One of his most memorable movie characters was Father O'Malley in *Going My Way* and *The Bells of St. Mary's*.

Biographer Gary Giddens stated that Crosby "was marked by a serenity that suggested an appealing indifference. He had something going for him that could not be touched by Hollywood envy and mendacity. He acted in the early years of his career as if he didn't give a damn, displaying an irresponsibility that would have ensured a less talented man's failure, and he learned to turn that knowing calm into a selling point. Other performers worked on the surface, but Bing kept as much in reserve as he revealed. He was as cool in life as he was in song or onscreen."

Mack Sennett and William Paley

The time spent at the Cocoanut Grove brought Crosby to the attention of three men who were key to his career: in addition to Jack Kapp, there was Mack Sennett and William Paley.

Mack Sennett was a movie producer who offered Crosby a movie contract for six pictures; those pictures brought Crosby to the attention of the movie industry and launched his career as a movie star.

In 1929, the movie business saw 95 million people visiting 23,000 theaters each week; in 1936 there were about 15,000 theaters. There would not be more than 20,000 movie theaters in the United States again until the 1980s, but the movie industry, though threatened, survived, then thrived; by the late 1990s, there was an average of 22 million ticket buyers attending movies each week.

Crosby filmed four movies for Sennett in the summer of 1931 and two more in 1932. Those movies allowed audiences to both see and hear Bing Crosby and allowed him to demonstrate his acting ability and appeal as a matinee idol.

Bing's brother, Everett mailed two records to William S. Paley, head of the CBS radio network: "I Surrender, Dear" and "Just One More Chance." Paley liked Crosby's voice and signed him to do a 15 minute show each night over CBS in New York. For six nights a week, Monday through Saturday, Crosby sang three songs, the band performed an instrumental, and no one talked except the network's announcer. The show began at the end of August, 1931, and was broadcast at 11 p.m. Eastern time, so it was on in prime time, 7 p.m., on the West Coast.

Crosby recorded "Star Dust," becoming the first to record the lyric of that song shortly before the radio series. He also recorded "Dancing in the Dark" and "I Apologize" as well as the theme song for his radio show "When the Blue of the Night (Meets the Gold of the Day)." A successful theme song was essential for a singer's identity, and that song remained Crosby's theme song his entire life.

Cremo Cigars became Crosby's first sponsor on CBS, and they would not allow him to talk on the air. The show established Crosby as a major radio singer and soon he was doing two shows a night, one at 7 p.m. for East Coast prime time and the other at 11 p.m. for West Coast prime time. In November, he began a five month set of appearances at the Paramount Theater; there he did four stage shows in addition to his two 15-minute daily broadcasts, as well as various charity shows, guest appearances, recording dates and concerts. Everett Crosby, Bing's brother and manager, took care of Bing's business interests.

Bing Crosby hit radio at the right time; in 1930, less than a third of all American homes had a radio. By the end of 1935, over two thirds of homes had a radio. Movie attendance fell; that led to theaters offering double features and creating the "B" picture. Crosby hit the movies at the right time as well.

In 1932, the movie studios produced 11 musicals, down from 78 in 1930. Only five were profitable: *One Hour With You* and *Love Me Tonight*, both starring Maurice Chevalier; *Horse Feathers* by the Marx Brothers; *The Kid From Spain* starring Leo McCarey and Eddie Cantor, and *The Big Broadcast*, starring Bing Crosby. That was the movie that made Bing Crosby a national movie star.

In New York, Crosby was signed by Chesterfield cigarettes to a 13 week contract, beginning on January 4, 1933. The show was called "The Music That Satisfies," and ran January through April, 1933. His recording career with the Brunswick label continued to be successful as he emerged as a top selling recording artist.

Guitarist Eddie Lang accompanied Crosby on his broadcasts and performances; Lang was also a friend and confidant. However, on March 29, 1933, the 29-year-old Lang died after a tonsillectomy. Crosby never had a regular guitar accompanist again. Musically, it meant that Crosby moved away from jazz and towards mainstream pop music, encouraged strongly by Jack Kapp, who wanted Bing Crosby to become the best-selling recording artist in America. In 1934 his radio shows were sponsored by Woodbury Soap and that sponsorship lasted until the end of 1935 when the "Kraft Music Hall" became interested in him after he made guest appearances with the Dorsey Brothers. Bing Crosby served as host of the Kraft show on NBC for eleven years, refining the image of the easy-going, genial Bing Crosby.

Swing Music and Benny Goodman

The arrival of "swing" music in the mid-1930s was ushered in by the Benny Goodman Band, whose energetic, light-hearted, outgoing music was in marked contrast to the bandleader, who was introverted, arrogant, egotistical and self-centered. Swing became "the theme music for a generation of adolescents struggling into adulthood during the critical days of the Depression and World War II...[the] audience was born between, let us say, the years of World War I and the early years of the Depression."

Benjamin David Goodman was born in Chicago on May 30, 1909, the son of Jewish immigrants from Europe. He had his first music lessons at the Kehelah Jacob Synagogue, where he learned the clarinet, while his brother Harry learned the tuba and brother Freddy took up trumpet. Goodman was a child prodigy who practiced constantly and believed in rehearsals. He played in various local groups in Chicago and by age 14 was a professional musician and dropped out of school. In April, 1925, he moved to Los Angeles where he joined Ben Pollack's band; he was 16 years old. In 1926, Pollack returned to his home town of Chicago, where he recorded sides for Victor. In 1928, Goodman left Pollack briefly for the Isham Jones band, then returned to Pollack when the latter moved to New York.

Goodman was an excellent musician who performed as a studio musician for radio shows and recording sessions; between 1929 and April 1934 he cut almost 500 records under different names for different labels in addition to playing with Pollack's band. In 1934 Pollack's band broke up, then reformed as the Bob Crosby Orchestra. That same year Goodman became a bandleader when he put together a band for Billy Rose's Music Hall in the old Manhattan Theater; he was 23 years old.

During the Golden Age of Radio, large orchestras were either hired by one of the networks or by an advertiser to put together a musical show. The McCann-Erickson Agency had the National Biscuit Company as an account and decided to put together a show called "Let's Dance" for Saturday nights. NBC had trouble selling Saturday nights because advertisers felt nobody was home listening; McCann-Erickson needed a showcase for its client's new product, Ritz crackers, so they decided to produce a show that featured three bands--a "sweet" band playing soft, commercial music, a Latin band, and a "hot" or dance band. The "sweet" band was Ken Murry's, the Latin band was Xavier Cugat's, and the "hot" band was Goodman's. The show ran 1934-1935 over the network and made Goodman a star; it ended when the employees of the National Biscuit Company went on strike. Among the songs Goodman made popular were "King Porter Stomp," "Down South Camp Meeting," "Sometimes I'm Happy," and "Wrappin' It Up," all arranged by Fletcher Henderson who, with Spud Murphy, provided arrangements for Goodman.

Goodman recorded for Columbia Records and was booked by the Music Corporation of America (MCA), who sent him on a cross-country tour after the radio show ended. In 1935 Goodman switched from Columbia to Victor, which was trying to capitalize on the pop music market created by Decca with its 35 cent records. The tour ended in Los Angeles at the Palomar where Goodman's shows drew large, enthusiastic audiences of young people. The one month engagement was extended to two months, then the band played in Chicago at the Urban Room, beginning in October.

Goodman continued to tour and perform on radio throughout 1936 as swing became popular with listeners and record buyers. On March 3, 1937, Goodman was scheduled to play at the Paramount Theater in New York. Goodman and the band arrived at 7 a.m. for a rehearsal and found thousands of fans lined up for tickets for that evening's performance; they quickly organized a show that began at 8:30 that morning and continued to play five shows a day. It was a teenage frenzy as fans came to the shows while others listened to Goodman on the radio--and the swing craze was in full bloom.

"Swing became a central facet of the teen culture. Adolescents felt it necessary to know about the bands, to be able to recognize this or that style, to dance the appropriate dances, to buy the records, to listen to them on the radio," according to Goodman biographer James Lincoln Collier. Teenagers danced the jitterbug with the girls wearing white buck shoes, short white "bobby sox," a pleated dress and blouses and sweaters while the guys dressed in "zoot suits," comprised of trousers with a small cuff and very wide knees which produced "pegged" pants as they narrowed to the ankle, a single-breasted jacket with very wide artificial shoulders and a narrow waist that was low. A vocabulary of slang developed for the "hepcats" who followed swing; the musicians were "cats," "the swingeroos were killer-diller, the band was in the groove, the ickies were square." It was teenage rebellion with a pseudo-sophistication; an in-crowd who knew the right clothes to wear and the right things to say and the "squares" were "out of it."

The swing band craze lasted from that point through World War II,. Goodman soon had competition from bands headed by Glenn Miller, the Dorsey Brothers, Artie Shaw and numerous others who all went after the teenage market. It was the beginning of the concept of "teenagers" and a teen culture where young people set the standard for the music. Benny Goodman, still in his 20s, was the leader of the movement, dubbed the "King of Swing."

Paul Whiteman

During the Depression, the Paul Whiteman band cut back on its personnel and the remaining players took a 15 percent pay cut. Whiteman was never successful as a radio personality and his "Old Gold" show was soon dropped from the air. By the early thirties, Whiteman was struggling to survive with his group. The problem of the economic Depression were exacerbated by Whiteman's drinking.

In 1934 Whiteman joined other top big band conductors, Rudy Vallee, Richard Himber, Guy Lombardo, and Abe Lyman, to form the Committee of Five for the Betterment of Radio. The purpose was to keep songs with suggestive titles and lyrics off the air. Each Friday the group met and looked over all the songs published during that week. Publishers were asked to revise songs they found objectionable; if they did not comply, the song was put on a list of black-balled songs that was mailed to orchestra leaders.

The sponsor of "Kraft Music Hall" wanted a variety show with music while Whiteman insisted on a music show that featured unknown as well as established acts. The conflict came to a head at the end of 1935 when, on December 5, Kraft announced that Bing Crosby would be the new star of their program. During the first four weeks of the show, the program had Whiteman performing with his band from New York while Crosby sang with Jimmy Dorsey's band from Hollywood. Finally, Woodbury Soap and Cosmetics, which sponsored Crosby's previous show, offered a contract to Whiteman for a show, "Paul Whiteman's Musical Varieties."

During 1936, Whiteman's show continued to lose its audience; in an attempt to gain ratings, Whiteman hired Judy Canova, her sister Annie and her brother Zeke, a hillbilly comedy act. It didn't work and, after 26 weeks, Whiteman's contract was not renewed. That forced Whiteman to tour with his 16 piece group in the Spring of 1937. By that time, "swing" music was the rage, with Benny Goodman, Tommy and Jimmy Dorsey, Glenn Miller, Red Norvo, Artie Shaw and others leading the way. The swing crowd never accepted Paul Whiteman and his group.

At the end of 1937, a new radio series, "Chesterfield Presents," featured Paul Whiteman's group, which gave his career a boost in popularity, but the flush of success caused him to drink more heavily. At the age of 50, Paul Whiteman could not keep the pace required of popular musicians who spent weeks on the road doing one-nighters so his career continued its decline.

The Golden Age of Radio Begins

The Depression cut deeply into the record business; in 1928 there were 34 million records sold but in 1931 only ten million were sold. If families had to choose between buying a phonograph or buying a radio, they bought a radio. There were 14 million radio sets in the country by 1930--seven times as many as there had been in 1925--and over 600 stations. Certain regions of the country had more radios than others; only 23.4 percent of West Virginians owned a radio by 1930.

Radio exposure created a demand for live performances and artists often played on a radio program for free in order to obtain bookings within a listening area. The most popular performers found sponsors who wanted to reach an audience. Sometimes a sponsor paid the performer, but usually paid the radio station so the performer could have time on the air. Sponsors also worked on the "PI" (per inquiry) plan whereby a performer advertised a product on the air, then received a commission on the sales via mail order from their shows.

For performers, radio had a profound impact; no longer were amateurs who played music on the side part of the game. Professional entertainers had emerged and had careers instead of an avocation. Because radio demanded a huge repertoire, no longer could a musician, or group, get by with a few tunes. Audiences no longer accepted the tunes they had been hearing for years; performers either had to compose new songs or find new songs from professional songwriters.

The new carbon microphones demanded a new type of singing; gone was the belt-em-out style and in was the crooning sound where singers sang softly with emotion. The most popular singers developed an easy-going, conversational vocal style that appealed to listeners who felt the performer was accessible and sincere.

Tape technology was not available during the 1930s, but in 1932 "transcription discs" were introduced. Harold C. Smith of the Vitaphone Company, created the transcription disc, which was an oversized record—sixteen inches in diameter—that played at 33/13 rpm, which meant that each side could hold fifteen minutes. During the 1930s, over 75 percent of radio stations played live programs recorded on transcription discs. There were usually spaces on the disc for local advertising inserts. The discs allowed popular radio performances to be broadcast over a number of stations when it fit their schedule. The discs solved the problem of time zone differences between the east and west coasts and popular shows and performers could then be heard without the performer being in the studio.

During the 1930s, a number of firms manufactured radios: Philco, Atwater Kent, Stewart-Warner, Victor, Spartan, Crosley, Musette, Clarion, Gloritone, Stromberg-Carlson, Silver-Marshall, Echophone, Zenith, Majestic, Fada, Temple, RCA, Eveready, Apex, Brunswick, Graybar, and Earl, to name the most popular. In 1931 the car radio was developed by Philco; those first radios, called a "transitone," were attached to the dashboard of the car.

Country Music on Radio

Country music during the 1920s was the era of early recordings, beginning with fiddle tunes, then to songs sung by New York singers, and then to field recordings, most significantly the 1927 sessions in Bristol, Tennessee. But country music during the 1930s was defined by radio.

During the 1930s, radio became the major way that country music was heard by listeners, replacing the phonograph. As a result, country music came of age on radio, primarily through "Barn Dances," or radio shows that were variety shows for the rural audience. Those shows, generally aired on Saturday nights, showed advertisers and station managers that country music could be profitable. In many areas, country music programs were also heard in the early morning and at the noon hour--the time when farmers came in from the fields for their mid-day meal. There were about 5,000 programs featuring country music in the United States by 1935, generating about $25 million a year in advertising revenue.

Country music blossomed during the 1930s because it was consistently on the radio. Ironically, many early rhythm and blues performers grew up listening to country music because country music could be heard on the radio; blues records were not on the radio.

Radio developed "programs" which appeared regularly at scheduled times; that also applied to country performers. The most popular time for country music programs on radio was early in the morning because the rural audience listened to radio before going to work. On weekdays, noon was important because farmers usually came in from the fields for their noon meal and listened to the radio before going back to work. Saturday night had once been radio's "dead" night but country music found a home there, playing to rural listeners after they'd finished their week's work. Most of the "barn dances" were on Saturday nights.

Radio soon became a way of life for Americans; author Wayne Daniel stated, "The radio was perceived as a vibrant, living thing--almost as another member of the family. A phonograph record was an historical document; a radio broadcast was the here-and-now. Radio performers communicated not only through their music, but through conversation as well. Listeners could write--were, in fact, encouraged to write--to their favorite entertainers, and in return they could hear their names read on the air...The radio, once turned on, would play without interruptions, allowing listeners to perform the chores of the household, shop, or farm while being entertained and informed. On the other hand, a person listening to the phonograph for any length of time had to be available to perform the inconvenient and annoying task of changing records about every three minutes. The radio also provided more than music. It gave the listener news, weather forecasts, comedy, and drama tailored to every age and taste."

In radio, the most important spot for country music during the early 1930s was WLS in Chicago. In 1928 the Prairie Farmer Publications purchased WLS from Sears and the station increased its wattage from 500 to 5,000. On March 19, 1932, The National Barn Dance on WLS moved to Chicago's Eighth Street Theater. One of the featured performers on the Chicago Barn Dance was "Oklahoma's Singing Cowboy," Gene Autry.

The market for country music tripled between 1930 and 1932. In 1936, half of the records produced were destined for jukeboxes, half of which were in the South. There were 225,000 jukeboxes which consumed 13 million records a year by 1939.

Gene Autry

After Jimmie Rodgers, Gene Autry was the most commercially successful country artist during the 1930s. In late September, 1927, 20-year old Gene Autry, a relief telegraph operator for the Frisco Railroad Line, and an aspiring singer living in Oklahoma, made his first trip to New York to audition for record labels. Autry did not have success landing a recording contract, but he did meet Johnny Marvin, who recorded with Victor, and his brother, Frankie Marvin, and auditioned for Edison, Brunswick, Columbia and Victor. At Victor, Autry auditioned for Nat Shilkret, who encouraged him to obtain experience on radio and learn to work with a microphone. Autry cajoled Shilkret into writing a letter, saying the young singer had potential, and used this to obtain a job singing on KVOO in Tulsa, beginning in 1928.

In 1929 Autry returned to New York, arriving just before the Stock Market Crash, and recorded several sides for Victor, "My Alabama Home" and "My Dreaming of You," and some for Grey Gull. He went to the American Record Company's offices, at 1776 Broadway, where he met Art Satherley. The American Record Company had been formed in July by consolidating several small labels, including the Regal and Cameo Recording complexes. ARC also had an agreement with Sears, Roebuck and Company to provide recordings to their mail-order catalogue company under Sears's imprint, Conqueror. Through this connection, Autry's records were released on Conqueror and sold in the Sears, Roebuck catalogue.

Autry was deeply influenced by Jimmie Rodgers, and ARC was looking for a singer to compete with Rodgers in the country market. On his first session for ARC, Autry recorded a Jimmie Rodgers song, "Blue Yodel #5" and one written by Carson Robison, "Left My Gal in the Mountains." In December he recorded several more times, doing Jimmie Rodgers' "Blue Yodel #4," "Waiting For a Train," "Lullaby Yodel," "Daddy and Home" and "I'm Sorry We Met," as well as "The Railroad Boomer," "Stay Away From My Chicken House," and "Slue Foot Sue" (released under the name Johnny Dodds) and three songs he was credited with writing, "Why Don't You Come Back To Me," "Hobo Yodel," and "No One To Call Me Darling."

Throughout 1930 and 1931, Gene Autry, sang on KVOO in Tulsa. Many of the recordings he did were released under pseudonyms (Sam Hill, Johnny Dodds) and sold through Sears. None of those records was a big hit, but sales were good enough for ARC to want him to continue recording.

During 1931 Autry and Jimmy Long, his supervisor at the Frisco Railroad where Autry was a telegrapher, wrote "That Silver-Haired Daddy of Mine," which they recorded on October 29; that became Autry's first big hit, selling around 30,000 in its first month. On December 1, Autry debuted on WLS on a morning show, "Conqueror Record Time," 8:15-8:30, sponsored by Sears to promote their recording label. Autry was introduced by Ann Williams and Sue Roberts as "That Fabulous Cowboy" and soon began making personal appearances in the listening area.

Barn Dances

On September 30, 1933, The National Barn Dance on WLS became a national barn dance when it went on the NBC Blue Network sponsored by Miles Laboratories, who wanted to publicize their new, then-unknown product, Alka-Seltzer antacid.

Other important "Barn Dances" on radio during the 1930s were "The Renfro Valley Barn Dance," broadcast originally from Cincinnati, then Renfro Valley, Kentucky; "Cross Roads Follies," on WSB in Atlanta; "The Grand Ole Opry" on WSM in Nashville; "Hillbilly Heart-Throbs" and "Log Cabin Dude Ranch," both broadcast on the NBC network from New York; and "The Hollywood Barn Dance" and "Lucky Stars" in Los Angeles.

The Carter Family and Dr. Brinkley

Country music received national exposure from broadcasts on "border stations." Located just across the Texas border in Mexico, XED began broadcasting from Renosa, Tamaulipas in 1930. The station was originally owned by Will Horwitz, a Houston theater owner and philanthropist and Jimmy Rodgers played there, then Dr. John R. Brinkley moved in.

Dr. John Romulus Brinkley grew rich and famous in Milford, Kansas, by pioneering the implementation of slivers of billy goat sex glands into males to "rejuvenate" their sex drive. In 1930 he ran for Governor of Kansas and almost won, but soon after the election was run out of the state by medical authorities. In 1931 he established XER (later XERA) just across the border from Del Rio, Texas in Villa Acuna, Mexico, a 100,000 watt station, then purchased XED and changed its call letters to XEAW.

In 1933 Brinkley gave up the goat gland business and began a controversial prostate treatment. His radio stations, and others on the Mexican border such as XEPN in Piedras Negras and XENT in Nuevo Laredo, operated because Mexico had been denied United States broadcasting licenses; Canada and the United States had divided those up amongst themselves, leaving Mexico out. Mexico welcomed those outlaw stations, which broadcast from 50,000-500,000 watts, blanketing the United States.

During the 1930s those stations played country records and transcriptions and were an important source of country music on the airwaves. Listeners could hear the Carter Family, Patsy Montana, the Pickard Family, Pappy O'Daniel's Hillbilly Boys, Roy "Lonesome Cowboy" Faulkner, Jesse Rodgers (a distant cousin of Jimmie) and others. Perhaps the most popular singing cowboy was Nolan "Cowboy Slim" Rinehart, whose theme song was "Roaming Cowboy."

Country music has traditionally been the music for the white working class and many in that audience left farms and rural areas for big cities during the 1930s. In 1933 the first major exodus of white workers from the South to the North occurred when the automobile companies in Detroit, nervous about their workers joining a union, chartered buses to bring workers from Kentucky, Tennessee and Alabama to Detroit, where they worked for 50 cents an hour on the assembly lines. By 1934 there were between 15,000 and 30,000 Southerners in Detroit; that exodus led other Southerners to move north to Detroit, Indianapolis, Chicago, Pittsburgh, Cincinnati and Cleveland to look for jobs in manufacturing plants.

The Carter Family had encountered domestic problems. Sara Carter fell in love with Coy Bays, a Poor Valley neighbor and cousin to A.P., who was often away for days at a time hunting songs for the Carter Family to record. A.P. found out about Coy and Sara's affair and was livid. Coy Bays' family decided he needed to leave Poor Valley so he and his mother moved to California in 1933. Sara moved back to her parent's house and did not want to record with the Carter Family again but was persuaded to by Anita Peer, Ralph Peer's wife. On that first session after the breakup they recorded the classic numbers "Will the Circle Be Unbroken," "I Never Will Marry," "Gold Watch and Chain" and 13 other songs.

The Carters continued to record but in October, 1936, the divorce between A.P. and Sara Carter became final.

In 1938, the Carter's received an offer to go to Del Rio, Texas, and do two shows a day on XERA for six months. Sara and Coy had written letters to each other during the six years they had not seen each other but family members intercepted the letters so they never reached the couple.

During a broadcast on XERA one evening, Sara said over the microphone, "I'm going to dedicate this song to Coy Bays in California." Coy heard it in California and knew he had to go to Texas and get Sara. The couple married and moved to California and Sara left her children behind in Poor Valley. She had not seen the children much, only visiting occasionally, after the breakup with A.P.

That was the end of the original Carter Family. From that point forward, the Carter Family was Mother Mabelle and her three daughters, Anita, Helen and June.

Blues on Radio

Although country music thrived on radio during the 1930s, blues did not fare as well. First, blacks--with few exceptions--were generally barred from radio broadcasts and, even when there wasn't an "official" policy against African-Americans on radio, business practices of the day excluded the exposure of music by blacks on radio.

The rate of unemployment for African-American males during The Great Depression was estimated to have been about 75 percent. That meant the demand for blues recordings virtually dried up and although the major record labels continued to record some blues during the Depression, they cut back significantly on their recordings and releases. The emphasis was on big band and pop music because that music received regular exposure on the radio and had a proven audience while blues had limited exposure, mainly on jukeboxes.

Because of the lower demand for blues records during the Depression, there were few record companies and few executives working in that industry. Because their time and attention was generally taken up with pop and big band music, those executives lost touch with the blues audience. The blues that was recorded was generally not the foundations of rhythm and blues that emerged after World War II, but the old Delta blues, which was becoming part of the past in the African-American community.

The major labels would pay a price for this neglect during the coming two decades, but it was a logical decision at the time. Blues survived in live clubs and on jukeboxes during the 1930s, unknown to most of the middle class white audience who listened to radio.

Country Music on Record

The sales of country hits declined during the 1930s; Jimmie Rodgers's first "Blue Yodel (T for Texas)" sold 500,000 and that was his best seller. During the 1920s Vernon Dalhart's "Wreck of the Old 97" b/w "The Prisoner's Song" sold over a million copies, but during the 1930s big hits like "Wildwood Flower" by the Carter Family of "Brown's Ferry Blues" by the Delmore Brothers only sold about 100,000.

Country hit songs of 1930 include "Roll Down the Line" by the Allen Brothers and "Wabash Cannonball" by the Carter Family; in 1931 hits included "White House Blues," "There"ll Come a Time," "If I Lose," "Sweet Sunny South," and "Budded Rose" by Charlie Poole and the North Carolina Ramblers.

Not all country musicians embraced the country image. Clayton McMichen was an original member of the Skillet Lickers in Atlanta, but never cared for string band music. McMichen was a master of old-time fiddling; he won the national fiddling championship eighteen times, broadcast over a number of stations, and performed in a number of shows. He toured with Jimmie Rodgers, played on his recordings and wrote his hit, "Peach Pickin' Time in Georgia." McMichen hated the hillbilly image; he was a serious musician who took his music seriously.

That was a major reason he disliked the Skillet Lickers; the band, put together by Columbia A&R man Frank Walker and comprised of Gid Tanner and Riley Puckett in addition to McMichen, perpetuated the image of southern musicians as moonshine drinking, hound dog hugging, uncouth backwoodsmen. In 1931, at the final Skillet Lickers session for Columbia, McMichen came with a new band, The Georgia Wildcats, and played a jazzy swinging fiddle on "Yum Yum Blues" and "When the Bloom Is on the Sage." However, those records did not sell as well as the Skillet Lickers string band music.

McMichen wanted hillbilly music to be more refined and so, according to author Charles Wolfe, "McMichen continued his long, lonely battle to take country music uptown, to open the music up to experimentation, to technical expertise, and to professional musicianship. The trouble was, the music didn't want to go uptown just yet." McMichen incorporated jazz and pop music into the Georgia Wildcats. That group included guitarist Slim Bryant, fiddler Carl Cotner, and guitarist Merle Travis but the "progressive" country never sold; McMichen had to stick to "swamp opera," as he called it, because "there's 500 pairs of overalls sold to every one tuxedo suit." Clayton McMichen remained frustrated with the musical limits imposed by country music at the same time he made a living in it. He continued to lean towards jazz and pop, but was too far ahead of his time and place, despite the fact that he was one of the most influential musicians and performers of his era.

The Death of Jimmie Rodgers

On May 26, 1933, Jimmie Rodgers died in New York after finishing his last recording session. On June 22, Gene Autry recorded "The Death of Jimmie Rodgers" and "The Life of Jimmie Rodgers" both written by Bob Miller; and on November 1 recorded "When Jimmie Rodgers Said Goodbye" written by Dwight Butcher and Lou Herscher and "Good Luck Old Pal (In Memory of Jimmie Rodgers)," which Autry wrote. In 1934 Little Jimmy Sizemore had a hit with "Little Jimmy's Good-bye to Jimmie Rodgers." In 1935 the first biography of a country artist appeared when Carrie Rodgers wrote, *My Husband, Jimmy Rodgers*.

Western Swing

The seeds of western swing were planted in Texas during the summer of 1930 when fiddler Bob Wills and singer Milton Brown, joined by guitarists Herman Arnspiger and Derwood Brown, performed as the Aladdin Laddies on WBAP in Fort Worth, Texas. Later that year, Burrus Mills began sponsoring a radio program with that group, who changed their name to the "Light Crust Dough Boys." W. Lee O'Daniel worked for the Burrus Mill and Elevator Company, who first performed on KFJZ before moving to 50,000 watt WBAP. In 1932 the Light Crust Dough Boys recorded for Victor at a session in Fort Worth.

In September, 1932, Milton Brown left the Light Crust Doughboys and formed the Musical Brownies, with Brown on vocals, brother Derwood on guitar, Jesse Ashlock on fiddle, Wanna Coffman on bass and Ocie Stockard playing tenor banjo. Soon, jazz pianist Fred "Papa" Calhoun joined, followed by swing fiddler Cecil Brower. The twin fiddle sound of Brower and Ashlock created the western swing sound. Another influential "sound" came when Bob Dunn brought his amplified steel guitar to Brown's group in 1934. Dunn was influenced by the Hawaiian music of Sol Hoopii and Sam Koki, who played an amplified steel or "Hawaiian" guitar. In 1932 Brown's group was on a daily radio show on KTAT.

In 1933, Bob Wills left the Light Crust Dough Boys to form his own group, the Texas Playboys. Singer Tommy Duncan, a classic western crooner, replaced Brown in the Light Crust Doughboys but in 1933 left that group to join Wills. Leon Huff replaced Duncan in the Light Crust Dough Boys while Leon McAuliff became the steel guitarist for the group.

In 1934 Bob Wills and the Texas Playboys moved to Waco, Texas, then Oklahoma City, before settling in Tulsa, Oklahoma, where they began performing on KVOO on February 9. Their daily program, at 12:30 p.m., was sponsored first by Crazy Water Crystals, then General Mills. That period--and that show--mark the beginning of the maturing of Western Swing. Wills made his band "big," adding brass and reeds, to sound more like the popular Big Bands coming over radio on the networks.

In 1934 the Blue Ridge Playboys were formed in Houston by Ted Daffan with guitarist Floyd Tillman and fiddler Leon Selph; that same year the Tune Wranglers were formed in San Antonio by fiddler Tom Dicket and guitarist Buster Coward and began playing on WOAI. The following year Adolph Hofner and his brother, Emil (guitar and steel), joined with fiddler Jimmie Revard, guitarist Curley Williams and jazz pianist Eddie Whitley to form the Oklahoma Playboys.

Western Swing was first recorded in Texas when labels came for their field recordings. On April 4, 1934, Milton Brown's group recorded for Bluebird and in 1935 Bob Wills's group began recording for the American Record Company. In 1934 the Light Crust Doughboys had hits with "Beautiful Texas" and "My Mary" and in 1935 Bill Boyd released his hit, "Under the Double Eagle" on Victor.

In 1935 Milton Brown and his Brownies had a daily radio show on WBAP in Fort Worth and also played local dances. They played a jazz akin to Cab Calloway and did songs such as "Right or Wrong" "Corrine Corrina" and "Sitting on Top of the World." That same year W. Lee O'Daniel left Burrus Mill Company and began his own flour firm, Hillbilly Flour. He started a new band after firing the Light Crust Doughboys. The old Light Crust Doughboys had a hit in 1936, "Ding Dong Daddy," sung by Dick Reinhart; they also appeared in a Gene Autry movie. That same year, Leon McAuliff recorded "Steel Guitar Rag" and Tommy Duncan sang "Right or Wrong" on recordings with the Bob Wills group; and during the summer fiddler Cliff Bruner formed his own group, the Texas Wanderers.

On April 13, 1936, Milton Brown was critically injured in an automobile accident that killed his passenger; five days later he died.

By that time the "sound" of western swing was pretty well defined; it was Texas string band music meeting Big Band jazz head on. Western swing fiddlers like Cecil Brower and Cliff Bruner were influenced by jazz violinists Joe Venuti and Stephane Grappelli and the groups were influenced by the Big Band sounds of the Dorsey Brothers, Benny Goodman, Duke Ellington and Paul Whiteman.

Old time fiddling was fading away; in 1935 the last old-time fiddling contest was held in Atlanta. Fans didn't miss them much because they could see fiddlers on live shows when radio performers toured. Times had changed; in his book *Pickin' On Peachtree*, author Wayne Daniel quoted one of the organizers of the Georgia Fiddling contest in 1935 who said, "Folks used to be satisfied with just straight fiddling...[but] The country folks ain't satisfied with the simple old fiddle tunes no more. They want this jazz band music."

Bob Wills and His Texas Playboys

Country music was influenced by the Jazz Age and the Big Band movement with the development of Western Swing and the most important pioneer in western swing was Bob Wills and His Texas Playboys.

Bob Wills was born on March 6, 1905, on a farm in Limestone County, Texas. The son of a Texas fiddler, Wills learned the fiddle when he was young and began playing for dances at ranch parties where the fiddler was required to play all night for people dancing far away from bright city lights. Among the songs he performed were "The Eighth of January," "Hell Among the Yearlings," "Sally Goodin'," "Done Gone," "Gone Indian,'" "Lost Chief," "Billy in the Low Ground," "Prosperity Special," "Stone Rag," "Waltz in D," "Put Your Little Foot" and "All Night Long." Wills was ten years old when he first performed publicly at a ranch dance; by 1929 Wills had become one of the best-known fiddlers in West Texas.

According to biographer Charles Townsend, the emphasis on music for dancing was the major reason the "country" or "folk" music Wills played was so different from music in the East that also had rural and folk roots; west of the Mississippi the country folk wanted music to dance to while east of the Mississippi the rural musicians performed a show or at a school house where people sat and listened. The lack of dancing came because of the strong religious influence in the South, which considered dancing sinful because it could lead to sex.

Wills was influenced by blues (Bessie Smith was his favorite singer) and began playing blues songs on his fiddle. The fiddle itself was going out of style with dance bands and city musicians; it was considered a rural instrument for backward whites or dirt poor blacks.

In 1929 Wills left West Texas for Fort Worth, where he worked as a barber and tried to find work as a musician. An ambitious, aggressive man, Wills had an audition at WBAP in Fort Worth and performed there as well as a musician and blackface comic on a medicine show and developed his showmanship and his wisecracking asides during performances. His first recording came in the fall of 1929 for Brunswick; on November 1 in Dallas he recorded "Wills Breakdown" and a Bessie Smith song, "Gulf Coast Blues."

During the Fall of 1930 he played on a show on WBAP sponsored by the Alladin Lamp Company; his group was known as the Alladin Laddies. The radio station, one of the most powerful in the southwest, led to bookings at Crystal Springs, a dance club where he added more members to his band.

In January, 1931 Wills began playing on a program sponsored by the Burrus Mill and Elevator Company, promoting their Light Crust Dough. W. Lee O'Daniel purchased an expensive automobile, painted it elaborately with signs and slogans about Light Crust flour and Light Crust Doughboys and installed a public address system; he also demanded the musicians spend 40 hours a week at the mill practicing for their broadcasts.

In 1932 O'Daniel added Tommy Duncan, who became the main vocalist with the band. In 1933 Wills was fired for drinking; he then went to Waco, Texas where he formed his own band, first called The Playboys on WACO. O'Daniel tried to destroy Wills' group so, to escape the clutches of O'Daniel, Wills moved to Oklahoma City, Oklahoma, where he began a show in February, 1934. O'Daniel offered the Oklahoma station the possibility of the Light Crust Doughboys if they would fire Wills, so Wills moved on to KVOO in Tulsa; O'Daniel did not fulfull his promise. In Tulsa there was an oil boom and Wills and his group were soon playing dances.

In the Spring of 1935 Wills added Leon McAuliff and his amplified steel guitar, adding a new sound to the band. He also began to add brass when announcer Everett Stover joined on trumpet. With that move, the string band started to become a brass band and "eventually Wills added enough brass and reeds to play popular dance music in a manner that rivaled the big swing bands." Wills had to play in Tulsa nearly two years before his boys were allowed to join the union because they were informed by the Tulsa local musicians union "that they 'were not musicians' and did not play what could correctly called 'music.' Only reading musicians, according tto the local, were considered musicians, and only they were allowed to join the union."

Wills continued to record and "sold more records on Brunswick's Vocalion label in 1936 than any other recording artist or group. They outsold Louis Armstrong, Bix Beiderbecke, Fats Waller, Fletcher Henderson, Gene Autry and other artists."

By 1938 Wills was recording with brass and drums, influenced heavily by the big band sound and swing music coming from the networks. That year, recording for Columbia, Wills rearranged his old song "Spanish Two Step" and named it "San Antonio Rose." By this time, the group played "four nights a week on the road and two nights at Cain's Dancing Academy in Tulsa, in addition to six radio broadcasts a week."

In 1938 they began to dress in western clothing--cowboy boots and hats--and the image of the band was distinctly western while the music, despite its big band leanings, still embraced his Texas roots. His band was the most popular in the Southwest and he began to develop a musical organization akin to the orchestras on network radio. Wills was influenced by bandleaders like Tommy Dorsey, Count Basie, Bob Crosby, and Glenn Miller and sought to emulate their organizations as well as their sound.

Wills insisted his musicians smile on stage and always presented an upbeat performance while, in his private life he was generally moody, depressed, given to heavy drinking, possessive and jealous of a string of wives.

"San Antonio Rose" was Bob Wills' biggest hit; the instrumental attracted the attention of Fred Kramer with the Irving Berlin publishing company. Because the song had not been published, Kramer wanted it; however, he insisted that lyrics be added. Wills and his band members wrote lyrics, gave them to Kramer for a $300 advance and Bing Crosby recorded it as "New San Antonio Rose." Wills also recorded the song with a big band sound and received a Gold Record for that recording in 1940. Crosby's recording, released in January, 1939, sold over a million and a half units and was a turning point in Wills' career.

Bob Wills developed his music for dancers; at the same time, he listened to network radio and heard the great dance bands playing and wanted to incorporate their sound and style. He did this with a West Texas fiddling background, with the fiddle a key part of the band.

Jukeboxes

Jukeboxes saved the recording industry during the Great Depression. Sales of recordings dropped; individuals and families purchased radios instead of phonograph players and the only consistent buyers of records were jukebox operators. One of the only public places you could hear blues were bars with jukeboxes and country music also found exposure on jukeboxes. People may not have been able to afford to buy records, but they could drop a nickel in a jukebox and hear their favorite song.

Jukeboxes were found in "joints" and "honky tonks" Those "juke joints" or barrooms became popular after Prohibition was repealed in 1933 after

President Franklin Roosevelt took office. Hillbilly recordings accounted for about a fourth of record sales during the Great Depression, and a significant number of them were sold to jukeboxes.

The roots of the jukebox go back to the coin-in-the-slot machines of the nineteenth century; however, those only played one recording. In 1906 the John Gabel Company came out with the "Gabel Automatic Entertainer," a coin-operated record player with an automatic changer system. That was a mechanical, acoustic machine that had to be wound up. By the end of the 1920s, the spread of electricity led to better jukeboxes, which were manufactured by Gabel, the Mills Novelty Company, Holcome & Hoke, the Automatic Musical Instrument Company (AMI) and Seeburg. Homer Capehart, an employee of Holcombe & Hoke, branched out on his own with the Capehart Automatic Phonograph Company.

In 1934 the Rudolph Wurlitzer Manufacturing Company introduced its first jukebox, the P-10; Rock-Ola began manufacturing jukeboxes in 1935.

Not only did jukeboxes save the music industry financially, they also provided the major exposure for blues and country music. Although a number of radio stations increasingly programmed the music (particularly country) for many people it was the jukebox that allowed them to hear non-mainstream music.

The South was the hardest hit of all areas during the Depression, and here is where most country and many blues buyers lived. Recording companies could not afford to do field recordings, so artists had to go to their facilities in New York or Chicago to record.

Hollywood and the Movies

The Hollywood movie business made a dramatic change in July, 1934. Four years earlier, in March, 1930, the Motion Picture Producers and Distributors of America pledged to abide by a Production Code, after much criticism was directed at Hollywood because of off-screen scandals and onscreen antics and innuendoes. Heading up the Motion Picture Producers and Distributors of America was Will H. Hays, the former postmaster general during the Warren Harding administration.

The Production Code was written by Catholic priest Daniel Lord and Martin Quiqley, a prominent Roman Catholic and editor of the *Motion Picture Herald*. The problem was that the Code had no effective enforcement; whenever the Code administrators made an unfavorable decision against a MPPDA member, those members appealed to the next level of executive authority. In other words, the movie producers and directors appealed to themselves; a "transit visa" was then granted for theatrical release. As a result, gangster movies and "flaming youth" movies with sexual themes were on movie screens in middle America.

Beginning in late 1933 and continuing through early 1934, the Catholic church launched a campaign against Hollywood immorality. A group called the Motion Picture Research Council published reports that linked bad behavior with bad movies. When President Franklin D. Roosevelt took office in March, 1933, he began bringing a number of businesses and industries under the scrutiny of the Federal government. One of the laws passed in 1934 was the Federal Communications Act, which said the radio airwaves should be used for the public interest, as determined by the Federal government.

At the end of 1933, the *Hollywood Reporter* published an article that stated the movie industry would have to clean up its act or else face the possibility of Federal censorship. During that period, a number of bills were proposed or introduced in Congress to regulate the movie industry with strong, bi-partisan support.

The Legion of Decency was formed in 1933 by Catholics to force Hollywood to present a more "moral" and wholesome vision on the screen. Catholic priests and bishops warned parishioners against Hollywood movies with priests sometimes standing outside a movie box office to confront parishioners wanting to buy a ticket.

All of those events--the Legion of Decency, FDR's New Deal legislation, the decline in movie attendance from the Depression--combined to force the Hollywood powers to put some teeth into the Production Code. They did this by hiring Joseph Breen to enforce the Code. The MPPDA's Board of Directors changed the Code with two alterations; they abolished the power of studio heads to reverse decisions but allowed Production Code Administration decision to be reversed by a court of appeals in New York, dominated by the bankers and financiers of the movie industry. A. P. Giannini, president of the Bank of America, sealed the deal when he announced that there would be no financing of a film without prior clearance from the Production Code Administration.

Nearly overnight, the Hollywood movie business became "wholesome." One of the first beneficiaries was Shirley Temple, a six-year old child star, who rocketed to fame in 1934. Temple sang in her films; in 1934's *Bright Eyes*, she sang "On the Good Ship Lollipop." Another beneficiary was Gene Autry, who began singing in western movies in 1935 and the following year starred in a string of "singing cowboy" movies. Both children and cowboys were considered quintessentially American and presented a moral image.

Beginning in 1934, the Hollywood musical was back; in 1935 it was in full swing as movies like *Top Hat*, starring Fred Astaire and Ginger Rogers, *Born to Dance*, a series of *Gold Diggers* movies, *Showboat* and numerous others were filmed.

The Production Code continued to be strictly enforced in Hollywood until the 1960s. Hollywood Musicals played a role in getting the United States out of the Depression and launched stars such as Bing Crosby, Fred Astaire, Mickey Rooney, Judy Garland, and Bob Hope. They also brought the songs of composers like Howard Arlen, Johnny Mercer, Rodgers and Hart, Rodgers and Hammerstein, Richard Whiting, Jimmy McHugh, the Gershwins, Jerome Kern, Cole Porter, Irving Berlin, Sammy Cahn, Nacio Brown and others to the public.

Perhaps the biggest impact on American popular music came in country music. The popularity of the singing cowboys, led by Gene Autry, then Roy Rogers and others, changed the "image" of country singers from mountaineers to cowboys. Autry became the top country music performer of the 1930s, leading to a string of hit recordings and then a network radio show in the 1940s. The songs written for the singing cowboys were essentially pop songs with western themes; this later influenced commercial mainstream country music and moved it away from its folk roots and towards the pop song format. Finally, the singing cowboys gave country music its first national, popular exposure; until this point, it was considered a regional music centered in the South. Gene Autry and the singing cowboys changed that.

The Singing Cowboys

In mid-1934 Autry and Smiley Burnette drove from Chicago to Hollywood, where they appeared as featured performers in the Ken Maynard western *In Old Santa Fe*; Autry called a square dance and sang "Down in Old Santa Fe" and "Someday in Wyoming" while Smiley sang "Mama Don't 'low No Music in Here."

In February, 1934 a 13 chapter serial, *Phantom Empire* starring Autry was released; he sang "That Silver-Haired Daddy of Mine" and a number of other songs (at least one in each chapter); the fan reaction was good so Mascot Pictures signed Autry to his first starring role in a western, *Tumbling Tumbleweeds* and the singing cowboy was born. In that movie Autry did the title song, as well as "That Silver Haired Daddy of Mine," "Ridin' Down the Canyon," and "Oh, Susanna."

It was the singing cowboy who created the first positive public image for country singers in America and the image of the music began to shift from mountaineers to cowboys. Because of the singing cowboy movies, the cowboy is the most enduring symbol of country music.

Sons of the Pioneers

When Gene Autry moved to Hollywood there was already a fertile western music scene that had been developed through live programs over the radio as well as a tradition of western songs in country music.

In 1931, Leonard Slye moved to Los Angeles from Ohio; the year before the Slye family had come to Los Angeles to visit Leonard's sister. In mid-1931 he entered an amateur program with his cousin Stanley; that led to an appearance on the "Midnight Frolic" on KMCS where Ebb Bowen invited Slye to join his group, the Rocky Mountaineers, who appeared on KGER. The instrumental group wanted a singer, so they hired Slye. Slye wanted harmonies, so he ran an advertisement in the *Los Angeles Herald* on September 30, 1931, for a "Yodeler...Tenor preferred." A number of singers answered the ad; one of them was Bob Nolan, who landed the job and the two began to rehearse. Nolan recommended a friend, Bill "Slumber" Nichols, for a third slot and the trio of Slye, Nolan and Nichols began singing on KGER in Long Beach in December, 1931.

In the summer of 1932 Nolan left the group and became a caddy at the prestigious Bel Aire Country Club; Slye ran another advertisement in the *Los Angeles Herald* for a "Harmony yodeler," which was answered by Tim Spencer, who joined the group in mid-August. The trio of Slye, Nichols and Spencer worked with the Rocky Mountaineers for a few weeks, then joined Benny Nawahi's International Cowboys, where they did personal appearances and appeared on KGER and KRKD in Los Angeles. In June, calling themselves the O-Bar-O Cowboys, the trio left for what would be a disastrous tour of the Southwest before returning to Los Angeles in September, 1933.

The trio broke up and Slye joined Jack and His Texas Outlaws. However, Slye still wanted a trio and persuaded Tim Spencer to give it another shot; those two drove out to the Bel Air Country Club and convinced Bob Nolan to try again. The Trio began rehearsing at a boardinghouse in Hollywood; within a few weeks, calling themselves The Pioneer Trio, they joined Jack and His Texas Outlaws and began appearing on KFWB on a morning show.

On a late afternoon show they performed again as the Gold Star Rangers, then played in the evening with the Jack Joy Orchestra. At the beginning of 1934, the trio of singers added an instrumentalist, fiddler Hugh Farr.

Early in 1934 they were introduced on the radio by announcer Harry Hall as "The Sons of the Pioneers." The group was upset with Hall, who told them the new name was more appropriate because they were all so young they looked more like "sons" than "pioneers." The name stuck and by March, 1934 it was official, just before their first recording session for Decca, on March 7. During that session they recorded "There's a Roundup In the Sky," and "Roving Cowboy." They recorded two more sessions that month then, on August 8, recorded "Way Out There," and Tumbling Tumbleweeds" for Decca.

"Tumbling Tumbleweeds" was written by Bob Nolan, who became one of the greatest and most influential songwriters in the history of Western music. Born in Canada, about six months after Gene Autry was born, Bob Nobles moved to Tucson, Arizona where he changed his name to "Nolan" because it sounded more "American." Nolan began to compose poems in high school in Arizona; there he wrote the poem that eventually became the song "Cool Water." After college Nolan traveled before moving to California where he joined a Chautauqua troupe and began to write songs and perform. He was working as a lifeguard when he read the advertisement in the newspaper placed by Leonard Slye for a singer who could yodel. He dropped out of the group in mid-1932 and landed a job as a golf caddy at the prestigious Bel Air Country Club. While at home in his apartment one day, he wrote "Tumbling Leaves," which later became "Tumbling Tumbleweeds." After the recording was released in 1934, the song became a huge hit.

The idea of "singing westerns" was an idea whose time had come and other movie studios quickly joined. In mid-1935 the Sons of the Pioneers were featured in their first movie appearance, *The Old Homestead* for Liberty Pictures, released in August, 1935--a few weeks before Autry's picture was released. In that picture they were known by a name they continued to use, "The Gold Star Rangers." They also appeared in *Slightly Static*, an MGM short, and *Way Up Thar* with Joan Davis, also in late 1935. They then appeared in two pictures for Columbia with cowboy star Charles Starrett as well as Autry's picture, *Tumbling Tumbleweeds*.

In addition to *Tumbling Tumbleweeds*, Gene Autry starred in three more movies in 1935: *Melody Trail*, *Sagebrush Troubadour*, and *Singing Vagabond*.

Other singing cowboys soon followed to the silver screen; first there was Dick Foran, then Tex Ritter.

In 1936 Gene Autry appeared on the silver screen in seven movies, including one named *The Singing Cowboy*. The Sons of the Pioneers were featured in four movies, and Tex Ritter made his debut as a singing cowboy on the movie screen. In a poll, Gene Autry was voted the number three favorite movie cowboy.

Roy Rogers

In mid-1937, Gene Autry walked out on Republic Studios, disgruntled over his contract. Herbert Yates at first refused to re-negotiate the contract and, instead, held auditions to develop another singing cowboy to replace him. Leonard Slye, founding member of the Sons of the Pioneers, auditioned and won the job; it was at that point that studio executives changed his name to Roy Rogers and cast him in his first starring role in *Under Western Skies* (1937). Although Autry later returned to the studio, Republic continued to use Roy Rogers and both proved popular with audiences.

The songs those singing cowboys sang were written mostly by professional songwriters, many who had moved from New York and Chicago to write for the movies. The "sound" of western music was defined by the harmonies of the Sons of the Pioneers as well as the vocals of Gene Autry and Roy Rogers, who were inspired by the first country music singing star, Jimmie Rodgers.

The Guitar on Early Country Recordings

Radio and recordings played a major role in making the guitar a popular instrument during the 1920s. Recordings of early string bands, led by the fiddle were often accompanied by a guitar, followed and in 1924 when Vernon Dalhart recorded "The Prisoner's Song" b/w "Wreck of the Old '97."

In 1927 in Bristol, Tennessee, the Carter Family, with Maybelle on guitar, Sarah on autoharp and Sarah's husband, A.P. as principal songwriter, recorded several songs for the Victor Company. Jimmie Rodgers, who accompanied himself on guitar, also recorded during those sessions and those acts became two of the most influential acts in early country music. Their recordings were helped by the invention of the microphone, which allowed the guitar to be heard as it accompanied a singer. Without the microphone, the sound of the guitar was buried underneath other instruments.

Bradley Kincaid's Houn' Dog Guitar

In 1926 Bradley Kincaid joined WLS and sang on daily programs as well as "The National Barn Dance" each Saturday night. Kincaid was born in Berea, Kentucky and received a guitar when his father traded a dog for a guitar. Kincaid sang old folk songs such as "Barbara Allen" accompanied by his guitar and became the first star of WLS. He was incredibly popular with listeners and became the first country radio star to publish a songbook, *Favorite Mountain Ballads and Old Time Songs* in 1928,

Sears owned the largest mail order business in the country; it was the nation's major retailer and sold radios, phonographs, phonographs, records, instruments, clothes and a host of other objects. Since Bradley Kincaid played a guitar, it seemed logical for Sears to market a guitar endorsed by Kincaid. In 1929 the "Bradley Kincaid Houn' Dog Guitar" was featured in the Sears catalog. The guitar was a standard-sized guitar with a solid spruce top and mahogany body and mahogany neck. The body featured a large mountain hunting scene decal (called "decalomania") on the belly. The fingerboard was ebonized hardwood with pearl dot inlays. The pin bridge was rosewood, and the ladder braced guitar was intended for steel strings."

The guitar was manufactured by Harmony, a company owned by Sears. If you ordered this guitar you also received a copy of Kincaid's songbook and a pick.

Gene Autry Roundup Guitar

Gene Autry joined WLS at the end of 1932; during that year, Sears introduced the Gene Autry Roundup Guitar, which was, essentially, the Bradley Kincaid Houn' Dog Guitar with a picture of a cowboy rounding up cattle and Autry's signature on the bottom of the guitar's body.

The guitar was a standard-sized guitar, manufactured by Harmony, and in 1935 Sears offered an "Old Santa Fe Archtop" guitar after Autry appeared in Ken Maynard's picture, *In Old Santa Fe*. There were some developments in the Gene Autry Roundup guitar, primarily increasing the size of the body. The 1935 model had a spruce top and birch body with a reddish mahogany finish. There were pearl dots on the inlays on the neck. The model lasted until 1930 when it was replaced by a larger guitar.

Guitars were popularized by the Singing Cowboys of the 1930s and 1940s who generally played a guitar on screen as they sang.

Pictures of the singing cowboys, especially Gene Autry, Roy Rogers and Tex Ritter, often show them holding a guitar and in their movies they are often shown playing the guitar as they sang. Young boys and girls watching those movies--or seeing these pictures--were often inspired to pick up a guitar and learn to play.

Gibson: The Guitar That Won the West

There has been no guitar more identified with the Singing Cowboys than the Gibson SJ-200. The roots of that relationship go back to the late 1930s and Ray Whitley.

It has long been acknowledged that Ray Whitley was the major figure in the development of the Super Jumbo 200 (SJ 200) guitar by Gibson and Eldon Whitford, a guitar historian as well as builder of guitars, said that evolved from "a relationship Ray Whitley had with Gibson through mail order catalog guitars." Those guitars were the "Ray Whitley Recording King" guitars sold in the Montgomery Ward catalogue.

Whitford also noted that "Whitley was the best musician of the singing cowboys" and "put more miles on the road than any of the others." In an article in *Vintage Guitar* magazine, Whitford and David Vinopal state that "every fall for over 20 years, Whitley was the star of Colonel W.T. Johnson's Rodeo in New York City and Boston, a role he sometimes shared with Autry and Roy Rogers." During one of his appearances at Madison Square Gardens in 1937, Whitley met Guy Hart, who worked for Gibson, and the two became friends.

Whitley had played Gibson guitars for a long time and told Hart that the company should build a flat-top guitar that was "fancy" with a bigger body to produce a louder sound with a deeper tone. Whitley also suggested a shorter neck--12-frets-to-the-body because country singers did not usually play up on the neck. According to Whitfield and Vinopal, Hart told Whitley that Gibson "would build him his dream guitar if he would be willing to help them promote it" and invited Whitley to come to Gibson's plant in Kalamazoo for a week to help with the development of this guitar.

Prior to Whitley's visit, the Gibson luthiers had experimented with a bigger bodied guitar and had built several guitars as part of their on-going experimentation to improve and enhance their models. There was also the matter of the competition. Martin had introduced the D-18 and D-28 guitars in 1934 and they had a wide waist, a 14 fret-to-the-body neck with a louder, deeper sound.

Whitley spent a week in Kalamazoo and Gibson made him a blonde, 12-fret-to-the-body neck and inlaid Whitley's name in pearl on the headstock. This was the first SJ-200 from Gibson for Whitley and he received it in

December, 1937. Later, he received a 14-fret version and another short neck, this one with a sunburst finish. Gibson also sought to make them "fancier."

The Gibson SJ-200 was soon seen in the singing cowboy movies, which created sales for Gibson. Singing cowboys who owned SJ-200s included Ray "Crash" Corrigan, Bob Baker, Jimmy Wakely, the Girls of the Golden West, and Rex Allen. Red Foley, who only appeared in one singing cowboy movie, owned a Jumbo 400 as well as a J-200. Others connected to singing cowboys who owned an SJ-200 were Merle Travis and Johnny Bond as well as country stars Eddy Arnold, Hank Thompson, Johnny Cash, Emmylou Harris and numerous others.

Gene Autry, Tex Ritter and Roy Rogers all played Martin guitars when they began and, after Whitley showed his SJ-200, Autry and Ritter switched. Roy Rogers also switched to a Gibson guitar during his 1940s movies, but it was a Super 400, an arch top guitar.

The Super 400 was introduced by Gibson in 1934; it cost almost $100 more than their popular L-5 guitar and came during the Great Depression when the Gibson factory had begun making wooden toys in order to stay in business. (The first Super 400 cost $400 with a case; the L-5 cost $305.)

Roy Rogers played a Super 400 acoustic arch top; perhaps the most famous electric Super 400 was the one played by Scotty Moore, Elvis's guitar player in the early days. Elvis himself played Scotty's Super 400 during his performance of "One Night" on his 1968 "comeback special" on NBC.

Gibson became "the guitar that won the west" by winning over western film stars. Those Gibson SJ-200s that audiences saw on the Silver Screen and in live appearances by western and country stars cemented the relationship between Gibson, western and country singers and fans. Those Gibson SJ-200s became as essential to the cowboy "look" as cowboy hats, boots, and fancy outfits.

Country Performers

Country music performers also accompanied themselves on the guitar. During the 1940s artists such as Ernest Tubb, Eddy Arnold and Red Foley were seen playing the guitar as they sang; in the 1950s artists such as Ray Price, Lefty Frizzell, Johnny Cash, Carl Smith and most other country stars played guitars when they sang. Elvis Presley the most popular performer of the 1950s started out as a country artist and the personal appearances, TV shows and movies where he was shown playing the guitar inspired numerous young men and women to pick up the guitar and learn to play.

After Elvis, sales of guitars skyrocketed and the guitar was well on its way to becoming the most popular musical instrument in America.

Blues in the 1930s

After 1930, as the Great Depression grew and spread, the recording labels reduced the number of blues recordings. In 1931 the Paramount label closed down while Columbia and Brunswick discontinued their "race" series. In 1932 Vocalion discontinued its race series; in 1934 Gennett went bankrupt and Okeh discontinued its race series. However, in 1934 Decca began a race series under J. Mayo Williams, who formerly worked for Paramount and Vocalion.

Chicago emerged as a major source of blues talent during the 1930s, primarily through Lester Melrose, who owned a record store and was a talent scout for labels who came to Chicago to record blues artists. Melrose generally published the songs those artists recorded and often kept the royalties, but he was an important source of talent as Chicago emerged as a center for blues musicians.

One of the most prolific blues recording artists found by Melrose was Big Bill Broonzy. During the 1930-34 period, Broonzy recorded for a number of labels under a variety of names. Broonzy was born in 1893 in Scott, Mississippi in a family with 21 children, 16 of whom survived. His earliest musical influences were string band music. In 1920 Broonzy moved to Chicago as a manual laborer, where he found a thriving jazz scene. Broonzy noted, "In New Orleans, they don't raise no cotton. They raise sugar cane. That's the difference between New Orleans and Mississippi blues. Only time New Orleans cats see cotton is in bales on a boat or train...They didn't play the blues in New Orleans; they played jazz. They didn't make blue notes. We push the strings; they made them clean." In 1926, Broonzy recorded his first sides for Paramount.

Important blues artists who recorded during the 1930s include Cryin' Sam Collins on Gennett; jazz guitarist Lonnie Johnson, who recorded with Duke Ellington, Louis Armstrong's Hot Five and his own Harlem Footwarmers, whose hits included "I Got the Best Jelly Roll in Town" and "Don't Wear It Out"; Robert Brown, known as Washboard Sam, whose hits included "C.C.C. Blues," "Levee Camp Blues," "Diggin' My Potatoes" and "Back Door"; Robert Johnson, called the "Shelley, Keats, and Rimbaud of the blues" only recorded 29 sides before he was killed by a jealous husband when he was only 25 or 26 years old and whose songs include "Me and the Devil Blues," "Hellhound on My Trail," "Dust My Broom," "Crossroad

Blues" and "Love in Vain"; Roosevelt Sykes, recorded under a variety of names until 1936 when he became known as "The Honey Dripper" for Decca (Honeydripper is a blues colloquialism for a virile male); Sonny Boy Williamson, harmonica bluesman who was murdered at the age of 32; and Speckled Red (Rufus Perryman), a partially blind albino who played boogie woogie piano.

During the 1930s blues musicians often cut their musical teeth in the lumber, levee, turpentine and sawmill camps of the South. Those camps were set up to harvest the South's rich crop of timber, and lumber companies set up a small "city" where workers were housed until the forests were cleared. The levee construction crews built levees, or earth barriers, to control rivers, particularly the Mississippi River. In 1927 there was a huge flood in Mississippi from that river, changing towns and boundaries and wiping out homes.

In those lumber encampments, black workers wanted entertainment and that was provided by traveling musicians, who usually played in a shack set up as a bar. The bar itself was rudimentary--generally two barrels with a board across it, hence the term "barrel house." The music the lumber workers liked was loud, raw and raucous, hence the term "barrel house" piano, which featured a driving, boogie woogie beat.

The songs often had blatant references to sex, which were toned down when the musicians played before mixed audiences or when the songs were recorded, but those lumber camps and barrel houses were proving grounds for a number of black musicians. One musician who worked those lumber and levee camps was Arthur "Big Boy" Crudup. In 1940 Crudup came to Chicago with a gospel group, The Harmonizing Four, and made his first recordings for Bluebird.

During the late 1930s the ground was laid for the recording of rhythm and blues in New York and Los Angeles when several independent record companies were formed. In Los Angeles, Exclusive and Excelsior were owned and operated by the Rene brothers, a black family from New Orleans. Otis, born in 1898, and Leon, born in 1902, were both college graduates; Otis graduated from Wilberforce with a degree in pharmacology while Leon attended Xavier and Southern in New Orleans before graduating from Wilberforce in Ohio. Around 1924 both moved to Los Angeles where Leon wrote "When It's Sleepy Time Down South" in 1931 and, later, "When the Swallows Come Back to Capistrano" in 1940. "When It's Sleepy Time Down South" was recorded by Louis Armstrong, and became his theme song.

Their first label, Exclusive, was formed out of frustration from trying to get Rene brothers songs recorded. During the 1940s they signed Herb Jeffries, Johnny Moore's Three Blazers and the Basin Street Boys.

During the late 1930s, Eli Oberstein left Victor Records and formed Variety and purchased the Paramount and Gennett catalogs. He signed the Mississippi Sheiks, who had a hit with "I'm Sitting on Top of the World," which was covered by a number of pop and country acts. A sound that became popular in the late 1930s was boogie woogie; "Roll "Em Pete" by Joe Turner and Pete Johnson was a big hit and one of the first recordings with this sound.

"From Spirituals to Swing" and John Hammond

On December 23, 1938, the "From Spirituals to Swing" concert was held at Carnegie Hall in New York. The concert was organized by John Hammond and fulfilled Hammond's lifelong ambition of "producing a concert that traced the history of American popular music from its contemporary roots as swing jazz back through its roots in the blues of the Deep South and finally to its origins in African culture."

Hammond began searching for talent during the Spring and found singer Sonny Terry, Mitchell's Christian Singers, and intended to book Robert Johnson, only to discover Johnson had died; Hammond booked "Big Bill" Broonzy instead. Others on the show were boogie-woogie pianists Albert Ammons, Meade "Lux" Lewis and Pete Johnson; blues singer Big Joe Turner, pianist and Harlem legend James P. Johnson (who wrote "The Charleston"), gospel singer Sister Rosetta Tharpe; saxophonist Sidney Bechet, and The Count Basie Orchestra.

The show was a breakthrough musically as well as socially because, in 1938, there was no club in New York City where black and white musicians performed together on stage. Black and white musicians did jam together in small, out-of-the-way clubs after hours, but no nightclub allowed a mixed band on stage.

The "From Spirituals to Swing" show was a huge success; the concert was sold out and reviews were favorable. John Hammond had just turned 28 when he produced that show.

John Hammond had loved jazz and blues since he was a child. Born to a wealthy family in New York, Hammond began collecting jazz and blues records as a teenager and made regular trips to Harlem, where he listened to jazz and blues performers.

Hammond attended an elite prep school, then Yale, but dropped out during his second year. In 1931 he traveled to England and became the American correspondent for *Melody Maker* magazine. When he returned to the United States, he purchased time at Columbia's studio in September and recorded pianist Garland Wilson. None of those sides were released, but his second session with Garland, in February, 1932, saw a record released on Okeh, a subsidiary of Columbia.

Because of his wealth, Hammond could afford to purchase studio time and pay musicians, which is how he became a producer. In December, 1932 he produced his first sessions on Fletcher Henderson's band; they recorded "Honeysuckle Rose," "Underneath the Harlem Moon" and a song that became a swing classic, "New King Porter Stomp." In addition to producing sessions, Hammond regularly wrote about jazz in *Melody Maker*, praising the musicians and the recordings.

Hammond traveled to Alabama to cover the second trial of the Scottsboro Boys, nine young black men accused or raping two white women. The young men were not represented by an attorney during their arraignment and were not allowed to communicate with family or friends. At the first trial an all white jury convicted them and sentenced them to die in the electric chair. The trial was reported by the *New York Times* and brought to the attention of the NAACP. The convictions were appealed but the Alabama Supreme Court upheld the verdicts.

In March, 1933, a second trial for the Scottsboro Boys was held in Decatur, Alabama and John Hammond went to cover it for *The Nation*. The articles he wrote of the trial, the town and the South, provided a forum for Hammond "to air his views on ignorance, intolerance, and institutional racism." Hammond and the magazine "made no attempt to hide their outrage and frustration" and his articles, "well written, sharply analytic, and clearly opinionated, helped put John Hammond on the map."

John Hammond was a dedicated integrationist who pushed for equality of the races. He saw the arts as a path towards social reform and pushed racial equality from his earliest involvement in music. He pushed Benny Goodman to record with black musicians although Goodman balked at first, fearing that he would be unable to obtain work if word spread that he had recorded with black musicians. That fear was not unfounded, and Hammond's biographer, Dunston Prial stated, "Black and white musicians regularly jammed together in clubs, speakeasies, and after-hours joints. But they rarely mixed in the studio. Many white bandleaders and musicians shied away from recording with black musicians for fear of being barred from lucrative radio work by racist producers...sponsors would pull their ads if they believed their products were being associated with black players."

Goodman finally relented and in November, 1933, recorded with black musicians on a session produced by Hammond, who had recorded pianist Teddy Wilson in October and during that fall served as producer for Billie Holiday's first record session and the last recording session for Bessie Smith. In July, 1935, Goodman and Teddy Wilson played on the Billie Holiday session that yielded "Miss Brown to You."

Hammond continued to record artists and write for *Melody Maker*. In the summer of 1934 he worked briefly with publisher and talent manager Irving Mills as associate editor of the magazine Mills published to promote his acts. While with Mills, Hammond recorded sessions with Benny Goodman, Red Norvo and Mildred Bailey. In June, 1935, Hammond became a columnist for *Down Beat* magazine and joined the NAACP, where he served on the Board with Eleanor Roosevelt, Adam Clayton Powell, Sr. and Herbert Lehman, former governor of New York.

Reporter Otis Ferguson profiled Hammond in New York's *Society Rag*, stating: "You can tell him by the crew haircut, which bobs approximately in time to the music, and also by a habit of standing with his legs crossed, and also by the fresh copies of the various trade, intellectual, and left-wing papers under his arm. Or just find the youngish chap with the crew haircut who is in the most earnest conversation with whoever is running whatever show it is, and that will be John ...[who] is either spilling over with enthusiasm (Isn't it *swell?*) or only partly concealing his disgust (It's a *crime*, it stinks).

Biographer Dunston Prial described John Hammond the producer in the studio: "Dressed casually but conservatively in tweed over a blue oxford shirt and a matching tie, he arrived at the studio each day looking more like an English professor than a record producer. Permanently tucked under one arm were at least a half-dozen newspapers and magazines. As the band tuned their instruments, Hammond would sit with one long leg crossed over the other, his face buried in *The New York Times*. When it was time to record, he would put the paper down and move into a corner of the studio where he could observe the entire band. Then he would lean one shoulder against a wall, fold his arms across his chest, and cross his legs at the knees. Motionless and wrapped around himself like that, he looked like a well-dressed barber's pole."

"Once the band was warmed up, Hammond would grow more animated, nodding his head and tapping his foot in time to the music. A particularly tasteful solo might produce a grin that left him squinting, his molars clearly visible somewhere back near his ears. 'That's mah-velous. Just mah-velous,' he would say."

In early 1938, John Hammond was hired as sales manager for Columbia's classical division; he lasted less than a month in that job but in 1939 when William Paley, head of CBS, arranged for the purchase of the American Record Corporation, which owned the Columbia label, he hired Edward Wallerstein to head the label. Paley also hired Goddard Lieberson and John Hammond as "associate recording director" and Hammond remained identified with that label for the rest of his career.

Robert Johnson

Recording labels often found tips about talent for recordings from store owners, who knew the local area and local musicians. H.C. Speir, owned a general store in Jackson, Mississippi and, around 1936, Robert Johnson contacted him about recording. Speir connected Johnson with Ernie Oertle, a salesman for the American Recording Corporation, who introduced him to Don Law, who worked in A&R. Law set up a session for Johnson in San Antonio at the Gunter Hotel on November 23, 1936. Brunswick Records, under the umbrella of ARC, set up a temporary recording studio in Room 414 where Johnson recorded 16 songs over three days.

During those three days, Johnson recorded "Come On in My Kitchen," "Kind Hearted Woman Blues," "I Believe I'll Dust My Broom" and "Cross Road Blues." He often did two takes of a song. The label first released "Terraplane Blues," which reportedly sold 5,000 copies.

Robert Johnson was born May 8, 1911, in Hazelhurst, Mississippi, to Julia Major Dodds and Noah Johnson. He lived in Memphis with Charles Dodds, Julia's husband, who changed his name to Charles Spender. When he was around eight, Johnson moved back to the Mississippi Delta around Tunica, Mississippi and rejoined his mother, who had married Dusty Willis, who was 24 years younger than her. Johnson was registered at school as Robert Spencer but, after he finished school, took his father's name.

Johnson began playing music early in life; he was adept at the harmonica and jaw harp. Johnson left the Tunica and Robinsonville area and moved to Martinsville, near where he was born. There, he perfected his guitar style, influenced by Son House, who he had met in Robinsville, and Isaiah "Ike" Zimmerman. In a short period of time, Johnson mastered the guitar "miraculously," which led to the legend that Johnson had made a pack with the Devil to play secular music, a view that Johnson apparently believed.

According to that "Devil Legend," Johnson had a burning desire to become a great musician. The Devil told Johnson to go to a cross-road near the Dockery Plantation. At midnight, the Devil (a large black man) took Johnson's guitar and tuned it, then played a few songs. When the Devil returned the guitar to Johnson, he was a master of the instrument.

The "Devil Legend" has been traced back to the story of blues musician Tommy Johnson and published in a 1971 biography of Tommy Johnson by David Evens. However, Robert Johnson was friends with Ike Zimmerman, who often played in graveyards. Robert Johnson lived with Zimmerman for about a year and Johnson reportedly joined him in graveyards as he learned to play the guitar.

In Martinville, Johnson had a child with Vergie Mae Smith, then, in May 1931, married Caletta Craft. The couple moved to Clarksdale, Mississippi, in 1943 but Caletta died in childbirth and Johnson became an itinerant musician.

Johnson traveled around the Mississippi Delta and up to Memphis. He traveled with blues musician Johnny Shines to Chicago, Texas, New York, Canada, Kentucky, Indiana and St. Louis, often staying with members of his extended family as well as various women. During that time, Johnson used at least eight different names.

In his travels, Robert Johnson often played on street corners or in front of a barbershop or restaurant for tips. When playing for money, he usually played pop standards, jazz or country songs. He was known to quickly develop a connection with an audience and provide them with what they wanted to hear.

Robert Johnson's second series of recordings was on June 19 and 20, 1937 in Dallas, Texas with Don Law overseeing the session in the Vitagraph Building at 508 Park Avenue; Brunswick had an office on the third floor. During those sessions, Johnson recorded 13 songs and during 1938, eleven records from that session were released.

In addition to the songs previously mentioned, Robert Johnson also recorded "Sweet Home Chicago," "Ramblin' On My Mind," "When You Got a Good Friend," "Phonograph Blues," "32-20 Blues," "Dead Shrimp Blues," "Last Fair Deal Gone Down," "Walkin' Blues," "Preaching Blues (Up Jumped the Devil)," "If I Had Possession Over Judgment Day," "Stones in My Passway," "I'm a Steady Rollin' Man," "From Four Till Late," "Hellhound on My Trail," "Little Queen of Spades," "Malted Milk," "Drunken Hearted Man," "Me and the Devil Blues," "Stop Breakin' Down

Blues," "Traveling Riverside Blues," "Honeymoon Blues," "Love in Vain" and "Milkcow's Calf Blues."

During those two separate recording sessions, about six months apart, Robert Johnson recorded 29 songs or a total of 41 recordings when alternate takes are included.

When John Hammond was putting together the musical lineup for his "From Spiritual to Swing" concert at Carnegie Hall in 1938, he instructed Don Law to find Robert Johnson. That's when it was discovered that Johnson had died.

The death of Robert Johnson, like most of the details about his life, are difficult if not impossible to prove conclusively. It is known that he died on August 16, 1938, near Greenwood, Mississippi at the age of 27. Historians and researchers have uncovered stories from those who knew him that paint a picture of an itinerant musician who had an eye for the ladies. The story that seems to be most accurate is that while Johnson was playing at a country dance he was flirting with a married woman. She gave him a bottle of whiskey poisoned by her husband and Johnson took a drink and then another. He soon became ill and was helped back to his room where, after three days of intense pain, he died.

Robert Johnson was a known, but not well-known, musician amongst other musicians in the Delta. He was certainly not a "star" during his time or even 20 years after he died. He was barely known among blues fans until 1961 when Columbia Records released an album, *King of the Delta Blues Singers*. British blues fans and musicians discovered Johnson when that album was released. Brian Jones, founder of the Rolling Stones, introduced Keith Richards and Mick Jagger to Johnson through that album. The Rolling Stones and other British musicians, such as Eric Clapton and Alexis Korner performed and recorded some of Johnson's songs. Americans learned about Robert Johnson from those and other British musicians.

Bob Dylan learned about Robert Johnson when John Hammond, who signed Dylan to Columbia, gave him the album.

It took about 25 years after his death for Robert Johnson to become known and accepted as one of the greatest bluesmen of all time.

Big Bill Broonzy

The addition of Big Bill Broonzy to the line-up of the "From Spirituals to Swing" concert brought one of the most accomplished and best known bluesman to the New York stage.

Big Bill Broonzy was born Lee Conley Bradley on June 26, 1903 (although that date, like many other dates connected to early blues musicians, is disputed—Broonzy claimed he was born in 1893) in Scott, Mississippi (although researchers have claimed he was born in Pine Bluff, Arkansas). He grew up in Pine Bluff where, at the age of ten, he made a fiddle from a cigar box and learned to play from his uncle, Jerry Belcher. He performed with Louis Carter, who played a handmade guitar, at local social and church functions, performing for both white and black audiences.

Broonzy married when he was in his late teens and became a sharecropper and a preacher. His crop and livestock were wiped out by a drought in 1916 and in 1917 he was drafted into the Army during World War I and served two years in Europe. He returned to Pine Bluff after his discharge but a racial confrontation with a white man led him to move to Little Rock and then, in 1920, to Chicago.

Bill Bill Broonzy was a fiddler when he arrived in Chicago but switched to the guitar, taught by Papa Charlie Jackson, a veteran performer on minstrel and medicine shows. In order to survive as a musician, Broonzy worked odd jobs, including Pullman porter, cook, foundry worker and janitor. He performed regularly at rent parties, held in apartments where an entry fee was charged in order to pay the rent. He wrote a solo guitar piece, "Saturday Night Rub," which became one of his signature tunes.

Papa Charlie Jackson, who recorded for Paramount, introduced Broonzy to J. Mayo Williams with Paramount. Broonzy, with singer John Thomas on vocals, was turned down on his first audition but persisted and several months later recorded "Big Bill's Blues" b/w "House Rent Stomp," credited to "Big Bill and Thomps," which was released in 1927. Sales were disappointing.

In 1930 he made his first record, "Station Blues," as Big Bill Broonzy. Lester Melrose, who served as a talent scout for various labels, recorded "Alabama Scratch" by the Harum Scarums, a trio of Broonzy, Georgia Tom and Mozelle Alderson, which was released on Paramount. In 1931 Broonzy recorded several sides as Big Bill Johnson. In March, 1932 Broonzy went to New York and recorded for the American Record Corporation and those records sold better. In Chicago, Broonzy worked regularly in clubs on the South Side and toured with Memphis Minnie

Broonzy began recording for Bluebird Records, a subsidiary of RCA Victor, with pianist Bob "Black Bob" Call in 1934. He joined with pianist Joshua Altheimer in 1937 and they recorded with a small group that included drums (called "traps"), double bass and horns or harmonica. In March, 1938, he began recording for Vocalion as he reputation grew. His appearances at the "From Spirituals to Swing" concerts at Carnegie Hall in 1938 and 1939 led to him having a role in *Swingin' the Dream*, a jazz adaptation of Shakespeare's *Midsummer Night's Dream* which featured Louis Armstrong, Maxine Sullivan and the Benny Goodman sextet.

Broonzy performed on the recordings of other musicians (including those by his half-brother, Washboard Sam) and became a popular songwriter. He was a versatile musician and during the 1940s his repertoire included ragtime, hokum blues, country blues, urban blues, folk songs and spirituals. After World War II, his recordings reflected the emergence of rhythm and blues with electric guitars as blues performers moved away from the traditional acoustic blues.

Charlie Christian

One of John Hammond's greatest achievements during the 1930s was pairing guitarist Charlie Christian with Benny Goodman. Christian, born 1916 in Bonham, Texas, was living in Oklahoma City when Hammond heard him play in a club. The electric guitar was heard primarily in western swing groups, and Christian heard western swing in Oklahoma, but the electric guitar was not popular with guitarists, who generally thought it was a gimmick.

Hammond told Benny Goodman about Christian and the bandleader reluctantly agreed to audition the guitarist in Los Angeles, but apparently had forgotten when the 23-year old Christian arrived at the L.A. studio where Goodman was recording his first sides for Columbia Records. Goodman was reportedly rude to Christian and angry at Hammond for the interruption. After a quick audition, where Christian played "Tea for Two," without plugging in his guitar, Goodman dismissed him but Hammond did not give up.

Goodman and his band played later that evening at the Victor Hugo nightclub. Hammond and an accomplice set Christian's amplifier on stage and set a chair on stage for Christian while Goodman was meeting members of the crowd. When Goodman mounted the stage for the quintet segment, he saw Fletcher Henderson on piano, Lionel Hampton on vibraharp, Artie Bernstein on bass, Nick Fatool on drums—and Charlie Christian with his electric guitar plugged in. Goodman gave Hammond a deadly stare and then decided to play a complicated song, "Rose Room," to extract his revenge on Hammond and embarrass Christian.

When they kicked off the song, "Christian played as if he'd been waiting for years for Goodman to call the song. Astounding everyone on the bandstand, Christian reeled off one sparkling lead after another. By some accounts, his solo lasted for more than twenty choruses as Goodman and the other musicians listened and followed him rapturously." The quintet became a sextet and Charlie Christian played in Benny Goodman's big band and small group for the remaining three years of his life.

Martin Block and Make-Believe Ballroom

On February 3, 1935, "Make Believe Ballroom" hosted by disc jockey and host Martin Block, began broadcasting on WNEW in New York. The show was a local show that received national attention. Bock, who got the idea of a record show in Los Angeles "Make Believe ballroom" hosted by Al Jarvis, convinced listeners that he hosted the top bands in his studio by playing recordings.

He later syndicated the show and became the first nationally known disc jockey.

Your Hit Parade

On April 20, 1935, "Your Hit Parade" began broadcasting on Saturday nights on NBC sponsored by Lucky Strike cigarettes. The hour long show became two shows in March, 1936, with one show on Saturdays on CBS and the other a 30 minute show on Wednesdays on NBC. The first announcer was Ben Grauer on NBC; Andre Baruch was the initial announced for CBS.

There were four vocalists on the show, two males and two females, who sang the top ten songs of the week, with vocalists alternating who sang what. The first orchestra was led by Lennie Hayton and then there were visiting orchestras.

The top ten songs on the first broadcast were 1. "Soon," 2. "Lullaby of Broadway," 3. "Lovely to Look At," "4. "I Won't Dance," 5. "When I Grow Too Old to Dream," 6. "Isle of Capri," 7. "Every Day," 8. "I Was Lucky," 9. "Everything's Been Done Before," and "10. "Easy to Remember."

The show was popular with listeners. During the 1930s the vocalists were Loretta Lee, Willie Morris, Gogo DeLys, Kay Thompson, Charles Carlisle, Stuart Allen, Margaret McCrea, Edith Dick, Buddy Clark, Len Stokes, Bob Simmons, Kay Lorraine, Patricia Norman, Fredda Gibson (Georgia Gibbs), Buddy Clark, Lanny Ross, Bea Wain, Barry Wood and "Wee" Bonnie Baker.

Tabulations for the top ten of the week were compiled in the offices of Lord and Thomas, which was the agency representing the American

Tobacco Company. Later, the company switched its agency to Batten, Barton, Durstine and Osborne. The agency based their ratings on radio requests, sheet music sales, dance-hall favorites and jukebox tabulations, which were done in secret. An announcer introduced each show, stating "Once again the voice of the people has spoken. You've told us by your purchases of sheet music and records, by your requests to orchestra leaders in the places you've danced, by the tunes you listen to on your favorite radio programs" which songs were the most popular that week.

The theme songs for the show were "Happy Days Are Here Again" during the 1930s and then "Lucky Day."

The show was originally broadcast from New York but moved to Hollywood in 1947. The show moved over to television in 1950 and did not ended until April 24, 1959, a period of 24 years.

CBS Buys Columbia Records and ARC

On January 4, 1938, the Columbia Broadcasting System, under William Paley, bought the American Record Company for $700,000; .ARC had paid $70,000 for it. CBS wanted a record company, like their rival NBC, which had RCA Victor Records, in order to have access to musical talent. They also wanted the Columbia name and ARC had three prime subsidiaries, the Columbia Phonograph Company, Brunswick Record Corp and Master Records. Included in the deal was Okeh, as well as the Brunswick and Vocalion catalogs, although the material recorded before 1932 by Brunswick and Vocalion was not included. Decca later acquired the pre-1932 Brunswick material, as well as the Brunswick name. CBS retired the ARC labels and activated the Columbia name, which became the flagship label. Art Satherley became A&R head for country and race music for Columbia.

Columbia continued to lease recordings to Sears to be sold through their catalog. The purchase made CBS a major player in the recording industry overnight.

The label was headed by Ted Wallerstein, who was described as "cordial and somewhat aloof" and someone who "didn't publicize his own accomplishments" but was key to the success of the record label.

Edward "Ted" Wallerstein was born in Kansas City, Missouri in 1891 and attended Haverford College where he majored in economics and was the quarterback on their football team. During World War I, Wallerstein was in the army but did not serve overseas. By the time he was 30, he was managing the east coast division of Brunswick, where he was promoted to sales manager before he was hired by RCA Victor and then Columbia.

In April, 1939, Columbia, bought the East Fifty-second Street Corporation, which served as one of the label's primary recording studios. Brunswick had been headquartered at a seven story building on 799 Seventh Avenue at 52nd Street and that became the offices for Columbia Records.

The Grand Ole Opry and Nashville

On January 7, 1939 R. J. Reynolds, sponsored a portion of the Grand Ole Opry promoting their product, Prince Albert tobacco. Prince Albert was a loose tobacco sold in a can; it could be used for pipes or to "roll-your-own" with cigarette papers. It was an inexpensive brand aimed for the blue collar class. The show was presided over by Judge Hay, who ran each show as talent organizer, master of ceremonies, and power to be reckoned with.

George Dewey Hay was one of those colorful, charismatic characters on which the history of country music is built. Known by the sobriquet "The Solemn Ole Judge," he was the major architect of the program that came to be known as the Grand Ole Opry. Hay played the major role in choosing the original talent and running the show and wanted the performers to "keep it close to the ground," which meant sticking with the rural hillbilly or mountain folk tunes. In 1925 he began the show as the "WSM Barn Dance" and in 1927 gave it the name "Grand Ole Opry."

Born in Attica, Indiana, on November 9, 1895, Hay was first exposed to country music during World War I while he was a newspaperman working for the *Commercial Appeal* in Memphis, Tennessee. Hay had gone to Mammoth Spring, Arkansas, to cover the funeral of a soldier who died in the War; after the funeral he attended a "hoedown" or "house dance" at a small cabin where he witnessed people dancing to a country fiddler. It was an experience he never forgot.

The *Commercial Appeal* in Memphis owned a new radio station, WMC, and Hay switched from being a newspaper reporter to a radio announcer. With a natural flair for show business, Hay began to blow on a steam whistle, which he named "Hushpuckena," and called himself "The Solemn Old Judge," which was also the name of the newspaper column he'd written. In 1924 he took the chief announcing job in Chicago at WLS and served as the announcer for a new country music program, "The National Barn Dance."

On October 5, 1925 the National Life and Accident Insurance Company's new radio station WSM (for "We Shield Millions") went on the air in Nashville and Judge Hay, because he was a prominent air personality, attended the opening festivities. The National Life executives offered Hay the position of Program Director for WSM and he took it; he began work the first week of November.

Prior to Hay coming to the Nashville radio station there were several appearances by country performers; Dr. Humphrey Bate, a physician from nearby Sumner Country, appeared with his string band as did Uncle Dave Macon, a lively banjo player and performer who'd appeared on the vaudeville circuit. The station's programming was often a hodgepodge of performers as radio was in its experimental stage, trying to determine who the audience was and what they wanted.

Hay instituted a regular Saturday night program of country music with fiddler Uncle Jimmy Thompson on December 26, 1925 after Thompson spent about a month performing a Saturday night program to enthusiastic listener response. Thompson's first Saturday evening performance was November 28, 1925, so that is the date given as the "birth" of the Grand Ole Opry, although the original name of the program that began on December 26 was "The WSM Barn Dance." In 1927, Hay told his audience, who had just heard the Metropolitan Opera, that while they had been listening to "grand opera," now they were going to hear "The Grand Ole Opry." And thus the name was born.

Hay organized groups such as the Fruit Jar Drinkers and the Gully Jumpers, combined or re-named existing groups, and insisted they carry the image of mountaineers, an image of country people perpetuated by vaudeville. The earliest Opry performers generally wore suits and ties; the first picture of the Opry cast shows them attired, but after that Hay insisted the Opry performers wear bib overalls and sit amidst bales of hay in order to present a "country" image. The following photographs taken of Opry performers show them to be dressed as hayseeds as the Opry actively promoted the idea that this was a rural-based show comprised of just plain country folks. Even Dr. Humphrey Bate, a physician who had graduated from Vanderbilt, changed the name of his group to "The Possum Hunters" and traded his suit and tie for the hillbilly look.

Hay was the decision maker for programming on WSM beginning at the end of 1925 but those responsibilities began to be transferred to Harry Stone, who the station hired as Assistant to Hay in 1928. Stone was born in Jacksonville, Florida and moved with his family to Savannah, Georgia and then Hamlet, North Carolina, where his father owned a Coca Cola plant for five years. The Stone family then moved to Nashville where he graduated from Hume-Fogg High School. During World War I he enlisted in the Army and was stationed at the Vanderbilt campus in Nashville for special training.

Stone became fascinated with radio in 1921 and began to work with a crystal set. In 1922 Stone began a radio station in Nashville and continued to work with radio until he was hired by WSM as an announcer as well as Assistant Program Director. In 1930 he was promoted to Program Director and became George Hay's boss. In 1932 Stone was named General Manager for the station but Hay retained a good amount of power--he was the host of the Grand Ole Opry and in charge of that program--although decisions about the talent hired for the Opry was generally decided by a group consisting of Hay, Harry Stone and Harry's brother, David Stone, also an announcer on WSM.

The "Prince Albert" segment of the Opry, begun at the beginning of 1939, continued for nine months, during which time the R. J. Reynolds executives, pleased at the success of the Opry promoting their tobacco, decided to sponsor a 30 minute show on the NBC "Red" network. That first network show for the Opry was at 9:30 p.m. Central Time on October 14, 1939.

It was a relatively small start--there were only twenty-six stations across the South that broadcast the Opry that evening. The NBC "Red" network was a secondary network for them. The major network was the "blue" one; later the "Red" network became ABC.

Although the first show was a bit rough and ragged, by the next week WSM executives Jack Stapp and Harry Stone assembled the cast of the "Prince Albert" segment on Saturday morning at the WSM Studios on Seventh Avenue for a rehearsal to make sure the program began and ended on the minute. The Grand Ole Opry seemed perfect for the audience that R.J. Reynolds wanted. In fact, the "Prince Albert" folks sponsored the Opry for 21 years--until 1960.

There were major changes at WSM in 1939, signaled by the Opry's connection to a national advertiser and network radio, that led to a decrease in the power of Judge Hay and an increase in the powers of Jack Stapp and Harry Stone. Hay was described as "too much in the clouds" to be an effective corporate executive, so first Stone, then Stapp, whose personalities made them effective in corporate offices, assumed more power. Further, the advertising agency--and sponsor--wanted a "star" to sell their product--not Judge Hay. Although Hay had a prominent role at the beginning of the "Prince Albert" show, Roy Acuff began to emerge as the dominant star. Another casualty was Uncle Dave Macon, a vibrant and colorful performer who was not comfortable with a microphone.

Jack Stapp was hired by WSM in 1939; they lured him away from CBS in New York to be Program Manager. Stapp was born in Nashville on December 8, 1912, but moved with his family to Atlanta in 1921 when he was nine; at 16 he obtained his first job in radio at the Weinkopf Hotel, programming a station that was piped into the hotel's rooms. Later, he went to Georgia Tech and became involved with the campus radio station, WGST, which became a commercial station while Stapp moved up and eventually became program manager. There he met Bert Parks and hired him as an announcer; the two remained lifelong friends and their friendship led to both going to New York to join CBS.

Stapp and Parks were both fascinated with network radio. Parks was the first to go to CBS in New York and audition; he came back to Atlanta and a few weeks later received notice he'd been hired. Stapp then immediately went to CBS in New York and applied for a job in production; he too received a wire a few weeks after he returned to Atlanta which told him he'd been hired.

Jack Stapp was successful at CBS in New York and rose through the ranks to become a top executive while Parks became a well known celebrity, but two things happened which caused Stapp to look south. First, Bert Parks was sent by CBS to Hollywood, so Stapp no longer had a roommate. Next, WSM executive Jack Harris came to New York and was given a tour at CBS; when he reached the studio where Stapp was rehearsing a show Stapp stopped the rehearsal and introduced Harris (whom he had never met) to the cast and crew and extolled his station, WSM. Although WSM was affiliated with NBC, Harris noted that Stapp and CBS had given him better treatment when he visited and he never forgot that. When WSM needed a program manager, Jack Harris called Stapp and offered him the job.

Jack Stapp welcomed the chance to return to Nashville. Before he left, he called on Phil Carlin, the production manager of NBC who had been Stapp's friendly competitor. Stapp wanted to stay connected to the networks and since NBC was WSM's network, he told Carlin he'd like to provide programming for the network from WSM in Nashville. Carlin was interested so he and Stapp agreed to stay in touch.

Hiring Stapp led to the development of live radio shows like "Sunday Down South," "Hospitality Time," "Mr. Smith Goes to Town," "Riverboat Rebels," and a children's program "Wormwood Forest," for the NBC network. The Opry was only part of the network connection to NBC at the beginning--although it was a network connection that put WSM in prime time on Saturday night.

The "Prince Albert Show" made WSM a major player in country music. Although WSM was a clear channel 50,000 watt station that reached most of the United States (and transcriptions were available for the West Coast) the top "Barn Dance" before World War II was "The National Barn Dance" on WLS in Chicago, which was a network regular before the Grand Ole Opry achieved that distinction.

During the period of the early to mid-1930s, the dominant star of the Opry was Uncle Dave Macon, a colorful character and superb entertainer in the vaudeville tradition. The rest of the Opry cast was a mixture of string bands and other "traditional" or "folk" musicians who had regular jobs during the week but played weekends on the Opry as well as acts with smooth, pop-type harmonies like the Vagabonds. Although the "hillbilly" entertainers formed the core of the Opry, it was essentially a variety show that incorporated musical styles that ranged from mountain music and cornball comedy to pop-type citified acts.

Several important things happened with the Opry because of their network connection. First, the Opry and WSM became nationally known for a country music show; next, they attracted national advertisers--and advertising agencies—that played a major role in future national exposure. Finally, they began to move away from the original idea of the Opry show as the major attraction to a star system where an act was promoted over the others. It had been the show that was central and artists were interchangeable; after this, the star became the central figure, although WSM and Opry executives continued to try and balance the idea that the Grand Ole Opry itself was essential and that's what people wanted to see and hear versus the idea that people paid for tickets in order to see and hear a particular star. The development of stars shifted the balance of power at the Opry hierarchy as the Opry progressed through the 1940s. One of the first casualties of the change was Judge Hay, who had to give way to Roy Acuff announcing the Prince Albert portion due to the demands of the advertising agency.

Judge Hay suffered from depression and occasionally left the station for periods of time; those absences, and Hay's inability to blend into the corporate mold in the corridors at National Life and Accident, the insurance company that owned the Grand Ole Opry, led to Hay's power being eroded and, finally, stripped away. Although George D. Hay lived until 1968, he moved to Baltimore in 1950 and came back to the Opry only for special performances, where he was introduced and recognized. He was certainly honored and the Opry never denied Hay's importance during the early years, but corporate politics had made Hay a figure for public consumption, not for the corridors of power.

The connection with a major advertising agency shifted the balance of power away from the WSM executives in Nashville to New York ad agency executives who approved the talent and wrote the shows. Jack Stapp was in charge of rehearsing the "Prince Albert Show" every Saturday morning for the evening performance, making sure it started and finished on time. Both Stapp and the Esty executives realized there had to be some latitude with the live show--hence the idea that nobody could "control" the Opry and that it had to stay loose and unstructured--but the fact was that while there was some amount of ad libbing and a relaxation of the practice that everything on the network had to be timed to the second, the "Prince Albert Show" was highly structured and controlled by the ad agency, who paid for the network exposure.

Nashville Begins to Emerge As a Music Center

The network connection for the Grand Ole Opry was important to musicians, and that played a major role in establishing Nashville as a major recording center after World War II.

The musicians union was connected to the AFL-CIO and each local office had control over who got in and who did not. Many union offices did not want country or blues musicians in their union; some even established a rule, enforced by a test, that you had to be able to read and write music in order to become a union member. Union officers did not want unemployed musicians in the union, so country musicians were regularly discouraged, but if an act was employed by a radio station then the union wanted them in; the reason was simple: the union collected dues from those musicians, which supported the union.

The union had an agreement with the networks that all musicians who appeared on network shows had to be union musicians. This meant that an act employed on the Grand Ole Opry, or other network shows, had to be in the union. When the major recording labels came to Nashville after World War II to record--and those labels also had agreements that all musicians on a recording had to be union members--there was no problem finding country musicians who were union members. The breakthrough came when Pee Wee King and the Golden West Cowboys joined the Opry in 1937; the group members insisted they be allowed to join the union and Nashville union head George Cooper agreed.

That was an important hurdle to overcome in order for Nashville to become a major recording center for country music, and that hurdle was surmounted in 1939 when the Opry first went over the network.

Having said that, due credit must also be given to George Cooper, who became President of Nashville's Musicians Union (Local No. 257) in 1937. Cooper liked the country musicians and welcomed them into the union; he had the vision to see a union not limited to big band musicians. Because of Cooper's open door policy with musicians, and his respect for country music musicians who were talented but musically illiterate, Nashville grew as a recording center.

Black Gospel During the 1930s

During the 1930s there was a widening gap between mainline churches and the Holiness/Pentecostal denominations that were creating a new style, music, language, and expression in their services. The Holiness/Pentecostals were more interested in personal salvation--"heaven or hell" was their rallying cry--than in assimilation. Their services were filled with emotional ecstasy, members gave dramatic testimonies, clapped their hands, stomped their feet, sang forcefully and made music with drums, tambourines, guitars, pianos or any other instruments they had. The music was loud, rhythmic and jubilant, and a song, accompanied by a "shouting session," could last half an hour or more. Women fainted and men jumped during those services; it was not uncommon for someone to be "slain in the spirit"--or "knocked out cold" for God--or for someone to dance in the aisle, oblivious to everything around them.

The reserved sense of decorum, the withholding of emotion in order to present a dignified appearance that was part of mainline services was ejected from the Pentecostal service. Stoic demeanor was replaced by an emotional release that proclaimed joy, strength, and jubilation.

In 1927 Sallie Martin moved to Chicago from Pittfield, Georgia; she worked as a domestic and joined Pilgrim Baptist, Thomas Dorsey's church, where Dorsey taught her music by ear. That same year, Theodore Frye moved from Fayette, Mississippi to Chicago and joined Dorsey's church. Frye was known as a singer who could "move a house"--get an audience emotionally involved in his song--and he influenced Dorsey, who played piano for him.

Mahalia Jackson was born in 1911 and moved to Chicago in 1927 after quitting school and began singing with the Greater Salem Baptist Church choir, often doing the lead vocal. Jackson supported herself as a domestic, doing laundry and serving as a maid. She joined the Johnson Gospel Singers, organized by Robert Johnson, son of the pastor of the church that she attended. Along with Robert's brothers, Prince and Wilbur, and Louise Barry Lemon, the five-member group became professional, earning their living with gospel music. According to gospel historian Tony Heilbut, their style was "advanced and free" and Johnson played a "distinctive boogie-woogie piano geared to the Dorsey bounce." They performed a series of plays Robert wrote, with Mahalia and Robert singing lead in those church dramas. During the early 1930s, the group played a number of local churches, but by the end of the decade the group had split and each member was singing solo.

Thomas Dorsey first heard Mahalia sing around 1928, during the time she was with Johnson's group. The group was thrown out of one church by a pastor who told them, "Get that twisting and jazz out of the church." Mahalia was a "shouter" and, according to Dorsey, she originally approached him wanting him to be her vocal coach. She also wanted to sing some of Dorsey's songs. Dorsey spent about two months teaching her his songs and trained her to sing them; he also worked on her timing and performance.

One of the keys to Dorsey's success was finding collaborators, and he found his best in Sallie Martin, Roberta Martin (no relation) and Mahalia Jackson. In 1932 Dorsey organized a gospel choir at the Pilgrim Baptist Church in Chicago; Roberta Martin was his first choir director and Sallie Martin was a principal soloist who also became a business partner. In 1932 Sallie Martin organized Dorsey's publishing business and made it profitable; until that time, Dorsey was a disorganized businessman who kept few records. Mahalia Jackson sang at Dorsey's church when she wasn't on the road performing concerts.

Thomas Dorsey toured throughout America between 1932 and 1944, performing concerts of the new gospel music he called "Evenings with Dorsey." The singers included Sallie Martin, Mahalia Jackson, Roberta Martin, Theodore Frye and others he had trained. Admission was nominal and sheet music was sold at the concerts for a nickel a song. It proved to be an effective way to build a publishing company as well as promote his songs, because he left copies at churches for others to perform wherever he went. In many ways, that knack for self-promotion was as great a gift as the songs themselves.

A key to the development of Thomas Dorsey as the "Father of Black Gospel" was his formation, in 1933, of the National Convention of Gospel

Choirs and Choruses. With several associates, Dorsey held conventions in various cities, attracting choirs and soloists he instructed. They also learned his songs. The National Baptist Convention was another key for Dorsey; that annual convention drew thousands of black Baptists from all over the country. In 1935 his song "Take My Hand, Precious Lord" was sung four times; it was the first step toward the song becoming a gospel standard. Another Dorsey song, "Peace in the Valley," also became a gospel standard.

Songs Dorsey wrote include "I Surely Know There's Been a Change in Me," "It's My Desire" (popularized by Guy Lombardo), "When I've Done the Best I Can," "How Many Times," "I'm Gonna Live the Life I Sing About in My Song," "Singing in My Soul," "Life Can Be Beautiful," and "The Lord Will Make a Way."

Throughout the 1930s, Mahalia Jackson sang at Dorsey's church; Dorsey accepted her as a great singer and gave her a "gospel home" whenever she was in Chicago. Throughout her career, a number of people wanted Mahalia to use her rich and powerful vocal talents to sing music other than gospel. The first of those was her first husband, Isaac Hackenhull, who she married in 1936. Hackenhull wanted her to sing classic pop songs and jazz and Mahalia made some attempts; however, the church was embedded in her too deeply. Wracked by guilt, she abandoned that music after a few attempts and returned to gospel, where she was clearly comfortable musically, spiritually, and emotionally.

Always a good businesswoman, Mahalia opened a beauty salon and then a florist shop, and both succeeded for a short time. Like a number of other gospel pioneers who survived in the field, it was her business acumen that was as much a key to her success as her talent. She was not the only one--Thomas Dorsey, Sallie Martin, and Sam Cooke also made smart business moves which assured them successful musical careers throughout their lifetimes.

Mahalia's first recording was "God's Gonna Separate the Wheat from the Tares" b/w "Keep Me Every Day" in 1937. The first song was one Mahalia had adapted from the wakes she had attended as a child in New Orleans, and the second an old Baptist hymn. That first record brought her national recognition and made her name equal to that of other great soloists in Chicago during that time like Willie Mae Ford Smith, Sallie Martin, Madame Lula Mae Hurst, Mary Johnson Davies, Roberta Martin and Louise Lemon. It was a rich time for female soloists and although Mahalia began as just one of a number, her strong southern influence, which manifested itself in the moaning, growling, strutting, and skipping stage performances, soon caused her talent to be in front of all the rest.

A number of black gospel quartets—the forerunners to the black quartets in Rhythm and Blues and Motown--were formed during the 1930s. The Dixie Hummingbirds were formed in Greenville, South Carolina by James Davis. The Soul Stirrers were formed in Trinity, Texas in 1934; bass singer Jesse Farley joined in 1935. From the beginning, the Soul Stirrers stood apart from most other quartets who sang spirituals and jubilee songs by singing newer "gospel" or original compositions. They were innovative in their use of lead singers, employing two and bringing the lead vocalist out front. Rebert Harris, their first lead singer, virtually revolutionized the gospel quartet tradition. Among Harris's innovations were the techniques of ad-libbing within a song and singing delayed time, off the regular meter, from the rest of the key lyrics. The group was among the first traveling quartets who were full-time performers and their early success with concerts caused many other quartets to adapt the newer "gospel" songs instead of the more traditional spiritual and jubilee songs.

Another influential performer was Sister Rosetta Tharpe. Born Rosetta Nubin in Cotton Plant, Arkansas, she was the daughter of a mother who traveled from church to church as a "missionary" (women could not be evangelists or preachers), and "Little Rosetta Nubin," the singing and guitar playing miracle" was a child prodigy. She was unique because she played the guitar instead of the piano; she and her mother joined evangelist P.W. McGhee and settled in Chicago during the 1920s, then moved to New York and settled in Harlem in 1934. Rosetta married Wilbur Tharpe and, though the marriage did not last, she kept his name throughout her life.

In 1937 the Golden Gate Quartet began recording for Victor. Inspired by the Mills Brothers, with their smooth vocal sound, the group did "Jonah" on that first session. On December 23, 1938, when John Hammond presented his first "From Spirituals to Swing" concert at Carnegie Hall, included in that concert were the Golden Gate Quartet, the Mitchell Christian Singers and Sister Rosetta Tharpe. Although numerous jazz historians have cited that event as pivotal to demonstrating the importance of African Americans in jazz, it was equally important for black gospel, showcasing that music to an audience who had never heard it, or had heard very little of it.

Tharpe began recording for Decca in October 1938 but the label would not allow her to sing with just her guitar. Instead, they put her with the

Lucky Millinder jazz orchestra and she did "Rock Me," "That's All," "My Man and I" and "Lonesome Road."

Although black gospel singers traveled during the 1930s and 1940s, most disliked to do so. In the South there were segregated restaurants, hotels and businesses. Most black-owned restaurants did not open before 6 p.m. or so because the owner generally had a day job. The groups could always find a meal and a place to stay in someone's home, and the church groups could count on a collection from the congregation to help them but the quartets were stranded if the promoter did not pay; they generally survived from concert to concert.

The 1930s were a difficult time in the United States, especially for blacks, whose unemployment rates for men reached 75 percent in many areas. Because there was less money to buy recordings, fewer recordings were produced and there was very little music from blacks on radio, which was dominated by Big Bands. When Prohibition ended in 1933, "blues" could be heard on jukeboxes in dives; but that was no place for black gospel. The saving grace was the church, and there black gospel grew and developed, aided by the Pentecostal/Holiness movement. That is where black gospel found the "voice" which would define the music throughout the rest of the 20th century.

Black gospel has a distinctive, identifiable sound. Thomas Dorsey was a leader in introducing jazz rhythms and blues singing in the church, adding gospel lyrics to the blues tradition. According to Mahalia Jackson, "The basic thing is soul feeling ... gospel music ... is soul music. When they talk about jazz, the Holiness people had it before it came in. They would take a song like 'What a Friend We Have in Jesus' and give it personal expression. They gave it a joyful expression ... expressed by things they couldn't speak. Some called it gospel music for years but it did not come into its own until way late ... when the Holiness people helped to emphasize the beat."

The emotional impact of gospel came from the Holiness Church and from Southern singers, who moved North. There, they found the opportunity to connect with a large, African-American community. Although the mainstream churches in a community originally rejected the Holiness sound, in time they embraced it as "black gospel," which developed its own unique sound, rooted in the black experience in the United States that came from a deep-felt emotionalism that was anchored in a certain hopelessness about their earthly life balanced by a shining hopefulness about the Heavenly life to come.

Southern Gospel Music During the Depression

During the 1930s the Stamps-Baxter Company in Dallas emerged as the top shaped-note publisher, eclipsing the James D. Vaughan Company. Those were not the only companies publishing shaped-note books; others included the Teachers' Music Publishing Company in Hudson, North Carolina, the Morris-Henson Company in Atlanta, Athens Music Company in Athens, Alabama, the Benson Company in Nashville, the Trio Music Company in Waco, Texas, the Central Music Company of Little, Rock, Arkansas, and the Tennessee Music and Printing Company in Cleveland, Tennessee. Those companies sponsored singing schools; the personal relationships that developed between teachers, students and company representatives led to loyalties to a particular company. Quartets aligned with those companies were not allowed to sing songs published by their competitors; they were required to sing only songs published by their sponsor.

There were changes on the horizon, primarily because of radio. As the quartets, which had depended on an affiliation with a shaped-note publisher, obtained radio shows, they reached larger audiences, which increased the demand for personal appearances and, as they played on the radio, they obtained recording contracts and records carried their music even further. The advent of radio also meant that people could be entertained in their homes by professionals, they did not have to depend on going to a singing convention, church, or concert to hear music. They also didn't need to learn to play or sing to have music around, which led to a decline in the demand for songbooks.

Southern Gospel quartets had a major advantage over their counterparts in black gospel because radio welcomed white performers but not black ones. A good white country or gospel singing group could obtain a regular broadcast while a black gospel quartet could not. Black gospel quartets had to depend on recordings--which declined during the Depression--and personal appearances.

Songs of black gospel quartets were heard by Southern white gospel groups, who began to learn and use those songs. The influence worked both ways--black gospel quartets heard southern quartets on the radio and learned some of their songs.

There was a conflict between rural and urban audiences that developed during the 1930s. The music that came from urban areas--particularly jazz and rhythm and blues--was deemed "dirty" by rural audiences, who extolled the virtues of rural living and insisted on "good, clean family entertainment."

That split between the sacred and the secular did not affect country and gospel music at that time; most country performers sang gospel songs and most white gospel groups included some country or "folk" songs in their repertoire but there was resistance within the church world toward gospel music. Many ministers saw the traveling quartets as a "threat" and criticized the lack of spiritual depth in the songs and performances. Increasingly, the gospel quartets put on a good show, which angered religious conservatives. New musical forms such as jazz also threatened those who liked traditional sounds. Finally, radio was deemed an enemy because, the argument went, entertainment led the serious-minded Christian astray.

The performers in both country and southern gospel music shared a rural heritage and a common motive for wanting to sing: it was a way off the farm and away from the southern agricultural life that was difficult, demanding and unpredictable. Performers were widely respected and many young farm boys and girls dreamed of the day when they could sing for a living, rather than walk crop rows with a hoe, chopping weeds.

The difference between country and gospel music was that country performers could charge admission for their concerts while gospel groups could not. The church frowned on "entertainment," and "paid concerts" were part of that world. Gospel acts had to depend on "free will" offerings wherever they sang. They took a collection and hoped there was enough money in the hat at the end of the evening to pay their way to the next church. A good collection meant that God had blessed the group and the evening.

A number of important white gospel groups formed during the 1930s. The Speer Family joined the Vaughan organization, while the Blackwood Brothers were affiliated with Stamps-Baxter. The Chuck Wagon Gang received their start on a 15-minute daily radio program on KFYO in Lubbock, Texas, in 1935. Dave Carter, born in Milltown, Kentucky in 1889, had moved with his family to north-central Texas; he married in 1909 after meeting his future wife at a singing school in Clay County, Texas. Carter obtained a job on the railroad and worked in Missouri and Oklahoma where, in 1927, he was hurt in a railroad accident and could no longer work so the family moved back to Texas where the couple sang wherever and whenever they could. They sang some gospel songs, but mostly country music. When one of his children got sick, Carter, out of desperation for money, walked into radio station KYFO and asked for a job singing on the air; he got it as well as an advance of money for medicine for his sick child.

In 1936 Carter landed a job on Fort Worth's WBAP on a show sponsored by Morton Salt. The family group sang mostly western tunes on a morning program, "The Roundup." Bewley Flour Mills sponsored a group, The Chuck Wagon Gang, on a program. The group traveled to local towns and sang, demonstrating the flour by cooking biscuits during their appearances. They couldn't make it back to the radio station each day for their on-air program, so another group was needed. Dave Carter agreed to do the radio program, and changed the name of his family group to "The Chuck Wagon Gang." For the next 15 years, they played on that program, heard on the Texas Quality Radio Network all over the state, and became one of the most popular groups on southern radio stations.

In November, 1936, the Chuck Wagon Gang made their first recordings for Columbia in San Antonio; the following year they recorded in Dallas. Although they originally recorded a mixture of secular and sacred songs, by April, 1940, they were recording only gospel.

The V.O. Stamps Quartet performed on KRLD in Dallas, opening each program with their theme song, "Give the World a Smile Each Day." They also sent transcriptions to XERL in Del Rio, Texas. In 1938 V.O. Stamps promoted his first "All-Night Singing" in Dallas at the State Fair Grounds; it was broadcast live over KRLD. Those "All-Night Sings" became increasingly popular after World War II.

By the mid-1930s, the groups affiliated with Vaughan were the Vaughan Office Quartet, the Speer Family, the Vaughan-Daniel Quartet, the Oliver Jennings Family, Vaughan's Sand Mountain Quartet (with Erman Slater), the Vaughan Melody Girls, the Vaughan Victory Four and the LeFevre Trio. In 1935 Vaughan closed down his recording label, and the groups who'd recorded with him moved on to other labels. Those groups increasingly found outlets on radio stations throughout the South, often on 15-minute programs in the morning.

Groups associated with Stamps-Baxter at the end of the 1930s included Virgil Stamps Original Quartet, Frank Stamps' All-Stars, W.T. "Deacon" Utley's Smile-A-While Quartet, the Daniel Stamps-Baxter Quartet, the Deep South Quartet, the Blackwood Brothers, and Herschel Foshee and Stamps-Baxter Melody Boys. Each of those groups sang regularly on a radio station.

During the summer of 1941, just before the United States became involved in World War II, over 500 students attended the Stamps-Baxter school in Dallas, but World War II changed a great many things in America. The changes in Southern Gospel music were already in the wind as the first generation of southern quartets, who needed an affiliation with a publishing firm during the 1920s and 1930s, became celebrities on radio and recordings. That marked a transition in southern gospel music from being part of the publishing industry to standing as an industry on its own.

On August 19, 1940, Virgil Stamps died in Dallas; less than six months later, on February 9, 1941, James D. Vaughan died in Lawrenceburg, Tennessee. The deaths of these two publishing giants marked the end of the first era of southern gospel music. The American involvement in World War II halted the development of the southern gospel music industry, which emerged after the war into its Golden Era.

50th Anniversary of the Recording Industry

In 1939 the recording industry celebrated its unofficial 50th Anniversary, although no one noticed it at the time. Recordings made in 1889 by Edison and Columbia were far different than the Big Band sound of 1939 and Sousa's Marine Corps Band was a distant ancestor to Benny Goodman's "swing" music. The major labels were Victor, now owned by RCA, which also owned the NBC network; Columbia, now owned by CBS; and Decca, whose 35 cent records rejuvenated the music business. In 1939 there were 50 million phonograph records sold in the United States; Decca sold 18 million of those.

Radio was now the carrier of the most popular music of the day and the music they played was "national" music as the electronic media, via radio, linked the nation. Radio had become a vital part of the music business and so had recordings while sheet music publishing was in a decline. Still, songwriters made most of their money from sheet music sales and those who wrote country or blues music were not accepted by ASCAP. A strike against ASCAP by broadcasters that would change that.

During 1939 the entertainment world saw the release of several great movies: *Gone With The Wind*, *Wuthering Heights*, Walt Disney's *Pinocchio*, *Mr. Smith Goes To Washington*, *Stagecoach* (which made John Wayne a star), and *Goodbye, Mr. Chips*. There were 388 movies released that year and the average American spent $25 annually to watch them.

The singing cowboys were still going strong. In 1938, Gene Autry starred in six films, Tex Ritter in eight and Roy Rogers in four. That year the *Motion Picture Herald* named Gene Autry the number one movie cowboy; William Boyd (Hopalong Cassidy) was a close second while Tex Ritter was ninth, Roy Rogers 13 and John Wayne number 18.

The image of country music was divided between hillbillies, or mountaineers, and cowboys. The singing cowboys seemed to be winning, but the movie industry kept releasing "hillbilly" movies as well, reinforcing the stereotype that most country musicians wanted to escape.

During the 1930s, movies that featured the hillbilly image of rural people included *Kentucky Kernels* (1934); the animated movies *Hill Billys* (1935), *When I Yoo Hoo* (1936), and *A Feud There Was* (1938) *Musical Mountaineers* (1939), *Naughty Neighbors* (1939); and *Kentucky Moonshine* (1938). Lum and Abner starred in *Dreaming Out Loud, Bashful Bachelor, So This is Washington* and *Goin' to Town*, while the Weaver Brothers and Elviry starred in 13 movies. In the comics of the newspapers were Al Capp's "Li'l Abner" and Billy De Beck's "Snuffy Smith."

Autry and the other movie singing cowboys had enhanced the "look" of movie cowboys by having custom made outfits done by Nathan Turk in Hollywood. Turk and Nudie Cohen added flash and pizzazz to the cowboy look, enhancing it with elaborate designs and embroidery. That look influenced country performers, who increasingly dressed like singing cowboy stars during the 1930s. Although the Grand Ole Opry in Nashville and the National Barn Dance in Chicago, promoted the "mountaineer" image for country performers, increasingly performers on those shows adapted cowboy outfits.

The End of the Thirties

On July Fourth, 1938, President Franklin Roosevelt announced that the South was the nation's top economic problem, putting the entire nation at risk. The South had 21 percent of the population, but earned only 9 percent of the nation's income; annual wages in the South were $865 compared to $1,291 nationally.

The year 1938 had begun with Mae West banned from network radio because she had made "vulgar" and "indecent" comments during her appearance on the Edgar Bergen-Charlie McCarthy radio show; those comments were sexually suggestive. In 1926, West had been arrested while starring in *Sexx*, a play she wrote. The Vice Squad busted West for "corrupting the morals of youth" when she appeared in a show as a prostitute who swung her hips, licked her lips, and moved her navel in a belly dance.

That year the "Fair Labor Standards Act" passed Congress, setting a minimum wage and working hours for the first time; the wage was 25 cents an hour, to be raised to 40 cents over time, with time and a half for overtime and a 44 hour workweek, to be reduced to 40 over time.

In 1939 the Supreme Court upheld the Constitutionality of the Tennessee Valley Authority (TVA), which was in competition with private enterprise. The suit was brought by the Tennessee Electric Power Company. The TVA was created by the federal government to improve the living standards of one of the nation's poorest regions; at the beginning of the project, only two out of every 100 farms in the area had electric power, many families lived on less than $100 a year, and the region was plagued with floods.

At the New York's World's Fair, called "The World of Tomorrow," NBC introduced television to the American public, but the public did not buy it. The Great Depression still hung over the country and the world at large witnessed the growing threat of Nazism in Germany. On September 1, 1939, Hitler's army invaded Poland and began World War II; Europe and Asia were both at war, although the United States was not directly involved.

1940

As the world's clock turned to 1940 there were wars and rumors of war throughout the world. Germany had already annexed Austria (in 1938), taken over Czechoslovakia in March, 1939 and defeated Poland in a blitzkreig in September 1939. Hitler had re-built Germany's armed forces so that, by September, 1939, there were 2.5 million men ready to fight. The armed forces of the United States stood at 174,000 men, with only 1,700 aircraft and was ranked 17th in the world.

In Asia, the Japanese Army occupied Manchuria in 1931 and attacked China in July, 1937, causing the fall of Peking (now called Beijing), Nanking, and Shanghai. Although the Chinese fought valiantly, the Japanese had the superior army and navy. In November, 1938, "Kristalnach" occurred in Germany as Nazis rounded up German Jews, breaking into their homes and businesses.

President Franklin Roosevelt declared the United States a "neutral" nation and public opinion demanded the United States not become involved in the European conflict. It was "their" war and most Americans felt no threat to Nazi or Japanese aggression. However, as a result of a diplomatic agreement that England and France made to support Poland, those nations declared war on Germany after the September invasion. At the end of 1939, Europe was at war.

On May 10, 1940, Winston Churchill became Prime Minister of Great Britain; Churchill stood virtually alone in England warning against Hitler and German aggression and had been labeled a "war-monger." Now the time had come for the visionary Churchill to assume leadership in the war he had warned against. Two weeks later, the British and French forces were trapped in Dunkirk, across the English channel in France, but in an amazing rescue, numerous British in small boats (there would be about 800 civilian craft who joined 222 naval vessels) ferried 338,226 men across the 70-mile body of water over a seven-day period when Hitler first stopped his assault, convinced the French and British were defeated, then engaged in an all out attack during the rescue.

In June, Germany invaded France where, on June 14, Paris surrendered. Mussolini declared Italy at war against England, Japan continued its advance toward the Chinese capital of Chungking and Britain prepared for a German invasion. At the end of July the Luftwaffe, Germany's air force, began bombing England. The "Battle of Britain" continued until mid-September when after over 50 days of continuous bombing--including bombing the city of London--600 British planes stopped the 2,500 German planes, causing Hitler to postpone a cross-Channel ground invasion.

In the United States, President Roosevelt proposed a "lend-lease" agreement whereby America would "lend" Great Britain military equipment in exchange for a lease on military bases. In September Congress passed the first peace time draft bill authorizing the activation of National Guard and Officers Reserve units for a year. That same month Japan signed an agreement to join the Axis--Germany and Italy--in an alliance.

In September and October, over half a million children were evacuated from London while most of the rest of London's population spent their nights sleeping in underground railroad stations. In November, Franklin Roosevelt was re-elected for an unprecedented third term as President of the United States; the following month, Ambassador to Great Britain Joseph P. Kennedy--who believed Hitler should be appeased and that Britain would lose a war with Germany--resigned and returned home.

At the end of 1940, Great Britain achieved her first victory in Northern Africa, but on December 30 London was fire bombed by German planes, which damaged much of the city.

There were 131.6 million people living in the United States in 1940; 13.5 million of them lived in New York, the most populous state. Pennsylvania had 9.9 million, Illinois had 7.7 million, Texas had 6.4 million, and California had become the fifth most populated state, going from over 2 million in 1930 to 5.7 million in 1940. During the previous decade 60,000 Oklahomans (and

50,000 from South Dakota) moved out of their state, mostly to California, because of dust storms. Thirty million homes, or 81 percent of American families, had radios; there were 765 radio stations on the air. A third of all farms now had electricity, a direct result of the Rural Electrification Act in 1936. Most people could read; the illiteracy rate was only 4.2 percent, and life expectancy had risen a couple of years to 63.

The State Department limited Jewish entry into the United States; only 33,000 Jews entered during the 1933-1937 period. American Jewish leaders pressed for more refugees to enter because of the abuses of Jews in Germany; however, in 1940 a ship carrying 900 European Jews was turned away at New York Harbor. In June, Congress passed the Alien Registration Act, requiring that all foreigners be registered and fingerprinted.

In January, 1940, the U.S. trade treaty with Japan expired and the United States declined to renew it. In June, Roosevelt spoke at the University of Virginia and stated, "We are convinced that military and naval victory for the gods of force and hate would endanger the institutions of democracy in the Western world, and that equally, therefore, the whole of our sympathies lie with those nations that are giving their life blood to combat against those forces." Roosevelt asked Congress for $1.3 billion to build up the Armed Forces and agreed to sell Great Britain American surplus supplies.

In July, Roosevelt banned all exports of oil and scrap metal to Japan, which was at war with China. In September, a gathering of the "America First" group, numbering 60,000, met in Chicago. That group of isolationists viewed Roosevelt as a "warmonger"; among its members was Charles Lindbergh.

In October, the draft lottery began; 16 million American men between the ages of 21 and 36 registered for the draft. In December, after Roosevelt's third election as president, he proclaimed the United States must be an "arsenal of democracy" during a Fireside Chat.

In 1940 the Willys Corporation introduced a four wheel drive vehicle called the "jeep," and the first American helicopter was demonstrated by its Russian-born inventor, Igor Sikorsty. Also in 1940 the first social security check, to Ida Fuller for $22.54, was issued.

Movies and Recordings

In Hollywood, Walt Disney produced *Fantasia* in 1940, which introduced fantasound to give a concert hall effect. Other movies that year were *My Little Chicadee*, starring Mae West and W. C. Fields, *The Grapes of Wrath*, starring Henry Fonda, Alfred Hitchcock's first American film, *Rebecca*, *The*

Great Dictator by Charlie Chaplin, and *A Wild Hare*, which introduced Bugs Bunny to American audiences.. On the movie range, Gene Autry starred in six singing westerns, Roy Rogers in seven, and Tex Ritter in eight.

The movie *Grand Ole Opry*, starring the Weaver Brothers and Elviry and featuring performances by Roy Acuff, Uncle Dave Macon, and Judge George D. Hay was released in 1940. Songs in that movie included "Take Me Back to My Carolina Home," "Bully of the Town," "Late Last Night When Willie Came Home," "Rock About My Saro Jane," "Buddy, Won't You Roll Down the Line," "When the Train Comes Along," and "Cumberland Mountain Deer Chase."

In the United States the song "Bluebirds Over the White Cliffs of Dover," a song in sympathy with Britain's plight, was a hit as the Big Band era continued. The biggest change that affected the American recording industry occurred in 1940 when the Supreme Court surprised both Victor and Columbia with a ruling that upheld a lower court decision that when a record was purchased at its list price, all property rights belonged to the buyer. Victor and Columbia had filed suit in order to make radio pay for the privilege of using recorded product on the air as part of their ongoing efforts to keep records off radio. With that decision, disk jockeys could purchase a recording at a retail outlet and play it on the air. That was the case which opened the airwaves to recordings and ended the arguments against radio airplay by the major labels; it eventually led to a new way of exposing music to the American public, with radio airplay of records becoming the major way consumers learned of new acts and new recordings.

The gains in record sales and the importance of music on radio led to important changes in music publishing. During the 1920s music publishers sold 500,000 to one million copies of sheet music of hit songs, but by 1931 sales had plummeted to 200,000 at best for a hit. Woolworth's closed down its sheet-music departments and Kresge's, the largest retail chain in the United States, replaced them as the major outlet for sheet music sales. Sales of hit recordings dropped and top artists were fortunate to sell 40,000. The major source of income for music publishers shifted from sheet music sales to "mechanicals," or money received when transcriptions were licensed to radio stations; a four minute song received 25 cents for each "sale" to radio, which was sent to the Music Publishers Protective Association (MPPA) and passed along to publishers.

The publishing industry was contracting; instead of branch offices in a number of cities, the industry concentrated on New York, Chicago and

Los Angeles. Free music, which had been sent to almost any performing band, was limited to those groups with sponsored shows on network radio. Bands, which had avoided touring, began to tour in large buses, playing one-night stands in ballrooms for a percentage of the gate.

The Formation of BMI

ASCAP and the MPPA were at war with the radio networks, NBC and CBS; basically, ASCAP wanted more money for radio airplay of transcriptions, which the networks provided to their affiliates, while the networks wanted to pay less.

ASCAP was controlled by publishers, who fought against giving songwriters an equal share of income or allowing songwriters to own their own copyrights. Members were voted into ASCAP and both publishers and songwriters were given a "ranking" or classification, which meant that the top classified songwriters and publishers received the most money. The classifications were not based on current success; the old line songwriters and publishers consistently received the highest ratings and most money, rankling newer songwriters and publishers. ASCAP excluded songwriters and publishers of "race" or "hillbilly" music, restricting its membership to Tin Pan Alley east in New York and west, in Los Angeles. By 1934, only 778 writers and 102 publishers were members of ASCAP and only those publishers and writers could collect money from radio airplay.

In 1938, Neville Miller, an attorney and former provost of Princeton University, was named to head the National Association of Broadcasters (NAB). One of his first orders of business was to bring up to date an idea first presented by the networks in 1935 to create a catalog of non-ASCAP music as leverage against ASCAP in negotiations. The original proposal was drawn up by Sydney Kaye, a member of the law firm that represented CBS. At Kaye's suggestion, the broadcasters pledged $1.75 million to get the new organization off the ground. The new organization, Broadcast Music, Inc. (BMI), agreed they would not pay dividends but would be a money-spending company. Twenty percent of the stock was allocated to NBC and CBS, with the remaining stock sold to other broadcasters. The deadline was April 1, 1940; if by that time at least $400,000 had been raised, the new organization would begin to collect money from broadcasters to be distributed to songwriters and publishers for the use of music on radio.

The new organization was originally intended to temper ASCAP's demand for more money from broadcasters, but ASCAP had created such animosity with broadcasters, as well as within its own ranks, that there was grass roots support among broadcasters. By January, 1940, only $250,000 had been raised; still, in February, BMI opened a "temporary" office in New York. BMI then received a stroke of luck; on February 11 Gene Buck, president of ASCAP, was arrested in Phoenix on a warrant claiming he had obtained money from broadcasters under false pretenses. Buck made key strategic mistakes, left out key people in negotiations with the broadcasters, and presented a contract that stated network stations would pay five percent of their income to ASCAP for the use of its music. After the new contract was read at a NAB meeting, Edward Klauber, executive vice-president of CBS, announced that the NAB would be the only organization his network would negotiate with. A massive walkout of broadcasters followed. ASCAP appealed to CBS President William Paley, who adamantly supported Klauber and BMI.

Carl Haverlin, who worked for KFI in Los Angeles during the 1920s, was brought in to go on the road and sell the idea of BMI to broadcasters; he was aided by ASCAP's demands that broadcasters sign the contract, which angered broadcasters and provided proof of the heavy-handed manner ASCAP had of dealing with the radio industry. BMI offered the broadcasters a better deal, asking for less money. By September, 1940, BMI had 220 full-time employees and affiliated with a number of non-ASCAP publishers. By the end of the year, BMI had contracts with Ralph Peer and Edward B. Marks, both of whom were dissatisfied with ASCAP. Peer had contracts with Latin American publishers and broadcasters, but ASCAP refused to deal with those compositions; BMI agreed to license that music in the United States. The advertising agencies in New York, who controlled most of network programming, went along with BMI after BMI brought a million-dollar infringement-suit insurance policy to protect itself against ASCAP.

The networks began a boycott of ASCAP, reducing the amount of ASCAP songs from 76 percent of commercial broadcasts to 31 percent. Bandleaders discovered they could make more money if they opened a BMI publishing company for their songs, and that brought them in line.

By the end of 1940, 660 stations, out of 796 commercial stations, had signed with BMI. The last week of that year there was no ASCAP music on the networks or its affiliates; thus began a war between ASCAP and radio. Ironically, ASCAP was saved by internal reforms demanded by the Justice Department, and because the networks fought against government control and regulation of their industry. The creation of BMI ended the monopoly of ASCAP, although the government felt that ASCAP, BMI, CBS and NBC controlled the radio music industry and wanted to break that control.

1941

In an address to the nation on January 6, 1941, President Roosevelt proclaimed the "Four Freedoms," which were freedom of speech and expression, freedom of every person to worship God in his own way, freedom from want, and freedom from fear. He also requested more money for the military, stating, "Never before Jamestown and Plymouth Rock has our American civilization been in such danger...if Great Britain goes down... all of us...would be living at the point of a gun."

In March, "lend-lease" was approved whereby the United States would "lend" $7 billion in war material, mostly to Great Britain, which Britain would send back when they had finished using it. In April the automobile industry slashed production of domestic vehicles by 20 percent, or one million units, and directed production to the war effort. By 1940, General Motors supplied half of all American automobiles sold; there were 31 million autos on the roads.

In May, United States Savings Bonds went on sale and the President declared that the last Thursday of November would be declared "Thanksgiving Day." In June, all German and Italian assets in the United States were frozen and all American consulates in territories under German and Italian control were ordered closed.

During the summer, baseball had a record breaking season; Ted Williams hit over .400 and Joe DiMaggio hit in 56 consecutive games; in the World Series, the Yankees defeated the Brooklyn Dodgers four games to one. In 1941 the aerosol spray can was introduced and on November 1, Mount Rushmore in South Dakota was dedicated; unfortunately designer John Gutzon de la Mothe Borglum had died in March.

Top movies that year included *Citizen Kane* by Orson Wells, *The Maltese Falcon*, starring Humphrey Bogart, *Dumbo* from Walt Disney, *Sergeant York*, starring Gary Cooper, *Dr. Jekyll and Mr. Hyde*, starring Spencer Tracy and Ingrid Bergman, and John Ford's *How Green Was My Valley*.

At the beginning of 1941, the war in North Africa continued. German U-boats (submarines) controlled the Atlantic and the German spring offensive targeted British cities; Liverpool suffered seven consecutive days of bombing while London was in flames. A major turn in the war occurred in June when Germany attacked Russia, causing the former allies to declare war against each other.

In Asia, the Japanese invaded Indochina in July, causing President Roosevelt to freeze all Japanese assets in the United States and Great Britain. That same month the Nazis ordered the "Final Solution" of "the Jewish question" by instigating the elimination of all Jews. After nearly defeating Russia--Hitler invaded in order to obtain a supply of oil in the Caucasus--the Russian winter arrived to defeat the German army. Access to oil was the reason Japan invaded French Indochina; however, the United States responded by refusing to sell American oil and gas to Japan. Japan began to plan for an attack on American bases in the Pacific as an act of "self-defense" while they continued to negotiate with the United States.

Major hit recordings for the year included "Take the 'A" Train" and "I Got It Bad and That Ain't Good" by Duke Ellington and his Orchestra; "Boogie Woogie Bugle Boy" and "I'll Be With You in Apple Blossom Time" by the Andrews Sisters; "God Bless the Child" by Billie Holiday; "Star Dust" by Artie Shaw and His Orchestra; "Chattanooga Choo Choo" and "Elmer's Tune" by Glenn Miller and His Orchestra; "New San Antonio Rose" by Bob Wills and His Texas Playboys; and hits by the bands of Tommy Dorsey, Charlie Barnet, Jimmy Dorsey, Sammy Kaye, Benny Goodman, Vaughn Monroe, and Kay Kyser as well as "I Don't Want to Set the World on Fire" by the Ink Spots.

For the record industry, the declaration of war meant a problem in obtaining shellac, which had been imported from India, and wax from Germany in order to press records. RCA Victor was the only label with a good supply in its warehouses, which caused labels to use acetate blanks, painted over an aluminum base, for their recordings instead of the old method of cutting on wax-based masters. Those problems caused labels like Columbia and Decca to stop pressing records for weeks at a time; still, in 1941, the industry sold 130 million records, their best year since 1921.

Consumers had begun to purchase recordings at a strong rate. In 1940, jukebox operators were responsible for purchasing 40 percent of disks manufactured.

During early 1941 there was no ASCAP music on the radio, except on the 200 independent stations that programmed records. In a meeting in Washington, an agreement was finally reached for a consent degree that was ratified on March 4, 1941, allowing both BMI and ASCAP to license music.

Country Music in 1941

In 1941 there were close to 400,000 jukeboxes in operation, and they bought most of the country recordings released. Warner Brothers decided not to get into the record business and sold the Brunswick/Vocalion labels and catalogue to Decca. Montgomery Ward Records ended that year, but Sears still sold records.

There were a lot of harmonicas sold in 1941 (and the rest of the 1940s) by Wayne Raney and Lonnie Glosson, a harmonica duo who performed on WCKY in Cincinnati and on a syndicated radio program; they sold harmonicas for $1.60 through the mail and eventually sold five million.

Jimmy Davis had his biggest hit, "You Are My Sunshine," then Gene Autry and Bing Crosby also released it and it became a hit song for them as well; Crosby's was number 19 on the pop charts. Davis recorded the song on February 4; he and guitarist Charles Mitchell had purchased it from Paul Rice, whose group had first recorded the song in 1939. Davis's name remained on the song as "songwriter" and he collected royalties his entire life.

In 1941, the original Carter Family broke up and stopped recording; Sara had divorced A. P. in 1932, then later married his cousin and moved to California. A. P. went back to Maces Springs but Maybelle and her daughters continued to perform. That same year the Mexican government confiscated XERA and tried to confiscate XEAW, but owner Carr Collins moved the equipment just north of the border into Texas before Mexican authorities arrived.

Bebop Jazz

Jazz became deliberately uncommercial with the introduction of "Bebop," a music with complex chord progressions, fast tempos with many changes of key and improvisation. It was a backlash against dance music, the popular form of jazz from the 1920s through the 1940s. The Bebop Revolution was a rebellion by young jazz artists who wanted to play music for musicians; it was not intended for the popular jazz audience. The basic line-up was either alto or tenor saxophone, trumpet, bass, piano and drums and the song structure consisted of musicians playing the melody before each soloist improvised a section until the song returned to the melody.

Jazz historians claim "Body and Soul" by Coleman Hawkins in 1939 was an important early influence on Bebop and on Charlie Parker, the leading proponent of Bebop in its early years. Young jazz musicians, who grew up on swing music that was made for dancing, wanted to create a music that an audience had to listen to—and that meant not dancing. The young jazz mavericks were inspired by soloists such as pianists Art Tatum and Earl Hines, saxophonists Coleman Hawkins and Lester Young and trumpeter Roy Eldridge.

At Minton's Playhouse in New York, many young players developed the Bebop style of improvisational solos that extended beyond the two and four bar solos in dance bands. Guitarist Charlie Christian, who played with Benny Goodman's band, was an early innovator with his improvised solos. Drummers in swing music played a straight beat on the snare and bass drums while Bebop drummers kept time with the cymbal, using the bass drum for accents. The bass was a key instrument, keeping the foundation of the song in 4/4 time.

One of the most influential Bebop musicians, saxophonist Charlie Parker, also known as "Yardbird," was a hipster who led the way in branding jazz as a music for intellectuals. The performance of jazz by jazz musicians meant they did not compromise their vision or musical integrity. This was a music to sit and listen to; it was not entertainment or played for dancing.

Charlie Parker

Charlie Parker was born in Kansas City, the son of a pianist, dancer and singer who performed on black vaudeville shows. Parker began playing the saxophone when he was 11; he joined his high school band at 14 and spent 14 to 15 hours a day practicing, mastering improvisation. Parker played in jazz clubs locally and then joined pianist Jay McShann's band in 1938. The band toured nationally and Parker's first recordings were with McShann's group. In 1939 he moved to New York City to further his music career.

Charlie Parker left McShann's band in 1942 and joined Earl Hines, whose band included Dizzy Gillespie. Parker often joined jazz musicians who jammed at Clark Monroe's Uptown House and Minton's Playhouse, after hours clubs in Harlem. Musicians in the after hours clubs included Gillespie, pianist Thelonious Monk, guitarist Charlie Christian and drummer Kenny Clark. The musicians wanted to develop a style that swing musicians couldn't play.

The new style of jazz was disliked and rejected by most traditional jazz musicians. The early development of Be bop is not documented with recordings because of the AFM's Musicians strike in 1942-1944. After 1945, the recordings by Parker, Dizzy Gillespie, Max Roach and Bud Powell had a major influence on jazz. Musicians and fans soon became aware of Be bop and followed the musicians. In November, 1945, Charlie Parker's Reboppers, comprised of Parker, Gillespie, trumpeter Miles Davis, bassist Curly Russell and drummer Max Roach recorded "Ko-Ko," "Billie's Bounce" and "Now's the Time" in what is often considered by jazz historians to be the "greatest Jazz session ever."

After a booking at a club in Los Angeles, Parker elected to stay in L.A. while most of the group returned to New York. That was a difficult time for Parker and he spent time in a mental hospital. Parker wanted to record with strings, blending jazz with classical music in a style dubbed "Third Stream." A recording of Parker with strings was done in November, 1949 for Verve Records.

During his teen years, Parker became addicted to morphine after an auto accident when he was hospitalized, which led to a life-long heroine addition. Because of his addiction, Parker was an unreliable performer and was considered unemployable. Although he often recorded and did excellent recordings, his behavior grew increasingly erratic. He recorded for Verve and then returned to New York, where he recorded for Dial and Savoy Records. Many of those recordings are considered "classic."

Charlie Parker died on March 12, 1955; an autopsy was conducted and the coroner estimated Parker's age at between 50 and 60; he was 34.

Pearl Harbor

The Japanese-American negotiations aimed at avoiding armed conflict ended on Sunday, December 7, 1941. The attack by the Japanese on Pearl Harbor was made just before 8 a.m. in Hawaii, which was 1 p.m. in Washington, D.C. In addition to the attack on Pearl Harbor, the Japanese armed forces attacked Malaysia, the Philippines, Hong Kong, and Thailand. At the United States Naval Base at Pearl Harbor in Hawaii, 19 warships and 188 aircraft were destroyed, killing 2,403 Americans.

The next day President Roosevelt addressed the nation by radio, calling it "a date that will live in infamy," and declared war on Japan. A few days later, Germany declared war on the United States and the United States reciprocated, bringing America into World War II.

Frozen in Time

During the World War II years, the United States, in many ways, was "frozen in time." There were no new cars, radios or appliances made. What you owned at the beginning of the war was, for the most part, what you owned at the end of the war. This was especially true with music. Consumers purchased records during World War II but the sound did not evolve; Big Band music was the most popular sound at the beginning of the War as well as at the end of the war.

However, there were also immense changes during World War II, most of them hidden from the public. There were developments in war related industries, such as aircraft, weapons and technology. American soldiers left home and went to Europe, Asia, Africa, the South Pacific and other places they never imagined they'd see.

That was the enigma of World War II; it was a time of immense changes while we were also "frozen in time."

1942

The war wasn't going well for the British--they suffered setbacks from Rommel's Afrika Korps in Africa and lost Singapore and Hong Kong; the United States forces in the Philippines, under General Douglas MacArthur, were lost to Japanese invaders, resulting in the Bataan Death March (about 20,000 men died during this 65 mile march) after only 2,000 men out of the 78,000 stationed there could be evacuated to Corregidor. In April, an air raid led by General Jimmy Doolittle launched a surprise attack on Tokyo, which required the innovative launching of large B-25 bombers from an aircraft carrier.

The Japanese captured the Burma Road, which had been used by the Allies to send supplies to China, and the Germans continued bombing England, but there were several breakthroughs for the Allies. The Russian Army finally turned back German forces and in the Coral Sea the American Navy won its first victory over Japan's Navy in May. In June, at the Battle of Midway, Americans used intercepted Japanese code messages to break the back of the Japanese Navy; although only about nine bombs hit their targets, the American planes destroyed four of Japan's six aircraft carriers, sinking 275 planes within 24 hours. That same month Major General Dwight D. Eisenhower was put in command of American troops in the European Theater of Operations (ETO).

British forces, led by General Bernard Montgomery, scored a decisive victory at El Alamein in Egypt in October, forcing Rommel to retreat. In November, the first American troops landed in North Africa to help the British.

In January, 1942, the Office of Production Management banned the sales of all new automobiles and trucks to consumers; that same month the Office of Civilian Defense began organizing civilian volunteers to help with national defense, watching shores and monitoring "lights out" nights to make sure no enemy plane could see a speck of light to guide it.

In May, the forced evacuation of every ethnic Japanese to internment camps began. About 110,000 Japanese (over two-thirds born in the United States) were given a week to ten days to wind up their affairs and bring a bed roll and no more baggage than they could carry and report for the internment. Many had to sell their property and businesses at a fraction of its worth. There were ten Japanese internment camps located in California, Idaho, Utah, Arizona, Wyoming, Colorado and Arkansas.

Ration books were issued to Americans, allowing them to purchase one pound of sugar every two weeks while each motorist was given coupons for 25-30 gallons per month. Citizens conducted scrap rubber drives, collecting old tires and rubber boots for the war effort. The Boy Scouts collected 150,000 tons of paper to be recycled and women began wearing trousers in factories. About 3.5 million women joined the work force during World War II and trousers were considered a badge of honor; sales of trousers increased five fold during 1942.

Introduced during 1942 were daylight savings time and blackout drills where all lights had to either be extinguished or dimmed behind blackout curtains in homes.

In June, the Senate took only 34 minutes to approve a $42.8 billion military budget and the United States entered the spy business, establishing the Office of Strategic Services (OSS) to collect secret intelligence overseas. That month the Office of War Information was created to unify the government's information activities. The term "G. I. Joe" was introduced by the Army's newspaper, *The Stars and Strips*, for the ordinary soldiers serving. (G.I. stood for "General Inductee.")

In July, Congress approved two units for women in the Armed Services; the Women Accepted for Volunteer Emergency Services (WAVES) and the Women's Army Auxiliary Corps (WAAC) served in non-combat roles. In December, President Roosevelt ended the Works Progress Administration; there was no longer any need to find jobs in civilian public works projects.

Movies

One of the biggest movies of 1942 was *Mrs. Miniver* starring Greer Garson, made in England, which brought home the War to Americans as they watched the story of a British family's struggles during the early days of World War II. Other top movies included *Casablanca* starring Humphrey Bogart and Ingrid Bergman, *Bambi* by Walt Disney, and *Holiday Inn*, which featured Bing Crosby singing a new song written by Irving Berlin, "White Christmas." Prominent actors gave up their movie careers to serve in the Armed Forces, including James Stewart, Caeser Romero, Spencer Tracy, Robert Stack, Douglas Fairbanks, Jr. and 41-year old Clark Gable, whose wife, Carole Lombard, was killed in January in a plane crash while on a war bond drive.

White Christmas

"White Christmas" was written by Irving Berlin, probably in either 1938 or 1939, possibly on the set of the film *Top Hat* starring Fred Astaire but it didn't fit that film. It was performed in the film, *Holiday Inn*, about an Inn that only opens on national holidays. Irving Berlin wrote the 12 songs in the movie; in addition to Christmas, there were songs for Lincoln's birthday, Valentine's Day, George Washington's birthday, Easter and Thanksgiving.

The movie was filmed from November, 1941 until January 1942. During the filming, Pearl Harbor was bombed with the result that the patriotic numbers were beefed up.

The song "White Christmas was introduced to the public by Bing Crosby on his radio show, the Kraft Music Hall, on Christmas Day, 1941.

Holiday Inn premiered on August 4, 1942. The song in the film thought to be the hit was "Be Careful, It's My Heart," which did well when the film was released. However, in October, "White Christmas" became popular and remained number one on the Hit Parade for eleven consecutive weeks.

Although the song is a Christmas favorite, it is a secular, not a Christmas song; Irving Berlin was Jewish. The song is not a "happy" songs, as most Christmas songs are. Instead, it is a bit wistful and melancholy. A possible reason for that may be because Irving Berlin's son, Irving Berlin, Jr., died when he was three weeks old on Christmas Day, 1928. Berlin and his wife visited their son's grave on each Christmas Day after that.

The Singing Cowboys in Hollywood

The singing cowboys were still popular in 1942; Tex Ritter and Roy Rogers each starred in eight movies that year while Gene Autry starred in six. Autry made a decision to enlist in World War II and was inducted on the air during a "Melody Ranch" radio show, broadcast in July over the CBS network. He continued to broadcast his "Melody Ranch" show from various bases where he was stationed while training as a pilot, until he was sent overseas.

With Autry in the Service, Republic Studios decided to give Roy Rogers a major publicity and promotional campaign. He was crowned "King of the Cowboys" and a movie by that title starring Rogers was released. He began to play a character named "Roy Rogers" and more songs were included in his films, making them more like Autry's. Lavish production numbers were incorporated into the films after studio head Herbert J. Yates saw the musical *Oklahoma* in New York. In effect, Rogers' pictures became Western musicals instead of cowboy movies with some singing.

In May, 1942 James Caesar Petrillo, head of the American Federation of Musicians, issued an ultimatum to record labels that a strike would start in August. Although President Roosevelt sought to stop the strike--Americans needed to be united in the War effort--Petrillo called one anyway. Labels had been aware of that threat and had stockpiled recordings. The strike continued until December, 1944, when labels could record again. In the meantime, American consumers heard only the music recorded before the strike began.

Capitol Records and Johnny Mercer

On April 8, 1942 a new record label, Liberty, was established in Hollywood. Formed by music store owner Glenn Wallichs, songwriter Johnny Mercer, and movie executive George "Buddy" DeSylva, the headquarters for the label was at Sunset and Vine, in offices above Wallich's "Music City" store. Wallichs was the owner of the largest radio and record store in L.A.; he also had a small, custom-recording service. DeSylva was an executive producer at Paramount Pictures and a former successful Broadway musical lyricist (he wrote lyrics for "April Showers" and "California Here I Come"). DeSylva put up $25,000 for the venture.

Johnny Mercer was born on November 18, 1909, in Savannah, Georgia. During the 1930s, he sang with Paul Whiteman's band. Mercer was primarily a lyricist, although he wrote the words and music to "I'm An Old Cowhand," "Dream," "G.I. Jive," and "Something's Gotta Give." Mercer won three Academy Awards for co-writing the themes to the movies *Days of Wine and Roses*, *Laura*, and *Charade*.

Other hits as a lyricist include "Blues in the Night," "One for My Baby," and "Accentuate the Positive" with Harold Arlen; "Day In, Day Out" and "Fools Rush In" with Rube Bloom; "Lazybones," "Skylark" and "In the Cool, Cool Cool of the Evening" with Hoagy Carmichael; "Namely You" with Gene De Paul; "Mister Meadowlark" with Walter Donaldson; "Satin Doll" with Duke Ellington and Billy Strayhorn; "P.S. I Love You" with Gordon

Jenkins; "I'm Old Fashioned" and "Dearly Beloved" with Jerome Kern; "Moon River" with Henry Mancini; "I Remember You," "Tangerine" and "Arthur Murray Taught Me Dancing in a Hurry" with Victor Schertzinger; "I Thought About You" with Jimmy Van Heusen; "Jeepers Creepers," "You Must Have Been a Beautiful Baby" and "On the Atchison, Topeka and the Santa Fe" with Harry Warren; and "Hooray for Hollywood" and "Too Marvelous for Words" with Richard Whiting.

As a singer and recording artist, Mercer had 29 hit singles between 1938 and 1952; those include "Strip Polka (1942), "The G.I. Jive" 1944), "Ac-Cent-Tchu-Ate the Positive" (1945), "On the Atchison, Topeka, and the Santa Fe" (1945), "Autumn Leaves" (1955), "Day In, Day Out" (1939), "Dream" (1945), "Fools Rush In (Where Angels Fear to Tread)" (1940) and "Goody Goody" (1936).

When Capitol was formed, Mercer was in charge of recording and song selection and Wallichs handled business details and other production. Because of a conflict with the Liberty Music Shops in New York, the label changed its name to Capitol in June.

In an effort to acquire an edge on the three established majors (RCA Victor, Columbia and Decca) Capitol instituted a policy of sending records free to disc jockeys in order to obtain radio airplay. Before Capitol instituted their policy, the majors Victor and Columbia had only sent free copies to music editors and record reviewers at general newspapers and magazines and the music and entertain trade papers--concentrating their efforts on the print media instead of radio exposure. The strategy worked well; in the first year, Capitol had pop hits with Johnny Mercer's "Strip Polka" and Freddie Slack's "Cow Cow Boogie."

Nat King Cole

African-American crooner Nat King Cole became one of the most popular singers on Capitol from the 1940s until his death in 1965.

Born in Montgomery, Alabama in 1919, Nathaniel Adams Cole was raised in Chicago where his father was a Baptist minister. Cole's mother, Perlina, was a church organist who taught him how to play organ; at 12 he began formal lessons on piano and learned jazz, gospel and classical music. Cole began performing as a teenager, using the name "Nat Cole." His older brother, Eddie, was the bass player in the band and their first recording, in 1936, was under Eddie's name. He acquired the name "King" while performing in a jazz club because it was connected to the nursery rhyme "Old King Cole." The name Nat King Cole stuck.

Nat King Cole began his career as a pianist; he was on a national tour of the musical *Shuffle Along* and when it ran out of money in Long Beach, California, Cole elected to remain there. "The King Cole Swingsters," featuring Cole on piano, Oscar Moore on guitar and Wesley Prince on bass, performed in clubs in Long Beach and recorded a number of transcriptions; their first appearance on national radio came in 1938 on NBC, followed by appearances on NBC's "Swing Soiree" and during the 1940s the group was on radio shows "Old Gold," "The Chesterfield Supper Club," "Kraft Music Hall" and CBS's variety show, "The Orson Wells Almanac."

Although the Cole Swingsters were a jazz instrumental group, Cole often sang during their performances. During World War II bassist Wesley Prince was replaced by Charlie Harris. Their first professional recordings were with Excelsior Records and they had a regional hit with "I'm Lost." Their first chart record, "That Ain't Right" was released on Decca in 1942; it reached number one on the Harlem Hit Parade in *Billboard*. The following year, Cole signed with Capitol Records and his first release was "All For You," originally released on Excelsior; it reached number one as well. Cole's third single, "Straighten Up and Fly Right" was number one on the Harlem Hit Parade for ten consecutive weeks.

"Straighten Up and Fly Right," written by Cole and publisher Irving Mills, was inspired by a folk tale that Cole's father used in a sermon. In the tale, a buzzard takes animals for an aerial joy ride and then drops them on the ground, killing them so he can eat them; however, the monkey knew this trick and wrapped his tail around the buzzard's neck, thwarting the buzzard's efforts to obtain a meal. The song was often sung by Tuskegee airmen as they went into battle and was in the 1943 film, *Here Comes Elmer*.

The lyrics have been cited as an example of race relations, particularly in the music business, with white executives being the buzzard and a canny black artist being the monkey.

During the 1940s Nat King Cole had a string of top five chart singles, including "I Can't See For Lookin,'" "Gee, Baby, Ain't I Good To You," "I'm Lost," "It's Only a Paper Moon," "(Get Your Kicks On) Route 66," "The Christmas Song (Chestnuts roasting by an open fire)," "(I Love You) For Sentimental Reasons," "Nature Boy." During the early 1950s he had "Mona Lisa" (number one for four weeks), "Too Young," and "Unforgettable." It was the success of Nat King Cole during the early years of Capitol Records that reportedly allowed the company to build the Capitol Tower, which looked like a stack of records.

The Cole trio paid for their 15 minute radio program, "King Cole Trio Time" in 1946, the first time a radio program was sponsored by a black recording artist. The transcriptions they made were sent to radio stations for broadcast and later the songs became commercial records. Nat King Cole aimed for the pop audience so many of his recordings had an orchestra backing him.

Cole angered jazz critics with his move into pop music but it showed the world that an African-American singer could be a major pop act. Although he was often confronted with boos and threats, particularly when performing in the South, Nat King Cole became the epitome of a class act.

Hit Songs and War Songs

The entry of the United States in World War II inspired a number of "war" songs that were recorded and/or released in 1942: "Get Your Gun and Come Along (We're Fixin' to Kill a Skunk)," "Mussolini's Letter to Hitler," "Hitler's Reply to Mussolini," "It's Just a Matter of Time" and "Plain Talk," all written and recorded by Carson Robison; "Shh, It's a Military Secret," "When Johnny Comes Marching Home" and "She'll Always Remember" by Glenn Miller and His Orchestra; "Three Little Sisters" and "He Wears a Pair of Silver Wings" by Dinah Shore; "This Is Worth Fighting For" by Shep Fields and His New Music; "News of the World," by Cliff Nazarro; "Pearl Harbor Blues" by Doctor Clayton; "Wartime Blues" and "One Letter Home" by Jazz Gillum; "Little Bo Peep Has Lost Her Jeep" by Spike Jones and His City Slickers; "Obey Your Air Raid Warden" by Tony Pastor and His Orchestra; "Dear Mom," by Swing and Sway with Sammy Kaye; "Johnny Doughboy Found a Rose in Ireland" by Freddy Martin and His Orchestra; "From the Coast of Maine to the Rockies" by Vaughn Monroe and His Orchestra, and "(We'll Be Singing Hallelujah) Marching Through Berlin," by Ethel Merman.

A song that became a standard during World War II was recorded in 1939 by Kate Smith. "God Bless America," sometimes referred to as our second National Anthem, was written by Irving Berlin for his World War I musical, "Yip, Yip Yaphank." Berlin pulled the song out of the musical, but remembered it twenty years later when Smith asked him for a song to sing on the tenth anniversary of the end of World War I. He donated all income from the song to the Boy Scouts.

On March 19, 1942, Elton Britt recorded "There's a Star Spangled Banner Waving Somewhere" for Bluebird in New York and it became one of the two biggest selling country recordings during World War II. The other was

"Pistol Packin' Mama," recorded by Al Dexter a day later, March 20, on the other side of the country, in Hollywood for Columbia. Both of those songs were covered by pop acts.

The biggest pop hits from 1942 were "Chattanooga Choo Choo" by Glenn Miller and His Orchestra, which sold over one million units, "White Christmas" by Bing Crosby and "Don't Sit Under the Apple Tree (with Anyone Else But Me)" by the Andrews Sisters. Other pop hits include "A String of Pearls" by Glenn Miller and His Orchestra, "Tangerine" by Jimmy Dorsey and His Orchestra, "Blues in the Night" by Dinah Shore, "Jingle Jangle Jingle," by Kay Kyser and His Orchestra, which covered the country hit by Tex Ritter, "Deep in the Heart of Texas" by Alvino Rey and his Orchestra, "Cow-Cow Boogie" by Freddie Slack and His Orchestra, "(There'll Be Bluebirds Over) The White Cliffs of Dover" by Kate Smith, "Flying Home" by Lionel Hampton and His Orchestra, and hits from the bands of Benny Goodman, Harry James, Vaughn Monroe, Tommy Dorsey, Johnny Mercer and Bing Crosby.

Gasoline and tire shortages meant that most musicians could not do personal appearances during World War II; it also stopped crowds from coming to shows. Additionally, a number of musicians were drafted or enlisted, forcing the breakup of bands.

Country Music

Country music was popular on the radio during World War II; the Grand Ole Opry was broadcast over the NBC network and attracted about 3,000 fans to each performance; the Renfro Valley Barn Dance attracted about 5,000 to its shows each Saturday night. However, the Wheeling Jamboree at WWVA moved to a studio and did not perform for a live audience during World War II; by that time it had become a 50,000 watt station. At the Hollywood Barn Dance, Foy Willing and the Riders of the Purple Sage and the Jimmy Wakely Trio played while Stuart Hamblen continued his "Lucky Stars" program on KFWB in Los Angeles. In New York, Esmereldy, "The Streamlined Hillbilly," hosted her radio show on WNBC and was a regular on NBC's "Mirth and Madness."

The "sound" in country music changed when Bill Monroe hired his first banjo player, Stringbean. But the "sound" that dominated country music came out of California with the western swing bands led by Bob Wills and Spade Cooley. Wills had moved to California from Tulsa in 1942 and began performing in the ballrooms in the Los Angeles area.

Another top act to emerge from those ballroom dances was Spade Cooley, whose western swing group ran head to head in popularity with Bob Wills and His Texas Playboys. Cooley's group featured vocalists Tex Williams and Deuce Spriggins, steel guitarists Joaquin Murphey and Noel Boggs, and guitarist Smokey Rogers. This group first popularized the term "western swing" and played more like an orchestra than a group based on Texas fiddling. The band dressed in matching outfits and had a lush sound, akin to the best Big Bands of the era, while doing "country" songs.

Fred Rose and the formation of Acuff-Rose

When Gene Autry decided to enlist in the Army Air Corps during World War II, songwriter Fred Rose, who wrote for Autry, was out of a job. He had written a number of songs for Autry and other singing cowboys, but decided to move back to Nashville in mid-1942 rather than stay in Hollywood because his wife, who was from Nashville, wanted to return home.

Rose was popular and quickly landed an afternoon show on WSM. He was approached by Roy Acuff about starting a publishing company because Acuff wanted to keep the rights to his songs (he reasoned that "if the New York and Chicago publishers wanted to buy them, they must be worth something") and because the songbook business was extremely profitable but also a burden--he needed someone to handle that part of his business. Acuff earned over $200,000 in 1942.

Fred Rose was an ASCAP songwriter with connections in New York, Chicago and Hollywood. He was a unique individual who had the talent to compose songs quickly on whatever topic and in whatever mood was needed. He thrived as an editor and talent scout and was an unselfish man who willingly helped other songwriters with their works. He was scrupulously honest, a direct result of his religion, Christian Science, which he practiced. Rose held himself to the highest ethical standards and when he went into business he treated other songwriters fairly and honestly. He signed songs to his company but not songwriters because he only took the songs he felt he could get recorded.

The Acuff-Rose Publishing Company was officially incorporated on October 13, 1942, and, because of the talents and abilities of Rose, soon had songs recorded by Opry acts, including Acuff. For start-up capital the company had $25,000 from Acuff (which was never touched) and $2,500 from BMI, which needed new publishing companies to supply songs to catch up with the twenty-five year head start from ASCAP. BMI practiced an "open door" policy with songwriters; anyone could join. That meant that for the first time country music had access to monies derived from performances on radio and live performances. Since radio had become the dominant medium during the 1930s, and became even more important during the war years as families sat beside the radio for entertainment as well as news from the war, this meant that, for the first time country music publishers could make money from radio airplay.

Fred Rose was in a unique position. He knew the people at WSM and the Opry, he had learned about the market for country music--and the money involved--through his work with Autry and the singing cowboys in the movies, and he was a pop songwriter who came to Nashville as country music was changing from a folk based music into a contemporary commercial music. Rose played a major role there, introducing the pop song format with country topics to replace the folk song format. That had already been done with western music, most of which was composed by Tin Pan Alley writers who used pop song structures with western themes. Fred Rose took that same process to Nashville and applied it to southern-based country music.

1943

In January, 1943, Roosevelt and Churchill met in Casablanca for a Summit to discuss war strategy; Russia continued to fight the German forces that had invaded while Stalin called for a second front from American and British forces in France to relieve the pressure Germany exerted on Russia.

In Stalingrad, the German Army suffered its first major defeat against Russian troops, although the city was in ruins. The Russians pursued the retreating German Army while the Allies stepped up their air war, bombing key cities in order to cripple German industry. An American P-38 fighter shot down and killed Japanese Naval leader Admiral Yamamota, causing a further setback to the Japanese Navy.

After cracking the German secret code, the Battle of Atlantic turned in favor of the American and British. Allied troops landed in Sicily in July, which led to the fall of Italy and Mussolini by the end of September. The United States also had victories in the Pacific and after Thanksgiving, Roosevelt, Churchill and Stalin met for the first time in Tehran to discuss a major cross-channel invasion the following year. General Dwight Eisenhower was named by Roosevelt to lead the Allied forces in that invasion.

By February, 1943, 60,000 Americans had been killed. Martial law ended in Hawaii, but the military still had control of civilian court cases.

The United States had truly become "the arsenal for democracy" by 1943; the factory at Willow Run, Michigan, which manufactured B-24 bombers, had 100,000 workers and was producing 500 planes a month. In 1942 it produced 47,000 planes and in 1943 produced 86,000; since Pearl Harbor, 150,000 planes had been manufactured in the United States. In 1943 1,949 ships were built; every four days a new ship came off the line. Additionally, 800,000 tons of synthetic rubber was produced by the end of the year.

"Use it up, wear it out, make it do or do without" became the slogan for American consumers. Butter was limited to four ounces a week and cheese to four pounds a week; coffee and flour were rationed and Tuesday and Fridays became "meatless" days. Tuna casserole became popular with meat limited to 28 ounces-a-week. Businessmen wore suits without vests and "victory pants" that had no cuffs.

Each American was allotted three pairs of leather shoes a year. Tin, metals, paper and nylon were recycled; kitchen fat was processed for explosives and rubber was scarce. A 35 mph speed limit was in effect but, with gas and tires rationed, cars tended to stay in garages or parked at home. There were long lines in grocery stores, restaurants, and bars because there were too few employees to wait on customers.

Factories needed workers so they introduced incentives like coffee breaks, piped in music, provided child-care for working mothers, and instituted fringe benefits and awards for good performances. President Roosevelt ordered all wages, prices and salaries frozen and a 48-hour work week. In the evening, Americans sat in front of their old radios; no new ones were made for civilian consumption during the War.

In May, Roosevelt ordered striking miners back to work and placed the mines under Federal control; United Miner Workers chief John L. Lewis had ordered 500,000 miners to strike. In December, Roosevelt seized the railroads to avert a strike; Federal troops operated the railroads until management and labor settled their differences.

In June there were race riots in Detroit and Los Angeles; in Detroit 35 were killed because Southern whites who came there to work in the defense plants objected to Negroes being hired. In August, there were race riots in New York.

Campbell's Soup had to stop sponsoring the popular "Amos'n'Andy" radio show, which had been on the air for 15 years and 4,000 performances, because of a shortage of tin cans.

During the year, penicillin was developed, which helped battlefield casualties.

American Entertainment

In New York, the musical *Oklahoma* opened and soon everybody was singing "Oh, What a Beautiful Morning," "The Surrey With the Fringe on Top," "People Will Say We're in Love," "Out of My Dreams," and the title song. That was an influential musical because songs propelled the story, instead of being dropped into a play.

The American entertainment industry joined the War effort in full force in 1943. In Hollywood, directors John Huston and John Ford made patriotic war films such as *Desert Victory, The Battle of Midway* and *Fires Were Started*. Actor Humphrey Bogart starred in *Casablanca* while Joan Crawford and Bette Davis starred in *Stage Door Canteen*. Actor Jimmy Stewart served as a pilot while a number of other actors, including Ronald Reagan and Clark Gable, starred in documentaries and propaganda war films for the Armed Forces.

The Big Band sound reigned, although Captain Glenn Miller served his country in the U.S. Army Air Force, leading a band entertaining troops. Major pop hits from 1943 include "American Patrol" and "I've Got a Gal In Kalamazoo" by Glenn Miller and His Orchestra; "Sunday, Monday or Always" by Bing Crosby; " "Don't Get Around Much Any More" by Duke Ellington and His Orchestra; "Besame Mucho by Jimmy Dorsey and his Orchestra; "Paper Doll" by the Mills Brothers, and the songs "Lili Marline," "I Left My Heart at the Stage Door Canteen," and "Pistol Packin' Mama," which was a pop hit by Bing Crosby, covering the country hit by Al Dexter on Capitol.

Frank Sinatra

During World War II, Frank Sinatra emerged as a star, capturing the hearts of teenage girls with his ballads. Virtually unknown when the War began, Sinatra was one of the biggest pop stars of that era when the War finished. An intense, determined, ambitious young man, Frank Sinatra was not easy to get along with and did not allow for anyone or anything to stand in the way of his climb to success and fame. Sinatra did not replace Bing Crosby as America's favorite singer; instead he gave audiences a different kind of singer to admire, one whose singing was an "art" and whose recordings captured the longing of love-starved teenage girls, yearning for romance.

Frank Sinatra's father, Marty, emigrated from Sicily with his parents, settling in Hoboken, New Jersey, where he married Dolly Gravente. Marty Sinatra worked as a boilermaker in a shipyard while Dolly ran a bar during Prohibition. Their only child, Francis Albert Sinatra, was born December 12, 1915.

Biographer Randy Taraborrelli observed that "From an early age, Sinatra had a petulant, spoiled streak that dictated that if he didn't get his way, not only did he not want to be in the game, he didn't even want to know the other players." The biographer further stated that "His near obsession with cleanliness, his unyielding stubbornness, and his legendary temper can be clearly traced to his mother...'he was as scrappy as they come.'"

Frank Sinatra grew up with pictures of Bing Crosby on his bedroom wall. He dropped out of high school, took business classes at a local business school then, at 16, went to work in the shipyards, unloading crates of books, then to United Fruit Lines where he worked on transport ships. But he always wanted to be a singer.

Sinatra bought a portable public-address system and sheet-music arrangements so he could work in local nightclubs. "I started collecting orchestrations," Frank once explained. "Bands needed them. I had them. If the local orchestras wanted to use my arrangements, and they always did, because I had a large and up-to-the-minute collection, they had to take singer Sinatra, too. Nobody was cheated. The bands needed what they rented from me, and I got what I wanted, too."

Sinatra started singing with small bands in clubs on evenings and weekends, continually listening to Bing Crosby. However, along the way, Sinatra made the decision to become "a different kind of singer...It occurred to me that maybe the world didn't need another Crosby. I decided to experiment a little and come up with something different. What I finally hit on was more the bel canto Italian school of singing...It was more difficult than Crosby's style, much more difficult."

The singer's first big break came in 1935 when he was 19 and auditioned for "Major Bowes and His Original Amateur Hour" on NBC radio, broadcast from the Capitol Theater in New York. A group, The Three Flashes, also auditioned and Bowe's decided to team them and call them "The Hoboken Four." They performed "Shine," a hit record for Bing Crosby and the Mills Brothers, and were a success, going on tour with Bowes's other amateurs.

Sinatra left The Hoboken Four at the end of 1935 and waited tables and sang at the Rustic Cabin, a roadhouse in Englewood Cliffs, New Jersey, and performed on radio programs. On February 4, 1939, the 23-year-old married and his wife, Nancy, worked as a secretary, enabling Frank to continue in the entertainment business.

Sinatra contacted bandleader Harry James, who was looking for a singer, and James went to the Rustic Cabin to see him perform. Impressed with Sinatra, James hired him and Sinatra made his debut with Harry James and his Music Makers on June 30, 1939, at the Hippodrome Theater in Baltimore, performing "Wishing" and "My Love For You." That same year, Sinatra recorded ten songs with the James band--his first recordings. Songs recorded included "From the Bottom of My Heart," "Melancholy Mood" and "All or Nothing At All," which sold few copies on its initial release but became a major hit when re-released a few years later.

At the Hotel Sherman in Chicago, the James group appeared with the Tommy Dorsey Orchestra; Sinatra, always ambitious, set his sights on joining Dorsey's orchestra when he found out that Dorsey wanted to replace his vocalist, Jack Leonard. Harry James generously let Sinatra leave his group, even though James had a contract with the young singer. Sinatra's first performance with the Dorsey band was in January, 1940; he joined singer Jo Stafford and the Pied Pipers, who also sang with Dorsey.

The contract Tommy Dorsey offered Sinatra called for the singer to be paid $75 a week for two years; after that, Sinatra would owe 10 percent of his income to Dorsey's agent and a third of his total earnings to Dorsey-- for the rest of his life. Sinatra, hungry for a break and eager to join Dorsey, signed the agreement.

Sinatra made his first recordings with the Dorsey band in February, 1940, then had a session in May where he recorded "I'll Never Smile Again," which became his first big hit, staying number one on the *Billboard* chart for 12 consecutive weeks.

Sinatra watched Tommy Dorsey play his trombone and wondered how Dorsey could play a musical phrase for as long as 16 bars. Sinatra "knew that if he could sustain a note as long as that, he would be able to sing a song with much more dramatic impact. (Many singers ruined their songs by taking breaths in the wrong place, thereby interfering with the melody as well as the lyric's message.)." Sinatra finally realized that "Dorsey had what he called 'a sneak pinhole in the corner of his mouth.' It wasn't an actual pinhole, of course, but rather a tiny place where Dorsey was sneaking in air."

According to biographer Taraborrelli, "Frank realized that in order to do this--to sustain those notes in a seamless fashion---he would need extraordinary breath control. So he began an intense swimming regiment in public pools, which he would find in cities on the tour. As he took laps underwater, holding his breath, he would sing song lyrics in his head and approximate the time he needed to sustain certain notes. That it all looked so simple was just part of the magic. 'It was easy,' Frank said later. 'It just wasn't simple.'"

Sinatra also ran laps, singing to himself, practicing holding notes. The result was that Sinatra "was able to sing six bars--sometimes eight--without taking in air. Other singers were lucky to be able to sing two or four. Frank learned to sneak in air from the sides of his mouth, and no one was the wiser...When he did decide to take that breath, he would do it in as dramatic a fashion as possible, effecting a gasp of anguish when he needed it, when it suited the lyric of the torch song being performed."

Sinatra also learned from Dorsey "that a vocalist didn't necessarily have to sing a song the same way every time he performed it, though that is what most singers did. Dorsey taught Sinatra how to personalize a melody so that it was unique to the moment, yet familiar to the fans just the same"

Sinatra, who stood five feet nine and weighed 138 pounds, with a 29 inch waist, not only used the microphone as his instrument in the band, he also found a way to "tenderly hold the microphone stand like a considerate lover during romantic ballads or jerk it roughly if he felt he needed that kind of impact on a brassier number. He would back away from the mike when a dramatic note needed to soar to the heavens and echo, or step into it if he wanted the crowd to hear just the slightest sigh or breath...The way Sinatra romanced a mike and mike stand was erotic and an important part of his appeal."

Sinatra appeared in his first movie, *Las Vegas* in October, 1940, singing "I'll Never Smile Again." During the summer of 1941, he was on the radio, on records, in the movies, on theater stages and in nightclubs, performing with the Dorsey group.

In January, 1942, *Billboard* and *Downbeat* both named Sinatra the top male vocalist, ending the six year reign of Bing Crosby. Sinatra desperately wanted to leave the Dorsey band and become a solo star, but there was the problem of his contract with Dorsey. Sinatra was also tied to RCA Victor by this time because of Dorsey's contract with that label. Finally, Dorsey agreed to let Sinatra leave, as long as the financial agreements in the contract remained in effect. Sinatra reasoned that he would deal with that thorny issue later and performed with Dorsey for the last time on September 3, 1942, in Indianapolis. When Sinatra left, Dorsey replaced him with Dick Haymes.

On December, 30, 1942, at the Paramount Theater in New York, Sinatra appeared in a program that also included the Bing Crosby movie, *Star-Spangled Rhythm*, and the Benny Goodman Band featuring vocalist Peggy Lee. The two week engagement was extended for two more months when crowds of 13-15 year old girls--known as "bobbysoxers"--showed up, screaming for Sinatra. Almost overnight, 2,000 fan clubs were formed for Sinatra, who hired a press agent, George Evans, who hired girls to scream whenever Sinatra sang a ballad. Evans also hired girls to faint, but it was discovered after one concert that 30 had fainted--but only 12 had been hired. Soon girls were throwing their bras onstage at Sinatra and he became a national sensation, dubbed "The Voice" by Evans.

George Evans got Sinatra media exposure, arranged interviews, photo sessions, autograph parties and visits to radio stations. In February 1943, Sinatra became a regular on the top rated radio show, "Your Hit Parade," sponsored by Lucky Strike cigarettes. That same year he recorded his first sides for Columbia and in August went to Hollywood where he sang five songs and appeared in *Higher and Higher* in his first acting role.

Sinatra was rejected for military service (punctured eardrum), so he pursued his career in the United States during the War. That caused many in the male audience--particularly those serving overseas--to intensely dislike Sinatra. Here was a young man who looked healthy and lived the good life back in the States while soldiers the same age put their lives on the line in Europe and the South Pacific. On top of that, the soldier's sisters, wives and girlfriends back in the States absolutely adored Frank Sinatra.

Sinatra was hot property, earning lots of money, which caused Sinatra and Dorsey to sue each other. Sinatra's booking agency, MCA, came up with $60,000 to pay Dorsey (although $25,000 of that came directly from Sinatra). MCA agreed to split the commissions on Sinatra with Dorsey's agency, Rockwell-O'Keefe, until 1948. Finally, Frank Sinatra was free and clear to purse a solo career.

After Sinatra signed with Columbia Records, the label re-released his earlier recording of "All or Nothing at All," which became a hit in 1943. In Hollywood, Sinatra signed a seven year deal with RKO to make movies.

During the 1942-45 period, Sinatra was constantly on the radio, either with his own programs or as a guest on the programs of other radio stars. He moved to Los Angeles and in 1944 starred in the movie *Anchors Aweigh* with Gene Kelly. In October, 1944, Sinatra appeared for three weeks at the Paramount Theater in New York, doing five shows a day, the first beginning at noon. Small riots broke out as teenage girls screamed while he sang. In 1945, the 29-year-old Sinatra recorded over 40 songs for Columbia.

Sinatra studied songs, particularly the lyric, because he "wanted to know what that song said and whether it appealed to him or not...'I'll leave the music to somebody else. I pick the lyrics.'" said Sinatra. According to biographer Randy Taraborrelli, Sinatra "always took his recording sessions seriously...[he was] involved in some way...in nearly every aspect of the session, from choosing the musicians to the fine-tuning of the arrangements." Taraborrelli added that "Instinct was always important" to Sinatra. "If the music or the recording didn't sound right to him, then it didn't matter if technically it was correct...It had to feel right. Or, as he would say, it had to 'swing.'"

By the end of World War II, life was good for Frank Sinatra, he was on top and thought his life and career would stay that way forever.

Billie Holiday

The voice of Billie Holiday was like a jazz instrument, manipulating the tempo and phrasing with her improvisational skills. Although she had a limited range and lacked a formal musical education, her voice captured the attention of an audience.

Billie Holiday was born Eleanora Fagan in 1915 in Philadelphia to an unmarried teenage couple. Her father abandoned the family to pursue a career in music (he played banjo and guitar). Holiday and her mother moved to Philadelphia where Billie stayed with her mother's half sister. Her first ten years were difficult; her mother was often absent and she was in the care of others. At the age of nine she was brought before juvenile court for skipping school and was sent to a Catholic reform school She was released nine months later, at the age of 11, dropped out of school, fought off an attempted rape by a neighbor and was placed in protective custody. She obtained a job running errands for a brothel when she was almost 12 and, around this time, first heard records by Louis Armstrong and Bessie Smith.

Holiday's mother moved to Harlem and in 1929 Billie joined her. Holiday's mother became a prostitute; at the age 13 Holiday also became a prostitute. When the brothel where they worked was raided in May, 1929, Holiday and her mother were sent to prison; in October Billie, age 14, was released, three months after her mother had been released.

She began singing in night clubs in Harlem, taking the name "Billie Holiday." She teamed with saxophone player Kenneth Hollan from 1929 to 1931, performing in a number of clubs. Her reputation as a singer grew and in 1932, the 17-year-old Billie became the singer at Covan's, a nightclub in Harlem, where producer John Hammond heard her and arranged for her first recording session in November, 1933, with Benny Goodman's group, singing "You Mother's Son-in-Law" and "Riffin' the Scotch."

In 1935 she signed with Brunswick Records through producer John Hammond and recorded "What a Little Moonlight Can Do" with bandleader Teddy Wilson. That was her first chart record. Hammond wanted her to record pop songs in a "swinging" style for jukeboxes and the success of "What a Little Moonlight Can Do" allowed her to record for Vocalion under her own name, instead of as a vocalist for the bandleader. Her sessions were produced by Hammond and Bernie Hanighen and her next chart single was "Twenty-Four Hours a Day," a pop tune which reached the top ten; those early recordings became jazz classics. Holiday was often accompanied by saxophonist Lester Young, who named her "Lady Day."

Holiday's recordings for Brunswick from 1935 to 1938 sold well and rescued the company, which was broke. Holiday received a session fee for her recordings, but did not receive royalties. She released a number of chart recordings, including "These Foolish Things," "Summertime," "The Way You Look Tonight," "I Can't Give You Anything But Love," "Pennies From Heaven" and her single, "Carelessly" reached number one on the *Billboard* chart and remained in that position for three weeks.

Billie Holiday was the vocalist for Count Basie's band for a brief period in late 1937, choosing her own songs and taking part in the arrangements. Songs she sang with Basie's band included "I Must Have that Man," "Travelin' All Alone," "I Can't Get Started," "They Can't Take That Away From Me" and the Gershwin's "Summertime," from the musical *Porgy and Bess*. A number of Basie's musicians played on Holiday's recordings.

In February, 1938, Holiday was fired by Basie (for being "temperamental and unreliable") and joined Artie Shaw's band, which put her in the unusual situation of being a black vocalist in a white band. Shaw stood up for her when they toured the segregated south where Holiday encountered taunts and jeers.

In March, 1938, Holiday was singing with Shaw's band on radio broadcasts; however, Shaw's songs were mostly instrumentals to she sang less than when she was with Basie. Under pressure, Shaw hired a white vocalist, Nita Bradley, who joined Holiday on the bandstand. Holiday left Shaw's group in November, 1938, after being asked to use the service elevator at the Lincoln Hotel after white patrons complained; she was also not allowed to be in the bar or dining room. Holiday only recorded one song with Shaw's band, "Any Old Time." Holiday's work with Basie's and Shaw's band led to her becoming an influential jazz singer and other jazz singers attempted to copy her style.

In 1939 Holiday recorded "Strange Fruit," a song based on a poem written by a Jewish school teacher, Abel Meeropol under the pseudonym "Lewis Allen." The poem, about the lynching of Negroes, was set to music and first performed at teachers' union meetings. Barney Josephson, who owned Café Society, an integrated nightclub in Greenwich Village, heard the song and introduced it to Holiday and she first performed it at Café Society.

Executives at Columbia did not allow her to record the song because of the sensitive subject matter but Milt Gabler, who owned Commodore Records, recorded it for his label on April 20, 1939. The song reached number 16 on the *Billboard* chart but did not receive much radio airplay; however, the record sold well—Holiday claimed it as her best selling record.

When Holiday performed the song at Café Society, the waiters first silenced the crowd then, as the intro played, the lights were dimmed and only a small spotlight shone on her face. After she sang the last note, the lights went out and, when they came back on, Holiday had disappeared from the stage.

After "Strange Fruit," Billie Holiday became a star; her two years at Café Society made her nationally known.

Holiday lent her mother, Sadie Fagan, money to support "The Duchess," a restaurant her Mom owned but when Holiday fell on hard times she went to the restaurant and asked her mother for money. Her mother turned her down and the two argued with Holiday angrily yelling, "God bless the child that's got his own." Later, she co-wrote the song, "God Bless the Child" with pianist Arthur Herzog, Jr. The song eventually sold over a million copies and numerous artists covered it.

In 1944, Holiday was signed with Decca Records by A&R man Milt Gabler, who continued to own the small independent Commodore Records.

Her first recording for Decca, "Lover Man (Where Can You Be)," became one of her biggest hits. For that song, Holiday insisted that a string section was added, which led to strings being added to her other Decca recordings.

In 1946, Holiday starred, with Louis Armstrong and Woody Herman, in her only major film, *New Orleans*. However, several scenes were deleted from the film because of the sensitivity of film producers who did not want to offend segregated audiences, although Holiday recorded the soundtrack.

Billie Holiday was addicted to heroin and spent most of her money— she earned over a thousand dollars a week performing at clubs—on drugs. In May, 1946, Billie Holiday was arrested in her New York apartment for possessing narcotics; her attorney refused to represent her at the trial so she pled "guilty" and was sentenced to the Alderson Federal Prison Camp in West Virginia; she was released in March, 1948.

A "comeback" concert at Carnegie Hall was scheduled the same month she was released from prison; it was a sold out performance. She sang 32 songs during that concert, including "Strange Fruit" and "Lover Man." That was followed by a Broadway show, *Holiday on Broadway*, which also sold out but lasted only three weeks.

In January, 1949, Holiday was arrested in San Francisco for drugs; her New York City Cabaret Card, which allowed her to perform in clubs in New York, was revoked because of her drug conviction so she could not perform anywhere that sold alcohol for the rest of her life. Those were the highest paying dates for singers and her main source of revenue.

During the 1950s, Holiday's records went out of print and she received few royalties; her attorney had neglected to register her songs with BMI (except for two songs) so she lost songwriting revenue. Her health deteriorated, a result of drug abuse, drinking and relationships with abusive men. Her vocal skills declined but she toured Europe in 1954. In 1956 her autobiography, *Lady Sings the Blues*, was published, accompanied by an album, *Lady Sings the Blues*.

Billie Holiday continued to record and perform during the 1950s but developed cirrhosis of the liver. She was taken to Metropolitan Hospital in New York for treatment of heart and liver disease on May 31, 1959; while she lay dying she was arrested and handcuffed for drug possession at the insistence of an agent with the Federal Bureau of Narcotics, which had targeted Holiday for a number of years. On July 17, she died a few hours after the police guard had been removed; in her bank account was 70 cents. She was 44 years old.

V-Discs

Although American recordings were sold abroad before World War II--there are examples of songs, musicals and artists having an international impact--it was that war that made American music truly international. Ironically, it did not come from the American record labels, who could not record from May, 1942, until the end of 1944, due to a strike from the American Federation of Musicians, but from V-Disks, sent abroad to American servicemen.

As part of the military build-up in the United States before it entered the War, a Morale Branch was created in July, 1940, under the direction of General James Ulio for the purpose of building the morale of soldiers who were away from home. In June, 1941, Captain Howard Bronson was assigned to be in charge of music; he recorded military bands and marching band music for the troops. In March, 1942, this section was renamed the Special Services Division; in April the Radio Section established offices in New York and Los Angeles. The California office was headquarters for production while the New York office had production responsibilities as well as the job of working as a liaison with Army units to obtain personnel and material. In May, 1942, Thomas H. A. Lewis, who had worked for the Young and Rubicam Advertising Agency before he entered the Army, was named head of the Radio Section.

In April, 1942, George Robert Vincent, a 1922 graduate of Yale who had worked with Thomas Edison at the inventor's West Orange, New Jersey, laboratory doing research into sound recording, was named technical officer for the Radio Section's New York office. In July, 1943, Vincent, then in his early 40s, initiated the V-Disk program where popular music was sent to troops; this was initiated with a $1 million allocation from the Pentagon. The first V-Disks were issued in October, 1943, and the program continued until May, 1949.

At first, the Army contracted with record companies to supply recordings and with radio stations to supply transcriptions of broadcasts; then the V-Disk program began organizing their own recording dates, a move partially brought on by the American Federation of Musicians strike organized by union head James Caesar Petrillo.

In addition to Robert Vincent, other members of the original V-Disk team included Steve Sholes, who had worked for RCA Victor and Morty Palitz from Columbia. The V-Disk program was headquartered in New York.

By the time the V-Disk program ended in 1949, over eight million records had been distributed around the world. Those recordings were first made on shellac 78 rpm records and 33 1/3 rpm transcriptions; however, the shellac was easily breakable and the earliest shipments suffered with 80 percent of the records broken. Since shellac was easily broken, and also because of its scarcity (the Malay Peninsula and French Indochina, the major sources for shellac, were occupied by the Japanese in early 1942), the V-Disks were made of Vinylite, which had been used for radio transcriptions since the 1930s Vinylite also became critical because the military needed it for electrical insulations, life rafts and other supplies, so Formvar, a Canadian polyvinyl acetal resin developed in early 1943, was the major material for V-Disks throughout most of the War, except for those pressed by Columbia, which continued to use shellac.

The V-Disks were shipped in shockproof boxes sturdy enough to withstand 500 pounds of pressure and were coated with wax and waterproof glues. In a single box were 100 Duotone or Microphonic steel needles and a letter from Captain Robert Vincent inviting requests and comments from the recipients. There was also a Hit Kit of Popular Songs (one Music Book and 50 Lyric Folders) beginning in November, 1944. On the outside of each box was a release sheet, which listed the release letter, artists, and selections.

The initial V-Disk shipment consisted of 1,780 boxes containing 30 records each, or 53,400 records. In addition to the V-Disks sent overseas, there were 7,200 V-Disks initially sent each month to domestic bases and hospitals; however, those shipments were soon discontinued. In February, 1944, the number of records per box was reduced from 30 to 20; however, that same year the production of V-Disks tripled because of increased Army demand and to accommodate the Navy, Marine Corps, Office of War Information (OWI), and Office of Inter-American Affairs (OIAA). The last two agencies used the disks during short-wave transmissions to Latin America and Europe, respectively. During the War approximately four and a half million V-Disks were sent to the military.

The Army reached agreements with the American Federation of Musicians, the Music Publishers Protective Association, and the American Federation of Radio Artists for all fees and royalties to musicians to be waived; in exchange, the Army agreed that V-Disks would be manufactured only for military personnel with no commercial exploitation. The military also agreed all V-Disks would be destroyed after they were used. That allowed the Army to pay only for pressing the recordings because all sessions were "free."

At first the program was part of the Army but in the spring of 1944 the Navy decided to join and the first Navy V-Disks were issued in July, 1944.

Musically, the V-Disks were dominated by popular music with big bands and vocalists supplying the bulk of the offerings. Bing Crosby, the Glenn Miller group, Duke Ellington's orchestra, and others heard regularly on network radio were the most popular choices for V-Disks.

Armed Forces Radio

Col. Thomas H. A. Lewis, formerly with the Young and Rubicam Advertising Agency, headed the Armed Forces Radio Service during the War after he joined the Army in 1942. While at Young and Rubicam, Lewis had developed and produced the "Kate Smith Show," the "Abbott and Costello Show," the "Aldrich Family," and "Screen Guild Theater." He also founded, with Frank Gallop, the Audience Research Foundation to test audience tastes and responses to shows as well as define demographic breakdowns of radio audiences.

Armed Forces Radio during the War was a small, portable affair; the stations were 50-watters. During World War II the Armed Forces Radio Service used transcriptions and shortwave broadcasts to provide over fifty hours of programming each week. The Armed Forces Radio Services also produced their own programs for service personnel; in 1945 there were forty-three programs produced. That same year, transcriptions of American radio programs, with advertising messages deleted, accounted for thirty-six hours of programming each week.

The USO

In addition to V-Disks and radio programs, touring shows were also organized for military personnel during World War II, carrying American entertainers abroad. The United Service Organizations (USO) was founded on February 4, 1941, an outgrowth of a group organized in 1918 to entertain American soldiers in France during World War I. Six of those organizations--the Young Women's Christian Association (YWCA), the Young Men's Christian Association (YMCA), the National Catholic Community Service, the National Jewish Welfare Board, the Traveler's Aid Association and the Salvation Army were brought together by Frank Weil, head of the National Jewish Welfare Board, in New York in October, 1940.

The organizations formed the United Service Organizations for National Defense, which was later shortened to the United Service Organization (USO) and Walter Hoving, a director of the Salvation Army, was named the first president while Thomas E. Dewey, a future nominee for President, was head of fund-raising. In January, 1941, the leaders of the USO were summoned to Washington by President Franklin Roosevelt and met with Paul McNutt, director of the Federal Security Agency; General George Marshall, Army Chief of Staff; Mrs. Frederick Osborn, chairman of the Joint Army and Navy Committee on Welfare and Recreation; and Admiral Chester Nimitz, chief of naval operations.

On February 4, the USO was incorporated in the state of New York and by the end of that year had raised over $16 million. After the initial fund-raising, Dewey resigned to run for Governor of New York (he won) and was replaced by Prescott Bush, with the firm of Brown Brothers Harriman & Company and later a United States Senator and father and grandfather to future Presidents named George Bush. During the rest of the War, the organization raised $33 million.

At first, USO centers were established in the United States where there were military training camps. Those centers served as havens of recreation that hosted dances, parties and other social activities. They were staffed by young women who served as volunteers. By the end of the War in 1945, over 1.5 million Americans had volunteered at USOs.

On October 30, 1941, Camp Shows, Inc. was created to stage live shows by professional entertainers. The president of Camp Shows was Abe Lastfogel, chairman of the board at the William Morris Agency. The first overseas tour was held at defense installations in the Caribbean and lasted two weeks. Performers included Laurel and Hardy, John Garfield, Ray Bolger, Chico Marx and Mitzi Mayfair. Soon, there were four circuits: the Victory Circuit brought fully staged Broadway shows to military bases stateside; the Blue Circuit featured vaudeville entertainers who performed at military bases that did not have facilities for large audiences; the Hospital Circuit provided entertainment for military hospitals, and the Foxhole Circuit took shows all over the world to soldiers and sailors.

By the end of the War over seven thousand performers, known as "Soldiers in Greasepaint" had performed on those tours. Well-known entertainers included Bing Crosby, Bob Hope, Ann Sheridan, the Andrews Sisters, Al Jolson, Clark Gable, Carol Lombard, Gertrude Lawrence, Walt Disney, Gary Cooper, Fred Astaire, James Cagney, Humphrey Bogart, Dinah Shore, Jimmy Stewart, Paulette Goddard. Joe E. Brown, Benny Goodman, Sammy Kaye, Martha Raye and Marlene Dietrich, who had been placed on Adolf Hitler's death list. They performed on 428,521 live shows to over

212,974,401 people (in the United States, men and women working in defense plants were also included).

The work was not without risks; thirty-seven entertainers were killed during the War, including Glenn Miller, who was killed on December 16, 1944, when his plane went down over the English channel. By the end of the War in Europe (May, 1945) the USO produced as many as 700 shows each day for American service personnel around the world.

King Records

In September, 1943, Decca settled with the American Federation of Musicians, but Columbia and RCA Victor continued to hold out. In Cincinnati, a new record label, King, was started by Sydney Nathan. Nathan had worked a variety of jobs--in a pawnshop, as a wrestling promoter, ran a shooting gallery and then a photo finishing operation--before he began selling used records. He soon realized there weren't enough race and hillbilly recordings to satisfy demand, and the major labels were not spending much time or effort recording country or, especially, blues music, so he established his own label and then developed a vertical organization that controlled publishing, a pressing plant, mastering and printing facilities, a recording studio, a national distribution network and his own trucking fleet to carry records to distributors.

Nathan established King Records in November and his first recordings were by country acts Merle Travis and Grandpa Jones as the Sheppard Brothers. The Boone County Jamboree at WLW gave him a pool of talent to draw from and he soon recorded Cowboy Copas, Moon Mullican and the Delmore Brothers.

The Roots of Rhythm and Blues

In January, 1943 an article appeared in *Billboard* stating that Negroes were not allowed to join most AFL unions; instead, cities had established two separate unions, one for blacks and another for whites. Los Angeles had two local unions; across the country there were 673 AFM locals and 32 were for blacks. There were 641 white locals and eight had segregated subsidiary branches. Most locals denied membership to blacks outright.

The *Billboard* article stated, "the role of the American Negro in the war effort cannot be mentioned on a sponsored program. Negro artists may not be introduced on any commercial network show with the appellation of 'Mr.' 'Mrs.,' or 'Miss" preceding his other name." There were a few exceptions, pointed out by NBC, which objected to the article. However, the fact remained that network radio, the major source of music during the 1930s and through the war years, was overwhelmingly off limits to African Americans.

There were recordings by blacks on the *Billboard's* "Harlem Hit Parade" at the beginning of 1943, dominated by Decca, which had eight of the top ten records with acts such as the Ink Spots, Lionel Hampton, Lucky Millinder, Bea Booze, Ella Fitzgerald, and Charlie Barnet. The only indie on the charts was Savoy with "Don't Stop Now" by the Bunny Banks Trio.

The most successful black artists on major labels during the War years were The Ink Spots, the Mills Brothers, Ella Fitzgerald, Louis Jordan and Nat King Cole, who all appealed to white audiences.

By 1942, the term "sepia" was generally used for the genre of African-American recordings, although when *Billboard* instituted its chart for black performers in October, 1942, it was called the "Harlem Hit Parade." That chart was dominated by black big band performers. The major artist to emerge during that period was Louis Jordan, whose biggest hits were "G.I. Jive" and "Is You Is, or Is You Ain't (Ma' Baby?)" which reached the pop charts. "Is You Is" was featured in four Hollywood movies.

Rhythm and Blues in Los Angeles

During the period 1940-1945, a number of defense plants were established on the West Coast, particularly the area in and around Los Angeles. When the Japanese attacked Pearl Harbor, citizens on the West Coast felt threatened, believing that the Japanese would continue east and attack the West Coast. That fear lasted throughout World War II and led to citizens regularly patrolling the beaches on the West Coast and the construction of munitions factories.

The need for workers in those defense factories led to a number of people moving to California for jobs. Whites settled in the north of Los Angeles, in the San Fernando Valley and then about 100 miles further north in Bakersfield. About 5,000 African-Americans a month moved to L.A., settling in the southern central areas of Watts and Compton. Central Avenue became a center of black entertainment with clubs such as the Plantation, the Downbeat, the Savoy, the Memo and the Chicken Shack. When Japanese citizens were evicted from their homes to concentration camps, blacks moved into the "Little Tokyo" area.

In 1942, the Exclusive label was formed by two Creole brothers, Leon and Otis Reno, who came from Louisiana to L.A. during the 1930s. Leon Reno wrote "When It's Sleepytime Down South" for Louis Armstrong and

"When the Swallows Come Back to Capistrano" by the Ink Spots. Their brother, Otis, founded Excelsior Records.

In July, 1944, Norman Granz began his "Jazz at the Philharmonic concerts.

In 1945, two important indie labels were founded. Jules, Saul and Joe Bihari formed Modern Music. The sons of a Lebanese grain merchant, they came to Los Angeles in 1941 and entered the restaurant and jukebox business.

Also in 1945, Philo was formed by brothers Leo and Eddie Messner, who had the Philharmonic Music Shop in downtown Los Angeles. The following year, Philo changed its name to Aladdin Records and during the following years had hits with Texas Boggieman Amos Milburn and Charles Brown.

Louis Jordan: The Father of Rhythm and Blues

Louis Jordan was the pivotal figure in the development of rhythm and blues "not only because he was the musical father of Bill Haley and, strange as it may seem, Chuck Berry, but because his fantastic success on disk, on the radio, in personal appearances, and on the screen fired the imagination of black artists and independent record producers. He demonstrated that, not only was there a market for black-oriented material and black-styled music, but it was a big market, white as well as black."

In an interview with Arnold Shaw, Jordan recounted that he majored in music at Arkansas Baptist College before joining the Rabbit Foot Minstrels. In 1936 he joined Chick Webb's jazz band in New York, playing at the Savoy. Jordan stated, "I really wanted to be an entertainer...I wanted to play for the people, for millions, not just a few hep cats." In 1938, after Webb's death, Jordan formed his own band, the "Tympany Five," although they usually had eight musicians in the group. Jordan received his big break in Chicago when he became the opening act for the Mills Brothers, then performed in a number of top clubs around the country. Jordan stated, "I made just as much money off white people as I did off colored...I had white audiences. Many nights we had more white than colored, because my records were geared to the white as well as colored, and they came to hear me do my records."

In 1938 Jordan began recording for Decca and had his first chart hits in 1942, "I'm Gonna Move to the Outskirts of Town" and "What's the Use of Getting Sober?" In 1943 Jordan had hits with "Five Guys Named Moe" and "Radio Blues" and in 1945 had a hit with "Caldonia." In 1945, Jordan had his biggest hit, "Choo Choo Ch' Boogie," written by Vaughn Horton and country songwriter Denver Darling. Jordan played a happy, infectious music and told Arnold Shaw, "My whole theory, my whole life, has been: when you come out to hear me, I want to make you happy. Now I hardly ever do any morbid tunes, or any sad tunes, or any tunes that would suggest that you cry. I wanted to make you smile or laugh."

Jordan's producer, Milt Gabler, told Shaw, "We favored good lyrics, topical and meaningful, and we got them from both white and black writers. When we found something we liked, an arrangement would be made up and we'd play it on the one-nighters. The songs that the public asked for again and again were the songs that we recorded. When we walked into a studio to do a record date, we knew that the four songs would be hits-- we had pre-tested the market." Record executive Berle Adams noted that Jordan's records "were never 'broken' through airplay. By the time they were released, we had a waiting public who had heard Louis do the tunes at his personals."

Jukeboxes

On May 1, 1942, the War Production Board took over the facilities of J.P. Seeburg and other jukebox manufacturers in order to produce war material. Jukeboxes were important to the armed services because no PX was without one. Called "Jukebox Clubs," they were set up in areas with jukeboxes generally donated by local civic clubs. The clubs were popular with soldiers, who listened to popular records while in the service. In the States, the clubs were viewed as an effort to combat juvenile delinquency.

By the summer of 1944, jukeboxes bought 75 percent of all records purchased and labels could not keep up with demand from consumers. The demand by jukeboxes for records by black artists was a major contributing factor in the development of rhythm and blues by indie labels during that period.

The Ink Spots

The Ink Spots, formed during the early 1930s in Indianapolis, Indiana, became an internationally known singing group during the 1930s and 1940s. The African-American group's original members were Orville "Hoppy" Jones, Ivory "Deek" Watson, Jerry Daniels and Charlie Fuqua; their smooth harmonies on ballads made them popular with both white and black audience.

The roots of the group go back to "Jerry and Charlie", a vocal duo of Jerry Daniels and Charlie Fuqua, who began singing in Indianapolis around 1931. "Hoppy" Jones and "Deek" Watson were in The Four Riff Brothers, a quartet that performed on WLW in Cincinnati. The group disbanded in 1933 so Watson, Daniels and Fuqua decided to form a new group that sang, did instrumentals and comedy; the following year Jones joined the group.

Originally named "King, Jack and Jester," the group changed their name to "The 4 Ink Spots" in mid-1934 when they began performing at the Apollo Theater in New York, opening for bandleader Tiny Bradshaw. Later that year they toured with Jack Hylton's Orchestra in the U.K., which gave them an international following. Three of the Ink Spots played guitar while Hoppy Jones played the cello like a stand-up bass.

In 1935, the Ink Spots made their first recordings for Victor Records but their first releases were not commercially successful. The following year, 21-year-old Bill Kenny replaced Jerry Daniels as lead singer; Kenny had won an amateur contest at the Savoy Ballroom in Harlem with his high tenor voice.

The group originally did comedic and "jive" songs but in 1938 they began using the "Top & Bottom" format developed by Bill Kenny. That format called for the lead singer (either Bill Kenny or Deek Watson) to sing the lead in the chorus of a song, followed by bass singer Hoppy Jones reciting the lyrics, then the tenor singer finishing the song.

The Ink Spots began recording for Decca in 1938; the ballad "I Wish You the Best of Everything" featured a guitar intro—which became a trademark of Ink Spot's recordings—but it did not sell well. In January, 1939, they recorded "If I Didn't Care," which became a hit and the first chart record for the group, selling over 19 million copies. That was the first recorded example of the "Top and Bottom" format, with Bill Kenny singing lead and Hoppy Jones doing the "talking bass"; it established their sound.

They followed that with a string of chart records in 1939: "You Bring Me Down," "Address Unknown" (their first number one), "My Prayer" and "Bless You." They continued their string of chart records until 1951; some of their biggest hits were "When the Swallows Come Back to Capistrano," "We Three (My Echo, My Shadow, and Me)" (number one in 1940), "I Don't Want To Set the World On Fire," "Don't Get Around Much Anymore," "I'm Making Believe" (number one in 1944), "Into Each Life Some Rain Must Fall" (number one in 1944), "The Gypsy" (number one for 13 weeks in 1946), "To Each His Own" (number one in 1946) and "The Best Things In Life Are Free."

During World War II, guitarist and baritone singer Charlie Fuqua was drafted; Bernie Mackey replaced him for two years, then Huey Long took over that role until October, 1945, when Fuqua returned and re-joined the group.

In October, 1944, Hoppy Jones died after collapsing on stage; he had suffered from cerebral hemorrhages during that year. He was temporarily replaced by Cliff Givens, then Bill Kenny's twin brother, Herb Kenny, assumed that role. Adriel McDonald became the bass singer for the Ink Spots from 1951 to 1954. The Ink Spots were the first African-Americans to appear on The Ed Sullivan Show; they made three appearances on that show, in 1948, 1950 and 1952.

At the end of their recording career, the Ink Spots had 46 chart songs. Since the original group broke up, there have been a number of groups which have used the name "Ink Spots" or some variation, the result of a number of court cases after various members left and formed a competing group. The final court decision, in 1955, stated that the original group was a partnership, not a corporation, and since Hoppy Jones died in 1944, the partnership had ended, therefore no other group could honestly use the name after that, so the door was open for over 100 groups that have used that name since then.

The Almanac Singers

Millard Lampell and Lee Hays rented an apartment in New York City, which they called "Almanac House," and Pete Seeger moved in with them in 1940. The apartment became a gathering center for left-wing intellectuals.

During 1941, Seeger and Hays performed at a benefit for Spanish Civil War Loyalists and Seeger, Hays and Lampell sang in Washington D.C. at a fund raiser for the American Youth Congress. Politically, the group was isolationist and for racial equality. A loosely organized group emerged that Lee Hays called "The Almanacs" because, in rural America, farmers "had only two books in their houses: the Bible, to guide and prepare them for life in the next world, and the Almanac, to tell them about conditions in this one." Those who sang with the group at various times were Josh White, Burl Ives, Sis Cunningham, the Hawes brothers, Peter and Butch, Butch's wife Bess Lomax Hawes, Cisco Houston, Arthur Stern, Jackie Alper, Jaime Lowden and Sam Gary.

The group dressed in street clothes instead of "show biz" outfits and performed acoustic folk music. They sought to present themselves as part of their audience and invited audiences to sing along with their songs. They performed at informal "hootenannies" as well as parties, rallies, union meetings and benefits.

An album of three 78s titled *Songs for John Doe* was their first release; the songs protested the Selective Training and Service Act of 1940 that drafted young men during peace time. The recordings were released in May, 1941; two songs were written each by Millard Lampell, Pete Seeger and Lee Hays. They were all connected to the Communist Party in the United States, although not all were members. They based their positive views of Communism on the Hitler-Stalin non-aggression pact of 1939.

Their recordings were released on Almanac Records, sponsored by Eric Bernay, who owned Keynote Records, had a small record store and was the former business manager of the magazine *New Masses*. Bernay insisted that performers Pete Seeger, Millard Lampell, Josh White and Sam Gary pay for the production. The release was controversial; the songs attacked large American corporations because the performers felt they had supported the rearmament of Germany and then sought government defense contracts. Those corporations were viewed as anti-union and racist because blacks could not obtain employment for the defense jobs. The folk singers were pacifists.

After Hitler broke the non-aggression pact and attacked Russia in June, 1941, Keynote destroyed all copies of *Songs for John Doe* and the CIO urged the group to support President Roosevelt, the draft and urged its members not to strike.

Black activist leaders planned a march on Washington protesting segregation in the army and the inability of blacks to obtain work in factories doing defense work but the march was called off after President Roosevelt issued "The Fair Employment Act that banned racial discrimination by corporations who had defense contracts.

The Almanacs released a collection of six labor songs in July, 1941, and two albums of traditional folk songs, *Deep Sea Chanteys* and *Whaling Ballads and Sod-Buster Ballads*.

After Pearl Harbor was bombed in December, 1941, the Almanacs released an album, *Dear Mr. President* that supported the war effort. The FBI and Army intelligence believed the anti-draft messages from the group were seditious and threatened recruitment. They were exposed for their Communist ties and received negative coverage in the press. In late 1942 or early 1943 the group disbanded.

1944

"Loose lips sink ships" was a popular slogan during 1944, indicative of the worry that Americans had about spies and espionage. Overseas, American soldiers scribbled "Kilroy was here" on every surface imaginable; it became a popular catch-phrase for Americans abroad.

About half of all the steel, tin and paper needed for the war effort was provided by civilians recycling what they used at home. A "black market," or underground economy, emerged to provide legally unavailable goods to consumers; by 1944, it was estimated that this underground economy earned $1.2 billion. In May, meat rationing ended (except for choice cuts of beef) and President Roosevelt approved the G.I. Bill of Rights, known officially as the "Servicemen's Readjustment Act," to provide schooling for returning servicemen. That enabled returning soldiers to attend college in record numbers, paid for by the Federal government, as a reward for those who had served.

In Europe, the Allied Forces planned their major cross-Channel invasion in 1944 but in January of that year the Allie's main offensive was in Italy while in the Pacific, American forces attacked the Marshall Islands. Although the War raged on a world-wide scale in 1944, the primary emphasis was the American military's build-up in England in anticipation of the D-Day landings in France.

Perhaps the biggest change in America's everyday international relations during the War occurred in the relationship with Great Britain. Before World War II the United States and Great Britain were, literally, worlds apart; after the War, the two countries were not only allies, but also knew one another in a way that was nearly impossible to imagine before the War.

Between January, 1942, and December, 1945, about three million American service personnel were in Great Britain. Most of those came during the build-up for the D-Day invasion on June 6, 1944; prior to that period the only Americans in Britain who were fighting were airmen. Although over a million Americans had gone through Great Britain during World War I, and almost four million Americans had gone to Europe during that War, the stay in England was brief and usually limited to a brief stopover on the way to France and the western front, where most of the action in World War I took place. However, during most of World War II, Great Britain served as the western front.

Americans had long held a distrust of Great Britain because they were viewed as colonizers with their British Empire; American school children were taught that the United States could only emerge after the British were defeated and routed from America so it could become a nation of its own and not a colony of Great Britain. The British also had preconceptions about Americans. According to David Reynolds in his book *Rich Relations*, at the start of World War II a survey of British citizens about Americans showed that "Americans were liked most for their 'friendliness,' a composite trait that included generosity, candour, kindness, and hospitality, and for their 'vigour,' whose cognate buzzwords were initiative, virility, zeal, and openness. Conversely, they were disliked most for their 'boastfulness,' ostentation, and a propensity for talk without action, and for their 'materialism,' greed and love of money. In general, the British thought Americans were "brash and uncivilized...[with] eternal superficiality."

The major build-up in Great Britain occurred in the six months before D-Day, at which time there were 1,650,000 members of the American armed forces in the British Isles.

By that time the British had characterized the Americans as "overpaid, oversexed and over here." There was some justification to that stereotype. An American GI received about 12 ounces of meat a day, twice what British soldiers received and three times the amount rationed to British citizens. An American private with less than three years service stationed in Britain received $60 a month in pay while British soldiers received the equivalent of about $20 a month. As a result, the American soldier was more attractive to young English women than British soldiers and a number of marriages-- as well as children outside marriages--resulted.

Entertaining the Troops

In terms of entertainment, Americans in England had to listen to the BBC, which was considered "an acquired taste" and considered inferior to American popular entertainment. The problem was an essential conflict between the differences in a basic philosophy of radio that evolved in Great Britain and the United States. In America, radio was seen as an entertainment and advertising medium; therefore, programs were developed to achieve the widest possible audience--to appeal to popular tastes and popular culture--and stations were licensed to individuals who pursued the profit motive in their programming. In Great Britain radio was seen as preserving and promoting national culture, to give people what they should have instead of just what they wanted. The BBC saw itself as a guardian and protector of British culture and morals and aimed their programming towards elite tastes. In the United States, radio provided entertainment whose purpose was to attract an audience; therefore, programmers aimed their fare at the "lowest common denominator."

For American soldiers, that was a clash of cultures and an affront to their basic beliefs; radio should primarily entertain, not educate; should satisfy individual desires, not protect social institutions; should promote fun, not promulgate duty. One of the first results of Great Britain's attempts to placate American soldiers--who the British wanted and needed in order to help win the War--was the broadcast of Jack Benny's and Bob Hope's radio shows over the BBC on Sunday evenings. That was not enough for Americans so, starting July 4, 1943, the Armed Forces Network (AFN) began operating in Great Britain from seven Army camps. Within a year it was operating 12 hours a day--from 11 a.m. to 11 p.m.--Monday through Saturday and 8 a.m. to 11 p.m. on Sundays. That network broadcast American recordings as well as a number of American radio shows, eliminating all references to commercial sponsors.

A number of American films were sent overseas to Great Britain and about 85 percent of the movies seen by British during the War were American. The films were regulated by the movie industry to assure distribution. Censorship was not new to the movie industry; films had been regulated since the Hays Office was established during the 1930s to regulate sex and violence in the movies.

The movie industry had imposed its own self-censorship during the 1930s but its production code was a response to criticism from the Catholic Church and primarily regulated scenes of sex and violence. After Pearl Harbor, censorship became political in content and governmental in operation. By 1943, the staff in the Office of War Information (OWI) office in Los Angeles had issued broad guidelines, sat in on story conferences, reviewed screenplays, rewrote scripts, and pressured studios to scrap whole pictures. The Office of Censorship could withhold export licenses for unacceptable films. The basic criterion of the *Government Information Manual for the Motion Picture Industry* was "Will this picture help win the war?" That meant highlighting the struggle ideologically as a crusade for democracy, embodied by America at home and assisted by its Allies abroad. Thus, a number of musicals *like Meet Me in St. Louis* were produced as well as a number of "war" movies that emphasized the importance and rightness of America's involvement in World War II.

The American military policy towards its soldiers abroad was to keep them entertained and make wherever they were stationed feel like "home" as much as possible in order to keep morale high. The American Red Cross set up clubs and social centers with an American atmosphere and dispensed American products like cigarettes and Coca Cola. The British set up "Welcome Clubs" for servicemen as well, hosting social gatherings and dances in order to keep soldiers entertained and occupied during their off-hours.

Those clubs reflected the basic view of the average American soldier in Great Britain: he was "not interested in Britain or the British. He is only interested in the day the war will end, so that he may return home. During the interim, he remains close to his own fellow Americans and seeks diversions in pubs and other public places of amusement." The British didn't exactly look at American soldiers with awe and envy; an article in *Time* stated they were "annoyed by the free-spending, free-loving, free-speaking U.S. troops" and thought of soldiers as "sloppy, conceited, insensitive, undiscriminating, noise."

Still, the stereotype of Americans by the British "remained 'youthfulness.' Those favorably disposed mentioned traits such as energy, enterprise, generosity, and efficiency. Those who basically disliked the United States cited boastfulness, immaturity, materialism, and immorality--...'the less pleasing qualities of adolescence.'"

Although American soldiers traveled internationally during World War II, they did not become "international." The emphasis on providing American home comforts and entertainment while they were abroad and the proclivity of Americans to be more concerned about the people back home rather than the people in other countries remained. In short, although the War was a defining point in the lives of Americans who participated in World War II, it did not internationalize them to any great extent. That was reflected in their preference for American entertainment.

D-Day to December, 1944

The D-Day landings on June 6 and 7 were difficult and brutal; on a stormy rainy dawn, after spending about 70 hours on ships, troops landed at five different points over a 50-mile wide area in Normandy, France, struggling ashore in cold water with high waves, weighted down with backpacks.

In all, 57,500 American troops, along with 72,215 British and Canadian troops, landed by sea (over 6,000 boats were involved) while 15,500 American troops and 7,900 British and Canadian troops landed by air. They faced a blistering barrage of firepower from the Germans entrenched there as they made their way ashore.

The Germans were caught by surprise, although they managed to inflict heavy casualties. Hitler had been deceived into believing the landings would occur at another point in France, causing him to hold reserves out of the action; that allowed the Allies to obtain a foothold in France and began driving in-land. The Allies were helped by the Russians, who attacked Germany from the east, forcing the German military to fight on two fronts instead of massing its armed forces in one place against the Allies. Hitler answered the Allied invasion by sending V-2 rockets screaming into London, killing thousands of civilians.

Once past the beaches, American troops became tangled in hedgerows of trees and brush where Germans troops were hidden. The hedgerows were dense, tangled growth that soldiers had to hack their way through in order to advance into France. It took several months before troops broke out of the Normandy area; it was not until August 25 that troops liberated Paris.

After that, the Allies moved quickly across France towards Germany at such speed that they outran their lines of supply and had to wait for gasoline and other essentials before they could continue. In the Pacific, General MacArthur fulfilled his promise to return to the Philippines in October as American troops re-captured Manila.

The fighting went well until mid-December when Allied troops were hit with a surprise offensive by German troops in the Ardennes. Unable to receive air support--or receive supplies air-dropped in because of fog--American troops were pinned down in Bastogne while a severe winter storm hit, covering the area with snow and ice. It was one of the coldest winters in Northern Europe and the troops were not prepared; huddled in fox holes, troops suffered freezing temperatures as the Battle of the Bulge unfolded. However, when the Germans demanded the surrender of the trapped, pinned down American troops, General Anthony McAuliffe replied "Nuts!"

The day after Christmas the Allies began a counter-attack, aided by clear skies that allowed air support, and the battle turned.

American Music

American popular music provided the soundtrack for World War II. Americans at home and G.I.'s abroad listened to the same music, although there was obviously a lot more of it back in the United States.

The Nazis hated American popular music, and in 1944 German authorities demanded that war be waged against jazz and other "un-German" influences, calling it an "interminable knee-buckling perversion" and "an irreverence appealing to the lowest instincts of the masses." The diatribes against popular music weren't confined to Germany; in England, Lord Winterton stood in the House of Commons and complained that female crooners on the BBC "remind one of the caterwauling of an inebriated cockatoo. I cannot believe that all this wailing about lost babies can possibly have a good effect on troops who are about to endanger their lives." However, a government official answered that "I do not think a certain amount of crooning is likely to have a serious effect on the British Army."

By 1944, the Big Bands had lost members to the Armed Services and many groups had to disband. The loss of musicians to war manpower coincided with a shift in national tastes away from Big Bands and towards singers. The record industry hadn't quite caught up with those changes; there were no recordings made throughout 1943 and most of 1944 because of the musician's strike. Hits that year included "The Trolley Song" by Judy Garland, "San Fernando Valley" and "I'll Be Seeing You" by Bing Crosby "Time Waits for No One" by Helen Forrest, "It Could Happen to You" by Jo Stafford, "It Had to Be You" and "Long Ago (And Far Away)" by Helen Forrest and Dick Haymes, "Mairzy Doats" by The Merry Macs, and "You Always Hurt the One You Love" by the Mills Brothers as well as hits from the orchestras of Guy Lombardo ("Speak Low When You Speak, Love"), Lawrence Welk ("Don't Sweetheart Me"), Harry James ("I'll Get By As Long as I Have You" and "Cherry") and Duke Ellington ("Do Nothin' Till You Hear From Me"). There were also hits by African—American artists, including "Straighten Up and Fly Right" by The Nat King Cole Trio and two hits by Louis Jordan and His Tympany Five, "Is You Is or Is You Ain't (Ma' Baby)" and "G.I. Jive."

A major change occurred for the "hillbilly" and "race" record industries in 1944 when *Billboard* and *Cashbox* began listing the top ten records in each genre weekly. The "Folk" (as the country charts were labeled) and "Race" charts provided pop vocalists with new material outside the mainstream. In addition to the recognition of songs by those charts, alerting pop singers and their producers to be aware of songs in those genres, the hillbilly and race fields were helped by the increased power of BMI, which licensed most of those songs, and the continued backlash against ASCAP by broadcasters.

Billboard was a little murky on exactly what constituted "Folk,"; the first number one on the charts was "Pistol Packin' Mama" by Bing Crosby and the Andrews Sisters, which held that position for five weeks. The next song to reach number one was Al Dexter's version of "Pistol Packin' Mama," then rhythm and blues bandleader Louis Jordan hit number one with "Ration Blues."

Billboard did a story of "folk shows," spotlighting the Renfro Valley Barn Dance, stating the show managed to keep two touring shows on the road, averaging about $5,000 in revenue each, despite wartime shortages. At the Chicago Rodeo, Red Foley attracted 210,000 people to Soldier's Field over a two day period. Country singer Jimmy Davis was elected Governor of Louisiana in 1944; he also appeared in the movie *Cyclone Prairie Ramblers*.

There was no country singer to rival Frank Sinatra, called "Swoonatra," "The Voice" and the "King of Swoon," who performed at the Paramount in New York while 10,000 teenage girls screamed for tickets, held back by 700 policemen.

1945

By mid-January, 1945, the Allies broke out of Bastogne and were on the offensive again, marching in the freezing weather towards the German lines. With the Russians pushing through Poland on the East, and the Allies coming from the West, both Armies moved toward Berlin. In February, Stalin, Roosevelt and Churchill met in Yalta to discuss the world alignment after the War. The Russians wanted to keep the lands they had captured--Poland and East Europe--while the Americans and British wanted the nations decimated by World War II to have self-government. That same month, in the Pacific, the Stars and Stripes were raised on the island of Iwo Jima, 650 miles from Tokyo, after a brutal fight.

On March 7, American troops entered Germany; three days later American bombers raided Tokyo, killing 80,000. In April, American troops landed on Okinawa while in Germany the Allied advance became a route.

On April 12, the world received news that President Franklin Roosevelt had died, shortly after his election to his fourth term. Roosevelt had been in office since 1933--over 12 years--and guided the United States through two of its most devastating crises, the Great Depression and World War II. Most of the soldiers in World War II had come of age during Roosevelt's tenure and could not imagine another leader. In the United States, thousands lined the railway tracks from Warm Springs, Georgia, where he died, to Washington, then on to Hyde Park, New York where he was buried. The new President was Harry S. Truman and many Americans were concerned their new President was "too small" for the office, especially walking in the footsteps of a giant like Roosevelt.

In April, the Allies tightened the noose around Berlin where, on April 30, Adolph Hitler committed suicide. Both Hitler and Roosevelt came to power in January, 1933; now they would both die within days of each other.

After a nine-day battle, the Allies captured Berlin and at 2:40 a.m. on the morning of May 7 the Germans surrendered; the next day, May 8 was declared "V-E" (Victory in Europe) Day as thousands of Europeans gathered in the streets to celebrate the ending of the War. However, the Allies, had to turn their attention to the Pacific to defeat Japan.

In May, the only American civilians killed during World War II occurred when picnickers found a bomb the Japanese had launched with a balloon. The balloon landed in a remote area of Oregon and five children and one woman were killed examining it. That same month, a German submarine was sunk off the coast of Rhode Island.

On July 16, 1945, the Americans tested their first atomic bomb in the New Mexico desert; President Harry S. Truman then authorized the use of that bomb on Japan. After Japan rejected calls to surrender, the first atomic bomb was dropped on the Japanese city of Hiroshima on August 6; three days later a second atomic bomb was dropped on Nagasaki. On August 14, Japan surrendered. V-J (Victory Over Japan) was declared for August 15 and World War II was finally over.

Although the fighting had officially ended, troops could not return home immediately; however, by Christmas a large number had managed to make it back. There was still much work to be done, keeping the peace and rebuilding devastated countries where homeless refugees wandered, foraging for food and shelter. Allied Prisoners of War were released--many were emaciated--and the world learned of the Nazi's concentration camps for Jews. It would be a brutal, trying time in the years ahead for Europe and Japan, but at least the German and Japan military forces had been stopped and World War II was over. Americans were relieved and joyous; no soldier could get home quick enough and friends, family and loved ones thought the wait interminable as they prepared for the first peaceful Christmas in four years.

By 1945, new toys were scarce; there were no bicycles, sleds, tricycles, skates or electric trains being manufactured. During the school day, students often participated in air raid drills. School children sometimes lent a hand in putting together packages for the Cooperative for American Remittances to Europe (CARE) to help Europeans devastated by War. Those CARE packages reminded civilian volunteers of the devastation of the War in Europe. Because of the shortage of fuel, a "dim-out" had been ordered in January, with a minimum of light used.

By the end of the year, rationing for gas, tires and most foods was coming to an end. In August, President Truman ordered the full resumption of consumer production, free markets and collective bargaining, calling for a "Fair Deal" for all Americans. However, the demand for public housing and jobs was escalating and labor unrest was occurring. In December, 325,000 General Motors workers went on strike, demanding a pay raise and the opening of General Motors financial books to the public. During the War, labor had their wages frozen while General Motors made tremendous profits; now labor wanted to be compensated for their sacrifices while management objected. The United Auto Workers shut down operations in 80 plants in 20 states with that strike.

Radio

In 1945, the National Association of Broadcasters (NAB) celebrated its twenty-fifth anniversary, and NAB President J. Harold Ryan (who was radio chief of the Office of Censorship during World War II) gave a speech stating emphatically that radio was a business--not "some kind of art center, a technical museum, or a little piece of Hollywood transplanted strangely to your home town" or an educational institution. The business of radio meant providing consumers with what they wanted to hear so that advertisers were attracted to spend money on radio ads, making the radio business profitable.

Ryan's brother-in-law, George Storer, was already a radio businessman, owning a number of stations that operated independently. Storer bought and sold radio stations regularly for large profits but his operations came under the scrutiny of the FCC. While the FCC agreed that radio was a business, it also believed that radio served the public interest and therefore should have a personal interest in the local community and should not be big business with absentee ownership. The memory of the trusts and trustbusting early in the century was still prevalent and the FCC did not want a radio station owner to establish a Standard Oil in radio, owning a large number of stations. James Fly, head of the FCC, decreed that no one could own more than six AM stations or more than one in any market.

The issue came to a head in 1945 when Powell Crosley, Jr., the Cincinnati based mogul who owned a number of radio stations as well as radio, refrigerator and other manufacturers, wanted to sell his business interests (except the Cincinnati Reds baseball team) to AVCO for $22 million. AVCO chairman Victor Emanuel testified before the FCC that he knew nothing about radio broadcasting; AVCO was a "holding" company involved in manufacturing airplane engines, ships, boilers, bombers, jeep bodies and other goods. That concerned the FCC commissioners who ruled that whenever station licenses were purchased, others could apply for the channel to be vacated so no station could be sold unless it was in the public interest--which contested the idea of radio stations being private property.

FCC Commissioner Clifford J. Durr began to question station license renewals and demanded to know what kind of programming was being offered to the public. Stations had increasingly declined public-affairs programs in order to program popular programs that listeners preferred. That led to a report issued by the FCC in March, 1946 titled "Public Service Responsibility of Broadcast Licenses," which became known as the "blue book" because its cover was blue. That report directed local broadcasters to provide balanced programming, provide non-commercial programs, serve minority interests, help non-profit groups and experiment with new techniques in order to have their licenses renewed.

Cries of "censorship" and "freedom of speech" went up from radio programmers and station owners, although newspapers and magazines often lauded the report because it forced radio to serve the public interest rather than just commercial concerns. Lee de Forest, often called the "father of radio," was appalled at radio programming for popular tastes and weighed in with his view, directed to the NRB: "What have you gentlemen done with my child?...You have sent him out in the streets in rags of ragtime, tatters of jive and boogie woogie, to collect money from all and sundry for hubba hubba and audio jitterbug. You have made him a laughing stock to intelligence, surely a stench in the nostrils of the gods of the ionosphere; you have cut time into tiny segments called spots (more rightly stains) wherewith the occasional fine program is periodically smeared with impudent insistence to buy and try."

In the end, commercial interests had their way, although each radio station had to show that it broadcast "in the public interest" before its license could be renewed. It was helped by the fact that a number of Congressmen acquired an interest in radio stations and radio offered Congressmen the opportunity to broadcast to local voters through transcriptions recorded in a Radio Room in Congress, which kept Congress on the side of the broadcasters.

The FCC issued a ruling in 1945 that would have a far-reaching impact on radio, although it would be twenty years before the fruits of that ruling were seen by the majority of Americans. The FCC moved FM radio waves to a different part of the spectrum from AM radio waves. That ruling made the pre-World War II FM radio sets obsolete and seemed, at the time, a setback for FM broadcasting. Edwin Armstrong had proven during the 1930s that FM radio waves provided a cleaner, clearer radio sound but Armstrong was contractually obligated to RCA for his work and his efforts to change AM to FM radio broadcasting were thwarted by David Sarnoff, president of RCA, who wanted to pursue TV broadcasting. Sarnoff preferred to invest in TV instead of radio and felt TV would soon replace radio so there was no point in improving radio when TV was the wave of the future.

Sarnoff had introduced television to the American public at the New York World's Fair in 1939, but it did not catch on. The public was still in the Great Depression and could not afford the new technology. During World War II the development of television halted in order to concentrate on the War effort. When the war ended, Sarnoff and William Paley at CBS preferred to take profits from radio and invest them in TV technology rather than improving radio. This meant that AM radio continued to dominate while television was being developed and that FM radio was put on the backburner. Many felt this would be the death of FM radio because radio itself would become obsolete with the introduction of television.

However, the FCC also ruled that stations could present the same programming over an AM-FM combination, which removed an incentive to purchase FM sets because they would receive nothing new from FM-- and they already had AM sets. The FM carrier wave was used to develop television transmissions.

When World War II ended, the networks continued their commitment to news and public affairs broadcasting. Edward R. Murrow broadcast for CBS from Europe during World War II and became one of the most respected and well-known news broadcasters during that period. In 1946 he returned to the United States, was appointed vice president in charge of news and public affairs at CBS and given a documentary unit for a show entitled "I Can Hear It Now."

Small radio stations solved the problem of presenting national news through their use of AP, UPI and INS news ticker services, which provided news stories directly to radio stations. A disk jockey or news announcer had only to "rip and read" the news, which came in on teletype machines and did not have to depend on hiring a news staff for its news division.

Small radio station owners welcomed the changes. No longer did they have to hire talent for live shows and staff to gather news; all they needed was a news service to provide the news, disk jockeys to play records and read the news, recordings to play on the air, salesmen to sell time and an engineer to keep the station running. Stations began hiring disk jockeys who specialized in a type of music--pop, hillbilly, rhythm and blues--because each of those shows delivered a market segment that advertisers wanted to reach.

The Record Business

In 1945 two new record labels were formed. The Majestic Radio Company began Majestic Records and the MGM-Lion Company started the MGM label. In 1942, before the Musicians Strike, MGM head Louis B. Mayer allotted $500,000 to enter the record business but, because of the strike, only a small label, Lion, was formed, headed by Jack Robbins. In 1945, MGM hired Frank Walker from Victor to head their record label. One of the first things he did was contact Fred Rose in Nashville to obtain country acts; Rose would serve as the producer and, among the first acts he recorded for MGM, was Hank Williams.

RCA Victor, Columbia and Decca had not been enthusiastic about their records broadcast on the radio, but the new upstart Capitol held no such compunctions. Capitol sent its recordings to radio stations free of charge with the result that disk jockeys played them and the promotion sold many records--moving Capitol into the ranks of the majors. The Capitol policy took advantage of a new reality, especially after World War II, that disk jockeys had become increasingly important in promoting singers and songs. They changed the music business; no longer would fans of Bing Crosby or Dinah Shore have to wait for their network program to hear the artist, now listeners could hear the most popular acts throughout the day from disk jockeys playing records.

The disk jockeys were among the first to realize that the public's tastes had shifted from big bands to singers and played records by Frank Sinatra, Margaret Whiting, Nat "King" Cole, Dick Haymes, Mel Torme, Eddy Howard, Georgia Gibbs, Helen Forrest, Peggy Lee and Perry Como, which led to an increase of record sales. It didn't take long before the labels realized that radio airplay led to record sales instead of the long held belief that radio airplay stopped people from buying records.

In 1945, Capitol went public, offering its stock on Wall Street and raised $8 million in its stock offering. That helped the label position itself as a major. At RCA Victor, Eli Oberstein returned to head the music division. Things were humming; there were 32 pressing plants in the nation manufacturing records.

By the end of 1945, the year had seen pop hits "Till the End of Time" by Perry Como," "Ac-Cent-Tchu-Ate the Positive" and "On the Atchison, Topeka and the Santa Fe" by Johnny Mercer, "Rum and Coca-Cola" by the Andrews Sisters, "Don't Fence Me In" by Bing Crosby with the Andrews Sisters, as well as hits by orchestras led by Vaughn Monroe, Les Brown, Russ Morgan, Harry James ("It's Been a Long, Long Time") and Benny Goodman and Les Brown ("Sentimental Journey").

The beginnings of what became rock'n'roll a decade later were heard in songs on the pop charts like "Caldonia" by Louis Jordan and His Tympany Five" and "Dig You Later (A Hubba-Hubba-Hubba)" by Perry Como.

Network radio was king and the top radio programs starred Bob Hope, Fibber McGee and Molly, Lux Radio Theater, Walter Winchell, Edgar Bergen, Jack Benny, Mr. D.A., Fred Allen, Abbott and Costello, Screen Guild, Take It or Leave It, Kraft Music Hall, Eddie Cantor, Jack Haley, The Aldrich Family, The Shadow, One Man's Family and the Family Hour.

Country Music at the End of the War

Western swing dominated commercial country music sound at the end of World War II. Bob Wills and Spade Cooley were on the West Coast, playing at large ballroom dances in the Los Angeles area. One hundred miles north of Hollywood, there were several dance halls in Bakersfield.

In Pasadena, California, Four Star Records was established by Dick Nelson to record country music as a sister label to Gilt, which did R&B. Located at 467 Larchmont Avenue, it was nearly bankrupt when Bill McCall invested $5,000 and gained controlling interest in the operation. Don Pierce, recently discharged from the Navy, bought an interest in the company. One of the first acts to record for Four Star was the Maddox Brothers & Rose, who were on KGDM in Stockton, California. The Maddox Brothers & Rose wore striking, elaborate stage outfits, created by Nathan Turk in Hollywood. They became known as "The Most Colorful Hillbilly Band in America."

Columbia Records reorganized their country division and divided the nation in two parts; Art Satherley was in charge of everything west of El Paso while Don Law was in charge of the country east of El Paso. Biggest sellers on Columbia were Bob Wills and Gene Autry (overseen by Satherley) and Roy Acuff in Nashville.

Cliffie Stone began working as an assistant to country A&R head Lee Gillette at Capitol in addition to his radio duties. At Decca, Paul Cohen moved to New York, where he headed the country music division of the company. At RCA Victor, Steve Sholes returned from working with the

V-Disk program to re-join the label; he was put in charge of country and race music, and immediately noticed a country artist in Nashville, Eddy Arnold, whose initial release in January, 1945, had done well.

E. T. Herzog, who worked as an engineer with WLW in Cincinnati, established the E.T. Herzog Recording Studio at 811 Race Street in that city in 1945. Herzog's studio recorded a number of records for King and became one of the first commercial studios to record country music. In Dallas, Jim Beck was released from the army and began working for KRLD as an announcer; he built his first recording studio with the Army as his first client. Beck soon began recording Texas country music acts.

On Saturday night, December 8, 1945, exactly four years after the United States officially entered World War II, the Grand Ole Opry was broadcast live from the Ryman Auditorium on Fifth Avenue in Nashville. At noon that Saturday there had been a one hour matinee featuring Opry acts; that night the radio listings again showed the times for the performers: at 6 was Wally Fowler; at 6:15 Pee Wee King and Lew Childre performed; at 6:45 it was Paul Howard and Minnie Pearl; at 7 Ernest Tubb entertained; at 7:30 it was the Golden West Cowboys; at 7:45 it was Ol' Times and Lew Childre; at 8 it was Eddy Arnold; at 8:15 Uncle Dave Macon performed; and throughout the rest of the evening in 15-minute segments that structured Opry performances were Clyde Moody, Paul Howard, Ernest Tubb, the Golden West Cowboys, Roy Acuff, the Duke of Paducah, Bill Monroe, Curly Fox and Texas Ruby, Roy Acuff, Eddy Arnold, Roy Acuff, Ernest Tubb, the Golden West Cowboys and, closing the show, the Fruit Jar Drinkers.

By this time Nashville had been the place for several recording sessions by major labels; the WSM Radio Studios had first recorded Eddy Arnold for RCA Victor on December 4, 1944, and there were other recording facilities. Brown Radio Productions was formed in Nashville by Charles and Bill Brown (Monogram Radio Productions was a companion firm). Located on Fourth Avenue N. downtown, it was one of the earliest studios in Nashville. The Brown Brothers had an advertising agency that handled the Purina account, which sponsored a segment of the Grand Ole Opry as well as noon shows starring Eddy Arnold and Ernest Tubb that broadcast from the Nashville Theater downtown and were fed to the Mutual Network via WSM.

In December, 1945, in Nashville, Bullet Records recorded its first record, "Zeb's Mountain Boogie" by Brad Brady, a pseudonym for bandleader Owen Bradley.

There were major publishing companies, led by Acuff-Rose (whose founder, Fred Rose, enticed his son, Wesley, from his first marriage to leave his job as an accountant for Standard Oil in Chicago and move to Nashville as general manager of the publishing company), and recording label executives increasingly came to Nashville to look for talent and record them.

In terms of country music in general, the biggest song to come out of the war was "There's a Star Spangled Banner Waving Somewhere" by Elton Britt. That song became popular after its release in mid-1942 and put country music on the pop charts. Country songs were recorded by a number of artists, including the premier pop singer, Bing Crosby. It was Crosby's hits with songs such as "Pistol Packin' Mama," "New San Antonio Rose," "You Are My Sunshine" and "Don't Fence Me In" that served to make country music widely accepted and acceptable in the pop music world.

The major changes for country music in Nashville were all connected to the Opry. The War had led the country to be united by radio, and WSM emerged as a major radio station. The Opry was a major performance outlet with a network program; that attracted advertising agencies with New York connections and money to promote tours. The Opry organized its booking agency to capitalize on the demand for live country music shows after the War.

Jack Stapp returned to WSM Radio as program manager after the War while Jim Denny was in a position to be a dominant executive in the day-to-day operations at the Opry. Harry Stone was still a strong voice as General Manager of the station. In addition to the power of WSM and its affiliation with NBC, the Mutual Network began national broadcasts of "The Checkerboard Jamboree" in November, 1945. Those were two half-hour shows on Saturday afternoon, one hosted by Ernest Tubb and the other by Eddy Arnold.

During the War years, 1941-1945, things changed a great deal in Nashville and in the country music community; some of those changes laid the groundwork for Nashville becoming the "Capital of Country Music," the city synonymous with country music. There were immense changes in the country as well that occurred during the four years the United States was actively engaged in World War II.

Musically, Roy Acuff was the major star on the Opry through the War years, and he presented the "mountaineer" image. Acuff's power came from the fact that he hosted the "Prince Albert Show" over the NBC network each

Saturday night, which gave him star power, but there were other musical stars ascending from the Opry like Ernest Tubb, who'd joined in 1943 and who represented the Texas honky tonk sound with his hit, "I'm Walking the Floor Over You."

Country Music and Post-World War II America

The history of country music since World War II seems to center on several things. First is the rise of Nashville as the center or capital of country music, the corporate as well as recording center for commercial country music. That is certainly an important and legitimate story.

The year 1945 was the last year of World War II and a pivotal one for country music. At that point, American country music was dominated by Western Swing--particularly Bob Wills and Spade Cooley--and by West Coast country music. Of the top songs in 1945 only one, "It's Been So Long, Darling" by Ernest Tubb, was by a Nashville act. The next year would be a virtual repeat of 1945 with Western Swing still dominating country music. The top country music recording acts, Bob Wills & His Texas Playboys, Tex Ritter, Al Dexter, and Merle Travis were all West Coast acts. While Nashville was important for its radio broadcasts from the Grand Ole Opry on WSM, it was certainly not a recording center nor were its acts well known for their success on records. All that was beginning to change.

Nashville had all the musical elements that would guide the future of country music by the end of 1945. On the Opry was Bill Monroe with his group the Blue Grass Boys; by the end of 1945 his group included Lester Flatt and Earl Scruggs, and that sound would define bluegrass in the coming years. There was also Ernest Tubb and his Texas "honky tonk" sound showed another direction country music would take, especially into the 1950s as this hard driving, barroom sound virtually defined the sound of "hard" or "traditional" country for the coming years. Hank Williams and Webb Pierce later represented that "traditional" country music, which stayed close to its rural roots.

The star of the Grand Ole Opry was Roy Acuff, whose mountaineer image fit with the Opry's image of country music from folk roots in the southern area of the United States and whose full throated sound was the prime example of the country music singing style. Uncle Dave Macon, with his vivid showmanship and vaudeville background also connected country music to its folk and live performance roots but his sound and style were already part of the past, although a past that would be treasured and revisited time and again in the future.

Also on the Opry was Pee Wee King and his Golden West Cowboys, whose tight organization headed by manager J. L. Frank, pioneered business practices in country music artist management and bookings in the years to come and whose outfits--they dressed in snappy cowboy clothes--defined the country music "look" after the mountaineer image was shunned and discarded (except by Acuff) after World War II.

Ernest Tubb

Ernest Tubb came to Nashville from Texas, where he was born in 1914. When he was 12 his parents divorced and he quit school; in 1929, at the age of 15 he had a life changing experience when his sister came home with a Jimmie Rodgers record, "In the Jail House Now." The "Blue Yodeler" was Tubb's first and most important hero; the young singer set out to emulate Rodgers. In 1935, two years after the death of Jimmie Rodgers, Tubb was living in San Antonio, hosting an early morning radio program over KONO. One day at home it dawned on him that Jimmie Rodgers had also lived in San Antonio just before his death; he picked up the phone book, leafed through it and found the phone number for Carrie Rodgers, Jimmie's widow, and called her. Mrs. Rodgers invited young Tubb over to her house and then began to listen to his radio program.

Through the influence of Carrie Rodgers, Ernest Tubb obtained his first recording session on October 27, 1936 at the Texas Hotel in San Antonio, for Victor Records, the same label Jimmie had recorded for. On that session he recorded two songs about Rodgers, "The Passing of Jimmie Rodgers" and "The Last Thought of Jimmie Rodgers." Both of those were written by Elsie McWilliams, Carrie Rodgers' sister and writer of a number of songs Jimmie had recorded, including "My Old Pal," "Mississippi Moon," "Never No Mo' Blues," "My Rough and Rowdy Ways," "I've Ranged, I've Roamed, I've Travelled" and "Nobody Knows But Me." Tubb also recorded four songs he wrote, "My Mother is Lonely," "The Right Train to Heaven," "Married Man Blues," and "Mean Old Bed Bug Blues."

Carrie Rodgers arranged Tubb's second session with Victor in March, 1937, as well, and the singer recorded "The T.B. Is Whipping Me." At that point Ernest Tubb was a Jimmie Rodgers imitator: he wore Rodgers's tuxedo in publicity pictures, played Rodgers' guitar on recordings, and sang a number of Rodgers's songs when he performed.

Tubb made his first recordings for Decca in April, 1940, recording "Blue-Eyed Elaine," and "I'll Get Along Somehow," both of which he wrote.

He and his wife, Elaine, moved to San Angelo where he opened a bar, "The E & E Tavern," where he performed and developed the Texas Honky Tonk sound that made him famous. In April, 1941 he went to Dallas and recorded his biggest hit, "I'm Walking the Floor Over You." That song crossed over into the pop market and reportedly sold a million copies.

Tubb appeared on KGKO, a 5,000 watt station in Fort Worth and toured northern Texas, sponsored by Universal Mills, which manufactured the Gold Chain brand of flour; Tubb was billed as "The Gold Chain Troubadour" on his radio show and tours. In July, 1942, he went to Hollywood where he filmed a cowboy picture with Charles Starrett for Columbia Pictures; in that movie he sang "Walking the Floor Over You." In late November, 1942, he returned to Hollywood and filmed his second western with Charles Starrett.

At the end of 1942, Ernest Tubb was a hot commodity, in demand on records and for personal appearances. He decided to leave Texas and had to choose between Hollywood (which he initially favored because of the possibility of future movie work) or Nashville, home of the Grand Ole Opry. The pendulum swung in Nashville's direction because J. L. Frank, whose reputation for booking country acts and promoting concerts was firmly established through his work with Gene Autry and Pee Wee King's Golden West Cowboys. Frank called Tubb in December, 1942, when the singer was in Birmingham for an appearance, and invited him to perform on the Opry. Tubb agreed and on January 16, 1943, made his debut at the War Memorial Auditorium in a guest spot that was beamed over the NBC network. The formal invitation to join the Opry was then extended to Tubb, who accepted.

During World War II, Tubb recorded "Soldier's Last Letter," a song written by Redd Stewart, Pee Wee King's fiddle player who was then serving in the Army; Stewart sent the song to J. L. Frank, who gave it to Tubb. Also during the War he recorded "Tomorrow Never Comes," "Careless Darlin,'" "It's Been So Long Darling," and "There's a Little Bit of Everything in Texas." By 1945 he was appearing regularly on the Opry, on a 15-minute daily morning program, and a half hour show on Saturday afternoon, "Opry House Matinee," which was broadcast over the Mutual Broadcasting System and sponsored by Ralston Purina. That Purina Show, broadcast live from the Princess Theater in Nashville, featured Eddy Arnold from noon to 12:30 and then Tubb from 12:30 to 1 p.m.--two separate shows, back to back, with the same sponsor.

Bill Monroe and His Bluegrass Boys

By 1945 the Opry was expanding from the sound of acoustic string bands to include the various tastes of its listening audience. Even Bill Monroe, who had a traditional string band line-up, was changing his music and sound.

Bill Monroe was born in 1911 in Rosine, Kentucky, where he picked up the mandolin because his older brothers, Birch and Charlie, had already claimed the fiddle and guitar. Monroe first performed gospel songs in churches, then at house dances backing his Uncle Pen (Pen Vandiver) during the 1920s.

During the Depression, the Monroe brothers, Bill, Birch and Charlie, moved to Chicago, where they worked at the Sinclair Oil refinery; during evenings and on weekends they played at dances and house parties. In 1932 they obtained a spot on the WLS "Barn Dance" as buck dancers. Two years later, Bill and Charlie began performing music full time; they were sponsored by the laxative, Crazy Water Crystals, on radio stations. In 1935 they left the midwest and moved to North Carolina. On February 17, 1936, they made their first recordings in Charlotte for RCA Victor, with Eli Oberstein overseeing the session. That began a two year association with Victor which saw the Monroe Brothers record about 60 songs, which were released on the Bluebird label. In 1938, the brothers split and went their separate ways; Charlie Monroe kept the RCA Victor contract while Monroe formed his own band, The Blue Grass Boys, and learned to sing lead (he'd always sung tenor harmony to Charlie's lead previously).

In 1939, Monroe and his group went to Nashville to audition for Judge Hay, Harry Stone and David Stone for the Opry; he became a member of the Opry in the Fall of that year. Monroe began to hone his sound, which was a basic string band sound, but played in overdrive. Monroe's group played their music fast and, though he did not have a drummer, with a beat. He changed members as he worked on his music and by the end of 1945 had assembled what many consider the best bluegrass group of all time: Lester Flatt on guitar and vocals, Chubby Wise on fiddle, Cedric Rainwater (real name: Howard Watts) on bass, and Earl Scruggs on banjo. Monroe's music had begun to be called "bluegrass," after the name of his group, and the addition of Scruggs, with his unique style of three-fingered picking, defined the sound of bluegrass. By the end of 1945 "bluegrass" music was named, defined and set out into the world.

The Oak Ridge Quartet began as an outgrowth of the Georgia Clodhoppers, led by Wally Fowler. Fowler made the Oak Ridge Quartet a gospel group, with himself on lead vocals, and other members Curly Kinsey, Lon "Deacon" Freeman and Johnny New. In September, they joined the Grand Ole Opry. They recorded "Propaganda Papa" and "Mother's Prayer" for Capitol; playing his first session on those recordings was lead guitarist Chet Atkins.

The hiring of Bill Monroe for the Grand Ole Opry represented the taste of Judge Hay, but the hiring of Ernest Tubb, Pee Wee King's Golden West Cowboys and Eddy Arnold, represented the vision and taste of Harry Stone, who saw the need for the Opry to expand beyond its initial "barn dance" sound into something more commercial for a diverse audience.

Roy Acuff was the biggest star of the Opry, and he held the coveted network spot each week. Bill Monroe, with his hard driving sound that evolved to become bluegrass, Ernest Tubb, with his Texas honky tonk sound, and Eddy Arnold, with his smooth countrypolitan sound, were important members of the Opry at the end of 1945. All of those men played key roles in the future of country music, although at times it seemed like they were leading the industry in four different directions.

In terms of national acceptance of country music, there was a fifth direction country music was headed led by the Western Swing bands of by Bob Wills and Spade Cooley on the West Coast. By the end of 1945, the Opry had emerged as the leading country music show on radio, although "The Renfro Valley Barn Dance," "The National Barn Dance" in Chicago, and "The Hollywood Barn Dance" were still going strong.

For the country as a whole, 1945 was a momentous year. President Franklin Roosevelt died on April 12 after being in office for over twelve years; many in the country could hardly remember the United States having a different President. His Depression era programs led most rural Southerners to become "Roosevelt Democrats" for the rest of their life.

Harry Truman became President just in time to see the death of Hitler, the defeat of Germany, and the discovery of the Jewish Holocaust. Truman signed the United Nations charter in August, establishing that organization, while General Douglas MacArthur became Military Governor of Japan as the United States committed itself to rebuilding that country.

Rhythm and Blues and World War II

During World War II, several important independent labels began which were important for the development of R&B. In 1942, Herman Lubinsky began Savoy. Lubinsky was running a small record store in Newark, New Jersey at 58 Market Street at the time he began the label. In 1942, Joe Davis began Beacon Records, which was renamed Joe Davis Records in 1945. Davis bought the masters of Varsity when that label went out of business. The reason for the purchase was because of wartime restrictions on shellac; Harry Gennett of Gennett Records had received a shellac ration so Davis lent him the money to reopen a defunct pressing plant and receive shellac. That meant Davis could have records pressed on a cost plus basis and have access to a catalog of recorded material. Davis developed The Five Red Caps, who had a ht with "Mama Put Your Britches On" by Savannah Churchill, and Una Mae Carlisle.

Other labels begun during the war years were DeLuxe, in Linden, New Jersey by the Brauns, and Apollo, begun by partners Hy Seigal, Sam Schneider and Ike Berman as an outgrowth of the Harlem Record Show. National, founded in Manhattan by A.B. Green, had Herb Abramson as A&R director; Abramson later co-founded Atlantic Records.

By 1944, indies were coming on strong in the R&B field; Beacon had the Five Red Caps, Exclusive had Ivy Anderson, Hit Records had Cootie Williams, DeLuxe had Billy Eckstine and Keynote had Lester Young, Lionel Hampton and Cozy Cole, all on the charts.

In 1944, Speciality Records was formed by Art Rupe in Los Angeles. "Boogie No.1" by the Sepia Tones was Rupe's first hit record. In an interview with Arnold Shaw, Rupe stated, "To a black man, boogie meant intercourse, sexual intercourse" and "There was a tremendous demand for this type of record. The majors weren't supplying music of this type. With the wartime shortage of shellac and other materials, their pressings went mostly to pop music."

Jukeboxes were the major way for a label to promote an R&B record; if it was a hit on the jukes, then radio might play it but a hit R&B record would never start on radio. The jukes were also important because they purchased records in volume; small operators might own twenty to thirty boxes while a large operator might have a thousand or more locations so, if a small label convinced jukebox operators to stock their record on jukeboxes, they received important exposure for consumer purchases as well as a cash flow from the operators. That connection with jukebox operators was essential for a label to operate profitably.

A recording session was relatively inexpensive. The emphasis was on cutting a hit single; the studio rental was around $25 for a three-hour session for four songs, the cost of the musicians was $30 each with the leader getting double, and most R&B recordings used three musicians. The label would then have 600 or 700 copies pressed for sale to the jukebox operators; if they bought, then the label pressed more. If the song was played extensively, the record had to be replaced, which increased sales.

Songs had to be three minutes or less because the jukeboxes had a mechanism that lifted the tone arm after about three minutes. Also, jukebox operators wanted short songs because that meant customers played songs more often.

As World War II was ending, there were several immediate problems with rhythm and blues. The first was that it was hard to find on record--the major labels had virtually abandoned it since they reduced blues recordings during the 1930s. The white-dominated labels were no doubt uncomfortable with R&B, but they also had their plates full with what worked for them--big band music, then the singers who came out of big bands. That void was filled by independent labels forming, particularly in New York and Los Angeles. Another problem was that musically rhythm and blues was heading in several different directions. First, there was the "crooning" style that was popularized by Nat "King" Cole, which was derived from white big band singers, then there was the "tenor-sax styled combos" that featured "jump" music--which was a smaller version of big band swing. "Boogie woogie" and "shuffle" were also popular and so was the "shout-styled blues," both of which would lead directly to rock'n'roll a decade later.

The final problem with getting rhythm and blues to jukeboxes and consumers was a lack of pressing and distribution for independent R&B labels. Most of the pressing plants were owned by the major labels who guarded the technology; there were few independent pressing plants and it took technological know-how and a fairly large capital investment to put together a plant to press 78s.

There were three independent distributors handling R&B by the end of World War II: Paul Reiner in Cleveland, Jack Gutshall in Los Angeles, and Julius Bard in Chicago. Those distributors sold primarily to jukebox operators, but several new indie distributors began: M.S. Distributing in Chicago was started by Milt Salstone, Melody Sales began in San Francisco, Joe Kaplan started Pan American in Detroit and Bill David founded Davis Sales in Denver.

Independent Labels

The impetus for independent labels recording R&B came with the hit single, "I Wonder," recorded by Pvt. Cecil Gant in Los Angeles for Gilt Edge

Records. Gant was born in Nashville in 1915 and was stationed in Los Angeles during the War, where he played for bond rallies. Gilt Edge was owned by Bill McCall of Los Angeles, who also had Four Star Records (although some contend it may have been owned by Bob Geddins of Oakland). The recording was done in L.A. and distributed to jukebox operators there; in New York it was distributed by the Apollo Record Distributing Company and soon reached number one on the Harlem Hit Parade.

Gant was a crooner, influenced by Leroy Carr, Bing Crosby and Frank Sinatra, with a sound that influenced Nat King Cole. He dressed in army khakis on personal appearances. "I Wonder," though an incredibly influential record in the R&B market, was Gant's only hit. The black artist with a crooning style that emerged as a pre-eminent artist was Nat King Cole, who released "That Ain't Right" and "Straighten Up and Fly Right" for Decca, then signed with Capitol.

Several independents important in the recording of rhythm and blues were formed in Los Angeles in 1945. Imperial Records was founded by Lewis Chudd, who formerly produced the radio program, "Let's Dance," which was a key factor in launching Benny Goodman's career. Chudd served in the Office of War Information during World War II, then started Crown Records, a jazz label, but sold it to Irving Felt. Chudd then started Imperial Records, initially eyeing the Mexican market by recording Hispanic music. When Chudd found Fats Domino, the label became a major force in R&B.

The Mesners began Philo Records at 4918 Santa Monica Boulevard in L.A. in 1945; the next year it changed its name to Aladdin and their first hit was by former Count Basie vocalist Helen Humes, "Be-Babb-Luba." In 1946, Aladdin had its biggest hit with Charles Brown's "Drifting Blues."

In Oakland, Bob Geddins ran a record store and wanted to start a label. He rented the studio at radio station KSFO in San Francisco and recorded The Rising Stars, a local gospel group, doing "If Jesus Has to Pray, What About You?" He played an acetate of the recording over his store's loudspeakers so people in the street could hear it. When someone wanted to buy a copy, Geddins required a fifty-cent deposit for future delivery; in that way, Geddins had the money to pay for the pressings and begin a label. The next year (1946) Geddins built a small pressing plant that could turn out 500 78 rpm disks a day.

In March, 1945, the Biharis--Jules, Joe, and Saul--formed Modern Records, which developed subsidiary labels RPM, Kent, Crown and Flair.

The label was founded because Jules Bihari was a jukebox operator and could not find enough R&B records for the jukeboxes he serviced. In 1947 they bought a record pressing plant from Mercury; their first record was "Swingin' the Boogie" by Hadda Brooks.

Joe Liggins

In 1945-46, Joe Liggins' had a reported million seller with his record "The Honeydripper" on Modern Records. Born in Guthrie, Oklahoma in 1915, Joe Liggins moved to San Diego in 1932, then to Los Angeles in 1939. He performed with Sammy Franklin's California Rhythm Rascals and other groups in L.A. Franklin did not want to record Liggins' jump blues song, "The Honeydripper," so Liggins started his own band, Joe Liggins and His Honeydrippers, in the basement of saxophonist Little Willie Jackson's home; Jackson was co-founder of the group. Liggins played piano and did vocals, Little Willie Jackson played alto and baritone sax, James Jackson, Jr. played tenor sax, Fred Pasley played guitar, Eddie Davis played bass and Preston "Peppy" Prince played drums and percussion.

The group recorded "The Honeydripper" for Exclusive Records, owned by Leon and Otis Rene. It was released in 1945 and during the 1945-1946 period it was number one on *Billboard's* "Harlem Hit Parade" chart for 18 consecutive weeks.

Liggins followed that with a string of hit recordings, "Left a Good Deal in Mobile," "Got a Right to Cry," "Tanya," "Blow Mr. Jackson," "Sweet Georgia Brown," "Dripper's Blues," "Roll 'Em," and "The Darktown Strutters Ball," all for Exclusive. In 1950 he signed with Specialty Records and had a string of singles, including "Pink Champagne," which was number one on the Harlem Hit Parade for 13 straight weeks, "Little Joe's Boogie" and "Frankie Lee."

In 1946, Louis Jordan had a million seller with "Choo Choo Ch' Boogie" with its boogie-shuffle; other big hits that year were "R.M. Blues" by Roy Milton, "Hey! Ba-Ba-Re-Bop" by Lionel Hampton, and "Stone Cold Dead in the Market" by Ella Fitzgerald and Louis Jordan. In 1946, Apollo Records recorded Dinah Washington on blues numbers as well as one of the greatest gospel singers of all time, Mahalia Jackson, who had hits on "How I Got Over," "Just Over the Hill" and "Move On Up a Little Higher." That same year Arthur "Big Boy" Crudup recorded "That's All Right, Mama" for Victor.

Woody Guthrie

In 1944, Woody Guthrie recorded "This Land is Your Land" for Moe Asch's Folkways label. He had written the song in February, 1940, as a response to the overplaying of Irving Berlin's "God Bless America," which Guthrie thought was unrealistic. For "This Land Is Your Land," Guthrie took the melody from "Oh, My Loving Brother," a gospel song, that had been adapted by the Carter Family for their song, "When the World's On Fire."

Woodrow Wilson Guthrie (his parents named him after presidential candidate Woodrow Wilson) was born July 14, 1912, in Okemah, Oklahoma. Woody's father, Charles Guthrie, was a businessman involved in Oklahoma politics. When Woody was seven, his home burned down. His mother, a victim of Huntington's disease and dementia, was institutionalized when he was 14; she died in 1930 when he was 18.

Charles Guthrie moved to Pampa, Texas, to earn money to pay off his debts from failed real estate deals; the children remained in Oklahoma, supported by oldest brother Ray.

Woody Guthrie loved music and learned old folk songs from neighbors; he often busked for money. His father sent for Woody to come to Pampa in 1929 but Woody disliked school and spent his time busking or reading in Pampa's library. He married when he was 19 and had three children, but left his wife and family during the Depression to move to California, looking for work.

During the late 1930s, Woody and Maxine "Lefty Lou" Crisman performed country and traditional folk music on KFVD; during his time at the station, Woody began writing and singing protest songs; some would later appear on *Dust Bowl Ballads*.

Guthrie met newscaster Ed Robbin at KFVD and Robbin introduced Woody to socialists and Communists in Southern California, including Will Geer and John Steinbeck. Robbin was Guthrie's political mentor. Woody never joined the Communist party but was a "fellow traveler," which meant he agreed with the Communist party's platform and wrote a column, "Woody Sez" from May, 1939 to January, 1940 for the *People's World*, a Communist newspaper.

After World War II began in Europe, Guthrie and Robbin left KFVD because the owners did not want the two providing pro-Soviet commentary. Guthrie and his family moved back to Texas, then Woody moved to New York City at the invitation of Will Geer.

Woody became part of the leftist folk music community in New York. Known as "the Oklahoma cowboy," he recorded songs and conversation for Alan Lomax for the Library of Congress and recorded an album, *Dust Bowl Ballads*, for Victor Records.

Woody Guthrie met Pete Seeger in March, 1940, when Guthrie performed at a benefit for migrant workers hosted by the John Steinbeck Committee to Aid Farm Workers. Guthrie and Seeger traveled to Texas, where Seeger met Woody's family, and in April they moved to New York city where they were roommates in Greenwich Village.

The Model Tobacco Company invited Guthrie to host their radio program, "Pipe Smoking Time" in September, 1940; they paid him a salary large enough for him to bring his family to New York. The job with "Pipe Smoking Time" only lasted seven broadcasts for Guthrie, who quit and moved his family to California, where he only stayed until May, 1941, when he moved to Portland, Oregon for a job as narrator for a documentary on the construction of the Grand Coulee Dam on the Columbia River. His role became much smaller when the Bonneville Power Administration, that was constructing the Dam, became nervous about Woody's politics.

Woody was hired by the Department of the Interior to write songs about the Columbia River and federal dams for the soundtrack to the documentary. Guthrie was inspired by his travels in the Pacific Northwest and wrote 26 songs in one month, including "Roll On, Columbia, Roll On," "Pastures of Plenty" and "Grand Coulee Dam."

Guthrie then returned to New York but his wife, tired of being uprooted, returned with their children to Texas. That marked the end of their marriage; they were divorced in December, 1943.

Guthrie joined Pete Seeger's Almanac Singers, a folk protest group, in New York where the singers hosted "hootenannies," or gatherings when singers sang folk and protest songs. The core members of the Almanac singers were Pete Seeger, Woody, Millard Lampell and Lee Hays. They lived as socialists, sharing meals, chores and rent with money raised from their Sunday hootenannies.

Woody Guthrie wrote constantly, writing poems, prose and songs, which led Alan Lomax to encourage him to write his autobiography. That led to Guthrie's book *Bound for Glory*, published in 1943.

Woody met Moe Asch, who had Folkways Records, in 1944 and recorded hundreds of songs, including "Worried Man Blues" in addition to "This Land Is Your Land."

During World War II, Guthrie believed that the best use for his talents was writing anti—fascists songs. He wrote songs and sang for a radio program, "Labor for Victor" on NBC as well as other radio programs, as a solo act and with the Almanac Singers. He joined the Merchant Marines in June, 1943, after failing to persuade the Army to enlist him as a USO performer. Guthrie served in the kitchen fixing food and washing dishes in addition to singing for the troops. During the D-Day invasion, Guthrie was on a ship that was torpedoed by a German submarine but was not hurt.

Because of his previous political activity with the Communist Party, Guthrie was dismissed by the Merchant Marine and drafted into the Army. After his discharge, he moved to New York with his new wife, Marjorie, and they had four children. It was during this time that Guthrie wrote and record a collection of children's song, *Songs to Grow on for Mother and Child*. He wrote a novel, *House of Earth*, in 1947 that was not published until 2013. The documentary, *Columbia River*, which contained Guthrie's songs, was released in 1949, eight years after the songs were written.

By the late 1940s, Woody Guthrie's health was in decline because of Huntington's disease. During the early 1950s, he laid low because of the anti-communist movement led by Senator Joe McCarthy and moved to California, where he married his third wife. In Florida, Guthrie hurt his arm in a campfire accident when gasoline exploded on a fire being built. He was never able to play the guitar again.

Guthrie wrote about songwriting, "I hate a song that makes you think that you are not any good. I hate a song that makes you think that you are just born to lose. Bound to lose. No good to nobody. No good for nothing. Because you are too old or too young or too fat or too slim, too ugly or too this or too that. Songs that run you down or poke fun at you on account of your bad luck or hard traveling. I am out to fight those songs to my very last breath of air and my last drop of blood. I am out to sing songs that will prove to you that this is your world and that if it has hit you pretty hard and knocked you for a dozen loops, no matter what color, what size you are, how you are built. I am out to sing the songs that make you take pride in yourself and in your work."

The United States and World War II

It is difficult to imagine the changes that World War II brought to the United States, both domestically as well as internationally. That war, more than any other single event, united us as a single nation and made America an international superpower.

During the American Civil War (1861-1865) the central issue was whether America was a single nation or a collection of States; a "union" or a "confederacy." The Southern states believed they could leave the United States if they wished; the national government, led by President Abraham Lincoln, believed that the United States is a single nation and the parts could not leave. The Civil War, or War Between the States, proved that the United States is a single nation--not a confederacy of States.

Although a dramatic war was fought over that issue, and although the idea of the "union" won, the United States remained a large nation of localities and regions until World War II. No one doubted the South was distinctly different than the West, which was quite different from the Northeast or the Midwest; even towns and communities within a region were perceived as unique and different. World War I did not truly unite the United States because the American involvement came late and did not last long. The resulting League of Nations, created from President Woodrow Wilson's Fourteen Points, was virtually ignored by the United States after Congress failed to ratify the League so the United States never joined.

That explains, in part, the isolationist stance of the United States before World War II, although isolationism was deeply ingrained in America's psyche since its inception, a product of geography and natural barriers to intruders as well as having non-threatening neighbors on its borders. There was no reason to believe that what happened in Europe or Asia had any affect on Americans until Japan and Germany both declared War on the United States in December, 1941. President Franklin Roosevelt had instituted a number of national programs to combat the Great Depression--Social Security, bank reform, the Works Progress Association, and the Civilian Corps to name a few--that affected all Americans--but it was World War II that caused Americans to stand united.

The Great Depression was still part of America at the outbreak of World War II. In 1939, the unemployment rate was 17 percent, down from 25 percent in 1933, but still large. In 1943, the jobless rate was 1.7 percent. A large number--12 million or 75 percent of all young men born between 1918 and 1927--served in the military. In all, 16.3 million Americans served in the military during World War II; about 10 million of those were drafted. That was in contrast to 350,000 in the armed services in 1939 before the draft. By 1945 there were 12.1 million in the military or about 18 percent of the work force. More than any other single reason, the armed services ended unemployment in the United States.

For most American conscripts, life in the armed services was better than life at home; here, for the first time, they had a steady job, regular paycheck, regular meals, new clothes and good housing. When the first draftees took their physicals in 1939, approximately 40 percent were turned down because of health, primarily malnutrition, and for many inductees it was the first time they'd worn new clothes. For some farm boys, it was the first time they'd ever worn shoes.

In 1940, over 20 percent of Americans still lived on farms and less than a third of those farms had electricity. Only ten percent of those farms had flush toilets. The rest of America was a little better off, although 56 percent of Americans were renters who did not own their own homes. Over half of all the households did not have a refrigerator and 58 percent did not have central heating; around 30 percent did not have running water.

During World War II, there were huge shifts in population as people from rural areas moved to cities where there were defense plants, engaged in producing for the War effort. Approximately 27 million Americans moved during the War and between 1940 and 1944 farm workers dropped by 16 percent. Since the population in 1940 in the United States was about 132 million, this meant that about 20 percent of Americans moved during the War. The South lost the most people; about 3.2 million left that region during the War, while California, with its strong defense industry, gained one million in population.

War time employment peaked at about 60 million, with about a third of the work force comprised of women. In 1940, the average worker earned less than $1,000 a year and only 7.8 million Americans made enough money to pay taxes; by 1945 the population had risen to 140 million and 50 million of those made enough to pay taxes.

The Army had men from all parts of the country and did not segregate them according to region; that meant a Southerner got to know a Westerner, a young man from New York became acquainted with someone from Alabama, and a young man from Kansas might befriend someone from Vermont. It seemed like, for the first time, Americans really got to know each other during World War II.

World War II ended the isolation of the South in America. Most of the Army's training camps were in the South because there were large tracts of land available to establish bases and because the climate allowed training year-round. About half of those who served in the military during World War II spent time in the South, which meant about six million non-Southerners were exposed to the region for the first time.

The movement of Americans had a profound impact on their self-image. According to David Reynolds, "the Army mixed up young Americans as never before in their lives, but its immediate effect was to enhance rather than blur their sense of ethnic, sectional, and racial differences. Seeing America made them more aware of its variety; it was seeing the world that made them more conscious of being American. Reynolds notes that, once overseas, "many GIs...came to accept that they were all Yanks...the similarities outweighed the differences."

The United States became the most productive nation in the world during World War II; Great Britain's wealth declined by a fourth while America's increased by 50 percent. Big business benefited the most; the top ten corporations received 30 percent of the $240 billion spent on War contracts and the top one hundred corporations received over two-thirds of the money spent by the government on the War effort. There were 17 million new jobs created in the U.S. during the War and the GNP jumped from $100 billion to $215 billion a year. Factories turned out over two million trucks, over 100,000 tanks, almost 300,000 planes, almost 100,000 ships, over 20 million guns and 44 billion rounds of ammunition during the War. Because so much of the production was diverted from consumer items to the demand for war supplies, and because Americans were forced to save, there was a huge amount of savings and pent up demand at the end of the War. That led to a tremendous growth in consumer goods in the period following World War II.

A single example will indicate those changes: at the end of 1941, when World War II began, the United States Army owned pigeons as part of its communications systems and 200,000 horses for its cavalry. In August, 1945, the War effectively ended with an atomic blast from a bomb dropped by a long range bomber.

Prior to the War Americans were united in entertainment, especially the movies and radio. Musically, the radio was dominated by the networks (CBS, NBC--which had two networks--and Mutual). The most popular music was the Big Band jazz or groups led by Benny Goodman, the Dorsey Brothers, Duke Ellington, Harry James and others. Although country music became a national music through the Singing Cowboys movies, with Roy Rogers, Gene Autry, Tex Ritter, the Sons of the Pioneers and others who developed a national following, the country music from the South was known as "hillbilly" music and mostly confined to the South. Blues music was not recorded a great deal from the beginning of the Great Depression until after World War II and it was limited to cities like Chicago, Detroit, New York and others with a large black population.

1946

In 1946, the year after the War, there were eight million records sold; country music accounted for 13.2 percent of sales--topped only by "popular" with 50 percent and classical with 18.9 percent; blues records did not account for enough sales to claim a full percentage. The 550,000 jukeboxes, which before the War accounted for most of the sales of country records, now accounted for only about ten percent of the total. Part of the reason for increased country record sales to consumers was the exposure country music received, either on local radio shows, on network shows, or through disc jockeys playing records on the radio.

World War II brought Americans together over the radio to hear news of the world. People were employed because of the defense-based economy and were making money they could not spend because of the rationing of goods, as well as limited availability of consumer items, and the heavy encouragement of savings by the government through their "War bond" drives to finance the War. There was pent up savings and pent up demand when the war ended in 1945; the result was that in 1946-1947 there were a large number of radio sets sold. By the end of that two year period, 93 percent of American households owned a radio. The year 1947 was also the beginning of the television revolution; just when radio was at the height of its popularity, TV made its first inroads to replace it as the dominate medium in the United States.

When the results were tallied at the end of the year, there had been 350 million records sold; about 300 million came from the major labels--RCA Victor, Columbia, Decca and Capitol. Those were impressive figures, but the industry had a four month sales slump during the year. Further, there was a trend bubbling under: 50 million records were sold by independent labels. In addition to "Near You" by Francis Craig on Bullet of Nashville (which sold four million), other big hits on indies included "Peg O'My Heart" by the Harmonicats, released on Vitacoustics of Chicago, and "How Soon" by Jack Owens, on the Los Angeles-based Tower label.

Late in 1946 all wage and price controls were dropped and the major labels raised their disk prices to 75 cents ($1 for classical).

On June 5, 1947, Secretary of State George Marshall announced a plan to send aid to Europe to rebuild after the devastation of World War II; that became known as the "Marshall Plan" and helped Europe get back on its feet with American help. The United States was already shipping food and grain to help the millions starving in Europe. In the first televised address to the American people by a President, Truman asked Americans to conserve food to aid starving peoples of the world.

The "cold war" became a widely used term to describe the battle between the Soviet Union and the United States to influence the world towards either communism or democracy. That was played out in Europe, which was divided between "East" and "West." The "west" was under democratic influence; the "east" was controlled by the Soviet Union. Germany was divided between the Federal Republic of Germany, or "West Germany" and the German Democratic Republic, or "East Germany."

Jackie Robinson broke the color barrier in baseball, although some Southerners in the Major Leagues threatened a mutiny and at least two teams threatened to strike. About 300,000 telephone workers did strike, the first national strike by that group.

There were half a million radios in Russia and the Voice of America beamed Russian-language broadcasts to them, as well as American jazz. In October, 24-year old pilot Chuck Yeager became the first person to break the sound barrier in a Bell X-1 secret rocket plane. In April, Henry Ford, who had been one of the most admired men in America, died.

In 1947, the record industry recorded sales of $214.4 million at retail--which exceeded the 1921 figures for the first time. There were 3.4 million record players produced. Columbia Records finally realized the importance of radio disk jockeys by opening an in-house department of publicity and promotion and bought advertising on radio for their records.

The major labels missed a major trend in music for blacks. The executives in charge of artists and repertoire and sales played a very conservative game, unwilling to risk their reputations and jobs on new sounds. They were puzzled that songs and artists outside the mainstream Tin Pan Alley, Broadway, Hollywood establishment circle were achieving success, but instead of exploring new music and new audiences, they remained entrenched in the sounds they had grown accustomed to from the mid-1930s on.

In 1948, radio was still the dominant mass medium in the United States; by the end of 1948, 94.3 percent of American families owned a set. There were changes at the network level for country music on radio after the War. In 1946, NBC cancelled the "National Barn Dance" on WLS in Chicago after star Red Foley left to join WSM and joined the Grand Ole Opry. Foley was replaced by Rex Allen, who left for Hollywood in 1949; at that time the WLS National Barn Dance moved to the ABC radio network but was cancelled there after about a year.

The Rise of the Indies

The music business was changing after World War II, primarily because the improved economic conditions made it possible for a number of new labels to open. The fact that major labels generally avoided hillbilly and race music in favor of middle-class oriented "pop" music meant there were large markets for entrepreneurs.

At the end of the war there were 32 pressing plants across the country and in 1946 independent labels sold 50 million records. Most of those records were hillbilly, race, and jazz. Those records cost about a dollar and received air play primarily on the 462 small 250-watt stations whose owners could not afford electrically transcribed programs.

There were overt signs that race and hillbilly music were gaining in popularity. The big difference came when numerous servicemen were exposed to that music during World War II, then came home ready to party and bop. Blacks had served in the Armed Forces with whites--although the services were not be fully integrated until the Korean War in 1952--and heard each other's music so exposure to different musics was an important factor in the music industry when all those servicemen returned home after the war.

Los Angeles was particularly important as a music center for R & B and country after the War. It became a boom town during World War II because of its war industries and defense plants. It was a remarkably open city and poor blacks and whites obtained jobs there. A number of them came from Texas, Louisiana, Oklahoma and Arkansas and L.A. soon had its turf divided with blacks settling in Watts and Compton while whites settled in Bakersfield and the San Fernando Valley. By the end of the War, over two million people had arrived in California--over 400,000 in the Los Angeles area.

Leadbelly

Leadbelly was born Huddie Ledbetter in either 1888 or 1889 on a plantation in Mooringsport, Louisiana; when he was five his family moved to Bowie County, Texas. By his mid-teens Leadbelly was performing in the brothels in Shreveport. He married young and received his first instrument, an accordion, during his time in Texas. He left home by his early twenties—after fathering two children—to make a living as a laborer and guitarist.

Leadbelly wrote the song, "The Titanic" after that ship sank in April, 1912; the song was written on his twelve-string guitar, which became his main instrument and created his signature sound. He performed in and around Dallas with Blind Lemon Jefferson.

Always hot-tempered, Leadbelly was convicted of carrying a pistol in 1915 and sentenced to the chain gang in Harrison County. He escaped but in January 1918 was sentenced to prison in Sugar Land, Texas for killing one of his relatives in a fight over a woman. He reportedly first heard the song, "Midnight Special," a traditional prison song, during that time. Leadbelly was pardoned in 1925, after serving seven years; he gained his release by writing a song to Governor Pat Morris Neff seeking his freedom. During his time in prison he often entertained the guards and fellow prisoners and reportedly sang the song to the Governor when the politician brought guests to a Sunday picnic at the prison.

Leadbelly was sentenced to the Angola Prison Farm in Louisiana in 1930 after stabbing a white man in a fight. In 1933, John and Alan Lomax were in the Angola prison collecting folk songs when they heard Leadbelly and recorded him on equipment from the Library of Congress. In July, 1934, they returned and recorded Leadbelly singing hundreds of songs; in August he was released after a petition from the Lomaxes was given to Louisiana Governor Oscar Allen. The Lomaxes also sent the governor a recording of Leadbelly singing "Goodnight Irene." (A prison official claimed Leadbelly was released because he had served his minimum sentence with "good behavior.")

Huddie Ledbetter probably acquired the name "Leadbelly" (or "Lead Belly") while in prison, a result of prisoners calling him a derivation of his family name, although there are other versions of that story. He used the name "Leadbelly" during his entire recording career.

In September, 1934, unable to find work and fearing his release from prison would be cancelled because he was unemployed, he asked John Lomax for a job as his driver; Lomax agreed and for three months Leadbelly drove Lomax around the south for the folklorist's song collecting.

In December, John Lomax had a speaking engagement at an academic conference for the Modern Language Association in Pennsylvania at Bryn Mawr College; Leadbelly went and participated in a group sing and was written up in the press. On January 1, 1935, Lomax and Leadbelly arrived in

New York where Lomax had an appointment with Macmillan, his publisher, about a book of folk songs. *Time* magazine and newspapers wrote articles about the "singing convict" and Leadbelly became well known. The next week, he recorded 40 songs for the American Record Corporation; only five were released and sales were not impressive, leaving Leadbelly short on money.

In February, Leadbelly recorded songs for Lomax's upcoming book, *Negro Folk Songs As Sung by Leadbelly* and did interviews about his life. In March, Lomax and Leadbelly went on a two-week lecture tour of colleges in the Northeast, ending at Harvard. Lomax concluded that he could not work with the singer any longer so he gave him and his wife, Martha (Leadbelly had married while in New York) money to return to Louisiana by bus. Leadbelly had earned money from three months of performing but, instead of giving him the entire amount (Lomax assumed Leadbelly would soon spend it all) gave it to him in installments.

Leadbelly sued Lomax for the entire amount and demanded a release from the management contract he had signed with Lomax. The two quarreled about the lawsuit but during the suit Leadbelly proposed they team up again; it did not happen and the book about Leadbelly, released the following year, was not a commercial success.

Leadbelly returned to New York in January, 1936, and performed twice daily at the Apollo Theatre in Harlem. A "March of Time" newsreel documented his time in prison. A long article, "Lead Belly: Bad Nigger Makes Good Minstrel," was published in *Life* Magazine, accompanied by pictures of him playing his guitar and singing.

Leadbelly's performances in Harlem were not successful but he became popular singing in concerts and benefits for left-wing groups and fans of folk music. He used the model of Lomax's college lectures to introduce and explain his songs and Southern black culture. His presentation of children's songs and games proved be popular.

Leadbelly was jailed in 1939 for stabbing a man during a fight. Alan Lomax, then 24, dropped out of graduate school to help him and organized an event to raise money for his legal expenses. After his release, Leadbelly became a regular on the CBS radio show, "Back Where I Come From" hosted by Alan Lomax and Nicholas Ray, and appeared regularly in New York clubs with Josh White. Leadbelly became friends with other folksingers, including Woody Guthrie, Pete Seeger, Brownie McGee and Sonny Terry and went to Los Angeles in 1944 where he recorded songs for Capitol Records.

Leadbelly appeared regularly on Henrietta Yurchenco's radio show broadcast over WNYC on Sunday nights in 1949. That year he also did his first European tour, but fell ill before it was completed and was diagnosed with Lou Gehrig's disease (ALS or amyotrophic lateral sclerosis). Through that European tour, Leadbelly became the first American folksinger or blues artists to have success in Europe.

Back in the U.S., his final concert was in Austin at the University of Texas. He died on December 6, 1949 in New York City; he was 61. He is buried in Mooringsport, Louisiana.

The defining sound of Leadbelly was him singing with his 12-string guitar. His song, "Goodnight, Irene," was a huge hit for The Weavers in 1950, the year after his death. It reached number one on the *Billboard* chart and remained in that position for 13 consecutive weeks. His song, "Midnight Special," has been recorded by a number of artists.

Muddy Waters Moves North

In May, 1943, Muddy Waters caught a train out of Clarksdale, Mississippi to Memphis; there he caught the Illinois Central to Chicago. The Illinois Central stopped at the train station at Twelfth Street and Michigan Avenue; from that point southward for about 15 miles was Chicago's famous South Side.

Muddy Waters obtained a job on the loading dock of a paper factory but soon became the King of the Blues in Chicago. His domain was the South Side, or the "Black Belt" which had displaced Harlem as the artistic center for blacks in America. Here was the home of the *Chicago Defender*, the largest and most influential newspaper for African Americans. Headed by publisher Robert S. Abbott, the *Defender* had a large circulation in the South, a result of an agreement with railroad porters to distribute the paper in southern towns. Chicago was the home of the largest black congregation, the Olivet Baptist Church headed by J. H. Jackson.

The South Side area was bordered on the North by the train and bus stations at Twelfth and Michigan and extended southward like a giant "V." The "black belt" was about 25 blocks from the train station, at the northern end of this South Side. The main street in that area is State Street and from Twenty-second to Fifty-first there were a number of small taverns with three piece blues bands or jukeboxes. The area between Thirty-first and Forty-third was the center of Muddy's domain; it was also where Polish immigrants Leonard and Philip Chess operated a nightclub.

Blacks lived in small, one or two room apartments with a hot plate and ice box; the bathroom was shared by residents in a number of apartments. There were three-story tenements along South Street, some barely inhabitable, all crowded.

Muddy Waters was part of The Great Migration, a period covering roughly from World War I until 1970. Between 1910 and 1970, over six and a half million black Americans left the South for the North, but the major migration occurred during the 1940s. In 1940, 77 percent of African-Americans lived in the South and 40 percent lived in the rural south; in 1970 about half of all African-Americans lived in the South and less than 25 percent lived in rural areas. After 1940, five million blacks moved north, a huge exodus with ramifications that were be felt in music and popular culture. Before World War II, most African-Americans were strongly tied to agriculture; after World War II African Americans inhabited cities to such an extent that "urban" became a euphemism for "black."

Muddy Waters in Chicago

Muddy Waters was born McKinley Morganfield (April 4, 1913) near Clarksdale, Mississippi on the Stovall Plantation—although the date and place of his birth are in dispute. (He may have been born in 1913 or 1915 in either Rolling Fork, Mississippi or in Jug's Corner in Issaquena Country). His mother died shortly after birth and his grandmother, Delia Grant, raised him and gave him the name "Muddy" because he loved to play in the mud.

During his early teens he learned to play a Stella guitar he bought from Sears and Roebuck for $2.50 after he sold a horse for $15. He was influenced first by the music of the Baptist church he attended and began performing in joints around the Stovall Plantation, which was owned by Colonel William Howard Stovall.

Alan Lomax, on a trip collecting folksongs for the Library of Congress, came to Stovall in August, 1941, and recorded Waters in his home as well as other blues musicians. Lomax sent him two acetates of those recordings and Waters took them to a joint and put one on the jukebox, playing it over and over. The recording gave him confidence that he could make a living playing music.

In July, 1942, Alan Lomax returned and those two field recording sessions were released on Testament Records as *Down on Stovall's Plantation*. They were later released by Chess Records on a CD as *Muddy Waters: The Complete Plantation Recordings.*

After he moved to Chicago in 1943, Waters drove a truck and worked in a factory while playing music at night. He opened shows for Big Bill Broonzy in rowdy clubs; Broonzy was a well-known bluesman in Chicago and that allowed Waters to play before large audiences.

Muddy Waters bought his first electric guitar in 1944 and formed a band; the clubs were rowdy and electric instruments were needed in order to be heard. In 1946, Waters recorded for Mayo Williams at Columbia Records with a clarinet, saxophone and piano. Those were released on the 20th Century label, owned by Ivan Ballen and based in Philadelphia under the name "Sweet Lucy" Carter and his Orchestra. He began recording for Aristocrat records, led by Leonard and Phil Chess, before they changed the name of the label to Chess.

Muddy Waters first hits came in 1948 when he recorded "I Can't Be Satisfied" and "I Feel Like Going Home" for Chess. He was a popular act in clubs and recorded "Rollin' Stone," his signature song, also in 1948.

The Chess brothers insisted that Muddy Water record with local musicians instead of his backing band until 1953. Waters' band was one of the most acclaimed in the history of the blues; it included Little Walter Jacobs on harmonica, Elga Edmonds (also known as Elgin Evans) on drums, Jimmy Rogers on guitar and Otis Spann on piano. During the early 1950s, Muddy Waters and his band recorded classics such as "Hoochie Coochie Man," "I Just Want to Make Love to You" and "I'm Ready."

During the late 1940s and early 1950s Muddy Waters became known as "the father of modern Chicago blues."

The Great Migration

The Great Migration, which was the movement of blacks leaving the South and moving to cities in the North, was made possible by the railroad, which was the major source of long-distance transportation during the first half of the twentieth-century. In 1892 the Illinois Central completed its rail link between Chicago and New Orleans. That line ran up the Mississippi Delta, parallel to Highway 51 and Highway 61, to Memphis and then on to Chicago with three famous lines: the Panama Limited, City of New Orleans and the Louisiana.

The Great Migration began during World War I when labor was needed for northern factories. On May 15, 1917, the *Chicago Defender* instituted the "Great Northern Drive" to persuade blacks to move to Chicago. They offered impressive enticements; blacks could make more money, could vote, did not have to face the Jim Crow laws of the South such as having to step off a sidewalk when a white person passed, and had legal rights as citizens that were denied them in the South. Abbott persuaded the railroads to offer special rates to blacks going north and spread the word in the *Defender*, handed out surreptitiously by black porters.

The Great Migration was helped during the 1920s when laws were enacted to restrict immigration into the United States. Americans had an increasing distrust of foreigners and had been reluctant to enter World War I. They wanted to ignore the troubling developments in Europe between the Wars that gave rise to Hitler in Germany during the 1930s. Without the heavy influx of immigrants, particularly from Eastern Europe, the northern cities needed cheap labor; they got it from blacks in the south. There was an appeal to southern blacks; since they came from rural farms, they were hard workers and since wages were low in the south, it made the northern wages look like a bonanza.

Before World War II a good cotton picker, dragging a 75 pound cotton sack through the fields and reaching down into the thorny stem to pull off the soft white cotton ball, could pick about 200 pounds of cotton a day, working from sunup to sundown with a half hour off for lunch. For that work they received 75 cents to a dollar for each hundred pounds, or about $2 a day. During World War II the labor shortage created a situation where farmers had to watch cotton rot in the field because of a lack of pickers. Wages went up to $2 for picking a hundred pounds of cotton, or about $4 a day. Women who worked as maids in the south--and every respectable white family in the Delta had at least one servant--earned about $2.50 a week, but in Chicago, a black worker could receive 75 cents an hour working in a laundry, hotel, restaurant or factory. That was more money for work that was easier than picking cotton; no wonder Chicago looked like the Promised Land to so many rural African Americans.

In 1910 there were 44,000 blacks living in Chicago; by 1920 that figure had grown to 109,000. During the eighteen months of World War I there were 50,000 blacks who moved to Chicago, but returning soldiers took a number of jobs and thus the migration was briefly stemmed. Then came the restrictions on immigration during the 1920s when northern firms recruited blacks from the south; during that decade the number of blacks living in Chicago swelled to 234,000. There was a slackening in black migration during the 1930s (the black population in Chicago grew only by 44,000 during that decade) because of the Depression but during World War II the pace of migration dramatically increased, a direct result of labor shortages for defense industries in major cities due to so many young men serving as soldiers.

Musically, there were changes from the music played by black farm workers in the Delta and the music played by musicians in Chicago. The old rural blues of a single person with a guitar gave way to a small three-piece group with guitar, bass and drums. The music was louder and more belligerent, indicative of "The Attitude" of blacks in Chicago. No one reflected this better than Muddy Waters.

The Chess Brothers

In February, 1946, Leonard Chess obtained a liquor license for the Macomba Lounge, a small club at Thirty-ninth and South Cottage Grove Avenue in Chicago. The brothers, whose real names were Lejzor and Fiszel Czyz, became Leonard and Phil Chess when they joined their father after they immigrated from Poland in 1928. Their father, Yasef Czyz, changed his name to Joseph Chess when he arrived in New York in December, 1922. Joseph Chess was a junk dealer and small businessman and the Chess brothers helped at his junk store.

Phil Chess was in the Army when Leonard established the Macomba; after his discharge Phil joined his brother.

Like other tavern owners, the Chess brothers knew that live music was key to attracting a crowd and selling drinks. Soon there was a house band at the Macomba, consisting of a piano, drum, bass and one or two horn players. The band played every night--Saturdays 10 p.m. until 4 a.m., then Tuesdays through Saturday 10 p.m. to 5 a.m.-- except Monday, which was an "off" night; on those evenings, musicians came in for informal jams and played for drinks. Actually, the club seldom closed; the blinds were closed but musicians continued to play.

According to Nadine Cohadas, Leonard Chess "apparently had an instinct for the right musical mix. He hired musicians who were liked and respected by their peers, and the lounge became a magnet for other musicians. It developed a reputation as one of the best after-hours places on the South Side."

Because the Macomba attracted musicians, Leonard met Sammy Goldberg, who worked for small labels Savoy and Aladdin as a talent scout. Goldberg brought Andrew Tibbs over to the Macomba; Tibbs had played at Jimmy's Palm Garden, around the corner, but began playing at Chess's lounge. Tibbs real name was Mervyn Andrew Grayson but his father was the well known minister Reverend S. A. Grayson, who did not approve of nightclubs, so Andrew changed his name to avoid embarrassing his father.

Leonard Chess learned that a new label, Aristocrat, was interested in recording Tibbs, and that created an interest in Leonard to begin making records as well. Aristocrat had made records with several other musicians who played at the Macomba—Tom Archia,, who was the main act there, and Jump Jackson.

On April 26, 1947, the formation of Aristocrat Records was announced in *Billboard*. The label was formed in Chicago by two couples--Charles and Evelyn Aron and Fred and Mildred Brount. Their office was at 7508 South Phillips Avenue in Chicago and the first artists signed were bandleader Sherman Hayes and a girl singer, "Wyoma." On October 11, *Billboard* announced that Leonard had joined Aristocrat's sales staff.

Aristocrat's first release was a cover of the pop tunes, "Chi-baba, Chi-Baba" and "Say No More" by the Sherman Hayes Orchestra. By the end of 1947 they had also recorded Muddy Waters and Sunnyland Slim. Since there were few record stores that carried R&B, they sold records to Pullman porters, beauty and barber shops, drug stores, furniture stores, grocery stores and anywhere else blacks shopped. Chess had 180 accounts in the South Side area of Chicago.

In December, 1947, Andrew Tibbs' record, "Union Man Blues" b/w "Bilbo is Dead" was released on Aristocrat, with Leonard Chess listed as co-writer on the songs. Leonard hit the road, driving to cities with a trunk full of records, selling them for Aristocrat.

Aristocrat was not the only label in Chicago recording rhythm and blues; others included Rhumboogie, Melody Lane, Hy-Tone, Sunbeam, Miracle, Sunrise, and Sultan. In late 1949 the Aron's sold their interest in the record company to the Chess brothers, who renamed the label "Chess" in 1950.

Recording rhythm and blues in Chicago had a long history, going back to the 1920s when the Melrose Brothers, Lester and Walter, both white, owned a record shop and served as talent scouts for the major labels. Most of the acts recorded by the Melrose brothers were released on either RCA Victor or Columbia but during World War II, the major labels lost interest in the blues market and independent labels moved in.

Atlantic Records

In October, 1947, Atlantic Records was formed by Ahmet Ertegun and Herb Abramson in New York, with offices located at the Jefferson Hotel on Broadway and Fifty-sixth. Abramson, a dentist, had been a part time

A&R man for National Records during the early 1940s. A Turkish dentist, and a family friend of the Erteguns, Dr. Vahdi Sabit, invested $10,000 in the fledgling record company.

Ahmet and Nesuhi were the sons of Munir Ertegun, the Turskish Ambassador to Switzerland, France and then England, where young Ahmet saw Cab Calloway and Duke Ellington at the London Palladium. In 1934, Munir Ertegun was stationed in Washington D.C. where young Ahmet "became fascinated with black America and, above all, with its music.

In 1944, Munir Ertegun died and his wife and daughter returned to Turkey; Ahmet and Nesuhi remained in the United States. Nesuhi, who was five years older than Ahmet, moved to Los Angeles where he managed a jazz and blues record shop, edited a music magazine, recorded jazz and blues albums and taught a course on the roots of American music at the University of California. Ahmet remained in Washington where he did postgraduate work at Georgetown University and hung out at Waxie Maxie's record shop.

Dentist Herb Abramson was a passionate fan of jazz and had owned part of National Records in Chicago. In 1947, ex-bandleader Jerry Blaine, who worked with Abramson at National, bought out Abramson's share of the newly formed Jubilee Records. That gave Abramson cash to invest in Atlantic. Abramson's wife, Miriam, took care of business affairs at Atlantic.

Because James Caesar Petrillo called a strike of the American Federation of Musicians beginning on January 1, 1948, Atlantic had to record prolifically and stockpile recordings at the end of 1947. Because they were located in New York, Atlantic first recorded a number of jazz and blues instrumental groups they found in New York clubs.

Unlike most of the R&B entrepreneurs, who were in the business as a way to make money, Ertegun and Abramson "were not executives so much as 'absolute fans' who respected their artists, and were even a little in awe of them." That set Atlantic apart from the rest of the independent labels right from the start. However, it did not help them achieve early success; during the first couple of years Atlantic struggled to survive.

Mercury Records

In late summer, 1945, The Mercury Radio and Television Company began releasing recordings. The company, named after the Mercury car, was headed by Irving Green, who owned a pressing plant. On March 1, 1947, the Mercury Record Corporation was formed, with several companies affiliated, including a pressing plant and a distribution company. The first president of the record label was Berle Adams, Louis Jordan's manager.

When the company began in 1945 there was a shortage of shellac, so Green arranged a deal with EMI India (where the key ingredients for shellac were found) to obtain enough shellac to press 700,000 records a week. The first releases in September that year were rhythm and blues, but by the end of the year they had recorded their first country music act, Tom Owen and His Cowboys.

The label soon diversified into jazz, Latin, Hawaiian, children's and polka music. Their first big hit was "To Each His Own," by Tony Martin in the summer of 1946. They also signed Frankie Laine, who had a string of pop hits as they entered the mainstream music market. Laine's early hits include "That's My Desire," "Shine" and "That Lucky Old Sun."

Chicago was a major center for country music in 1945; radio stations WLS and WJJD were heavy into country music with WLS's "National Barn Dance" on network radio. In August, 1947, Mercury became the first label to establish an office in Nashville when Les Hutchens was named label representative. Hutchens only remained a few months before leaving to manage Cowboy Copas. In March, 1948, Mercury named Murray Nash to be head of their country division. Nash, who grew up in Nebraska, Australia, Canada and Tennessee, lived in Knoxville, where he worked for the RCA distributor. Nash signed Pee Wee King to RCA Victor and remained in Knoxville, where he signed the Sons of the Soil (featuring Don Gibson), Carl Story, Bill Carlisle and Flatt and Scruggs after they left Bill Monroe's Bluegrass Boys.

Like most label reps in charge of country music, Nash was also in charge of southern R&B and blues. When the label wanted Nash to move to New Orleans in 1951 and establish an office there, he resigned and joined Acuff-Rose Publishers in Nashville. In November, 1951, the label hired Walter "D" Kilpatrick to head the Nashville office. Kilpatrick joined the Marines during World War II, then became a salesman for Capitol after the war. He moved to Nashville in 1950 with that label. Kilpatrick became the first full-time A&R man in Nashville for country music, with an office in the Hill Building on 4th Avenue. Kilpatrick stayed in Nashville until 1955, when he moved to Chicago, then returned in 1956.

Country music was always profitable, but never with huge hits. Each record made a little money but the Mercury label was never a major player in Nashville. According to Kilpatrick, "Country music is an attitude and Mercury was pop and R&B. The sales force wasn't oriented to it--they went where the buck was."

King Records

In 1945, Syd Nathan began King Records in Cincinnati in a defunct icehouse and first recorded country music. Since WCKY in Cincinnati, a clear-channel 50,000 watt station programmed country music four to five hours and day and had the Midwestern Hayride on Saturday nights, Nathan had access to country music talent.

A number of country artists recorded for King and a number of others used his studio to record for other labels, but Nathan soon discovered there was an even bigger opportunity in the R&B market for an independent label. In 1947 he had a hit on his subsidiary, Queen, set up to record R&B, by Bull Moose Jackson and His Bearcats, "I Love You, Yes I Do."

Nathan's label mixed country and R&B music for the different markets. Nathan had his black artists recording songs written and originally done by white country artists, and his country artists cut boogie-woogie tunes for their market. Since consumers were segregated, the white audience would not buy an R&B tune unless done by a white artist and the black audience wouldn't buy a country tune unless it was done by a black artist. Henry Glover, an African-American, was the in-house producer and produced a number of country and R&B recordings. Black musicians often played on the country recordings while white musicians played on recordings by black artists.

A country act, the York Brothers recorded many of the day's R&B hits in 1947-48 but the label was more successful having black artists cover country hits. "Bloodshot Eyes" was a country hit for Hank Penny before Wynonie Harris covered it. A major reason for songs reaching both markets through different artists was that Syd Nathan was usually the publisher who owned the copyrights to the songs, so there was a financial incentive for him to have a song released in each market.

That was basically the cross-fertilization that produced rock'n'roll in the 1950s, but Syd Nathan was ahead of his time. Also, Nathan was a profane, cigar-chomping businessman who did not have the creative vision of a Sam Phillips; Nathan simply wanted to make money--and relentlessly pursued profits.

Rhythm and Blues

On March 1, 1947, the number one race record on *Billboard* was "Open the Door, Richard" by Dusty Fletcher, a comedian who had developed the routine. Soon, there were 14 different versions--five by black artists: (Count

Basie (Victor), Tiger Haynes' Three Flames (Columbia), Dusty Fletcher (National), Louis Jordan (Decca) and Jack McVea (Black & White), who recorded the first version, all vying for sales.

That was a break-through song, receiving acceptance in the white as well as black markets. Also in 1947 T-Bone Walker recorded "Stormy Monday" for the Black & White label, which sold the master to Capitol. That was a breakthrough record for one of the most influential electric guitarists in R&B.

The development of the electric guitar was a major component in the development of R&B. According to Arnold Shaw, "Without amplification there would, perhaps, have been no R&B, certainly not as we know it. Starting with the guitar, electrification enveloped bass and organ as well. The bluesman who was pivotal in the development of the electric guitar was Aaron Walker, known as T-Bone Walker, who pioneered the introduction of electric guitar into combo blues." Walker also pioneered showmanship with the electric guitar, playing it behind his head and back and placing it between his legs in a sexually suggestive way.

The Electric Guitar

The electric guitar was developed to solve the basic problem of how to make a guitar louder so it could be heard over horns and other instruments in an orchestra or band. The acoustic guitar simply could not be heard over horns--the main instruments in big bands--and even had difficulty competing with the banjo and fiddle in string bands. The microphone helped, especially on radio and in the recording studio, but the acoustic guitar could still not compete in volume with other instruments when played in a concert hall.

Guitar manufacturers worked to solve this problem by replacing "gut" strings with ones made of steel and by building bigger guitars. Some guitar manufacturers felt the answer was in electrical guitars, which made the guitar louder. But that created a problem: How do you "amplify" the sound of a guitar?

The solution to that problem meant that manufacturers had to invent two things: an "electric" guitar and an "amplifier" which could broadcast that sound. That led to another problem because critics complained that the electrical inventions distorted the natural sound of a guitar.

The development of electric guitars and amplifiers came during the 1920s and 1930s. The breakthrough for electric guitars occurred in 1931 when George Beauchamp and Adolph Rickenbacker created an electromagnetic pickup. That pickup consisted of a coil of wire wrapped around a magnet which a electrical current passed through and amplified the vibrations of the guitar's strings. The first guitar they used this on was called "The Frying Pan," which was a lap steel guitar.

The first commercially successful electric guitar was the Gibson ES 150 in 1936. Other guitar companies had experimented with electric guitars but Gibson had the respect and the clout to make their guitar successful. The ES 150 was a Spanish style arch top guitar whose pickup was close to the neck. That became the best known early electric guitar.

The success of the electric guitar depended on well-known guitarists adopting the instrument. Charlie Christian, a jazz guitarist from Oklahoma City, who joined Benny Goodman's Band in 1939, was the first electric guitar "star." He played a Gibson ES 150; blues guitarist T-Bone Walker also played an ES 150.

The electric pick-ups created a problem when attached to hollow body guitars because the vibrations of the wood from the strings created distortions and feedback. That led to experiments with solid body guitars and in 1939 Slingland became the first company to introduce a commercially viable solid body electric guitar.

Les Paul built an instrument he called "The Log" in 1940, which consisted of a guitar made of a solid block of pine wood. Unfortunately, the guitar was much too heavy to play comfortably--but it did minimize the vibrations from the body of the guitar. Les Paul had been trying to develop an electric guitar for a number of years and continued to work towards that end.

In Los Angeles, Paul Bigsby and Leo Fender began experimenting with solid body guitars during the 1940s. Paul Bigsby built a solid body guitar designed by Merle Travis with a headstock that put all the tuning pegs on one side.

Leo Fender designed the first commercially successful solid body guitar in 1946. The guitar had one magnetic pickup and was named the "Esquire." The version with two pickups developed by Fender was called the "Broadcaster"; however, the name was soon changed to the "Telecaster." The "Stratocaster" was developed by Fender in 1954; that guitar contained three pickups and had a contoured body. In 1951, Fender produced the first commercially successful electric bass guitar, the Fender Precision Bass."

Traditionalists did not like the electric guitar; it's sound was quite different from the sound of the acoustic guitar, which was considered the "true" guitar. But the fact that performers needed the louder sound led guitarists to adapt the electric guitar.

The electric guitar created a new sound that became the sound of rock'n'roll during the 1950s; in fact, the electric guitar and electric bass are as important in the creation of rock'n'roll as any performer.

T-Bone Walker

T-Bone Walker was a pioneer blues guitarist; his playing "was bluesy in a jazz like way: crisply articulated notes interspersed with sexy slurs in the manner of a jazz trumpeter. His storming chordal vamps, often echoed by the horn section, were a six-string imitation of blaring brass and reeds," stated Lawrence Cohn in *Nothing But the Blues: The Music and the Musicians.* "He created an approach to guitar that seemed intended to compensate for an absence of horns, despite there being plenty on his records."

Cohn added that "his imitators were legion, though few ever equaled Walker's impeccable phrasing, subtle syncopation, and the thoughtful depth of his lean guitar monologues."

Walker was a consummate showman, totally at home on the stage, who played the guitar behind his back, with his teeth, and did splits while he played.

T-Bone Walker was born Aaron Thibeaux Walker on May 28, 1911, in Linden, Texas; "T-Bone" evolved from "Thibeaux." His father was African-American and his mother was a full-blooded Cherokee. Both his parents were musicians. They divorced and his mother married Macro Washington, who taught T-Bone to play guitar, ukulele, banjo, violin, mandolin and piano.

As a boy, T-Bone often led Blind Lemon Jefferson, a family friend, to street corners where T-Bone held Lemon's tin cup and danced as Lemon played.

By the time he was 15, T-Bone Walker was a professional performer. In 1929 he made his first recordings, "Wichita Falls Blues" b/w "Trinity River Blues" for Columbia Records as Oak Cliff T-Bone. (Oak Cliff was the section of Dallas where he lived.)

T-Bone Walker played in a number of bands in a number of clubs before he moved to Los Angeles in 1925 and worked in the clubs on Central Avenue.

During the 1930s, he was tutored by Chuck Richardson in Oklahoma City; Richardson also tutored Charlie Christian. Both were influential guitarists; what Christian did for jazz, Walker did for blues, opening new pathways for those who followed.

Joe Louis and Charlie Glenn, joint operators of the Rhumboogie Club in Chicago, heard and saw Walker at the Alabam Club in Los Angeles and brought him to Chicago where he performed in lavish productions at the Rhumboogie. Walker recorded his early hits for the Rhumboogie label before he recorded them for Black and White. Walker returned to the Rhumboogie Club a number of time to perform.

From 1946 to 1948 T-Bone Walker recorded for the Black and White label; he recorded his biggest hit, "Stormy Monday" for that label. Those recordings "established T-Bone's reputation as the father of the electric blues."

T-Bone Walker was a major influence on B.B. King, Chuck Berry and countless other blues guitarists who came after him. His sound was described as "both incisive and delicate, and it was served by a superb sense of dynamics, which gave it a very personal, dramatic quality. The intensity of his rhythm punctuations was varied to great effect, and the character of his melodic line could range quickly from nostalgic and biting single-note lines to chords powerfully exultant. Moreover, he seemed wholly at ease in any tempo from slow to what in jazz is termed 'up,' and he had an almost infallible gift for choosing tempos perfectly appropriate to the content of his lyrics."

Roy Acuff Leaves Grand Ole Opry

At the beginning of 1946, country music from Nashville received national exposure on the NBC radio network from the Opry shows sponsored by "Prince Albert" tobacco and "Ralston Purina."

In April, Roy Acuff left the Grand Ole Opry and the "Prince Albert" show. Acuff was frustrated because of the Opry's requirement that he return every Saturday night to perform on the show. Saturday nights were the biggest night for personal appearances and Acuff's popularity kept him in constant demand for appearances--at much higher fees than what the Opry paid--so Acuff went to the West Coast to tour and appear in movies. He was replaced by Red Foley, a smooth-voiced singer who had been on the Opry's major competitor, "The National Barn Dance" on WLS out of Chicago.

Red Foley

Red Foley, born June 17, 1919 in Blue Lick, Kentucky, began his career as a vocalist with the Cumberland Ridge Runners on WLS's National Barn

Dance during the 1930s, then hosted the WLS road shows in the late 1930s and early 1940s. In 1941 he began recording for Decca and his first hit was "Old Shep."

Red Foley was more popular with Opry audiences than with Opry members when he started the "Prince Albert" segment. Opry regulars coveted the spot vacated by Acuff and many resented it going to an outsider, but the WSM brass knew Foley had network experience; further, the Esty advertising executives, who had the Prince Albert account, wanted Foley and they got him. Foley represented the smooth sound of a country crooner who could be popular with city audiences as well as rural customers.

Hank Williams

In September, 1946 Acuff-Rose signed a songwriter, Hank Williams, and Fred Rose soon obtained a recording contract for him with a small label, Sterling.

Hank William was born September 17, 1923, in Mount Olive, Alabama. Hank's father was confined to a Veteran's hospital when Hank was six because of a brain aneurysm, and his mother, a strong, domineering woman, moved the family to Montgomery in 1937. For the next ten years Hank lived in Montgomery where he formed a band and developed his songwriting and performing skills. Hank had a show on WSFA in Montgomery from July, 1941, until August, 1942, but was fired for habitual drunkenness--a problem that plagued him his entire life.

During World War II, Hank worked at a shipbuilding company in Mobile, Alabama; he met Audrey Sheppard and the two married in December, 1944. Hank met several country performers while he was in Alabama, including Roy Acuff, and in 1943 sold Pee Wee King a song, "(I'm Praying for the Day That) Peace Will Come" for fifty dollars. King assigned the song to Acuff-Rose Publishers in December, 1943.

In 1945, back in Montgomery, Hank published his first songbook, *Original Songs of Hank Williams*, and began to perform on WSFA, where he developed a large following. Hank came to Nashville to audition for the Opry--and was turned down--before he came to Nashville on Saturday, September 14, 1946, to audition his songs for publisher Fred Rose. Rose signed six of Williams's songs, then got Hank a recording contract with the small, New-York based label, Sterling Records.

Hank's first recording session occurred on December 11, 1946, when he did "Wealth Won't Save Your Soul," "Calling You,"" Never Again" and

"When God Comes and Gathers His Jewels." When the year ended Hank Williams was still living and performing in Montgomery, Alabama.

Jim Bulleit and Bullet Records

At the end of 1945, Jim Bulleit, a booking agent in Nashville, and Wally Fowler, a gospel singer and entrepreneur, discussed starting a record label with C.V. Hitchcock, who owned Hermitage Music, a store that supplied phonographs and records for jukeboxes. In January, 1946 they issued their first releases. Their first release in the "Popular" series came in January, 1947. That was "The Bullet Bounce"/"Babe, You Know You Like It That Way" by the Eddie Wiggins Sextet, a group based in Chicago. That was followed by Francis Craig and His Orchestra, who recorded "Red Rose" on the "A" side and "Near You" on the "B" side. Both songs featured vocalist Bob Lamm.

"Near You" put Bullet Records and Nashville on the map as a recording center. The song sold more than two million records and was number one on the *Billboard* chart for seventeen consecutive weeks. It became the theme song for Milton Berle's popular radio and TV shows.

Francis Craig had a popular dance band in Nashville but quit performing and took a job with WSM as a disc jockey and oversaw their music library. Craig wanted to record "Red Rose," which was his theme song. During a session on January 20, 1947, the group recorded "Red Rose," "Hot Biscuits," and "Sometimes I Wonder" in the WSM Studio with Bob Lamm, a blind trumpet player who had sung with Craig's group since 1943. The session was engineered by Aaron Shelton, with Owen Bradley overseeing production.

The group had enough time for one more song and the decision was made to record "Near You," written by Craig with lyrics by Kermit Goell. "Red Rose" was the "A" side but when it was released in April, Cal Young, a disc jockey in Griffin, Georgia, played the "B" side. Soon, other stations began playing it, and the record started selling.

"Near You" debuted on the "Most Played on Air" chart in *Billboard* on August 9 and reached number one on that chart on August 30. The song was covered by the Andrews Sisters on Columbia, Elliott Lawrence on Columbia, Alvino Rey on Capitol, and Larry Green on RCA, but the Bullet release had a head start. Craig and Lamm went on a national tour promoting the song, and it officially sold two million records, although there were unreported sales from manufacturers selling directly to distributors without accounting to Bullet.

"Near You" was the first million selling record recorded in Nashville.

The biggest country records of 1946 were "Guitar Polka" by Al Dexter and "New Spanish Two-Step" b/w "Roly-Poly" by Bob Wills--both on Columbia; "Divorce Me C.O.D." by Merle Travis on Capitol; "Rainbow at Midnight" by Ernest Tubb on Decca; and "Sioux City Sue" by Zeke Manners on Victor. None of them were recorded in Nashville.

Castle Recording Studio

The first professional recording studio in Nashville was the Castle Recording Studio. It was formed by three engineers at WSM, Aaron Shelton, Carl Jenkins, and George Reynolds. The studio was built by using equipment purchased to broadcast Eddy Arnold's and Ernest Tubb's syndicated shows, which were recorded in WSM's Studio B. The three engineers began by using WSM Studios in the National Life Building at the corner of Seventh Avenue North and Union Street to record and then sent the signal over the telephone line to a lathe at Fifteen Avenue South and Weston, which was the location of WSM's backup transmitter.

The engineers obtained a $1,000 loan from Third National Bank, pooled their resources, and moved to the Tulane Hotel on Church Street, between Seventh and Eighth Avenues North. The name "Castle" came from the WSM logo, which advertised the radio station as the "Air Castle of the South." The first recording was a musical advertisement for Shyer's Jewelry Store, sung by Snooky Lanson.

The studio began in 1946, the first full year after World War II, and recorded sessions for the national Decca and MGM labels as well as local independents Dot and Bullet and Cincinnati-based King Records. Besides recording sessions for record labels, the studio recorded local advertising jingles and radio shows for regional networks. Among the early hits recorded there were "Chattanoogie Shoeshine Boy" by Red Foley and "You Win Again" by Hank Williams.

Decca Records in Nashville

On August 11 and 13, 1947, Paul Cohen, head of country A&R for Decca Records, came to Nashville and recorded Ernest Tubb, Red Foley, and Milton Estes at the Castle Recording Studio in Nashville's downtown Tulane Hotel. Before that session, most of Decca's country sessions were recorded in Chicago, although there were other country recordings made in Los Angeles and New York. Ernest Tubb was Decca's best-selling artist after Bing Crosby, and the fact that he insisted on recording in Nashville was a key factor in Nashville's establishment as a recording center. Owen Bradley always attributed the growth of the Nashville recording industry to Tubb's decision. "If Ernest had said no, we wouldn't have done it. He was that big," said Bradley. During the first six months of 1947, it was reported that Tubb received more than $50,000 in royalties from Decca.

Those sessions marked the beginning of major labels regularly recording in Nashville.

Musicians Union

When major label recordings began in Nashville in 1947, musicians were paid union scale, which established the practice of Nashville becoming a union town for recording musicians. Led by Local 257's president, George Cooper, the fact that musicians were paid union scale instead of receiving whatever they could negotiate with a label meant that musicians from other cities were attracted to Nashville, where they could make a living playing sessions. The Nashville union led the way in developing a place where a core of professional musicians could be assured of being paid well for their recordings. It was a major reason why Nashville became a center for recording.

Steve Sholes and RCA Victor

In 1945 Steve Sholes was discharged from the Army, where he had worked compiling V-Disks, and rejoined RCA Victor Records.

Stephen H. Sholes first joined Victor as an errand boy in 1929, soon after he graduated from high school. Sholes' father worked for Victor after the family moved in 1920 to Camden, New Jersey, then headquarters for the Victor Company and site of their manufacturing facility.

Sholes was born in Washington, D. C. on February 12, 1911, and lived there until he was nine, when the family moved to Merchantville, New Jersey. After high school, he attended Rutgers University and continued to work at RCA Victor part-time; beginning in 1935 he joined the firm full-time and worked first in the factory storeroom of the radio department and then in the sales department at RCA Victor under label president Edward Wallerstein.

Sholes came of age in the Big Band era and played saxophone and clarinet in local bands. That musical background was advantageous when he moved from the radio to the record department in 1936, taking a $25 a week cut in salary to do so. There, he worked as a sales clerk for Wally Early and was assigned to listen to test pressings (recordings were made direct to disk at this time) to ensure the "takes" were acceptable quality.

Eli Oberstein came from the accounting department at Okeh Records and was brought to RCA Victor's accounting department by Ralph Peer, but an enmity developed between Oberstein and Peer over Peer's publishing interests and outside income that led to Peer's departure from the company. Oberstein remained and in October, 1936, was promoted to head of the A & R Department where he was in charge of signing and recording talent. In that role he traveled the country recording country and blues acts. He let Sholes record jazz artists Mezz Mezzrow, Tommy Ladnier, Jelly Roll Morton, Sidney Bechet and others. During the War, in the Army's V-Disk division, Sholes recorded Jan Peerce, Eileen Farrell, Mischa Elman, Artur Rubinstein, Primrose and a number of other classical and jazz acts.

In 1938 Frank Walker became president of RCA Victor Records when Ted Wallerstein joined Columbia, which was part of the American Record Company group and had just been purchased by William Paley at CBS. The elevation of Walker led Eli Oberstein to leave the company, although Oberstein had brought Benny Goodman, Tommy Dorsey, Larry Clinton, and Glenn Miller to the label--in addition to his role recording hillbilly and race music.

Oberstein left the label and immediately headed a new label, the United States Record Corporation, which ended in bankruptcy. The departure of Oberstein left RCA Victor without a strong presence in the country music field, until Steve Sholes rejoined the label and was put in charge of country and blues music.

To be put in charge of hillbilly and race music was not a prestigious position for a New York record man; the prestige and power was in pop music. The Big Band era was coming to a close and the single vocalist would emerge as major stars after Frank Sinatra exploded as a bobby sox idol in 1943. To be put in charge of hillbilly and race music was the bottom rung of the pecking order for A & R men, and most turned up their noses and barely tolerated it, even though both hillbilly and race music were profitable. Steve Sholes was a rare man; he developed a love and respect for the people in country music as well as the music itself. His first success was Eddy Arnold.

Eddy Arnold

When Frank Walker signed Eddy Arnold unseen and unheard in 1943, RCA Victor desperately needed a successful country act. Victor had led the way in country music, beginning with Uncle Eck Roberston's fiddle tunes, then Vernon Dalhart and through the 1930s with Jimmie Rodgers. It was in danger of being replaced by Columbia, who had Gene Autry and Roy

Acuff, and Decca, who had Ernest Tubb, Red Foley and Bill Monroe, as the top country label. Eddy Arnold changed that.

Arnold had done two recording sessions for Victor--both in Nashville at the WSM studios--before Steve Sholes called him in 1946 and invited him to record in Chicago. Arnold and Sholes picked songs, among them "That's How Much I Love You," written by Arnold and Wally Fowler. Since country recordings did not use drums, and Arnold wanted more "bottom" to his sound, he invited a piano player to come along. That was Owen Bradley's first recording session for a major label and he added piano to the song, which was released in late 1946. Soon, the record began to take off; it was the first hit of Eddy Arnold's career.

Eddy Arnold's smooth vocal style--reminiscent of a country Bing Crosby--led country music to a more commercial sound and his image of a well-dressed southern gentleman pulled country music away from the rural, hayseed image towards a more urban, urbane, sophisticated look.

There is a difference between what is influential and what is popular. The criticism of what is most "popular" is that it satisfies only the current tastes of the public, often at the expense of artistic integrity or breaking new ground musically. The theory is that for something to be "popular" it must appeal to the lowest common denominator, the basest tastes of the public, and hence is discardable.

On the other hand, in an open market capitalist economy, what is most commercial defines popular culture. In business--and the music industry is a business--record companies must achieve success from sales of recordings in order to be profitable. The incentives for recording an act or a kind of music rests with this profit motive. The capitalist system serves as a gatekeeper for which musical acts are available to the public.

Since World War II, country music has proven itself to be commercially successful. Even before World War II, going back to Fiddlin' John Carson in Atlanta, to Vernon Dalhart in New York, and through Jimmie Rodgers and the Carter Family as well as the singing cowboys Gene Autry, Roy Rogers and Tex Ritter, country music has done well as a business. That led to major corporations recording and releasing this music. That, in turn, led to the possibility of broad exposure for the music--and access to the electronic media and distribution network that brought the product to the consumers.

Before World War II the music was called "hillbilly," a degrading term that signified backwoods bumpkins. Just prior to World War II there were two distinct images for country--the singing cowboy and the musical mountaineer.

Another image gradually evolved--that of a sophisticated singer who had a country background but assimilated the ways of the city. A singer who did not sing with a twang, who sang with violins instead of fiddles, and who dressed in tasteful sports coats and slacks (and later, tuxedoes)--not cowboy hats, rhinestones or dungarees. This is what Jim Reeves and Eddy Arnold did for country music--they moved it up town and into the middle class.

Just as the country's population shifted from rural areas to urban areas, especially beginning in World War II, country music shifted--both musically and visually--from the rural, country image to one of the suburban gentleman who kept his down home roots and rural values but acquired city sophistication along the way. That is the story of the generation that grew up in rural America during the Depression and then left the farm during World War II. They were proud of their heritage, but wanted something more--they wanted respect, wanted to be part of mainstream America and wanted to join the American middle-class; in short, they wanted to be more worldly and less provincial.

The importance of Eddy Arnold in the five years after World War II center on several things: (1) his commercial success as a recording artist, which helped make country music big business and was a factor in RCA Victor establishing a permanent office and studio in Nashville, which helped to establish Nashville as the major corporate and recording center for country music; and (2) his connection with the urban middle class with rural roots that emerged after World War II. More than any other artist-- country or pop--Eddy Arnold represented the great body of Americans who came from farms and rural areas around World War II and who moved to urban areas and began their ascent into the middle class, both financially and culturally.

The Disc Jockeys

An important reason for the rise in sales of country and blues records were disk jockeys, particularly at small radio stations, who grew in stature and importance after World War II. Disk jockeys didn't just cue up records and play them anymore, they provided commentary about the song or artist, thought about format and spacing, and had special programs for requests, new releases, a single vocalist, or oldies. The local disk jockey was a leading contributor to the demise of the network programs of Bing Crosby, Frank Sinatra and Dinah Shore.

The music business began to take disc jockeys seriously after World War II; by the end of 1947 about 90 percent of radio stations had a disc jockey show. A survey showed that 24 percent of people said the disc jockey was the reason they purchased a record. Responding to a survey, the biggest buyers of pop music were families with teenagers while teenagers directly accounted for 10 percent of purchases of records; a major reason was the increased number of radio stations.

The leading disc jockey in 1947 was Martin Block, who earned $750,000 a year. Also in 1947, the first radio station with an all-black format and black disc jockeys--WDIA in Memphis--went on the air. It became a success virtually overnight, appealing to an African-American audience.

In response to the changes in the music business--particularly the importance of disc jockeys on radio, Columbia became the first major label to initiate an in-house department for publicity and promotion.

Goddard Lieberson

Goddard Lieberson began working for Columbia Records in September, 1939, shortly after William Paley purchased the company from the American Record Corporation. The company's offices were moved from 57th and Broadway to 799 Seventh Avenue at 52nd Street, a seven story building where Brunswick Records had been headquartered. Label president Edward Wallerstein hired John Hammond as associate director of popular recordings and Hammond recommended hiring 28-year-old Lieberson to assist Moses Smith, who had covered classical music for the *Boston Globe* and now headed Masterworks, Columbia's classical division.

Goddard Lieberson, according to Gary Marmorstein his his book, *The Label: The Story of Columbia Records*, always had big plans which "would place him in New York's most exclusive social circles, clear the way for a climb up the CBS corporate ladder and make him wealthy. He would socialize with the Western world's finest musicians, as well as society and showbiz types...A musician himself, he possessed a deep love of literature and was the quickest wit in the land. In addition to a gleeful, continually punning deployment of English, he could string together a few sentences in four languages: French, German, Japanese and, later in life, Italian—and, when the joke called for it, a smattering of Yiddish. As a boss, he knew how to delegate; he left his people alone to do their jobs."

Goddard Lieberson was born in England in 1911 and, at seven, moved with his family to Canada and then Seattle. One of his brothers taught him basic piano and, during high school, he enjoyed playing popular music for friends. Before he finished high school he was composing and received a scholarship to the University of Washington, based on a composition, and then transferred to the Eastman School in Rochester, New York where he quickly impressed his professors. "His professors could hear his musical gifts, and he was already great company, his banter rife with literary as well as musical references," stated Marmorstein. At Eastman, two of his classmates were Mitch Miller and Alec Wilder.

In addition to composing at Eastman, Lieberson worked as editor of the *International Encyclopedia of Music and Musicians* and wrote for the *Rochester Evening Journal* and *Musical America*, covering classical music. Although he had not obtained a degree, he taught music in an elite high school and wrote string quartets and music to literary works. By 1939 he was in New York where he wrote for *Modern Music* magazine, covering radio and "overflowed with punning wit."

By the time he was introduced to Columbia Records President Ted Wallerstein, Lieberson "had written, composed and socialized his way into position" where "everyone knew Lieberson was talented, witty, and plugged in—a good man to have in the classical division."

Lieberson's first marriage ended around the time he moved to New York and he set out "to know everyone worth knowing." In 1943, Lieberson replaced Moses Smith as head of Masterworks, a position which "fit Lieberson like a bespoke suit." He "wasn't a workaholic—not at the office, anyway," according to Marmorstein, "for much of the requirements of his job were blended into an active social life." In his role as head of Masterworks, Lieberson "Consoled, cajoled, and entertained-all to keep his Masterworks artists happy....Letter writing alone could take up a whole day's work, never mind recording sessions and garden variety hand-holding when artists appeared in the office."

By 1946, Lieberson was well known for his "wit, erudition, a debonair handsomeness, executive responsibility and accomplishment, perhaps even talent." He met and married ballet dancer Vera Zorina. In that year he was named Vice President at Columbia. By the following year he "had a wife, a son a published novel (*Three for Bedroom C*), a handsome East Side residence, and an impressive corporate title and salary." He was known as someone who could trade "profane insults with writers and musicians" and then put on a tux for dinner at Elsa Maxwell's."

Broadway Musicals

During the 1940s, Decca Records recorded the top Broadway shows, such as *One Touch of Venus, Bloomer Girl, Carousel, Call Me Mister, Annie Get Your Gun, Call Me Madam, Guys and Dolls* and *Oklahoma!* Lerner and Loew's

Brigadoon was recorded by RCA but they soon stopped after they recorded a series of flops.

The first musical Goddard Lieberson produced came in 1947 with the Kurt Weill and Langston Hughes musical *Street Scene*. CBS engineers were developing the LP and Lieberson saw the LP as the perfect vehicle for musicals. He had good contacts with composers and searched for older musicals that had been overlooked. Lieberson was a musical scholar and could be a fearless but effective producer, staying within a budget while adding musicians to the orchestra. Seeking recognition, Lieberson arranged to have "Produced for Records by Goddard Lieberson" on the recordings he produced. For consumers who purchased cast recordings the name "Goodard Lieberson soon became well known; it had class. However, on the cast recording of *South Pacific*, show producers Josh Logan and Leland Hayward objected to Lieberson's name on the album so Lieberson removed it.

The groundwork for Columbia's series of Broadway musicals was paved by Mannie Sacks who, as head of pop music Artists and Repertoire, was responsible for finding and supervising the recording of musicals. In 1947, Sacks obtained *Finian's Rainbow*, with the score written by Burton Lane and Yip Harburg, for the label, then *Kiss Me Kate* by Cole Porter, *South Pacific*, *Miss Liberty* by Irving Berlin and then the musical *Gentlemen Prefer Blondes* by Jule Styne and Leo Robin.

Manie Sacks left Columbia for RCA Victor and was replaced by Mitch Miller in 1950. Miller was assigned to produce the Cole Porter musical *Out of This World*, but Miller did not have a deep interest in producing musicals and, after that one, did not produce another. Goddard Lieberson, who did have a deep interest and love of musicals, took over the production of musicals starting with *A Tree Grows in Brooklyn*. That was followed by a series of musicals under conductor Lehman Engle until he had amassed a large catalogue of musicals for Columbia.

Author Gary Marmorstein stated "In this series Lieberson, for all his Renaissance-man talents and interests, discovered his deepest musical passion. He spent an increasing amount of time researching older musicals, found out what was available and went to work, trying to get them on record and sometimes restoring songs that had been cut from either the show or an earlier version...re-creating older works." The cost of producing older musicals were much lower because the label did not have to pay Actors Equity minimums and a lower rate was negotiated for arrangers and copyists. In 1951, Columbia recorded *Porgy and Bess,* which was originally staged in 1935. As usual, Lieberson used the original score and recorded the complete libretto.

The Introduction of Tape

A great leap in recording technology came at the end of World War II when the head of the Russians Radio Berlin unit showed American civilians a captured German Magnetophon in September, 1945. The tape machine had 14-inch reels which could produce symphonic works on magnetic tape with such fidelity that they could not be distinguished from an actual concert. It was also used for Hitler's speeches.

The importance of that discovery was not immediately apparent to the recording industry, who felt the future belonged to wire recorders. Sears had one on the market for $169 and some predicted wire recordings would eventually replace records. However, the magnetized wire was fragile, had poor fidelity and tended to rust--all of which was overlooked at the time. For that reason, recording sessions continued to be direct to disc with musicians playing while an acetate was being cut. If a mistake was made, the entire song had to start over from the beginning. There was no tape splicing, overdubbing, or mixing after the song was recorded. It all had to be done right on a single take.

The Magnetophon was an improved development from the original dictating machine by Allgemeinische Elektrische Gesellschaft and which I. G. Farben offered for sale originally in 1935. In the United States, General Electric held the rights under a cartel arrangement which divided the world's markets.

Tape technology received its biggest boost from Bing Crosby in 1946. Crosby was negotiating with NBC for his radio show, and wanted to tape his show, sponsored by Kraft, so the shows could be edited. It left him more time to play golf because he could tape several shows at a time, freeing up days for the golf course. NBC objected but ABC accepted the arrangement. That allowed ABC to repeat the program and saved overtime costs. The other networks soon saw the advantages of taped shows and followed suit.

1948

In 1948 the United States was hit by skyrocketing inflation as the cost of goods and services increased dramatically. New imports included Honda motorcycles, Land Rovers, Porsche sports cars, Michelin radial tires, Nikon

35 mm cameras as well as domestic introductions of Dial soap, Baskin-Robbins ice cream, and the board game Scrabble.

The world was perceived to be a scary place for Americans, prompting the Nixon-Mundt bill which required Communists to register with the government. In December, Alger Hiss was convicted of espionage in a case pursued and brought to national attention by California Representative Richard Nixon, who lambasted the Truman administration for being soft on Communism.

In Berlin, the Soviets blocked all land access to that city, so the Berlin Airlift was instituted to fly food in. Japanese war leaders were convicted as war criminals and hung. In May, the State of Israel was created, with the former Palestine divided into a Jewish and Arab state. In June, the draft was re-instituted for young men 18 to 25. President Truman ordered the integration of the Armed Forces, despite objections from many military leaders. Six billion dollars was allocated for the Marshall Plan,

In the November elections, Harry Truman was not given much of a chance to win; popularity polls showed him to be one of the most unpopular Presidents of the century. But Truman went on a whistle-stop campaign on a train across the country, lambasting the Republican "do nothing Congress," describing Republicans as "Bloodsuckers with offices on Wall Street, princes of privilege, plunderers." In South Carolina, Senator Strom Thurmond headed the Dixiecrat party, opposed to integration, that attracted a million votes. On November 3 a Chicago newspaper ran the headline "Dewey Wins" to celebrate the victory of Republican nominee Thomas Dewey, but they got it wrong; "Give 'em Hell Harry" had won the Presidential election.

One of the most far-reaching inventions of 1948 went virtually unnoticed. Dr. William Shockley at the Bell Labs invented the transistor, but the Lab thought the only commercial use was for hearing aids.

The Musicians Strike of 1948

At midnight on December 31, 1947, as bands all over the country played "Auld Lang Syne," musicians performing in the midst of that celebration on New Year's Eve were both rejoicing at the good times and bracing for tough times. American Federation of Musicians head James Petrillo had called a strike to begin January 1, 1948.

When all the sales figures were in, it was discovered that 1947 was the best year for the music industry since 1921, the previous best year. In 1947, the recording industry sold $214.4 million worth of disks at retail and 3.4 million record players were produced.

In 1948 there would be virtually no recording the entire year--it was not until mid-December before the strike was resolved--but during that year, there were major technological breakthroughs which altered the music and the industry.

First, ABC Radio network announced it was going "all tape" for nighttime programming. That followed Bing Crosby's decision to tape his radio shows for ABC. Crosby's production crew chose a tape developed by the Minnesota Mining and Manufacturing Company and a recording machine manufactured by Ampex. 3M had experimented with tapes developed by the Germans and developed a quality tape that recorded at seven and a half inches per second. (The German tapes recorded at 30 ips and had 14 inch reels.) With that announcement by Crosby and ABC, the networks ordered 3M tape and Ampex recorders, replacing their old wire recorders.

The record labels were aware of the strike looming and worked hard to stockpile releases. Columbia and Victor spent about $2 million in last minute recording, storing 2,000 masters. When the strike began, releases continued regularly and the strike appeared to have little effect, until sales began to plummet.

The 1948 strike was Petrillo's last hurrah. First, the country disliked him calling a strike during World War II, even after President Roosevelt had requested that he not do so. Further, some alleged he was a member of organized crime and Congress accused him of being a racketeer. Finally, the Taft-Hartley Act, passed over President Harry Truman's veto in June, 1948, limited the power of unions.

The strike signaled the end for Big Bands. In 1948 a number of Big Bands disbanded, including the Dorsey Brother's Band, and other top names. With changing musical tastes, the decline in network radio because of the rise of television as well as the rise of small radio stations, and problems with the economics of touring (having to support a large number of musicians on the road) and, finally, the strike which ended the money from recording sessions, the days of the Big Bands were over.

Radio had its biggest year in 1948, collecting $616.5 million in revenue from advertising sales. That year, a number of radio comedy programs--which led in network ratings--moved from NBC to CBS. In one fell swoop CBS acquired top rated shows like Edgar Bergen and Charlie McCarthy, Jack Benny, Amos'n'Andy, Red Skelton and Burns and Allen for their Sunday night line-up, which was the biggest night for listening to radio. That had far-reaching effects when those radio programs moved to network television because CBS dominated in that time slot.

The year 1948 was the first full year of network television programming; among the shows launched were "Toast of the Town," a CBS variety show hosted by newspaper columnist Ed Sullivan, Kate Smith's variety show, and Bing Crosby's musical variety show. Smith had been on radio for 15 years and Crosby for 17 years; the philosophy of radio programming was that people became comfortable with entertainers and shows and wanted to hear them year after year. That was why so many long-running radio shows were still around when television debuted, and why they were moved over to television when that medium was introduced.

A musical game show premiered in 1948, launched by Louis G. Cowan. "Stop the Music!" featured Harry Salter's orchestra, that played popular songs until host Bert Parks shouted "Stop the music!" A phone call was placed to a household in the United States and if the person could identify the interrupted song, he/she received a number of expensive gifts. By the beginning of 1949 that was a top-rated TV show, which led to a number of game shows on TV.

The 33 1/3 Album and 45 Single

Peter Goldmark was born in Budapest, Hungary in 1906 and educated in Berlin and Vienna, where he earned his doctorate in physics from the University of Vienna. In 1933, Goldmark emigrated to the United States and soon established himself as an engineer. He applied to work at RCA, but they turned him down; his application to join CBS was successful and he joined that company in 1936.

CBS had a research division and Goldmark "quickly assumed command of the research lab," where he received financial backing for his experiments. Goldmark loved classical music but was frustrated when he listened to classical works on 78 rpm records because he could not hear most classical works in their entirety without changing records. That led Goldmark to develop the long playing (LP) record.

In his experiments, Goldmark found that the length or duration of a record depended on (1) the diameter of the disc, (2) the speed or revolutions per minute (rpm) and (3) the number of grooves per inch that were covered by the needle. In his research, he discovered that almost all (90 percent) of all classical works fit within 45 minutes of playing time. A 12-inch disc would hold most classical pieces and fit the turntables used at that time.

Transcription discs had been used since the days of silent movies and, after the "talkies" came in, those transcription discs were used to record radio shows to send to radio stations to air. Transcription discs ran at 33 1/3 rpm so Goldmark used that speed as his starting point.

(In 1931, RCA, under Edward Wallerstein, had introduced a 33 1/3 rpm disc but it did not survive.)

Records had been made out of shellac, a hard, brittle plastic that broke easily, especially when shipped. During World War II shellac, which came from India, was not available. Record labels recycled old discs to provide new releases. After World War II, Goldmark found a synthetic replacement for shellac in vinylite, or vinyl, which made lighter, better sounding records that could bend.

Goldmark took his idea of a 12-inch record made of vinyl that could hold 22 minutes of music on each side to Edward Wallerstein, president of CBS Records, who told Goldmark to stick with his work on television (Goldmark was working to create color television at the same time he was working on the LP). However, Bill Paley, head of the CBS Corporation, gave Goldmark permission to continue working on the long playing record.

When the new format was ready for the market, CBS tried to find a name for the new disc. None of the suggestions were satisfactory. Goldmark has been using the term "LP" (for long player) and, when talking with Wallerstein, used the term. Wallerstein excitedly said "that's it!" and that's how the LP was named the LP.

The term "album" came from Bell Laboratories, who had developed a ten inch record for film soundtracks. Popular artists were released on 78 rpm records that were slipped into paper sleeves like a photo album of multi-disc sets.

CBS and Wallerstein planned to debut the new format at the annual record dealer's meeting in August, 1948, but the press got wind of it so he moved up the date to June 18. On that day, Wallerstein stood between a stack of the new LPs and the old 78s: it took eight feet of the old format to provide only 15-inches in the new format. The picture was sent out across the country. At the press conference when the LP debuted, Columbia released 101 albums in the new format which were dominated by classical music but also included releases by Frank Sinatra, Dinah Shore and Harry James.

Prior to the presentation of the LP, Bill Paley had invited his chief competitor, David Sarnoff, head of the RCA Corporation, to attend a demonstration of the new format with his engineers. Sarnoff was impressed with the sound, quality and "unbreakable" vinyl disc. Paley offered to join forces with Sarnoff to market the new disc but Sarnoff called back a few days later and declined. Instead, he ordered the engineers in his research division to create a new format that would be different than the LP.

The RCA engineers decided on the speed of their new disc to be 45 rpm; they arrived at that figure by subtracting 33 from 78, which equaled 45. Instead of using the established 10 inch in diameter disc of the 78 or the 12 inch disc of the 33 1/3, the RCA engineers came up with a seven inch disc with a large hole in the middle that held four minutes of sound. RCA introduced the new 45 rpm record in January, 1949.

RCA and CBS both manufactured and marketed phonographs so if CBS prevailed, then they would sell a lot of hardware and RCA would have to license the new technology, creating a windfall profit for their chief competitor. That was unacceptable so RCA engineers created a disc that could not play on any phonograph except those manufactured by RCA. That led to a "Battle of the Speeds." The 78 rpm record still dominated releases and that was another format that had to be accommodated.

Engineers solved that problem by creating a multi-speed phonograph that played 78, 33 1/3 and 45 rpm records by adjusting a knob. Adapters were developed so that 45s could be played on the thin spindle that played small hole records.

In 1950, RCA gave in to the LP format and began manufacturing them; the next year, Columbia gave in to the 45 rpm format. The 33 1/3 was good for the classical market as well as original cast recordings of Broadway and movie musicals. The first million selling LP was the cast recording of *Oklahoma!* on Decca in 1949. The 45 was perfect for pop and, later, rock'n'roll and by 1953 RCA had sold ten million 45 rpm phonographs.

Not everyone loved the new LP format. Some listeners liked the idea of "active" listening when they had to regularly change records.

Discount Selling

Discount selling hit the recording industry just before World War II when Sam Goody of New York began selling records to his line of novelty and magic trick paraphernalia he offered at his store near the financial district. Goody bought records from southern jukebox operators at a cut rate and sold them for 30 percent less than suggested retail.

Records were available to Goody because many operators were overstocked, a result of major companies allocating new releases based on past sales. Goody received a 40-50 percent discount on those records and sold them at a discount. By selling vast quantities, he turned a handsome profit.

The major labels didn't like it. First, they were used to controlling the market, deciding who would and who wouldn't sell their records. Too, they kept a tight control on prices, insisting that their dealers sell records for "suggested retail price." Discount selling upset this and Columbia reacted by bringing litigation against Goody.

From Big Bands to Singers

Musically, there was a change at the major labels as Columbia, Victor and Decca found that consumers now wanted singers instead of dance bands. A major reason for that change was the disk jockey, who had gained in importance. Radio audiences liked the jocks programming records by Nat "King" Cole, Frank Sinatra, Margaret Whiting, Dick Haymes, Mel Torme, Eddy Howard, Georgia Gibbs, Perry Como, Peggy Lee and Helen Forrest instead of a steady diet of shows.

Victor began to accept the importance of the disc jockeys on radio because disk jockeys influenced about 85 percent of record sales of popular music, spinning disks on over 1,200 stations. With that fact staring them in their face, Victor began sending out free disks to 850 radio stations, covering about 2,800 program directors, disk jockeys and music librarians.

Country Music in 1948

In country music, 1948 was the year of Eddy Arnold, who held the number one position on the *Billboard* charts for every single week except two and, going back to the end of 1947, Arnold had the number one record in *Billboard* for sixty consecutive weeks. His number one hits in 1948 were "Anytime," "Bouquet of Roses," "Texarkana Baby," "Just a Little Lovin' (Will Go a Long, Long Way)" and "A Heart Full of Love (For a Handful of Kisses)." The only number one that year that was not an Eddy Arnold record was "One Has My Name (The Other Has My Heart)" by Jimmy Wakely.

On April 3, 1948, the Louisiana Hayride was first broadcast from 50,000 watt KWKH in Shreveport, Louisiana. The station was owned by a newspaper, the *Shreveport Times*, which was owned by the Ewing family. The commercial manager of the station was former Vagabond member Dean Upson, who secured sponsors, with Johnnie and Kyle Bailes working as announcers and talent recruiters. Producer and emcee of the show was Horace Logan, who introduced a line-up of Harmie Smith, Hoot & Curley, Pappy Covington, Tex Grimsley, Johnnie & Jack with Kitty Wells, and the Bailes Brothers that night. In August, Hank Williams made his first appearance on the Hayride, then became a member.

Gene Autry starred in only one singing cowboy movie but continued his "Melody Ranch" radio show on CBS sponsored by Wrigley's Doublemint gum, and began a series of tours. Those one-night stands featured two-shows a day. The fall tour usually ended at the Madison Square Garden and Boston Gardens rodeos. Each performance was a full two-hour show with music interspersed with comedy, rope tricks, acrobats and dog acts.

In the fall of 1948 the Big D Jamboree began in Dallas, an outgrowth of the Texas State Barn Dance and Lone Star Jamboree (established in 1946 and 1947 respectively). The original host for the Texas State Barn Dance, KLIF DJ Big Al Turner, was joined by KRLD's Johnny Hicks, who co-produced the show. The show featured the Callahan Brothers, Riley Crabtree and Gene O'Quin; the house band was the Light Crust Doughboys, who were billed as the Country Gentlemen.

Publishing was becoming increasingly important to Nashville because of the increasing power of BMI over ASCAP, who still shunned country and blues music, and the decline in sheet music sales in the publishing industry. Monies from record sales and radio airplay were becoming the way publishers and songwriters made most of their money. The country music industry was growing and needed new, fresh songs for the increasing number of country recordings released.

In Nashville, publisher Acuff-Rose, pioneered the "Nashville plan" with the musicians union, headed by George Cooper. Under that plan, songwriters received money from airplay directly from the performance licensing organization BMI. The publisher had previously received that money to pay songwriters. That meant songwriters and publishers each received money directly from BMI for radio and television airplay.

Rhythm and Blues

In 1948, Dinah Washington began recording for Mercury and soon switched from blues to ballads--a black singer doing what white singers were doing, but selling to a black audience. That same year Paul Williams recorded a hit, "The Huckle-Buck" for Savoy and Wynonie "Blues" Harris had a hit on King Records with "Good Rockin' Tonight." The only African-American singer hitting big in the pop music market was Nat King Cole. In 1947 Nat King Cole had a major pop hit with "I Love You (For Sentimental Reasons)," then in 1948 had "Nature Boy" and "Mona Lisa," which won a Academy Award in 1949.

In Los Angeles, Johnny Otis opened the Barrel House, a club in the Watts section of the city. According to Otis, at the Barrel House "we began to develop something within something. It was a hybrid form that began to emerge. It surely wasn't big band; it wasn't swing; it wasn't country blues. It was what was to become known as rhythm and blues, a hybrid form that became an art form in itself. It was the foundation of rock'n'roll."

The Hunt for Communists

During his presidential campaign of 1948, President Harry Truman was attacked by Republicans as a communist sympathizer and had to campaign hard against Communists, creating a furor that culminated when Senator Joseph McCarthy instigated an era of "witch-hunts" for communists and communist sympathizers in 1950.

The Communist Scare dominated news in 1947 as the nation searched for traitors. In October, 1947, the House Committee on Un-American Activities opened public hearings on communism in the film industry which soon spread to the entertainment industry. Although R&B and country music were ignored, a number of prominent entertainers, writers and directors were declared "red" and blacklisted by Hollywood. Those who were named on this "blacklist," found that networks determined who they would or would not book were Leonard Bernstein, Lee J. Cobb, Aaron Copeland, Jose Ferrer, Morton Gould, Dashiell Hammett, Lillian Hellman, Lena Horne, Burgess Meredith, Orson Wells , Arthur Miller, Zero Mostel, Dorothy Parker, Edward G. Robinson, Artie Shaw and folk singers Burl Ives, Pete Seeger, and Josh White.

1949

In January, 1949, for the first time in recorded weather history, it snowed in Southern California--a foot! Pizza was introduced to American consumers, although the appeal was primarily to Italian families and adventurous college students at first. On Long Island, William Levitt developed the first mass-produced suburban housing development, Levittown, with houses selling for $7,990 to buyers eager to own their own home. There was a catch; only whites were eligible to buy a house in that first suburban development.

During the War, American automobile factories re-tooled to produce 20 percent of military goods used in the war; by 1949 they were back in full domestic production, manufacturing six million cars a year. General Motors reported a profit of $500 million that year.

In New York, the cornerstone was laid for the United Nations Building, which would be headquarters for the peace-keeping organization. Congress passed a bill creating the North Atlantic Treaty Organization (NATO) to defend Europe in military conflicts between nations. In September, news came that the Soviets had detonated their first atomic bomb. In China, the Communists, led by Mao Tse Tung, took over mainline China while Chiang Kai-shek fled to Formosa (now Taiwan).

The United Steel Workers union gained pension and welfare benefits for its members, although executives at United States Steel argued those benefits would "strike a blow at the principle of self-help and dignity."

Bringing the news to Americans were 1,780 daily newspapers that reached a circulation of 53 million.

Rhythm and Blues

On June 25, 1949, *Billboard* changed the name of its charts from "Race" to "Rhythm and Blues." This marked the acceptance of the term "rhythm and blues" within the music industry as well as an acknowledgement that R&B was a dynamic musical force in American music. (It also changed the "Folk" chart to "Country and Western," a reflection of a more accurate description of commercial country music as well as a desire from the country music community to separate themselves from folk singers and folk music, which had connections with Communist politics.)

The development of rhythm and blues came from a variety of sources. According to Arnold Shaw, "If the blues was trouble music and urban blues adjustment songs, then R&B was good-time dance music. If the blues was rural song and urban blues city music, R&B was black ghetto music. If the blues was loneliness and self-expression song, and urban blues nostalgia and growing music, then R&B was group and joy music. If the country bluesman wailed and the urban bluesman sang, the rhythm and bluesman shouted--and soul men howled and screamed. Country and delta blues were a man and his guitar (sometimes with harmonica added); urban bluesmen were backed by guitar and/or piano, bass, and drums; rhythm and bluesmen sang to combo accompaniment and electrified instruments."

Shaw added, "Economically, R&B was a product of the jukebox, the shortage of disks in black locations, and the rising purchasing power of black people during and after World War II. Technologically, R&B was made possible by the development of tape recording, a process that brought the cost of making masters within the reach of small entrepreneurs.

Psychologically, it was an expression of a people enjoying a new sense of freedom, hemmed in though that freedom was by ghettos."

Shaw also noted that R&B was "liberated music, which in its pristine form represented a break with white, mainstream pop. Developing from black sources, it embodied the fervor of gospel music, the throbbing vigor of boogie woogie, the jump beat of swing, and the gutsiness and sexuality of life in the black ghetto."

A number of black musicians, particularly within the jazz community, thought R&B was a fad and passing phase and jazz, the more sophisticated music, would dominate. R&B was too simple and vulgar for jazz musicians. Many blacks in the middle class disliked R&B as well; they felt it was too "raw" and did not "elevate" the Negro.

Within the black community in cities, singing was an escape and an easy way to make money. However, young performers had little understanding of the music business and often fell prey to older, shrewder entrepreneurs. A personal manager was necessary, but he or she might take 10 to 50 percent of the money earned while a booking agency would take 10-15 percent. A group needed a choreographer for club dates and choreographers often turned down a flat fee and demanded a percentage of personal appearance income--usually around five percent. An arranger was needed for recording sessions as well as to put together a club show. When all the accounts were settled, a group might be left with half of what they had earned--and that had to be split four or five ways.

By 1949 there were important independent labels recording rhythm and blues: Chess in Chicago had Muddy Waters, Howlin' Wolf, Little Walter, Bo Diddley, Willie Mabon, Sonny Boy Williamson, and Lowell Fulson. An act like Muddy Waters (like many on the Chess label) would not cross over because his "hard" R&B appealed primarily to a black market. Those artists generally migrated from the South.

In New Orleans, Lewis Chudd, founder of the Imperial label, found Fats Domino and began recording him in 1949; Domino soon crossed over into the white market. That same year Don Robey began Peacock Records in Houston, Texas because, as Gatemouth Brown's manager, Robey was frustrated when Brown's label, Aladdin, would not release the artist's records.

The problem of finding a pressing plant seemed to be solved by 1949; Syd Nathan built a pressing plant in Cincinnati while Los Angeles had the RGR pressing plant. That plant was developed during World War II after

Allied Records, the only indie pressing plant in the area, would not press more than 200 records for an indie label. The breakthrough came when indie owners found Jimmy Beard, who worked in the maintenance department at Allied, and built them a record press for a thousand dollars. The indie labels scoured the area for discarded records, which they melted down because of the shortage of shellac. That was the impetus that created the RGR pressing plant and soon, several others. By that time, Beard worked for the new companies because Allied fired him when they found out what he'd done.

The development of the 45 single on vinyl by RCA led to the demise of the 78s. Those heavy ten-inch records were costly when shipping and extremely breakable. The 45s were made of vinyl, lighter and did not break easily; however, the pressing plants had to retool--a costly venture--and the retail price of records dropped to 75 cents from $1.05, which forced some independents out of business.

Radio and Television

In 1948 the most powerful station broadcasting the music of African-Americans was WLAC in Nashville. Led by disc jockeys "Daddy" Gene Nobles and "John R" Richbourg, it became a key station because of its 50,000 watts, which allowed listeners all over the South to hear its broadcasts.

In 1949 NBC and CBS began to allow "canned music" on the air, following a ruling by the Federal Communications Commission that allowed transcribed network programs. That came as a result in the increased fidelity of sound recordings. A major factor was that CBS was losing between $250,000 and $400,000 in morning income, when there was no audience for advertisers.

In 1949, Paul Whiteman hosted a local dance show on television for teenagers in Philadelphia. "Paul Whiteman's TV-Teen Club" was broadcast over WFIL-TV and ABC-TV. Whiteman was in charge of music for the ABC network and the production costs were covered by Whiteman. That was the first TV dance show for teenagers, and would be a forerunner for Dick Clark's American Bandstand several years later.

Frank Sinatra

Entertainers and other public figures were punished for public indiscretions during the 1940s and 1950s. Frank Sinatra's public affair with actress Lana Turner in 1945 and 1946, during a time when he was still married to his high school sweetheart, Nancy, caused the public to turn against him. In January, 1947, Sinatra went to Havana where he met Mafia leaders Lucky Luciano and Frank Costello and his association with those major crime figures made the news. In April, 1947, Sinatra slugged reporter Lee Mortimer, who sued him and that, too, made headlines.

In September, 1947, journalist Westbrook Pegler wrote about Sinatra socializing with gangsters; in 1948 the singer began a very public affair with actress Ava Gardner, which meant his concerts drew few fans. He continued his downward spiral through the 1940s, living lavishly but did not keep up with his taxes. In 1950, still married to Nancy with two small children at home while the media covered his public affair with Ava Gardner, Sinatra attempted some concerts--his first in two years--and discovered he couldn't sing because of throat problems.

The throat problems were not helped by the fact that he usually stayed up all night, drinking and smoking; still, he performed three shows a night at the Copacobana in New York and five radio shows, in addition to his recording sessions, because he needed the work and the money.

In December, 1950, a Congressional committee, the Special Committee to Investigate Crime in Interstate Commerce, held hearings that were televised nationally. For the first time, the spotlight shone on organized crime and Frank Sinatra was questioned about his associations with figures in organized crime by that committee.

In 1951, Louis Mayer, head of MGM, terminated Sinatra's contract with the movie studio and told him "I want you to leave this studio here, and I don't ever want you to come back again." His close associate heading Columbia Records, Manie Sacks, resigned and was replaced by Mitch Miller. A low point in Sinatra's recording career came on a session produced by Miller where the singer and blond comedienne Dagmar recorded "Mama Will Bark" and Sinatra barked like a dog on the recording.

In 1951, Frank and Nancy Sinatra divorced; their divorce was final on October 31 and he married Ava Gardner on November 7. The following year Sinatra appeared at a nightclub in Chicago that seated 1,200 but only 150 showed up. In June, 1952, Frank Sinatra was dropped by Columbia Records and the agents at MCA who booked him were having difficulty finding bookings. Sinatra's last session for Columbia occurred on September 17.

1950

Network radio in 1950 collected over $183 million from ad sales. There were 108 different series which had been on the air for ten years or more and twelve series that had been on the air for 20 years. Jack Benny led the ratings, followed by Bob Hope, Edgar Bergen & Charlie McCarthy and Burns &

Allen. In music, Bing Crosby led ratings with his variety show while Arthur Godfrey had the top rated "amateur hour" show. "The Lux Radio Theater" was the top rated drama series while "The Romance of Helen Trent" and "Ma Perkins" led daytime shows. "Amos'n'Andy" remained one of the most popular shows after twenty-one years on the air.

Television made inroads during the 1948-1952 period but the FCC did not issue any TV licenses because of "interference problems." At that point there were 108 TV stations but only 24 cities had two or more stations. There was only one station in Houston, Kansas City, Milwaukee, Pittsburgh, and St. Louis. A number of cities (Austin, Denver, Little Rock, Portland, Oregon) had no television stations. Only in New York and Los Angeles--which had seven stations each--was TV in full bloom.

The "freeze" in issuing television licenses lasted three and a half years, prolonged by the Korean War. Although television was having a rocky start, it affected movie attendance, which dropped 20 to 40 percent in cities where there was a TV station. There was a major shift in sports, as minor league baseball teams, located in a number of cities, suffered declining attendance. Wrestling did well on TV; baseball did not do so well. Less people went to nightclubs and restaurants when TV came, bookstore sales declined and jukeboxes collected less money. Radio listenership declined as well.

Network sponsors wanted national exposure, so they remained with radio through 1952 and many of the network radio shows remained on radio as well as television. However, the shift to television caused most network executives to pay less attention to radio.

Between 1948 and 1952, a number of "Negro radio stations" came on the air, playing rhythm and blues; among those were WSOK in Nashville and WERD in Atlanta. The Atlanta station discovered that 20 percent of its listening audience was white. That marked the beginning of the influence of black music on pop and country music because mainstream listeners to those musics--as well a future artists—were able to hear music directly from African-American recording artists for the first time in their own homes.

The movie industry suffered a major setback in a Supreme Court case when Paramount, Loew's (including Metro-Goldwyn-Mayer), RKO, Twentieth Century-Fox, Warner Brothers, Columbia Pictures, Universal and United Artists were ordered to sell their movie theaters--divorcing their production from their distribution. The Big Studios had a vertical integration of the movie industry; they produced their movies, with a cast of talent under contract who had to appear in their movies, then sent the pictures to movie theaters they owned. That kept smaller studios and foreign firms from getting their movies shown, except in small towns and independently owned theaters.

In 1952 the FCC split the TV band, assigning Channels 2 to 13 to VHF (very high frequency) and other channels to UHF (ultra high frequency). In July, 1952, the FCC began processing new applications for TV stations.

At the beginning of 1952 there were 15 million TV sets in 64 cities. Among the top rated shows were "Texaco Star Theater" starring Milton Berle, "I Love Lucy," "Your Show of Shows" starring Sid Caesar and Imogene Coca, "Toast of the Town" hosted by Ed Sullivan, "Arthur Godfrey's Friends and Talent Scouts," the puppet show "Kukla, Fran and Ollie," the variety show "Garroway at Large," the talk show "The Faye Emerson Show" and the drama series, "Philco Playhouse" and "Goodyear Playhouse."

The Presidential election of 1952 pitted Dwight Eisenhower with his vice-president candidate Richard Nixon, against Democratic nominee Adlai Stevenson. Nixon soon became involved in a controversy over a secret fund of money from rich backers for his use. Nixon went on television where he delivered his famous "Checkers" speech, claiming he had received no special gifts except a little dog, "Checkers," that his children loved and which he would not give back. That heart-rending speech saved his candidacy and he remained on the Republican ticket.

Several things happened before the election which defined the early 1950s period. On February 9, 1950, Senator Joseph McCarthy from Wisconsin claimed, in a speech he gave in Wheeling, West Virginia, to have a secret list of "card-carrying Communists" in his pocket. For the next several years McCarthy held Senate hearings on Communists in America that kept the nation enthralled. This was followed by a book, *Red Channels: The Report of Communist Influence in Radio and Television* that named people suspected of Communist involvement and resulted in a number of writers, directors and performers who were unable to get on the networks because they were listed.

On June 25, 1950, Communist forces in northern Korea invaded southern Korea, igniting the Korean War. General Douglas MacArthur organized American forces to repel the invaders and a line was drawn to divide Korea into "North" and "South." MacArthur ignored warnings from the Joint Chiefs of Staff and President Truman and pushed American forces further north, getting them trapped and engaging Chinese forces. Finally, American forces were pulled back below the 38th parallel and a stand-off ensued.

Mitch Miller

In the Fall of 1949, Goddard Lieberson was promoted to executive vice president. He was disappointed when he was passed over for the position as President of Columbia Records in 1950 but remained with the company and hired Mitch Miller as a record producer.

Mitch Miller was born on July 4, 1911, to Russian-Jewish immigrants who had emigrated to Rochester, New York, where he grew up. The family obtained a Chickering piano and Miller took piano lessons. He attended a public school that received money from George Eastman (before he established the Eastman School) for music instruction on Saturday mornings. Miller enrolled in the program and chose the oboe because it was the only instrument available when it came time for him to choose.

Miller was talented and played oboe for the Syracuse Symphony and the Rochester Philharmonic. He entered Eastman School of Music and graduated in 1932; two years later he moved to New York and played oboe regularly for the CBS Symphony and CBS's "Swing Club" on CBS radio. During the late 1930s and early 1940s Miller worked steadily on radio and in recording studios and "was held in such high regard around town that musicians alerted each other when he was part of a program."

Miller had extensive experience as a musician in recording studios, which served him well as a producer. He supervised classical recordings for Keynote Records and supervised popular recordings from October, 1947. (The term "producer" came later; the term "musical supervisor" was used for those who supervised sessions.) During the AFM's recording strike in 1948, Miller became musical director for Golden Records, a children's label that was part of the children's "Golden Books" series, a subsidiary of Simon & Schuster. Keynote had been absorbed into Mercury Records and Miller took Mercury artist Frankie Laine into the studio in April, 1949 and recorded "That Lucky Old Sun," which became the signature song for Laine.

Miller insisted that Laine record "Mule Train," although Laine did not want to, and the song became a hit. Miller also produced recordings by Patti Page (including "Tennessee Waltz") and Vic Damone.

Mitch Miller worked with Goddard Lieberson for a number of years and stated "People don't realize what a guiding genius [Lieberson] was. He was like a great parent. It's not what he did that mattered; what he did was plenty. It's what he *didn't* do. He never second-guessed you, he backed you up; he encouraged you to experiment, because if you're not going to shoot for something big, you'll never make something big. You can always imitate. The sales department would say, 'Ooh, Capitol has a record like this, let's copy it,' and he'd say, 'No, why waste an artist and come in second best? We'll make our own.' And they would lose some immediate sale, but they would gain a much greater sale later and this was nothing but straight common sense."

"Go to Sleep, Go to Sleep, Go to Sleep" a duet by Arthur Godfrey and Mary Martin was the first record Miller produced for Columbia and it charted in May, 1950. It was banned from radio because listeners might conclude the two were in bed together; in films and on TV, married couples were required to be in separate beds.

At Columbia, Miller worked with Frankie Laine (who left Mercury to join him), Rosemary Clooney, Jo Stafford and Tony Bennet. Miller had an appreciation for country music; he recorded "You Belong To Me" and Hank Williams' "Jambalaya" on Rosemary Clooney and Hank Williams' "Cold Cold Heart" on Tony Bennet. In 1950, Miller brought Percy Faith to Columbia; Faith was an arranger and orchestrated strings for singers before he began a recording career of his own.

Miller could be difficult and dictatorial, but he produced hits. Tony Bennett did not want to record "Cold, Cold Heart" but Miller insisted-and it was a number one hit (for six weeks) in 1951. Bennett also hated "Rags to Riches" but Miller "laid down the law," said Bennett; it became a number one record for eight weeks in 1983.

Miller was blamed for Frank Sinatra leaving Columbia in 1953 and signing with Capitol. According to Gary Marmorstein, Miller "kept Sinatra away from the songs he was right for and instead forced him to sing novelty songs." The prime example was the Sinatra duet with Dagmar on "Mama Don't Bark," where Sinatra barked on the record.

Patti Page and "How Much Is That Doggie in the Window"

Patti Page was a popular singer whose first chart records were in 1948. In 1950 she had "All My Love," which was number one for five weeks, then "The Tennessee Waltz, which was a number one song for 13 weeks in 1950-1951. In 1952 she had a number one hit (for ten weeks) with "I Went To Your Wedding" and the next year had a number one hit (for eight weeks) with "(How Much Is) That Doggie in the Window." The last song has been the whipping boy for numerous rock'n'roll historians, who cite it as an example of a bland, insipid and shallow songs that set the stage for the coming excitement of authentic rock'n'roll.

The song is cute and, rather than a song that should be dismissed with a sneer, serves to demonstrate that young baby boomers were attracted to music at an early age. It is a song that personified the family-friendly image of the 1950s; it became popular with young baby boomers and sold over two million records.

Pete Seeger

"Goodnight, Irene" by The Weavers entered the *Billboard* pop chart on July 1, 1950; it reached number one and remained in that position for 13 consecutive weeks and sold over two million copies. The Weavers were led by Pete Seeger; other members of the group included Lee Hays, Ronnie Gilbert and Fred Hellerman.

Pete Seeger was born in New York City (May 3, 1919) and traced his ancestry back to the American Revolution. His father, Charles Seeger, was a Harvard trained composer and musicologist and founded the American Musicological Society; his mother, Constance de Clyver was a classical pianist who trained at the Paris Conservatory of Music and later taught at Juilliard.

Pete's parents divorced when he was seven and his father remarried; the second marriage produced four children, Peggy, Mike, Barbara and Penelope, who all became folk singers.

Beginning when he was four, Pete attended boarding schools; his first instrument was the ukulele. Pete attended Camp Rising Sun in 1935 and the international leadership camp held each summer in upstate New York influenced his life's work.

In 1936, he first heard the five-string banjo at the Mountain Dance and Folk Festival, held near Ashville, North Carolina. Seeger considered the exposure to old time folk songs and ballads as a conversion experience. After that festival, Seeger learned old folk songs such as "Cindy," "Old Joe Clark" and "John Henry."

In 1937, Seeger entered Harvard on a partial scholarship but dropped out the following year because his grades suffered from his active involvement in politics and folk music. He had a job assisting Alan Lomax at the Archive of American Folk Song in the Library of Congress in Washington and Lomax encouraged Seeger's folk singing. Seeger sang on the weekly radio show "Back Where I Come From" hosted by Lomax and Nicholas Ray that also featured performances by Woody Guthrie, Burl Ives, Leadbelly and Will Geer.

Pete Seeger joined the Young Communist League in 1936, when he was 17, and became a member of the Communist Party USA in 1942. In the Spring of 1941, Seeger became a member of the Almanac singers; other members included Millard Lambell, Cisco Houston, Woody Guthrie, Butch and Bess Lomax Hawes and Lee Hays. The Almanacs recorded several albums, including *Songs for Joe Doe* in 1941, which was an anti-war protest album against the draft.

The American Communist party objected to the United States becoming part of the European war until Hitler invaded Russia; after that, the Communist Party directed its members to support the draft and forbid strikes. During World War II, Pete Seeger served in the Army, stationed in the Pacific where, although trained as an airplane mechanic, he was reassigned to entertain the troops with music.

After serving in World War II, Seeger and others established People's Songs, a national organization dedicated to promoting and distributing labor songs; Seeger was the director.

Pete Seeger was a political activist during the 1940s; he campaigned for political prisoners, civil rights, union organizing and world peace. The Almanac Singers functioned as a singing newspaper promoting the Industrial unionization movement, racial and religious inclusion and other progressive causes. The Weavers grew out of The Almanac Singers.

Beginning in 1950, the Weavers performed in tuxedos (the Almanacs had performed in everyday clothes) and their managers forbid them to perform at political venues. Their first single was an old Leadbelly song, "Goodnight, Irene" with the Israeli folk song, "Tzena, Tzena, Tzena" on the "B" side.

After "Goodnight, Irene," the Weavers had hits with "The Roving Kind," "So Long (It's Been Good To Know Ya)," "On Top of Old Smokey," "Kisses Sweeter Than Wine" in 1951 and "Wimoweh" and "Midnight Special" in 1952.

At the peak of their popularity in 1953, after Seeger was blacklisted, radio stations refused to play their songs and they could not obtain bookings. Seeger continued to campaign for civil and labor rights, racial equality, anti-militarism and international understanding but left the Communist Party USA in 1949.

Seeger's political activism caused him to be subpoenaed before the House Un-American Activities Committee (HUAC) on August 18, 1955. In 1950 the "Hollywood Ten" had been convicted and imprisoned for contempt of Congress after pleading the Fifth Amendment, which stated that someone does not have to testify if their testimony incriminates them. Seeger refused to name personal and political associates or organizations based on First Amendment grounds, stating "I am not going to answer any questions as to my association, my philosophical or religious beliefs or my political beliefs, or how I voted in any election or any of these private affairs. I think these are very improper questions for any American to be asked, especially under such compulsion as this."

In March, 1957, Seeger was indicted for contempt of Congress and during the coming years had to inform the federal government whenever he left the Southern District of New York. In May, 1962, his conviction was overturned.

Alan Freed in Cleveland

Leo Mintz owned the Record Rendezvous, a large record retailer in Cleveland, located near the black inner city area, and sponsored a show on WJW. In 1951 he met Alan Freed in a bar. Over drinks, Mintz offered to sponsor a show by Freed if he would only play rhythm and blues records. Freed turned him down.

Cleveland had a black population of about 130,000 and Mintz's shop saw steady sales of race records. Hardly any whites knew of this music and Freed disliked the fact that many of the lyrics were blatantly sexual, that the arrangements were crude (Freed was a product of the Big Band era) and there was virtually no white audience. Mintz saw the potential for this market and persisted with Freed; finally, Freed agreed to the arrangement and played what Mintz told him to. As his show progressed, Freed began to like the music.

Freed took the name "Moon Dog" and called his show "The Moon Dog Show." He joined a number of other disc jockeys playing rhythm and blues on the radio: Dewey Philips in Memphis; Gene Nobles and John Richbourg (John R) in Nashville; Zenas "Daddy" Sears in Atlanta; Ken "Jack the Cat" Elliott and Clarence "Poppa Stoppa" Hamman, Jr. in New Orleans; George "Hound Dog" Lorenz in Buffalo; "Jumpin'" George Oxford in Oakland-San Francisco; Phil McKernan in Berkeley; Hunter Hancock in Los Angeles; and Bob "Wolfman Jack" Smith in Shreveport and Del Rio, Texas.

Alan Freed's show made its debut on WJW on July 11, 1951. His theme song was "Blues for the Red Boy," an instrumental which Freed called "Blues for the Moondog." On the air Freed used a cowbell and phone book, which he pounded to keep beat with the records. He used jive language and howled like a hound in thrall with the moon.

The necessity of a white disc jockey--and later, white singers--to make rhythm and blues acceptable to the white audience cannot be underestimated. In his biography of Alan Freed, author John A. Jackson stated, "Because it was regarded by whites as the music of blacks, rhythm and blues ultimately needed a white as its champion in order to gain mass acceptance in American society...Freed performed the feat of building a large white audience for records that had previously been of interest only to blacks."

In some ways, Alan Freed was an unlikely prophet for rock'n'roll; on the other hand, he seemed to be born for that time and mission.

Aldon James Freed was born in western Pennsylvania on December 21, 1921. His father was a Lithuanian-born Jew who emigrated to the United States in 1901. Freed grew up in Salem, Ohio and graduated from high school in 1940. In high school, he idolized Benny Goodman and loved swing music. In the Fall of 1940 he entered Ohio State University, where he studied journalism, then mechanical engineering. Ohio State did not give him a degree but it did give him his true love: radio. Freed fell in love with the medium when he saw the campus radio station, WOSU.

After dropping out of Ohio State in early 1941, Freed enlisted in the Army but received a medical discharge later that year, just before Pearl Harbor. He then attended Broadcasting School at WKBN in Youngstown, Ohio and in October, 1942, landed a job on WKST in New Castle, Pennsylvania, where he was a one-man operation and announced a classical music program in the evening.

In February, 1943, Freed was hired to be a staff announcer on WKBN in Youngstown, Ohio, where he was a newscaster and sports announcer 1943-1944. He then moved to WAKR in Akron, Ohio where he hosted the program "Request Revue" that featured jazz and popular recordings and soon became the top moneymaker at the station.

The 29-year-old Freed had been on WJW for eight months, playing rhythm and blues records and, although he knew the program had followers, wasn't aware of the number listening or who comprised the audience. In partnership with Leo Mintz and booking agent Lew Platt, the Cleveland Arena was booked for the "Moondog Coronation Ball." The event was set for March 21, 1952, and that night the 10,000 capacity arena was packed to capacity, full to overflowing and police would not allow any more in. Further, the audience was mixed—black and white.

In an attempt to get into the arena, a mob of about 6,000 youths burst past the police and broke down the arena's doors. Police Captain William Zimmerman called off the dance and the next day the *Cleveland Plain Dealer* carried the headline, "Moondog Ball is Halted as 6,000 Crash Arena Gate." The event made national news and some have cited that date—March 21, 1952—as the beginning of the rock'n'roll era.

Although Freed was blamed for the unruly mob, WJW increased his airtime by six hours; less than a year after he began playing rhythm and blues records on the radio in Cleveland, he was on late night radio every night except Sundays.

Dick Clark, Bob Horn and Bandstand in Philadelphia

In 1951, Dick Clark obtained his first job on WKTV, Utica-Rome, New York after graduating from Syracuse with a degree in Business Administration; he was host of "Cactus Dick and the Santa Fe Riders," a country music program. On May 13, 1952, he began work at WFIL in Philadelphia and soon had a regular show, "Dick Clark's Caravan of Music" each weekday 1:45 to 6 p.m. where he played easy listening standards.

On WPEN-AM (950 on the dial) the station had a show where the studio audience could dance to the recordings as they were broadcast. Hosted by Joe Grady and Ed Hurst, the show originated in 1945 and by the early 1950s the "950 Club" was the most popular radio show in the afternoon in Philadelphia. The show attracted a number of teenagers to dance as well as performers, who stopped by for on-air interviews.

In 1945 Bob Horn returned to Philadelphia, where he obtained a job on WPEN and developed an evening show, "Bandstand" that featured teenagers dancing to popular recordings; in 1951 Horn moved to rival WIP, taking his hour-long "Bandstand" show with him.

Paul Whiteman started a TV show in Philadelphia for teenagers in March, 1949. Broadcast from a National Guard Armory, "TV-Teen Club" featured eight or nine teen acts introduced by Whiteman and his daughter, Margo. Whiteman, who was a vice-president at the ABC network in charge of music programming, also did a show from New York, "Paul Whiteman's Goodyear Revue" during the 1951-52 season. Whiteman's shows were never as popular as Milton Berle's "Texaco Star Theater" on NBC or Ed Sullivan's "Toast of the Town" on CBS, or Jack Benny's show--which played opposite Whiteman's show on Sunday evenings.

Whiteman continued his teenage dance show on TV until March, 1954, and, although it was never really successful on a national scale, inspired

Horn to want to take his show to television. That prompted him to join WFIL-TV before there were any openings for his television show because, he reasoned, if a slot opened up, he would be in the right spot to take advantage of it.

Horn lobbied WFIL's management for a television show that combined Grady and Hurst's "950 Club" format with his own "Bandstand" show. Management agreed if Horn enlisted the support of a co-host; Horn reluctantly consented and Lee Stewart was assigned to co-host the show, which was named "Bandstand" and produced by Tony Mammarella.

On October 6, 1952, "Bandstand" made its debut on WFIL-TV; on the show Horn introduced "Rate-a-Record" and recording artists regularly stopped by and lip-synched their latest recording. The show was immediately popular and membership in the "Bandstand Club" soon approached 10,000--primarily teenagers--who danced to records by artists such as Frankie Laine, Connie Boswell, Georgia Gibbs and Joni James.

In 1955, Horn was allowed to host the show alone; the Horn-Stewart combination was a mismatch of epic proportions and the management knew it. Other TV stations around the country tried to duplicate the "Bandstand" show, but none were as successful. Several factors contributed to this success: the fact that Philadelphia was known as a "break-out" city for records, the fact that it had a music industry in the town, and its proximity to New York, as well as its ethnic mix--there were Italians and blacks--blue collar and working class--as well as whites.

To capitalize on the show's success, Horn, along with Bernie Lowe and attorney Nat Segal formed the Teen and Sound record labels and covered rhythm and blues hits with local white talent. Beginning in 1953, Horn took payments from local record distributors who were promoting records they hoped Horn would play.

Horn was arrogant and flush with cash; he had a yacht and cruised the city in a Cadillac. He became a major celebrity in Philadelphia and had a following with his teenage audience, although he was 37, a bit overweight with a wife and children. Occasionally, Dick Clark stood in for Horn on the "Bandstand" TV show when Horn was on vacation.

Alan Freed's Live Shows

Disc jockeys during the 1950s often promoted concerts and dances locally to meet their fans and earn extra money. Alan Freed developed a traveling live show that featured artists whose records he played on his radio show. In 1953, Alan Freed took his live shows on the road. The "Biggest Show of

'53" began a six week tour of the South and Southwest in February. On the bill were Ruth Brown, Billy Eckstine, and Count Basie. The next tour, which started July 9, featured Ruth Brown, Wynonie Harris, the Clovers, Joe Louis and his band, the Lester Young Combo, and Buddy Johnson's Orchestra.

On August 22, 1953, Freed emceed the "Big Rhythm and Blues Show," which starred Fats Domino and Joe Turner. During that summer, Freed and Lew Platt formed Champagne Records and recorded the Moonglows, originally known as the Crazy Sounds, in the WJW studio. Using the name Al Lance, Freed received songwriting credit on the record, "I Just Can't Tell No Lie," which he played on his radio show.

In addition to the tours, Freed regularly promoted dances in and around Cleveland, some of which were broadcast live.

Rhythm and Blues was gaining in popularity; in February, 1953, the trade magazine *Variety* noted that over 500 disc jockeys on 260 radio station were programming R&B. One of those stations was WNJR in Newark, New Jersey, just across the river from New York City. Alan Freed's taped show was heard on that station.

Songwriters of America Lawsuit

In November, 1953, the Songwriters of America filed a $150 million antitrust suit against BMI, the three major broadcasting networks (NBC, CBS and ABC) and two affiliated record companies (RCA Victor and Columbia). The suit claimed that radio stations blocked ASCAP songs from being aired because BMI controlled the nation's airwaves.

The "Songwriters of America" was a group of 700 ASCAP members (33 filed the suit) who were angry that their songs were no longer receiving the airplay they had previously received. During that period the charts were filled with rhythm and blues and country songs, licensed by BMI. The ASCAP writers reasoned that since broadcasters owned the radio stations, they only allowed BMI songs to be played. Further, in their minds, the R&B and country songs that were played were much inferior to ASCAP's "pop" offerings, so payola had to be responsible for that music getting on the air.

ASCAP announced it would not credit any performances of songs if one of its writers collaborated with a BMI writer; that took effect January 1, 1955. The ASCAP writers charged that R&B songs were dirty and had "leer-ics." They insisted that "all rhythm and blues records are dirty and as bad for kids as dope" and the airplay was "fouled by marketing filth."

Years later it is easy to sit back and see that a major shift in music tastes was taking place during the 1948 to 1956 period and that the ASCAP writers saw a conspiracy where none existed. Further, it is easy to ridicule the ASCAP group for being so out of step with the times, but to ASCAP members, who for years had written "pop" songs that dominated the airwaves and who were clearly offended by the sound of R&B, which was raw, unsophisticated, and aimed for an audience of young teenagers of loosened inhibitions, something had to be amiss for their market to dry up virtually overnight.

Country Music in Nashville and Beyond

The first "Disc Jockey Convention" for country disc jockey was held in Nashville on November 22, 1952. The idea originated with Murray Nash, who promoted records of songs published by Acuff-Rose. It was a way to get closer to disc jockeys who played those records. Additionally, disc jockeys often promoted concerts by country artists and that helped the Artists Services Bureau, which booked Opry artists on shows. Less than a hundred disc jockeys came to that first event—there was only a two week notice—but in November, 1953, the second Disc Jockey Convention for country D.J's was held and planned well in advance with support from executives at WSM, the station that broadcast the Grand Ole Opry. Over 400 D.J.'s attended and BMI president Bob Burton presented the first songwriter awards. Since ASCAP would not license country music, the involvement with country music gave BMI a boost and led to BMI licensing early rock'n'roll and R&B, which ASCAP refused to do.

During the second convention an organization, the Country Music Disc Jockeys Association (CMDJA) was formed "to further a greater and more widespread public acceptance of country music through the betterment of country music disc jockey programs." WCKY's (Cincinnati) DJ Nelson King was named president. During the following years that event became the major convention for those engaged in the business of country music.

In 1952, there were still more listeners to radio than there were viewers of television. Country music continued to be heard on barn dances until the mid-1950s. In 1952 there were 176 stations carrying the "Prince Albert Show" from the Grand Ole Opry over the NBC radio network each Saturday night. In July, 1954, the Ozark Jubilee began on KWTO in Springfield, Missouri; it was broadcast over the ABC radio network, then became a TV show on ABC. There were also barn dances or country jamborees throughout the country: The "Big D Jamboree" was on KRLD in Dallas and the "Saturday Night Shindig" was on WFAA, also in Dallas; Houston had the "Hometown Jamboree" on KNUX while the "Hollywood Barn Dance" came from Los

Angeles on KNX. The "Hometown Jamboree," begun around 1949 by Cliffie Stone on KLXA in Los Angles and the "Hayloft Jamboree" from WCOP in Boston also began in the 1950s. One of the most popular country music shows was the "Town Hall Party" from Los Angeles, which was carried by the NBC network.

Other barn dances were "Hayloft Hoedown" on WFIL in Philadelphia; "Hoosier Hope" from WOWO in Fort Wayne, Indian, "Roundup of Stars" in Tampa over WDAE, and the "Old Dominion Barn Dance" on WRVA in Richmond, Virginia; other cities with regular radio barn dances included Cleveland, Indianapolis, Yankton, South Dakota and Omaha, Nebraska.

Les Paul

At the end of the 20th century, Les Paul was most famous for having his name on the Gibson electric guitar that was popular with many rock'n'roll performers. Many of those who played a Les Paul guitar had never heard one of the legendary performer's records or were aware of the breakthroughs he had pioneered in recording technology.

Les Paul was born Lester William Polfuss in Waukesha, Wisconsin, on January 9, 1915. Polfuss loved country music before he heard jazz guitarists Eddie Lang and Nick Lucas.

Red Hot Red was Polfuss's first stage name; as a youngster he performed at Rotary Club and PTA meetings, then formed "Red Hot Red and His Five Aces" when he was 14, playing mostly country music and novelty numbers.

In the Spring of 1931, Polfuss met guitarist Sunny Joe Wolverton; Polfuss soon joined Wolverton in Rube Tronson's Cowboys, a country act that played on WLS in Chicago. In Fall, 1932, the 17 year old Polfuss dropped out of school (he had reached the tenth grade) and moved to St. Louis, where he joined Wolverton and took the name "Rhubarb Red."

From St. Louis, Rhubarb Red and Wolverton moved to Springfield, Missouri, then to Chicago where, in August, 1934, Wolverton and Polfuss split.

Les remained in Chicago, first at WLS, then at WGN, then WJJD and WIND, which were both owned by Ralph Atlass. Les performed as "Rhubarb Red" but during that period heard the recordings of Django Reinhardt and was soon performing songs he learned from Reinhardt's records, such as "Avalon," "Tiger Rag," "Smoke Rings," "Nagasaki," and "Nuages."

Polfuss made his first recordings in 1936 as Rhubarb Red. He was fascinated by technology and in the mid-1930s asked guitar makers Carl and August Larson to build him a semi-solid body electric guitar. Prior to this, Les had played an acoustic guitar.

In Chicago, Polfuss formed a jazz quartet, but still performed country music. In mid-1938 he moved to New York where he joined Fred Waring's group, which performed on NBC every Saturday night during prime time. At the end of the 1930s, there were only about a dozen guitarists playing the electric guitar in New York; Les formed the Les Paul Trio and jammed with jazz artists after his Waring engagements.

Les Paul moved back to Chicago, where he was named music director for WJJD and WIND, the stations owned by Ralph Atlass. Paul then moved to WLS, where he performed as Rhubarb Red, then landed a full-time job as staff musician at WBBM, where he was billed as "one of America's electric guitar virtuosos." During World War II, Les Paul served in the Armed Forces Radio Service, performing as a guitarist in the orchestra.

After his stint with the Army, Les Paul moved to Los Angeles where he became a staff musician at NBC and made guest appearances on a wide variety of shows. Paul's big dream was to play with Bing Crosby, whose show, "Kraft Music Hall," was broadcast live each Thursday evening. Paul managed to meet Crosby and was soon appearing with him; he made his first recordings with Crosby in July, 1945, when he backed the singer on his hit, "It's Been a Long, Long Time."

Les Paul loved tinkering with guitars and at his home on North Curson Avenue in L.A. Paul experimented in his garage with guitar sounds and recording techniques. He was in demand as a producer; by the summer of 1946 he was producing acts such as Andy Williams, Judy Canova, Tex Williams, Perry Como and W. C. Fields as well as recording advertising spots and transcriptions for radio stations.

A man of enormous energy, Les Paul also appeared on a number of shows on NBC (half of them as Rhubarb Red), recorded for Decca and performed in Hollywood nightclubs. The Les Paul Trio served as an opening act for a tour by the Andrews Sisters.

Les Paul devised a system of "overdubbing" on recordings. The recordings during the 1940s were done all in one take; if there was a mistake, the musicians had to start again at the beginning. If a producer or artist decided later that another instrument would improve the recording, he had to gather all the musicians together again, with the addition of that new musician, and record the song from the beginning.

Paul had two direct-to-disc machines. He would record a guitar part on one, then play that back and add another guitar part. In the Fall of 1947, Les Paul recorded eight guitar parts on "Lover." Paul took that recording to Capitol where label head Jim Conkling signed Les Paul to a long term contract with that label and released the single.

Les Paul was not the first musician to overdub, but he perfected the technique far beyond the others. Biographer Mary Alice Shaughnessy in *Les Paul: An American Original*, noted that "Although he was not responsible for introducing overdubbing to commercial recordings, he was certainly the first to make it a major selling point of his disks. This studio technique, which took him roughly two years to perfect, would ultimately force the industry to reexamine its approach to recordings--and make Les Paul a fabulously wealthy man."

In January, 1948, Les Paul was in an automobile accident near Davenport, Iowa which shattered his right arm in three places; many thought he would never play the guitar again. The following month, Capitol released "Lover," which broke in the United States, then Great Britain. In the hospital, doctors grafted a bone from Paul's leg to his arm and rebuilt his right elbow with a metal plate so that his right warm was frozen at an almost 90 degree angle.

During his recovery, Bing Crosby came by Paul's home and gave him an early Ampex reel-to-reel tape recorder. The recorder, based on a model brought from Germany by engineer Jack Mullin, was similar to the one Crosby began using in 1947 for his show sponsored by Philco. Paul began experimenting with the tape recorder and pioneered more advances in recorded sound.

There was resistance to Les Paul's work in multi-track recordings and overdubs. Musicians viewed it as a threat that would put many out of work; if one guitarist could overdub several parts, what was the need for several guitarists in the studio? Record company executives felt it was too costly because it meant re-training their engineering staff. So, despite Les Paul's breakthroughs in multi-track recording processes, the engineers at most studios continued to use the same techniques for another decade. They would record an artist several times, then take a razor and splice the tape to put together the best performances on one recording.

Les Paul and Mary Ford

Before his accident, Les Paul met Colleen Summers, a member of the country music group "Colleen and the Sunshine Girls." Summers had grown up in Pasadena and joined the country music circuit in southern California, appearing on "Hollywood Barn Dance," "Dinner Bell Roundup" and Gene Autry's "Melody Ranch" radio programs. They were soon dating regularly.

At first, Paul was reluctant to record Summers on his pop songs because he thought she was "too country." However, he continued to experiment in the studio, changed her name to "Mary Ford" (because Colleen Summers was too well known as a country singer in L.A.) and began recording her vocals.

During their live appearances, Les did the talking and worked on numbers that had crowd appeal. Paul wanted to release commercial recordings, records that people liked and bought. He noted, "The people you're playing for work all day. They don't go to music schools and study harmony. They pay their dough, they come, they listen. If they don't understand what you're doing, they walk out. What are you supposed to do, tie 'em to a chair with a rope while you explain you're performing great music?"

"The Les Paul Show with Mary Ford" became a regular show on NBC and the duo began recording for Capitol and toured extensively. In May, 1950, their record "Nola" was released and became a hit. During the late 1940s and early 1950s, Les Paul was described as "wild." Biographer Mary Shaughnessy stated that Paul "lived an uninhibited life-style. Les listened to nobody but Les. His family, his work, his pleasures were all wrapped up in one. There was no separation. He would go eighteen, twenty hours a day, record all night, and get to bed at five in the morning, and he expected Mary to do the same." .

One of the results of his manic recording was "How High the Moon," which had 12 overdubs. Capitol president Jim Conkling did not want to release "How High the Moon" because it was an old jazz tune that he felt had been done too much. However, in early 1951, Conkling accepted the position of president of Columbia Records. He was scheduled to leave Capitol in March so, after constant badgering by Paul, decided to release "How High the Moon." That record reached number one on the charts in April, 1951, and became one of the biggest sellers on Capitol Records.

During the early 1950s Les Paul and Mary Ford sold over six million disks and had a number of hit singles. They bought a home in New Jersey where Paul set up a studio with an echo chamber and generally worked from midnight until four or five in the morning. The manic energy and punishing schedule took a toll on his marriage.

"There was no separation between his work and pleasure," said Dick Linke, a publicist at Capitol who was close to Paul. "He'd brag about staying up eighteen hours a day, every day, and he expected everyone to keep up with him. ...Mary simply didn't have the constitution to withstand this physically punishing regime."

Payola Hearings Begin

In 1952 the House of Representatives in Congress formed the House Subcommittee on Legislative Oversight "to probe the morals of radio and television programs." There was virtually no rhythm and blues on television, which was still in its infancy. On the radio, R&B was acceptable as late night programming, but was not heard in prime-time because of fear of offending daytime sponsors.

By 1953, rhythm and blues was offending many in the white middle class as well as middle class blacks, who were ashamed and embarrassed by the primitive sound. Rhythm and blues had been on the outside of mainstream American music but, in 1953, several R&B records became hits: "(Mama) He Treats Your Daughter Mean" by Ruth Brown; "Goin to the River" by Fats Domino; "Crying in the Chapel" by the Orioles; "Shake a Hand" by Faye Adams; and "Marie" by the Four Tunes.

Those hits generated a lot of money: previously, an R&B hit meant sales of about 250,000 singles; however, "Goin' To The River" and "Crying in the Chapel" both reportedly sold over a million copies each. R&B accounted for less that five percent of total record sales, but that meant about 15 million singles sold in 1953. The best-selling single, "Hound Dog" by Willie Mae Thornton, wasn't even on the pop charts.

The early small label entrepreneurs distributed their records by putting them in the trunk of their cars, then driving to stores, jukebox dealers and radio stations. The label owner would take the record in, play it, and hope the radio disc jockey liked it enough to play it or the store owner liked it enough to purchase copies. Soon, distributors--whose major market had been jukeboxes--came to be the key factor in getting records in stores nationally. Although the distributors tended to be local, if it was a big city, or regional, they were the key link between the record company and retail stores, which allowed consumers to purchase them. Distributors soon realized that if radio played a record, sales would generally follow, and so they channeled their efforts to getting their records on the radio, because a payoff in sales followed.

With the advent of big sales, which generated big dollars, a lot was suddenly at stake in promoting rhythm and blues records.

Distributors provided the bulk of payoffs because they were the middlemen, the key link between the labels and the retail outlets. If a record did not reach the store shelf, it could not be sold--and if it did not have radio airplay, nobody knew about it, so the distributors began to court disc jockeys, giving them "gifts" in appreciation for what had been done and greasing the wheels for future exposure.

Those "gifts" could include cash payments--the most popular and accepted--as well as watches, trips, dinners, and even the publishing or songwriting credit on a record. As the most powerful disc jockeys became more sophisticated, they formed their own labels, distribution companies, talent agencies and publishing companies, each supplying a piece of the pie. Since the disc jockey controlled access to the airwaves, he controlled which records had a shot at being a hit.

Not every record played was a hit--some were played and no consumer demand was created and some received little airplay but sales were brisk; however, overall, airplay was the gateway to a record's sales. It was a model that was followed throughout the rest of the twentieth century: get a record on the radio, play it a lot of times, and consumers would most likely buy it in large numbers. The system wasn't fool-proof, but it was the best bet going.

Those "gifts" from the record companies and distributors were not a major factor in the early attention from Congress. The major factor was the lobbying by ASCAP to investigate BMI. Congress was more intent on investigating television, but the ASCAP lobbyists pushed hard for them to investigate radio because ASCAP songwriters were not receiving airplay while the "trash" called rhythm and blues was increasingly dominating the radio airwaves.

The RIAA

The payola issue was a popular topic with newspaper columnists, as well as the "Battle of the Speeds" after RCA and CBS issued new phonographs and records that required speeds different than the long-used 78. Those factors led to the formation of the recording industry's first trade group, the Recording Industry Association of America (RIAA). The organization was established in September, 1951, and officially designated to "deal with legislation, the allocation of materials, preparation of industry statistics and such matters as the government's request...for a voluntary price cutback."

Paul Puner, head of Allegro, an independent label, had originally suggested the idea of a trade organization but the growing payola controversy led Milton Rackmill of Decca, Frank Walker of MGM, Glenn Wallichs of Capitol, James Conkling of Columbia and Paul Barkling of Victor to unite in the formation of the organization.

After its formation, the RIAA spoke for the thirty-two most important manufacturers in the recording industry, representing at least 85 percent of the income earned from record sales.

The major labels—Decca, MGM, Capitol, Columbia, Victor—led the industry in sales. There were 800 record labels registered with the American Federation of Musicians in 1952 but less than forty-five earned over $20,000 in sales.

Sun Records

On January 1, 1950, a small recording studio, "The Memphis Recording Service" opened on Union Avenue in Memphis, Tennessee. It was owned by Sam Phillips, who had worked as a disk jockey at Memphis station WREC and, at that time, a disk jockey also served as an engineer. Phillips generally worked the Saturday afternoon shift, hosting a program called "Songs of The West." WREC often broadcast big band shows from the Skyway Ballroom at the Peabody Hotel, providing a network feed to CBS.

Sam Phillips, the youngest of eight children, was born January 5, 1923, and grew up on a farm outside Florence, Alabama. In 1942 he began his radio career working at WMSL in Decatur, Alabama, then moved to WLAC in Nashville before joining WREC in Memphis in June, 1945. Phillips was an energetic, ambitious man, who dreamed of opening his own recording studio; at the beginning of 1950 that dream was realized.

There was a independent record distributor in Memphis at the time, "Music Sales," which was formed by Robert E. "Buster" Williams and Clarence Camp in January, 1946. In 1949 Williams opened "Plastic Products," a record pressing plant, in Memphis. Music Sales distributed the rhythm and blues recordings by Atlantic and Chess and pressed and distributed Phillip's recordings, warehousing and shipping them from its Memphis location.

The recording studio was simple and basic. "I had a little Presto five-input mixer board," said Phillips. "It was portable and it sat on a hall table, The mixer had four microphone ports, and the fifth port had a multi-selector switch where you could flip it one way and get a mike and flip it another to play your recordings back. That was my console...I had a Presto portable tape recorder, a PT 900 companion piece to the mixer. Before that I had a

Crestwood tape recorder...The second was...a Bell Recorder." When Phillips began his studio he cut directly to disk but in late 1951 switched to tape.

There was a market for Rhythm and Blues Records ignored by the major labels but filled by small labels like Chess and Atlantic. The music gained an outlet on radio stations that programmed black music, such as WLAC in Nashville, WERD in Atlanta, WDIA in Memphis, and WEDR in Birmingham. Also in Memphis was the "Red Hot and Blue" radio program on WHBQ, hosted by Dewey Phillips (no relation to Sam), that began in 1948. Those stations soon discovered that about 20 percent of their listeners were white.

Howlin' Wolf

Howlin' Wolf scared the hell out of a lot of people. He was a big man; he stood six feet three inches, weighed about 300 pounds and his voice rumbled with a deep, raw power. He was a difficult child, which is how he came to be called Howlin' Wolf. He was not a stranger to the rough and tumble violence found in blues clubs on the other side of town. A lot of people were afraid of him.

His real name was Chester Arthur Burnett--named after President Chester Arthur--and he was born in White Station (near West Point), Mississippi on June 10, 1910. His moniker came from his grandfather.

Howlin' Wolf knew legendary Delta blues singer Charley Patton, who taught him some guitar chords. He was also influenced by the Mississippi Sheiks, Tommy Johnson and country star Jimmie Rodgers, the "blue yodeler." Howlin' Wolf adapted some of Rodgers "blue yodels" to his own style.

During the 1930s Howlin' Wolf farmed, then was drafted into the Army in 1941, during World War II, and was stationed in Seattle. After his discharge, he returned to farming, then formed a band and moved to West Memphis, Arkansas where he had a 15 minute show on KWEM in 1950.

Sam Phillips spoke to record labels about supplying them with recordings he made in his studio. The idea was that Sam would find the talent, record them and lease the master to a label, which would press the record and make it available to radio, jukeboxes and retailers. His first success came in March, 1951 when he recorded Ike Turner's group. Turner was a disc jockey on WROX in Clarksdale, Mississippi and came to Memphis to audition after a recommendation from B.B. King. Jackie Brenston was the singer in Turner's band and the group recorded "Rocket 88." Phillips made a copy of the recording and sent it to Chess Records in Chicago where Leonard Chess released it in April. The song became a huge hit; it was released under the name "Jackie Brenston and his Delta Cats" and hit number one on *Billboard's* R&B chart and remained in that position for five weeks.

Phillips had leased recordings of B.B. King to RPM Records, a subsidiary of Modern Records owned by the Bihari Brothers in Los Angeles. The deal with Chess angered the Bihari's, who felt Sam should have brought Turner's band to them instead of to Leonard Chess.

That was the background when Sam Phillips heard Howlin' Wolf on KWEM in West Memphis and invited him to his Memphis Recording Service Studio for a session in Spring, 1951. On that first session, Howlin' Wolf brought his band, comprised of guitarists Willie Johnson and M.T. Murphy, Junior Parker on harmonica, drummer Willie Steele and a now unknown pianist, to the studio and they recorded "How Many More Years" and "Baby Ride With Me." Phillips sent dubs of those songs to the Biharis, who agreed to sign Howlin' Wolf but their dispute over "Rocket 88" led Phillips to also send the masters to Chess Records, who agreed to sign Wolf. Phillips took Howlin' Wolf back into the studio and re-recorded "How Many More Years" and "Moanin' at Midnight," which became his first single with Chess. Meanwhile, Ike Turner produced a session on Wolf which he sent to RPM; "Moanin' at Midnight" became "Morning at Midnight."

Howlin' Wolf's song "How Many More Years" on Chess entered the *Billboard* R&B chart in December, 1951 and rose to the number four position; "Moanin' At Midnight" reached number ten.

Howlin' Wolf recorded several more sessions in Memphis at what became known as the Sun Studios at 706 Union; his last session was in October, 1952. The conflict between Chess and the Biharis was resolved when the Biharis agreed to keep Roscoe Gordon, another artist produced by Phillips, while Chess signed Howlin' Wolf to their label.

In late 1952 or early 1953 Howlin' Wolf gave up farming for good and moved to Chicago where he was signed directly to Chess Records and where he achieved his greatest fame as one of the seminal American blues singers in the twentieth century.

Randy's Record Shop

Randy Wood was discharged from the armed forces after World War II and opened an electrical appliance store in Gallatin, about thirty miles northeast of Nashville. Wood began stocking records in his store after Nashville-based Bullet Records was founded. Wood discovered that Rhythm and Blues discs were the best-sellers. In February, 1947, he purchased an on-air spot advertising R&B and gospel records on WLAC that was so successful that Wood changed the name of his store to Randy's Record Shop and sold records by mail through on-air advertising. When Wood fulfilled an order, he enclosed a list of their entire stock, which led to more sales.

Wood featured "Randy's Specials," which were five records for $2.98. Those included "Gospel Specials" (which featured five records by Mahalia Jackson, the Golden Gate Quartet, Sister Rosetta Tharpe, and other gospel stars), and "All Time Favorites," which featured five pop releases. Wood soon expanded his business with advertisements on stations in Memphis, Chattanooga, Cincinnati, Atlanta, and other stations and developed a national and international clientele. He was soon selling four thousand records a week.

Wood not only bought spots on WLAC, he also regularly conferred with disc jockey Gene Nobles about which records to program that would enhance sales.

Dot Records

Around 1949, Gene Nobles encouraged Randy Wood to release a record of "Gene Nobles Boogie" backed with "Gene Nobles Blues" written by Richard Armstrong; the recordings had previously been released on Nashville-based Cheker Records. Wood named the label "Randy's Records" and also released gospel recordings.

That led Wood to found Dot Records, with distribution initially through Bullet. The firm was incorporated on April 12, 1950, with the idea that he would press records to sell by mail order from Randy's Record Shop. The first release was "Bluejack Boogie"/"Late Hour Blues" by the Blue Jacks in late 1949. The second, also released at the end of 1949, was "Boogie Beat Rag"/"Honest Heart" by George Toon and the Tennessee Drifters.

Johnny Maddox was an employee at Randy's Record Shop (he had joined in 1947) as well as a ragtime pianist who had a dance band in Gallatin. On May 19, 1950, Maddox recorded "Crazy Bone Rag" at the WHIN studio in Gallatin and it sold well for Dot. He followed with other ragtime tunes recorded at WHIN and at Castle Studio in Nashville that had good mail order sales. In September 1951, Dot began a series of popular releases beginning with Maddox's recording of "San Antonio Rose."

The big sales for Dot were in R&B, and that label released over a hundred R&B and black gospel records between 1950 and 1957. Their first hit was "I'm So Crazy for Love" by the Cap-Tans, released in September 1950. Most of those recordings were purchased or leased from other labels.

Dot's Country Releases

Dot's country releases came primarily from Nashville talent. One of its major acts was Big Jeff Bess who recorded "Juke Box Boogie," "Fast Women, Slow Horses, and Wine," and "Step It Up and Go." Lonzo & Oscar and Jamup & Honey also recorded for Dot. Wood signed Mac Wiseman as an artist as well as A&R man, and Wiseman began with a hit "'Tis Sweet to Be Remembered" released in June 1950. Wiseman's hits on Dot included "I Wonder How the Old Folks Are at Home" and "Love Letters in the Sand." Dot also had hits with Jimmy C. Newman and Jimmy Work, whose biggest hit was "Makin' Believe," covered later by Kitty Wells.

Randy Wood wanted to record pop music and began that series with Johnny Maddox. He then recorded Beasley Smith, Billy Vaughn, and the Hilltoppers, a group from Western Kentucky State University in Bowling Green, Kentucky.

The Hilltoppers

The first hit from the Hilltoppers was "Trying," which became a Top Ten pop hit in August 1952. The Hilltoppers had been formed by Billy Vaughn, and the group included Vaughn, Jimmy Sacca, Don McGuire, and Seymour Spiegelman. Their first release was recorded on a portable tape recorder with one microphone in the college auditorium of Western Kentucky. They followed that with two million sellers: "P.S. I Love You" and "I'd Rather Die Young" and toured Europe in 1955. Vaughn had left the group by then and became Dot's musical director. He recorded with his own orchestra and had hits with "Melody of Love" in 1953 and later "Shifting, Whispering Sands."

At the end of five years, Randy's Record Shop stocked 125 different labels and sold sixty thousand records a month in over thirty-five states. Dot Records was worth more than a million dollars.

Sinatra's Comeback

In 1953, Frank Sinatra began filming a movie, *From Here to Eternity*, which became his ticket to a comeback. The novel had been published in 1951 and became a best-seller. Columbia Pictures bought the rights but studio head Harry Cohn and director Fred Zinneman turned down Sinatra's request for consideration. Finally, the William Morris Agency arranged for Sinatra to take a screen test and Cohn and Zinneman agreed to give him the part of Magglio in the movie.

The major recording labels all turned down Frank Sinatra; finally, Capitol Records offered him a one-year deal that gave him no advance with all costs for arranging, copying and musicians paid by Sinatra. Sinatra's first recordings for Capitol occurred in April, 1953, and he worked with arranger Nelson Riddle.

At Columbia, Sinatra had recorded ballads; at Capitol he recorded "swing" with producer Voyle Gilmore. In May, 1953, Sinatra did a three month tour of Europe, then in August, *From Here to Eternity* opened in movie theaters. The following year, when the Academy Awards were held, Sinatra won the award for "Best Supporting Actor" while the movie won eight awards, including "Best Picture."

The finances of Sinatra brightened in 1953 when he purchased a two percent interest in the Sands Hotel in Las Vegas; he eventually owned nine percent of the hotel, and that investment made him a multi-millionaire during the next several years.

At Capitol, Sinatra recorded "My Funny Valentine" in November, 1953, then did an album *Songs for Young Lovers*. Although his professional life had picked up, his personal life suffered a setback when Ava Gardner left him at the end of 1953 and filed for divorce the following year.

In 1954, Sinatra was named the "Top Male Vocalist" by *Billboard*, *Downbeat* and *Metronome* magazines. He was in a series of successful films during 1954 and 1955: *Suddenly, Young at Heart, For Daughters, Not as a Stranger, The Tender Trap* and *Guys and Dolls*. In February, 1955, he recorded the concept album *In the Wee Small Hours*; hit songs during 1954 and 1955 included "Luck Be a Lady Tonight," "What Is This Thing Called Love?," "When Your Lover Has Gone," "I Get Along Without You Very Well," "Glad to Be Unhappy," "In the Wee Small Hours of the Morning" and "Mood Indigo."

In the summer of 1955, Sinatra was on the cover of *Time* magazine and at the end of that year the movie, *The Man With The Golden Arm* was released. It looked like Frank Sinatra was back on top.

SECTION III:
1954 TO 1979

1954

The year 1954 was a transitional year for the music industry. In many ways, it was the last hurrah for the type of pop music dominated by white singers with a Big Band background. The great radio shows were shifting to television and radio increasingly had disc jockey shows where records were played instead of live entertainment. Rhythm and blues was heard on radio stations and attracted a white as well as black audience; in 1954 there were 700 radio stations broadcasting to a black audience. In April, Bill Haley and the Comets recorded "Rock Around the Clock" and in July Elvis Presley recorded "That's All Right, Mama." The next year, 1955, marked the beginning of what became known as the rock'n'roll era.

When the year 1954 began, the number one song on the *Billboard* pop chart was "Oh! My Pa-Pa" by Eddie Fisher; it remained number one for eight weeks. Number one on the "Rhythm and Blues" chart was "The Things That I Used To Do" by Guitar Slim and His Band and number one on the Country and Western chart was "Bimbo" by Jim Reeves. On "Your Hit Parade," the popular radio show sponsored by Lucky Strike cigarettes where a quartet of singers sang the ten top songs of the week, the number one song was "Ebb Tide" by the Frank Chacksfield Orchestra.

Number one hits that year on the *Billboard* Pop chart were "Secret Love" by Doris Day, "Make Love To Me!" By Jo Stafford, "Wanted" by Perry Como, "Little Things Mean A Lot" by Kitty Kallen, "Three Coins in the Fountain" by the Four Aces, "Sh-Boom" by the Crew Cuts, "Hey There" and "This Ole House" by Rosemary Clooney, ""I Need You Now" by Eddie Fisher and "Mr. Sandman" by the Chordettes.

R&B number ones were "I'll Be True" by Faye Adams, "You'll Never Walk Alone" by Roy Hamilton, "Work With Me Annie" by The Midnighters, "Shake, Rattle and Roll" by Big Joe Turner, "Honey Love" by The Drifters, "Oh, What a Dream" by Ruth Brown, "Annie Had a Baby" by The Midnighters, "Hurts Me To My Heart" by Faye Adams, "Mambo Baby" by Ruth Brown, "Hearts of Stone" by The Charms and "You Upset Me Baby" by B.B. King.

Number one hits in 1954 on the Country and Western Chart were "Slowly" by Webb Pierce, "Wake Up, Irene" by Hank Thompson, "I Really Don't Want To Know" by Eddy Arnold, "(Oh Baby Mine) I Get So Lonely" by Johnnie & Jack, "I Don't Hurt Anymore" by Hank Snow, "Even Tho" by Webb Pierce, "One By One" by Kitty Wells & Red Foley and "More and More" by Webb Pierce.

During 1954 the number one hits on "Your Hit Parade" were "Stranger In Paradise" by Tony Bennett, "Secret Love" by Doris Day, "Wanted" by Perry Como, "Young At Heart" by Frank Sinatra, "Little Things Mean a Lot" by Kitty Kallen, "Three Coins in the Fountain" by the Four Aces, "Hernando's Hideaway" by Archie Bleyer, "Hey There" by Rosemary Clooney, "I Need You Now" by Eddie Fisher, "If I Give My Heart To You" by Doris Day, and "Mister Sandman" by The Chordettes.

There were a number of important independent labels, including Minit (New Orleans), Duke (Houston), Chess (Chicago), King (Cincinnati), Atlantic (New York) and Modern and Aladdin (Los Angeles). The major labels were RCA, Columbia, Decca and Capitol.

In February, 1954, RCA used two-track tape and Ampex equipment to record Charles Munch and the Boston Symphony's interpretation of "Berlioz's "The Damnation of Fault" for the first "true stereo" recording.

During the summer, Goddard Lieberson with Columbia investigated the idea of a record club to reach those in rural areas who did not have access to record stores. The Book-of-the-Month Club had been established and Lieberson wanted to replicate that idea with records. Columbia set in motion a plan to terminate the independent distribution system they used and replace it with wholly owned branches that distributed their records. They also worked with rack jobbers, who got their records stocked in drug and department stores. Columbia introduced the 12 inch pop album; previously pop albums were ten inches and only classical LPs were 12 inches.

Television was making headway; at the end of 1954 there were 354 TV stations.

Country Music

The end of 1954 marked the end of a golden era in country music, and the beginning of some dark days. Hank Williams died at the beginning of 1953 and Fred Rose died on December 1, 1954. During 1953 Hank Williams had number one records with "I'll Never Get Out of This World Alive," "Kaw-Liga," "Your Cheatin' Heart" and "Take These Chains Form My Heart."

Country music's biggest star in 1954 was Webb Pierce, who had the number one record for 47 weeks. "Slowly," which was number one for 17 weeks, was the first country hit record to feature the pedal steel guitar. Bud Isaacs played steel on that recording, which inspired numerous musicians to take up the instrument.

By the end of 1954, Nashville was emerging as a major recording center. The Castle Studio, located downtown in the Tulane Hotel, was a busy studio. In November, RCA began recording in the TRAFCO Studio on McGavock Street. The building was rened to the Methodist Television, Radio and Film Commission, who shared the building with RCA.

Paul Cohen, head of country A&R for Decca Records, contemplated moving their recording sessions to Jim Beck's Studio in Dallas, which had echo. Owen Bradley approached Cohen and offered to build a studio—with echo—if Decca guaranteed 100 sessions a year; Cohen. On the last day of 1954, Owen Bradley bought a house at 804 16th Avenue South for $7,500 and began renovations in early 1955 to convert it into a studio. There were columns in front of the house that were removed and the middle floor of the house (it had a basement and upstairs) was knocked out so there was a high ceiling. Bradley purchased a Quonset Hut for $7,500 which was assembled beside the house, creating a 35 by 78 foot metal wing. The Quonset Hut was intended for video productions while the basement studio was for recordings.

The previous year, Owen Bradley and his brother, Harold, opened "Bradley's Film and Recording Studio" in Hillsboro Village, off Twenty-first Avenue in an alley across the street from McClure's Department Store. The studio made promotional films for Genesco, Springfield Woolen Milles and others but the building had low ceilings. Sound bounced off the low ceiling so recordings were not optimal; however, Kitty Wells recorded there.

Chet Atkins met Ray Batts, a radio repairman from Cairo, Illinois who built an amplifier, the Echosonic, that re-created the echo effects used by Les Paul by using a tape loop. Atkins bought the amp, which made his guitar play back a fraction of a second later to create an echo effect. Scotty Moore, just starting to work with Elvis Presley, heard Chet's new sound. Scotty purchased an Echosonic amp from Butts in 1955 and used it on some of Elvis's last Sun material. Carl Perkins and Luther Perkins of Johnny Cash's Tennessee Two subsequently purchased Echosonics, which helped define the Sun sound.

News in 1954

For years, Parents had feared their children would contact polio but the eradication of polio began in 1954 with a polio vaccine developed by Dr. Jonas Salk.

On May 17, the Supreme Court declared, in Brown vs. Board of Education, that school segregation was unconstitutional and ordered schools to be integrated "with all deliberate speed." Although this was a landmark decision that eventually ended school segregation, "deliberate speed" moved quite slow in most school districts.

The anti-Communist hearings led by Senator Joseph McCarthy were watched on TV during 1954; however, McCarthy evoked the ire of his fellow Senators, one of whom confronted him, saying "Have you no sense of decency, sir, at long last have you no sense of decency" after brutal remarks from McCarthy. In December, the Senate censured McCarthy, ending his reign of Communist witch hunts.

The New York Stock Exchange had its best year since 1933 and 70 percent of Americans owned their own car, signs that the United States had recovered from the Great Depression.

President Eisenhower signed a law that altered the Pledge of Allegiance, changing the wording of "One nation indivisible" to "one nation "under God."

The girls of 1954 liked boys with flat tops and crew cuts who drove a sporty car while guys like blondes who wore felt skirts with poodle appliques. The "raccoon look" of heavy mascara on girls was also O.K.

The Music Business in 1955

In 1955 *Billboard* magazine began publishing three pop charts, "Most Played by Jockeys," "Best Sellers in Stores" and "Most Played in Juke Boxes"; that marked the beginning of their "Hot 100 Chart."

The British firm, EMI, purchased Capitol Records in January for $8.5 million, , giving the company a direct outlet into the American market. There was an attempt by the major labels--particularly Operation TNT by

Victor--to phase out 78s and institute 45s as the dominant configuration by raising the prices of 78s.

The jukebox industry was thriving in the United States; there were approximately half a million in use, or one for every 300 in the population. Stereo recordings, known as stereosonic, were first introduced commercially.

A TV hero at the beginning of 1955 was Davy Crockett, with Fess Parker starring in the Walt Disney produced television series. The spread of "Crockett-mania" (a number of youngers bought coon-skin caps that year) led to the biggest song of that year. There were 17 versions of the "Ballad of Davy Crockett," with Bill Hayes, Fess Parker and Tennessee Ernie Ford all having versions reaching the top ten.

The biggest *record* of that year was "Rock Around the Clock" from the film *Blackboard Jungle* starring Glenn Ford in a movie about juvenile delinquency. An important reason for the success of that movie was because "Rock Around the Clock," which had previously been released and flopped, had been added to the soundtrack. The recording quickly reached the number one position on the charts by the end of June.

Bill Haley and the Comets

William Haley was born in Highland Park, Michigan on July 6, 1925; his family soon moved to Chester, Pennsylvania, where young Haley grew up with Gene Autry as his hero. Because Haley was blind in one eye, he avoided the World War II draft.

Haley joined a band, the Downhomers, in Wilmington, Delaware, after answering an ad in *Billboard* for a "singing yodeler." He returned to Chester, Pennsylvania and was a country music disc jockey on WPWA; he also had a band, the Four Aces of Western Swing, who played locally and recorded for Cowboy Records. The group's first record, in 1948, was the Hank Williams song "Too Many Parties, Too Many Pals," b/w "Four Leaf Clover Blues." Their second release was a cover of George Morgan's "Candy Kisses" on one side and Red Foley's "Tennessee Border" on the other.

After those releases, Haley changed the name of his band to the Saddlemen and had a string of releases, mostly country. In February, 1951, Haley recorded a cover record of "Rocket 88," which had been produced by Sam Phillips in Memphis and was an R&B hit for Jackie Brenston on Chess. Haley's version was released on Holiday Records.

Haley performed "Rock the Joint" to open his set at a local club, the Twin Bar in Philadelphia near the Navy Yard and the song was a crowd favorite. Under the prodding of Jack Howard, a country music promoter in Philadelphia, Haley recorded the song for Essex Records, owned by Dave Miller. The song was a hit. In 1953 Haley got rid of his sideburns and cowboy hat and renamed his group Bill Haley and the Comets. They recorded "Crazy, Man, Crazy," a song filled with jive phrases and buzz words, which became a hit in the summer of 1953.

Veteran songwriter Max Freedman had written a song with Jim Myers, "We're Gonna Rock Around the Clock Tonight," that was a proven crowd pleaser when Haley played it at the Broomall Cafe during 1953. Miller did not want Haley to record the song for Essex, so when Haley's contract with the label was up, Jim Myers took the group to Milt Gabler at Decca. Gabler had recorded Billie Holiday, Eddie Condon, Peewee Russell, and Meade Lux Lewis before Jack Kapp hired him in 1941. At Decca he recorded Louis Armstrong, Ella Fitzgerald, the Ink Spots and Louis Jordan; however, by 1954, Jordan had left the label.

Gabler signed Haley and recorded "Thirteen Women and Only One Man in Town" as the "A" side and "Rock Around the Clock" (the title was shortened) as the "B" side on April 12, 1954 at the Pythina Temple Studio in New York. "Thirteen Women" was a song about a nuclear disaster that left only 14 people alive. "Thirteen Women" did not chart but "Rock Around the Clock" entered the *Billboard* chart on May 23, 1953 and reached number 23, only staying on the chart one week; it sold 75,000 copies. Myers reportedly sent 200 copies of "Rock Around the Clock" to people connected to the film industry in Hollywood that he thought could get the song in a movie. Haley recorded his follow-up, "Shake, Rattle and Roll" and "ABC Boogie" on June 7; "Shake, Rattle and Roll" entered the *Billboard* chart on August 21, 1954 and reached number seven, remaining on the chart for 27 weeks.

Glenn Ford had been signed to star in the film *Blackboard Jungle*, which was based on a novel by Evan Hunter and directed by Richard Brooks. Filming began on November 15, 1954. Brooks sometimes went to Glenn Ford's home to discuss the film. During one of those visits he heard Ford's son, Peter, playing "Rock Around the Clock," a single the youngster purchased that fall. Previously, eleven year old Peter Ford had purchased Haley's single, "Crazy, Man, Crazy" which was released in 1953. Brooks borrowed Peter Ford's record and in mid-December played it for Joel Freeman, the assistant director of the film. They agreed the song would fit the movie and MGM purchased the rights to the recording, which was played over the opening and closing credits of the film.

Blackboard Jungle, starring Glenn Ford, was released in March, 1955. In the film, Ford plays a teacher who tries to win over a class of juvenile delinquents by playing his jazz '78s in class. The kids mock him for listening to "square" music and then smash his valuable record collection. The movie had a message for both adults and kids. For adults, it showed that kids had no respect for time-honored music and that rock'n'roll led to rebellion. For the kids, it delivered the message that a new era had arrive: the era of rock'n'roll.

After the film was released, Decca re-serviced the record to radio stations where it became a hit, landing at the number one spot on *Billboard's* pop charts on June 19, 1955 and sold over six million copies. That record marked the official start of the rock'n'roll era. Haley celebrated by buying five Cadillacs for his band and a yacht for himself.

The term "rock'n'roll" or "rock and roll" became popular in 1955 after Alan Freed lost his "Moondog" moniker in a lawsuit instituted by a street musician. Freed changed the name of his show to "The Rock'n'Roll Party" and copyrighted the term; the copyright was filed on behalf of Seig Music, which was owned by Freed, Morris Levy, Lew Platt and WINS. Freed wanted to capitalize on the term "rock'n'roll" so he constantly promoted it, hoping to eventually get paid each time someone else used the term. However, the term became so ubiquitous and widely used that the copyright was worthless; it simply couldn't be enforced.

By the end of 1955 rock'n'roll was a household word and its most famous practitioner was Bill Haley & the Comets. A movement and a music now had a name.

Your Hit Parade

On July 10, 1950, the long running radio show, "Your Hit Parade," sponsored by Lucky Strike cigarettes, began broadcasting on NBC TV on Monday nights. The TV show continued the same format as the radio show; four singers—two male and two female—sang the most popular song as compiled by the advertising agency for the cigarette company. The announcer from 1950-1957 was Andre Brauch and singers during 1955 included former Big Band singers Snooky Lanson, Dorothy Collins, Russell Arms and Gisele MacKenzie. The Hit Paraders, a chorus and dancers, also performed on the show.

On July 9, 1955, the singers and the orchestra performed "Rock Around the Clock" for the first time. Other songs on the "Hit Parade" that week wee "Unchained Melody," "Cherry Pink and Apple Blossom White, "The Ballad of Davy Crockett" and "Whatever Lola Wants." The singers took turn singing songs that were on the chart for multiple weeks, so a different singer sang "Rock Around the Clock" the following week, and the week after that for sixteen consecutive weeks. The final performance of "Rock Around the Clock" by a singer with an orchestra was on October 22. During that show, other songs on the "Hit Parade" were "Ain't That a Shame?," "The Yellow Rose of Texas" and "The Bible Tells Me So."

A Tipping Point

The success of "Rock Around the Clock" was a tipping point for the music industry as power began to shift from publishers, who marketed sheet music, to record companies, who sold records. Publishers owned the copyright to songs and song pluggers pushed for multiple singers to record a song. The record companies owned the copyright to the recordings and promoted a record in the marketplace. There were already a number of recordings by rhythm and blues artists that were covered by white artists, which made song publishers happy but many African-American artists upset that their song had been "stolen." Record companies segregated the marketplace for "pop," "country" and "R&B" audiences and it was difficult if not impossible for "country" or "R&B" records to reach the mainstream pop audience. The only way to do it was for pop artists to record the country and R&B songs.

Overall, it was business as usual for A&R men who wanted hit songs for their artists to record. That meant that a number of different artists recorded a hit song during the sheet music days. The emerging R&B field allowed those A&R men to hear new songs from new sources and they took advantage of that.

This was the transition of a record being the definitive version of a song instead of a variety of singers covering a song, which increased the sale of sheet music.

Chuck Berry

On May 21, 1955, Chuck Berry recorded "Maybellene" 36 times before he had the "take" that everyone was satisfied with. The song, originally called "Ida Red," was on a demo tape of four songs Berry put together for Chess Records. Berry didn't believe the song was as strong as his "Wee Wee Hours," a blues number that was also on that tape.

Born Charles Edward Anderson Berry on October 28, 1926 in St. Louis, Berry had three sisters and two brothers and grew up in a religious household. Berry was in the church choir and part of a gospel quartet; he also learned to play the guitar. In 1934 he was placed in a reform school because he and some friends had gone on a robbery spree. In reform school he organized a gospel quartet that performed outside the prison. Just after he turned 21--after spending three years in reform school--Berry was released and moved back to St. Louis, where he played in clubs.

Berry worked as a janitor at WEW and bought his first electric guitar for $30; he also bought a tape recorder. At the end of 1952 he was invited by Johnnie Johnson, pianist and leader of the Johnnie Johnson Trio, to perform with the group at their New Year's Eve show in East St. Louis. Berry received his biggest response when he did country songs.

Early in May, 1955, Berry went to Chicago where he heard Howlin' Wolf, Elmore James and Muddy Waters during a weekend at the clubs; he approached Waters about making a record and Muddy told him, "See Leonard Chess." On a Monday morning, Berry parked his car in front of the Chess offices at 4720 Cottage Grove on Chicago's South Side and waited for them to open. When they did, he approached Leonard Chess and asked about making records.

Chess asked him for a tape; Berry did not have one. Chess told him they were looking for current songs for the rock'n'roll market, so Berry went back to St. Louis, wrote four songs, put them on tape and came back. Leonard Chess was immediately impressed with "Ida Red" but since there was already a song called "Ida Red" Leonard suggested Berry change the title to "Maybelline."

At the session, Berry recorded "Wee Wee Hours," "Thirty Days" and "You Can't Catch Me" in addition to "Maybelline." On July 30, "Maybelline" was released on Chess Records. During that summer, "Maybelline" sold over one million copies and reached number five on *Billboard's* pop charts. It was the first rhythm and blues record that overshadowed the pop cover versions done by white artists that were released.

On Friday, September 2, Chuck Berry was the opening act for Alan Freed's road show. At the end of the year he was declared "Most Promising New Artist" by both *Billboard* and *Cashbox* and finished number 15 on *Billboard's* "favorite artist" list.

It was a good year for Chess: Bo Diddley finished second to Berry on *Cash Box's* "new artist" honor; The Moonglows (with their hit "Sincerely"), Little Walter, Muddy Waters, Lowell Fulson, Willie Mabon and Howlin' Wolf also did did well in the trade polls.

Atlantic Records

Herb Abramson, one of the original owners of Atlantic Records, was drafted into the Army as a dentist during the Korean War. He was stationed in Germany and, after his discharge, returned to New York with a pregnant girlfriend, which led to a divorce from his wife, Miriam. Abramson and Ahmet Ertegun never quite got along and Abramson was unhappy with Atlantic's abandonment of jazz for R&B, so he insisted on being bought out. Ahmet's brother, Nesuhi, bought part of Abramson's stock and became a partner in the company. The rest of the stock went to Miriam Abramson in lieu of alimony and child support. Miriam soon married Freddie Bienstock and that infusion of cash helped him build his publishing firm, Chappell.

As part of the buy out, Abramson was named the head of Atco, a subsidiary of Atlantic. One of the acts for Atco, 21-year old Bobby Darin (real name Walden Robert Cassoto) was dropped from the label but Ertegun signed Darin to Atlantic and recorded "Splish Splash." That record was the breakthrough that allowed Atlantic to reach the pop market but it was the final straw for Abramson, who left the company.

In an interview with Arnold Shaw, Ertegan spoke about the reasons for the success behind Atlantic, noting that "Black people were clamoring for blues records" during the late 1940s when records were their primary source of home entertainment. Most network radio stations would not play rhythm and blues records, saying those records were "too loud" or "too rough" or the record "doesn't fit our format." No one said they wouldn't play the record because the artist was black although the same R&B song was played if it was recorded by a white artist.

The breakthrough came, according to Ertegun, in the South where artists such as Fats Domino, Ivory Joe Hunter, Roy Milton, Ruth Brown and Amos Milburn were played on radio stations because white teenagers heard them on small stations and requested them. The recordings were produced well and Atlantic's artists "weren't down-home bluesmen," said Ertegun, "they didn't come from red-clay country. And our backup groups were either studio musicians or jazzmen" who were "sophisticated cats."

"We worked at getting a strong and clean rhythm sound," said Ertegun. The engineers that Atlantic worked with miked the drums, bass and guitar separately and used written arrangements, which was different from recordings by other independent R&B labels. "Atlantic grew and survived when most other independents disappeared because it had great flexibility and responded to change," said Ertegun. "We established a reputation early for paying established artists top royalty--and we did pay. This trade secret attracted many performers to our doors. And after we signed them, we worked to make them feel at home and to search out the best material we could find for recording."

Jerry Wexler became a partner in Atlantic in June, 1953 and was a driving force in rhythm and blues. He noted that during World War II blues musicians migrated to Chicago from Mississippi and Alabama, which meant that recordings on Chess were influenced by Delta blues. The blues musicians went to California from Oklahoma, Texas and the Southwest, according to Wexler where they were influenced by honky-tonk and jazz while blue musicians from the Carolinas, Florida, and Georgia migrated to New York, influenced by gospel and pop. "The majors had a lock on black music until World War II," said Wexler, "then they walked away from it and gave the small independents like Atlantic the opening to move in. But the majors established the parameters of R&B--good-time bands playing shuffle on non-blues changes."

Wexler obtained a degree in journalism after serving in the Army, then worked at BMI, as a *Billboard* reporter and then with MGM publishing before he joined Atlantic. Wexler helped Atlantic emerge as a major label. In an interview he stated, "What differentiates R&B from jazz and pop is a strong bass line--that's what we always looked for in recording R&B...we did what we dug. We were fans of the music we recorded, fans who had the rare privilege of making records that we liked and enjoyed. And the weird thing is that we made money--lots of money--out of doing our thing. We built a pretty big company, an eighty million dollar giant, without the help of banks or any outsiders...We weren't segmented, as at the big companies, where different departments with different philosophies and tastes make a mishmash product. We picked the pictures used on albums, selected the liner note writers, and approved the album covers."

Rhythm and Blues

The period 1950-1955 was a blossoming of rhythm and blues, especially from independent labels. Major labels had continued to record "country blues," but blacks living in cities--especially young blacks--looked down on this music, calling it "field nigger music." They wanted a music that was citified and found it in R&B.

The executives leading the way were usually Jewish. According to Arnold Shaw, "The 40s were still a time when even bright Jews could not easily find a place in the WASP world of communications--advertising, book publishing, journalism, broadcasting, and even higher education. In motion pictures, they could make it as administrative and creative people, but not too readily as actors...The music business, however, was wide open for Jews as it was for blacks."

During the early 1950s, the major labels "discovered" R&B; in 1951 Columbia activated its Okeh label while RCA established Groove Records in 1954. Decca did not get into R&B until 1958 when it revived its Brunswick label, although Decca had Louis Jordan before that time. The indies had a strong foothold by then; Atlantic had over 100 Top Ten R&B hits from 1950 to 1966. In 1953 it grossed $1 million.

R&B was considered a threat to mainstream America throughout the 1950s. In Houston, the Juvenile Delinquency and Crime Commission issued a list of objectionable disks and urged radio stations to ban them. Those disks included "Honey Love" by the Drifters, "Too Much Lovin'" by the Five Royales, "Work With Me, Annie" by the Midnighters, "I Got a Woman" by Ray Charles, and "Every Day I Have the Blues" by Lowell Fulson. Critics have pointed out that the thirty "objectionable disks did not include a single record that was not by a black artists on an R&B label. What ostensibly made them objectionable was off-color lyrics" (or Leer-ics as they became known). .

In 1954 a sign was seen in Alabama: Don't Buy NEGRO RECORDS "If you don't want to serve negroes in your place of business, then do not have negro records in your juke box or listen to negro records on the radio. The screaming idiotic words, and savage music of these records are undermining the morals of our white youth in America. Call the advertisers of radio stations that play this type of music and complain to them!"

An important independent label began in late 1952 or early 1953 in Chicago. Vee Jay Records, a black-owned company, was located in a building directly across the street from Chess Records. It was founded by the husband-wife team of James and Vivian Carter Bracken with Vivian's brother, Calvin Carter, who named the label after Vivian and James' initials. The Brackens owned record stores in the Chicago area and, frustrated at trying to stock records, began their own company.

Important records during that time include "The Glory of Love" by the Five Keys (1951), "Lawdy Miss Clawdy" by Lloyd Price (1952), "Crying in the Chapel" by the Orioles (1953), and "Shake Rattle, and Roll" by Big Joe Turner (1954). In the summer of 1954 hits included "Gee" by The Crows on Rama, "I Understand" by the Four Tunes on Manor, and "Sh-Boom" by The

Chords on Cat. The major labels and pop singers responded by recording R&B hits while songwriters and publishers began to panic because their Tin Pan Alley tunes weren't being recorded.

White Artists Recording R&B

That era, 1950-1956 has become known as a time of whites "ripping off" black music. That view has been perpetuated by rock writers who looked at the number of white artists covering black recordings and concluded that the blacks had their music "stolen." In truth, it was business as usual for the music business. There had always been cover tunes, and pop artists routinely covered songs that were hits. Black artists had often covered white material in the past and white artists covered songs by blacks when they were hits.

During that period white pop artists found a rich mother lode of new hit songs from black artists on independent labels. Artists must sell records and consumers buy hit songs. It was only natural that those songs would be covered. In the segregated world of the 1950s, black artists could not reach the large, lucrative white mainstream market with R&B, but white acts could. At the same time a number of white teenagers "discovered" R&B because radio stations were increasingly playing it.

While it may be argued that black artists might have had a shot at the white market without the white artists covering them, that was a long-shot during the early 1950s. On the other hand, the cover records by the white artists brought attention to R&B that it might not have received--or taken a long time to receive. It is a matter of selective aesthetic taste by rock critics to single out artists like Pat Boone and Perry Como as "rip off" artists for covering R&B songs in soulless white bread versions while artists such as Elvis Presley and, later, the Beatles and Rolling Stones, were applauded for their covers because that helped bring attention to black artists and were aesthetically better.

But the music business does not operate on aesthetics; it operates on profits and money was to be made with the cover records, so they were done. That blunts the criticism of Pat Boone covering Little Richard's hits like "Tutti Frutti" and "Long Tall Sally" because, at the time, Boone outsold Little Richard. In the long run, Little Richard was recognized and appreciated for his recordings and, after the music broke racial barriers, Little Richard received his due.

Something else was happening during this period and that was the popularity of a recording became greater than the popularity of a song. In the past, sheet music of songs sold greater than recordings and a great song was sung and recorded by a number of singers. As rhythm and blues, and then rock'n'roll became popular, the record became the defining version of a song. A song on sheet music could be sung by anyone; a recording could only be re-created by the artist or group who did the original or hit version. During the 1950s, records replaced sheet music as the carrier of music and the performance on a recording came to define a song. Hence, Little Richard's recording of "Tutti Fruitti" was "authentic" because he did it first and, arguably, did the defining version. All other artists after Little Richard who recorded "Tutti Fruitti" were compared to his version and found lacking.

The turning point came when white disk jockeys, led by Alan Freed and others began playing R&B records on the radio and found a large, enthusiastic, young audience. That led to concerts that featured both black and white artists playing before mixed audiences, which threatened white middle-class America. The new generation of teenagers wanted a wild, vibrant music even though their parents preferred more sedate fare.

The Bradley Recording and Film Studios

Owen Bradley and his brother, Harold, built a studio in the basement of a house in Nashville they bought at 804 16th Avenue, the first studio in the area that became known as "Music Row." They purchased a Quonset Hut and constructed a studio which they hoped to use for film production.

Al Gannaway began filming "Stars of the Grand Ole Opry" in February, 1955 and continued filming through 1956; Gannaway needed a movie set so a stage was built at the north end of the Quonset Hut where a backdrop showed a barn door with hay bales scattered around. However, after Gannaway, there wasn't much film business so, increasingly, recordings began to be held in the Quonset Hut.

Country Music on TV

The "Ozark Jubilee," a country music TV show based in Springfield, Missouri, began broadcasting on January 22, 1955 on the ABC network. "The Grand Ole Opry" TV series premiered on October 15.

Chet Atkins and RCA

In 1955, Chet Atkins was named manager of RCA's new Nashville studio on McGavock Street by Steve Sholes, head of country A&R in New York.

Country Hits in 1955

Webb Pierce continued to dominate country music during 1955; he had the number one record for 46 weeks; his hits included the old Jimmie Rodgers song, "In the Jailhouse Now," "I Don't Care" and "Love, Love, Love." Eddy Arnold had two number one's, "The Cattle Call" and "That Do Make It Nice" while Tennessee Ernie Ford had "Sixteen Tons" at the end of the year.

TV vs. Radio

A key factor in the increased popularity of Rhythm and Blues was the rise in television and the decline in network radio. As advertisers shifted their money to TV, radio faced declining revenues. Network shows declined on radio and moved to TV and network executives turned their attention to TV. Live shows were eliminated--too costly to pay live talent--and records replaced departed shows. Radio owners were mostly white, middle-class businessmen who may not have liked R&B but needed revenue. Advertisers soon discovered that while Mom and Dad were watching TV, the young teenage members of the family were likely to be in their rooms listening to radio. Increasingly, they were listening to R&B or, later, rock'n'roll.

Although television has received credit for being a revolutionary technology, changing American family life with its entertainment, the fact is that radio—specifically "Top 40" radio--was equally revolutionary. The first station to play all rock'n'roll was WHB in Kansas City, owned by Todd Storz. This was "formula radio" or radio that was programmed to a play list and young fans heard a steady stream of rock'n'roll. Radio needed rock'n'roll to replace the radio shows that went to TV, but rock'n'roll needed radio because that's how rock reached a young audience.

In its fight for survival, radio created a "new" medium, dominated by recordings and aimed at young people. While the American family became increasingly sedentary in front of the television, teenager became increasingly active with the radio, changing their dress, behavior and language because of the music they heard.

As radio became increasingly important, jukeboxes became less important in terms of breaking a record. At first, small labels sought out isolated stations playing black music who were influential and tried to convince them to play their records. If they did, an immediate boost in sales resulted, so a lot of money was on the line connected to radio airplay. Record promoters soon began offering "incentives" to disk jockeys--free records they could sell, then some cash, then dinners, trips, a supply of credit, and "perks" such as "piece of the action," which might mean an influential disk jockey's name as a co-writer or a piece of the publishing or rights to book an artist on a concert for a low fee so the jockey could make a profit promoting a show.

The independent labels argued this was doing business the American way and pointed out that big business regularly courted its favored customers with such incentives. It was also like lobbying Congress where special interests donated money to a politician's campaign and then expected the Congressman to listen to their concerns. However, because this music was considered a "threat" to American values, it came under investigation.

The cause of concern was "dirty" lyrics, suggesting sex. However, ASCAP songwriter Al Stillman pointed out in a *Variety* article, "As far as I can remember, practically all lyrics, except 'Barney Google,' have been dirty--with the carriage trade practitioners, Cole Porter, Larry Hart etc ...Actually the object of all leericists,..has always been to get as close to the Main Subject as possible without stating it and/or 'cleaning it up' by marrying 'em in the last line. The current rock'n'rollers are not beating around the bush. But without condoning 'em, it's at least a less hypocritical approach."

R&B record executive Ralph Bass basically agreed with that assessment but pointed out the racial overtones. He stated, "If Freed knew what the hell he was saying, it would never have been called it rock'n'roll. I did 'Work with Me, Annie,' and my buddy Henry Glover did 'We're Gonna Rock All Night Long' with Wynonie Harris. We weren't talkin' about rock'n'rollin''; we were talkin' about sex...The problem was that white kids were listening to these things for the first time. It was all right so long as blacks were listening, but as soon as the whites started listening, it was no good. Then it became a big, political thing. When Freed named it, he just took the idea from a Wynonie Harris lyric. If whites had known at that time, they would not have permitted the name 'rock'n'roll' to be used."

The American mainstream wasn't buying it--they couldn't control their kids so the music must be to blame. Although they were not aware that the term "rock'n'roll" was a term blacks used for the sex act, and that "rockin' all night long" did not mean having a party, they sensed there was a strong sexual element in the music. And they were right.

Social Roots of the Rock Revolution

Although June, 19, 1955 when "Rock Around the Clock" by Bill Haley and the Comets reached number one on the *Billboard* Hot 100 Chart marks the beginning of the rock revolution for many rock historians, it does not mean that rock'n'roll dominated the music industry from that date forward. In fact, the truth is that rock'n'roll had a long way to go before it dominated the pop charts. Perhaps more significant than the actual music or charts was the attitude the rock revolution ushered in because, when all is said and done, rock'n'roll is not just a music, it is an attitude.

The audience most attracted to rock'n'roll was teenagers and the teenagers of 1955 were born before World War II. Their neighbors and relatives went off to fight in a global conflict and the United States was victorious, emerging after World War II as the major world power. That gave them a feeling of confidence and security. That is important because individualism is the product of a secure society.

The Rock'n'roll Revolution was a revolution about individualism, about rebellion, about a new world order. It was a new way of thinking that discarded the past and created a new future not bound by restrictions of the past. It was almost like a new, secret language that insiders shared. That new individualism expressed itself in the younger generation breaking away from previous generations for new forms of entertainment and new forms of music. It was a demand for individualism, made possible by the strength and security of the Allied victory in World War II. The teenagers of 1955 were also beneficiaries of an economic boom that came after World War II.

By the 1950s, a significant portion of the adult population had settled down, married, gotten good jobs and began heading towards the American dream with a vengeance, anxious to make up for the time lost during World War II. It created a new prosperity.

The end result was that teenagers could afford to buy recordings and wanted young stars they could relate to. They also wanted their own individuality to shine through. They found those heroes in movies and recordings and on TV but the soundtrack of their lives was music on the radio.

Sam Phillips and Early Sun Records

According to biographer Peter Guralnick, Sam Phillips, founder of Sun Records, "believed--entirely and without reservation--in differentness, in independence, in individuation, he believed in himself, and he believed--even to the point of articulating it in public and private utterances from earliest adulthood on--in the scope and beauty of African-American culture." He worked hard, 18-hour days on his business, traveling between 65,000 and 75,000 miles each year, stopping by each of his 42 different distributors who handled his product, and met jukebox operators, disc jockeys, record-store owners, and anyone else who could help him sell records.

The first hit for Sun was "Bear Cat," a rewrite of Big Mama Thornton's hit, "Hound Dog" (written by Jerry Leiber and Mike Stoller) by Rufus Thomas, which entered the national charts on April 18, 1953. In the summer of 1953 Phillips recorded Little Junior Parker's hit, "Mystery Train." He also recorded "The Prisonaires," inmates at the Tennessee State Prison in Nashville, with lead singer Johnny Bragg, doing "Just Walkin' in the Rain," a song he had written.

On July 15, 1953, an article about the Prisonaires appeared in the *Memphis Press-Scimitar*, which promoted "Just Walkin' in the Rain." A recent high school graduate, Elvis Presley, probably saw the article and decided to go down to Phillips' studio and record something himself.

Young Elvis Presley

Elvis Presley was born January 8, 1935 in Tupelo, Mississippi and spent his first 13 years there. His family was poor and in November, 1948 they packed everything they owned in a 1937 Plymouth and moved to Memphis. In Tupelo, Guralnick wrote that "Many of the other children made fun of him as a trashy kind of boy playing trashy "hillbilly music." He graduated from Humes High School on June 3, 1953; the next day he went to the Tennessee Employment Security Office and applied for a job; on June 5 he started work with M.B. Parker Machinists' Shop at $33 a week.

In Memphis, Elvis sang country and gospel songs with friends at Lauderdale Courts, a low-income housing project administered by the Memphis Housing Authority. He sang songs by the Sons of the Pioneers ("Cool Water" and "Riders in the Sky"), Hank Snow ("I'm Movin' On") and lots of Eddy Arnold songs as well as pop hits by Bing Crosby, Kay Starr, Eddie Fisher, Perry Como and his favorite, Dean Martin.

On his first trip to Sam Phillips' studio, which had a custom recording business, he paid to record the 1948 pop hit "My Happiness," and a song recorded by the Ink Spots in 1941, "That's When Your Heartaches Begin," accompanied only by his guitar. In January, 1954 he returned and recorded "I'll Never Stand in Your Way," a Joni James hit, and "It Wouldn't Be the

Same Without You," a hit for western singing star Jimmy Wakely. He met Phillips' secretary, Marion Keisker, who was impressed enough to put his name in a file and remind Sam Phillips about him.

Sam found a song in Nashville, "Without You," and needed a singer. That was sometime in May or June, 1954, and Marion called Elvis to come to the studio and record it. It didn't work but Sam thought he saw some talent.

On May 25, 1954, a country group, "The Wranglers," with guitarist Scotty Moore and bassist Bill Black, came into the studio and recorded. Keisker recommended Elvis as a singer for the group and on July 4 Elvis went to Scotty's house where they jammed on some songs. They decided to record "Harbor Lights" and "I Love You Because" the next day at Sam's studio.

In addition to Sam Phillips, there were two other owners in Sun Records, his brother Jud and Jim Bulleit, who had previously owned Bullet Records in Nashville. At the end of 1953 Sam and Jud pressured Bulleit to sell his share of Sun; in February, 1954 Jud bought him out. Jud then decided to let Sam have the whole company, but Sam couldn't pay him off immediately. Also in 1954, Sam installed two Ampex 350 recorders: one console model and another mounted on a rack behind his head for the tape delay echo, or "slapback," for which Sun became famous.

On July 5, 1954 Elvis, along with Scotty Moore and Bill Black, spent the evening in Sam's studio recording "Harbor Lights" and "I Love You Because." It wasn't quite working so they decided to call it a night. Elvis, a young man full of energy, began pounding his guitar and singing the old Arthur "Big Boy" Crudup hit, "That's All Right, Mama." Sam felt an excitement and got them to work it up so it could be recorded. Later (perhaps a few days), they recorded the old Bill Monroe bluegrass hit, "Blue Moon of Kentucky" in the same frenzied, souped-up style.

"That's All Right" b/w "Blue Moon of Kentucky" was released as Sun #209 on July 19, 1954. On July 30 the trio played at the Overton Park Bandshell in Memphis. The record caught on quickly and the group was soon playing all over Memphis.

The first record by Elvis was a founding document on the roots of rock'n'roll. On one side was a blues song, "That's All Right, Mama," originally recorded by Arthur "Big Boy" Crudup and the other side was a country song, "Blue Moon of Kentucky," originally recorded by Bill Monroe and his Bluegrass Boys. It was country music coming from southern whites and blues and rhythm and blues music coming from African-Americans that melded into rock'n'roll, a music with two deep tap roots.

Things happened quickly. On October 2 the group performed "Blue Moon of Kentucky" on the Grand Ole Opry in Nashville, but Opry Manager Jim Denny wasn't impressed; the wild-haired kid just didn't seem to fit the Opry mold. On November 6 Elvis signed with the Louisiana Hayride for a year's worth of appearances. By January, 1955, Sam Phillips had virtually quit recording other artists and was concentrating on Elvis.

Elvis's records were selling briskly, but a big hit causes a problem for a small label. Phillips didn't make much on each single sold, and he had to plow that money back into more pressings while hoping distributors would soon pay up. The cash flow problem was enormous. Distributors would not pay before 90 days, and then perhaps a partial payment to keep the product coming. Meanwhile, Phillips had to pay all his creditors--from publishers to pressing plants to trade papers. He was barely successful, but felt like he was going under.

Elvis and Nashville

Sam Phillips was experiencing success with Elvis as well as a new singer, Johnny Cash, who released "Cry, Cry, Cry" b/w "Hey Porter" early in 1955. The cash flow problem was putting Sam Phillips on the edge of being out of business but there was hope on the horizon; several major labels were interested in purchasing Elvis's contract from Sun.

At the 1955 DJ convention in Nashville, Elvis came and met Steve Sholes, who was head of RCA's country division, as well as Colonel Tom Parker, a manager and booking agent who had been working with Hank Snow, and Julian Aberbach, head of the Hill and Range publishing company. Parker structured a deal whereby Sam Phillips received $35,000 from RCA Victor, who acquired all of Elvis's Sun masters and assumed payment of all back royalties, which enabled Sam Phillips to carry on with Sun Records.

Fats Domino

Fats Domino (born February 26, 1928) began his professional career in 1947 when he joined the Solid Senders, led by New Orleans bandleader Billy Diamond, who performed at the Hideway Club in New Orleans. He was given the name "Fats" (his real name was Antoine) by Diamond because he reminded the bandleader of pianists Fats Waller and Fats Pichon.

Domino's first release on Imperial, "The Fat Man" was released in 1949 and entered *Billboard's* R&B chart in early 1950, rising to number two. He followed this with a string of top ten records, including "Every Night About This Time" in 1950; "Rockin' Chair" in 1951; "Goin' Home" (number 1),

"Poor Poor Me" and "How Long" in 1952; "Going To The River," "Please Don't Leave Me" and "Rose Mary" in 1953; "Something's Wrong" and "You Done Me Wrong" in 1954; and then "Ain't It A Shame," which was number one for eleven weeks on *Billboard's* pop chart in 1955 (it reached number 10). Pat Boone covered this as "Ain't That a Shame," in 1955 and it landed at number one on the pop chart.

Producer Dave Bartholomew was an integral part of Fats Domino's success; he was co-writer on most of his songs and guided the recording sessions. Domino's first album, *Carry On Rockin'* was released by Imperial in 1955 and the following year was re-released as *Rock and Rollin' with Fats Domino*, which was a top 20 on *Billboard's* pop album chart.

Fats Domino covered pop hits "My Blue Heaven" (Paul Whiteman) and "Blueberry Hill" (Glenn Miller and Gene Autry) in 1956, the latter reaching number two on *Billboard's* pop chart. His hit "Blue Monday" was released in late 1956 and "I'm Walkin'" was a hit on the pop chart in 1957, along with "It's You I Love" and "Valley of Tears."

Fats Domino was one of the earliest R&B artists to cross over to the pop market during the mid-1950s. He was one of the first R&B artists whose songs were covered by white singers and then became one of the first R&B artists to have his own recordings on *Billboard's* pop chart.

In addition to his success on radio and jukeboxes, Domino was in two early rock'n'roll films, *Shake, Rattle & Rock* and *The Girl Can't Help It*, both in 1956.

Record Labels

In 1955, Liberty Records was formed by Si Waronker and Herb Newman, Del-Fi was formed by Bob Keane. Specialty, formed during the 1940s by Art Rupe, had Little Richard, Larry Williams and the Soul Stirrers with lead singer Sam Cooke.

Stereo sound popularized the LP format, which was initially marketed on reel-to-reel format for audiophiles.

In August, the Columbia Record Club debuted with a series of advertisements in major national magazines. The record club was possible because of the LP format, which was on vinyl. The club would not have been possible with the 78 format on shellac because breakage would have made mailings prohibitive. Columbia established the distribution center for their record club in Terre Haute, Indiana, where LPs were pressed. Retailers objected to the club, so Goddard Lieberson—who selected most of the initial offerings of the Record Club, did not offer a recording on Columbia until at least six months after it had been released commercially.

The Record Club quickly became popular, especially with rural customers, and during the first year they signed 125,000 members.

In the News

On July 18, 1955, Walt Disney opened Disneyland. Congress voted an increase in the minimum wage from 75 cents to $1; it would take effect in March, 1956.

Charismatic actor James Dean died in a car wreck on September 30. The film *Rebel Without a Cause*, which starred Dean, was released a month after his death. That film, and Dean's character, would often be cited as a cause of juvenile delinquency.

On December 1, Rosa Parks,a seamstress in Montgomery, Alabama, was riding on a city bus, on her way home from work. A white man entered the bus and the driver ordered Parks to move back so the white man could have a seat. She refused and was arrested. Black citizens in Montgomery called for a boycott of the city's buses and Reverend Martin Luther King, Jr., pastor of Dexter Avenue Baptist Church in Montgomery, was elected to head the campaign to publicize the boycott to the 50,000 black citizens of Montgomery who comprised about 75 percent of bus passengers. The boycott began that December.

1956

Elvis and Heartbreak Hotel

On January, 10, 1956—two days after this twenty-first birthday--Elvis went into the RCA Victor studios in Nashville located in the United Methodist Publishing Company on McGavock Street and recorded "I Got a Woman," "Heartbreak Hotel" and "Money Honey." The next day he recorded "I'm Counting on You" and "I Was the One." He was backed by band members Scotty Moore on guitar, Bill Black on Bass and D.J. Fontana on drums along with session musicians Chet Atkins on guitar and Floyd Cramer on piano. Elvis had requested the Jordanaires for backing vocals but Chet Atkins, who booked the session, only hired one member of the Jordanaires, Gordon Stoker, to sing with Ben and Brock Speer, members of the family gospel group The Speers, who were signed to RCA.

RCA released "Heartbreak Hotel on February 22 and it entered the *Billboard* country chart on March 3 and rose to number one, where it remained for 17 consecutive weeks; at the end of March it entered *Billboard's*

Hot 100 chart and reached number three and the R&B chart, where it reached number three.

His first album, *Elvis Presley,* entered the *Billboard* album chart on March 31 and reached number one, where it stayed for ten weeks; it spent a total of 48 weeks on the album chart.

Colonel Tom Parker

Colonel Tom Parker managed one of the greatest acts in the history of the recording industry--Elvis Presley. He took over management after Presley had signed with RCA and released his first RCA recordings in 1956 and built his client into a worldwide superstar. While many have criticized Parker for Presley's lack of artistic development as a recording artist and actor--a criticism that ignores what Elvis wanted in his career --the fact remains that Parker and Presley became a team which brought millions of dollars into both of their pockets.

Alanna Nash, who wrote a biography of Parker, noted that the manager was "the man who almost single-handedly took the carnival tradition first to rock and roll, and then to modern mass entertainment, creating the blueprint for the powerful style of management and merchandising that the music business operates by today." An important aspect of this "carnival tradition" was making the quick buck, taking as much money as you can get today because you can never count on tomorrow. It was a short-term view of life and careers, and intensely capitalistic, but Elvis agreed with it, particularly during the first part of his career.

When Elvis first signed with Sun Records, his guitar player, Scotty Moore, served as his manager but Bob Neal, a local disc jockey, became Elvis's manager, effective January 1, 1955. Tom Parker had worked with singer Gene Austin and managed Eddy Arnold for about seven years; in fact, the work he did for Arnold and the connections he made--with Steve Sholes at RCA Records, the Aberbach Brothers with Hill and Range, and agents at the William Morris Agency who handed television appearances-- would all be used when he managed Elvis. Eddy Arnold had hit records on RCA, did lucrative personal appearances, appeared in several Hollywood movies, and made appearances on major network shows on radio and television. That would also be the career path that Elvis followed.

Elvis and Colonel Tom Parker

Parker used his contacts with RCA Victor and the William Morris Agency to obtain a $40,000 advance from Hank Saperstein, a Beverly Hills movie merchandiser, to license articles with Elvis's name on them; they included charm bracelets, lipstick, dolls, plastic guitars, scarves and teddy bears.

Although Parker had contacts with the William Morris Agency, there was no written contract--the Morris agents as well as many others in the music industry felt that Elvis was possibly a fad that would pass quickly. Parker did not disagree with that assessment, which is why he set out to make as much money as he could, for Presley and himself, as quickly as possible. A prevailing idea was that Elvis would soon burn out so it was best to get as much as you could as quickly as you can.

Parker contacted Steve Yates, an independent agent, who booked Elvis for four consecutive weeks on "Stage Show," the CBS-TV variety show hosted by former big band leaders Tommy and Jimmy Dorsey on Saturday nights. That is where Elvis debuted "Heartbreak Hotel," his first single for RCA. The response to his performances was so overwhelming that Elvis did six appearances on that show.

Meanwhile, the William Morris office drew up a contract, signed January 31, 1956, for exclusive representation of Elvis. Parker negotiated the contract and it was signed six weeks before the management contract between Parker and Presley was signed. That contract gave Parker final approval on all contracts involving Elvis, which meant that Parker had total control of Elvis's entire career.

Elvis was 21 years old in 1956, immature and underdeveloped as a personality; he had a high school education but had grown up poor, lived in a housing project and was un-worldly and inarticulate. Parker decided to not allow Elvis do long interviews, which ended up giving him a mystique and the object of teenage fantasies. On the practical side, it hid the fact that the young man who was an exciting, hypnotic performer, was not as exciting in person.

The biggest TV appearance for Elvis was on "The Ed Sullivan Show" on CBS on Sunday nights; when Elvis appeared for the first of his three appearances, in September, 1956, 82 percent of American TV sets were tuned into the show.

On personal appearances, promoters had traditionally booked an act for a set amount, say $500, then charged what they could for tickets and if they sold a lot of tickets, could make a handsome profit. For example, if a promoter charged $3 a ticket, and sold 4,000, they would gross $12,000. Promoters justified this because they also booked shows that lost money, so the big money makers carried them past the money losers. Colonel Tom

Parker routinely adjusted the cost of Elvis so the promoter could not make a big profit.

Parker's management commission was 25 percent on all monies that Elvis received, including royalties, fees and profits, and he also charged the act for all expenses occurred so that Parker never paid anything out of his own pocket.

Elvis did not argue with his arrangement; he wanted to sing and wasn't interested in the business agreements. Parker had the total trust of Elvis and the manager noted that "As long as Elvis can write a check for something he wants, he doesn't care how much money is in the bank"

Parker's primary interest was not in generating money from fans, but in making deals with deal-makers. Parker wanted to "sell the sellers," so his concerns were the executives who controlled the TV and radio networks, the record companies, the press and the movies. He loved negotiating and getting the best deal he could--for both Elvis and himself.

In doing business, Parker believed that everything costs so he hated giving away anything free, even show tickets to key executives who, he felt, could pay and he always wanted to know where the money was before he made the deal. Trying to determine how much money fans would spend was too iffy and nebulous; Parker preferred dealing with people who could write a big check.

Parker always "dressed down," believing that if he dressed poorly he would be perceived as homespun and give him an edge in business deals. Parker believed (and said) "You don't have to be nice to people on the way up if you're not coming back down" and lived that mantra.

Colonel Parker made a deal with Hal Wallis to get Elvis in the movies. Wallis owned an independent film company whose films were distributed by Paramount. Although Elvis's big dream was to be a movie star, he was never allowed to develop his acting ability. Parker did not believe that Elvis had the ability to become a serious actor; instead, he saw the movies as a way to sell more concert tickets and records.

Hal Wallis did not see Elvis as a serious actor either; instead, he viewed the singer as a way to make money with low-budget pictures so he could invest in "serious" films with major stars.

Parker and Wallis made a seven movie deal for Elvis; he received $15,000 for the first film, which escalated to $100,000 for his seventh. There were no perks in the contract--no script approval or billing structure. There was a "loan-out" clause that said Elvis could make one picture a year for another movie company so the first movie for Elvis was *Love Me Tender*, which was produced by Twentieth Century-Fox. Wallis preferred that another firm test the waters first.

Elvis's first film role came in *Loving You*, a film where the co-stars made significantly more than the star. Thousands of fans lined up when it premiered at New York's Paramount Theater on November 15, 1956, with a 40 foot cutout of Elvis on the front of the theater. The original movie contract was a bad deal, and Parker soon realized it; he set himself the goal of having Elvis earn $1 million for each movie.

While Parker negotiated deals for Elvis, he also negotiated deals for himself. That generally meant that Parker was provided an office and secretarial staff on the movie lot, as well as a car and driver at his disposal. He also received on-screen credit for all of Presley's movies. As biographer Alanna Nash observed, "Parker saw himself and not Elvis as the client."

Elvis was both loyal and dependent on Parker; the singer was isolated from the business dealings and showed no interest in the behind the scenes machinations. That suited Parker, who preferred to keep Elvis away from those business deals as well as out of contact with executives who might be rivals to Parker's power.

When Elvis protested, usually for some creative control over the movies or recordings, Parker replied, "We do it this way, we make money" and Elvis always replied, "Okay, let's make money." Elvis was also constantly admonished by his father to listen to and follow the Colonel's dictates.

Carl Perkins

Another Sun artist, Carl Perkins, beat Elvis to the charts in 1956. On February 18 "Blue Suede Shoes" entered the country chart and reached number one, where he remained for three weeks; on March 3 it entered the *Billboard* Hot 100 and reached number two, where it remained for four weeks; on March 10 it entered the Rhythm and Blues chart and rose to number two, where he remained for four weeks, the first record to be an across the board hit in country, pop and R&B. The executives at RCA were concerned they had signed the wrong artist but Sam Phillips assured them they had chosen the right one in Elvis.

Carl Perkins (born April 9, 1932) was the son of sharecroppers and grew up on a farm near Tiptonville, Tennessee. He heard southern gospel music in church and blues from black field workers in the cotton fields; for entertainment the family listened to the Grand Ole Opry in Nashville, about 200 miles east southeast of Tiptonville. His first guitar was built by his Dad from a cigar box and broomstick; his next was a Gene Autry guitar sold by Sears. His earliest influences were Opry stars Roy Acuff and Bill Monroe and an African-American fieldworker, John Westbrook. Uncle John played the blues and told Perkins that when he played the guitar to "Get down close to it. You can feel it travel down the strangs, come through your head and down to your soul where you live. You can feel it. Let it vib-a-rate.'"

In January, 1947, when Perkins was 14, the family moved to a farm near Jackson, Tennessee, about 100 miles east of Memphis and he wrote "Let Me Take You To the Movie, Magg." Perkins and his brother, Jay, began playing local clubs around Jackson and were joined by their brother Jay on bass fiddle. The group began performing on WTJS in Jackson and by the late 1940s had a 15-minute show on the radio.

Playing music was a weekend and evening job while Perkins picked cotton, worked at a dairy, in a mattress factory, a battery plant and then as a pan greaser for the Colonial Baking Company. He married his wife, Valda, in January, 1953 and when his job at the bakery was reduced to part time, Valda encouraged him to work the clubs and bars full-time. Later that year the group added W.S. "Fluke" Holland on drums.

During the summer of 1954 Carl and Valda heard "Blue Moon of Kentucky" by Elvis on the radio and Perkins realized "There's a man in Memphis who understands what we're doing. I need to go see him." Perkins had been playing—and writing—what came to be known as rockabilly before Elvis made his first recordings. In October, Perkins and his band auditioned for Sam Phillips, who recorded them doing"Movie Magg" and "Turn Around" and released it on Flip Records, a label Phillips also owned, in March, 1955.

The record was a regional hit and Perkins and his band were booked with Elvis and Johnny Cash on dates. In October, 1955, Sun released "Gone, Gone, Gone" b/w "Let The Juke Box Keep On Playing" and it was also a regional success. Perkins wrote "Blue Suede Shoes that autumn; he was inspired to write the song after witnessing a dancer become angry at his date for scuffing up his shoes. (The idea also came from Johnny Cash who had a dapper friend when he was in the Air Force stationed in German.) On December 19, Perkins recorded "Blue Suede Shoes" at the Sun Studio in Memphis; the idea to add "Go, cat, go" came from Sam Phillips. The record was released on January 1, 1956.

In March Perkins performed "Blue Suede Shoes" on two TV shows, "The Ozark Jubilee" on ABC and "Stage Show" on CBS. Carl Perkins was on the cusp of stardom but on March 22 the Perkins brothers band were headed to New York for a scheduled appearance on NBC's "Perry Como Show" when they had an automobile accident near Dover, Delaware. Carl landed face down in a water-filled ditch and was saved from drowning by "Fluke" Hollard; he suffered a severe concussion, three fractured vertebrae in his neck, a broken collar bone and a body filled with lacerations. He was unconscious for a whole day. Carl's brother, Jay, had a broken neck and severe internal injuries.

While Carl Perkins recovered, Elvis released "Heartbreak Hotel," which was also a hit on the country, pop and R&B charts; Elvis also recorded "Blue Suede Shoes," which was a top 20 pop record for him that spring, and performed it on the Milton Berle Show on April 3.

A month after the accident, on April 21, Carl Perkins resumed performing; prior to touring he went into the Sun Studio and recorded "Dixie Fried," "Put Your Cat Clothes On," "Right String, Wrong Yo Yo," "You Can't Make Love to Somebody," "Everybody's Trying to Be My Baby" and "That Don't Move Me."

During 1956 Sun released Perkins' "Boppin' The Blues," "All Mama's Children," "Dixie Fried," "I'm Sorry, I'm Not Sorry," "Matchbox" and "Your True Love." During the session on December 4 when Perkins recorded "Matchbox," Jerry Lee Lewis was in the studio, Elvis dropped by and Johnny Cash was called and came by and the four were recorded singing a variety of songs. That session was later released as "The Million Dollar Quartet," a name the newspaper headline gave the session when the article was published.

Johnny Cash

The independent Sun label was red hot in 1956; in addition to Elvis and Carl Perkins, Johnny Cash had a number one hit with "I Walk the Line."

Johnny Cash (born February 26, 1932) grew up in Dyess, Arkansas, where his family had moved when Cash was three. Influenced by gospel music, Cash began writing songs when he was twelve. In July, 1950, shortly after high school graduation (and a brief job at a car manufacturing plant in Detroit) Cash enlisted in the Air Force and served four years, mostly in Landsberg, Germany where he was a Morse Code operator in a division that intercepted Soviet Army transmissions sent in Morse code. During his time in Germany he formed a band, The Landsberg Barbarians.

Cash was discharged in July, 1954, married Vivian Liberto, who he had met in San Antonio during basic training, and moved to Memphis where he obtained a job selling appliances. During the evenings he played music with guitarist Luther Perkins and bassist Marshall Grant, then auditioned for Sam Phillips at the Sun Records Studio. During the audition, Cash sang gospel songs and was told by Phillips that he could not sell gospel; Cash went home and wrote "Hey, Porter" (from a poem he had written during his time in Germany) and "Cry! Cry! Cry!." Phillips recorded those songs and released them on Sun in June, 1955; "Cry! Cry! Cry" entered the *Billboard* country chart in November and rose to number 14.

Cash's next release was "Folsom Prison Blues" b/w "So Doggone Lonesome"; both sides charted, each reaching number four and remained on the chart for five months. "I Walk the Line," his third release on Sun, entered the *Billboard* country chart in June, 1956 and reached number one, where it remained for six consecutive weeks, staying on that chart for 43 weeks. "I Walked the Line" entered the *Billboard* Hot 100 chart in September and reached number 17 but remained on that chart for 22 weeks. That was the breakthrough hit for Johnny Cash, who also had chart hits with "Get Rhythm," and "There You Go" in 1956.

Elvis's Hits

Elvis's first chart records were on the country chart during the time he was with Sun; in 1955 "Baby, Let's Play House," "I'm Left, You're Right, She's Gone," "I Forgot To Remember to Forget" (number 1) and "Mystery Train" were all top ten records on that chart.

After "Heartbreak Hotel," his next chart record for RCA was "I Was the One," which he had recorded in Nashville and then "I Want You, I Need You, I Love You," also recorded in Nashville which reached number one on the country chart and number three on the pop chart.

Elvis continued to be stronger on the country chart; "My Baby Left Me" reached both the country and pop charts but then "Hound Dog" became a number one pop hit for six straight weeks and number one for ten straight weeks on the country chart. "Don't Be Cruel" entered the country chart before it was on the pop chart and became a number one record on the country chart for ten weeks and reached number one on the pop chart, where it remained for six weeks.

"Love Me Tender" entered the country and pop charts at the same time, October 20, but reached number three on the pop chart and only number 18 on the country chart. "Love Me" was the first record by Elvis that entered the pop chart in *Billboard* before it entered the country chart; it was number seven in pop and number ten in country.

By the end of 1956, Elvis had released eight records that reached the *Billboard* pop chart and 13 that reached the country chart.

Top 40 Radio

In 1956, the year Elvis and rock'n'roll hit, the Top 40 radio format was perfected. The Top 40 format was a key to the success of rock'n'roll.

The legend goes that Todd Storz, owner of KOWH in Omaha, Nebraska, and his program director, Bill Stewart, were in an Omaha bar in 1953, waiting for Storz's girlfriend, a waitress, to finish work. They were discussing the impact TV was having on radio and questioned how to improve KOWH's ratings when they noticed that the bar's customers played the same few songs on the jukebox over and over while some songs weren't played at all. After the customers left, the waitresses dropped nickels into the jukebox and played those same songs again. That led Storz to go to the jukebox and write down the titles of the songs played most often and discovered he could narrow his playlist to 30 songs.

Program Director Bill Stewart eliminated the classical music, country records, music, network shows, transcriptions and other programs (rock'n'roll had not come in yet) and programed the top pop songs for homemakers. It boiled down to disc jockeys playing songs from a playlist rather than playing whatever they felt like playing. The ratings for KOWH soared.

That story is probably true but it goes a bit deeper than that. When Todd Storz was in the army during World War II, he observed that customers in restaurants played the same songs over and over on the jukebox. In 1949, Storz and his father purchased KOWH in Omaha and then purchased WTIX in New Orleans in 1953. On the New Orleans station, Storz had initiated a program, "Top 40 at 1450" for the station. By 1956 Storz owned three other stations, WHB in Kansas City, WDGY in Minneapolis and WQAM in Miami. All of the stations were successful with this "formula radio" format.

Storz knew of research that showed that the reason people listened to radio was to hear music, so programming more music made sense. His stations also offered a number of contests and promotions that advertised and promoted the stations.

The success of WHB in Kansas City—the first station to play all rock'n'roll--attracted the attention of Gordon McLendon, who operated three powerful stations in Texas. McLendon visited the Kansas City station and copied the format for his Dallas station, reportedly giving the format the name "Top 40." He then expanded the format to his stations in Houston and San Antonio.

In addition to programming music, McLendon created catchy contests and promotions which made his stations popular, involving listeners to his stations.

By the time rock'n'roll exploded with Elvis in 1956, the "Top 40" format was a proven winner. Neither Storz nor McLendon cared for rock'n'roll but both wanted their stations to attract an audience so they could sell advertising, which is how radio made money. The "Top 40" format helped make rock'n'roll popular because radio listeners who loved rock'n'roll could hear a steady diet of their favorite songs.

Cast Recordings and Soundtracks

For albums, the year 1956 was the era of movie soundtracks or Broadway cast recordings. The year began with the movie soundtrack of *Oklahoma* on the charts (it entered the *Billboard* album chart in September, 1955 and remained on the chart for 283 weeks, or over four years). Other movie soundtracks were *The Man With the Golden Arm*, *Picnic*, *The Eddy Duchin Story*, *The King and I* (277 weeks on the chart) and *High Society*.

Goddard Lieberson's production of *My Fair Lady*, recorded the Sunday after the musical premiered, was an outstanding commercial success for Columbia, who owned majority stock in the musical. It held the number one chart position for 15 weeks and remained on the album chart for 480 weeks, or over nine years. The original cast recording of *Li'l Abner* also charted. Both of those were released by Columbia Records.

That was followed by the musicals *The Most Happy Fella*, *L'il Abner*, *Bells Are Ringing* and *Candide*. *Bells Are Ringing* was the first cast recording released in true stereo. *Candide* had a very brief run and many producers would not have bothered with it but Lieberson recorded it and, in the long run, it became a classic. A big winner was *West Side Story*, which Lieberson originally was not enthusiastic about but recorded it and that album reached number one on the *Billboard* album chart and remained there for 54 consecutive weeks; Columbia also did the film soundtrack for *West Side Story*. The film *The Ten Commandments* starring Charlton Heston debuted in October and the song, "Que Sera Sera (Whatever Will Be Will Be)" by Doris Day from the Alfred Hitchcock film, *The Man Who Knew Too Much*," was popular.

Goddard Lieberson and A Clash of Cultures

In June, 1956, Jim Conkling, president of Columbia Records, decided to retire from the label and move back to Los Angeles; Conkling and his wife disliked New York. He was replaced as president by Goddard Lieberson.

Columbia Records was a "Gentleman's Club" and Goddard Lieberson personified the urbane, sophisticated gentleman who had a deep commitment to classical music, produced Broadway musicals and served as an elegant, suave representative of Columbia Records. Many of the Columbia executives had backgrounds in classical music and thought of themselves as "Gentlemen."

Rock'n'roll did not fit into a Gentleman's Club and when rock hit full force in 1956, there was undisguised disdain for it, especially from Mitch Miller who was outspoken in his hatred of rock'n'roll. Although Miller, the head of A&R for Columbia, was an outspoken critic of rock'n'roll, Lieberson, who headed the classical division at Columbia, was more open-minded. Lieberson cared about his Masterworks division and knew that success in other genres would help support it.

Clare Booth Luce was a prominent author, playwright, politician and wife of Henry Luce, who owned the magazines *Time, Life* and *Fortune*. Luce was a strong conservative and anti-Communist who was Ambassador to Italy in 1955 when *Blackboard Jungle* was released. Luce threatened to boycott the Venice Film Festival if *Blackboard Jungle* was shown and urged Gordon Lieberson to mount a campaign against rock'n'roll.

A committee of powerful figures in the music industry was formed and Sammy Davis, Jr., asked Lieberson to join in condemning juvenile delinquency and its connection to rock'n'roll. Lieberson declined, stating that he had reservations that a committee of music industry heavyweights "to fight juvenile delinquency somehow conveys the idea of a tacit admission that music, and pop music in particular, is connected with juvenile delinquency. I emphatically do not believe this to be the case. Perhaps it is true that juvenile delinquents do like certain types of pop music extant, but I do not believe that music can contribute to juvenile delinquency. Anyone who has a scientific interest in the subject knows that the origins are much deeper and are rooted in the psychological, sociological, and economic foundations of the family unit. Therefore, a song entitled 'Don't Be a Juvenile Delinquent' is not going to stop juvenile delinquency any more than a song entitled 'Don't Have Cancer' is going to prevent cancer.'"

Columbia, as long as Mitch Miller was there, was never a rock'n'roll label. The prestige might not have been there for rock'n'roll, but there was a young audience willing to spend money buying 45s. RCA and other manufacturers provided small, lightweight phonographs that could be easily carried to someone's house for a night of playing rock'n'roll records.

Classical music and Broadway musicals provided high earnings per sale of LPs, but their sales would decrease as rock'n'roll took hold through the 1950s and into the 1960s.

Country Music Showdown

Some of the early ventures in Nashville's music business were started by employees of WSM, which owned the Grand Ole Opry. In August, 1955, WSM President Jack DeWitt sent a memo to employees that if they wished to remain with WSM, they needed to relinquish their outside interests. Jack Stapp, co-owner of Tree Publishing (which had published "Heartbreak Hotel") sold his interest to his partner, Lou Cowan, and the three engineers who had started Castle Recording Studio, George Reynolds, Carl Jenkins and Aaron Shelton, agreed to end their venture and stay with WSM. The hold-out was Jim Denny, who managed the Opry and booked Opry members on personal appearances and had a publishing company, Cedarwood. All of those involved in WSM, the Grand Ole Opry and the music industry in Nashville watched and waited for over a year to see the outcome of the DeWitt-Denny confrontation.

The big showdown occurred on September 24, 1956 when Jim Denny was called into DeWitt's office and fired. A few days later Denny called a meeting of the artists he represented and outlined his plans to establish an outside booking agency. The artists, whose income depended on their bookings, agreed to go with Denny. They knew and trusted Denny, and knew he could get them work; further, they were concerned about an inexperienced person being named to the Opry Artist Agency which would put their livelihoods in jeopardy.

The artists sent a telegram to DeWitt and told him of their plans; DeWitt's response was that if they went with Denny, there would be no Opry membership for them. However, Denny controlled about 70 percent of the top talent in country music and the Opry could not afford to lose them. The artists were obviously fraught and caught in a quandary; they did not want to lose their Opry affiliation but the Opry provided mainly exposure, and they had families to feed. Further, Jim Denny had negotiated with the Philip Morris Tobacco Company for a package tour of Opry acts while still employed at the Opry; the tobacco executives were impressed with Denny and decided to stay with him for the tour, even after he'd left WSM. The result was that Denny booked a hugely successful tour that lasted sixteen months and established his firm, The Jim Denny Agency, as the premier booking agency for country music. It also broke the back of the Opry's hold on country music in Nashville. After that point, the Opry would never be the dominant force in country music like it had been; now, there was outside competition. The way was now paved for independent entrepreneurs to set up shop and create a country music industry outside the Opry.

That was both a blessing and a curse in the events of 1955-1956. On one hand, this led to Nashville becoming a more diverse city with country music and broke the hold of the Opry. On the other hand, the success of Elvis and the rock revolution threatened country music. The Opry suffered declining attendance for a number of years, unable to attract new, young followers who went to rock instead. Radio stations that had programmed country switched to rock, the young artists who would have sung country now sung rock, and the audiences for country switched to rock. There was publishing money coming in which kept the industry alive. In fact, a number of the new young rock acts--such as Elvis, the Everly Brothers, Roy Orbison and others--had strong Nashville connections in publishing so the money from a number of early rock hits came back to Nashville.

Country Music's Identity Crisis

During the 1956-1958 period, country music suffered an identity crisis. The early rock'n'roll stars—Elvis, Carl Perkins, Johnny Cash, the Everly Brothers and Jerry Lee Lewis-- were white southerners and originally viewed as country artists. The music by those early rock'n'roll pioneers certainly had country roots but it did not sound like the country music of the late 1940s and early 1950s.

Elvis Presley was signed as a country act; he was a white southerner with a "country" background and his first *Billboard* chart records came on the country chart. In 1956, the chart compilers at *Billboard* still considered Elvis a country act in addition to his success on the Hot 100. During 1956, Elvis had number one country hits with "Heartbreak Hotel," "I Want You, I Need You, I Love You," "Don't Be Cruel" and "Hound Dog." Carl Perkins' hit, "Blue Suede Shoes" and Johnny Cash's "I Walk the Line" were also number one country hits on *Billboard* but those country hits did not *sound* like country music. It seemed like country music was being buried by rock'n'roll, although "Crazy Arms" by Ray Price was a major country hit. Marty Robbins' "Singing The Blues" sounded rock'n'roll as well, although Columbia covered that song with Guy Mitchell, who had the number one pop hit with it.

Elvis had appeared on the Grand Ole Opry, been a member of the "Louisiana Hayride" since 1954—a country music radio show based in Shreveport, Louisiana, and toured with country music musicians in "package shows." Until "Heartbreak Hotel" and the following hits, Elvis's core audience was country fans but his records did not sound like the country music of 1954 or 1955 when artists such as Webb Pierce, Jim Reeves, Eddy Arnold, Hank Snow, Carl Smith, Faron Young and Porter Wagoner dominated the charts.

The musical future of rock'n'roll was found primarily on the R&B charts in *Billboard* where there were number one hits by Little Richard ("Long Tall Sally" and "Rip It Up"), Fats Domino ("I'm In Love Again" and "Blueberry Hill"), the Platters ("The Great Pretender" and My Prayer"), Ray Charles ("Drown In My Own Tears") and Shirley and Lee ("Let the Good Times Roll"). However, the R&B charts were also a mixture with Elvis number ones with "Don't Be Cruel" and "Hound Dog."

Interestingly, a top ten hit in 1956 was "Rock Island Line" by British singer Lonnie Donegan. This "folk" music as called "Skiffle" in England and young skiffle bands were forming all over England, inspired by Lonnie Donegan and the craze for skiffle music. One of those skiffle bands, with members John Lennon, Paul McCartney and George Harrison, who later became The Beatles.

The Rock'n'Roll Tsunami

Rock'n'roll fully arrived with Elvis Presley in 1956. That year he sold ten million records and a force in American culture as preachers, parents and political leaders condemned him and rock'n'roll, linking it with juvenile delinquency. The generation who grew up during the Great Depression and served in World War II could not understand, much less accept, the appeal of rock'n'roll. The music industry establishment, particularly ASCAP songwriters, looked at rock'n'roll as the music of white trash and black trash.

The pop acts established before rock'n'roll did not do well; many lost their careers vitually overnight. Les Paul lamented that "People like me and Crosby were confused because everything we had learned was just thrown out the window." Paul, like many other pop acts, railed against the new sounds. "We were all big-band people," said Paul. "However, the sounds of big band, and the pop singers who dominated popular music 1945-1955 were suddenly out of style. Almost overnight, artists like Les Paul and Mary Ford were buried under the avalanche of rock'n'roll.

Pat Boone

Pat Boone (born June 1, 1934) is the whipping boy of every writer who ever wrote a history of rock'n'roll. Boone competed with Elvis on the pop charts and had more hits on the *Billboard* Hot 100 chart than Ricky Nelson, the Platters, Aretha Franklin and the Beach Boys, but he will never enter the Rock and Roll Hall of Fame.

Boone was a bridge between the era of the Big Band era singers like Bing Crosby, Frank Sinatra, Perry Como, Eddie Fisher and Tony Bennett and young rockers like Elvis, Buddy Holly, Gene Vincent and Eddie Cochran. Boone was one of the first artists to cover R&B songs and often had greater success on the pop charts than early R&B performers who originally recorded those songs. It did not help his legacy that his recordings of songs by Fats Domino ("Ain't That a Shame"), Little Richard ("Tutti Fruitti," "Long Tall Sally"), Ivory Joe Hunter ("I Almost Lost My Mind") , the Eldorados ("Crazy Little Mama") or Wynonie Harris ("Good Rockin' Tonight") were done in a more bland style that the rip it up R&B singers. Still, Boone was a bridge in the segregated world of 1950s America whose recordings of R&B songs allowed white radio stations to play them and white audiences to hear them when the original versions could not get on mainstream pop radio.

Other artists (Elvis, Ricky Nelson and, later, the Beatles and Rolling Stones) covered R&B songs but they dod not face the same ridicule and criticism as Boone, probably because their versions were more soulful. Boone may not have been a great vocalist for those early R&B covers, but the songs that fit his voice and image, such as "Friendly Persuasion," "Love Letters in the Sand," "April Love" and "It's Too Soon to Know," were hits during the 1955-1958 period of early rock'n'roll and show a great singer with the right material.

Boone's first recordings with Republic Records in 1954 did not chart but when he signed with Dot Records his first releases, "Two Hearts," "Ain't That a Shame" (which reached number one on the pop chart), "At My Front Door (Crazy Little Mama,)" and "Gee Whittakers" all charted in 1955. During 1956 he had chart records with "I'll Be Home," "Tutti Fruitti" (number 12), "Long Tall Sally" (number 8), "I Almost Lost My Mind"

(Number 1 for four weeks), "Friendly Persuasion" (number 5) and "Chains of Love" (number 10) were all competitors to Elvis's releases.

Boone's success with the covers of R&B songs encouraged other Big Band-type singers to record R&B covers, which allowed more listeners of pop radio the chance to hear those songs; acts such as the Crewcuts, Doris Day and Frank Sinatra all covered R&B songs and the publishers and songwriters of those songs generally benefitted.

Boone was shunned by the rock'n'roll crowd for his clean-cut image in the era of rock'n'roll rebellion but a survey of high school students in 1957 preferred him two to one over Elvis with boys and three to one over Elvis with girls. Pat Boone was "safe" in an era that we look back on and celebrate the wild and reckless. Boone was also an outcast from the rock'n'rollers because of his strong religious beliefs, his conservative political beliefs and his embrace of the traditional family. In short, Pat Boone has not been given his due as a bridge between black and white music with rock historians because of politics and religion.

Boone's label, Dot Records, founded by Randy Wood, was responsible for Boone recording so many R&B hits. Wood was a record retailer and saw first hand that R&B songs sold to a black audience when sung by a black performer and then sold to a white audience when covered by a white performer. It was good business for a label to make records that sold and Wood did a great job of this during the mid-1950s.

Dot Records and Pat Boone

Dot artist Johnny Maddox first heard Pat Boone at West End High School in Nashville in 1952 when Maddox played for a school assembly that featured student Pat Boone singing pop songs. Randy Wood wanted to record him for Dot, but Boone was signed to Republic Records at the time.

Boone and his family moved to Denton, Texas, where he intended to enroll at North Texas State University. By that point, Boone had won the *Ted Mack Amateur Hour* TV show contest three times and then won the *Arthur Godfrey's Talent Scouts* show contest. Stopping in Nashville, Boone met Randy Wood through disc jockey Hugh Cherry and agreed to record for Dot.

In January 1955, Pat Boone's first release was "Two Hearts"/"Tra La La," the latter a cover of an R&B hit by the Griffins, which had been released on Dot. Boone recorded it in Chicago. In June, Dot released "Ain't That a Shame," an R&B hit for Fats Domino, backed with "Tennessee Saturday Night," which had been a country hit for Red Foley. In January 1956, Boone covered Little Richard's "Tutti Fruitti" for Dot, and that record—a sanitized version of Little Richard's release--sold over a million records. In April, Boone covered Little Richard's "Long Tall Sally."

During 1955-1959, Pat Boone had a string of hits that included the number one hits "I Almost Lost My Mind," "Love Letters in the Sand," "April Love," and "Moody River." During his career on Dot, Pat Boone had sixty-five chart records on the *Billboard* Hot 100.

Dot Records also had pop hits with the Fontane Sisters in 1955, who covered the R&B hit "Hearts of Stone" and Gail Storm, whose hit "I Hear You Knocking" was a cover of the R&B hit by Smiley Lewis. In 1955, Johnny Maddox's record of "Crazy Otto Blues" sold over two million units.

Randy Wood had success selling R&B music during his early years with Randy's Record Shop and Dot Records, but he preferred "middle-of-the-road" music because it appealed to a wider audience.

Dot Moves to Hollywood

Randy Wood hosted a dinner at the Hermitage Hotel in Nashville on July 6, 1956, to celebrate Pat Boone's success and announced that Dot Records was moving to Los Angeles. Wood, feeling that Nashville was limited as a recording center, had opened offices in New York and Hollywood in 1955. He had wanted to sell Dot to a movie company, but the film executives who visited Gallatin, Tennessee, were not impressed with his shoestring operation. In 1957, after the move to Los Angeles, Randy Wood sold Dot Records to Paramount Pictures for around $3 million and was named president of the label.

Little Richard

Little Richard (born Richard Penniman on December 5, 1932) grew up in Macon, Georgia in a religious family; his father was a church deacon and owned a night club and his mother sang in the New Hope Baptist Church. He first sang in church and his early influences were gospel performers Sister Rosetta Tharpe, Mahalia Jackson, Marion Williams and Brother Joe May, a singing evangelist. In high school he learned to play the saxophone.

Little Richard's first significant public performance was in October, 1947 when he opened a gospel concert for Sister Rosetta Tharpe at the Macon City Auditorium. Tharpe had heard the 14-year old sing two of her songs before the concert and invited him to sing on stage. He did, the crowd cheered and he was hooked on performing. He sang with shows that visited Macon and then, in 1948, joined Dr. Hudson's Medicine Show where he sang Louis

Jordan's hit, "Caldonia," the first secular song he sang. His deeply religious family had banned rhythm and blues music from their home.

After the medicine show he joined Buster Brown's Orchestra where he began calling himself "Little Richard." He sang with the band until 1950 when he joined vaudeville groups Sugarfoot Sam from Alabam, the Tidy Jolly Stepper & the King Brothers Circus and Broadway Follies where he performed in drag. In Atlanta, he saw Roy Brown and Billy Wright perform, then performed on the "Chitlin Circuit" where, in 1951, he was introduced to Zenas Sears, an Atlanta disc jockey who managed Billy Wright. Sears recorded Little Richard at the radio station's studio, which led to a contract with RCA; his first single, "Every Hour," was a local hit. Little Richard then toured with Perry Welch and his Orchestra and learned to play boogie-woogie piano from Esquerita. In February, 1952, he was dropped by RCA. That month his father was killed outside his nightclub.

Needing money, Little Richard worked as a dishwasher for Greyhound Lines, hired Clint Brantley as his manager and formed a band, The Tempo Toppers, that performed on blues package tours. The Temp Toppers signed with Peacock Records, owned by Don Robey, in February 1953 but none of those recordings were released. Little Richard had confrontations with Robey, disbanded the Temp Toppers and left Peacock, then formed the Upsetters, an R&B band that was booked by Brantley. Singer Lloyd Price was with Specialty Records and encouraged Little Richard to send a demo to Art Rupe, head of Specialty. Rupe liked the recordings and lent Little Richard the money to buy his way out of the Peacock contract and put him in the studio with producer Robert "Bumps" Blackwell.

Little Richard began recording with session musicians who backed Fats Domino in New Orleans at the J&M Studios owned by Cosimo Matassa, The first session did not go well so the musicians took a break and Little Richard and Blackwell went to the Dew Drop Inn where Little Richard sang "Tutti Fruitti," a risque song that began with an a cappella vocal that resembled a drum opening and then the lyrics "tutti fruitti, good booty." Blackwell loved the sound but knew the song could not be released to the public so he hired songwriter Dorothy LaBostrie to provide some replacement lyrics. "Tutti Frutti" was recorded in three takes and released in November, 1955 and entered the *Billboard* pop chart in January, 1956, around the same time Elvis was recording "Heartbreak Hotel" in Nashville.

"Tuitti Frutti" reached number two on *Billboard's* Rhythm and Blues chart (and remained there for six weeks) and number 17 on the pop chart.

The follow up single, "Long Tall Sally," entered the R&B chart in April and rose to number one, where it remained for eight weeks; it reached number eight on the pop chart. A string of hits followed in 1956, all produced by Bumps Blackwell, including "Slippin and Sliddin'," "Rip It Up," "Ready Teddy," "Heebby Jebbies" and "The Girl Can't Help It" in 1956 and "Lucille," "Send Me Some Lovin'," "Jenny, Jenny," "Keep on Knockin'" in 1957 and "Good Golly, Miss Molly" in 1958.

Little Richard toured with his high energy, explosive performances on stage, playing piano while standing up and attracting white as well as black audiences.

Technology, Business and Politics

The year 1956 was a leap year, which meant that the Olympics were held in Italy (winter), Melbourne and Stockholm (summer). On television, the peacock made its debut on the NBC network while the DuMont Network, formed in 1946 and at one time a serious competitor to NBC and CBS, went out of business.

In technology, the videotape machine, developed by Ampex, was first demonstrated in April at the broadcasters convention in Chicago. The first snooze alarm clock was put on the market, IBM developed the first hard drive and, at the end of June, President Eisenhower signed the Federal Highway Act which created the Interstate system. That network of roads would benefit tourists as well as musicians in the coming yeara but it was funded by the Department of Defense and a key reason for building it was national defense: in case of war, troops and military equipment could be moved quickly across the country so the original four lanes were constructed so planes could land on them.

The Nobel Prize for Physics was awarded to William Shockley, John Bardeen and Walter Houser Brattain for their work developing the transistor and research on semi-conductors.

"In God We Trust" became the national motto in July and in October the Yankees beat the Brooklyn Dodgers in the World Series where Yankee pitcher Don Larsen threw a perfect game.

The poem "Howl" was written by Allen Ginsberg and published by City Lights Press, part of the City Lights Bookstore in San Francisco owned by Lawrence Ferlinghetti. That led to an obscenity trial ("Howl" was eventually declared to be not obscene and later became an American classic). Ginsberg was part of a group of writers in the "Beat Generation" and their members and followers became known as "Beatniks."

It was an election year in 1956 and the presidential race was a rematch between Dwight Eisenhower and Adlai Stevenson. On November 6, voters re-elected Eisenhower and the "Eisenhower era" continued through the end of the 1950s.

Civil Rights

The Supreme Court ruled the doctrine of "separate but equal" had no place in education, that separate meant inherently unequal in 1954 when it handed down its ruling in the Brown v. Board of Education suit. That ended the legal legitimacy of segregation, but it did not end segregation right away; however, it did begin a decade of turmoil and violence connected to Civil Rights.

The Southern states had been spending twice as much to educate white children, and four times as much for white school facilities, as they had for black children. There was basically no transportation for black children to and from school and the salaries of black teachers were approximately 30 percent lower than their white counterparts. At the college level, Southern states spent $5 million on black colleges while they spent $86 million on white colleges. The Southern political establishment kept blacks from voting through a poll tax; in the presidential election of 1940, only 2.5 percent of the black population in the deep South voted.

In August, 1955, Emmett Till, a 14-year old African American from Chicago visiting relatives in Tallahatchie County, Mississippi, was killed for allegedly talking "fresh" with Carolyn White, a 21-year old white woman. Her husband, Roy Bryant, with his friend, J. W. Milam, took Till into the woods, stripped him, shot him, and threw him in the river. That murder made national news and brought the code of Southern segregation into American living rooms via graphic pictures in the print media.

In 1956, Central High School in Little Rock, Arkansas was scheduled to become integrated for the first time but Governor Orval Faubus called out the Arkansas National Guard to stop the integration; that forced President Eisenhower to federalize the National Guard and call in the Army's 101st Airborne to protect the African-American students. That, too, became another turning point in the struggle for Civil Rights.

It was the practice of buses in Montgomery, Alabama, to require blacks to sit in the back and whites to sit up front; further, if a white person got on and there was no seat, a black was required to give up his/her seat for the white rider. On December 1, 1955, a 42-year old seamstress, Rosa Parks, was riding home on a city bus in Montgomery. When the driver ordered her to get up from her seat and move further back, she had reached the limits to her endurance and simply refused. That incident sparked the Montgomery Bus Boycott, which brought the first national fame to Reverend Martin Luther King, the 26-year old pastor of the Dexter Avenue Baptist Church who had been in Montgomery for 15 months.

King was arrested and his home was bombed in 1956 but, as he stated, "There comes a time when time itself is ready for a change." That time had come.

The Montgomery Bus Boycott lasted until November 13, 1956 when the Supreme Court ruled that segregated city buses were illegal. In May of that year, 96 Congressmen signed a "Southern Manifesto" protesting the Brown vs. Board of Education decision.

Elvis and Race

Racial tensions during 1956 were a major reason for the backlash against Elvis and rock'n'roll. Elvis became not just a singer, but a threat to white middle class American culture. His stage movements were considered sexual by many and the fact rock'n'roll contained musical roots in Rhythm and Blues led to accusations that rock'n'roll caused juvenile delinquency, viewed as a major national threat during that time.

Girls did not just applaud when Elvis sang; they screamed and fainted. Whenever and wherever Elvis performed, it was pandemonium. He made TV appearances on The Steve Allen Show, the Milton Merle Show and the Ed Sullivan Show before huge TV audiences.

On Wednesday, November 21, Elvis's' first movie, *Love Me Tender*, was released nationally; it broke box office records in Memphis and elsewhere. The next day, Elvis began a series of performances, first in Toledo, Ohio, then Cleveland, Troy, Ohio and on Sunday, November 25 at the Jefferson County Armory in Louisville. The next day he drove back from Louisville to Memphis, where he dropped into a Loew's theater for a matinee showing of *Love Me Tender*.

On Monday, December 3, Elvis bought a new 1957 two-door hardtop Eldorado Cadillac Seville for $8,400. The next day, driving around with his current girlfriend Marilyn Evans, Elvis stopped by the Sun Records studio where he first went into the control room and spoke with Sam Phillips, then listened to a playback of "Matchbox," a song that had just been recorded by Carl Perkins. Perkins had recorded the song with his band, comprised of brothers Jay and Clayton with W.S. "Fluke" Holland on drums and a new

Sun artist, Jerry Lee Lewis, on piano. Jerry Lee's first single on Sun would soon be released.

Elvis went into the studio, sat down at the piano and began singing, with Perkins and Jerry Lee joining in on old gospel and country songs. Johnny Cash was called and he stopped by. Engineer Jack Clement had the presence of mind to record the session which became known as the "Million Dollar Quartet."

In the News

In Moscow, Soviet Premier Nikita Khrushchev told Western diplomats "Whether you like it or not, history is on our side. We will bury you."

There were 7,000 drive-in movie theaters across the country, three times as many as there were in 1950. In 1956, 11percent of cars sold were station wagons.

The problem of juvenile delinquency plagued the nation. It was reported that, in New York City, half the thieves arrested were under 21 while in Los Angeles, police reported that 20 percent of crimes were committed by teenagers. A majority of auto thefts in larger cities was attributed to youth. A book, *The Juvenile Offender in America Today* by professors at Brookely College and the University of Chicago attempted to explain the reasons for juvenile delinquency. Among the reasons they cited were endocrine glands, comic books. broken homes, the media and movies. The film *Rebel Without a Cause* was cited as an instigator of crime.

1957
Rock'n'Roll and 45s

Rock'n'roll was a singles business; the hits were on 45s. Albums were for grown-ups and successful albums were from Broadway musicals or acts such as Johnny Mathis and Harry Belafonte. The single 45s were for teenagers and the technology for teens was the portable record player sold by RCA Victor in 1957 for $39.95. These small, lightweight players could be closed and carried from gathering to gathering.

Stereo benefited from standardization enforced by the RIAA, which established a uniform recording curve that assured all LPs would sound good on all record players.

The success of Elvis and other rock'n'rollers in 1956 inspired young artists to become rock stars and labels signed them, trying to copy the success of Elvis. One of the first to emerge in 1957 was Ricky Nelson.

Ricky Nelson

Ricky Nelson was born (May 8, 1940) into a show business family. His father, Ozzie, was a Big Band leader and his mother, Harriet, was a Big Band singer; he had an older brother, David. The family moved from Teaneck, New Jersey to Hollywood and first appeared on Red Skelton's radio show, "The Raleigh Cigarette House" and, after Skelton was drafted, the show's producer created "The Ozzie and Harriet Show," which first went on the air on 1944. In 1949, Ricky and his brother, David, made their debut on the show; their roles were previously played by child actors. "The Adventures of Ozzie and Harriett Show" then went to television where it was a popular sitcom beginning October, 1952; the show lasted until September, 1966.

Ricky Nelson loved the artists on Sun Records and was especially influenced by Carl Perkins. In 1957, 17-year-old Ricky began his recording career; his first chart single was "A Teenager's Romance," followed by a cover of a Fats Domino song, "I'm Walking," then "Be-Bop Baby" and "Stood Up," which were all top five records in 1957. On "The Ozzie ad Harriet Show" the family played themselves and Ricky generally sang a song on each episode. His first number one record in *Billboard* came in 1958 with "Poor Little Fool."

Guided by his father, Ozzie, Nelson had creative control over song selection, artwork and other details in his career. His first album, Ricky was released in October, 1957 and reached the number one position on *Billboard's* album chart before the end of the year.

At the end of 1958 Nelson formed his first band, which featured 18-year old James Burton on lead guitar, James Kirkland on bass, Richie Frost on drums and Gene Garf on piano. During his early recording sessions, Joe Maphis played lead guitar.

Ricky Nelson promoted his records, produced by Jimmy Haskell, through regular appearances on "The Adventures of Ozzie and Harriet" television show.

Sam Cooke

Sam Cooke's (born January 22, 1931) roots were in gospel music. He was born in Clarksdale, Mississippi, the fifth of eight children, to Reverend Charles Cook, minister of the Church of Christ (Holiness) and Annie Mae Cook. In 1933 the family moved to Chicago where he began singing with his brothers and sisters as The Singing Children. He joined the Highway QC's as lead singer at the age of 14 and in 1950 joined The Soul Stirrers, where he replaced lead singer R.H. Harris. The group was signed to Specialty Records, owned by Art Rupe. During his time with the Soul Stirrers he recorded "Jesus Gave Me Water," "Peace in the Valley" and "How Far Am I From Canaan?" as well as others.

Gospel singers were not supposed to sing secular music so Cooke recorded his first secular single, "Loveable" under the name Dale Cook in order not to alienate his (and The Soul Stirrers) gospel audience. Art Rupe was upset with Bumps Blackwell for producing a secular song on Sam Cooke and fired Blackwell.

Bumps Blackwell, Keen Records and Sam Cooke

Robert "Bumps" Blackwell began his career in Seattle, Washington, leading a jazz band that included Ray Charles on piano and Quincy Jones on trumpet. He moved to Los Angeles and became head of A&R for Specialty Records and produced Little Richard's hits.

As part of the separation from Specialty, Blackwell was allowed to keep the masters he recorded on Cooke. Blackwell took the masters to Keen Records, an independent label started in April, 1957, by aerospace industry executive John Siamas and his brother, Alex, as a side business. Keen released "You Send Me," which entered the *Billboard* Hot 100 chart on October 21, 1957 and remained in the number one position for three consecutive weeks. That was followed by a string of chart records on Keen that included ""Only Sixteen" and "Wonderful World" before he signed with RCA in 1960.

Bumps Blackwell joined Mercury in 1959 and produced Little Richard's gospel albums and then became his manger.

The Everly Brothers

The Everly Brothers, Don (born February 1, 1937) and Phil (born January 19, 1939) were the sons of Ike Everly, a fingerpicking guitarist whose style influenced Merle Travis and Chet Atkins. The family lived in Shenandoah, Iowa where Ike had a radio show with his wife and sons. In 1953 they moved to Knoxville, where they met Chet Atkins and in 1955 moved to Nashville. Atkins arranged for the Everly Brothers to record for Columbia but they had no success.

Chet Atkins then introduced them to Wesley Rose, head of Acuff-Rose Publishing, where they signed as songwriters. Rose introduced them to Archie Bleyer with Cadence Records, who was looking for young talent for the teenage market. In February, 1957, they recorded "Bye, Bye Love," written by Acuff-Rose songwriters Felice and Boudleaux Bryant; that song entered the *Billboard* pop chart in May and was followed by "Wake Up Little Susie" and "All I Have to Do Is Dream," both number one hits written by the Bryants.

The Everly's had a string of hits on Cadence, including "Bird Dog," "Devoted to You," "Till I Kissed You," "Let It Be Me," and "When Will I Be Loved" before they signed with Warner Brothers in 1960.

During 1957 and 1958 the Everlys toured with Buddy Holly.

Buddy Holly

Buddy Holly (born September 7, 1936) grew up in Lubbock, Texas in a musical family; he loved the music of Hank Williams, Hank Snow, Jimmie Rodgers, Bob Wills and his Texas Playboys, the Louvin Brothers and the Carter Family. Holly and Bob Montgomery joined forces as "Buddy and Bob" and performed on KDAV in 1953 and were influenced by rhythm and blues. Inspired by an early performance of Elvis Presley in Lubbock, Holly opened for Elvis during a performance in October, 1955 and then for Bill Haley and the Comets, where he was seen by Eddie Crandall, a manager who contacted Jim Denny, manager of the Grand Ole Opry to seek a recording contract. At that time his band consisted of Larry Welborne on bass and J. I. Allison on drums.

Pappy Dave Stone, a DJ at KDAV who booked Elvis and Bill Haley in Lubbock, sent a tape of Holly to Jim Denny, who forwarded it to Paul Cohen, head of the country division of Decca, who signed Holly (misspelling his original name, Holley) in February 1956. Holly's first recording session was produced by Owen Bradley in Nashville. Two singles, "Blue Days, Black Nights" and "Modern Don Juan" were released and Denny booked him as an opening act for some country artists but neither record hit so in January, 1957, Holly was dropped from the label.

Holly contacted Norman Petty in Clovis, New Mexico, who had produced "Party Doll" by Buddy Knox and "I'm Stickin' With You" by Jimmy Bowen. Holly, on lead guitar, with bassist Joe B. Mauldin, rhythm guitarist Niki Sullivan and drummer J.I. Allison went into Petty's studio and recorded "That'll Be the Day"; Petty sent the tape to Brunswick Records in New York. Holly had recorded "That'll Be the Day" during his Nashville sessions and, under his contract, could not release any of the songs he had recorded for Decca for five years, which meant that releases from Holly would be released as a band name, "The Crickets." The label released the demo of "That'll Be the Day"; it entered the *Billboard* pop chart in August,

1957 and became a number one hit. That was followed by "Oh, Boy" later that year and then, in 1958, the Crickets released "Oh, Boy" and then "Maybe Baby," "Think It Over," and "Fool's Paradise" in 1958. "Peggy Sue" was released as a record by Buddy Holly in 1957; this was followed by "Rave On" and "Early in the Morning" in 1958. An album, *The Chirping Crickets* was released in November, 1957; on December 1 Holly and the Crickets performed "That'll Be the Day" and "Peggy Sue" on The Ed Sullivan Show.

Buddy Holly died, along with Richie Valens and J.P. Richardson ("The Big Bopper") in an airplane crash on February 3, 1959 outside Mason City, Iowa.

Country Music: 1957

Country music responded to the onslaught of rock'n'roll by developing "The Nashville Sound." There are several definitions of the Nashville Sound. For musicians, the Nashville Sound meant recording using "head arrangements" instead of sheet music. A group of Nashville studio musicians, who became known as "The A Team," were talented and versatile and became adept at hearing a song for the first time in the studio, creating an arrangement and then recording it; they usually recorded four songs during a three hour session. Another definition came when someone jingled coins in his pocket for Chet Atkins, telling him "that's the Nashville Sound." It was profitable.

The final definition was a musical one. It meant that country music increasingly eschewed the fiddle and steel guitar for violins and a piano, creating a much "smoother" sound, akin to the pop music of the late 1940s and early 1950s.

In 1957 there were several "crossover" hits recorded in Nashville that fit the idea of the Nashville Sound. Early in the year, "Young Love" by Sonny James reached number one on both the country and Hot 100 in *Billboard*. Later in the year, "Gone" by Ferlin Husky reached number one on the country chart—and remained there for ten weeks—and reached number four on the pop chart. On that song, producer Ken Nelson with Capitol added a female singer to a male quartet, which inspired Elvis to do the same, adding soprano Millie Kirkham to the Jordanaires to create a unique sound.

Bobby Helm had "Fraulein" and "My Special Angel" in 1957, both were number one (for four weeks) on the country chart and crossed over (number 36 and number 7, respectively) to the pop chart.

The best example of the Nashville Sound in 1957 was "Four Walls" by Jim Reeves. That record, produced by Chet Atkins, featured smooth voiced Jim

Reeves backed by the Anita Kerr Singers. The song was number one on the country chart for eight weeks and reached number 11 on *Billboard's* pop chart.

All three of those songs were recorded in Nashville with "A Team" musicians.

Country music was still plagued by the sound of rock'n'roll replacing a more country oriented sound on the country chart; during 1957, "All Shook Up" by Elvis was a number one record on the country chart and "A White Sport Coat (And a Pink Carnation)" by Marty Robbins was number one country and number two on the pop chart; it was produced by Mitch Miller in New York.

Although the Nashville music industry struggled to keep its rural country image, during the 1950s there were a number of rock'n'roll hits recorded there. In addition to the early hits by Elvis, "Be-Bop-A-Lula" by Gene Vincent was recorded in Bradley's basement studio, Buddy Holly recorded several sessions in Nashville, although there were no hits, and the album, *Johnny Burnette and the Rock'n'Roll Trio*, a landmark rockabilly album, was recorded in Nashville.

The perennially favorite Christmas songs, "Rockin' Around the Christmas Tree" by Brenda Lee and "Jingle Bell Rock" by Bobby Helm were both recorded in Nashville.

Chet Atkins and RCA's Studio in Nashville

In November, 1957, Chet Atkins was named Operations Manager of RCA's Nashville office when Steve Sholes was promoted to head RCA's pop singles division after the success of Elvis. Atkins had been playing on recording sessions for Shoals and, as Sholes recognized Atkins ability as a session leader, he began hiring him to set up studio time and organize recording sessions when Sholes came to Nashville. When Sholes could not come, Atkins produced the sessions.

A studio built especially for RCA was opened in late October on Music Row at the corner of 17th Avenue South and Hawkins, just a block west of Owen Bradley's studio. The establishment of Chet Atkins as "Operations Manager" for RCA in Nashville meant that RCA was the first major label to establish a permanent office in Nashville.

In the News

The Soviet Union was winning the space race; they launched two Sputnik satellites in 1957 while an American rocket exploded on the launching pad in Cape Canaveral.

In September the first compact car, the Rambler, was manufactured by the American Motor Company. Also in September, the first underground nuclear tests by the United States began.

On May 2, former Senator Joseph McCartney died; it was announced that the American Communist Party was in decline.

Congress passed a Civil Rights Act on August 29 after Senator Strom Thurmond of South Carolina filibustered for 24 hours and 18 minutes, the longest personal filibuster in history. The Act, which had been proposed by President Eisenhower the year before, allowed the Justice Department to bring suits on behalf of Negro voters who were denied the right to vote. It also established a commission to obtain facts, suggest future legislation and amend the U.S. Code to affirm the right to vote or sit on a jury regardless of race, color or previous condition of servitude.

Arkansas Governor Orval Faubus attempted to stop the integration of Little Rock High School in September but President Eisenhower called out 10,000 Arkansas National Guardsmen and 1,000 paratroopers to assure integration. About a thousand whites stood outside the school after the soldiers left, taunting the students and threatening to lynch them. The mob remained for two days until, at the insistence of the black community, Federal troops returned to provide protection.

1958
Elvis: 1958

In 1958 Elvis's pop chart hits were "(You're So Square) Baby I Don't Care," "Don't," "I Beg of You," Wear My Ring (Around Your Neck), "Doncha Think Its Time," "Hard Headed Woman," "Don't Ask Me Why" and "One Night."

In March, 1958, Elvis was inducted into the Army. After boot camp, and prior to advanced training (in tanks), Elvis went to Nashville and recorded "I Need Your Love Tonight," "A Big Hunk O'Love," "Ain't That Loving You Baby?," "A Fool Such as I" and "I Got Stung," which were released during the next two years while Elvis was out of the country, serving in Germany. Many considered it a miracle and example of excellent management that Colonel Tom Parker managed to keep his records on the radio and Elvis in the public eye during that period.

Harry Belafonte

Harry Belafonte popularized Caribbean flavored folk songs, beginning with his hit, "Jamaica Farewell" in 1956.

Harold George Bellafanti Jr. was born in Harlem New York (March 1, 1927); his parents were both mixed race (white and black) and born in Jamaica. Belafonte lived in Jamaica from 1932 to 1940 then returned to New York City and, after high school, joined the Navy and served during World War II. After seeing a production at the American Negro Theater and meeting actor Sidney Poitier, the two regularly saw plays at the Theater. Belafonte took acting classes at the Dramatic Workshop of The New School in New York and performed in plays at the American Negro Theater.

In order to pay for his acting classes, Belafonte became a club singer of pop songs. He recorded for the Roost label in 1949 but then developed an interest in folk music and learned material through the Library of Congress American folk song archives. Accompanied by guitarist Millard Thomas, Belafonte began singing at The Village Vanguard, a legendary jazz club. He signed with RCA Victor in 1952 and his first single was "Mathilda." In 1956 he had two albums that reached number one on the *Billboard* album chart. His album *Belafonte* entered the chart on February 25 and remained number one for six weeks and remained on the chart for 61 weeks. His album *Calypso* entered the album chart on June 16 and reached number one where it remained for 31 consecutive weeks and remained on the chart for 99 weeks. The *Calypso* album introduced American audiences to calypso music, which originated in Trinidad and Tobago. On that album were "Jamaica Farwell" and "Banana Boat (Day-O)."

Those albums were followed by *An Evening With Belafonte* and *Belafonte Sings of the Caribbean*, both released in 1957 that reached number two and number three on the charts respectively. Harry Belafonte became known as a singer of Caribbean and folk songs and his albums were top sellers.

In "Jamaica Farewell," Belafonte sang that he "had to leave a little girl in Kingston Town." Kingston, the capitol of Jamaica, inspired a folk group to name themselves "The Kingston Trio."

Folk Music

The Urban Folk movement began when the Kingston Trio released "Tom Dooley" in September, 1958; it reached number one on the *Billboard* pop charts and remained on the charts for 21 weeks after its debut in September of that year and was awarded a Grammy for "Best Country and Western Recording" at the first Grammy Awards in May, 1959.

The "unofficial" beginning of folk music dates back to the European and African cultures--particularly the British culture--and the ancestors of colonial Americans. Old songs and stories were passed by oral tradition from generation to generation and those songs and stories were brought to this country by the early settlers. Once in this country, those old stories and songs continued to be told and sung, sometimes with changes in the lyrics, sometimes with new lyrics, sometimes with changes in the melodies. Those traditions remained part of the "folk" who continued to pass them along.

In some parts of this country, particularly the Appalachian areas of southern Virginia, east Tennessee, western North Carolina, some of those old songs remained virtually the same as when they arrived, a product of the fact that those mountainous areas were isolated, with few outside visitors and entertainment provided by natives who played and sang those songs like their parents, grandparents and great-grandparents. Early recording pioneers recorded many of those old songs and singers and preserved them. Those were generally called "hillbilly" songs at the time, since rural, white Southerners recorded them, and they provided the first examples of commercial country music.

Commercial country music became "Country and Western" and then "Country Music," adding instruments to make a full sound with harmony vocals, and corporate marketing. Bluegrass music stayed closer to the traditional folk music, using old songs and traditional acoustic instruments like the banjo, guitar and fiddle, but what became known as "folk" music ventured into other areas in the 1930s, namely songs of the radical left.

As unions were being organized, there was singing involved and the music was usually "folk" music, using new lyrics to old melodies for a cause or function.

Folk music has often been a political music. It is a lyric-oriented music and the lyrics tended to lean left, embracing civil rights, gender equality and labor rights.

Along the way, a critical distinction arose between folk music and its offshoots like country and bluegrass. The distinction: folk music is generally a music a performer sings with an audience while country and other types of music is a music a performer sings to an audience. In folk, the audience is part of the performance; in country (and most other commercial music) the audience is passive.

The Kingston Trio

The origins of the Kingston Trio began with Dave Guard and Bob Shane, who were friends in junior high school in Honolulu, Hawaii, where they performed as a duo at local functions. After high school, Guard enrolled in Stanford University and Shane enrolled at Menlo College, where he became friends with Nick Reynolds, who played guitar and knew a lot of folk songs. Eventually, the three came together and began performing at various functions as "Dave Guard and the Calypsonians."

After college, Shane returned to Hawaii but Guard and Reynolds remained in the San Francisco area and formed "The Kingston Quartet" with bassist Joe Gannon and vocalist Barbara Bogue. They met Frank Weber, who agreed to manage them with the condition that the group drop Gannon. Guard and Reynolds agreed and Bogue left with Gannon; they then invited Shane to re-join the group. In February, 1957, Shane returned to San Francisco and the group decided on the name "Kingston Trio" because it was associated with the popular calypso music and Kingston, Jamaica.

The group entered into intensive rehearsals and vocal training and in June, 1957, obtained a week-long engagement at The Purple Onion, a small club in San Francisco after comedienne Phyllis Diller cancelled her engagement. Weber and the group promoted the engagement by inviting everyone they knew to come and put up posters throughout the city; the engagement was a success and the Kingston Trio played for six months at the Purple Onion. In early 1958 Weber booked them into clubs in Chicago, New York, Boston and the Hungry I in San Francisco. They signed with Capitol Records and their first album, *The Kingston Trio*, was released in June, 1958. The album sold well but Salt Lake City DJ Paul Colburn began playing "Tom Dooley" from the album, which led Capitol to release a single of that song in August, 1958.

The song was based on the murder of Laura Foster by Tom Dula in Wilkes County, North Carolina in 1866. (Dula was pronounced Dooley.) Dula was convicted of her murder and hung on May 1, 1886; shortly after the hanging, local poet Thomas Land wrote a song about the murder. Dula was a Confederate veteran who had been the lover of Anne Foster, Laura's cousin, before the Civil War. During the War, Anne married and became Anne Foster Melton; however, after the war she became Dula's lover again before he became Laura Foster's lover. Laura and her unborn baby were killed by a large knife and, although Dula was convicted and hung, there was speculation that Anne Foster Melton, in a jealous rage, had actually killed Laura.

The song was first recorded by Grayson and Whitter in 1929; it was later recorded by Frank Proffitt and Frank Warner. The Kingston Trio learned the song from Warner's recording.

In late November, it was number one on the *Billboard* Hot 100 chart and their debut album also reached number one and was certified "Gold."

That album remained on *Billboard's* pop album chart for 195 weeks; their follow-up album, *From the Hungry I*, was on the album chart for 178 weeks and their third album, *The Kingston Trio At Large*, released in 1959, held the number one position on the pop album charts for 15 consecutive weeks and remained on the chart for 118 weeks.

The Kingston Trio had a succession of singles, including "Raspberries, Strawberries," "The Tijuana Jail," "M.T.A.," "Where Have All the Flowers Gone," "Scotch and Soda," "Reverend Mr. Black" and "Last Night I Had the Strangest Dream" but none, except "Reverend Mr. Black," cracked the top ten on the singles chart. However, their albums were consistent top sellers. Their fourth album, *Here We Go Again!* held the number one position for eight weeks; *Sold Out* remained number one for 12 weeks and *String Along* was number one on the *Billboard* album chart for ten consecutive weeks. In December, 1959, there were four Kingston Trio albums in the top ten of the *Billboard* pop album chart and the group accounted for 15 percent of Capitol's sales.

James Conkling

James Conkling was a major executive in the record industry during the late 1940s and throughout the 1950s. Conkling was with Capitol during the 1940s, and founded their two publishing companies Blackwood Music (BMI) and Ardmore Music (ASCAP) before succeeding Ed Wallerstein as President of Columbia Records.

Conkling was born in 1915 in East Orange, New Jersey and graduated from Dartmouth, where he majored in Economics with a minor in Political Science. At Dartmouth, he played trumpet in the college's Barbary Coast Orchestra; during the summers, Conkling played trumpet with a band on cruise ships.

During World War II, Conkling received a medical discharge and was hired at Capitol by Paul Weston in 1943; the 29 year old produced Stan Kenton and other acts. Conkling stayed at Capitol for seven years, then joined Columbia Records in 1951 where, at the age of 36, he became president of that label.

When the Recording Industry Association of America (RIAA) was formed in 1952 Conkling was elected its first President. In 1956, at the age of 41, Conkling retired and moved back to California. The following year, he was a founding member of the National Association of Recording Arts and Sciences (NARAS), which created the Grammy Awards.

The Creation of Warner Brothers Records

Television scared the movie industry, which lost ticket buyers to the TV set. In 1956, Warner Brothers sold it's entire pre-1948 library of movies--784 features and 1,800 shorts--to Elliott Hyman, president of Seven Arts and Associated Artist Productions, which licensed movies to TV networks, who were desperate for cheap entertainment to fill the airwaves.

The financiers of Warner Brothers, Charles Allen and Serge Semenenko, who extended the company credit, joined the Board of Directors in 1956 and urged the Warner brothers to sell their company. Harry Warner, president of the studio, was 75 years old, Abe, the treasurer, was a few years younger, and the bankers thought the company needed new blood. Harry Warner was reluctant to sell, but finally agreed if all three Warners sold their shares and left together.

On May 13, 1956, the Warner Brothers sold 90 percent of their shares for $22 million, but Jack Warner had negotiated a secret side deal. The next day, Jack bought back 600,00 shares and was named President. When Harry Warner read the news of his brother's betrayal in the newspaper, he fell on the floor with a stroke. A semi-invalid, Harry Warner died in 1958; Jack didn't attend the funeral. Abe Warner never spoke to Jack for the rest of his life.

Two years later, in 1958, Jack Warner decided to enter the record business again; Warner intensely disliked the fact that other labels, like Columbia and RCA Victor, licensed the music from Warner's films, then made a profit selling the recordings.

Initially, Warner decided to purchase Imperial Records from Lew Chudd for $2 million but, on the day of the contract signing, Chudd did not show up (he vanished to Hawaii for a spell). Warner then decided to start its own label, but Herman Starr, still on the Board and with a long memory of the 1930 financial disaster when Warners attempted to enter the recording business, resisted. Finally, Starr said he would go along with starting a record label if Jim Conkling was named president.

Jim Conkling had been president of both Capitol and Columbia; he was a major success in the recording industry, marketing the LP and introducing the first record clubs at Columbia. In addition, Conkling had been one of the founders of the RIAA--and its first President, as well as founder and first Executive Director of NARAS. At the age of 41, he had retired, moved from New York back to California, and had to be persuaded to take over a start-up label.

Conkling drew up a $2 million budget, envisioning Warner's as a major label, because that was his background. On March 10, 1958, Jim Conkling became president of Warner Brothers Records, with a three year contract that paid him $1,000 a week, plus profit sharing and stock options; Jack Warner was Chairman of the Board of Warner Brothers Records.

The Warner Brothers office was at 3701 Warner Boulevard and Conkling assembled a team of executives for the label. Immediately, he faced pressure from the movie and TV company, which wanted the label to record their studio contract artists, whether they could sing or not. The first act signed to Warner Brothers was Tab Hunter, a teen movie idol who "could not carry a tune in an armored car."

Because of the introduction of rock'n'roll, the record business had changed a great deal within a few years, but Conkling still thought in terms of the past. The label issued its first releases on September 1, 1958 and featured actress Connie Stevens of "Hawaii Five-O" singing "Conchetta," Jack Webb, star of "Dragnet" doing recitations, the Warner Brothers Military Band, and three of Conkling's brothers-in-law: Alvina Rey (under the name of "Ira Ironstrings"), Buddy Cole (his album was *Have Organ, Will Swing*), and Del Courtney, a San Francisco big band leader. The first single from the label was "The Star Spangled Banner."

The first "hit" from the label was from Edd Byrnes, star on the TV show "77 Sunset Strip," who performed "Kookie, Kookie, Lend Me Your Comb." (Byrnes played a young man who was always combing his full head of hair; he couldn't carry a tune so Connie Stevens did the singing.)

By the end of 1959, Warner Brothers Records had lost $3.5 million and Conkling was ordered to liquidate the label. In February, 1960, the label began the day with 130 employees; at the end of the day, there were 29.

Warner Brothers had signed the Everly Brothers, who'd had a string of hits ("Bye Bye Love," "Wake Up Little Susie," "All I Have To Do Is Dream" and "Devoted To You" for Archie Bleyer at Cadence Records. The Nashville-based duo signed for $1 million with Warner Brothers and their first single, "Cathy's Clown," became a number one hit, selling three million copies world-wide. Conkling thought the Everly Brothers should add an orchestra to their recordings to broaden their appeal, and the next releases didn't do well. Also, the brothers enlisted in the Marine Corps Reserve because they were scheduled to be drafted.

James Conkling flew to Chicago, where he visited the Warner distributor. At the warehouse, Conkling listened to a Chicago accountant, Bob Newhart, who did comedy phone call routines; the comic brought a portable tape recorder and played his routines; Conkling believed he had commercial potential and signed him. Herman Starr hated the idea of a comedy record and told Conkling they would have to record him "live" to save money but the comic did not have any dates booked--he wasn't really a performer. Finally, the Warner Brothers staff arranged an appearance at a club in Texas where *The Button-Down Mind of Bob Newhart* was recorded. The album quickly reached the number one position on the charts and stayed there for 14 weeks. Newhart won two Grammys, including "Album of the Year," for his initial effort.

After two years at Warner Brothers, Conkling was replaced by Mike Maitland, who had been head of sales at Capitol. Warners was distributed by independent distributors and Columbia did their manufacturing. Maitland hired a Yale graduate and Boston disc jockey, Joe Smith, to head up radio promotion; Smith supplemented his regular promotion team with off-season sports celebrities, who had no trouble gaining access to radio programmers.

Fender Guitars and Guitar Instrumentals

Rock'n'roll was music made by and for the guitar. During the early days of the recording industry, it was the piano that defined the sound of pop music but, from the time of Elvis—who played a guitar—the sound of rock'n'roll was rooted in the guitar.

Guitar instrumentals and guitar groups were popular on the West Coast during the early years of rock'n'roll. The style was often called "surf guitar" because of the influence of surfing in southern California. Another major reason was that Fender guitars, the first mass-produced solid-body guitars, were manufactured in Southern California.

Fender Guitars were developed by Leo Fender, born August 10, 1909 in Anaheim. Fender was fascinated by electronics from an early age, which led him to learn how to repair radios. Fender studied accounting at Fullerton Junior College and then worked as a bookkeeper. A local band needed a public address (PA) system and asked Fender to construct one; he ended up building six.

Fender continued to work as an accountant but lost jobs during the Depression. Fender and his wife returned to Fullerton in 1938, borrowed $600, and established "Fender Radio Service" to repair radios, which ran on vacuum tubes at that time Band leaders and musicians came to Fender to amplify guitars; the "lap steel" or "Hawaiian guitar" had become popular in country and western swing music.

Fender went into business during World War II with a lap steel player, "Doc" Kauffman, who was also an inventor. Kauffman had worked for Rickenbacker, a firm that had a history of building lap steel guitars. Fender and Kauffman formed K & F Manufacturing Corporation to build electric lap steel guitars and amplifiers and they began selling the electric lap steel in 1945 with an amplifier.

Guitarists with Big Bands usually played hollow body guitars but those guitars created feedback when played loudly. A solid body guitar could play louder and musicians who played in bars and honky tonks needed a louder guitar. Rickenbacker had developed the Spanish Electro guitar, Les Paul had developed "The Log," which was too heavy to play, and Paul Bigsby had built a solid body guitar under the direction of Merle Travis that had all of the tuning keys on one side of the head.

Leo Fender began working on a solid body guitar that could play loudly in dance halls and released it in 1950 as the Esquire, which had one pickup. The name was changed to the Broadcaster and then the Telecaster, which had two pickups, and this became widely used, first with country and later rock musicians. Fender developed the Stratocaster with help from draftsman Freddie Tavares after country musician Bill Carson complained about the Telecaster's straight edges, which made it uncomfortable to play.

Bass players had played a stand up bass but, with the introduction of electric guitars, could no longer compete for volume. There was also the problem of carrying the large bass around. Fender solved that problem by creating the Fender Precision Bass, which was released in 1951. He also developed the Fender Bassman, an amplifier for the electric bass that had a 15-inch speaker.

Early Guitar Instrumental Hits

Les Paul had worked with Gibson and Chet Atkins worked with Gretsch to develop guitars during the early 1950s. Paul and Atkins, along with Merle Travis, were probably the best known guitarists during the early 1950s. All were rooted in country music and, except for Travis, a middle-of-the road type sound that was complex. The first wave of rock guitarists would play more simply and louder.

The first guitar hit in rock was by a keyboard player; Bill Doggett was a jazz and rhythm and blues musician who had worked with Louis Jordan, Johnny Otis, Ella Fitzgerlad, Wynonie Harris, the Ink Spots and Lucky

Millender as pianist or organ player. In 1956, his combo worked up "Honky Tonk, Parts 1 and 2" during appearances at clubs. The guitar part on "Honky Tonk" was played by Billy Butler, credited as co-writer of the song, and the saxophone section was played by Clifford Scott. The song reached number one on the R&B chart and number two on the Hot 100 in 1956.

"Honky Tonk" was recorded in New York for King Records; Doggett recorded "Slow Walk" and "Ram-Bunk-Shush" where the organ was more pronounced as follow-ups.

In 1957, Bill Justis recorded "Raunchy" in Memphis at the Sun Studio in Memphis. Justis worked for Sam Phillips at Sun as a producer and arranger. He worked up the song with guitarist Sidney Manker, who is credited as co-writer. Manker's guitar opens the record before Justis plays his saxophone. The song was released on Phillips International, an offshoot of Sun created by Sam Phillips and entered the *Billboard* Hot 100 in November and reached the number two position on the Hot 100. It lasted 20 weeks on the singles chart, peaking in 1958. Like the Doggett record, this was a "guitar hit" by someone who was not a guitarist.

"Tequila," by The Champs, a studio group, begins with an acoustic rhythm guitar and then an electric lead before the saxophone takes over. Again, it is a "guitar hit" but the guitar parts are discernable, although subdued.

Dick Dale

The "King of the Surf Guitar" was Dick Dale, who combined his love of surfing with his guitar playing to pioneer a unique, powerful sound.

Born Richard Anthony Mansour on May 4, 1937 in Boston, Dale was of Arab descent and his family was involved in the Arab immigrant community. His earliest love was Hank Williams and country music and Dale first learned to play ukulele and then the guitar. Dale grew up in Quincy, Massachusetts until his senior year in high school when Dale's father took a job in the Southern California aerospace industry and the family moved to El Segundo. In southern California, Dale learned to surf and wanted to merge surfing with his guitar playing. Dale imagined a soundtrack for his experiences surfing and that led to him to develop a unique style of rapid picking on tunes heavily influenced by Arab music.

Dick Dale played a Fender Stratocaster and Fender amp and worked with Leo Fender to develop a 100 watt amp with overpowering sound.

Dale's first chart record, on his own Deltone label, was "Let's Go Trippin'," which set the tone for his following chart singles, "Night Rider," "Miserlou" and "Tidal Wave."

Dick Dale was a major influence on the West Coast music scene that connected the Southern California lifestyle of surfing with a music that married the surfer's big wave.

Duane Eddy

Duane Eddy was the first solo guitar instrumentalist to become a rock star. His first release, "Movin'n'Groovin'" started a career that lasted over 60 years.

Born in Corning, New York (April 26, 1938) he began playing guitar when he was five. His family moved to Arizona in 1951, when Eddy was 13, and he formed a duet with Jimmy Delbridge, performing on KCKY where they met disc jockey Lee Hazlewood. In 1955, Hazlewood produced the duo's first single, "Soda Fountain Girl" in Phoenix.

Eddy and Delbridge joined a country music band, Buddy Long's Western Melody Boys" in Phoenix. Eddy played a Chet Atkin's model Gretsch and developed a style where he played the melody on the bass strings of his guitar, creating a "twangy" sound. The instrumental, "Movin'n'Groovin," written by Eddy and Hazlewood, was recorded in November, 1957 at the Phoenix radio station. Eddy signed a recording contract with Lester Sill and Lee Hazlewood in 1958; they recorded at Audio Recorders Studio in Phoenix and leased the masters to Jamie Records, based in Philadelphia. "Movin'n'Groovin" reached number 72 on the *Billboard* Hot 100 in 1958.

Eddy's next single, "Rebel Rouser," debuted on the *Billboard* Hot 100 in June, 1958 and rose to number six and sold over a million copies. That single featured Gil Bernal, a session musician in Los Angeles, playing saxophone. That was followed by two other chart singles in 1958, "Ramrod" and "Cannonball." In 1959 Eddy had chart records with "Yep!" "Forty Miles of bad Road," "The Quiet Three," "Some Kind-A Earthquake" and "First Love, First Tears."

Duane Eddy formed a band with Steve Douglas, Jim Horn (saxophone) and Larry Knectel, who later became members of L.A.'s "Wrecking Crew," a group of musicians who played on a number of pop and rock songs recorded in Los Angeles.

Eddy's first album, *Have 'Twangy Guitar Will Travel*, was released in January, 1959 and reached number five on the *Billboard* album chart, remaining on that chart for 82 weeks.

Duane Eddy was regularly featured on "Dick Clark's American Bandstand" and by the early 1960s was the best known solo rock guitarists, billed as "The Guitar Man." This made him the first "Guitar God" in the rock'n'roll era.

Link Wray and the Raymen

A month after "Movin'n'Groovin' entered the *Billboard* chart, another guitar instrumentalist made his debut. "Rumble" by Link Wray and the Ray Men begins with "power chords" and was such a powerful sound that city officials banned the record in New York and Boston because they were afraid it would incite teenage violence.

Link Wray was born in Dunn, North Carlina, a descendent of Native Americans. In 1951 Wray was drafted and spent time in Korea during the Korean War where he caught tuberculosis, which caused the removed of one of his lungs and left him unable to sing. After the service, he formed a band and developed "Rumble" when he was asked to play a "stroll" during a dance. He recorded the song for Cadence Records and label head Archie Bleyer named the song "Rumble." It entered the *Billboard* Hot 100 on April 28, 1958 and reached number 16. Wray's follow-up single, "Raw-Hide" (or "Rawhide") was recorded for Epic and reached number 23 on the Hot 100 in 1959.

Santo and Johnny

Santo and Johnny had a number one hit with "Sleep Walk" in 1959 with the steel guitar in the lead. Santo and Johnny Farina were born and raised in Brooklyn. During World War II their father was stationed in Oklahoma where he first heard the steel guitar played. He told his wife that he would like his sons to learn the steel.

Santo, the eldest, obtained a Gibson six-string steel guitar after World War II and found a teacher who gave him lessons. Santo's brother, Johnny, accompanied him on an electric rhythm guitar. Santo then bought a Fender steel guitar that had three necks with each neck having eight strings and developed different tunings. "Sleep Walk" came while the brothers were jamming one night, unable to sleep. The song was recorded in New York and released on the Canadian American label. It entered the *Billboard* Hot 100 on July 27, 1959 and reached number one, where it remained for two weeks.

Davie Allan

Davie Allan became known as the "King of the Fuzz Tone Guitar" from his work on teen movie soundtracks.

Allan grew up in Southern California and met Mike Curb when both were in the school choir. Curb formed a number of groups, the Sudells, the Heyburners, the Zanies and others with Allan on guitar. Curb had an independent label, distributed by Tower, a subsidiary of Capitol, that produced soundtracks for films produced by Roger Corman's American Independence Pictures.

Curb and Allan first came to recognition from a short film, *Skaterdater*, that featured Allan's guitar playing. Their breakthrough film was *The Wild Angels*, starring Peter Fonda. Allan's single, "Theme From the Wild Angels" charted and "Blues Theme," from the film, was a top 40 single. On "Blues Theme," Allan developed the distorted "fuzz tone" sound that defined his style of playing.

Allan's biggest hit for him and his band, The Arrows, was "Apache '65," which debuted on the *Billboard* hot 100 on February 13, 1965.

Chet Atkins

Chet Atkins had several guitar instrumentals chart during the late 1950; "Boo Boo Stick" charted in 1959 while "One Mint Julep" and "Teensville" charted in 1960. Chet Atkins was admired by other guitarists but his style was too complex for rock'n'roll. Instead, it was Duane Eddy who had the most rock hits until the Ventures.

Other Guitar Hits

A number of guitar hits, mostly influenced by the "surf guitar" sounds from Southern California were popular with bands all over the country. Those include "Ghost Riders in the Sky" by the Ramrods, "Limbo Rock" by the Champs, "Red River Rock" by Johnny and the Hurricanes, "Let's Go" by the Routers, "Wipe Out" by the Sufaris, "Pipeline" by the Chantay's, "Out of Limits" by the Marketts, and "Telstar" by the Tornadoes.

The Ventures

The Ventures came together in Tacoma, Washington in 1958 after Don Wilson and Bob Bogle met and discovered a common interest in guitars. They purchased used guitars for $10 from a pawn shop and formed a group, the Versatones, that played clubs, bars and parties in the Northwest with Bogle playing lead and Wilson on rhythm. They became "The Ventures" when they attempted to register the name "Versatones" and discovered it had already been taken; Wilson' mother suggested "The Ventures" so that's what they became in 1959. Bassist Noke Edwards and drummer Skip Moore soon joined them.

The Chet Atkins' album, *Hi-Fi in Focus* contained the song, "Walk, Don't Run," which the group decided to record for Dolton Records; it entered the *Billboard* Hot 100 on July 18, 1960 and rose to number two, remaining on the chart for 18 weeks, reportedly selling over a million copies.

Drummer Skip Moore dropped out of the group and was replaced Howie Johnson; that group stayed together until 1962 but Bogle and Edwards switched instruments with Bogle taking over on bass while Edwards took over as lead guitarist.

The Ventures released a string of chart singles as well as successful albums. In 1960 they had the single "Perfidia" and the album *Walk Don't Run*; in 1961 they had chart singles with "Ram-Bunk-Shush" "Lullaby of the Leaves (Theme From Silver City)," and "Blue Moon" and the albums *Another Smash!!*, *The Ventures*, and *The Colorful Ventures*.

In 1963 and 1964 the group had chart singles with "Skip To M'Limbo," "Fugitive" and their biggest single, "Walk, Don't Run '64," a remake of their early hit that landed right in the midst of the British Invasion. Their strength, however, was in albums, which often had a theme, and soundtracks. During that period that had chart albums with *Surfing*, *Bobby Vee Meets the Ventures*, *The Ventures Play Country Classics*, *The Ventures in Space* and *Walk Don't Run, Volume 2*.

The Ventures were an all Fender guitar line-up (Jazzmaster, Stratocaster and Precision Bass) until 1963 until their album *The Ventures in Space*. Mosrite, a guitar manufacturer in California started by Semie Moseley, produced solid body guitars, some with multiple necks, and developed "The Ventures Model."

The Ventures recorded a number of TV and movie themes; the most popular was the theme to the TV show "Hawaii-Five-O."

Revenues

The profits from the recording industry were certainly appealing as they rose every year except one during the 1950s. In 1951 the recording industry sold $191 million worth of recordings; in 1959 that figure had risen to $514 million. The major reason: rock'n'roll and the number of teens buying records. In fact, the only year the recording industry moved backward--1954 when sales dropped to $195 million from the previous year's $205 million--was the year before the rock revolution hit. Prior to 1955 the growth was slow and steady: $202 million in 1952, $205 million in 1953. But in 1955 the amount was $227 million; in 1956 it was $331 million, then jumped to $400 million in 1957, $438 million in 1958, and $514 million in 1959.

At that point, about 100 singles a week were released and 60 percent came from independent labels. In 1958, 76 percent of the hit singles on *Billboard's* charts were from independent labels, the four majors accounted for only 24 percent. The industry was concerned and alarmed and set about protecting its turf from the brash, new upstarts.

In July, 1958 the National Association of Record Dealer's formed the National Association of Record Merchandisers (NARM) was formed to counter the trends of discounters, record clubs and rack jobbers.

The rack jobbers supplied "racks" in a variety of locations, particularly grocery stores, mass merchandisers and variety stores. They assumed responsibility for deciding which recordings to put up and kept them stocked regularly. The store got a bit less profit and a whole lot less worry. The rack operations were pioneered by two brothers from Detroit, Joe and David Handleman, who had supplied chain stores with drug and beauty items.

Technically, the industry was moving towards stereo sound, first introduced by Walt Disney for the *Fantasia* movie. FM Radio began broadcasting in stereo, although their audience was limited to "good music" and appealed to affluent, upper class audiences at home; there was no FM radio in cars.

After World War II it was generally conceded that FM Radio was the wave of the future, but the "future" would not really arrive until the late 1960s--over 20 years later.

AM radio thrived from its beginnings in 1920 through the golden years of the 1930s and 40s--before TV--and as the medium for the new sounds of rock'n'roll in the 1950s and most of the 60s. Station owners purchased an FM outlet as well and often simulcast. However, the advent of stereo caused a demand for classical recordings to be re-recorded to take advantage of the new technology. In 1959 stereo sales increased by 21 percent; in 1960 they increased by 26 percent and in 1961 by 30 percent over the previous year.

By the end of the 1950s the appeal of the LP had become obvious to consumers. As far back as 1888 when the recording industry began, it had been a singles business. Albums were developed, essentially, for cast recordings and classical works; the idea that this format would embrace pop music with ten or twelve recordings of different songs took awhile, but by the late 1950s consumers realized that a $3.98 LP with twelve songs and approximately 40 minutes of music was a better "buy" than a single, which cost 98 cents and contained two songs with five or six minutes of music.

Owen Bradley takes over Decca's Nashville Office

In early 1958, Paul Cohen left Decca's country division to head pop production for Coral, Decca's subsidiary and then started his own label, Todd. Owen Bradley took over as head of Decca's country division with offices, first at the Bradley studios.

Elvis in Nashville

In March, 1958, Elvis Presley was inducted into the Army. After basic training, he had two weeks before he reported for his tank training course at Fort Hood, Texas and then on to Germany. Elvis had been recording in New York and Los Angeles after those first Nashville recordings in 1956 but there wasn't time to go to a studio in either of those places. RCA had their new studio in Nashville—only seven months old--but Chet Atkins and engineer Bill Porter had recorded hits on Don Gibson there so Steve Sholes decided to record him in Nashville. On June 10, Elvis came to Nashville and, backed by A-Team musicians Hank Garland and Chet Atkins on guitars, Bob Moore on bass, Floyd Cramer on piano and Buddy Harman on drums, with Elvis' band member D.J. Fontana also on drums, they recorded "I Need Your Love Tonight," "A Big Hunk o'Love," "Ain't That Loving You Baby?," "(Now and Then There's) A Fool Such as I" and "I Got Stung." During Elvis' time in the Army, "I Got Stung," "(Now and Then There's) A Fool Such as I," and "A Big Hunk O'Love" were all released and became hits. Interestingly, it was on this session that Ray Walker joined the Jordanaires as their bass singer.

Country Music Association Formed

In July, 1958, the Country Music Association was formed; it was the first trade organization for a specific genre of music.

In August, *Billboard* reported that a "Caretaker Committee" had been formed and appointed Wesley Rose of Acuff-Rose Publications as temporary president and chairman of the committee. W.D. Kilpatrick, manager of the Grand Ole Opry, was appointed temporary treasurer and Hubert Long, personal manager of Faron Young and Ferlin Huskey, was named secretary and publicity director. Nashville music executives Don Pierce, Chet Atkins, Jim Denny, Ken Nelson, Connie B. Gay and disc jockey Cracker Jim Brooker were appointed to a committee to draft a set of bylaws for the new association, "The purpose of the CMA," it was explained, "is to further promote and publicize country music and to do everything maintain its individuality. Every effort will be made by the association to add more country music to the programming of radio and TV stations throughout the country, and to act as a governing body for country music as a whole." Hubert Long volunteered a small cubicle in the old Exchange Building on lower Church Street and lent a typewriter. That was the first office for the CMA.

The organization was formed because country music was fighting for survival; rock'n'roll had cut into country records sales, road show receipts and radio exposure.

Harry Stone was hired as the first executive director of the Country Music Association and Jo Walker was hired for bookkeeping, typing and general office duties. Stone only lasted ten months because there was not enough to pay him; Jo Walker remained because "I could type and Harry couldn't" remembered Walker.

Don Gibson: "I Can't Stop Loving You" and "Oh, Lonesome Me"

Don Gibson had been dropped by RCA Victor because his records were not selling. However, Chet Atkins, impressed with Gibson's songwriting, signed him in late 1957 and on December 3 they went into the new RCA studio and the first two songs they recorded were "Oh, Lonesome Me" and "I Can't Stop Lovin' You," which was the "A" and "B" side of his single. The record was released in February, 1958 and "Oh Lonesome Me" became a number one record on the country chart, staying in that position for eight weeks and crossing over to the pop chart where it reached number seven. "I Can't Stop Lovin' You" reached number seven on the country chart and number 81 on the pop chart after its release. Kitty Wells covered "I Can't Stop Loving You" after Gibson released it and her version reached number three on the *Billboard* country start and remained on that chart for 19 weeks.

Mitch Miller Blasts Rock and Roll

Mitch Miller's musical taste led to profitable years for Columbia Records. The biggest pop sellers on Columbia during the 1950s, in addition to the Broadway and film musicals, were Ray Coniff and Johnny Mathis. Coniff had a group, "The Ray Coniff Singers," who recorded smooth, middle of the road pop songs. Johnny Mathis had an appeal to teens with his soft, romantic ballads that were released as singles. The popularity of Mathis led Columbia to release a "greatest hits" package, which soon became a popular album format. Johnny's Greatest Hits was released in 1958 and other artists soon followed.

In March, 1958, Todd Storz hosted the first convention for radio and record executives at a hotel in Kansas City. Mitch Miller was the featured speaker at the convention and he gave voice to his strong feelings about rock'n'n'roll.

Miller told his audience of radio programmers and disk jockeys who, for the most part, cheered him, that they had "abdicated" their birthright by playing music for "The eight to fourteen year olds, the pre-shave crowd that makes up 12 percent of the population and zero percent of its buying power, once you eliminate the ponytail ribbons, popsicles and peanut brittle."

Miller attacked "the high percentage of radio shows and records aimed at teenagers. He wanted the delegates to agree that 'much of the juvenile stuff pumped over the air waves these days hardly qualifies as music.'"

Mitch Miller saw the music buying audience as adults who wanted soothing music, not a music that agitated them.

Sing Along With Mitch

Four months after Miller railed against rock'n'roll, his first "Sing Along" album entered the *Billboard* pop chart and reached the number one position, where it remained for eight weeks and a total of 204 weeks—or four years— on the chart. Using songs from the late nineteenth and early twentieth centuries, Miller enlisted Jimmy "Jigsie" Carroll to create the arrangements and then gathered a chorus of 25 men to sing. Most of the singers had worked with Miller since 1948.

The "sing along with" albums by "Mitch Miller and his gang became a phenomenon. The original idea came from Stan Kavan, head of Columbia's national merchandising, who suggested Miller record an album of songs that servicemen sang during World War II and call it "Barracks Ballads." There was also a sing-along show on CBS radio hosted by the Landt Trio. In 1955, Miller had a hit single with "The Yellow Rose of Texas," which was number one for six consecutive weeks. He had eight chart singles with his group before his first sing along album, that contained the single, "March From The River Kwai and Colonel Bogey," from the film *The Bridge Over the River Kwai*.

Beginning in 1958, Miller released 23 "sing along" albums that charted— most in the top ten on *Billboard's* album chart. He developed a television show, "Sing Along With Mitch," where viewers could "watch the bouncing ball" as it moved over the lyrics that scrolled across the screen. The "sing along with Mitch" albums were a huge success for Columbia and reinforced Miller's insistence that people wanted his definition of "good" music.

Gold Records and Grammys

The Recording Industry Association of America or RIAA created the "Gold Record" in 1958, which brought it good publicity as well as more attention to the recording industry. Originally awarded only to singles that generated a million dollars worth of business (or sold a million units) it was extended to albums the following year. The first single to be awarded a "Gold" record was "Don't Let the Stars Get In Your Eyes" by Perry Como.

The first Grammy Awards were presented in 1958, a result of a promotion of James Conkling, who had long wanted an industry awards evening. The awards came about when the Hollywood Beautification Committee decided to include recording artists on the Walkway of Stars on Hollywood Boulevard. The question of "criteria" came up and record sales were immediately cited; however, at that time the young rock'n'rollers were selling the most records, an untenable situation for the Hollywood Beautification Committee as it was for recording industry stalwarts. The National Association of Recording Arts and Sciences (NARAS) was formed to reward "artistic creativity" in the recording field. This was an award for excellence, voted on by its members, and not an award based on sales.

Their first meeting was held in June, 1957 and Conkling was elected temporary Chair. In May, 1958, the first awards were presented in Los Angeles. Given awards were artists Frank Sinatra, Ella Fitzgerald, Henry Mancini, Count Basie, and Domenico Mondugno. The top song was "Volare" ("Nel Blue Dipinto di Blue"). Ignored were Elvis Presley, the Platters, the Coasters and songs like "Hound Dog," "Teddy Bear" and "Yakety Yak." (The first Grammy for "Country" music was given to the Kingston Trio for "Tom Dooley." There were no Grammys for R&B music.)

The "Grammy" was named by a woman in New Orleans in a contest; she reasoned the award looked like "a replica of the old-fashioned gramophone" and was awarded 24 LPs for her prize.

The awards soon proved popular and grew; in 1958 there was a second awards show in November, the first to be televised, although it was taped and broadcast later. There were 28 awards handed out; in 1959 there were 34, in 1964 there were 47.

The National Association of Recording Merchandisers (NARM) was formed in 1958, a direct result of the problems the music industry was facing with Congressional investigations into payola and the threat of rock'n'roll. The industry had come under government scrutiny in 1955 from an accusation by the Justice Department over unfair trade practices. The four majors were accused of shipping too many free records to radio stations, unfair dealings with indie distributors, "discriminatory LP price practices, price cutting" and other business practices..

1959
Middle-of-the-Road Pop Music

It is easy for rock'n'roll historians to dismiss the mainstream middle-of-the-road music that came from former big band singers once the rock era, which tends to start either in 1955 when "Rock Around the Clock" hit number one on the *Billboard* singles chart or 1956 when Elvis sold ten million records and the cultural impact of this artist was felt all over the country.

Rock and roll was a singles business; the impact of rock and roll during the early years, 1955-1963, was on songs hitting the radio airwaves and the singles charts. In terms of albums, it was classic singers and Broadway soundtracks that dominated the charts. Record labels made more profits from albums, so it is understandable why they could ignore--or at least scratch their heads in wonder--about rock when it hit.

There is no doubt the rules changed in the music industry when rock and roll hit. The top executives at major labels had learned how to do business with pop singers and soundtracks and they could not see rock on the horizon because they were out of touch with rhythm and blues. Further, those executives had, for the most part, grown up during the Great Depression and came of age during World War II. Looking at their consumers, they concluded that the wage earner bought recordings because they were the ones who made the money. It was a simple, obvious conclusion that proved wrong because, by the mid-1950s, there was more discretionary income in the family as teenagers received allowances or worked odd jobs and spent the money on themselves. During the Depression, when young people worked, they brought the money home and put it in the general pot in order to keep the family going. That was no longer necessary for most families by the mid-1950s; the wage-earners (primarily the father) earned enough to support the family on a single salary so teenagers did not have to contribute to the family's survival.

In 1955, the top selling album was the movie soundtrack to *Love Me or Leave Me* by Doris Day; albums by Sammy Davis, Jr. Jackie Gleason and

Mario Lanza also reached the number one position. In 1956, the top selling albums were *Calypso* by Harry Belafonte, and the Original Cast recording of *My Fair Lady*. There were two albums by Elvis that topped the charts in 1956, the same as Harry Belafonte. Further, the soundtracks to *Oklahoma!* and *The King and I* were top selling albums.

In 1957, Elvis had two albums that reached number one--a Christmas album and the soundtrack to *Loving You*. But the soundtrack to *Around the World in 80 Days* and a Bing Crosby Christmas album also reached number one. The top selling album for all of 1958 was the soundtrack to *South Pacific*, followed by the Original Cast Recording from *The Music Man* and the soundtrack to *Gigi*. Frank Sinatra and Mitch Miller each had two albums that reached number one, and Van Cliburn's *Tchaikovsky: Piano Concerto No. 1* and a Johnny Mathis album also reached number one. In the youth market, Ricky Nelson and the Kingston Trio both had number one albums, but those two albums only topped the charts for a total of three weeks.

The Music From Peter Gunn by Henry Mancini, the Original Cast recording of *Flower Drum Song*, a Mantovani album and a Johnny Mathis album each reached number one in 1959. The Kingston Trio had two number one albums that year and those two albums had the number one spot for a total of 23 weeks. There were no rock and roll acts with an album at number one the entire year of 1959.

The World of Folk Music

By the time the Kingston Trio had their hit with "Tom Dooley" in 1958, folk music encompassed several facets. First was the commercial folk music, which usually consisted of smooth vocal harmonies for urban--most often college--audiences. Another kind of folk music featured traditional songs like "Barbara Allen" and "Streets of Laredo" and sung by singers to an urban, usually more intellectual audience generally gathered in night clubs. Finally, there was the folk music being created by folk singers, who usually patterned themselves after Woody Guthrie, who emerged as a sort of guru to the whole folk movement.

During the 1930s, Woody Guthrie was a radical singer whose appeal was limited to urban intellectuals and left wingers or union organizers. He had very little, if any, effect on most mainstream country music but at the end of the 1950s and beginning in the early 1960s, as he lay dying of Huntington's Disease in New Jersey, he was "re-discovered" by a host of young, generally urban folk singers, the most notable being Bob Dylan.

After the Kingston Trio hit, the folk music movement blossomed, with publications, clubs, and folksingers as well as television shows all jumping in on the action. A folk-oriented TV show, "Hootenanny" was on ABC-TV.

The center for the folk scene was the east coast, particularly Greenwich Village in New York and Cambridge, Massachusetts. Here is where Bob Dylan, Peter Paul and Mary, Phil Ochs, and other core members of the movement lived. There was also a lively folk music "scene" in Boston.

The Newport Folk Festival

The popularity of folk music in 1958 gave George Wein, a founder of the Newport Jazz Festival, the idea to create a folk festival in Newport after he invited Odetta to perform on Sunday afternoons at Storyville, his jazz club in Boston.

The Newport Jazz Festival began in 1954, funded by socialite Elaine Lorillard and her husband, Louis Lorillard, who financed the festival for a number of years. Lorillard hired jazz impresario George Wein to organize the festival. Wein wanted to expand the Newport Jazz Festival to include an afternoon of folk music and in 1959 invited Odetta, Pete Seeger and the Weavers and the Kingston Trio to perform. The demand for folk music was so overwhelming that Wein decided to stage an entire festival of folk music.

Wein enlisted the aid of Albert Grossman, who managed Odetta to help plan and produce the festival in the summer of 1959. The first Newport Folk Festival featured Pete Seeger, Earl Scruggs, the Kingston Trio, John Jacob Niles, Sonny Terry & Brownie McGhee, Odetta, The New Lost City Ramblers and Bob Gibson, who brought 18-year old Joan Baez on stage.

In 1960 the festival was extended to three nights.

The Second Grammys

The second Grammy Awards were held six months later, on November 29, at the Beverly Hilton in Los Angeles and the Waldorf-Astoria in New York. Record of the Year was "Mack the Knife" by Bobby Darin Album of the Year was *Come Dance With Me* by Frank Sinatra; New Artist was Bobby Darin; "Song of the Year" and "Best Country and Western Performance" was "Battle of New Orleans," written by Jimmy Driftwood and recorded by Johnny Horton; Male Vocalist was Frank Sinatra for *Come Dance With Me*; Female Vocalist was Ella Fitzgerald for "But Not for Me"; Vocal Performance by a Group or Chorus was The Mormon Tabernacle Choir for "The Battle Hymn of the Republic"; Best Performance by a Top 40 Artist was Nat "King" Cole for "Midnight Flyer"; Rhythm and Blues Performance was Dinah Washington for "What a Diff'rence a Day Makes"; and "Best Country and Western Performance" was "The Battle of New Orleans by Johnny Horton.

"Battle of New Orleans"

Jimmie Driftwood, a teacher and principal in Arkansas, wrote songs to help students learn history. "The Battle of New Orleans" was about Andrew Jackson's victory over British troops in 1815. The tune used was an old fiddle tune, "The Eighth of January." Johnny Horton recorded the song at the Quonset Hut, with Harold Bradley playing the banjo intro, and entered *Billboard's* country chart on April 27, 1959 and reached number one on the country chart, where it remained for ten weeks and number one on the pop chart, where it remained for six weeks. Driftwood had been "discovered" by Don Warden, who worked with Porter Wagoner. Driftwood recorded an album of 12 songs for RCA, produced by Chet Atkins; "Battle of New Orleans" was on that album. The song won the Grammy for "Song of the Year" and inspired an comedic "answer" song, "The Battle of Kookamonga" by Homer and Jethro.

"El Paso"

The song "El Paso was on Marty Robbins' album, *Gunfighter Ballads and Trail Songs*, released in September, 1959. "El Paso was released on October 26 and rose to number one on both the country and Hot 100 charts in *Billboard*. The song was produced by Don Law for Columbia and recorded at the Quonset Hut. The Mexican flavored guitar was played by Grady Martin and harmonies were by Jim Glaser and Bobby Sykes. The song was 4:38 in length—much longer than the three minute records that disc jockeys regularly played—so Columbia released it on a two-sided single, with an edited version on one side and the full version on the other; the DJ's preferred the longer version. Robbins wrote two follow-up songs for "El Paso"; "Faleena (From El Paso)" in 1966 and "El Paso City" in 1976. The Grateful Dead often performed "El Paso" during their concerts. "El Paso" received the 1959 Grammy for "Best Country Song."

"The Three Bells"

The Browns—Jim Ed and his two sisters, Bonnie and Maxine—were frustrated with their recording career. They had two top ten hits for Fabor Records but after signing with RCA Victor in 1956 they were not having success. They had decided to quit music but their RCA contract required them to do one more ssession. Chet Atkins encouraged them to do any song they loved; they loved "The Three Bells" and on August 3, 1959, "The Three Bells" by The Browns entered *Billboard's* Country chart and rose quickly to number one, where it remained for ten weeks. It also reached number one on the pop chart and held that position for four weeks. The smooth voiced trio followed "The Three Bells" with Scarlet Ribbons," which also crossed over to the pop chart.

"He'll Have to Go"

"He'll Have to Go" by Jim Reeves, produced by Chet Atkins and backed by the Anita Kerr Singers, was released at the end of 1959 and during 1960 I was another example of the Nashville Sound as the smooth-voiced Jim Reeves sang the ballad. It was number one for 14 weeks, remained on the country chart for 34 weeks, and crossed over to the pop chart where it remained at number two for three weeks.

Transistor Radios

In 1959 there six million transistor records imported into the United States; by the end of the year, there were 12 million in use. Transistor radios were popular with teenagers because it made their music portable; they could listen to the radio outside the home or cars.

The transistor was developed by William Shockley, Walter Houser Brattain and John Bardeen with Bell Labs; the transistor was first publicly demonstrated on December 23, 1947. Several companies, including the German firm Intermetall and Texas Instruments, developed prototypes in 1953 and 1954 but were not manufactured commercially.

In October, 1954, Texas Instruments with Industrial Develop Engineering Associates (I.D.E.A.) marketed the TR-1, the first transistor radio. The price was high and sound quality was low. In 1955, Raytheon marketed a transistor radio that was larger, with better sound.

In 1952, Masaru Ibuka, cofounder of the Tokyo Telecommunications Engineering Corporation came to the United States and learned of the transistor. Ibuka and his co-founder, Akio Morita, licensed the transistor for $25,000 and Ibuka used ideas from other transistor radio manufacturers to create TR-63, the first commercially successful transistor radio. Ibuka and Morita changed the name of their company to "Sony" and, in 1957, 100,000 transistor radio were exported into the United States.

A revolution in electronics was occurring with the transistor replacing vacuum tubes. The transistor radios were small, less expensive that phonographs or standard radio and ran on small batteries (9 volts) that did not generate light or head. The transistor was soon be installed in television sets and other electronics as the days of the vacuum tube passed.

Payola Investigation in Fall, 1959

In the Fall of 1959, the Internal Revenue Service announced that it would scrutinize business expense deductions for gifts and promotions in the record business. The Federal Trade Commission (FTC) believed that payola was a deceptive business practice because the public didn't know that money had changed hands to play a record. It was, they felt, a form of commercial bribery.

The FTC ruled that labels who paid disc jockeys to play recordings, created an unfair advantage over competition. RCA and the FTC came to an agreement: RCA did not admit doing anything wrong, but promised never to do it again.

In the meantime, the Quiz show scandals hit in 1958 with proof that some of the shows were "rigged," the answers provided to contestants ahead of time.

The biggest loser in the recording industry was disc jockey Alan Freed, one of the most visible members of the young rock establishment. Freed openly admitted accepting "gifts" for playing a record but vehemently denied taking anything in order to play a recording, saying "I'd be a fool to. I'd be giving up control of my program." Still he was hounded constantly and lost his radio show.

Another disc jockey, this one on TV, fared much better. Dick Clark had taken over "Philadelphia Bandstand" after creator Bob Horn was fired from the TV station. The move was supposedly temporary but Clark fit the picture perfectly with his all-American good looks and personality. In August, 1957, American Bandstand went on network TV for 90 minutes each day and was a major boost to having rock accepted nationally.

By 1959 Clark was worth a considerable amount of money, and the Bandstand show was bringing in $12 million. That contrasted sharply with Freed's $40,000 salary and the $200,000 a year in billings for Freed's New York station. Behind closed doors in front of a Congressional committee, Dick Clark testified he had never received payola, even though he had made half a million dollars during a 27 month period. The sources of his income: music publishing, talent representation, record manufacturing, pressing and distribution. Clark agreed to dispose of all those interests and did so.

The payola investigations effectively ended the independent labels control of rhythm and blues because most of them were driven out of business, slapped with fines and taxes from the IRS. The major labels stepped in and embraced rock'n'roll and rhythm and blues; these were large and respectable companies that carried political clout. Also, they saw there was money to be made in R&B and rock'n'roll. Increasingly, they hired younger executives who understood the music. In this way, rock'n'roll shifted from an "outlaw" music into the mainstream, a symbol of innocent, restless youth.

In October, 1959, there were public revelations about the rigging of TV quiz shows. Further, the Federal Trade Commission (FTC) Chairman, Earl Kinter, announced plans to charge several record companies for "unfair trade practice," violating a section of the FTC act that prohibited "unfair methods of competition" [and]...unfair or deceptive acts or practices in commerce." In November, a formal investigation into payola in the music industry by the government began. The impetus behind that was ASCAP.

On Monday, November 2, 1959, Charles Van Doren stood before the House Subcommittee on Legislative Oversight in hearings televised on the networks and stated that his success on "Twenty-One" was ill-gotten. He tearfully confessed that he had been given answers for the show. He was immediately fired by Columbia University, where he was on the faculty, and by NBC-TV, where he appeared regularly. The sponsor of the Barry-Enright produced shows, Revlon, dropped its sponsorship and within a week all shows produced by that organization were dropped from the air.

On November 6 the House subcommittee finished its TV quiz show investigations. Chief counsel Robert Lishman then presented the committee a letter from ASCAP alleging that commercial bribery was the primary reason that radio selected which songs were played. They charged that the public was "surreptitiously induced to buy" those songs from this tainted airplay. Included in those accusations were 13 pages of articles from *Billboard* and *Cashbox* from the past eleven years that alleged a conspiracy of broadcasters, disc jockeys, and BMI "to suppress genuine talent and to foist mediocre music upon the public."

On November 11, ABC demanded that Dick Clark either give up his American Bandstand and Saturday night television shows or relinquish all his music-related companies. On Friday, November 13, Alan Freed received an affidavit with three questions relating to payola. Those three questions dealt directly with payments received by Freed for broadcasting records, his refusal to play recordings unless a payment was received and his ownership or interest in music copyrights or performance rights. If he answered "yes" to any of the three questions, Freed was required to supply details. The affidavit was required to be signed, notarized and returned to the legal department at ABC.

Alan Freed realized he could not sign the document, so he didn't. Instead, he sent a letter to ABC accusing them of "malicious, unfounded accusations" and that if signing such a payola affidavit was a "necessary prerequisite" for him remaining at ABC, the company should have required him signing it before he was hired. Freed found it "impossible to accede" to the network's request "for to do so would violate my self-respect."

Dick Clark, who received the same affidavit, was allowed to have his attorney draw up an affidavit with different wording, which he signed.

At that time, "payola" was not a Federal crime; however, the FCC could suspend a broadcast license and an individual who did not report the payments as income was subject to federal tax evasion charges. It was not a crime in most states, but in New York there was a law on the books which made this practice illegal.

Alan Freed refused to sign the affidavit from ABC and was fired on Sunday, November 22; by the end of the week he was not on the air on any station in New York. Freed's firing led to a national purge of disc jockeys from radio stations.

On December 4, 1959, the Federal Trade Commission (FTC) accused three record manufacturers and six independent record distributors of deceiving the public and restricting competition by making payoffs to radio and TV disk jockeys. Charged were RCA, London, both based in New York, and Bernard Lowe, who owned the Cameo label in Philadelphia. The distributors charged were Edward Barsky, Lips Distributing, Davis Rosen, Universal Record Distributors, Sparks Music Distributors (all in Philadelphia) and Main Line Cleveland, located in that city. There were no disc jockeys named.

Albums 1956-1959

It is revealing to see the albums who spent the most time on *Billboard's* album chart during the 1956-1959 period. They were led by *My Fair Lady* which spent 480 weeks or a combined total of over nine years on the album chart with 173 weeks in the top ten and 15 weeks at number one. The South Pacific movie soundtrack spent 31 weeks in the number one position, 90 weeks in the top ten and 262 weeks overall. Next, in terms of longevity on the album chart is Oklahoma!, which spent two weeks at number one, 112 weeks in the top ten and 283 weeks over all.

Harry Belafonte's album *Calypsos* also spent 31 weeks in the number one position on the Billboard chart and a total of 99 weeks, 58 of those in the top ten. Johnny Mathis' greatest hits album spent 490 weeks on the chart—over nine years—and 57 weeks in the top ten. Other albums with chart longevity were *Heavenly* by Johnny Mathis (295 weeks). The Music Man original cast recording (245 weeks), *Sing Along With Mitch* (204 weeks). The top folk group was the Kingston Trio; their *At Large* album spent 15 weeks at number one, 31 weeks in the top ten and 118 weeks on the chart overall while their *Here We Go Again* album spent eight weeks at number one, 26 weeks in the top ten and 126 weeks on the chart.

Here are the top 25 albums for the 1956-1959 period:

1. *South Pacific* (movie soundtrack)
2. *Calypso* by Harry Belafonte
3. *My Fair Lady* (original cast recording)
4. *The Kingston Trio At Large*
5. *The Music Man* (original cast recording
6. *Around the World in 80 Days* (movie soundtrack)
7. *Gigi* (movie soundtrack)
8. *Elvis Presley*
9. *The Music From Peter Gunn* by Henry Mancini
10. *Loving You* by Elvis (movie soundtrack)
11. *Sing Along With Mitch* by Mitch Miller & The Gang
12. *Love Is the Thing* by Nat "King" Cole
13. *Here We Go Again!* By the Kingston Trio
14. *Tchaikovsky: Piano Concerto No. 1* by Van Cliburn
15. *Belafonte* by Harry Belafonte
16. *Heavenly* by Johnny Mathis
17. *Elvis* by Elvis Presley
18. *Frank Sinatra sings for Only the Lonely*
19. *Exotica* by Martin Denny
20. *Come Fly With Me* by Fran Sinatra
21. *Elvis' Christmas Album*
22. *Johnny's Greatest Hits* by Johnny Mathis
23. *Flower Drum Song* (original cast recording
24. *Oklahoma!* (movie soundtrack)
25. *Ricky* by Ricky Nelson

Dollars generated by sales of recordings at retail during the 1950s

1951: $191 million
1952: $202 million
1953: $205 million
1954: $195 million
1955: $227 million
1956: $331 million
1957: $400 million
1958: $438 million
1959: $514 million

In the News

Alaska and Hawaii became the forty-ninth and fiftieth states in the United States in 1959.

In April, Fidel Castro, who had led a band of troops to defeat Cuban dictator Fulgencio Batista, came to the United States and spoke before the American Society of Newspaper Editors. The United States had recognized the new regime in January, a week after Castro had paraded victorious through the streets of Cuba.

1960
1960s: The Beginning

The popular rock music of the 1960s was rooted in rock'n'roll and folk music, influenced by Elvis, Chuck Berry and the rockabilly and rhythm and blues performers as well as folk performers such as the Kingston Trio, Bob Dylan and Joan Baez. Most of the 60's rock bands were originally 50's cover bands who developed their talent before audiences, generally playing dances.

The repertoire of the '50s cover bands came from hits by Elvis, the Everly Brothers, Carl Perkins, Jerry Lee Lewis, Fats Domino, Chuck Berry, Duane Eddy, Ray Charles and Gene Vincent to name a few.

Folk performers developed their talents at "hootenannies" and other gatherings of folk singers. They performed traditional American songs, most rooted in Appalachia, as well as new compositions in a traditional style on acoustic instruments. Influential folk performers include Pete Seeger, Woody Guthrie, the Weavers, Odetta, Joan Baez, Bob Dylan, Phil Ochs, Tom Paxton and Dave Van Ronk, to name a sample.

The 60s rock performers developed their own material after they had a firm foundation performing live. In England, some of the musicians were influenced by the folk blues of artists like Robert Johnson and Muddy Waters. As the 1960s progressed, British performers often introduced early blues and rhythm and blues to white musicians and audiences. The path for both American and British performers was from acoustic groups to electric groups.

The first three years of the 1960s saw the success of folk music groups, inspired by the Kingston Trio, Peter, Paul and Mary and the folk singers based in Greenwich Village, New York. On the West Coast the sounds of "surf" music emerged, first with guitar instrumentals and then with the Beach Boys and other west coast surfing groups.

The singer-songwriter first emerged in folk music. As the 1960s progressed, it was the era of bands, some of whom wrote their own songs although, as the decade progressed, more and more bands featured a songwriter as a lead singer. The Lovin' Spoonful, the Beatles, the Rolling Stones, the Doors, Creedence Clearwater Revival and the Young Rascals are a few examples.

The year 1960 began with "El Paso" by Marty Robbins in the number one slot of the *Billboard* Hot 100, followed by "Running Bear" by Johnny Preston, "Teen Angel" by Mark Dinning, ""The Theme From 'A Summer Place'" by Percy Faith and "Stuck On You" by Elvis Presley during the first four months of the year.

The number one album in *Billboard* at the beginning of the year was *Here We Go Again!* by the Kingston Trio, followed by the original Cast Recording of *The Sound of Music* during the first quarter.

On the Rhythm and Blues chart, "Smokie—Part 2" by Bill Black's Combo began the year at number one, followed by "Baby (You've Got What It Takes)" by Dinah Washington & Brook Benton, "Fannie Mae" by Buster Brown and "White Silver Sands" by Bill Black's Combo during the first four months.

On the country chart in *Billboard*, "El Paso" by Marty Robbins held the number one position and, during the next four months, the number one song was "He'll Have to Go" by Jim Reeves," which held that position for 14 weeks.

For the recording industry, the year 1960 began with record companies and disc jockeys under a Federal investigation into payola.

Payola: 1960

The Federal Trade Commission filed charges of payola against 15 companies, including Atlantic, Jay-Gee Records, Jerry Blaine's Cosnat Distributing Corporation and Morris Levy's Roulette Records at the beginning of 1960. On January 12, ASCAP again attacked broadcasters and BMI. At a public hearing ASCAP president Stanley Adams asked the FCC to deny licenses to 557 radio stations because they owned conflicting interests in the music field; the FCC ultimately rejected that claim.

On January 31, the FTC added nine more to the payola list, including Sam Weiss, president of Superior Record Sales Corporation, Inc. and George Goldner, president of Gone Recording Corp. and End Music, Inc. That brought the total to 37 named in the payola scandal; however, RCA signed a consent decree with the FTC in mid-December.

The first session of the payola hearings began in Washington in January, 1960. The disc jockey witnesses generally stated they never asked for money, it was simply offered to them. They contended that since they made no agreements concerning airplay before they received the money, there was no payola. While the disc jockeys insisted they didn't play records for money, the label owners all felt that's exactly what their money was buying.

That was the crux of the payola problem. Label owners felt they were paying money in order to stay in good graces with the disc jockey and obtain radio airplay for their records. The disc jockeys felt they were being "thanked" for past airplay and the money was simply a "gift" with no strings attached. At the same time, the disc jockeys couldn't easily say "no" to someone who'd given them money, although occasionally they did not play a record. The label owners accepted the fact that not every record was a hit and were betting that, overall, they'd receive favorable treatment from the DJs, even if they didn't get favorable treatment on a particular record. The label owners were well aware that for every "hit" that was generated, there were others that "stiffed" or didn't sell even when they received airplay.

On February 2, the Grand Jury in New York began its investigations into payola. The District Attorney's office decided to prosecute those who took payola, using testimony from those who received payola, but left alone those who gave payola. That decision sealed the fate of Alan Freed and other disc jockeys, who became the scapegoats in the payola trials. Meanwhile, those who took part in this bribery by paying disc jockeys insisted they did not condone those practices.

Alan Freed was the most visible figure at those trials; he also had the most enemies who wanted to see him fall. Add to that Freed's own self-destructive tendencies and his arrogant behavior and you have the makings of a tragedy played out on a national stage. On February 7 Freed was charged by the Grand Jury with "requesting and accepting" $10,000 from Roulette Records on February 28, 1958.

The problem was worse for Freed because had been on radio in New York, which had laws against payola, while disc jockeys from other states did not face commercial bribery laws. However, those disc jockeys lost their jobs, careers and reputations as the hearings unfolded.

In Washington, the House subcommittee conducting hearings on payola concluded on February 19, although Alan Freed and Dick Clark had not yet testified. Freed's testimony came on Monday, April 25 while Clark's came on April 29. At the hearings, using the alibi that he was a "consultant," Freed openly admitted that he was on the payroll of a number of record companies and distributors--although that was a potential incrimination with the New York Grand jury.

Freed's strategy was that "consultation fees" were not illegal payments; however, during the hearings, Freed admitted he had taken money to give records airplay. Still, Freed insisted he'd never taken a bribe and although he accepted a "gift" if he'd helped someone, he "wouldn't take a dime to plug a record. I'd be a fool to. I'd be giving up control of my own program." At the end of Freed's testimony, the members of the subcommittee felt they had received honest answers.

Dick Clark hired influential Washington attorney Paul Porter for his defense. Dressed in a conservative blue suit, white shirt and dark blue tie, Clark began with an offensive. He read a 34 page statement where he claimed "he had taken no payola. He had followed normal business practices under the ground rules that existed at the time" but that he had been "convicted, condemned and denounced even before he had a chance to tell his story."

At the time of his testimony, Clark's TV and film enterprises consisted of three wholly owned corporations. Drexel Television Productions, formed in July 1958, and the wholly owned subsidiary Drexel Shows, Inc, formed in January, 1959 produced Clark's Saturday night television show and his World of Talent. Drexel Pictures Corporation produced Clark's first movie, *Because They're Young* for Columbia. The third corporation, Drexel Films Corporation, had a movie contract with United Artists to produce two films.

There were allegations that ABC had a double standard when it came to Clark and Freed. At the time of the hearings, Clark was grossing about $12 million annually for ABC while Freed was grossing about $250,000. The fact that ABC allowed Clark to draw up his own affidavit (he admitted he could not have signed the original affidavit) while Freed and other ABC employees were required to sign the internal documents certainly lends credence to that argument. There was also a double standard from the Congressional subcommittee.

Dick Clark stated that during the hearings, while the TV cameras were rolling, the Congressmen acted like attack dogs but when the cameras were off, they tried to ingratiate themselves with the celebrity. According to Clark. the chief counsel, Robert Lishman, "allowed his kid to skip school and took me into the anteroom [during lunch break] to say would I please take pictures with him and give him [an] autograph...The kid had cut school to get my autograph, and his father didn't seem to mind." At a different time, six congressmen sent their wives and children to New York to attend Clark's Saturday night show.

During 1960, "American Bandstand" remained popular and Clark maintained high visibility. "American Bandstand" was produced by Clark through his Click Corporation and the Saturday night show was produced by Clark's Drexel Television Productions, so Clark had a base to expand his business opportunities in TV production after the hearings.

When Dick Clark sold his music-related companies, he took the money and developed a diversified portfolio, investing in a soft drink company, fast food restaurants, radio stations, real estate and oil wells. He also began to develop his TV and movie production companies. He kept one of his most lucrative enterprises, the Dick Clark Caravan of Stars, which toured America, presenting rock'n'roll in a safe setting that helped broaden the music's appeal.

On May 19, 1960, Alan Freed and seven others were arrested in New York City and charged with commercial bribery; Freed was charged with 26 counts, including accepting $10,000 in payola from Roulette Records in 1958. In addition to Freed, the others arrested were Mel Leeds, Peter Tripp, WWRL's Tommy "Dr. Jive" Smalls, WLIB's Hal Jackson and Jack Walker and record librarians Joe Saccone of WMGM and Ron Granger of WINS. They were booked at the Fifth Precinct Elizabeth Street station house in Manhattan.

In June, 1960 the "Communications Act Amendments, 1960" was approved by Oren Harris's Commerce Committee, then by the House Rules Committee. Designed to eliminate payola, quiz show rigging and free plugs for products on the air, the bill contained provisions which authorized the FCC to suspend broadcast licenses for up to ten days and impose fines of up to $1,000 a day for violations. On September 13, President Eisenhower signed the bill into law.

The major effect the payola bill had on radio was that disc jockeys no longer had control over what they played on the air; their kingdoms were crushed. Instead, the program directors at the radio stations tightened their playlists, limited the number of records played, and took over the selection of those records. No longer could a record industry promotion person walk into a major station and have a disc jockey play a new record on the air. The record would have to be submitted to a Program Director and/or a Music Director, who decided whether or not it was aired and, if it was, another record generally had to be dropped.

Indictment of Alan Freed

Three days before his arrest, on May 19, 1960 in New York, Freed started work at KDAY in Santa Monica, California. During his time in California, Freed drank heavily; on November 26, 1962 he was fired from the station. On December 10, in New York, Freed pled guilty to two of the 29 counts of commercial bribery against him and was sentenced to six months--suspended--and a fine of $500. The fine was reduced to $300 after Freed's attorney pleaded lack of funds.

On March 8, 1963 Freed, in an alcoholic haze with huge legal fees hanging over him, paid his $300 fine but still faced the possibility of federal tax evasion charges.

Alan Freed was indicted by a Federal grand jury of evading income tax from 1957 to 1959 on March 15, 1964. He spent his final days in Palm Springs, calling old friends and asking them to send him money while he drank steadily. In the end, Randy Wood and Morris Levy continued to support him. His health deteriorated and on January 20, 1965--the same day Lyndon B. Johnson was sworn in as President--Freed died. He was cremated in Los Angeles at Woodlawn Memorial Park, then his ashes were returned to New York, where they were interred in Hartsdale, New York. A public memorial was held in New York on February 6.

On June 20, 1961 the Federal Trade Commission dismissed payola charges against the distributors of Columbia, Capitol and Dot Records.

Bandstand

In early 1963 Dick Clark began taping all five of his afternoon "American Bandstand Shows" on Saturday, to be broadcast the following week. That caused the show to lose much of it's spontaneity. In the summer of 1963 Bernie Binnick acquired the rights to a single, "She Loves You," by a British group called The Beatles. Binnick convinced Clark to play the song on the "Rate-a-Record" segment on American Bandstand; it was rated a "stiff," in the low 70s and the disc jockeys didn't play it.

In August, American Bandstand moved to Saturday afternoons from its normal weekday afternoon slot.

Elvis Discharged from the Army

Elvis Presley received his discharge from the Army in March, 1960, and within a few days was in RCA's Nashville studio to record six songs backed by his old band members, Scotty Moore and D.J. Fontana, with A-Team musicians Hank Garland, Bob Moore, Buddy Harman, Floyd Cramer and vocals by the Jordanaires. Songs they recorded during the all night session were "Make Me Know It," "Soldier Boy," "Stuck on You," "Fame and Fortune," "A Mess of Blues" and "It Feels So Right." "Stuck on You" was the first single after Elvis' time in the Army.

RCA did not know what songs Elvis would record—or the name of the single—so they printed a 45 sleeve with Elvis's picture. They rushed the finished master to New York, pressed and shipped it within days of Elvis recording it. It reached number one on *Billboard's* Hot 100 and remained there for four consecutive weeks.

Motown Records

Berry Gordy, Jr. first entered the record business after he left the Army; in 1953 he borrowed $700 from his father and brother and opened a record store in Detroit, "3D Record Mart--House of Jazz" that closed its doors in 1955. It seemed that people were less interested in buying jazz than blues and rhythm and blues. Gordy went to work in a Ford auto plant, then quit to become a songwriter. Teaming with Billy Davis, he wrote "Jim Dandy Got Married" for LaVern Baker, "All I Could Do Was Cry" (with Davis and his sister Gwen Gordy) for Etta James, and a string of hits for Jackie Wilson, including "Reet Petite" and "Lonely Teardrops."

Gordy wrote for the Pearl Music publishing company, run by Nat Tarnopol and one day the Matadors, a group of high school students, came by and auditioned; Tarnopol passed but Gordy liked them, introduced himself and met William "Smokey" Robinson.

The Matadors were founded by Smokey Robinson in 1954 while they were students at Morgan High School in Detroit; members included Warren "Pete" Moore (bass), Ronnie White (baritone), Bobby Rogers (tenor) and his brother Emerson Rogers (tenor) in addition to Robinson, who sang lead. In 1956 Claudette Rogers replaced her brother, Emerson, who joined the Army.

After Smokey Robinson and Berry Gordy joined forces, with Gordy serving as the group's manager, they struggled with bookings and recordings. The group changed their name to "The Miracles" and recorded "Got a Job," an answer song to the Silhouettes "Get a Job," which Gordy placed with George Goldner's End Records

Gordy's songwriting partner, Billy Davis, and his sister Gwen Gordy decided to start a label and invited Berry to join; he declined. Finally, he borrowed $800 from his family and started his own label, Tamla. The first releases were by Marv Johnson and Eddie Holland, but neither hit. Gordy set up a small studio, "Hitsville," and the first song he recorded there was "Money" by singer Barrett Strong, a song Gordy co-wrote. Released on both Tamla and Anna (his sister's label) the recording reached number 23 on the *Billboard* Hot 100 in 1960 and number two on the R&B chart (where it stayed for six weeks).

The Tamla label was the beginning of the Motown empire and "Shop Around" by Smokey Robinson and the Miracles became the defining record for the Motown sound; it was the first number one record from Motown on *Billboard's* R&B chart.

That was R&B aimed for a white audience, smooth, hip and classy. By the end of 1961, Smokey Robinson was a vice president at Tamla and the Motown era had begun.

Pop in L.A.: Late 1950s & Early 1960s

The pop/rock music scene in Los Angeles during the late 1950s and early 1960s featured a number of actors who came from TV shows. Annette Funicello was on the popular "Mickey Mouse Club" show that ran from 1955 to 1958. In 1959 she had a top ten single with "Tall Paul" on Disneyland Records. She was then signed to Buena Vista Records (Disney owned the label) and had 12 chart singles for that label. Shelley Fabares, who starred on "The Donna Reed Show," had a number one hit with "Johnny Angel" on Colpix in 1962; she had four more chart singles. Paul Peterson, who also starred on "The Donna Reed Show" had a top ten single with "Mid Day" on Colpix; he had five other chart singles. Johnny Crawford, who starred on "The Rifleman" TV series with Chuck Connors, had a top ten single with "Cindy's Birthday" on Del-Fi in 1962; he had nine other chart singles. Connie Stevens, who starred on "Hawaiian Eye" had a top five hit with "Sixteen Reasons" on Warner in 1960 and a top five hit with Ed "Kookie" Byrnes, who starred in the TV series "77 Sunset Strip." Stevens sang the chorus on "Kookie, Kookie (Lend Me Your Comb)," a top five hit in 1959. On her own, Stevens had five other chart singles.

Although there were pop and rock songs in films—the prime example being "Rock Around the Clock" by Bill Haley and His Comets in *Blackboard Jungle*, released in 1955, the film connection to rock'n'roll came primarily through a series of films released by American International Pictures.

The Brill Building

"The Brill Building" became known as the last bastion of Tin Pan Alley songwriting in New York. The key years were 1958-1963 or the early years of rock'n'roll until the Beatles hit. The term is actually a misnomer; there were two buildings in New York on Broadway where a number of publishers, songwriters and independent labels had offices. The Brill Building was located at 1619 Broadway while 1650 Broadway also housed publishers and songwriters writing songs for young rock acts. Ironically, it was the 1650 Broadway building and not the Brill Building where most of the songwriters and publishers who provided songs for young rock'n'rollers were housed.

The Brill Building, which opened in 1931, was named for its owners, who had a men's haberdashery on the ground floor. In 1958 there were 90 music publishers in the building, mostly ASCAP writers and publishers. Two blocks uptown and on the other side of the street was 1650 Broadway, which opened in 1922. In 1958 there were 66 music publishers in that building.

New York had a long history of "Tin Pan Alley" songs, or songs written by professional songwriters for the commercial market. During the late 1950s and early 1960s the demand for songs came from the teen market. A local group might come up with a hit, but could not create a string of hits. The acts thought of themselves as singers and entertainers; they were touring, singing their hits and their source of songs came from professional songwriters.

There were a number of songwriters in New York during that time but there were seven songwriting teams who were the core of what became known as "Brill Building songwriters." Those teams were: Jerry Leiber and

Mike Stoller; Doc Pomus and Mort Shuman; Burt Bacharach and Hal David; Neil Sedaka and Howard Greenfield; Carole King and Gerry Goffin; Barry Mann and Cynthia Weil; and Jeff Barry and Ellie Greenwich

Interestingly all of the songwriters were Jewish except one (Ellie Greenwich) and she was half Jewish (her mother was Jewish and her father was Catholic). Most were born or grew up in Brooklyn; all were New Yorkers.

The songwriter's rooms in the Brill Building and at 1650 Broadway were about six feet by seven feet with a piano, a table, a couple of old chairs and no window. The general idea was that the rooms were so uncomfortable--with no window to look out of for distractions--that songwriters wrote quickly in order to leave them, thus producing a large number of songs.

Leiber and Stoller

Songwriters Jerry Leiber and Mike Stoller began their career in Los Angeles, where both had lived since the mid-1940s. Steeped in blues and R&B, Leiber and Stoller were the "hep cats," the "coolest" by any measure during the 1950s and early 1960s. Leiber (b. April 25, 1933) grew up in Baltimore in a Jewish neighborhood; Stoller (b. March 13, 1933) was born on Long Island but moved to Queens when he was four. Stoller grew up on classical music and heard black music when he attended interracial summer camps. In 1945 Lieber's family moved to L.A.; in 1949 Stoller's family made the move West.

In Los Angeles, Stoller was interested in classical music and modern jazz but both he and Leiber loved black music, which they sometimes referred to as "alley music." During World War II the black population in Los Angeles more than doubled, so there were opportunities for Leiber and Stoller to hear black music. Both dropped out of Los Angeles City College. During the 1950s they wrote songs for a number of R&B performers, including Johnny Otis, Jimmy Witherspoon, Charles Brown, Little Esther and Little Willie Littlefield. Their first hit was "Hound Dog" by Big Mama Thornton in 1952, which became a number one hit on the R&B chart. Later, Elvis covered the song. They also wrote "K.C. Lovin'" in 1952 which became a hit for Wilbur Harrison as "Kansas City" in 1959.

In L.A. Leiber and Stoller formed a record company, Spark, and recorded the Robins; the first Leiber-Stoller song released as a single was "That's What the Good Book Says." Because of problems with distribution, the Robins records were not heard in the East. Leiber and Stoller took members of the Robins and formed The Coasters and produced them. At the end of 1957

Jerry Leiber and Mike Stoller moved from Los Angeles to New York, after writing a number of songs for Elvis Presley, including "Jailhouse Rock" and the songs for Elvis' *Jailhouse Rock* movie.

Leiber and Stoller moved to New York because that's where the pop music business was headquartered. There were headquarters for the major labels RCA, Columbia, and Decca; the major publishers were also there as well as a number of start-up independent labels. The TV networks were located there, the performance rights organizations (ASCAP and BMI) and the radio stations who commanded the largest audiences.

In 1959 Leiber & Stoller had 12 songs on the pop charts. In an article in *Time,* Leiber lamented that "At least 60% of our stuff is rock'n'roll and we're sick of it. But consumers dictate the market: kids nine to 14 make up our market and this is the stuff they want." (**Emerson 64**) Leiber and Stoller wanted to write Broadway musicals, the pinnacle for songwriters, but their audience was teenagers, not the Broadway audience. Ironically, years later a Broadway musical, *Smokey Joe's Café,* was comprised of their songs.

The hit songs of Jerry Leiber and Mike Stoller include rock and roll classics such as "Hound Dog," "Charlie Brown," "Stand By Me," "Spanish Harlem," "Yakety Yak," "Along Came Jones," "This Magic Moment," "Bossa Nova Baby," "Don't," "Girls, Girls, Girls," "His Kiss," "I (Who Have Nothing)," "Is That All There Is?," "Jailhouse Rock," "Kansas City," "Little Egypt," "Love Me," "Love Potion #9," "Loving You," "On Broadway," "Poison Ivy," "Ruby Baby," "Searchin'," "Smokey Joe's Cafe," "There Goes My Baby," "Treat Me Nice," "(You're So Square) Baby I Don't Care" and "Young Blood."

Aldon Publishing

The publishing company at the forefront of "Brill Building" rock'n'roll was Aldon, founded by Don Kirshner and Al Nevin, although they were actually located at 1650 Broadway.

Don Krishner grew up in the Bronx, the son of a tailor; he spent a year at City College then went to Upsala College in East Orange, New Jersey, where he graduated with a degree in Business Administration. Kirshner met Robert Walden Cassotto, a sickly child who was not expected to live past 16; Cassotto, a Hunter College dropout, wanted to be "the most important entertainer in the world" and patterned his career after Frank Sinatra. Kirshner and Cassotto joined forces and Cassoto changed his name to Bobby Darin; his first hit was "Splish Splash."

Kirshner approached Al Nevins, a music industry veteran, to become a partner in a publishing venture and Nevins agreed. Their first songwriters were Neil Sedaka and Howard Greenfield who told them that if the publishers placed one of their songs with a recording artist in the next three months the songwriters would sign a long-term contract with the firm.

Concetta Maria Franconero had been renamed Connie Francis by Arthur Godfrey; at the time, she'd had her first hit, "Who's Sorry Now." Kirshner knew her from his connection with Bobby Darin and pitched her Sedaka and Greenfield's "Stupid Cupid." She recorded the song and it was a chart single for her. That put Aldon in the music publishing business.

The songwriter's lives at Aldon were built around writing songs and making demos. At the end of the day they all went into Kirshner's office and played their songs. Kirshner was always encouraging and optimistic and songwriters loved him; he was also a great song plugger and consistently got their songs recorded by artists. Kirshner could neither read nor write nor play music but he knew a great song when he heard it and he knew how to inspire songwriters. The songwriters that Aldon signed included Sedaka, Greenfield, Gerry Goffin, Carole King, Barry Mann and Cynthia Weil. Those songwriters--and Kirshner--turned rock'n'roll into a profession rather than just a vehicle for rebellion.

Kirshner served songwriters as well as A&R men with record labels. "If you were an A&R person, he could make you feel he had the answer to your problems," said producer Richard Gottehrer. "And your problem, if you were signing teenage talent, was what in the hell were they going to record?"

Neil Sedaka and Howard Greenfield

Neil Sedaka (b. March 13, 1939) and Howard Greenfield (b. March 15, 1936) both grew up in Brooklyn. Sedaka's father was a Turkish immigrant and Sedaka was a musical prodigy; he studied classical piano at the Juilliard School of Music.

During the period 1960-1962 Sedaka and Greenfield wrote "Oh, Carol," "Stairway to Heaven," "Calendar Girl," "Breaking Up Is Hard to Do," "Little Devil," "Happy Birthday, Sweet Sixteen" and "Next Door to an Angel," most of which were hits for Sedaka.

Neil Sedaka obtained a recording contract with RCA Victor and in 1958 his first single, "The Diary" was released. His third single, "Oh! Carol," reportedly written for singer/songwriter Carole King, was released the following year and became his first top ten single. That was followed by a string of hit singles into the early 1960s.

Sedaka was musically talented and was soon on the road performing his hits, leaving Greenfield without a co-writer until he joined with Jack Keller. Greenfield and Keller wrote every Monday and Wednesday for six years; they started at 10 in the morning with coffee and then continued throughout the day. They wrote "Everybody's Somebody's Fool" and "My Heart Has a Mind of Its Own," which were Connie Francis's first and second number one singles. Those songs were covered by Ernest Tubb, Patti Page and Brenda Lee.

Keller and Greenfield also wrote "Venus in Blue Jeans" for Jimmy Clanton while Greenfield and Carole King wrote "Crying In the Rain" for the Everly Brothers. Goffin and Keller wrote together on Tuesdays and Thursdays.

Barry Mann and Cynthia Weil

Cynthia Weil (b. October 18, 1940) grew up in Manhattan, attended the University of Michigan for a year, then graduated from Sarah Lawrence with a major in theatre. Weil loved Broadway musicals and began writing for Frank Loesser, the Broadway writer who wrote *Guys and Dolls* and *How To Succeed In Business Without Really Trying*. Loesser hated rock'n'roll and called teenage rock'n'roll fans "pimple farms."

Barry Mann was born Barry Imbermann (February 9, 1939) in Brooklyn; he grew up loving the radio show "Make Believe Ballroom" hosted by Martin Block and his musical idols were Frankie Laine, Johnny Ray and Patti Page. Mann dropped out of the Pratt Institute in 1957 and began writing songs with Larry Kolber; they wrote "Patches," a hit for Dickie Lee in 1962.

Nevins and Kirshner pitched Barry Mann as an artist to ABC-Paramount, who signed him and released "Who Put the Bomp (in the Bomp, Bomp, Bomp)," a spoof of doo wop lyrics, written by Mann and Goffin (who wrote the lyrics).

Mann-Weill hits include "(You're My) Soul and Inspiration" by the Righteous Brothers; "Blame It on the Bossa Nova" by Eydie Gorme; "Come Back Silly Girl" by The Lettermen; "Come on Over to My Place" by The Drifters; "Hungry" and "Kicks" by Paul Revere and the Raiders; "Johnny Loves Me" by Shelley Fabares; "Looking Through the Eyes of Love" by Gene Pitney; "Saturday Night at the Movies" by the Drifters; "Uptown" by The Crystals; and "We Gotta Get Out of This Place" by The Animals.

Their most famous song is "You've Lost That Lovin' Feeling" by the Righteous Brothers (written with Phil Spector). Mann and Weil also wrote "I Love How You Love Me" by the Paris Sisters and "Walking in the Rain" by the Ronettes with Spector.

Gerry Goffin and Carole King

Carol Klein (b. February 9, 1942) became Carole King when she released her first single for ABC-Paramount. Klein entered Queens College with the intention of following in her mother's footsteps and become a teacher. Blessed with perfect pitch, she recorded a number of demos for songwriters, including some for classmate Paul Simon. In college she married another classmate, chemistry major Gerry Goffin (b. February 11, 1939) after she became pregnant.

King dropped out of college and worked as a secretary after their marriage (she was 17, he was 20) while Goffin worked at a chemical plant.

Gerry Goffin wrote lyrics and he and Carole wrote songs in the evening after work. Michael Anthony Orlando Cassivitis, who became known as Tony Orlando, recorded some of their demos..

One day in the fall of 1960, Goffin came home sometime after nine; he had worked all day and then bowled in a bowling league. King was at a friend's house playing mah-jong. On the tape recorder was a note that Carole left stating that Don Kirshner needed a song by the next day for the Shirelles, a group who had just had a hit with "Tonight's the Night." Goffin listened to the tape and liked the melody that King had composed. The melody had no bridge--just three verses. Goffin started writing and "The lyric came out so easy," said Goffin. King came home around midnight and the two worked on the bridge and finished "Tomorrow."

The next day Kirshner heard the song and was excited; he thought it was a great song and took it to Mitch Miller for Johnny Mathis but Miller turned it down. Tony Orlando wanted to record it but Kirshner realized by this time that the song was more a "girl" song that a "guy" song.

The Shirelles, comprised of Shirley Owens, Addie "Micki" Harris, Beverly Lee and Doris Coley, began singing together in 1957 when they were students at Passaic High School in Passaic, New Jersey. Known originally as the Poquellos ("birds"), the group needed an original song for a talent contest and wrote "I Met Him on a Sunday." In February, 1958 they recorded for Tiara Records, which changed their name to the "Shirelles" (a derivative of "Shirley") and released the record, then sold the master to

Decca. "I Met Him on a Sunday" was a chart record on *Billboard's* Hot 100 but the next two singles failed to chart so Decca dropped the group.

Tiara Records was owned by Mary Jane Greenberg, the mother of a classmate of the Shirelles; Greenberg started Scepter Records in 1959 and, after the Shirelles were dropped by Decca, she recorded them. Their first single was "Dedicated to the One I Love," originally recorded by the 5 Royals. Greenberg hired Luther Dixon to head A&R for the label and Dixon wrote "Tonight's the Night," which was a chart record for the group.

Scepter Records had an office in the Brill Building and either Kirshner or King and Goffin played "Tomorrow" for Luther Dixon, who played it for the Shirelles; the group didn't like it because they thought it sounded too much like country music.

Dixon insisted they record it and changed the title to "Will You Love Me Tomorrow" (leaving out the "still" before "tomorrow"). The song entered the *Billboard* Hot 100 at the end of November, 1961 and reached number one--the first record by a female group to hit number one since the McGuire Sisters in 1958 and the first ever by a African-American female group--and stayed at number one for two weeks. The song then entered the R&B chart where it stayed at the number two position for four weeks.

The second number one single for Goffin-King was "Take Good Care of My Baby" by Bobby Vee.

Other hit songs by Carole King and Gerry Goffin include "Chains" by the Cookies (and later, the Beatles); "Don't Bring Me Down" by the Animals; "Every Breath I Take" by Gene Pitney; "Go Away, Little Girl" by Steve Lawrence; "I Can't Stay Mad at You" by Skeeter Davis; "I'm Into Something Good" by Herman Hermits; "One Fine Day" by the Chiffons; "Point of No Return" by Gene McDaniels; "Some Kind of Wonderful" for The Drifters; "Up on the Roof" by The Drifters; and "Walkin' With My Angel" by Bobby Vee. The duo wrote "(You Make Me Feel Like) A Natural Woman" with co-writer credit to Jerry Wexler; King and Howard Greenfield wrote "Crying in the Rain" for the Everly Brothers; and King wrote the James Taylor hit, "You've Got a Friend" by herself.

Ellie Greenwich and Jeff Barry

Ellie Greenwich (b. October 23, 1940) was born in Brooklyn but at age 11 moved to Long Island. She attended Queens College, then graduated from Hofstra and intended to teach high school English. Listening to Alan Freed on the radio, she fell in love with rock'n'roll. She joined Trio Music and was mentored by Leiber and Stoller. Greenwich was a popular singer of demos.

Jeff Barry was born Joel Adelberg (April 3, 1938) in Brooklyn but moved to New Jersey when he was seven. Barry studied Industrial Design at City College of New York before he dropped out to write songs. Adelberg took the name "Barry" when he recorded for RCA; his first big songwriting hit was "Tell Laura I Love Her" for Ray Peterson that he wrote with Ben Raleigh.

On October 28, 1962, Ellie Greenwich and Jeff Barry married and Barry left E.B. Marks Publishing and joined Greenwich at Trinity Music in the Brill Building. Unlike the writers at Aldon, Barry and Greenwich were not enamored with Broadway musicals or the Great American songbook and they had little background or interest in classical or jazz. Their interest was in teenage rock'n'roll records and that's what they set out to write.

They were joined in their writing efforts by Phil Spector; the three wrote "He's Sure the Boy I Love, " "Da Doo Ron Ron" "Then He Kissed Me" and "Little Boy" all for The Crystals; "Chapel of Love" for the Dixie Cups; "River Deep, Mountain High" for Ike and Tina Turner; and "Be My Baby," and "Baby I Love You" for the Ronettes.

Barry-Greenwich hits include "Do Wah Diddy Diddy" by Manfred Man; "The Kind of Boy You Can't Forget" by The Raindrops; "All Grown Up" by the Crystals; "Hanky Panky" by Tommy James and the Shondells; "Maybe I Know" by Lesley Gore; and "You Don't Know What You're Missing ('Til It's Gone)" by the Exciters. Greenwich and Barry with George Morton wrote "Leader of the Pack" by the Shangri La's.

Doc Pomus and Mort Shuman

Jerome Felder (b. June 27, 1925) grew up in Brooklyn and was crippled by polio when he was six. He became "Doc Pomus" during his late teenage years. The son of Austrian immigrants, Pomus dropped out of Brooklyn College of Music and began performing; he grew up on big band music but loved blues and jazz. Mort Shuman (b. November 12, 1936) was the son of Polish immigrants; he attended City College but dropped out to write songs. Shuman loved Latin music (there were a number of Latinos in New York and Cuban music and the "cha-cha" dance were popular during the early 1960s) but Pomus and Shuman mainly loved the blues and their songs were heavily influenced by blues and early rhythm and blues.

In 1961 Elvis recorded three Doc Pomus-Mort Shuman songs during one session: "Kiss Me Quick," "Little Sister" and "(Marie's the Name of) His Latest Flame." In total, Elvis recorded 16 Pomus-Shuman songs, plus several others each wrote alone or with someone else.

Doc Pomus-Mort Shuman hits include "I Count the Tears," "Save the Last Dance for Me" "Sweets for my Sweet" and "This Magic Moment" by The Drifters; "A Teenager in Love" by Dion and the Belmonts; "Suspicion" by Terry Stafford; and "Hound Dog Man" by Fabian. With Phil Spector the duo wrote "Clinging Vine" by Bobby Vinton and Pomus wrote "Lonely Avenue" for Ray Charles.

The roots of the song "Save the Last Dance for Me" came from Doc Pomus's wedding. Pomus' polio meant that he walked with difficulty and could not dance. He married a beautiful young woman and during the wedding reception, as he watched her dance with other men, he jotted down the idea for "Save the Last Dance For Me."

Talking about his songwriting, Doc Pomus once said, "Every hit song I've ever written has been rejected by ten or fifteen artists."

Hal David and Burt Bacharach

Hal David (b. May 25, 1921), son of an Austrian immigrant, moved to Brooklyn when he was one. His brother Mack David was nine years older and had already established himself as a songwriter when Hal dropped out of New York University, where he studied journalism, to work for the *New York Post*. Mack David had written "I Don't Care if the Sun Don't Shine" and "Cherry Pink and Apple Blossom White." Both Davids were mainly lyricists.

Burt Bacharach (b. May 12, 1929) moved to Queens when he was one and studied music composition at McGill University in Montreal before moving to New York as a songwriter. The publisher Famous Music put Bacharach and David together in 1957; they developed a routine where they met every morning at 11 a.m. and wrote through the day. Their earliest hits were "The Story of My Life," a country hit for Marty Robbins; "Magic Moments" for Perry Como and "Another Time, Another Place" for Patti Page.

Bacharach had an intense dislike for rock'n'roll, and once announced "I never wrote a rock and roll song in my life." He also wasn't "cool"; Bacharach struck people as a college preppie, an Ivy League kind of guy.

Both Bacharach and David had written hits with others before their successful collaborations. David and Paul Hampton wrote "Sea of Heartbreak" for Don Gibson; David and Sherman Edwards wrote "Johnny Get Angry" for Joanie Sommers. Bacharach and Bob Hilliard wrote "Tower of Strength" and "A Hundred Pounds of Clay" for Gene McDaniel.

Bacharach began hanging out with Leiber and Stoller, learning how to produce. He still wrote with Hal David three days a week as well as with other lyric writers. The big breakthrough for Bacharach and David came when Bacharach met Dionne Warrick in 1961 at a session for the Drifters produced by Leiber and Stoller. The Drifters recorded "Mexican Divorce," written by Bacharach and Bob Hilliard and Warrick was a back-up vocalist. Warrick came from East Orange, New Jersey and, at the time they met, was a 21-year-old music major at Hartt College in Connecticut. Dionne's aunt was Cissy Houston and her sister was Dee Dee Warrick; the three performed as the Gospelaires.

Bacharach and David had success with Gene Pitney: "The Man Who Shot Liberty Valance," "Only Love Can Break a Heart" and "Twenty-Four Hours from Tulsa." Greenberg signed Warrick to Scepter and engaged Bacharach and David in a package deal to write songs and produce her. At first, Warrick sang demos for Bacharach and David, who were unable to come up with a song just for her. Out of frustration one day she yelled at them, "Don't make me over, man!" and walked out of the studio. A week later she came back and they had written her first hit, "Don't Make Me Over," released at the end of 1962. On that first single her name was misspelled, so she became Dionne "Warwick."

Dionne Warwick established Bacharach and David as pop songwriters; their string of hits with her include "Anyone Who Had a Heart," "Walk On By," "You'll Never Get to Heaven (If You Break My Heart)," "A House Is Not a Home," "Reach Out For Me" and "(There's) Always Something There To Remind Me."

Phil Spector

Producer Phil Spector played an important part in the success of the Brill Building songwriters because those songwriters wrote many of the hits for Spector's productions.

Phil Spector (b. December 26, 1939 in the Bronx), son of a Russian immigrant family, spent his first 12 years in New York. On April 20, 1949, Spector's father committed suicide. In 1953, Spector moved to Los Angeles with his mother.

During high school, Spector, Marshall Leib, Sandy Nelson and Annette Kleinbard formed the Teddy Bears. Spector had written a song, "To Know Him Is Love Him," which was the epitaph on his father's tombstone. The record reached number one on December 1, 1958. This was one of the first Los Angeles recordings to be a national pop hit.

Stan Ross, who co-owned Gold Star Studios, tutored Spector on record production. Spector found his niche in the studio as a record producer.

Former promotion man Lester Sill sent Spector to New York to work with Jerry Leiber and Mike Stoller and Spector co-wrote "Spanish Harlem" for Ben E. King with Leiber. Spector also worked as a session musician, playing guitar. In New York, Specter produced sessions on LaVern Baker, Ruth Brown, Billy Storm and Ray Peterson before he returned to Los Angeles. Lester Sill formed Gregmark Records with Lee Hazlewood and Spector produced "I Love How You Love Me" by the Paris Sisters for that label.

In 1961 Spector and Sills founded Philles Records and Spector found the Crystals through Hill and Range Publishers. He produced a number one hit, "He's a Rebel," attributed to the Crystals on Philles, although the actual singers were Darlene Love and the Blossoms. Spector signed the Ronettes to Philles and produced "Be My Baby" on them, which was a hit in 1963.

Spector produced hits in both New York and Los Angeles, creating his famous "Wall of Sound" where he overdubbed a number of instruments to create a mini-symphony for teenagers. His production techniques changed pop music production and his "Wall of Sound" became a defining sound for the records he produced. In a car, records from that era were heard on a three-inch speaker in the middle of the dashboard.

In 1962 Spector bought out Sill's part in Philles Records and continued producing hits. For the Crystals he produced "Da Doo Ron Ron," "Then He Kissed Me," and "He's Sure the Boy I Love"; for the Ronettes he produced "Be My Baby," "Baby I Love You" and "Walking In the Rain"; for Darlene Love he produced "(Today I Met) The Boy I'm Gonna Marry" and "Wait Til My Bobby Gets Home"; and for the Righteous Brothers he produced the classic "You've Lost That Lovin' Feeling."

Aldon's Record Labels

Jerry Leiber and Mike Stoller formed labels and production companies in order to produce their songs on artists and control the creative process. Kirshner and Nevins decided to follow in their footsteps.

During the summer of 1962 Kirshner and Nevins created two record labels: Companion and Dimension. The first release on Companion was "It Might As Well Rain Until September" by Carole King and the first release on Dimension was "The Loco-Motion," written by Carole King and Gerry Goffin and recorded by their 19-year-old babysitter, Eva Narcissus Boyd. The song was written as an answer to all the "Twist" songs that were coming out. Boyd, who had sung backup for the Kookies on a few sessions, was chosen to sing the demo because she sounded like Dee Dee Sharp and King and Goffin wanted to take the demo to Cameo-Parkway, the label releasing the "twist" records.

The demo came off so well that Kirshner and Nevins released it on Dimension; the record became number one on the pop chart in August, 1962. The song it replaced at number one was "Breaking Up Is Hard to Do" by Neil Sedaka.

During 1962, Aldon Publishing had two number one hits, eight top ten songs and 18 top twenty songs on the *Billboard* Hot 100 chart.

Aldon Sold

Don Kirshner and Al Nevins sold Aldon Music, Dimension Records and their production company to Screen Gems, the recording and publishing subsidiary of Columbia Pictures, for $2.5 million in April, 1963. Kirshner, who had just turned 29, became a millionaire with the sale; he was named executive vice-president in charge of all Columbia Pictures-Screen Gems publishing and recording activities. Nevins became a consultant for Columbia Pictures.

The new company left the Aldon offices at 1650 Broadway and moved to 711 Fifth Avenue. The new offices were large and elaborate, but the songwriters felt they had lost their intimate connection with Kirshner.

In Ken Emerson's history of the Brill Building songwriters, *Always Magic in the Air*, he quotes Richard Gottehrer, who states that Kirshner's writers did not show up for work in the morning saying, "Well, I'm going to write a great song today. It was 'I'm going to write a song for the Shirelles,' and you'd have five groups of people writing songs for the Shirelles. They would go in and make the demos, Donnie would screen them, pick the ones he wanted to present, and that was it."

Most of the pop songwriters of that era "thought their songs were as short-lived as their initial stint on the charts. Few if any suspected that some of their work would outlast the puberty of the teenagers who bought it and become standards like the best songs of the previous generation." Artie Butler stated, "We never, ever, ever--any of us--thought that this music would be on the radio thirty-five years later." Mike Stoller said, "What we wrote were records and [we felt] that these records were like newspapers or magazines in that they'd last a month and then they'd be gone...All the standards had been written, we thought."

The beginning of the end for the Brill Building songwriters was when Bob Dylan hit in the early 1960s, then the British Invasion, led by the Beatles, meant that most artists and groups wrote their songs. The music industry shifted to the West Coast during the 1960s as Warner Brothers, based in Los Angeles, became the leading rock label and the pop and rock music business shifted to L.A.

Time Magazine **and the Nashville Sound**

An article on Jim Reeves in *Time* magazine in 1960 referred to the "Nashville Sound," a term that was increasingly picked up by the media when discussing the recordings coming out of Nashville. The first documented use of the term was in 1958 in a trade magazine, *Music Reporter*. The article, "Hoedown on a Harpischord," stated "Nashville has even nosed out Hollywood as the nation's second biggest (after New York) record-producing center," stating further that "20% or one out of five" pop hits was written and recorded in Nashville." Discussing the Nashville Sound, the magazine noted "As nearly as anybody can define it, the Sound is the byproduct of musical illiteracy."

Songs From Nashville

There were only four songs that reached number one on *Billboard's* country chart in 1960 and all four were crossovers that became hits in the pop field, showing the world the commercial appeal of Nashville music.

"He'll Have to Go" by Jim Reeves was released at the end of 1959 and during 1960 it was a prime example of the Nashville Sound as the smooth-voiced Jim Reeves sang the ballad. It was number one for 14 weeks, remained on the country chart for 34 weeks, and crossed over to the pop chart where it remained at number two for three weeks.

Bob Ferguson wrote "Wings of a Dove," a country gospel song that Ferlin Huskey recorded. That song was number one for ten consecutive weeks on the country chart and number four on the *Billboard* Hot 100. The song was recorded in Bradley's studio.

"Alabam" by Cowboy Copus was number one for 12 weeks on *Billboard's* country chart but only number 84 on the *Billboard* Hot 100.

Other big songs from Nashville in 1960 were "I'd Be a Legend in My Time," "Sweet Dreams" and "Just One Time" by Don Gibson, a "history song," "Since the Bismark" by Johnny Horton, a song inspired from western TV shows, "Big Iron" by Marty Robins, the smoth "The Old Lamplighter" by the Browns, Loretta Lynn's first release, "Honky Tonk Girl" on the Zero label, "Please Help Me I'm Falling" by Hank Locklin featured pianist Floyd Cramer playing in a "slipped note" style. The origin of that style came from Don Robertson, who wrote the song and recorded the demo, using that "slipped note" style. Producer Chet Atkins played the demo for Cramer and encouraged him to use it in a song. That led Cramer to write and record "Last Date," which also became a hit in 1960, reaching number two on the "Hot 100" chart and number 11 on the country chart.

Cramer's next two singles, "On the Rebound" and "San Antonio Rose," were both pop hits in 1961, played in the "slipped note" style that defined the sound of Floyd Cramer. After Cramer's release of "Last Date," Skeeter Davis recorded "My Last Date (With You)" with lyrics by her and Boudleaux Bryant. In 1963 Duane Eddy recorded "Last Date" with Floyd and in 1972 Conway Twitty recorded "(Lost Her Love) On Our Last Date." Cramer's recording is in the Grammy Hall of Fame.

"Are You Lonesome Tonight?"

Elvis Presley recorded "Are You Lonesome Tonight" in Nashville's RCA Studio B at 4 a.m. on April 4. Written by Lou Handman and Roy Turk, the song was first recorded on May 9, 1927 for Harmony Records; there were other early recordings by Charles Hart, Vaughn De Leath, Henry Burr and the duet of Jerry Macy and John Ryan. In 1950, the Blue Barron Orchestra recorded it. Gene Austin used to perform the song during his shows when Colonel Tom Parker managed Austin; this is how it came to be Parker's wife, Marie's, favorite song. The only time Parker requested Elvis to do a song was when he requested the singer record "Are You Lonesome Tonight."

Elvis was discharged from the Army in March, 1960 and returned to RCA's Nashville studio to record songs for his album, *Elvis is Back*. Elvis recorded six songs on March 20, then appeared on a TV special with Frank Sinatra in Miami before returning to the studio for more recordings on April 3. Elvis recorded eight songs that evening before he tackled "Are You Lonesome Tonight." Engineer Bill Porter was editing "Such a Night," the song Elvis had just recorded, when producer Steve Sholes told him to "roll the tape." Porter replied that he hadn't heard the song but Sholes countered "roll the tape." Elvis had requested that all the lights be turned off for this song so Porter could not see what was going on in the studio; he quickly realized there was no piano, just an acoustic guitar, bass and the Jordanaires. Scrambling, Porter began turning the other microphones in the studio off but still had a lot of echo on Elvis's voice when he began the recitation. Porter thought he's get it right on the next take but Elvis did not want to do the song again—telling Sholes to throw the recording away. The Jordanaires had made a mistake on the last chord of the song and Porter wanted to record it again. Sholes told Porter to keep the take and Porter requested that Elvis and the Jordanaires just sing the ending. They did and Porter spliced the tape for the "fix," so on "to" is on one side of the splice and "night" is on the other side.

During the recording Elvis had bumped a mic stand in the dark but that did not stop the song reaching number one on the Hot 100 and remaining in that position for six weeks after it was released on November 1, 1960. The song debuted on the country chart on December 12; it had reached number one on the pop chart on November 28, where it remained until January 9, 1961. It reached number three on the R&B chart and was a number one record in the U.K.

"Rockin' Around the Christmas Tree"

Brenda Lee recorded "Rockin' Around the Christmas Tree" on October 19, 1958 and it was released that year but did not chart until the 1960 Christmas season. Written by Johnny Marks, who also wrote "Rudolph the Red-Nosed Reindeer," "A Holly Jolly Christmas" and "Run Rudolph Run," the recording was produced by Owen Bradley for Decca with Grady Martin providing the guitar intro, Boots Randolph on saxophone and Buddy Harman on drums. The record was not a hit until Lee had hits with "Sweet Nuthin's," "I'm Sorry" and "I Want to Be Wanted."

Fred Foster and Monument Records

In 1960, Fred Foster, owner and head of Monument Records, moved his company from Washington, D.C. to Nashville and settled in Hendersonville, a suburb north of downtown Nashville. "Gotta Travel On" was a big hit for Billy Grammer on Monument in 1959; it reached number four on *Billboard's* Hot 100 Chart and number five on the country chart.

Foster produced Roy Orbison, another artist on his label and "Only The Lonely (Know The Way I Feel)" was released in 1960. This was the beginning of a series of pop and rock hits by Roy Orbison for Monument that were recorded in Nashville. Those songs include "Running Scared," "Crying," "Dream Baby (How Long Must I Dream), "It's Over" and, in 1964, "Oh, Pretty Woman."

Sit-Ins

On February 1, 1960, African-Americans staged a sit in at a lunch counter in Woolworth's store in Greensboro, North Carolina. That led to sit-ins in a number of stores in Greensboro and kicked off the sit-ins during the Civil Rights movement.

There had been sit-ins two years before; in July, 1958 in Wichita, Kansas, and the next month in Oklahoma City sit-ins led to the desegregation of lunch counters.

The sit-ins at lunch counters in downtown stores in Nashville, beginning on February 13, led to violent reactions from whites when black students attempted to be served. The Nashville sit-ins, organized by the Nashville Student Movement and Nashville Christian Leadership Council, was a non-violent movement, inspired by the teachings of Gandhi and Reverend Martin Luther King but the non-violence by the black students was met with whites verbally and physically attacking the students. Over 150 non-violent protesters were arrested.

On April 19, the home of Z. Alexander Looby, an attorney who defended the protesters, was bombed but no one was hurt. The next day, Tennessee State student Diane Nash led 4,000 marchers to the Nashville Court House to confront Mayor Ben West. On the Court House steps, Mayor West agreed that lunch counters should be desegregated. On April 21, Reverend Martin Luther King, Jr. spoke at Fisk University and praised the Nashville sit-in movement for its organization. During his talk, before an audience of 4,000, King said, "We will say, do what you will to us, but we will wear you down by our capacity to suffer."

The sit-ins, and boycott of downtown Nashville stores, ended on May 10 after merchants agreed to serve African-Americans at their lunch counters.

The sit-ins inspired wade-ins at all white beaches, read-ins at libraries and kneel-ins at racially segregated churches. There was violence; in Texas, a civil rights protestor was found hanging upside down from a tree with "KKK" carved in his chest.

"The Twist"

On August 1, 1960, "The Twist" by Chubby Checker entered the *Billboard* Hot 100 Chart; it reached number one and remained on the chart for 18 weeks. The dance created a national craze. Writer Lillian Roxon described the dance, stating "You put one foot out and you pretend you're stubbing out a cigarette butt on the floor with the big toe. At the same time, you move your hands and body as though you're drying every inch of your back with an invisible towel."

The song was written by Hank Ballard who, with his group The Midnighters, had a string of R&B hits dating back to 1953 that included "Work With Me Annie," "Sexy Ways," "Annie Had a Baby" and "Finger

Poppin' Time." Hank Ballard and the Midnighters had a top 20 R&B hit with "The Twist" in 1959; it reached number 16 on the R&B chart and in 1960, entered the Hot 100 two weeks before Chubby Checker's but only reached number 28.

Ballard had reportedly written "The Twist" after watching the dance moves by teen dancers on "The Buddy Dean Show," a local dance show in Baltimore akin to Dick Clark's "Bandstand" show out of Philadelphia. The popularity of "The Twist" led to interviews with leading music industry executives who, for the most part, agreed that the Twist was here to stay.

"The Twist" led to songwriters writing—and performers performing—a number of "twist" songs; there was "The Peppermint Twist" by Joey Dee and the Starlighters, "The Alvin Twist" by the Chipmunks," "Twistin' Bells" by Santo and Johnny, "The Hully Gully Twist" by Bill Doggett, "Tequila Twist" by the Champs and "Twist and Shout" by the Isley Brothers (later made popular by The Beatles). There were albums *Twist with the Ventures*, *The Ventures Twist Party* and Duane Eddy's *Twistin''n'Twangin'* dedicated to the Twist.

Chubby Checker was born Ernest Evans in South Carolina and grew up in Philadelphia, He recorded a song, "The Class," for Dick Clark where he imitated a number of singers. Clark sent the record out as a private Christmas greeting and received enthusiastic response. Clark's wife gave Checker his last name, after he had done an impersonation of Fats Domino. That led to the 18-year-old singer recording "The Twist."

"The Twist " inspired a number of dance records and Checker recorded a number of them. In 1961 Chubby Checker had "Let's Twist Again" and in early, 1962, his recording of "The Twist" became a number one record again. Checker also recorded the dance records "The Fly," "Slow Twistin'," "Teach Me To Twist," "Limbo Rock" and "Twist It Up."

Westerns on TV

Westerns had been popular on television since TV was introduced to the American public in 1946. Early TV stars like Hopalong Cassidy, Gene Autry and Roy Rogers came out of the singing cowboy movies. During the 1957-1958 season, "Gunsmoke" was the top rated show, with "Tales of Wells Fargo, "Have Gun, Will Travel,," "The Life and Legend of Wyatt Earp," and "The Restless Gun," all in the top ten. Other popular westerns were "maverick," ""Cheyenne," "Colt .45," "The Rifleman," "Wagon Train," "Rin Tin Tin," "Wanted: Dead or Alive," "Rawhide," This inspired country artists to write and record western songs. Johnny Cash signed with

Columbia Records in Nashville and one of his first releases was "Don't Take Your Guns to Town," which was number one for six straight weeks in 1959. In 1960, Cash released the album *Ride This Train*. Marty Robbins released an album, *Gunfighter Ballads*, and his singles, "The Hanging Tree, "El Paso" (number one for seven weeks in 1959) and "Big Iron" were all western songs that charted 1959-1960.

Newport Jazz Festival

Nashville musicians Chet Atkins, Hank Garland, Boots Randolph, Brenton Banks, Floyd Cramer, Bob Moore, Buddy Harman and Gary Burton went to Newport, Rhode Island during the July Fourth weekend in 1960 to perform at the Newport Jazz Festival. However, a large number of teenagers and college students came and discovered that all seats were sold and no rooms were available. On Saturday night, July 2, fueled by alcohol, a riot broke out and the performance by the Nashville musicians was cancelled. However, the group began jamming on the front porch of a mansion RCA had rented for them. The album, *After the Riot* in Newport by the Nashville All Stars, was issued later in 1960 and showed the Nashville musicians in a jazz setting. The group recorded a Chet Atkins original, "Nashville to Newport," the Gershwin's "S' Wonderful" and "All the Things You Are" by Oscar Hammerstein and Jerome Kern. They also recorded "Riot Chorus," written by Hank Garland and Boots Randolph as well as "Relaxin'" by Jimmy Guinn. Those two songs were also on Hank Garland's album *Jazz Winds From a New Direction*.

Third Grammy Awards

The third Grammy Awards, for records released in 1960, was held on April 12, 1961 at the Beverly Hills Hotel in Los Angeles and the Hotel Astor in New York. Album of the Year was a comedy album, *The Button-Down Mind of Bob Newhart*. "El Paso" by Marty Robbins won "Best Country and Western Performance" and "Best Rhythm and Blues" Grammy went to "Let the Good Times Roll" by Ray Charles. Ella Fitzgerald won best female single for "Mack the Knife" and best female album for *Ella in Berlin*. Best male single and album was "Georgia On My Mind" and *The Genius of Ray Charles* by Ray Charles, who also won "Best Performance of a Pop Single" for "Georgia On My Mind." Best vocal group was Eydie Gorme and Steve Lawrence ("We Got Us") and best "Chorus" was Norman Luboff for Songs of the Cowboy.

Summing Up 1960

Nineteen sixty was an election year with Richard Nixon, vice president under Eisenhower, representing the Republican party and Senator John Kennedy the Democratic nominee. The big issue during the campaign was the Cold War; tensions were high after the Soviets shot down a U-2 spy plane over Russia in May and captured the pilot, Gary Powers. The State Department at first claimed that it was a weather plane but then had to admit it was a spy plane. The spy plane incident came two weeks before a Summit with Eisenhower, Soviet Premier Nikita Khrushchev, British Prime Minister Harold Macmillan and French President Charles de Gaulle who were scheduled to meet in Paris. At the Summit, which ended abruptly after two days, President Eisenhower refused to apologize but then agreed to stop flights by spy planes over the Soviet Union.

During the Fall, there were TV broadcasts of the Kennedy-Nixon debates which, some believed, turned the tide to Kennedy. On Tuesday, November 8, John Kennedy was elected by a narrow margin—less than one percent of the popular vote.

It was an Olympic year and the winter games were held in Squaw Valley, California and the summer games held in Rome where the Soviets won more points than the United States but Wilma Rudolph captured three gold medals in track , Rafer Johnson set a record in the decathlon and Cassius Clay won a gold medal in boxing's light heavyweight division.

Golf had become popular; President Eisenhower enjoyed it and golf had a charismatic champion in Arnold Palmer.

The population of the United States was almost 180 million, 23 percent of women over 14 were working, the birth control pill had been approved for the market, and there were 2,000 computers in use.

1961
Early 1961

On January 3, 1961, President Dwight Eisenhower ordered that diplomatic relations with Cuba end. On January 17, he gave his "Farewell Address" where he cautioned the nation about "the acquisition of unwarranted influence by the military-industrial complex" and warned Americans to guard their liberties.

On January 20, a cold day in Washington, John F. Kennedy was inaugurated as the 35th President of the United States. In his inaugural speech he proclaimed, "Ask not what your country can do for you, but what you can do for your country." On March 1, the President signed an Executive Order that created the Peace Corps and the 42-year old President, who appeared active and energetic, promoted physical fitness.

The Cold War dominated American policy and the United States was in the process of creating a huge arsenal of intercontinental ballistic missiles with over 100 Atlas and Titan nuclear-tipped rockets with plans to build 700 Minutemen missiles.

On April 24, the United States invaded Cuba at the Bay of Pigs on the southern shore of Cuba but the invasion was met by Cuban forces, who repelled the attack and captured the invaders. The Bay of Pigs was a disaster for America and an embarrassing defeat for the Cuban militants who conducted the raid. The invasion had been planned under the Eisenhower administration and the American military wanted those plans to be executed. After the botched invasion Kennedy took responsibility but learned a valuable lesson to not give blind acceptance to military plans.

"Sing Along With Mitch" on TV

On Friday, January 27, 1961, the first telecast of "Sing Along With Mitch" on NBC TV was broadcast at 9 p.m., Eastern time. The show was an immediate hit as viewers watched a bouncing ball land on lyrics as the song played and Mitch Miller became a national celebrity.

During the first season, Miller's show alternated with "The Bell Telephone Hour" but the high ratings meant that it was a weekly show on Thursday nights in the Fall of 1961.

The show featured "The Sing Along Gang" and "The Sing Along Kids" who performed old favorites as well as some new numbers. During 1961, Mitch Miller had six "sing along" songs enter the national album chart on *Billboard*. The albums were *Happy Times! Sing Along With Mitch*, *Mitch's Greatest Hits*, *TV Sing Along With Mitch*, *Your Request Sing Along With Mitch*, *Holiday Sing Along With Mitch* and *Christmas Sing Along With Mitch*. All of the albums reached the top ten on *Billboard's* album chart and one, *Holiday Sing Along With Mitch*, reached number one.

Miller's TV show and album were incredibly popular and profitable for Columbia Records but Miller's success and busy schedule caused him to leave as head of Columbia's A&R division in the Spring of 1961. Miller's departure opened the door at Columbia for the label to sign rock acts, but it would be awhile before the label abandoned it's middle of the road acts who generated significant income.

The Marvelettes

The first number one on the *Billboard* Hot 100 chart for Motown was "Please Mr. Postman" by the Marvelettes.

The line-up for the Marvelettes was Gladys Horton , Georgia Dobbins, Georgeanna Tillman, Juanita Cowart and Katherine Anderson. They were high school students at Inkster High in Detroit who received an audition at Motown after entering a talent contest. Gordy and Robinson both listened to them and were impressed, but told them they needed to find original songs. Since none of the group were writers, Georgia Dobbins asked a songwriting neighbor, William Garrett, if he had anything. Garrett showed them a blues song, "Please Mr. Postman." Dobbins re-wrote the entire song overnight, keeping only the title, gave it to the group to learn, then dropped out to take care of her mother. The group added Wanda Young and Gordy named them "The Marvelettes." They released "Please Mr. Postman" in the summer of 1961 on Tamla.

Distribution

The Handleman Company was formed in Troy, Michigan in 1937 by Philip Handleman and his sons, Joseph, Paul and Moe. In 1946, another brother, David, joined the organization.

The company was formed to distribute pharmaceuticals and soon moved into health care. During the 1950s Handleman moved into the distribution of records as a rack jobber, providing records and inventory control to outlets that did not stock recordings, such as drug stores, grocery stores, department stores and mass merchandisers. The rack jobbers were an asset to record companies because they provided additional retail outlets were records were sold, and they were an asset to retailers because they managed the displays and inventories so retailers did not have to manage which records to buy (or not buy).

Rack jobbers bought albums from record companies for a lower wholesale cost, undermining traditional independent companies, and were efficient in their management of stock for retailers. Customers increasingly preferred the cheaper prices at racks than the stand-alone record stores. By 1961, rack jobbers like the Handleman Corporation had become national distributors and the music business was a substantial part of their income.

TV A Vast Wasteland

In 1961 Newton Minow, head of the Federal Communications Commission (FCC) called television "A vast wasteland" of game shows, violence, formula comedies about totally unbelievable families, blood and thunder, mayhem, violence, sadism murder.

Man in Space

Astronaut Alan B. Shepard blasted off from Cape Canaveral on May 5, and went 115 miles up into space, then returned to earth safely after the 15-minute flight. It was America's first human space launch but the Soviets were ahead. In April, Soviet cosmonaut Yuri Gargarin orbited the earth.

Freedom Rides

The summer of 1961 was a bloody one as African-Americans challenged the accepted practices of segregation on busses and bus terminal bathrooms, water fountains, waiting rooms and restaurants. The Freedom Rides lasted from May through September and forced the Kennedy administration, state and local governments and police forces to take an important step towards ending segregation.

The first Freedom Riders left Washington on May 4, 1961 on two buses bound for New Orleans. There had been rulings against segregation on interstate travel but the Interstate Commerce Commission (ICC) had not enforced them. In the case of Boynton v. Virginia in 1960, the Supreme Court outlawed segregation in restaurants and waiting rooms serving buses that crossed state lines but, again, the ICC failed to enforce it.

The first Freedom Ride was led by James Farmer, director of the Congress of Racial Equality (CORE), and was comprised of 13 riders, seven black and six white. Their plan was to leave Washington, D.C., travel through Virginia, the Carolinas, Georgia, Alabama, and Mississippi and arrive in New Orleans on May 17, where a civil rights rally was planned.

There were minor problems in Virginia and North Carolina but in Rock Hill, South Carolina, Freedom Rider John Lewis was attacked and Riders were arrested in Charlotte and Winnsboro, South Carolina.

The two buses separated and on May 14, Mother's Day, in Anniston, Alabama, one bus arrived and were attacked by the Ku Klux Klan, who beat the riders and slashed the tires on their bus. The bus limped out of town but was stopped by the Klan, who firebombed it, then shut the doors with the Freedom Riders inside. The Riders managed to escape but were left semi-conscious.

In Birmingham, Bull Conner arranged with the Ku Klux Klan to allow the Klan fifteen minutes to beat the Freedom Riders with baseball bats, iron pipes and chains before police arrived. One Rider was beaten so badly that he was taken to a hospital but the hospital refused to treat him. Attorney General Robert Kennedy sent his assistant, John Seigenthaler to Birmingham but Seigenthaler was also beaten.

Nashville student activist Diane Nash organized a Freedom Ride from Nashville to Birmingham on May 17; when that bus arrived, the Riders were arrested. On May 20 the Freedom Riders continued to Montgomery with police escorts but, just outside the city, the police left and the Riders were brutally beaten.

On Sunday, May 21, Reverend Ralph Abernathy, pastor of the First Baptist Church of Birmingham, organized a service to honor the Freedom Riders; Reverend Martin Luther King, Jr. spoke at the service. Outside the church, 3,000 angry whites attacked the congregants.

Civil Rights activists were determined to continue the Freedom Rides and new Riders joined the journeys. In Jackson, Mississippi, so many Freedom Riders and civil rights activists were arrested that the local jails were too full to accommodate any more so about 300 of those arrested were sent to the Mississippi State Prison, known as "Parchman Farm." Those arrested were locked in the Death Row section of the prison where they sang Freedom Songs. The guards threatened to take away their mattresses if they continued singing; the prisoners threw their mattresses out the door and kept singing.

President Kennedy wanted a "cooling off" period because the Freedom Rides had embarrassed the United States internationally; even the Soviet Union criticized American racism. That call to "cool off" was answered by James Farmer, who said, "We have been cooling off for 350 years and if we cooled off any more we'd be in a deep freeze."

The Freedom Rides continued throughout the summer with over 60 Freedom Rides criss-crossing the South. About 450 participated in the Rides; about 75 percent were male and under 30 and the racial split was fifty-fifty white and black.

At the end of September, the Interstate Commerce Commission (ICC) issued a ruling, effective November 1, 1961, that ended segregated buses that traveled across state lines and forced the removal of "white" and "colored" signed from bus terminal water fountains, toilets, waiting rooms and restaurants. It took six years after a Supreme Court ruling that ended segregated interstate bus travel until the ICC finally enforced it.

Fuzz Tone

Marty Robbins' number one hit in 1961, "Don't Worry 'Bout Me," featured a "fuzz tone" guitar. That "fuzz tone" effect came during a session at the Quonset Hut studio when one of the pre-amps in the console went out and Grady Martin's amplifier began to distort. Engineer Glen Snoddy couldn't fix the problem. Other artists and producers heard that record (it reached number three on the *Billboard* Hot 100) and wanted it use it but Snoddy had fixed the original distortion problem. However, he was now faced with another problem: how to create and control that "fuzz tone" distortion. Snoddy solved the problem by building a guitar pedal with a button that, when pressed, provided that distorted sound. Snoddy met with Gibson guitar president Maurice Berlin in Chicago and showed him the invention. Gibson then acquired the patent and named the invention "The Maestro Fuzz-Tone FZ-1" and began marketing it in 1962. At first, sales were slow but when the Rolling Stones released "(I Can't Get No) Satisfaction" in August, 1965 with that opening riff played by Keith Richard, sales took off and Glen Snoddy received royalties for seven years.

Nashville Music Business 1961

By 1961 it was reported that there were over 100 music publishers, 1,100 professional musicians, 200 songwriters, 12 talent agencies, 15 recording studios and 1,600 artists and sidemen in Nashville, which was also home to the Country Music Association, radio syndicators, jingle companies, arrangers, copyists, record pressing firms and offices for the three performing rights organizations, ASCAP, BMI and SESAC.

In their first survey of country radio in 1961, the Country Music Association found there were only 81 stations playing country music full time.

Overall, it was a good year for country music. The Grand Ole Opry played a show at Carnegie Hall for the Musicians Aid Society on December 29, 1961. The show was a sell-out; 2,700 watched performances by Patsy Cline, Grandpa Jones, Jim Reeves, Bill Monroe, Faron Young, Marty Robbins, the Jordanaires, and Minnie Pearl.

An article, "Country Music: Nashville Style" by Richard Mareck in *McCall's* Magazine came out in 1961 and stated that country is "the most popular music in American today" adding that "the new sound at the Opry is less authentic country music, more akin to the popular styles of today (although not strictly pop songs)."

Patsy Cline and "Crazy"

Patsy Cline's classic "Crazy," written by Willie Nelson with some help from his friend, Oliver English, was recorded on August 21, 1961 and released on October 16. The song was first pitched to Billy Walker, who turned it down because it was "a girl's song." Cline did not like Nelson's demo of the song because it seemed more spoken than sung, but Owen Bradley loved the song and arranged it as a ballad. Cline had been in a car wreck a short while before the recording session and found it difficult to hit the high notes in the song. After a trying for four hours, she went home and came back a week later and sang it perfectly on the first take. Patsy's previous release was "I Fall To Pieces," which was number one on the country chart and stayed on that chart for 39 weeks. "Crazy" entered the country chart on November 13, 1961 and reached number two; it was also number two on the "Easy Listening" chart.

1961 Grammys

The Fourth Annual Grammy Awards were held on May 29, 1962 in venues in New York, Los Angeles and Chicago for releases in 1961. The Record and Song of the Year was "Moon River," written by Henry Mancini and Johnny Mercer and performed by Mancini and his orchestra. Best new artist was Peter Nero.

"Big Bad John" by Jimmy Dean won the Country Grammy, The Belafonte Singers won the Folk Grammy, Ray Charlies won the R&B Grammy for "Hit the Road Jack," and Mahalia Jackson won the Gospel Grammy for "Everytime I Feel the Spirit." Under the "Pop" category, Judy Garland and her album Judy at Carnegie Hall won in the Female category while Jack Jones won in the Male category for "Lollipops and Roses."

1962

Folk Music

Folk music was an integral part of the foundation of 1960s rock music. Many of those who emerged as rock'n'rollers during the 1960s had their roots in folk music. Many young people were initially inspired to join a folk music group, especially after the popularity of the Kingston Trio.

Politics directly affected young people during the 1950s and 1960s in ways that were unknown to later generations. The threat of the nuclear bomb during the Cold War was a real threat and the idea that the United States could be under attack with nuclear weapons by Russia was felt with school drills. The issue of Civil Rights was real and protests against the injustices of segregation was known by young people. The draft, which forced young men to plan their lives with a military interruption was a fact of life, and then the war in Vietnam, a war that was considered unjust by the young men who had to fight it, was also part of life decisions. It was natural, since folk is a lyric-oriented music, that these issues would be part of folk songs and the folk music culture.

The political side of folk music was uncomfortable with the consumer society that emerged after World War II; activists were idealists who believed in social justice and wanted to be seen as "authentic" in their political beliefs. Many tended to look down on those who did not actively share those same beliefs. The non-political side wanted to have a good time singing folks songs together. The folk songs that were hits on radio tended to be the smooth, non-political songs; radio was not comfortable with songs about civil rights, labor and leftist politics.

During the mid-1950s, Harry Belafonte recorded a number of songs from the Caribbean; his album *Belafonte* was number one on the *Billboard* album chart for six weeks; his album Calypso was number one for 31 weeks. He had hit singles with "Jamaica Farewell," "Banana Boat," "Marianne" and other songs.

Harry Belafonte had strong political beliefs but his albums and songs fit comfortably with middle America. He was a major record seller for RCA, even during the early Elvis years of 1956-1958.

In November, 1958, the Kingston Trio had a hit with "Tom Dooley" and that led to a series of best selling albums. Aside from a few hit singles from folk acts, urban folk music was a music of albums. It attracted a young audience who came of age when folk music was popular and thus became a major influence on their musical lives.

The artist who brought folk music into rock was Bob Dylan

Bob Dylan

Bob Dylan was born Robert Allen Zimmerman in Duluth, Minnesota on May 24, 1941. The Zimmerman family moved to Hibbing, in northern Minnesota, a region known for its iron ore mines, when Bob was six. He grew up there, son of a Jewish merchant who sold appliances. In grade school he began writing poems--childhood verses--and the first stage of his development as a poet began. He liked the idea of writing poetry and felt a need to express himself in writing.

In 1951, Dylan's father bought a piano and Bob taught himself to play that instrument as well as guitar, harmonica, and autoharp. He formed his first band, The Golden Chords, as a freshman in high school and they played basic rhythm and blues, early rock, and whatever else was on the radio. Later he formed other bands and made the usual rounds of school dances, youth club outings, and talent shows.

The early poems he wrote at ten or eleven gave way to song lyrics as he entered high school and began playing in rock'n'roll bands and began to dream of becoming a rock star. That would be important later as he returned to these early roots after his success as a folk singer.

Dylan graduated from Hibbing High School in 1959 and entered the University of Minnesota, where he was enrolled for three semesters. However, his heart was not in school and he was soon hanging out in Dinkytown, a bohemian/student section of Minneapolis where he began to call himself Bob Dylan and fabricate stories about his past. He also began singing folk songs, playing coffeehouses and developed an image and persona.

Young Bobby Zimmerman wanted to be someone other than the son of a middle-class merchant. Too, he had a desire to be a big star and Zimmerman wasn't a name you could easily see in lights. So, as Jonathan Cott observes, he "began to create a self for himself, much as a novelist creates a character."

A turning point in young Dylan's life occurred in 1960 when he read *Bound for Glory*, the semi-autobiographical novel by Woody Guthrie. After reading that book, Dylan assumed Guthrie's persona, learned his songs and made an equally fascinating past for himself. In his biography of Dylan, *No Direction Home*, author Robert Shelton states: "Even his speech patterns began to change. That Oklahoma twang, which became much more extreme after he left here, came into his voice. That incredibly harsh gravel sound in his voice became more and more a part of him. It really became much more than identification. He was the people he identified with, especially Guthrie."

Shelton also noted that "to a few close friends, Dylan admitted that the change of summer 1960 grew out of a genuine need for a new identity: He simply wasn't pleased with his former bland, directionless self."

Woody Guthrie was in Greystone Hospital in East Orange, New Jersey, dying from Huntington's disease and Dylan was determined to meet him. He first tried to make contact by telephone before heading to New York in December, 1961.

When Dylan arrived in New York, not yet twenty years old, he began visiting Guthrie and managed to meet Guthrie's friends and family while singing songs for them. He also began making the rounds of coffeehouses, auditioning and playing wherever he could, trying to make connections as well as find a place to sleep. Although he had written songs before he left Minnesota, now he began writing songs in earnest, under the influence of Guthrie, picking up ideas around him and filling his pockets with pieces of paper full of scribbles. His performances during that time generally consisted of traditional material--especially Woody Guthrie songs--but he had a knack for composing novelty songs which came off as comic routines in his set. Dylan also began to grow as a person, meeting other people, seeing other performers, learning new songs, struggling for survival and developing relationships. Shelton quotes an early friend of Dylan who described the singer as enthusiastic "about the whole, wonderful world of songs."

Dylan: Politics and Folk Songs

In addition to being influenced by the songs of folk singers, Dylan was also influenced by their politics, which were generally left-wing, and their tastes in literature and poetry, which led to exposure to the Beat poets and the French symbolists. Many of the Beat poets were in New York's Greenwich Village and Shelton noted they were "working alongside the folk-guitar pickers." Discussing the early influences of poetry, Dylan stated "There used to be a folk music scene and jazz clubs just about every place. The two scenes were very much connected, where the poets would read to a small combo, so I was close up to that for a while. My songs were influenced not so much by poetry on the page but by poetry being recited by the poets who recited poems with jazz bands."

When he arrived in New York, he began developing as a performer. Biographer Anthony Scaduto states "Dylan was singing before Village audiences every chance he got, hitting the coffee houses primarily. No one would hire him at first, and he was forced to sing for nothing more than the exposure, getting up on the stages of the coffee houses in the afternoons and evenings, before the paid professionals would come on, singing for a sandwich and some coffee, mostly."

Dylan performed mainly traditional folk songs like "Pastures of Plenty," "Jesse James," "Gypsy Davey," "On the Trail of the Buffalo," "Remember Me," "Jesus Met the Woman at the Well," and "San Francisco Bay Blues."

Robert Shelton noted that "Bob sensed how much more he had to learn about performing, how much harder he would have to develop his songs" and stated that, as he developed, "he moved through New York and Boston folk circles like a sponge, sopping up everything he heard and saw"

The stage that propelled Dylan to his first level of recognition was Gerde's Folk City, at that time located on ll West 4th Street. Owned by Mike Porco, who bought it in 1959, the club first featured jazz. Folk enthusiasts Izzy Young and Tom Prendergast persuaded Porco in 1960 to turn the place into a folk club. By that summer, the club had been renamed "Gerde's Folk City." Soon after, the Monday night hootenannies began as a way of getting the Village folkies to play for free one night a week, attract large crowds of paying customers, and give amateurs a chance to showcase. The hoots soon caught on and when Dylan arrived they were in full swing, providing him an opportunity to be heard by the Village folkies. Those were significant performances for Dylan and, according to Scaduto "It was an important engagement for him. It brought no reviews, no public acclaim, no mobs lining up outside, waiting to get in. But it cemented the impression of the Village folkies that he was something special, possibly a genius, and it resulted in a good deal of talk along the folk underground about this strange little kid who was knocking them dead in the Village."

Robert Zimmerman to Bob Dylan

Robert Allen Zimmerman knew that name did not fit him. According to his autobiography, Zimmerman saw the name "Allyn" and thought he would become "Robert Allyn" but then saw the name "Dylan" and that appealed to him. Deciding whether to be "Robert," "Bobby" or "Bob" boiled down to liking the sound of "Bob" and feeling it fit him best, visually and by sound.

Dylan in the *New York Times*

There was a buzz about the young Bob Dylan in Greenwich Village and the singer came to the attention of New York Times music critic Robert Shelton. Shelton watched several performances of Dylan at Gerde's Folk City and wrote a glowing review, stating that the 20-year-old singer had "one of the most distinctive stylists to play in a Manhattan cabaret in months."

"When he works his guitar, harmonica or piano and composes new songs faster than he can remember them, there is no doubt that he is bursting at the seems with talent," wrote Shelton. He continued, "Mr. Dylan's voice is anything but pretty. He is consciously trying to recapture the rude beauty of a Southern field hand musing in melody on his back porch."

"Mr. Dylan is both comedian and tragedian. Like a vaudeville actor on the rural circuit, he offers a variety of droll musical monologues," wrote Shelton, noting that Dylan performed "Talking Bear Mountain," "Talking New York," "Talkin' Hava Negilah" which "burlesques the folk-music craze and the singer himself."

"Mr. Dylan's highly personalized approach toward folk singing is still evolving. He has been sopping up influences like a sponge," stated Shelton, who stated further that Dylan's "music-making has the mark of originality and inspiration, all the more noteworthy for his youth."

Although Shelton extolled Dylan's talent and performance, he also noted that "Much of the Village music coterie reacted with jealousy, contempt, and ridicule" about the singer.

Bob Dylan did several more nights at Gerde's and then attended a recording session for Carolyn Hester where he met legendary Columbia producer John Hammond, Sr. "I shook his hand with my right hand and I gave him your review with my left hand," Dylan told Shelton. "He offered to sign me without even hearing me sing!"

That is how Bob Dylan got on Columbia Records.

Dylan Signed to Columbia by John Hammond

Dylan was signed by John Hammond to Columbia Records, a major pop label, giving him exposure he would never have had on a small, folk label. In his autobiography, *On The Record*, Hammond states "I think it was his air of being willing to take on the world that grabbed me. It was bold, it was witty...and it was very attractive." Hammond added that he "watched him for a while and found him fascinating, although he was not particularly good on either guitar or harmonica."

Bob Dylan entered the Columbia Studios in October, 1961, and recorded twenty songs with just vocal, guitar, and harmonica. The album cost $400 to produce and was released in early 1962. Soon after the release, Dylan signed with Albert Grossman for management and Grossman guided the young singer's career for the next seven years, assuring him of both fame and fortune. Dylan's talent was the force that made this combination work; still, Grossman--who also managed Peter, Paul and Mary--made significant contributions with management, business affairs, publishing, and bookings that helped secure early success for the young Dylan.

On his first album, Dylan included only two self-penned songs, "Talkin' New York City Blues" and "Song to Woody" and filled the rest of the album with traditional folk material. However, his second album, *The Freewheelin' Bob Dylan*, saw the young singer emerge as a songwriter as he composed all the material on the album. The album was filled with "protest songs," which provided much of Dylan's initial fame, and included "Talking World War III Blues," "Masters of War," "A Hard Rain's A-Gonna Fall," "Don't Think Twice, It's Alright," and "Blowin' in the Wind."

Freewheelin', unlike the debut album, *Bob Dylan*, sold well from the beginning and Peter, Paul and Mary recorded "Blowin in the Wind," which rose to number two on the *Billboard* charts in 1963, giving Dylan his first national exposure on pop radio. Accompanying the album were "ll Outlined Epitaphs" as liner notes, ll poems by Dylan which "coupled folk and beat poetry.".

Dylan as Songwriter

Dylan's songwriting consisted of using a number of "borrowed" melodies--"Bob Dylan's Dream" came from "Lord Franklin," "Restless Farewell" was a bluegrass tune, "Little Moses," and "Blowin' in the Wind" were derived from "No More Auction Block"--with lyrics coming from a reporter's perspective, with the addition of Dylan's own unique insights. Those were mostly topical songs which often proved timeless because of Dylan's perspectives and language, which were complex, insightful, poetic and mystical.

Scaduto states that during this time Dylan "sat and wrote a poem, and later found a tune, stole it, rewrote it, or composed one. And, he deliberately smoothed the transition from standard folk to his own songs by pinning his lyrics to a traditional framework." Dylan was quoted at that time saying "I'm using the old melodies because they're there. I like the melodies. Besides, if they can hear the old melodies in my new songs, they'll accept the songs more. It ain't the melodies that're important, man, it's the words. I don't give a damn 'bout melodies."

With his second album, Dylan's genius emerged and was recognized, and Shelton noted that "Because Dylan frequently developed songs out of the folk tradition, he was often branded a song thief...By the end of 1963 the folk scene was bitterly divided over whether Dylan was a song cribber or a composer working in the accepted tradition of building on skeletal remains." Shelton also quoted noted musicologist Charles Seeger (father of Pete) who stated "Conscious and unconscious appropriation, borrowing, adapting, plagiarizing and plain stealing...always have been part and parcel of the process of artistic creation. The attempt to make sense out of copyright law reaches its limit in folk song. For here is the illustration par excellence of the Law of Plagiarism. The folk song is, by definition, and, as far as we can tell, by reality, entirely a product of plagiarism."

Dylan himself answered those claims by asking "What did I steal? Did I steal the word 'the', the word 'a', the word 'so'? Everybody has to get their words from somewhere. Woody didn't write ten original melodies, but nobody ever called him a thief."

Several things made Dylan unique among songwriters. First, he used the folk tradition and saw creativity as synthesis rather than coming up with something totally his own. Since the 1910 Copyright Act, it has been essential that songs be original--and the American tradition since that time insists that a song must be wholly original--putting pressure on songwriters to create something from within themselves, ignoring all that has gone before them for fear of a lawsuit. Yet the folk tradition always synthesized all that had gone before. (Shakespeare himself used old plots and stories.) Dylan, by synthesizing, became part of a long tradition of songwriting, rather than just a songwriter standing alone.

Too, Dylan spent as much time reading and studying poets--particularly Allen Ginsberg and the Beat poets and Rimbaud and the French poets-- as he did listening to Hank Williams, Elvis, or anybody else. The result was a strong literary background as well as a strong musical one. Many songwriters only listen to songs--they don't read or listen to poetry. Dylan was different.

The Times They Are A-Changin' was Dylan's third album, filled with more protest songs in the folk tradition. His early records consisted of only his voice, guitar, and harmonica and he was increasingly being hailed as a "poet" because of his lyrics. He was also being hailed as the "Voice of a Generation" because he articulated, in his songs, what the youth of America were thinking and feeling, heralding the protest movements that swept college campuses in the mid-60s.

Dylan was increasingly uncomfortable with the protest image and genre and wanted to move on so his fourth album, *Another Side of Bob Dylan*, did not have any protest songs, just love songs (or "anti-love" songs) like "All I Really Want To Do," "It Ain't Me, Babe," and "I Don't Believe You." That would be his last all-acoustic album. Dylan had stated that he did not want to be a "spokesman" and that "From now on I want to write from inside me, and to do that I'm going to have to get back to writing like I used to when I was ten--having everything come out naturally. The way I like to write is for it to come out the way I walk or talk.".

The folk singer period was vital to Dylan's development as a performer and a poet. While he was immersed in that world he gave himself to it completely--it is Dylan's nature that when he does something, he does it totally--yet he also saw that period opportunistically, as a way to become famous, be a singer, and eventually be a rock star like he dreamed about in high school. Dylan told Robert Shelton "I latched on, when I got to New York City, because I saw a huge audience was there...I knew I wasn't going to stay there. I knew it wasn't my thing." Dylan added that "Folk music was just an interruption, which was very useful."

Broadside

In addition to audiences in clubs and gatherings of friends and folk enthusiasts to play songs he had just written, Dylan also had a print outlet for his compositions. *Broadside* began in the Village in 1961 by Sis Cunningham with the help of Pete Seeger and Gil Turner. A four page mimeographed publication that tried to come out twice a month, it featured new songs from folk songwriters. The offices also served as a gathering place and sounding board for folkies. The first publication in February 1962 printed "Talkin' John Birch Paranoid Blues" by Dylan; later editions were the first exposure for songs like "Blowin' in the Wind" (which was published in *Broadside* #6 in May, 1962).

Robert Shelton noted that *Broadside* "clearly stimulated Dylan's writing in 1962 and 1963" and that "for a year and a half, the first place one saw Dylan's songs, even before performance" was in this publication, which listed Dylan as "contributing editor." Shelton continued that "with Broadside's encouragement, Dylan flowered before he was accepted by the public, and sharpened his craft. The roots of the revolution in popular music that Dylan led lie partly in those monthly staff meetings and the crudely mimeographed pages of Broadside."

Albert Grossman

Most acts who achieved superstar--and legendary--status had a manager who played a key role in their ascendancy. A manager represents the artist to the business. For Bob Dylan, that person was Albert Grossman.

Albert Grossman was the son of a Russian Jewish immigrant, born in Chicago who earned a degree in Economics from Roosevelt College.

In Chicago, Grossman was a public housing administrator who became friends with folksinger Bob Gibson in 1955, which led to Grossman and a partner, Les Brown, opening a folk music club, the Gate of Horn, in 1957. Grossman then formed a partnership with Ed Sarkesian and George Wein to form Production and Management Associates (PAMA) which promoted shows by folksingers. From there, he moved into management.

Bob Dylan's first manager was Roy Silver and Grossman purchased the management contract from him for $5,000 in 1962. Dylan had signed a publishing deal with Leeds/Duchess for $1,000; once Grossman had the management contract, Artie Mogull of Witmark, the publishing arm of Warner Brothers, paid Leeds/Duchess that advance, releasing Dylan from his contract, then signed him to Witmark for a $5,000 advance. During the summer of 1963, that advance and much more was earned back when Peter, Paul and Mary had major pop hits with two of Dylan's songs, "Blowin' in the Wind" and "Don't Think Twice, It's Alright."

In addition to Dylan and Peter, Paul and Mary, Grossman also managed, during his long career, Janis Joplin, The Band, Richie Havens, the Electric Flag, Gordon Lightfoot, the Paul Butterfield Blues Band, Ian and Sylvia, Todd Rundgren and Odetta.

There was a pecking order amongst folksingers; the "true" singers were the old timers who were on the political left and non-commercial; they sang because they held strong political beliefs. Next were the commercial folk actss. The core folk crowd dismissed groups like the Kingston Trio because they were commercially successful and non-political. The commercial folksingers were viewed as pretty boys and girls with pretty voices; their core belief was in successful careers, not political causes.

Albert Grossman aggressively pursued commercial success for the folksingers he managed, but did it in a way that the singers were known as "artists" and retained their artistic integrity. Grossman protected and defended his artists, provided support for them and insisted that they be known as "artists." Along the way, Grossman managed to book his folksingers out of clubs and into concert halls.

Albert Grossman and Peter, Paul & Mary

Albert Grossman managed folksinger Peter Yarrow for about a year, then presented the idea to him of a folk singing trio, consisting of an attractive female and a second male singer who could do comedy. Yarrow agreed with the idea and they found Mary Travers and Noel Stookey (whose middle name was Paul) and thus "Peter, Paul and Mary" was formed.

Soon after they were formed, Grossman took the group to Atlantic Records where they sang "Where Have All the Flowers Gone" for Jerry Wexler, who signed them to a deal for a single with an option for an album, but before the session, Grossman called and cancelled; Artie Mogull at Warner Brothers had offered a publishing and recording contract that gave the group a $30,000 advance. That's how Peter, Paul and Mary ended up on Warner Brothers.

As part of that contract, Peter, Paul and Mary had creative control of their recordings and packaging, a revolutionary concession at the time. Most artists were "owned" by their record company and worked for them, recording the songs the A&R men or producers found for them. Although an artist could turn a song down, or find one on their own, for the most part the record companies decided what songs to record and how they should be recorded. Under Grossman's rules, the record company worked for the artist, taking the material given to them and developed a marketing and promotion plan. With the success of Peter, Paul and Mary and other acts in both folk and rock, it soon became apparent that record companies needed artists who could deliver hits and the power swung from the record company to the artist for superstars. Managers like Albert Grossman used this leverage to negotiate better deals for their clients.

Grossman regularly charged his artists a 25 percent management commission when other managers charged 15 percent. When Bob Krasnow at Warner Brothers asked him why his rate was so high, Grossman answered, "Because every time you talk to me you're ten percent smarter than before. So I just add that ten percent on to what all the dummies charge for nothing."

A good manager puts together a team--often called an "artist development team"--and the success of each team member is directly correlated to the success of the artist. A manager and those team "members" receive the rewards of their efforts when the artist succeeds in the commercial arena.

A key member of Albert Grossman's team was attorney David Braun, whom he hired in 1962. The attorney helped Grossman negotiate deals for artists; Grossman had the vision but Braun provided the nuts and bolts negotiating skills and business acumen to translate that vision into black and white and incorporate it into contracts. In doing that, the pop record business was re-defined during the early 1960s.

Grossman insisted that his "clients"--the artists--have control of their careers and their work. Grossman negotiated artist-owned publishing and production companies for his artists as well as well-paid fees for performances. Grossman had a saying: "If the bird ain't happy, the bird don't sing."

To those who worked with him, Grossman was known as "the Cloud. You could see it--it's huge, gray and august--but when you went up to touch it, it wasn't there."

Milton Glaser noted that "He was quite inarticulate, actually...Albert would absolutely run out of things to say."

Warner Brothers executive Bob Krasnow stated that Grossman "could wait anyone out...He could just take command of a room and make everybody kind of come to him." Nick Gravenites said of Grossman, "He'd enter into some kind of business discussion and say five words. And the other person would talk, and Albert would say nothing. He'd pick at his tooth with his little finger. Then there'd be silence, and the other person would start talking again, revising the deal. Without Albert saying anything!"

Mike Friedman added that "he would come in with a piece of paper and say what he wanted, and these guys didn't know how to talk to him because you couldn't really talk to him. He'd look vaguely at the ceiling and say things like 'Well...maybe we oughta be looking around a little bit... if he was negotiating with you, it was almost passive-aggressive behavior: he tells you what he wants, and whatever you want you never get. It wasn't a negotiation. But you just couldn't get enough of it."

"It was the most intimidating experience in the world to come into this guy's office," continued Friedman. "It was so Albert. Dark? It was a cave. There was a mahogany desk and a Tiffany lamp with like a twenty-watt bulb. Files piled so high on the desk you couldn't see Albert behind them and a visitor's chair so low that when a guest sat in it, he couldn't see Albert anyhow...And Albert had a voice like the voice of God coming from the walls...You couldn't see anything! His house was the same way."

Bob Dylan's girlfriend, Suze Rotolo, said "Albert never denied who he was, but he had that way of observing and not being forthcoming. Bob never gave a straight answer. He couldn't at that time. He was creating his own legend and his own fiction of himself...They got along because they both were observers and very smart and could, in a very few words, figure things out."

Albert B. Grossman Management (ABGM) was located in New York at the corner of East Fifty-fifth, between Madison and Park Avenues. Those offices contained an in-house booking company, publishing companies, press office, road managers, business managers and a bevy of secretaries and bookkeepers.

Mike Friedman, who worked in those offices as a management associate of Grossman's stated, "It was essentially a business of children and outcasts when I came into it. It was such a primitive business; nobody really knew how to do it. The rules were being created, and he was just making it up as he went along." Booking agent Dan Weiner noted that "Everybody looked to him to find out how it should be done."

The keys were the initial commercial success of Peter, Paul and Mary and the visionary songs of Bob Dylan.

Albert Grossman was the first modern manager in rock music. He taught the rock world to "appreciate, empower and follow the artist" because he "recognized the artistic credibility and impact of his clients, and he translated it into creative freedom and financial power." Grossman did not dictate artistic decisions to his artists; instead, he allowed them to make creative decisions, then created a "scene" where they could achieve their artistic visions.

That world created "a perverse culture of personality that surrounded both the manager and his artists, delineated by an effete hipness and exclusivity."

"This whole thing was based on us and them," said Mike Friedman. "Hip people versus lame people. That's what it was all about...it was having a great time and doing whatever you wanted to do and getting away with it because you were so hip."

"Bobby Neuwirth and Dylan and that crew were mean. Cold," said Peter Coyote. "There was this thing that revolved around Albert...the hippest of the hip. There was a meanness, an edgy kind of competition. People had to be on their toes. You got the feeling of ins and outs; when you were on top it was fine, but you could lose status quickly and suddenly be excluded...it was like weasels driving intruders away."

Friedman added that this "scene" was part of the reason "why people go into the music business. Because it's fun and it's hip. They don't talk about art and poetry. It's about getting laid and being cool and privileged. It was America's royalty in a sense. There was a real sense of 'us'--you either get it or you don't get it. If you got it you were okay, and if you didn't get it you weren't okay."

The one area where he was not successful was in trying to educate his artists about planning for their financial futures so they could one day be self-sufficient. Most did not want to hear it. As Barry Goldberg observed, "Everyone was too young and wild. No one had learned the rock and roll lesson yet--that if you just went along with the moves, in a few years you could control your own fate. It was totally because of drugs and craziness that it became too much."

"We Shall Overcome"

Music played an important role in the Civil Rights Movement, from the songs of the African-American church to old well-known folk songs. "We Shall Overcome" became an anthem for the Civil Rights Movement, a rallying cry for those who marched and sang for Civil Rights. The song dates back to a 1901 hymn by Charles Albert Tindley, a minister in the African Methodist Episcopal Church. Tindley's lyrics were "I'll Overcome Someday" but his melody was not the same as the one sung during the 1960s. The old spiritual "No More Auction Block For Me" provided the basic structure for the melody.

In 1946, Lucille Simmons led a strike against the American Tobacco Company and, at the end of each day picketing, led the pickers in singing "We Will Overcome." Zilphia Horton, wife of Miles Horton, one of the founders of the Highlander Folk School in Monteagle, Tennessee, learned the song from Simmons and Pete Seeger learned the song from Horton. Seeger changed "we will" to "we shall" and added verses. Frank Hamilton learned Seeger's version of the song and taught it to his friend, Guy Carawan. In 1959, Guy Carawan became music director at Highlander, succeeding Zilphia Horton, and he sang it at the school. The young student-activists picked up the song and used it as a source of strength when Tennessee police raided Highlander and put the students in jail during the 1959-1960 period. As they sang the song, the young students changed the rhythm and melody to the song we known today as "We Shall Overcome."

In 1960, Guy Carawan attended the founding meeting of the Student Nonviolent Coordinating Committee in Raleigh, North Carolina and sang the song to that group; the song then took on a life of its own as it spread throughout the civil rights community.

The Beach Boys

By 1962, surfing was a popular pastime in southern California and the beaches in the region attracted about 30,000 surfers each weekend. Records that appealed to surfers began with instrumentals; Dick Dale became known as "King of the Surf Guitar" and his recording of "Let's Go Trippin'" is considered the first surf/guitar song. Later he had "Jungle Fever," "Surf Beat" and his signature song, "Misirlou." Other instrumentals that appealed to surfers were "Pipeline" by the Chantays and "Wipe Out" by the Surfari's. Southern California became a fantasy land with baggies and bikinis on the beaches and teen movies that showcased the California lifestyle.

The laid-back casual lifestyle of Southern California sunshine and surfing found its voice in the Beach Boys, whose early songs of surfing and cars brought the Southern California lifestyle to middle America. The group was led by songwriter and arranger Brian Wilson, who was later proclaimed "a genius" for his elaborate, complex record production and songwriting skills.

The Wilson family-father Murry, mother Audree and sons Brian, Carl and Dennis—lived in Hawthorn, California. Their father, Murry, was a songwriter and musician who experienced limited success in his musical career.

From an early age, Brian was drawn to music; he loved vocal harmonies, especially those of the Four Freshman, a jazz vocal group formed at Butler University in 1948 by brothers Ross and Don Barbour with their cousin Hal Kratzsch and Marvin Pruitt. In 1953 Kratszsch left and was replaced by Ken Errair. They were "discovered" in 1950 by Stan Kenton in Dayton, Ohio when he caught their performance and recommended them to Capitol Records, who signed them later that year. In 1960 the group recorded "Their Hearts Were Full of Spring," which became a Beach Boys song, "A Young Man is Gone" in 1963 after a new set of lyrics was used.

Brian Wilson received a reel-to-reel tape recorder on his birthday in 1958 and learned to overdub; he often dissected songs and taught backing harmonies to his family. Carl Wilson had received a guitar the previous Christmas.

Brian, with Mike Love, a cousin of the Wilsons, and two classmates had performed at Hawthorne High School and Brian invited Al Jardine, another classmate to join them. Carl Wilson, Mike Love, Al Jardine and Brian formed a group and Mike Love gave them the name The Pendletones after Pendleton shirts, which were heavy, jacket-like shirts that surfers liked.

Brian Wilson was not home when Al Jardine and a friend, Gary Winfrey, came by to ask for help recording a folk song, "Sloop John B." so Jardine spoke with Murry about recording the song. Murry's song publisher was Hite Morgan and Murry set up a meeting where the group performed "Their Hearts Were Full of Spring." Morgan was not impressed.

Brian Wilson began writing songs after listening to Johnny Otis's R&B show on KFOX and loved the simplicity of R&B. Young brother Dennis had encouraged Brian to write about surfing and cars because that's what interested young people. Dennis was the only Wilson who surfed and he knew about life on the beach. When Morgan said he was not interested, Dennis spoke up and said the group had an original song, "Surfin," which interested Morgan.

Brian finished the song, with input on surfing lingo from Dennis, and then wrote "Surfin' Safari" with Mike Love. The group rented instruments and practiced the songs for three days while Murry and Audree were away.

In October, 1961, the Pendletones recorded demos of "Surfin'" and "Surfin' Safari" at the Keen Recording Studio and Murry took those demos to Candix Records owner Herb Newman, who signed the group and pressed the single, which was released in December.

When the box of singles arrived at the Wilson home, the group discovered that their name had been changed to the Beach Boys. Newman had wanted to name the group "The Surfers" but Russ Regan, who worked in promotion for Era Records, which Newman also owned, told them there was already a group named "The Surfers" and suggested "The Beach Boys."

"Surfin'" received airplay on KFWB and KRLA, two stations popular with the young audience and was an immediate local and regional hit, then entered the *Billboard* Hot 100 chart on February 17, 1962 and rose to number 75. Young Californians loved the song about their favorite pastime and the record sold over 40,000 units.

In February, Al Jardine left the group and was replaced by David Marks, a neighbor of the Wilsons that Brian and Carl had jammed with. The new group recorded "Lonely Sea" and "409" at Western Studios in April and re-recorded "Surfin' Safari." Murry took the tape to Dot and Liberty, who both turned him down, then went to Capitol where he played them for Nick Venet.

Venet had been hired by Capitol to find new acts that appealed to youth; when Venet heard the Beach Boys he felt like he had struck a gold mine and signed the group, then took them into the Capitol Records studio to re-record their songs.

In June, Capitol released "Surfin' Safari" and on August 11 it entered the *Billboard* Hot 100 and rose to number 14, remaining on that chart for 27 weeks. The "B" side was "409" written by Brian with Gary Usher,that charted at number 78. The Beach Boys and producer Nick Venet then went into the studio and recorded an album, *Surfin' Safari*, that entered the *Billboard* album chart on November 24 and reached number 32 but stayed on the chart for 37 weeks. The Beach Boys ended 1962, their first year as a professional group, with three chart singles and a chart album.

In January, 1963, Venet and the Beach Boys were back in the studio to record their second album.

Brian had emerged as the creative force in the Beach Boys, writing the songs and providing arrangements, but he did not like to tour and perform live.

The Beach Boys single, "Surfin' U.S.A." entered the *Billboard* album chart on March 23 and reached number three on the Hot 100. The writer of that song is listed as Chuck Berry, whose tune, "Sweet Little Sixteen," was pinched by Brian; Berry let them know and the issue was resolved when he received sole songwriter credit. Their next single, "Shut Down," entered the *Billboard* singles chart on April 27 and reached number 23. Their second album, *Surfin' U.S.A.* was released in March and reached number two, where it stayed for two weeks; the album remained on the chart for 78 weeks—over a year and a half.

Jan and Dean

Jan Berry and Dean Torrence were both Los Angeles natives who met in junior high school, where they were both on the football team. At University High School they were again on the football team with adjoining lockers and began harmonizing together after football practice. They formed a doo-wop group, The Barons, and rehearsed in Berry's parent's garage, where Berry's father had installed two two-track Ampex reel-to-reel tape recorders and a piano.

After a high school talent contest, the group broke up but Berry, Torrence and group member Arnie Ginsberg decided to record a song "Jennie Lee," written by Ginsburg; however, Torrence was called into the United States Army Reserves so Berry and Ginsburg recorded "Jennie Lee," which was released on Arwin Records as "Jan & Arnie." It entered the *Billboard* Hot 100 on May 19, 1958 and reached number eight, a surprise hit. Billy Ward and the Dominoes released an R&B cover of the song that reached number 55 on the pop chart. Their follow-up single, "Gas Money," only reached number 81.

Jan & Arnie appeared on The Dick Clark Show on ABC, performed on the Summer Dance Party that toured the East Coast in July, 1958 and appeared on the first rock'n'roll show at the Hollywood Bowl, hosted by Dick Clark.

Their last single did not chart and Arnie recorded a single with The Rituals which may never have been released although some promotional copies were pressed.

Dean Torrence returned from his six-month stint with the Army Reserves and reunited with Jan Berry but Ginsberg decided to quit the music business enrolled in college.

Jan and Dean went into the studio with producers Herb Alpert and Lou Adler and recorded "Baby Talk" for Dore Records; the single entered the *Billboard* Hot 100 on August 3, 1959 and reached the number ten position. They released four more singles on Dore, two on Challenge and four on Liberty Records from 1959 to 1963 but none charted higher than 25 until "Surf City." During that time they performed with a number of acts, including the Beach Boys and Berry had co-written, arranged and/or produced songs for a number of acts.

Music was not a full-time job for Jan and Dean during that period; Torrence studied advertising design at USC while Berry was at UCLA taking science and music classes, then entered the California College of Medicine and completed two years of medical school.

Jan Berry began collaborating with Brian Wilson and the two wrote "Surf City," which was released on Liberty Records and reached the number one position on the *Billboard* Hot 100 where it stayed for two weeks. That further enhanced Southern California's image as a "surf city" and a mecca for those wanting hot fun in the California sunshine.

"The Beverly Hillbillies"

"The Beverly Hillbillies" TV show premiered on September 26, 1962 on the CBS network at 9 p.m. on Wednesday evenings; the theme song was "The Ballad of Jed Clampett," written by the show's creator, Paul Henning and recorded by Lester Flatt and Earl Scruggs and the Foggy Mountain Boys. However, the version heard on TV was sung by Jerry Scoggins, former member of Gene Autry's backing group, The Cass County Boys. The single featured Lester Flatt singing the lead and was released on November 26, 1962 and reached number one on *Billboard's* country chart in 1963, where it remained for three weeks. That show and song brought attention to bluegrass and Nashville. Flatt and Scruggs were regular guests on the show and those appearances often featured Scrugg's banjo playing, which inspired numerous young men and women to pick up the banjo.

"The Beverly Hillbillies" was an immediate hit when it was first broadcast and was ranked the number one show on TV during its first two season. However, the "rural purge" by CBS, where the network was pushed by advertisers to develop shows for a young, non-rural audience, caused a number of shows, including "Hee Haw," "The Lawrence Welk Show," and other shows to be dropped, even though they continued to draw large numbers in the non-rural audiences.

Ray Charles and the Modern Sounds of Country and Western Music

The album *Modern Sounds in Country and Western Music* was released by Ray Charles in April, 1962 and reached the number one spot on the *Billboard* album chart, remaining there for 14 weeks. His album *Modern Sounds in Country and Western Music (Volume Two)* was released at the end of that year and rose to number two. The single "I Can't Stop Loving You," written by Don Gibson, came on the *Billboard* Hot 100 chart in May and reached number one, where it remained for five consecutive weeks. Other chart singles from those albums were "Born To Lose," "You Don't Know Me," "Careless Love," "You Are My Sunshine," "Your Cheating Heart," "Take These Chains From My Heart," "No Letter Today" and "Making Believe." None of those singles was on the *Billboard* country singles chart (*Billboard* did not have a country album chart until 1964) but it had a profound effect on country music, bringing attention to the "Nashville Sound" and increasing the popularity and awareness of country music with non-country audiences.

Ray Charles had been warned against recording an album of country songs; it was not considered "hip" for a black artist to do so. But Ray Charles had grown up, like so many early R&B performers, hearing country music because country music was on the radio. Blues and early rhythm and blues were not heard on the radio until after World War Ii and, even then, it was difficult to find stations playing R&B music until the early 1950s.

From Country and Western to "Country"

In the November 3, 1962 issue of *Billboard* magazine, the name of the chart was changed from "Hot C & W Sides" to "Hot Country Singles." The change represented a move towards a more pop-oriented "Nashville sound" in country music and away from the cowboy image of country.

Columbia buys the Bradley's Recording Studio

Columbia Records bought the Quonset Hut studio in Nashville and surrounding property in 1962 for $300,000 and moved their headquarters for their country division to offices there under the direction of Don Law.

The purchase included a non-compete clause whereby Owen Bradley could not build another studio within a 30 mile radius of the Quonset Hut.

After the purchase of the Quonset Hut studio in 1962, Decca established their Nashville office under the leadership of Owen Bradley at 805 16th Avenue South, less than a block away from the Bradley's studio. Assisting Bradley in the new offices was Harry Silverstein, head of country promotion. In addition to Decca Records, the building housed the label's two publishing companies, Northern and Champion Music. The roster for Decca included Ernest Tubb, Kitty Wells, Red Foley, Webb Pierce, Bill Monroe and Jimmy Davis. New artists recently signed to Decca include the Wilburn Brothers, Goldie Hill, Bobby Helms, Roy Drusky, Jimmy Martin, Grady Martin, Bob Beckham, Loretta Lynn and Connie Hall. Burl Ives, Brenda Lee and Patsy Cline all recorded their recent hits in Nashville.

"The End of the World"

On December 15, 1962, "The End of the World" by Skeeter Davis entered the *Billboard* country chart; on January 26, 1963 it entered the Hot 100 chart. The song peaked in March, 1963 when it was number two on the pop and country charts, number one on the "Easy Listening" chart and number four on the R&B chart. The song was also a hit in the U.K. and Australia. The song was written by Arthur Kent and Sylvia Dee and inspired by Dee's father's death. The song was recorded on June 8, 1962 and produced by Chet Atkins and featured Floyd Cramer's piano.

Skeeter had been part of The Davis Sisters with Betty Jack Davis (although Skeeter's name was Mary Frances Pennick) and they were signed to RCA by Steve Sholes and had a hit, "I Forgot More Than You'll Ever Know" which was number one for eight weeks on the country chart in 1953. However, on August 1, 1953, Betty Jack Davis was killed in an auto accident and Skeeter was severely injured. After trying to resume her career with Betty Jack's sister, Skeeter decided to quit the music business in 1956. She returned in 1958 with an "answer" song, "Lost To a Geisha Girl," then had ten chart records before she recorded "End of the World." Chet Atkins always considered Skeeter's record of "End of the World" was his greatest achievement as a producer because Davis had a limited vocal range and was the harmony singer for the Davis Sisters.

Albums 1960-1962

The top selling album of 1960 was the Original Cast recording of *The Sound of Music*, followed by *The Button-Down Mind of Bob Newhart*. Frank

Sinatra, the Kingston Trio, Billy Vaughn and the Mormon Tabernacle Choir all had number one albums that year, which also saw the soundtrack album to *G.I. Blues* by Elvis top the chart.

In 1961 Elvis was again the only rock and roll artist who had a number one album (he had two); other albums that reached number one were the soundtrack to *Exodus* and the Original Cast Recordings to *Camelot* and *Carnival*. Judy Garland, Bob Newhart, Bert Kaempfert and Judy Garland also had number one albums that year.

West Side Story was the most successful album of 1962 and, in fact, the top album (determined by the most weeks in the number one spot on the *Billboard* album chart) during the 1955-1985 era. Other top albums were by Mitch Miller, Ray Charles, Peter, Paul & Mary and Allan Sherman with the Henry Mancini soundtrack to *Breakfast at Tiffany's* also reaching number one. In 1963, albums by Andy Williams, the Singing Nun, Peter, Paul & Mary, Allan Sherman, Frank Fontaine and a jazz album by Stan Getz and Charlie Byrd all reached the number one position. "Little Stevie Wonder" had a number one album that year, but it was number one for only one week.

It is easy to look back and claim that the major recording labels were out of touch during the 1955-1963 period when rock and roll first hit, but that is not a totally accurate perception. True, the Beatles and other rock acts began to dominate the album charts in 1964, but during the early years of rock and roll, it was business as usual for the major labels for a pretty good economic reason: it worked.

Having said that, the development of the teenage and young buyer market was obviously there and independent labels dominated the singles charts. But this was a "new" music that was unpleasant and even offensive for many middle class Americans who had grown in the era of Big Band and pop vocalists. Compounding the problem was that most of the mainstream acts were outspoken in their dislike of rock and roll; there are numerous quotes from top acts about how bad rock and roll was and how it would only be a passing fad that couldn't pass soon enough.

Because acts like Bing Crosby, Frank Sinatra and other top artists dismissed this music, the young rock and roll fans dismissed them. For the rock and rollers, the music of Crosby, Sinatra and their middle-of-the-road (MOR) pop music was irrelevant--and became irrelevant overnight. That fact is reflected in the histories of rock and roll written by those impacted by rock, but does not acknowledge the fact that those MOR artists continued to have an active, record buying audience throughout the rock and roll era. Or that Original Cast recordings and movie soundtracks constituted the bulk of album sales during the 1955-1963 period.

An American in Orbit & Other News of 1962

John Glenn, in the spacecraft he named Friendship 7, blasted off from Cape Canaveral on February 20, 1962 and circled the earth three times before he returned safely to earth.

The Supreme Court ruled on June 25 that reciting a prayer written by a state agency for use in public schools violated the establishment clause of the First Amendment." Government did not have the "power to prescribe by law any particular form of prayer," they stated in their ruling.

Screen bombshell Marilyn Monroe died on August 5 at the age of 36 in an apparent suicide. Former First Lady and leading social activist Eleanor Roosevelt died on November 7.

The Civil Rights struggle in the South put a spotlight on James Meredith, a 29-year old African-American and former Air Force sergeant who enrolled at the University of Mississippi on October 1. Meredith eventually managed to enroll although a mob tried to stop him; over 200 were arrested during riots that lasted throughout the night.

1963
Broadcasting Magazine

In January, 1963, "A Special Report" was published in Broadcasting Magazine that noted that Nashville "whose musical attainments once scarcely drew a sneer from Tin Pan Alley has now burgeoned into a $40 million economy" and added that Nashville was "Second only to New York as a source for popular music." The article stated that "one out of every two records now sold in the U.S. and a heavy proportion of the records played on U.S. radio come from a Nashville studio. The article noted that "some of the biggest names in pop music are turning to country style songs" and many "are starting to record in Nashville because the studios produce a relaxed type of music support." Discussing the "Nashville Sound," the article stated "the term has become a symbol of prestige in an industry that once belittled Nashville as the corn crib of the music industry."

The article attributed Nashville's success to several reasons, included the reservoir of musical talent on the Grand Ole Opry, the willingness of the performance rights organization BMI to license songs that ASCAP refused to license, and the success of Ray Charles' *Modern Sounds in Country & Western Music Vol 1 and 2* which opened pop music's eyes world to the sales potential of country songs.

The magazine could not resist some digs at country music, stating it was popular despite "some misgiving by those of sophisticated tastes" and country "may be anathema to music's social leaders and their followers" but "more people are corny than sophisticated."

Time Magazine

An article in *Time* magazine, "Country Music: The Nashville Sound," appeared in 1964 and stated, "Country and Western music, known in the trade as C&W, has never been more widely popular." It noted that "Nashville, with 21 recording studios, produces 30 percent of the nation's hit singles" and attributes that to "the tenacious loyalty of C&W fans, who through the years have made country music the most durable sound on the popular market." Trying to define the Nashville sound the article stated, "More than the drawling, sow-belly accents and nasal intonations of the singers, it is the background music provided by the sidemen on twangy electric guitars."

The Jimmy Dean Show

Country music got a classy TV show when the hour-long "The Jimmy Dean Show" began on ABC in September, 1963. The show was broadcast from New York and Jim Henson's muppet "Rowlf" was a continuing character on the show and provided a major break for Henson's career. The show was a major booster of country music and featured a number of Nashville-based acts. Prior to starring on his ABC show, Dean had a hit, "Big Bad John," which was number one in 1961 on both the country and Hot 100 charts in *Billboard*. It was number one on the country chart for two weeks and number one on the Hot 100 for five consecutive weeks, spilling over into 1962. He had also had a hit with "P.T. 109," a tribute to President John Kennedy's World War II exploits, in 1962.

"Six Days on the Road"

Dave Dudley's recording of "Six Days on the Road" entered the country chart in June, 1963 and began a trend of truck driving songs in country music. Dudley, who later recorded in Nashville, was the leading singer of truck driving songs with hits such as "Truck Driving Son-of-a-Gun," "Trucker's Prayer," "There Ain't No Easy Run" and "Keep On Truckin'."

Nashville Tragedies

Patsy Cline sang at a benefit on March 3, 1963 in Kansas City, Kansas for disc jockey "Cactus" Jack Call, who died in a car crash. Cline, Hawkshaw Hawkins, Cowboy Copas and pilot Randy Hughes left on March 5 to fly back to Nashville in a small plane. The plane stopped to refuel in Dyersburg, Tennessee. They were advised not to attempt to fly to Nashville because of heavy winds and a driving rain but decided to take a chance. Randy Hughes was not trained in instrument flying and the plane crashed near Camden, Tennessee, about 90 miles east of Nashville. All four were killed. A Memorial service was held on March 8 and Jack Anglin, a member of the duo Johnnie and Jack, died in a car accident on the way to the service. It was a terrible tragedy for country music.

Grammy Awards: 1962

The Grammy Awards honoring recordings released in 1962 was held on May 15, 1963 at events in New York, Los Angeles and Chicago.

Record of the Year was "I Left My Heart in San Francisco" by Tony Bennett, Song of the Year was "What Kind of Fool I Am" written by Anthony Newley and Album of the Year was *The First Family* by Vaughn Meador, a comedy record that spoofed the Kennedy family in the White House. The Grammy for Best Rock and Roll Recording went to Bent Fabric for "Alley Cat," The Grammy for Country was "Funny Way of Laughing" by Burl Ives; for Folk was "If I Had a Hammer" by Peter, Paul and Mary; for Rhythm and Blues it was "I Can't Stop Loving You" by Ray Charles; and for Gospel was *Great Songs of Love and Faith* by Mahalia Jackson.

In the Pop category, "I Left My Heart in San Francisco" by Tony Bennett won for Best Male Vocal, Best Female Vocal was Ella Fitzgerald for *Ella Swings Brightly with Nelson*, Best Group was Peter, Paul and Mary for "If I Had a Hammer" and Best Chorus was the New Christy Minstrels for *Presenting the New Christy Minstrels*. Best "New" artist was Robert Goulet.

Newport Folk Festival: 1963

The 1963 Newport Folk Festival was the apex of the folk music movement. Guided and MC'd by Pete Seeger, the show featured Bob Dylan--then at the height of his career as a folk singer--Joan Baez ("the Queen of Folk Music"), Tom Paxton, Phil Ochs and others all gathered to sing songs of social significance to an audience who wanted to be involved activists and change the world.

The event was held shortly after the police in Birmingham had turned fire hoses on Civil Rights demonstrators in an effort to "put out a fire that would not die" (as stated by *Life* magazine, whose pictures dramatized the brutality of the Alabama police and the plight of southern blacks). The Cuban Missile Crisis had occurred in October, 1962--less than a year before--and school children were regularly drilled to huddle against the school wall with their arms over their heads or under their desks in the event of a nuclear attack.

A number of people built bomb shelters in their neighborhoods and stocked them and many felt a nuclear war was just around the corner. It was the height of the Civil Rights struggle--and folk music was an important part of that movement--while the anti-war movement had not yet latched onto Viet Nam. Anti-war meant anti-atomic bomb, but the seeds were planted to oppose any form of war. When the Viet Nam war escalated and became part of the nightly viewing habits of Americans watching the six o'clock news, the anti-war movement came to fruition, fueled by opposition to the draft where young men were forced to serve in a war they questioned.

If rock'n'roll freed the body, then folk music freed the mind, causing youth to question their elders, rebel intellectually as well as physically about assumptions, presumptions and the notion they should do what they were told and act like adults felt they should act. Rock and folk combined to give youth the courage of their convictions, which included social justice and civil rights as well as the right to rock and party all night long.

The Freedom Singers performed at the 1963 Newport Folk Festival and linked folk music with the Civil Rights Movement. The Freedom Singers were a student quartet, formed at Albany State College in Albany, Georgia in 1962. The original quartet was comprised for Rutha Mae Harris, Bernice Johnson Reagon, Cordell Reagon and Charles Neblett. The group was formed by Cordell Reagon, who was born in Nashville and had seen the power of songs during the sit-ins in Nashville. On the first night of the Newport Folk Festival in 1963, the Freedom Singers performed and on the second night joined a march led by Joan Baez and other activists that marched through Newport, walking past mansions in the upscale town.

Peter, Paul and Mary were scheduled to close the festival but Albert Grossman, who managed Peter, Paul and Mary as well as Bob Dylan, persuaded promoter George Wein to allow Bob Dylan to close the evening. Dylan performed "With God on Our Side," "Talkin' John Birch Society Blues" and "A Hard Rain's Gonna Fall," then Peter, Paul and Mary returned for an encore of "Blowin' in the Wind."

The Freedom Singers then joined Dylan, Joan Baez, Pete Seeger and Theo Bikel on stage and they crossed arms and held hands in a single line and sang "We Shall Overcome."

Hootenanny

The TV show "Hootenanny," which presented folk music to the nation on the ABC network had its first broadcast on April 6, 1963. Hosted by Jack Linkletter and taped before a live audience at different college campuses, the show featured performances by the Limeliters, the Chat Mitchell Trio, the Smothers Brothers, Josh White and the Carter Family. Several folk acts refused to appear on the network show because Pete Seeger and the Weavers were still blacklisted and could not appear on network television. Those who refused to appear included Joan Baez, the Kingston Trio and Peter, Paul and Mary.

The show's theme was "Hootenanny Saturday Night." It began as a 30-minute show but in September it was extended to an hour.

Civil Rights: 1946-1963

There is a nobility in the story of the Civil Rights movement and those involved in it that affects those who came of age during that period. The issue was clearly defined in terms of right and wrong better than most issues that confront Americans. Who can deny the basic humanity of African-Americans, or the wrongs perpetrated on them, particularly in the South during the days of segregation? Who can deny the moral authority and courage of conviction of a Martin Luther King, Jr. or other Civil Rights leaders? Who can defend people like Alabama Governor George Wallace and Birmingham police chief Bull Conner who fought against that movement when the post-1960s history has shown them to be blatantly wrong?

Still, the issue was clouded in complexities at the time, and the struggle was a difficult, bloody one before it was over.

The "separate but equal" doctrine that sanctioned segregation, was challenged in courts by the NAACP, who argued that schools for Negro children were inferior to schools for whites, receiving less funding and having to read textbooks discarded by white schools. On May 23, 1951, NAACP lawyers filed Brown v. Board of Education of Topeka in Kansas on that issue. On May 17, 1954, the Supreme Court ruled for the NAACP, ending the legal precedent of school segregation.

The year 1960 marked the Presidential campaign that saw the Republicans nominate Eisenhower's vice-president, Richard Nixon, to run against Democratic nominee, John Kennedy. There was increased racial tension and Reverend Martin Luther King, Jr. was arrested and put in jail, then transferred to a prison. During the campaign Kennedy was persuaded to call King's wife, Coretta, and offer condolences and support for her. News of that phone call spread quickly throughout the Negro community and during the November election the Negro vote, which had split 60-40 for the Republican party in 1956, went 70-30 for the Democrats.

The civil rights struggle was began to achieve the status of a sacred cause for civil rights activists.

Vietnam: 1954-1963

The story of the involvement of the United States in the small, southeast Asian country of Vietnam, went back to the end of World War II, when the French attempted to regain its colonies in that region. The United States provided foreign aid to the French in their efforts. However, on May 7, 1954 French troops were defeated by the Vietnamese at Dien Bien Phu and at the conclusion of the Geneva Conference on July 21 the French agreed to surrender the Northern half of the country to the Viet Cong (then called the Viet Minh).

The United States Army and CIA became involved and engineered the appointment of Ngo Dinh Diem as prime minister of South Vietnam in mid-1954.

The South Vietnam government of Diem was supported by American forces. However, in 1957 guerilla forces from the North began to attack the Saigon forces of Diem. By December, 1961, President Kennedy had to commit American arms to South Vietnam in order to stop the Diem government from being overthrown; prior to that time there were only American "advisors" in South Vietnam, whose job was to train and advise the South Vietnamese army. In 1962 Vietnam was viewed as a "test" of who would rule the globe: the Free World or the Communist world. This was not idle speculation; in January, 1961, Soviet Premier Kruschchev announced that the Soviet Union would not engage in an atomic war with the United States, but would support popular uprisings and liberation wars in Third World countries in an effort to spread the communist doctrine.

In 1962 the United States had 850,000 military men and civilian officials serving in 106 countries overseas. That was a result of the post-World War II strategy of trying to contain Soviet aggression and fight the Cold War through a military presence, which deterred actual fighting. In October, 1962 the Cuban Missile Crisis occurred when President Kennedy confronted

Soviet Premier Kruschchev over Soviet attempts to place missiles with atomic warheads in Cuba, 90 miles from Miami. The United States had "lost" Cuba in 1959 when a popular uprising led by Fidel Castro overthrew the American backed regime of President Fulgencio Batista and ended American involvement in Cuba. Cuba then aligned itself with the Soviet Union. The Soviets finally backed down, after the world stood on the brink of a nuclear war; that was proof of the Soviet threat and justification for American military involvement in the world at large.

On June 11, 1963 a Buddhist monk set fire to himself in Saigon, South Vietnam and committed suicide as an act of protest; the picture of the monk in flames appeared in newspapers all across the United States.

There was a crisis in South Vietnam and the American government decided it had to oust President Diem in order to "win" the war. That fall, Lt. Colonel Lucien Conein led the effort to arrange a coup d'etat against the South Vietnam ruling family. That coup was carried out by the South Vietnamese army on November 1, 1963; the next day Diem and his brother, Ngo Dinh Nhu, were assassinated. Three weeks later, President John F. Kennedy was assassinated in Dallas, Texas.

The Beach Boys

At Brian Wilson's request, Al Jardine re-joined the Beach Boys in April, 1963 as they began a tour of the mid-west. Brian disliked performing and stayed home as much as possible, writing songs and recording.

Their single "Surfer Girl" entered the *Billboard* Hot 100 on August 3 and rose to number seven; the flip side, "Little Deuce Coupe," written by Brian and Roger Christian, reached number 15. The album *Surfer Girl*, released in September, reached number seven and remained on the album chart for over a year. That album was the last by the six member Beach Boys—the three Wilsons, Jardin, Love and David Marks. Marks left in October due to conflicts with Murry; that departure caused Brian to tour and perform again.

The Beach Boys finished strong on the *Billboard* Hot 100 in 1963. "Be True to Your School" and "In My Room" (written by Brian and Gary Usher) both entered the singles chart on November 2 with "Be True to Your School" reaching number six and "In My Room" reaching number 23. "Little Deuce Coupe" entered the chart on November 9 and reached number four.

In September, "Honolulu Lulu" by Jan and Dean was released and reached number 11 on the *Billboard* chart. On December 7, "Drag City," written by Berry, Brian Wilson and Brian Wilson entered the *Billboard* Hot 100 and reached number ten.

The Beach Boys were not the only ambassadors for surfing; there were records made in L.A. of "The Lonely Surfer," "Tell 'Em I'm Surfin," "Summer Means Fun," "Beach Ball," "The Okie Surfer," "the Monster Surfer, "Surfin' Hootenanny," "Sufrin' South of the Border," "Surfin' Bongos," "Ski Surfin'," "Look Who's Surfin" and even a Christmas song, "Santa the Sidewalk Surfer."

California beckoned those who loved sun, fun and surfing and young people from all over America headed West to become part of the California lifestyle.

Warner Brothers Purchases Reprise Records

Frank Sinatra had recorded hit records for Columbia and Capitol but always recorded under a producer who had final say in the material recorded, although Sinatra had some freedom in choosing his material. The fact that Sinatra did not have full creative control of his work and the freedom to record whatever, whenever, wherever he wanted to irked him.

Sinatra signed a seven year control with Capitol Records in 1953 and worked with arranger and orchestra conductor Nelson Riddle. At the end of his contract, frustrated with Capitol executives, he sought to buy the jazz label, Verve, but that deal did not go through. That led to him forming the Reprise label in 1960.

The era of Big Band singers had passed and, although Sinatra continued to be commercially successful, many others from that era could not find a recording contract. Sinatra signed many of those artists, including Dean Martin, Sammy Davis, Jr., Bing Crosby, Jo Stafford, Dennis Day, the McGuire Sisters, Dinah Shore, Rosemary Clooney and his daughter, Nancy. He also signed black stand up comedian Redd Foxx, whose albums were risqué.

Sinatra guaranteed the artists signed to Reprise that they would have complete creative control of their recordings and would have ownership of their masters and the publishing. The label released some good albums but was not profitable.

In September, 1963, Warner Brothers purchased Reprise Records for $1.5 million in cash and one third ownership in the combined record companies. The deal was structured so that Warners paid Sinatra $2 million but Sinatra then paid $500,000 for a third of the combined labels.

Jack Warner saw the deal as a way to acquire Sinatra as an actor for Warner Brothers films. Sinatra had starred in *Ocean's Eleven* in 1960 and that movie had grossed $10 million.

Jack Warner did not inform the executives at Warner Brothers Records about the acquisition or terms of the new deal; he viewed it as a deal for an actor and the movie company. As part of the deal, Warner Brothers Records acquired the services of Mo Ostin, who had previously handled administration and accounting for Reprise.

Mo Ostin graduated with a degree in economics from UCLA in 1950 and then attended law school at night. In 1954 he became the bookkeeper for Verve Records, which was owned by jazz impresario Norman Granz. Verve was a leading jazz label, with an artist roster that included Charlie Parker, Dixy Gillespie, Lester Young, Count Basie, Oscar Peterson, Louis Armstrong, Roy Eldridge and Ella Fitzgerald but the label was in financial trouble.

Attorney Mickey Rudin's major client was Frank Sinatra; Ostin contacted Rudin to represent Verve. After Sinatra's attempt to purchase Verve fell through, the label was sold to MGM for $2 million. Ostin had come to the attention of Mickey Rudin and Frank Sinatra so Ostin was asked to head Reprise when it was sold to Warner Brothers; he agreed.

Rhythm and Blues: 1960-1963

By the 1960s the music that had been called "race" at the beginning of the century had evolved through a half century of recordings. Musically, the sounds of rhythm and blues, and rhythm and blues-influenced music, were quite diverse and integrated. Then the music--and the race--ran headlong into the 1960s with the Civil Rights Movement. As James Brown sang, "Say it loud, I'm black and I'm proud."

The music that came from Motown in Detroit and the studios of Memphis and Muscle Shoals was made by a mixture of black and white musicians, producers and engineers. Although many Americans were fighting integration in schools and neighborhoods, on the radio integration had been accomplished. The *Billboard* Hot 100 and Rhythm and Blues (R&B) charts were such a mirror of each other that on November 30, 1963 *Billboard* stopped publishing an R&B chart because it was almost an exact replica of their Hot 100 chart.

R&B found its voice on small, independent labels but it became difficult for those small indies to remain in business after the payola scandals broke in 1960. A number of disc jockeys--including Alan Freed--lost their jobs and many small labels could not afford legal representation for the various court cases. The IRS demanded payment of back taxes from deductions they ruled illegal and assessed fines that put many entrepreneurs out of business. Although small labels continued to operate, and several labels--Motown, Stax, Vee-Jay and Atlantic--established themselves as R&B labels, the era of the major labels was only a decade away.

Vee Jay Records

Vee Jay Records was started by Vivian Carter Bracken ("Vee"), her husband, James Bracken ("Jay") and her brother, Calvin Carter. The Brackens owned a record store in Gary, Indiana and often came to Chicago for records; Vivian also worked as a disc jockey. From selling records they moved into recording them because they found talented youngsters wanting to sing. Their first record was "Baby, It's You" by the Spaniels, which was released in Fall, 1953 on Vee Jay, then re-released on Chance, a Chicago label that did not last long. Their first R&B top ten was "At My Front Door" by the El Dorados, which was a number one R&B record in late 1955. Their next hit was "Oh What a Night" by the Dells, which reached number four on the R&B chart in early 1957. By that time the Brackens had moved from Gary to Chicago where they owned a building on Michigan Avenue, across the street from Chess Records.

Vee-Jay became a successful black-owned record label and signed Jimmy Reed, Eddie Taylor, John Lee Hooker and Jerry Butler.

The Four Seasons

Frankie Valli always had one of the most defining and powerful voices in rock. His first commercial release, under the name Frankie Valley, came in 1953 with "My Mother's Eyes." The next year he formed the Variatones with guitarist Tommy DeVito and three others as The Four Lovers. They were signed to RCA Victor but only one release charted; during the 1956-1959 period they performed and recorded under a variety of names.

They began working with producer and songwriter Bob Crewe in 1959 and in Baltimore that year shared a stage with the Royal Teens, who had a hit that summer with "Short, Shorts," written by 15-year-old Bob Gaudio. A short while later, Gaudio joined the Four Lovers on keyboards and guitar. After they failed an audition for a lounge in a bowling alley in New Jersey, they decided to take the name of the lounge, "The Four Seasons" for themselves. They signed with Crewe's production company and released several singles that did not chart in addition to serving as a backing vocal group on Crewe's sessions for his Topix label. During this period Gaudio and Crewe wrote "Sherry," which the group recorded.

Seeking a label, Frankie Valli approached Randy Wood (not the founder of Dot) who was West Coast sales manager for Vee Jay. Wood took the recording to the label and they became the first white artists signed to Vee Jay. "Sherry" became a huge hit in 1962; it was number one for five weeks. That same year they released "Big Girls Don't Cry," which was also number one for five weeks. In 1963 they had a three week number one with "Walk Like a Man" and "Candy Girl," reached number three.

During 1962 and 1963 the Beach Boys and the Four Seasons were the top selling rock acts.

Stax Records

Stax Records was formed during the late 1950s by Jim Stewart ("St") and Estelle Axton ("ax"), a white brother and sister who lived about thirty miles east of Memphis. They had a record store and label, "Satellite," where they recorded a wide variety of music. However, in 1960 they moved into an old movie theater in Memphis and began recording R&B.

Stewart and Axton were an unlikely pair to start an R&B label; he had played fiddle in western swing bands and worked at a bank in Memphis when the label started; Estelle also worked at a bank so business was conducted in the evenings and on weekends when the label started.

Rufus Thomas was a popular disc jockey on WDAI in Memphis and emcee at a local nightclub; he had Sun Records' first hit, "Bear Cat," an answer to Big Mama Thornton's "Hound Dog" and was a local legend in Memphis. He recorded "Cause I Love You," a duet with his daughter, Carla, a senior at Hamilton High School. That was the first record for Stax that received significant airplay and caught the attention of Jerry Wexler of Atlantic, who leased the record for his label.

The label needed a follow-up and Rufus suggested Carla record "Gee Whiz," a song she had written several years before, then tucked away in a notebook. Rufus had originally taken a demo of the song to Vee Jay in Chicago and they liked it but did nothing for a year, so in November, 1960, Carla recorded the song for Stax in Memphis. The song was originally released on Stax but Jerry Wexler heard the record and insisted it be released on Atlantic because that label had better distribution.

The song was produced by Chips Moman in the Stax Studio and engineered by Jim Stewart. The record was released when Carla was a college student at Tennessee State University in Nashville and Wexler and Carla's parents had to convince school officials to allow Carla to leave campus to tour.

Stax Records developed a studio group that played on most of their records; the group, known as the Mar-Keys was comprised of Booker T. Jones, Steve Cropper, Al Jackson, Jr. and bass player Lewis Steinberg and had a regional hit with an instrumental, "Last Night." The group coalesced in 1962 with Booker T. Jones, a multi-instrumentalist known primarily for his keyboard work; Steve Cropper on guitar; Donald "Duck" Dunn on bass; and Al Jackson Jr. on drums. The Stax group was "transracial" and there was a mixture of blacks and white in the organization. Of these four studio musicians, two were white (Cropper and Dunn) and two were black (Jones and Jackson).

One a Sunday afternoon in the summer of 1962, a session was booked by Dale Bowman for Billy Lee Riley, the rockabilly artist known for his hit "My Gal is Red Hot (Your Gal Ain't Diddly-Squat)" but Riley never showed up. The studio group began jamming and recorded a blues instrumental, "Behave Yourself." Stax owner Jim Everett was excited about the recording and wanted to release it but needed a "B" side. The group then worked up an idea Cropper and Jones had worked on, which became "Green Onions." The label credited the group Booker T. and the MG's. It entered the *Billboard* Hot 100 in August, 1962 and reached number three.

The name "the MGs" has often been cited as an acronym for "Memphis Group." However, Chips Moman insisted they took their name from his sports car, a Triumph MG; the group was previously known as The Triumphs.

Civil Rights struggles in the South

Birmingham, Alabama was Ground Zero for the civil rights movement in 1963. In April and May there were weeks of demonstrations and riots; on May 3, millions of Americans watched TV as public safety director Eugene "Bull" Connor turned fire hoses and vicious police dogs on children demonstrating. Dr. Martin Luther King, Jr. was jailed in April where he wrote his "Letter From the Birmingham Jail," a 20 page message to clergymen that explained his view towards civil disobedience. In the letter he stated "I submit that an individual who breaks a law that conscience tell him is unjust, and who willingly accept the penalty of imprisonment in order to arouse the conscience of the community over its injustice, is in reality expressing the highest respect for the law."

Alabama Governor George Wallace vowed to "stand in the schoolhouse door" to block school integration at the University of Alabama on June 11.

Two African-American students, Vivian Malone and James Hood, had been accepted to register for classes.

On June 12, President John Kennedy gave a speech, broadcast nationally on TV and radio, and stated that he would begin the push to take action on civil rights. That night, Medgar Evers, a field aide for the NAACP, was killed just after midnight after he drove into the driveway of his home in Jackson, Mississippi. Five days before, Evers spoke at a rally and said he would gladly die to make a better life for his family. The killer, a white man, Byron de la Beckworth of Greenwood, Mississippi, was put on trial twice but each time the result was a hung jury.

On August 18, James Meredith became first black to graduate from the University of Mississippi.

The March on Washington and the "I Have a Dream " speech

Plans for a March on Washington for Jobs and Freedom began in December, 1961 when A. Philip Randolph and Bayard Rustin had a vision of two days of protests, sit-ins and lobbying followed by a mass rally at the Lincoln Memorial. That wanted to focus on public works programs that would employ blacks. They made their plans public early in 1963.

Randolph, who was president of the Brotherhood of Sleeping Car Porters and president of the Negro American Labor Council, and Rustin had a long history of organizing. In 1941 they planned a march on Washington with 100,000 black workers marching for jobs; the march was called off after President Franklin Roosevelt issued an Executive Order that established the Committee on Fair Employment Practice and banned job discrimination in the defense industry.

Randolph and Rustin planned several large marches on Washington during the 1940s but all were called off. In 1957, they organized the Prayer Pilgrimage for Freedom at the Lincoln Memorial that featured speakers Martin Luther King, Jr., Roy Wilkins, Adam Clayton Powell and a performance by Mahalia Jackson.

During 1963 there were a number of demonstrations and marches for civil rights; it was also the 100th anniversary of President Lincoln signing the Emancipation Proclamation. A number of organizations put aside differences to unite in the March on Washington, including the National Association for the Advancement of Colored People (NAACP) and the Southern Christian Leadership Conference.

In June, the council for United Civil Rights Leadership was formed by leaders from different organization to coordinate fund raising and messaging. That coalition included A. Phillip Randolph; president of the Congress of Racial Equality James Farmer; chairman of the Student Nonviolent Coordinating Committee John Lewis; president of the Southern Christian Leadership Conference Martin Luther King Jr.' president of the NAACP Roy Wilkins and president of the National Urban League Whitney Young. The leaders did not want Bayard Rustin to lead the march because he was a former Communist, a draft resister and a homosexual but accepted him as deputy organizer with Randolph named as the lead organizer.

The six leaders met with President Kennedy on June 22 and Kennedy pushed them to call off the march because an air of intimidation would occur if a large crowd of blacks were brought to Washington. The leaders insisted on holding the march. The issue of civil disobedience was debated and the decision was reached to not allow it. The public announcement of the march was made at a press conference on July 2; on July 17, President Kennedy stated that the assembly would be peaceful and there was cooperation with the police force in Washington.

A team of two hundred activists and organizers, led by Rustin, publicized the march and recruited marchers.

The goals of the march included passage of a meaningful civil rights bill, the elimination of school segregation immediately, a program of public works that included job training, a federal law prohibiting racial discrimination in hiring, a minimum wage of $2 an hour and authority for the Attorney General to bring injunctive suits when constitutional rights were violated.

The leaders agreed that both blacks and whites would march instead of a black only march.

Plans for the march were met with claims of Communist involvement and bomb threats in the homes and offices of civil rights activists.

The march was held on Wednesday, August 28, 1963. On that morning, bomb threats grounded five airplanes, a caller in Kansas City phoned the FBI and stated he would "put a hole between King's eyes" (the FBI did not respond) and Roy Wilkins would be assassinated if he did not leave the country.

Marchers began arriving early in the morning and continued to arrive throughout the day. Many of the marchers traveled great distances to be there and almost all of them were concerned about what awaited them. Would there be violence? Would the police protect them? Would the protests make a difference? D.C. residents were also nervous about violence. The marchers were surprised by the civility they found when they arrived in Washington and the protection provided but Washington police, National Guard troops and soldiers stationed in the area.

At the insistence of Bayard Rustin, an expensive sound system was acquired; however the system was sabotaged on Tuesday but was rebuilt by the U.S. Army Signal Corps overnight.

The march did not come off as planned. Randolph and Rustin envisioned the streets in Washington full of marchers but the crowd began marching on the mall from the Washington Monument to the Lincoln Memorial because the march leaders were meeting with members of Congress. The leaders finally made it to the front of the march where they joined arms for pictures showing them leading the event.

Speakers at the event included A. Philip Randolph, Roy Wilkins, John Lewis and Walter Reuther, head of the AFL-CIO.

The National Anthem was scheduled to be sung by Marian Anderson, but she did not arrive on time so it was sung by Camilla Williams. Anderson sang "He's Got the Whole World In His Hands," Mahalia Jackson sang "How I Got Over," Joan Baez sang "We Shall Overcome" and "Oh, Freedom," Bob Dylan sang "When the Ship Comes In" with Baez and "Only a Pawn in Their Game" alone, Peter Paul and Mary sang "If I Had a Hammer" and "Blowin' in the Wind" and Odetta sang "I'm On My Way."

The tenth speaker that day was Martin Luther King. His speech had been written in advance and the group of leaders had approved it. However, near the end of the speech, Mahalia Jackson shouted "Tell them about the dream, Martin!" King had used the phrase "I have a dream" in previous speeches, particularly one to a North Carolina high school in November, 1962 and in Detroit two months earlier.

King departed from his prepared speech with the phrase "I have a dream" where he stated that dream included that "my four little children will one day live in a nation where they will not be judged by the color of their skin but by the content of their character" and "in Alabama little black boys and black girls will be able to join hands with little white boys and white girls as sisters and brothers."

It was a memorable speech which provided an unstoppable impetus for the passing of the Civil Rights bill the next year.

Phil Spector and the "Wall of Sound"

Producer Phil Spector's "Wall of Sound" reached its zenith in 1963 with a string of hits that included "Da Doo Ron Ron," "Then He Kissed Me" and "He's Sure the Boy I Love," all by the Crystals and "Be My Baby" by the Ronettes. The year before, "He's a Rebel" was a hit by the Crystals, which often featured Darlene Love doing the vocals.

Spector recorded his hits in Los Angeles and used L.A. studio musicians "The Wrecking Crew" to layer sound on sound for his teen masterpieces. Musicians who were part of the "Wall of Sound" included Glen Campbell guitar; Leon Russell piano, Larry Knechtel, keyboards; bass; Jim Gordon, drums; Carol Kaye, bass; Billy Strange, guitar; and Harold Battiste, sax with full orchestra string sections. Spector's sessions usually began at 4 p.m. and lasted until daybreak. Musicians laid down basic tracks and then doubled, tripled and quadrupled them so there were often two drummers, three pianists, and four guitarists on one track, "all of them blending into one blast of noise."

News in 1963

During 1963, President Kennedy spoke before a crowd of 150,000 at the Berlin Wall, stating "All free men, wherever they may live, are citizens of Berlin. And therefore, as a free man, I take pride in the works 'Ich bin ein Berliner'" ("I am a Berliner").

Betty Friedan published *The Feminine Mystique* where she stated "women are unfulfilled and must develop their identities" and emphasized they could do that working outside their homes.

California became the most populated state, passing New York, and the five digit ZIP Codes (Zone Improvement Plan) was instituted.

End of 1963

Time froze in America on the afternoon of Friday, November 22, 1963; anyone old enough to remember remembers exactly where they were and what they were doing when they heard the news of the assassination of President John F. Kennedy in Dallas, Texas. Pop songs on the radio during that time included the Beach Boys "Be True to Your School," "Can I Get a Witness," by Marvin Gaye, "Dominique" by the Singing Nun, "Louie Louie" by the Kingsmen," "Twenty-Four Hours From Tulsa" by Gene Pitney" and "You Don't Have To Be a Baby to Cry" by The Caravels.

That very same day in England another famous man died. C. S. Lewis, the noted Christian apologist and sixteenth century scholar passed away at his home in Oxford. That evening, at about the same time President Kennedy was assassinated, the Beatles were at the Globe Cinema on High Street in Stockton-on-Tees, Durham performing a concert. They were in the midst of an English tour--their fourth in 1963--where they played in 34 different towns, two shows a night; the following night they performed at City Hall in Newcastle-upon-Tyne.

Their second album, *With the Beatles*, was released that day; it had advance orders in England of 270,000 but few people in the United States were aware of the Beatles, Beatlemania in England, that album or any of their hit singles that year. The Beatles had released six singles in England by the end of 1963: the first, "My Bonnie"/"The Saints" was with Tony Sheridan and they were billed as "The Beat Brothers." The next five singles were "Love Me Do"/"P.S. I Love You," "Please Please Me"/"Ask Me Why," "From Me To You"/"Thank You Girl," "She Loves You"/"I'll Get You" and "I Want to Hold Your Hand"/"This Boy."

1964
1964 Begins

The year 1964 began with President Lyndon Johnson stating, in his State of the Union Address, that he was committed to a "War on Poverty." His Surgeon General announced that "smoking may be hazardous to your health." Congress passed the 24th Amendment to the Constitution outlawing the poll tax as a requirement for voting. In Austria, the Winter Olympics were being held.

There had been less joy at Christmas; it had only been a month since the assassination of President Kennedy and the nation still mourned.

The Musical Year of 1964 Begins

In America, the musical year of 1964 began with "There! I've Said It Again" by Bobby Vinton sitting in the number one position on the *Billboard* Hot 100 chart; it was a popular song and remained in that position for four weeks—all of January. It replaced "Dominique" by the Singing Nun, which was also number one for four weeks at the end of 1963. The number one pop album was *The Singing Nun* by The Singing Nun, which held the number one position for ten straight weeks, starting in December. The number one R&B song was "Louie Louie" by the Kingsmen, which reached number one at the end of 1963 and remained in that position for six consecutive weeks.

"Love's Gonna Live Here" by Buck Owens was the number one country song at the beginning of 1964; it had stayed in the number one position for 16 weeks, since October, 1963.

On January 11, 1964, *Billboard* debuted its first Country Album chart. Prior to that time, country music, whose primary market was singles for jukeboxes, did not warrant enough album sales to be tracked. Before 1964 there were albums by Eddy Arnold, Jimmy Dean, and Chet Atkins (who had nine) on the pop album chart in Billboard. During 1964 there were two number one albums by Buck Owens, two by Johnny Cash, and one each by Ray Price, Chet Atkins, Hank Snow and Jim Reeves.

On January 18, "I Want To Hold Your Hand" by the Beatles on Capitol Records entered the Billboard Hot 100.

The Beatles: Early 1964

"The Beatles Christmas Show" on the BBC, which featured the group doing skits as well as singing, began on December 24, 1963 and extended until January 11 in London. On Saturday night, January 12, they appeared on "Val Parnell's Sunday Night at the London Palladium," one of the most popular—and prestigious—TV shows in England.

The Beatles then left London for Paris where they performed at the Olympia Theatre from January 16 until February 4, an 18 day run of two and three shows daily as part of a line-up with eight other acts. On January 29, they recorded two of their hits in German, "Komm, Gib Mir Deine Hand" ("I Want To Hold Your Hand") and "Sie Liebt Dich ("She Loves You") as well as the basic tracks for "Can't Buy Me Love" in a studio in Paris.

During their time at the George V Hotel, they first heard Bob Dylan's album, *The Freewheelin' Bob Dylan*, which was given to them by a French D.J. The album, which had been released in the United States at the end of May, 1963, contained songs such as "Blowin' in the Wind," "Masters of War," "A Hard Rain's a-Gonna Fall," "Don't Think Twice, It's Alright" and "Girl From the North Country." The Beatles listened to it constantly.

The Beatles were in their suite at the George V Hotel when they received the news that their single, "I Want To Hold Your Hand," was number one in the United States. They were ecstatic. They were already scheduled to perform on "The Ed Sullivan Show," but a number one record increased their excitement.

The Beatles Arrive in America

On February 7, the Beatles boarded a plane in London for New York. When they landed they were met by screaming fans; at first, the Beatles did not know those fans were screaming for them. A round of interviews followed and then rehearsals for the Sullivan show.

The Beatles rehearsed for the Sullivan Show on February 8 and the next evening, at 8 p.m. Eastern time on February 9, 1964, they opened the show with "All My Loving," then sang "Till There Was You" and "She Loves You." Watching the Beatles were 73 million Americans in 23,240,000 homes. At the end of the show, the Beatles returned and sang "I Saw Her Standing There" and "I Want to Hold Your Hand."

Two days later, the Beatles took a train to Washington in a snow storm and performed at the Washington Coliseum for 8,092 fans. The concert was "in the round" so the Beatles adjusted their amplifiers and drum kit after several songs to face a different segment of the audience. After the concert there was a reception at the British Embassy where someone cut a lock of Ringo's hair, causing the Beatles to leave early.

The Beatles at Carnegie Hall

On February 12, the Beatles performed two shows at Carnegie Hall, with an audience of 2,900 for each show.

The performance at Carnegie Hall had already been booked by a fluke chance. Sid Bernstein was a booking agent with the General Artists Corporation (GAC) in New York; he attended a night class at the New School in the Village where the professor, noted journalist Max Lerner, told his students to read a British newspaper to find out how the government in England worked.

The first newspaper Bernstein saw contained a story about the Beatles. The class was required to look at a newspaper each week and the second week Bernstein picked up a paper, it had another story on the group. Same thing on the third week. Bernstein sent memos to London, urging the GAC office there to sign the Beatles but was rebuffed. He then called a friend, who happened to have been hired by Beatles manager Brian Epstein to promote Beatles records in the United States; the friend gave him Epstein's home phone number.

In February, 1963, Sid Bernstein called Brian Epstein in Liverpool, wanting to book the Beatles at Carnegie Hall; he offered $6,500 for two shows in a one day booking. Bernstein suggested the show be held in three months but Epstein thought that was too soon; they finally settled on a date in February, 1964. The agreement contained a proviso: if the Beatles did not have a hit in the United States by November, the deal could be called off. Bernstein then contacted Carnegie Hall and discovered he needed a $500 deposit to secure the date; he borrowed the money and sent it in.

The Beatles had not had any success with a hit record in America during 1963. Brian Epstein shopped the group to RCA, Columbia and Decca, who all turned them down. Finally, he found a small label in Philadelphia, Swan, which released a single. Then he made an agreement with Chicago-based VeeJay records for an album--but nothing hit.

In November, 1963, while Epstein was in New York, he placed a call to Alan Livingston, then head of Capitol in Los Angeles, and asked if the executive had heard the group. When Livingston replied that he had not, Epstein requested he listen and then call him back about releasing a single in the United States.

Livingston listened to "I Want to Hold Your Hand," the fifth single as The Beatles that had been released in England, and decided that Capitol would release it in the United States. Epstein insisted that a promotion budget of $40,000 be used to promote the single. That was an unheard of sum for an unknown group at that time, but Livingstone agreed because the group was scheduled to perform on "The Ed Sullivan Show" three times. The single was released on December 26, 1963; on January 18, 1964 "I Want to Hold Your Hand" b/w "I Saw Her Standing There" entered the *Billboard* charts; it went quickly to number one.

During the fall of 1963, an airline stewardess flying the Washington to London route picked up a copy of their latest single, "I Want to Hold Your Hand" and brought it back to the United States and gave it to her boyfriend, a disc jockey in Washington D.C.. He put it on the air--and the phone lines lit up. He phoned a disc jockey friend in Chicago, sent a tape, and the Chicago disc jockey put it on the air with the same reaction. A call from the Chicago D.J. to his D. J. friend in St. Louis resulted in the tape being put on the air in that city. The seeds of Beatlemania in the United States were sown.

Second Appearance on "The Ed Sullivan Show"

The Beatles second appearance by the Beatles on the Sullivan show came a week later on February 16 while they were in Miami. On that show, before an audience of 3,500 at the Deauville Hotel, the Beatles performed "She Loves You," "This Boy," "All My Loving," "I Saw Her Standing There" and "I Want to Hold Your Hand." Their third appearance, on February 23, was taped. On that date they were back in London where they worked on their next single, "Can't Buy Me Love" and began filming *A Hard Day's Night* as well as writing and recording songs for the film.

By the time the Beatles left the United States, Beatlemania had arrived in America and they had several hits on the radio: "I Want to Hold Your Hand," "I Saw Her Standing There," "She Loves You," and "Please Please Me" (the last two had been re-released by Swan and Vee-Jay, respectively).

British Music Before the Beatles

British influence on American music started long before the Beatles arrived. The early folk songs of the British Isles—England, Scotland, Ireland and Wales—were brought by settlers during the 16th and 17th centuries and formed the basis for American popular music.

During the mid-nineteenth and early twentieth century the Music Hall was a major source of popular entertainment in the United Kingdom. It was a variety show that featured musical acts as well as comedy and specialty acts, much like American vaudeville. The Music Hall developed into larger establishments during the late nineteenth century, with room for 500 to 5000 people and evolved into a "theatre of varieties" with grand designs, spotlights, splendid and luxurious interiors and theatre seating.

The demand for songs for the Music Hall led to the application of copyright law for the compositions of songwriters and music publishers. During the days of the Music Hall, the sheet music business thrived and music publishers became profitable businessmen.

The movies, then radio and the phonograph became popular during the early twentieth century, which led to a decline in the Music Hall, although stars such as George Formby, Gracie Fields, Max Miller and Flanagan and Allen emerged.

The audience was primarily working class Brits and the songs were written for them. Many of the most popular songs were distinctly British, such as "Boiled Beef and Carrots," "Burlington Bertie from Bow," "Daddy Wouldn't Buy Me a Bow Wow," "I'm Henry the VIII, I Am," "Ta Ra Ra Boom-de-ay," and "Run, Rabbit, Run." Some of those songs, such as "I'm Henry the VIII" later became pop hits during the British Invasion (recorded by Herman's Hermits).

During World War II American music became international through the V Discs issued by the American Special Services Division of the Armed Forces. After the War, a number of American recordings were imported into the U.K.

Traditional Jazz, or "Trad" emerged from the Big Band era. This jazz, known as "Dixieland" in the United States was the earliest jazz developed in New Orleans, before it became popular in England.

Skiffle

The skiffle craze began in England in 1956 when Lonnie Donegan released "Rock Island Line" on Decca. "Rock Island Line" was originally recorded by folk song collector John Lomax at the Arkansas State Prison in Tucker, Arkansas in 1934. The song was sung by Kelly Pace, a convict in the prison, who reportedly wrote the original version. Blues singer Leadbelly accompanied Lomax on the trip to Arkansas and later took the basic song, re-arranged it, added new lyrics, and recorded it. The Donegan version was released as a single and became a huge hit, reaching number eight on the British pop charts. It was also released in the United States in 1956 and reached number eight on the *Billboard* Hot 100.

Skiffle was called "folk music" in the United States, although there were some differences. In skiffle, a tea chest bass was used. In American folk music, musicians did not use a tea chest bass; instead, it was primarily acoustic guitars with some groups having a banjo and/or an acoustic bass.

In addition to "Rock Island Line," Donegan had a series of skiffle hit singles during 1956-1958 in the U.K. Donegan's biggest skiffle hits came in 1957, around the same time that John Lennon bought a mail-order guitar and decided to form a skiffle group. The group that evolved into the Beatles was originally The Quarry Men, led by John Lennon with some of his school friends.

"Lonnie Donegan had a much bigger influence on British rock bands than he was ever given credit for," said Beatle George Harrison. "In the late Fifties, he was virtually the only guitar player that you could see. He was the most successful person, and had the highest profile. He had a great voice, a lot of energy and sang great songs—catchy versions of Leadbelly tunes and things. I loved him. He was a big hero of mine. Everyone got guitars, and formed skiffle bands because of him."

The Quarry Men

Future Beatles John, Paul and George first gravitated to skiffle; it was easy to play and skiffle songs were among the first they performed as each learned the guitar.

John Lennon had originally formed The Quarry Man (named after the school he attended) with school friends; along the way, he invited Paul McCartney and George Harrison to join.

However, by the end of 1957, early rock'n'roll, particularly recordings made by Bill Haley and the Comets, Elvis, Carl Perkins, the Everly Brothers and Buddy Holly, were the group's major musical inspiration.

Rock and Roll first reached England in December, 1954 when Bill Haley's "Shake, Rattle and Roll" entered the British pop chart. Haley's "Rock Around the Clock" charted in January, 1955, then was re-released in the Fall. The re-released "Rock Around the Clock" entered the British pop chart in October, 1955 and remained on the chart until late winter, reaching the number one position. "Rock Around the Clock" had a huge impact on John, Paul, George and Ringo; it was their first exposure to rock'n'roll.

In 1956 Elvis was a phenomenal, cultural shaking hit; that year he sold over ten million records in the United States. His first release in Britain was "Heartbreak Hotel" and it, too, made a huge impact on John, Paul, George and Ringo.

Buddy Holly and the Crickets

"That'll Be the Day" by The Crickets was released in the U.K. in September, 1957, came on the British chart and rose to number one, then dropped off and re-entered in January, 1958. Other records released under "The Crickets" included "Oh Boy," "Maybe Baby," "Think It Over" and "Love's Made a Fool of You." Records were also released in the U.K. under "Buddy Holly" ("Peggy Sue," "Rave One," "It Doesn't Matter Anymore") but it was The Crickets who had the greatest influence on young British groups.

"That'll Be the Day" "was as much a sensation among British boys as anything by Elvis Presley or Little Richard," said Mark Lewisohn in his book, *Tune In*. "If one can nail down a specific moment that the white pop group business—the whole rock band industry—kicked off in Britain, it was when the needle dropped into the first groove of 'That'll Be the Day' and boys were grabbed by its distinctive ringing guitar intro. The record came at the perfect time, just when skiffle was fading, limited by sameness of repertoire and sound." He continued, "The Crickets were so much bigger in Britain...The only group of note was the Coasters...just vocalists with session musicians. The Crickets were another kind of group: vocals, electric guitar, bass, drums. When thousands of skifflers heard 'That'll Be the Day,' those eternally uplifting two minutes, they were converted. It was like a well-drilled, willing and equipped army being given a new battle plan."

Early Influences of the Beatles

The early records of Carl Perkins, The Everly Brothers, Jerry Lee Lewis and Johnny Burnette and the Rock'n'Roll Trio were influential with the early Beatles .

The group comprised of John Lennon, Paul McCartney and George Harrison evolved through several names ("Johnny and the Moon Dogs" and "The Silver Beatles") until they settled on The Beatles, a name derived from Buddy Holly's group, The Crickets. George and Paul bought electric pick-ups for their acoustic guitars and they became a 1950s cover band. They backed singer Johnny Gentle on a Scotland tour and had several drummers (Tommy Moore, Norman Chapman) play with them for short stints until Pete Best joined, just before they headed to Hamburg, Germany in August, 1960 to perform at the Kaiserkeller, a club in the red light district. They added a bass player, Stuart Sutcliffe, before their trip and performed in Hamburg until December of that year.

Before they returned to Hamburg in Spring, 1961, they played at the Cavern Club on Matthew Street in Liverpool, which became their base in Liverpool; their first appearance was on February 9, 1961. They eventually performed at the Cavern Club 292 times.

The Beatles first recording was an amateur affair done in Liverpool. The group did Buddy Holly's "That'll Be the Day" and a song written by Paul McCartney (credited to Paul and George), "In Spite of All the Danger." Their first professional recording session was on June 22, 1961 in Hamburg, Germany, during the time they performed at the Top Ten Club with Tony Sheridan. During that session they backed Tony Sheridan on "My Bonnie," ("My Bonnie Lies Over the Ocean"); "The Saints," ("When The Saints Go Marching In," which had been recorded by Jerry Lee Lewis) "Why" (written by Sheridan); "Take Out Some Insurance," (originally done by bluesman Jimmy Reed); and the old Hank Snow song, "Nobody's Child," that had been a favorite song of Ringo's. Ringo was not in the group at the time; Pete Best was the drummer. The Beatles as a group recorded "Ain't She Sweet" and the instrumental "Cry For a Shadow."

The Beatles Meet Brian Epstein

In November, 1961 The Beatles met Brian Epstein after he heard about their German recordings.

Great Britain was an entrenched "class" society during the early 1960s and Brian Epstein was part of the "respectable middle" class of Liverpool while the Beatles were "lower or working" class, except John Lennon. Epstein's father was a store owner and Epstein, after trying his hand at acting school in London, moved back to Liverpool and began working in the record department of one of his father's stores, NEMS, which stood for North End Music Stores.

Brian Epstein was born September 19, 1934. He was urbane, worldly, well-dressed, elegant and had an air about him that discouraged over-familiarity. Americans described him as "stuffy" and "snobbish" but those in England saw him as very "British."

Epstein's shop at NEMS advertised itself as the place where a customer could get any record released; if they were out of stock, he promised to get a copy to the customer within 24 hours. The inventory was impressive; since Liverpool was a sea port, there was a large population of seamen who traveled all over the world, including the United States, where they became aware of new music in a variety of genres--rhythm and blues, rock and roll, country and pop.

A number of young people from Liverpool came into Epstein's shop and asked about the Beatles record done in Germany, so Alistair Taylor, an employee at the shop, ordered a box of 25. Epstein placed a hand written notice "Beatles Record Available Here" in the window and the store sold out. Taylor ordered another 25, which also quickly sold out.

One day Epstein came into the shop and told Taylor that there was a poster announcing the Beatles were performing at the Cavern on Matthew Street during the lunch hour. Since their record had sold well, Epstein was curious about the group. During that lunch hour, Epstein and Taylor--both fans of classical music--went to the Cavern to see the Beatles. As they watched the group they discovered that the members were from Liverpool and had, in fact, been into the NEMS store. After seeing the group, Epstein wanted to manage them, feeling there was something special about them.

The Beatles were flattered that someone like Brian Epstein--successful, confident, immaculately dressed, polished, an authority figure who commanded respect, distinguished, with money who gave the impression that he was in charge of everything--would want to manage them. Further, by signing a contract with him, it sent a message through the Liverpool music community--there were about 300 beat bands performing at the time--that the Beatles were headed on the way up. Not that the Beatles didn't always believe that they would somehow, sometime hit it big, but now they had someone to take care of the business aspects that were necessary in order to get to the top.

The Beatles dressed in black leather--outfits they had picked up in Germany--smoked and swore on stage, and were a sloppy, undisciplined act. They were, essentially, a 1950s and early 1960s cover band. The first thing Epstein did was dress them in suits and impose a stage discipline; there would be no more smoking, drinking, joking or swearing on stage. He had them groom their hair and take a deep bow after each performance.

Derek Taylor, who worked with Epstein later, noted, "He was an absolute stickler for information, for clarification. From day one in management all our artists had to have gig sheets which told them the date of a gig, where the band were playing, who the contact was, what equipment was being supplied, how many electric points there were, what time they were supposed to be there, which hotel they were staying in and so on." Taylor also stated that "Brian's attitude was that an artist should only have to worry about his performance on stage. Everything else we took care of and that was unique."

Gerry Marsden, whose group "Gerry and the Pacemakers" was later managed by Epstein, stated that, at that time "Liverpool groups didn't have managers. My dad looked after us, which meant he'd be on the phone to take the bookings down and tell the clubs how much we wanted...When Brian came on the scene as a manager we realized what a manager meant because Brian then took the bookings, sorted out the money, got us a few quid, sorted out the tax, sorted out the publicity...Before that you did your own. If you had a manager he drove you to the gig, collected your money and paid out. He didn't think of publicity.

Brian Epstein had a devotion and faith in the Beatles because he believed they were going to be a major act, if they could only obtain the opportunity. The first order of business was to secure a recording contract, so Epstein took the train from Liverpool to London a number of times, making appointments with record companies and pitching the Beatles. He finally obtained an audition with Decca Records for the Beatles.

On January 1, 1962, at the Decca studio in London, they performed 15 songs: "Like Dreamers Do," "Money (That's What I Want)," "Til There Was You," "The Sheik of Araby," "To Know Her Is To Love Her," "Take Good Care of My Baby," "Memphis," "Sure To Fall (In Love With You)," "Hello Little Girl," "Three Cool Cats," "Crying, Waiting, Hoping," "Love Of the Loved," "September In The Rain," "Besame Mucho" and "Searchin.'"

The Decca executives turned down the Beatles. In January, 1962, Epstein requested an audition for the Beatles with the BBC.

The Beatles on the BBC

The BBC had a half hour show at five o'clock on weekdays on the Light Programme aimed at young listeners. In February, the Beatles auditioned for Peter Philbeam, the producer of those programs (there was a different name for the program each day). The Beatles passed the audition and Philbeam noted on the audition form, "An unusual group, not as 'Rocky' as most, more C&W." In March they made their BBC debut at the Manchester facility, singing "Memphis," "Please Mr. Postman" and the Roy Orbison hit, "Dream Baby."

On a trip to London, Epstein went into the HMV record shop on Oxford street with a reel-to-reel tape of the Decca audition to have it transferred to disc. At that time, record companies wanted to listen to an acetate--which looked like a record but would not last as long. The engineer thought the group sounded promising and introduced Epstein to Sid Coleman, who worked for EMI publishing in an office upstairs from HMV. Coleman listened and asked Epstein if the group had been pitched to EMI; Brian replied they had but had been turned down. Coleman recommended an acetate be taken to George Martin at Parlophone. Epstein did not know who Martin was, but knew Parlophone was a small label that recorded mostly jazz and comedy. Epstein agreed to meet with Martin and Coleman made an appointment.

Martin listened to the discs and was intrigued enough to want to meet the group for a live audition. "When I met them and saw them, worked with them," remembered Martin. "I got the same kind of feeling that he'd got. It was a kind of falling-in-love business because they had this tremendous charisma, which nobody else seemed to have recognized, and I was puzzled by it. But there we are."

The Beatles First Professional British Recordings

During the Spring of 1962 the Beatles signed a recording contract with Parlophone. Producer George Martin offered them one cent per two-sided record with a requirement to record eight songs per year. It was not a terribly lucrative contract, but the group needed to get their foot in the studio door and Epstein had been worn down by so many rejections.

It was a learning process for both Epstein and the Beatles; neither really knew the music business so there was a lot of trial and error. Both the group and their manager dreamed big and knew they would eventually "make it," but no one could have foretold the level of success the Beatles would obtain. Looking back, it looks like Epstein made a number of bad business agreements but, at the time, he was dealing with a ground-breaking phenomena that would change the recording industry and make old ways of doing business obsolete in the years ahead,

The Beatles audition session on June 6 was at the EMI Studio on Abbey Road. During that session, they recorded "Besame Mucho," "Love Me Do," "P.S. I Love You" and "Ask Me Why." The last three were Beatles originals. None were released and another recording session was set for September.

After the first session, George Martin informed Brian Epstein that Pete Best was not acceptable as a drummer for recordings. Bert Kaempfert in Berlin, who recorded them in Hamburg, told the group the same thing. That, and personal considerations, according to McCartney, led John, Paul and George to dismiss Best. The Beatles actively recruited Richard Starkey (known as Ringo Starr), the drummer for Rory Storm and the Hurricanes, a popular group in Liverpool; Ringo was hired in August, shortly before their next recording session.

The Beatles did not have a music publisher so Martin suggested three; the first one Epstein went to see was Dick James, a former singer with a small publishing company, who signed them. James also offered Epstein and the Beatles a unique arrangement: a co-publishing agreement where James would set up a company, Northern Songs, that would be owned by the two principal songwriters, John Lennon and Paul McCartney (who each owned 20 percent), Brian Epstein (ten percent) and Dick James (50 percent). Epstein and the Beatles agreed.

During that second recording session, the Beatles recorded "Love Me Do," "P.S. I Love You" both credited to Lennon-McCartney, and "How Do You Do It," a song written by Mitch Murray. Producer George Martin believed the latter song was a hit but the Beatles disliked it, although they recorded it, then requested it not be released and Martin acquiesced. (Martin was correct in believing it was a hit; he later produced it on Gerry and the Pacemakers and it reached number one in Britain during the summer of 1963 and number nine in the United States in the summer of 1964.)

"Love Me Do"

The Beatles toured extensively to promote "Love Me Do," which was recorded on September 11, 1962 and released on October 5. It reached number 17 on the British pop chart. For the follow-up session, on November

26 , George Martin liked a song the Beatles had written and initially played for him on September 11. "Please Please Me," but the song seemed to drag- -it resembled a soaring ballad by Roy Orbison. Martin encouraged them to increase the tempo and "Please Please Me" was recorded; it became the Beatles first number one hit in England.

Meanwhile, Epstein continued to promote the group in England, where girls screamed whenever they played. That was the start of "Beatlemania," a wild outpouring of emotion from young females for the band. The success of "Please Please Me" led to more touring where "Beatlemania" spread throughout England during 1963.

The decision was made for the group to record an album. On Monday, February 11, 1963, the Beatles recorded ten songs between 10 a.m. and 10:45 p.m. They were, in order, "There's a Place," "Seventeen" (later re-named "I Saw Her Standing There"), "A Taste of Honey," "Do You Want to Know a Secret," "Misery," "Hold Me Tight," "Anna (Go To Him)," "Boys," "Chains," "Baby It's You" and "Twist and Shout."

The Beatles and Capitol

Capitol, the American label for EMI, had the right of first refusal for any product from their British counterparts; however Dick Dexter, head of international A&R for Capitol, turned down every Beatle record offered during 1963 so the first Beatle singles released in the United States were released on small, independent labels. "From Me to You" and "Please Please Me" were released on Vee Jay and "She Loves You" on Swan. Without adequate promotion, the singles did not make an impact ("From Me To You" was the only one that reached the *Billboard* Hot 100, landing at #106. Del Shannon's recording of "From Me To You" reached number 77 on the *Billboard* chart in America during the summer of 1963)

There wasn't much initial interest in the Beatles in America during 1963. Dick Clark, host of the popular week-day TV show "American Bandstand" had a segment where new records were played and teenagers "rated" them. Clark played "She Loves You" on one of his "Rate-a-Record" sessions and it was declared a "stiff," rated in the low 70s.

At the end of October, 1963, the *Washington Post* published a story about "Beatlemania" in England but few readers took notice. The "CBS Morning News" with Mike Wallace on November 22, featured a story on the Beatles. It was scheduled to be re-broadcast that evening but the assassination of President John Kennedy that day caused the story to be shelved.

England: 1963

The Beatles were all the rage in London and the U.K. by the end of 1963. The group was comprised of John Lennon, rhythm guitarist, age 23; Paul McCartney, bass, age, 21; George Harrison, lead guitarist, age 20; and Ringo Starr, the stage name for Richard Starkey, drummer, age 23.

At the beginning of the year their second single for Parlophone, "Please Please Me" reached the top of the charts on February 22. The year was filled with concert appearances as they moved from their Liverpool base to become a national group. They appeared on the BBC a number of times, did extensive press interviews, TV shows, and headlined several tours. One tour, with American acts Tommy Roe and Chris Montez, marked the first time a British group headlined over American acts.

On February 11, "From Me To You," their third single, was released and quickly rose to number one. That led London recording executives and talent scouts to travel to Liverpool to sign a number of acts, including Gerry and the Pacemakers, Billy J. Kramer, Cilla Black, the Searchers, the Fourmost, the Mersey Beats and the Swinging Blue Jeans. By the end of the year the Beatles had the number one record for 40 of the 52 weeks.

During that summer the Beatles had their own radio show, "Pop Go the Beatles" for 15-weeks on the BBC. Their first album, *Please Please Me* was released in May. From mid-May through early June they toured with Roy Orbison. In July they recorded their second album, *With the Beatles* as well as their fourth single, "She Loves You." Their final performance at the Cavern Club, the local Liverpool establishment where they received their first fame, occurred on August 3.

On October 17, the Beatles recorded "I Want to Hold Your Hand" and "This Boy," which ws released as a single on November 29.

Beatlmania became "official" on Sunday October 13 when they appeared on a TV show, "Val Parnell's Sunday Night at the London Palladium." Their shows consisted of 20-25 minute sets with audiences screaming and the Beatles prisoners of their fame; they could no longer hear themselves when they played.

Their first foreign tour, to Sweden, was followed by their return to London Airport on October 31 and resulted in their first famous "airport reception" of thousands of screaming fans. Also at the airport was Ed Sullivan, host of the "The Ed Sullivan Show," whose flight had been delayed. Sullivan was intrigued and impressed; the following week, on Tuesday, November 5, Sullivan and his producer, Bob Precht, met with Beatles manager

Brian Epstein, who had flown to New York for the meeting, to discuss an appearance on the show by the Beatles. Sullivan, always interested in international acts for his variety show, was taken aback when Epstein insisted on top billing, but Sullivan agreed because Epstein offered a deal to take less money--$10,000--for three appearances. (The normal amount would have been $7,500 for each appearance.) Sullivan agreed to pay air fare and hotel room expenses in New York and Miami for the Beatles.

Sullivan's show was a throwback to vaudeville, an old time variety show that featured singers, dancers, acrobats, circus acts, comedians, and other talent to fill up an hour on Sunday nights on CBS. The Beatles fit in Sullivan's scheme to book interesting musical acts, particularly international ones.

Sullivan was not a fan of rock music, but he knew that rock acts drew young viewers and helped his ratings. Elvis Presley played on Sullivan's Show in 1956 and the host, a former New York newspaper entertainment reporter, continued to book rock acts, albeit reluctantly.

The Capitol Roster

Capitol Records, based in Los Angeles, was flush with success with the Beach Boys, who made beach music popular in Kansas, Texas, Tennessee, Michigan and other places where there was no surf. The label also had Nat "King" Cole, the Kingston Trio, Frank Sinatra and Buck Owens, who was outselling many of the artists on the label.

Capitol was owned by EMI (Electrical Music Instruments) of Great Britain and that label also owned Parlophone, the label the Beatles recorded for. Sir Edward Lewis, head of EMI, had called the head of Capitol in America and alerted him about the Beatles in England and encouraged him to release singles in the United States but was turned down. There was a reason for that; no commercially successful rock'n'roll record had ever come out of England. That was where American records were sold; it was not a source of music for the American market. Even the biggest star of England, Cliff Richard, had failed to make a dent in the American market.

Finally, Capitol was persuaded to release a Beatles recording at the beginning of 1964, accompanied by a $50,000 promotion campaign. That decision came about partly because the Beatles were scheduled to appear on the Ed Sullivan Show for three appearances on three successive Sunday nights beginning February 9. Additionally, a promoter, Sid Bernstein had secured a contract to promote a short tour of the Beatles while they were in the United States.

The British Invasion

The success of the Beatles in 1964 led to the British Invasion of America. Since the Beatles had been popular in England for over a year, a number of young rock groups, inspired by the Beatles, had formed and many had obtained recording contracts on British labels. When the Beatles hit in America, the pipeline was primed for other British acts to follow. By the end of the year, the most successful British acts were the Rolling Stones and the Dave Clark Five. Those two groups were a replay of the Elvis-Pat Boone division in the 1950s. The Rolling Stones were rock's bad boys, the kinds you didn't want your daughter to date, who were arrested in England for urinating in public. The Dave Clark Five were wholesome and clean cut; they advertised their favorite drink as milk and proclaimed themselves healthy in mind, body and spirit. Somehow the Beatles were above the fray; their long hair made them suspect, but their suits and charming demeanor disarmed critics and parents.

On April 4, the Beatles had the top five songs in the country: "Can't Buy Me Love," "Twist and Shout," "She Loves You," "I Want to Hold Your Hand" and "Please Please Me."

The British Invasion led directly to an interest in traditional black music in the United States. Although blues and rhythm and blues artists were recorded in the United States, they were generally shunned by the mainstream white market. The British were always keen to promote R&B; The Rolling Stones had taken their name from a Muddy Waters song. When the Stones came to America in 1964 the place they most wanted to visit was the Chess studios in Chicago, where Muddy Waters had recorded so much of his material.

Dave Clark Five

The second group in the British Invasion was the Dave Clark Five, led by drummer Dave Clark. The group began in 1957 as the Dave Clark Quintet; in addition to Clark, the group had Dave Sanford on lead guitar, Chris Walls on bass, and Don Vale on piano. There were personnel changes before the group emerged as the Dave Clark Five with Clark on drums, Rick Huxley on bass, Mike Smith on piano and lead vocals, Lenny Davidson on lead guitar and Denny Payton on tenor and baritone saxophone.

Clark was a savvy businessman; he often performed on drums in front of the stage with the other musicians to his sides and back. He signed agreements with record labels that allowed him to own his masters and was listed as co-writer for all their original songs.

The first American hit for the Dave Clark Five was "Glad All Over," which entered the *Billboard* Hot 100 on February 15, 1964 and rose to number six. This was followed, two months later, with "Bit and Pieces," which reached number four. During 1964 they had eight songs on the Billboard chart, including "Can't You See That She's Mine," which reached number four, "Because," which reached number three and "Any Way You Want It," which entered the chart at the end of the year and peaked at number 14 the following year.

The Dave Clark Five appeared on "The Ed Sullivan Show" 18 times, more than any other British act, and was the first British act to do a full tour of the United States. Their film, *Catch Us If You Can*, inspired by the Beatles *Hard Day's Night*, was released in the United States as Having a Wild Weekend.

The Rolling Stones

The first record by the Rolling Stones in the American chart was "Not Fade Away," a cover of the Buddy Holly song, which entered the *Billboard* chart on May 2, 1964 but only reached number 48. Their follow up, "Tell Me (You're Coming Back)" reached number 24, "It's All Over Now," a cover of the Valentino's song by the Womack brothers, reached number 28 and then "Time Is On My Side," which entered the *Billboard* chart on October 17, 1964, reached the top ten, peaking at number six.

The Rolling Stones were a blues band, founded by Brian Jones in London in 1962 with an original line-up of Jones (guitar, harmonica), Ian Stewart (piano), Keith Richards (guitar), Mick Jagger (vocals), Bill Wyman (bass) and Charlie Watts (drums). In 1963, Ian Stewart was dropped from the original line-up by manager Andrew Loog Oldham, who felt he did not fit the band's image. However, Stewart continued to play piano off and on with the group.

Childhood friends Mick Jagger and Keith Richards both loved the blues. The two had lived in Dartford, Kent until the Jaggers moved away but the two met again at the Dartford railway station.

Mick Jagger had formed a group with Dick Taylor and the two, with Richards, began meeting at Jagger's house to listen to blues records. In 1961, they were joined by Alan Etherington and Bob Beckwith and formed "The Blue Boys." The group met Brian Jones at the Ealing Jazz Club in April 1962 while Jones was in Alexis Korner's R&B band, Blues Incorporated. Future Rolling Stones Ian Stewart and Charlie Watts were also in group. Soon, Korner, Jagger and Richards began jamming with Blues Incorporated.

Brian Jones placed an advertisement for musicians in the Jazz News; Stewart joined him and soon Jagger, Taylor and Richards left Blues Incorporated to join the new group. The line-up in June, 1962 was Jagger, Richards, Jones, Stewart, Taylor and drummer Tony Chapman. Brian Jones named the band the Rolling Stones after a Muddy Waters song and album.

The Rolling Stone played their first gig in July, 1962 at the Marquee Club on Oxford Street in London. They were a blues cover band, performing Chuck Berry and Bob Diddley songs. In December, 1962 Bill Wyman joined the group and the next month, Charlie Watts became their drummer. The established a residency at the Crawdaddy Club in Richmond and hired Andrew Loog Oldham as a publicist; the Beatles had been a previous client.

The Rolling Stones were signed to Decca Records after Beatle George Harrison recommended them to a Decca executive looking for a band to sign. They recorded their first U.K. album at Regent Sound Studios.

Manager Andrew Loog Oldham, who started working with the Rolling Stones when he was 19, promoted the Stones as the "bad boys" against the Beatles more wholesome image.

Their first single, "Come On," a cover of the Chuck Berry song, was released in the U.K. in June, 1963 and reached number 21 on the UK sales chart.

The Rolling Stones began to tour and in Fall, 1963, were on a bill with Bo Diddley, Little Richard and the Everly Brothers. During that tour, the Stones recorded "I Wanna Be Your Man," written by John Lennon and Paul McCartney who gave them the song. That was their next single and reached number 12 on the UK chart. Their third single was Buddy Holly's "Not Fade Away," which reached number three in the U.K. after it was released in February, 1964.

Seeing the success of the Beatles Lennon-McCartney songwriting team, Andrew Loog Oldham pushed Mick Jaggar and Keith Richard to writer songs. On their first album, released in the United States as *England's Newest Hit Makers*, Jagger-Keith wrote one song, "Tell Me (You're Coming Back)" and two songs were credited to Nanker Phelge, which was the name used when songs were written by the entire group, but the rest were covers.

In 1964, the Rolling Stones had their first American tour in June, but they had not had any hits by then so the crowds were small. They made their American TV debut on "The Hollywood Palace," where guest host Dean Martin ridiculed them. However, they did record in the Chess Studios in Chicago where many of their important influences had recorded. At the

Chess studio, they recorded "It's All Over Now," originally done by the Valentinos, led by Bobby Womack. That was their first number one in the U.K. but it only reached number 21 in the States.

The Rolling Stones appeared on "The TAMI Show," a theatric release that featured Jan and Dean and James Brown.

The Rolling Stones finished 1964 with their second number one hit in the U.K. a cover of Willie Dixon's "Little Red Rooster." It was not released as a single in the U.S.

NARAS in Nashville

In March, 1964, just prior to the Grammy Awards in April for recordings made in 1963, three emissaries from NARAS arrived in Nashville to encourage the creation of a NARAS chapter. By that point, it was obvious that Nashville was a major music center and needed to be more involved with the organization. "The Jimmy Dean Show" on ABC was receiving excellent ratings, "The Ballad of Jed Clampett" by Lester Flatt and Earl Scruggs was heard each week on "The Beverly Hillbillies" TV show and Johnny Cash and Buck Owens were selling better than many pop acts.

The group met with Wesley Rose, head of Acuff-Rose Publishing and, after negotiations, NARAS agreed to add six awards in the country categories of album, single, song, new artist, male and female vocalists, giving country more awards than rock'n'roll, R&B and jazz combined. They also agreed to have the country awards presented in Nashville. When the NARAS group arrived in Nashville there were 50 members of NARAS from the Nashville community; by May, after intensive recruiting, there were 100.

Grammy Awards for 1963

The Grammy Awards for 1963 was held on May 12, 1964 in venues in Los Angeles, New York and Los Angeles.

Record of the Year and Song of the Year was "Days of Wine and Roses" by Henry Mancini, Album of the Year was *The Barbra Streisand Album*.

The Grammy for "Rock and Roll" was "Deep Purple" by April Stevens & Nino Tempo; for Country it was "Detroit City" by Bobby Bare; for Rhythm and Blues it was "Busted" by Ray Charles; for Folk it was "Blowin' in the Wind" by Peter, Paul and Mary; for Gospel it was Soeur Sourie for "Dominique," and for Comedy it was "Hello Mudduh, Hello Faddah" by Allan Sherman.

In the "Pop" category, the award for Male Vocal was presented to Jack Jones for "Wives and Lovers," for Female Vocal it was Barbra Streisand for

The Barbra Streisand Album; for Vocal Group it was Peter, Paul and Mary for "Blowin' in the Wind" and for Chorus was *Bach's Greatest Hits* by the Swingle Singers.

Country Music: 1964

In Country Music, the year 1964 began with "Love's Gonna Live Here" by Buck Owens in the number one slot on *Billboard's* country chart. Despite the claims that "the Nashville Sound" dominated country music during the 1960s, it was Buck Owens and the "Bakersfield Sound" that appealed to a significant number of country fans. During 1964, Buck Owens had four number one singles, in addition to "Love's Gonna Live Here," there was "My Heart Skips a Beat," "Together Again" and "I Don't Care (Just As Long As You Love Me)." The year before, Owen's record of "Act Naturally" was his first number one.

In 1964 *Billboard* magazine introduced the country album chart. The country music business had been a singles business—the major buyers were jukeboxes—but albums were becoming increasingly important. The first album in the number one position on the first country chart was *Ring of Fire (The Best of Johnny Cash)*, who had another number one album, *I Walk The Line*, that year. Buck Owens had two albums that reached number one. Other country artists with number one albums were Ray Price, Chet Atkins, Hank Snow and Jim Reeves, who had two.

Buck Owens

Buck Owens was born in Texas but grew up in Mesa, Arizona, where his family moved in 1937. In 1945 he had a local radio show and during the late 1940s he played in a band in Mesa. His wife, the former Bonnie Campbell, was frustrated with Buck's wandering ways so she moved to Bakersfield with their two sons; Buck soon followed. Bonnie Owens began singing in clubs and began a singing career of her own; she later married Merle Haggard.

In Bakersfield, Buck played guitar for Bill Woods' Orange Blossom Playboys for seven years at the Blackboard Café, then left and became the lead guitarist in Tommy Collins' band. Collins recorded for Capitol Records and Buck played on those recordings, which brought him to the attention of Ken Nelson, head of Capitol's country division. Owens signed with Capitol in 1957 but then moved to Puyallup, Washington, where he had a show on KTNT-TV and met Don Rich, who joined his band in 1960.

In October, 1959, Owens recorded "Second Fiddle" for Capitol and it entered the Billboard chart the next month, rising to number 24. His next single, "Under Your Spell Again" reached number four and then "Above and Beyond," written by Harlan Howard, reached number three in 1960; during that year he had a top five hit with "Excuse Me (I Think I've Got a Heartache." In 1961 he had chart hits with "Foolin' Around," "Loose Talk" and "Under the Influence of Love." Owens continued to release chart records in 1962 and 1963 before "Act Naturally" reached number one.

The British Invasion and Roger Miller

The British Invasion hit America in 1964 after the Beatles appeared on Ed Sullivan's TV show in February. During that year there were numerous British groups on the Billboard Hot 100 chart. However, in January, 1964, a month before the Beatles arrived, Roger Miller went into the Quonset Hut studio and recorded an album over two days. In June, the first single from that album, "Dang Me" was released; it became a number one country single and held that position for six weeks. It crossed over to the pop side and reached number seven while the follow-up single, "Chug-A-Lug" reached number three on the country chart and number nine on the pop chart. That meant that during the first year of the British Invasion, a Nashville artist was sharing the charts with them.

There was a "Nashville Invasion" of Britain during the 1964-1965 period with Nashville connected artists such as Jim Reeves, Brenda Lee, Roy Orbison, Elvis Presley and album releases from Starday that featured country artists all present in the U.K.

Jim Reeves dies

On Friday, July 31, 1964, Jim Reeves died in a plane crash. Earlier that day, ground was broken for a new RCA Studio and office building on Music Row. Reeves had convinced arranger Bill Walker to move to Nashville from South Africa, where he had headed a label that released Reeve's records. Walker arrived in the New York the same day Reeves died.

Country Music Foundation

The Country Music Foundation was chartered by the Country Music Association in 1964 as "a tax-exempt educational and charitable organization." The new organization was established to "collect, preserve, and publicize information and artifacts relating to the history of country music." The CMF would operate the Country Music Hall of Fame, which had not yet been built. The Foundation was the first archive established for a genre of music.

Your Cheatin' Heart **movie**

Your Cheatin' Heart, a movie about Hank Williams starring George Hamilton as Hank, Susan Oliver as his wife, Audrey and Arthur O'Connell as Fred Rose, was released in 1964. Although the movie was criticized for its many inaccuracies, it was popular in the South and showed Hank Williams as a songwriter hero. The soundtrack was sung by Hank Williams, Jr. and the soundtrack album marked the beginning of his recording career.

Johnny Cash and *Bitter Tears*

The great majority of country albums in 1964 were a hit single or two and then "filler" songs that were recorded in hopes they'd be a single or hit songs from other artists. There were seldom any "concept" albums but Johnny Cash recorded several. His album *Bitter Tears (Ballads of the American Indian)* was comprised of eight songs about Native Americans, five written by Peter La Farge and two by Cash and one by Cash and Johnny Horton. Cash believed that his ancestors included members of the Cherokee tribe (that was later disproved).

Cash met Peter La Farage, a New York-based folk singer, at a "hootenanny" hosted by Pete Seeger at Carnegie Hall in September, 1962. During that concert, La Farge performed "As Long as the Grass Shall Grow." The concert led to him recording folk albums for Moses Asch's Folkways label. Cash's album, Bitter Tears, his twentieth, was recorded between March 5 and June 30, 1964, released on October 1 and entered the *Billboard* country album chart on November 14, where it reached number two.

The album spotlighted the unfair and harsh treatment of Native Americans and Cash encountered a backlash, possibly because of the harsh and unfair treatment African-Americans had received (this was during the Civil Rights era of the 1960s). The only single from the album was "The Ballad of Ira Hayes," which entered the country chart on July 11, 1964, ahead of the album's release, and reached number three. Hayes was a Pima Indian who served in the Marines during World War II and helped raised the flag at Iwo Jima but, when he returned home to his reservation, faced prejudice. Hayes died drunk and in poverty, two weeks after he turned 32. When radio proved reluctant to play the controversial single, Cash rented a billboard that asked "Where are your guts?" That same year, Cash performed at the Newport Folk Festival.

Roy Orbison and "Oh, Pretty Woman"

The biggest rock hit single to originate in Nashville during 1964 was "Oh, Pretty Woman" by Roy Orbison. The song was written by Orbison and Bill Dees and that iconic opening riff was played by guitarists Orbison (on a 12-string Epiphone), Jerry Kennedy, Billy Sanford and Wayne Moss—all playing the exact same lick. Joining them was Bob Moore on bass, Floyd Cramer on piano, Boots Randolph and Charlie McCoy on saxophone with drummers Buddy Harman and Paul Garrison. The song was produced by Fred Foster and released in August; on September 26 it reached number one on the *Billboard* Hot 100 and remained there for three consecutive weeks. Earlier in 1964 Orbison had another top ten single, "It's Over." The song was recorded at Fred Foster's studio, located at the top of the Cumberland Lodge Building on Seventh Avenue N.

"Pretty Woman" wasn't the only rock hit to come out of Nashville in 1964. "Bread and Butter" by the Newbeats was recorded at the Acuff-Rose studio for Hickory Records. The Newbeats were singers Larry Henley, Dean and Marc Mathis. "G.T.O." by Ronny and the Daytonas, which sounded like the Beach Boys, was recorded in the Monument Studio in downtown Nashville. Ronny was lead singer John "Bucky" Wilkin, son of Nashville songwriter Marijohn Wilkin (she co-wrote "Long Black Veil") with vocalists Johnny McRae, Bobby Russell, Bergen White and Buzz Cason.

The British Invasion in Entertainment

The British Invasion was more than hit records on the radio; the American public had earlier loved the James Bond films starring Sean Connery; the first was released in 1962. The film *Lawrence of Arabia* starring Peter O'Toole swept the Oscars in 1963. In August, 1964 *Mary Poppins* starring Julie Andrews, was released and at the end of the year the film version of *My Fair Lady*, also starring Julie Andrews was released. A number of other British films were released, introducing American audiences to British actors Richard Burton, Michael Caine and others..

The Beach Boys

The Beach Boys toured Australia and Asia in January and February, 1964; when they returned, they learned about the Beatles and the British Invasion. The addition of the Beatles to the Capitol roster caused the label to slack off promotion of the Beach Boys which, in turn, caused Murry Wilson to fight for attention for the group from the label for the group.

In February, 1964, the Beach Boys finished their album *Shut Down Volume 2* that contained the single "Fun, Fun, Fun" with "Why Do Fools Fall in Love" on the flip side. "Fun, Fun, Fun" entered the *Billboard* chart on February 15 and reached number five while "Dead Man's Curve" written by Brian Wilson with Jan Berry, Roger Christian and Arnie Kornfield for Jan and Dean reached number eight. The album *Shut Down, Volume 2*, reached number 13. The album also included "Don't Worry Baby," written by Brian with Roger Christian.

"I Get Around," written in April, was the last surfing song that Brian Wilson wrote. Brian's songs increasingly required studio musicians and he hired L.A. session musicians, later known as "The Wrecking Crew," to work on "I Get Around," which entered the *Billboard* chart in May and reached number one, where it remained for two weeks and 15 weeks total. In the midst of the British Invasion and the dominance of the Beatles on the *Billboard* Hot 100, Brian Wilson and the Beach Boys showed they could compete.

That summer, Jan and Dean's "The Little Old Lady From Pasadena" reached number three and in September, "Ride the Wild Surf" by Jan and Dean, written by Berry, Christian and Brian Wilson, entered the chart and reached number 16; it was the theme song for a film starring Tab Hunter and Fabian.

In October, a live album, *Beach Boys Concert* was released and reached number one. The *Beach Boys Christmas Album*, recorded in June with a forty-one piece orchestra and vocal arrangements by Dick Reynolds, who had arranged for the Four Freshman was released in December with a single, "The Man With All the Toys."

At the end of 1964, Brian suffered a panic attack on a flight from Los Angeles to Houston; he had just performed with the group on the TV show "Shindig!" In January, 1965, Brian announced he would no longer tour with the group, concentrating instead on songwriting and record production. Glen Campbell was Wilson's replacement in the group for the rest of 1964 until April, 1965, when his solo career required his full time attention. Bruce Johnston replaced Campbell and, unable to find a replacement, became a full time member of the Beach Boys in May. Johnston's first recording session with the group came in June when they recorded "California Girls."

Brian became a full-time studio artist in 1965 and the album *The Beach Boys Today!* which featured the singles "Dance, Dance, Dance" backed with "Good To My Baby" and "Please Let Me Wonder" backed with "She Knows Me Too Well," both ballads.

Capitol Records promoted them as "America's Top Surfin' Group" but they did not follow that lead. Their album, *Summer Days (And Summer Nights!)* was released in June, 1965 and included "Help Me, Rhonda," which reached number one in the spring, knocking "Ticket To Ride" by the Beatles from the number one slot.

"California Girls' was also from *Summer Days*; it reached number three that summer while the album, *Summer Days (And Summer Nights!)* reached number two on the album chart.

Capitol pressed the Beach Boys for an album for the 1965 Christmas season and the group recorded *Beach Boys' Party!"* which was primarily an acoustic album with a "live" feel. The album was recorded in the studio with chatter from family and friends added later. The album contained three Beatles songs, "I Should Have Known Better," "Tell Me Why" and "You've Got to Hide Your Love Away," the Bob Dylan song "The Times They Are a-Changin,'" "Hully Gully" (originally by The Olympics), "Papa-Oom-Mow-Mow" (originally by the Rivingtons), "Devoted to You" (originally by the Everly Brothers), "Alley Oop" (originally by the Hollywood Argyles), "There No Other Like My Baby" (originally by the Crystals), a medley of "I Get Around" and "Little Deuce Coupe," and "Barbara Ann," (Originally by the Regents). That last song became a number two chart hit in 1966.

The Beatles

The filming for *A Hard Day's Night* was finished by June 1 and on June 12, the Beatles began a tour of Copenhagen, the Netherlands, Hong Kong, Australia and New Zealand with drummer Jimmy Nichol because Ringo was sick in the hospital.

The premier of *A Hard Day's Night* was in July and in August the Beatles began recording their next album. On August 19, the Beatles returned to the United States for a tour; during their 25 date tour they performed in San Francisco, Las Vegas, Seattle, Vancouver, Los Angels (The Hollywood Bowl), Denver, Cincinnati, Forest Hills (New York), Atlantic City, Philadelphia, Indianapolis, Milwaukee, Chicago, Detroit, Toronto, Montreal, Jacksonville Florida (where they refused to play before a segregated audience), Boston, Baltimore, Pittsburgh, Cleveland, New Orleans, Kansas City, Dallas and finished on September 20 at the Paramount Theatre in New York for a charity concert.

On September 21, they flew back to England where they continued working on their next album.

The British Invasion

Beatles records were all over the radio; on the April 4, 1964 Hot 100 in *Billboard* the Beatles had the top five singles. No other artist had done that before or since. Suddenly, American audiences, who had no desire to hear British artists couldn't get enough.

The next British artist to have a chart hit in the United States was Dusty Springfield with "I Only Want to Be With You." She was followed by a string of artists: the Dave Clark Five, the Rolling Stones, Peter and Gordon, The Who, The Zombies, The Hollies, the Animals, Billy J. Kramer and the Dakotas, Herman's Hermits, The Searchers, Gerry and the Pacemakers, Manfred Mann, Petula Clark, Freddie and the Dreamers, Wayne Fontana and the Mindbenders, The Bachelors, Chad & Jeremy, The Honeycombs, Them (with lead singer Van Morrison), Tom Jones, The Yardbirds (with guitarist Jimmy Page), The Spencer Davis Group and The Small Faces, .

In 1965, half of the number one singles on the *Billboard* Hot 100 chart were British acts.

Motown: The Supremes

In 1959 two 15-year old high school girls met at a talent show; Florence Ballard of Northwestern High School sang "Ave Marie" while Mary Wilson of Northeastern High School sang Frankie Lymon's "I'm Not a Juvenile Delinquent." Milton Jenkins of the Primes--the group whose members Eddie Kendrick and Paul Williams later became members of the Temptations-- wanted a sister act for their doo-wop group for live shows. Flo brought in 16-year old Betty Travis while Paul Williams recommended 15-year old Diane Ross of Cass Technical High School. All of the girls lived in the Brewster Projects, a set of eight 14-story buildings that had been constructed in the mid-1950s. The female group became The Primettes.

There were early problems connected to school; Betty Travis had to leave because her parents insisted she spend more time on her studies. Barbara Martin then joined but had to leave--with Flo--for the same reason; those two rejoined the group after their grades improved.

Although Flo, Mary and Diane could all sing lead, Flo was considered the best lead vocalist. In 1960 they met Smokey Robinson, a neighbor of Diane's, and auditioned for him; they also auditioned for Berry Gordy, who told them to return after they finished high school. The group began hanging out at Motown's offices and signed with a competing label, Lupine, in 1960 and released two sides that flopped.

Berry Gordy signed the group in January, 1961 and insisted they change their name; Flo came up with "The Supremes," which the other girls apparently disliked. Diane Ross also changed her name, becoming "Diana." Their first single came in April, 1961 on Tamla, "I Want a Guy," followed by "Buttered Popcorn," both with Flo singing lead; both flopped. The struggles continued; Barbara Martin became pregnant and left. By mid-1962 it looked like the group was going nowhere; Diana took a job in Hudson's Department Store and Barbara left to get married. Still, the trio persisted.

Their first top 25 single was "When the Lovelight Starts Shining Through His Eyes," released in Fall, 1963. But their breakthrough single came with "Where Did Our Love Go," written by the songwriting/production team of Holland-Dozier-Holland; ironically, the Marvelettes had turned down the opportunity to record the song with their lead singer, calling it "junk."

"The Funk Brothers" was the house band for Motown and played on all the hits coming out of the small studio in Detroit. Comprised of Earl Van Dyke (piano and bandleader), James Jamerson (bass), Benny "Papa Zita" Benjamin (Drums), Beans Bowles (sax), Hank Cosby (flute), Eddie Willis, Robert White or Joe Messina (guitar) and Joe Hunter (keyboards), the group had learned their chops playing a wide variety of music in Detroit clubs. The Funk Brothers were integral to the sound and success of the Supremes; their tight, driving commercial sound defined the Motown Sound.

The Supremes finished the recording of "Where Did Our Love Go" on April 8, 1964; it entered the *Billboard* Hot 100 and R&B charts on July 11 and remained number one for two weeks on each chart. It was the first of five consecutive number ones (11 weeks in that position) on the Hot 100 and a total of 13 number ones and 10 top tens for the group.

Motown: The Four Tops

Levi Stubbs, Abdul "Duke" Fakir, Renaldo "Obie" Benson and Lawrence Payton were childhood friends who first sang together at a birthday party in 1954; from that impromptu performance The Four Aims emerged. The Aims played school parties, church socials, clubs and served as a back-up group for Billy Eckstine, Brook Benton, Della Reese and others. In 1956 they changed their name to the Four Tops in order to avoid confusion with another group, The Ames Brothers.

The group signed for a single with Chicago's Chess Records, then signed with the legendary John Hammond at Columbia for a single in 1960--but neither hit. In 1962 they recorded "Pennies From Heaven" for the Riverside label while backing Billy Eckstine but that, too, failed to hit.

They signed with Motown in 1964--pursued by Berry Gordy, Jr.--and originally recorded as a jazz group for Gordy's Workshop Jazz label; that album was never released. Continuing to tour, they performed standards, show tunes and big ballads and backed the Supremes on "When the Lovelight Starts Shining Through His Eyes." They recorded a Holland-Dozier-Holland song "Baby, I Need Your Loving," which entered the *Billboard* Hot 100 chart in August and reached number 11. Their next singles, "Without The One You Love (Life's Not Worth While)" and "Ask the Lonely" were respectable, but not huge hits; however, those records set up their breakthrough song. "I Can't Help Myself (Sugar Pie, Honey Bunch)" which entered the *Billboard* Hot 100 and R&B charts on May 15, 1964 and captured the number one spot on the pop chart for two weeks and held that position on the R&B chart for nine consecutive weeks. The Four Tops became one of the most enduring groups in pop or R&B music; they never changed personnel, the original group remained together their entire career.

Motown: The Temptations

In Birmingham, Alabama, four high school students, Eddie Kendricks, Paul Williams, Cal Osborne and Wiley Waller formed The Cavaliers; after high school they moved to Cleveland and met Milton Jenkins, who became their manager. The group then moved to Detroit and changed their name to "The Primes."

Otis Miles, Edbridge Bryant, Melvin Franklin (real name: David English), Richard Street and Albert Harrell formed the Elegants in 1959; that Detroit group changed their name to The Questions, then The Distants. In 1960 they recorded for the Northern label.

At a house party in Detroit, the Primes met the Distants and the groups merged; Otis Miles (now calling himself Otis Williams), Melvin Franklin, Eddie Kendricks, Paul Williams and Elbridge "Al" Bryant became "The Elgins." Berry Gordy, Jr. saw the group perform at a club and signed them to the Miracle label, a subsidiary in his developing Motown stable. Otis Williams and Billy Mitchell, an employee with the label, came up with the name "Temptations."

The first five singles from the group did not do much; in early 1963 there was a personnel change and David Ruffin replaced David Bryant. In early 1964 Smokey Robinson wrote and produced "The Way You Do The Things You Do" for the Temptations with Eddie Kendrick singing a falsetto lead. That song was a breakthrough single.

Smokey Robinson had written "My Guy," a number one pop hit in 1964 for Mary Wells. Gordy prodded him to come up with a male version and Robinson wrote "My Girl," which he produced on the Temptations. That song became the first number one for the Temptations; it entered the R&B and *Billboard* Hot 100 charts in January, 1965 and reached number one on both charts, remaining number one on the R&B charts for six weeks.

Black Gospel, Civil Rights and Fanny Lou Hamer

The black church and politics were often linked with preachers serving as a lightning rod for political issues. A number of African-American political leaders came from churches and the Civil Rights Movement of the 1960s owed a major portion of its victory to the grassroots support of church members. Since music is a focal point for the black church, it is logical that black gospel music would play a pivotal role in the Civil Rights Movement. Although there are a number of television clips of people singing "We Shall Overcome," "Blowin' in the Wind," and other songs while their arms locked together, it was the old black gospel standards which provided the foundation for that movement and people like Fanny Lou Hamer, who had the courage to become leaders in that movement.

Rural Mississippi in 1964 was not the most comfortable place to live if you were black. The public bathrooms were marked "Men," "Women" and "Colored." There were "White" water fountains and there were "Colored" water fountains. All public places, including restaurants, movie theaters, and bus stations, were either segregated with special places for blacks or reserved for whites only.

During the summer of 1962, the Student Non-Violent Coordinating Committee (SNCC) came to Ruleville, Mississippi to work on a voter registration drive. Blacks were required to pass a literacy test in order to vote--a requirement not applied to white voters. The literacy tests required them to copy and interpret an arcane section of the Mississippi state constitution to the satisfaction of the county examiner. The SNCC volunteers knocked on doors to recruit African Americans to go to the courthouse in Indianola, about 26 miles away. After a week, they held a mass rally to stimulate community interest; finally, registration day arrived and 18 people boarded a bus for the trip to the courthouse.

According to Charles McLauring, who was in this group of volunteers, a "short, stocky lady" was the first to step off the bus and go in to register. The others followed---all taking the literacy test and all failing.

That lady was 43-year old Fanny Lou Hamer and she had lived on the Marlowe plantation in Sunflower County with her husband and two adopted daughters for 18 years. After the group took the test, they boarded the bus to return home. A police car stopped them on their way out of town and informed the driver he was under arrest for driving a bus the color of a school bus. The police took the driver to jail while everyone else was "shaking with fear," according to McLaurin. No one knew if they would be arrested and put in jail or whether they would just be left on the road.

Then a voice was heard singing old hymns and spirituals. It was Fanny Lou Hamer. Somebody on the bus said, "That's Fanny Lou, she know how to sing." And she did know how to sing as she sang with a power in her voice that calmed and comforted the others on the bus. It was a voice that carried the power of Jesus and she sang the gospel songs that expressed a faith that was like a rock in her life.

When the police came back to the bus, they informed everyone that the driver needed $52 to pay his fine; a collection was taken, the money was raised and all went home except the driver, Robert Moses, who was jailed. There were also problems waiting for Fanny Lou. The plantation owner where the Hamers lived as sharecroppers was told that she tried to register and informed her husband, Pap Hamer, that Fanny Lou had to go back to the courthouse and withdraw her name or she would have to move. With that, Fanny Lou packed her belongings and moved into Ruleville, where she stayed with friends. That night, nightriders shot up the home where she was staying. They also fired into the homes where other SNCC members were staying. Fanny Lou Hamer would never again go back to that sharecropper's shack that had been her home.

Several weeks later Fanny Lou went to Nashville for an SNCC conference. There she was asked to sing and began singing "This Little Light of Mine," "Ain't Gonna Let Nobody Turn Me Around" and other songs that became part of motivating people in the Civil Rights movement. The "Freedom Singers" were born that night and toured college campuses in the north to raise money for the SNCC.

Living the Christian life is risky business and carrying the message of the gospel is dangerous; Fanny Lou Hamer and many others proved that during the Civil Rights movement in the 1960s. Although she eventually performed gospel music while she was in her 40s in a concert setting before warm, appreciative audiences, most of Hamer's life was spent singing gospel music because that was where she found her strength.

Fanny Lou Hamer demonstrated to people the power of gospel music. She also showed them the power of love. She and other SNCC workers faced constant threats and beatings by southern police; once in Charleston, South Carolina, Hamer and a group of workers were held for three days in a jail and brutally beaten. She suffered kidney damage and developed a blood clot in her left eye that permanently impaired her vision. Still, she refused to consider hate or revenge. "It wouldn't solve any problem for me to hate whites just because they hate me," she once said. "There's so much hate. Only God has kept the Negro sane."

Fanny Lou Hamer chose to stand up for her civil rights and believed God had created blacks equal to whites. When her husband and two daughters left the plantation to join her in town, the plantation owner confiscated all their belongings, claiming they owed him money. The next day after Hamer attended a Mississippi Freedom Democratic Party meeting, her husband was fired from his job.

The sharecropper's life was tough--they were provided with a house and food, seed, fertilizer and farm equipment on credit from a company store owned by the plantation owner. After the crops were harvested, the owner received half the income and the sharecropper the other half. However, the bill at the company store always managed to exceed what sharecroppers received for their crops.

After the Hamers left the plantation, they were destitute so Fannie Lou applied at the welfare office for emergency surplus food, but the clerks would not accept her application until someone appealed to the Federal government in Washington. Because of her stand, she was destitute, homeless and her life, and the lives of her family, were in constant danger.

Fanny Lou Hamer was the youngest of twenty children. She was semi-literate, except in the area of biblical wisdom. As she became active in Civil Rights, she sought to help others; she attended seminars and workshops until she received a certificate stating she was qualified to teach literacy and citizenship.

On Thanksgiving Day, 1963, less than a week after President John Kennedy had been assassinated, Fanny Lou Hamer was at Howard University in Washington for a SNCC Conference. The day before, Lyndon Johnson had given a speech to a Joint Session of Congress, stating he would push forward on Civil Rights. At the conference, Fanny Lou Hamer sang "Go Tell It On the Mountain." In Hattiesburg, Mississippi, during "Freedom Day" marches, Fanny Lou led the crowd singing "Which Side Are You On?"

At countless other gatherings, she sang gospel songs in her strong, powerful voice, giving herself--as well as others—the courage to face the challenges of changing the South.

Fanny Lou Hamer knew more than her share of troubles. When she distributed food and clothing to destitute African American families while encouraging them to register to vote, the Mayor of Ruleville complained to the Mississippi State Sovereignty Commission--a state agency funded by the legislature to defend white supremacy after the Brown decision--and wanted bribery charges brought against her.

When Hamer decided to run for Congress, her campaign manager was Charles McLaurin. While McLaurin was driving in Mississippi, he was stopped by a Highway Patrol officer in Starkville, who found campaign leaflets for Fannie Lou in his trunk. The officer took McLaurin and another man riding in the car into the Lowndes County jail where they were beaten until McLaurin admitted he "was a nigger rather than a Negro."

At a hearing in Washington, Fanny Lou said, "Not only have I been harassed by the police, I had a call from the telephone operator after I qualified to run as congresswoman. She told me, 'Fannie Lou, honey, you are having a lot of different callers on your telephone. I want to know do you have any outsiders in your house? You called somebody today in Texas. Who was you calling, and where are you going? You had a mighty big bill.'"

Hamer's politics were linked directly to the gospel. She wrote in 1968, "I think the sixth chapter of Ephesians, the eleventh and twelfth verses helps us to know...what it is we are up against. It says, 'Put on the whole armor of God, that ye may be able to stand against the wiles of the devil. For we wrestle not against flesh and blood but against principalities, against powers, against the rulers of darkness of this world, against spiritual wickedness in high places.' This is what I think about when I think of my own work in the fight for freedom."

Fanny Lou once stood up in a meeting and said, "I've been sick and tired for so long that I'm sick and tired of being sick and tired." That phrase---"sick and tired of being sick and tired"---stuck with her during the Civil Rights movement and is now etched on her tombstone in Ruleville, Mississippi. She died in 1977 and was buried on land purchased by the Freedom Farm Cooperative.

Shindig

Rock'n'roll came to TV when "Shindig" premiered on the ABC network on September 16, 1964; the half hour show stayed on the air until January,

1966. Host of the show was DJ Jimmy O'Neill, who began his radio career in Oklahoma and then Pittsburgh before joining KRLA in Los Angeles in 1963, the moved over to KFWB in L.A. The show was approved by Chuck Barris, head of daytime programming at ABC. The Shindig Dancers were regulars on the show.

The premiere featured performances by Sam Cooke, the Everly Brothers, the Righteous Brothers and The Wellingtons. Acts who appeared on the show included Bobby Sherman (the "Shindig discovery"), Donna Loren, Glen Campbell and Sonny & Cher performing their latest hits. During the second season the show was on two nights a week and began with the Rolling Stones. During the second season, the Beatles appeared via video; other performers included the Beach Boys, Chuck Berry, Neil Sedaka and Louis Armstrong. The producers wanted Elvis but the performer never appeared.

Frank Barsalona

The major booking agencies were not accustomed to booking or promoting rock'n'roll shows; they were experienced with pop singers.

Frank Barsalona started in the mail room at General Artists Corporation (GRC) and then became an agent, booking rock'n'roll acts. Barsalona's dissatisfaction with the lack of respect those acts were shown led him to be fired. He then formed Premier Talent in 1964 to handle rock acts; his first clients included Mitch Ryder and the Detroit Wheels, Little Anthony and the Imperials, Del Shannon, the Ronettes, the Chiffons and the Shangri-La's. His first British acts were Freddie and the Dreamers, Wayne Fontana and the Mindbenders, Herman's Hermits and the Who. (25) (Goodman, Mansion)

Barsalona and Premier Talent set the standard for the booking of rock acts during the 1960s.

Technology: Synthesizers

In 1964 Robert Moog invented the Moog Synthesizer, a computer that produced music. The major innovation from Moog was that the computer was played through a piano keyboard, rather than a computer keyboard, which allowed a computer to become a musical instrument.

Moog demonstrated his synthesizer at the Audio Engineering Society Convention in New York in September, 1964; the invention made a huge impact and, at the end of the convention, there was a demand for Robert Moog to produce synthesizers for studios.

Robert Moog had a long history with cutting edge technology. When he was 15, Moog built a "theremin," after reading an article in *Radio & Television News* about how to build one. The theremin was first built by Dr. Leon Theremin, a Russian physicist who created the instrument, which is played by waving your hands around the instrument. Moog published an article in the same journal demonstrating his own theremin design.

Moog built and sold theremins during the time he attended the Bronx High School of Science, helped by his father. He continued to build theremins during his time at Queens College and Cornell University.

Raymond Scott was a composer of music for Warner Brothers cartoons during the 1940s and 1950s. In 1952 he created the Clavivox, an electronic instrument the size of a table top that had a small keyboard with a row of knobs and buttons on the side; he enlisted the help of Robert Moog, who designed the Clavivox's circuits.

Robert Moog published an article in *Electronics World* in January, 1961, demonstrating the Moog Melodia, an extension of the theremin concept, which was mounted on a microphone stand.

Moog was involved in early electronics work at the Columbia-Princeton Electronic Music Center. He developed voltaze controlled oscillators and ADSR envelope generators with Herbert Deutsch. That led to the creation of the first voltage controlled subtractive symthesizer which used a keyboard as a controller. This is what he demonstrated at the AET convention in 1964.

The Beatles

On October 9, the Beatles began a British tour, their only one in 1964. After more time in the studio recording, the Beatles did a short tour of Scotland, performing in Edinburgh, Dundee and Glasgow.

On December 4, their album *Beatles For Sale*, was released in the U.K. It was their fourth album in 21 months.

Civil Rights

The Civil Rights movement saw progress made through legislation when Congress finally passed the Civil Rights bill in June after a 75 day filibuster by Southern senators. The law prohibited racial discrimination in public accommodations, employment, unions and federally funded programs. It was the most sweeping civil rights legislation in American history.

The transformation from segregation to integration was not smooth and there was violence in the air during 1964. In July, there were race riots in New York after an off-duty police officer killed a 15-year old black youth in

Harlem. That led to a thousand arrests and six deaths. African-Americans attacked the police and white owned stores with fire bombs before it spread from Harlem to Brooklyn. Late in August, there were race riots in Philadelphia.

In early August, police found three civil rights workers buried in an earthen dam near Philadelphia, Mississippi. The three had been missing since June 21 after they were arrested for speeding and taken to the Neshoba County jail. The workers were in Philadelphia to investigate the bombing of a black church.

The Beatles joined the push for Civil Rights on September 11 when they announced they would not perform before a segregated audience at their concert in Jacksonville, Florida.

At the end of the year, Reverend Martin Luther King, Jr. went to Oslo, Norway to accept the Nobel Peace Prize.

Student Demonstrations

Students were active in 1964; the first student demonstrations against the Vietnam War were held in May in New York and then in San Francisco. Twelve students burned their draft cards. At the University of California, Berkeley, 1,300 students blocked a police car from taking away a civil rights worker. After the university banned political activities by students, there was a 32 hour sit-in and students took over the administration building. That was the beginning of the "Berkley Free Speech" movement.

There was an escalation in the Vietnam war in August when it was reported that there were attacks by the North Vietnamese against American destroyers in the Tonkin Gulf. President Johnson pushed for broad, emergency powers and the "Gulf of Tonkin Resolution" gave him full authority to use any means necessary to protect American troops in Vietnam.

In November, 1964 President Lyndon Johnson won a landslide victory (over 61 percent of the vote) over the Republican nominee, Arizona Senator Barry Goldwater. Johnson vowed to continue the Kennedy commitment to Civil Rights and wanted to conduct a "War on Poverty" to eradicate poverty in America.

Phil Spector and "You've Lost That Lovin' Feeling"

In the Fall of 1964, producer Phil Spector flew Brill Building songwriters Barry Mann and Cynthia Weil to Los Angeles to write a song for the Righteous Brothers. Spector had first heard the Righteous Brothers in San

Francisco where his act, the Ronettes performed. The Righteous Brothers—Bill Medley and Bobby Hatfield—had started in 1962 as part of a five member group, The Paramours. The duo recorded for Moonglow Records but Spector arranged for them to record for Philles, his label.

In their hotel room at the Marmont Hotel, inspired by the Four Tops hit, "Baby, I Need Your Loving," Mann and Weil wrote "You've Lost that Loving Feeling." Mann had written the line "I love how your eyes close whenever you kiss me" for "I Love How You Love Me," which was a top five hit for them in 1961. He altered that to "You never close your eyes any more when I kiss your lips" for the first line in "You've Lost That Lovin' Feeling."

Spector added "gone, gone, gone, whoa, whoa, whoa" and slowed the song down to a deep ballad so he became the third songwriter.

When they played it for Righteous Brothers Bill Medley thought it would be good for the Everly Brothers, but wasn't the high powered R&B "blue eyed" sound that defined him. Also, the song was written in "F," which was too high for Medley's bass voice. The song was re-arranged for "C sharp."

In L.A.'s Gold Mine Studio, musicians Tommy Tedesco and Barney Kessel (guitars), Don Randi (piano), Carol Kay and Ray Pohlman (bass) and Earl Palmer (drums) began by recording four tracks of acoustic guitars, then three of piano and three of bass, then added horns—two trumpets, two trombones and three saxes—and, finally drums. This was the epitome of Phil Spector's "Wall of Sound."

After the tracks had been laid down, the Righteous Brothers spent two days—around eight hours—on vocals. Tenor Bobby Hatfield was upset that the song began with Medley alone and asked Spector what he should do while Medley sang and Spector replied, "You can go directly to the bank!"

The background vocals by the Blossoms with Cher were then added, then strings were overdubbed. The total cost for those sessions was $35,000, an enormous sum for a single record.

The song was long—three minutes and forty-five seconds—so, knowing radio would not program a song that long, Spector listed the time as 3:05 on the record label.

The song entered the *Billboard* Hot 100 chart on December 12, 1964; it reached the number one slot the next year and at the end of the 20th century, BMI announced that it had received more radio airplay (over 8 million plays) than any other song in the history of radio or the music industry.

The success of "You've Lost That Lovin' Feeling" led Phil Spector to buy a mansion at 1200 La Collina Drive in L.A., form Phil Spector Productions in an office at 9130 Sunset and drive around Los Angeles in a Rolls Royce that cost $100,000. An article by Tom Wolfe in the New York *Herald Tribune* in 1965 labeled Spector "the first Tycoon of Teen."

Films for Teens

During the early 1960s, there were a number of films for the teen-age audience. Most of the films were low-budget films produced by independent companies that centered on the beach, hot rods, surfing, motorcycles and, as the decade continued, drugs. The leading indie for those films was ARC.

The American Releasing Corporation (ARC) was formed in April, 1954 by James H. Nicholson and Samuel Z. Arkoff; Roger Corman and Alex Gordon were the major film producers with Corman directing a number of the low-budget pictures aimed at the teenage market. The company changed its name to American International Pictures and their first release was *The Fast and the Furious*, a car chase movie.

The company released a series of "Beach Party" movies starring Annette Funicello and Frankie Avelon begin in 1963 with *Beach Party*. During the next three years, Annette and Avelon starred in *Muscle Beach Party* (964), *Bikini Beach* (1964), *Pajama Party* (1964), *Beach Blanket Bingo* (1965), *How to Stuff a Wild Bikini* (1965) and *The Ghost in the Invisible Bikini* (1966). Annette released a number of singles from those films.

AIP's early films included a number of hot rod movies then, during the 1960s they produced a number of motorcycle and "druggie" films. Les Baxter's big band sound provided the music in a number of films but during the 1960s a number of soundtracks were done by Mike Curb for his Sidewalk label.

Mike Curb began his career scoring the film *Skaterdater* for Warner Brothers. AIP films where Curb provided the soundtrack include *The Wild Angels*, which had the chart single "Blue's Theme" by Davie Allan and the Arrows. Others include *Riot on Sunset Strip*, *Devil's Angels*, *Mondo Hollywood*, *The Glory Stompers*, *Born Losers*, *Hell's Belles*, *Mary Jane*, *The Hellcats*, *The Hard Ride*, *The Devils 8* and The *Cycle Savages*. *The Trip* featured tracks by the Paul Butterfield Blues Band, the Electric Flag and Cream; *Psych-Out* featured the Strawberry Alarm Clock. The film *Wild in the Streets* contained the hit single "Shape of Things to Come" by Max Frost and The Troopers and a soundtrack of songs written by Barry Mann and Cynthia Weil.

The T.A.M.I. Show

T.A.M.I. stood for "Teenage Awards Music International" as well as "Teen Age Music International." The T.A.M.I show was a concert filmed by American International Pictures on October 28 and 29, 1964 at the Santa Monica Civic Auditorium. Emcees for the show were Jan and Dean and the theme song, sung by Jan and Dean, was "Here They Come (From All Over the World," which was written by L.A. songwriters P.F. Sloan and Steve Barris. The show's music director was Jack Nitzsche and featured a line-up that included The Beach Boys, Chuck Berry, Marvin Gaye, Gerry & the Pacemakers, Lesley Gore, Billy J. Kramer and the Dakotas, Smokey Robinson and the Miracles, The Supreme, The Rolling Stones and James Brown. The house band was comprised of L.A. studio musicians Tommy Tedesco and Glen Campbell (guitars), Lyle Ritz (bass), Leon Russell (piano) Jimmy Bond (electric bass) and Hal Blaine (drums).

The film was one of the first to capture rock'n'roll in high-quality film. The landmark show was closed by the Rolling Stones after James Brown had performed, capturing the audience with his dazzling dancing. Rolling Stone Keith Richard later stated that following Brown was the biggest mistake of their careers.

The film was released on December 29.

1965
The Year 1965 Begins

On January 4, 1965, President Lyndon Johnson pledged the creation of a "Great Society" that would help the politically and economically impoverished and eradicate poverty and racial injustice. The President told Congress and the nation that he wanted federal support for urban renewal, health care, education and the basic needs of the poor.

On February 21, Malcolm X was assassinated in New York City by three members of the Nation of Islam. Malcolm X had become disillusioned with the Nation of Islam and its leader, Elijah Muhammed the previous year and left to form Muslim Mosque, Inc. and the Organization of African-American Unity. He was killed just before he was to address an audience of 400; he was 39 years old. Malcolm X was a controversial figure, openly criticizing whites for racism and injustice.

An elderly woman poured gasoline on her clothes publicly set herself on fire in Detroit on March 7 to protest the growing involvement of America in Vietnam.

In Selma, Alabama on March 7, a crowd of 25,000 began a 54 mile march to Montgomery, the capital of Alabama to protest for their right to vote. The Selma to Montgomery march was inspired by the beating and death of Jimmy Lee Johnson in February. The 26-year-old African American was in a peaceful voting rights march in Marion, Alabama, when he was attacked and beaten.

At the Edmund Pettus Bridge near Selma, State Troopers, some on horses, charged through the group, trampling and beating the marchers as TV viewers across the nation watched. Viola Liuzzo, the wife of a Detroit union official, was attacked and killed by whites as she took a group of marchers back to Selma. During that march, which lasted until March 25, a white Unitarian minister, Reverend James Reeb was clubbed and died two days later.

Hullabaloo: Rock and Roll on TV

"Hullabaloo," a one-hour weekly show on NBC, premiered on January 12, 1965. The show was a big budget show aimed at youth; top pop recording artists, backed by elaborate production, performed their songs. Suspended in a cage and dancing were the mini-skirted Hullabaloo Dancers. During the first three months of the show, a special segment was taped in England and hosted by Brian Epstein, who presented British acts such as Gerry and the Pacemakers, Marianne Faithful, Herman's Hermits and the Moody Blues. (Epstein never hosted the Beatles but they appeared after he left.)

There was a different host each week; those included Paul Anka, Jack Jones, Frankie Avalon and Annette Funicello and Jerry Lewis with his son, Gary. The show ended on August 29, 1966. Acts who performed on the show included the Supremes, the Ronettes and Sonny and Cher.

King of the Road

At the beginning of 1965, "King of the Road" by Roger Miller was released on Smash Records. The song, which had been recorded in the Quonset Hut, was Roger Miller's biggest hit; it was number one country for five consecutive week and reached number four on the pop chart. In England, "King of the Road" replaced "Ticket to Ride" at the top of the British chart; it also received the most airplay on the BBC and sold the most sheet music during the week it was number one. That same year Miller released "Engine Engine #9," "One Dyin' and A Buryin'" and "Kansas City Star."

Grammy Awards: 1964

The Seventh Annual Grammy Awards for records released in 1964 was held on April 13, 1965 in four different locations: the Beverly Hilton Hotel in Los Angeles, the Astor Hotel in New York, at a club in Chicago and, for the first time, in Nashville at the Carousel Club in Printer's Alley where the Country & Western Grammys were presented. There were now six categories for Country, the same number as "Pop," while Jazz had three and Folk, Gospel, R&B had Rock and Roll had one each (The Rock award was in the Pop category).

In those six "Country" categories, Roger Miller and his songs, "Dang Me" and "Chug-a-Lug" won five: "Best Country & Western Vocal Performance, Male," "Best Single," "Best Song," "Best Album" and "Best New Country & Western Artist." The only award in the country category that he did not win was for "Best Female Vocal," which was won by Dottie West for "Here Comes My Baby."

The "Record of the Year" was "The Girl From Ipanema" by Astrud Gilberto & Stan Getz, "Best Album" was *Getz/Gilberto* by Joao Gilberto and Stand Getz, "Best Song" was "Hello Dolly!" written by Jerry Herman and performed by Louis Armstrong, and The Beatles won for "Best New Artist."

The Grammy for "Folk" was awarded to Gale Garnett for her album *We'll Sing in the Sunshine*; for "Gospel" it was Tennessee Ernie Ford for *Great Gospel Songs*, for "R&B" it was "(You Don't Know) How Glad I Am" by Nancy Wilson, and the "Best Rock and Roll" Grammy went to Petula Clark for her song, "Downtown."

In the "Pop" category, "Best Vocal, Female" went to Barbra Streisand for "People"; "Best Vocal, Male" went to Louis Armstrong for "Hello, Dolly!"; "Best Performance by a Vocal Group" went to The Beatles for their album *A Hard Day's Night*; "Best Performance by a Chorus" went to *The Swingle Singers Going Baroque*; and "Best Instrumental Performance" went to Henry Mancini for "The Pink Panther Theme."

Needless to say, members of the recording academy in Los Angeles, New York and Chicago were upset that the Country category had gone from one entry to six. The Board of NARAS vowed to fix that problem for the next Grammy Awards.

TV: Where the Action Is

"Where the Action Is" was a rock and roll TV show that was a spin-off of "American Bandstand." The afternoon show premiered on June 27, 1965 on ABC and featured Freddy "Boom Boom" Cannon singing the theme song, "Action," which was written by Steve Venet and Tommy Boyce. The regulars on the show were Paul Revere and the Raiders and the show generally featured two or three acts lip synching their hit. The show was taped in Southern California at various locations, giving viewers a taste of California scenery as they watched the performers.

Bob Dylan

Bob Dylan's first album where he recorded with a band was *Bringing It All Back Home*, released in 1965, and on it were songs like "Subterranean Homesick Blues," "Love Minus Zero/No Limit," "Like a Rolling Stone" and "Maggie's Farm." On the second side of the record, Dylan recorded four acoustic tunes: "Mr. Tambourine Man," "Gates of Eden," "It's Alright Ma (I'm Only Bleeding)," and "It's All Over Now, Baby Blue," which were the last acoustic songs appearing on his Columbia studio albums for two decades.

Dylan noted that "Until *Bringing It All Back Home* songwriting was a sideline. "I was still a performer. Then I knew I had to write songs...Get some of those literary people, some of those poetry people to sit down with my records," he told biographer Robert Shelton. That album and his next one, *Highway 61 Revisited*, did that. Robert Shelton stated "*Back Home* and *Highway 61* changed pop lyrics by successfully amalgamating oral literature, folk tradition, and rock experimentation... toward three aesthetic and philosophical concepts: exploration of the grotesque and the absurd in art; existentialism; dreams and hallucinations as mirrors of consciousness." Anthony Scaduto stated about *Highway 61* "As living poetry the album demonstrated that Dylan's talent had matured to the point that it seemed capable of expressing in word-rhythms the depth of his visions."

It was other artists recording Dylan's songs that brought him to the attention of middle America, first "Blowin' in the Wind" and "Don't Think Twice, It's Alright" by Peter, Paul and Mary, then "Mr. Tambourine Man" by the Byrds, "All I Really Want to Do" by Cher and "It Ain't Me, Babe" by the Turtles and Johnny Cash. Dylan's vocal talents were always limited and many record buyers could not fathom his voice on their stereo. The songs were another story, and when someone else did them, they shone like gems. His earliest works had been recorded by numerous folksingers on albums and they sang them in concerts; however, it was the hit singles on pop radio that brought his poetry to the masses.

Bob Dylan himself was never an artist who depended on hit singles to the extent other artists did; he was primarily an album artist and people bought his records despite the fact there was no hit single on them. However, he did have hit singles in the 60s which allowed the radio audience to hear him and led to major album sales and further identified him as the "voice of a generation."

The first chart single for him as an artist was "Subterranean Homesick Blues," which peaked at number thirty-nine on the *Billboard* charts in spring, 1965. Then "Like a Rolling Stone" followed, reaching number two and "Positively Fourth Street" reached number seven, all in 1965. In 1966, his recording of "Rainy Day Women #12 and 35" reached number two, "I Want You" reached number twenty, and "Just Like a Woman" reached number thirty-three.

The question arises: are songs poems? Are songwriters poets? The answers are less obvious. Yes, some songs may be considered poems and yes, some songwriters may be considered poets. On the other hand, most songs should not be considered poems and most songwriters should not be considered poets.

The genius of young Dylan was largely intuitive and he could not explain it, no matter how many times he was asked. He said about his songwriting, "I got nothing to say about these things I write, I mean, I just write them" and "The point is not understanding what I write but feeling it." In a conversation with William Burroughs, he told the novelist he "had a knack for writing lyrics and expected to make a lot of money." A vital part of genius is sub-conscious or unconscious and Dylan acknowledged this with his own work during interviews. Early in his career he stated "I don't even consider it writing songs. When I've written it I don't even consider that I wrote it when I got done...I just figure that I made it up or I got it some place. The song was there before I came along. I just sort of came and just sort of took it down with a pencil, but it was all there before I came around."

Bob Dylan and "Like a Rolling Stone"

Bob Dylan returned to the United States exhausted and disillusioned after a grueling tour of England in Spring, 1965. In June he wrote 20 pages (although some claim it was 10) of prose, poems and, to use Dylan's term, "vomit." "Like a Rolling Stone" was not a song—only words--until Dylan sat at a piano and a tentative melody came. Dylan called blues guitarist Paul

Butterfield to his home in Woodstock to go over material for his upcoming session on June 15; the two worked up a rough arrangement.

Producer Tom Wilson hired musicians Paul Griffin (piano), Joe Macho, Jr. (bass), Bobby Gregg (drums) and Bruce Langhorne (tambourine) to join Butterfield for the June 15 session at Columbia's Studio A on 799 Seventh Avenue in New York. The group tried the song in three-quarter time but it wasn't working so they quit and resumed the next day.

Wilson had invited Al Kooper to drop by the session and Kooper at first sat in the studio with his guitar but was intimidated by Butterfield's guitar playing so he went into the control room. When Wilson moved Griffin from Hammond organ to piano, Kooper said he had an organ part for the song. Wilson dismissed him but did not stop him from going back to the Hammond organ.

As Kooper played his iconic riff on the organ, Dylan became enthused while listening to a playback and wanted the organ brought up in the mix; Wilson demurred, saying Kooper wasn't an organ player but the session continued. On the fourth take, led by drummer Bobby Gregg's snare gunshot, the group captured the song in the key of "C" (it had originally been in "A flat") and that was the master that was released; however, the group recorded it 11 more times.

The song was over six minutes long and executives at Columbia dismissed it as too long for radio airplay. Columbia exec Shaun Considine took an acetate of the song to a new disco, Arthur, that had recently opened and asked the disc jockey to play it. The audience demanded he play it again and again. The next day, a disc jockey and program director of a top 40 station in New York called Columbia and demanded a copy.

Columbia released the song on a two sided 45; the first three minutes of the song on one side and the rest on the back, but disc jockeys protested and some taped it, then spliced the tape for a six minute single.

The song was released on June 20; it entered the *Billboard* Hot 100 on July 24 and rose to number two for two weeks—the Beatles single "Help!" held the top slot—and remained on the chart for 12 weeks.

"Like a Rolling Stone" was a turning point in Bob Dylan's career; he felt that the song said what he wanted it to say. It convinced the folk audience that rock and roll could be authentic and legitimate and young folksinger began drifting to rock. The song itself was one of the most influential songs in the history of rock and roll; years later *Rolling Stone* named it the greatest song ever recorded.

Dylan Goes Electric at the Newport Folk Festival

On Saturday, July 24—the same day "Like a Rolling Stone" entered Billboard's Hot 100 chart, Bob Dylan performed at s workshop at the Newport Folk Festival. During that workshop, Dylan performed three acoustic numbers, "All I Really Want to Do," "If You Gotta Go, Go Now" and "Love Minus Zero/No Limit." At another Festival workshop the Paul Butterfield Blues Band played and Dylan was bothered by condescending remarks made about Butterfield's band by Alan Lomax, one of the Festival's organizer. Reportedly on a whim, Dylan decided to have the band perform with him on the Sunday night concert. That night, Dylan gathered the band members together and rehearsed at the home used by George Wein, a Festival organizer.

On Sunday evening, after Cousin Emmy performed, Paul Butterfield came on stage and plugged in his guitar, Jerome Arnold plugged in his bass, Barry Goldberg sat at the piano, Al Kooper went to the organ and Sam Lay mounted his drums. Master of Ceremonies Peter Yarrow of Peter Paul and Mary announced, "Ladies and gentlemen, the person's that's going to come up now has a limited amount of time..His name is Bob Dylan." Dylan, with a plugged in electric guitar, then stepped to the microphone and launched into "Maggie's Farm." There was both booing and cheering as Dylan sang.

Dylan then performed "Like a Rolling Stone" and "Phantom Engineer," which was later re-written and re-named "It Takes a Lot to Laugh, It Takes a Train to Cry." The memories of Dylan's performance—whether he was positively received by the audience or loudly booed—are mixed. It seems there was both a positive and negative response to Dylan going electric. However, all agree it was a pivotal moment in the folk movement and Dylan's career. According to one report, Dylan "electrified one half of his audience and electrocuted the other."

After those three songs, Dylan left the stage to a mixed response of booing and clapping. Peter Yarrow then returned and asked Dylan to continue so Dylan came back and, after discovering he needed a different harmonica, asked the audience for an "E" harmonica; a number of harmonicas were thrown on stage. Dylan, with just his acoustic guitar, then did "Mr. Tambourine Man" and "It's All Over Now, Baby Blue," then walked off to thunderous applause.

Pete Seeger, Alan Lomax, Theodore Biken and other old guard folk singers had a dream of seeing activist left-wing politics embraced by young students. When Bob Dylan the folksinger came along, they thought they had found their link to the young masses, their dreams come true, but it was not to be. Bob Dylan had no intention nor desire to be a spokesman for left-wing political causes; he wanted to be a rock'n'roll star and that performance at the Newport Folk Festival in 1965 was a giant step in that direction. Dylan's audience—or at least many of them—followed.

Albert Grossman

Bob Dylan's manager, Albert Grossman, had offices at the corner of East Fifty-fifth Street, between Madison and Park Avenues, by the mid-1960s. Grossman's management company included an in-house booking agency, music publishing companies that his company administered or owned, producers, a press office and bookkeepers, along with a number of secretaries.

"It was essentially a business of children and outcasts when I came into it," remembered Mike Friedman, who worked there. "Everybody looked to him to find out how it should be done," remembered booking agent Dan Weiner.

While Dylan challenged the established music industry with his songs, Grossman challenged the established industry with his ways of doing business. Film producer Jonathan Taplin stated, "Albert was the first guy I ever knew who was willing to renegotiate in the middle of a contract."

Mike Friedman described Grossman's office: "Dark? It was a cave. There was a mahogany desk, and a Tiffany lamp with like a twenty-watt bulb. Files piled so high on the desk you couldn't see Albert behind them and a visitor's chair so low that when a guest sat in it, he couldn't see Albert anyhow....Albert had a voice like the voice of God coming from the walls... You couldn't see anything! His house was the same way."

"Albert understood the role of the manager was to supply the link to the commercial world so these artists would not have to deal with it," said David Braun. "With Dylan, of course, he reached the apogee. Because Dylan didn't want to deal with anyone. And Albert was extremely protective of Bob—more so than of the others. The insularity that Dylan demanded and that Grossman so masterfully provided—along with the belief that anyone he deemed inauthentic was not entitled to polite behavior—gave birth to a perverse culture of personality that surrounded both the manager and his artists, delineated by an effete hipness and exclusivity."

Beatles Second Full American Tour

On August 14, the Beatles began their second full tour of the United States (or third overall) with a concert in New York at Shea Stadium where they performed before 55,600 fans—the largest audience to see at concert at that time. They also taped a short segment for "The Ed Sullivan Show."

After Shea Stadium, the Beatles performed in Toronto, Atlanta, Houston, Chicago, Minneapolis, Portland (Oregon), San Diego, two concerts at the Hollywood Bowl in Los Angeles and finished on August 31 with a concert at the Cow Palace in San Francisco. Back in London, they began work on their *Rubber Soul* album in October. They were under a deadline because the album had to be in U.K. stores by Christmas. They met their deadline.

The Beatles had done a series of TV appearance to promote each single but in November, 1965, they decided to film video clips of their singles that could be sent to TV stations in England as well as the United States, Australia and New Zealand. The first songs filmed for video clips were "We Can Work It Out," "Day Tripper," "Help!", "Ticket to Ride" and "I Feel Fine."

The Byrds

The Byrds were the first link between the folkies and the rock and rollers, between Bob Dylan and the Beatles.

Jim McGuinn, born in Chicago on July 13, 1942, heard Elvis's record, "Heartbreak Hotel" when he was around 14 and asked his parents to buy him a guitar. During his early years he was also attracted to artists such as Johnny Cash, Carl Perkins, Gene Vincent and the Everly Brothers. In 1957, when he was around 15, he enrolled in Chicago's Old Town School of Folk Music where he learned to play the five-string banjo.

McGuinn was a folkie during the Urban Folk Revival years and joined the Chad Mitchell Trio in 1962, then became a guitarist and backing singer for Bobby Darin. When Darin retired from singing he opened a publishing company, T.M. Music in New York's Brill Building, and hired McGuinn as a songwriter. During 1963 he did studio work in New York, playing for Judy Collins and Simon & Garfunkel.

After he moved to Los Angeles, McGuinn landed a spot performing at Doug Weston's Troubadour club at 9081 Santa Monica Boulevard. Monday nights were open to singers and McGuinn often sang Beatle songs. There were two folk clubs in Los Angels at that time, the Troubadour and the Ash Grove on Melrose. Gene Clark was another folkie Beatle fan and he and

McGuinn became a duet. David Crosby, another folkie Beatles fan, joined and the trio called themselves Jet Set.

Jim Dickson had produced a Lord Buckley's album for Elektra in 1955 and in 1962 produced a bluegrass album, *Dian and the Greenbriar Boys*. Dickson loved bluegrass and produced three albums for Elektra on the Dillards, who were on Andy Griffith's television show. Dickenson was one of the first in Los Angeles to produce bluegrass albums; he also loved Bob Dylan's songs and encouraged bluegrass acts to do them. In late 1963 and early 1964 Dickson produced an album for Elektra on The Hillman, a bluegrass group that included Chris Hillman. (The album was not released until 1969)

Dickson worked as an independent producer and was recording demos on David Crosby at World Pacific Studios when Crosby introduced him to Jim McGuinn and Gene Clark. Dickson, who became the manager of the group with Ed Tickner serving as accountant and financial manager. The group soon added Michael Clarke as drummer; Dickson produced sessions on Jet Set as they incorporated their folkie roots with Beatles and Dylan songs.

Dickson arranged for Jet Set to record a single for Elektra; the single, "Please Let Me Love You" b/w "Don't Be Long" used session musicians Ray Pohlman on bass and Earl Palmer on drums in addition to McGinn, Clark and Crosby. In an attempt to sound more "British," the group changed their name to the Beefeaters. The single was released in October, 1964, but did not chart.

Dickson obtained a publisher's demo acetate of Bob Dylan's "Mr. Tambourine Man," which Dylan later released on his album *Bringing It All Back Home*. Dickson encouraged the band to rehearse the song and invited Dylan to the studio to hear it; he loved it.

The Beatles film, *A Hard Day's Night*, premiered in July, 1964. Jim McGuinn (he had not become Roger yet) and David Crosby saw the film and then grew their hair long, like them. Those Beatles fans bought instruments like the Beatles played; Jim McGuinn bought a 12-string Rickenbacker and Michael Clark got a Gretsch Tennessean (although Crosby later claimed it) because George Harrison played those models. A Ludwig drum kit, like the one used by Ringo Starr, was acquired by drummer Michael Clarke. They recruited Chris Hillman to play bass; Hillman was a veteran bluegrasser and a member of the Green Grass Group who had previously been a member of the bluegrass groups the Scottsville Squirrel Barker and the Hillman, also known as the Golden State Boys.

By the end of October, 1964, the group's line-up was in place and in November they signed with Columbia. During a Thanksgiving dinner at Eddie Tickner's house a few weeks later the group decided to change their name to The Byrds, again copying the Beatles with a "y" replacing the "i" in Byrds.

Their debut single, "Mr. Tambourine Man," used only the second verse in Dylan's original song, which had four verses. It was recorded on January 20, 1965 at the Columbia Studio in Hollywood but McGuinn, who played the lead "jangly" opening, was the only Byrd who played on it. Producer Terry Melcher, unsure of the musical abilities of the group's members, used L.A. session musicians Hal Blaine on drums, Larry Knechtel on bass, Jerry Cole on guitar and Leon Russell on electric piano. McGuinn, Crosby and Clark sang the song.

During March and April, before the song was released, the Byrds played a residency at Ciro's Le Disc nightclub on the Sunset Strip, which allowed them to improve their musical skills and expand their repertoire. They soon became a "must see" act on the Strip with musical and movie luminaries dropping by, including Bob Dylan, who performed Jimmy Reed's "Baby What You Want Me to Do" with the band on stage.

"Mr. Tambourine Man" was released on April 12, 1965, and entered the *Billboard* Hot 100 on May 15, where it rose to the number one position. Their album, *Mr. Tambourine Man*, was released on June 21, entered the *Billboard* album chart a week later, and rose to number six, remaining on the chart for 38 weeks. The album featured the Byrd's playing their instruments and included three more Dylan songs, "Spanish Harlem Incident," "All I Really Want to Do" and "Chimes of Freedom"; five songs by Gene Clark, the classic "I'll Feel a Whole Lot Better," "Here Without You," "I Knew I'd Want You," "It's No Use" and "You Won't Have To Cry," the last two co-written by McGuinn. "The Bells of Rhymny" by Pete Seeger and Idris Davies; a Jackie DeShannon song, "Don't Doubt Yourself, Babe," and "We'll Meet Again" by Ross Parker and Hughie Charlies rounded out the album.

Folk rock had arrived.

The Byrd's second single was another Dylan song, "All I Really Want to Do." It was rush released on June 14 (while "Mr. Tambourine Man" was still climbing the chart) because Cher had released a competing version; the Byrd's version entered the *Billboard* Hot 100 on July 3 and only reached number 40 while Cher's version rose to number 15. The flip side was Gene Clark's "I'll Feel A Whole Lot Better (When You're Gone)" that only reached 103 on the chart but is now considered a classic.

The Byrds did a tour of England during the summer of 1965 and met the Beatles, who proclaimed their love for the Byrds.

The third single from the Byrds was Pete Seeger's "Turn! Turn! Turn," with lyrics based on the Book of Ecclesiastes, which McGuinn had previously arranged for Judy Collins' 1963 album *Judy Collins 3*. The single was released on October 1, entered the *Billboard* Hot 100 on October 23 and reached number one, where it remained for three consecutive weeks.

Their second album, *Turn! Turn! Turn!* was released in December. On the album were two Dylan songs, "Lay Down Your Weary Tune" and "The Times They Are a-Changin,'" the old country classic "Satisfied Mind," three songs by Gene Clark, "Set You Free This Time," "The World Turns All Around Her" and "If You're Gone." "It Won't Be Wrong" was written by McGuinn and Harvey Gerst and "Wait and See" was written by Crosby and McGuinn. There were two old folk songs with new arrangements, the Stephen Foster song "Oh Susannah" and the traditional gospel number "He Was a Friend of Mine."

The album entered the *Billboard* album chart on the first day of 1966 and rose to number 17, remaining on the chart for 40 weeks.

At the end of 1965, the Byrds, in their first full year as a group, had risen to the point where their name could be spoken in the same sentence as the Beatles, the Rolling Stones and Bob Dylan.

Derek Taylor

In March, 1965, Derek Taylor, a former press officer for the Beatles, moved to Los Angeles; he would prove to be a vital link between London and Los Angeles. Taylor was described as "dapper and witty" and became a "conduit" to British talent and the London scene. He kept British acts, including the Beatles in London, about what was happening in Los Angeles and the L.A. crowd about London. He became a major and essential contact for both sides of the Atlantic.

"Eve of Destruction"

The most overtly political song in America in 1965 was "Eve of Destruction" by Barry McGuire, a former member of the New Christy Minstrels, for Dunhill Records. The song was written by P.F. Sloan, who had been given a copy of Dylan's "Like a Rolling Stone" by producer Lou Adler to inspire the songwriter.

McGuire recorded the song in one take on a Thursday morning, reading the lyrics off a crumpled piece of paper. There were plans to re-do the vocal but a Los Angeles disc jockey received a copy of the rough version on disc and began playing it. On the following Monday, McGuire was awakened by a phone call telling him the song was on the radio.

The Byrds had turned the song down and the Turtles recorded it for an album, but "Eve of Destruction" was not released as a single until several years later.

"Eve of Destruction" entered the *Billboard* Hot 100 chart on August 21 and quickly rose to number one. It was another example of folk-rock, combining the folk tradition of protest with a rock'n'roll production that articulated the anger of youth living in a dangerous world. It was widely criticized by conservatives.

The Turtles

A folk-rock-surf group, the Crossfires, had a two month residency at DJ Reb Foster's Rebellaire Club in Manhattan Beach during the summer of 1965. Foster managed the band, led by Howard Kaylan and Mark Volman. The group changed their name to the Turtles and were signed to White Whale Records, formed by Lee Laseff and Ted Fagan. Their first hit single, a cover of Bob Dylan's "It Ain't Me, Babe," entered the *Billboard* Hot 100 chart in August and became a top ten single. Earlier that year, Johnny Cash had a top five country hit with the song.

By the end of the year, the Turtles, along with the Byrds and the Lovin' Spoonful, were performing regularly at L.A. clubs Ciro's and the Whiskey A Go Go on the Sunset Strip.

The Beach Boys

The Beach Boys had a string of hit singles in 1965: "Do You Wanna Dance," "Help Me Rhonda," "California Girls" and "The Little Girl I Once Knew" as well as three chart albums: *The Beach Boys Today!*, *Summer Days (And Summer Nights!)*, and *Beach Boys' Party!*, which all reached top ten positions on the *Billboard* album chart. But 1965 would be a transitional year for them.

The Wilson's father, Murry, was dismissed as manager in 1964. On December 23, after an appearance on the "Shindig" TV show, Brian Wilson had a panic attack on a plane traveling from Los Angeles to Houston. On January 1, 1965, Brian announced that he would no longer tour with the band but would concentrate on songwriting and production in the studio. Glen Campbell was hired as a temporary replacement but left in April because his own career was gaining steam. In May, Bruce Johnson joined the group as a temporary replacement but, after the Beach Boys could not find anyone else suitable, became a full time member of the group.

On the album *The Beach Boys Today*, the group left the surf and car songs behind and expanded their repertoire; on that album were the hit singles "Do You Wanna Dance," "Help Me, Rhonda," "When I Grow Up To Be a Man" and "Dance, Dance, Dance." It marked the beginning of an album era for the group, but their album did not meet the sales expectations of Capitol executives.

Their next album, *Summer Days (and Summer Nights)* contained "California Girls" and "Help Me, Ronda" (again). Bruce Johnston's first recording session with the Beach Boys came when he sang on "California Girls." That song was another anthem for the sunshine, surf and sand of Southern California, which was becoming a paradise for youth. The album went Gold.

The final Beach Boys album for 1965 was *Beach Boys Party*, which was an acoustic album of mostly cover songs to meet the demand from Capitol for an album during the Christmas selling season. The album was recorded in the studio, then friends gathered in the studio to give it a spontaneous "live" feel. The Beach Boys recorded three Beatle songs, "I Should Have Known Better," "Tell Me Why" and "You've Got to Hide Your Love Away," a Bob Dylan song ("The Times They Are a-Changin' In") and an Everly Brothers song, "Devoted To You." The hit single from the album was "Barbara Ann."

The Rolling Stones

The Rolling Stones began 1965 with a song written by Mick Jagger and Keith Richard, "Heart of Stone," entering the *Billboard* Hot 100 on January 9; it reached number 19. Their second album, released in the UK as *The Rolling Stones No. 2* reached number one on the U.K. chart. It was released as *The Rolling Stones, Now!* In the U.S. and reached number five. The album was recorded at the Chess Studios in Chicago and the RCA Studios in New York.

The Rolling Stones single, "The Last Time" reached number one on the U.K. singles chart. The song, written by Mick Jagger and Keith Richard, entered the *Billboard* Hot 100 ion March 27 and peaked at number nine.

The breakthrough hit for the Rolling Stone, "(I Can't Get No) Satisfaction" came from Keith Richards guitar riff played through a fuzz tone. The song was recorded in May, 1965 during the band's tour of North America. It entered the *Billboard* Hot 100 on June 12, 1965 and reached number one, where it remained for four weeks. It was also number one on the U.K. singles chart. Their album, *Out of Our Heads*, entered the *Billboard* album chart in on August 7, 1965 and reached number one, where it remained for three weeks and stayed on the album chart for over a year (66 weeks).

That song and album established the Rolling Stones as a premier rock'n'roll band.

In 1965, the Dave Clark Five had six records on the *Billboard* singles chart, including "I Like It Like That," "Catch Us If You Can" and their only number one, "Over and Over."

From New York to Los Angeles

The creative center for pop music moved from New York to Los Angeles during the 1963-1965 period. In 1963, pop songs recorded in New York were number one on the charts for 26 weeks while those made in Los Angeles were number one for only three weeks. In 1965, pop songs recorded in Los Angeles held the number one position for 20 weeks while only one recording made in New York, "Hang On, Sloopy" by the McCoys, reached number one for one week.

A partial reason for the shift from New York to Los Angeles was a problem performers encountered with the "Cabaret Law" in New York, which required performers to acquire a "Cabaret Card" in order to perform in New York. The law, passed in 1926 and enforced by the New York City Police Department had caused problems with jazz artists Billie Holiday, Chet Baker, Charlie Parker and Lenny Bruce. The police denied a card to Lord Buckley, a recording artist and humorist (who Bob Dylan called "the hipster bebop preacher who defied all labels").

Performers who applied for a Cabaret Card were required to be fingerprinted, submit extensive financial records and meet other requirements. When Lord Buckley's card was confiscated, a backlash against the card promoted many of the Greenwich Village folk singers to pack their guitars and head west to Los Angeles, where there were several venues, such as Doug Weston's Troubadour and the Ash Grove on Melrose, which did not require a card and welcomed them. There was also sunshine and fun to be had in the L.A. paradise.

However, the real reason for the shift starts with Phil Spector, who took the Brill Building style of songwriting and moved it West, creating a pop sound for teenagers. Next came the Beach Boys and their songs of beaches and cars that painted southern California as a teenage utopia. Other pop songwriters and producers then built on the foundation laid down by Phil Spector and Brian Wilson.

Soul Music

Many Blacks disliked the music of their past until "soul" music emerged during the 1960s and 1970s. The Fisk Jubilee Singers initially disliked the old Negro Spirituals because they were slave songs and they wanted to put that past behind them. Blacks referred to early blues as "field nigger" music after they migrated to cities.

When Rhythm and Blues emerged after World War II, black jazz musicians hated the simple song structures, so different from the complexity of jazz, and the black middle class disapproved because it did not elevate the Negro race. African Americans wanted equality with white society and R&B music did not seem to lead in that direction.

Rhythm and blues became popular, led by Louis Jordan during the 1940s. During the mid-1950s, R&B merged with country music to create rock'n'roll, but that music was linked to juvenile delinquency and crime. R&B was viewed as "black trash" music and country was viewed as "white trash" music so rock'n'roll was a "mongrel trash" music. Middle class white rejected it because it mixed the races; middle class black audiences disliked it because they felt it degraded their race.

That changed during the 1960s when the Civil Rights era arrived. Soul music came out of the black experience in the United States. It was a music that proclaimed a pride in being black and stressed the importance of African-American identity and culture. R&B labels Motown, Stax and Atlantic led the way. Detroit's Motown had an R&B sound that appealed to white as well as black audiences. Motown's goal was to be commercial, and they succeeded with a roster that included the Supremes, Smokey Robinson and the Miracles, the Four Tops, the Temptations, Marvin Gaye and Stevie Wonder.

Stax, based in Memphis, had a roster that spoke directly to the black audience, although young white audiences also liked it. Stax had a line-up that included Otis Redding, Booker T. and the MGs, Sam and Dave and Isaac Hayes.

Atlantic had a long history in R&B before the mid-1960s. By the mid-1960s their roster included Aretha Franklin, Wilson Pickett, Solomon Burke and the rock act Cream

During 1964 and 1965 important Civil Rights legislation was enacted. Reverend Martin Luther King led peaceful protests and won the Nobel Peace Prize but young blacks became more militant and this was reflected in songs.

James Brown

James Brown had a long history of R&B hits on *Billboard's* R&B chart but in 1965 he had his first top ten Hot 100 hits with "Papa's Got a Brand New Bag" and "I Got You (I Feel Good." Brown's records, which featured a pulsating bass and drums with horns that stabbed the lyrics

James Brown's roots, like those of soul music, go deep into gospel music. He was born (May 3, 1933) in Barnwell, South Carolina and grew up in poverty. When Brown was three or four, his family moved to Augusta, Georgia, but his mother left a difficult marriage and moved to New York. James Brown only attended school through the sixth grade. In 1944, Brown won a talent contest in Augusta, performed locally, and learned to play piano, guitar and harmonica. Inspired by Louis Jordan's record, "Caldonia," Brown decided to become an entertainer.

When he was 16, Brown was convicted of robbery (he stole car batteries) and sentenced to a juvenile detention center of Toccoa, South Carolina. Brown joined a gospel quartet in the facility with Johnny Terry; he was paroled on June 14, 1954 and worked several manual labor jobs. After his release from juvenile detention, Brown met Bobby Byrd and joined his group, which performed under two different names: the Gospel Starlighters sang gospel while the Avons were an R&B band. The group changed their name to the Toccoa Band and then the Flames.

Their first manager, Barry Trimier, booked them at parties and they gained a reputation as a great live act. In Macon, Georgia, the group met Little Richard, who wrote the phrase "Please, Please, Please" on a napkin. James Brown was determined to write a song with that title and, with Johnny Terry as co-writer, did it.

Little Richard connected Brown's group with his manager, Clint Brantley, and he agreed to manage them. Brantley sent the group into a radio station to record a demo and they recorded "Please, Please, Please." The song was re-recorded after Federal Records, a subsidiary of King Records owned by Syd Nathan, agreed to release it. It entered the *Billboard* R&B chart in March 1956, reached number five and reportedly sold over a million copies. Brown and his group's next single, "Try Me," entered the *Billboard* R&B chart in November, 1958 and reached the number one spot the following year.

Brown's early records did not have strong crossover appeal, although "Try Me" made it to number 48 on the *Billboard* Hot 100 and "Think," reached number seven on the R&B chart but only 33 on the Hot 100. During the early 1960s, James Brown had a string of top ten records on the R&B

chart but he reached a major breakthrough with the mainstream market with his album, *Live at the Apollo*.

King Records owner Syd Nathan opposed the idea of Brown recording a live album because King had released two albums of Brown's singles and a live album would just be another collection of singles. Also, Nathan's experience and gut told him that live records were lousy sellers.

Frustrated with Syd Nathan's opposition to the album, James Brown financed the recording of his show at the Apollo on October 24, 1962. Brown convinced Nathan to release the record in June, 1963 and it entered the *Billboard* Album Chart on July 6 and reached the number two position. It remained on the album chart for 33 months—over two and a half years.

It was not until 1965 that Brown had his major breakthrough on the singles chart when "Papa's Got a Brand New Bag" reached number eight on the Hot 100 and "I Got You (I Feel Good)" entered the Hot 100 chart in November and reached number three the next year. "Papa' Got a Brand New Bag" was number one for eight consecutive weeks on the R&B chart and "I Got You (I Feel Good)" was number one on the R&B chart for six straight weeks. Both of those singles stayed on the R&B chart for over a year.

"Green, Green Grass of Home"

"Green, Green Grass of Home," written by Curley Putnam, was recorded by Porter Wagoner and released in 1965, where it rose to number four on the country chart, remaining on that chart for 19 weeks. The song was then recorded by Tom Jones and released at the end of 1966; during 1967 the song reached number 11 on the *Billboard* Hot 100 and became a standard, recorded hundreds of times by different artists.

CBS Records and Columbia A Studio in Nashville

The old Victorian house in Nashville that was purchased by Owen and Harold Bradley in 1955 was demolished by CBS in 1965. The company kept the Quonset Hut studio but built a three story wing for offices and new recording studio, Columbia A with up-to-date equipment.

Journal of American Folklore

Inspired by the urban folk revival, which began in 1958 with "Tom Dooley" by the Kingston Trio, academics began to look at country music as a serious art form, rooted in folk music. In 1965, the Journal of American Folklore published their "hillbilly issue" with articles on country music by

Archie Green, Norman Cohen, L. Mayne Smith, Ed Kahn and D.K. Wilgus. This issue was a wake-up call for those in the academic community who had previously dismissed country music. After this issue, there were more studies of bluegrass and country music from the academic community.

Chet Atkins

Chet Atkins was an executive, the head of RCA's Nashville office, a producer for most of the acts on that label and an artist who was perhaps the most well-known guitarist in America. In 1965 he had his first big hit on country radio, "Yakkety Axe," which entered the *Billboard* country chart on June 26, 1965 and reached the number four position; it was number 98 on the Hot 100. "Yakety Axe" was an instrumental written by saxophonist Boots Randolph and guitarist James "Spider" Rich. Randolph had a pop hit (number 35 on the Hot 100) in 1963 on the song, inspired by the Coaster's "Yakey Yak," which featured snippets of a number of old fiddle tunes.

"Flowers on the Wall"

The Statler Brothers toured with the Johnny Cash show and often recorded with him. One day Cash left the studio (or didn't show up) so producers Don Law and Frank Jones asked if anyone had any songs to record. Lew DeWitt, the tenor singer for the Statlers, volunteered a song he had written, "Flowers On The Wall" so they recorded it. The song entered the *Billboard* country chart on September 25, 1965 and peaked in January, 1966, when it reached number two and remained there for four weeks; it reached number four on the Hot 100. The song launched The Statler Brothers as a recording act and there was a rush by Columbia to sign them—they didn't have a contract when the song was released. The song was number one in Canada and number two in New Zealand.

"Make the World Go Away"

On October 9, 1965, Eddy Arnold's record, "Make the World Go Away," entered the country chart and reached number one, where it remained for three weeks, then crossed over into the pop field where it reached number six on the Hot 100 and number one on the Adult Contemporary chart. The song was also a hit in the U.K. and Canada. This was a definitive example of "the Nashville Sound" with Nashville A-Team players Grady Martin (electric guitar), Velma Smith (rhythm guitar), Henry Strezelecki (bass) Floyd Cramer (piano) and Jerry Carrigan (drums) playing on the song. The record was produced by Chet Atkins and Bill Walker did the string arrangements with the Anita Kerr Singers providing background vocals. The song was written by Hank Cochran who also wrote Arnold's follow-up hit, "I Want to Go With You."

Arnold had a hit earlier in 1965 with "What's He Doing in My World" and decided to do an album titled *My World* with "world" songs. "Make the World Go Away" had been a hit in 1963 for Timi Yuro (pop) and Ray Price (country) and "Make the World Go Away" was originally intended to be an album cut for Arnold.

The song revitalized Eddy Arnold's career. He had been the top selling country artist during the late 1940s and early 1950s but his career waned when rock'n'roll came in. "Make the World Go Away" led to a second stage of stardom for Arnold, who became a defining artist for "the Nashville Sound."

Columbia Records: 1965

The corporate offices for CBS in New York were at 485 Madison Avenue while the record labels, Columbia and Epic, were located at 799 Seventh Avenue, which had formerly been the offices for Brunswick records. The decision was made to have all of the CBS offices in one building and on May 3, 1965, all of CBS moved into the Eero Saarimen Building, better known as "Black Rock," at 51 West 52nd Street. Their telephone number was 765-4321. (**370**)

The new building, according to those with Columbia and Epic, ushered in a new, metallic corporate tone. It "marked the end of the record division's collegial feeling," according to Gary Marmorstein in his book *The Label*. (**365**). William Paley sat on the 35th floor, watching over everything. The "corporate" atmosphere was "very strict, very formal, very severe" which made it "more of a business than a creative affair. People felt like they were coming into cells each day." Mitch Miller hated rock'n'roll so Columbia and Epic were behind other majors in signing rock acts.

Goddard Lieberson hired the Harvard Business School to provide an analysis of the organization. CBS had expanded; they had purchased Fender Guitars and toy company, Creative Playthings. The Harvard report recommended that A&R and Marketing be in one department; Lieberson was in control there and he promoted Clive Davis to answer only to him.

Lieberson often found executive talent in the law firm of Rosenberg, Goldmark, Colin & Kaye; the firm had sent Clive Davis, Walter Yetnikoff, Norman Adler and Harvey Schein to work for CBS. Lieberson liked attorneys because "they think logically and clearly, most of them, and I think the training they've had gives them some cultural background, in addition to a very clear way of thinking that's not...messed up with emotionalism or other things."

Clive Davis dropped his Brooklyn accent when he was at Harvard Law School, but he was still a "street wise" New Yorker. Goddard Lieberson left the office each day at 5 p.m.; Clive stayed until 8 p.m. or so.

During the Fall of 1965, Goddard Lieberson went to Los Angeles to see Russian classical composer and conductor Igor Stravinsky at his home. Billy James had been a Columbia publicist in New York then, in 1965, moved to Los Angeles first did publicity and was then named head of Artist Development for Columbia. James loved jazz but was not a hippie; he wasn't a fan of pop music but he knew that Columbia needed acts that were commercially successful and more record were sold by rock artists than the middle-of-the-road acts like Andy Williams, Percy Faith and Ray Coniff who were on Columbia, although Williams and Faith were out-selling most other Columbia acts.

Columbia had some success with rock during 1965. Bob Dylan went electric and "Like a Rolling Stone" debuted on the *Billboard* chart in the summer of 1965 and reached number two. A few months earlier, "Mr. Tambourine Man" by the Byrds reached number one. Paul Revere and the Raiders were also on Columbia, but they hadn't had any major hits by 1965. The Columbia brass had turned down other acts that James had brought them, including Jefferson Airplane, Tim Buckley and Jackson Browne.

James was surprised to receive a phone call from Goddard Lieberson, who asked to be shown around Hollywood. The two walked along Sunset Strip and was intrigued. Lieberson loved Broadway musicals and classical music; he really didn't like rock and roll and, further, did not respect the music or musicians. Lieberson was open to signing commercially successful acts but reluctant to abandon what had worked for him in the past and what he liked. The problem was that Columbia's favored acts, like Coniff and Faith, were in their fifties and were arrangers. For the kids of 1965, those acts were out of touch.

Premier Talent

Premier Talent, headed by Frank Barsalona, represented the San Francisco group, the Beau Brummels but his strength was with British groups. Barsalona sought out managers and record executives and established relationships with Kit Lambert and Chris Stamp, who managed the Who, Island Records head Chris Blackwell, Denny Cordell of Regal Zonophone and Chrysalis executives Chris Wright and Terry Ellis. That led him to represent Procol Harum, Spencer Davis, Traffic, Savoy Brown, Joe Cocker, Spooky Tooth and Ten Years after. "The British bands were far more willing to treat rock and roll like a business, perhaps because it afforded working-class kids one of the few ready opportunities to overcome England's more rigid class system," stated Fred Goodman in his book, *The Mansion on The Hill*. "The work ethic of the British bands was, in general, decidedly different from that of their San Francisco counterparts. Both the bands and their handlers were hungry for success in a way that few American bands of the period were."

Herb Alpert and the Tijuana Brass

In the midst of the British Invasion, you would not expect to see a mariachi flavored Big Band to be popular with young audiences, but Herb Alpert and the Tijuana Brass had an album, *Whipped Cream and Other Delights* that was number one on the *Billboard* chart for eight consecutive weeks and an instrumental single, "A Taste of Honey," that reached number seven on the Hot 100.

Herb Alpert and the Tijuana Brass had three albums on the *Billboard* chart in 1965; in addition to *Whipped Cream and Other Delights*, they had *South of the Border*, which reached number six, and *Going Places*, which entered the album chart in October and reached number one where it stayed for eight weeks. Further, *South Of The Border* remained on the album chart for 163 weeks, *Whipped Cream and Other Delights* remained on the chart for 185 weeks and Going Places stayed on the chart for 164 weeks.

In 1965, Herb Alpert and the Tijuana Brass reportedly sold more albums than the Beatles.

Bill Drake and "Boss Radio"

A revolution in radio programming came in 1965 when Bill Drake introduced "Boss Radio," which took the "Top 40" format and sped it up, limited disc jockey chatter and promised more music for their listeners. In doing that, Drake introduced the concept that radio did not promote the music or the disc jockeys, it promoted the station. The first station to program "Boss Radio" was KHJ in Los Angeles.

"Boss Radio" was tightly programmed and ran according to a "Hot Clock." The "Hot Clock" dictated that music was playing on the hour and half hour. Because of ratings methodology, a station received credit for music played each quarter hour—from 12 to 3, 3 to 6, 6 to 9 and 9 to 12 so if listeners were listening on the quarter hour the station was credited with an audience for two quarter hours. Bill Drake did not want anything that was a "tune out" factor; i.e. anything (a record, a commercial, news) that caused a listener to punch the button for another station.

The "Hot Clock" said there was music playing from one minute before the hour until seven minutes after, then there was a commercial(s) or "spot" as it was known. Drake insisted that commercials be short—30 seconds at the most and preferably less—even three or four seconds. There was music until 14 minutes after the hour, then two minutes for "sports," a "spot" at 17 minutes after the hour, then music until 29 minutes after the hour, then music until 44 minutes after the hour, when there was sports and a "spot," then music from 47 minutes until 54 minutes after the hour, then news, which ended at 59 minutes after the hour.

Chuck Blore, another pioneering programmer who worked with KFWB in Los Angeles, did not want news on the hour because the network owned radio stations always gave news on the hour and half hour so he wanted to program music against that. If the listener tuned out news, they'd find music on Blore's station.

Drake's Hot Clock on "Boss Radio" was similar but more complex. Drake insisted that disc jockeys—who used to ramble on—only talk when they had something to say. That meant research into "liners" or "one liners" that were informative, humorous or both when the disc jockey talked. The jock always said the station's name when giving time and temperature ("72 KHJ degrees; it's 10:50 KHJ time).

Music was either "currents," "recurrents" (recent hits), "oldies," "hitbounds" (record climbing the charts) or "extras."

Bill Drake (real name Phil Yarborough—radio DJs often took or were given catchy names that were easy to remember) was from Atlanta, where he became program director of WAKE. Owner Jane Swain sold WAKE and sent Drake to KYA in Fresno, a sister station, where he was program director and morning DJ. Drake studied commercial radio, read research reports and was intent to program a station that attracted an audience. He did not just show up when it was time to go on the air—like many disc jockeys did—but carefully prepared for his radio show.

When Drake moved to KHJ in Los Angeles, the station was at the bottom of the ratings. The station bought billboards to advertise the change and, since they couldn't advertise themselves as "Number One" in the market, decided to call the station "Boss Radio," which sounded like "Number one," when they went on the air in May, 1965. The station constantly promoted itself with their "Boss Jocks" in "Boss Angeles" and announced "KHJ" before a record.

Drake did not like dead air or long songs and sometimes edited a song down (perhaps one with a long instrumental introduction) to fit the station's programming. He had an early portable phone and constantly listened in and called the DJ's on the air to reprimand or just let them know he was listening.

"Boss Radio" was programmed for a specific audience: listeners 18-34 years old, which is what advertisers wanted. It dominated the airwaves in Los Angeles during the late 1960s and throughout the 1970s. Drake went into the radio syndication business with his former boss, Gene Chenault and they formed Drake-Chenault.

Bill Drake was not the only influential person in radio during the 1960s. Other program directors and stations who played important roles in changing radio during that time were WABC in NY; Chuck Blore on KFWB; Gordon McLendon, KLIF in Dallss; WLS in Chicago; KQV in Pittsburgh; Scott Shannon on WMAC in Nashville; and Ron Jacobs with KHJ in Los Angeles.

Summer of 1965

President Lyndon Johnson signed the Medicare Social Security bill into law on July 30 in Independence, Missouri with former President Harry Truman in attendance. Truman was the first president to recommend a federal program to provide health insurance for seniors under Social Security. The Medicare legislation expanded established insurance programs by providing hospital and nursing home care and out-patient diagnostic care for seniors.

The Voting Rights Act was signed into law by President Johnson and prohibited states from using poll taxes, literacy tests or other technical requirements used to keep blacks from voting.

Africa-Americans reported police brutality and voiced complaints about impoverished and humiliating lives. The arrest of 21-year old Marquette Frye, a black male, for drunken driving by police, who brutally beat him, led to five days of rioting in Watts, the black section of Los Angeles. The phrase "burn, baby burn" was heard as racial tension led to rioting that decimated Watts and resulted in 34 deaths, over 1,000 injures and 4,000 arrests. About 200 businesses were destroyed and 700 were severely damaged, with damage estimated to be $40 million. Governor

Edmund Brown activated 20,000 members of the National Guard to stop the riots and instituted a curfew from 8 p.m. until sunrise over a 35 mile area.

In Chicago, a black women was killed by a fire engine driven by a white driver on August 12, which led to three days of rioting. There were over 1,000 rioters and 140 arrests before 500 policemen subdued the riot.

On September 9, President Johnson created a cabinet level post for the Department of Housing and Urban Development, which was formed to provide financial aid for low-income residents.

Vietnam

A vast bombing campaign in Vietnam in February, directed against military targets and dubbed "Operation Rolling Thunder," led to a dramatic buildup of combat personnel in March. By the beginning of 1965, American troop strength in Vietnam had increased from 23,000 to 154,000. In December, American Armed Forces moved from an advisory role to offensive combat operations that engaged the Vietcong in battalion sized offenses.

In Detroit, a 72-year old woman sat in the middle of the street, doused herself with gasoline, then set herself on fire to protest the Viet Nam War.

In the News

In 1965 things turned nasty in the news. Malcolm X was killed in February, Dr. Martin Luther King led a march from Selma to Montgomery, the Watts area of Los Angeles went up in flames as race riots spread across the country, and It was a time when drugs were becoming widespread--the same year Dr. Timothy Leary encouraged everyone to "turn on, tune in, drop out" in his book *Psychedelic Reader*.

During 1966, the term "Flower Power" was coined by Allen Ginsberg at anti-war rally and Timothy Leary, a psychologist and former Harvard professor who was a proponent of the psychedelic drug LSD popularized the term "turn on, tune in and drop out."

Astronaut Edward White became the first American to walk in space. In April, NASA launched the first commercial satellite to relay telephone and television signals.

Ralph Nader published a book, *Unsafe at Any Speed,* which was an indictment of the automobile industry for their lack of safety standards.

In November, the greatest electric failure in history occurred, which blacked out seven states for two days.

College Students 1964-1965

There were five million students in college in 1965 which represented a ripe market for entertainment. One artist manager noted that "There's more money on college campuses than there is in Las Vegas," stating that it cost about $15,000 to put on a show in Las Vegas but a college show only required lighting and sound, which was generally provided by the college.

Top name acts generally received a guarantee of $4,000 or $5,000 against a 60 percent gross if tickets were sold. If it looked like there would be a large crowd, an agent might negotiate for no guarantee but 75 percent of the gross. Tickets were usually priced so that $5 was the top price. However, many college dates were for a flat fee to the artist so students attended concerts free as part of the college's slate of entertainment and cultural enrichment. In 1964, the college audience purchased around 18 million albums and six million singles with a little over half of college students owning their own phonograph at school. In a survey done by *Billboard* magazine, about 17 percent of the college audience listed "pop vocalists" and "pop instrumentalists" as their favorites. About 16 percent were folk music fans while a little over 14 percent preferred rock and roll, just ahead of either classical or jazz at 13 percent each. About 7.5 percent liked country music. However, most college students liked several kinds of music and crossed genres.

On average, college students listened to music--on radio, phonographs or at dances--about 22 hours a week. The average owner of a phonograph owned 36 albums and 61 singles; however, students in 1964 purchased three times as many albums as they did singles, an indication of the shift in buying patterns of college students during the 1960s. In high school, they had purchased singles; however, as folk and rock became popular, buying patterns of young consumers shifted towards albums and away from singles. In folk, it was the albums of Bob Dylan, Joan Baez and other folk artists who were not singles oriented that ignited demand for albums. In rock it was The Beatles, whose hit singles inspired fans to purchase an album of ten or 11 songs from the group.

A report stated that concert artists on campus could be divided into two groups. The first group, labeled "the pop group," covered folk, jazz, country, R&B and big bands. These were usually booked by student organizations who sold tickets. The second group, which covered symphony orchestras, chamber music, classical soloists and dramatic artists, were generally booked by the college administration. The latter artists were paid from university funds, generated from student activity fees.

Campus Tastes in 1965

Colleges during the 1960s and early 1970s were training grounds for young entrepreneurs who wanted to get into concert promotion and booking. Ken Kragan, who later managed Kenny Rogers and Lionel Richie, got his start this way. Colleges and university booked acts to enhance the "cultural" and "artistic" experiences for students; that meant they generally booked classical music. Rock'n'roll was not deemed a legitimate reason to spend a college's money.

The Urban Folk movement was still alive and well on college campuses in 1965 so folk acts were popular. Also--and this is generally a shock to many who view the 1960s college crowd as all politically liberal wild dope smoking hippies--the tastes of this group were often surprisingly conservative. As the Beatles and other groups became popular after 1964, college students increasingly gravitated to them. But there was also a strong sentiment among mainline college students for traditional middle-of-the-road acts.

A poll of the favorites acts of college students yielded these results:
Favorite Male Vocalist:
1. Andy Williams
2, Johnny Mathis
3. Frank Sinatra
4. Jack Jones
5. Robert Goulet
6. Tony Bennett
7. Dean Martin
8. Ray Charles
9. Elvis Presley
10. Nat King Cole
11. Roy Orbison
12. Steve Lawrence
13. Perry Como
14. Harry Belafonte
15. Sammy Davis Jr.
16. Bobby Vinton
17. Gene Pitney
18. Bobby Darin
19. Trini Lopez
20. Rick Nelson

Favorite Female Vocalist:
1. Barbra Streisand
2. Connie Francis
3. Nancy Wilson
4. Brenda Lee
5. Doris Day
6. Lesley Gore
7. Ella Fitzgerald
8. Julie London
9. Eydie Gorme
10. Peggy Lee
11. Mary Wells
13. Petula Clark
14. Judy Garland
15. Joan Baez
16. Dusty Springfield
17. Patti Page
18. Gale Garnett
19. Nina Simone
20. Joanie Sommers

Favorite Vocal Group:
1. Beatles
2. Lettermen
3. Beach Boys
4. Kingston Trio
5. Four Seasons
6. Peter, Paul & Mary
7. Four Freshmen
8. Supremes
9. Dave Clark Five
10. Ray Conniff Singers
11. Brothers Four
12. Rolling Stones
13. New Christy Minstrels
14: Platters.
15. Ray Charles Singers
16. Four Preps
17. Kingsmen

18. Impressions
19. Everly Brother
20. Drifters

Favorite Male Vocalists: Folk
1. Harry Belafonte
2. Bob Dylan
3. Pete Seeger
4. Johnny Cash
5. Burl Ives
6. Glenn Yarbrough
7. Josh White Sr.
8. Leon Bibb
9. Theodore Bikel
10. Trini Lopez

Favorite Female Vocalists: Folk
1. Joan Baez
2. Odetta
3. Miriam Makeba
4. Judy Collins
5. Barbra Steisand
6. Mary Travers (PP&M)
7. Gale Garnett
8. Carolyn Hester
9. Judy Henske
10. Joan Collins

Favorite Group: Folk
1. Peter, Paul & Mary
2. Kingston Trio
3. New Christy Minstrels
4. Chad Mitchell Trio
5. Brothers Four
6. Smothers Brothers
7. Limeliters
8. Serendipity Singers
9. Lettermen
10. Weavers

1966
Simon and Garfunkel

On the first day of 1966, "The Sound of Silence" was in the number one spot on the *Billboard* Hot 100 chart. Simon and Garfunkel had a long history of recording before they had their first hit.

Paul Simon and Art Garfunkel met in Junior High School in Queens, New York. Influenced by the Everly Brothers, they began singing together and formed a doo-wop group, The Peptones, then began performing as a duo. At Forest Hills High School they wrote their first song, "The Girl for Me" and then wrote "Hey Schoolgirl," which they recorded at a studio in Manhattan. A promoter, Sid Prosen, signed them to Big Records , an independent label and, under the name Tom & Jerry, "Hey Schoolgirl" was released in 1957.

Disc jockey Alan Freed began playing the song on his radio show after Prosen gave him $200; the record reportedly sold over 100,000 copies and reached number 47 on the *Billboard* Hot 100. Three more singles followed, but none were successful.

Paul Simon's first solo release was "True or False" on Big Records while he and Garfunkel were still a duo, upsetting Garfunkel.

After Big Records went bankrupt, the duo had a song they record for that label released on Bell Records, but it did not sell. After graduation in 1958, Simon enrolled at City University of New York and majored in English; Garfunkel enrolled at Columbia and majored first in architecture, then art history.

During their college years, Garfunkel recorded for Octavia Records under the name Artie Garr while Simon recorded solo under the names Jerry Landis and Paul Kane and with two groups, the Mystics and Tico & The Triumphs. Simon was active in the music industry, writing and performing demos for artists.

After college graduation in 1963, Simon and Garfunkel reunited (Garfunkel was still at Columbia) and, influenced by folk music, performed as Kane & Garr at Gerde's Folk City in Greenwich Village folk; there is where they first performed "The Sound of Silence." Tom Wilson, who was Bob Dylan's producer at the time for Columbia, heard them. After an audition with Columbia, where they performed "The Sound of Silence," they were signed them to the label.

Simon and Garfunkel (Simon insisted they use their real names) recorded an album *Wednesday Morning, 3 A.M.* in March which was released in

October, 1964; they were accompanied by Barry Kornfield on acoustic guitar and Bill Lee on acoustic bass and engineered by Roy Halee. Simon wrote five of the 12 songs on the album: "Bleeker Street," "Sparrow," "He Was My Brother," "Wednesday Morning, 3 A.M." and "The Sound of Silence." They also recorded a Bob Dylan song, "The Times They Are a-Changin'," and six songs familiar to the folk audience. Their first appearance as Simon and Garfunkel was a showcase on March 31 at Folk City; neither the showcase nor the album did well.

Paul Simon moved to England and performed at small folk clubs. He signed a publishing contract with Lorna Music and an artist contract with Oriole Records and released "He Was My Brother" as a single. During the summer, Simon invited Garfunkel to join him in England but, at the end of the summer, Garfunkel returned to Columbia and Simon entered Brooklyn Law School for a semester, then returned to England in January, 1965.

Simon's landlord compiled a tape of songs recorded for Lorna, which led to airplay on the BBC. Oriole folded into CBS and an album *The Paul Simon Songbook* was released; the album featured "I Am a Rock" and "April Come She Will," which were later recorded by Simon and Garfunkel. Tom Wilson flew to England to produce the album, which was released in August but sales were poor. At that point, Simon decided to remain in England.

"The Sound of Silence" was played by a late night disc jockey in Boston at WBZ-FM and became popular with college students. Other radio stations on the East coast also played the song, which led Tom Wilson, influenced by the Byrd's singles "Mr. Tambourine Man" and "Turn! Turn! Turn" to take "The Sound of Silence" back into the studio and add electric guitar, electric bass and drums. The new version of "The Sound of Silence" was released in September, 1965 and entered the *Billboard* Hot 100 in November.

Simon and Garfunkel were not aware of Wilson's new version of the song and Simon was reportedly "horrified" when he first heard it. Garfunkel, who graduated in 1965, enrolled in Columbia for a Masters in mathematics.

After "The Sound of Silence" was a radio hit, Simon returned from England and re-united with Garfunkel. Columbia wanted a new album titled *The Sound of Silence*, which was recorded quickly and released in mid-January. On that album were "Homeward Bound" and "I Am a Rock," which were both top five hit singles on the *Billboard* Hot 100 in 1966. During 1966 Simon and Garfunkel released "The Dangling Conversation" and "A Hazy Shade of Winter," which also made the Hot 100 chart. Their next album, *Parsley, Sage, Rosemary and Thyme* was released in October.

The Mamas and Papas

The Mamas and Papas became spokesmen for sunshine utopia with their record "California Dreamin'," which entered the *Billboard* Hot 100 on January 8, 1966 and rose to number four. It was the quintessential song of the southern California dream, a love song to sunny California that captured the youth of 1966.

John Phillips first recorded with a folk group, The Smoothies. He married Michelle Gilliam and met Denny Doherty in New York at a hootenanny in 1963 and in 1964 they became a quartet with the addition of Cass Elliott (born Naomi Cohen). They performed in Greenwich Village and then spent two months on St. Thomas Island, part of the Virgin Islands, singing songs Phillips wrote, including "California Dreamin.'" In 1965 folk-rock became the big, new trend so they went to Los Angeles, got rooms at the Landmark Hotel on Franklin Avenue and were referred to Nik Venet with Capitol, who auditioned them in his home. Barry McGuire sent them to see Lou Adler, head of Ode Records, who signed them for $3,000.

The name "Mamas and Papas" came from a term used by Hell's Angels.

The group sang background on Barry McGuire's second album and McGuire recorded "California Dreamin'" with the Mamas and Papas singing backup. However, the group wanted to release the song so, using the same tracks, they recorded their vocals.

Studio musicians on the album included Glen Campbell (guitar), Joe Osborn (bass), Larry Knechtel (piano) and Hal Blaine (drums). The flute was played by jazz musician Bud Shank. The song was written by John Phillips and Michelle Phillips and represented her longing for her home in California.

The Mamas and Papas followed "California Dreamin'" with "Monday, Monday," which entered the *Billboard* Hot 100 in April and became their first number one, remaining in that position for three weeks. In July, the group's third single, "I Saw Her Again," written by John Phillips with Denny Doherty, entered the Hot 100 on July 2 and reached number five.

The group had four more songs reach the Billboard Hot 100 in 1966: "Look Through My Window," "Words of Love" and "Dancing in the Street."

Crawdaddy

The underground press, comprised of small print publications and initially sold in "head shops" that sold albums and drug paraphernalia, played a major role in exposing and promoting the music of the 1960s. Those publications, or alternative media, covered the youth culture extensively, reviewing albums, interviewing artists and writing critically about the songs and the artists.

The first underground magazine, *Crawdaddy*, was started by a Swarthmore college student, Paul Williams and premiered on February 7, 1966; 400 copies were printed on a mimeograph machine. It was named after the Crawdaddy Club in London where the Rolling Stones and the Yardbirds made their debuts. Williams was a science fiction fan and had initially written a "fanzine" on science fiction when he was 14.

Crawdaddy was the first publication that took rock and roll seriously and published critical reviews of rock releases. It became a training ground for many rock writers; early contributors included Jon Landau, Sandy Pearlman, Richard Meltzer and Peter Knobler. Williams edited the magazine until 1968 when he left was replaced as editor by Peter Knobler.

Crawdaddy moved from fanzine roots to become one of the first rock music "prozines" with a standard sized magazine format and newsstand distribution. Initially, there were artist and musician profiles and rock criticism but extended to coverage of filmmakers, athletes, politicians and celebrities.

The magazine stopped publication in 1969 but resumed in 1970 and continued for the next several decades.

A Confederate Coup at the Grammys

The media reported that the 1965 Grammys, held on March 15, 1966, at locations in Los Angeles, New York, Chicago and Nashville was "a Confederate Coup" that was "embarrassing."

NARAS officials had come to Nashville in 1964 seeking more involvement in their organization. They offered more awards for country, which were introduced for the 1964 Grammys, held in 1965. That upset a number of NARAS members so more categories were added for the 1965 Grammys—but the categories did not prohibit an artist from nominations in multiple categories. A large influx of new members from Nashville resulted in another sweep by Roger Miller, whose hit, "King of the Road" in 1965 led him to win six Grammys in both country and pop categories.

Roger Miller was nominated in ten of the 47 Grammy categories, including four nominations in the rock'n'roll categories. Roger's "King of the Road" defeated "Yesterday" by Paul McCartney for "Best Rock'n'Roll Single" and "Best Male Vocalist" in the Rock'n'Roll categories. He was also nominated in the "Pop Record of the Year" (that was won by Herb Alpert for "A Taste of Honey") and "Best Vocal Performance, Male" (that was won by Frank Sinatra for "It Was a Very Good Year") categories.

Additionally, the Anita Kerr Quartet, studio singers in Nashville who occasionally recorded an album, triumphed over The Beatles in the "Best Performance by a Vocal Group." The Statler Brothers, with their hit "Flowers on the Wall," beat the Beatles, Herman's Hermits and The Supremes for "Best Rock and Roll Performance by a Group." Eddy Arnold and the Statler Brothers were also nominated in the "pop" and "rock" categories. Acts who won no Grammys that evening included Bob Dylan, the Beach Boys and the Rolling Stones.

In the "Country & Western" categories, Roger Miller had a clean sweep—album, single, song, and male vocalist; Miller was ineligible for "Best New" artist (The Statler Brothers won) or "Best Female" which was won by Jody Miller (no relation to Roger) for "Queen of the House," an answer song to "King of the Road."

For the 1965 Grammys, "Album of the Year" was *September of My Years* by Frank Sinatra; "Song of the Year" was "The Shadow of Your Smile" by songwriters Johnny Mandel and Paul Francis Webster and performed by Tony Bennett, "Best New Artist" was Tom Jones.

In the "Folk" category, Harry Belafonte and Miriam Makeba won for *An Evening With Belafonte/Makeba*; in the "Gospel" category Anita Kerr and George Beverly Shea won for *Southland Favorites*; and the R&B Grammy went to James Brown for "Papa's Got a Brand New Bag."

Under the "Pop" division, there were three more Grammys for "Rock & Roll." In the "Pop" division, "Best Female Vocal" was won by Barbra Streisand for *My Name Is Barbra*; Best Vocal Male went to Frank Sinatra for "It Was a Very Good Year"; Best Performance by a Vocal Group went to the Anita Kerr Singers for "We Dig Mancini"; "Best Performance by a Chorus" went to the Swingle Singers for *Anyone for Mozart?*; "Best Instrumental Performance was won by Herb Alpert and the Tijuana Brass for "A Taste of Honey"; "Best Contemporary Rock and Roll Vocal, Female " was won by Petula Clark for "I Know a Place"; "Bet Contemporary Rock and Roll Vocal, Male" went to Roger Miller for "King of the Road"; "Best Contemporary Rock and Roll Performance, Group" went to The Statler Brothers for "Flowers on the Wall"; and "Best Contemporary Rock and Roll Single" was awarded to Roger Miller for "King of the Road."

After those Grammy Awards, NARAS changed the rules, limiting nominees to a single category.

Beatles Recordings in 1966

On Wednesday, April 6, 1966 the Beatles began a new album, later to be named *Revolver*, by recording "Tomorrow Never Knows," which showed the direction the Beatles were headed in exploring new sounds. The song only had one chord and became last cut on their Revolver album.

During the next several months they recorded "Got To Get You Into My Life," then "Love You To," "Paperback Writer," "Rain," "Doctor Robert," "And Your Bird Can Sing," "Taxman," "I'm Only Sleeping," "Eleanor Rigby," "For No One," "Yellow Submarine," "I Want to Tell You," "Good Day Sunshine," "Here, There and Everywhere," and then "She Said She Said." "Love You To" was the first Indian flavored composition on a Beatles album, inspired by George Harrison's discovery of Indian music and his interest in the Sitar. On "Eleanor Rigby," there are no Beatles playing, just an orchestra background while the Beatles sang.

All except two songs, "Paperback Writer" and "Rain" appeared on the British version of the album; those two were on a single. Three of the songs, "Doctor Robert," "I'm Only Sleeping" and "And Your Bird Can Sing" appeared on the American album *Yesterday...And Today*, which was scheduled to be released in the United States on June 20. Capitol, their recording label, released American albums that were different from the Beatles British albums. The first American album, *Meet the Beatles*, was actually a combination of their first two British albums and Capitol always put less songs on the American albums than were on the British albums. (There were usually 14 songs on the British albums but only 11 on the American ones.) In the spring of 1966 Capitol had eight Beatle songs that had not been released in the United States and wanted three more from the Beatles for a summer release. The Beatles complied but posed for a cover photograph of themselves in butcher's coats with raw meat--symbolic of their albums being butchered. The cover was Lennon's idea and he later insisted it was "as relevant as Viet Nam."

During the spring recording sessions the Beatles took a break on Sunday, May 1 to appear at the *New Music Express* Annual Poll-Winners' All-Star Concert at Empire Pool in Wembley. They performed five songs--"I Feel Fine," "Nowhere Man," "Day Tripper," "If I Needed Someone," and "I'm Down" but did not appear on the ABC Television show of the awards because of contractual disagreements; the Rolling Stones also appeared at the concert but not on the TV show. The Beatles received awards from the publication, based on fan ballots, and John Lennon received an individual award. That concert was the last concert the Beatles did in England. They were living two different lives as a group by this point; on one hand they were still a band doing live shows but at the same time they were increasingly becoming a studio group recording material too difficult and complex to perform live.

The Beatles finished recording the songs for *Revolver* on Wednesday, June 22, at the EMI Studios in London and then left for a tour of Germany, where they performed three shows. Also on the tour were support acts Cliff Bennett and the Rebel Rousers, the Rattles and Peter and Gordon. The Beatles had not rehearsed any of their new songs for the German tour, performing instead songs they had previously done live, "Rock and Roll Music," "She's a Woman," "If I Needed Someone," "Day Tripper," "Baby's in Black," "I Feel Fine," "Yesterday," "I Wanna Be Your Man," "Nowhere Man," "Paperback Writer" and "I'm Down." Their stage repertoire generally consisted of eleven songs and John, Paul, and George even had to huddle together onstage for the lyrics to "I'm Down" but Paul still muddled the verses on stage. Interestingly, "Yesterday" was performed by the whole band.

Perhaps the most significant appearance for the Beatles was in Hamburg, where they had honed their performing talent at the Star Club. At that performance they ran into a number of old friends, including Astrid Kirchherr who had taken the photographs that inspired the four head shots half lit on their *Meet the Beatles* album cover. On June 27 they flew back to London, then departed immediately for Japan where they performed five shows in Tokyo with Japanese singers Yuya Uchida and Isao Bitoh also on the shows.

On August 5, Revolver was released in the U.K.

Beatles on Tour: The Philippines

On Monday, July 4 the Beatles performed at a football stadium in the Philippines before 80,000 fans, but there were problems. Filipino First Lady Imelda Marcos had invited them to a special garden reception at the Presidential Palace, but Brian Epstein had not thought it very important or necessary to attend. This inadvertent snub led to newspaper headlines the following day that read "Beatles Snub President." Filipino concert promoters refused to pay the Beatles their concert fees and there were death threats phoned to the British Embassy. Epstein tried to make amends with an apology on TV in Manila but there was heavy static during the transmission--which amazingly cleared up as soon as Epstein was finished.

On July 5, when the Beatles departed for Manila airport, there was no police protection for them and their entourage and they were nearly torn to shreds before they finally boarded their plane, but they could not depart until Epstein paid a Philippines tax official 7,000 pounds sterling. The Beatles were livid with Epstein for the snafu and were increasingly frustrated, angry, and tired of their tours. In Japan, they had not been allowed to leave their hotel rooms and security was so heavy that at each of their concerts there were 3,000 security guards for 10,000 fans.

From the Philippines the Beatles flew to New Delhi, India to absorb Indian music for a few days before they returned to London on July 8, where they taped interviews, then boarded a plane for the United States for their American concert tour.

Beatles North America Tour

The 1966 American tour was their third full concert tour--and fourth if the February 1964 tour was counted. It was a tour they were not looking forward to.

By the time the Beatles boarded the plane from London to America in August, 1966 they had a string of pop hits on American radio. Beginning with "I Want to Hold Your Hand" b/w "I Saw Her Standing There," which entered the charts at the beginning of 1964, the Beatles' hits on American radio included "She Loves You," Please Please Me," From Me To You," "Twist and Shout," "All My Loving," "Roll Over Beethoven," "Can't Buy Me Love," "Do You Want To Know a Secret," "Love Me Do," "P.S. I Love You," "A Hard Day's Night, "I Feel Fine," "She's a Woman"--all released in 1964. In 1965 there were "Eight Days a Week," "Ticket to Ride," "Help," "Yesterday," "We Can Work It Out," and "Day Tripper." In 1966 there were "Nowhere Man," and "Paperback Writer," which was their current single when they arrived in the United States.

More Popular Than Jesus Controversy

The album *Yesterday...And Today* had run into problems. Scheduled to be released June 20, advance review copies had been sent out and an outcry ensued, prompting Capitol to recall the album, put another photo on the cover of the Beatles posed with a trunk as a prop, and re-release it.

The real controversy swirled around an interview with John Lennon by Maureen Cleave in March of that year, conducted in England and published in the *London Evening Standard*. Lennon had been reading the controversial best-seller, *The Passover Plot* by Hugh J. Schonfield which treated the

Easter resurrection as a hoax. In response to a question about his beliefs in organized religion Lennon told Cleave, "Christianity will go. It will vanish and shrink. I needn't argue with that; I'm right and I will be proved right. We're more popular than Jesus now. I don't know which will go first--rock and roll or Christianity." Lennon noted he had nothing against Jesus but the disciples were "thick" and "They're the ones that ruin it for me."

The quote attracted no attention in England when it was originally published; however, a major storm arose in the United States after a teen magazine, *Datebook*, published the article on July 29 under a syndication arrangement. On the front of the magazine was a headline trumpeting the interview, quoting John saying "I don't know which will go first--rock'n'roll or Christianity." A radio station in Birmingham, Alabama announced it would no longer play Beatle recordings; 22 other radio stations followed suit. In Nashville, Tennessee, the first public burning of Beatles albums occurred; that was followed by public burnings of Beatles records, books, merchandise and other memorabilia in other cities.

The reaction concerned Brian Epstein enough to consider canceling the tour for fear of their safety. Before the tour the Beatles manager flew to New York and held a press conference in an attempt to play down Lennon's remarks but the flames kept growing higher, especially in the South.

The Beatles landed in Boston on August 11, 1966, made a connecting flight and arrived in Chicago at 4:55 p.m. They had established a pattern where they came into a city and held a press conference; usually, the same questions were asked--light fluff, really--and the Beatles used their charm and wit to get through. During the press conference in Chicago the light questions were put aside and John Lennon was grilled about his remarks about Christianity.

When asked about his claim that the Beatles were more popular than Jesus, Lennon stated "I pointed out that fact in reference to England that we meant more to kids than Jesus did, or religion at that time. I wasn't knocking it or putting it down. I was just saying it for the fact. And it's true more for England than here. I'm not saying that we're better or greater or comparing us with Jesus Christ as a person or God as a thing or whatever it is, you know. I just said what I said and it was wrong or was taken wrong and now it's all of this."

"All of this" was quite a lot; there were Beatle boycotts, radio stations refused to play Beatle records, and Beatle bonfires where their records were burned. There were also death threats and Lennon was visibly shaken; at the Chicago press conference he appeared nervous and obviously wanted the whole thing to be over. What had started out as fun and games, living the rock'n'roll dream, playing music and getting paid for it with fame thrown in to boot, had all turned rather ugly and distasteful. The three TV networks, NBC, CBS and ABC were all at the press conference so it made the national evening news. Britain's Independent Television News was also there. It wasn't exactly the kind of publicity everyone was hoping for at the beginning of a tour.

Later, Lennon vented some of his ire at the ordeal and stated "In England they take what we say with a pinch of salt" and characterized the Beatle protesters as "middle-aged DJs and 12-year-olds burning a pile of LP covers." But he had to take those protestors seriously; it was a violent time in America--race riots and anti-war rallies were the order of the day--and revolution was in the air.

After the August 12 concert in Chicago, the Beatles did concerts in Detroit, Cleveland, Washington, Philadelphia, Toronto, Boston, Memphis, Cincinnati, St. Louis, their second Shea Stadium concert in New York (which was not a sell-out—there were 11,000 tickets left unsold), Seattle, Dodger Stadium in Los Angeles and Candlestick Park in San Francisco, where their final concert began at 8 p.m. before 25,000 fans.

Beatle Solo Projects

On Wednesday, August 31, the Beatles were back in London after their American tour where each member had several months off to pursue individual projects. John Lennon went to West Germany and then Spain where he appeared in a movie *How I Won The War* as Private Gripweed. The firlm was directed by Richard Lester, who had directed the Beatles in *A Hard Day's Night* and *Help!* For that part, Lennon was issued National Health spectacles—granny glasses, which became part of his image—and had his long hair cut short, which made news around the world.

Paul McCartney took the time immediately after the tour to compose the score for a movie, *The Family Way*, which starred Hayley Mills. George Harrison went to India to study the sitar, yoga and India philosophy while Ringo Starr stayed home in Surrey with his wife and three children, just puttering about.

On November 7 John Lennon flew back to London from Madrid and two nights later attended the opening of a new art gallery where he met the avant garde artist Yoko Ono for the first time.

Back in the Abbey Road Studio

In late November, the Beatles went into the Abbey Road Studios of EMI and began working on some of their most ambitious recordings. The first song recorded was "Strawberry Fields Forever," a song Lennon had written in Spain about a Salvation Army children's home, located behind his boyhood home in Liverpool. In early December they recorded "When I'm 64," a song written by McCartney back in their Cavern Club days in Liverpool before they'd become world famous.

There were numerous rumors about the Beatles breaking up so they did brief interviews with London's ITV just before Christmas to squelch the stories of their dissolution. After Christmas they recorded "Penny Lane" as they contemplated recording an album of songs about growing up in Liverpool.

Bill Graham and the Fillmore Ballroom

Bill Graham gave up his $21,000 a year salary as regional manager for Allis-Chalmers—a heavy industrial equipment manufacturer—to take a job with the San Francisco Mime Troupe in San Francisco for $1,400 a year. Graham loved the theater and wanted to be independent; he followed his heart.

Born Wolodia Grajonca in Berlin in 1931, just before Hitler came to power, the Jewish boy escaped to the United States in 1941 and was taken in by foster parents Alfred and Pearl Ehrenreich in the Bronx. Re-named "Billy," the young boy became fluent in English in nine months. He Americanized his name to "Graham" and was drafted into the Army during the Korean War. After his discharge, he wandered around, trying to break into acting and ended up in San Francisco in 1963 at the age of 31.

The San Francisco Mime Troupe was a left wing group who performed in San Francisco's parks as well as at local events. Graham acted in the Troupe, emceed, served as manager and obtained coverage in the San Francisco newspapers. On the posters and handbills drawn up to advertise the Troupe, he insisted that "Bill Graham Presents" appear before "The San Francisco Mime Troupe." He was described as "very high energy... incredibly smart, energetic and ambitious."

"The Family Dog" was a hippie commune whose "simple aim was to brighten up San Francisco's dull nightlife and get people together to dance." Family Dog members Alton Kelly and Luria Castell informed Graham that the Fillmore Auditorium, located in a seedy section of town, could be rented for $60 a night. Graham immediately contacted the leaseholder and negotiated a four-year option for first rights to the auditorium whenever it was available for $45 a night.

On November 6, 1965, about three thousand "hippies, beats, and radicals" crowded into the Mime Troupe's loft, which had a capacity of 600, to see The Committee, Jefferson Airplane, The Fugs and poets Allen Ginsberg and Lawrence Ferlinghetti. Sensing an opening in the San Francisco entertainment scene, Bill Graham began promoting concerts.

Early in 1966, Graham left the Mime Troupe and formed "Bill Graham Presents." One of the first events that Graham "presented" was Ken Kesey's "Trips Festival." Kesey and his followers, The Merry Pranksters, had traveled around the country in a brightly colored van on a rolling LSD trip. In San Francisco, Kesey was busted for possession of marijuana and banned from attending his own festival.

The Trips Festival was held at Longshoreman's Hall over three days, January 21-23, and two bands performed at a psychedelic show: Big Brother and the Holding Company played the first half of the show and the Grateful Dead, who had just changed their name from the Warlocks, played the second half.

The Festival grossed $4,000 and Graham saw future opportunities for making money and a position of power in the developing rock, blues and poster art world in San Francisco.

Bill Graham had no contacts with rock performers in San Francisco, other than those who volunteered to help the Mime Company. Chet Helms managed Big Brother and the Holding Company and approached Graham about two acts, Big Brother and The Great Society, playing free gigs. Helms also had commitments from the Jefferson Airplane and out-of-town bands the Paul Butterfield Blues Band, Love and the Sons of Adams to perform. Helms and John Carpenter, who managed The Great Society, were well connected to San Francisco's music scene, which provided opportunities for Graham.

In February, 1966, the First Family Dog Show at the Fillmore featured Tribal Stomp, the Jefferson Airplane and Big Brother and the Holding Company; admission was $2 and the concert was successful. The third concert, featuring The Paul Butterfield Blues Band, posed an initial problem. Helms and Carpenter had paid the Butterfield Band $2,500 for the weekend and decided to go to Los Angeles to see Butterfield's show there. At the club in L.A. there was Butterfield's group, the bartender, the two promoters—and no one else. Helms and Carpenter went back to San Francisco, called everyone they knew, put up posters and handbills up and aggressively promoted the Butterfield show. It was a success; over three nights, 7,500 people attended and the show grossed $18,750.

Bill Graham was against the booking; he had never heard of Butterfield and knew nothing of the blues. However, at 6 a.m. on the morning after the last show, Graham placed a person-to-person call to Butterfield's manager, Albert Grossman, in New York and secured all Butterfield dates in San Francisco for the next two years. Helms and Carpenter were livid; they thought they had been betrayed and demanded a meeting with Graham. At the meeting, Graham was unapologetic, stating, "Look, I get up early."

In his biography of Graham, John Glatt states that "Graham had this New York style of doing business where anything you can get away with is okay as long as you didn't break your word…His word was his bond. But it was all the things that were left unsaid."

The Fillmore Ballroom held 3,000; Graham wanted to establish the venue as San Francisco's leading ballroom but there was a public backlash because rumors had spread about wild drug orgies on the Ballroom's floors. Police were also pressured by parents about the growing hippie scene in Haight-Ashbury in San Francisco. Graham ran into problems with the Musician's Union, whose rules required a certain number of musicians for each gig depending on the size of the hall, even if those musicians just stood around and did nothing. Graham stated those rules did not apply because he held dances, not shows or concerts.

Graham always played by his own rules and as he scheduled more "dances" at the Fillmore, he developed a schedule of rising at six in the morning, so he could be at his desk in his office in the Fillmore at seven in order to talk to New York booking agents when they arrived in their offices.

Working with Graham was his girlfriend Bonnie MacLean, who began working for him in 1963 when he was employed by Allis Chalmers. MacLean's job was to obtain the necessary permits from the city, schedule the acts and events, and put the upcoming events in poster form. According to author Glatt, Graham "brought an organization in the midst of chaos to the Bay Area…[he] had a lot of street smarts and a lot of savvy" and "completely understood the astonishing power of that lost generation who had all the confusions of the Vietnam War and the Free Speech Movement piled on top of an increasingly popular drug culture. And those were the elements that turned out to be a multibillion-dollar music industry."

Bill Graham was a workaholic who pushed himself relentlessly, working 20 hours a day booking bands, staging the shows and promoting concerts through posters, print media and radio. He developed Sunday afternoon auditions to find local talent and discovered Carlos Santana at one of those auditions. The posters became collectable art.

During his concerts, Graham placed a large barrel, filled with apples, at the top of the stairs and posted a sign, "Take One or Two." He blew up hundreds of balloons with a large, industrial vacuum cleaner so the audience could play before the show started. Graham studied crowds and noticed the hall did not clear at the end of a show when the lights were turned fully up so he had the lights turned up halfway and played "Greensleeves" over the sound system. The audience filed out peacefully.

The bands during the early 1960s were happy to play for any amount of money; the era of Big Money concerts had not been imagined. The early headlining acts at the Fillmore, like Quicksilver Messenger Service and The Grateful Dead, received only $200-300 a show. Between ticket sales— admission was around $2—and concessions, Graham could gross about $25,000 for a weekend of shows. The overhead was minimal and the money was all in cash, so the income was not traceable. There were no tickets sold; the people who came paid at the door. The facility was built to hold about 3,000 but on some shows there could be three times that amount; Graham "never paid attention to the regulations."

Bill Graham was a shrewd businessman who was "not a guy to spend money on himself....He used to wear the same clothes all the time. Sweatshirts, jeans, baggy pants and tennis shows...But he always had finely tailored suits from Vienna in case he had a business meeting where he had to dress up."

When Chet Helms opened The Avalon, a competing ballroom, Graham drew up contracts that blocked groups from playing the Avalon—or any other club in San Francisco—for a year after they played the Fillmore. If Graham booked an act into the Fillmore, that act could not play anywhere else for a radius of several hundred miles, which established his territory. Big Brother and the Holding Company did not play the Fillmore because they were the house band at the Avalon.

Graham was in his mid-thirties and "hated the hippie movement and all it stood for." (Singer Nick Graventis observed that Graham "was a good businessman, and he knew he had a hot thing going, but he was absolutely not part of the scene. He was outside it, and in fact he denigrated it," adding

"He thought we were kind of foolish and stupid, and he looked down on us in every way. He wasn't part of the hippie gang because he was a businessman."

Graham did not tolerate drug use because he knew the authorities would shut him down if they found drugs. He developed a business designing and printing posters—a key way to advertise his concerts—and that became quite profitable as well as an artistic success.

In addition to promoting concerts, Bill Graham took over management of Jefferson Airplane, which made him a major force on the San Francisco music sense.

Muscle Shoals Studios

Rick Hall, Billy Sherrill and Tom Stafford started FAME (Florence Alabama Music Enterprises) studio in the late 1950s in a room above City Drug Store. In the early 1960s, the studio moved to a former tobacco warehouse and Hall split from his two partners.

The first hit recorded in Muscle Shoals was "You Better Move On" by Arthur Alexander in 1961. With the money he made from that record, Hall build a studio at 603 East Avalon Avenue in Muscle Shoals.

Rick Hall did not mind working with black musicians and singers, or having mixed race sessions in his studios, during a time when race was a major problem in the South and any affinity for the black race by a white was against social custom and could be dangerous.

A studio becomes successful when they cut hit records and there were a number of hit records recorded in the FAME studio. Alexander's "You Better Move On" was a top 25 hit on the *Billboard* Hot 100 in 1962; on the flip side he had "A Shot of Rhythm and Blues." He had chart records with "Where Have You Been All My Life" and "Anna" also in 1962. IN 1963 Alexander had Hot 100 chart records With "Go Home Girl," "Pretty Girls Everywhere" and "Every Day I Have to Try Some."

Other hits recorded at FAME were "What Kind of Fool Do You Think I Am" by the Tams, "Hold On To What You've Got" by Joe Tex, "Tell Mama" by Etta James, "Mustang Sally" and "Land of 1000 Dances by Wilson Pickett and "Sweet Soul Music" by Arthur Conley.

The original studio band at FAME was Norbert Putnam (bass), David Briggs (keyboards), Peanuts Montgomery (guitar) and Jerry Carrigan (drums).

The session musicians who formed the Muscle Shoals Rhythm Section, known as "The Swampers," were Barry Beckett, keyboards; Jimmy Johnson, guitar; Roger Hawkins, drums; and David Hood bass. In 1969, those musicians, with start-up funding from Jerry Wexler with Atlantic Records, founded the Muscle Shoals Sound Studio at 3614 Jackson Highway in Sheffield. The first hit in that studio was "Take a Letter, Maria" by R.B. Greaves.

The song that put Muscle Shoals on the national map was "When a Man Loves a Woman" by Percy Sledge, which hit in 1966. Sledge, born in Leighton, Alabama, was the first Southern soul singer to reach the top of the pop charts and inspired a number of acts to leave the studios of Los Angeles and New York and venture to the small Southern town to record with a group of white musicians who provided the bulk of recordings from the studios there.

Percy Sledge was a 25-year old hospital orderly at Colbert County Hospital who had been a stand-out baseball player for local teams. Sledge loved to sing and joined a group, The Esquires. One night Quin Ivey heard Sledge at a club spontaneously sing out "Why did you leave me, baby?" and invited him to his studio. "Why did you leave me, baby" became the basic idea for "When a Man Loves a Woman" and the group worked on the song during fall, 1965, changing the lyrics and shaping the melody.

The song was finally recorded around Christmas, 1965, engineered by Jimmy Johnson with Spooner Oldham on Farfisa organ, Roger Hawkins on drums, Marlin Greene on guitar and Junior Lowe on bass; vocals and horns were overdubbed later.

Songwriting credit was given to Sledge, Cameron Lewis, the bass player in Sledge's group, and Andrew Wright, who played organ in Sledge's group; Quin Ivey declined songwriting credit despite making a number of suggestions.

Ivy was convinced the record was a smash; he played it for Rick Hall who called Jerry Wexler at Atlantic and told him about the record and encouraged him to release it on Atlantic, although Hall would not benefit from the song.

The song hit in the spring and summer of 1966; it entered the *Billboard* Hot 100 on April 9, 1966 and was number one for two weeks; a week later it entered the R&B chart and held the number one spot for four weeks.

Artists and producers are always looking for a "new" sound, a new infusion into their recordings and, starting in the 1960s, many came to the small town of Muscle Shoals in northern Alabama to find that sound, which has been characterized as a soulful, dusky sound.

The FAME and Muscle Shoals Sound studios hosted recordings by Aretha Franklin, Otis Redding, Wilson Pickett, the Rolling Stones, Clarence

Carter, Solomon Burke, Percy Sledge, Tommy Roe, the Tams, Joe Tex and Etta James and the Allman Brothers. Duane Allman reportedly pitched a tent in the parking lot at FAME in order to be close to the studio and make himself available for sessions.

Artists who recorded at Muscle Shoals Sound Studio include Cher, Boz Scaggs, Herbie Mann, the Rolling Stones, the Staple Singers, Paul Simon, Rod Stewart, Canned Heat, Bob Seger, Cat Stevens, Lynyrd Skynyrd, Bob Dylan, Helen Reddy, Julian Lennon and the Black Keys.

Stax: Sam and Dave

Samuel Moore (born in Miami) had sung with the Melionaires, a gospel group; he met David Prater (born in Ocilla, Georgia), a solo act, in Miami in 1961. The duo first recorded for Alston in 1962, produced by Isaac Hayes and David Porter.

David Porter and Isaac Hayes were a songwriting team at Stax in Memphis; Porter was a life insurance salesman and Hayes a packer at a meat plant when they met and decided to write songs together. Porter hung around Stax until he was hired; he became their first black employee. Hayes auditioned for Stax with several different groups: Sir Isaac and the Do-Dads, the Teen Tones and Sir Calvin Valentine and His Swinging Cats. Hayes became the studio keyboard player when Booker T. Jones left for college.

Stax signed Sam and Dave and assigned Porter and Hayes to write for the duo. Their first success was "You Don't Know Like I Know." At a songwriting session for the next recording date, Hayes became impatient waiting for Porter, who was in the bathroom; Porter yelled out "hold on, man, I'm coming" and as soon as he said the words knew they had the title to a song. The song was written quickly; it entered the R&B chart for Sam and Dave on April 9, 1966 and rose to number one; two weeks later it entered the *Billboard* Hot 100 and reached number 21.

The Monkees

In 1966 rock'n'roll hit TV with a comedy sit-com,"The Monkees," a group created for TV based loosely on the Beatles and inspired by the film *A Hard Days Night*. Almost 500 applied for the roles, which were cast in Fall, 1965. Actors selected for the Monkees were David Jones (guitar), Peter Tork (bass), Micky Dolenz (drums) and Mike Nesmith (guitar). After the selections were made, the members were coached and rehearsed until they could appear as competent musicians. Tork and Nesmith had previous music experience but Dolenz was an actor (he had previously appeared as a child star on "Circus Boy" 1956-1958) and could play guitar, although he was a drummer on the show. Jones was an actor who had appeared in the Broadway musical *Oliver*. .

The show premiered on NBC on September 12, 1966 with Don Kirshner the musical supervisor. The show featured film techniques such as fast and slow motion, distorted focus and one-liners, all at a fast pace. In the show the Monkees got into awkward situations, saved girls from danger and defeated villains.

In addition to their roles on TV, the Monkees were signed as a recording act, although they were not allowed to play their instruments on their first album. They were signed to the Colgems label, a joint venture between Columbia Screen-Gems and RCA. Kirshner assigned Tommy Boyce and Bobby Hart, two veteran songwriters to write songs for the group and Boyce and Hart with Jack Keller produced their first album, *The Monkees*, which was released in October.

Their first single, "Last Train to Clarksville," was written by Boyce and Hart and released in August, just before the TV show premiered. It entered the *Billboard* Hot 100 on September 10 and reached number one. The lead singer for the single was Micky Dolenz. Their second single, "I'm a Believer" was written by Neil Diamond and also featured Dolenz on lead voctal.

Their first album, *The Monkees*, entered the *Billboard* album chart on October 8 and reached the number one position, where it remained for 13 weeks and stayed on the chart for 78 weeks. Six of the songs featured Dolenz on lead vocal, three were by Davy Jones, two by Michael Nesmith and one where Dolenz and Jones shared lead vocals. The album sold over five million copies.

The first live appearance was in December in Hawaii and they used the Candy Store Prophets for musical support.

8-Track Tapes

Inventor William Lear conceived the idea of 8-track tapes that contained a continuous loop tape with four sets of paired stereo tracks. The Ford Motor Company installed 8-track Motorola tape machines as a luxury item in their 1966 cars.

Eight-track tapes were successful in cars but were never fully accepted for listening at home. Their biggest problem was the gaps in sound when the tape switched from one pair of stereo tracks to the next, often in the middle of a song. Record labels never attempted to solve the problem by rearranging the order of songs; they simple used the LP order for the tapes.

The transistor radio had made music portable so music fans could listen to radio wherever they went. The 8-track tapes took it a step further, allowing listeners to hear their favorite albums traveling in a car.

The Beach Boys and *Pet Sounds*

Pet Sounds by the Beach Boys, released on May 16, 1966, was one of the most revolutionary and visionary albums of the 1960s but Brian Wilson was the only Beach Boy on the album.

The recording of *Pet Sounds* began in July, 1965 and lasted until April, the following year. Brian Wilson had stopped touring with the band and concentrated on songwriting and producing. The Beach Boys had stopped writing and recording songs about surfing and cars with the sixth album, *All Summer Long*. The following albums, *Today!* and *Summer Days (and Summer Nights)* and their single, "California Girls" showed Brian Wilson experimenting with songwriting and studio production under the influence of psychedelic drugs.

In July, 1965, Wilson, at the urging of Beach Boy Al Jardine, laid down tracks for an old Caribbean folk song, "Sloop John B." He then had to concentrate on their album *Beach Boys Party* because Capitol, their label, wanted a Christmas release. Wilson returned to "Sloop John B" and also recorded "The Little Girl I Once Knew," which was released as a single.

Wilson had written songs with Beach Boy Mike Love but for this album he had Tony Asher, who wrote jingles for an advertising agency, worked on lyrics. There were long, philosophical discussions between Wilson and Asher about what Brian wanted, which was about stages of relationships as well as deep inner feelings that Wilson had.

Their first collaboration came from an instrumental track that Brian had, "In My Childhood," that Asher changed; the end result was "You Still Believe in Me." Wilson knew what he wanted to say lyrically in a song, but Asher shaped those ideas into lyrics. Asher, who also had input musically, stated that, as a co-writer, he was Brian's "interpreter."

The writing sessions usually began with Brian having a melody or a chord pattern, then discussing with Asher what he wanted to say. The discussion were often long and rambling about a variety of topics while the actual work sessions were shorter.

Many critics consider *Pet Sounds* the first rock concept album; however, there was really no unifying theme lyrically or musically, although an emotional theme runs through the album. Brian felt that there was a production concept to the album.

Wilson was influenced by the Beatles album, *Rubber Soul,* during his time writing Pet Sounds and wanted to be at the same level as the Beatles. He spent hours in the studio working on the album and Beach Boys did not hear what he's been working on until they returned from a three-week tour of Japan and Hawaii. The songs were different from what they had done and there was concern about performing the songs live. The biggest dissension came from lead singer Mike Love, who found some of the lyrics offensive and nauseating.

Brian used Hollywood session musicians on the tracks done at United Western Recorders; many of those musicians were also used by Phil Spector, a huge influence on Wilson's producing. There were also session done at Gold Star Studios and Sunset Sound Recorders. The Beach Boys came into the studio and sang their parts after Brian showed them what to sing.

The album had 13 songs. Side one of the LP, began with "Wouldn't It Be Nice," credited to Wilson, Tony Asher and Mike Love, "You Still Believe in Me," "That's Not Me" and "Don't Talk (Put Your Head on My Shoulder," all written by Brian and Asher. The fifth song was "I'm Waiting for the Day," which had been written several years early by Wilson and Love, then "Let's Go Away for Awhile," written by Brian alone. The final song on side one was "Sloop John B."

Side two began with "God Only Knows," written by Wilson and Asher, then "I Know There's an Answer" written by Wilson, Love and Terry Sachen, then two songs written by Wilson and Asher, "Here Today" and "I Just Wasn't Made for These Times." Wilson wrote "Pet Sounds" alone and he and Asher wrote "Caroline, No." (Mike Love received credit for "Wouldn't It Be Nice" and "I Know There's an Answer" only after a court case.)

Brian Wilson dominated the lead vocals; he sang led on "You Still Believe in Me," "Don't Talk (Put Your Head on My Shoulder)," "I'm Waiting for the Day," "I Just Wasn't Made for These Times" and "Caroline, No." He shared lead vocals with Mike Love on "Wouldn't It Be Nice," "That's Not Me," and "Sloop John B." Mike Love has the lead vocal on "Here Today." Wilson, Love and Al Jardine share lead vocals on "I Know There's an Answer" and Carl Wilson and Bruce Johnston shared lead vocals with Brian on "God Only Knows." The remaining two songs were instrumentals. The cost of recording the album was around $70,000.

Pet Sounds was the eleventh album by the Beach Boys; it reached number ten on the *Billboard* chart and remained on the chart for 39 weeks.

To promote the album, Derek Taylor was hired; he came up with the phrase "Brian Wilson is a Genius" that has labelled Wilson and his work ever since.

"Good Vibrations"

The writing and recording of *Pet Sounds* led Brian Wilson to change his method of songwriting. Wilson no longer had a complete song when he entered the studio; instead he would record a track of chord changes, have an acetate made and listen to it at home, where he would refine the melody and write lyrics. He had been labeled a "genius" and with "Good Vibrations" he proved that he was. He was 23 years old when he wrote it.

Brian Wilson first enlisted lyricist Tony Asher to work on the song with him. Wilson began singing "good, good, good, good vibration" and began working on the melody on the piano. The final lyrics for "Good Vibrations" were written by Mike Love, who reportedly wrote them on his way to the studio.

By this time, Wilson was writing fragments of songs and working them into songs. He used L.A. studio musicians again and reportedly spent over 90 hours and between $50,000 and $75,000 recording the song.

The first version of "Good Vibration" was recorded in February, 1966, while he was working on the *Pet Sounds* sessions. Wilson wanted a Theremin on the song and he also had a cello, not instruments anyone would expect on a rock record. Brian worked on the song off and on and the lead vocal was intended for Dennis Wilson but a last minute case of laryngitis by Dennis lead to Carl Wilson doing the vocal during August and September. There were numerous overdubs—instrumental and vocal—as the song took its final shape.

"Good Vibrations" was released on October 10, 1966 and entered the *Billboard* Hot 100 chart on October 22 and reached number one, remaining on the chart for 14 weeks. It is considered one of the most important recordings in the twentieth century. The production of the records was widely influential and a landmark in the history of rock music.

L.A. vs. San Francisco

There was a bit of a riff between Los Angeles and San Francisco during the mid-1960s. San Francisco was a city of beatniks, hippies, street theater and political engagement. The San Francisco crowd saw Los Angeles as plastic, slick and phony. If San Francisco was on the cutting edge of music, drugs and lifestyle, Los Angeles, according to that train of thought, was viewed as teeny bopper pop. San Francisco claimed itself to be "real" while Hollywood and Los Angeles was shallow and plastic.

Those involved in the Haight-Asbury and hippie scene in San Francisco did not believe the L.A. bands could cut it at the Fillmore because the San Francisco bands were engaged in "communal mind expansion" while those in Los Angeles played for mindless stardom.

Nashville and Country Music

In 1966, country music was doing quite well, although the city tended to be isolated from New York and Los Angeles, the other two recording centers in America. Country music artists and records had a national impact, but it wasn't with the same audience as pop and rock artists and Nashville was viewed as a bit backward and behind the times to those in Los Angeles and New York. However, there several country songs during 1965 that crossed over and were heard on pop radio.

The biggest country record of 1966 was "Almost Persuaded" by David Houston; it entered the *Billboard* country chart on June 25, 1966 and reached number one, where it remained for nine weeks. No country song lasted that long at number one until Taylor Swift's "We Are Never Ever Getting Back Together" topped that—46 years later. In 2014 Florida Georgia Line bested that with 20 weeks at number one.

The song was written by Billy Sherrill and Glenn Sutton and produced by Sherrill for Epic. Houston had six more number one's after "Almost Persuaded," including a duet with Tammy Wynette on "My Elusive Dreams." The record won Grammys for "Best Country Record, "Best Country Song" and "Best Country Male Vocal."

Jeannie Seely was an attractive newcomer to country music; dressed often in mini-skirts—not the accepted dress of the conservative country audience—and undeniably sexy, her first chart single for Monument Records was "Don't Touch Me," which entered the *Billboard* country chart on April 16, 1966 and rose to number two, where it remained for three week; however, it was number one on the country charts in *Record World* and *Cashbox* magazines. Seely's husband, Hank Cochran, wrote the song, which was recorded on March 12. The song was also released by Wilma Burgess, which reached number 12 but Seely's version prevailed.

Jack Greene's record of "There Goes My Everything," written by Dallas Frazier, was number one for seven weeks and number 65 on the *Billboard* Hot 100 in 1966. The song entered the *Billboard* country chart on October 22 and, during the first Country Music Association (CMA) Awards, was voted

"Single of the Year" and "Song of the Year" while his album won "Album of the Year" and he was voted "Male Artist of the Year." In 1967 Engelbert Humperdinck's version of "There Goes My Everything" was number 22 on Billboard's Hot 100 chart and number two in the U.K.

Johnny Cash: *Mean As Hell (Ballads From The True West)*

While most Nashville based artists were embracing "the Nashville Sound" during the 1960s, dressed in sports coats, suits and tuxedos and backed by strings section, Johnny Cash was putting the "western" back into country music. His twenty-second album, *Mean As Hell! (Ballads From the True West)* was a follow-up to his *Bitter Tears* album but in this album he embraced the cowboys as well as the Indians.

The double album debuted on *Billboard's* country chart on April 2, 1966 and reached number four; it remained on that chart for 18 weeks; the album did not enter the pop chart in *Billboard*. The album contained traditional western songs like "I Ride an Old Paint," "Streets of Laredo," "Bury Me Not on The Lone Prairie" and "Sweet Betsy From Pike" as well as songs written by Carl Perkins ("The Ballad of Boot Hill"), Ramblin' Jack Elliott ("Mr. Garfield"), Tex Ritter ("Sam Hall"), Harlan Howard ("The Blizzard), Shel Silverstein ("25 Minutes to Go") Peter La Farge ("Stampede") Merle Kilgore ("Johnny Reb") and songs Cash wrote, "Hiawatha's Vision," "Hardin Wouldn't Run," "Mean As Hell" and "The Road to Kaintuck."

Magazine Coverage

Nashville received significant coverage in national magazines during 1966. In the *Saturday Evening Post* was an article, "That New Sound from Nashville" by Charles Portis that featured Roger Miller on the cover. The article stated "Country music is prospering and so is Nashville's recording industry, which now does a brisk non-country trade." The article noted that "Few country singers manage to get themselves taken seriously in Nashville...generally, the Athenians of the South go one way, and the country music people another" and added "Hillbilly is characterized by a squonking fiddle introduction, a funeral steel guitar and an overall whiney, draggy sound that has never set well with urban ears" but then noted, "this music has a new acceptance and a new dignity...It's not, you know, the old hillbilly stuff, the nasal voices, those guitars thumping and all."

An article, "The Gold Guitars" in *Newsweek* reported that in 1965 "country music raked in $70 million, or about 10 percent of the total sales of all records, adding that about 25 percent of major labels releases are country.

It concluded "What has made the Nashville Sound an all-American sound is the evolution of country music toward popular taste. The raw, nasal 'hillbilly' sound, alien to urban ears, has gradually been discarded."

An article in *Business Week* titled "Country Music Snaps Its Regional Bounds" stated "The Nashville Sound" has hit the $600 million popular music business, and it's the hottest thing around." The article noted that country was "every bit as important as rock'n'roll" and that "four out of every ten records sold are either country music or show its influence."

The Roger Miller TV show

"The Roger Miller Show" premiered on September 12, 1966 on Monday nights at 8:30 on NBC. The 30 minute variety show's theme song was "King of the Road," which had been a hit for Miller in 1965. The 30 minute variety show featured "The Doodle Town Pipers" and guests included Bill Cosby, Wes Harrison, the Geezinslaw Brothers, Peter, Paul & Mary, Arthur Godfrey, Soupy Sales, New York Yankee manager Casey Stengel, George Carlin, the Kingston Trio and others. Roger sang songs on the show backed by his band, Thumbs Carllile on guitar, Don Bagley on bass and Jerry Allison on drums. The show ended on December 26, 1966 after only one season.

The genius of Roger Miller was his wit and spontaneity—but that was not possible for a scripted television show. Also, Roger was going in ten different directions and couldn't really concentrate on the TV show; he was too busy making records, touring and having fun.

Bob Dylan records in Nashville

Nashville and country music was off the radar screen for most of those in Los Angeles in New York, who tended to look down on country music and country artists as redneck hillbillies who were the epitome of everything un-hip and un-cool. Roger Miller was living in Los Angeles and socialized with the Hollywood crowd but the other country artists were far removed in Nashville.

As the issues with Civil Rights and Vietnam grew, Nashville and country artists were considered on the wrong side of the political divide. Not only did most of those involved in the pop and rock music worlds in L.A. and New York not know much about Nashville or country music, they did not want to know anything about the southern city and its music. They dismissed it because it wasn't "progressive."

Then Bob Dylan came to Nashville

Bob Dylan recorded his first six albums in New York and began work on his seventh in October, 1965 with producer Bob Johnston in Columbia Studio A in New York.

After his electric appearance at the Newport Folk Festival in July, Dylan went on tour, backed by Levon and the Hawks, after guitarist Mike Bloomfield and keyboard player Al Kooper bowed out after early dates. The new band had been formed in Canada to back Ronnie Hawkins; members were Levon Helm, Robbie Robertson, Rick Danko, Richard Manuel and Garth Hudson.

In the studio with the Hawks, Dylan attempted several songs but nothing jelled, although they managed to finish "Can You Please Crawl Out Your Window" for a single.

During December, Dylan performed concerts in December, then took off the first three weeks in January after his son was born. On January 23 he returned to the New York studio with musicians Robie Robertson, bassist Rick Danko, pianist Paul Griffin, organist Al Kooper and drummer Bobby Gregg (Levon Helm had quit the band, dissatisfied at being in a back-up band) and recorded "Leopard-Skin Pill Box Hat" and "One of Us Must Know (Sooner or Later)." "One of Us Must Know (Sooner or Later)" was completed and released as a single.

The musicians did not click with Dylan, leaving him dissatisfied and frustrated. Producer Bob Johnston suggested they record in Nashville; Johnston was head of Columbia in Nashville and lived there. Albert Grossman, Dylan's manager, hated the idea of going to Nashville to record and told Johnston to never mention Nashville to Dylan again. Grossman thought the charm was in the New York studio, but Dylan agreed to Johnson's suggestion.

On February 14, 1966, Bob Dylan went into Columbia Studio A in Nashville with Robbie Robertson, Al Kooper and Nashville session musicians hired by Johnston. Charlie McCoy, a versatile musician who played a number of instruments, including harmonica, guitar and bass was there with guitarist Wayne Moss, guitarist and bassist Joe South and drummer Kenny Buttrey. Baffles were set up in the studio to isolate the musicians so there would be no "bleed" into microphones for the vocal or other musicians. Dylan asked that they be removed so the musicians could sit as a tight group and play off each other.

On that first session, Dylan recorded "Visions of Johanna," which he had tried in New York as "Freeze Out." He also recorded "4th Time Around" and then "Leopard-Skin Pill Box Hat," which didn't work.

In his hotel room, Dylan had a piano installed that Kooper played while Dylan worked on lyrics and the arrangement of a song. Kooper would go to the studio ahead of Dylan and teach the musicians the song(s) they planned to do so they could be ready when Dylan arrived.

At 6 p.m. the next day, the musicians played cards, napped and generally killed time while Dylan worked on the lyrics to "Sad Eyed Lady of the Lowlands." Finally, at 4 a.m., the musicians were called in and Dylan told them the arrangement of the song.

Dylan counted off for the musicians, who then began playing what would be an eleven minute and twenty-three second song. Drummer Kenny Buttrey stated "If you notice that record, that thing after like the second chorus starts building and building like crazy, and everybody's just peaking it up 'cause we thought, 'Man, this is it—this is gonna be the last chorus and we've gotta put everything into it we can. And he played another Harmonica solo and went back down to another verse and the dynamics had to drop back down to a verse kind of feel. After about ten minutes of this thing we're cracking up at each other, at what we were doing. I mean we peaked five minutes ago. Where do we go from here?"

That song took up the entire side of a vinyl LP.

A pattern had been established. Dylan would spend the afternoon working on lyrics, the session would begin around six and go into the wee hours of the next day. On that third day, Dylan and the musicians worked on "Stuck Inside of Mobile with the Memphis Blues Again" and, after several starts and stops, the fourteenth take was deemed good.

Dylan's tour, backed by the Hawks, resumed after those three days of sessions. On March 8, he was back in the studio and recorded "Absolutely Sweet Marie," "Just Like a Woman" and "Pledging My Time."

Beginning on March 9 and extending into the morning of March 10, Bob Dylan recorded six songs in 13 hours. First up was "Most Likely You Go Your Way and I'll Go Mine," "Temporary Like Achilles" (which Dylan had attempted in New York under the title "Medicine Sunday"), "Rainy Day Women #12 and 35," "Obviously Five Believers," "Leopard-Skin Pill-Box Hat" and "I Want You," with the lead guitar played by Wayne Moss.

The tapes of the Nashville sessions were taken to Los Angeles for mixing before Dylan left for a tour of Australia. As the album was mixed, Bob Johnston asked what the album should be called and Dylan answered "Blonde on Blonde." The initials spell out "BOB," Dylan's first name.

The album, released in May, entered the *Billboard* album chart in July and reached number nine, remaining on the chart for 34 weeks. "One of

Us Must Know (Sooner or Later)" had been recorded in New York and released as a single but was included on the Blonde on Blonde album. The first Nashville recorded song recorded during the *Blonde on Blonde* sessions and released as a single was "Rainy Day Women #12 and 35," (they couldn't call it "Everybody Must Get Stoned!) which entered the *Billboard* Hot 100 on April 16 and rose to number two. The next three Dylan singles, "I Want You," "Just Like a Woman" and "Leopard-Skin Pill-Box Hat" all came from the *Blonde on Blonde* sessions in Nashville.

After Bob Dylan recorded in Nashville, other pop and rock artists came to Nashville to record. Dylan opened up the gates that let in singers and songwriters who now felt Nashville was a "hip" place to record.

Dylan: After the Accident

A turning point for Bob Dylan occurred in July, 1966, when he suffered a broken neck in a motorcycle accident. Before the accident he had been living a hectic life, touring constantly, writing constantly, living in the fast lane and the accident put him in the hospital, unconscious for a short while, and the recovery period gave him the opportunity to stop and re-evaluate himself and his work. He stated in several interviews about writing songs that he "used to be able to do it in an unconscious way" but with the later songs "I was trying to do it in a conscious way." He told Jonathan Cott in a Rolling Stone interview in 1978 "Right through the time of *Blonde on Blonde* (recorded in Nashville just before the accident) I was [writing songs] unconsciously. Then one day I was half-stepping, and the lights went out. And since that point, I more or less had amnesia. Now you can take that statement as literally or metaphysically as you need to, but that's what happened to me. It took me a long time to get to do consciously what I used to be able to do unconsciously."

Dylan told biographer Robert Shelton "I always felt that I've stumbled into things." and in a long interview about his songs and songwriting with Bill Flanagan for his book *Written in My Soul* he stated "Not a whole lot of real thought goes into this stuff. It's more or less remembering things and taking it down. Sometimes you're just taking notes on stuff and then putting it all together."

Dylan also told Flanagan, "I'm just writing from instinct. I do that most of the time anyway. I just write from instinct and however it comes out is how it comes out. Other people can make of it what they choose to. But for me I can't expound too much on what I'm doing because I really don't have any idea what I'm doing." Dylan added that "anything I try to write about, I can't do it. If I try to write about something...I can't get anywhere with that."

It was difficult for Dylan to have any kind of perspective when he was in his 20s (or even early 30s) because he was in the eye of the hurricane with things happening around him he couldn't quite grasp and found it hard to deal with. Things like pop stardom, with all its frills and trappings, and being analyzed in the press for what he was writing, or people seeing things in his songs he didn't see himself and being called a "genius" for works he had created on the run. In his 40s, Dylan, who had always been reclusive and evasive, did a spurt of interviews and seemed to have a much better handle on himself and his songs. Somehow the years had given him a perspective and he had a new experience as a songwriter--trying to create consciously what he had previously created unconsciously. No longer was songwriting something that "just happened," it was now something he thought about and knew people would analyze as he created it.

He noted that "My songs are not for me to understand. I don't make that a part of it. While I'm doing them I have an understanding of them, but that's all." This was a further admission that he was a vehicle for the songs--a vessel they come through--and that the songs are already there, just waiting to be written down, a thought he has stated since his earliest days in New York.

In a *Rolling Stone* interview, Dylan stated, "I'm not reluctant to talk about my songwriting, but no one has ever really asked me the right things. I just tried to be brief, remember kind of how things happened. I'm not really a nostalgia freak." Then he added, "It's still hard for me to talk about playing, about songwriting. It's like a guy digging a ditch. It's hard to talk about how the dirt feels on the shovel."

In an interview in 1985 in *Spin* magazine he expressed the frustration of trying to explain himself as a songwriter. He stated "I've never been to college and taken a literary course. I can only try to answer these questions, because I'm supposed to be somebody who knows something about writing, but the actual fact is, I don't really know that much about it. I don't know what there is to know about it, anyway."

In several interviews, Dylan stated that he began songwriting only after singing a number of other people's songs. He implied that one of the problems with young songwriters is they begin by singing their own songs rather than someone else's and believes his own success as a songwriter came from the necessity to find songs to perform that hadn't already been written. He stated "I began writing because I was singing. I think that's an important thing. I started writing because things were changing all the time and a certain song needed to be written. I started writing them because I wanted to sing them. If they had been written, I wouldn't have started to write them. Anyway, one thing led to another and I just kept on writing my own songs, but I stumbled into it, really. It was nothing I had prepared myself for, but I did sing a lot of songs before I wrote any of my own. I think that's important too."

Vietnam and Protestors

In 1966, American forces claimed victory in two search-and-destroy missions in the Mekong Delta region of South Vietnam in March. The operation began in January and American troops destroyed an entire Vietcong battalion and the headquarters of a second battalion

In mid-May, anti-war protests swept the country as thousands of young men and women marched to protest American involvement in Vietnam. Protestors surrounded the White House and vowed to rid Congress of those who supported the war. At the University of Chicago, hundreds of students seized the administration building and held it for three days. In New York, students sat outside the office of the president of City College and raised their voices in protest.

Around 400,000 students took a Selective Service qualifying test; those who scored under 70 risked losing their 2-S student deferment. Critics claimed the test created a burden for the poor and uneducated. President Johnson labelled his critics "nervous Nellies" and accused them of "turning on their leaders, their country and their fighting men."

At Princeton University, President Johnson told protestors to "cool it" and was met with a stony silence. The protestors held up signs that read "This war is unconstitutional" and "Who are we to police the world?"

In April, American forces bombed targets on the border with Laos; in May, bombers, flying at 50,000 feet could not be seen or heard until the 36 2,000 pound bombs hit a target. At the end of June, B-52 bombers bombed Hanoi and Haiphong in North Vietnam, the first time those cities were blasted with bombs. Pentagon Generals had warned that striking cities in North Vietnam might provoke intervention by Russia or China or both. The Defense Department thought that the block-busting bombs would be the decisive force to defeat North Vietnam.

At the end of October, Secretary of Defense Robert McNamara warned that neither the heavy bombing campaigns nor the pacification program where members of the Armed Forces attempted to win over the "hearts and minds" of the South Vietnamese had enticed North Vietnam leaders to peace talks. The political and military situation in South Vietnam was deteriorating.

Country Songs About Vietnam

During the Spring of 1966, there were songs related to the Viet Nam War on the country chart, including "Ballad of the Green Berets" by Sgt. Barry Sadler, "Dear Uncle Sam" by Loretta Lynn, "The One on the Right Is On the Left" by Johnny Cash, "Private Wilson White" by Marty Robbins and "Viet Nam Blues" by Dave Dudley. Johnny Wright's album, *Hello Vietnam*, named after his hit single the previous year, and Dave Dudley's album *There's a Star Spangled Banner Waving Somewhere*, named after the popular World War II song that Dudley recorded, were on the country album chart. Country music artists tended to be more supportive of the Viet Nam war than their contemporaries in the rock field.

Civil Rights and Race Riots in 1966

Julian Bond, a 25-year-old African-American activist (he had headed the Student Non-Violent Coordinating Committee or SNCC) was elected to the Georgia legislature in 1966 but the legislature refused to seat him in January. Legislators claimed that Bond was disloyal to the United States because he said he admired draft card burner. The vote was 184-12 to deny him his seat in the House.

The Congress of Racial Equality (CORE) endorsed the slogan "Black Power" in July but the NAACP rejected it. Roy Wilkins of the NAACP stated that his organization "will have none of this…It is the raging of race against race on the irrelevant basis of skin color. It is the father of hatred and mother of violence." CORE responded that "Black Power is not hatred. It is a means to bring Black Americans into the covenant of brotherhood…a unified Black voice reflecting racial pride in the tradition of our heterogeneous nation."

The phrase "Black Power" became popular when Stokely Carmichael used it when he spoke during a Mississippi voter registration march in June.

In September in Atlanta, a race riot began after police shot an African-American suspect they claimed was fleeing. Militant African-Americans shouted "Black Power" as they attacked cars and police vehicles with concrete blocks. Atlanta Mayor Ivan Allen, Jr. blamed Stokely Carmichael, national chairman of the Student Non-Violent Coordinating Committee, for the riots because Stokely had popularized the "Black Power" slogan. Carmichael was arrested and charged with inciting violence.

The rioting was criticized by Martin Luther King, Jr., before he left Atlanta for Chicago to lead marches demanding better housing for the poor. As King led a march in Cicero, Illinois, roving gangs of whites attacked the marchers with bottles and rocks. Shouts of "Kill 'em" and "Tar and feather 'em" were heard. Days after King launched his crusade, rioting broke out in Chicago and the National Guard was called in after three days of looting and burning.

In June, James Meredith was shot in the back during a Civil Rights march and in Grenada, Mississippi, mobs of whites assaulted Negro children and their parents at newly integrated public schools

Controversial Books

Two books were controversial in 1966. The previous year, *Unsafe at Any Speed* by Ralph Nadar had been published. The book pointed out safety flaws in automobiles. General Motors responded by hiring private detectives to discredit him by prying into his sexual life and political beliefs. GM president James Roches and other GM officials later admitted this in testimony before a Congressional committee investigating the charges.

Human Sexual Response was by gynecologist William Masters and psychologist Virginia Johnson. They filmed and studied over 600 male and female volunteers from 18 to 89 engaged in sexual activities. The study provided detailed measurement of the sexual cycle, orgasms and physiological patterns necessary for treating sexual problems. This was the first book that utilized extensive experiments on human subjects to study sexual behavior.

NOW and Supreme Court Rulings

The National Organization of Women (N.O.W.) called for "true equality for all women in America" and NOW leader Betty Friedan said that women are "in relatively little position to influence or control major decisions." NOW announced plans to organize women's voting and work on legislation to fight sex discrimination.

In June the Supreme Court ruled that when someone was arrested, they had "the right to remain silent" and "nothing you say may be used against you in a court of law." An arresting policeman was required to inform a suspect of their rights, including the right to have an attorney present.

This became known as the Miranda Ruling because it was brought to the Supreme Court in the Miranda vs. Arizona case.

Mass Murders

There were several gruesome mass murders in 1966. In July, Richard Speck, Jr. was arrested in Chicago for killing eight student nurses after he had forced his way into their dormitory with a knife and gun, tied their hands with bedsheets, then strangled five and stabbed three. A ninth nurse survived by hiding under a bed.

On August 1, Charles Whitman went to the top of the 27 story tower at the University of Texas and began shooting people below. Whitman killed 16 and wounded 30 during a 90 minute rampage that ended when he was killed by an off duty policeman. Whitman, a 25-year old honor student and former Marine, had killed his wife and mother the night before.

Other News

President Lyndon Johnson signed the Child Nutrition Act, which guaranteed that federal funds would be available to feed impoverished students. This would also helps schools because a good meal can make a difference in the lives, attitudes and learning of school children. Four days later Johnson signed a bill to established the Department of Transportation.

In November, Johnson signed the "Model Cities Act" which provided almost $1 billion in federal funds over two years for 60 to 70 "demonstration cities for reconstruction of their cores." This was an experiment in inter-governmental administration.

In November, actor Ronald Reagan was elected Governor of California. On December 15, Walt Disney died in Hollywood.

College Campuses

In 1966, the amount of students on college campuses had grown by almost a million; there were now 5.9 million.

The taste in music of the students surveyed had changed; 18.8 percent said that "rock" was their favorite music, followed by 17.7 percent who preferred pop vocalists and 16.6 percent who favored pop instrumentalists, which meant that over 34 percent of college students preferred "pop" to "rock. Those who preferred folk music accounted for 16.6 percent of the survey but the appeal (and sale) of folk music was in decline.

Jazz was the favorite of 11.5 students while 11.6 students preferred classical and six percent listed country as their favorite. Almost 64 percent of students owned their own phonograph and owned an average of 40 albums and 79 singles and purchased an average of 13 singles and eight albums a year.

A listing of the favorite acts of college students in 1966:

Favorite Male Vocalist:
1. Andy Williams
2. Frank Sinatra
3. Johnny Mathis
4. Dean Martin
5. Robert Goulet
6. Jack Jones
7. Sammy Davis Jr.
8. Elvis PResley
9. Tony Bennett
10. Gene Pitney
11. Ray Charles
12. Roy Orbison
13. Bob Dylan
14. James Brown
20. Tom Jones
21. Roger Miller
22. Nat King Cole
28. Paul McCartney

Favorite Female Vocalist:
1. Barbra Streisand
2. Petula Clark
3. Connie Francis
4. Nancy Wilson
5. Dionne Warwick
6. Lesley Gore
7. Brenda Lee
8. Julie Andrews
9. Ella Fitzgerald
10. Eydie Gorme
11. Doris Day
15. Joan Baez
17. Cher Bono

Favorite Groups:
1. Beatles
2. Rolling Stones
3. Supremes
4. Beach Boys
5. Letterman
6. Righteous Brothers
7. Four Seasons
8. Peter Paul & Mary
9. Dave Clark Five
10. Kingston Trio
11. Byrds
12. Sonny and Cher
13. Four Freshmen
14. Brothers Four
15. Animals
16. Ray Conniff Singers
17. Herman's Hermits
18. New Christy Minstrels
19. Kingsmen
20. Four Tops

Favorite Male Vocalist: Folk
1. Bob Dylan
2. Harry Belafonte
3. Glenn Yarbrough
4. Pete Seeger
5. Donovan
6. Josh White Sr.
7. Phil Ochs
8. Theodore Bikel
9. Trini Lopez
10. Johnny Cash

Favorite Female Vocalist: Folk
1 Joan Baez
2. Judy Collins
3. Mary Travers
4. Odetta
5. Buffy Sainte Marie

6. Carolyn Hester
7. Judy Henske
8. Miriam Makeba
9. Marianne Faithful
10. Gale Garrett

Favorite Group: Folk:
1. Peter, Paul & Mary
2. Kingston Trio
3: New Christy Minstrels
4. Mitchell Trio
5. Brothers Four
6. Ian and Sylvia
7. Smothers Brothers
8. Serendipity Singers
9. The Lettermen
10. Limeliters

American Radio and Album Sales

American radio played a wide variety of artists and songs during 1966. During the 52 weeks of the year, there were 27 songs that reached number one on the *Billboard* Hot 100 chart.

Two songs by the Beatles ("We Can work It Out" and "Paperback Writer") reached number one, although they had five others that reached the chart. During the year artists Petula Clark, Nancy Sinatra, SSgt Barry Sadler, The Righteous Brothers, The Young Rascals, The Mamas and the Papas, Percy Sledge, The Rolling Stones, Frank Sinatra, The Troggs, Tommy James & the Shondells, The Lovin' Spoonful, Donovan, The Supremes, The Association, the Four Tops, the Monkees, Johnny Rives and the Beach Boys all had number one records.

Six of the songs that reached number one during 1966 were by British acts; the Beatles, the Rolling Stones, Donovan, The Troggs ("Wild Thing") and the New Vaudeville Band, who had a novelty hit with "Winchester Cathedral."

On the *Billboard* album chart, The Beatles had three albums that topped the chart, Herb Alpert and the Tijuana Brass had two, and the Supremes, Frank Sinatra and the Monkees each had one. The album, *Ballad of the Green Berets* by SSgt Barry Sadler, a patriotic album also reached number one, as did the soundtrack to *Dr. Zhivago*.

1967
1967 Begins

The Monkees single, "I'm a Believer," written by Neil Diamond, was the number one song on the *Billboard* Hot 100 when 1967 began. They also held the number one spot on the *Billboard* album chart. On the country chart, "There Goes My Everything" by Jack Greene was number one and on the R&B chart it was "(I Know) I'm Losing You" by The Temptations that was number one. The next song to reach the top spot on the R&B chart was "Tell It Like It Is" by Aaron Neville, which captured a theme of those who came of age during the 1960s and pushed for more honest in a world they felt was dishonest and deception.

The first Super Bowl was held on January 15 in Los Angeles and the Green Bay Packers, under legendary coach Vince Lombardi, defeated the Kansas City Chiefs 35-10. The stadium was only two-thirds full.

The self-confessed "Boston Strangler," Albert De Salvo, received a life sentence for the murder of 13 women in the Boston area.

On January 27, three astronauts were sitting in their Apollo capsule atop a rocket, rehearsing for their space flight, when a flash fire swept through the capsule, killing Virgil Grissom, Edward White and Roger Chaffee.

In May, the one millionth telephone was installed in an American home; half of all the telephones in the world were in the United States.

Muhammad Ali was stripped of his heavyweight boxing title in April for resisting the military draft. Ali had claimed that, as a Black Muslim minister, he was exempt from the draft.

Thurgood Marshall became the first black Supreme Court justice when he was approved by the Senate on August 30.

Recording *Sergeant Pepper's Lonely Hearts Club Band*

When the new year of 1967 came in, John Lennon and Ringo Starr were both 26, Paul McCartney was 24, and George Harrison was 23. It had been exactly five years since their audition for Decca Records--held on January 1, 1962--and over four and a half years since their recording session in September which yielded their first single in Britain, "Love Me Do." It was almost impossible to imagine how much had happened to them or how far they had come to arrive at the point where they were in the process of recording what many consider to be one of the greatest rock'n'roll albums of all time: *Sergeant Pepper's Lonely Hearts Club Band*.

The Beatles began 1967 in the Abbey Road studios finishing "Penny Lane." On January 19, they recorded the basic tracks for "A Day in the Life."

The single "Strawberry Fields" backed with "Penny Lane," both recorded in Fall, 1966, was issued as a single in the U.K. and the Beatles did film clips of the two songs to promote the two-sided single.

On February 1, the Beatles recorded the song "Sergeant Pepper's Lonely Hearts Club Band," written by Paul McCartney, which gave the album they were recording a name. With that song, McCartney conceived the idea of the Beatles recording as a different band—as Sergeant Pepper's Lonely Hearts Club Band—so they wouldn't have to be Beatles.

The Beatles spent February and March in the studio recording, laying basic tracks and then overdubbing various effects, altering the songs and trying various mixes. After "Sergeant Pepper," they laid down basic tracks for "Good Morning, Good Morning" (written by Lennon), "Fixing a Hole" (McCartney), "Only a Northern Song" (Harrison), "Being For the Benefit of Mr. Kite" (Lennon), "Anything" (a 22 minute recording of Ringo playing drums), "Lovely Rita" (McCartney), "Lucy in the Sky With Diamonds" (Lennon), "Getting Better" (McCartney), "Within You, Without You" (Harrison), "She's Leaving Home" (McCartney) and then, on March 29, "With a Little Help From My Friends" (written by Lennon and McCartney and sung by Ringo).

On March 30, the photo shoot for the Sergeant Pepper's album was held at the crosswalk in front of the Abbey Road studio. After the photo, the Beatles did a reprise of "Sergeant Pepper's Lonely Heart Club Band" to finish the concept before the album's final song, "A Day in the Life."

In April, returning from a trip to the United States, Paul McCartney had the idea to do a film based on Ken Kesey's "Merry Pranksters" tour where Kesey loaded a bus with friends and fiends and traveled across America, promoting LSD. On April 25, the Beatles recorded "Magical Mystery Tour" for the new film and album.

Grammys: 1967

The Grammy Awards for recordings released in 1966 were again held in four locations, Los Angeles, New York, Chicago and Nashville on March 2, 1967.

"Record of the Year" was "Strangers in the Night" by Frank Sinatra, produced by Jimmy Bowen; "Song of the Year" was "Michelle," written by John Lennon and Paul McCartney; and "Album of the Year" was Frank Sinatra's *A Man and His Music*, produced by Sonny Burke.

In the "Rock and Roll" category in the "Pop" division, "Best Male" was Paul McCartney for "Eleanor Rigby"; Best Group Vocal or Instrumental" was "Monday, Monday" by the Mamas & the Papas; and "Best Recording" was "Winchester Cathedral" by the New Vaudeville Band.

In the "Pop" category "Female Vocal" was Eydie Gorme for "If He Walked Into My Life"; "Male Vocal" was Frank Sinatra for "Strangers in the Night"; Vocal Group" was the Anita Kerr Singers for "A Man and a Woman"; "Best Chorus" was the Ray Conniff Singers for "Somewhere My Love (Lara's Theme from *Dr. Zhivago*"; and Best Instrumental (other than jazz) was Herb Alpert & the Tijuana Brass for "What Now My Love."

The R&B category had been extended to three: "Best Solo Male or Female" was Ray Charles for "Crying Time"; Best Group was the Ramsey Lewis Trio for "Hold It Right There"; and "Best Rhythm & Blues Recording was Ray Charles for "Crying Time."

The Country category had been shrunk to four: "Female Vocal" was Jeannie Seely for "Don't Touch Me"; Male Vocal was David Houston for "Almost Persuaded"; Best Recording" was "Almost Persuaded" by Houston; and "Best Song" was "Almost Persuaded," written by Billy Sherrill and Glenn Sutton.

"Best Folk Recording" was Cortelia Clark for *Blues in the Street*; and "Best Gospel" was Porter Wagoner and the Blackwood Brothers for Grand Ole Gospel.

Vietnam

The biggest military operation at that point in the Vietnam war began on February 22 after assaults by the North Vietnamese army from January 8 to 26 north of Saigon. North Vietnamese headquarters north of Saigon in the "Iron Triangle" was destroyed.

President Lyndon Johnson signed the largest defense appropriation bill--$70 billion—in the 177 year history of the United States in September. He increased income taxes in order to finance the Vietnam war and decided to send 47,000 more combat and support soldiers to Vietnam.

On October there was a major anti-war demonstration outside the Pentagon in Washington D.C. Protestors started bonfires and jeered at the helmeted police force that protected the Pentagon. Tens of thousands of protestors, who vowed to shut down the Pentagon, streamed from the Lincoln Memorial, across Memorial Bridge to the Pentagon, many carrying "Dump Johnson" banners. Students came from across the country to be part of the protest, which began peacefully before thousands of guards with rifles and tear gas grenades confronted the crowd.

There were hundreds arrested in the Washington protest, organized by the National Mobilization Committee to End the War in Vietnam, which capped a week of protests in San Francisco, Los Angeles, New York and Madison, Wisconsin.

Warner Brothers Records & The Grateful Dead

Warner Brothers was a struggling label when executive Stan Cornyn went to San Francisco to check out the "psychedelic scene." He returned to L.A. and told Mo Ostin and Joe Smith what he had seen; Cornyn and Ostin then went to San Francisco and realized they could find acts that were inexpensive to sign that would not compete with what the other majors had. The idea was to sign acts that could sell locally, then regionally and then perhaps make the leap to national success.

Mike Maitland was overall head of Warner Brothers and Joe Smith was head of their Reprise label while Mo Ostin headed the Warner Brothers label. Maitland gave each a budget to sign one psychedelic act. Reprise signed an L.A. band, the Electric Prune and Warner Brothers signed a San Francisco act, the Grateful Dead.

In San Francisco, Tom Donahue took Smith and Ostin to see the Grateful Dead at the Avalon ballroom. "Dealing with the Grateful Dead and San Francisco's psychedelic consciousness proved a cultural and financial turning point for the label," stated Fred Goodman in his book, *Mansion on the Hill*. The "group was bankrolled by LSD chemist Stanley Owsley.. musicians lived and conducted business communally. Joe Smith, a graduate of Yale, noted the group members were all intelligent, adding "all of the Grateful Dead went to college. Of course, when they started gassing up with acid it was a little difficult to talk to them."

The Grateful Dead evolved out of a jug band to form the Warlocks, then changed their name to the Grateful Dead. They began in 1965 in Palo Alto, California and were part of the San Francisco Haight-Asbury scene known for drug experimentation and the founding home of the hippies.

Jerry Garcia, the leader of the group, started out playing bluegrass and had roots in folk music before he took up the electric guitar. Other original members included Bob Weir, guitar; Phil Lesh, bass; Ron "Pigpen" McKernan, keyboards and harmonica; and Bill Kreutzmann, drums. They were known for lengthy instrumental jams and attracted a core group of dedicated followers known as the "Deadheads."

The Grateful Dead controlled all creative decisions from the material they recorded to their album cover art. They recorded a double live album for their initial release and titled the album *Skull Fuck*. During discussions, Joe Smith, reminded the band that they were in debt $120,000 to Warner Brothers and they had to pay back the label through album sales before they received any money. Smith did not tell them to change the name of their album but told them all of the places where the album could not be sold and "found them remarkably pragmatic when the subject was their career." The title of their debut album was *The Grateful Dead*.

Warner Brothers Introduces the Grateful Dead

In March, 1967, Warner Brothers executives Stan Cornyn and Joe Smith, wore their dark blue Warner Brothers blazers with "WR" emblazoned on the breast pocket to Fugazi Hall in San Francisco to celebrate the first release of the debut album by the Grateful Dead. The two stood out in a crowd dressed in jeans, t-shirts, tie-dyed headbands and "hippie dress."

Joe Smith stood on stage and told the crowd that he was honored "for Warner Brothers Records to be able to introduce the Grateful Dead and its music to the world." Grateful Dead member Jerry Garcia then took the stage and said, it was an honor "for the Grateful Dead to introduce Warner Brothers Records to the world."

That event marked the death of the Warner Brothers blue blazers.

The Grateful Dead made Warner Brothers hip and became a great asset, although their early albums did not sell well. "They were authentic American Bohemians, the acid-munching standard-bearers of the underground. The Dead challenged convention—and now, by inference, Warner Bros. did as well," stated Stan Cornyn.

Summer of Love: 1967

The year 1967 had begun in San Francisco with a New Year's Eve bash that ended 1966 and ushered in the New Year with a concert by the Grateful Dead and Jefferson Airplane. After Graham did his New Year's countdown, the Grateful Dead began their set with "The Midnight Hour," the 1965 hit by Wilson Pickett.

In January, 1967, a "Be-In" was held in San Francisco which saw 20,000 people gathered to celebrate peace and love. The idea of a "Be-In" spread to New York, Los Angeles and other cities. The image of San Francisco as the counterculture's Mecca came from stories about the Hippies in Haight-Ashbury, the "Be-In" and the concerts at Bill Graham's Fillmore Ballroom.

Soon, there were other ballrooms in other cities; the Electric Ballroom, founded by Larry Magid, opened in Philadelphia; the Kinetic Playhouse, founded by Aaron Russo opened in Chicago; the Boston Tea Party opened by Don Law in Boston; the Psychedelic Supermarket opened by George Popodopous in New York; and in London, the Middle Earth Ballroom was opened. All of them modeled their operations after Bill Graham's Fillmore. Graham had achieved a position of wealth and power in San Francisco, although he had only been in business for a year.

Graham planned to open the Fillmore six nights a week, instead of just weekends, during 1967 and set up a free legal aid center that advised those busted for drugs, evading the draft or any other legal problems faced by young people. Graham co-opted the Haight-Ashbury Medical Clinic and his new role as a charitable benefactor enhanced his power and social status by giving him more prestige as well as leverage when dealing with city authorities.

Flowers in Your Hair

In May, 1967, the song "San Francisco (Be Sure To Wear Some Flowers In Your Hair)" by Scott McKenzie reached the national charts; that became the anthem for the Summer of Love and embrace the essence of "hippiedom." The song was written by John Phillips of the Mamas and Papas and McKenzie had sung with Phillips in a folk group, The Journeymen. The song reached the top five in the *Billboard* charts during the Summer of Love.

The Counterculture and The Hippies

Many of the young people coming into their teen years during the 1960s—the Baby Boomers—rejected the values of their parents and the 1950s and developed a "counterculture" in opposition to "the Establishment." That "counterculture" grew out of the Beat Generation, a literary movement during the 1950s led by Jack Kerouac, Allen Ginsberg and other "hipsters" who embraced a non-churched spirituality that championed individualism and idealism.

The Hippies (the term derives from "hipsters") also had a vision of non-churched spirituality that embraced individualism, idealism, a disdain for materialism and an anti-capitalism that sought a higher meaning to life than making money and accumulating possessions. During the 1960s, the counterculture stood against segregation and against the Vietnam War, which they felt was an unjust war. The social issues of civil rights, women's rights, gay rights, an eco-friendly view of the earth and a disdain for traditional authority were defining political positions for the counterculture.

The hippies were a relatively small part of the counterculture (although those outside the counterculture tended to view all those with long hair as "hippies") who embraced the philosophies of personal freedom, sexual liberation, drug use to attain a higher state of consciousness, astrology and Eastern philosophy as spiritual concepts, and communal living. Phrases such as "turn on, tune it and drop out," "whatever turns you on" and "do your own thing" were popular. At it's best, the Hippie Culture was filled with gentle souls who embraced the belief that love and peace would overcome all of the world's problems.

The Hippies used psychedelic drugs as a way to expand consciousness and expressed their views through street theater, alternative arts and music—from folk to psychedelic rock. Their lives were living protests of middle class values and the belief that the established culture was corrupt.

Monterey Pop Festival

The Great Dividing Line for the music of the 1960s came in March, 1967 when the Monterey Pop Festival was held at the Monterey Fairgrounds, about 100 miles south of San Francisco. From that point forward, Los Angeles—not New York—was the creative center for pop and rock music.

The idea for the festival originated with Alan Paraiser who had promoted a fund-raising concert in 1966 featuring the Byrds and Buffalo Springfield. Benny Shapiro, a booking agent in L.A. was his partner. Pariser hired Derek Taylor, former publicist for the Beatles who had recently moved to L.A. Taylor connected Pariser with John Phillips of the Mamas and Papas to see if that act would be a headliner. The group was hot; by this point they'd had hit singles with "California Dreamin'," "Monday, Monday," "I Saw Her Again," "Words of Love" and their current single, "Dedicated To The One I Love" was on the chart.

After Phillips became involved, he contacted Lou Adler, head of Ode Records, and the Mamas and Papas producer, and the two managed to gain control of the festival from Pariser, who had raised $50,000. They bought out Shapiro for $8,000.

The concept of the festival was that it was a fundraiser and the acts would perform free. Phillips and Adler formed a power packed committee to advise them that included Paul McCartney, Brian Wilson and Mick Jagger. They contacted filmmaker D.A. Pennebaker to film the event.

There were two different music scenes in California. In Los Angeles, the emphasis was on pop and rock recorded in studios. In San Francisco, the anti-business vibe prevailed in a mostly live music scene. San Francisco was home to great bands such as the Grateful Dead, Steve Miller Blues Band, Quicksilver Messenger Service, Country Joe and the Fish, Big Brother and the Holding Company, Moby Grape and Jefferson Airplane. Great bands, but no hits and, for many, no recording contracts. Los Angeles had acts who had hits. There was tension between the two communities but Bill Graham and Ralph J. Gleason, with the *San Francisco Chronicle*, acted as intermediaries and soothed tensions. Albert Grossman played an important role, delivering a package of talent that included the Paul Butterfield Blues Band, the Electric Flag, Al Kooper and the Blues Project.

The event began on Friday, June 16 and the first problem that arose came from a drug, "Monterey Purple," that was circulating. Festival organizers opened a "bummer tent" to take care of those who encountered problems with the drug. The Friday evening set began with a three song set by the Association, then The Paupers, Lou Rawls, Beverley Kutner, Johnny Rivers (who did ten songs), Eric Burdon & The Animals and finished with Simon and Garfunkle.

On Saturday afternoon, the line-up was Canned Heat, Big Brother and the Holding Company, Country Joe and the Fish, Al Kooper, The Butterfield Blues Band, Quicksilver Messenger Service, Steve Miller Band and The Electric Flag. The Saturday evening line-up was Moby Grape, Hugh Masekela, The Byrds, Laura Nyro, Jefferson Airplane, Booker T. & the M.G.s and Otis Redding. Rolling Stones manager Andrew Loog Oldham and convinced Phil Walden, Otis Redding's manager, to let Otis play to the audience of "white hippies" and Otis delivered to what he called "the love crowd."

On Sunday afternoon, Ravi Shankar performed Indian ragas for over three hours. That evening, the line-up was the Blues Project, Big Brother and the Holding Company, The Group With No Name, Buffalo Springfield, The Who, Grateful Dead and The Jimi Hendrix Experience, comprised of Hendrix, Mitch Mitchell and Noel Redding. During his performance that day, Hendrix played his Fender Stratocaster behind his back, made it scream, put it between his legs and humped it. As he played the Trogg's "Wild Thing," Hendrix poured lighter fluid on his guitar, set fire to it and then smashed it while the guitar shrieked before he flung it into the audience.

Closing the show was The Mamas & the Papas, who brought on Scott McKenzie to sing his hit, "San Francisco (Be Sure to Wear Flowers in Your Hair)" before they closed with "Dancing in the Street."

Jimi Hendrix

Mo Ostin and Joe Smith were aware that acts were breaking in England before they were released in the United States so they regularly read *Music Week*, the British trade magazine, to be aware of new British acts. That's how they learned about Jimi Hendrix and agreed to sign him before they'd heard him. The first time they saw Hendrix was at the Monterey Pop Festival and they were not sure exactly what they had signed. To put it mildly, Jimi Hendrix was *different*.

Jimi Hendrix was born Johnny Allen Hendrix in Seattle, Washington on November 27, 1942, the oldest of five children. His father, Al, was in the Army, stationed in Alabama, when Hendrix was born; he was refused a leave of absence for the impending birth and Al's commanding office had him locked in the stockade so he would not go AWOL to see his son. Al was in the stockade when he received a telegram announcing the birth.

Al was in the army for three years; he was discharged in September, 1945. Two months after his discharge Al saw his son for the first time. Al and his wife, Lucille (Jimi's mother) lived in poverty and moved often; he was often taken care of by family members; his three younger brothers and sister were given up to foster care and adoption. Jimi's father became violent when drinking and Jimi sometimes had to hide in a closet when his father drank.

Young Jimmy often carried a broom, pretending it was a guitar. His father refused to buy him a guitar and a social worker was unable to obtain a guitar for him. In 1957 Jim found a ukulele in garbage he was helping his father clear. Although the ukulele had only one string, Hendrix learned to play Elvis Presley songs on that one string.

In 1958 Hendrix's mother, Lucille, died but his father would not take Jimmy and his brother Leon to her funeral. That same year Jimmy finished Washington Junior High and began attending Garfield High school; he did not graduate. Around the middle of 1958, when Jimmy was 15 years old, he acquired his first guitar, an acoustic, and spent hours practicing, getting tips from those who knew how to play a guitar and listening to blues records by Muddy Waters, B.B. King, Howlin' Wolf and Robert Johnson. The first song he learned to play was "Peter Gunn," the theme from the TV show. Hendrix was left-handed but played a right-handed guitar; he did not re-string it for a left hander.

Hendrix met Billy Davis. the guitarist for Hank Ballard & the Midnighters, after he attended one of their concerts. Davis showed him some licks and helped him obtain a short gig with the Midnighters. Hendrix formed a band, the Velvetones, but, without an electric guitar, he was buried under the sound. In mid-1959, Hendrix's father bought him a Supra Ozark guitar but he was fired from the band because he showed off too much. Later, he joined the Rocking Kings but after a gig his guitar was stolen. His father then bought him a red Silvertone Danelectrro, a guitar made by Sears.

By the time he was 19, Jimmy Hendrix had been caught twice riding in a stolen car by authorities and had to choose between prison or joining the Army—a fairly common choice for young men in trouble. Hendrix chose the army and enlisted on May 31, 1961. After basic training at Fort Ord, California, he was assigned to the 101st Division in Fort Campbell, Kentucky, about an hour away from Nashville; he arrived on November 8. He wrote to his father, asking him to send his guitar and he did.

Hendrix played the guitar constantly, often ignoring his army duties.

Billy Cox was also in the service at Fort Campbell. Walking past an army club, Cox heard Hendrix playing his guitar and was intrigued. Cox met Hendrix and they jammed with Cox on bass; that led to weekend performances at base clubs with a group, the Casuals.

Hendrix completed his paratrooper training and received the Screaming Eagles patch in January, 1962 but his conduct—particularly playing guitar and ignoring his duties—led to criticism from his superiors. A Captain made the case for Hendrix to be discharged because his problematic behavior could not be solved by counseling or hospitalization.

During a parachute jump, Hendrix suffered an ankle injury, which gave the upper brass a good reason to discharge him, although his superiors and fellow enlistees agreed he was not cut out to be a soldier. Jimmy Hendrix received an honorable discharge on June 29, 1962.

Billy Cox was discharged in September, 1963. Cox and Hendrix lived in Clarksville, Tennessee and formed a band, the King Kasuals. Hendrix learned some tricks from other guitarists; he saw Butch Snipes in Seattle play the guitar with his teeth. That same trick was used by the other guitarist in Hendrix's band, Alphonso "Baby Boo" Young so Hendrix learned the same gimmick.

The band moved to Nashville where Jefferson Street was the main artery for the black section of town. Jefferson Street and the area in North Nashville where the clubs for blacks were located had a thriving R&B scene. During the next two years, Hendrix played in clubs in Nashville or in southern venues known as the "Chitlin' Circuit." Hendrix also worked as a backing musicians for acts that came through Nashville, such as Wilson Pickett, Slim Harpo, Sam Cool, Ike & Tina Turner and Jackie Wilson.

After two years in Nashville, where Hendrix developed his skills as a guitarist, he moved to Harlem in January, 1964. The next month, Hendrix won first prize in the Apollo Theater amateur contest. He played in various bands in Harlem and was hired by the Isley Brothers to be in their backing band, the I.B. Special.

Jimmy Hendrix was on several significant recording sessions; he was on the song "Testify" by the Isley Brothers and on "Mercy Mercy" by Don Covay. He toured with the Isleys until October, then left, and joined Little Richard's band, the Upsetters. In February, he played guitar on a Little Richard single, "I Don't Know What You Got (But It's Got Me)." In Los Angeles Hendrix played on a single by Rosa Lee Brooks, "My Diary," written by Arthur Love.

The first television appearance by Jimi Hendrix came in July, 1965, when he appeared on Nashville's "Night Train" on Channel 5 with Little Richard's band backing Buddy and Stacy.

Hendrix was fired from Little Richard's band (tardiness and stage antics, which upset Little Richard) and rejoined the Isley Brothers and recorded a single with them, "Move Over and Let Me Dance." In Fall, 1965, Hendrix joined Curtis Knight and the Squires and stayed with them for eight months; he played guitar on their single "How Would You Feel." He signed a three-year recording contract with Ed Chalpin, an entrepreneur, toured with Joey Dee and the Starliters, worked with King Curtis and played on a single by Ray Sharpe. His first composer credits came on two instrumentals, "Hornets Nest" and "Knock Yourself Out" that were released in 1966 as a Curtis Knight and the Squires single.

Jimi Hendrix moved to Greenwich Village in New York in 1966 and formed a band, Jimmy James and the Blue Flames and began developing the guitar style and material he later used with the Experience. He befriended Linda Keith, girlfriend of Keith Richards of the Rolling Stones, and she recommended him to Andrew Loog Oldham, manager of the Stones, and producer Seymour Stein but they rejected him. She then introduced him to Chas Chandler with the Animals, who wanted to quit the band to manage and produce him. Chandler loved the song, "Hey Joe" and thought it could be a hit with the right artist. Chandler brought Hendrix to London in September, 1966, signed him to a management and production contract with his partner Michael Jeffery, former manager of the Animals. Hendrix also acquired a girlfriend, Kathy Etchingham.

Chandler sought out musicians that complemented Hendrix's guitar playing for the Jimi Hendrix Experience. He recruited guitarist Noel Redding to play bass. Mitch Mitchell, who had been fired from Georgie Fame and the Blue Flames, was recruited to play drums. Chandler then convinced Jimmy Hendrix to become Jimi Hendrix.

On October 13, 1966, the Jimi Hendrix Experience performed their first concert in France as the opening act for French superstar Johnny Hallyday. They were signed to a recording contract with Track Records, owned by the Who's managers Kit Lambert and Chris Stamp. Hendrix came back to London and recorded "Stone Free," which he wrote, on November 2. The Jimi Hendrix Experience performed at the Bag O'Nails club in London; in the audience were Eric Clapton, John Lennon, Paul McCartney, Jeff beck, Pete Townshend, Brian Jones and Mick Jagger. The show was an astounding success and led to media coverage; Hendrix was quoted saying the group didn't want to be put in any category but if it must be labelled "I'd like it to be called 'Free Feeling.' It's a mixture of rock, freak-out, rave and blues."

Track Records negotiated a distribution agreement with Polydor for the U.K. and released the first single of the Jimi Hendrix Experience, "Hey Joe" in December. The group appeared on two TV shows, "Ready Steady Go!" and "Top of the Pops" and "Hey Joe" entered the charts and rose to number six.

In March, 1967, the Jimi Hendrix Experience had a hit in Britain with "Purple Haze" and then "The Wind Cries Mary" in May. Seeking media attention, journalist Keith Altham suggested the band do something more dramatic than the Who, who smashed their guitars during their show. Altham said it was unfortunate that Hendrix couldn't "set fire to your guitar." A can of lighter fluid was procured and at the end of their performance Hendrix sprayed lighter fluid on his guitar and set it on fire. Word quickly spread that Hendrix was a "Wild Man of Borneo."

The Jimi Hendrix Experience began work on their debut album, *Are You Experienced*, which was released on May 12, 1967, in the U.K. It contained the song "I Don't Live Today" where Hendrix displayed his feedback improvisation. It reached number two on the U.K. charts and remained on the chart for 33 weeks. The album ahead of it was *Sgt. Pepper's Lonely Hearts*

Club Band. During an appearance at the Saville Theater in London three days after Sgt. Pepper was released, Hendrix opened the show with the song "Sgt. Pepper's Lonely Hearts Club Band" with Paul McCartney and George Harrison in attendance. The two Beatles were blown away.

The first single released in the U.S. by the Jimi Hendrix Experience was "Hey Joe," released on May 1, 1967. Paul McCartney recommended Hendrix and his group to the organizers of the Monterey Pop Festival. McCartney told the organizers that the event "would be incomplete" if Hendrix didn't play and agreed to join the Board of Advisors if the Experience was booked to perform.

Taking the stage at the Festival, Hendrix opened with "Hey Joe," then did a B.B. King song, "Rock Me Baby," then Chip Taylor's "Wild Thing" and "Like a Rolling Stone" by Bob Dylan. Hendrix also performed four originals, "Foxy Lady," "Can You See Me," "The Wind Cries Mary" and "Purple Haze." At the conclusion of his set, Hendrix set fire to his guitar, then sat in front of the guitar with his hands raised while the guitar burned. After destroying his guitar, Hendrix threw pieces of it into the audience. Hendrix's performance at the Monterey Festival left the audience dazed in disbelief; they were stunned by the sound of Hendrix and the sight of him burning his guitar.

A picture of Hendrix in front of his burning guitar made national news. It became an iconic photo and gained him national attention.

Are You Experienced was released in the U.S. by Reprise Records on August 23; it reached number five on the *Billboard* album chart.

Albert Grossman and Jimi Hendrix

Albert Grossman signed Jimi Hendrix to a management contract for $100,000, then negotiated a recording contract with Warner Brothers. Bill Graham watched Albert Grossman operate and was impressed; it inspired him to work even more hours overseeing the Fillmore. Graham also booked the Winterland Auditorium and began promoting concerts at this larger venue on weekends.

Because Graham had trouble finding enough bands to play at the Fillmore, he began to book jazz, blues and R&B artists and mixed them with rock artists on a show. When the British Invasion of bands arrived in the United States, Graham quit booking jazz artists. Albert Grossman and Paul Butterfield encouraged him to book blues artists, who needed the exposure and were used to playing for low wages. During the first half of 1967, Graham booked Jimmy Reed, Otis Rush and His Chicago Blues Band,

B.B. King, Chuck Berry, Howlin' Wolf and Bo Diddley. Graham also held open auditions on Sundays and found Carlos Santana and Tower of Power at these open mic events.

After Monterey

The Monterey Pop Festival came during a time when FM "underground" radio was emerging and was staged a little over two weeks after the release of *Sergeant Pepper's Lonely Hearts Club Band*, who moved rock from teenage toe-tapping to "art." The influence of Sergeant Pepper was all over the Festival. Musically, the Festival had roots in folk, pop and soul but what really emerged was rock music, led by the Grateful Dead, Jimi Hendrix and Janis Joplin with Big Brother and the Holding Company.

The Monterey Pop Festival was a showcase of West Coast acts for New York as well as West Coast music executives. At the Festival from New York were Clive Davis of Columbia and Jerry Wexler of Atlantic Records. Mo Ostin and Joe Smith with Warner Brothers, Jerry Moss with A&M records and Lou Adler with Ode, who had the Mamas and Papas, were there from the West Coast.

Warner Brothers had signed the Grateful Dead and Jimi Hendrix. After the Festival, Clive Davis signed Big Brother and the Holding Company with singer Janis Joplin, the Electric Flag and songwriter Laura Nero. Capitol signed Steve Miller and Quicksilver Messenger Service.

In addition to signing acts, major labels began hiring in-house hippies or "company freaks" to communicate with the acts, who would not and could not relate to music executives in suits and ties. Among those "in-house hippies" were Andy Wickham at Reprise, Derek Taylor at A&M and David Anderle at Elektra. Label executives began shedding suits and ties until the executives looked like the rock acts. The look as well as the sound of music was changing.

After Monterey, there was no doubt that the creative center of rock music had shifted from New York to California but there were changes. The innocence of beach music and pop in Los Angeles met the business minded New York way of doing business while in San Francisco, the hippie dreams in Haight-Asbury were invaded by con-men, drug dealers and motorcycle gangs.

Clive Davis

Clive Davis was born in Brooklyn, New York (April 4, 1932); his father was an electrician and salesman. When he was a teenager, first his mother, then his father died so he lived with his married sister. He received a full scholarship to attend New York University, where he majored in Political Science, and then a scholarship to Harvard Law School, where he graduated in 1956. Davis practiced for a small, New York firm for two years, then joined Rosenman, Colin, Kaye, Petschek and Freund, which represented CBS. The law firm served as a quasi-farm club for CBS executives; Harvey Schein had been with the law firm before he joined CBS as general counsel and he hired Clive Davis to join CBS as assistant counsel for Columbia Records. A year later, Davis was made general counsel for Columbia.

In 1965, William Paley and Goddard Lieberson decided to reorganize CBS. At that point, CBS had the network, Columbia and Epic record labels, Fender Guitars, Leslie Speakers, Rogers Drums, Steinway Pianos and Creative Playthings, which made musical toys. Prevailing wisdom said that large firms should own a diverse collection of companies that were somehow connected to the parent company. That's why musical instruments became part of a company with two record labels and also why it was decided to establish a musical instruments division.

Clive Davis had done much of the legal work on contracts with the companies under the CBS umbrella, which led Goddard Lieberson to offer Davis the position as head of the musical instruments division. Davis hesitated giving an answer; since Fender, the centerpiece of the instruments division was in California, it might mean moving to California and Clive Davis was a New Yorker.

Davis was spared making the difficult decision when Lieberson called him shortly after making the offer and said that executive vice president Norman Adler, head of the record club, liked the idea of heading the new instruments division and wanted to move to California. Lieberman then offered Davis the position of administrative vice president of Columbia Records, which meant Davis would oversee all of Columbia Records.

"Columbia was a hotbed of political maneuvering," stated Davis in his autobiography, *The Soundtrack of My Life*. He felt that Lieberson named him to head Columbia, although he lacked a musical background or training, because he was "unlikely to make rash or unnecessarily provocative moves simply because I now had the power to do so" and "while I wasn't a music expert, I obviously enjoyed music and got along well with both creative people and executives."

In his book, Davis noted that Goddard Lieberson had led Columbia "to pre-eminence in the worlds of classical music and Broadway show recordings" and was "a towering figure in New York's cultural life" with his wife, Vera Zorina and the two were "a glamorous power couple."

"Goddard was elegant, informed, incredibly witty, and very articulate," wrote Davis. "as attractive a figure to the high-end media as many of the artists on the label. He was always very handsomely turned out. Matching his pocket handkerchief with his English-made shirts was a signature element of his style," which, Davis added, "I have adopted to this day."

Lieberson admired and socialized with Leonard Bernstein and Richard Rodgers "without being pretentious or arrogant about it," wrote Davis. "He was as accomplished and well known a producer as he was an executive. His stature reflected on the entire company, and when he spoke at Columbia's annual conventions, he was invariably eloquent and always hilarious, and we were rapt. Everyone at Columbia was devoted to him, proud to have him as our standard-bearer."

Davis added that Lieberson, although he became president of the record label in 1956 "never relinquished his identity to the corporation. He was his own person, exactly who he was at all time" whose "charm, individuality, and personal command rendered him a superb counterexample of that stereotype of anonymity" and "remade Columbia Records in his own image, rather than the other way around."

Davis stated that, as he worked with Lieberson, "my respect for him only grew. Along with, in my experience, John Hammond at Columbia and Ahmet Ertegun and Jerry Wexler at Atlantic, Goddard was one of the very rare people who responded to music with a completely unalloyed passion. When he was listening to something he loved, all distinctions of age, class, race and background evaporated."

Clive Davis was 33 when he was named to head Columbia and noted that "a lot of executives feel that they need to kick the applecart over as soon as they take their job, but I think it's essential to take some time and diagnose the situation thoroughly. Even in circumstances that have gone bad, not everything or everyone is a problem. You want to make the right moves, not just make moves for their own sake. So at first my approach was simple: listen, watch, observe."

The first problem he had to deal with was Mitch Miller, who's *Sing Along With Mitch* series of albums were no longer selling in acceptable numbers and his TV show was no longer popular; it had been cancelled in 1964 and Miller left Columbia the following year, during the time of the CBS reorganization.

Lieberson and Miller went back a long way; they met when both were at the Eastman School of Music and Lieberson hired him to head Columbia's A&R department in 1950. During the 1950s, Miller worked with Tony Bennett, Ray Conniff, Percy Faith, Johnny Mathis, Doris Day and Rosemary Clooney during a golden age of pop music and those artists sold well. Their music was the music Miller loved but his musical taste would not allow him to accept the appeal rock'n'roll. In the mid-1950s when rock'n'roll made its mark, Columbia only had Johnny Cash on their roster. Miller defended his dismissal of rock'n'roll but a deeper problem was that he was outspoken in his distaste of rock,

Mitch Miller proclaimed that rock'n'roll was "musical baby food" that was "the worship of mediocrity." He loudly proclaimed that "much of the juvenile stuff pumped over the air waves these days hardly qualified as music." As a result, Columbia Records was perceived as hostile to the music that defined the teenage culture in the mid-50s and 1960s.

Bob Dylan "went electric" in 1965 and Columbia signed the Byrds and Simon and Garfunkel but the best selling rock act in mid-1965 was Paul Revere and the Raiders, who were regulars on the Dick Clark produced TV show "Where the Action Is." Epic Records had the Dave Clark Five and the Yardbirds but at Columbia, "We were very thin in the music of tomorrow," stated Davis. "When the music scene changes, you can't be content with just doing more of what you've been doing all along, however good you may be at it. You can't just relive your former glory. That's the hardest thing for executives, even very creative executives," said Davis, who added that it was difficult for artists as well because "You've got to know when you've got to build for the future."

That led Clive Davis to "my lifelong habit of bringing home and listening to all the major records on the charts every week, just to develop a clear sense of what's going on....You can never take your understanding of the market for granted. To break the rules creatively you have to know what the rules are. Your own taste is not the issue," stated Davis. "Music is always evolving, and it's essential to understand how and when it does, and what you need to do about it."

Clive Davis spent a lot of time listening to the Top 40 stations in New York, absorbing the new sounds and, in 1966, signed his first act, Donovan, a British singer on Pye Records who'd had three chart records in the United States with Hickory Records, based on Nashville. Donovan was touted in England as the next Bob Dylan so, wanting to avoid a conflict with Dylan,

Davis signed Donovan to Epic where he had a number one song, "Sunshine Superman.," followed by "Mellow Yellow" in 1966.

Lou Adler was the producer of the Mamas and Papas, Barry McGuire, Johnny Rivers and Jan and Dean. He and three others owned Dunhill Records, which they sold to ABC, which created the ABC-Dunhill label. Adler then started Ode Records; his attorney was Abe Somer who had also done business with Clive Davis. Somer represented the duo Chad and Jeremy, who were on Columbia. Somer suggested a distribution agreement whereby Columbia would distribute Ode; Davis agreed.

The first release in that agreement was for "San Francisco (Be Sure to Wear Flowers in Your Hair)" by Scott McKenzie. Since singer/songwriter John Phillips and Lou Adler were among the organizers and producers of the Monterey Pop Festival, Adler and Somer encouraged Davis to attend the Festival, which had Columbia acts Simon and Garfunkel and the Byrds on the bill. Davis agreed and that's how Clive Davis experienced a life-changing event for both himself and Columbia Records.

Clive Davis at Monterey

In the sea of humanity attending the Monterey Festival, most of the crowd wore head scarves, cut-offs, flowing robes, jeans, t-shirts or no shirts), sandals (or no shoes) and an assortment of face paint, beads and bells. Clive Davis wore "a V-neck tennis sweater in the traditional white, maroon, and black, over white pants. I was totally unprepared for what was happening in Haight-Ashbury, which seemed to have transported itself in toto to Monterey for the weekend as easily as I had flown in from New York," wrote Davis. "Monterey proved to be an eye-opener that was stunning in its impact."

The headliners were in the evening but the new, fresh talent played during the daytime. Clive Davis's ideas of meeting business associates, catching some shows and relaxing in California ended as an awakening occurred. "I was in the audience simply because there was nowhere else to go," remembered Davis.

Clive Davis was impressed with the Electric Flag, led by Mike Bloomfield and then, on Saturday afternoon, saw the set by Big Brother and the Holding Company, led by vocalist Janis Joplin. "Big Brother played a short set, five songs, and were onstage for perhaps thirty minutes," remembered Davis. "But they took the crowd in an emotional journey that made it seem as if they had performed for hours" while Joplin "radiated a desperate sexual heat."

Joplin's performance "bought the entire meaning of the festival itself home to me," stated Davis. "I thought, how could it be that none of us in the East knew that this was taking place?" He realized "This has got to be my moment...I've got to sign this band."

No one knew except the accountants and top executives that Columbia Records was barely breaking even; it was a label on the brink of irrelevance if they did not establish themselves as a rock'n'roll label in tune with the young audience in the 1960s. Davis had not originally planned to sign any acts at Monterey but, watching those performances, he knew he had to act and act quickly.

Albert Grossman managed the Electric Flag; Columbia had recently re-signed Bob Dylan so Davis and Grossman had a working relationship. Signing the Electric Flag was relatively easy; Grossman then suggested Columbia sign the Steve Miller Band and Quicksilver Messenger Service. Davis agreed but Grossman was unable to obtain managerial rights so those deals fell through.

Big Brother and the Holding Company was managed by Julius Karpen; Davis met him backstage and asked about signing the group. Karpen referred him to Bob Gordon, the group's attorney, who informed Davis that Big Brother had signed a contract with Mainstream Records, a small, independent label owned by Bob Shad who had produced some demo sessions on the band. The performance at Monterey led Shad to plan an album release but he did not want the band to work on the rough recordings they had made, which made the band dissatisfied. Shad released the album, which made the negotiations to sign with Columbia more difficult.

Albert Grossman took over management of Big Brother after they fell out with Julius Karpen. Grossman bought Big Brother out of its contract with Shad for $200,000, which Grossman expected the label to reimburse. Half of that would be the label's investment and the other half was recoupable, which meant the band would have to earn that money back through record sales before they received any royalties. Columbia advanced the band $50,000—another recoupable—to record the album while Mainstream received a two percent override on the band's first two Columbia albums. That meant that Columbia had put up $250,000 for a relatively unknown band with no track record of hits or sales success. It took almost a year from the time Clive Davis first saw the band at Monterey until the deal was finally finished.

Then Clive Davis needed to meet the band.

"When dealing with artists or creative people generally, it's wise to make sure that you put them at ease," said Davis. "They tend to be wary of business people, even as they also want to be absolutely sure that you know how to take care of them professionally and don't want to be around them just because it's cool. Keeping boundaries clear while being as warm and friendly as possible always works best for me. I have always been available to artists from 9:30 a.m. to 8 p.m. every working day. I rarely do social dinners with artists. But up until the evening meal—usually around 8:30—I always take their calls and I'm ready with the best advice or information my expertise can offer."

Before they met, Albert Grossman had relayed the request that Joplin wanted to "ball" him to cement the deal. "That would be her way of showing this is a more meaningful relationship," said Grossman. As politely as he could, Davis declined having sex with Janis Joplin.

During their meeting, Davis told them that he wanted to be an artist friendly label and that, despite being housed in the formidable "Black Rock" building, the company was informal. At the end of the meeting, before a press conference, one of the members said he needed to get dressed. Another band member threw him a shirt and as he stood up to put on the shirt, Davis realized he had been sitting at the table naked. "This is how informal we are," said Joplin to Davis.

Shortly after Monterey, Clive Davis was named president of Columbia Records.

"All You Need is Love"

On June 14, the Beatles were in Olympic studio where they recorded the tracks to "All You Need Is Love." There had been an announcement on May 18 that the Beatles would be on a TV program where they would perform live for a worldwide audience via a satellite link-up. The Beatles had to come up with a song for this landmark event and Lennon wrote "All You Need Is Love."

The event, titled "Our World," was scheduled to be shown in 118 countries with a potential audience of 500 million, although 150 million potential viewers were lost when 23 Communist countries dropped out. The show was scheduled for Sunday, June 25.

Work continued on "All You Need is Love" with overdubs on basic tracks and an orchestra, which was overdubbed on June 23.

On Sunday, the Beatles arrived at the studio at 2 p.m. and rehearsed the song from 3 to 5 p.m. The group played to a pre-recorded rhythm track but the vocals, McCartney's bass guitar, George Harrison's lead guitar, Ringo's drums and the orchestra were all live. Lennon decided not to play guitar but concentrated on his vocal. In the control room were Beatles producer George Martin and engineer Geoff Emerick, who fed a mono mix directly to a BBC van and then the world.

The session took on the aspects of a party. The orchestra musicians performed in tuxedos but the Beatles and their friends were casually, but colorfully dressed. In the studio audience were Mick Jagger, Marianne Faithfull, Keith Richard, Keith Moon, Eric Clapton, Pattie Harrison, Jane Asher, Mike McCartney, Graham Nash and his wife, Gary Leeds and Hunter Davies, the Beatles first official biographer. George Martin, in a white suit, was in the control room.

After the event, John Lennon re-recorded some of his vocal track.

On July 7, "All You Needs Is Love" was issued as a single, backed with "Baby, You're a Rich Man." It was five weeks after the *Sergeant Pepper's* album, but there were no singles issued from that album.

"All You Need Is Love" (not on the album) became a number one single, their fifty-third single on the *Billboard* Hot 100. It was the perfect message for the "Summer of Love" and the perfect coda for the Monterey Pop Festival when it was performed a week after the Festival ended.

Death of Brian Epstein

On August 22, the Beatles recorded basic tracks for "Your Mother Should Know" for the Magical Mystery Tour project. The Beatles manager, Brian Epstein, attended an overdub session the next day. On August 24 the Beatles met the Maharishi Mahesh Yogi and the next day left for Bangor, in north Wales, for a weekend studying Transcendental Meditation with the Yogi. On August 27, the Beatles were informed that their manager had died on Saturday evening, from a reported accidental overdose.

The Doors

In July, 1965, Jim Morrison, who had attended the UCLA School of Theater, Film and Television, met Ray Manzarek, who had also attended that school, on a Venice Beach. During their conversation, Morrison told Manzarek he had been writing songs and poems and Manzarek encouraged him to sing one; he sang "Moonlight Drive."

Ray Manzarek played keyboards and, with his brothers Rick and Jim, was in a band, Rick & the Ravens. John Densmore was a drummer with the Psychedelic Rangers; he had met Manzarek in meditation classes. Morrison became lead singer, Densmore joined the group and, with bass player Patty Sullivan the group recorded a six song demo in September. Manzarek's two brothers and Sullivan left and guitarist Robby Krieger joined the group, which changed its name to "The Doors" after *The Doors of Perception*, a book by Aldous Huxley. That book title came from The Marriage of Heaven and Hell by William Blake, which said "If the doors of perception were cleansed, everything would appear to man as it is: infinite."

The group became the house band for the London Fog, a club in Los Angeles which had a small clientele. The Doors used the sparsely crowded club to write and polish their songs, "The End," "When the Music's Over" and "Light My Fire." The Doors were then hired by the Whisky a Go Go as the house band. They opened for acts such as Them, led by Van Morrison.

The group wanted to land a recording contract and Jim Morrison had visited a number of labels without success. Their only recording demo was the one done for Aura Records, a subsidiary of Pacific Jazz Records owned by Richard Bock. Arthur Lee, leader of Love, recommend the group to Jac Holzman who, with producer Paul Rothchild, saw them perform several times at the Whiskey a Go Go. On August 18, 1967, the Doors were signed to Elektra Records. Three days later, the group was fired from the Whiskey after Morrison added a profanity laced verse to "The End.".

On August 24 The Doors went into Sunset Sound Recording Studios with producer Paul Rothchild and engineer Bruce Botnick and began recording their first album, which included a 12 minute version of "The End" as well as "Break On Through (To The Other Side)," "Light My Fire," a cover of Willie Dixon's "Back Door Man" and seven others.

The album was released on January 4, 1967. Their first single, "Break On Through (To The Other Side)" entered the *Billboard* Hot 100 on April 8 but only lasted one week, peaking at number 126. Their second single, "Light My Fire" entered the Hot 100 on June 3 and rose to number one, where it remained for three weeks. The song was originally seven minutes long, with extensive instrumental breaks but producer Rothchild edited the song down to three minutes before its release. They released two more singles in 1967, "People Are Strange" and "Love Me Two Times."

The debut album, *The Doors*, entered the *Billboard* chart on March 25 and reached the number two spot, where it remained for two weeks and stayed on the chart for 121 weeks. They second album was also released in 1967 and entered the *Billboard* chart on November 4, reaching number three.

Ed Sullivan had signed The Doors for seven appearances on his show. On September 17, they performed on "The Ed Sullivan Show." Network executives insisted that the word "higher" not be sung but during the show Morrison sang the song in its entirety; he either never intended to delete the term or forgot because of nervousness. Sullivan was upset, cancelled the remaining six scheduled appearances and told the group they'd never appear on his show again. Morrison reportedly replied, "Hey man. We just *did* the Sullivan Show."

Jim Morrison was arrested during a performance in New Haven, Connecticut on December 9. Morrison was in a shower stall before the concert, making out with a girl, when a police officer—unaware that Morrison was the singer of the band about to go on--told them both to leave. Morrison replied "Eat It." The policemen pulled out a can of mace and told Morrison, "Last chance," to which Morrison replied "Last chance to eat it." The police then sprayed mace on both Morrison and the girl; Morrison could not immediately perform and the show was halted for an hour to allow Morrison to recover. After he took the stage, Morrison taunted the police, making up a song about "little blue men" that contained profanity. The police charged Morrison and dragged him off stage to the police station while the crowd became unruly. Morrison was booked on charges of inciting a riot, indecency and public obscenity.

Several weeks later the charges were dropped.

The Doors were a very literate band; producer Paul Rothchild stated that, during the time he was their producer, he never saw the members without a book they were reading. That was reflected on Morrison's poetry and his use of myths and literature in his songs.

The Doors were one of the most charismatic acts that emerged during the Summer of Love. In his performances, Morrison captured life lived on the edge, but he succumbed to self-destructive behavior and drug use. At the end of the Summer of Love, Jim Morrison only had a few more years to live.

"Never My Love"

"Never My Love" was written by Don and Dick Addrisi and recorded by The Association; it entered the *Billboard* Hot 100 on August 26, 1967. The single followed "Windy," which was a number one song for the group. Their previous hits included "Along Comes Mary" and "Cherish," which also reached number one.

"Never My Love" reached number two on the Hot 100 chart and became a standard; by December, 1967 16 other artists had recorded it and the Fifth Dimension had a hit with it in 1971. It was the second most played song on radio during the twentieth century, behind "You've Lost That Lovin' Feeling" and ahead of "Yesterday."

The roots of the Association go back to 1962 when Jules Alexander and Terry Kirkman met in Hawaii while Alexander was in the Navy; in 1963 they reunited in Los Angeles and began performing. In 1964 they were members of the Inner Tubes with Doug Dillard, a folk group that featured, at different times, Cass Elliott and David Crosby. In February, 1965, they were part of a 13-piece rock band, The Men, which disbanded but six members formed The Association. They rehearsed for five months, then landed a gig at The Ice House in Pasadena. They auditioned for labels, released a single, "Babe, I'm Gonna Leave You" on Jubilee and then the Dylan song, "One Too Many Mornings" on Valiant. Jules Alexander heard "Along Comes Mary, written by Tandyn Almer, when he played on the demo and the song entered the Billboard Hot 100 on June 6, 1966 and rose to number seven. The follow—up, "Cherish," written by Kirkman, entered the chart on August 27 and reached number one, where it remained for three weeks. Valiant was bought by Warner Brothers and "Windy" entered the Hot 100 on May 27, 1967 and reached number one and remained in that position for four weeks.

Changes

After the 1960s, people—at least young whites--sat and listened and the acts that developed came through the recording studio, not the dance hall. The music changed; the *Sergeant Pepper's* album by the Beatles forced critics who did not like rock music to take it seriously while fans began to view rock music as "art" and not just entertainment. Musicians became more serious, more introspective, more intent on expressing and pleasing themselves rather than pleasing a crowd.

When the music industry became Big Business it became serious because of the money involved. It also became serious because young, white musicians were no longer playing for dancers having fun; instead, they played for sitting listeners intent on extracting meaning and purpose from the songs.

Race Riots

Police raided an after-hours nightclub in Detroit in July where Black Power advocates often met and arrested 75. That led to race riots in Detroit that were declared to be the "worst in U.S. History" with property damage estimated at $500 million. Four days of violence, fire bombing and looting left 38 dead and parts of the city in charred ruins. Rioting in Newark, New

Jersey from racial strive led to rioting in 70 cities, including Atlanta, Boston, Philadelphia, Birmingham, New York and Cincinnati. The new president of the Student Non-Violent Coordinating Committee, H. Rap Brown, called on African-Americans to "wage guerrilla war on the honkie white man," adding, "I love violence."

In July, Brown was arrested when fires broke out in Cambridge, Maryland after he urged a crowd of 400 young blacks to "burn this town down."

Blacks were protesting high unemployment, poor housing conditions and the hopelessness they felt in city ghettos.

Charley Pride

There were racial tensions and race riots during 1967. White southerners, who fought against integration and civil rights legislation were often at the forefront of efforts to continue segregation practices, and yet the first black country music star emerged during that time.

Manager Jack Johnson was looking for an African-American country singer when he met Charley Pride at the Cedarwood Publishing offices on Music Row. Jack Clement persuaded Chet Atkins to sign Pride to RCA and in 1967 Pride had his first chart record, "Just Between You and Me." Early releases of Pride did not include his picture; it was only after he had established himself with several chart singles that country radio and country fans knew that Charlie Pride was African-American.

Stax: Otis Redding

During his short life, Otis Redding was the heart and soul of Stax Records. He came to the attention of the label because he drove his friend, guitarist Johnny Jenkins, from Macon, Georgia to Memphis so Jenkins could record a session. Jenkins had a regional hit with "Love Twist," an instrumental that Atlantic distributed. Since Atlantic had an option on his next record, Jenkins went to Memphis to record.

Otis was the singer in the Pinetoppers, which featured Jenkins. Jenkins was managed by 22-year old Phil Waldon, a recent graduate of Mercer College in Macon; Waldon became the manager of Otis Redding. Born in Dawson, Georgia, Redding moved to Macon and dropped out of school in the tenth grade to perform in clubs. In Macon, Redding regularly won the talent contest at the Douglass Theatre, which was broadcast on WIBB as "The Teenage Party." Jenkins, a local celebrity, saw Redding perform at the Douglass and began playing behind him.

Jenkins had recorded "Love Twist" for the Tifco label, created by Phil Waldon and a local banker. Atlantic's southeastern rep, Joe Galkin, took the record to Jerry Wexler at Atlantic, who distributed it. Galkin then arranged for the session at Stax and insisted that Redding be recorded. Otis did "These Arms of Mine," which was released on Volt, an R&B subsidiary of Stax, in October, 1962. It hit the charts the following March from extensive airplay by John R. at WLAC in Nashville, after the disc jockey had been cut in for a share of the royalties.

Redding had a string of hits and became the top selling artist in the Stax family. In 1967 a Stax-Volt tour ended in March; in June he played the Monterey Pop Festival and the Fillmore in San Francisco. Redding had been listening to the *Sergeant Pepper* album by the Beatles, which had been released in June, and was a long-time fan of Sam Cooke's *Live at the Copa* album.

During the week of the Fillmore engagement, Redding lived on a houseboat in Sausalito with his road manager, Speedo Simms. That was where he first developed the idea for "Sittin' On the Dock of the Bay."

Redding returned to Macon exhausted; he had to have throat polyps removed and was off the road for two months in the Fall of 1967. He wrote a number of songs during that time and in early December took 30 new songs into the Stax studio to record over the next two weeks.

Redding finished "Dock of the Bay" in the studio with guitarist Steve Cropper helping him; the song was recorded with Booker T. Jones on piano, Duck Dunn on bass, Cropper on guitar and Al Jackson on drums. It was quite different from previous Redding songs and most of those close to Redding initially did not like the song. Jim Stewart, head of Stax, did not want the song released, but Redding loved it.

The recording sessions ended on Thursday, December 7, 1967; on Saturday, Redding flew to Cleveland for a TV show. On Sunday, he had a performance scheduled at the Factory Club in Madison, Wisconsin. The winter weather was terrible and all commercial flights had been grounded; however, Redding insisted the date be fulfilled so the plane took off. At 3:28 that afternoon it crashed into the icy waters of Lake Monona, just outside Madison.

The Bar-Kays were formed in Memphis in the mid-60s and were the second string studio group for Stax; they also became known as one of the top back-up groups on the road. Comprised originally of Jimmy King, guitar; Ron Caldwell, organ; Phalin Jones, sax; Carl Cunningham, drums;

Ben Cauley, trumpet; and James Alexander, bass, the group was with Otis Redding in December, 1967 when their plane crashed, killing Redding and four members of the group. Ben Cauley was the only survivor of that plane crash; James Alexander was spared when he missed the flight.

The funeral was held at Macon's City Auditorium where 4,500 people, including a who's who of R&B music attended.

After the death of 26-year old Otis Redding, the label released "Sittin' On the Dock of the Bay." It entered the *Billboard* Hot 100 on January 27 and rose to number one--Redding's first pop number one--and remained in that position for four weeks. It entered the R&B chart a week later and remained at number one on that chart for three weeks.

Aretha Franklin & The Muscle Shoals Sessions

Aretha Franklin was born in Memphis and raised in Buffalo and Detroit where her father, famed preacher Rev. C. L. Franklin pastored the New Bethel Baptist Church. "The Queen of Soul" had a strong gospel background; she first recorded in 1956 for JVB/Battle and was then signed to Columbia in 1960 by legendary A&R man John Hammond. At Columbia she had her first chart record on the Hot 100 in 1961 but mainly recorded show tunes and pop songs.

Jerry Wexler signed Aretha to Atlantic Records and wanted her to record in Muscle Shoals; in January, 1967 Wexler, engineer Tommy Dowd, Aretha and her husband, Ted White, went to Rick Hall's studio for a week's worth of recording. Wexler had arranged for guitarist Chips Moman and bass player Tommy Cogbill to come down from Memphis and join the rhythm section at Fame Studio, joining Jimmy Johnson (rhythm guitar), Spooner Oldham (keyboards) and Roger Hawkins (drums).

The first song recorded was "I Never Loved a Man (The Way I Love You)," with Aretha playing piano. The second song, "Do Right Woman," written by Chips Moman and Dan Penn, did not come off well; Dan Penn did the scratch vocal because Aretha couldn't hook the melody in the studio.

That evening, at the hotel, an argument broke out between Rick Hall, Ted White, Aretha and Jerry Wexler. The next day, Aretha and her husband were back in New York; she never returned to Muscle Shoals to record again. However, Jerry Wexler, who knew they had captured magic in Muscle Shoals, flew the Muscle Shoals players to New York to finish the recording sessions with Aretha.

"Respect" was part of the "Muscle Shoals sessions" that were actually recorded in New York with Muscle Shoals musicians. The song is credited to Otis Redding, who originally intended to produce the song on Speedo Simms and The Premiers. The group had actually developed the song as a ballad; Otis re-wrote the song but Simms could not pull it off in the studio. Like many other singers, Simms was a great live performer but could not master the recording studio. Finally, Redding decided to do the song; his version entered the *Billboard* Hot 100 and R&B charts on September 4, 1965. Aretha's recording, which became the definitive version of that song, entered the Billboard Hot 100 on April 29, 1967 and climbed to number one; it entered the R&B chart on May 6 and remained number one for eight weeks.

Redding reportedly said, after he heard Aretha's version, "I've lost my song."

Columbia Record Club

In 1967 the Columbia Record Club had over a million members and was an important way to sell records to rural customers or those who chose to stay home and shop for records by mail order. Their competitors were the RCA and Capitol Records clubs but none of the clubs sold records made by their major competitors. Columbia had expanded to manufacture and sell the Verve, Mercury, Warner Brothers, Kapp, Vanguard and United Artists labels and controlled 60-70 percent of the very lucrative mail order business.

Buffalo Springfield

Neil Young formed The Squires in Winnipeg, Canada in 1963; in 1965 they performed at the Fourth Dimension in Thunder Bay, Ontario where he met Stephen Stills, who was on tour with The Company, a spin-off of the Au Go Go Singers. At the end of the tour, Still moved to Los Angeles where he scrambled for work as a guitarist and singer. Producer Barry Friedman encouraged Stills to form a band and Stills invited Richie Furay and Ken Koblun, who had been with the Au Go Go Singers when he was a member, to move to Los Angeles, and they did. However, Koblun soon decided to leave and join another group.

In 1966, Neil Young was invited to join a Toronto group, the Mynah Birds by bassist Bruce Palmer; the group needed a lead guitarist. The Mynah Birds singer was Ricky James Matthews, later known as Rick James. The group was scheduled to record an album for Motown but Matthews was arrested by the U.S. Navy for being AWOL so their album was cancelled.

Young and Palmer decided to go to Los Angeles; Young drove down in his car, a large black converted hearse. Sitting in a traffic jam on Sunset

Boulevard, Stephen Stills and Richie Furay, driving in the opposite direction, recognized Young and flagged him down.

Stills, Furay, Young and Palmer added drummer Dewey Martin and bassist Chris Hillman to form Buffalo-Springfield. The group first performed at the Troubadour and then became the opening act for the Dillards and the Byrds during a short tour in California.

Buffalo Springfield became the house band at the Whisky a Go-Go on the Sunset Strip for seven weeks—from May 2 to June 18, 1966—after Hillman convinced the owner to hire them. Their performances attracted attention and Barry Friedman, who had been their manager, was shoved out of the picture and management was taken over by Charlie Greene and Brian Stone, who managed Sonny and Cher. Greene and Stone negotiated with Ahmet Ertegun to sign the band to Atlantic for a four-album contract with a $12,000 advance.

The group recorded their first album at the Gold Star Studio in Hollywood. Their first single, written by Young, was "Nowadays Clancy Can't Even Sing," which entered the Billboard Hot 100 on August 20, 1966 but only reached the 110 position.

On Saturday, November 12, 1966—Neil Young's birthday—radio stations announced the closing of Pandora's Box Club on Sunset Strip. Flyers were sent out, inviting youth to demonstrate because of the club's closing and because the Los Angeles Police Department, responding to complaints from local residents and businesses about the crowds and congestion along the Sunset Strip from young people visiting clubs and hanging out. The police had treated the young protestors roughly.

The demonstration on Saturday, November 12 attracted around a thousand people and began peacefully but trouble soon erupted. The demonstrations continued through the rest of November and into December.

About a week later, Stills was at a party where he wrote "For What It's Worth (Something's Happening Here)." The title came when Stills said to Ahmet Ertegun, "I've got a song here, for what it's worth, if you want it." Ertegan added ("Hey, Stop, What's That Sound") so it would be more recognizable.

The song was first performed at the Whisky a Go Go on Thanksgiving night and was recorded on December 5, 1966; the guitar line was played by Neil Young. Atlantic released it in January and it caught on immediately in Los Angeles. It entered the *Billboard* Hot 100 on January 23, 1967 and rose to number seven.

Their debut album, *Buffalo Springfield*, had been released but had not had any success until the album was withdrawn and "For What It's Worth" was added; the album entered the *Billboard* album chart on March 25, 1967 and reached number 80.

In January, 1967, Bruce Palmer was deported for possession of marijuana; the group used several bassists until he returned in June. There was dissension and bickering between Young and Stills and each insisted on producing their own compositions for their second album. There was also dissatisfaction with their management team of Greene and Stone. At the Monterey Pop Festival, Young was absent and David Crosby sat in for him, causing a conflict between the Byrds and Crosby.

In October, Young returned to the group, which severed ties with Greene and Stone. Ahmet Ertegun oversaw their second album, *Buffalo Springfield Again*, which was released in November. The ten song album contained four songs written by Stills, three written by Young and Furay each; songs included "Mr. Soul," "Broken Arrow," "Bluebird" and "A Child's Claim to Fame."

Bruce Palmer was deported again in January, 1968 and the band was an opening act for the Beach Boys. After Palmer's deportation, Jim Messina, who engineered their second album, was hired as bassist for the Springfield.

Conflicts between Stills and Young escalated with Young increasingly absent. They had recorded the songs for their final album by the end of March and in April, 1968, Young, Furay and Messina were arrested for disturbing the peace for making too much noise at a party with Eric Clapton.

The band members met with Ahmet Ertegun after a performance at the Long Beach Arena to discuss their break-up. It was agreed that Young would go to Warner Brothers while Stills and Furay would remain with Atlantic. Their final album, *Last Time Around*, was comprised of tracks recorded from mid-1967 until early, 1968. That album entered the *Billboard* album chart on August 17, 1968 and reached number 42 on that chart.

The Pop Market

Just like the rock revolution of the 1950s, the British rock invasion of the early and mid-1960s had another side: the white middle class market. It seems odd to look back and realize that in 1965, when the Beatles were outselling every other act in the America, the next best selling act was Herb Alpert and the Tijuana Brass.

Alpert had begun his own record label, A & M, in 1962 with partner Jerry Moss. The label had begun with a hit single, "The Lonely Bull," which featured two trumpets playing in harmony with the Mexican mariachi sound. In 1965 the five LPs released by the group sold 5.3 million and their singles sold 2.5 million.

In 1966 the Tijuana Brass sold 13 million copies of their LPs.

Radio and the Record Business

Business for the recording industry was going well: it was announced that in 1967 the industry passed the billion dollar mark for the first time. The LP was still the dominant configuration but tape sales were $234 million. In mid-1967 the price of all monaural records was raised to equal that of their stereo counterparts; soon monaural records would be a thing of the past.

Stereo had received a major boost when the FCC approved FM stereo broadcasting in 1962; however 60 percent of the 990 FM stations broadcast the same thing as their AM counterparts as station owners duplicated their programming. On October 15, 1965 the FCC ruled that all jointly owned AM/FM stations located in markets with over 100,000 people had to present non-duplicated music at least half the time. That ruling would go into effect on January 1, 1967.

FM was floundering at that time; at the end of 1966 advertising revenues were up to $32 million a year, a far cry from AM's ad sales of $580 million. By Spring, 1967, FM radio was primarily playing middle-of-the-road music (61 percent). But FM changed forever with the advent of "underground radio," ushered in by "Big Daddy" Tom Donahue at KMPX-FM in San Francisco.

FCC Ruling

On January 1, 1967 a ruling from the FCC, passed in 1964 but delayed by broadcasters, limited the amount of simulcasting from radio stations who broadcast AM and FM. The lack of growth by FM stations led to the ruling and the effect was to force station owners to develop separate programming for their AM and FM stations. At the time, radio was dominated by AM programming (car radios only had AM receivers) and the first success came with "underground" or "album oriented" stations that appealed to the college rock audience. The growth in high quality components led to a demand for a higher quality radio signal and FM fit the bill. As pop/rock music moved over to the FM dial, this opened up AM stations, which needed programming to replace the pop/rock station. That provided an opportunity for country music to gain exposure because stations often used country to fill in the AM slot. The growth of country radio can be attributed to the fact that more people could now hear country and the more they heard, the more they wanted to hear. The success of country music on AM led to station owners moving the format over to FM so that, by the mid-1980s, country music was primarily heard on FM. Until this FCC ruling, country music was usually blocked from growing as a radio format.

Tom "Big Daddy" Donahue

Tom "Big Daddy" Donahue had been a rock'n'roll DJ at WIBG in Philadelphia during the 1950s. The deep voiced Dohanue ("400 pounds of solid sounds") would announce "I'm here to clear up your face and mess up your mind" as he played records by black artists—which upset his family—as well as white rock'n'rollers. After the payola investigations, DJ's fled west. (The Congressional committee didn't have enough money to investigate radio west of the Mississippi so DJ's left the east coast stations in droves). Donahue started his career in radio at a station in Charleston, West Virginia, then to WIBG and then to KYA in San Francisco.

In San Francisco, Donahue was joined by Bobby Mitchell, another former WIBG dee jay, and they set up businesses for concert booking (he booked the Beatles last concert in August, 1966 at Candlestick Park), management and booking. They started a record label, Autumn, a psychedelic nightclub, operated a radio consultant tipsheet ("Tempo") and even groomed race horses. They both drove Cadillacs.

After he was fired from KYA in May, 1965, Donahue remained in San Francisco. He hired Sly Stone (then Sylvester Stewart) as the label's producer. Hits from that label included "C'mon and Swim" by Bobby Freeman, "Laugh, Laugh" by the Beau Brummels, "I Still Love You" by the Vejtables and "Dance With Me" by the Mojo Men. He also produced The Great Society with Grace Slick as the lead singer, but they had no hits.

Donahue and his wife were with friends one night on his birthday, stoned, playing records for each other—those that were not on the radio—when he had a revelation: play records on the radio that were not Top 40 hits. The FM airwaves had opened up, in stereo, because of the FCC ruling against simulcasting. That led Donahue to call FM stations and he found one, KMPZ, with a disconnected phone. That triggered the thought that "a drowning man doesn't care who's throwing the rope."

KMPX operated as a barter station, allowing air time to whoever paid for it. The station carried some foreign language programs. On the all-night shift, DJ Larry Miller played blues, folk and folk rock and Donahue—who disliked programmed radio that had been pioneered by

Todd Storz, Bill Stewart, Gordon McLendon and Bill Drake—wanted to do a program like that.

Big Daddy Donahue began the evening shift on April 7, 1967 (he replaced a Chinese language program) and his show of free form radio became popular. He then used that formula on anther FM station, KMPX in Los Angeles.

Those stations with their free form programming became so popular that *Rolling Stone* magazine—whose offices were in San Francisco—ran an essay by Donahue in their November, 1967 edition. The headline read, "Top 40 radio, as we know it today and have known it for the last ten years, is dead, and its rotting corpse is stinking up the airways." The Top 40 stations, said Donahue, "were replete with jingles, sirens and explosions introducing the news and disc jockeys who worked at a frantic pace and never, never lost their jollity."

Donahue was low key and he played album cuts (it was later known as "AOR" or "Album Oriented Radio) on the station and took the music seriously. The idea of playing an hour of songs back to back came from this FM format, initially because the station had no advertising. Listeners liked the idea of hearing large blocks of uninterrupted music and that method of programming radio later became standard in pop radio as stations moved from the AM to the FM dial.

The "Underground Press" was a major part of the alternative culture during the 1960s. The "Underground Press" offered an alternative to the established daily newspapers and printed news of interest to young, primarily college-students: another version of the news, left-wing commentary, and, of course, record reviews and stories of rock acts. It treated its readers as intelligent insiders; the media could be trusted because it "interpreted" the network news, provided coverage to "real" news that traditional media outlets didn't have a clue about, and created a network of like-minded activists.

When that idea was translated by Donahue to radio, it meant a radio station did not yell at its audience--like Top 40 with its hyper disc jockeys screaming at the top of their lungs--and that it played artists who didn't get played on AM radio but played album cuts--or even whole albums--instead of just hit singles over and over again. That kind of radio was more free form that the highly programmed AM Top-40 stations, featured more music, less hard sell commercials, and ignored the traditional AM hoopla of jingles, games, gimmicks and other razz-ma-tazz. The emphasis was on the music, and FM underground gave its listeners plenty of it, presented tastefully and understated.

That was the breakthrough for FM radio to reach college students and other music aficionados to move away from the hit singles on AM radio to FM. It led to FM becoming the leading channel for rock, then all other genres of music.

In his book, *The Hits Just Keep On Coming*, Ben Fong-Torres stated, "The Beatles had changed the rules. Their dominance of the sales charts and radio airwaves, as well as their influence on making albums viable hits in their entirety rather than just packaging for a hit or two and ten tracks of filler, forced some Top 40 radio stations to change. Top 40 had never played album cuts. Now, because of the Beatles—and, soon, the Stones, Dylan, the Byrds and others—the format had to adjust."

Major Labels

There were five major labels in 1967, controlling over half the market: Columbia, Warner-7 Arts, RCA Victor, Capitol-EMI, and MGM. Warner was gaining strength.

Bill Graham

Graham established a hierarchy of acts for his shows: "headliners, second on the bill, and third-line bands. Status was dictated by their popularity and drawing power and, like any business, new bands would start at the bottom and have to work their way up until they were able to sell out the Fillmore."

The British bands that Graham booked into San Francisco were The Yardbirds, The Who, Eric Burdon & The Animals, Cream, Donovan, Pink Floyd and Pocul Harum. Since Albert Grossman now managed Janis Joplin, Big Brother was booked into the Fillmore.

Each band booked into the Fillmore played two forty-five minute sets each night; the first show started at 8 and the second show began at 11:30 with the headliners taking the stage at 12:30 a.m. There were three acts and Graham was adamant that his shows run on schedule.

Graham demanded discipline from the musicians and noted that "What the new musician refuses to admit is that he's a professional entertainer. They don't want to say that. They want to tell you, 'I'm an artist looking for myself. I'm searching for the truth, for reality. I want to share and relate to the audience."

Dave Getz, the drummer for Big Brothers, observed that "Bill was really into power and if he needed you, the power would be transposed into charm and graciousness and helping you. Bending over backwards. If, at some point, he just decided that he didn't need you, he could just cut you in ribbons and throw you away like a piece of garbage."

Sergeant Pepper's

During the Summer of Love, the Jefferson Airplane hit with "White Rabbit," the Rolling Stones had "Ruby Tuesday," Procol Harum had "A Whiter Shade of Pale," The Turtles had "Happy Together," and The Doors had "Light My Fire."

Bill Graham

Bill Graham ended his six nights a week schedule for the summer on September 8, 1967, with Cream performing the final six nights before sold out shows. From that point, the Fillmore had shows on weekends.

The demand for drugs led to crime which led to San Francisco community leaders declaring "The Death of the Hippie" in October, 1967, with a special ceremony where they proclaimed the flower-power movement a failure. That month, police raided the Grateful Dead's house and busted several members of the Dead family for drugs; a year earlier, LSD had been declared illegal.

As the Summer of Love ended, things were changing in the world of pop and rock music, especially in the area of live concerts. San Francisco writer Herbert Gold wrote "The first people who went to the Fillmore were doing something original and expressing themselves freely. The second generation was following a lead, and the musicians became canonized. It became a pilgrimage, and you don't dance when you're visiting the saint's chapel. A lot of the fun went out of rock music." The fun went out when the dancing stopped. The bands who came of age during the Summer of Love developed through live performances at dances. A band had to play songs from other groups—and play them like the record—which forced musicians to learn other styles and broadened their playing skills. When a band played a dance, they had to play four or five hours a night, and that gave them an education in what songs worked for a crowd of dancers. It also honed their skills and they became better, sharper, more practiced musicians. After the 1960s, people—at least young whites--sat and listened and the acts that developed came through the recording studio, not the dance hall. The music changed; the *Sergeant Pepper's* album by the Beatles forced critics who did not like rock music to take it seriously while fans began to view the music as "art" and not just entertainment. Musicians became more serious, more introspective, more intent on expressing and pleasing themselves rather than pleasing a crowd.

When the music industry became Big Business it became serious because of the money involved. But it also became serious because young, white musicians were no longer playing for dancers having fun; instead, they played for sitting listeners intent on extracting meaning and purpose from the songs.

Rolling Stone Magazine

In 1967, *Rolling Stone* magazine was founded in San Francisco by Jann Wenner, a drop out from the University of California at Berkeley, and Ralph Gleason, a music critic for the *San Francisco Chronicle*. The name came from the Muddy Waters song, "Rolling Stone," the same song that gave The Rolling Stones their group name. Wenner borrowed $7,500 from his family and fiancé to begin the magazine, which initially reported on the San Francisco and hippie culture.

Wenner had been active in the Free Speech Movement at the University of California in Berkley and wrote for the student newspaper, *The Daily Californian*. Before starting *Rolling Stone*, Wenner worked at *Ramparts*, a magazine where Ralph Gleason was a contributing editor.

Rolling Stone was founded during a period when the "underground press" was emerging. The "underground press" was alternative newspapers who wrote for a young audience—the '60s generation—who distrusted the mainstream media and did not report on or represent the issues and topic they felt were important. Rolling Stone, like other alternative newspapers, covered music and musicians, but they held high journalistic standards and covered politics and social issues as well. The magazine soon became the most important print outlet for the counterculture generation with its taste defining coverage of musicians who came to define the era. Rolling Stone covered the most relevant musicians and ignored the irrelevant and, in doing so, showed music fans who they should listen to and why.

Country Music Hall of Fame opens

A gala celebration was held on April 1, 1967 for the opening of the Country Music Hall of Fame and Museum, a building with a barn-shaped roof. Fund raising, led by Roy Horton, began in 1963 and featured a multi-artist album—one of the first to be marketed on TV—to raise funds. The Hall of Fame was built on land that was formerly Tony Rose Park, which Mayor Beverly Briley had arranged to be donated. The Hall of Fame was located at the northern end of Music Row and the plaques for Hall of Fame inductees were moved from the Tennessee State Museum to the new building. This was the first Hall of Fame dedicated to a genre of music.

Gospel Music Association

The Gospel Music Association (GMA) was founded in 1964; among the founding members were James Blackwood, J.D. Sumner, Cecil Blackwood, Don Light and Don Butler. The Country Music Association in Nashville served as the role model for the organization. The GMA was an outgrowth of the National Quartet Convention, first held in Memphis in 1956, where it grew from a four day to a ten day event. The convention was a joint business venture of the Blackwoods and Statesman quartets.

In 1967, a committee of the Gospel Music Association comprised of Brock Speer, Ron Page, Don Light, Bob Benson and J.D. Sumner hired LeWayne Satterfield as the first executive director of the GMA and opened offices on Music Row. By 1970, it had over a thousand members.

The GMA membership categories were enlarged to include artists, musicians, promoters, record companies, radio-TV personalities, publishers, trade papers, composers, performing rights organizations and directors at large, representing consumers.

They produced an album with 14 quartets singing their biggest songs; the album brought in needed revenue; the organized also published a monthly newspaper, *Good News*.

Dolly Parton joins Porter Wagoner

In 1967 Norma Jean left the Porter Wagoner TV Show TV to get married; she was replaced by Dolly Parton, who had an album on Monument, *Dumb Blonde*. Wagoner arranged for Dolly to leave Monument and sign with RCA so they could record duets and he could have a hand in producing her albums. This was a critical break for Parton, and a first step in her becoming a star.

"Gentle on My Mind"

"Gentle on My Mind" was never a big hit on the radio, but became a standard. The song was written and originally recorded by John Hartford, who was inspired to write it after seeing the film *Dr. Zhivago*. Glen Campbell heard the record on the radio and decided to record a demo on May 17, 1967; on the demo was Campbell giving directions to the musicians between verses. Campbell sent the demo to Al De Lory, head of Capitol and De Lory loved it and decided to edited out the vocal instructions and release the record on June 19, 1967. Campbell's version entered the *Billboard* country chart on July 29 and only reached number 30; it entered the *Billboard* Hot 100 on September 14, 1968 and only reached 39 on that chart. Campbell loved the song and used as the introduction to his TV show, "Glen Campbell's Goodtime Hour" which ran from 1969 to 1972. Hartford was a regular on that show. Dean Martin and Patti Page both covered the song and it reached the Hot 100 chart but Martin's version was a hit in the U.K. in 1968

"Everlasting Love"

Nashville songwriters Buzz Cason and Mac Gayden wrote "Everlasting Love," which was originally recorded in Fred Foster's studio by Robert Knight on the Rising Son label, which was owned by Cason and Gayden, who produced the record. Knight, an African-American artist, had recorded for Dot but had no hits. He attended Tennessee State University and sang with a vocal trio, the Fairlanes; it was during a performance with the Fairlanes at a Vanderbilt fraternity party that he came to the attention of Gayden. In 1967, Knight's version reached number 13 on *Billboard's* Hot 100 chart and number 14 on the R&B chart. In 1968, Love Affair released the song in England, where it reached number one. The Town Criers released the song in Australia where it reached number two on the Australian chart. In 1974 "Everlasting Love" was a hit for Carl Carlton, reaching number six on the Hot 100 and 11 on the R&B charts. That version was produced by Papa Don Schroeder and Tommy Cogbill at Creative Workshop, owned by Buzz Cason in the Berry Hill subdivision of Nashville. Rex Smith and Rachel Sweet recorded a duet version of the song in 1981 that reached number 32 on the Hot 100. "Everlasting Love" was a worldwide hit for Sandra in 1987-1988. It was also chart releases by Worlds Apart and Gloria Estefan.

The song has been covered by numerous artists include U2, the Drifters, Steve Ellis and country artists Narvel Felts, Hank Locklin, and Louise Mandrell.

First Country Music Association Awards Show

The Board of Directors of the Country Music Association were against giving awards for a number of years; there were awards from the Trade magazines—Billboard and Cashbox—but the Board felt that, since only one person received an award and the rest would be unhappy, it was best not to venture into the political side of giving awards. They finally relented and the first Country Music Association (CMA) Awards Show was held on Friday, October 20, 1967 at the Municipal Auditorium during the annual Disc Jockey Convention. The show was preceded by the annual CMA banquet.

The trade magazines were initially against the idea but, deciding they could gain additional advertising revenue from the awards show, *Billboard* publisher Hal Cook promoted the idea. Hosted by Sonny James and Bobbie Gentry. This first CMA Awards was broadcast over the radio but not on television. Eddy Arnold was voted the first Entertainer of the Year but the big winner was Jack Greene and his song, "There Goes My Everything." Other awards winners were Chet Atkins (Instrumentalist), Loretta Lynn (female vocalist) The Stoneman Family (vocal group) and Don Bowman (comedian).

Tex Ritter announced the new members of the Country Music Hall of Fame, were Jim Reeves, J.L. Frank, Red Foley and Steve Sholes.

November, 1967

President Johnson signed the Public Broadcasting Act on November 7, which established a corporation that would use public and private funds to subsidize noncommercial TV and radio stations. The announcement of the Act stated that "news, public events and cultural and educational programs will be offered." The initial federal funding of this "network of knowledge" was $9 million.

On November 29, Robert McNamara resigned as Secretary of Defense and was named president of the World Bank. The next day, Minnesota Senator Eugene McCarthy announced he would run as an anti-Vietnam candidate in the Democratic primaries in the spring for President. McCarthy was an out-spoken critic of the Vietnam war.

Nashville Songwriters Association

A trade group for songwriters, The Nashville Songwriters Association, was formed after songwriter Eddie Miller encouraged Buddy Mize and Bill Brock to launch the organization. The initial organizational meeting was in December, 1967; among those attending were Liz Anderson, Kris Kristofferson and Marijohn Wilkin. Within a year the group had a charter from state of Tennessee and in 1970 the Board of Directors established the Nashville Songwriters Association Hall of Fame. In April, 1976, the organization added "International" to its name, making it the Nashville Songwriters Association International (NSAI).

John Wesley Harding

Bob Dylan returned to Nashville in October, 1967, to record his eighth studio album, *John Wesley Harding*. The name of the album was the name of a Texas outlaw, John Wesley Hardin, but Dylan misspelled his name.

It had been a year and a half since Dylan had released *Blonde on Blonde*. He had moved to Woodstock in upstate New York with his wife and young children. About two months after the release of *Blonde on Blonde* Dylan had suffered a broken neck after a motorcycle accident.

During his time in Woodstock, he regularly went over to the house known as "Big Pink" where members of The Band lived. In the basement of that house, Dylan recorded on a tape recorder songs he had just written, old folk, country and blues songs and fragments of songs. None of those songs were released commercially until 1975 when a selection was released on an album, *The Basement Tapes*. None of the songs recorded in the basement during that time were on the songs he brought to Nashville.

Dylan's producer, Bob Johnston, visited Dylan in his hotel room at the Ramada Hotel after he arrived and listened to the new material. Dylan told Johnston he only wanted a guitar, bass and drums on the album—a sparse production—so Johnston hired Charlie McCoy to play bass and drummer Kenny Buttrrey for the session; both had been on the *Blonde on Blonde* sessions.

The first session was held in Nashville's Columbia Studio A on October 17. In three hours, Dylan recorded "I Dreamed I Saw St. Augustine," "Drifter's Escape" and "The Ballad of Frankie Lee and Judas Priest."

Dylan returned to Nashville on November 6 and recorded "All Along the Watchtower," "John Wesley Harding," "As I Went Out One Morning," "I Pity the Poor Immigrant" and "I Am a Lonesome Hobo."

Robbie Robertson recalled that after the second session, Dylan played the songs for him and Garth Hudson and asked them to overdub on the tracks but Robertson liked what Dylan had done and could not come up with anything to add that would enhance the songs.

Bob Johnston suggested they include a steel guitar on the next session on November 29. Dylan agreed and Johnson called Pete Drake for the session. On "I'll Be Your Baby Tonight" and "Down Along the Cove," Drake and his steel guitar joined Charlie McCoy and Kenny Buttrey. Those two songs finished the album.

Dylan requested that Columbia not issue any publicity about the album when it was released on December 27. Dylan also requested that no singles be released from the album and none were.

Despite a lack of publicity or any singles and a sparse production, the album gained immediate attention. It entered the *Billboard* album chart a month after its release, On January 27, 1968, and rose to the number two positon on the chart, remaining there for four weeks. The album ahead of it was the Beatles soundtrack to *The Magical Mystery Tour*.

Paul Whiteman

The Big Band days were over; Tommy and Jimmy Dorsey died in 1956 and 1957, respectively, but Paul Whiteman held on for another decade. In March, 1970 he was on a TV tribute, where Bing Crosby contributed songs, but the recognition was fleeting; it bothered Whiteman that he was no longer famous, that his fame had disappeared with the new generation. That caused him to sink into a deep depression and drink more heavily.

Paul Whiteman died on December 29, 1967. Although he left a number of recordings, he did not leave a musical legacy because he never developed a distinctive "sound" with his group; or perhaps, the distinctive sound he pioneered was soon outdated and overshadowed by the group of Big Band leaders who blossomed in the Swing era. During his time he was a showman, both popular and influential, but his showmanship was topped by the musicianship of others like Louis Armstrong, Glenn Miller, Benny Goodman and others who were disciplined musicians as well as showmen.

The jazz critics and historians who emerged after World War II overlooked Paul Whiteman and his contributions to the genre. To them, Whiteman was an imposter who did not belong in the same arena as Louis Armstrong and Duke Ellington. The later jazz critics and historians looked to New Orleans and the African-American culture as the source of "true" jazz, and ignored the development of jazz from the white orchestras that played hotel ballrooms, clubs and cabarets during the early years.

The end result is that most jazz historians ignore Paul Whiteman and his contributions when chronicling the "true" history of jazz and its emergence on the American musical landscape during the 20th century.

1968

The year 1968

There were times when it felt like America was coming apart during 1968. It was a year of violence, political turmoil, civil unrest, racial tensions and an ongoing war in Vietnam that increasingly lost the support of the nation and led to the deaths of thousands of young men for a cause that politicians knew was lost.

It was a year of extremes, demonstrated by the songs and acts who were popular that year. The year began with "Hello Goodbye" by the Beatles at number one; the next single to top the chart was "Judy In Disguise (With Glasses)" by John Fred & His Playboy Band, a light pop number, then "Green Tambourine" by the Lemon Pipers, a light pop number about busking, and then "Love Is Blue," an easy listening middle-of-the road instrumental by Paul Mauriat, a French orchestra leader.

The number one album at the beginning of the year was *Magical Mystery Tour* by the Beatles; after eight weeks in that position it was replaced by *Blooming Hits* by Paul Mauriat, which remained number one for five weeks and was replaced by the movie soundtrack to The Graduate, which featured songs by Simon & Garfunkel.

The entire musical year was like that with R&B songs, MOR easy listening songs, country and rock all alternating in the number one position.

Vietnam

Secretary of Defense Robert McNamara announced in January that the Vietnam War was winding down because the North Vietneme were losing their will to fight.

On January 31, the North Vietnamese and Vietcong forces launched a massive offensive in South Vietnam. The "Tet Offensive" was 84,000 Communist combat troops with support forces who struck major cities in South Vietnam. A suicide squad of Vietcong blew a hole in the wall of the United States Embassy and occupied the Embassy yard for five hours.

That was the Vietnamese "New Year" and a truce was in effect for the holiday period, but the Vietcong used the lull to overrun the South; about 5,000 Marines faced 20,000 North Vietnamese troops. The annual cost of the Vietnam War was approaching $25 billion.

A counteroffensive by American and South Vietnamese troops began on February 24 and there were major air strikes against Hanoi. General William Westmoreland requested 206,000 additional troops. In January 14,000 Air Force and Naval reservists were called up.

Draftees made up 42 percent of the soldiers, but suffered 58 percent of the casualties. A thousand young men were killed each week and even more were injured. By the end of the year there were over 500,000 American troops in Vietnam.

On March 6 popular CBS News Anchor Walter Cronkite announced on TV that he was against the Vietnam War. Cronkite drew that conclusion after he told his audience that a trip to Vietnam left him deeply disillusioned and he believed the war was futile and immoral. President Johnson was distraught; he felt that if he lost Walter Cronkite he'd lost the support of the public.

10th Annual Grammys

The tenth annual Grammys, honoring recordings from 1967, took a step away from MOR/easy listening music and embraced contemporary rock and pop as the defining music of America at their awards. The awards were held February 29, 1968 in four locations: Los Angeles, New York, Chicago and Nashville.

"Record of the Year" was "Up, Up and Away" by the 5th Dimension, "Album of the Year" was *Sgt. Pepper's Lonely Artist Club Band,* by the Beatles; "Song of the Year" was "Up, Up and Away" written by Jimmy Webb, and "Best New Artist" was Bobbie Gentry, who had a major hit with "Ode to Billie Joe."

In the "Pop" division, there was no separate category for "Rock and Roll"; instead they renamed that section "Contemporary."

"Best Vocal, Female" was Bobbie Gentry for "Ode to Billie Joe"; "Best Vocal, Male" was Glen Campbell for "By the Time I Get to Phoenix"; "Best Performance, Vocal Group" was the 5th Dimension for "Up, Up and Away"; "Best, Performance, Chorus" was the Johnny Mann Singers for "Up, Up and Away"; "Best Instrumental Performance" was Chet Atkins for *Chet Atkins Picks the Best;* "Best Contemporary Female" was "Bobbie Gentry for "Ode to Billie Joe"; Best Contemporary Male" was Glen Campbell for "By the Time I Get to Phoenix": "Best Contemporary Group" was the Fifth Dimension for "Up, Up and Way"; "Best Contemporary Single" was ""Up, Up and Away" and "Best Contemporary Album" was *Sgt. Pepper's Lonely Hearts Club Band* by the Beatles, George Martin, producer.

There were four Grammys for R&B: "Best Vocal Female" was Aretha Franklin for "Respect"; Best Vocal, Male" was Lou Rawls for "Dead End Street,"; "Best Group Performance" was Sam & Dave for "Soul Man" and "Best R&B Recording" was Aretha Franklin for "Respect."

There were five Grammys for country: "Best Vocal, Female" was Tammy Wynette for "I Don't Wanna Play House"; "Best Vocal, Male" was Glen Campbell for "Gentle on my Mind": "Best Duet or Group" was Johnny Cash & June Carter for "Jackson"; "Best Recording" was "Gentle on My

Mind," By Glen Campbell, Al De Lory, producer; and "Best C&W Song" was "Gentle on My Mind" by Glen Campbell, written by John Hartford.

"Best Folk Performance" was John Hartford for "Gentle On My Mind."

"Best Gospel Performance" was Porter Wagoner & the Blackwood Brothers Quartet for *More Grand Ole Gospel*; "Best Sacred Performance" was Elvis Presley for *How Great Thou Art*.

The Beatles in India

In February, the Beatles went to Rishikesh in northern India to study Transcendental Meditation with the Maharishi Mahesh Yogi. It was a way to retreat from the hectic world they were living in. The Beatles were the most influential music group and their visit to India to study Transcendental Meditation led a number of others to embrace Indian music and spirituality.

Ringo Starr only stayed ten days, Paul McCartney stayed a month but John Lennon and George Harrison stayed for six weeks. Harrison had already become interested in Indian music and was a leader in guiding the other Beatles to India.

During their time in India, each of the Beatles wrote a number of songs (and Ringo finished one song he had for awhile, "Don't Pass Me By"). Those songs were recorded later that year on the double sided "White" album.

In May, after their return, Lennon and McCartney announced the formation of Apple Corps, Ltd.

Civil Rights

A civil rights protest against a white only bowling alley in Orangeburg, South Carolina resulted in the death of three students on February 8. Five days later there were disturbances at the University of Wisconsin-Madison and the University of North Carolina-Chapel Hill.

At Howard University in Washington March 19-23, there were five days of rallies, protests and sit-ins as students seized the administration building, demanding an end to the ROTC program and a more Afro-centric curriculum March 19-23.

Presidential Primaries

On March 12, President Johnson won the New Hampshire primarily by only 7,000 votes. Senator Eugene McCartney, running on an anti-Vietnam platform, received 42 percent of the vote, helped by thousands of student volunteers.

Four days later Senator Robert Kennedy announced his intention to seek the Democratic nomination.

President Johnson gave a televised speech to the nation from the Oval Office on March 31. He addressed the nation about the Vietnam war. At the end of the talk, in a surprise announcement, he told the TV audience, "I shall not seek and I will not accept the nomination of my party as our president. In a Gallop poll, only 26 percent of Americans approved of Johnson's handling of the Vietnam war.

The Death Martin Luther King, Jr.

Four days after Johnsons' announcement that he would not run for re-election, the nation was stunned with another announcement: Reverend Martin Luther King, Jr. had been killed in Memphis.

King had flown into Memphis on March 29, delayed by a bomb threat. King was organizing the "Poor People's Campaign" to address the issues of economic injustice. He wanted to recruit a multi-racial army of the poor to culminate in a march on Washington. He had flown into Memphis to support a strike by sanitation workers that began on March 12; the workers demanded higher wages and better treatment.

On the evening of April 3, King gave his "I've been to the mountaintop speech" at the Mason Lodge, world headquarters for the Church of God in Christ. In that speech King told his followers that peaceful demonstrations were the best course of action.

At the end of the speech he said "I don't know what will happen now. We've got some difficult days ahead. But it really doesn't matter with me now, because I've been to the mountaintop. And I don't mind. Like anybody, I would like to live a long life; longevity has its place, but I'm not concerned about that now. I just want to do God's will and He's allowed me to go up to the mountain and I've looked over and I've seen the Promised Land. I may not get there with you but I want you to know tonight, that we, as a people, will get to the Promised Land. So I'm happy, tonight. I'm not worried about anything. I'm not fearing any man. Mine eyes have seen the glory of the coming of the Lord."

Reverend King was staying at the Lorraine Motel in Room 306 but the next day, April 4, he was on the second floor balcony, talking to a musician, Ben Branch, who was scheduled to play that evening. King told him to play "Precious Lord, Take My Hand" when a shot rang out from across the street at 6:01 p.m.

King fell and those around him comforted him until he was taken to St. Joseph's Hospital, where he died at 7:05 p.m.

After King's Death

When news of the death of Dr. King reached the public there was an outpouring of riots in Memphis and 124 other cities. Before it ended there were at least 40 blacks and five whites who were dead, $45 million in property was destroyed, and over 20,000 arrested. In Washington, D.C. there were seven dead, over 1,000 injured and over 7,000 arrested. There were major outbreaks in Baltimore, Chicago and Pittsburgh; it took over 15,000 troops to stop the rioting.

On April 9, Dr. Martin Luther King, Jr was buried in Atlanta after a funeral march through the city that was televised.

Two days later, President Johnson signed the Civil Rights Act of 1968, which curbed discrimination in housing. He also signed a law that made it a crime to cross state lines for the purpose of inciting a riot.

Most of the rioting had ended by April 15 but in Chicago Mayor Richard Daley ordered his police force to "shoot to kill" anyone suspected of looting, rioting or arson.

James Brown

The year 1968 was transitional in many ways for rhythm and blues. The racial unrest, the race riots, the death of Martin Luther King and the emergence of Black Power made some artists militant and artists started speaking directly to and for the black audience rather than seeking white crossovers. They were helped by the fact that the pop/rock audience was increasingly open to listening to and buying music from black artists.

The old school of choreographed steps by black performers while they sang was still alive; the first number one R&B single was "I Second That Emotion" by Smokey Robinson and the Miracles while "I Wish It Would Rain" by the Temptations and "We're a Winner" by the Impressions also reached number one early in 1968.

The core of soul music was "funk" and James Brown led the way, beginning with "Cold Sweat" in 1967, which reached number one on the R&B chart and number seven on the Hot 100. In 1968 Brown had a hit with "I Got the Feeling" but it was "Say It Loud, I'm Black and I'm Proud" that was the anthem for soul music as well as racial identity during that year. The song is half shouted and half sung, which would increasingly dominate Brown's sound, along with the funky drum and bass.

James Brown wasn't just a performer, he was a spokesman and cutting edge artist. The sound of "funk" spread throughout R&B music and James Brown became be "Soul Brother Number One."

Motown: Marvin Gaye

Although Marvin Gaye was a powerful soul and R&B singer, he aspired to be a romantic, ballad singer in the vein of Frank Sinatra. An enigmatic, gifted songwriter and singer with a three-octave vocal range, he was born in Washington, D.C., son of a preacher in the Apostolic Church. He enlisted in the Air Force and, after his release, joined the Rainbows, then formed the Marquees in 1957 where he was spotted by Harvey Fuqua, founder of the Moonglows ("Sincerely," "Please Send Me Someone To Love," "Ten Commandments of Love") who invited Gaye's group to become a re-constituted Moonglows in 1958.

Berry Gordy first met Marvin Gaye and heard him sing at the first Motown Christmas party in 1960; Gordy signed Gaye in 1961 and the singer married Gordy's sister, Anna.

Gaye became a studio musician and played drums on the early hits of Smokey Robinson and the Miracles. He also released singles; his four releases were "Stubborn Kind of Fellow" in 1962 (the first to chart) followed by "Hitch Hike," "Pride and Joy" and "Can I Get a Witness." He recorded a series of duets with Mary Wells, Kim Weston and then Tammi Terrell. The duet recordings of "Ain't No Mountain High Enough," "Your Precious Love" and "You're All I Need To Get By" became classics.

Berry Gordy had a stable of songwriters and producers at Motown who actively competed with each other. Norman Whitfield had written "I Heard It Through the Grapevine" and produced the demo on Barrett Strong, the artist who'd hit with "Money." Whitfield then produced a master on Marvin Gaye and at the weekly Friday morning meeting, where songs were screened, that cut competed against another Gaye recording, "Your Unchanging Love," produced by Holland-Dozier-Holland. The staff voted to go with "I Heard It Through the Grapevine" but Gordy overruled the staff and released "Your Unchanging Love." Since Gaye wanted to be a romantic singer, Gordy felt that "Your Unchanging Love" fit the singer's image better than the driving soul of "I Heard It Through the Grapevine."

Whitfield believed strongly in the song and, after the rejection by Gordy, produced it on Gladys Knight and the Pips, whose version entered the charts on October 21, 1967 and rose to number two on the Hot 100 chart and number one--for six weeks--on the R&B chart.

Whitfield still loved the Gaye recording, which had a different arrangement, but Gordy refused to release it, citing the fact that the Gladys Knight version had been a hit only a year earlier. Finally, Whitfield convinced Gordy to include the cut on an upcoming Gaye album; the DJs at radio stations quickly picked up on the cut and played it and Motown was forced to release it as a single.

Marvin Gaye's version of "I Heard It Through the Grapevine" entered the *Billboard* Hot 100 chart on November 23, 1968 and the R&B chart a week later; it became number one on both charts--and held that position for seven weeks.

Student Protests

Students took over Columbia University at the end of April, occupying five buildings, including the office of University president Grayson Kirk and ransacked it. Around 5,000 students took part in the demonstration, led by Mark Rudd, president of the Students for a Democratic Society. On April 30, police ended the week long takeover by arresting 700; there were 148 hurt.

Poor People's Campaign

The "Poor People's Campaign" that Dr. King had been working on began on May 12 when his widow, Coretta Scott King, led a group to the Washington Mall, where they camped. During the next six weeks, caravans of poor people came from across the country; there was a Mule Train from Marks, Mississippi. They build a shantytown and named it "Resurrection City" and demanded an "Economic Bill of Rights."

The Poor People's Campaign made poor people visible in the media and to Congressmen and Senators, but the nation's politics were caught up in the Vietnam War. But at least the poor had made themselves known and felt.

"Honey"

Bobby Goldsboro's recording of "Honey," produced by Bob Montgomery, entered the *Billboard* Hot 100 on March 23, 1968 and the country chart a week later. The song, recorded in Nashville, was number one on the Hot 100 for five consecutive weeks and number three on the country chart. The song was written by Bobby Russell, who also wrote "Little Green Apples," which was also on Goldsboro's album but was a single by Roger Miller. Russell was married to Vicki Lawrence, who had a number one pop hit on

Russell's song, "The Night the Lights Went Out in Georgia." Russell also wrote "Camp "Wethahekhwee" for Ray Stevens. "Honey" was Goldsboro's only number one song. Goldsboro later had a popular syndicated TV show, "The Bobby Goldsboro Show from 1973-1975.

Hair

The musical *Hair* premiered off-Broadway in Joseph Papp's Public Theater off-Broadway on October 17, 1967 and opened on Broadway on April 29, 1968. The book and lyrics were written by Gerome Ragni and James Rado and the music was by Galt MacDermont.

The idea for the musical came from James Rado and Gerome Ragni in 1964 and they began writing it. The show was a celebration of 1960s youth and their connections to drugs, political activism, protesting, the back to nature movement, hippies, the counterculture and the changes going on in society which were embraced by those youth. What drove the musical— and the counterculture-was the music.

The Original Cast Recording of *Hair* debuted on the *Billboard* album chart on August 3, 1968 and rose to the number one position, where it remained for thirteen consecutive weeks. It remained on the Billboard chart for 151 weeks, or almost three years and sold over three million albums. The show lasted on Broadway for 1,750 performances. The show opened in London on the West end the following year and ran for 1,997 performances.

There were four songs that became hit singles when released by recording artists. "Age of Aquarius/Let the Sun Shine In" was a hit for the 5th Dimension, "Hair" was a hit for the Cowsills, "Easy to Be Hard" was a hit for Three Dog Night and "Good Morning Starshine" was a hit for Oliver.

Assassination of Robert Kennedy

The political campaigns for the Democratic nominee for President reached California, where the primary was held on Tuesday, June 4. Robert Kennedy won that primary and it looked like he was on the way to the nomination at the Democratic convention at the end of August.

At the Ambassador Hotel in Los Angeles, Kennedy thanked his supporters then, a little after midnight, went through the kitchen on the way to the press room. As he stopped to shake the hand of a busboy, Juan Romero, a 24-year old Palestinian, Sirhan Sirhan, opened fire with a .22 caliber pistol. Kennedy was hit three times and five others were injured; Sirhan was wrestled to the ground and his pistol confiscated.

As he lay on the kitchen floor, cradled in the arms of Juan Romero, Kennedy asked if everything was all right. Medics came, placed him on a stretcher and took him away by ambulance. Early in the morning of June 6, about 25 hours after he had been shot, Robert Kennedy died.

Olympic Protest

The summer Olympics of 1968 were held in Mexico. Americans Tommy Smith and John Carlos finished first and third, respectively, in the 200 meter dash. After the medals were handed out, the "Star Spangled Banner" was played as Smith and Carlos raised their dark-gloved fist up in a black power salute. They had their heads bowed, refusing toe look at the American flag.

After their act of defiance, the two were suspended from the Olympic games and expelled from Olympic Village.

During the Olympic games, the United States won 45 gold medals while the Soviets won 30.

Vietnam: 1964-1968

In 1965 the American public's confidence in government was at an all-time high since 1945; there was a great amount of prestige connected with "public service." The country was in good shape: unemployment was 4.5 percent, inflation was only 1.6 percent.

On January 4 President Johnson became the first president to deliver a State of the Union speech to a nationally televised audience during prime time. He laid out ambitious plans for "The Great Society" that kept Congress busy enacting laws and statues. Among the Acts of Congress were those that created the Legal Services Corporation, the National Endowment for the Arts and the National Endowment for the Humanities, Medicare, a new Department of Housing and Urban Development and the Elementary and Secondary Education Act were passed.

Civil Rights was a major issue. In March, 1965 there was march from Selma (where only one percent of the voters but 42 percent of the population was black) to Montgomery. During that march (March 9-March 25), a white civil rights activist, Viola Liuzzo, was murdered while she was driving and a Boston minister, James Reeb, was beaten to death. Americans watched that march and confrontation on their television sets.

In late May, the Voting Rights Act passed overwhelmingly. That act led to great progress in the following period. In 1964 there were 1.5 million blacks registered to vote in the eleven states of the former Confederacy; by 1969 there were 3.1 million. There were less than 100 black elected officials in the entire South; in 1973 Mississippi alone had 191.

On the last day in May, 1965, riots broke out in the Watts section of Los Angeles after a white policeman arrested a black man for drunk driving. The rioting left 34 dead and Watts in charred ruins. In a speech in June at Harvard, the President first expressed the idea that would evolve into the Affirmative Action program.

In March, Johnson initiated Operation Rolling Thunder, a bombing campaign against North Vietnam. He had also taken the first steps in planning that sent artillery, armor, fleets of fighter-bombers and hundreds of thousands of troops to Vietnam to defeat the Communists. Those would be the first American combat troops in Vietnam, led by General William Westmoreland; by June there were over 50,000 military personnel in that country.

The war was not going well so in mid-July, Johnson agreed to a request from Westmoreland for 200,000 more troops. Westmoreland noted he needed another 100,000 and reserved the right to request more; by Christmas, 1965 there were almost 185,000 Americans in Vietnam.

The military and civilian leaders assured the American public that victory was coming into view and the War would soon be won but events contradicted those assessments. In early 1967 Johnson agreed for Westmoreland to have 470,000 Americans in Vietnam; in March the general requested 550,500 for a minimum essential force, saying he preferred about 678,000 servicemen.

In October, 1967 the percentage of voters who wanted the United States to get out of Vietnam stood at 30 percent--up from 15 percent at the beginning of the year. That same month 50,000 demonstrators marched on the Pentagon calling for an end to the War.

Tet Offensive

A major turning point in the Vietnam War occurred on January 31, 1968 when the North Vietnam launched their Tet offensive. "Tet" was the Vietnamese New Year and the Vietnamese army planned to overrun Saigon and topple the South Vietnamese government. About 20,000 Americans had been killed in Vietnam and another 50,000 had been seriously wounded. The United States forces barely survived the Tet offensive, but by this point, even a number of those in the military conceded that the war was unwinnable. It was also costly; by January, 1968 the war was costing $33 billion a year. Still, a draft call went out for 33,000 more young men.

Campus demonstrations against the war created turmoil. Neil Sheehan observed, "The threat of being conscripted for a war that was the object of widespread moral revulsion made marchers and shouters out of young men who might otherwise have been less concerned over the victimization of an Asian people and the turning into cannon fodder of farm boys and the sons of the working class and the minorities. The appeal of the cause aroused women students in equal number and with equal passion." One of the essential problems was that the white, middle class, which had previously avoided the draft through college deferments, was now being drafted. Even prominent and influential families were asked to surrender their sons to that war.

In March, 1968 Senator Eugene McCarthy, campaigning against the Vietnam War, won the New Hampshire primary; on March 22 Johnson announced he was bringing Westmoreland home to become Army Chief of Staff then, on March 31, after a speech discussing peace negotiations with North Vietnam, President Johnson announced he would not seek re-election. Less than a week later, on April 4, Martin Luther King was assassinated in Memphis, Tennessee, which led to large race riots in a number of cities. In May there were 536,000 American servicemen in Vietnam. Robert Kennedy joined the Presidential primaries as an anti-war candidate, but was assassinated in June in Los Angeles, just after he won the California primary. In the summer of 1968 the Democratic convention was held in Chicago where the police ran roughshod over demonstrators, beating them with billy clubs. Even reporters covering the Convention were beaten. At the end of the convention, party regulars denied McCarthy the nomination and gave it to Johnson's vice president, Hubert Humphrey. At the Republican convention, Richard Nixon was nominated. Democrat George Wallace, who had won a number of primaries on his anti-Civil Rights platform, ran as an independent.

By the end of 1968 General Westmoreland had been recalled from Vietnam and named Chief of Staff of the Army. Richard Nixon won the Presidential election, intimating that he had a "secret plan" to end the war in Vietnam. Later in life he admitted he had no plan.

By the end of 1968, 14,589 Americans had been killed in Vietnam.

Rock'n'Roll and American Culture

In *The Greening of America*, a book that captured the consciousness of the 1960s (it was published in 1970), author Charles A. Reich stated "Music has become the deepest means of communication and expression for an entire culture." Reich went on to assert that the music of the 1960s "achieved a height of knowledge, understanding, insight, and truth concerning the world, and people's feelings, that is incredibly greater than what other media have been able to express."

Reich was supportive and enthusiastic about rock music; Allen Bloom in *The Closing of the American Mind* was not. However, Bloom was equally perceptive about the role of music in the youth culture, stating in his book about the 1980s generation that "nothing is more singular about this generation than its addiction to music." Bloom continued "Today, a very large proportion of young people between the ages of ten and twenty live for music. It is their passion; nothing else excites them as it does; they cannot take seriously anything alien to music...Nothing surrounding them--school, family, church--has anything to do with their musical world...The music of the new votaries, on the other hand, knows neither class nor nation. It is available twenty-four hours a day, everywhere.".

It is obvious from those books, although they had opposing views of contemporary music in the youth culture, that a mass media poet had to work in the world of popular music. Bob Dylan could not have achieved his fame as a poet without being in the pop music culture; certainly his poetry could not have had the impact it had on the youth culture of the 1960s or American popular culture in general without the melodies to carry the words or the musical performances to excite audiences.

Bob Dylan

It is essential to understand Bob Dylan the performer in order to understand Bob Dylan the poet. It was this conflict that defined him. Dylan told Robert Shelton he was "subservient to [my] songs...The writing part is a very lonely experience, but there's strength in that loneliness. But I'm a performer too, and that's an outward thing. One is the opposite of the other, and it makes me crazy sometimes, because I can't write with the energy that I perform with. I can't perform off the energy that I write with. There just has to be time for both."

The love of performing was ignited in high school when he was performing with his rock'n'roll bands and one of his classmates observed about that period. "You could see something happening to Bob at this time... He was starting to really dig being a performer. Being up there on the stage and have kids scream over him...I got a strong feeling that he badly wanted the other kids to dig it, to approve of it. And the more he got the more he damned well was going to get."

The desire to perform continued when he entered college and began developing as a folksinger. According to Anthony Scaduto "Bob was persistent and sang as often as he could. His friends say he was not a very good guitar player at this point, and his voice and style were an imitation of so much around that they didn't ring true. 'He just wanted to get into a situation where he could learn where his talent and his feel for the music could develop,' one friend says. 'He learned things quickly and tried everything, and developed at a remarkable speed. But those first few months he was nowhere at all. Just a kid trying damned hard to learn.'"

The period of Dylan's early folk singing was reflected in his first album, *Bob Dylan*. Dylan's next two albums, *Freewheelin'* and *The Times They Are a-Changin'* reflected his emergence as a folk poet or poet working in the folk song tradition. *Another Side of* demonstrated a development away from the folk song idiom and protest songs to a desire by Dylan to write about himself, to have his art come from within him rather than outside stimuli like the Civil Rights and protest movements. During that transition, he moved away from Woody Guthrie and other folk singers as dominating influences to poets--both the Beat poets and French symbolists. Here, Dylan began to view himself more and more as a poet working in the folk singing market rather than a folksinger who wrote lyrics in order to have new songs to sing. The shift is subtle but nonetheless there: the young man's self-image is the guiding force from folksinger to writer of folk songs to a poet using music to perform his poems before audiences.

Several performances served as turning points. His concert at Town Hall in New York on April 12, 1963 show him still a folksinger but merging into a poet. Here he sang some of the traditional folk songs, some of his own compositions in the protest vein, and recited his poem, "Last Thoughts on Woody Guthrie" to the audience.

The performance in July, 1963 at the Newport Folk Festival was another turning point. Here, as Anthony Scaduto put it, "was the scene of the transformation of Bob Dylan--hobo minstrel, into Bob Dylan--the eclectic poet-visionary-hero who was orchestrating a 'youth revolution'" Dylan closed the show here to an enthusiastic audience reception. Scaduto stated "He had become more certain of himself as an artist, as a poet; not simply a folk-poet, in the Guthrie tradition, but an artist from whose grave-dark mind began to spring epic images. Bombarded by visionaries such as Rimbaud, Brecht, Byron, Ginsberg, and the anonymous authors of the Bible, among others, the songs that were beginning to flow from him were growing more transcendent, less concretely objective, increasingly filled with the shapes of vivid fantasy, with the motifs out of the collective unconscious."

After the *Another Side* album, released in August 1964, Dylan added instrumentation to his songs and moved into rock music, achieving much notoriety during his 1964 Newport Folk Festival appearance when he did an amplified set before an audience expecting folk music, although as Robert Shelton noted, "Dylan had never really abandoned his high-school rock'n'roll, his schoolboy radio music...he alone decided to leap back into rock, taking with him folk song's storytelling and comment" adding that "Dylan's creation of 'folk-rock' was a turning point in popular culture. Before Dylan's new work, most rock musicians, including The Beatles, had been using insipid, frivolous lyrics."

Dylan's fifth album, *Bringing It All Back Home*, combined his electric rock'n'roll music with folk--one side was acoustic and the other electric--as that album served as a transition from Bob Dylan folksinger to Bob Dylan rock'n'roller, carrying his poetry from folk into rock. It was rock that reached an even wider audience; still, what launched Dylan to the next level of recognition and success was the songs themselves, which had begun to be recorded by numerous others. Scaduto states "It was Dylan's work as a composer rather than performer, the startling imagery of his writing,that brought him his first wide audiences. For Dylan by now had transcended all his earlier influences and had taken the topical folk song beyond journalism--the topical song, at first, because that was the idiom in which he felt he had to work. Very deliberately, he was trying to bring poetry to what was usually only rhyme in the hands of most writers. He was conscious of himself as a poet. "The words to the songs aren't written out just for the paper," he would later tell an interviewer. "They're written so you can read it, you dig? If you take away whatever there is to the song--the beat, the melody--I could still recite it."

Dylan continued to fuse poetry with rock music in his songs through *Highway 61 Revisited* and his double album, *Blonde on Blonde*. This period--a very intense period of creativity--ended with his motorcycle accident in July, 1966 when he broke his neck and was forced to stop performing and spend time recovering. By this time he was a rock star, and his performances in concert were before large audiences who came as much for the music as for the poetry. His key performances during this time came during his tour of England in 1965 when the Beatles endorsed him and announced they were his fans. This put him in their league and, with the Rolling Stones, into the top echelon of rock performers.

The words, poetry--Dylan believed he could pull it off, writing poetry for a wide audience, for the people of the streets. Rimbaud had done it, and there was much of Rimbaud in Dylan and his contemporaries...Dylan used his guitar and harmonica--and, later, a rock band--to lend nuance to the poems, to end the divorce of music and poetry brought about by the printed page. In his liner notes, long letters, program notes, even a piece written for a folk magazine, *Hootenanny*, Dylan's writing was in the form of poetry.

Bob Dylan's songs are poetry, yet the role of a song in performance causes him to look at them as songs first, poetry later. Although there is a definite link between his songs and poetry, there is also a definite separation. He noted this when talking about his *John Wesley Harding* album with biographer Robert Shelton. He states: "I only look at them musically...as things to sing. It's the music that the words are sung to that's important. I write the songs because I need something to sing. It's the difference between the words on paper and the song. The song disappears into the air, the paper stays. They have little in common. A great poet, like Wallace Stevens, doesn't necessarily make a great singer. But a great singer always--like Billie Holiday--makes a great poet...I've always tried to get simple. I haven't always succeeded...I used to think that myself and my songs were the same thing. But I don't believe that anymore. There's myself and there's my song, which I hope is everybody's song."

The Introduction of Tape

Technically, the major breakthrough for consumers in the mid-1960s was the tape cartridge. The first label to release tapes was Victor, whose executives realized a changing trend in the music industry. With the transistor radio, listeners were not longer chained to their home stereos to listen to music. Now they could go anywhere with their small, portable radios. Tape had an even greater affect, making recorded music portable for the first time and changing the way people listen to music. In the past, when someone listened to an album, they had to sit down in their living room (or wherever their stereo system was), put on a record and listen. Further, the same room that held the phonograph often had the TV in it as well, so families could not listen to the TV and the phonograph at the same time.

Tape changed all that. After tape was accepted, people could listen to their favorite albums riding in the car, walking on the street or even jogging in the park. It allowed people to exercise with music, carry their favorite albums wherever they went, and created demands for new kinds of music.

The inventor of the first tape cartridge was Cleveland inventor George Eash. His "Fidelipac" was designed to be an automobile accessory. The Fidelipac came to the attention of Earl "Madman" Muntz, a Midwestern entrepreneur who began working on marketing the Fidelipac in 1958 and met Eash in 1961, where they agreed to open a Muntz stereo-pac headquarters in California in 1963.

There were problems with the Fidelipac, which were solved by William Lear (who also invented the Lear jet) who doubled the playing time and increased the tracks to eight. Lear made a deal with the Ford Motor company to install eight track playback systems in their 1966 line of higher priced autos. That contract went to the Motorola Company.

In 1967 General Motors, Chrysler and American Motors all announced they would include the 8-track into their models.

The Lear-designed 8-track system was available to consumers for the 1966 Christmas season. At the same time, Philips began marketing their compact cartridge system, distributed through Mercury Records. Philips called the unit a "cassette" and it played 1 7/8's ips, using one-eighth-inch-wide tape. The advantage of the Philips units was that it could record as well as play back and was available for home units as well as autos but there were several drawbacks, chief being the loud surface noise on cassettes.

The cassette had been introduced initially in Germany in 1962; the following year it was introduced into the United States by Norelco. It was originally intended as a business machine for dictation; ironically this was the same reason the phonograph invented by Thomas Edison was originally marketed.

The cassette had a number of things going against it when it was first introduced. The 8-track tape had a $60 million advertising campaign, financed by car companies and a noise reduction unit would not be made available to the public until 1970 when Ray Dolby invented one for the cassette but people had begun buy eight-track tape players and cartridges, locking in that early market.

David Geffen

David Geffen became a powerhouse manager during the 1960s after beginning his career at a booking agency. Along the way, he taught the music industry the "art of the deal" because he was a consummate deal maker. He played hardball and always held one overriding goal: win at all costs.

David Geffen was born in a blue-collar section of Brooklyn in 1943; his father died when he was 17. Geffen grew up dreaming of power and glamour, of being a mogul in Hollywood. After high school, he attended the University of Texas, but flunked out after his first semester. He stayed with his older brother in Los Angeles, a student at UCLA, then returned to New York and spent a semester at Brooklyn College. In 1964, at the age of 21, David Geffen walked into the offices of the William Morris Agency in New York and filled out an application.

William Morris stood alone at the top of the world of booking agencies in 1964; the previous year their top competitor, Music Corporation of America (MCA), gave up its talent agency when the United States Justice Department found it guilty of violating anti-trust laws with its purchase of Universal Pictures and Decca Records to go with its TV and movie production arm. MCA was forced to choose and they chose to concentrate on their movie, record and television companies.

On the application, Geffen stated that he had been a theater arts major at UCLA. He was hired and started work in the mail room; since he knew that William Morris regularly checked applicant's resumes, Geffen made sure he was the first to arrive in the mail room each morning so he could intercept a letter from UCLA that contradicted his claim; he found it so it never reached William Morris's personnel department.

William Morris had "trainees" for their organization; they began in the mail room and learned the organization. William Morris agents wore tailored suits and lived in a fast, hectic world. Geffen moved into the television division--the agency's most important--as an assistant, selling comedy writers to TV shows.

Booking rock and roll acts was not really part of the Morris organization, which did not consider it "prestigious" so agents did not view it as an important career track. However, Ros ???? Ross, a music agent for GAC, joined William Morris and led them into the rock and roll business. At that point, there were few music promoters so agents often called wrestling promoters to entice them to book and promote rock and roll acts. Ross had a key client: he represented the Rolling Stones who were not the legends they later became, but were still young stars on the ascendant.

David Geffen saw this situation and thought the music department might be a faster career track than television, so he switched departments. At first, he was the New York contact for a West Coast band, the Buffalo Springfield, then became the agent for several of Albert Grossman's acts, including Peter, Paul and Mary and Janis Joplin. Somewhere along the line, Geffen, whose musical tastes tended to run to Broadway musicals and classical music, found he admired, loved and respected those acts. David Geffen also learned that, whether it was television, the movies or music, a star is a star.

Geffen's first big act he found on his own was Laura Nyro, who had been signed by Artie Mogull for management, production and publishing and landed her a recording contract with Verve, a jazz label. Geffen booked Nyro into the Monterey Pop Festival in 1967 but the singer-songwriter bombed.

In 1968 Geffen left William Morris and joined a competitor, Ashley Famous Talent. That fall, he urged Nyro to hire an attorney to get out of her contract with Mogull. The move succeeded and Geffen became Nyro's manager, then created a publishing company, Tuna Fish Music, where he and Nyro were partners.

Since publishers control song copyrights, in essence "owning" the songs, the artist-owned publishing company allowed songwriters to control their own copyrights, building assets with each song. Those publishing companies were generally administered by a large, established company, who took either a fee or a percentage of the publishing income. Since income was split between a songwriter and a publisher 50/50 for income from airplay ("performances") and the sales of recordings ("mechanicals") songwriters who owned their own publishing company could receive 100 percent of the income of a song instead of 50 percent. In the case of Tuna Fish Music, Nyro received 50 percent of a song's income as the songwriter and an additional 25 percent as co-owner of the publishing company; Geffen received 25 percent of the income or half the publisher's share.

In 1968 Laura Nyro had her first big hit as a songwriter: "Stoned Soul Picnic" by the Fifth Dimension. She then signed a recording contract with Columbia and released her first album, *Eli and the Thirteenth Confession*. Nyro continued writing hit songs: "Eli's Coming" by Three Dog Night, "And When I Die" by Blood Sweat and Tears," "Wedding Bell Blues" by the Fifth Dimension, and "Stoney End" by Barbra Streisand were all hits. In the middle of her contract with Columbia, Geffen negotiated an extension with label head Clive Davis. Part of the contract extension involved selling Tuna Fish Music to April-Blackwood, CBS's publishing arm, for 75,000 shares of CBS Stock. Geffen then paid Artie Mogull $470,000 for the rights to the songs that publisher held.

The end result, when the ink was dried from these contracts, was that David Geffen, at the age of 27, was a millionaire.

The Graduate and Simon & Garfunkel

The film, *The Graduate*, was released on December 22, 1967 and became a major movie during 1968, helped by the Simon and Garfunkel soundtrack.

The film starred Dustin Hoffman in his first starring role, Anne Bancroft and Katharine Ross. The plot involved a recent college graduate (Hoffman) who was drifting after graduation, not knowing what he wanted to do. At a pool party at his parent's house to celebrate his graduation, his father's law partner's wife (Anne Bancroft) insisted he drive her home. At her home, she tried to seduce him but he resisted; however, shortly afterward they engage in an affair. The conflict occurred when he fell in love with her daughter (Katharine Ross). She planned to marry someone else but, at the wedding, he whisked her away, making true love a rebel act of freedom. The young audience loved it.

The hit song from the film was "Mrs. Robinson," written by Paul Simon and recorded by Simon and Garfunkel. The song entered the *Billboard* Hot 100 on April 27 and rose to number three, remaining there for three weeks.

The song was a major breakthrough for Simon and Garfunkel, whose next single was "The Boxer," which entered by Hot 100 on April 12 and reached number seven.

The soundtrack for *The Graduate* entered the *Billboard* chart on March 1 and rose to number 1 and remained there for nine consecutive weeks. Simon and Garfunkel's album, *Bookends*, released about the same time, entered the chart on April 27 and reached the number one position, staying there for seven consecutive weeks.

Steppenwolf and Iron Butterfly

In 1968 there was a heavier sound coming out of Los Angeles from Steppenwolf and Iron Butterfly.

Steppenwolf was formed in L.A., an outgrowth of Jack London and the Sparrows; the new group took their name from a Hermann Hesse novel. Group members were John Kay, lead vocals; keyboard player Goldy McJohn, guitarist Michael Monarch, bassist Rushton Moreve and drummer Jerry Edmonton.

Their third single, "Born to Be Wild" was in the film *Easy Rider* starring Peter Fonda, Dennis Hopper and Jack Nicholson. That song played as Fonda's motorcycle took off, forever linking that song with motorcycles. It entered the *Billboard* Hot 100 on July 13 and rose to number two. Their next single, "Magic Carpet Ride," entered the Hot 100 on October 5 and rose to number three.

Their first album, *Steppenwolf*, entered the *Billboard* chart on March 9 and rose to number 6, remaining on the chart for 87 weeks. Their second album, titled *The Second*, entered the *Billboard* chart on October 5 and rose to number three.

Iron Butterfly is best known for their single, "In-a-Gadda-da-Vida," a 17 minute long song that was edited down to 2:52 for radio airplay.

The band started in San Diego, then moved to Los Angeles. There were personnel changes and their first album, *Heavy*, was not successful. The line-up for their second album, *In-a-Gadda-da-Vida* was Doug Ingle, vocals and organ, Lee Dorman, bass, Ron Busby drums and Erick Bann, guitar and vocals. The single entered the Hot 100 on August 4 and reached number 30; their album entered the album chart on July 20 and reached number 4.

"In-a-Gadda-da-Vida" reportedly came from a long recording session. The line originally was "In the Garden of Eden" but as the session dragged on and on, the lyrics became less pronounced until the lyric became "in-a-gadda-da-vida."

FM disc jockeys on the new free form radio loved the 17 minute album cut because it gave them a long break during their shift and no doubt contributed to the popularity of the song.

Second CMA Awards Show

The Board of Directors for the Country Music Association wanted to have their show on network television so WSM executive Irving Waugh and Tree Publishing president Jack Stapp went to New York and met with the J. Walter Thompson advertising agency, which handled Kraft Foods, to sponsor a telecast on the CMA Awards for their "Kraft Music Hall" program. They were convincing and Kraft was convinced.

Kraft was set to sponsor a show by Roy Roger and Dale Evans from Texas but decided to let the husband and wife host the CMA Awards Show instead. Convinced that a live awards show would not draw a large audience because there were no big name "stars," the show was taped in black and white and shown in November, a month after the awards presentations.

Roy and Dale hosted the first televised "CMA Awards Show" at the Ryman Auditorium where Glen Campbell was voted "Entertainer of the Year." "Song of the Year" was "Honey," given to songwriter Bobby Russell, "Single of the Year" was "Harper Valley P.T.A." by Jeannie C. Riley, Male Vocalist was Glen Campbell, Female Vocalist was Tammy Wynette, Best

Vocal Group was Porter Wagoner and Dolly Parton, Best Album was Johnny Cash's *Live at Folsom Prison*, Best Instrumentalist was Chet Atkins, Best Instrumental Group was the Buckaroos (Buck Owens' band), Best Comedian was Ben Colder (the alter ego of Sheb Wooley) and Bob Wills was the new inductee into the Country Music Hall of Fame.

During the show there were performances by Johnny Cash, who sang "Folsom Prison Blues," Jeannie C. Riley sang "Harper Valley P.T.A.," Tammy Wynette sang "D-I-V-O-R-C-E" and Bobby Goldsboro sang "Honey."

Country Music in Los Angeles

There were roots for country music in California planted during the Great Depression when large populations of Okies from Oklahoma, Texas and Kansas moved to California in a desperate search for a better life. The Singing Cowboy movies starring Gene Autry, Roy Rogers and Tex Ritter were made in Hollywood. During the 1940s, there was more country music recorded in Los Angeles than anywhere else.

During the 1960s a number of young performers began their musical careers playing folk and bluegrass, including Jerry Garcia of the Grateful Dead. Long hair was a political statement during the 1960s that ran counter to the conservative politics of Nashville. The L.A. musicians revered country music, especially artists like Merle Haggard and the Louvin Brothers, but played country music with a fresh edge and heavier beat that the Nashville produced country.

The L.A. musicians who played country music during the 1960s were viewed by Nashville as part of the counterculture, part of rock'n'roll but were not really country as defined by Nashville. L.A. country music did not obtain airplay on country radio or have a following with Nashville country audiences. The L.A. musicians felt like outsiders and the country music establishment, based in Nashville, seemed to view them as "not one of us." It was a clash of cultures defined by politics, long hair and drugs even though they were united by a music.

Chris Hillman

Chris Hillman grew up in northern San Diego County and became interested in folk and country music through his older sister, who returned from college with an album by the New Lost City Ramblers. The TV shows, "Town Hall Party," The Space Cooley Show" and "Cal's Corral" were broadcast in the Los Angeles area and Hillman watched them, furthering his interest in country music. He learned to play guitar and became interested in bluegrass; at 15 he attended a show by the Kentucky Colonels at the Ash Grove in Los Angeles, which sparked his interest in the mandolin. When Hillman was 16, his father committed suicide.

Hillman took banjo lessons from Scott Hambly and developed into a proficient musician; he joined the Scottsville Squirrel Barkers, who recorded an album, *Blue Grass Favorites*. The group disbanded in 1963 and Hillman joined the Golden State Boys, whose members included the brothers Vern and Rex Gosdin and banjoist Don Parmley; Vern Gosdin later became a country star and Parmley later joined the Bluegrass Cardinals. They changed their name to The Hillmen and Hillman performed as Chris Hardin to hide the fact he was underage when they performed in bars. The group appeared regularly on TV in the L.A. area. After the Hillmans broke up, Chris joined the Green Grass Revival, a spinoff of the New Christy Minstrels.

Jim Dickson was the Hillman's producer and manager and invited Hillman to join Jim McGuinn, David Crosby, Gene Clark and Michael Clarke in a new band that became known, after several name changes, as The Byrds. In the Byrds, Hillman played bass, which he had never played before, and in 1965 the group hit with "Mr. Tambourine Man." The early Byrd's recordings featured Jim McGuinn and Michael Clarke on lead vocals with Crosby adding harmony, but after Clark left in 1966, Hillman developed as a singer and songwriter. On the *The Notorious Byrd Brothers* album, Hillman co-wrote seven of the 11 songs.

Chris Hillman met Gram Parsons in 1967 in a bank; business manager Larry Spector had told Hillman about Parsons.

Gram Parsons

Gram Parsons was born Ingram Cecil Connor III in Waycross, Georgia on November 5, 1946; his mother, Avis, was the daughter of Avis Connor a wealthy citrus fruit magnate; his father, Cecil (known as "Coon Dog") was a World War II flying ace. When Gram was 12, his father committed suicide during the Christmas season. His mother then married Robert Parsons and Gram and his sister adopted their step-father's name. Gram graduated from the prestigious Bolles School, a private school in Jacksonville, Florida on June 5, 1965; that same day his mother died from a life of heavy drinking.

During his teenage years, Parsons played in rock'n'roll cover bands in clubs owned by his step-father. When he was 16, inspired by the Urban Folk revival led by the Kingston Trio, Parsons began playing folk music with a group, Shiloh. The group disbanded in spring, 1965.

Parsons was accepted at Harvard but only spent one semester there. At Harvard, Parsons heard Merle Haggard for the first time and became interested in country music. He formed a group, the International Submarine Band and in 1967 moved to Los Angeles where the band was signed to LHI Records by producer Lee Hazelwood and recorded an album, *Safe At Home*, which was released in 1968.

The Byrds bring L.A. Country to Nashville

The Byrds only had two original members, Chris Hillman and Roger (formerly Jim) McGuinn at the beginning of 1968. Gram Parsons was invited to audition for the band after David Crosby left and joined. Chris Hillman and Gram Parsons became the two key figures in the country music movement in L.A., although Rick Nelson had recorded an album, *Bright Lights and Country Music*, that was released in 1966. Hillman played bass and mandolin in the revised Byrds, who recorded the landmark *Sweetheart of the Rodeo* album.

Shortly after the album's release, Parsons left the group and Hillman recruited guitarist Clarence White, who had been with the Kentucky Colonels. After a few more changes, Hillman left the group and formed The Flying Burrito Brothers with Parsons before Parsons left to pursue a solo career.

The Byrds *Sweetheart of the Rodeo* album and appearance on the Grand Ole Opry

On March 15, 1968, the Byrds played on the Grand Ole Opry, performing Merle Haggard's "Sing Me Back Home" and Gram Parson's "Hickory Wind." The Byrds had success in folk-rock, recording hits such as "Mr. Tambourine Man," "Turn, Turn, Turn" and "Eight Miles High." Gram Parsons, a new member of the Byrds, pushed them to record in Nashville and on March 9-15, 1968 they recorded in Columbia Studio A, the same studio where Bob Dylan recorded. Their *Sweetheart of the Rodeo* album became an influential album amongst rock artists and fans who found an appeal in country music. The Byrds brought attention to Nashville and country music but they never had a country hit; they were considered "rock" and cutting a country album did not change that. The Byrds—Parsons, Roger McGuinn, Chris Hillman and Kevin Kelley—were joined by Nashville musicians Lloyd Green, John Hartford, Clarence White, Roy Husky and Earl Ball on the sessions. The album was released on

August 30—after Parsons left the group—and their single, "You Ain't Going Nowhere," reached the pop but not the country chart.

"Harper Valley P.T.A."

There have never been many "protest" songs in country music but a song protesting hypocrisy in a small town was considered fair game by the country audience. "Harper Valley P.T.A." was recorded by Jeannie C. Riley, a receptionist on Music Row for the independent label, Plantation, owned by Shelby Singleton, who was the former head of A&R for Mercury Records. It entered the country chart August, 24, 1968 and was number one on Billboard's country chart for three consecutive weeks. The song entered the Hot 100 chart the same week and rose to number one three. In the midst of a counterculture year, a country song became popular on pop radio.

The song was written by Tom T. Hall and produced by Shelby Singleton for his Plantation Records label. This song led to a play and film.

"Stand By Your Man"

Country music was the "counter" to the "counterculture" of the 1960s. Nashville represented conservative politics in the midst of a liberal/ progressive era. It was an era when country represented the "traditional values" of a nuclear family and booze while the counterculture represented feminism, free love and marijuana.

"Stand By Your Man," recorded by Tammy Wynette and written by Tammy and her producer, Billy Sherrill, was a prime example of country music being part of the "counter" to the "counterculture." The song looked at love in the traditional way, although Tammy was married five times.

"Stand By Your Man" entered the *Billboard* country chart on October 19 and reached number one, where it remained for three weeks. It also reached the Hot 100, rising to number 19.

It was truly an unusual year with different music genres and different lifestyles all finding their way onto pop radio.

Johnny Cash: Live at Folsom Prison

On January 13, 1968, Johnny Cash recorded his live concert at Folsom Prison. Cash had battled drugs and, at the end of 1967, had gotten himself clean. Cash had written "Folsom Prison Blues" after seeing the film *Inside the Walls of Folsom Prison* in 1953 when he was in Germany serving in the Air Force. "Folsom Prison Blues" was Cash's second single for Sun Records in 1955. During the show Cash was joined by June Carter, the Tennessee

Three (Marshal Grant, W.S. Hollard and Luther Perkins) and the Statler Brothers. The album was released in May and reached number one on the Country Albums chart and number 13 on the pop chart; the single, "Folsom Prison," was number one on the country singles chart for four consecutive weeks and the album was certified "Gold" before the end of the year.

Joan Baez in Nashville—the first time

When Joan Baez came to Nashville to record at Columbia Studio A in 1968, there was security posted around the studio because it was feared that resistance to Baez's political views might create problems. It is probable that many (most?) of the session players did not agree with Baez's political views but they put politics aside and backed her on two albums, *Any Day Now* (released in December, 1968) and *David's Album* (released in May, 1969. Backed by Jerry Kennedy (guitar), Jerry Reed (guitar), Grady Martin (guitar), Harold Bradley (guitar and dobro), Fred Carter (mandolin), Pete Drake (steel guitar), Johnny Gimble (fiddle), Tommy Jackson (fiddle), Buddy Spicher (fiddle) Fred Carter (mandolin), Roy Huskey, Jr. (bass), Norbert Putnam (bass) Harold Rugg (guitar, dobro) and Kenny Buttrey (drums) with pop musician Stephen Stills on guitar, Baez recorded 16 songs written by Bob Dylan; this was the *Any Day Now* album.

Baez's husband, David Harris, was an anti-war activist scheduled to be imprisoned for resistance to the draft and a fan of country music; that was the reason Baez came to Nashville to record. The ten songs on *David's Album* included traditional numbers "Will the Circle Be Unbroken," "The Tramp on the Street," "Poor Wayfaring Stranger," the gospel song "Just a Closer Walk With Thee" and the A.P. Carter song, "My Home's Across the Blue Ridge Mountains" as well as the country hit, "Green, Green Grass of Home," "Hickory Wind" by Gram Parson and Bob Buchanan, "Rock Salt and Nails" by Utah Phillips and a new song, "If I Knew" by Nina Dusheck and Pauline Marden.

"Rocky Top"

"Rocky Top" is a song that every bluegrass band has to play. The song was originally recorded by The Osborne Brothers and entered the country chart on February 3, 1968 and reached number 33. It was written by Felice and Boudleaux Bryant, who had been assigned by Chet Atkins to write an album's worth of songs for Archie Campbell album, *Golden Years*, about aging adults. The Bryants had purchased the Gatlinburg Inn in the Great Smoky Mountains and retreated there to write the Campbell album. The songs were slow and Felice suggested they write something "light" to break the spell of writing slow songs. They wrote "Rocky Top" in about ten minutes. The song was popular during Osborne Brothers concerts but did not achieve national popularity until Lynn Anderson released her version in 1972 (it reached number 17 on the country chart). The Osborne's were voted CMA's "Vocal Group of the Year" in 1971 due the popularity of the song. The song was first played at halftime during a Tennessee-Florida football game when the University of Tennessee's "Pride of the Southland" marching band performed it; it's been played at Tennessee football games ever since. The "real" Rocky Top is a sub-peak of Thunderhead Mountain in the Great Smokes on the Tennessee-North Carolina border. The song is one of Tennessee's ten official state songs. The song is so popular at bluegrass concerts that bluegrass groups dread hearing it requested.

Bonnie and Clyde and Earl Scruggs

Earl Scruggs' banjo rang out loud and clear playing "Foggy Mountain Breakdown" during the film, *Bonnie and Clyde*, starring Warren Beatty and Faye Dunaway, when it was released on August 13, 1967. The song was originally recorded the song in 1949 with the Foggy Mountain Boys, led by Lester Flatt and Scruggs, for Mercury Records. The original recording featured Scruggs playing a Gibson Granada five-string banjo in the "Scruggs" or "three finger" style of playing that he popularized. A new version of "Foggy Mountain Breakdown" by Flatt and Scruggs and the Foggy Mountain Boys" was recorded for Columbia, their label in 1967 and that version reached number 58 on the country chart and number 55 on the pop chart in 1968. That inspired a number of young people to learn the banjo

Republican Convention: 1968

The 1968 Republican was held August 5-8 in Miami Beach, Florida. Richard Nixon had been the Republican nominee in 1960 but lost to John Kennedy. The "new Nixon" had devised a "Southern strategy" based on the South's opposition to integration and liberal/progressive policies and programs of the Democratic party under President Lyndon Johnson. A key phrase he used was "law and order," which implied a crackdown on campus demonstrations and racial unrest.

Richard Nixon was elected to be the Republican nominee for the Presidency on the first ballot, defeating Nelson Rockefeller and Ronald Reagan. He selected Maryland Governor Spiro Agnew as his vice-presidential running mate.

The Convention was relatively un-eventful. There was a picture of entertainer Sammy Davis, Jr. hugging the President when he walked on stage during Davis's performance; clearly visible in the background is Mike Curb at a keyboard.

Democratic Convention: 1968

The 1968 Democratic Convention was held August 26-29 in Chicago. It was a fractious convention.

Going into the convention, the Democratic party was divided. Senator Eugene McCarthy had entered the Democratic primaries on an anti-Vietnam platform and attracted a number of activist youth volunteers who were opposed to the Vietnam war. In March, Robert Kennedy, Senator from New York and formerly Attorney General under his brother's presidency, entered the race. President Johnson declared he would not run at the end of March and vice-president Hubert Humphrey inherited his delegates, although he never competed in any of the primaries. After Kennedy was assassinated on June 5, his delegates were uncommitted. By the time the convention began, the candidates were McCarthy, the "peace" candidate; Humphrey, who was part of the Johnson administration that was waging the Vietnam War; and Senator George McGovern, who appealed to some of the Kennedy supporters.

There were massive protests outside the convention hall. Young people belonging to The National Mobilization Committee to End the War in Vietnam and the Youth International Party (Yippies) as well as the Students for a Democratic Society—in addition to a number of demonstrators not affiliated with any organization—numbered around 10,000. Mayor Richard Daley, determined to show the country a peaceful, orderly Chicago, met the demonstrators with 23,000 police and National Guardsmen who beat them and sprayed them with tear gas. Not only did the 23,000 assigned to keep order beat demonstrators, they also beat the media outside the convention covering the event. There were even news media accosted by the police inside the convention center, including CBS TV reporter Dan Rather.

The Yippies used humor and satire to gain attention. Yippie leader Jerry Rubin and folk singer Phil Ochs organized a a mock convention and nominated Pigasus—a real pig. Rubin, Ochs and Pigasus were all arrested. The Yippies threatened to put LSD in Chicago's water supply. If they had done that, the LSD would have been diluted so there was really no threat although Chicago residents felt threatened.

About 10,000 protestors gathered in Grant Park for a demonstration on August 28. . During the afternoon, a young man lowered the American flag and police began beating him; the crowd responded by hurling food, rocks and chunks of concrete at the protestors. The protestors then dispersed throughout Chicago while police sprayed them with tear gas. Police assaulted demonstrators in front of the Hilton Hotel was shown on live television and was a visual demonstration of the violence inflicted upon protestors in Chicago by the police. The police were forceful, indiscriminate in who they beat or tear gassed and unrestrained in their clashes with demonstrators.

By the end of the Convention, Hubert Humphrey had been elected as the Democratic candidate for President; his running mate was Senator Ed Muskie.

The anti-Vietnam protestors believed that Americans would be on their side after seeing police clashes but surveys of public opinion showed that the majority of Americans sided with Mayor Daley. Media reports later concluded that the Chicago riots had a major effect in electing Richard Nixon as president.

The Chicago Seven

After the Democratic Convention, the Justice Department charged seven individuals with conspiracy and incitement to riot in Chicago. Those named were Abbie Hoffman, Tom Hayden, David Dellinger, Rennie Davis, John Froines, Jerry Rubin, Lee Weiner and Bobby Seale. During the trial there were constant demonstrations outside the courthouse, protesting the charges against those seven.

Nixon elected president

On Tuesday, November 5, Richard Nixon won the Presidency with a razor thin edge in the popular vote, collecting 43.4 percent of the vote against 42.7 percent for Humphrey. George Wallace, who ran an anti-civil rights campaign, won 13.5 percent of the vote, winning the states of Arkansas, Louisiana, Alabama, Mississippi and Georgia.

The Elvis Comeback

Elvis Presley missed the early years of the British Invasion. He had a string of chart records but, except for "Crying in the Chapel" they weren't big hits. Instead, Elvis was in Hollywood during those years making movies.

They were not "must see" movies except for the most dedicated Elvis fans. Even Elvis grew tired of those formulaic low-budget releases.

Elvis's manager, Colonel Tom Parker, approached Tom Sarnoff, West Coast VP of NBC about an Elvis special sponsored by Singer Sewing Machines to be called "Singer Presents." Parker conceived a Christmas Special but Elvis disliked the idea. Elvis met with producer Bob Finkel and a new idea emerged: A TV special centered on Elvis that would provide a soundtrack album and a Christmas single would also be recorded.

Finkel brought in director Steve Binker, who had directed the *T.A.M.I. Show* film and worked on "Hullabaloo" and wanted to introduce Elvis to a new, young audience. He enlisted the help of Bones Howe and they met with Colonel Parker, who gave them complete creative control but all publishing rights on songs had to be under the publishing companies owned by Presley. Binder agreed.

Binder and Howe put together a team to tape the special and record the soundtrack. In June, 1968, rehearsals began in Hollywood but during those two weeks there was dissention in the crew and different ideas for the special were presented. The group moved to the NBC studios in Burbank on June 17. After seeing Elvis interact with his entourage, playing songs and kibitzing, Binder and Howe decided on sit-down concert with two of Elvis's band members from his early days, , Scotty Moore and DJ Fontana along with Charlie Hodge and Alan Fortas from Elvis's entourage who all sat on a small stage that looked like a boxing ring. There was no script but Binder and Howe gave Elvis a list of topics to cover, such as his early years.

Recording began at United Western Recorders on June 20 with L.A. session players Tommy Tedesco and Mike Deasy on guitars and Hal Blaine on drums in addition to members of the NBC orchestra.

During the taping of the sit-down section, Elvis sang songs and joked while wearing a leather outfit—something he had never done before, but it fit his image. Presley and the group took a break and then returned for another sit-down session.

The show was scripted to end with Elvis making a spoken statement and then a Christmas song, "I'll Be Home For Christmas." but Binder decided the show should close with another song. He told music director Billy Goldenberg and lyricist Walter Earl Brown to write one that reflected Elvis's beliefs. . The night before the session, they wrote "If I Can Dream" and used phrases and imagery from Martin Luther King's speeches. Goldenberg and Brown played the song for Colonel Tom Parker, who disliked it and thought it wasn't an "Elvis song" but they then played it for Elvis, who decided he liked it.

After Elvis decided to record it, Colonel Parker demanded 100 percent publishing rights. Goldenberg then took his name off the song and told Parker that Brown had written it, and that's how . Walter Earl Brown came to be listed as the sole songwriter.

"If I Can Dream" was performed at the end of the taping with Elvis in a white suit and a big red ELVIS on a black background. Using a hand held microphone, Elvis's performance was emotional and intense. The show ended with Elvis saying "Good night, thank you very much."

During the tapings in June, Elvis told Colonel Parker that he wanted to return to touring and performing live concerts.

When the taping had finished, there were four hours of tapes that had to be trimmed to 50 minutes for the TV show. During the summer and fall, those edits were made and Elvis approved of the final cut.

On Tuesday, December 3, 1968 at 9 p.m. Eastern time, "Singer Presents... ELVIS" was broadcast. It came in first place in the ratings, ahead of the popular "Rowan & Martin's Laugh-In." Of all those watching TV that evening, 42 percent watched Elvis; it was the most watched TV show that season.

The single, "If I Can Dream" was released before the special aired and entered the Billboard Hot 100 November 30; it peaked at number 12. The album Elvis—TV Special, contained 23 songs, although five were medleys as well as some dialogue, entered the Billboard chart on December 21 and reached number eight the following year.

Elvis was back!

1969

The Beatles and the Get Back sessions and rooftop concert

The Beatles were contractually obligated to film another movie. Paul McCartney suggested that if they filmed a documentary rehearsing for a TV special and upcoming live performance in addition to recording their next album, their contract would be fulfilled. Those ideas emerged in various forms as the filming progressed. The project would satisfy their movie obligation as well as get the Beatles performing together live again, something they had not done since they quit touring in 1966.

After some discussion and dissention, the group agreed and on January 2, 1969, they were in Twickenham Film Studios to begin rehearsals.

Although George Martin was involved in production, but McCartney wanted engineer/producer Glyn Johnson involved, overseeing the sound, although his role was never fully defined. As a result, he was given credit as an engineer but, although he often acted in the role of producer, he was never given producer credit on the album that emerged.

Filming was done by Michael Lindsay-Hogg and Tony Richmond was director of photography with the Beatles as "Executive Producers," which meant they paid for the filming.

On Wednesday, January 2, Beatles roadie Mal Evans was filmed bringing in the Beatles musical equipment bright and early. At 11 a.m. John Lennon, George Harrison and Ring Starr arrived; McCartney arrived at 12:30 p.m.

The group had a simmering anger with disagreements that could surface at any time. They were at the studio Monday through Friday, generally starting between 11 a.m. and 1 p.m. without a clear musical direction. The soundstage was cold and the Beatles bickered, although there were also moments of laughter as the Beatles jammed on over a hundred songs, from "Baa Baa Black Sheep" to the Elvis rocker "All Shook Up" to songs they recorded, such as "Help!' and new songs they were working on such as "All Things Must Pass," "Back Seat of My Car," "Child of Nature," "Every Night," "Give Me Some Truth," "Maybe I'm Amazed" and "That Would Be Something." Some of these songs, such as "All Things Must Pass" and "Maybe I'm Amazed" were on later Beatles solo projects.

Along the way, George Harrison quit the group but came back.

On January 22, the Beatles moved to their Apple Studios in the basement of their Savile Row building. If they were going to record an album, it had to be in a recording studio, although film cameras would also be there. It would be a back to basics recording session for the Beatles, with technical trickery but every song performed live for the tape.

That day, keyboardist Billy Preston, who the Beatles first met in Hamburg, Germany when Preston was in Little Richard's band, dropped by the Savile Row offices and was invited by George Harrison to join the sessions to help alleviate the tense atmosphere.

The sessions were not pleasant experiences for the individual Beatles, who found it difficult to focus on a song but instead headed off in jam sessions. That first day, the Beatles did a run-through Lennon's "All I Want Is You" (which later became "Dig a Pony"), John and Paul's "I've Got a Feeling," Lennon's "Don't Let Me Down," an instrumental listed as "Rocker," "McCartney's "Bathroom Window" (later known as "She Came in Through the Bathroom Window"), as well as a Drifters hit, "Save the Last Dance For Me" and "Going Up The Country," which was recorded by Canned Heat.

The sessions generally ended at 5 p.m. because of requirements of the film crew, but a few went on to 10 at night.

On January 23, the Beatles recorded a number of takes on McCartney's song, "Get Back." The next day they ran through "On Our Way Home" (later titled "Two of Us"), McCartney's "Teddy Boy," the old Liverpool skiffle song "Maggie Mae" (from an impromtu jam between takes of "On the Way Home"), Lennon's "Dig It' and "Dig a Pony" and "I've Got a Feeling."

On Saturday, January 25, the Beatles recorded an short instrumental "Untitled Jamming," the Everly Brothers "Bye Bye Love," McCartney's "Let It Be" and Harrison's "George's Blues," later titled "For You Blue."

Sunday, January 26, the Beatles recorded a 12 minute and 25 second version of "Dig It." The Beatles then strung together some old rock'n'roll songs. They did Big Joe Turner's "Shake, Rattle and Roll," Wilbur Harrison's "Kansas City," Little Richard's "Miss Ann," Lloyd Price's "Lawdy Miss Clawdy," Carl Perkins "Blue Suede Shoes," and Smokey Robinson and the Miracle's "You've Really Got a Hold On Me." George Harrison then began the Miracle's "Tracks of My Tears," which evolved into a mostly instrumental. The group then taped McCartney's "The Long and Winding Road" and Harrison did a demo with just his guitar of a song that became "Isn't It a Pity."

The next day, the Beatles with Billy Preston recorded "Untitled Jamming" (for almost 11 minutes), "Get Back," "Oh! Darling," "I've Got a Feeling" and "The Walk," which was a hit in 1958 for Jimmy McCracklin. The old rock'n'roll songs the Beatles put down on tape were songs they did when they were a 50s cover band, performing in Germany and Liverpool.

Since the death of Brian Epstein, the Beatles had been managing themselves. They knew they needed a new manager and discussed several. On Sunday, Allen Klein met with John Lennon to discuss Klein's management of the Beatles and on Monday met with the other Beatles. George Harrison and Ringo Starr agreed to go with Klein but McCartney preferred Lee and John Eastman.

On Tuesday, January 28, the Beatles recorded "Get Back" and "Don't Let Me Down," which would be the two sides of their next single. They also recorded their first single, "Love Me Do" and ""The One After 909," which they had recorded on their first session but never released. They also did "Dig a Pony," "I've Got a Feeling" and "Teddy Boy." There were also two Billy Preston demos, "Billy's Song (1) and "Billy's Song (2) that were never released.

A conversation between the Beatles was captured on tape, with opinions expressed about whether they should be recording or rehearsing, when the filming would end, what songs they should do—or whether they should just forget the whole thing. Obviously, things were not going well.

On Wednesday the group recorded "Teddy Boy," "The One After 909," Lennon's "I Want You" (later titled "I Want You (She's So Heavy)," two Buddy Holly songs "Not Fade Away" and "Mailman, Bring Me No More Blues" and "Besame Mucho," which had been a Cavern Club favorite they had recorded on their first session but never released.

A cold wind blew through London on Thursday, January 30. Four days earlier, the group had the idea to perform a set live on the roof of the Apple Building on Savile Row. That morning Michael Lindsay-Hogg set up for filming, then the Beatles did "Get Back," then did it again, which led into "Don't Let Me Down," followed by "I've Got a Feeling," "The One After 909," a false start on "Dig a Pony," then John asking for the lyrics before they did the full song."

Engineer Alan Parson had to change tapes. The Beatles and Billy Preston did a quick version of "God Save the Queen," the British national anthem. With the second tape on the machine, the Beatles did "I've Got a Feeling," then "Don't Let Me Down" and a third version of "Get Back" as police come onto the roof to shut the concert down.

The lunch time concert had lasted 42 minutes and was thought to be the end of the "Get Back" project. That evening, Glyn Johns mixed the session at Olympic Studios and had acetates cut for each of the Beatles.

It was decided to issue the January 28 studio recordings of "Get Back" and "Don't Let Me Down" as a single, accompanied by promotional video clips from Lindsay-Hogg's film work.

On Friday, January 31, the Beatles recorded "The Long and Winding Road," "Let It Be" and "Two of Us" in the Apple studio. They also jammed on "Lady Madonna." For those recordings, the Beatles set up in stage formation on and around a platform.

That ended the "Get Back" film and recording project but it would be a long time before the film and album were released.

Grammy Awards

On March 12, 1969 the 11th Annual Grammy Awards were held in Los Angeles, New York, Chicago and Nashville to honor recordings released in 1968.

"Record of the Year" was "Mrs. Robinson" by Simon & Garfunkel, produced by Paul Simon and Roy Halee; "Album of the Year" was *By the Time I Get to Phoenix* by Glen Campbell, produced by Al De Lory; "Song of the Year" was "Little Green Apples," written by Bobby Russell and recorded by Roger Miller and O.C. Smith on separate releases; and "Best New Artist" was Jose Feliciano.

There were five categories in "Pop": "Best Vocal, Female" was Dionne Warwick for "Do You Know the Way to San Jose?"; Best Vocal, Male" was Jose Feliciano for "Light My Fire"; Best Vocal Duo or Group" was Simon & Garfunkel for "Mrs. Robinson"; Best Chorus" was the Alan Copeland Singers for "Mission Impossible/Norwegian Wood Medley"; and "Best Pop Instrumental" was "Classical Gas" by Mason Williams.

There were four R&B Grammys: "Best Vocal, Female" was Aretha Franklin for "Chain of Fools"; "Best Vocal Male" was "Otis Redding for "(Sittin' On) The Dock of the bay" (posthumously); "Best Do or Group" was the Temptations for "Cloud Nine" and "Best R&B Song" was "(Sittin' On) The Dock of the Bay" written by Otis Redding and Steve Cropper and performed by Otis Redding.

There were four Country Grammys: "Best Vocal, Female" was Jeannie C. Riley for "Harper Valley P.T.A."; Best Vocal, Male was Johnny Cash for "Folsom Prison Blues"; "Best Duo or Group" was Flatt & Scruggs for "Foggy Mountain Breakdown" and "Best Country Song" was "Little Green Apples," written by Bobby Russell and recorded by Roger Miller and O.C. Smith, separately.

There were three Gospel Grammys: "Best Gospel Performance" was The Happy Goodman Family for *The Happy Gospel of the Happy Goodmans*; "Best Soul Gospel Performance" was Dottie Rambo for "The Soul of Me" and "Best Sacred Performance" was Jake Hess for "Beautiful Isle of Somewhere."

The Grammy for "Folk" went to Judy Collins for "Both Sides Now."

Beatles personal's lives

On Wednesday, March 12, Paul McCartney and Linda Eastman were married at the Marylebone Register Office. At the same time, police were at George Harrison's home, arresting him and his wife, Patti, for possession of cannabis. John and Yoko were at the Abbey Road studio listening to their "Peace Song."

Eight days later, on March 20, John and Yoko were married in Gibraltar, then spent their honeymoon in Paris at the Amsterdam Hilton on a "bed in" for peace. Journalists gathered and filed newspaper and video reports of the two in bed, talking about peace for 18 hours a day for seven days.

The Beatles did media interviews except Ringo, who was filming *The Magic Christian* on location.

On Monday, April 14, John Lennon and Paul McCartney were in the EMI Studios on Abbey road and recorded "The Ballad of John and Yoko (They're Gonna Crucify Me)" about John and Yoko's life and marriage. Lennon played acoustic and lead guitar, Paul played piano, bass, drums and maracas. On April 16, the Beatles recorded "Old Brown Shoe," written by Harrison as well as their first stab at recording another Harrison song, "Something."

"The Ballad of John and Yoko" b/w "Old Brown Shoe" were released at the end of May, the first stereo single by the Beatles. Meanwhile, mixes and overdubs and new recordings were done on "Oh! Darling," "Two of Us," "Octopus's Garden," "You Know My Name (Look Up My Number" and "Let It Be" during April.

On May 10, "Get Back" entered the *Billboard* Hot 100 and reached number one, where it remained for five weeks.

Good by to Get Back

The Beatles had finally given up on the "Get Back" album project on May 28 after engineer Glyn Johns finished mixing and sent copies of the proposed LP to each of the Beatles, who rejected it. The line-up for that album was: Side A—"The One After 909," "Rocker," "Save the Last Dance for Me," "Don't Let Me Down, "Dig a Pony, "I've Got a Feeling, "Get Back" and Side B—"For You Blue," "Teddy Boy," "Two of Us," "Maggie Mae," "Dig It, "Let It Be," "The Long and Winding Road" and a reprise of "Get Back."

For the cover of the album, the Beatles posed at EMI headquarters in an identical pose for their first album cover.

Elvis returns to performing

In January, 1969, Elvis' single, "If I Can Dream" reached number 12. He recorded his next album, *From Elvis in Memphis*, produced by Chips Moman at the American Recording Studio in Memphis with Memphis session musicians. On May 3, "In the Ghetto" entered the *Billboard* Hot 100 and reached number three. On September 13, "Suspicious Minds" entered the *Billboard* Hot 100 chart and rose to number one, his first number one single on the Hot 100 since "Good Luck Charm" in 1963. A third single in 1969, "Don't Cry Daddy" entered the Hot 100 on November 29 and reached number six.

His album *From Elvis in Memphis* entered the *Billboard* chart on June 14 and rose to number 13.

Elvis returned to live performing on July 1 with a four week stand in Las Vegas that saw him perform 57 shows over four weeks. Scotty Moore, D.J. Fontana and the Jordainaires did not accompany him because they had too much session work in Nashville so Elvis formed a new band, led by guitarist James Burton and featuring two gospel groups, the all-male Imperials and all-female Sweet Inspirations. Bill Belew designed new stage costumes, which gave him a distinctive look that defined his image from that point on.

On his first show in Las Vegas, he entered the stage unannounced and was given a standing ovation by the audience of 2,200 before he sang a note.

Woodstock

In 1969 it was a summer of festivals for rock and roll. The "father" of those festivals was the Monterey Pop Festival, held in 1967; in 1968 the movie *Monterey Pop* was released and served as an inspiration for concert promoters, artists, fans, and filmmakers to try and re-create the magic of Monterey. However, there were a number of problems that occurred.

The Monterey Festival was profitable; although only 7,100 tickets were sold, the artists all performed for expenses, which meant that there was about $250,000 cleared when it was over.

The idea of thousands of fans in an open field enjoying a line-up of great acts was appealing, so concert promoters set about staging that kind of event. During Easter week, there was a two day festival in Palm Springs, California; the first night John Mayall, the Butterfield Blues Band and Procol Harum performed at a drive-in theater and the next night Ike and Ina Turner played in a minor-league baseball stadium. A riot ensued as concert goers clashed with police outside the baseball stadium on the second night. An essential problem that had not occurred to concert organizers was that the dominant drug at Monterey--marijuana--was a drug that tended to make people mellow. During the ensuing two years, other drugs, including hallucinogenics which made people more prone to violence, became popular.

Two weekends later, there was an L.A. Free Festival in Venice that resulted in a number of arrests. In May there was the Aldergrove Beach Rock Festival in British Columbia, then the Newport 1969 Festival just outside Los Angeles was held in June. That three day festival attracted 150,000 fans who heard Jimi Hendrix, Creedence Clearwater Revival, Steppenwolf, Jethro Tull and Booker T. and the MGs. There was another clash with police and arrests; at the Denver Pop Festival a week later the same basic line-up attracted 50,000 fans.

Things ran smoother in Toronto (50,000 fans watched The Band and Procol Harum) and the Atlanta Pop Festival (140,000 for Joe Cocker, Creedence Clearwater Revival, Johnny Winter, Paul Butterfield, Led Zeppelin and Janis Joplin). In July, somewhere between 300,000 and 650,000 gathered in London at Hyde Park to see a free concert by a line-up that was headlined by the Rolling Stones, who toured America later that year.

And then came Woodstock, held on August 19-21 on Max Yasgur's farm in Bethel, New York. The Woodstock Festival was actually not in Woodstock. The event was advertised for Woodstock but the town denied permits to the organizers so they were forced to move it, but it was still called the Woodstock Music and Arts Festival.

Recording rights to the festival were with Atlantic Records, although they only had one act, Crosby, Still, Nash and Young, on the festival. Warner brothers Pictures secured the film rights.

The line-up of acts was impressive: The Jimi Hendrix Experience, Blood, Sweat and Tears, Joan Baez, Creedence Clearwater Revival, The Jefferson Airplane, The Band, Janis Joplin, Sly and the Family Stone, Canned Heat, the Who, Richie Havens, Crosby, Stills, Nash * Young, Arlo Guthrie, Ravi Shankar, Johnny Winter, Ten Years After, Country Joe and the Fish and the Grateful Dead. The build-up to the Festival was intense; young fans quickly concluded this was THE festival to attend. Unfortunately, a whole lot went wrong for the concert promoters.

The organizers planned for 150,000 to attend, but about 400,000 showed up. There were 300 off-duty New York City police to handle security but, at the last minute, the New York Police Department applied pressure so the trained police canceled. An improvised, untrained security force was hired quickly. On Friday, the roads into Woodstock were jammed with automobiles and the crowd over-ran the barriers and fences set up, so ticket collection had to be abandoned. Because of the much larger than anticipated crowds, there was inadequate food, water and toilets. And then it started to rain.

There seemed to be a shortage of everything except drugs and music but a community came together that weekend. In the end, there were three deaths and three births at the festival, and a film crew to document it. There for all the world to see was the essence of the cultural gap between Americans: some were fighting in the mud in Vietnam while others were fornicating in the mud at Woodstock. Middle America looked on disapprovingly as long-haired, free spirited youth imbibed drugs and partied for a long weekend.

In the end, the festival gave a name to that generation: Woodstock Nation. It became the most visible image of that generation, especially when the movie was released the following year.

Crosby, Stills & Nash

The Byrds ousted David Crosby from the group in mid-1967 and the Buffalo Springfield disbanded in 1968. Stephen Stills and Crosby often met to jam together and wrote "Wooden Ships" when the two, with Paul Kanter of Jefferson Airplane, were in Florida on Crosby's schooner. In 1966, Graham Nash, with the Hollies, met Crosby when the Byrds toured England; when the Hollies performed in California in 1968, Graham and Crosby renewed their friendship.

In July, 1968, Crosby, Stills & Nash were at a party at Joni Mitchell's house. Stills had written a new song, "You Don't Have To Cry" and Crosby had sung harmony with him; Nash asked them to sing the song again and added a third part harmony. Everyone agreed that the trio's voices blended perfectly, which led to Nash quitting the Hollies.

Crosby, Stills and Nash chose to use their own names instead of a group name because they had all been frustrated with the group experience. They were, essentially, three singer-songwriters performing together. Stills was still signed to Atlantic from his membership in Buffalo Springfield but Crosby had been released from his contract with Columbia after he left the Byrds. Nash, however, was signed to Epic because of his membership in the Hollies, which were on that label.

Elliot Roberts and David Geffen became the managers of the new group and Geffen went to Clive Davis and brokered a deal between Ertegun and Davis whereby Davis released Nash and received Richie Furay and his new band Poco. That allowed Crosby, Stills & Nash to record as a group for Atlantic.

In May, 1969 Atlantic released their debut album, *Crosby, Stills and Nash*, which debuted on the *Billboard* album chart on June 28 and rose to number six, remaining on that chart for 107 weeks. There were two singles from that album, "Marrakesh Express," written by Nash reached number 28 and "Suite: Judy Blue Eyes," written by Stills, reached number 21 on the *Billboard* Hot 100, but they were an album act and, although they released singles, that was not their focus.

The group needed a keyboard player and Stills asked Steve Winwood about joining, but he was with his new group, Blind Faith. Ahmet Ertegun suggested Neil Young who, although primarily a guitarist, was also proficient on keyboards. Stills and Nash also played keyboards so they could alternate. The group was apprehensive about Young joining but, after several meetings, agreed for him to join; Young retained his freedom to record solo albums and perform with his band, Crazy Horse, for a different label.

The original bassist was Bruce Palmer but, due to personal problems, he was dismissed and Greg Reeves, a teenage bassist at Motown was hired.

The group began a tour on August 16, 1969 in Chicago with Joni Mitchell the opening act. Their second show was the next morning at the Woodstock Festival. They were well received and, later, recorded "Woodstock," written by Joni Mitchell. David Geffen demanded that the recording by Crosby, Still, Nash and Young be included in the film or else the group would not be allowed in the film. The agreement was made and their single, "Woodstock," entered the *Billboard* Hot 100 on March 28, 1970 and rose to number 11.

The Manson Murders

On August 9, 1969, the Manson Family, a cult directed by Charles Manson, murdered six people, including actress Sharon Tate, who was eight months pregnant, at 10050 Cielo Drive in Los Angeles. Manson used the Beatles song, "Helter Skelter," which he heard as a guiding voice for an impending race war. The Manson Family had committed murder before the Tate murder as well as after the Tate murder. The Tate murder made national news and the Los Angeles community lived in fear until the end of the year, when Manson and members of his family were arrested.

Charles Manson had met Dennis Wilson of the Beach Boys and members of the Cult lived at Wilson's house for a period. Wilson paid for studio time so Manson could record songs he wrote and the Beach Boys recorded one of his songs.

Mike Curb and MGM Records

Mike Curb was a young entrepreneur from Los Angeles who started his own record label, Sidewalk Records, when he was 19 years old. He produced commercials and soundtracks for low-budget surfing and motorcycle movies in L.A., then merged his company with MGM Records and became part-owner and president of MGM when he was 24 years old--the youngest president to ever head a major label.

MGM Records was part of the MGM organization, with the MGM movie company serving as the umbrella. The company had been purchased by Kirk Kerkorian in 1969; at that point, the label had lost $17 million the previous year.

Curb set about signing acts; his most successful act was the Osmonds, which he co-produced. The Osmonds, who became the white version of the Jackson 5, produced a string of hits in the early 1970s, including "One Bad Apple" and "Down By the Lazy River." In 1971, Curb made lead singer Donny Osmond a solo act and had a string of hits with him, including "Go Away Little Girl" and "Puppy Love." In 1974 he teamed Donny with his sister, Marie, to produce a string of hits including "I'm Leaving It (Up To You)" and "Morning Side of the Mountain." Curb produced or co-produced all of Donny and Marie's hits and was named Producer of the Year by *Billboard* in 1972.

Curb then went into politics, serving as Lieutenant Governor (and Acting Governor for a year) of California, then moved to Washington to work as Finance Chairman of the Republican Party during the Reagan administration.

Joni Mitchell

In June, 1969, Joni Mitchell's second album, *Clouds*, entered the *Billboard* album chart; on the album were the songs "Both Sides Now," "Chelsea Morning" and "Big Yellow Taxi," which would be her first chart single the following year. Mitchell had established herself as a songwriter, "The Circle Game," and "Urge for Going" had both been recorded and "Both Sides Now" had been a top ten hit for Judy Collins in 1968,

Roberta Joan Anderson was born in Alberta, Canada on November 7, 1943; when she was nine her family moved to Saskatoon. She began writing poems in high school and, inspired by country music, wanted to learn to play the guitar. Mitchell started with the ukulele but she had contacted polio when she was young, which meant she had problems fingering chords. That disability led her to play in alternative tunings.

Mitchell began singing in folk and jazz clubs in and around Saskatoon and enrolled in an art college but soon dropped out. She continued to play at folk venues and moved to Toronto. In 1964, she became pregnant by her ex-boyfriend and decided to put the baby girl up for adoption after it was born in February, 1965. This would remain a deep secret of Mitchell's until 1993 when an art school roommate sold the story to a tabloid magazine. In 1997, Mitchell met her daughter for the first time.

In 1965 Mitchell began singing songs she had written in Toronto. She met Chuck Mitchell and they performed together, then married and she took the name "Mitchell." The two moved to Detroit and she continued writing songs in alternative tunings. Her marriage ended in 1967 so she moved to New York and she performed in coffee houses along the East Coast.

Joni Mitchell wrote "Urge For Going," which was recorded by Tom Rush, then covered by George Hamilton IV, and it became a top ten record on the country chart. Buffy Sainte-Marie recored "The Circle Game," Dave Van Ronk recorded "Both Sides Now."

Buffy Sainte-Marie brought Elliot Robinowitz, a junior agent with Chatkoff-Winler in New York to see her and he was so impressed that he quit his job and went with her to the Gaslight South, a club in Coconut Grove, Florida. During her appearance in Florida, David Crosby came in and was captivated by her talent.

Crosby took her to Los Angeles where she was signed to management by Elliot Roberts, formerly Elliot Rabinowitz, who formed a management company with David Geffen. David Crosby suggested Mitchell meet with Andy Wickham with Reprise Records and he signed her. Her first release was a solo acoustic album, *Song to a Seagull*. Mitchell toured to promote the album, then recorded Clouds, which was released in April, 1969. Mitchell painted the album cover, a self-portrait of herself.

Clouds won a Grammy for "Best Folk Performance."

Kinney buys Warner 7 Arts

In June, 1969, Kinney National bought Warner 7 Arts. Jack Warner felt it was time to sell; most of the movies they produced were losing money. Included in that deal was Atlantic Records, who had to face a new bureaucratic corporate world. Jerry Wexler remembered "Man, we never had a budget. Never had a recording production budget, a promo budget, a publicity budget."

Mike Maitland was president of Warner Brothers Records but Ahmet Ertegun convinced Steve Ross that the strength of the record company was in Joe Smith and Mo Ostin—not Maitland. Ostin replaced Maitland as president of Warner Brothers Records, Smith headed Reprise and Ertegun was promoted to Executive Vice-President. With this team in place, over a two year period, 1969-1970, Ostin and Smith signed Black Sabbath, Doug Kershaw, Jethro Tull, Gordon Lightfoot, Van Morrison, James Taylor, Fleetwood Mac, Ry Cooder, Deep Purple, Alice Cooper and Small Faces with Rod Stewart.

Sinatra sells Reprise to Warner Brothers

Frank Sinatra, Mickey Rudin and Daniel Schwartz were partners who owned 107,500 shares in Warner 7 Artists. Sinatra owned 20 percent of Reprise Records but sold it to Warner Brothers for $22.5 million. Mickey Rudin received 25,000 shares of Kinney stock and a finder's fee of $1.5 million, paid out over ten years. Sinatra and Steve Ross signed the papers in Fort Lee, New Jersey at the home of Sinatra's mother, Dolly, who had prepared a large, Italian dinner. The transaction was signed in New Jersey for tax reasons.

Big Band Meets Rock'n'Roll

In March, the single "You've Made Me So Very Happy" by Blood, Sweat and Tears debuted on the *Billboard* Hot 100. In August, "Questions 67 and 68" by Chicago debuted on that chart. Both acts were on Columbia, which found itself with horn heavy big bands—although not as big as those from the Big Band era—with a non-rock'n'roll sound for rock'n'roll radio.

Both of the groups formed in 1967, Blood, Sweat and Tears, led by Al Cooper, in New York City and the Chicago Transit Authority in Chicago. Both acts were produced by Jim Guercio.

Al Kooper, who had played on Bob Dylan albums (including the Hammond B3 organ on "Like a Rolling Stone") and was with the Blues Project, was the leader of Blood, Sweat and Tears but left after their first album was released. He was replaced by vocalist David Clayton-Thomas.

The six member Chicago Transit Authority changed their name to simply "Chicago" after their first album, a double album that reportedly sold over a million copies. Lead singer for the group was Peter Cetera.

Country Music on network TV in 1969

Country music was on television with three network shows during 1969. "The Glen Campbell Goodtime Hour" show debuted on the CBS network on January 29 on Wednesday evenings then moved to Sunday nights in December. Campbell opened the show with "Gentle On My Mind" written by John Hartford. The hour-long variety show came after a number of appearances by Campbell on "The Smothers Brothers Show" and hits such as "By the Time I Get to Phoenix," ""Dreams of the Everyday Housewife" and "Wichita Lineman." Regulars on the show included Jerry Reed, and the Mike Curb Congregation, who were featured weekly singing an inspirational song. The Campbell show featured Nashville talent but was taped in Los Angeles.

"The Johnny Cash Show" premiered on the ABC network on June 7. Cash opened the show with "Folsom Prison Blues" and closed it with his earliest hit, "I Walk the Line." Regulars on the hour-long variety show included Mother Maybelle and the Carter family (Helen, Anita and June), the Statler Brothers and Carl Perkins. The show featured country music guests who performed as well as guests from the rock, folk and pop worlds such as Bob Dylan, Arlo Guthrie, Jose Feliciano, Glen Campbell, Rod McKuen, Pete Seeger, Linda Ronstadt, Merle Haggard, James Taylor and Minnie Pearl. "The Johnny Cash Show" came at a time when country music was increasingly popular with middle America.

"Hee Haw," was an hour-long musical/comedy/variety show on CBS hosted by Roy Clark and Buck Owens that premiered on CBS on Sunday, June 15. The show was patterned after "Rowen and Martin's Laugh-In" on NBC.

The country music community in Nashville initially disliked "Hee Haw" because it reinforced every stereotype many had of country music, full of corny jokes, haystacks, cornfields and regulars wearing bib overalls. The show cut across the grain of an urbane, middle-America image of country music that the country industry was trying to project. However, the show proved extremely popular with audiences so top country artists regularly performed on the show and stood in the cornfield where they announced the name and population of their home town, accompanied by a Hee Haw "sah-lute!"

CMA Awards Show

The CMA Awards Show was shown live on television for the first time on Wednesday, October 15, 1969. Johnny Cash was the big winner, winning five CMA Awards for "Best Album" (*San Quentin*), "Single" ("A Boy Named Sue"), "Vocal Group" (Johnny and June Carter), Male Vocalist and Entertainer of the Year." During 1969 Cash had two big hits, "Daddy Sang Bass" and "A Boy Named Sue" and he performed both on the show.

This was "country music's big night" and Bob Schwaratz, director of "The Ed Sullivan Show" and Vince Calandra, Sullivan's talent coordinator came to watch. This show was really a "test" to see whether country music on television could attract a large audience. The CMA Awards Show passed the test in flying colors.

George Jones and Billy Sherrill

Billy Sherrill signed classic country singer George Jones to Epic Records and produced Jones' records with a "countrypolitan" sound; among the hits Sherrill produced on Jones were "A Picture of Me (Without You)," "What My Woman Can't Do," "The Grand Tour," "The Door," "Once You've Had the Best," "Bartender's Blues," "Her Name Is..." and "He Stopped Loving Her Today." Sherrill also produced the George Jones and Tammy Wynette duets "We're Gonna Hold On," "Golden Ring," "Near You" and "Two Story House."

Bob Dylan's *Nashville Skyline*

Bob Dylan's came back to Nashville in February, 1969, to record his *Nashville Skyline* album in Columbia Studio A. The album included the songs "Lay Lady Lay," "I Threw It All Away" and a duet with Johnny Cash on "Girl From the North Country." Nashville session musicians Norman Blake (guitar) Kenny Buttrey (drums), Fred Carter, Jr. (guitar), Charlie Daniels (guitar), Pete Drake (steel guitar) and Charlie McCoy (utility and bass) provided the back-up.

Johnny Cash at San Quentin

Johnny Cash's album, *Live at San Quentin*, was recorded on February 24, 1969 at the California prison. It was released on June 4, entered the *Billboard* country album chart on July 5 and was the number one country album for 20 consecutive weeks. It reached number one on the *Billboard* 200 Album Chart and remained there for four weeks; the album remained on *Billboard's* pop album chart for 70 weeks and the country album chart for 55 weeks.

The concert was filmed by Granada Television and Cash became frustrated when a camera man blocked his view of the audience so he gave him the finger; that iconic photograph appeared later on ads.

The album was certified "Gold" on August 12 and Platinum and Double Platinum in 1986. It was one of the top selling albums for the Columbia label that year.

The concert was long so the vinyl album was edited and songs were left out. That was the first album Cash did without his long-time guitarist, Luther Perkins, who died in a fire several months before the performance.

The single "A Boy Named Sue" was written by Shel Silverstein, who played it during a "guitar pull" at Cash's house where Bob Dylan performed "Lay, Lady, Lay," Graham Nash performed "Marrakesh Express, Joni Mitchell sang "Both Sides Now" and Kris Kristofferson sang "Me and Bobby McGee." After Silverstein sang the song, Cash asked for the lyrics. Cash had not rehearsed the song before the concert but June Carter encouraged him to do it so, after running over it quickly backstage, he read the lyrics as he sang it during the concert. The song was number one on *Billboard's* country chart for five weeks and number two on the Hot 100 for three consecutive weeks.

The album received a Grammy nomination for "Album of the Year" and won a Grammy for "Best Male Country Vocal" for "A Boy Named Sue."

Sun Records

On July 1, 1969, Shelby Singleton purchased Sun Records, the legendary label founded by Sam Phillips in Memphis that made the earliest recordings of Elvis Presley, Howlin' Wolf, Carl Perkins, Jerry Lee Lewis, Johnny Cash, Roy Orbison and other Sun Records pioneer artists. The Sun recordings by Elvis were not included; they had been acquired by RCA when they signed Elvis at the end of 1955. Sun Records moved out of Memphis and became a Nashville-based label, located on Belmont Boulevard.

"Me and Bobby McGee"

During the summer, Roger Miller's recording of "Me and Bobby McGee" was released. The song, written by Kris Kristofferson, reached number 12 on the country chart. Fred Foster, head of Monument Records who had signed Kristofferson, gave him the title "Me and Bobby McKee"; the real Bobby McKee worked for songwriter Boudleaux Bryant. Kristofferson but mis-heard the name as "McGee." He wrote most of the song in New Orleans when he was flying helicopters to off-shore oil rigs.

The recording by Roger Miller was popular during the summer of 1969 and New York folk singer Bobby Neuworth heard it on the radio and taught it to Janis Joplin, whose version was released after her death.

Man on the Moon!

On July 24, 600 million around the world watched on television as astronauts Neil Armstrong and Edwin Aldrin landed on the moon while

Michael Collins circled the moon in the Apollo XI control ship. Thirty-eight year old Armstrong emerged from the capsule and said "That's one small step for man, one giant leap for mankind." It took the astronauts four days to reach the moon and Armstrong and Aldrin spent two hours on the lunar surface, collecting sample rocks, setting up instruments and planting an American flag.

Richard Nixon and Vietnam

The number of American servicemen in Vietnam reached its peak during Richard Nixon's first year in office; there were 543,000 in April, 1969. On November 3, 1969 President Nixon ordered the withdrawal of 60,000 American troops and declared in a speech that the United States would have "Peace with honor." During that year 11,527 Americans were killed in Vietnam.

During the fall of 1969 Daniel Ellsburg, a former Marine and advisor who had served in Vietnam, was working for the Rand Corporation, a think tank charged with helping formulate policy. He began copying a top-secret 7,000 page report, called "The Pentagon Papers," that documented American involvement in Vietnam. In June and July, 1971, the Pentagon Papers was published in the *New York Times*, then picked up by several other newspapers. That gave fuel to the anti-Vietnam campaign because the report highlighted the lies, cover-ups and history of Vietnam War.

Give Peace a Chance

John Lennon and Yoko Ono wanted to hold their second "Bed-in" for peace in New York at the end of May but US authorities would not grant Lennon a visa because of his drug conviction in November, 1968. They flew to the Bahamas but decided against that location because of the heat. They finally decided on Montreal because of its close proximity to the United States and their peace message could be heard in the United States.

From May 26 until June 2 at the Hotel Reine-Elizabeth John and Yoko stayed in bed under the sheets and welcomed TV broadcasters and journalists who showed up and did phone interviews with American radio stations as they urged the world to adopt peace.

On Sunday June 1, Lennon led the recording of "Give Peace a Chance," which he had written (although the song is credited to Lennon-McCartney). Lennon played acoustic guitar while a room full of media, friends and visitors sang along on the chorus. It is the most well known and effective peace song ever recorded.

Anti-War Demonstrations

On November 15, 250,000 anti-war marchers, led by Senators Eugene McCarthy and George McGovern, Coretta Scott King, Benjamin Spock and Arlo Guthrie marched from the Capitol to the Washington Monument; it was the largest anti-war demonstration in the history of Washington, D.C. In San Francisco, around 200,000 anti-war demonstrators gathered in San Francisco's Golden Gate Park and sang John Lennon's "All we are saying is give peace a chance." President Richard Nixon had criticized campus demonstrations and vowed that he would ignore the demonstration in Washington.

That Fall, Vice President Spiro Agnew embarked on a speaking tour and denounced war protestors as "anarchists and ideological eunuchs" and said of the news media that "A spirit of national masochism prevails, encouraged by an effete corps of impudent snobs who characterize themselves as intellectuals." Agnew labelled journalists "nattering nabobs of negativism."

Merle Haggard and "Okie From Muskogee"

Merle Haggard's parents came to California from Checotah, Oklahoma in 1934 after their barn burnt down. It was during the Great Depression and his parents, Flossie and James, with their two children, Lowell and Lillian, came to Bakersfield, where James began working for the Santa Fe Railroad. James converted a railroad boxcar in Oildale that a woman owned into a home that he bought. That is where Merle Haggard was born on April 6, 1937.

Merle Haggard had a troubled childhood; his father died from a brain hemorrhage in 1945 when Merle was he was eight, which affected him deeply and left him with a reservoir of resentment. Merle's mother worked as a bookkeeper to support the family. When he was 12, his brother, Lowell, gave him his guitar and he learned to play. Haggard's influences were country performers like Lefty Frizzell, Hank Williams and Bob Wills.

Merle was rebellious and soon became a juvenile delinquent. He was arrested for minor offenses, sent to a juvenile detention center and, at 14, with a friend, escaped and ran away, hitchhiking to Texas. Back in California, Haggard worked manual labor jobs in Modesto, then returned to Bakersfield where he was arrested and sentenced to a juvenile detention center. Another escape landed him in a high-security jail where he served 15 months. More trouble meant another lock-up.

Haggard attended a Lefty Frizzell concert and, after hearing Haggard sing along to his songs backstage, Frizzell insisted that Haggard appear on his show. A positive reception from the audience led to Haggard's decision to pursue a career in music.

In 1957, Haggard was married but in financial difficulty, which led him to attempt to rob a bar; he was caught, sent to the Bakersfield Jail, escaped but was caught, and was then transferred to San Quentin Prison on February 21, 1958, where he turned 21 in prison. In prison, Haggard learned that his wife had given birth to a child with another man. Haggard was incorrigible, fired from prison jobs and planned another escape but was talked out of it by other inmates, who told him he could have a future singing songs.

Prison guards caught Haggard drunk—he was brewing booze and operated a gambling ring—and sent him to solitary confinement. There, he met Caryl Chessman, who was on Death Row. Meanwhile, the prisoner he planned to escape with, "Rabbit," was caught, shot a policemen and returned to San Quentin and sentenced to death. Those encounters and experiences convinced Merle Haggard he needed to change his life. He earned a high school equivalency diploma, worked a job in the prison's textile plant and became a model prison. On January 1, 1959, Johnny Cash performed a concert in San Quentin and Merle Haggard was in the audience. That concert inspired Haggard to join a country music band in the prison.

In 1960, Haggard was released from prison and obtained a job digging ditches for his brother, who had an electrical contracting company. He had met Lewis Talley, who owned a record label in Bakersfield, before his prison sentence and Talley gave him encouragement. After his time in prison he recorded "Singing My Heart Out" for Talley's label, but the record was not a success. In 1962 he took a job playing guitar in Wynn Stewart's band in Las Vegas; there he heard Stewart's song "Sing a Sad Song" and asked permission to record it. It entered the *Billboard* country chart on December 28, 1963 and rose to number 19 the following year.

Haggard's next single was "Sam Hill," written by Tommy Collins and reached number 45 in 1964. "Just Between the Two of Us," a duet with Bonnie Owens, who soon became his wife, reached number 28 in 1964.

Late in 1964, a reluctant Haggard visited Liz Anderson's home and she played him "(All My Friends Are Gonna Be) Strangers," which became his first top ten country hit in 1965.

In 1966, Merle Haggard had hits with "Swinging Doors" and "The Bottle Let Me Down." "The Fugitive," written by Liz and Casey Anderson, entered the *Billboard* country chart at the end of 1966 and became his first number one the following year. He followed that with a string of hit songs;

in 1967 he had "Someone Told My Story in a Song," "I Threw Away the Rose" "Branded Man" and "Sing Me Back Home," all of which he wrote. In 1968 he had hits with "The Legend of Bonnie and Clyde" and "Mama Tried" (which was number one on the country chart for four weeks),

In 1969, Haggard's "I Take a Lot of Pride in What I Am" reached number three, then "Hungry Eyes" and "Workin' Man Blues" both reached number one. Haggard was in great demand, touring constantly with his band, the Strangers. On a bus traveling down Interstate 40, Haggard saw a sign "Muskogee 19 miles." That prompted the line, "I'll bet they don't smoke marijuana in Muskogee" from Haggard or his drummer, Eddie Burris. That began a series of lines that stated what the silent majority were saying and feeling about the counterculture; it was a song protesting the protesters. It became a series of lines that started out funny but seriously articulated what many Americans were feeling about their country in the midst of student demonstrations, race riots and the open promotion of drugs by the youth culture.

The next day, Haggard performed the song at Fort Bragg, North Carolina and the response was overwhelming; before the show finished, he had performed it four times. "Okie From Muskogee" became one of the most important songs of the 1960s and 1970s because it was an anthem for the white working class. Just as Bob Dylan became the voice of his generation, Merle Haggard became the voice of the "silent majority" with a song that protested the protestors and stated in clear, simple terms what they believed.

Abbey Road

By the end of June, 1969, the Beatles had decided they would unite and record an album at Abbey Road studio with George Martin as producer. They booked Studio Two at Abbey Road every weekday from 2:30 until 10 p.m. from July 1 until August 29.

On July 1, Paul McCartney was the only Beatle in the studio; he overdubbed the lead vocal for "You Never Give Me Your Money." John Lennon was in a hospital in Scotland after an automobile accident; he would not leave Scotland until July 6.

On July 2, Paul recorded a 23 second song, "Her Majesty" before George and Ringo arrived. The idea, fostered by producer George Martin, was to link together a series of short songs into a long piece, like what was done in classical music.

When George and Ringo arrived, they recorded a number by Paul, "Golden Slumbers," which was original a 16th century prose piece by

Thomas Dekker. "Carry That Weight" was also part of that proposed section of linked songs and the two songs were recorded as one. Overdubs were done during the next two days.

On July 7, the first session for "Here Comes the Sun," written by George Harrison was recorded by George, Paul and Ringo. Overdubs on the song were done the next day.

John Lennon came to the studio on Wednesday, July 9 and the group recorded "Maxwell's Silver Hammer." Yoko accompanied John to the studio and lay in a bed set up in the studio because she was pregnant and still nursed injuries from their automobile accident. Overdubs were done on "Maxwell's Silver Hammer" and "You Never Give Me Your Money" during the next several days as the Beatles established a pattern or recording the basic track of a song one day and then added overdubs and changes during the next several days.

They worked on "Something," "Octopus's Garden" and "Oh! Darling" and on July 21, the group recorded the basic tracks for "Come Together" as long-time engineer Geoff Emerick returned. On July 23, "The End" was first recorded.

Paul McCartney had written a song, "Come And Get It" which he intended for the group The Iveys (who changed their name to Badfinger) on Apple. He recorded the demo alone on July 24 before the rest of the Beatles arrived. The group recorded "Sun King"/"Mean Mr. Mustard," written by Lennon; the two pieces were recorded as one song. The Beatles also jammed on Gene Vincent's "Ain't She Sweet," which they had originally recorded in Germany as The Beat Brothers, "Who Slapped John" and "Be-Bop-A-Lula." On July 25 they recorded "Polythene Pam" and "She Came in Through the Bathroom Window" as one piece.

The short song pieces were put together on July 30 and titled "The Long One/Huge Medley"; the line-up was "You Never Give Me Your Money," "Sun King/Mean Mr. Mustard," "Her Majesty," "Polythene Pam"/"She Came in Through the Bathroom Window," "Golden Slumbers"/"Carry That Weight" and "The End." McCartney decided to delete "Her Majesty" but engineer John Kurlander was determined to save it, so he taped it on the end of the tape after 20 seconds of silence.

On August 1 the Beatles recorded "Because," written by Lennon, with three-part harmony by Lennon, McCartney and Harrison. The harpsichord was played by George Martin, bass by Paul and electric guitar by Lennon. The final version would have three sets of that triple harmony.

In November, 1968, George Harrison bought a Moog synthesizer in the United States and had it brought to London, where he recorded "Electronic Sounds, released in May, 1969 on the Zapple label, a division of Apple to experimental music. On August 5, the synthesizer was brought into the EMI studio and the large bank of wires and two-tiered keyboard was programmed by Mike Vickers. The Moog synthesizer, played by Harrison, was overdubbed on "Because."

From August 6 on, the Beatles often came into the Abbey Road studio as individuals to overdub or correct parts of songs. The synthesizer was overdubbed on "Maxwell's Silver Hammer." On "The End, " McCartney, Harrison and Lennon each played a guitar passage.

On Friday, August 8, photographer Iain Macmillan stood on a step-ladder and photographed the four Beatles walking across the pedestrian crossing in front of the Abbey Road studio six times—three times each way. Paul McCartney picked the one used on the album cover.

After the photo shoot, the Beatles added synthesizer overdubs to "I Want You," which became "I Want You (She's So Heavy)" on August 11.

On August 15, an orchestra came to the studio to overdub on "Golden Slumbers"/"Carry That Weight," "The End," "Something" and "Here Comes The Sun." George Martin wrote the arrangements and conducted the orchestra of 12 violins, four violas, four cellos, one string bass, four horns, three trumpets, one trombone and one bass trombone.

Wednesday, August 20, saw all four Beatles in the studio to hear the songs sequenced; it was the last time all four Beatles were together in the EMI studio building.

The *Abbey Road* album was released on Friday, September 26 in the U.K.; on October 31 the first single from the album, "Something"/"Come Together" was released in the U.K.

"Something" and "Come Together" both entered the *Billboard* Hot 100 on October 18; "Come Together" reached number one and "Something" reached number two. That same day, the *Abbey Road* album entered the *Billboard* album chart and quickly rose to number one, remaining in that slot for 11 weeks and on the chart for 129 weeks.

Moog Symthesizer

An important step for the Moog Synthesizer came in 1969 when Wendy (formerly Walter) Carlos released an album, *Switched On Bach*, comprised of Bach selections played on the synthesizer. The album won three Grammys, including "Classical Album of the Year" in 1969.

During 1969 Moog Synthesizers could be heard on rock'n'roll records by the Beatles, the Rolling Stones, the Byrds and the Monkees.

In 1971 the Moog Synthesizer, played by Wendy Carlos, was used on the soundtrack for the film, *A Clockwork Orange* and in 1973 Stevie Wonder won the Grammy for Album of the Year for *Innervisions,* which made extensive use of the synthesizer.

Production of the Mini-Moog Model D began in 1971 and that became the first easily obtainable, portable and affordable synthesizer and solidified the synthesizer's image as a "piano keyboard" computer. It became the most popular synthesizer during the 1970s and sold approximately 13,000 units.

CREEM magazine

Billed as "America's Only Rock'n'Roll Magazine, CREEM (as it called itself) was first published in March 1969 and grew out the frustration Barry Kramer felt when his concert review for another publication was turned down.

Barry Kramer owned Full Circle, a record store in Detroit, and a head shop/bookstore, Mixed Media. Kramer had been an unsuccessful concert promoter and band manager before he decided to create a publication to publish his article. He enlisted Tony Reay, a clerk at his record store, to be a partner and editor in the publication; Reay named the magazine after Cream, his favorite band.

The first issue was a tabloid-sized newspaper only distributed in Detroit but Kramer soon found distribution, although a number of early issues were ordered by porn shops who were misled by the title. Within two years, *Creem* became a glossy color magazine with national distribution due to the efforts of circulation director Richard Siegel.

For the first two years, the offices were at 3729 Cass Avenue in Detroit but Kramer moved to a farm in Walled Lake, Michigan after the offices were robbed. Lester Bangs, considered to be one of the greatest rock critics of all time, joined the magazine just before it moved. Bangs had been fired by Jann Wenner, publisher of *Rolling Stone,* for what the publisher claimed was "disrespecting musicians." Bangs had written a harsh review of Canned Heat.

The Walled Lake farmhouse was home to many of the *Creem* staff. Dave Marsh, another legendary rock critic, joined the magazine when he was 19 and Charlie Auringer was photo editor and designer. After some disagreements and altercations between house members, *Creem* moved into offices in downtown Birmingham, Michigan. Lester Bangs loved Detroit and proclaimed it "rock's only hope."

The magazine poked fun at rock stars with humorous photo captions and adopted an irreverent tone towards the rock elite in Los Angeles and New York. Their location meant that they covered Detroit-area acts such as Alice Cooper, The MC5, Mitch Ryder, Bob Seger, The Stooges, Iggy Pop and Parliament-Funkadelic, giving those acts national exposure from a midwestern base.

Creem was an important glossy monthly for rock'n'roll coverage; it joined *Crawdaddy* and *Rolling Stone* to give authentic coverage of a music that was mostly ignored by the mainstream press.

The Who and *Tommy*

Roger Daltrey, Pete Townshend and John Entwistle all went to Acton Grammar School in west London. Townshend and Entwistle formed a traditional jazz group in school; Townshend then attended Ealing Art College. Daltrey, a year ahead in school, was expelled when he was 15 and then worked in construction. Daltrey started a rockn'n'roll band, the Detours, in 1959. He recruited Entwistle to play bass when he spotted him on the street carrying one. (Entwistle had switched from French horn to guitar to bass because his fingers were too large for a guitar.) Entwistle suggested Pete Townshend as rhythm guitarist in mid-1961. The line-up was now Daltrey on lead guitar, Entwistle on bass, Harry Wilson on drums, Townshend on rhythm guitar and Colin Dawson on vocals. The group was a cover band, covering everything from rock and roll instrumentals, pop songs and traditional jazz numbers. Roger Daltrey was the acknowledged leader of the group.

There were personnel changes until the group's line-up became Daltrey on lead vocal, Townshend on lead guitar and Entwistle on bass. They obtained a management contract with promoter Robert Druce through connections Townshend's mother had. They became the opening acts for a number of acts and in February, 1964 discovered there was another group named the "Detours." They changed to "The Who" after Townshend came up with that name.

The Who played regularly in and around London, changed managers (Helmut Gorden took over) and auditioned for Chris Parmeinter with Fontana Records, who disliked the drumming. Doug Sandom had been the drummer since mid-1962 but, in a heated exchange with Townshend, quit the band, although he allowed his drum kit to be used by any stand-in or replacement.

The band members met Keith Moon at a date in Oldfield in late April. Moon grew up in Wembley and was in a part-time band, the Beachcombers, but wanted to play full time. Moon sat in with the Who, who offered him the job of drummer. After a few more dates with the Beachcombers, Moon joined the Who full time.

Another change in managers brought Peter Meadon into that role, who changed the name of the group to the High Numbers, gained another audition with Fontana and they recorded a single, "Zoot Suit"/"I'm the Face" that Meadon wrote. The single was not successful and the band reverted to calling themselves The Who and developed an energetic stage act with Daltrey swinging the microphone and jumping into the crowd, Moon juggling drumsticks while he played and Townshend playing guitar with a windmilling motion.

Kit Lambert and Chris Stamp, two filmmakers, took over management and filmed the group playing at the Railway Hotel in Wealdstone, which was their regular gig. Lambert encouraged Townshend to write songs and the band evolved from playing Motown covers and R&B.

Townshend accidentally broke the head of his guitar during a performance at the Railway; angered by laughter from the audience, he smashed his guitar on stage—then picked up another guitar and continued playing. The next week, a crowd was at the Railway to see another act of musical instrument destruction; Moon obliged them by kicking over his drum kit and the destruction of instruments became part of the Who's set.

In late 1964, American producer Shel Talmy, who produced the Kinks, produced a session on The Who, who recorded "I Can't Explain," written by Townshend. The song was popular on Radio Caroline, the pirate radio ship and led to an appearance on the TV show 'Ready, Steady, Go," which led to another single, "Anyway, Anyhow, Anywhere" written by Townshend and Daltrey so the group had two singles on the UK chart.

There was tension in the group; manager Lambert encouraged the group to do original material but Daltrey resisted, wanting to do only R&B covers. In October, they released "My Generation" in the UK; it entered the *Billboard* Hot 100 on January 5, 1966 and reached number 75; it reached number two on the U.K. chart. The song featured the line, "Hope I die before I get old," which became a rallying cry for the '60s generation.

The Who's recording contract with Brunswick in the U.K. (a subsidiary of Decca) and Decca in the U.S. ended when the group fell out with Talmy. The Who's album, *My Generation*, was tied up by Talmy, who would not relinquish the master tapes.

The Who had several more successful singles in the U.K., which also reached the Hot 100, but managers Lambert and Stamp, needed to break into the U.S. market in a big way so they arranged a short package tour with promoter Frank Barsalona. Their American appearances featured them smashing guitars and kicking over drum sets and audiences loved it. They performed at the Monterey Pop Festival in 1967 and their single, "Happy Jack," reached number 24 on the Hot 100. After Monterey, The Who opened for Herman's Hermits and drummer Keith Moon gained a reputation for destroying hotel rooms and setting off fire bombs in toilets.

The Who recorded "I Can See For Miles," written by Townshend, which was their first top ten record in the U.S.

Their album, *The Who Sell Out*, was a concept album that paid tribute to pirate radio, which had been banned in August, 1967 in the U.K. The album featured humorous jingles between songs, a mini rock opera and they declared themselves a "pop art" group.

The Who began receiving attention in the underground press in the United States and Townshend, who had quit using drugs, told *Rolling Stone* editor Jann Wenner about a new album project, inspired by the teachings of Meher Baba, that was called, at various times, *Deaf Dumb and Blind Boy* and *Amazing Journey*; he finally settled on *Tommy*. The album told the story of a boy who was deaf, dumb and blind but tried to communicate with others. Originally scheduled to be released for Christmas, the release was delayed after Townshend decided to make it a double album. The group continued to tour and record songs that Townshend wrote.

The album was released in May, 1969 with "Pinball Wizard" the first single. It entered the *Billboard* chart on June 7 and rose to number four, remaining on the chart for 126 weeks or two and a half years. "Pinball Wizard" entered the Hot 100 on April 5 and reached number 19. Their second single from the album, "I'm Free," made it to number 37 on the *Billboard* Hot 100.

The 24 songs on the double album featured Daltrey singing lead on five, Townshend singing lead on five and the two sharing lead vocals on ten of the songs, with Entwistle also joining the vocals on several songs.

The first complete performance of the rock opera *Tommy* was on April 22, 1969 in Dolton, Devon, U.K.

Tommy was an influential rock opera, a step for rock music into the world of serious music. Like *Pet Sounds* and *Sgt. Pepper's Lonely Hearts Club Band*, the album broke new ground had an impact that lasted for years.

Creedence Clearwater Revival

On January 25, 1969, "Proud Mary" by Creedence Clearwater Revival entered the *Billboard* Hot 100. The group had two chart singles in 1968; "Suzy Q" and "I Put a Spell on You," both cover records ("Suzy Q" had been a hit for Dale Hawkins in 1957 with the opening guitar riff played by James Burton and "I Put a Spell on You" was released by Screamin' Jay Hawkins in 1956). "Proud Mary" marked the beginning of John Fogerty as a great songwriter as well as Creedence Clearwater Revival as a rock'n'roll act.

John Fogerty, Doug Clifford and Stu Cook attended Portola Junior High School in El Cerrito, California. The formed a band, the Blue Velvets, that played instrumentals and cover songs. Tom Fogerty, John's older brother, was a singer and they backed him for some shows and then Tom joined the band. The line-up was Tom, lead singer, John, guitar, Clifford on drums and Cook on piano. They signed with Fantasy Records, an independent jazz label based in San Francisco. Max Weiss, co-owner of Fantasy, changed the name of the group to the Golliwogs.

As the band progressed, John took over as lead vocalist and lead guitarist, Tom played rhythm guitar, Cook moved from piano to bass and Clifford remained the drummer. However, John Fogerty and Doug Clifford were both drafted so Fogerty enlisted in the Army Reserve whil Clifford enlisted in the Coast Guard Reserve.

Saul Zaentz bought Fantasy records in 1967and made the band an offer: change your name to something other than the Golliwogs and you can record an album. They agreed and became Creedence Clearwater Revival in January, 1968. During that year, John Fogerty and Clifford completed their military duties and the band members quite their jobs and began rehearsing and playing local gigs.

The chart singles in 1968 led to touring to promote their album and then working on their second album, *Bayou Country*. Recorded in Los Angeles at the RCA Studios, their first single from the album was "Proud Mary" b/w "Born on the Bayou." Their next single, "Bad Moon Rising," also reached number two on the Hot 100. The flip side, "Lodi," reached number 52.

On August 2, 1969, "Green River," the title song of their third album entered the Hot 100 chart and became their third consecutive single that reached number two. The flip side, "Commotion," reached number 30. Their fourth single, "Down on the Corner," entered the *Billboard* Hot 100 on October 25 and reached number three; the flip side, "Fortunate Son," did not chart but received considerable airplay.

All of those songs were written by John Fogerty.

Creedence appeared at Woodstock but were not included in the film (Fogerty did not feel the band's performance was of high enough quality) and the Atlanta Pop Festival. Their fourth album, *Willy and the Poor Boys*, was released in November. By the end of 1969, Creedence Clearwater Revival had established itself as a major American act that also had success on the British charts. Their sound was unique and different from British rockers, showing the influence of country music as well as R&B along with Cajun influences.

Altamont

The end of 1969 featured a concert at Altamont Speedway in California headed by the Rolling Stones that brought a violent end to the decade. The concert was originally scheduled at the Sears Point Raceway but, at the last minute, that facility became unavailable. A concert at Altamont Speedway--whose largest crowd up to that point had been 6,500--had to be organized in less than 24 hours; the Stones, at the suggestion of the Grateful Dead, hired the local Hell's Angels to supply security for $500 worth of beer. There were 300,000 fans who showed up to watch a line-up of Santana, The Flying Burrito Brothers, Jefferson Airplane and Crosby, Still, Nash & Young. The Grateful Dead, who played a major role in organizing the concert, refused to play because of the escalating violence.

The Rolling Stones were the headliners and closed the concert. During their peroforman, a fan was killed by the Hell's Angels in front of the stage while the group performed "Sympathy for the Devil." Two other fans were killed by a hit and run car accident and one fan died from an LSD induced drowning.

The Hell's Angels beat a number of fans that evening and the concert was filmed so all could see a violent end to the decade of the 1960s. That incident is shown in the film *Gimme Shelter*.

American Radio

During the last week of 1969, the number one song on the radio was "Someday We'll Be Together" by Diana Ross and the Supremes; it was the last single for the Supremes; Diana Ross embarked on a solo career after this.

The songs that stayed longest at number one in 1969—six weeks each—were "Aquarius/Let the Sunshine In" by the Fifth Dimension and "In The Year 2525" by Zager and Evans.

During 1969, 16 songs reached the number one slot on the *Billboard* Hot 100. One song, "Get Back" by the Beatles, was number one for five weeks while songs that remained number one for four weeks were "Everyday People" by Sly & the Family Stoe, "Dizzy" by Tommy Roe, " "Honky tonk Women" by the Rolling Stones, "Sugar, Sugar" by The Archies. "Love Theme From Rosmeo & Juliet" by Henry Mancini and the folk sounds of Peter, Paul and Mary on "Leaving On a Jet Plane (written by John Denver) also reached number one.

Perhaps the most appropriate song during the decade that ended the 1960s was "Na Na Hey Hey Kiss Him Goodbye" by Steam, which was number one in early December.

There were only eight albums that reached number one during 1969, led by the original cast recording of the Broadway musical, *Hair*, which remained number one for 13 weeks and The Beatles, whose *Abbey Road* album held the number one spot for eleven weeks.

Other albums tha reached number one on the *Billboard* album chart were *TCB* by Diana Ross & The Supremes with the Temptations, *Blood, Sweat & Tears* by Blood Sweat & Tears, *Johnny Cash At San Quentin*, *Blind Faith* and *Green River* by Creedence Clearwater Revival.

Led Zeppelin II by Led Zeppelin was the number one album when 1969 ended; it had been number one for seven weeks.

Rhythm and Blues: 1964-1969

British rockers such as The Rolling Stones, who recorded songs originally done by bluesmen such as Muddy Waters, Howlin' Wolf, Robert Johnson and others, told audiences of their respect and admiration for those blues and R&B pioneers, and sought out blues and R&B artists when they toured the United States, often inviting those acts to open for them on tours.

Many British rockers saw their future by looking back to early American blues and R&B but the R&B field did not like looking back; while ten years earlier a number of R&B acts reached back to old pop songs for chart records;

during the 1964-1969 period, the songs of R&B acts were usually new and captured the spirit of the times.

While American rock and roll turned away from its southern roots and looked towards England for inspiration, R&B reached down to its gospel roots. Acts such as the Four Tops and Temptations were reminiscent of black gospel quartets, first formed at Fisk University in Nashville. As "Soul" emerged as the dominant sound of black America, the singers, such as Wilson Pickett, Percy Sledge, Otis Redding and Aretha Franklin sang more like preachers than velvet-voiced pop singers.

The radio airwaves were integrated, but Soul Music and the Black Power movement saw a musical separation emerge; a large group of African-American artists increasingly concentrated on reaching a black audience with their messages rather than trying to please white audiences with crossovers. That led to January 30, 1965, when *Billboard* re-instated their R&B chart, which it had discontinued in the November 30, 1963 issue of that magazine.

The R&B music of the 1964-1969 Civil Rights era had strong roots in the South; Memphis and Muscle Shoals, Alabama were centers for recording activity and labels such as Stax, Motown, Atlantic and and Vee Jay specialized in R&B, although by the end of the decade Chicago-based Vee Jay was out of business, Atlantic had been purchased by Warner Brothers, and Memphis-based Stax was on a path that led to its bankruptcy in 1975.

Country Music During the 1960s

Country music moved from a musical form on the fringes of American society to part of mainstream American popular music during the 1960s. A major reason for that success was the development of the "Nashville Sound," which added string and pop-type arrangements to country recordings, moving it away from its "twangy" sound into one palatable to the tastes of middle-class fans.

The story of country music from before World War II until the present time mirrors, in many ways, the story of the United States itself. While this country had been changing from a rural, agricultural based nation into an urban, industrial based nation before World War II, the War certainly sped up this process and brought it to fruition. During the War, the population shifted from rural areas to cities, where defense plants were set up--and which hired workers. It was not unusual for people from the South--still recovering from the Great Depression--to move to a major city during the War for jobs in defense or defense-related plants. In the Services,

Southerners were mixed with those from other parts of the country, so country music reached a wide-variety of people. Also American music became an international music during World War II, primarily through the V-Disks sent out during the War to servicemen and Armed Forces Radio. Country music left the South for good and became a national music because southern servicemen exposed others to country music in the Armed Forces and because Southerners moved from the South in large numbers and fanned out across the country in search of defense-related jobs.

The importance of "the Nashville Sound" during the 1960s was based on several things: (1) its commercial success, which helped make country music big business and (2) its connection with the urban middle class with rural roots that emerged after World War II.

In short, the Nashville Sound made people proud they were country music fans and, in a more general sense, it moved country music uptown, gave it self-respect and dignity. The Nashville Sound proved that you didn't have to be a hillbilly to sing country music. Because of its commercial success--as well as the commercial success of country music in general--the Nashville Sound helped move country music into the American popular music mainstream. This led to country music becoming an accepted part of the corporate culture in the American entertainment industry by improving what corporate America looks at closest: the bottom line. By improving that bottom line, country music improved itself and became a major player in the world of music.

The Post World War II World

In 1956 a book was published entitled *The Organization Man*. That title came to identify the generation who came of age during World War II and who were born during the period 1915-1929. For that group of white males the United States was a great place to come of age and have a career. Although the ethic of this group stressed "hard work," and the idea of working hard for what they got was an integral part of their self-image as well as the reason most cited for doing well in the post-World War II economy, they also had advantages that generations before them did not have and that generations that came after them would not have. It was that group who gave birth to the Baby Boomers, a generation who came to be known as *The New Individualists*, which was also the name of a book about a generation which came to describe that group.

The first group was united by World War II, a war that was popular at home and which united the country in a single cause like it had never been united before and would not be united again. For that group, patriotism and manhood were defined by their willingness to fight in the Armed Services and the support they received at home while they were away and when they returned, it defined their view of the world for years to come. That group found it nearly impossible to understand their own children, who came of age during the Vietnam War, a war that divided rather than united the country. For many in the Baby Boom generation, it was more patriotic to not fight and protest the war; for the older generation that was unthinkable. The biggest social revolution and generational split occurred from two different wars which shaped and defined two different generations.

The World War II generation of "organization men" shaped America until 1992 when Bill Clinton, the first Baby Boomer was elected President. Until that time every President since 1941 when the United States declared war on Japan and Germany was profoundly shaped by this war. From Franklin Roosevelt, who was President when Pearl Harbor was bombed and war was declared to Harry Truman, who assumed the Presidency after Roosevelt died in 1945 and who was responsible for the ending of the war by dropping two atomic bombs on Japan, and the peace accords which defined the world for the next 50 years, and then through a series of Presidents who all served in the Armed Forces during World War II: Dwight Eisenhower, John Kennedy, Lyndon Johnson, Richard Nixon, Gerald Ford, Jimmy Carter, Ronald Reagan and George Bush. All of those men, as well as the country they led, were shaped by their view of the world developed during the Great Depression and World War II.

In addition to a popular war that united the country, that group of men had other advantages past and future generations did not have. During the 1920s there was an anti-immigrant movement that culminated in a series of acts that severely restricted immigration into the United States. That was the reason it was so difficult to get Jews into the United States during World War II when their lives were in danger. From 1924 until after the War, the limit on immigration caused the work force to be mostly restricted to those born in America. Further, the birth rate of the 1930s during the Great Depression was the lowest of any time in the history of this nation; thus the "organization man" came of age when the competition for jobs was extremely limited. Accepted discriminatory practices against women and blacks further enhanced the position of the white male, who had a booming economy that demanded workers in order to grow and thrive.

After the War the GI Bill provided an opportunity to higher education for those who served in the Armed Services. That led to the popularization of mass higher education; prior to that, colleges and Universities were generally limited to the privileged and elite. After World War II the concept that a college education was available to anyone who wanted it was widely accepted. That led to an educated work force at the management level after the War, a decided advantage in an economy shifted from being a blue collar industrial and manufacturing economy to a white collar information-based economy during the following fifty years.

The government built roads from cities out to the suburbs during the post-World War II period and the idea of mass construction of housing developed by William Levitt in Long Island created the suburbs. The sales agents and developers of those suburbs openly advertised that no blacks or other minorities could buy in the area in order to entice whites to buy. Further, the government granted low interest home loans to veterans as well as others through the Veterans Home Administration (VHA) and Federal Home Administration (FHA) to help buyers with their first homes. There was a catch to most of these loans: you had to buy a new house.

The government's programs encouraged housing construction and ownership in the suburbs, which caused the country to shift to a nation of suburbs in the next 50 years. The cities were left to those who could not afford to move or who were denied access to loans; increasingly that meant blacks were left in the inner cities while whites moved to the suburbs. By the 1990s the term "urban"--which means "city"--was used to describe African-American music; this was appropriate since most African-American music by that time came out of the inner cities, which were populated primarily by blacks.

During World War II women entered the work force in large numbers because male workers were overseas fighting and "Rosie the Riveter" was born. After the War the majority of those women were replaced by men when servicemen came back home. There were a great deal of marriages and couples then moved to the suburbs and began raising families. The "role" of women at that point was as a homemaker, and the popular media and advertisers consistently reinforced those images. The images on TV shows of "Ozzie and Harriet," "Leave It to Beaver," "Donna Reed" or "Father Knows Best" where the husband left the suburbs every day to work while the wife stayed home to take care of the house and kids was widely accepted as the "ideal" life for the middle class. It was made possible by an economy which allowed one male wage earner to support a growing family with one income. Women generally accepted their role--in surveys after World War II and into the 1950s most women described the "ideal" life as being married to a successful man--but their daughters increasingly saw their fathers, not their mothers, as professional role models.

Some women began to rebel in the 1960s after examining their life in the suburbs carrying kids around in a station wagon and realized they felt unfulfilled. The most famous example here is Betty Friedan, who wrote *The Feminine Mystique,* which led to the feminist movement during the 1960s becoming a major social force. But, by and large, most of the women married to organizational men were happy with their lives and their roles. For later generations, that was hard to grasp and many women openly asked themselves why should they stay married to a man they did not like, or remain locked in a life that seemed unfulfilling. For that generation, the divorce rate soared as they refused to accept the values of the post-World War II women and became more independent and assertive. The post-World War II women provided a commitment and stability that was important to the growing society and economy of that period.

For the organization men, a stable marriage meant free child care and that the home life was taken care of so they could pursue their career full force and they did pursue their career with dedication and commitment. That was augmented by a business culture that virtually guaranteed lifetime employment for loyal employees with the promise that things would get better every year. That generation grew up with pessimism, nurtured by the Great Depression, so they were cautious and learned optimism slowly. The following generations were born with an optimism that things would always get better and learned a pessimism as they grew older. That became an essential difference in the World War II generation and those born later. The World War II generation believed in saving money; the post-World War II generations believed in spending it. That basic difference in values, as well as the fact that the post-World War generation acquired wealth through home ownership and the dramatic rise in property values after World War II as well as the generous Social Security benefits when they retired meant that by the 1990s the wealthiest part of the American population was the over-65 group while the younger generation just starting their careers had to face the fact they might never own a home, that businesses could fire them on a whim or a corporate takeover of their firm might mean unemployment whether they worked hard and were doing a good job or not, and that a good portion of the money they earned went to support retirees through Social Security pensions. For the young generation, an estimated third would never be out of debt their entire life (primarily because of credit cards), another third would hover at the break-even point, and only the final third would have a positive net worth during their life. If that generation managed to purchase a home, it was usually because the older generation had lent them the money for a down payment.

The business climate could not have been better after World War II. The sensitivity to the environment or energy was not there; there was no concern (and generally no knowledge) about the harmful effects of pollution. Auto and gas manufacturers thought of new ways to sell big cars with no concern for the price of gas because it was so cheap. It was not until the 1973 Arab oil boycott that the United States had to face, for the first time, a severe restriction on the supply on energy.

In the meantime, Americans bought bigger and bigger cars; the 1950s and early 1960s models with their long tail fins represented affluence and the price of gas made mileage insignificant. General Motors and Standard Oil bought up public city transportation systems and tore up the rails so cities would buy busses, which ran on gas. That left most cities without an adequate public transportation system and forced Americans to rely even more on cars. At this point, this was not a problem; Americans liked owning their cars and car manufacturers conceived the idea of a new model every year and planned obsolescence in order to have a larger turnover in cars. Things were so good for car manufacturers, especially General Motors, that they grew fat, lazy and arrogant and insensitive to changing public tastes. That led to the Japanese motor companies acquiring about a fourth of the American car market during the 1970s and 80s.

At the end of World War II the United States was the only major economy that had not been directly affected by the ravages of War. Europe was in ruins and so was Japan. It took massive rebuilding efforts for Germany and Japan to get back on their feet, and the first steps for that rebuilding was done through the Marshall Plan during the late 1940s when the United States provided massive aid to Europe and Asia. The aid was to help those countries become capitalist economies with democratic governments so America had places to sell their goods and keep the peace. It worked well for a number of years and the United States became the world's dominant economic power in the post-World War economy.

The 1950s brought other massive changes in our society. In New York, Eugene Ferkauf developed "Korvettes," a mass merchandising chain. Stores were placed in the suburbs instead of the inner cities and profits were made by high volume. That led to a nation of K-Marts, Wal-Marts and other mass merchandisers; it also led to the death of small town stores on the square, owned locally and run by people you knew. Small stores need a high mark-up on individual products in order to survive; large chains can drive the family owned store out of business simply by providing much more merchandise at lower prices and make their profits through high volume. That changed the face of America--particularly small town America.

In California Ray Kroc purchased a hamburger stand from the McDonald brothers and created McDonald's a national chain. In Memphis, Kemmons Wilson took his family on a summer vacation and was appalled at the problem of trying to find a decent motel to stay in at night; from that experience he developed Holiday Inn motels. Both Holiday Inn and McDonald's helped traveling Americans because now citizens felt safe to travel; they knew what to expect--a McDonald's and Holiday Inn--everywhere they went and thus were cushioned against the problems of the unknown when they traveled.

The Interstate Highway System, developed beginning in 1956, came from the Defense Department's attempts to provide a way to move the Armed Forces around this country quickly. But the Interstate Highway system also provided a way for tourists to get quickly from one part of the country to another. Gone were the small two way streets with stop lights in every town; it was replaced by superhighways where people could travel a high speeds for miles and miles without stopping or even slowing down. It also provided a way for musicians to tour nationally more easily; the superhighways particularly made it easy for the big busses to get all over the country carrying their stars in comfort without worrying about small congested roads.

The birth control pill gave women an advantage they never had; the ability to have sex without worrying about pregnancy. That allowed them greater control in their lives and careers and ushered in the sexual revolution of the 1960s, as well as increased women in the workplace and in careers, as opposed to "jobs." The sexual revolution was also aided by Hugh Hefner and the introduction of *Playboy* magazine. *Playboy* was more than a magazine with naked women; it was a magazine that allowed middle class youth to learn about "taste" in clothes, wine, stereo equipment and other material goods previously limited to the upper class. In the past it was the elite schools which provided upper class youth the knowledge of social graces; after the 1950s *Playboy* provided middle class youths this information. It was a change as radical as the pictures of beautiful nude women available to any American boy. It began with Marilyn Monroe as the first centerfold who posed with nothing on but the radio. The social revolution hit full speed when Elvis Presley, "who sang like Marilyn Monroe walked," was heard on the radio by thousands of teenagers who heard more than a voice; they heard a social revolution.

1970

The year 1970 began with "Raindrops Keep Fallin' On My Head" by B.J. Thomas, from the soundtrack of Butch Cassidy and the Sundance Kid, in the number one position on *Billboard's* Hot 100, where it remained for four consecutive weeks.

The Beatles had two singles top the Hot 100 chart that year, "Let It Be" (2 weeks) and their final single as a group, "The Long and Winding Road," which was number one for two weeks in June. That same month, Ringo Starr went to Nashville and recorded a country album.

The biggest single hit of 1970 was "Bridge Over Troubled Water" by Simon & Garfunkel, which held the number one position for six straight weeks. Other big single hits during 1970 were by The Jackson 5 who had four: "I Want You Back," "ABC" (2 weeks), "The Love You Save" (2 weeks), and "I'll Be There" (5 weeks). Sly and the Family Stone had "Thank You (Faletittinme Be Mice Elf Again)," "Everything is Beautiful" by Ray Stevens (2 weeks), "American Woman" by the Guess Who (3 weeks), "Mama Told Me (Not to Come)" by Three Dog Night (2 weeks), "(They Long To Be) Close To You" by the Carpenters (4 weeks), "War" by Edwin Starr (three weeks)," "Ain't No Mountain High Enough" by Diana Ross (3 weeks) "The Tears of a Clown" by Smokey Robinson& The Miracles, "I Think I Love You" by the Partridge Family (3 weeks) and "Cracklin' Rosie" by Neil Diamond.

The year 1970 ended with former Beatle George Harrison's "My Sweet Lord" in the number one positon. His three disc album, *All Things Must Pass*, also reached number one on the *Billboard* album chart and became the best selling album from a solo Beatle after their breakup.

James Taylor

The album, *Sweet Baby James* by James Taylor was released by Warner Bros. and entered the *Billboard* album chart on March 14, 1970; it reached the number three spot, where it remained for three consecutive weeks. The first single, "Fire and Rain" entered the *Billboard* Hot 100 on September 12, 1970 and stayed on the chart for 16 weeks, reaching number three where it remained for three straight weeks. It was an album filled with sensitive, acoustic songs of self-expression and self-discovery.

The singer-songwriter era had arrived.

James Taylor was born in Boston on March 12, 1948; his family moved to Chapel Hill, North Carolina in 1951 when his father, a physician, took a job as professor at the University of North Carolina School of Medicine. James learned to play the guitar in 1960, after lessons on the cello, and developed a finger-picking style. He attended the Milton Academy in Massachusetts and, during summer vacation on Marta's Vineyard, met Danny Kortchmar, who was also learning guitar. The two began playing and performing together.

Taylor dropped out of the elite college preparatory school and enrolled in high school in Chapel Hill and joined a band where he played electric guitar; during his senior year he returned to Milton Academy and began to suffer depression. He entered McLean, a mental health facility in Massachusetts, and was rejected for the draft because of physiological reasons. He graduated from Arlington School, affiliated with McLean.

Taylor moved to New York City and formed a band, The Flying Machine, with Danny Kortchmar and they performed a number of Taylor's songs, often at the Night Owl Café in Greenwich Village. In New York, Taylor became a heroin addict. At the end of 1966, his band recorded two of Taylor's songs, "Night Owl" and "Brighten Your Night With My Day" that were released on Jay Gee Records. The song reached number 102 on the *Billboard* chart.

The Flying Machine broke up and Taylor's drug addiction deepened. His father drove to New York and took James back to North Carolina where he spent six months getting treatment.

In 1967, financed by a family inheritance, James Taylor moved to London and recorded demos as a solo artist. Danny Kortchmar connected Taylor to Peter Asher, formerly of Peter and Gordon who had hits with "A World Without Love" and "I Go to Pieces." Asher was the head of A&R for Apple, the Beatles label, and gave a demo tape to Paul McCartney and George Harrison; on that tape was "Something In The Way She Moves." The tape impressed the Beatles and Taylor was called in for an audition and became the first non-British act on Apple. Peter Asher later became Taylor's manager.

Taylor wrote more songs, rehearsed with a backing band, and recorded his first album at Trident Studios between July and October, 1968 while the Beatles recorded *The White Album*. Tayor resumed his drug habit during those sessions and underwent treatment in London, then back to New York and a treatment center in Stockbridge, Massachusetts.

His debut album, *James Taylor*, was released by Apple in December, 1968 and in the U.S. in February, 1969. Taylor, because of his drug treatments, was unable to tour to promote the album and it sold poorly, although it received good critical response.

James Taylor headlined a six-night stand at the Troubadour in Los Angeles in July, 1969 and then performed at the Newport Folk Festival and was well received; however, a motorcycle accident left both hands and both feet broken. He could not play for several months but continued writing and signed a new recording contract with Warner Brothers in October, 1969.

James Tylor moved to Los Angeles and so did Peter Asher, his manager and producer. Sessions for his second album, *Sweet Baby James*, were held with Carole King participating. The album was released in February, 1970 and sold over 1.5 million copies during its first year (and eventually over three million copies). The album was nominated for a Grammy for "Album of the Year."

Taylor appeared in the film, *Two-Lane Blacktop* with Beach Boy Dennis Wilson and performed at a Greenpeace benefit with Joni Mitchell, Phil Oches and Chilliwack, a Canadian band.

On the March 1, 1970 edition of *Time Magazine*, James Taylor was the cover story. That was positive affirmation that the singer-songwriter was now part of mainstream American music.

Taylor's next album on Warners, *Mud Slide Slim and the Blue Horizon*, entered the *Billboard* album chart on May 8, 1971 and reached number two, where it held for 45 weeks. Taylor's single, "You've Got a Friend," written by Carole King, was his only number one single and won Grammys for "Song of the Year" and "Pop Male Vocal." He had a series of chart single, "Long Ago and Far Away" (with then-girlfriend Joni Mitchell on backing vocal), "Don't Let Me Be Lonely Tonight," "Mockingbird" (with wife Carly Simon), "How Sweet It Is (To Be Loved By You)," "Mexico," "Shower the People" and "Handy Man" (which won a Grammy for Pop Male Vocal) but James Taylor was an album artist and his albums, *One Man Dog, Walking Man, Gorilla* and *JT* sold well. He was the epitome of the male singer-songwriter.

Crosby, Stills, Nash & Young

The group, now Crosby, Stills, Nash and Young, released their album, *Déjà Vu* and it entered the *Billboard* album chart in April, 1970 and rose to number one, remaining on the chart for 97 weeks. In addition to the single, "Woodstock," the album contained the singles "Teach Your Children" and "Our House," both written by Graham Nash.

During their second American tour, while staying at a house in San Francisco, Young and Crosby heard the news about the shooting at Kent State where four students died during an anti-war demonstration. Young wrote "Ohio" in response to the tragedy at Kent State University that left students dead.

The song was recorded and rush released as a single; it entered the *Billboard* chart on June 27 and reached number 14, and became an anthem for anti-war demonstrators.

There were conflicts, disagreements and dissatisfaction in the group as the tour progressed, exacerbated by drugs, alcohol and megalomania, resulting in the group firing Stephen Stills in July 1970 during a performance in Chicago. Stills was reinstated and the tour ended on July 9, 1970 but the group broke up

Laurel & Topanga Canyons

The music industry in Los Angeles had been centered in Hollywood and in the clubs along Sunset Strip until the end of the 1960s. Around 1970 musicians began to move out of Hollywood and into the canyons and hills that surrounded it.

Two canyons, Laurel Canyon and Topanga Canyon, became the homes and gathering places for rock musicians in Los Angeles. Some musicians lived in both places at different times of their life. Topanga Canyon, twenty miles west of Hollywood in the Santa Monica Mountains, , became the homes of Neil Young, Stephen Stills, Chris Hillman, Barry McGuire, Linda Ronstadt, Neil Diamond, the Flying Burrito Brothers, Gram Parsons, Joni Mitchell, and Van Morrison.

Laurel Canyon, is located in the Hollywood Hills and Santa Monica Mountains. The main thoroughfare is Laurel Canyon Boulevard, which extends to Mulholland Drive, where side roads from the thoroughfare dead end. Musicians who lived there include Carole King, the Byrds, Buffalo Springfield, members of the Eagles,, Mickey Dolenz and Peter Tork of the Monkees, and Neil Diamond.

The Concert Business After Woodstock

Woodstock forever changed the concert business in America. Promoted by Michael Lang, it was the largest concert ever staged at that point. Before Woodstock, the largest crowd to attend a concert was 55,000, who watched the Beatles perform a 28-minute set at Shea Stadium in New York.

Bill Graham hated Woodstock as well as outdoor concerts in general. He felt festivals and outdoor shows were unsafe for audiences because they were uncontrollable and did not provide a good concert experience because the sound was bad and it was hard to see the performers. Young concert goers tended to love outdoor festivals because of the atmosphere, the feeling of being where they action was and sharing the experience with thousands of others. It was cool to be surrounded by like-minded people of the same age at a major event. It felt like one was truly present and part of a huge, important moment. If you were there, you weren't left out.

At Woodstock, the ticket price was $15. Jimi Hendrix, the headliner, received $30,000; The Band, Janis Joplin and Crosby Stills, Nash & Young each received $12,500; Joan Baez and Creedence Clearwater Revival each received $10,000; The Grateful Dead got $7,500, Ten Years After got $6,500 and Joe Cocker and Santana each received $2,500. After Woodstock, the prices for these and other superstar artists soared.

Musicians and their managers realized they, not the promoter, were responsible for the crowds who attended concerts and they wanted a bigger slice of the profits from concerts. Managers and artists made demands as the power shifted from promoters—who took a financial risk when they decided who to book a venue and promote a concert—to the "stars," who felt it was all them and nobody else that attracted a paying crowd. Further, an act with the power to draw a large audience could play larger markets, play for less time on stage, and bring home more money. It wasn't the same rock'n'roll attitude—or business—of the early 1960s.

The first act to flex their muscle was Led Zeppelin, who demanded a 90/10 split with promoters during their 1971 American tour. Promoters were forced to accept the act's demands; Led Zepplin, who played two-and-a-half to three-hour shows dispensed with an opening act. It was a no risk tour; if the promoter put an advertisement in the newspaper, the show sold out quickly. At Pontiac Stadium, the concert gross was $980,000 and Zeppelin's manager demanded to be paid in cash. It was not unusual for the band to travel with millions of dollars in ready cash.

Promoters became "The Man" and when acts demanded high ticket prices or did not show up for a concert, the promoter was blamed.

The old concert business of ballrooms like the Fillmores, which held less than 3,000, was over. When bands realized they could play arenas and stadiums for hundreds of thousands of dollars, that's where they played. With the huge crowds came a huge arrogance with many groups. Tempers got shorter and the list of demands got longer.

In October, 1970, the Aragon Ballroom shut its doors; in December, the Electric Factory in Philadelphia closed. The Boston Tea Party closed in January, 1971 and by the summer of 1971, the Fillmores were not generating profits like they had in the past.

Rock'n'Roll had become Big Business by 1972. *Variety* estimated that $2 billion had been spent by concert goers the previous year and the number of record buyers in 1972 was between 25 and 30 million Americans. Over 20 artists sold over a million albums of their latest release; seven or eight years before, big stars had sales of 200,000-300,000 for a hit album.

In 1972, the Rolling Stones tour of 39 North American cities grossed almost $4 million; Bill Graham promoted some of those concerts. When Bob Dylan decided to tour with The Band in 1974, Bill Graham promoted that tour, which established new rules for a rock'n'roll tour. The tour, which featured 40 concerts in 21 cities in 43 days, was the first national tour organized by a single promoter. The Dylan tour was followed by a stadium tour of Crosby, Stills, Nash & Young promoted by Graham that featured the first collapsible outdoor stage and room. The third tour Graham promoted that year was by former Beatle George Harrison. That, too, was a national tour and those three tours grossed over $22 million.

The Emerging Structure of Concerts

During his first several years as a concert promoter, Bill Graham had no real organization or business structure; he booked acts into the Fillmore, advertised, put up posters, collected the money, paid the acts, and went on to the next show.

Prior to Graham, the most important rock'n'roll shows were staged by Alan Freed or Dick Clark, who organized "caravans" where eight to ten acts performed their hits in a package show format. Outside of those caravans, rock acts played in clubs, in college auditoriums and, increasingly, in "ballrooms" modeled after the Fillmore in San Francisco.

Rock concert promoters began to emerge in different cities; they were generally young people who, knowing about Graham's Fillmore, basically copied him by renting a venue, hiring an act, publicizing the show and hoped that people showed up. Young rock acts usually played for a set fee. Most acts were initially thrilled to receive $1,000—it was an incredible amount of money to play for a evening or even several evenings. Tickets were priced around $2 because young people did not have a lot of money. Advertising consisted of a newspaper ad and posters, put up around town. The promoter courted the media so a story about the upcoming show would run in the newspaper and the disc jockeys mentioned the show on the radio. The cost of advertising might run $150.

If the venue seated 2,500 people, and everyone bought a ticket, that was $5,000. Subtract the $1,000 for the act and $150 for advertising and that meant the promoter could take home almost $4,000 for a weekend show. The burden was on the promoter to make sure there was a crowd; if nobody showed up, the promoter received no money and had to pay the act. If more than 2,500 showed up, the profits increased. The real skill lay in knowing how to alert the public that a show was taking place and entice them to come.

As rock concert promoters emerged, the best acquired "territories" where they promoted concerts. In the Midwest, it was the Belkin Brothers, Jules and Michael; in Denver it was Barry Fey, in the Los Angeles market it was Steve Wolf and former William Morris agent Jim Rissmill; in New York it was Sid Bernstein until 1967, when he decided to go into management with The Rascals. Bernstein had booked the Beatles during their first visit to the States in 1964; they were paid $6,500 for two shows in one day at Carnegie Hall. The next year, the Beatles did one twenty-eight minute show at Shea Stadium and Bernstein paid them $180,000. That Shea Stadium concert alerted concert promoters that there could be big money at big venues for big acts. It also meant that the days of a young upstart promoting rock concerts on a wing and a prayer were over.

Bill Graham expanded into New York City in 1968. He put together investors that included Albert Grossman, Grossman's partner Burt Block, broker Mike Rogers and promoter Ron Delsener, and rented a venue, which he named "Fillmore East." Opening night was March 8, 1968; singer Tim Buckley and bluesman Albert King opened for Janis Joplin and Big Brother and the Holding Company. The move into New York made Bill Graham a national figure as he continued to operate Fillmore West, shuttling back and forth between the two coastal cities.

A "circuit" for touring rock bands emerged. They played the Fillmore East in New York, the Kinetic Playground in Chicago, the Electric Factory in Philadelphia, the Boston Tea Party in Boston, the Grande Ballroom in Detroit and the Fillmore West in San Francisco. Outside of those venues, acts often played college campuses.

The major booking agencies, like William Morris, were used to handling Big Bands or Las Vegas acts; they had no experience booking rock acts. Frank Barsalona, who was Sid Bernstein's assistant at General Artists Corporation (GAC) formed Premier Talent just as the British rock acts descended on America. Among the acts that Barsalona signed were Jimi Hendrix, Joe Cocker and The Who.

Barsalona and Premier Talent developed a system where records were released at intervals of nine months to a year, coordinated between the record company, the act's management and concert promoters. A single was promoted to radio and the act toured to promote the album.

In his biography of Bill Graham, author John Glatt stated that "When a band wanted to go on tour, its manager would hire a booking agent like Premier to set it up. The agents, who usually took 15 percent to 20 percent, were responsible for routing the tours, advising bands on what markets to play and, depending on their drawing power, whether to play clubs, arenas, or stadiums. Agents worked like real estate brokers; they didn't buy, but only sold, running no risk. The agent then negotiated with promoters like Bill Graham to fix a price for the band."

"In the late sixties it was standard for a headline act to take 60 percent of the gross and be responsible for all the promoter's local expenses," continued Glatt. "Other promoters worked on a formula basis where they would pay a guarantee of $10,000 and then split the gross 60/40, with the band paying its touring expenses out of its share. Once the deal was signed, the promoter assumed all risk for the show and was responsible for newspaper and radio advertising and other promotions needed to sell seats. He also did the ticketing, hired the hall, if necessary, and organized security, medical services, and catering. As the band got a guarantee upfront, the only party at risk if a show failed was the promoters."

Glatt noted that "As the concert promotion business became more sophisticated, a complicated maze of relationships evolved among promoters, agents, and managers. These all-important alliances, often years in the making, became the oil that kept the concert machine running and generating money." Those relationships meant that established promoters had the inside track when it came to booking top acts for their territory; it also meant each knew a network of support providers for everything from lights, sound, instruments and hotels to unions, drug runners and groupies. A concert promoter had to be a team manager because it took an entire team to promote a successful concert.

Bill Graham was a master at promoting concerts and pioneered the contemporary concert promotion business. On his office well, he posted a clipping on his office wall titled "How to Argue and Win." It read, "Keep up a stream of illogical thinking. Employ fallacies, prejudices and if you find that doesn't work go heavy on emotionalism and inappropriate analogies. Be completely irrational and avoid facing the truth. This method so frustrates your opponent that though he may be completely right, you appear to have won. Signed Bill Graham."

Asylum Records

David Geffen managed Jackson Browne and wanted him signed to Atlantic, but Ahmet Ertegun refused to sign him. Instead, Ertegun told Geffen that he should start his own label and even offered that Atlantic would help finance the label and handle distribution. Geffen wanted to be assured that he would eventually be sole owner of the new label so he negotiated a three year agreement, at the end of which time the label would be Geffen's.

Geffen named the label "Asylum," which was "fueled by Geffen's philosophy: to protect his artists from the rest of the world," stated Stan Cornyn. "This was an identity in vivid contract to the more exploitive behaviors of older companies. To artists, Geffen's company would offer asylum."

Vietnam

A Gallup Poll in 1970 revealed that "56 percent of people believe we made a mistake sending troops to fight in Vietnam" and "citizens who think we were wrong to commit our forces in Vietnam has more than doubled over the last five years." Still, the Vietnam War continued.

In Paris on October 8, a Communist delegation from North Vietnam rejected President Nixon's peace proposal, calling it "a maneuver to deceive world opinion." Four days later, Nixon announced that 40,000 American troops would be withdrawn from Vietnam before Christmas. At the end of October a monsoon that caused large floods did what diplomats could not do: it halted the Vietnam War, at least briefly.

It was reported that during the week of November 5, "only" 24 soldiers died in Vietnam, the lowest weekly death toll in five years and the fifth consecutive week that the death toll was less than 50; however, 431 were wounded that week.

Later that month, Lieutenant William Calley went on trial for the My Lai Massacre, where hundreds of Vietnamese citizens—mostly old men, women and children—were slaughtered in 1968. The day after that trial began, President Nixon asked for $155 million from Congress for the Cambodian government to prevent the overthrow of Premier Lon Nol.

Anti-war Demonstrations

There were numerous demonstrations against the Vietnam War on campuses across the United States and in June, 1970, a survey by the Gallup Poll was released that listed "campus unrest as the nation's number one problem," ahead of the Vietnam war, racial strife, the high cost of living and crime." Columnist Clayton Fritchey quoted a poll "which found that college demonstrators were more hated than prostitutes, atheists, and homosexuals" and noted "there is no doubt that the students have generated an unreasoning fury on the part of their elders."

The Chicago Seven, charged with inciting a riot during the Democratic Convention in Chicago in 1968 were found "not guilty" of that charge but five were found guilty of the lesser charge of crossing state lines to incite a riot.

On May 4, an anti-war demonstration on the Kent State campus led to the deaths of four demonstrators and the wounding of nine others when Ohio National Guardsmen opened fire. The demonstration began when President Nixon ordered U.S. forces to cross into Cambodia, a neutral nation, to widen the Vietnam war. That incident inspired Neil Young to write and record "Ohio." The single, by Crosby, Stills, Nash & Young, debuted on the Hot 100 in June, 1970 and reached number 14.

On May 8 the "Hard Hat Riot" occurred at New York City Hall when unionized construction workers attacked about 1,000 students demonstrating against the Kent State shootings. The next day, about 100,000 gathered in Washington, D.C. to protest against the Vietnam War.

Demonstrations against the Vietnam War began at Jackson State University in Jackson, Mississippi on May 13; the next day state law enforcement officers fired into the demonstrators, killing two and injuring 12. An anti-war rally in September in Valley Forge, Pennsylvania was attended by John Kerry and actors Jane Fonda and Donald Sutherland.

A Chicano Moratorium against the Vietnam War was held in East Los Angeles where police opened fire and killed three people, including journalist Ruben Salazar.

In New York, women marched down Fifth Avenue for a Women's Strike for Equality.

Radical groups such as the Weathermen had formed in the United States. In March, a bomb being constructed by the group and intended for a military dance in New Jersey, accidently exploded and killed three members of the group. In August, anti-Vietnam protestors bombed Sterling Hall at the University of Wisconsin, Madison.

Conservative America

On July 4, 1970, an "Honor America" day was held in Washington to celebrate the nation's 194th birthday. The main speaker was Reverend Billy Graham, who gave a somewhat conciliatory, uplifting speech before an estimated crowd of 35,000 on the Washington Mall. Graham addressed the audience, saying "We will listen respectfully to those who dissent in accordance with the constitutional principles, but we strongly reject violence and the erosion of any of our liberties under the guise of a dissent that promises everything and delivers only chaos.

The "Second Annual Atlanta International Pop Festival," held in Byron, Georgia, about 90 miles south of Atlanta, attracted 500,000 for the three day festival that featured the Allman Brothers, The Radars, Grand Funk Railroad, John Sebastian, Ten Years After and Cat Mother and the All-Night News Boys. Temperatures soared past the 100 degree mark during the festival.

Georgia Governor Lester Maddox, who began his political career by vowing to never serve Negros in his fried chicken restaurant, called the festival "a shame and disgrace...and something to be expected among savages."

The Mayor of Byron, Ed Green, called the festival "the worst thing that ever happened in this area of the country" and "I don't know if we will ever recover."

Newspaper reporters reported "tales of nude swimming, naked strollers, open fornication and widespread drug use during the festival." The Byron Mayor vowed that he "would take legal steps—and possibly appeal to the legislature—to prevent the festival's return next year."

Long haired young men

Long hair on men became a political statement during the 1960s and early 1970s. When the Beatles arrived in 1964, America was a crew cut nation. After the Beatles, young men began to grow their hair long, although many in high school were disciplined for having long hair and forced to have it cut in order to remain in school. Long hair became disruptive for the older generation, who were part of a short hair generation. Long haired young men were often called "Communists" or "sissies" and accused of having an anti-American attitude that harbored a danger radicalism which threatened the core values of America.

Young men with long hair were regularly denounced by religious leaders, citing I Corinthians 11:14 from the Bible, which states "Does not even nature itself teach you that if a man has long hair it is a disgrace to him, but that if a woman has long hair, it is her glory?"

AP reporter Richard Blystone, in an article titled "About That Rug on Your Neck, Pal," stated that young men with long hair were disqualified from receiving unemployment checks in Monterey, California, "under a ruling that too much hair restricts availability for jobs." In Detroit, two young "dissidents" took a sheriff to court after he ordered their heads shaved in the county jail.

There were numerous confrontations between young long haired men and the older, short-haired generation during that period. It was a volatile time and the Generation Gap between the youth of the 1960s and early 1970s grew wider. The two groups could not communicate; they could only rebel and chastise the other side.

"Rose Garden"

At the beginning of 1970—on January 7—"(I Never Promised You a) Rose Garden" by Lynn Anderson entered the *Billboard* country chart; it would reach number one and stay there for five weeks; it reached number three on *Billboard's* Hot 100. The song had been released in October, 1969 on Columbia, produced by her husband, Glenn Sutton. The song was written by Joe South (who also wrote "These Are Not My People," "Games People Play," "Down in the Boondocks" and "Walk a Mile in My Shoes") and was first recorded by Billy Joe Royal in 1967. "Rose Garden" was Anderson's first single on Columbia after several years recording for Chart Records. During 1967 she had been a regular on "The Lawrence Welk Show." "Rose Garden was a hit in Australia, Canada, New Zealand, Ireland and Norway; Anderson won a Grammy for "Best Female Vocal."

Kris Kristofferson: Songwriter

During 1970, Kris Kristofferson became the most successful and well-known songwriter in Nashville and a new voice in country songwriting. The previous year Roger Miller had a hit with "Me and Bobby McGee" and Ray Stevens released his version of "Sunday Morning Coming Down."

On June 27, 1970, "For the Good Times," written by Kristofferson and recorded by Ray Price entered the *Billboard* country chart and rose to number one, then went to number eleven on the *Billboard* Hot 100. Kristofferson wrote the song in 1968 while driving from Nashville to the Gulf of Mexico where he worked as a helicopter pilot taking workers to oil rigs. The first recording of the song was by Bill Nash, which did not chart. Price's version of the song was produced by Don Law and Frank Jones and was originally on the "B" side of the single, "Grazin' in Greener Pastures" but "For the Good Times" soon caught radio's attention. Price won a Grammy for "Best Country Vocal" with "For the Good Times." Later, Perry Como had a hit in the U.K. with the song.

Kristofferson's "Sunday Morning Coming Down" recorded by Johnny Cash entered the *Billboard* country chart on September 5 and rose to number one, where it stayed for two weeks; it reached number 19 on the *Billboard* Hot 100. The song was recorded live by Cash during one of his TV shows. Record label executives and ABC TV executives objected to the line "wishing Lord that I was stoned." They implored Cash to change the line to "wishing Lord that I was alone" and stated the song could not be released or broadcast with the offending line. Cash listened but was noncommittal; no one knew what he was going to sing when he sang the "stoned" line. As he sang that line as it was written, he looked at Kristofferson, seated in the upper balcony of the Ryman. The song was released and broadcast as Cash sang it. It won the CMA's "Song of the Year" award.

On December 19, "Help Me Make It Through the Night" written by Kristofferson and recorded by Sammi Smith on a new Nashville label, Mega, entered the Billboard country chart and reached number one in 1971, where it remained for three weeks. It crossed over to the pop chart, where it reached number six. Kristofferson reportedly wrote the song in the basement of Dotty West's home on Shy's Hill Drive. Kristofferson offered the song to West but she thought it was too suggestive. Kristofferson had gotten the title of the song from an article on Frank Sinatra he read in *Esquire* magazine where the singer answered the question to what he believed and stated he used "Booze, broads, or a Bible—whatever helps me make it through the night." West later recorded it on an album; other artists who soon covered the song included Joan Baez, Lynn Anderson, Jerry Lee Lewis, Loretta Lynn, Olivia-Newton-John, Andy Williams, Glen Campbell, Skeeter Davis, Tammy Wynette and Gladys Knight and the Pips; Johnny Cash and June Carter recorded it as a duet. The recording won Grammys for "Country Song" and "Country Female Vocal" and was later inducted into the Grammy Hall of Fame.

The day after Christmas, 1970, the Kristofferson penned "Come Sundown" by Bobby Bare entered the Billboard country chart and reached number seven. In the span of about 18 months, four songs written by Kris Kristofferson were released that would become standards.

Kristofferson: The Album

Fred Foster, who owned Monument Records, produced the album *Kristofferson*, which was released in 1970, established Kris Kristofferson as the premier Nashville singer-songwriter. On that album was "Blame It on the Stones," "To Beat the Devil," "Me and Bobby McGee," "Best of All Possible Worlds," "Help Me Make It Through the Night," "The Law Is for Protection of the People," "Casey's Last Ride," "Just the Other Side of Nowhere," "Darby's Castle," "For the Good Times," "Duvalier's Dream" and "Sunday Morning Coming Down."

Andy Williams Presents Ray Stevens TV show & "Everything is Beautiful"

Andy Williams had a top rated television show on NBC that began in July, 1958 and ended in July, 1971. During the summer of 1970 he named Ray Stevens, who had been a frequent guest on his TV show, to host a summer replacement show. The show was taped in Toronto and was a comedy/variety show that featured a number of guests from Nashville. Regulars on the show included Steve Martin, "Mama Cass" Elliot, Lulu, Dick Curtis, Carol Robinson, Billy Van and Solari and Carr. The show began on June 20, 1970 and ended on August 8. The hour-long broadcast was aired n NBC on Saturday evenings 7:30-8:30 p.m. (eastern).

"Everything Is Beautiful" was written by Ray Stevens as a theme song for his TV show. Stevens struggled to write the song at his home in Nashville. After several days of effort, he picked up a book of Chinese proverbs he had on a shelf and saw the phrase "everything is beautiful in its own way." The song was recorded at Jack Clement's studio, in Nashville, engineered by Charlie Tallent. For the opening of children singing "Jesus Loves the Little Children," Stevens went to his daughter's elementary school and taped the young students singing the song. The song entered the *Billboard* Hot 100 chart on April 4, 1970 and rose to number one, where it remained for two weeks; it was a top 40 song on the country chart. "Everything Is Beautiful" won the 1970 Grammy for "Pop Male Vocal."

The A Team

The "A Team" refers to the Nashville studio musicians who appeared on numerous recordings during the 1950s through the 1980s. The "A Team" was not comprised of a single set of musicians but rather a relatively small group whose members dated back to the WSM staff orchestra. During that period, guitarists included Chet Atkins, Hank Garland, Grady Martin, Ray Edenton, Harold Bradley, Velma Williams Smith, Paul Yandell, Pete Wade, Jerry Kennedy, Norman Blake, Jimmy Capps, Fred Carter, Jr., Billy Sanford, Wayne Moss, Jimmy Colvard and Mac Gayden. Bass players included Bob Moore, Ernie Newton, Henry Strzelecki, Junior Huskey, Floyd "Lightnin'" Chance and Joe Osborn. Keyboard players included Owen Bradley, Floyd Cramer, Hargus "Pig" Robbins, Ray Stevens and Bill Purcell. Fiddlers included Tommy Jackson, Johnny Gimble, Buddy Spicher, Dale Potter, Vassar Clements and Brenton Banks, an African-American musician who recorded with string sections. Steel guitarists included Pete Drake, Buddy Emmons, Jerry Byrd, Ralph Mooney, Lloyd Green, Shot Jackson, Hal Rugg and Weldon Myrick. Drummers include Buddy Harman, Ferris Coursey, Jerry Carrigan, Larrie Londin and Kenny Buttrey. Although mandolinists were generally not included, Jethro Burns was a top flight mandolinist when called. The banjo wasn't normally included either (guitarists often played the banjo during sessions) but Earl Scruggs, Buck Trent, Sonny Osborne and Bobby Thompson were top flight banjoists who were often called for sessions. Charlie McCoy was a "generalist" who could play a variety of instruments (his specialty was harmonica) and Farrell Morris was an on call percussionist. Boots Randolph and Bill Justis were key saxophone players.

Around 1970, musicians from the Muscle Shoals and Memphis studios moved to Nashville and became A-Team players. Those included Reggie Young (guitar) Norbert Putnam (bass), Jerry Kerrigan (drums), David Briggs (keyboards), Tony Migliore (keyboards), Sonny Garrish (steel guitar) and Dave Pomeroy (bass).

Joan Baez in Nashville

Joan Baez returned to Nashville in October 1969 and recorded her album, *One Day at a Time* at Bradley's Barn in Mt. Juliet, Tennessee, a suburb of Nashville; it was released in January, 1970. Backed by Nashville session musicians, Baez recorded country songs "Long Black Veil," "Take Me Back to the Sweet Sunny South," "Jolie Blon" and the Willie Nelson song "I Live One Day At a Time" as well as "Seven Bridge Roads" by Steve Young, "No Expectations" by Mick Jagger and Keith Richards) and "Joe Hill," a song about a legendary union organizer. Two Merle Haggard songs were recorded but were not released on the original album.

In 1971 she recorded her album, *Blessed Are...*at Quad Studios in Nashville with producer Norbert Putnam. That album, her last for Vanguard, her long-time label, contained the hit single, "The Night They Drove Old Dixie Down." The song was written by Robbie Robertson of The Band and was originally released as a single by that group in September 22, 1969. Baez's version was released in August, 1971 and reached number one on the *Billboard* Adult Contemporary chart, number three on the Hot 100 and number three on the *Cashbox* Top 100 (it did not appear on the country chart). The record impressed Clive Davis, head of Arista Records, so he asked Norbert Putnam to produce Dan Fogleberg's *Nether Lands* album on Full Moon/Epic.

Baez's 1972 album, *Come From the Shadows*, was self-produced and also recorded at Quad Studios.

Hank Williams, Jr.

Hank Williams, Jr. stepped out of the shadow of his famous father during the 1970s when he released his first number one country single, "All For the Love of Sunshine." The song was written by Mike Curb, Harley Hatcher and Lalo Schifrin and recorded in April, released in July and entered *Billboard's* country chart on August 1; it reached number one and remained in that position for two weeks. The recording was produced by Mike Curb and the Mike Curb Congregation backed Hank, Jr. on the record; it was featured in the movie, Kelly's Heroes, starring Clint Eastwood, Telly Savalas, Carroll O'Connor, Don Rickles and Donald Sutherland.

"Coal Miner's Daughter"

Loretta Lynn's autobiographical song, "Coal Miner's Daughter" told of growing up poor in Kentucky's coal mining country. The song was recorded on October 1, 1969 with producer Owen Bradley, released on May 10, 1970 and entered the *Billboard* country chart on October 31; it reached number one on the country chart and number 83 on the Hot 100. The record was released in the midst of a string of hit recordings by Lynn and led to her autobiography and then a movie by that name.

CMA Awards: 1970

The Fourth Annual Country Music Association Awards was held on October 15, 1970, and broadcast nationally on NBC from the Ryman Auditorium. The show was hosted by Tennessee Ernie Ford and the big winner was a California artist. "Entertainer of the Year" was Merle Haggard. "Song of the Year" was "Sunday Mornin' Comin' Down" by Kris Kristofferson, "Single" and "Album of the Year" was *Okie From Muskogee*, "Male Vocalist" was Merle Haggard, "Female Vocalist" was Tammy Wynette, "Vocal Duo" was Porter Wagoner and Dolly Parton, "Vocal Group" was Tompall and the Glaser Brothers, "Instrumentalist" was Jerry Reed, "Instrumental Group" was Danny Davis and the Nashville Brass, "Comedian of the Year" was Roy Clark and the Carter Family and Bill Monroe were inducted into the Country Music Hall of Fame.

Earth Day and Apollo 13

On April 22, 1970, the first "Earth Day" was celebrated. Earlier that month, President Nixon signed into law the Public Health Cigarette Smoking Act which banned television advertisements for cigarettes. Also that month, the Apollo 13 space capsule with astronauts Jim Lovell, Fred Haise and Jack Swigert aboard was launched. They were headed for a moon landing but an oxygen tank exploded, which forced the crew to return. Fortunately, that made it back after a harrowing four days and splashed down in the Pacific Ocean on April 17.

Led Zeppelin

The Yardbirds were formed in London in 1963; in October of that year Eric Clapton joined as lead guitarist; in 1965 Clapton left and was replaced by Jeff Beck. In June, 1966, session guitarist Jimmy Page joined the Yardbirds as bassist, although he and Beck sometimes played dual lead guitars. In October, 1966, Beck left and Jimmy Page became the sole lead guitarist. In July, 1968 the Yardbirds broke up and Page wanted to form a "supergroup" with Jeff Beck, Keith Moon and John Entwistle of the Who with vocalists Steve Winwood and Steve Marriott; however, that group was never formed.

Page and Chris Dreja formed a group to fulfill the Yardbirds final contractual obligations and hired Robert Plant as lead singer and drummer John Bonham, both former members of Band of Joy, before Dreja dropped out and John Paul Jones, who played bass and keyboards, joined. The group jelled and played on a session for P.J. Proby before they embarked on a Scandanavian tour as the New Yardbirds.

In September, 1968, the group recorded an album financed by Page but could not use the name New Yardbirds so they chose the name Led Zeppelin. In November, they signed with Atlantic Records; their contract gave them autonomy in deciding what they recorded, when they released albums and toured, the artwork on each album and which tracks would be singles. They formed a independent publishing company for their song copyrights.

Their first tour began in October in the U.K. and at the end of the year they toured the United States. In January, 1969, during their American tour, their first album, *Led Zeppelin*, was released and reached number 10 on the *Billboard* album chart. The album reached number six in the U.K. The group toured extensively and released *Led Zeppelin II*, which was recorded in American studios during their tour. That album peaked at number one on the *Billboard* album chart.

The group viewed their albums as complete works and disliked singles, although "Whole Lotta Love" from their second album was released as a single and peaked at number four on the *Billboard* Hot 100 chart in January, 1970.

Lez Zepplin saw themselves as a live, touring act who released albums, not singles, and preferred touring, where their audiences grew from clubs and ballrooms to large auditoriums. Their shows were long—sometimes four hours—and their songs were not limited to three minute tracks for singles.

During 1970, Jimmy Page and Robert Plant retreated to a cottage in Wales to write songs for *Led Zeppelin II*, which was a more acoustic album than their previous two. Against their wishes, a single, "Immigrant Song," was released in the United States at the end of 1970; it reached number 16 on the *Billboard* Hot 100 in January, 1971. Their third album reached number one on the American and U.K. album charts.

Led Zeppelin became an influential, trend setting group during the 1970s with their flamboyant clothing. They traveled by chartered plane and performed long concerts without an opening act. They were an album act who sold millions of albums without the benefit of hit singles.

Music News: 1970

The World Intellectual Property Organization (WIPO) was formed in April, 1970 and in June the Patent Cooperation Treaty became international law; it created a unified procedure for filing patent applications and protected invention.

In June, "American Top 40" countdown, hosted by Casey Kasem, debuted on five American radio stations.

Elvis Presley began his first concert tour in 12 years on September 9, 1970, when he performed at the Veterans Memorial Coliseum in Phoenix, Arizona.

In sad news, Jimi Hendrix died on September 18 and Janis Joplin died on October 4; both were 27 years old.

In 1970, "Monday Night Football" debuted on ABC on September 21; it was reported that the program lowered crime in cities. The North Tower of the World Trade Center in New York topped out at 1,368 feet, making it the tallest building in the world and the National Educational Television networked ended on October 4 and the next day the Public Broadcasting System (PBS) began.

Beatles Break Up in 1970

The Beatles officially broke up in 1970. Their last time in the studio was January 3, 1970 when George Harrison, Paul McCartney and Ringo Starr gathered in the Abbey Road Studio to record "I Me Mine." (John Lennon was in Copenhagen at the time of the session.) That last recording session was necessary because during the filming of what became their last released album, *Let It Be*, Harrison was filmed singing the rift "I, Me, Mine" and needed to complete the song for the soundtrack.

In April, unable to come to an agreement over who their manager should be—Lennon, Harrison and Starr agreed it should be Alan Grubman while McCartney wanted his father-in-law, Lee Eastman, to represent them—McCartney released his debut solo album, *McCartney*, and announced it with a Question-and-Answer press release that let the world know that the Beatles had broken up. There was no single released from that album.

George Harrison recorded a three disc set, All Things Must Pass, which was released at the end of the year; it entered the *Billboard* album chart on December 9 and reached the number one position the next year, where it remained for seven consecutive weeks. The debut single, "My Sweet Lord," entered the Billboard Hot 100 on November 28 and reached number one, where it remained for four weeks. Other singles released from that album were "Isn't It a Pity" (the flip side of "My Sweet Lord") and "What Is Life."

Ringo Starr records in Nashville

In June, 1970, Beatle Ringo Starr came to Nashville and recorded an album, *Beaucoups of Blues* with producer Pete Drake. In Nashville, Ringo visited Ernest Tubb's Record Shop and bought albums. He bought toys for his children at the Sears, Roebuck store. The sessions were held at Music City Recorders and engineered by Scotty Moore; musicians on the session were D.J. Fontana, Charlie Daniels, Dave Kirby, Jerry Reed, Jerry Shook, Roy Huskey, Jr., Buddy Harman, Charlie McCoy, George Richey, Shorty Lavender, Jim Buchanan an Ben Keith.

The Beatles together and apart

John Lennon released *The Plastic Ono Band—Live Peace in Toronto 1969* the previous year but it charted in 1970. His single, "Instant Karma (We All Shine On)" entered the *Billboard* Hot 100 on February 28 and reached number three.

The Beatles final album, *Let It Be*, which had mostly been recorded before the Abbey Road album, was released on May 8 after producer Phil Spector was called in organize the recordings and prepare a release. Spector added strings to some of the songs and sequenced them. The film *Let It Be*, which showed the Beatles bickering in the studio, premiered in London and Liverpool on May 20 but none of the Beatles attended either screening.

In December, John Lennon was interviewed by Jann Wenner for *Rolling Stone* magazine which was long, intensely personal and provocative. During the interview, Lennon gave his account of the Beatles breakup.

On December 31, unable to resolve the differences of management between himself and the other Beatles, McCartney filed a lawsuit suing the other three Beatles in London court in order to legally break up the group. .

1971
Grammy Awards: 1970

The 13th Annual Grammy Awards for 1970 was the first to be televised live. They were held on March 16, 1971 at the Los Angeles Palladium, the first time the Grammys had been held in one place, and hosted by Andy Williams on the ABC network.

The winners were:

Record of the Year: "Bridge Over Troubled Water," produced by Roy Halee, Art Garfunkel and Paul Simon.

Album of the Year: *Bridge Over Trouble Water*, Produced by Roy Halee, Art Garfunkel and Paul Simon

Song of the Year: "Bridge Over Trouble Water," written by Paul Simon for Simon & Garfunkel

Best New Artist: The Carpenters

Best Pop Contemporary Vocal, Female: Dionne Warwick for "I'll Never Fall in Love Again"

Best Pop Contemporary Vocal, Male: Ray Stevens for "Everything Is Beautiful"

Best Pop Contemporary Vocal, Duo or Group: The Carpenters for "Close to You"

Best Pop Contemporary Instrumental: Henry Mancini for *Theme From Z and Other Film Music*

Best Country Vocal, Female: Lynn Anderson for "Rose Garden"

Best Country Vocal, Male: Ray Price for "For the Good Times"

Best Country Vocal by Duo or Group: Johnny Cash & June Carter for "If I Were a Carpenter"

Best Country Instrumental: Chet Atkins & Jerry Reed for *Me and Jerry*

Best Country Song: "My Woman, My Woman, My Wife" by Marty Robbins

Best R&B Vocal, Female: Aretha Franklin for "Don't Play That Song"

Best R&B Vocal, Male: B.B. King for "The Thrill Is Gone"

Best R&B y Duo or Group: The Delfonics for "Didn't I (Blow Your Mind This Time)"

Best R&B Song: "Patches" written by General Johnson and Ronald Dunbar for Clarence Carter.

The "Best Spoken Word Recording" was "Why I Oppose the War in Vietnam" by Martin Luther King, Jr.

Motown Moves to L.A.

In 1971, Berry Gordy, Jr. moved Motown from Detroit to Los Angeles. Along the way he lost a number of acts, including Gladys Knight and the Pips, the Four Tops, Ashford and Simpson, Mary Wells, Martha Reeves, the Spinners, the Isley Brothers, Jimmy Ruffin and the songwriting/production team of Holland, Dozier & Holland.

Gordy wanted to get into movies and he did this with *Lady Sings the Blues*, a bio-pic of Billie Holliday starring Diana Ross. In L.A. he signed Sammy Davis Jr. and Diahann Carroll and established the Mowest label with Thelma Houston, Frankie Valli and the Four Seasons.

He saved Motown's credibility by keeping the Jackson Five, Marvin Gaye and Stevie Wonder.

Clive Davis head Columbia Records

In July, 1971, Clive Davis was named president of the Columbia Records Group; Walter Yetnikoff was named president of the International division. Davis was known as a supreme micro-manager, giving his executives little autonomy and directing everything to flow back to him.

Davis's plan was to plunder talent from other labels and embarked "on the heaviest talent raiding campaign ever conducted in the history of the music business." He already had on the roster Blood, Sweat & Tears and Chicago and Simon & Garfunkel's Bridge Over Troubled Waters, although the duo was splitting. From Nashville, there was Ray Price's third Columbia album *For the Good Times"*and Lynn Anderson's "I Never Promised You a Rose Garden." Davis saw the revenue generated by Nashville and thought that could increase, which led CBS to acquire the rights to distribute Monument Records, which had Roy Orbison and Kris Kristofferson.

Davis worked long, hard hours and assembled a roster of hit makers.

The Sonny and Cher Comedy Hour

"The Sonny and Cher Comedy Hour" premiered on the CBS network on August 1, 1971 and brought contemporary music to television, although the acts on the show were, for the most part, pretty tame. During the show's run, musical guests included the Jackson 5, Jerry Lee Lewis, Bobby Darin, the Righteous Brothers, the Supremes, Chuck Berry, and Glen Campbell. The show was a variety show, so there were ongoing skits with Sonny and Cher as well as a steady stream of Hollywood celebrities such as Tony Curtis, Farah Fawcett, George Burns, Roandl Reagan and Phyllis Diller; Steve Martin was a regular.

The theme song for the show was "And the Beat Goes On," written by Sonny which had been a top ten hit in 1967.

Janis Joplin and "Me and Bobby McGee"

On January 30, 1971, Janis Joplin's version of "Me and Bobby McGee" entered Billboard's Hot 100 chart, three months after her death. It reached number one for two weeks. The song was taught to her by Bobby Neuwirth, who heard Roger Miller's version on the radio. Songwriter Kris Kristofferson did not know she had recorded it until the day after she died. The song became Joplin's best known song and is in the Grammy Hall of Fame.

During 1971, Joplin's album, *Pearl*, held the number one spot on the album chart for nine weeks. The biggest album of the year was *Tapestry* by Carole King, which held the number one position for 15 consecutive weeks.

Country Radio Seminar

On April 23 and 24, 1971, the first "Nashville Country Music Radio Seminar" was held; it proclaimed itself a "conference" and not a "convention" and sought to avoid the problems of the October event where fans had come. Registration was $50. A Board of Directors were formed and, since no big name acts could be enticed to perform, the organization featured "new faces." This was the first organized radio conference for a specific genre of music that became an annual event.

In 1971 the number of full-time country stations dropped to 525.

"American Trilogy"

Mickey Newbury answered the challenge that "Dixie" could never be sung publicly because of it's tarnished past as the unofficial anthem of the Confederacy by writing "American Trilogy," which featuring "Dixie," then "All My Trials," a Bahamian lullaby associated with African-American spirituals and "Battle Hymn of the Republic," with was the marching song of the Union Army during the Civil War. His version entered *Billboard's* "Adult Contemporary" chart on November 6, 1971 and reached number nine. Elvis heard the song and began using it in his concerts; his single entered the *Billboard* Hot 100 in May, 1972 and reached number 66. "American Trilogy" is featured in the *Elvis on Tour* film and Elvis sang it on his "Elvis—Aloha From Hawaii" concert. Mickey Newbury was considered "a songwriter's songwriter) and also wrote "Funny Familiar Forgotten Feelings" for Don Gibson, "Just Dropped in (To See What My Condition My Condition Was In" for Kenny Rogers and the First Edition, "Sweet Memories" for Andy Williams and "Here Comes the Rain, Baby" for Eddy Arnold.

"American Trilogy" was included on Newbury's album, *Frisco Mabel Joy* and featured on his first concert album, *Live at Montezuma Hall* in 1973.

"Easy Loving,"

The biggest country song in 1971 was "Easy Loving," written and recorded by Freddie Hart and produced by George Richey. It entered the *Billboard* country chart on July 10, 1971 and reached number one, where it remained for three weeks; it reached number 17 on the Hot 100. This was Hart's 17th single and a breakthrough record for him. Capitol had decided to drop Hart when a disc jockey on WPLO in Atlanta began playing "Easy Loving" to great response; Capitol then put their promotional team on the song. "Easy Loving" won the CMA's "Song of the Year for 1971 and 1972 and Hart was the Academy of Country Music's "Top Male Vocalist" and "Entertainer of the Year."

"Coat of Many Colors"

The second single from Dolly Parton's album, *Coat of Many Colors*, was the single, "Coat of Many Colors," an autobiographic song that became a signature song for Parton and probably her best known work. It entered the *Billboard* country chart on October 30, 1971.

Dolly wrote the song in 1969 on Porter Wagoner's tour bus on the back of a dry cleaning receipt because she could not find any paper. The song was recorded in April, 1971, in RCA Studio B and was inspired by an incident in Parton's life when she was a young girl. The song reached number four on the *Billboard* country chart.

CMA Awards: 1971

The fifth annual Country Music Association Awards was held on October 10 at the Ryman Auditorium; Tennessee Ernie Ford was host for the NBC telecast. Entertainer of the Year was Charley Pride, Song of the Year was "Easy Loving" by Freddie Hart, Single of the Year was "Help Me Make It Through the Night" by Sammi Smith, and Album of the Year was "I Won't Mention It Again" by Ray Price. Male Vocalist was Charley Pride, Female Vocalist was Lynn Anderson, Vocal Duo was Porter Wagoner and Dolly Parton, Vocal Grop was the Osborne Brothers, Instrumentalist was Jerry Reed, Instrumental Group was Danny Davis and the Nashville Brass and Art Satherley was inducted into the Country Music Hall of Fame.

Vietnam

South Vietnamese troops, backed by air and artillery support by American armed forces, invaded Laos on February 13. On April 24, there were demonstrations against the Vietnam War in Washington, D..C. where over 500,000 marched and San Francisco, where 125,000 demonstrated. A Harris Poll in May claimed that 60 percent of Americas were again the Vietnam War. During the 1971 May Day Protests against the Vietnam War, anti-war militants attempted to disrupt government business; police and military units arrested approximately 12,000. The "Vietnam Veterans for a

Just Peace, which represented veterans who had served in Southeast Asia, spoke out against war protests on June 1.

Australia and New Zealand announced on August 18 that they had decided to withdraw their troops from Vietnam. The total number of American troops in Vietnam dropped to 196,700 at the end of October, the lowest number since January, 1966. President Nixon set a deadline of February 1, 1972 for the removal of another 45,000 American troops.

On March 1, a bomb exploded in the men's room at the Capitol in Washington; the radical group Weather Underground claimed responsibility and a group calling itself the "Citizens' Commission to Investigate the FBI" broke into the FBI offices in Media, Pennsylvania and stole all their files.

Lieutenant William Calley was found guilty of 22 murders in the My Lai Massacre and was sentenced to life in prison, but he was later pardoned.

The Pentagon Papers

On June 13, the New York Times began publishing the Pentagon Papers, a study of the war authorized by Secretary of Defense Robert McNamara which detailed the lies and deceptions from the government about the Vietnam War. The government sued the New York Times but on June 30 the Supreme Court ruled that the study may be published and rejected claims from the government as unconstitutional prior restraint.

News of the World: 1971:

A ban on cigarette advertising on radio and television went into effect on January 2, 1971. . On January 12, the landmark TV series, "All in the Family" starring Carroll O'Connor as Archie Bunker, debuted on CBS. The last broadcast of "The Ed Sullivan Show" occurred on March 28.

On July 5, the 26th Amendment to the United States Constitution, lowering the voting age from 21 to 18, was formally certified by President Nixon.

Walt Disney World opened on October 1 in Orlando, Florida. and on November 15, Intel released the world's first microprocessor, the Intel 4014. Also in 1973, Ray Tomlinson sent the first ARPANET email between host computers. The ARPANET evolved into the Internet.

A man calling himself D.B. Cooper hijacked a Northwest Orient Airlines plane, received $200,000 in ransom money, and parachuted out over Washington State during a severe storm. He was never seen again and the hijacking has never been solved.

Greenpeace was formed on October 13 in Vancouver, Canada and the humanitarian organization "Doctors Without Borders" (Medecins Sans Frontieres) was formed by two groups of French doctors who merged their groups.

Musicals

The musicals *Godspell* and *Jesus Christ Superstar* both opened in New York in 1971; Godspell ran for 2,600 performances (572 on Broadway) and Jesus Christ Superstar ran for 711 performances.

Concert for Bangla Desh

At the beginning of 1971, George Harrison's "My Sweet Lord" was in the number one slot on the Billboard Hot 100 chart; his album, *All Things Must Pass*, was number one for seven weeks on the album chart. During 1971, he had chart singles with "Isn't It a Pity" (the "B" side of "My Sweet Lord") and "What Is Life."

In early 1971, Harrison's friend and musical mentor, Indian musician Ravi Shankar, told Harrison about the conflicts in Bangladesh during dinner at Friar's Park, Harrison's home, in Henley-on-Thames.

When India was a colony of Britain, the colony included both India and Pakistan. India was a country with Hindu and Muslim populations that had a long history of conflict. When India became an independent nation in 1947, Pakistan became an independent Muslim nation, although it was divided by India—Pakistan, to the west of India, and East Pakistan to the east of India. East Pakistan sought to become a separate nation under the name of Bangladesh in 1971 and the Bangladesh Liberation War was fought.

The turmoil caused approximately seven million people to flee Bangladesh and move into India. The new country had faced a devastating cyclone in November, 1970, that resulted in the deaths of nearly half a million people. Then, the Pakistani army slaughtered approximately 250,000 civilians, which created a mass exodus of refugees to Calcutta in India, where they encountered starvation and the outbreak of diseases.

In April, Harrison and Ravi Shankar were in Los Angeles to work on the soundtrack to the film *Raga*, a documentary film on the life of Ravi Shankar. Harrison then returned to England and produced tracks for the *Straight Up* album by Badfinger and played on sessions for John Lennon's *Imagine* album. Shankar kept Harrison informed about the problems in Bangladesh, which had grown worse in March when torrential rains and flooding caused even more people to be displaced.

Harrison and Shankar finished the *Raga* soundtrack by the end of June. By that point, Pakistani journalist had written an article published in the *London Sunday Times* telling of the atrocities in Bangladesh. Shankar appealed to Harrison for help to relieve the suffering. Harrison began making phone calls during the last week of June to organize a fund-raising concert for Bangladesh, set for Sunday, August 1, at Madison Square Garden in New York.

Apple Corps, owned by the Beatles, allowed Harrison to organize a film and album in addition to the concert in New York. Harrison spent days on the phone from his rented home in Nichols Canyon in Los Angeles working on this; he was helped by Chris O'Dell, a former Apple employee.

In early July, George Harrison recorded a single, "Bangladesh" in an L.A. studio; the session was co-produced by Phil Spector. Harrison suspended his work on Badfinger's album but flew to New York to work with Lennon. Back in L.A., Harrison produced an EP, *Joi Bangla*, which was Ravi Shankar's Bangladesh benefit record. All proceeds from Harrison's and Shankar's efforts were earmarked for the George Harrison-Ravi Shankar Special Emergency Relief Fund, to be distributed by UNICEF.

A short mention of a concert by "George Harrison and Friends" set for August 1 was in the *New York Times*, which resulted in sold out ticket sales and a second show being scheduled.

By the end of July, Harrison had assembled a backing band of Billy Preston on keyboards, the four members of Badfinger (Pete Ham, Joey Molland, Tom Evans and Mike Gibbins) on acoustic guitars, Klaus Voormann on bass and Jim Keltner on drums. Saxophonist Jim Horn recruited a horn section of himself with Chuck Findley, Jackie Kelso and Lou McCreary.

Leon Russell and Eric Clapton agreed to be part of the concert and so did John Lennon. Harrison insisted that Lennon perform without his wife, Yoko Ono, which, after Lennon agreed, caused a rift between the couple and resulted in Lennon leaving New York two days before the concert.

Ringo Starr flew in from Spain, where he was working on a film, *Blindman*. Paul McCartney declined to participate, citing bad feelings caused by legal proceedings from the Beatles break-up.

On July 26, Harrison and the musicians began rehearsals for the concert but it wasn't until the night before the concert that there was a somewhat complete run-through of the songs.

The single, "Bangladesh," was released in the U.S. on July 28 (with "Deep Blue" as the "B" side); two days later it was released in the U.K.

The final rehearsal for the concert was during the soundcheck on July 31; by that time Bob Dylan had agreed to perform.

George Harrison served as "Master of Ceremonies" for the concert and the matinee performance at 2:30 began with his introduction of Ravi Shankar, accompanied by Indian musicians, who performed for 45 minutes. After a short intermission, when a Dutch film about the Bangladesh atrocities were shown, George Harrison took the stage, backed by Ringo Starr, Eric Clapton (who was suffering from heroin withdrawal), Leon Russell, Billy Preston, Klaus Voormann, Jim Keltner and 18 others, including background singers. Harrison began with "Wah-Wah," followed by "Something" and "Awaiting on You All," then Billy Preston performed "That's the Way God Planned It." Ringo Starr was next with his hit, "It Don't Come Easy," then Harrison performed "Beware of Darkness." After introducing the band, Harrison performed "While My Guitar Gently Weeps," with a guitar "duel" between Harrison and Clapton. Leon Russell, who insisted on performing with his own band, did a medley of the Rolling Stones "Jumpin' Jack Flash" and the Coasters "Young Blood."

George Harrison and Pete Ham, on acoustic guitars with Don Nix's gospel choir, performed "Here Comes the Sun." Harrison then put his white Fender Stratocaster back on and, looking at the set list taped to the guitar, saw "Bob?" Harrison looked over and saw a very nervous Bob Dylan waiting to go on. Dylan, backed by Harrison with Leon Russell on bass and Ring on tambourine, sang, "A Hard Rain's A-Gonna Fall," "Blowin' in the Wind," "It Takes a Lot to Laugh, It Takes a Train to Cry," "Love Minus Zero/No Limit" and "Just Like a Woman."

Harrison and the band then performed "Hear Me Lord," "My Sweet Lord" and his new single, "Bangladesh."

Before the 8 p.m. show, Harrison, Dylan and others in the group discussed changing the set list. For the evening show, Harrison again opened with "Wah Wah," then played "My Sweet Lord" and "Awaiting on You All, dropping "Hear Me Lord." Bob Dylan dropped "Blowin' in the Wind," "It Takes a Lot to Laugh," and "Love Minus Zero" and replaced them with "Mr. Tambourine Man." After he performed "Just Like a Woman," Dylan held up both fists in a salute.

Harrison closed the show with "Something" and then performed "Bangladesh" as an encore.

The concert was peaceful, with no police around, although about 200 non-ticket holders broke through the doors of Madison Square Garden during the evening concert. The concert received positive reviews with the British publication *NME* declaring it "The Greatest Rock Spectacle of the Decade." *Rolling Stone* declared it a "revival of all that was best about the Sixties."

On September 18, the British version of the Concert for Bangladesh took place in London's Wembley Stadium; it featured the Who, the Faces, Mott the Hoople, America and Lindisfarne.

When George Harrison and his wife, Patti Boyd, returned to England on September 22, he had to meet with Patrick Jenkin of the British Treasury about a purchase tax levied on the album. Jenkin reportedly told Harrison "Sorry! It is all very well for your high ideals, but Britain equally needs the money!"

The two shows at Madison Square Garden raised $243,418.50 and in December, Capitol Records presented a check for $3,750,000 for advance sales of the three-record set of the *Concert for Bangladesh* live album.

The event was not registered as a UNICEF benefit beforehand so it was not granted tax-exempt status, which meant that most of the money generated for Bangladesh was held in an Internal Revenue Service escrow account for ten years. That figure was somewhere between eight and ten million dollars. In 1972, approximately $2 million was sent to the Bangladesh refugees via UNICEF before Apple was audited. In 1981, $8 million was added to the UNICEF fund after the audit.

By June, 1985, almost $12 million had been sent to Bangladesh for relief.

The Concert for Bangladesh was the first major fund raising event by rock'n'roll artists. The next big event to raise funds by the rock'n'roll community came in 1985 when the Live Aid event was held. Prior to that concert, held to benefit victims of the famine in Ethiopia, George Harrison gave "meticulous advice" to Live Aid organizer Bob Geldorf about making sure that funds raised for victims of a tragedy got to the intended recipients.

1972
The Fragmenting of Rock Music

In the world of rock music, The Beatles provided a unity; although there were different types of rock music emerging during the 1960s--psychedelic, soft rock, underground--most fans liked The Beatles. The Beatles, because of their experimentation, showed the rock world that a variety of sounds--everything from rockabilly to Indian sitar music to psychedelic to old fashioned rock and roll--could come under the banner of "rock."

During the 1960s, led by The Beatles, rock music moved from something that challenged mainstream American culture to being part of mainstream American culture. By the time the Beatles broke up in 1970, there was an acceptance of rock as a voice of American popular culture. Previously, "show business" meant Las Vegas, Hollywood, and pop singers; Elvis and the early rock and rollers challenged that view but that definition of "show business" remained with mainstream America. After the Beatles era, 1964-1970, a rock concert was show business.

Part of the reason is the number of young people first attracted to rock in the 1950s, then the 1960s, were getting older and entering American society. Although they may have taken traditional jobs in corporate America, they did not turn loose of their roots of rock and roll when they joined the American middle class.

During the 1970s, the major corporations caught on to rock; executives no longer wondered if and when the fad would pass; instead, they accepted that it was part of the musical landscape and, further, a major part of their profits. However much older top level executives may have preferred Bing Crosby or Broadway musicals, they were businessmen and businessman have to watch the bottom line. Throughout the 1960s, it was rock music that filled that bottom line.

The first musical trend to emerge in the early 1970s was the singer-songwriters but increasingly rock split into several different sub-genres: hard rock, heavy metal, art rock, country rock, disco, reggae, punk, and oldies.

Hard Rock and Heavy Metal

Early rock and roll was rooted in the blues and country music. Country music thrived as its own genre in the 1960s, growing musically; at the same time, it represented a conservative part of America that was antithetical to the counterculture of the 1960s and early 1970s. Most rockers rejected country music until the late 1970s. The singer-songwriters reflected the folk movement, which paralleled, then replaced, rock briefly at the end of the 1950s.

The musics that returned rock and roll to its blues roots were hard rock and heavy metal. In some ways, the musicians in hard rock and heavy metal were the opposite side of the coin from the singer-songwriters, whose music was mostly acoustic, gentle, soft and filled with quiet self-discovery, best performed in a small, quiet, intimate setting. Hard rock and heavy metal were meant to be played loudly in large arenas.

Improved sound systems made arena rock possible; developments in amplifiers and electric guitars meant a group could play in huge stadiums and large arenas and be heard. The Big Bands of the 1940s needed to add more musicians in order to be heard in large ballrooms; a three piece rock group only needed to turn up their amps to blast a venue much bigger than any that Big Bands played in.

Acts like Lynyrd Skynyrd, J.Geils Band, Grand Funk Railroad, Aerosmith and the James Gang all became big within the rock culture, but never really had an impact on mainstream culture. Those groups did not receive much radio airplay or appear on television, but through their constant touring developed a core of faithful fans who consistently went to their shows and bought their albums.

Because radio splintered into various rock formats, the Album Oriented Rock (AOR) format became popular, especially for young males. Acts such as Journey, Styx, REO Speedwagon, Rush, Kansas, Supertramp, Ambrosia, Gentle Giant and Nazareth were called "faceless bands" because individual personalities did not matter; it was the image of the group that was appealing and became popular.

The most influential hard rock group was Led Zeppelin. This British group was voted England's most popular group by the publication *Melody Maker* in 1970, marking the first time the Beatles had not won this honor. In 1971, the group released the album "Led Zeppelin IV" which contained what became the most requested rock song of all time, "Stairway to Heaven."

Heavy Metal and Critics

Most music critics did not take heavy metal seriously; neither did a majority of major label record executives but heavy metal was a music that refused to die. A concert-based music that appealed primarily to young males, particularly in the 16-24 demographic, the music was loud, crude and hostile and embodied teenage rebellion. Although early fans grew older, they were always replaced by a a group of young fans who continued to perpetuate the music. Unlike many other forms of music, where young fans demand new acts to follow, in heavy metal young fans are often attracted to the same groups--and albums--became established years before.

During the early 1970s, heavy metal was defined by groups like Deep Purple, Black Sabbath, Humble Pie, Mahogany Rush, James Gang, Bad Company and Blue Oyster Cult; later Ozzy Osbourne, formerly a member of Black Sabbath, and Metallica, joined that line-up, replacing some of the earlier groups who disbanded or fell by the wayside.

Black Sabbath

Guitarist Tony Iommi and drummer Bill Ward were in a band, Mythology, which broke up in 1968; they recruited bassist Geezer Butler and singer Ozzy Osbourne (who had played in a band, Rare Breed) to form a band in Birmingham, England. Originally known as the Polka Tulk Blues Band, they became Earth but in December Iommi briefly joined Jethro Tull. In January, Iommi returned and in August they became Black Sabbath, named after a Boris Karloff film; Osbourne and Butler wrote the song "Black Sabbath."

In November, 1969, the group was signed to Philips Records and their first single, "Evil Woman," was released in January, 1970; the single was released on Fontana, a subsidiary of Phillips. The single did not chart but their first album, *Black Sabbath*, was released in February and reached number eight on the UK album chart. In May, the album was released in the U.S. and Canada on Warner Brothers and reached number 23 on the *Billboard* chart; it stayed on that chart for over a year. Although it was successful commercially (it reached platinum status in the U.S. and U.K.), many critics disliked it.

In June, 1970, the band recorded their second album, *Paranoid*; the single, "Paranoid" was released in September and reached number four on the singles chart and number one on the album chart in the U.K. In January, 1971, the *Paranoid* album was released in the U.S. and the group made their first American tour; the album sold over four million in the U.S. and reached number 12 on the *Billboard* album chart. This was an era when heavy metal bands did not record singles for radio airplay but instead recorded albums and toured; "Paranoid" was only one of two singles that reached the *Billboard* Hot 100 and that single only reached number 61. Their second single, "Iron Man," reached number 52 in early, 1972.

In February, 1971, the band recorded their third album, *Master of Reality*, which was released in July; a world tour followed and it became a top ten album on the U.K. and U.S. album charts. The band's next album, *Black Sabbath Vol. 4*, was recorded in Los Angeles in June, 1972, but the group had developed severe problems with substance abuse. The album was released in September and, again, was commercial (their fourth consecutive album to sell over a million units in the U.S.) but critics disliked it. A single, "Tomorrow's Dream" was released but did not chart; there was a worldwide tour in 1973.

The band returned to Los Angeles to record their fifth album but heavy drug use kept them from writing or recording so they returned to England

and recorded *Sabbath Bloody Sabbath*; it was released at the end of 1973 and received critical success as well as platinum sales. That album featured synthesizers and orchestras. A world tour followed in 1974 and they signed with British manager Don Arden.

In February, 1975, the group recorded their sixth album, *Sabotage*, in England; it was released in July. The album received positive reviews but was their first to not go platinum; a single, "Am I Going Insane," did not chart. The group's tour to support the album was cut short when singer Ozzie Osbourne had a motorcycle accident. In December, Warner Brothers released *We Sold Our Soul for Rock'n'Roll*, a greatest hits album, which went double platinum in 1976.

Black Sabbath's next album, *Technical Ecstasy*, was recorded in Miami in June, 1976; the band added keyboardist Gerry Woodruffe to the band (he was also on Sabotage) but Ozzie Osbourne's drug use had gotten to the point that he entered an asylum when the album was completed. Released in September, 1976, it did not achieve platinum sales although the group toured from November, 1976 until April, 1977.

Grammy Awards: 1972

The 1972 Grammy Awards was held on March 14, 1972 in the Felt Forum in New York. The show was hosted by Chuck Berry and was the last live telecast on ABC.

Three Nashville songs were nominated for "Song of the Year": "Help Me Make It Through the Night" and "Me and Bobby McGee," both written by Kris Kristofferson and "Rose Garden," written by Joe South. (The winner was "You've Got a Friend" by Carole King.) Here's the list:

Album of the Year: Tapestry (produced by Lou Adler and Carole King)

Record of the Year: "It's Too late" (produced by Lou Adler and Carole King

Song of the Year: "You've Got a Friend (written by Carole King for James Taylor)

Best New Artist: Carly Simon

Best Original Score for Movie: Isaac Hayes or Shaft

Pop Vocal, Female: Carole King for Tapestry

Pop Vocal Male: James Taylor for "You've Got a Friend

Pop Vocal by Duo or Group: The Carpenters for Carpenters

Pop Instrumental Performance: Quincy Jones for "Smackwater Jack"

Country Vocal, Female: Sammi Smith for "Help Me Make It Through the Night"

Country Vocal, Male: Jerry Reed for "When You're Hot, You're Hot"

Country Vocal by Duo or Group: Loretta Lynn & Conway Twitty for "After the Fire is Gone

Country Instrumental: Chet Atkins for "Snowbird"

Best Country Song: "Help Me Make It Through the Night," written by Kris Kristofferson for Sammi Smith

R&B Vocal, Female: Aretha Franklin for "Bridge Over Troubled Water"

R&B Vocal, Male: Lou Rawls for "A Natural Man"

R&B Vocal by Group: "Proud Mary" by Ike & Tina Turner

Best R&B Song: "Ain't No Sunshine" by Bill Withers.

The Grammy for "Best Sacred "Performance" was awarded to Charley Pride for his album *Did You Think to Pray* on RCA; the Grammy for "Best Gospel Performance" was awarded to Pride for his song "Let Me Live" and nominated for "Best Soul Gospel" was Dottie Rambo, whose song, "Pass Me Now," was recorded in Nashville.

Philadelphia International Records

The "Sounds of Philadelphia" reached the *Billboard* Hot 100 in 1972 when Philadelphia International Records had three hits on the chart: "Back Stabbers" by the O'Jays entered the Hot 100 Chart on July 22 and reached number three; "If You Don't Know Me by Now" by Harold Melvin and the Blue Notes entered the Hot 100 on September 30 and rose to number three; and "Me and Mrs. Jones" by Billy Paul entered the Hot 100 on November 4 and rose to number one in 1973, remaining in that position for three weeks. "Love Train" by the O'Jays entered the Hot 100 on January 20, 1973 and reached number one.

Founders of the "Philly soul" or "The Philadelphia Sound" (also known as TSOP) were Kenneth Gamble (b. October 14, 1943 in Philadelphia) and Leon Huff (b. April 8, 1942 in Camden, N.J.)

Kenneth Gamble was connected to music in Philadelphia his entire life. He helped DJs on WDAS, ran a record store and sang with the Romeos. In 1964, at the age of 17, he connected with manager Jerry Ross, who had Gamble signed to Columbia in 1963; he released "You Don't Know What You Got Until You Lose It." Gamble connected with keyboard player Leon Huff in the studio during a session for Candy & The Kisses. Gamble and Ross co-wrote the song "I'm Gonna Make You Love Me," which was recorded by Jay & The Techniques, Diana Ross and the Supremes and the Temptations. Gamble and Ross produced the 1967 hit "Expressway to Your Heart" by the Soul Survivors and worked with Atlantic Records artists Wilson Pickett,

Archie Bell & the Drells, Aretha Franklin, Dusty Springfield, the Sweet Inspirations and Mercury artists Jerry Butler and Dee Dee Warwick.

In 1971, Gamble and Huff formed Philadelphia International Records, patterned after Berry Gordy's Motown song factory. They approached Atlantic Records for backing but that label turned them down. Clive Davis with CBS Records agreed to back the new label and provide distribution.

Philadelphia International was established with in-house songwriters, producers and arrangers. Thom Bell, Bobby Martin and Norman Harris were the in-house arrangers who created a style of lush strings, heavy basslines and piercing horns. The sound was influenced by earlier R&B and funk and was described as "putting a bow tie on fun."

Other key songwriters, producers and arrangers at Philadelphia International were Linda Creed, Dexter Wansel, McFadden & Whitehead. They worked with an in-house band known as MFSB (Mother, Father, Sister, Brother). The band recorded several instrumental albums and a hit single, "TSOP (The Sound of Philadelphia)" which became the theme song for the TV show "Soul Train."

Philadelphia International addressed social and political issues in the black community on many releases, emphasizing Black Power and Black Pride in songs such as Billy Paul's "Am I Black Enough For You?' in 1977 and "Let's Clear Up the Ghetto" in 1977

Technology

The first hand-held calculator, the HP-35, was introduced on January 4; it cost $395.

Home entertainment centers grew as components became the major type of home system. This was made possible because of the development of transistors, which replaced tubes in electronic equipment. The transistors made electronic equipment smaller, lighter and long-lasting. In 1965 home equipment sales were $159 million; in 1972 they were $800 million. The "hi-fi" systems were made for living rooms; the component systems, where phonographs and tape players were stacked on amps that held an AM/FM radio were made for dorm rooms. College students during the 1960s demanded good sound and components, which large speakers, provided.

The video game system, Mangavox Odysessy, went on sale to the public in August, 1974, and Atari released their first generation of video games on November 29 with their arcade version of Pong, the first commercially successful video game.

Anti-copying Law

There was no federal law against copying recordings until February 15, 1972 when copyright protection was given. Prior to that time, some states had copyright protection. Copying recordings became a major problem with the introduction of tape; vinyl records needed a manufacturing facility to reproduce those recordings but personal cassette units were on many components.

"The Happiest Girl in the Whole U.S.A."

Donna Fargo's "Happiest Girl in the Whole U.S.A. premiered on the *Billboard* country chart on March 25, 1972, and rose to number one where it stayed for three weeks; it reached number 11 on the Hot 100 chart. Fargo (real name Yvonne Vaughn) was a teacher in California when she wrote the song and finished the school year as a teacher while the record was hitting. It peaked at number one in June, so Fargo quit her job and became a full-time performer. She had started the song as "The Happiest Girl in the World" but it didn't meter out so she changed it to "U.S.A." The song was produced by Jim Foglesong for Dot Records and won a Grammy for "Country Female Vocal" and was CMA's "Single of the Year." Fargo followed his was "Funny Face," "Superman," "You Were Always There" Little Girl Gone" and "You Can't Be a Beacon (If Your Light Don't Shine)—all number one's and all crossed over to the pop chart.

Opryland U.S.A. opens

On May 27, 1972, the Opryland USA theme park opened in Nashville. Created by the National Life and Accident Insurance Company, which owned The Grand Ole Opry and WSM, the organization included a convention hotel, the theme park, the Grand Ole Opry, WSM Radio, Country Music Radio Network, the Ryman Auditorium, the Opry House Theater, Springhouse Gold Club, Opryland Music Group (Acuff-Rose Pub), the General Jackson Showboat and Nashville's Wildhorse Saloon.

The theme park presented a number of live shows, who's talented members often became part of the Nashville music community.

The First Country Music Fan Fair

The First Annual International Country Music Fan Fair—sponsored by the Country Music Association and WSM, Inc.—was held April 12-15, 1972, in two locations: the Municipal Auditorium and at Opryland in Nashville. The idea for a "Fan Fair" came the previous year because so many fans came to Nashville for the annual Opry Birthday Celebration (DJ Convention), which was an industry event, and the annual meeting of the Country Music Association. That industry event was drawing 6,000 registered attendees. The Planning Committee for Fan Fair was comprised of Hubert Long, Irving Waugh, Danry Davis, Jack Geldhart, Harold Hitt and Frances Preston. Chair Hubert Long stated at the announcement for the event, "We have felt for a long time that the country music fan needs an annual country music event designed for him. Plans have been arranged so that we can have great shows, featuring top artists, tape and autograph sessions and fan club business meetings.

Neil Young: *Harvest*

Barry Mazor, co-owner of Quad Studios, convinced Neil Young to record his fourth album, *Harvest*, in Nashville during the time Young was in town to appear on "The Johnny Cash Show." On Saturday, February 6, 1971, Young, backed by his band and studio musicians Ben Keith (steel guitar), Tim Drummond (bass) and Kenny Buttrey (drums) began recording, putting down several songs, including "Old Man." Young admired the group Area Code 615 but they could not be found for a quick session on a Saturday night. After he taped his appearance on the Cash show on Sunday, February 7 he returned to the studio with James Taylor and Linda Ronstadt who added vocal harmonies to "Heart of Gold."

"Heart of Gold" was recorded during the period February 6-8, 1971; musicians on the song were Young (acoustic guitar and harmonica), Teddy Irwin (guitar), Ben Keith (steel guitar), Tim Drummond (bass), Kenny Buttrey (drums) with James Taylor and Linda Ronstadt on backing vocals. The single entered the *Billboard* chart in February, 1972 and quickly rose to number one on the *Billboard* Hot 100 chart; it was also number one in Canada and a top ten in Norway, the Netherlands and the U.K. This was Neil Young's only number one song.

Although "Needle and the Damage Done" was recorded during a live performance in Los Angeles, and "A Man Needs a Maid" and "There's a World" were recorded in London, the rest of the *Harvest* album was recorded in April at Quad Studios in Nashville.

The album was released on February 1, 1972 and became a world-wide hit, reaching number one on the *Billboard* chart in the U.S. and number one on charts in the U.K. and Australia. It was the top selling album in the U.S. in 1972.

CMA Awards: 1972

The sixth annual Country Music Association Award was held in Fall, 1972 at the Ryman Auditorium and broadcast over CBS with Glen Campbell as host. Entertainer of the Year was Loretta Lynn, Song of the Year was "Easy Loving" by Freddie Hart, Single of the Year was "The Happiest Girl In the Whole USA" by Donna Fargo and Album of the Year was *Let Me Tell You About a Song* by Merle Haggard. Male Vocalist of the Year was Charley Pride, Female Vocalist was Loretta Lynn, Vocal Duo was Conway Twitty and Loretta Lynn, Vocal Group was The Statler Brothers, Instrumentalist was Charlie McCoy and Instrumental Group was Danny Davis and the Nashville Brass; Jimmie Davis was inducted into the Country Music Hall of Fame.

Will the Circle Be Unbroken

The Nitty Gritty Dirt Band had decided to go to Nashville and record with some of the pioneers of country music and honor old songs and old timers. Since they had long hair and wore jeans—part of the youth culture—they were met with skepticism from many in the Nashville country music community. (Bill Monroe refused to participate.) The album featured performances by guests Roy Acuff (who did not record with them until the last day), Mother Maybelle Carter, Doc Watson, Earl Scruggs, Merle Travis, Pete "Oswald" Kirby, Norman Blake, Jimmy Martin and Vassar Clements.

The album *Will the Circle Be Unbroken* was recorded during 1972 and entered the country chart at the very end of the year—December 30. It reached number four on the country chart and number 68 on the *Billboard* 200 chart.

The album's title came from and old Carter Family song. The album was released on three LPs and three cassette tapes.

The album was influential and successful so the Dirt Band recorded Volumes two and three later. The album had a big impact on the rock audience as they brought old time country and string band songs and artists to ears that had never heard those songs or artists.

Vietnam

The last draft lottery was held on February 2, 1972, due to a wind-down of military conscriptions and the Vietnam War.

In Paris, the peace talks to end the Vietnam war suffered a setback in February when North Vietnamese negotiators walked out in protest of American air raids. The Easter Offensive in Vietnam began after the

Demilitarized Zone (DMZ) dividing North and South Vietnam was crossed by North Vietnamese forces. The United States resumed bombing Hanoi and Haiphong after an offensive assault by the North Vietnamese army. In May, President Nixon ordered the mining of Haiphong Harbor; a few days later American fighter plans began major bombing operations against Northern Vietnamese forces.

The USS Kitty Hawk riot occurred on October 12 when African-Americans led an anti-war protest aboard the aircraft carrier, which was en route to the Gulf of Tomkin. The protest, which was viewed as a race riot by some, involved over 200 sailors. Over 50 of whom were injured. The United States Army turned over the Long Binh military base to South Vietnam on November 11.

Singer/activist Joan Baez and human rights attorney Telford Taylor were caught in the Christmas bombing of Hanoi while they delivered mail and Christmas cards to American prisoners of war. President Nixon and the United States were criticized widely for the Christmas bombing.

China

A breakthrough in U.S.-China relations came when President Richard Nixon visited China, February 21-28, opening dialogue and relations with that country that had been halted for about 20 years. During the eight day visit, Nixon met with Chinese leader Mao Zedong. Taiwan had been recognized as "China" until that time; the U.S. and China agreed that Taiwan would become part of China at some time in the future, but did not establish a date.

Politics

On June 17, five men were arrested for breaking into the offices of the Democratic National Committee at the Watergate hotel complex. Six days later, President Nixon and White House chief of staff H.R. Haldeman were taped discussing using the CIA to obstruct the investigation of the Watergate break in by the FBE.

During the spring, Alabama Governor and independent presidential candidate George Wallace was shot by Arthur Bremer in Laurel, Maryland at a political rally; Wallace remained paralyzed for the rest of his life.

The Republican National Convention was held in Miami Beach, Florida beginning August 10 and re-nominated President Richard Nixon and Vice President Spiro Agnew for a second term. On November 7, President Nixon was re-elected for a second term, defeating Democratic nominee George

McGovern. Only 55 percent of eligible voters voted, the lowest turnout since 1948.

On December 26, former President Harry S. Truman died in Kansas City.

1973
Grammy Awards lands in Nashville

The 15th Annual Grammy Awards was held at the Tennessee Theater on Church Street in Nashville on Saturday, March 3, 1973. This was the third live telecast of the Grammys; the first two had been in Los Angeles and New York and, since Nashville was such a powerful chapter, the decision was made by the NARAS organization to hold it in Nashville. That created a great deal of controversy which led ABC, which had broadcast the first two awards, to refuse to participate. NBC did not like the location either so they, too, refused to participate. That left CBS who, after much prodding by the NARAS organization, reluctantly agreed to broadcast the show. After the show received a 53 share of the audience (over half the people watching TV that night were tuned into the 90-minute Grammy telecast) ABC realized it had made a major mistake. CBS fell into a Gold Mine and had the contract to broadcast the popular Grammy show from then on. ABC, trying to recover, decided to create the American Music Awards show, produced by Dick Clark who hosted "American Bandstand" on that network.

Prior to the telecast, an article in the *Nashville Banner* quoted Grammy Pierre Cossette saying "The efficiency of the Nashville people is amazing. Everybody—the stage hands, musicians, technicians, citizens—has been cooperative. The theater is perfect for the show, too."

Cossette admitted that "I battled NARAS (National Academy of Recording Arts and Sciences) about having it here. I had nothing against Nashville. I just thought Los Angeles was the proper, logical place to have it. I didn't believe Nashville had the facilities or manpower to do such a show [but] I am now a believer. We have had absolutely no problems here. Everything has run so smoothly that it has us who are in charge a little worried. Why, we could have had the show last night. That is how ready everything is."

Cossette concluded, "I tell you how sold I am on Nashville. I wouldn't oppose having it originate from here next year or any year." (Red O'Donnell, **Nashville Banner** March 3, 1973)

Actually, there was a major problem on Sunday evening when the show was held; at eight minutes before the show went on the air the electrical power was lost. However, at one minute before time to go on the air, it came back on.

Grammy Awards for 1972

The Grammy Awards Sow was emceed by Andy Williams, who performed a medley during the show. Don McClean, whose "American Pie" had been a big hit the previous year, was nominated for three Grammys but did not win. The Album of the Year award went to *Concert For Bangla Desh*, which was organized by George Harrison and held at Madison Square Garden in New York and was the first rock benefit concert ever held. Grammys for this three disc album were given to all the artists on the album, which meant that Bob Dylan, Eric Clapton, Billy Preston, Leon Russell and producer Phil Spector received their first Grammys. Ringo Starr, in a blue velvet tux with a pink and blue bow tie, accepted the award.

Ringo was the only Beatle to attend the show. Paul McCartney refused to attend because he was involved in a lawsuit to dissolve the Beatles and John Lennon turned down his invitation to perform because it excluded a performance by his wife, Yoko Ono.

Roberta Flack won "Record" and "Song" of the year for "First Time Ever I Saw Your Face"; her duet with Donny Hathaway on "Where Is The Love" won for "Best Pop Vocal by a duo or group." The group America won "Best New Artist," Nilsson won "Best Pop Vocal Male" for "Without You." "Papa Was a Rolling Stone" by the Temptations won for Best R&B song and "Best R&B Vocal by a duo or group" while Billy Paul won "Best R&B Vocal Male" for "Me and Mrs. Jones" and Aretha Franklin won "Best R&B Vocal Female" for "Young, Gifted & Black."

Helen Reddy won the "Best Female Pop Vocal, Female" for "I Am Woman" and during her acceptance said she wanted to thank God "because She makes everything possible," spurring a torrent of protest letters from religious fundamentalists.

There were performances by the Fifth Dimension, the Staple Singers, Don McClean, Mac Davis, Charley Pride and Donna Fargo. The show was running overtime—due to extensive applause by the audience, so the performance by classical guitarist Laurindo Almeida had to be cut.

Country Grammys

Charley Pride won "Best Country Vocal, Male" for his album Charley Pride Sings Heart Songs. Also nominated were Merle Haggard for "It's Not

Love (But It's Not Bad); Waylon Jennings for "Good Hearted Woman; Jerry Lee Lewis for "Chantilly Lace" and Charlie Rich for "I Take It On Home."

"Kiss and Angel Good Morning" won the country Grammy for best song; the award went to songwriter Ben Peters. Other nominees for "Best Country Song" were "Delta Dawn" written by Alex Harvey and Larry Collins; "Funny Face" written by Donna Fargo; "Happiest Girl in the Whole U.S.A." written by Donna Fargo; and "Woman (Sensuous Woman)" written by Gary S. Paxton.

Donna Fargo won "Best Country Vocal, Female" for "Happiest Girl in the Whole U.S.A." Also nominated were Skeeter Davis for "One Tin Soldier; Loretta Lynn for "One's on the Way"; Dolly Parton for "Touch Your Woman; Tanya Tucker for "Delta Dawn"; and Tammy Wynette for "My Man."

The Grammy for "Best Country Vocal but duo or group" went to the Statler Brothers for "Class of '57"; other nominees were the Nitty Gritty Dirt Bands with Mother Maybelle Carter, Earl Scruggs, Doc Watson, Roy Acuff, Merle Travis and Jimmy Martin for the album Will the Circle Be Unbroken; Johnny Cash and June Carter for "If I Had a Hammer"; George Jones and Tammy Wynette for "Take Me"; and Conway Twitty and Loretta Lynn for ""Lead Me On."

The "Best Country Instrumental" Grammy went to Charlie McCoy for his album *The Real McCoy*; other nominees were Chet Atkins for the album Chet Atkins Picks on the Hits; Chet Atkins and Jerry Reed for the album Me and Chet; Danny Davis and the Nashville Brass for "Flowers on the Wall"; and Lester Flatt for "Foggy Mountain Breakdown."

Nashville related Grammys and Grammy Nominees

Elvis Presley won his second Grammy for his album *He Touched Me*, recorded in Nashville, in the "Best Inspiration Performance" category; Ray Stevens was nominated in that category for "Love Lifted Me."

Clara Ward was nominated for "Best Soul Gospel" for her album Last Mile of the Way on the Nashville based Nashboro Records.

In the "Best Gospel Performance Other Than Soul," the Blackwood Brothers won for "L-O-V-E." Other nominees were Wendy Bagwell and the Sunliters for By Your Request; the Oak Ridge Boys for Light; The Rambos for Soul in the Family; and the Thrasher Brothers for America Sings. All were on Nashville based labels and most were recorded in Nashville.

Joe Tex was nominated in the "Best R&B Vocal, Male" category for "I Gotcha" on the Nashville-based Dial Records and Gladys Knight and the Pips were nomined for their single "Help Me Make It Through the

Night" written by Kris Kristofferson and published by Nashville based Combine Music.

The Grammy for "Best Jazz Performance" went to vibraphonist Gary Burton, who formerly lived and recorded in Nashville.

Tom T. Hall won in the "Best Album Notes" category.

Post telecast Grammys

After the Grammy telecast, there was a show and dinner at the Municipal Auditorium hosted by Roger Miller and Brenda Lee. The late night/early morning breakfast of country ham, scrambled eggs and champagne was served. The 35 Grammys not presented during the telecast were presented during this event.

The Eagles

Linda Ronstadt recorded her second album, *Silk Purse*, in Nashville at Cinderella Studios. The album was produced by Elliot Mazer and contained a Hank Williams song, "Lovesick Blues," a Mel Tillis song, "Mental Revenge," a Mickey Newbury song, "Are My Thoughts With You?," the Goffin-King song, "Will You Love Me Tomorrow" (that was a hit by the Shirelles), "He Darked the Sun" by Gene Clark and Bernie Leadon, the old traditional gospel songs, "Life Is Like a Mountain Railway," and "Long, Long Time," written by Gary White. The album was scheduled to be released in March, 1970 and Ronstadt needed a band to back her.

Her manager, John Boylan, recruited Don Henley, a Texas native who moved to Los Angeles with his band, Shiloh, and Glenn Frey, a Michigan native who was in the group Longbranch Pennywhistle. The two had met at the Troubadour and both were on the independent label, Amos, owned by Jimmy Bowen. Bassist Randy Meisner, who was with Ricky Nelson's Stone Canyon Band, then joined.

Henley and Frey were both ambitious and wanted to be stars. During the tour, they told Ronstadt they wanted to form a band and Ronstadt suggested they include Bernie Leadon with the Flying Burrito Brothers. He was added after discussing it with the other band members. The four backed Ronstadt only once, in a concert at Disneyland in July.

Jackson Browne introduced Glenn Frey to David Geffen, who had started a new label, Asylum, and he signed the group in September, 1971, after buying out Henley's and Frey's contract from Amos. Henley and Frey knew what they wanted; Frey stated that "Everybody had to look good, sing good, play good and write good. We wanted it all. Peer respect. AM and FM success. No. 1 singles and albums, great music, and a lot of money."

The group needed to jell as a band so Geffen sent them to Aspen, Colorado, where they were booked at The Gallery and performed as "Teen King and the Emergencies" beginning in October, 1971. They played four shows a night, every night, until they were a tight band. There are conflicting stories of how they picked the name "Eagles," suffice it to say that before they recorded the first album they were Eagles.

Geffen sent them to England to record their debut album with producer Glyn Johns. Johns was a legendary engineer and producer who had engineered and/or produced Led Zeppelin, the Rolling Stones, The Who, The Beatles (on their "Get Back" sessions) and other members of Rock Royalty.

The Eagles album was recorded in February, 1972, and released on June 1 and contained three hit singles. "Take It Easy," written by Jackson Browne and Frey, entered the *Billboard* Hot 100 on June 3 and rose to number 12; "Witchy Woman," written by Don Henley and Bernie Leadon entered the *Billboard* chart on September 9 and reached number nine; and "Peaceful Easy Feeling," written by Jack Tempchin, entered the *Billboard* chart on December 30 and reached number 22 in 1973.

The album entered the *Billboard* album chart on August 24, and reached number 22, remaining on the chart for 49 weeks.

The Eagles second album was a concept album of the Old West and the Doolin-Dalton Gang. It was again produced by Glyn Johns in England. The album contained two chart singles, "Tequila Sunrise," which entered the *Billboard* Hot 100 on June 23, 1973 and rose to number 65 and "Outlaw Man," which entered the chart on September 15 and reached number 59. The album also contained "Desperado," which was never released as a single but became one of the most well-known and well-loved songs in the Eagle's repertoire.

The album, *Desperado*, entered the *Billboard* chart on May 5 and reached number 41. Although it was less successful as a commercial release, the *Desperado* album was transitional because on this album Henley and Frey began writing together; songs they wrote were "Tequila Sunrise," "Desperado," "Out of Control" (with Tom Nixon), "Certain Kind of Fool" (with Randy Meisner), "Saturday Night" (with Meisner and Leadon) and "Doolin-Dalton (with J.D. Souther and Jackson Browne). Bernie Leadon wrote two alone, "Twenty One" and "Bitter Creek" and David Blue wrote "Outlaw Man."

Pink Floyd and Dark Side of the Moon

From May, 1972 to January, 1973, Pink Floyd recorded *The Dark Side of the Moon* at Abbey Road Studios, produced by Chris Thomas with EMI staff engineer Alan Parsons helping. The songs were written during the time the band toured the U.K., Japan, North America and Europe. The album cover was created by Hipgnosis and featured a refracting prism designed by George Hardie with a beam of white light going through the prism (which represented society) and emerging as colored light, which symbolized unity defracted, which leads to an absence of unity. It was released in 1973 and remained on the rock album chart in *Billboard* for 15 and a half years.

The lyrics on *The Dark Side of the Moon* were written solely by Roger Waters.

The roots of Pink Floyd go back to 1963 when Roger Waters and Nick Mason met in school and played in a group, Sextet, with Keith Noble, Clive Metcalfe, Sheilagh Noble and Richard Wright; the group went through several names, including Meggadeaths, the Abdabs, Leonard's Lodgers and The Spectrum before settling on Tea Set. Metcalfe and Keith Nobel left in 1964 and Syd Barrett moved in with Waters and guitarist Bob Klose; Waters and Barrett had been childhood friends. Singer Chris Dennis joined in December, 1964, and the group, without Wright, went into a studio and recorded a session. Dennis left the group and was replaced by Barrett as front man and the group became the resident band at a London club, playing three sets of 90 minutes each night.

In 1965, Bob Klose quite the group and Barrett became lead guitarist; Barrett named the band "Pink Floyd" after two blues musicians whose albums he owned, Pink Anderson and Floyd Council. The group played rhythm and blues and were spotted by Peter Jenner, a lecturer at the London School of Economics after a performance at the Marquee Club in March, 1966. Jenner and Andrew King, a friend and business partner, became their managers; King's inheritance allowed them to create Blackhill Enterprises and purchase about £1,000 worth of instruments and equipment.

The group became popular in the London clubs that featured "underground music." The group originally extended songs during their 90 minute sets as Tea Set and continued to expand songs with long instrumental breaks accompanied by light shows from colored slides. The social connections of Jenner and King led to more appearances and publicity. In 1966 the band became equal partners with Blackhill Enterprises; by late 1966 the group performed more Syd Barrett originals than R&B covers.

Barrett was an energetic, charismatic performer although the band's music, described as "psychedelic" in one newspaper, turned off many listeners until the group obtained a regular gig at London's UFO Club and began building a fan base.

Pink Floyd recorded a session, paid for by UFO club manager Joe Boyd and their booking agent, Bryan Morrison, and were signed to EMI three days later; their first single, released in March, 1967, was "Arnold Layne" with "Candy and a Currant Bun" on the "B" side. The single reached number 20 on the U.K. chart. Their second single, "See Emily Play" was released in June, 1967, on the EMI-Columbia label; it reached number six on the U.K. chart. The group appeared on BBC's "Look of the Week" and "Top of the Pops" three times but Syd Barrett was been using LSD regularly and his life had begun to unravel.

The first album by Pink Floyd, *The Piper at the Gates of Dawn*, was released in August , 1967 and reached number six on the U.K.'s album chart; it was released on Tower Records, a subsidiary of Capitol, in the United States. The group drew large crowds at the UFO club but Barrett suffered a mental breakdown; his erratic behavior caused cancellation of several shows, including one at the prestigious National Jazz and Blues Festival. Psychiatrists were called in but Barrett's behavior and mental condition did not improve.

Pink Floyd toured Europe in September, 1967, and made their first American tour in October. Barrett's condition continued to deteriorate and the group was sent back to England, where they opened for Jimi Hendrix on a British tour. In December, David Gilmour, a school mate of Barrett's, joined Pink Floyd, making it a five man group.

Working with Barrett became difficult and then impossible; in January, 1968, the group decided not to collect Barrett for a show in Southampton; in March Barrett agreed to leave the group. Considered the creative genius of the band by Pink Floyd's managers, Jenner and King, they decided to leave Pink Floyd and continue with Barrett; they sold their company and O'Rourke became their manager. Roger Waters assumed the role of creative director in the band and David Gilmour, who had sung Barrett's song, increasingly began to sing the songs written by Roger Waters and Richard Wright.

Pink Floyd recorded their second album, *A Saucerful of Secrets*, at Abbey Road studios in 1968; on the album was the final song Syd Barrett wrote for the group, "Jugband Blues." Norman Smith encouraged the group to self-produce their sessions and taught them how to use the equipment but was not convinced of their artistic vision.

The album was released in June, 1968, with a psychedelic cover created by Hipgnosis (Storm Thorgerson and Aubrey Powell), the first of several Pink Floyd album covers designed by the firm. The album reached number nine on the U.K. album chart but with mixed reviews. The group performed at the first free "Concert in Hyde Park" that day after the album was released and in July returned to the United States for a tour, along with The Who and the Soft Machine. Their single was not successful.

A double album, *Unmagumma*, was released on the Harvest label (a subsidiary of EMI); it was comprised of live performances on the first record and an experimental work by each of the members on the second album. Reviews were positive and the album reached number five on the U.K. album chart. *Atom Heart Mother* was released in October, 1970, but disagreements over production left the band dissatisfied with the release. Ron Geesin was brought in to help and did not involve the band. The album, which featured a choir, reached number one on the U.K. chart although band members disliked it.

Tours in America and Europe during 1970 followed; Roger Waters built a home studio in a converted tool shed and in January, 1971, began working on material for a new album but sessions were usually unproductive. Their album, *Meddle*, was released in October, 1971 and showed the emergence of lead guitarist David Gilmour as the creative center of the group; it remained on the U.K. album chart for 82 weeks, peaking at number three.

Dark Side of the Moon was released in March, 1973 and was an immediate hit in the U.K. and Europe, embraced by critics and fans. Pink Floyd toured to support the album, including an American tour. The album entered *Billboard's* pop album chart on March 17, 1973 and reached number one for a single week but remained on the chart for over fourteen years, selling over 45 million copies worldwide. In the U.K., the album peaked at number two but remained on that chart for 364 weeks or seven years. Their American single, "Money," entered the *Billboard* Hot 100 in May and reached number 13. The album's success brought enormous wealth to the members of Pink Floyd, who were dissatisfied with Capitol, their American label, and signed with Columbia Records for an advance reported to be $1 million.

Elton John

In October, 1973, Elton John released his album, *Goodbye Yellow Brick Road*, which had the hit singles, ""Bennie and the Jets," "Goodbye Yellow

Brick Road," "Candle in the Wind and "Saturday Night's Alright for Fighting." That album made Elton John a rock star. He toured, dressed in lavish costumes, one of the first "glam rock" stars, and formed a label, The Rocket Record Company and signed Neil Sedaka ("Bad Blood") and Kiki Dee (a duet with Elton, "Don't Go Breaking My Heart"). He signed an $8 million contract with MCA Records and the following year released his *Greatest Hits* album, which was number one on the *Billboard* album chart and sold 16 million copies.

From that point on, Elton John was one of the world's biggest rock stars. He continued to have hits with a career built on a firm foundation.

Reginald Kenneth Dwight was born in Middlesex, England, on March 25, 1947. He was raised in a council house and both parents were musically inclined; his father played with a semi-professional big band, the Bob Miller Band, at military dances (Stanley Dwight was a flight lieutenant in the Royal Air Force). His mother often purchased records and the young boy heard popular singers and musicians of the day, including Elvis Presley and Bill Haley.

At the age of three, "Reggie" began playing piano by ear and began formal piano lesson when he was seven. When he was 11, Dwight won a junior scholarship to the Royal Academy of Music; during the next five years, during Saturday classes, he studied classical music.

When young Dwight was 14, his parents divorced and his mother married Fred Farebrother. They moved into an eight-unit apartment building where he wrote his first songs. When Reggie was 15, he became a pianist in a pub, playing popular standards as well as self-written songs. He and some friends formed a band, "Bluesology," in 1962 and they backed American R&B musicians such as the Isley Brothers, Major Lance and Patti LaBelle and the Bluebells when they toured England. In 1966, Bluesology became Long John Baldry's backing band.

Ray Williams, the A&R manager for Liberty Records, placed an advertisement in the British magazine *New Musical Express* in 1967 for songwriters. Reggie answered the ad and was given an envelope of lyrics written by Bernie Taupin, who answered the same ad. Reggie wrote melodies to the lyrics and mailed them to Taupin; that was the beginning of their songwriting collaboration.

Six months after that meeting, Reggie was known as "Elton John." His name was a tribute to two members of Bluesology, saxophonist Elton Dean and vocalist Long John Baldry. In January, 1972, he legally changed his name to Elton Hercules John.

Elton John and Bernie Taupin became staff songwriters for Dick James's DJM Records in 1968. During the next two years, they wrote songs for other artists, mostly easy listening fare. Their method of working was that Taupin would write lyrics in under an hour and then John would spend about half an hour writing melodies; if nothing came in half an hour, the lyrics were discarded. Elton John also played recording sessions and sang backup vocals for other artists.

John and Taupin began writing songs for John to record for DJM; their first single, in 1968, was "I've Been Loving You." A second single, "Lady Samantha" and an album, *Empty Sky*, followed. In April, 1970, he recorded the album *Elton John*, released on DJM Records/Pye Records in the UK and Uni Records in the U.S.

At the suggestion of music publisher Steve Brown, John and Taupin began writing more complex songs for Elton to record. On the Elton John album the single "Border Song" was released and charted in the U.S., then "Your Song" was top ten in the U.K. and the U.S.; it was his first hit single and first hit album.

In August, 1970, Elton John performed his first concert in the U.S. at the Troubadour in L.A. In October, 1970, his concept album, *Tumbleweed Connection*, was released and it reached number five on the *Billboard* album chart. That was followed by a live album, *11-17-71* was released in the U.S.

John and Taupin wrote the soundtrack to a film, *Friends,* and then wrote the album *Madman Across the Water*, which had the hit songs "Levon" and "Tiny Dancer." Elton John's first number one album in the U.S. was *Honky Chateau*, which held that position for three weeks and included the singles "Rocket Man" and "Honky Cat." The album *Don't Shoot Me I'm Only the Piano Player*, released in 1973, included the singles "Crocodile Rock"—his first number one on the *Billboard* Hot 100, and "Daniel," which reached number two.

That was Elton John's solid foundation that built a life-long career.

Geffen sells Asylum

David Geffen agreed to a three year distribution deal with Atlantic Records in 1970 for his label, Asylum, with the proviso that at the end of the three years he would wholly own Asylum, which Atlantic helped finance.

Steve Ross, head of Warner Communications International (WCI), approached Geffen about selling Asylum to Warners. Asylum was a hot, prosperous label with six acts: the Eagles, Jackson Browne, Joni Mitchell, Jo Jo Gunne, The Byrds and Linda Ronstadt. Ross asked "how much?" and

Geffen blurted out "the biggest number I could think of," which was $7 million. A hard lesson learned: when negotiating a price, never name your price first.

Ross extended his hand and said, "Okay," then dictated his terms: there would be $2 million in cash plus $5 million in WCI stock. With that handshake, Asylum was now wholly owned by Atlantic.

There was another proviso for the sale: Geffen had to sign a seven year employment agreement to run Asylum for $150,000 a year. Within a few months, WCI's stock share, valued at $45 a share at the time of the agreement, had dropped to $8 a share and Geffen's $7 million sale had dropped to $3 million, pre-tax.

Geffen was not pleased and made it clear that he wanted out of the deal; his act, The Eagles, also did not like the deal because they felt it was a family operation at Asylum. Also, the Eagles received no revenue from that buyout of a label they had made profitable. During the feud with Geffen, the Eagles moved to Irving Azoff as their manager.

Steve Ross knew that David Geffen was a talented record label executive and wanted to combine Asylum with Electra and have Geffen run both labels, so he sweetened the deal by offering Geffen a salary of $1 million a year to run the combined labels. Additionally, for the next five years, WCI would pay Geffen 20 percent of the WCI stocks value. The 30-year-old Geffen agreed.

Elektra's roster was bloated with 45 acts; Geffen reduced that to 13: those included Carly Simon, David Gates & Bread, Judy Collins, Mickey Newbury, Ian Mathews and Harry Chapin.

Clive Davis fired

In July, 1973, Clive Davis was fired as president of Columbia Records and replaced by Irwin Segelstein. Davis was accused of using company money to pay for his son's bar mitzvah and other financial shenanigans. Davis protested his innocent but he was gone. That evening, he watched his dismissal was on TV news. Goddard Lieberson was named president of the CBS/Records Group; Walter Yetnikoff remained head of the International division.

"Drift Away"

Dobie Gray's recording of "Drift Away," written and produced by Mentor Williams, entered the *Billboard* Hot 100 on February 24 and reached number five; it became a rock'n'roll anthem with its line "give me the beat boys and free my soul, I wanna get lost in your rock'n'roll." It was reported that one rock station played it over and over after they received it. A country version was recorded by Narvel Felts and it reached number eight on the country chart. Dobie Gray had a hit with "The In-Crowd" in 1965 and in 1962 signed with Decca to make an album in Nashville with Mentor Williams. The song was recorded at Quadraphonic Sound studio and the opening guitar riff was played by Reggie Young.

"Behind Closed Doors"

Charlie Rich's record of "Behind Closed Doors," written by Kenny O'Dell, entered the *Billboard* country chart on February 10 and reached number one, remaining there for two weeks; it crossed over to the pop market, reaching number 15. Produced by Billy Sherrill at the CBS studios on Music Row, the song won a Grammy for "Best Male Country Vocal" and was CMA's "Song" and "Single" of the year.

The Ryman to be torn down

In March, 1973 officials with National Life reported that renovations for the Ryman would cost over $3 million and it might be necessary to tear down the 90 year old building and start over. The Tennessee Historical Sites Foundation announced it was not satisfied with the announcement and wanted a study done by an expert. In addition to the structural problems with the Ryman, the National Life executives were concerned about the "abundance of crime" in the area, especially during the weekends, citing a number of pornography places "just down the street." A real estate executive stated that the block which had the Ryman was in need of re-development and "If the Ryman is left standing in its present position, although it is less than ten percent of the block in which it stands, it would be damaging to any effort to redevelop that area." National Life planned to tear down the Ryman when the new Opry House was opened at Opryland but concerned citizens were rallying against the destruction of the Ryman.

"Country Sunshine"

Dottie West's record of "Country Sunshine," written by West, Billy Davis and Dianne Whiles, entered the *Billboard* country chart on September 15 and reached number two on that chart and number 49 on the Hot 100. The song was written for the McCann-Erickson Advertising Agency as a TV commercial for Coca Cola; the agency had developed "I'd Like To Teach the World To Sing (In Perfect Harmony)," "It's the Real Thing" and "Things Go

Better With Coke." McCann-Erickson had recruited West after hearing her 1968 single, "Country Girl." The ad was so popular that additional lyrics were added and the song was released as a single. After the song was a hit, Dianne Whiles' name was added because she had be-friended West and played her a song she had written, "Country Sunshine." The song revived West's career—she had not had a hit in five years—and she won a Clio Award for it.

"The Outlaws"

The term "outlaws" to described Waylon Jennings, Willie Nelson, Tompall Glaser and other artists who were breaking Nashville tradition by having creative control of their recordings as well as growing their hair long and jettisoning suits, sports coats and wearing jeans and cowboy hats was popularized by publicist Hazel Smith. Smith said she looked up "outlaws" in the dictionary and it seemed to fit; there was also a hit song and album, "Ladies Love Outlaws" written by Lee Clayton and recorded by Waylon Jennings that lent itself to the term. In 1973, Waylon released albums *Lonesome On'ry and Mean* and *Honky Tonk Heroes*; the latter album consisted of all but one song written by Billy Joe Shaver.

Second Annual Fan Fair

Attendance for the second "Fan Fair" tripled over the previous year with over 10,000 registrants paying $20 for registration. Over 160 artists performed with over 30 labels represented. The five-day event saw over 120 artists perform. There were 206 booths at Municipal Auditorium and there was an increase in record sales at the event. Artists sold pictures as well as T-shirts. Visitors from Australia, Japan and Canada attended and Nashville found itself short of hotel rooms so some attendees stayed about 60 miles away. There were at least 12 radio stations who did remote broadcasts and E.W. "Bud" Wendell, manager of the Opry and chairman of Fan Fair imported barbecue from Odessa, Texas to feed the crowds.

CMA Awards 1973

The seventh annual CMA Awards was the last held at the Ryman Auditorium; it was hosted by Johnny Cash for CBS on October 15, 1973. Entertainer of the Year was Roy Clark, "Behind Closed Doors" written by Kenny O'Dell was "Song of the Year, "Behind Closed Doors" recorded by Charlie Rich was "Single of the Year" and Behind Closed Doors by Charlie Rich was Album of the Year. Male Vocalist was Charlie Rich, Female Vocalist was Loretta Lynn, Vocal Duo was Conway Twitty and Loretta Lynn, Vocal Group was The Statler Brothers, Instrumental was Charlie McCoy and Instrumental Group was Danny Davis and the Nashville Brass; Chet Atkins and Patsy Cline were inducted into the Country Music Hall of Fame.

Musical Notes: 1973

On January 14, "Aloha From Hawaii Via Satellite" starring Elvis Presley was broadcast to over 40 countries around the world. More people watched the telecast than watched the Apollo moon landings.

A rock-oriented TV show, "The Midnight Special," premiered on February 2 on NBC. The Friday night 90 minute show did not have a host the first two years, then Helen Reddy hosted 1975-1976. Performers included Johnny Rivers, Mac Davis, Paul Anka, Lou Rawls, Ray Charles, Jerry lee Lewis, Chubby Checker, Al Green, Curtis Mayfield, David Bowie and Charlie Rich. The show ran until May, 1981. A syndicated TV show, "Don Kirshner's Rock Concert," premiered on September 27 with a concert by the Rolling Stones.

A syndicated radio show, "The King Biscuit Flower Hour" (named after the blues show "The King Biscuit Hour") premiered on February 27. The show taped a live performance of an artist, mixed it down and then sent it to radio stations; at one time there were over 300 stations broadcasting the show, which ran until 1981.

The first release on Virgin Records, founded by Richard Branson, was "Tubular Bells" by Mike Oldfield on May 25.

Singer/songwriter Jim Croce, whose hits included "You Don't Mess Around With Jim," "Operator (That's Not The Way I Feel)," "Bad, Bad Leroy Brown" and "Time in a Bottle," died in an airplane crash in Louisiana, along with his guitarist Maury Muehleisen and four others on September 20.

Neil Bogart began Casablanca Records and on November 1 signed his first act, Kiss.

In September, Gram Parson died. His body was scheduled to be sent back east but friends managed to capture the coffin and took it to Joshua Tree National Monument and burned it. On November 5, two of Parson's friends who had kidnapped the body and burned it On

The CBGB Club (the initials originally stood for "Country, Bluegrass and Blues"), which became an important performance venue for punk and new wave acts, opened in New York City on December 3. A syndicated TV show, "Don Kirshner's Rock Concert," premiered on September 27 with a concert by the Rolling Stones.

News in the World: 1973

At President Richard Nixon's inauguration on January 20, Mike Curb, head of MGM Records, hosted the "Youth Inaugural Concert in Washington, D.C. Artists featured on the concert were Solomon Burke, Tommy Roe, Jimmy Osmond, Ray Stevens, the Sylvers, the Don Costa Orchestra and the Mike Curb Congregation.

Two days after the Inauguration, later the Supreme Court ruled in Roe v. Wade that state bans on abortion were illegal. That same day, former President Lyndon Johnson died at his ranch in Texas.

The Vietnam War continued, although it was winding down. President Nixon suspended offensive action in North Vietnam after citing progress in peace negotiations. On January 27, the Paris Peace Accord were signed, signaling and end to American involvement in Vietnam, but there were still American troops, "advisors" and civilians there.

The bombing of Cambodia ended on August 15, concluding 12years of combat activity in Southeast Asia. In September, Henry Kissinger, former National Security Advisor, became Secretary of State.

The first prisoners of war were released in Vietnam on February 11. They began to leave Vietnam on March 17.

A protest by Native Americans led to the occupation at Wounded Knee by American Indian activists. The stand-off between the activists, who occupied the Pine Ridge Reservation in Wounded Knee, South Dakota, and federal authorities lasted 71 days before the militants surrendered on May 8.

The Watergate scandal, which began in June, 1972 when the headquarters for the Democratic Party were burglarized, provided fresh information to the court when one of the burglars, James W. McCord, sent a letter to Judge John Sirica admitting that he and other defendants in the case had been pressured to remain silent and named former Attorney General John Mitchell as the "overall boss" in the operation. On April 30, President Nixon that White House Counsel John Dean had been fired and that Attorney General Richard Kleindiest and his two top aids, H.R. Haldeman and John Ehrlichman had resigned.

On June 25, John Dean began his testimony before the Senate Watergate Committee and on July 16, former White House aid Alexander Butterfield told the Committee that President had secretly recorded conversations in the White House that were potentially incriminating.

The "Saturday Night Massacre" occurred on October 20 when President Nixon ordered Attorney General Elliot Richardson to fire Archibald Cox, the Watergate Special Prosecutor. Richardson refused and resigned, along with Deputy Attorney General William Ruckelshaus. Their third in line at the Justice Department, Robert Bork, carried out the order to fire Cox, which led to calls for the impeachment of Nixon for obstructing justice.

In an address before 400 Associated Press managing editors in Orlando, Florida on November 17, President Nixon told them "I am not a crook." Four days later, Nixon's attorney, J. Fred Buzhardt, revealed the existence of an 18 and a half minute gap in a tape recorded conversation related to Watergate.

Vice President Spiro Agnew was found guilty of income tax evasion during his time as Governor of Maryland and resigned the Vice Presidency on October 10. House Minority Leader Gerald Ford was named to replace him.

The Yom Kippur War began on October 6 when Egyptian and Syrian forces attacked Israeli forces in the Sinai Peninsula and Golan Heights on a Jewish holy day. On October 17, OPEC began an oil embargo against countries supporting Israel, which mean oil shortages in the United States. The war ended on October 25. In December, OPEC doubled the price of crude oil.

1974
Bitter Youth

Each year during the 1970s, one million American children lost their families because of divorce. There were 480,000 divorces in the entire United States in 1965; in 1969 that figure had risen to 640,000. The figure climbed to 773,000 in 1971 and over a million in 1975.

Marriage did not have the same value as previous generations; 84 percent of Americans in their 40s were married in 1972 while only 67 percent of that same age group were married in 1982. Individuals changed their attitudes about marriage and the roles of husband and wife during a fifty year period; in the 1920s, 52 percent of the teenage girls thought that "being a good cook and housekeeper" was the most desirable quality in a mother. By the mid-1970s, 76 percent disagreed with that statement. By 1973, barely half of college-educated youth regarded being a "good provider" as an important quality in a man.

The stigma of having children outside wedlock was mostly gone by the end of the decade; by 1979, it was "morally acceptable," according to three-quarters of all Americans, to be single and have children. The most admirable trait for an individual to have in the 1970s was to put one's own needs first.

Women during the 1970s wanted either small families or no family at all. Both men and women felt that having children would inhibit their personal freedom and compromise their own individuality; both sexes were adamant that their own personal needs came first.

In a survey conducted during the late 1970s, two thirds of American adults agreed that "parents should be free to live their own lives even if it means spending less time with their children." The insistence that the personal needs of the parent were more important than the needs of a child was reinforced by psychologists. Wayne Dyer stated, "If you make your children more important than yourself, you are not helping them, you are merely teaching them to put others ahead of themselves, and to take a back seat while remaining unfulfilled...Only by treating yourself as the most important person and not always sacrificing yourself for your children will you teach them to have their own self-confidence and belief in themselves."

The birth rate through the 1970s showed a declining trend through most of the decade; there were fewer babies born in 1971 than in 1970, fewer in 1972 than in 1971, fewer in 1973 than in 1972. The lowest number of births occurred in 1974, when 3.1 million babies were born, down from 4.3 million who were born in 1957. The birth rate in the United States was the lowest since the Great Depression during the 1930s; it was half the level of birth rates during the 1950s.

The nation of low-birth children were labelled "Generation X." Many of the children who came of age during the 1970s were angry and cynical and aware that they were unwanted and had a low priority in their parent's lives.

In the nation, the early 1970s gave everyone cause of cynicism; the Vietnam War finally wound down in 1975 after splitting the nation along generational--and even intra-generational lines. Watergate led to the resignation of the President of the United States in 1974; the vice-president, Spiro Agnew, had resigned in disgrace the year before. Motorists were angry that the Arab oil boycott drove up prices for gas, if gas could even be found after spending time in a long line at the gas pump.

Those factors help explain the angry sounds of punk music during the late 1970s.

The Rise of Tape in the Seventies

In 1974 tape--both 8 track and cassette combined--accounted for over one fourth of all recorded sales, which totaled $2.2 billion that year. The industry was changing: international giant Polydor, a division of the German firm Phonogram International, entered the United States market in 1970. Apple Records, the Beatles ill-fated label, closed its doors in 1975. In between, a major recession hit the country.

The quality of tape was improving. At first, the music industry didn't take tape seriously: labels released tape after vinyl albums, at a higher price with less quality. The notion was that this was the record business and tape was a bit of a nuisance. That cavalier attitude led to a massive amount of bootlegging, first with 8-track tapes being manufactured and sold on the black market, and then consumers taping albums onto blank cassette tapes.

At first, the 8-track tape was the dominant type of tape configuration preferred by consumers. Eight tracks were on the market first and were the beneficiary of a major advertising campaign from car companies, who advertised 8-track tape machines for their new cars. Too, the 8-track could be played at home or in the car, had a longer playing time with fully automatic operation than the cassette and the sound quality was better. The major problem was the click in the middle of a song when it switched tracks, which created a listening gap. That problem could have been solved if labels had paid more attention to sequencing and formatting those tapes; instead, labels merely dubbed the vinyl album onto 8-track and let the gaps fall where they may.

Eight tracks eventually accounted for about 90 percent of all auto installations at the factory. Cassettes meanwhile had seemingly insurmountable problems: the slow speed of cassettes was erratic and did not lend itself to high quality, and it did not seem capable of handling the high vibrations and variations of voltage in the automobile's electrical system. The Lear system--designed originally for 8-tracks--eventually conquered those problems. Still, 8-track had a head start and it looked like cassette might never catch up.

All that changed when physicist Ray Dolby invented a miniaturized B-type noise reduction unit, which allowed cassettes to become a serious hi fi component. Marketing savvy also came from cassette manufacturers, who dropped prices of units as they improved the cassette to undercut the 8-track manufacturers, who felt that format had too great a lead in the battle of the tapes to ever be overcome.

The cassette had other major advantages that soon became apparent to consumers. First, the tape could be run quickly forward or backward to find a song again; next, people could easily record on cassettes, which could not be done on 8-tracks.

In 1975 the sales of recorded product saw 29 percent go to tapes, mostly 8-tracks. But that same year there were 150 million blank cassette tapes sold, a harbinger of things to come for the tape industry as cassettes replaced 8-tracks as the configuration of choice because of the capabilities of home taping.

One technological breakthrough during the early 1970s that did not catch on was quadrophonic sound. RCA anticipated phasing out stereo completely, projecting that the industry would be all-quad in five years, but the quadrophonic system was too troublesome and never caught on with consumers.

Led Zeppelin

The album known as *Led Zeppelin IV* did not have a name; there was no album title or the band's name on the front cover; their popularity was so great that fans knew about the album and purchased it without key information on the cover. The album was released in November, 1974. It sold over 23 million copies during the next 35 years and featured "Stairway to Heaven," perhaps their best known song, which it was never released as a single. It was, however, played on album-oriented rock stations. During the two years after the album's release, Led Zeppelin toured all over the world.

The group's fifth album, released in March, 1973, did not have the band's name or album title on the cover but was controversial because of the images of four nude children on the cover. Led Zeppelin broke attendance records during their tours following their fifth album's release, performing in stadiums across America; their appearances at Madison Square Garden on this tour were filmed for a movie, *The Song Remains the Same*, which was released in 1976.

Led Zepplin's tours not only set attendance records and sold millions of albums, they also became legendary because of tales of riotous behavior, the destruction of hotel rooms, and debauchery that have grown (and possibly been enhanced) through the years.

Although the band ceased touring during the mid-1970s, the band and their albums remain a current phase for boys around 12-14, who generally go through a "Led Zeppelin phase" during their teen years—although some never grow out of it.

Led Zeppelin played a blue-based rock, basic chords pounding behind a high pitched male tenor. The lyrics were a combination of hostility, mysticism, and sex and their primary audience was young males. Following

Led Zeppelin were groups like Aerosmith, Ted Nugent, Kiss, and Motley Crue whose main connection to their fans was in high decibel concerts.

Technology

The Universal Product Code, or "bar code," was scanned for the first time on June 26 to sell a page of Wrigley's chewing gum in Troy, Ohio at the Marsh Supermarket.

The World Intellectual Property Organization (WIPO) became an agency of the United Nations on December 17.

The Roland RE-201 and 101 Space Echo tape based audio analog delay effects units were introduced and the Rubik's Curb was created by Emo Rubik, a Hungarian architecture professor.

Paul McCartney Comes to Nashville

In June, 1974, Paul McCartney and his family came to Nashville for six weeks where he rehearsed his new band, Wings. McCartney wrote and recorded two songs at the Sound Shop studio in Nashville, "Sally G." and "Junior's Farm," which became a number one pop hit. McCartney also recorded a song his father wrote, "Walking in The Park With Eloise" with Nashville musicians Chet Atkins, Bobby Thompson, Vassar Clements, Johnny Gimble, George Tidwell, Dennis Goode, Norm Ray and Billy Preutt. It was credited to The Country Hams.

Last Grand Ole Opry Show at the Ryman

On the evening of Friday, March 15, 1974, the last "Grand Ole Opry show at the Ryman was held with "Will the Circle Be Unbroken" the last song sung from the Opry stage; it was followed by Jimmy Snow's Grand Ole Gospel Program. After this show, the Ryman would be vacated and remain empty for the next 20 years.

On Saturday evening, March 16, the first performance of the Grand Ole Opry at the new Opry House in Opryland was held with President Richard Nixon as a "special guest." Nixon bounced a yo-yo with Roy Acuff and played the piano.

"I Will Always Love You"

Dolly Parton wrote "I Will Always Love You" as a "gift" to Porter Wagoner as she left the duo to embark on a solo career. The song entered the *Billboard* country chart on April 6, 1974; later it became a hit as a duet between her and Vince Gill and a pop hit recorded by Whitney Houston for the film *The Bodyguard*.

"The Streak"

Ray Stevens was long known for writing wry, comedic songs and he wrote "The Streak" based on a magazine article in read on an airplane trip that discussed the explosion of "streaking" (running naked) on college campuses. It was the first song he recorded in a new studio he had built in Nashville and was released on March 27; it was the first single from his album *Boogity Boogity*. The song entered the *Billboard* Hot 100 o April 13 and reached number one for three weeks; it reached number three on the country chart and number 12 on the Adult Contemporary chart. The song was a hit in Canada, the U.K., New Zealand, Ireland and Australia.

CMA Awards 1974

The eighth annual CMA Awards was held for the first time in the new Grand Ole Opry House on October 14, 1974; host for the show was Johnny Cash. Entertainer of the Year was Charlie Rich, "Country Bumpkin" written by Don Smith was "Song of the Year," "Country Bumpkin" recorded by Cal Smith was "Single of the Year, A Very Special Love Song by Charlie Rich was Album of the Year, Ronnie Milsap was Male Vocalist, Olivia Newton-John was Female Vocalist, Vocal Duo was Conway Twitty and Loretta Lynn, Vocal Group was The Statler Brothers, Instrumentalist was Don Rich, and Instrumental Group was Danny Davis and the Nashville Brass; inducted into the Country Music Hall of Fame were Owen Bradley and Pee Wee King.

Association of Country Entertainers (ACE)

Upset that Olivia Newton-John, a non-country act, won the CMA's "Female Vocalist" award and the crossover records that were on the country charts but deemed "not country," a group of veteran country entertainers gathered in November and formed the Association of Country Entertainers (ACE) to promote "real" country music and "real" country artists. Gathered in the home of George Jones and Tammy Wynette were Bill Anderson, Jim Ed Brown, Brenda Lee, Barbara Mandrell, Dolly Parton, Cal Smith, Hank Snow, Mel Tillis, Conway Twitty, Porter Wagoner, Dottie West and Faron Young, determined to make contemporary country music "real country."

Musical Notes: 1974:

Bob Dylan had not performed in public for almost eight years—since 1966—so there was high demand for tickets when he kicked off his 40-date concert tour with The Band in Chicago on January 3.

The first American Music Awards, created by Dick Clark for the ABC network because their contract had expired, was broadcast on February 19, two weeks before the Grammys.

The premiere of Ladies and Gentlemen: The Rolling Stones, a concert movie filmed during their 1972 tour, was held at the Ziegfeld Theatre in New York on April 14.

The TV show, "Happy Days" and the film, American Graffiti both used "Rock Around the Clock" by Bill Haley and His Comets, which led to that record re-entering the Billboard Hot 100 chart, 20 years after it was first released. The record peaked at number 39 in 1974.

What many consider to be the first punk rock single, "Hey Joe" by Patti Smith, was recorded June 5. The single did not chart.

Mama Cass Elliot, formerly with the Mamas and Papas, died in London on July 29 after performing two sold-out concerts at the London Palladium.

The Ramones first appearance at New York's CBGB club occurred on August 16; the club and the band both came to the forefront of the Punk music movement during the next several years.

On November 2, the George Harrison and Friends tour in North America began in Vancouver, Canada. It was Harrison's first tour since the final Beatles tour in 1966.

News of the World: 1974:

Patty Hearst, heiress to the Hearst newspaper chain founded by William Randolph Hearst, was kidnapped on February 4 outside her Berkeley, California apartment by the Symbionese Army. On April 15, a photograph of her as "Tania" holding an M1 carbine while robbing a bank in San Francisco appeared. During a two hour shootout between the Los Angeles Police Department and the Symbionese Liberation Army, SLA leader Donald DeFreeze and vie other SLA member were killed.

OPEC ended their embargo of oil to the United States, Europe and Japan on March 8, after it had caused an oil crisis.

Because of the Watergate Scandal, President Nixon announced his resignation from the Presidency would be effective at noon, August 9; after the resignation, Gerald Ford was sworn in as the 38th President of the United States.

On September 8, President Ford pardoned former President Richard Nixon. It was a controversial move but Ford insisted he needed to do it in order to put the Watergate Scandal behind. During the November elections, the Democratic party made big gains in elections for the House of Representatives, the Senate and in state Governor's races.

Muhammad Ali knocked out George Foreman in the eighth round of "The Rumble in the Jungle" on October 30 in Kinshasa, Zaire. With that knockout, Muhammad Ali regained the Heavyweight title that had been stripped from him eight years earlier.

1975
The Eagles: 1973-1975

The Eagles had established themselves as a country-rock band but they wanted to move more towards rock so, after recording two songs with Glyn Johns, they hired Bill Szymczyk to produce the rest of their album. Szymczyk had produced the James Gang, Joe Walsh and the J. Geil Band.

The Eagles spent six weeks in London with producer Glyn Johns but only came home with two songs, "Best of My Love" and "You Never Cry Like a Lover." All was not lost; "Best of My Love" became their first number one single.

At the Record Plant in Los Angeles they finished the album, *On the Border*, which was released on March 22, 1974. It entered the *Billboard* chart on April 20 and reached number 17. Their first single, "Already Gone" entered the *Billboard* Hot 100 on May 4 and reached number 32; "James Dean" entered the chart on September 21 and reached 77 and "Best of My Love" entered the Hot 100 on November 30 and rose to the number one slot in 1975, remaining on the chart for 19 weeks. The song was written by Henley, Frey and J.D. Souther.

During those sessions, the Eagles added a new member to the group, Don Felder. Bernie Leadon thought of Felder, a childhood friend, when Szymczyk wanteded a harder ege on the guitar part for "Good Day in Hell." Felder had jammed with the group backstage in 1972 and was nicknamed "Fingers" by Frey because of his dexterity. Felder added slide guitar to "Good Day in Hell" and they band was so impressed that the next day they invited him to join, which made the Eagles a five man group.

One of these Nights, the Eagles fourth album, was released on June 10, 1975; it would be their first number one album, debuting on the *Billboard* chart on June 28, 1975 and holding the number one position for five weeks and last 58 weeks on the chart. Their first single, "One of These Nights," written by Henley and Frey, entered the Hot 100 on May 31 and reached number one. Their second single, "Lyin' Eyes," also written by Henley and

Frey, came on the chart on September 13 and held the number two position for two weeks; it won the Grammy for "Pop Vocal Group." "Take it To The Limit," written by Henley and Frey with Randy Meisner with the lead vocal by Meisner, entered the Billboard chart on December 20 and reached the number four position.

The Eagles mounted a world-wide tour to promote the album.

That was the last Eagles album with Bernie Leadon as a member. He had written three songs on the album, including the instrumental "Journey of the Sorcerer" and "I Wish You Peace" which he had written with then-girlfriend Patti Davis, daughter of Ronald and Nancy Reagan.

The Eagles released their *Greatest Hits* album in early 1976; the album entered the *Billboard* chart and rose to number one and held that position for five weeks. It remained on the chart for 133 weeks or over two and a half years. It would be the best selling album in the history of the recording industry in the coming years.

Bruce Springsteen

Bruce Springsteen became a superstar during the mid-1970s with music that was lyrically articulate, a sound that had deep roots in rock'n'roll and showmanship led him to do three and four hour concerts when the norm was an hour and fifteen minutes on stage.

Bruce Springsteen grew up in New Jersey in a working class family; when he was 14 he discovered the guitar and at 15 joined a local band, the Castiles. Springsteen continued to perform at bars in New Jersey, playing every night he could in order to make a living, and began writing songs.

Sound man Carl "Tinker" West was impressed with Springsteen and in 1971 brought him to Wes Farrell's office in New York where Mike Appel worked as a songwriter. Farrell was a hit songwriter; he co-wrote "Boys" (covered by the Beatles), "Hang on Sloopy" and a number of others. He produced the Partridge Family, co-wrote their theme song and a number of songs for their TV show.

Springsteen was shy and depended on a girlfriend--there were a series of them--to do the talking for him. Appel began managing Springsteen and obtained an audition with John Hammond, the legendary A&R man at Columbia, who had signed Billie Holiday, Count Basie, and Bob Dylan. Hammond listened to songs that Springsteen played on an acoustic guitar, then arranged for a showcase that night at the Gaslight in the Village. Hammond also asked Springsteen to return the next day to record studio demos.

In 1972, Hammond signed Springsteen to Columbia; Appel signed the singer to concurrent management, production and music publishing agreements. Springsteen was happy to have a recording contract; he had no interest in the business or money so he never bothered to look at the contracts or hire an attorney--he just signed whatever was placed in front of him.

Appel produced Springsteen's first album, *Greetings From Asbury Park, New Jersey*, which was recorded during the summer of 1972 and released in January, 1973. Springsteen also signed with the William Morris Agency, where he was booked by Sam McKeith, who was in charge of the northeast territory for clubs and colleges. McKeith offered a number of dates for the singer in that area, beginning in November, 1972. The debut of Springsteen's group, the E Street Band, occurred at that time.

Springsteen was an energetic and captivating performer. In his book, *The Mansion on the Hill: Dylan, Young, Geffen, Springsteen, and the Head-on Collision of Rock and Commerce*, author Fred Goodman states: "Performing was a way for Springsteen to be the person he had never been as a kid. In real life, he felt like he was a loser, the poor kid from the wrong side of the tracks who always seemed to be walking with his head down, the disappointing son, the teenager left behind by his family, the guarded, socially inept young man who preferred to let his girlfriends do his talking. But in front of a crowd, with a guitar strapped across his shoulder, Bruce Springsteen was dynamic, self-assured, and powerful. The transformation grew out of a deep need to repudiate a painful past and bleak future and seemed, to those who met him, purely emotional."

Greetings From Asbury Park, New Jersey sold a disappointing 20,000 copies; the follow up album, *The Wild, the Innocent, and the E Street Shuffle*, did not sell well either. CBS wasn't terribly excited about Springsteen at that point, but his live shows continued to create a growing reputation.

Bruce Springsteen had written a song, "Born to Run" and wanted to create the "wall of sound" made famous by Phil Spector. Springsteen and Appel worked on that song for three months in the studio.

In 1974, critic Jon Landau saw Bruce Springsteen perform in Cambridge, Massachusetts at "Charley's," a small club. In his review, printed in *Rolling Stone*, Landau made the statement: "I saw rock and roll's future and its name is Bruce Springsteen." Columbia then bought an ad in *Rolling Stone's* July 18 issue that printed that quote in bold letters. That was the impetus for Columbia to begin a marketing campaign for Springsteen--and for Springsteen himself to make some changes.

Columbia did not want to release the single "Born to Run" because there was no album yet; manager Mike Appel sent tapes of the recording to disc jockeys, who played it. Meanwhile, Springsteen continued to play colleges and clubs in the northeast.

Problems came from Springsteen's manager, Mike Appel, who purchased his partner's half of the contract with Springsteen in early 1974 for $1,500. Appel's relationship with Springsteen deteriorated as the artist became bigger than the manager; also, Springsteen brought in Jon Landau to co-produce the *Born to Run* album against Appel's wishes.

In his desire to be a power broker, combined with Springsteen's indifference to the business side of the music industry, Appel signed the artist to a contract that was exploitive and short-sighted. Landau moved to New York and became Springsteen's confidant and sounding board, further eroding Appel's influence. In addition, Appel, according to many of those involved, had an abrasive personality and confrontational style when he needed to be more diplomatic.

The *Born to Run* album was released in September, 1975, with a large marketing and promotion effort. It sold 700,000 copies in the first two months and became the first album certified with RIAA's new "Platinum" award for album sales over a million units.

In October, 1975, Springsteen achieved the rarest of honors: he was featured on the covers of *Time* and *Newsweek* on the same week. That firmly established him as the dominant rock star in America at the end of 1975.

Springsteen's follow-up album, *Darkness at the Edge of Town*, was not released until 1979. After the *Born to Run* album, Springsteen and Mike Appel were involved in litigation that was not resolved until 1977, when Appel gave up management of Springsteen's career (Jon Landau then became his manager).

Prince

Prince's album, *Purple Rain*, and film by the same title was released in 1984. The album sold over 13 million copies in the U.S. and spent 24 weeks in the number one position of the *Billboard* 200 chart. Prince received an Academy Award for "Best Original Song Score" and the film grossed over $68 million. Singles from the album were "When Doves Cry," which was number one for five straight weeks on the *Billboard* Hot 100, and "Let's Go Crazy," which was number one for two weeks. The single, "Purple Rain," reached number two on the Hot 100. Two others singles from the album, "I Would Die 4 U" and "Take Me With U" also charted.

On the Purple Rain album was a song, "Darling Nikki," that had sexually explicit lyrics and a reference to masturbation. Tipper Gore, wife of then-Senator Al Gore, heard the song when her daughter played it at home, which led to Congressional hearings about "offensive lyrics" and the dangers of rock music. That led to the formation of the Parents Music Resource Center which, in turn, led to albums labeled "Parental Advisory: Explicit Lyrics" if they contained offensive lyrics.

It wasn't the first time that Prince had written a song with sexually explicit lyrics, but it was the first time they led to a Congressional hearing. It marked his image as a songwriter and performer who seemed obsessed with sex, which often overshadowed the talents of Prince.

Prince Rogers Nelson was born on June 7, 1958, in Minneapolis, Minnesota, the son of a father who was a pianist and songwriter and a mother who was a jazz singer. His father, John Lewis Nelson, used the stage name Prince Rogers when he performed with his wife in a jazz group, The Prince Rogers Trio. Prince did not originally like his name and was known as "Skipper" during his childhood.

Prince's father encouraged his and his sister, Tyka's interest in music When he was ten, his parents divorced and his mother remarried. Prince shifted between his father's and mother's homes; his father bought him his first guitar but then kicked him out of the house. Prince then moved into the basement of the Anderson family's home and became friends with the Anderson's son, Andre, who later became known as Andre Cymone.

At school, Prince played football, basketball and baseball and was in the Minnesota Dance Theatre. Pepe Willie formed a band, 94 East, with Marcy Ingoldstad and Kristie Lazenberry and hired Andre Cymone and Prince to record tracks for an album. Pepe Willie wrote the songs, Prince played guitar and wrote "Just Another Sucker" with Andre Cymone.

Prince recorded a demo tape with producer Chris Moon in 1976. The recordings were made in Moon's Minneapolis studio. Moon took the tape to several record labels but none were interested. Minneapolis businessman Owen Husney, who owned an advertising agency, was interested and signed Prince to a management contract and produced another set of demos in a Minneapolis studio. Husney's ad agency created a press kit, which created interest from several labels, including Warner Bros. .

Prince signed a three album deal with Warner Bros Records; the label gave him creative control for his albums and allowed Prince to keep publishing rights. Prince and Husney moved to Sausalito, California, and recorded

Prince's first album, *For You*, at the Record Plant Studios. The album was released on April 7, 1978, and featured Prince producing, arranging, writing and playing all 27 instruments except for the song, "Soft and Wet," where Chris Moon co-wrote the lyrics. The album was expensive; it cost twice as much as Prince's initial advance. Two songs landed on the *Billboard* charts, "Soft and Wet" and "Just as Long as We're Together."

Prince formed a band in 1979 comprised of Andre Cymone on bass, Dez Dickerson on guitar, Gayle Chapman and Doctor Fink on keyboards and Bobby Z. on drums.

Prince's second album for Warner Bros, *Prince*, was released in October, 1979, and reached number four on the R&B album chart and number 22 on the *Billboard* 200 album chart. The album sold over a million units and had two singles hit on the R&B chart, "Why You Wanna Treat Me So Bad" and "I Wanna Be Your Lover."

Prince released the album, *Dirty Mind*, which contained the songs "Head" and "Sister" in 1980. That album's songs had sexually explicit lyrics; it achieved Gold status and the single, "Uptown" was a top five on the Hot Soul Singles chart. His next album was *Controversy*, released in 1981, and Prince toured as the opening act with the Rolling Stones. He formed the Time, a side project band that released four albums; Prince wrote the songs and provided most of the instrumentation and background singing. His double album, *1999*, released in 1982, sold over three million copies.

Starting in 1984, Prince called his band "The Revolution" and it supported his tour promoting the *1999* album. The success of that album led Prince to seek a starring role in a major motion picture, which led to the film *Purple Rain* in 1984.

Changes in Distribution

The way recordings got to consumers changed during the 1970s. RCA pioneered the "dual" (or multiple-distribution) system in 1969 by creating an in-house distribution system to go along with their agreements with rack jobbers, who supplied records to drug stores and other retail outlets outside record stores. During the next few years, all the other major labels also created in-house or branch distribution systems which allowed labels greater control over their product.

That was the beginning of the end for the independent distribution system, which had previously dominated the industry. The independent distribution system made it possible for small labels to compete with the majors. The indie system was a series of independently owned companies in most major cities whose job was to take records that companies manufactured and get them into retail outlets--primarily record stores. Meanwhile, the rack jobbers took care of getting those same records into racks in mass merchandisers, discount stores, and department stores but with the major labels creating their own distribution system, staffed by company employees, the indies power began to decline, although during the early 1970s they still accounted for about one third of all records distributed. Gradually, however, the major labels began offering their distribution network to independent labels and the independent network held less and less power. Meanwhile, the major labels grew bigger and stronger, controlling not only their own product, but also the product of a number of former independent labels until their distribution system eventually accounted for over 80 percent of all recorded product sold domestically.

Another way of doing business was changing in the early 1970s: royalties paid to artists by recording companies. During the 1950s and 60 the standard royalty rate was 4-5 percent; by the mid-70s, a 10 percent rate was now standard.

Aerosmith

Steven Tyler formed the Strangeurs, later re-named Chain Reaction, in 1964 in New Hampshire; Tyler was the drummer and backup vocalist. Joe Perry and Tom Hamilton formed the Jam Band and moved to Boston where they met drummer Joey Kramer, a Berklee College of Music student. The two bands played at the same gig in 1970 and Tyler proposed that the two join together; they agreed. Tyler insisted he be the lead vocalist, which led to Joey Kramer becoming drummer for the new group. The group members moved in together in a house in Boston and the band decided to name themselves Aerosmith after Kramer suggested the name.

The group added Ray Tabano, a friend of Tyler's, on rhythm guitar and played their first gig in November, 1970. There was a change in the line-up in 1971; Tabama was replaced by Brad Whitford and Aerosmith's members became Tyler, Perry, Hamilton, Kramer and Whitford.

The band's shows became popular and they signed a management agreement with Steve Leber and David Krebs in 1972; the managers invited Columbia Records president Clive Davis to see the band perform at Max's Kansas City in New York and by mid-1972 the band was signed to Columbia; their first album, *Aerosmith*, was released in January, 1973 and did not do well initially on the album chart and their single, "Dream On" only reached number 59 on the *Billboard* Hot 100. Later, the album sold over two million copies (double platinum).

The band toured constantly and released their second album, *Get Your Wings*, produced by Jack Douglas, in 1974 but it was their third album, *Toys in the Attic* that established them as a major rock band, in league with the Rolling Stones and Led Zeppelin. The first single from *Toys in the Attic* was "Sweet Emotion," which reached number 36 on the pop chart and then "Dream On" was re-released and became a top ten single on *Billboard's* Hot 100. "Walk This Way" was also a top ten single and the album went multi-platinum, which re-ignited sales for their previous two albums.

In 1976 Aerosmith released *Rocks*, their fourth album which contained the singles "Last Child," "Back in the Saddle" and "Home Tonight"; the album went multi-platinum. In 1977 they released *Draw the Line*, their fifth album. Aerosmith became known as an album band that toured heavily; their singles received limited play on radio and did not reach the top ten but their albums sold in multi-platinum numbers.

Kiss

Gene Simmons and Paul Stanley were in Wicked Lester, a New York city band that recorded one album for Epic Records that was not released. In 1972, Simmons and Stanley hired drummer Peter Criss for Wicked Lester and began wearing make-up and tried various stage outfits. Epic Records did not want to continue with Wicked Lester so in January, 1973, the group hired lead guitarist Ace Frehley and changed their name to Kiss after Paul Stanley noted that he had previously been in a band called "Lips." Their iconic logo, with the two "S's" looking like lightning bolts was created by Frehley. The new logo created problems in Germany, where it looked too much like the outlawed Nazi symbol so it was not used in that country, Israel and middle European countries.

Kiss first performed in January, 1973 in Queens, New York with no make-up; their first performance with their iconic look was in Amityville, New York during shows on March 9 and 10. The group recorded a demo with producer Eddie Kramer and hired a manager, Bill Aucoin, who placed them with Casablanca Records, headed by Neil Bogart. In October, they entered a New York studio and recorded their first album, *Kiss*.

In February, 1974 they began a tour in Canada and their album was released. In addition to their tours, they appeared on "Dick Clark's In Concert" on ABC and "The Mike Douglas Show," where Simmons claimed he was "evil incarnate."

Their debut album did not sell well; in August they recorded their second album, *Hotter Than Hell*, in Los Angeles; it was released in October but did not do well. Kiss then entered the studio with Neil Bogart as producer and recorded *Dressed to Kill*, which was released in March, 1975 and contained "Rock and Roll All Nite,"which became the group's signature song.

Although their first albums did not sell well, the group's performances attracted attention with Simmons spitting "blood" (actually a concoction with red food coloring) and "breathing fire" (done by spitting flammable liquid at a torch) and Frehley's guitar bursting into flames (from smoke bombs inserted in the guitar). Drummer Peter Criss's drum riser produced sparks and Stanley smashed his guitar while pyrotechnics created a spectacle.

Kiss's label, Casablanca, was near bankruptcy in late 1975 but was rescued with Kiss's live album, a two disc offering compiled from concerts during May through July. *Alive!* went Gold and their single, "Rock and Roll All Nite" reached number 12 on *Billboard's* Hot 100 chart. The band then recorded *Destroyer* with producer Bob Ezrin; their single "Beth," which had been released as the "B" side of their single "Detroit Rock City," reached number seven on the pop chart. That single led to album reaching platinum status.

The band received wide exposure when they appeared on "The Paul Lynde Halloween Special" which featured a comedic interview. Their next albums, *Rock and Roll Over*, released in November, 1976, and *Love Gun*, released in June, 1977 as well as a second live album, *Alive II*, released in October, 1977, all went platinum soon after their release. During 1977, Kiss was named the most popular band in America by a Gallup poll.

Hard rock and heavy metal were woven together during this early stage, although later they became more defined as new bands staked out either one territory or the other with their image and sound. Heavy metal was loud, arena rock music which attracted a core group of faithful fans who bought albums in large numbers; record labels learned that a successful heavy metal band's albums had staying power in the commercial market-- their sales could be on-going for years.

The best example of this is Pink Floyd's album, *Dark Side of the Moon*, which was released in 1973 and remained on the rock album chart in *Billboard* for 15 and a half years. In 1979, the group released *The Wall*, which also showed strong staying power.

Geffen leaves Elektra-Asylum

David Geffen decided to leave as head of Elektra-Asylum in 1975. When he stepped down, the label had highest net profit of any record company in the world. For Geffen, the record business was his whole life. He arrived at the office in the morning before anyone else and stayed long after everyone had left.

Irving Azoff, known in the industry as "the Poison Dwarf," managed Joe Walsh and Dan Fogelberg. He had joined the management firm of Geffen-Roberts and when Elliot Roberts became ill during a Neil Young tour of the United States and Europe, it opened the door for him to take over management of the Eagles.

Geffen wanted to get into the movies and, after he left Elektra-Asylum became Vice President of Warner Brothers Pictures. Geffen's departure for the film industry led to the Geffen-Roberts empire being carved up, with Roberts keeping Neil Young and Joni Mitchell, John Hartman took Poco and America and Azoff had the Eagles. Joe Smith replaced Geffen as head of Elektra-Asylum.

Boom Boxes

During the 1960s, the transistor radio made music portable. During the 1970s the boom box or "ghetto blaster" made music portable. The speakers on the boom box were bigger than those on a transistor radio, so it was louder. It could play the radio or tapes and was carried either like a suitcase or perched on a shoulder.

A quality sound came from a record player, and those who were serious about sound and music had a record player at home, usually with large speakers, an AM/FM amplifier and dual tape deck in addition to the phonograph. But the record player was stationary and young people were on the move. Headphones plugged into a boom box made listening even more personal and solitary.

Curb and Warner Brothers

The labels under Warner Communications Inc. became the coolest labels in America; they had the singer-songwriters and other album artists that listeners loved. The problem was that the Warner labels needed singles for radio airplay to keep the labels balanced. Mo Ostin had known Mike Curb for a long time; in the early 1960s he had released a single on Curb's group. Since that time, Curb had headed MGM, where the Osmonds group as well as the solo acts of Donny Osmond and Marie Osmond (who also recorded duets) put out a string of hit singles

Osten contacted Curb about a production agreement marketed as Warner/Curb and Curb responded with hit singles by the Bellamy Brothers, Shaun Cassidy, Exile and Debby Boone. Curb was known to have an ear for hits; he was unabashedly commercial. With Curb, Warners now had rosters that produced both hit albums and hit singles.

In 1978, Mike Curb ran for Lieutenant Governor of California and, to the surprise of many in the music industry, won. That meant that Curb would not be active in the music industry during the four years he held that office.

Goddard Lieberson and *A Chorus Line*

Goddard Lieberson was the premier producer of Broadway musicals during the late 1940s and 1950s; Columbia's original cast recordings often accounted for 20 percent of sales during that period. But those days were gone, replaced by rock musicals like those written by Andrew Lloyd Webber and Tim Rice.

Goddard Lieberson's last Broadway musical was *A Chorus Line*, which was released in mid-1975. The musical was a success on Broadway but the cast recording entered the Billboard album chart in August and never rose higher than 98, although it remained on the album chart for 49 weeks.

In the Fall of 1975, Goddard Lieberson retired from Columbia. He was 64 years old and had been with Columbia for 36 years.

Technology

In a letter to his business partner Paul Allen on November 29, Bill Gates used the term "Micro-soft" for microcomputer software. The term "Microsoft" became a registered trademark on November 26, 1976.

The Sony Betamax was introduced in 1975 but soon lost out to the VHS recorders that could record louder. Sony insisted that its video recorder was a higher quality and he was right, but we are a nation of convenience and the new VHS recorders were more convenient and the quality was not noticeable to the average viewer.

Nashville: From Music Row to Music Square

In 1975, Sixteenth and Seventeenth Avenues South from Division Street to Grand Avenue were re-named Music Square East and West. James Hamilton, who owned the Pilcher-Hamilton House at the northern end of Music Row was the Metro Councilman who had fought against the

Music Row Boulevard plan because his house was threatened, wanted his property to be the only "Number One" on Music Square, so the lots are numbered in a crazy quilt that goes across the blocks and bounces back, so if you find "number 20" you probably won't find "number 21" across the street or "number 22 next to it. Instead, the numbering begins with Hamilton's house as "number 1," goes across the street to "number 2," continues west to "number 3" and "number four" is on the east side of Music Square East; the numbers then bounce back and forth all the way down to Grand Avenue.

Music Square Park (later renamed Owen Bradley Park) was created at the intersection of Division Street, Demonbreun Street and 16th Ave. S. Construction cost $675,769 and was part of a federal grant. The park replaced a service station at that location.

Although it legally became "Music Square," citizens of Nashville as well as the music industry continued to refer to the area as "Music Row" and it went from Demonbreaun on the North to Wedgewood on the South and extended over to 18th and 19th streets in addition to the original 16th and 17th Avenues South.

"Convoy"

During the early and mid-1970s a "CB" (Citizens Band radio) craze swept the nation and drivers installed CB radios in their cars to talk to other motorists and truckers, who had long used the technology to communicate. Bill Fries, creative director for the Bozewell and Jacobs advertising agency in Omaha, Nebraska created a TV ad for "Old Home Bread" for the Metz Baking Company that featured a truck driver, C.W. McCall. "Old Home Filler-Up An' Keep On Truckin' Café" was a single on MGM that was released from that ad and Fries became C.W. McCall. That single was followed by "Wolf Creek Pass" and then "Convoy" that told the story of truck drivers beating the police using CB terminology. (The speed limit had been reduced to 55 because of the energy crisis.) "Convoy entered the *Billboard* country chart on November 29, 1975 and reached number one, where it remained for six weeks; it was also number one on Billboard's Hot 100 chart. The song was so popular that it became a movie. C.W. McCall released singles for the next several years but in 1977, after having a number two hit with "Roses for Mama," McCall/ Fries decided he didn't want to be a country star and went back to his ad agency studio in Omaha.

Willie and Waylon

In 1975 Willie Nelson released his album, *Red Headed Stranger*, which was not recorded in Nashville but was released on Nashville-based Columbia Records. The album had a profound impact on country music with its stripped down production at a time when Nashville records were heavily produced. The first single from the album, "Blue Eyes Crying in the Rain," entered the Billboard country chart on July 19 and reached the number one slot; it reached number 21 on the Hot 100 chart. Waylon Jennings' record of "Are You Sure Hank Done It This Way" with "Bob Wills is Still the King" on the flip side entered the country chart on September 6 and reached number one and number 60 on the pop chart. Waylon and Willie's single, "Good Hearted Woman, entered the *Billboard* country chart after Christmas and reached number one on the country chart in 1976.

A film called *Nashville*

The film, *Nashville*, premiered in Nashville on September 21, 1975. Directed by Robert Altman, this was the first big budget picture to be filmed in or about Nashville (the budget was $2.2 million). Written by Joan Tewkesbury and starring Keith Carradine, Karen Black, Ronee Blakley, Lily Tomlin, Ned Beatty, Geraldine Chaplin, Henry Gibson and Shelly Duval, the film was controversial because of its Hollywood portrayal of the country music industry in Nashville. The film won a number of awards, including Oscars for the best original song, "I'm Easy" written by Keith Carradine and "Best Picture" for Robert Altman. The were Oscar nominations for "director" (Altman) and best supporting actress for Ronee Blakley and Lily Tomlin, and a Grammy nomination for the best film score for a film, but there were no accolades from the Nashville country music community. The Nashville audience expected to see themselves portrayed with respect and admiration; they were sorely disappointed.

CMA Awards 1975

The ninth annual CMA Awards was held at the Grand Ole Opry House in Nashville on October 13, 1975 and hosted by Glen Campbell and Charley Pride. Entertainer of the Year was John Denver, Song of the Year was "Back Home Again" written by Denver, Single of the Year was "Before the Next Teardrop Falls" by Freddy Fender Album of the Year was A Legend in My Time by Ronnie Milsap, Male Vocalist was Waylon Jennings, Female Vocalist was Dolly Parton, Vocal Duo was Conway Twitty and Loretta Lynn, Vocal

Group was The Statler Brothers, Instrumentalist was Johnny Gimble and Instrument group was Roy Clark and Buck Trent.

The evening became controversial when Charlie Rich came on stage to announce John Denver as the winner of the "Entertainer of the Year" award and set fire to the card that carried the announcement. After several tense moments, Charley Pride came onstage and led Charlie Rich off to the backstage area. John Denver was not there to accept his award; he thanked the audience via a telecast from Australia, where he was on tour.

Musical Notes: 1975:

On January 6, about 1,000 rowdy Led Zeppelin fans, waiting for tickets to go on sale for their February 4 concert, trashed the lobby of the Boston Garden, broke chairs and doors and caused an estimated $30,000 in damage. Boston Mayor Kevin White cancelled the Led Zeppelin show. The next day, tickets for three Led Zeppelin shows at Madison Square Garden in New York sold out in four hours.

On August 9, the first "Rock Music Awards," produced by Don Kirshner, were held in Los Angeles. The event was co-hosted by Elton John and Diana Ross.

On October 7, the New York Court of Appeals overturned John Lennon's deportation orders, allowing him to remain in the United States. Two days later—on Lennon's 35th birthday, Sean Ono Lennon was born to him and Yoko One. The birth of Sean Lennon led to John Lennon's temporary retirement from the music industry for five years as he dedicated himself to raising his song.

During 1975, the Broadway musicals *Chicago*, *A Chorus Line* and *The Wiz* opened on Broadway. Musical films the premiered in 1975 included *Funny Lady*, *The Rocky Horror Picture Show*, *The Magic Flute* and *Tommy*.

Vietnam

In Vietnam, North Vietnamese troops were on their way to capturing Saigon. South Vietnam President Nguyen an Thieu ordered the evacuation of the Central Highlands, which led to a mass exodus of troops and civilians. Communist Khmer Rouge guerillas forced the surrender of the Khmer Republic after they captured Phenom Penh, ending the Cambodian Civil War. A mass exodus of American troops and Cambodian civilians ensued as the Khmer Rouge forced a mass evacuation of Phnom Penh and began a genocide.

The North Vietnamese Army advance towards Saigon, the capital of South Vietnam, forcing the closure of the Australian Embassy on April 25 and "Operation Frequent Wind," where Americans and their allies are evacuated by helicopter, beginning on April 29. The next day, April 30, 1975, the Vietnam War ends with the fall of Saigon. The last Americans and South Vietnamese civilians are evacuated by helicopters from the roof of the American Embassy. South Vietnam surrenders unconditionally to the North Vietnamese.

The radical student group The Weather Underground, bombed the main office of the Department of State in Washington, D.C.

News of the World: 1975

John Mitchell, H.R. Haldeman and John Ehrlichman were all found guilty of the Watergate cover-up in January. They were sentenced to between 30 months and eight years in prison.

In London, 49-year-old Margaret Thatcher won the leadership of the Conservative Party in the U.K.

Bill Gates and Paul Allen found Microsoft on April 4 in Albuquerque, New Mexico.

At the Pine Ridge Indian Reservation in South Dakota, two FBI agents and one member of the American Indian Movement are killed in a shootout on June 26.

The first broadcast of "Saturday Night Live" aired on NBC on October 11. The show was hosted by George Carlin and the first musical guests were Billy Preston and Janis Ian.

Former California Governor Ronald Reagan entered the race for the Republican presidential nomination on November 20, challenging the incumbent, Gerald Ford.

The City of New York went bankrupt in 1975; on December 8, Congress voted to approve a bailout of $2.3 billion each year through 1978 or a total of $6.9 billion.

1976
Bicentennial Celebrations

The United States celebrated its 200th birthday in 1976 and during the July 4 weekend (July 4 was on a Sunday) the Bicentennial saw a number of music festivals. At Shaffer Stadium in Foxboro, Massachusetts, Elton John performed before 62,000 fans; at the Tampa Stadium in Florida, the Eagles and Fleetwood Mac performed for 36,000, at the Memphis Memorial

Stadium, Lynyrd Skynyrd and ZZ Top performed for 35,000, at a free concert in Central Park in New York there were 50,000 fans who watched in the rain as Jefferson Starship performed. Elvis Presley performed for 11,974 in the Mabee Center in Tulsa and in Gonzales, Texas at Willie Nelson's Annual Fourth of July Picnic, Willie, Waylon Jennings, Jessi Colter, Jerry Jeff Walker, Asleep at the Wheel and Leon Russell performed before an audience of 80,000.

The Recording Industry: Late 1970s

By 1976 CBS had an income of $484.3 million and Warner Brothers had an annual income of $313.8 million. That was greater than the entire recording industry 25 years earlier. The industry as a whole had an income of $2.73 billion.

The major labels in 1974 were MCA, CBS, Capitol-EMI, PolyGram, RCA and Warner Communications; together they accounted for 81 percent of the market. There were four major independents: A & M, Motown, 20th Century Fox and United Artists, who also had a major impact. Artist royalties had reached an average of 15 percent, with some artists receiving an 18 percent royalty rate.

The top independent to emerge during the 1970s was RSO Records, a product of the entrepreneurial talent of Robert Stigwood (RSO stood for Robert Stigwood Organization.) Stigwood got his start working for Brian Epstein, manager of the Beatles. When Epstein died in 1968, the ownership of NEMS/Nemperor, Epstein's organization, passed to his brother and mother and Stigwood was frozen out of the company so the Australian began his own management company, eventually managing the Bee Gees, Eric Clapton, Joe Cocker, Eric Burden, Procol Harum and T-Rex. He also ran the music publishing company which owned the copyrights of all his artists and ventured into theatre production, producing the British version of *Hair*, as well as Andrew Lloyd Webber and Tim Rice's first two musicals, *Joseph and the Amazing Technicolor Dreamcoat* and *Jesus Christ Superstar*. Those musicals changed the way the recording industry did business with Broadway shows: the album was first produced, then came the concert hall, the stage and, finally film.

In the early 70s Warner Communications offered $11 million to take over the Robert Stigwood Organization. That capital led Stigwood into a partnership with Allan Carr, the American film producer, which resulted in plans for their first film, *Grease*, from the Broadway musical. However, before that play was filmed, Stigwood became convinced their first film should be about a phenomena in Brooklyn about blue collar whites addicted to disco dancing that had recently been profiled in a magazine article. Thus was born *Saturday Night Fever*.

The center for disco was New York and by the mid-70s, the disco industry accounted for $4 billion. The disco disc jockey, like the early rock'n'roll disco jockeys, changed the music as they defined it, moving away from three minute singles and into long, extended versions of songs with special mixes, highlighted by a heavy bass and drums and accompanied by advanced lighting.

Frampton Comes Alive!

On January 6, 1976, the album *Frampton Comes Alive!* was released; at the end of January it entered the *Billboard* album chart and became number one on April 10 and remained in that position for ten straight weeks.

The double LP was recorded during four concerts in 1975. On June 16, his performance was recorded in San Rafael, California at the Marin Country Civil Center; the next night his performances was captured at the Winterland Ballroom in San Francisco. On August 24, his performaces was recorded at the Long Island Arena in New York and on November 22, his concert at the SUNY-Plattsburgh in New York.

Originally intended to be a single LP, executives at A&M Records suggested that more songs be recorded and the project extended to two LPs. The performances were caught live with only a few corrections made in the studio. In the studio, the first verse of "Something's Happening, the rhythm electric guitar on "Show Me the Way" and the piano into to "I Wanna Go to the Sun" were the only non-live parts of the record.

Peter Frampton was born in Kent, England (April 22, 1950). When he was seven, he found his grandmother's banjolele in the attic and taught himself to play, then moved to guitar and piano. Beginning at eight, he took classical music lessons. Early influences were Cliff Richard & the Shadows, Buddy Holly, Eddie Cochran and, later, the Ventures, the Beatles, Jimi Hendrix and the gypsy jazz guitarist Django Reinhardt.

Frampton joined his first band, The Little Ravens, when he was 12. His band played on the same bill at Bromley Technical High School as David Bowie's band, George and the Dragons. Bowie attended the same school as Frampton and Frampton's father, Owen, was head of the Art Department and Bowie's art instructor.

When he was 14 Frampton was in a band, The Trubeats, then joined The Preachers, which were produced and managed by Bill Wyman, bassist for the Rolling Stones. At 16 he was in The Herd as lead guitarist and singer. The group was first signed to Polydor and released three singles with no success. They then signed with Fontana Records and, with a new manager and producer, had four hit singles on the U.K. chart, "I Can Fly," "From the Underworld," "Paradise Lost" and "I Don't Want Our Loving to Die," which reached number five.

At the end of 1968, Frampton and Steve Marriott of Small Faces formed Humble Pie. They had several successful singles in the U.K. before their first chart single in the United States, "I Don't Need No Doctor." They signed with A&M and released the album *Rock On*, then a live album, *Performance—Rockin' the Fillmore*, that reached number 21 on the *Billboard* album chart.

Frampton left Humble Pie before the live album was released and began his solo career. His first album, *Winds of Change*, featured Ringo Starr and Billy Preston and was released in 1972. That was followed by *Frampton's Camel* and *Somethin' Happening*, which charted in the bottom half of the *Billboard* 200 album chart, then released *Frampton* in 1975, which reached number 32 on the album chart. His next album was *Frampton Comes Alive!*

The double album had a reduced list price of $7.98 and was pressed with sides one and four on one disc and sides two and three on the other. There were three hit singles on the album, "Show Me the Way," which reached number eight on the *Billboard* Hot 100, "Baby I Love Your Way" (number 12), "Do You Feel Like We Do" (number 10), which was edited down from 14:15 on the album to 7:19 for the single.

Peter Frampton played on George Harrison's first solo album, *All Things Must Pass* and met Nashville steel guitarist Peter Drake during those sessions. Drake had created a "talk box" and recorded an album of "talking steel guitar" album where he talked/sang along with the instrumental track. Drake gave the "talk box" to Frampton, who developed it and used it on the singles "Show Me the Way" and "Do You Feel Like We Do."

Frampton Comes Alive! sold over ten million copies and was one of the most successful albums of 1976.

The Copyright Act of 1976

The copyright to songs were set in 1909 and provided each song received two cents for each copy sold. The amount was actually fixed for player piano rolls and known as "mechanicals" but, as player pianos died away and records became the major way songs were sold, there was a need to update the copyright law for songs on recordings.

In addition to needing to be updated because of technological changes in sound recording, television, movies and radio, a new copyright law was needed because the United States had agreed to participate in the Universal Copyright Convention (UCC) in 1955 and projected participation in the Berne Convention. The United States needed to conform with UCC standards.

The original bill to reform copyright was drafted in 1964 but there were numerous revisions during the 12 years before the copyright law was passed on September 22 and signed into law by President Gerald Ford on October 19, 1976.

The law went into effect on January 1, 1978.

Among the changes in copyright that affected the music industry, there was protection granted for copyrights when they were in "fixed form." Registration with the Copyright Office was not required in order for a work to be protected. Copyright registration with the Copyright Office required forms to be filled out and one or two copies of the work.

The law also required that the payment for songs sold on recordings be re-visited an possibly increased during the following years. By 2018, a song earned 9.1 cents ($.091) for each recording sold.

100 Club Punk Special

The 100 Club on Oxford Street in London was known for jazz in 1976. The Sex Pistols had acquired a lot of attention during 1976 and in early September, concert promoter Ron Watts approached Malcolm McLaren, manager of the Sex Pistols about headlining an event at the club.

McLaren agreed and two other acts, The Damned and The Clash joined the line-up. Manchester was a hotbed for punk music; after the Sex Pistols performed at the Lesser Free Trade Hall on June 4, a number of audience members formed punk groups. Among the groups formed were Joy Division, New Order, the Smiths, Simply Red, The Fall, Buzzcocks and Magzine as well as the record company, Factory.

The two day event at the 100 Club began on Monday, September 20 and featured Subway Sect, Siouxsie and the Banshees, The Clash and the Sex Pistols. On Tuesday the line-up was Stinky Toys, Chris Spedding & The Vibrators, The Damned and Buzzcocks. Most of the acts were unsigned to a record label.

The 100 Club Punk Special, also known as The 100 Club Punk Festival, was a landmark in punk music. Boosted by extensive promotion by journalist Caroline Coon in *Melody Maker*, the punk movement moved from an unknown underground movement to one in the pop music mainstream.

The Outlaw Movement

The album, *Wanted! The Outlaws*, which featured recordings by Waylon Jennings, Willie Nelson, Tompall Glaser and Jessi Colter, entered *Billboard's* country album chart in February, 1976 and was the apex of in the "Outlaw Movement" in country music. The "outlaws" were mainly country artists who defied the Nashville rules by producing their own recordings and recording in studios that they—not the label—chose. The spiritual center for the outlaw movement was in Texas (Waylon and Willie were both Texas natives) and the music reached a young audience.

The term "outlaws" was coined by Hazel Smith, who worked at the Glaser Brothers studio and publishing company and seemed to fit the lifestyle and the music. The music had a heavier beat and Waylon and Willie both had a series of hit singles and albums at the height of the outlaw movement. The "lifestyle" involved drugs as "sex, drugs and rock'n'roll" entered the world of country music during the 1970s.

Wanted! The Outlaws reached number one on the *Billboard* country album chart and remained there for six week; it remained on the chart of 253 weeks. The songs on the album had been previously released but the timing was right for this compilation that featured "Good Heated Woman (Waylon & Willie); "Heaven or Hell (Waylon & Willie); "Honky Tonk Heroes" (Waylon); "I'm Looking For Blue Eyes" (Jessi Colter); "Me and Paul" (Willie); "Put Another Log On The Fire ((Male Chauvinist National Anthem)" (Tompall Glaser); "Suspicious Minds" (Waylon & Jessi); "T For Texas (Tompall Glase) r; "Yesterday's Wine (Willie); "You Mean To Say" (Jessi). The album was released on January 12, 1976 and, because the recordings had taken place over a long period of time, there was a long list of producers that included Waylon Jennings, Richie Albright, Chet Atkins, Danny Davis, Tompall Glaser, Ray Kennedy, Willie Nelson, Ray Pennington and Shel Silverstein.

The album reached number ten on *Billboard's* Top 200 album chart and had two hit singles, "Suspicious Minds" and "Good Hearted Woman," whose "live" cut came from Waylon's 1976 album, *Waylon Live* with Willie's voice overdubbed on the edited tracks.

The album was compiled by Jerry Bradley, head of RCA's country division, who saw that Willie's album, *Red Headed Stranger* had sold over a million copies and that "I'm Not Lisa" by Jessi Colter had been a hit on

Capitol. Waylon approved of Bradley's idea for the album and the choice of *Rolling Stone* magazine's Chet Flippo to write the liner notes.

The Cowboy in Country Music

The cowboy has been an enduring symbol of country music, dating back to the Singing Cowboys when Gene Autry and Roy Rogers were major stars. However, during the "Nashville Sound" period, a number of singers performed in tuxedos (Jim Reeves, Eddy Arnold and Ray Price) or in sports coats or suits. The "outlaw movement" brought country music back the cowboy image.

Gene Autry, Roy Rogers and other singing cowboy wore a white hat; the outlaws wore black hats. The Singing Cowboys took the cowboy away from tending cattle and dressed him in outfits that no one would wear on a working ranch. The outlaws took the horse away; instead, cowboys drove pick-up trucks.

In 1975 there were a number of western themed songs on the country charts; "Bandy the Rodeo Clown" by Moe Bandy, "Bob Wills Is Still the King" by Waylon Jennings, ""Cowboys and Daddys" by Bobby Bare, "Hoppy, Gene and Me" by Roy Rogers," "I Love a Rodeo" by Roger Miller, "Let's All Help the Cowboy (Sing the Blues)" by Waylon, "Rhinestone Cowboy" by Glen Campbell," "Ride 'Em Cowboy" by Paul Davis and "Western Man" by LaCosta.

In 1976 there was an explosion of songs with a western theme, including "Can You Hear Those Pioneers" by Rex Allen, Jr. (a tribute to the Sons of the Pioneers), "Cherokee Maiden" by Merle Haggard," "El Paso City" by Marty Robbins and "Faster Horses (The Cowboy and the Poet)" by Tom T. Hall. This led to the label "The Hat Acts" because many of the country artists wore cowboy hats.

CMA Awards 1976

The tenth annual CMA Awards was hosted by Johnny Cash and Roy Clark on October 11, 1976 at the Grand Ole Opry House. Entertainer of the Year was Mel Tillis, "Rhinestone Cowboy" written by Larry Weissas Song of the Year, "Good Hearted Woman" was Song of the Year and Wanted! The Outlaws was Album of the Year. Male Vocalist was Ronnie Milsap, Female Vocalist was Dolly Parton, Vocal Duo was Waylon Jennings and Willie Nelson, Vocal Gorup was the Statler Brothers, Instrumentalist was Hargus "Pig Robbins, Instrumental Group was Roy Clark and Buck Trent; Paul Cohen and Kitty Wells were inducted into the Country Music Hall of Fame.

ACE

A press conference was held by the Association of Country Entertainers (ACE) in November, 1976, that addressed problems with radio, specifically the short play lists and the desire for more country formats that allowed older and "real" country artists to continue to receive radio airplay. The most active members of this organization addressing these problems were Grandpa Jones, Ernest Tubb, Vic Willis, Jean Shepard, Hank Snow, Roy Wiggins, Patsy Stoneman, Justin Tubb, Del Wood, Oscar Sullivan, George Morgan, Wilma Lee & Stoney Cooper, Connie Smith, Barbara Mandrell, Charlie Louvin, Bill Carlisle, Jesse McReynolds, Billy Grammar and Little Jimmy Dickens.

Disco

Disco--the term derives from the French term "discotheque"--was a music designed and created to make people dance. It became a self-contained genre during the 1970s and, to many mainstream rock fans, was the most despised music to emerge from the 1970s. Critics complained about the throbbing beat that discouraged any adventurism in music and the pure commercial aspects--this was music for the body, not the mind.

Dancing has always been an important function of music; before the recording industry was developed, people saw music functioning in two major social settings: the concert and for dances. Jazz and Big Band developed as music for dancing; the early blues and country music was music that was made for dancing as well. Early rock and roll bands played for dancers but during the 1960s folk music was a music to sing along with or listen to--not dance.

The music of the rock counterculture, particularly beginning in 1964 with the British Invasion, was played to audiences who did not dance. That was partly because of drugs; when people danced at music festivals, it was often someone alone, lost in the ecstasy of music and drugs.

By the 1970s, the audiences for rock music had moved from clubs into concert halls. Clubs are smaller and more intimate; concert halls are large and impersonal. When disco arrived in the mid-1970s, it returned music to two of its major roots: night clubs and dancing.

Although disco returned music to clubs, it used the technologies developed for large concert halls and studios; there were elaborate sound systems that bathed the room with music. The rhythm and blues roots were obvious in disco, but technological advances such as synthesizers and drum machines also played an important part of this musical subculture.

The star of the disco was the disc jockey, who used two turntables to create a music that was hypnotic and manipulated a crowd on the dance floor to lose themselves in physical release. The disc jockey attempted to have the music build, creating a tension, until it peaked--like the sex act itself--letting the participants, sweaty and exhausted, moan in pleasure.

Disco developed in clubs patronized by gays, blacks and women; the audience tended to be older than the rock audience, and the aura of the club lent itself to high fashion--sharp dressed men and women--instead of the jean clad, t-shirt wearing audience for rock during the 1970s. Disco featured slick, polished production, an extension of Motown and then the sounds of Philadelphia International Records, led by Kenneth Gamble and Leon Huff, that was either up tempo with a pulsing beat or in ballads with lush, orchestral arrangements. In many ways it was a romantic music when "romance" wasn't the guiding ethos in the world of rock music during the 1970s.

Disco music spread from club to club, disc jockey to disc jockey. It was not a music made for radio, although there were a few disco hits on the radio. "Rock the Boat" by the Hues Corporation and "Rock Your Baby" by George McCrae in early 1974 were hits on both radio and the dance clubs; so was "The Hustle" by Van McCoy and "Shame, Shame, Shame" by Shirley and Company, both in 1975. That year (1975) there were an estimated 200-300 disco clubs in New York and about 2,500 in the United States. The clubs and the music were an urban phenomena; disco was a product of city life, a genre for the "beautiful people" who sought to be trendy and elegant.

Disco was a music dominated by producers and disc jockeys; few individual artists emerged from disco because most singers were a faceless part of an overall sound. KC and the Sunshine Band was a group that emerged in 1975 with "Get Down Tonight." KC was Harry Wayne Casey who, along with Richard Finch, had written and produced "Rock Your Baby" at TK Studios in Miami. "Get Down Tonight" became a number one hit in 1975 and that style was dubbed "the Miami Sound." Other hits followed, including "That's The Way (I Like It)," which also was a number one hit in 1975.

Europe was an important source of early disco and the biggest disco act to emerge, Donna Summer, recorded her initial disco hit, "Love to Love You Baby" in Munich, Germany in 1976. Produced by Giorgio Moroder, the vocals of the then-unknown singer were really a series of moans simulating sex over a heavily layered production. Moroder played the recording for

Neil Bogart, head of Casablanca Records, who decided to release it on his label after playing it at a party at his home and receiving an enthusiastic reaction. Casablanca, the home of Kiss, soon became the pre-eminent disco label with Donna Summer and others.

Disco existed outside the musical mainstream; the traditional method for marketing recordings--airplay and artist tours--did not apply. Major labels tended to ignore it at first, so the genre developed its own publicity and distribution system. Because the songs were long--dancers wanted 10-20 minute records to dance to, the recordings were put on 12 inch (instead of 7 inch) singles.

The white rock audience, put off by the cult following of disco in gay and African-American cultures, remained largely dismissive of it until the Bee Gees album *Main Course*, released in 1975 that featured the hit "Jive Talkin'." The Bee Gees, a trio of brothers (The Brothers Gibb) originally from Australia, had hits in the 1960s during the British Invasion, but found new life in the disco movement.

It was the Bee Gees, especially on the soundtrack to the movie *Saturday Night Fever*, released in 1977, that brought disco music into the musical mainstream.

Donna Summer

Donna Summer (b. LaDonna Adrian Gaines) was born in Boston and moved to New York where she landed a role in the Broadway musical *Hair* and then moved to Munich, Germany for a production of the show. She became fluent in German and appeared in several musicals there before she moved to Vienna, Austria. In 1968, she released her first single, "Aquarius" from *Hair* on Polydor under the name Donna Gaines; she released singles on Decca and then on Philips Records. In 1973 she married Helmuth Sommer, an Austrian actor and sang back-up on several singles by Veit Marvos on Ariola Records. She continued to perform in musicals, as a model and backup singer in Munich and met German producers Giorgio Moroder and Pete Bellotte; in 1974 she released an album on Groovey Records where a mistake on her first album, *Lady of the Night*, spelled her name as Donna Summer. Two of the songs on the album, "Lady of the Night" and "The Hostage" were hits in Europe.

Summer and Giorgia Moroder wrote "Love to Love You" in 1975 for another artist but Moroder decided Summer's demo of the song should be released. The recording was sent to Neil Bogart at Casablanca Records who decided to release it on that label after playing the song at a party and receiving an enthusiastic response from the crowd. At Bogart's request, Moroder produced a longer version of the song for discos; the longer version was 17 minutes long. In November, 1975, Bogart released the shorter version as "Love to Love You Baby" after signing Summer to his label. The single rose to number two in 1976 and remained on the *Billboard* Hot 100 for 18 weeks; it sold "Gold" status although some American station refused to play it because of Summer's sexual moans. The album went platinum, reaching number 11 on the *Billboard* album chart. This single and those that followed led to her becoming known as "The Queen of Disco."

A second album, *A Love Trilogy*, contained the singles "Could It Be Magic" and "Try Me, I Know We Can Make It" was released. Her third album, *Four Seasons of Love* was released and two singles from that album, "Spring Affair" and "Winter Melody" charted on the *Billboard* Hot 100. Both of those albums went "Gold."

Her fourth album on Casablanca, *I Remember Love*, contained the single, "I Feel Love," which reached number six on the *Billboard* Hot 100 and remained on the chart for 23 weeks; it was number one on the U.K. singles chart. That single went "Gold" and the album went "Platinum." Her next album was a *Once Upon a Time*, a concept album about her life story; it went "Gold."

In the 1977 film *The Deep*, Summer recorded the theme song, "Deep Down Inside" and appeared in the film, *Thank God It's Friday*; on that soundtrack was "Last Dance," which reached number three on the *Billboard* Hot 100 and won Grammys for "R&B song and "R&B Female Vocal" and an Oscar. That single went "Gold" and the album was "Platinum." The songwriter for "Last Dance," Paul Jabara, won an Academy Award and Golden Globe Award for that song.

Technology

On April 1, the Apple Computer Company was formed by Steve Jobs and Steve Wozniak. Microsoft was officially registered in Albuquerque, New Mexico by the Office of the Secretary of the State of New Mexico.

The first commercially developed supercomputer, The Cray-1, was released by Seymour Cray's firm, Cray Research and the first laser printer, the IBM 3800, was introduced by IBM.

Musical Notes: 1976

Beatles in the News: Mal Evans, the Beatles former road manager was shot dead by a Los Angeles policeman on January 5; the police thought he had a danger weapon when he only had an air gun; on January 19, concert promoter Bill Sargent offered the group $30 million if they would unite for a concert; they turned him down. EMI Records reissued all 22 previously released singles plus "Yesterday," in the U.K.

Lorne Michaels, producer of Saturday Night Live, offered to pay the Beatles $3,00 to unite live on the show. In an interview later, John Lennon stated that he and Paul McCartney were in New York watching the show when Michaels made his request and considered walking down to the studio "for a gag" but were "too tired."

The Eagles album, *Their Greatest Hits (1971-1975)* was the first album certified "Platinum" by the RIAA. The new certification by the RIAA became necessary become so many albums were selling muti-millions. The new award meant an album had to sell a million albums to be "platinum" ("Gold" remained a half a million copies) and singles had to sell two million copies ("Gold" remained at one million).

On April 14, Stevie Wonder announced that he had signed a contract with Motown for "$13 million plus."

In an effort to meet his hero, Bruce Springsteen jumped the wall at Graceland and strode towards Elvis's house before he was caught and ousted. The caper occurred on April 29 when Springsteen was in Memphis during his tour.

On May 3, Paul McCartney and Wings began their "Wings Over America" tour on May 3 in Fort Worth. This was McCartney's first public performances in the United States since the 1966 Beatles tour.

A United States District Court ruled on August 31 that George Harrison had "subconsciously" copied the hit, "He's So Fine" by the Chiffons when he wrote "My Sweet Lord."

Elton John publicly disclosed his bisexuality during an interview with *Rolling Stone* magazine on September 8. The magazine published the remarks in the edition on October 7.

"Hard Rain," a one hour concert special by Bob Dylan, was broadcast on NBC on September 14; it coincided with the release of his album by the same name.

"The P-Funk/Rubber Band Earth Tour" featuring George Clinton and Parliament Funkadelic began in Houston on October 31. The concert featured special lighting, elaborate costume and special effects, including "the Mothership," which arrived and landed on stage. It was a revolutionary stage show at high volume that lasted three to five hours.

The last official public concert by The Band was on November 25; it was filmed by Martin Scorsese.

"Anarchy in the U.K.," the first single by the Sex Pistols, was released on November 26 in the U.K. On December 1, there was a national outcry after the group swore on a TV show.

The first commercially available 12-inch single, "Ten Percent" by Double Exposure, was released. Prior to this release, 12-inch singles were only available to club DJs.

News of the World: 1976

At the Democratic National Convention on July 15, former Georgia Governor Jimmy Carter was voted the Democratic nominee for president. On August 19, President Gerald Ford defeated Ronald Reagan to become the Republican nominee for president. On November 2, American voters elected Jimmy Cater to be President of the United States.

1977

1977: An Overview

Jimmy Carter is inaugurated as the thirty-ninth President of the United States on January 20. The next day he pardons all Vietnam War draft evaders. The day before his inauguration, snow fell on Miami for the first time in its history.

The groundbreaking min-series, "Roots" broadcast its first episode on January 23.

During 1977, voters in Miami-Date County, Florida vote overwhelming vote to repeal the county's "gay rights" ordinance after heavy campaigning by Anita Bryant and her anti-gay "Save Our Children" campaign. On June 26, about 200,000 marchers in San Francisco paraded through the streets protesting Anita Bryant's anti-gay remarks about the murder of Robert Hillsborough.

Anita Bryant was pied in the face by four gay rights activities on October 14 during a press conference in Des Moines, Iowa and in San Francisco, citizens elected the first openly gay elected official in the United States on November 8 when they elected Harvey Milk as City Supervisor.

The New York City blackout, which lasted 25 hours, began on July 13. During the blackouts there was looting and disorder.

The Pinwheel Network, a children's cable channel, began broadcasting on December 1; it later changed its name to Nickelodeon.

The Eagles and Hotel California

The Eagles replaced Bernie Leadon with Joe Walsh, former member of the James Gang whose producer was Bill Szymczyk and was managed by the Eagles manager, Irving Azoff. Don Felder played Leadon's parts on their tours, which meant he had to learn banjo, mandolin and pedal steel guitar.

Their album *Hotel California* was released in early 1977 and reached the number one position, which it held for eight consecutive weeks and spent 109 weeks on the chart. It was nominated for a Grammy for "Album of the Year" but lost to *Rumours* by Fleetwood Mac.

The first single, "New Kid in Town" entered the *Billboard* chart on December 18, 1976, and reached number one in 1977. The next single, "Hotel California," written by Henley, Frey and Felder, debuted on the *Billboard* chart on February 26 and reached the number one positon and won the Grammy for "Record of the Year." Don Henley sang the lead vocal and Felder and Walsh did a guitar duet.

Their third single from the album, "Life in the Fast Lane," written by Henley, Frey and Walsh, entered the Hot 100 on May 14 and reached number 11.

The Eagles had toured continuously for eleven months and after the tour ended in 1977, founding member Randy Meisner left the group. Meisner was plagued by stomach ulcers and had struggled to hit high notes on "Take It To The Limit," a signature song with the group. The final straw was a vocal and physical confrontation with Glenn Frey, which led to him being frozen out of the band.

When Meisner left Poco he was replaced by Timothy Schmidt; now Schmidt would replaced him again, this time in the Eagles.

Grammys

The 19th Annual Grammy Awards were held at the Hollywood Palladium in Los Angeles on February 19, 1977. The event, hosted by Andy Williams on CBS, recognized musical achievements of 1976.

Record of the Year: "This Masquerade" by George Benson; produced by Tommy LiPuma

Album of the Year: *Songs in the Key of Life* by Stevie Wonder

Song of the Year: "I Write the Songs, written by Bruce Johnson and recorded by Barry Manilow

Best New Artist: Starland Vocal Band

Best Pop Vocal Female: Linda Ronstadt for her album *Hasten Down the Wind*

Best Pop Vocal Male: Stevie Wonder for his album, *Songs in the Key of Life*

Best Pop Vocal by Duo or Group: "If You Leave Me Now" by Chicago

Best Pop Instrumental: "Breezin'" by George Benson

Best Country Song: "Broken Lady" by Larry Gatlin

Best Country Vocal, Male: Ronnie Milsap for "(I'm a) Stand By My Woman Man"

Best Country Vocal, Female: Emmylou Harris for her album *Elite Hotel*

Best duo or group: The Amazing Rhythm Aces for "The End Is Not in Sight (The Cowboy Tune)"

Best Country Instrumental: Chet Atkins and Les Paul for their album *Chester and Lester*

Best R&B Vocal, Female: Natalie Cole for "Sophisticated Lady (She's a Different Lady)"

Best R&B Vocal, Male: Stevie Wonder for "I Wish"

Best R&B Vocal by a Duo or Group: Billy Davis Jr. and Marilyn McCoo for "You Don't Have to Be a Star (To Be in My Show)"

Best R&B Instrumental: George Benson for "Theme From *Good King Bad*"

Best R&B Song: "Lowdown, written by Boz Scaggs and David Paich and performaced by Boz Scaggs.

Best Ethnic or Traditional Recording: John Hartford for *Mark Twang*

Best Gospel Performance (other than soul): The Oak Ridge Boys for "Where the Soul Never Dies"

Best Soul Gospel Performance: Mahalia Jackson for her album *How I Got Over*

Best Inspirational Performance: Gary S. Paxton for his album *The Astonishing, Outrageous, Amazing, Incredible, Unbelievable, Different World of Gary S. Paxton.*

1977 was The Year of Punk.

On January 1, The Clash headlined at The Roxy, London's only punk club.

EMI dropped the Sex Pistols on January 27 after releasing only one single because of band member's disruptive behavior at London's Heathrow Airport. On February 15, Sid Vicious joined the Sex Pistols as bassist after Glen Matlock left.

On February 7, the International Times in London proclaimed that "punk is dead."

A&M Records signed the Sex Pistols on March 10 in a ceremony at the front of Buckingham Palace. Six days later the group was dropped from the label after they vandalized property and verbally abused employees during a visit to the label's office.

The Clash released their debut album on April 8 on CBS Records.

On May 11, the Stranglers and opening act London began a 10-week national tour of the U.K. The next day, Virgin Records announced they had signed the Sex Pistols. On June 7, the Sex Pistols played "God Save the Queen" on a boat in the River Thames in an attempt to disrupt Queen Elizabeth's Silver Anniversary celebrations.

On October 27, the Sex Pistols released their album, *Never Mind the Bollocks, Here's the Sex Pistols* on Virgin Records. Major U.K. retailers refused to stock it but it debuted at number one on the U.K. album charts. To promote the album, the group performed on a boat on the River Thames; the police made several arrests, including Malcolm McLaren, the band's manager, when the boat docked. Elvis Costello made his American television debut on "Saturday Night Live" on December 17 but was banned after performing "Radio, Radio" instead of the scheduled "Less Than Zero."

During 1977, a number of punk bands were formed, including The Avengers, Bad Brains, Black Flag, Crass, Discharge, Fear, the Flesh Eaters, the Germs, the Misfits, 999, The Pagans, The Plasmatics, VOM, The Weirdos, X and X-Ray Spex.

Several albums by punk bands were released that defined the genre. Those albums included *The Clash* by The Clash, The Damned's *Damned, Damned, Damned*; the Dead Boys' *Young, Loud and Snotty*; Johnny Thunders and the Heartbreakers' *L.A.M.F.*; The Jam's *In the City*, the Ramones' *Rocket to Russia*; Richard Hell and the Voidods' *Blank Generation*, the Sex Pistols' *Never Mind the Bollocks, Here's the Sex Pistols*; Television's *Marquee Moon*; and *Pink Flag* by Wire.

These albums kick-started the punk movement from the underground into the musical mainstream and are often considered "masterpieces" by the punk community.

"New Wave" was not punk but was associated with the punk movements. Influential "New Wave" albums released during 1977 included *My Aim Is True* by Elvis Costello; *Suicide by Suicide*; *Talking Heads: 77* by the Talking Heads; and Iggy Pop's second solo album, *Lust For Life*.

Punk Music

Punk Rock was never commercially successful during its early life; however, its influence reached beyond commercial sales. In some ways, punk contained the essence of early rock and roll with its rebellious snarl shaking up the conservative music establishment. By the mid-1970s, rock music had become mainstream entertainment; some people dismissed it as "corporate rock," a bland, shallow music made by an elite group for multinational corporations.

Punk's message was that "anybody can play this." One of its downfalls was that musical ability wasn't required--the attitude was more important than musical ability—so it could not reach a mass public. Not that it wanted to reach a mass public. Ever since music has been a business there have been the arguments over judging it on commercial versus aesthetic grounds. The punk fan--some would say the true rock fan--felt that the capitalist economic system was no way to measure music. The music business, of course, measures the success or failure of artists by commercial standards: are they selling records or not? If it doesn't sell, it smells.

The Punk Movement had a conflict with capitalism and adulthood, a juvenile self-loathing living in eternal puberty. For punk rockers, music had no place in the capitalist culture. The underlying belief is that if an act sells a huge amount of recordings, that act must be terribly shallow and trite because the vast majority of Americans have no real musical taste or appreciation. What is most important is reaching a core group of true believers.

The other part of the punk aesthetic is finding a voice for the powerlessness against a musical establishment whose sounds dominate the culture. It is a way of saying "I count!" to an industry who, most punks believe, couldn't care less.

The Sex Pistols and British Punk

The Sex Pistols were formed by manager Malcolm McLaren, who had a boutique, "Sex," on King's Road in London. McLaren recruited John Lydon, a musically illiterate unemployed janitor and changed his name to Johnny Rotten. Rotten was an apt description of his attitude, which was belligerent, cynical, sarcastic and in-your-face. Other musicians were Steve Jones, Glen Matlock and Paul Cook, all of whom were still learning to play when they became part of the group. Bassist Matlock dropped out and was replaced by Sid Vicious.

The Sex Pistols held the established rock world in contempt, believing that world, on the whole, was too tame. The Sex Pistols were angry and intent on showing it. That anger was aided by a depressed economy and massive unemployment in England during the 1970s which, under Prime Minister Margaret Thatcher, was moving away from a social capitalism into a free market capitalism. Free market capitalism can be brutal to those on the lower end of the economic scale, and the British punk rockers certainly fit that description.

The Sex Pistols were signed by EMI on Oct 10, 1976, shocking and disappointing their fans who felt that was a sell-out. Their first single, "Anarchy in the U.K." was performed by the group on the British TV show "Today" hosted by Bill Grundy. Grundy provoked Rotten to curse on television--which didn't take much provoking--and Rotten obliged. The result was that the Sex Pistols were dropped by EMI. However, because they had achieved so much publicity--a good start in selling records--they were signed to A&M in March, 1977. Their single, "God Save the Queen" was a straight ahead attack on the monarchy during Queen Elizabeth's Silver Jubilee year of celebrations.

"God Save the Queen" was immediately banned in Britain, which caused it to become the number one best selling single in the nation. The Sex Pistols only recorded one album, *Never Mind the Bollocks, Here's the Sex Pistols*, released in 1977. Warner Brothers decided to release the album in the United States, but it did not sell well.

New York Punk

The roots of punk may be traced back to the Velvet Underground in the 1960s. When that group broke up in 1970, Lou Reed signed on as a solo artist and made records through the 1970s. Reed was a street-smart New Yorker filled with cynicism, a rock star who was blatantly non-commercial. His voice was mostly monotone and he had rudimentary musical skills.

In 1975, a club in New York, CBGB (which originally stood for "Country, Bluegrass and Blues") opened its doors to the rock and roll avant garde. Owner Hilly Kristol let Patti Smith perform and she provided "new wave" (which was what the music was called) its first solid image. The club booked a number of new wave acts: Tuff Darts, Blondie, Stumblebunny, the Ramones, Television and the Talking Heads. Richard Hell wrote "Black Generation" for his group, the Voidoids, in 1977 and the movement had an anthem.

The Ramones made the definitive new wave/punk music with their 1976 debut album. They played loud, fast and furious--most sets lasted only thirty minutes but the crowd was both exhilarated and drained at the end. Formed in 1974 in Forest Hills, New York, the Ramones became America's most well-known punk group.

Another group whose music was classified variously as new wave, punk and art rock was the Talking Heads, a group formed in Rhode Island by David Byrne, Chris Frantz and Tina Weymouth who moved to New York in 1975.

Meanwhile, in London the most famous punk band of all time was forming.

L.A. Punk

The punk movement was influential, especially in Los Angeles, where a post-punk scene emerged with middle class teens who claimed punk in order wear ragged clothes, put safety pins on their face and get hostile while they got drunk. Slam dancing became a trademark of "hard core punk"; this dancing consisted of slamming into any and all who were near to a person.

The second wave of punk saw genuine musical talent emerge, although most punk bands felt that snarls, sneers, and self-absorption was a musical statement. In a way, they were not unlike the singer-songwriters of the early 1970s like James Taylor in that they ignored the world at large and focused on themselves. For a decade described as the "Me Decade," punk rock fit the prevailing view of oneself at the center of the universe.

Acts that did show musical ability, aside from Elvis Costello and Graham parker, were Chrissie Hynde and her band, The Pretenders, the Clash and Devo.

ADD: Elvis Costello

The Year of the Punk was 1977, when the Sex Pistols wreaked havoc on the British social scene; the era ended in 1979 when Sid Vicious died. But the influence of punk continued because their look of defiance from spiked hair, body piercings and torn, second hand clothes and their attitude of rebellion and in-your-face rejection of mainstream music continued to be an attribute of a number of acts during the rest of the 20th century.

Punk Fashion

The fashion statement made by the British punkers was an outgrowth of their economic condition: they bought their clothes at second-hand stores, the clothes were usually ripped and torn, there were leather bondage bracelets and arm bands, part of the S&M culture, and they shaved their heads like prisoners.

Commercial Punk

The most commercially successful punk group to come out of England was the Clash, formed by Joe Strummer after he had been to a performance by the Sex Pistols. The Clash's debut album was released in England in 1977 by CBS, but the CBS office in the United States deemed it "too crude" for American tastes. In 1979, CBS in the United States released *London Calling*, which became a hit album, led by the single "Train in Vain." The breakthrough airplay came from college radio stations, who were growing in numbers and importance throughout the 1970s.

Punk offered young women the opportunity to perform. With its "anybody can do this" ethos, young women, who had generally been discouraged from playing rock and roll, felt encouraged to start a punk band and write songs. Also, the women's liberation movement had empowered young women to try things that previous generations of women had been barred from doing.

Punk rock led to the creation of independent labels because the major labels steered clear of this music, which could be offensive both musically and lyrically. Stiff Records and Rough Trade both came out of the punk movement. Two artists who were initially considered punk acts who did become commercially successful: Elvis Costello and Graham Parker and the Rumour. However, in the long run, those two acts transcended punk and showed they had true musical ability.

Punk openly condemned rock as big business and, for many young musicians, cleared the slate for the star making machines but, in the long run, punk was a reason that the British invasion declined. When countless amateurs and mediocre musicians claim the stage, professionalism takes a hike. The idea that "anybody can do this so everybody should try" might be a good idea for the young amateur, but the paying public didn't want to spend money on acts who defined "talent" as being loud, abrasive, and having more nerve than musical ability.

The end of the initial punk movement came on February 2, 1979 with the death of Sid Vicious in New York. The self-destructive music had claimed a victim.

Black Music in the Seventies

In 1977, CBS had a 15 percent share in the rhythm and blues music business. That was not only a major change in the way major labels had done business in the past; it represented a whole new era of corporate thinking.

When rhythm and blues exploded after World War II, it did so on independent labels. Radio stations that broadcast African-American music were few and far between, although a few powerful ones, like WLAC in Nashville, were extremely influential.

In 1958, only 70 radio station in America were aimed directly at a black audience. By 1972, black radio was so important to pop music that pop records were often started or "broken" on black radio before reaching the pop audience.

In the late 60s the term "soul" came to be the new term for African-American music and in 1972 CBS created a division for "Soul" music. The corporation also deliberately set out to improve its image in the black community.

The real power for R&B came with the emergence of disco music in night spots, clubs, and even lofts during the mid-70s. Disco clubs provided a marketing outlet which saw this music grow in popularity despite a lack of airplay and even without marketing or advertising. The key ingredient was the disc jockeys at disco clubs, who played records for the dancers on the floor. If a record "worked," people knew it immediately, and disco patrons were quick to purchase the best recordings. The result was that a whole new industry sprang up virtually overnight. By the 1974 recession, when the music industry suffered severe losses in revenue, disco was the one music that survived and thrived: by then there were about 1,500 discotheques in the country.

Disco music also affected technology. Dancers wanted recordings longer than three minutes, so disc jockeys used tape loops and other electronic wizardry to expand the length of a song. Soon artists recorded songs that lasted much longer than the typical pop record. Out of that came the 12-inch single, first introduced by the Salsoul label, owned by the Latin record company Cayre Corporation.

Technology

The Commodore PET, the first all-in-one home computer, was introduced in January during the Consumer Electronics Show in Chicago. Apple Computer is incorporated on January 3. On June 10, the first Apple II series computers went on sale. The Tandy Corporations TRS-80 Model I computer is announced at a press conference on August 3.

A resolution against copyright infringement of video tapes was issued on September by Interpol. That copyright notice remains cited in warnings during pre-credits of DVDs and video cassettes.

On November 28, the first digitally recorded album to be released commercially in the United States, On Green Dolphin Street, was recorded by jazz saxophonist Archie Shepp.

"Lucille"

Kenny Rogers' recording of "Lucille" was a huge hit in 1977; it reached number one for two weeks and won the Grammy for Country Male Vocal and the CMA Awards for "Single of the Year" and "Song of the Year." The song was written by Roger Bowling and Hal Bynum and produced by Larry Butler; in addition to it's success on the country chart, it reached number five on the Billboard Hot 100. The song was an international hit, reaching the top of the charts in Canada, Yugoslavia, the U.K., Ireland, Scotland, Switzerland, Australia, Austria and the Netherlands.

Nashville going pop

During the summer of 1977 there were several newspaper articles reporting that the music industry was in decline. There was also the issue with some long-time music industry citizens that Nashville was abandoning its country roots and going "pop." In one article, Wesley Rose stated, "Apparently there are discontented people who don't like the idea of Nashville being the country music leader. Personally, I'm very happy with it. We have a few people in this town who, because of a lack of understanding of country music, decided recently they want this town called 'Pop City' instead of "Country Music City" They don't realize there are 20 Pop Cities in the nation and there's only one Country Music City. And this is it." He continued that things will be straightened out when "the discontented people learn not to muddy up the water and get back to cutting country songs."

Nashville and contemporary Christian music

The 1960s counterculture led to a Christian counterculture during the 1977-1978 period. Jimmy Carter, a "born again" Christian was sworn into office in January, 1977. The early days of this "born again" movement featured young people singing "Jesus music," which had fundamentalist Christian lyrics to rock and pop songs.

In 1977, Debbie Boone had a hit with "You Light Up My Life," which was a pop hit that many linked to the Christian message. B.J. Thomas, who'd had a number of pop hits ("Raindrops Keep Falling On My Head," "Somebody Done Somebody Wrong Song" and others) had a born again experience and recorded his album, *Home Where I Belong*, produced by Chris Christian.

Alleluia, a Praise Gathering for Believers by the Bill Gaither Trio, recorded in Nashville and released in 1977 on Nashville-based Benson Records, became the first million selling Christian album. Gaither, one of the most important figures in the history of Christian music, lived in Alexandria, Indiana but recorded his early albums in Nashville.

Also in 1977, 17-year old Amy Grant released her debut self-titled album. "Old Man's Rubble," "What a Difference You've Made in My Life" and "Beautiful Music" quickly received airplay on Christian radio stations.

A leading center for contemporary Christian music in Nashville was the Belmont Church (formerly the Belmont Church of Christ) located on Music Row and led by pastor Don Finto. Across the street was the Koinonia Coffee House where a number of Christian singers performed. Amy Grant, Michael W. Smith, Dogwood and other artists attended Belmont Church and performed at Koinonia during those early years.

Contemporary Christian Music: A Brief History

Contemporary Christian music was an outgrowth of "Jesus Music" from the Jesus Revolution, which was a product of the 1960s counterculture; it was also the counterculture of mainstream Christianity. It was an idealistic attempt to return religion to a "purer" Christianity. The early participants in the Jesus Revolution were young and innocent and the music they produced was filled with hope and idealism and, just like in the American countercultural movement, there was also a strong anti-establishment bias.

Within Christianity, the fundamentalist counterculture entered the mainstream in 1976 when Jimmy Carter, a "born-again" evangelical, was elected President. That brought immense amount of media coverage to the evangelical movement in the United States. In a 1976 survey, the Gallup Poll found that one out of every three Americans considered themselves a "born again" Christian; that same year, for the first time since World War II, church attendance increased rather than decreased.

During the mid-1960s the church had been on the decline with attendance decreasing and interest from the youth waning. The Jesus Revolution of the late 60s and early 70s took the gospel back to the street, largely via music.

America underwent a spiritual awakening and Christianity that was fundamental in its beliefs, active in its faith, and in touch with the contemporary culture became acceptable. The term "born again" became known, accepted, and practiced, with many Americans undergoing a rebirth in their spiritual lives. That was highlighted in 1977 by the publication of the book *Born Again* by Nixon's former hatchet man, Chuck Colson, and the beginning of Jimmy Carter's presidency. Carter's campaign and presidency made the born-again movement known and accepted to a wide cross-section of Americans who had looked with disfavor on the contemporary Christian culture. It also forced the press to seriously examine the Christian culture.

Christian bookstores, which sold Bibles, Christian books, sheet music, trinkets and other Chritian-themed objects, moved into malls and away from their former head shop image, Christian books proliferated, and Christian music became widely accepted. The Christian culture became big business as it moved from retail outlets into homes via recordings, books, and assorted trinkets and artifacts worn or hung on walls, in addition to increased church growth. Television evangelists became leading populist figures and magazines by, about, and for Christians delivered their messages straight to the living room.

By 1976 there was an infrastructure in place for contemporary Christian music to grow. A marketing network of Christian bookstores, represented by a trade organization, the Christian Booksellers Association, was firmly in place. The Christian Bookseller's Association had begun in 1950 with about 25 stores; in 1976 they represented 2,800 members, who generated $500 million in sales, up from $100 million in 1971. Average annual revenue jumped 17.4 percent per year, almost twice the growth of secular bookstores, which was listed at nine percent per year.

The early Christian bookstores were mostly family-owned but evolved from a store that was primarily a ministry which offered some religious books for sale into one which was recognized as a family business, concerned deeply with ministry but also aware of the need to institute sound business practices in order to survive.

When the Christian Bookseller's Association began, it represented stores that sold Bibles and books; gradually the stock began to diversify with music, Sunday school curriculums, greeting cards, jewelry, and gifts. Their growth came because they provided Christian product unavailable in other outlets.

By 1976 a trade organization for the gospel music industry, the Gospel Music Association, was well-established. The GMA had developed the "Dove Award" for gospel music performers, and those awards brought recognition and attention to Christian music. The roots for this organization and those awards went back to the previous decade.

The Gospel Music Association was an outgrowth of the National Quartet Convention, first held in October 1956 in Memphis. It was a joint venture between the Blackwoods and Statesman quartets, who owned it and viewed it as a business venture. This group obtained a charter for the GMA from the state of Tennessee in 1964, joining forces with a group in Nashville to elect the first board of directors. Among the founding fathers were James Blackwood, J.D. Sumner, Cecil Blackwood, and Don Butler; Tennessee Ernie Ford was elected the first president.

The idea of an awards ceremony honoring those in gospel music was first presented by Bill Gaither at a GMA quarterly board meeting in 1968; the first ceremony occurred on October 10, 1969, in the penthouse of the Peabody Hotel in Memphs.

The name "Dove" came from Bill Gaither while the design came from Les Beasley, who worked with an artist on the concept. The Dove Awards continued to grow and moved to Nashville, where the gospel music business was increasingly centered.

The year 1977 marked the beginning of a new era in music and religion--the era of Contemporary Christian Music.

The first "star" in contemporary Christian music was Evie Tornquist but she married, stopped touring and recording for awhile and devoted herself to being a wife and mother. When she did return to gospel, she directed her energies to the church.

B.J. Thomas had a celebrated conversion in the mid-70s; he had been a pop star before his conversion (he had reportedly sold 32 million records with hits such as "Raindrops Keep Falling On My Head," "Somebody Done Somebody Wrong Song," and others) and afterwards began recording Christian music for Word Records. Problems soon developed at his concerts when two sets of fans showed up--one wanting the old pop hits and the other wanting just Christian songs. Finally, the conflict proved too much and he moved out of gospel.

In 1977 Debbie Boone had one of the biggest hits of the year--"You Light Up My Life"--and was on her way to being the star who could bridge the gospel and secular worlds. She won a Grammy for "Best New Artist" and followed this with a number one song on the country music charts but, again, a husband and family took precedence as she withdrew from her performing career to a more low-key life with occasional performances and records.

Amy Grant became the first artist to be comfortable as a Christian entertainer with success in the mainstream secular field. In 1976, when she released her debut album, she was a young high school student. Her second album was *My Father's Eyes* and Amy's brother-in-law, Dan Harrell, joined Mike Blanton, the head of Word's Nashville office and instrumental in orchestrating the marketing of the second album, in forming a management firm with Amy as their first artist.

The NARAS (National Academy of Recording Arts and Sciences) board of directors was beginning to recognize gospel music as a significant style of American music; in 1976 there had only been three categories for gospel music; in 1977 the Grammys expanded to five awards.

Also in 1977 was the first album on a Christian label to be certified "Gold." *Alleluia, A Praise Gathering for Believers* by the Bill Gaither Trio on HeartWarming, the Benson Company's record label, achieved this honor.

Gospel Music Association and Dove Awards grow

The popularity of contemporary Christian music led the Gospel Music Association to extend their award categories to contemporary Christian and black gospel artists. In 1977, the Ninth Annual Dove Awards was a turning point for the GMA; for the first time there were categories for "Pop/ Contemporary" an "Soul/Black gospel" performers. Those categories continued to grow. The event had been held in the Fall since its inception but there was no Dove Award ceremony in 1979 so the Dove Awards could transition from a Fall to a Spring ceremony.

Contemporary Christian music continued to grow and so did sales of black gospel with increasing numbers of contemporary Christian artists living and working in Nashville and on Christian record labels, publishing companies, booking agencies and other connected Christian businesses settling in Nashville.

"Take This Job and Shove It"

An anthem for the working man, "Take This Job and Shove It" by Johnny Paycheck, was recorded on August 24, 1977 and released in October. It entered the Billboard country chart on November 5, 1977 and became Paycheck's only number one (it stayed there for two weeks). The song was written by David Allen Coe and produced by Billy Sherrill. The song inspired a movie with the same title in 1981

CMA Awards: 1977

The eleventh annual CMA Awards were hosted by Johnny Cash on October 10, 1977 at the Grand Ole Opry House. Entertainer of the Year was Ronnie Milsap, "Lucille," written by Roger Bowling and Hal Bynum was Song of the Year and "Lucile" recorded by Kenny Rogers was Single of the year; Album of the Year was Ronnie Milsap Live by Milsap, Male Vocalist was Ronnie Milsap, Female Vocalist was Crystal Gayle, Vocal Duo was Jim Ed Brown and Helen Cornelius, Vocal Group was The Statler Brothers, Instrumental was Roy Clark and "Instrumental Group was the Original Texas Playboys; inducted into the Country Music Hall of Fame was Merle Travis.

The Deaths of Elvis and Bing Crosby

On August 16, 1977, Elvis Presley died at his Graceland mansion in Memphis, Tennessee. The final concert by Elvis Presley occurred on June 26 in Indianapolis at the Market Square Arena. Earlier that day, RCA presented him with a plaque commemorating his two billionth pressing at their pressing plant in Camden, New Jersey.

Elvis was scheduled to resume his tour in August and the band members who lived in Nashville were at the airport, waiting to board a plane to take them to a concert scheduled in Maine when they heard the news of his death. At the time of his death, Elvis' records were doing better on the country chart than on the pop charts. Early in 1977 he had a hit with "Moody Blue" and, at the time of his death, "Way Down" was on the *Billboard* country chart; it became a number one record and reached number 18 pop after his death.

The next day, August 17, RCA Studio B—where Elvis had recorded over 260 songs—was closed because of a dispute with the engineer's union. A contributing factor was that artists wanted creative control to choose which studio where they recorded instead of having to record in the label's studio. RCA Studio A was also closed for that same reason.

Almost overnight a huge demand for Elvis's recordings came from fans and his recordings sold millions that year. It was the end of an era, in a way, because the first stage of rock'n'roll was definitely over. By the time of Elvis' death he was back where he started, on the country charts, and although large crowds still came to see him perform, he was bloated and overweight. Musically, he was far removed from disco, which was the new rock dominating the charts (although it was, again, a case of predominantly black music being sold to a predominantly white audience). His final years saw him as a mainstay in Las Vegas, the antithesis of rock's rebellion.

The funeral of Elvis Presley was broadcast live on NBC, ABC, and CBS—preempting the Saturday morning children's program—on June 20. The Florists Transworld Delivery (FTD) reported that the number of flowers ordered the day after the death of Elvis and delivered to Graceland exceeded the number ordered for any other event in the history of the company.

A TV concert filmed during the final tour of Elvis, "Elvis in Concert," was broadcast on CBS on October 3.

In October, Bing Crosby died on a golf course in Spain. That brought the end to another major giant and era in the recording industry. Crosby had been the major star of the 1930s Depression years; the affluence of the 60s and 70s had almost wiped those memories away from the American public.

A Bing Crosby Special at Christmas had become a tradition and "Bing Crosby's Merrie Olde Christmas," the final TV special by Bing Crosby, aired on CBS on November 30. On the special, David Bowie joined Crosby for a duet of "Peace on Earth/Little Drummer Boy."

The video technology Crosby's company had developed in the early 50s was an integral part of TV production. This technology became part of consumer's homes, and those video cassette recorders changed the way TV was watched.

There were two other deaths in the music industry in 1977. On May 29, Goddard Lieberson died at his home and on December, 7, Peter Goldmark, who is credited with creating the LP, died in an automobile accident.

Saturday Night Fever

The movie *Saturday Night Fever* starred John Travolta and featured the music of Robert Stigwood's acts, particularly the Bee Gees, who wrote most of the music. In the Fall of 1977 Stigwood and RSO's boss, Al Coury, introduced new marketing techniques to the movie soundtrack business. Four singles were released from the album in the four months prior to the LPs release--a radical departure from most record company practices which saw the soundtrack album released at the same time--or after--a film and then singles coming after that.

The singles released from the *Saturday Night Fever* soundtrack were hits and spurred interest in the film. The Dolby encoded sound reflected consumer's growing attention to quality.

This was before MTV so there were no music videos on TV—or TVs in record stores. Coury released a thirty-second trailer of the Bee Gees singing "Stayin' Alive" to 1,500 theaters across the country, further whetting the appetites of theater-goers. He also had videotape machines installed in a number of retail outlets in November and December of 1977 which showed the 30 second trailers as well as the Bee Gees in concert. By February, 1978, all four singles released were in the top ten.

In 1978, RSO and Casablanca, the two major disco labels, sold $300 million worth of recordings and RSO had five Gold or Platinum albums--half of the total they released.

The *Saturday Night Fever* soundtrack eventually sold 15 million LPs in the United States, with the Bee Gees receiving a royalty of $1.20 for each album. The Grease soundtrack sold 22 million units in the world.

The return of rock music to movie theaters was accompanied by--even made possible by--the new sound technology in theaters and movies theaters.

The Bee Gees and the *Saturday Night Fever* Soundtrack

The Bee Gees agreed to be part of the soundtrack for the film, *Saturday Night Fever*, although they were not involved until after the filming. Their manager, Robert Stigwood was the producer of the film and commissioned the Bee Gees to write the soundtrack (during filming the actors danced to recordings by Stevie Wonder and Boz Scaggs) and the Bee Gees wrote those songs during a weekend in France although they had only a rough script of the film but had no real concept of the movie. The supervisor for the soundtrack, Bill Oakes, stated that *Saturday Night Fever* did not create the disco craze but prolonged it; however, for many middle-class Americans, this was their introduction to disco.

The Bee Gees first single from the soundtrack, "How Deep Is Your Love," was number one in the US for three weeks (and number three in the UK) in 1977; their second single, "Stayin' Alive," was number one for four weeks in 1978; their third single, "Night Fever," was number one for eight weeks. "If I Can't Have You," written by the Bee Gees, was a number one hit for Yvonne Elliman and "More Than a Woman" was a chart hit for Tavares (it was an album cut on the Bee Gees album). For 32 weeks--from Christmas, 1977 until the end of August, 1978 the Bee Gees wrote the number one song for 25 weeks; their own records held the number one position for 15 weeks. Barry Gibb became the first songwriter to have four consecutive number one hits in the US: "Stayin' Alive," "(Love is) Thicker Than Water" for young brother Andy Gibb; "Night Fever" and "If I Can't Have You" for Yvonne Ellison.

The *Saturday Night Fever* soundtrack sold over 40 million copies, making it the biggest selling album at that time. During a two year period, The Bee Gees won five Grammys for the album.

By the time the Bee Gees recorded the *Saturday Night Fever* soundtrack, they had a long history in the music industry.

The Gibbs brothers, Barry, Maurice and Robin were born on the Isle of Wight in the U.K.; in 1955 the family moved to Manchester, England and the three brothers formed a band, The Rattlesnakes, with local friends. The Rattlesnakes disbanded in May, 1958 and in August the family moved to Queensland, Australia, where the brothers began performing at Redcliffe Speedway in 1960. Bill Gates, a DJ at a Brisbane radio station, reportedly named them the "BG's," after the initials of Bill Goode, who promoted races at the speedway, and Barry Gibb. (They were also named for the Brothers Gibb.)

The Bee Gees were featured on local TV shows and at resorts in Australia. In 1963, they were signed to Festival Records after an Australian star, Col Joye, was impressed by Barry Gibbs' songwriting. The group released several singles and Barry wrote songs for other artists. Their first album, *The Bee Gees Sing and Play 14 Barry Gibb Songs*, was released in 1965. Festival was ready to drop the Bee Gees when they met Nat Kipner, an American born songwriter and producer; he had joined Spin Records in their A&R department and became the Bee Gee's manager. He signed them to Spin and co-produced the group with engineer-producer Ossie Byrne at the St. Clair Studio in Sydney. With unlimited use of the studio, the group recorded a number of original songs, including "Spicks and Specks," their first hit. They also recorded cover versions of songs by overseas acts such as the Beatles.

In 1966, the Bee Gees returned to England after their father, Hugh Gibb, sent their demos to Beatles manager Brian Epstein. Epstein gave the tapes to Robert Stigwood, who worked for Epstein's organization, NEMS; the Bee Gees auditioned for Stigwood in February, 1967, and signed with Polydor in the U.K. and Atco Records in the U.S.

The group recorded their first album and Stigwood promoted them as "The Most Significant New Talent of 1967." Their second British single, "New York Mining Disaster 1941" was released without their names on the label—only the song's title. DJs thought it might be the Beatles and played the song in heavy rotation, which led to the song reaching the top 20 in the U.K. and U.S. In the US it entered the *Billboard* Hot 100 in May, 1967, and rose to number 14.

Their next single, "To Love Somebody," had been written for Otis Redding, who died in December, 1966; it entered the *Billboard* Hot 100 in July, 1967, and rose to number 17. It was followed by three more top 20 singles, "Holiday" and "(The Lights Went Out in) Massachusetts" in 1967 and "Words" in 1968. Their debut album, *Bee Gees 1st*, reached number seven in the US and eight in the U.K.

Their first promotional trip to the United States was in January, 1968, for their second album, *Horizontal*, which reached number 12 in the US and number 16 in the U.K.

Their single "Jumbo" b/w "The Singer Sang His Song" reached the *Billboard* Hot 100 but peaked at 57, then "I've Gotta Get a Message to You" reached number eight and "I Started a Joke" reached number six in the US; "I Started a Joke" was a number one hit in the U.K. Both singles were from their album, Idea, which was number 17 in the US and number four in the UK.

Their next album, *Odessa*, was a double album and reached number 20 in the US; their single from that album, "First of May," only reached number 37 in the US in 1969. Creative differences led to Robin, the lead vocalist, leaving the group in mid-1969 for a solo career. Their album, *Best of the Bee Gees* entered the *Billboard* album chart in July and reached number nine on the *Billboard* chart, but their single, "Tomorrow Tomorrow" only reached 54 in the US and number 23 in the UK.

The group released a string of singles that did not do well on the American charts and in December, 1969, Barry and Maurice split.

In August, 1970, the group re-united and released *2 Years On* in the US in October; their first single, "Lonely Days," peaked at number three in 1971; the album reached number 32 and the group made a number of TV appearances.

The album *Trafalgar*, was released in late 1971and contained the hit single, "How Can You Mend a Broken Heart," which became their first American number one, staying in that position for four consecutive weeks. That was followed by a string of singles, only one of which cracked the top 15.

The group was in a slump when they signed with manager Robert Stigwood's label, RSO. Their first album and single did not do well; their next album was not released and their Best of the *Bee Gees Volume 2* barely made it on the chart. In 1974, they recorded their album, *Mr. Natural*, with well-known soul producer Arif Mardin. Mardin's production took the group away from an emphasis on ballads to an R&B direction. The single and album, *Mr. Natural* barely made it onto the *Billboard* charts but, with Martin's encouragement, they continued to write and record in an R&B vein.

The Bee Gees moved to Miami in 1975 (at the suggestion of Eric Clapton) and began writing and recording disco songs. "Jive Talkin'" entered the *Billboard* Hot 100 in May, 1975 and reached number one; their follow-up, "Nights on Broadway" reached number ten and their album, *Main Course*, produced by Arif Mardin, reached number 14 and remained on the album chart for 75 weeks. On those records, Barry Gibb sang in falsetto, which became a defining sound for them. Their next album, *Children of the World*, was produced by Albhy Galuten and Karl Richardson and the first single, "You Should Be Dancing," reached number one in 1976. The following singles, "Love So Right" and "Boogie Child" were hits in 1977; the album reached number eight on *Billboard's* album chart, lasting 63 weeks on that chart. *Bee Gees Gold*, a compilation album containing their hits from 1967 to 1972 was released but only made the top 50 on the chart.

Their young brother, Andy Gibb, who was produced by Barry, had three straight number one's: "I Just Want To Be Your Everything" (four weeks), "(Love is) Thicker Than Water" (two weeks) and "Shadow Dancing" (seven weeks). Barry and Robin wrote "Emotion" for Samantha Sang, which reached number three and Barry wrote the film version of *Grease* for Frankie Valli.

In 1978, the Bee Gees starred with Peter Frampton in the film, *Sgt. Pepper's Lonely Hearts Club Band*, inspired by the Beatles album; the film, album and single ("Oh, Darlin'" credited to Robin Gibb) all flopped.

The Bee Gee's album, *Spirits Having Flown*, contained three number one singles: "Too Much Heaven" (two weeks), "Tragedy" (two weeks) and "Love You Inside Out" (one week); the album was number one for six weeks and remained on the album chart for over a year.

When the disco bubble burst, the Bee Gees career went into a tailspin; they never had a number one record after 1979. Their success during the 1980s came from producing and writing.

Musical Notes: 1977

Jimmy Buffett's album, *Changes in Latitudes, Changes in Attitudes*, which contained the single "Margaritaville," was released on January 20.

The twenty-fifth anniversary of American Bandstand was celebrated with a TV special on February 4. The special, hosted by Dick Clark, featured an all star band of Chuck Berry, Seals & Croft, Gregg Allman, Junion Walker, Johnny Rivers, the Pointer Sisters, Charlie Daniels, Doc Severinsen, Les McCann, Donald Byrd, Chuck Mangione and members of Booker T and the MG's performing "Johnny B. Goode."

Singer/songwriter Jesse Winchester, who fled to Canada to avoid the draft in 1967, returned to the United States and performed a concert in Burlington, Vermont. He was able to do that because President Carter had granted amnesty to all draft evaders.

The film *Star Wars*, directed by George Lucas, premiered on May 25.

Kiss was named "most popular band in America" by the Gallup poll on June 22.

On October 20, a plane carrying the Lynyrd Skynyrd group, crashed in Mississippi, killing lead singer and songwriter Ronnie Van Zant, guitarist Steve Gaines, background vocalist Cassie Gaines and assistant road manager Dean Kilpatrick. Other members of the band were severely injured but survived.

A TV special, "10 Years of Rolling Stone," honoring the first decade of that magazine, was broadcast on CBS on November 25, Guests included Bette Midler, Art Garfunkel, Billy Preston, Melissa Manchester and Keith Moon.

1978

The Disco Revolution

Disco changed the music business because it was technologically driven by engineers and producers who were often songwriters.

Disco had its roots in small, gay clubs in New York City. Sometimes the crowds, often a mixture of blacks, whites and Latinos, united by their sexual orientation, met at a juice bar or a loft or apartment for a private party and danced the night away while a Disc Jockey played records. One of the most influential early gay clubs was The Sanctuary, a former Baptist Church located n New York's "Hell's Kitchen." There, DJ Francis Grasso, "the only straight guy in the place" played records as he "improvised solutions and innovations that would help shape the next twenty-five years of popular music."

Grasso became the master of working two turntables—"wheels of steel"--with one hand on the volume fader. Grass perfected "slipcuing" where one disc played for the dancers while he listened through headphones to another record until he found a spot to jump to the second record. He held the second record with his thumb while the turntable continued to turn. When the right moment came, Grasso lifted his thumb from the second record so the music kept going and the song didn't end. That was perfect for dancers who wanted to get lost in the music for longer periods of time than a three minute single.

The music changed. Rhythm was more important than melody and lyrics were not even necessary. As disco developed and spread, the music was marketed on 12-inch singles that were heard in clubs filled with pleasure seekers.

The sound of disco was electronic and repetitive. It was made by synthesizers and drum machines with a heavy bass line that pulsed. The audience, not the singer, was the star and the spotlight was on the turntable. During the mid-to-late 1960s and especially with the singer-songwriters in the early 1970s, the audience was passive; it sat and listened. In disco, the audience was active; they danced.

Disco used new technology like the Technics 1200SL turntable and they provided a forum to create new technologies. As disco clubs grew, extensive and elaborate sound systems became an essential part of the disco sound and experience.

Rock and pop music had become album oriented formats by the mid-1970 and in 1975 singles were less than eight percent of the market. Disco brought back the single, but not just any single; the disco market wanted long singles while the record labels pressed for three minutes singles. Consequently it was new labels, such as Casablanca, that was at the forefront of disco music.

In disco, the emphasis was on the song and the groove rather than the singer; only Donna Summer, the Village People and Gloria Gaynor were disco stars. For disco fans, the songs were the stars.

Donna Summer

In 1978, Summer's recording of "MacArthur Park," written by Jimmy Webb, was her first number one on the *Billboard* Hot 100. It remained there for three consecutive weeks and was nominated for a Grammy for "Best Female Pop Vocal Performance; the song was on her live album, *Live and More,* which reached number one on the *Billboard* album chart. It went double platinum. Her single, "Heaven Knows" with Joe "Bean" Esposito of Brooklyn Dreams reached number four and her following single, "Hot Stuff" came from her album, *Bad Girls,* produced by Moroder and Bellotte, reached number one in 1979 and remained in that position for three weeks. The single "Bad Girls," from that album replaced "Hot Stuff" at number one for five consecutive weeks and a third single, "Dim All the Lights" reached number two. The album was number one for six consecutive weeks and was triple platinum. This meant that Summer had the number one album and number one single at the same time for three weeks and meant that in

1979 she had three number one singles that were in that position a total of eleven weeks.

Her duet with Barbra Streisand, "No More Tears" (Enough Is Enough)" also reached number one (for two weeks) giving her four number ones over a 12 month period. The follow up single, "On the Radio" was a top five single in 1980. She won a Grammy for "Best Female Rock Vocal Performance" for "Hot Stuff" in 1980 and performed eight sold-out shows at the Universal Amphitheater in Los Angles.

Her greatest hits album, *On the Radio: Greatest Hits Volumes I & II* was released on 1979 and reached number one *on Billboard's* album chart, remaining on that chart for 39 weeks. In 1980 she starred in her first televised special, "The Donna Summer Special."

RSO

Robert Stigwood formed RSO Records (the initials stand for Robert Stigwood Organization) in 1973 in London. It was distributed first by Atlantic, then Polydor and then by Polygram. The label released the soundtracks to *Saturday Night Fever, Grease, Fame* and *Star Wars* (*The Empire Strikes Back* and *Return of the Jedi*) and 12 albums by the Bee Gees as well as albums by Eric Clapton, Andy Gibb and Yvonne Elliman.

In addition to the label, RSO was a management firm, managing the careers of the Bee Gees, Yvonne Elliman, Eric Clapton and Andy Gibb.

They heyday of the label was in 1978 and 1979 when the *Saturday Night Live* and *Grease* soundtracks sold 70 million albums and the label had a string of hit singles from those soundtracks. In 1978, RSO had six consecutive number one singles that held that position for a total of 21 consecutive weeks; during calendar year 1978 RSO released nine number one singles. However, during 1978 RSO produced the film version of *Sgt. Pepper's Lonely Hearts Club Band* that was both a critical and commercial failure.

Stigwood dissolved his involvement in RSO in 1981 and the label was absorbed into Polygram except the *Star Wars* soundtracks, which went to Sony Classical, and the Bee Gees catalog, which reverted to the Gibb family, who negotiated a distribution agreement with Warner Brothers.

Growth

In the mid-1960s, Warner Brothers Records had about 200 people working for them. In 1978 there were 2,000 and the single job of 170 of those employees was to get records played on the radio.

Radio was a key factor in album sales. A record label released a single and the team of promotion men and women took it to radio stations and tried to convince radio station programmers to put it on the air. The promotion department was broken down into National, Regional and Local. The National promotion person was responsible for the whole nation in his field; for example, there was a Rock promotion person, an Easy Listening, an R&B and a Country national promotion person. Labels generally divided the country into five to eight regions; there would be the South, West Coast, Mid-West, Northeast and Northwest with perhaps the mid-Atlantic and a Southeast representatives. The regionals handled all of the company's roster so the person who was head of National promotion for rock constantly pushed for the regional promotion person to make his records a priority. The other national promotion people did the same.

The local promotion person also handled the entire roster and worked to get airplay on local radio stations. The strategy was to get a record on the radio and push it up the chart by constantly calling radio programmers and disc jockey, visiting stations and taking them out to lunch or dinner. Artists were expected to visit radio stations as well as do "listener appreciation" concerts. A single record in high rotation on radio, inspired consumers to go to a store and buy the album. The artist was also expected to tour in order to generation attention which would create more album sales.

Not every record received airplay on radio. Some who received initial airplay did not last on the playlist because listeners did not like it or there wasn't enough effort from the promotion person. There were also singles that received a lot of airplay but the album did not sale.

In general, about 20 percent of all the albums released by a major label either broke even or made a profit and only five percent of the albums released made a profit. In other words, only five percent of all albums released made the label profitable.

Technology

The first computer bulletin board system (CBBS) was created in Chicago and released on February 16.

Phillips, an electronics firm in the Netherlands, released a proto type compact disc player, then teamed with the Japanese company, Sony, to develop and market a standardized CD with compatible machines and software.

Casablanca

Neil Bogart, with partners Cecil Holmes, Larry Harris and Buck Reingold, began Casablanca Records in 1973; all the investors were formerly employed by Buddah Records. The label was financed by Warner Brothers and Bogart wanted to call the label Emerald City from *The Wizard of Oz* but Warner Brothers owned the rights to the movie *Casablanca*, so it was easier to get the rights to that name. Casablanca was a major outlet for disco music and released records by Cher, Kiss, Donna Summer, The Village People and Parliament featuring George Clinton.

In 1977 PolyGram acquired 50 percent of Casablanca but three years later, because of poor label performance—the label released four KISS solo albums that were not commercially successful--Bogart was ousted from the label. After Bogart's departure, the label released Robin Williams debut comedy album *Reality, What a Concept!* (1981). After leaving Casablanca, Bogart formed Boardwalk Records, which signed Joan Jett but in 1982 Neil Bogart died of cancer. Donna Summer sang at his funeral.

By the end of 1978, Casablanca, headed by Neil Bogart, had Donna Summer, the Village People and KISS and RSO, headed by Stigwood had the Bee Gees and the *Saturday Night Fever* soundtrack. Those two labels sold over $300 million worth of records that year. Both labels were jointly owned by the German conglomerate Polygram.

The two labels were not built on firm foundations. Cocaine ran rampant through the disco and record business culture during the 1970s and label executives often did not pay attention to good business practices. One of Neil Bogart's mantras was "whatever it takes," which led to money pouring out of the company to buy ads or curry favors with gatekeepers. Bogart regularly overshipped albums, sending out more than market demand and then claiming a platinum record for the wall.

Stores had no limits on returns; they could send back any number of albums and claim a full refund or credit to apply to a hot selling album on the label. That meant retailers would accept any size shipment. When Casablanca released a solo album on each member of KISS, each member received a platinum album for their wall, but the accounting department received notice that most of those solo albums were returned.

Things were a little better with RSO thanks to the Saturday Night Fever and Grease soundtracks. At the end of the year, those two albums accounted for about nine percent of revenue from record sales in 1978 and it was estimated that one in five American homes owned a Saturday Night Fever album.

Willie Nelson and *Stardust*

In April, 1978, Willie Nelson released *Stardust,* an album of ten pop standards that were favorites of Nelson. It may not have seemed like a logical choice at the time, but Nelson proved himself visionary again with that album.

Willie Nelson had released a number of country albums and singles on RCA during the 1960s but nothing really hit. He recorded two albums for Atlantic that were critically acclaimed but seemed to get lost in the shuffle of executives coming and going. He signed with Columbia and, aganst the wishes of his label—executives thought the tracks sounded like "demos" and could not compete with the country sound then popular on the radio—he released the sparse album Red Headed Stranger. The single "Blue Eyes Crying in the Rain" became a number one hit and Willie Nelson, who had moved back to Texas from Nashville after his house burned down, became a leader in the "outlaw" movement and hosted an annual Fourth of July festival.

The album *Wanted: The Outlaws* came out in 1976 on RCA and featured Nelson with Waylon Jennings, Jessi Colter and Tompall Glaser. It ignited the "outlaw movement" in country music. Willie Nelson had become a country star so it is no doubt that Columbia executives would be apprehensive when they learned of Nelson's plan to record an album of pop standards.

Nelson wanted to record "Moonlight in Vermont" but did not like the arrangement on the sheet music that he had. He asked his neighbor in Malibu, Booker T. Jones (formerly with Booker T. and the M.G.'s who hit with "Green Onions" during the 1960s) to work on an arrangement. Pleased with the arrangement provided by Jones, Nelson asked him to produce and arrange the album.

There were ten songs on the album: "Stardust," "Georgia on My Mind," "Blue Skies," "All of Me," "Unchained Melody," "September Song," "On the Sunny Side of the Street," "Moonlight in Vermont," "Don't Get Around Much Anymore" and "Someone To Watch Over Me."

The singles from the album, "Blue Skies" and "All of Me" were hits on country radio and the album reached number one on the Billboard country album chart and remained on that chart for ten years. It spent two years on the Billboard 200 album chart.

"Mama Don't Let You Baby's Grow Up to Be Cowboys"

The most famous cowboy song of the outlaw movement was "Mama, Don't Let Your Babies Grow Up to Be Cowboys," written by Ed and Patsy

Bruce; Ed Bruce released the song in late 1975 and it reached number 15 on the country chart, but the most famous version was by Waylon Jennings and Willie Nelson, released in January, 1978. That went to number one and remained in that position for four straight weeks. It was the second number one by Waylon and Willie and followed "Good Hearted Woman, which was a number one record for three consecutive weeks in 1976. The song won a Grammy for "Country Vocal Duo" for Waylon and Willie.

"The Gambler"

The biggest country song of 1978 was "The Gambler" by Kenny Rogers, which entered the *Billboard* country chart on October 28 and reached number one, where it remained for three weeks; it reached number 16 on the pop chart. The song won a Grammy for "Country Song" and "Country Male Vocal" and the CMA Award for "Song of the Year. "The Gambler" was written by Don Schlitz in August, 1976, after meeting with Bob McDill, who showed him the "open D" tuning; Schlitz then went home and wrote three songs, including "The Gambler," which he did not finish. Schlitz was working at Vanderbilt University as a computer operator on the graveyard shift and pitching songs during the day. He met with songwriter Jim Rushing six weeks later and played him some songs; Rushing encouraged him to finish "The Gambler"; it took him several weeks to complete the final eight lines.

Schlitz recorded a demo of the song and Bobby Bare recorded it on his album, Bare, but it was not released as a single so Schlitz released the demo on Crazy Mama Records; it entered the Billboard country chart on May 6, 1978 and reached number 65. on the country chart. Johnny Cash then recorded the song on his album *Gone Girl* before producer Larry Butler was handed a demo of the song by Merlin Littlefield, an executive with ASCAP. Butler and Kenny Rogers were aware of the song; they changed a few words, added a new guitar intro and added a key change when they recorded it.

It came at a good time for Kenny Rogers; he was hot and had previous number one's with "Lucille," "Daytime Friends" and "Love or Something Like It"; after "The Gambler" he had number one's with "Don't Fall in Love With a Dreamer," "Love the World Away" (on the Urban Cowboy soundtrack), "Lady," "You Decorated My Life" and "Coward of the County." The album *The Gambler* was number one on the country album chart for 23 straight weeks and on the country album chart for 137 weeks; it won the CMA's Album of the Year away.

Musical Notes: 1978

In February, a new band, Van Halen, released their debut album and guitarist Eddie Van Halen introduced a powerful new sound and technique to rock audiences.

The film *The Buddy Holly Story*, starring Gary Busey, was released in May and won Academy Awards for "Best Music," "Best Original Song Score and Its Adaptation" and was nominated for "Best Sound" while Busey was nominated for "Best Actor in a Leading Role."

The film *Grease*, adapted from the Broadway musical, was released in June.

On September 7, The Who's drummer, Keith Moon, died in London from an overdose of subscription drugs at the age of 32;

The Winterland Ballroom in San Francisco closed after a New Year's Eve show that featured the Grateful Dead, the New Riders of the Purple Sage" and the Blues Brothers."

For 22 years, CBS had aired a show on New Year's Eve starring Guy Lombardo; the show aired for the last time on December 31, 1978, two years after Lombardo's death.

In Review: 1978:

The Copyright Act of 1976 took effect on January 1, 1978. The act replaced the two cents per song payments from records sold with an escalading scale.

"Dallas" a TV show that captured huge American and international audiences, premiered on April 2.

The first test tube baby was born in England on July 26.

On August 6, Pope Paul VI died and on August 26, Pope John Paul I succeeded him. After only 33 days as Pope, John Paul I died and was replaced on October 16 by the first Polish pope in history, Pope John Paul II, who became the first non-Italian pop since Pope Adrian VI, 1522-1523.

President Jimmy Carter brought Egyptian President Anwar Sadat and Israeli Prime Minister Menachem Begin together at Camp David to broker peace in the Middle East. Their agreement, the Camp David Accords, brought peace between Egypt and Israel. Sadat and Begin won the Nobel Peace Prize later that year for the landmark agreements.

Reverend Jim Jones began the Peoples Temple, a cult religion that embraced "apostolic socialism" in Indianapolis, Indiana in 1955; in 1964 he moved to Redwood Valley, California. During the 1970s the Peoples Temple expanded into Los Angeles and San Francisco and Jones was became a public figure, appointed to head the San Francisco Housing Authority by Mayor George Moscone, who Jones and the Temple had campaigned to elect.

Reverend Jones established the Peoples Temple Agricultural Project in Guyana in 1973. There were articles critical of Jones and his movement published in the San Francisco newspapers as well a media investigations and Temple defectors that led .Jones to lead several hundred of his followers to Guyana in the summer of 1977. Friends and relatives of those who followed Guyana were concerned about the cult, which led Congressman Leo Ryan to lead a group to Guyana to investigate.

Reverend Jones had prepared his followers to drink Kool-aid with cyanide if his commune was threatened; there had already been several drills to "test" his followers. On November 18, 1978, Congressman Ryan and his group arrived in Guyana; Jones ordered his followers to drink the prepared Kool-aid and 918 died—304 of them children—in an unprecedented mass suicide.

1979

1979: The Year of Disco

On May 12, eight of the top ten spots on the *Billboard* Hot 100 chart were disco records; at the top of the chart was "Reunited" by Peaches and Herb.

Not everyone loved disco and its success created a backlash that reached its apex on July 12, 1979, when a Chicago disc jockey burned a pile of disco records in center field at Comiskey Park during a double-header between a Detroit Tigers-Chicago White Sox.

The most visible reminder of the music came from the Village People, six well-built males who appealed to the gay audience. Their recordings were produced by Jacques Morali 1977-1979, and their most enduring song was "Y.M.C.A" which became part of mainstream American culture everywhere from sporting events, where crowds stand and sing along, to dance clubs. The song with its hand gestures, debuted on January 6 on the TV show, "American Bandstand."

The Bee Gees hit, "Love You Inside Out," became their sixth consecutive number one single on June 9, tying the Beatles with that achievement. A week later, Donna Summer's single, "Hot Stuff" and album *Bad Girls* were number one on their respective charts. This made Summer the first female to have the number one single and album at the same time—twice. On June 30, she became the first female artist to have two of the top three songs on the *Billboard* Hot 100 with "Hot Stuff" at number one and "Bad Girls" at number three. They remained in the top three for four weeks.

On July 14, for the third time in an eight month period, Donna Summer had the number one single ("Bad Girls") and number one album (*Bad Girls*) at the same time. The album *Bad Girls* remained at number one for six consecutive weeks. One week later, Summer had the number one slot on three *Billboard* charts—Hot 100, Hot Soul Singles and *Billboard* 200 album chart--with "Bad Girls. That same week, the top six positions and seven of the top ten slots on the *Billboard* Hot 100 were disco records.

On November 3, Donna Summer became the first female artist to have five top ten hits in the same calendar year. Two weeks later, Summer again had two songs, "Dim All the Lights" and "No More Tears (Enough is Enough)" with Barbra Streisand in the top three slots on the *Billboard* Hot 100. On November 24, "No More Tears (Enough is Enough)" reached number one and Donna Summer became the first female artist to have three number one singles in a calendar year.

On August 10, Michael Jackson released his breakthrough album, *Off the Wall*, that sold seven mission copies in the U.S.

Studio 54

Studio 54 in New York was a disco filled with celebrities; doormen blocked those not sufficiently beautiful, rich or cool. Founded by Long Island restauranteur Steve Rubell and his partner, Ian Schraeger, Studio 54 was exclusive, elegant and gay and often in the national news. In 1979, drug and tax evasion led to the convictions of Rubell and Schraeger, who each spent time in jai.

Bob Dylan and *Slow Train Coming*

Perhaps the most surprising, confounding and significant event for the gospel music world in 1979 was the arrival of Bob Dylan's Christian album, *Slow Train Coming*. The conversion of major celebrities and artists had always been seen as an affirmation of the appeal of Christianity; perhaps the most prized catch of all was Bob Dylan and his conversion was expected to change American pop music. The belief in the Christian community was that a Christian conversion someone of Dylan's magnitude--the "voice of a generation" who had the ears of almost every major rock artist, critic, and follower--would cause massive conversions from the rock 'n' roll world and the Christian fold would be multiplied mightily. Alas, it would not be so.

Dylan's *Slow Train Coming* album—his nineteenth studio album—was released on August 20, 1979. Word of Dylan's conversion had spread and the album was eagerly anticipated, although Dylan's actual conversion experience was not well-known at the time.

Dylan's previous albums, *Street Legal* and *Bob Dylan at Budokan*, had not been well-received by critics. He was touring constantly and in November, 1978, during a concert in San Diego, someone threw a silver cross on stage that Dylan picked up and put in his pocket. He continued to perform, although he was ill, and in his hotel room in Tucson he took the cross out of his pocket and "Jesus did appear to me as King of Kings, and Lord of Lords. There was a presence in the room that couldn't have been anybody but Jesus," said Dylan. He continued, "Jesus put his hand on me. It was a physical thing. I felt it. I felt it all over me. I felt my whole body tremble. The glory of the Lord knocked me down and picked me up."

During the last month of the tour, Dylan wore the silver cross and began placing Christian lyrics in some of his old songs as well as writing new songs. During soundcheck, he worked on "Slow Train" and played "Do Right to Me Baby (Do Unto Others)" for the first time at a concert in Florida.

Dylan's band had born again Christians in it; Steven Sole and David Mansfield were members of the Vineyard Fellowship church in southern California; T-Bone Burnett had introduced them. Dylan's girlfriend at the time, Mary Alice Artes, was also a member of the Vineyard Fellowship.

Kenn Gulliksen was the pastor at Vineyard Fellowship and Artes told him about Dylan and Gulliksen sent two pastors, Larry Myers and Paul Emond, to Dylan's home. Dylan then attended a three month course—with classes four days a week—at the Vineyard School of Discipleship. He stated later that he didn't feel he could devote that much time to the course, but woke up one morning, early, and felt impelled to attend.

The course connected Dylan to the Bible in ways he had not been connected before; he was also influenced heavily by *The Late Great Planet Earth*, a 1970 book by Hal Lindsey, who was also associated with the Vineyard Church.

The songs he wrote for the *Slow Train Coming* album after his conversion frightened him; "I didn't plan to write them [and] I didn't like writing them," said Dylan. "I didn't want to write them."

Bob Dylan met Mark Knopfler after Knopfler's band, Dire Straits, did a concert at the Roxy in Los Angeles and asked the guitarist to play on his next album; Knopfler agreed. Dylan asked Jerry Wexler to produce the album in Muscle Shoals and Wexler agreed; he co-produced the album with session pianist Barry Beckett.

Dylan wanted a funkier sound on his album. He used two background singers on his tour, Helena Springs and Carolyn Dennis, Dire Straits drummer Pick Withers, bassist Tim Drummond, keyboardist Barry Beckett and the Memphis Horns.

The recording sessions began on April 30 with basic tracks and then overdubs, until the last session on May 11; his final song was "When He Returns."

Dylan promoted the album with an appearance on "Saturday Night Live" on October 18, 1979, then did a fourteen date stand in San Francisco where he only did his new, Christian material. After that he toured North American for six months.

Dylan had attracted a base of Christian fans with *Slow Train Coming* who cheered him on, but his long-time fans were frustrated and often angry about his conversion, wanting old Dylan songs in the concert. Those fans heckled and booed him.

Dylan's single from the album, "Gotta Serve Somebody," entered the *Billboard* Hot 100 on September 8, 1979, and reached number 24, staying on the chart for twelve weeks. He won a Grammy for "Rock Male Vocal" for the song.The Slow Train Coming album entred Billboard's album chart on September 8 and reached number three, where it stayed for four straight weeks; the album remained on the chart for 26 weeks.

Eagles: The Long Run Ends

It took two years to complete *The Long Run*, the Eagles seventh studio album. The album was released in September, 1979, reached number one and held that spot for nine consecutive weeks. The album contained three hit singles; "Heartache Tonight" was another number one single for the Eagles and won a Grammy for "Rock Vocal Group." "The Long Run" peaked at number eight in 1979 and "I Can't Tell You Why," which was featured in the film *Inside Moves* starring John Savage, also peaked at number eight.

There were bitter feuds in the group, intense confrontations and conflicts and Frey and Felder threatened to beat the other in a fist fight. It was time for the Eagles to come to an end and they did, although they had to deliver a live album from the tour to their label, Elektra.

The album, *Eagles Live*, entered the *Billboard* chart at the end of 1980 and reached number six, only remaining on the chart for 26 weeks. One single, an a capello version of Steve Young's "Seven Bridges Road" was released at the end of 1980 and reached number 21 on *Billboard's* singles chart. By that point, Glenn Frey had quit the band.

The *Eagles Greatest Hits, Volume 2* was released at the end of 1982 but only reached number 52 on the charts. It would be over a decade before the Eagles recorded again as a unit.

EMI/Capitol

In 1955 EMI, originally formed in London in 1931, took control of American-owned Capitol Records, which had initially been formed in 1941 in Los Angeles by Johnny Mercer, Buddy DeSylva and Eli Wallichs. EMI originally purchased 96 percent of Capitol; in 1968, EMI increased its ownership of Capitol to 98 percent. That same year, Capitol formed Capitol Industries, Inc., after merging with Audio Devices, Inc., which manufactured computer tape. That reduced EMI's stake in the new firm to 68 percent. Subsidiary labels for Capitol were Tower Records (1969-1970), Uptown and Sidewalk.

The company became Capitol Industries—EMI, Inc. in 1972 as EMI increased its holdings to over 70 percent then, in 1976, EMI purchased the remaining 30% to own the entire company.

In 1977 EMI merged with Thorn Electronics to form Thorn-EMI. The two companies had done business before; EMI sold its manufacturing division (radios and phonographs) to Thorn in 1954 and EMI acquired Thames Television (which was part of the Associated British Picture Corporation) in 1969. In 1979 EMI Music Worldwide became the parent company of Capitol Records.

EMI purchased United Artists, an American label, in 1979 and changed the name to Liberty in 1980.

In other label news, MCA Records purchased ABC records on January 15, 1979, for a reported $20 million.

Technology

The Fairlight CMI (Computer Musical Instrument), the first true music sampling machine, was developed by Australians Peter Vogel and Kim Ryrie and released in 1979. The device had a large TV monitor and a large tabletop keyboard; it could reproduce any sound. This machine was essential to the developing rap and hip hop genres as well as European pop music.

In March, Philips publicity demonstrated a prototype of an "optical digital audio disc," later known as the "compact disc" in Eindhoven, Netherlands.

The Sony Walkman went on sale in Japan on July 1. You could only listen on headphones to cassettes on the 14 ounce machine; it retailed for $199.99. In four years, new releases on 8-tracks disappeared.

It was almost a 50/50 split for consumers buying vinyl and tape in 1979, although tape was in two different formats. Vinyl LPs accounted for $2.1 billion sales, with pre-recorded cassettes and 8-track tapes each accounting for about $1 billion in sales. There were 40 million buyers of blank tape.

VisiCalc emerges as the first commercial spreadsheet program.

Slim Whitman

Suffolk Marketing filmed a TV commercial with Slim Whitman for release of his album, *All My Best* on TV. Whitman, who was considered a minor star, more popular in Europe than the U.S., surprised everyone by selling four million albums. The album was sold over TV—not in record stores—so it never charted on the *Billboard* country album chart, but Whitman outsold every country act with this album, the most successful TV marketing of an album ever done.

"The Devil Went Down to Georgia"

The Charlie Daniels Band hit, "The Devil Went Down to Georgia," was part of the Southern Rock wave of the late 1970s and early 1980s. The song featured Daniel's fiddling, influenced by Vassar Clements basic melody that was recorded an octave lower; Daniels put words to the melody and songwriting credited to the entire Charlie Daniels Band members: Daniels, Tom Crain, "Taz" DiGregorio, Fred Edwards, Charlies Hayward and James W. Marshall; the record was produced by John Boylan. The song became number one on the country chart, number three on the Hot 100 and number 30 on the Adult Contemporary charts; it was a hit in Australia, Canada, Ireland and the Netherlands. The song was censored for the single release but the uncensored version was heard on the Urban Cowboy soundtrack. The song and album were re-released on CD in 1998.

CMA Awards: 1979

The thirteenth annual CMA Awards were hosted by Kenny Rogers at the Grand Ole Opry House on October 8, 1979. Entertainer of the Year was Willie Nelson, "The Gambler" by Don Schlitz (recorded by Kenny Rogers) was "Song of the Year," "The Devil Went Down to Georgia" by the Charlie Daniels Band was Single of the Year, The Gambler by Kenny Rogers ws Album of the Year, Male Vocalist was Kenny Rogers, Female Vocalist was

Barbara Mandrell, Vocal Duo was Kenny Rogers and Dottie West, Vocal Group was The Statler Brothers, Instrumentalist was Charlie Daniels and Instrumental Group was the Charlie Daniels Band; inducted into the Country Music Hall of Fame were Hubert Long and Hank Snow.

Iranian Hostages

On January 16, after a series of demonstrations, Shah Mohammad Reza Pahlavi fled Iran with his family and relocated in Egypt. On February 1, Ayatollah Ruhollah Khomeni, who had spent 15 years in exile, returned to Tehran and established the Council of Islamic Revolution two days later. Four days later, supporters of Ayatollah Khomeini took over Iranaina law enforcement, the courts and government administration as the final session of the Iranian National Consultative Assembly was held.

The Iranian army withdrew to its barracks on February 10-11, which left power in the hands of Ayatollah Khomeni and effectively ended the Pahlavi dynasty.

By a vote of 98 percent in favor, Iran's government became an Islamic Republic on April 1, which marked the official overthrow of the Shah.

Ayatollah Khomeini urged his followers to demonstrate on November 4 and launch attacks against the interests of the United States and Israel. On that day, about 500 Iranian radicals, mostly students, invaded the American Embassy in Tehran and took 90 hostages, 53 of whom were American. They demanded that the United States send the former Shah of Iran to Tehran to stand trial.

On November 12, President Carter halted all oil imports from Iran to the United States. Two days later, President Carter issued an Executive Order freezing all Iranian assets in the United States and in U.S. banks.

The Ayatollah ordered the release of 13 female and African-American hostages in the American Embassy on November 17.

The United States entered the Thanksgiving and Christmas seasons with a heavy heart, frustrated from an inability to solve the hostage crisis and alarmed at the beginning of the Islamic Revolution that would dominated the Middle East during the coming years.

The Crash of 79

In 1978 the recording industry sold $4.1 billion worth of recordings at retail. Most of those sales came from vinyl records, which accounted for $2.1 billion in sales, but cassettes and eight-tracks each accounted for $1 billion in sales.

In 1979 the recording industry suffered a major crash, a reflection of an economic recession in the United States as well as bad business practices from the industry itself. Growth had been so certain that people assumed more recordings would be sold each year, that no matter how much money was wasted, thrown away or misspent, somehow it would all be recouped and nobody would notice. That ended in 1979.

Changes were instigated. Prior to that time, an album was awarded "Gold" or "Platinum" status on the amount of product shipped or sold. Label executives, whose bonuses depended on the amount of product shipped, regularly pressured retailers to take on stock that was unwanted or unneeded to boost their sales figures. It was a paper profit that looked good in the short term. The retailers had little to lose: most agreed to do so because they could return the product at full value or in exchange for another product at full value. A warehouse full of albums by unknown acts could be exchanged on an equal basis for the Bee Gees albums (if they were on the same label).

When interest rates skyrocketed--they eventually reached 22 percent--in 1979 the retailers could not afford to hold the surplus stock and sent it back in droves. The label executives lost millions of dollars in those transactions. Ironically, when the dust cleared it was discovered the industry had grown a bit that year in real terms--equal to about the growth in population--but took an overwhelming loss due to their returns policy and short-term business practices of executives.

Over 3,000 middle-and lower management positions were terminated by the recording labels and the generous offering of jackets, t-shirts, promotional albums and other record company goodies came to an end. From that time forward, accountants gained more power and kept a close eye to the bottom line.

By 1979, CBS and Warners had spent of $20 million for new manufacturing facilities to meet anticipated demands for albums; However, the amount of LPs returned in 1979 led them to alter their 100 percent return policy. There was also a problem with counterfeit albums among the returns.

Normally, retailers returned about 17 percent of albums shipped to them; the music industry worked on consignment with records being paid for only after they were sold. Unsold albums were sent back when the bill became due. The returns were costing the record industry about $200 million a year, according to RIAA.

The industry tried a revived price category, reducing the price of an some albums with sluggish sales to $5.98 with singles at $1.29.

In 1978, the soundtrack to *Saturday Night Fever* sold millions of albums; in 1979 hundreds of executives lost their job from lack of sales. Atari video games were blamed for distracting the kid audience and home taping also plagued the industry. Whether or not they were the reasons, the fact is that in 1979 the record industry crashed.

Albums as the Dominate Format for Rock

During the 1970s, the album became the dominant format for rock music. There were three movie soundtrack albums that were in the top 25 of the 1980s but only two could be labeled "rock" (*Saturday Night Fever* by the Bee Gees and *Grease* in addition to *A Star Is Born* by Barbra Streisand). Ten of the top 25 albums were by British acts, although many of those were recorded in the United States.

The albums that dominated the charts were *Rumours* by Fleetwood Mac, which spent 31 weeks in the number one position and a total of 134 weeks on the chart, *Saturday Night Fever*, which spent 24 weeks at number one and 120 weeks on the chart, and *Tapestry* by Carole King, which spent 15 weeks at number one and 302 weeks—or album six years—on the Billboard album chart. Those three albums show the continuing importance of British acts on the American charts, the popularity of disco—especially during the final years the 1970. Those top selling albums illustrate the shift of the creative center of the pop music business from New York to Los Angeles and the emergence of the singer songwriter.

Top 25 albums of the 1970s as compiled by Billboard magazine from their album chart:

1. *Rumours* by Fleetwood Mac
2. *Saturday Night Fever* by the Bee Gees/ (movie soundtrack)
3. *Tapestry* by Carole King
4. *Songs in the Key of Life* by Stevie Wonder
5. *Grease* (movie soundtrack)
6. *Frampton Comes Alive!* By Peter Frampton
7. *Bridge Over Troubled Water* by Simon & Garfunkel
8. *Greatest Hits* by Elton John
9. *The Long Run* by the Eagles
10. *Cosmo's Factory* by Creedence Clearwater Revival
11. *Pearl* by Janis Joplin
12. *Chicago V* by Chicago
13. *Goodbye Yellow Brick Road* by Elton John

14. *Hotel California* by the Egles
15. *52nd Street* by Billy Joel
16. *Wings At the Speed of Sound* by Wings
17. *In Through the Out Door* by Led Zeppelin
18. *American Pie* by Don McLean
19. *Captain Fantastic and the Brown Dirt Cowboy* by Elton John
20. *All Things Must Pass* by George Harrison
21. *Abraxas* by Santana
22. *Breakfast in America* by Supertamp
23. *A Star is Born* by Barbra Streisand/ (movie soundtrack)
24. *Spirits Having Flown* by the Bee Gees
25. *Bad Girls* by Donna Summer.

End of the Year

The year 1979 ended with "Escape (The Pina Colada Song)" by Rupert Holmes in the number one position. The biggest chart single hit that year was "My Sharona" by The Knack," which remained in the number one position for six weeks during the summer of 1979. Other big single hits that year were by Donna Summer, who had three, "Hot Stuff" (3 weeks at number one), "Bad Girls" (5 weeks at number one) and a duet with Barbra Streisand "No More Tears (Enough Is Enough)" two weeks at number one. The Bee Gees had three number one singles during 1979: "Too Much Heaven," (2 weeks), "Tragedy" (2 weeks) and "Love You Inside Out" (1 week). Rod Stewart's "Da Ya Think I'm Sexy" was number one for four weeks, "I Will Survive" by Gloria Gaynor was number one for three weeks, "Reunited by Peaches & Herb was number one for four weeks and there were number one hits on the Billboard Hot 100 by the Bee Gees, The Doobie Brothers, Amii Stewart, Blondie, Anita War, Chic, Robert John, Michael Jackson, Herb Alpert, the Eagles, the Commodores and Styx.

SECTION IV:
1980 TO 2010

1980: In the News

The 1980s began with the United States in a severe recession; interest rates were in the 20s and inflation was a major problem—costs outpaced salaries and income. The year 1980 started with President Jimmy Carter declaring a grain embargo against the Soviet Union and then bailing out the Chrysler Corporation with the bankrupt car company receiving $1.5 billion in loans.

At the end of January the "Canadian Caper" saw six American diplomats posing as Canadians board a flight to Zurich to escape Iran and the hostages held at the American Embassy by Iran terrorists. In Iran, Ayatollah Ruhollah Khomeini announced that the Iranian Parliament would determine the fate of the American hostages. In April, the United States severed diplomatic relations with Iran and imposed economic sanctions. Three weeks later, a commando raid dubbed "Operation Eagle Claw" was sent to Iran to free the hostages but was aborted because helicopters suffered mechanical problems; eight U.S. troops were killed after a mid-air collision of helicopters.

The Winter Olympics were held in Lake Placid, New York where the "Miracle on Ice" saw the United States hockey team defeat the Soviet team. President Carter declared that the United States would boycott the summer games in Moscow because of the Soviet invasion of Afghanistan. Due to threats from the Soviet Union, President Carter ordered a males 18-25 to register for a peace time military draft.

The eruption of Mount St. Helens in Washington state on May 18 resulted in the death of 57 and the loss of $3 billion in damages.

The United States Census, held every ten years, showed that there were 226,545,805 living in the United States. In May it was announced that smallpox had been eradicated by the World Health Organization.

The Recording Industry: 1980

By the time 1980 arrived, the major record companies felt like they had very little control in the music industry. The retailers—not the labels—stocked product on consignment, then chose what to return and only paid for what they sold. The labels lobbied for floor space and had to pay for Point of Purchase (POP) materials, such as posters on the walls of retail outlets, mobiles that hung from the ceiling or displays at the front of the store. In radio, program directors, and/or musical directors or sometimes a small group at the radio station—not the labels—decided what or what not to play. Labels pandered to those radio gatekeepers, providing artists for free "appreciation" shows or albums to give away to listeners. The labels had to absorb the cost of manufacturing, advertising and tour support as well as paying both in-house and independent promotion men (and women) to call radio stations, visit them, take the PDs to dinner at huge expense while neither the label nor the artist received any money from radio airplay. The cost of manufacturing depended on what the OPEC nations charged for oil, which was a component of vinyl.

(NOTE: Of all the developed countries, only the United States did not pay record labels and artists for radio airplay, only songwriters and publishers received payment, a result of the power of the publishers during the early years of the recording industry and the power of the broadcast lobby later.)

Artists demanded creative freedom to record whatever songs they wanted to record, pick the order of songs on the albums, pick the singles (most of the time), and pick the album cover. That freedom meant a lot of non-productive time in expensive studios as they searched for song ideas or, for many artists, took drugs that made them non-productive or just screwed around.

Promotion

Radio airplay was essential for an artist and label to have a hit single, which stimulated sales of the album and the bottom lines of record labels depended on a lot of albums being sold.

Obtaining radio airplay was the job of promotion or the "promotion man" (there were not many women in promotion). The stereotypical promotion man was a gregarious extrovert, everybody's best friend, who spent his days on the telephone, calling program and music directors, presenting them with factual reasons the artist's record should be added or moved up the radio station's chart. ("It broke in Cleveland," "the artist will play your town on this date," "your competition is playing it," "it's selling like hotcakes in Atlanta" are just a few examples). The promotion man also cajoled, begged, offered goodies (free albums to give away in a station contest, concert tickets to give away and/or a meeting with an artist). There were long term relationships between some radio station PDs and promotion men that extended back years and involved dinners, phone calls and "favors."

During the crash of 1979, labels had to lay off a number of their promotion staff and most of those laid off set up shop as an independent promotion man or joined a group of promotion men.

A group of independent men, known as "The Network," was led by Joe Isgro and Fred DiSipio. The Network was effective in getting radio airplay and, because of their effectiveness, major labels bid for their services and the costs kept rising. The labels were certain there were shady dealings but they didn't want to know; further, the Network stood between the label and the radio station so the label was protected from any illegal activities.

The Network was comprised of six to twelve individuals who were key to obtaining radio airplay; if the Network wasn't hired, it was difficult to obtain airplay and, without airplay, the single would not hit and the album would not sell. Since there might be 200 singles released in a week (from majors and independents) and radio only added three to five, the labels desperately needed the Network. The problem was that the Network's help came at a high price.

To promote a priority release, the label might have to pay the Network $100,000 or perhaps $200,000. There was no guarantee that a record would become a hit—the public always had the final say in that—but the Network could make sure that a record did not have the opportunity to become a hit.

It did not take long until each major label was spending millions of dollars a year for the Network to promote records. CBS, the heaviest user, reportedly spent $10 million in 1980 for the Network; Warner Brothers spent $5 million. That was too much money to spend on promotion—when there was no guarantee of a hit—but the major labels were trapped; they had pay for the services of the Network in order to compete with the other majors. The key was to set up a firewall between the major labels and the Network by not paying the Network directly; instead, the majors sent their acts "marketing advances" so the artist and manager hired the Network to promote their record while the label credited that as a "recoupable" expense, which mean the artist had to earn that money back from record sales before they received any royalties.

Cassettes and Piracy

The recording industry looked on the cassette as a plague and instigator of piracy. Someone would buy an LP but then make a tape of it for their car, or lend it to friends so they could make a cassette copy for their car. Consumers even compiled their own cassettes, a song from this artist, two songs from that artist and various songs from other artists in a mixed bag of favorite songs to listen to on their car's cassette player.

It had not been illegal to copy music until 1974, when Congress passed the anti-copying bill. Prior to that time, someone had to have a manufacturing plant in order to copy an LP or 45. Piracy was not practical when vinyl dominated music purchases.

A cottage industry of mass producing cassettes developed because duplication machines were more affordable than pressing plants. It was believed that for every album sold, one was taped, costing the recording industry $2.85 billion a year.

Labels responded by offering a tier of prices; a new LP's list price was raised to $8.98 while a mid-price tier for an older album was $5.98 and then a lower tier of $2.98 or $3.98 for "budget" albums. There were "cutouts," albums that did not sell and were eliminated from the label's catalog that were bundled into boxes and shipped to retailers for the "cutout bin." Retailers received those at rock bottom prices but had no choice of what was in the boxes; some albums might sell for $1 and some couldn't be given away.

If an artist was especially popular with a strong record of sales, the label might move the price up to $9.98 for a new release. Labels also nudged up wholesale prices and instituted returns policies that stopped retailers from ordering large quantities of albums and then returning them for equal value if they did not sell.

LPs vs. Cassettes

A survey by CBS in 1980 blamed home taping for millions of dollars in lost revenue. The Copyright Tribunal did a study on home taping which concluded that "home tapers purchased the most recorded music and possessed the deepest pocketbooks" and that home tapers would continue to buy vinyl albums and pre-recorded tapes. That conclusion indicated that the record industry's biggest enemies were its biggest allies. A campaign was launched, "Home Taping is Killing Music" and the RIAA lobbied for a tax on both tape recorders and blank tape. (**Coleman:** Playback, 159)

There was a physical glut of vinyl LPs by 1980, which led to a more restrictive returns policy and a market flooded with cutout LPs selling for vastly reduced prices. Cassettes were a threat to the LP, even though they were inferior sonically and less durable than LPs. Cassettes did not scratch or skip but they deteriorated quickly and were often chewed up by playback machines; however, they were portable and convenient.

There was also another "enemy" to the recording business. In 1980, the revenue for Warner Brothers Records was $445.9 million while Atari and Company, owned by Warner Communications, had revenues of $512 million. Young, male buyers increasingly spent their money on video games rather than records.

The Grammys

The 22nd Annual Grammy Awards were held at the Shrine Auditorium in Los Angeles and broadcast live. It honored the recordings released in 1979.

Record of the Year was "What a Fool Believes" by the Doobie Brothers, produced by Ted Templeton; Album of the Year was *52nd Street* by Billy Joel (Phil Ramone producer); Song of the Year was "What a Fool Believes," written by Kenny Loggins and Michael McDonald for the Doobie Brothers; and New Artist was Ricky Lee Jones.

This was the first year that "Rock" was a designated category at the Grammys. In the Rock category, Best Female Vocal was "Hot Stuff" by Donna Summer; Best Male Vocal was "Gotta Serve Somebody" by Bob Dylan; Best Duo or Group was "Heartache Tonight" by the Eagles; and Best Instrumental was "Rockestra Theme" by Paul McCartney and Wings.

In the R & B category, Best Female Vocal was "Déjà Vu" by Dionne Warwick; Best Male Vocal was "Don't Stop Till You Get Enough" by Michael Jackson; Best Duo or Group was "After the Love Has Gone" by Earth, Wind and Fire; Best Instrumental was "Boogie Wonderland" by Earth, Wind and Fire; and Best R&B Song was "After the Love Has Gone" written by Bill Champlin, David Foster and Jay Graydon for Earth, Wind and Fire.

In the Country category, Best Female Vocal was Emmylou Harris for *Blue Kentucky Girl*; Best Male Vocal was Kenny Rogers for "The Gambler"; Best Duo or Group was "The Devil Went Down to Georgia" by the Charlie Daniels Band; Best Instrumental was "Big Sandy/Leather Breeches" by Doc and Merle Watson; and Best Song was "You Decorated My Life" written by Debbie Hupp and Bob Morrison for Kenny Rogers.

The Grammy for Disco went to Gloria Gaynor for "I Will Survive."

Singles and Albums: 1980

The year 1980 began with disco music still going strong. "Please Don't Go" by KC & The Sunshine Band was in the number one position on the Hot 100 in *Billboard* but was replaced by Michael Jackson's "Rock With You," which held the number one position for four weeks. Other major number one records in 1980 were "Crazy Little Thing Called Love" by Queen (four weeks), "Another Brick in the Wall" by Pink Floyd (four weeks), "Call Me" by Blondie (six weeks), "Funkytown" by Lipps, Inc. (four weeks), "Coming Up (Love At Glasgow)" by Paul McCartney & Wings (three weeks), "It's Still Rock and Roll to Me" by Billy Joel (two weeks), "Magic" by Olivia Newton-John (four weeks), "Upside Down" by Diana Ross (four weeks), "Another One Bites the Dust" by Queen (three weeks), "Woman In Love" by Barbra Streisand (three weeks) and "Lady" by Kenny Rogers (six weeks).

Albums that reached the number one position on the *Billboard* album chart were *On the Radio—Greatest Hits Volumes I & II* by Donna Summer, *Bee Gees Greatest*, *The Wall* by Pink Floyd (number one for 15 weeks), *Against the Wind* by Bob Seger (six weeks), *Glass Houses* by Billy Joel (six weeks), *Emotional Rescue* by The Rolling Stones (seven weeks), *Hold Out* by Jackson Browne, *The Game* by Queen (five weeks), *Guilty* by Barbra Streisand (three weeks), *The River* by Bruce Springsteen (four weeks), *Kenny Rogers' Greatest Hits* (two weeks) and *Double Fantasy* by John Lennon and Yoko Ono.

The sales of *Double Fantasy*, a come-back album by the former Beatle, who had been exiled from the recording studio for a number of years, was aided by the tragedy of Lennon being killed on December 8, 1980. With that gun shot, the dream that the Beatles would sometime, somehow reunite ended.

Another Brick in the Wall

Another Brick in the Wall was Pink Floyd's second landmark album. The single, "Another Brick in the Wall Part II" debuted on *Billboard's* Hot 100 chart in January, 1980, and rose to number one, where it remained for four weeks, remaining on the singles chart for 25 weeks. The album *The Wall* entered *Billboard's* album chart in December, 1979 and rose to number one in 1980, remaining in that position for 15 weeks and remaining on the chart for 123 weeks or over two years. The album sold over 23 million units in America; its white brick cover did not contain the name of the band and was their first album since *The Piper at the Gates of Dawn* not designed by Hipgnosis.

Roger Waters had recorded his vision of Pink Floyd's album, *Bricks in the Wall* in July, 1978, with a 90 minute demo. The album was co-produced by Bob Ezrin, who composed a forty-page script based on Pink, a character based on the childhood experiences of Waters, who lost his father during World War II. The development of the character included a drugged out victim of the music industry, partly inspired by Syd Barrett. In the end, Pink tore down the wall and became a normal person.

During their tour to support *The Wall*, Pink Floyd used large, inflatable puppets that represented the characters in the album. The album also inspired a film, which starred Bob Geldof; the film was screened at the Cannes Film Festival in May 1982 and released in July, 1982, in the U.K.

Sugar Hill Records

Sugar Hill Records was owned by Joe and Sylvia Robinson. Sylvia had tasted success in the music industry in 1957 when, as part of the duo Mickey and Sylvia, their record "Love is Strange" reached number 11 on the pop charts. Recording as a solo act under the name Sylvia, she had a hit with "Pillow Talk" that reached number three on the pop chart. That song was recorded for Vibration Records and Sylvia Vanderpool married the label owner, Joe Robison, and that label evolved into Sugar Hill. Sylvia wrote and co-produced "Shame, Shame, Shame" and "Cry, Cry, Cry" for Shirley and Company in 1975; Shirley was Shirley Goodman, formerly of Shirley and Lee whose hit "Let the Good Times Roll" reached number 20 on the pop charts in 1956.

Joey Robinson, son of Joe and Sylvia, who later recorded with the West Street Mob, brought home locally recorded rap songs. When Shirley asked Joey and his friends what kind of music they liked, they replied "rap," which led Sylvia to look into that music. She didn't have to look far; Sugar Hill is in the Harlem section of New York.

In October, 1979, "Rapper's Delight" by the Sugar Hill Gang was released; it was a hit in the black community and rose to number 36 on the national chart in *Billboard*. The Sugarhill Gang followed with two more chart records on the *Billboard* Hot 100.

The major labels were unaware of rap or the hip hop culture. Although all of the majors had a black division, during the late 1970s and early 1980s, their emphasis was on rhythm and blues that could cross over to the white audience. Rock and R&B had gone corporate, and corporations need huge sales to generate huge amounts of money. Also, major label executives did not live in the 'hoods where rap music was being created.

After "Rapper's Delight," the MCs got the title "rappers" and the music was labeled "rap." "Christmas Rappin'" by Kurtis Blow on Mercury was the next big hit from rap, then Sugar Hill released "The Message" and "The Adventures of Grandmaster Flash on the Wheels of Steel." During those early years of rap, 1979-1983, Sugar Hill became the dominate label in rap music.

Kool DJ Herc

Clive Campbell moved to New York from Kingston, Jamaica in 1967 when he was 12. During the 1970s, he began working as a DJ at parties and became known as Kool DJ Herc. Coming from Jamaica, he knew reggae music and became the link between Reggae—which wasn't popular at the time--and the funky soul of acts like James Brown. Herc used two turntables and often had two copies of the same album so he could play a section of a song over and over, placing the needle to start one record while the other continued playing so there was non-stop dancing. The manual edits were known as "break beats" and the "break boys" were the mostly male audience. "Break dancing" was hyperathletic, gymnastic moves on the dance floor. This was the origin of Hip Hop.

Hip hop was a culture; it included paint can graffiti on walls and buses. The sound of hip hop came from the turntable. Kool DJ Herc knew about moveable sound systems from his time in Jamaica; the reggae culture used large sound units that could be moved and set up to create a party. The DJs did not play an instrument; the record was the instrument and the speakers were huge.

Kool DJ Herc recruited two other DJs, Clark Kent and Coke La Rock, and they played for dancers in public parks and local hangouts. Other DJs from that era were Grandmaster Flowers, Pete "DJ" Jones, and DJ Hollywood. Herc shouted out phrases as the music played and established a following that loved his deep funk and quick cuts. He found percussion breaks on different records that he could meld together; he played the break "Give It Up or Turn It Loose" by James Brown and switched to "Bongo Rock" by the Incredible Bongo Band" and then "The Mexican" by the British Group Babe Ruth to keep the music flowing and dancers dancing.

Kool DJ Herc was the pioneer who planted the seeds of Hip Hop but Grandmaster Flash and Africa Bambaataa improved it and made it national. Bombaataa, a former gang member, created Zulu Nation; the name came from the film, *Zulu*, starring Michael Caine. Bambaataa had wide-ranging, eclectic taste; he play the Beatles, Monkees, Grand Funk Railroad and Thin Lizzy in addition to James Brown and other funk artists. To protect his sources, he disguised the labels on his records.

The music and Djing crew more creative and complex as Hip Hop evolved from a music of the street and the record to recordings on cassette. Cowboy (Keith Wiggins) began using rhymes instead of just phrases with the beats and brothers Melvin and Nathaniel Glover (Melle Mel and Kid Creole) made their rhymes more literate. Melle Mel and Kid Creole united with Grandmaster Flash and, inspired by Motown groups like the Temptations, created fancy costumes and added dance steps. Cowboy is credited with coining the term "hip hop" when he was teasing a friend who had joined the Army. Cowboy emulated a soldier marching, saying "hip hop hip hop" When Hip Hop got on record, it became "rap."

Geffen Records

Warner Brothers Records courted David Geffen to start his own label, which would be co-owned by Warners with profits split 50/50. Geffen Records would be the fourth label owned by Warner Communication, joining Warner Brothers, Atlantic and Elektra.

Geffen opened an office on Sunset Boulevard, decorated it with used furniture scrounged from Warner Brothers and, dressed in his usual attire of jeans, Reebocks and a flannel shirt over his t-shirt, quickly signed Donna Summer, John Lennon & Yoko Ono and Elton John. An A&R executive, John Kalodner, signed Asia. Geffen signed with CBS International for international distribution, bypassing Warner's international group.)

Technology

The Global Positioning System time epoch began at 00:00 UTC and the Rubik's cube debuted in London at the British Toy and Hobby Fair. In May, Pac-Man, the best selling arcade game, debuted in Japan.

In June, Tim Berners-Lee began work on "ENQUIRE," a computer system that led to the creation of the World Wide Web.

The Roland TR-808 drum machine was released by the Roland Corporation in 1980. That drum machine became one of the most influential instruments in pop music and a foundation for the genres of dance music and hip hop.

Country Music

In 1980s, there were 1,534 full time country music stations. In the Spring of 1980, the Country Radio Seminar had 400 registrants representing 140 country stations.

The American General Insurance company bought National Life & Accident Insurance Company, which owned WSM-AM, WSM-FM, WSM-TV, the Grand Ole Opry and the Ryman Auditorium.

Selling country music through TV packages was successful in 1980; Boxcar Willie sold over three million copies of his album, *King of the Road*, in 1980.

Urban Cowboy

The film *Urban Cowboy* was released in 1980 and started a "cowboy craze" with people all over America wearing cowboy boots, hats, and riding mechanical bulls. It was a new version of the Singing Cowboy films with the "cowboy" wearing a black hat without a horse or ranch in sight; instead, the lead character lived in Houston, worked for an oil refinery, drove a pick-up truck and rode a mechanical bull. Starring John Travolta and Debra Winger, the plot featured Gilley's Club in Pasadena, Texas. The soundtrack album was successful—it reached number one on the *Billboard* Country Chart and spawned several hit singles, including "Lookin' For Love" by Johnny Lee and "Stand By Me" by Mickey Gilley. The album was not traditional country; on the soundtrack were songs by the Eagles, Jimmy Buffet, Dan Fogleberg, Anne Murry, Linda Ronstadt and Boz Scaggs.

Alabama

In the rock world, the Beatles ushered in an era when bands became major acts instead of solo male or female singers. Alabama became the Beatles of Country Music beginning in 1980 when they had their first number one record, "Tennessee River." There had been groups who sang in country music—the Statler Brothers and the Oak Ridge Boys are prime examples—but after Alabama there would be a number of bands emerge in country music. During the 1980s Alabama had a string of 20 consecutive number one records on the country charts. That string continued into the 1990s when Alabama became the top band in country music.

Coal Miner's Daughter

The Loretta Lynn bio-pic, *Coal Miner's Daughter*, was released in 1980. The story told the rags to riches story of Lynn with Sissy Spacek playing the singer, Tommy Lee Jones as her husband Doolittle, and Levon Helm as her father. There were appearances by Ernest Tubb, Roy Acuff and Minnie Pearl in the film. Spacek sang Lynn's song and the album was produced by Owen Bradley, Lynn's long-time producer.

Country Music in the Movies & TV

Smokey the Bandit II starred Burt Reynolds and Sally Field with appearances by Jerry Reed, the Statler Brothers, Don Williams, Mel Tillis and Brenda Lee. The soundtrack included those artists as well as Tanya Tucker, Glen Campbell and Roy Rogers with the Sons of the Pioneers who sang "Ride, Cowboy, Ride."

The film, *Any Which Way You Can*, a follow-up to *Any Which Way But Loose*, was released in 1980. Starring Clint Eastwood and Sondra Locke, the soundtrack album, which reached number five on the *Billboard* Country Album Chart, featured "Beers to You" by Eastwood and Ray Charles, the hit single "You're the Reason God Made Oklahoma" by David Frizzell and Shelly West, and songs by Glen Campbell, Johnny Duncan, Jim Stafford and Gene Watson.

The song "Theme From the Dukes of Hazzard (Good Ol' Boys)" was written and recorded by Waylon Jennings and featured at the opening and closing of the popular TV show. The TV series starred John Schneider, Tom Wopat and Catherine Bach and was based on the 1975 film *Moonrunners*; Waylon had been the narrator for that film so when "The Dukes of Hazzard" premiered on CBS in 1979, Jennings was asked to reprise his role as narrator and write a song for the show. "Just a Good Ole Boy" entered the *Billboard* country chart on August 23, 1980, and reached the number one position. Waylon's drummer, Richie Albright, produced the record and there were two versions; the one used for the TV show and a single for radio that was longer with a musical bridge and another verse and did not have a banjo. "Theme From the Dukes of Hazzard" was Waylon's twelfth number one and his only Gold single; in addition to the U.S., the song was a hit in New Zealand, Canada and Yugoslavia.

"He Stopped Loving Her Today"

George Jones' record of "He Stopped Loving Her Today" is often considered the greatest country song of all time. Written by Bobby Braddock and Curly Putman and produced by Billy Sherrill, the song went through numerous re-writes (at the insistence of Sherrill) before it was recorded. Sherrill first showed it to Jones in 1978 but Jones disliked the song; he thought it was too morbid. Johnny Russell was the first artist to record the song but his label, Mercury, wouldn't release it. Sherrill recorded it on George Jones on February 6, 1980; it was commercially released on April 14, two days after it entered the *Billboard* country chart, and reached number one. It was George Jones' first number one in six years and brought Jones back onto country radio in a big way. George Jones won a Grammy for Best Male Country Vocal, the Academy of Country Music voted it "Single of the Year" and "Song of the Year" for 1980 and it was the Country Music Association's "Song of the Year" for 1980 and 1981.

Singing background "ooohs" on the song while Jones did his recitation was Millie Kirkham, best known for her vocal on Elvis Presley's "Blue Christmas" when she sang "oooo-a-ooooa" after each of Elvis's lines.

9 to 5

The 1980 film *9 to 5* starred Dolly Parton with Jane Fonda, Lily Tomlin and Dabney Coleman; the plot centered on the three getting even with their sexist, autocratic boss. The film was a huge success and so was the title song, written and recorded by Dolly Parton. The song "9 to 5" entered the *Billboard* Hot 100 and country charts on November 29, 1980; it reached number one on both charts, remaining in that position for two weeks on the Hot 100 and stayed on that chart for 26 weeks. In 2009, the musical *9 to 5*, with songs written by Dolly, opened on Broadway.

Pac Man

Video games were found in arcades for most of the 1980s and proved popular, especially with young men. The Pac-Man game, one of the most popular video games of all time, was released in 1980.

During the 1980s, video games were viewed as a competitor by the music industry and many blamed lack of sales of recordings to video games.

Political Changes

On November 4, Ronald Reagan was elected the 40th President of the United States. That marked the beginning of a conservative political movement in the United States as the communitarian ideals of the 1960s were buried under a pro-business movement where money wasn't a dirty word anymore. In May, the term "yuppie," which labeled "Young Urban Professionals," was first used by journalist Dan Rottenberg in an article for *Chicago* magazine. The term characterized a generation whose ambition was to get rich and "Yuppie Greed" soon became a catch-word for the new, pro-corporate movement. The 1960s counterculture had finally ended.

The Dream Dies

The dream of the Beatles getting back together died on December 8, 1980, when John Lennon was assassinated at 10:45 p.m. outside his home in the Dakota Apartments in New York City. John Lennon and Yoko Ono's album, *Double Fantasy*, had been released earlier in the year and his single, "Just Like Starting Over" would reach number one on the Billboard Hot 100 in 1981. Lennon was killed by Mark Chapman, a deranged Beatles fan who had earlier that evening obtained Lennon's autograph.

On December 14, over 100,000 mourners gathered for a public vigil for Lennon in Central Park. At 2 p.m., ten minutes of silence was observed.

1981
Iran Hostages released and
President Ronald Reagan Inaugurated

On January 19, 1981, Iranian and United States officials agreed to release the 52 American hostages after 14 months of captivity; the next day, as Ronald Reagan was inaugurated as the 40th President of the United States, the hostages were released after 444 days in captivity.

About two months later, on March 30, President Reagan was shot in the chest by John Hinckley, Jr. outside a Washington D.C. hotel; also wounded were Press Secretary James Brady and two police officers. Reagan had emergency surgery and survived after several months of recuperation.

On May 13, Pope John Paul II was shot by Mehmet Ali Agca, a Turkish gunman as the Pope entered St. Peter's Square in the Vatican to address a general audience. The wound was almost fatal but he survived.

Cable Television and MTV

Cable television made significant inroads with American consumers during the 1980s.

The big breakthroughs for cable came in 1979 when ESPN went on the air and 1980 when CNN went on the air.

There was a demand for sports on TV—particularly by men—that the networks did not satisfy and an all-sports station appealed to those consumers. There was also a huge demand for news—the networks had only a 30 minute broadcast twice each night, which, because of commercials, meant there was only 22 minutes of news twice each evening. CNN came on the air during the Iran Hostage Crisis and during an election year when President Jimmy Carter ran against former California Governor Ronald Reagan. At the end of 1980, there were 28 cable networks and the successful ones realized that the key to success was in presenting something the networks were not presenting. The idea of network re-runs, which was the first stage in the programming of super stations, was not appealing enough to a broad base of consumers for them to pay.

ESPN and CNN paved the way for MTV. The audience for MTV was young people; without their parents paying for ESPN and CNN, there would have been no MTV, which came along in the package that delivered ESPN and CNN.

MTV (Music TeleVision) initially presented video clips of music 24 hours a day. Created by Warner Communications, the channel was an instant success with young people. Video had been projected to be "the next big thing" back in the early 1970s, but somehow it never quite materialized; in 1981 it materialized, but it would never have happened without ESPN and CNN paving the way.

Cable television was not a new technology, but the earliest cable stations offered only what had previously been on the networks or on local stations at a cost. The offer of a "better picture" was not enough to entice consumers to pay for something that they could get for free unless they were in rural areas where reception via antenna was weak or non-existent.

The first cable TV system was developed in June, 1948, the first full year of television programming and by 1952 there were 70 cable systems with 14,000 subscribers. In 1962, there were approximately 800 cable systems with 850,000 subscribers and a decade later, in 1972, the FCC relaxed some of their signal importation rules against cable. In November, 1972, the first commercially successful pay cable service, Home Box Office (HBO) began in Wilkes-Barre, Pennsylvania. HBO was the first to use a satellite to distribute programming.

The second station to use satellite service was WTBS in Atlanta, owned by Ted Turner, which became the first "superstation." Turner marketed his baseball team, the Atlanta Braves nationally and also broadcast old television shows and movies. Because of the popularity of those old TV shows and movies—which were unavailable to consumers unless they were re-run on network stations—WTBS because a huge success. By the end of the 1970s, approximately 16 million households had cable.

In 1984, the Cable Act established a regulatory framework that led to the growth of cable television. During the period 1984-1992, the cable industry spent over $15 billion wiring America. At the end of the 1980s there were approximately 53 million households that subscribed to cable.

Music shows came on the air—TNN and CMT broadcast country music, BET broadcast to the urban audience, and VH-1 was a video channel created by demand from older viewers while MTV was for teenagers.

Along the way, those music channels realized they had to change. After the initial novelty wore off, the demographic for MTV was 14-16 year old boys; further, people often didn't "watch" videos like they watched regular TV—with all their senses focused on the screen—but instead "listened" to MTV like they did a radio until a catchy song came on, then they might focus on the TV. As a result, advertisers were increasingly reluctant to buy time on cable music stations. What emerged was a programming model where videos were shown less while programs aimed at a broad range of consumers were introduced. Thus "Beavis and Butthead" and other shows premiered on MTV and the channel became a "lifestyle" channel with the lifestyle centered around music and popular culture.

During the decade from 1986 to 1996 the number of households with cable grew from 39.2 million or 45.6 percent of households to 62.6 million or 65.9 percent of households.

"Elvira"

Dallas Frazier wrote "Elvira" in 1966; the song was inspired because "Elvira" was the name of a street in Nashville. Frazier recorded the song on his album and it reached number 72 on the *Billboard* country chart. Kenny Rogers and the First Edition recorded it, as well as a few others, but it was the Oak Ridge Boys recording, with Joe Bonsall singing lead, Richard Sterban singing the deep bass with Duane Allen and William Golden doing the harmonies that made this a number one country hit and number five on the Hot 100 over the 1981 Memorial Day Weekend. The song had entered the country chart on April 4 and the pop chart May 16.

Tenth Annual Fan Fair

The tenth annual Country Music Fan Fair was held in Nashville in June, 1981, and over 15,000 registered for the event. During the event, the CMA and Grand Ole Opry announced that the 1982 Fan Fair would move from the Municipal Auditorium to the Tennessee State Fairgrounds. That would allow Fan Fair to accommodate approximately 30,000 registrations, twice the number that Municipal Auditorium could hold. There would also be space for 100 additional booths and 10-12,000 parking spaces would be available.

Technology

The Sony "Walkman" became the "Walkman II" in 1981; the new device was less expensive and 25 percent smaller. You could only hear the music on earphones, which made the device intimate, individual and somewhat isolating; music was private and not social.

During 1981 the E-mu Emulator was released; it had a sampler keyboard and used floppy discs; it was unveiled at the NAMM International Sound and Music Expo in Chicago and Model 001 was issued to Stevie Wonder.

The first IBM PC, the IBM 51.50, debuted in 1981; it became the dominant computer for professionals. The most popular home computers were the Commodore and the Macintosh, the first to use a graphical use interface and mouse.

"Donkey Kong" was developed by Nintendo and released by Mario; it was an instant success in arcades. The first Scientific Solutions PC add-in cards was introduced for the IBM PC and Luxor released the first ABC 800 computer. The development of "Synth-pop" was advanced by the new technology.

In 1981, Atari's profits were $1.2 billion.

The Business of Music

Major labels were part of giant corporations by the 1980s and, as the music industry developed into major sources of revenue for those corporations, there was a trend to appoint attorneys and accountants as heads of major labels, or in positions of power in the industry. That was especially true during the deep recession of the early 1980s when record sales dropped. Observing that trend, Mo Ostin, head of the Warner Brothers group, stated "I don't believe the problems of this business can be solved by business people. I think the problems must rest with the music and will be solved by music people. If you believe in the future of this business, you've got to bet on the music."

Other News

During 1981, the Centers for Disease Control and Prevention reported that in Los Angeles five homosexual men had a rare form of pneumonia which was only seen in patients with a weakened immune system. These were the earliest cases of what came to be identified later as AIDS (Acquired Immune Deficiency Syndrome).

On July 29 a worldwide audience of over 700 million people watched the wedding Prince Charles and Lady Diana Spencer at St. Paul's Cathedral in London. Later that year, the Church of England (Episcopal in the United States) voted to admit women to holy orders.

During 1981, Sandra Day O'Connor became the first woman named to the Supreme Court. In September, about 250,000 people joined a Solidarity Day March in support of organized labor in Washington, D.C.

In Egypt, President Anwar Sadat was assassinated while watching a military parade; he was killed by members of the Egyptian Islamic Jihad, angered by his meeting with Israeli leaders. He was succeeded by Vice President Hosni Mubarak.

The first use of crack cocaine, a smokeable form of cocaine that was cheaper than pure cocaine, was reported in the United States and the Carribbean in 1981.

1982
MIDI

As different manufacturers developed computers, computer related hardware and electronic music devices in the late 1970s, it soon became apparent that the new devices were often not compatible with each other. In 1981, Dave Smith proposed a standard at the meeting of the Audio Engineering Society, which resulted in the development of a Musical Instrument Digital Interface (MIDI) that enabled computers and electronic equipment from different manufacturers to "communicate" with each other.

The first sampling instrument, the E-Mu 1, was introduced in 1981 and in 1983 the first Drumulator came on the market. The E-Mu was linked to the Macintosh Computer and that device made sampling easy for rap/hip hop musicians and was a key factor in the development of rap and hip hop music that made use of previously recorded music as "samples" within a new creation.

Technology

Commodore International introduced the Commodore 64 8-bit home computer at the annual Consumer Electronics Show in Las Vegas in January, 1982. The first computer virus, the Elk Cloner, written by 15-year old Rich Skrenta, infected Apple II computers through floppy disks

Sony launched the first Compact Discs in Japan in 1982; the first plant to mass produce CDs was in Hanover, Germany. The LP could hold 40 minutes of music; the CD could hold 74 minutes and 42 seconds. Unlike the tone arm and needle, the laser did not wear out the disk which, at five inches in diameter, made it easier to carry and store.

In 1982 there were 125 million cassettes and 273 million LPs sold.

Time Magazine's "Man of the Year" for 1982 was a computer the first time it had now been a human.

In 1982, the Weather Channel debuted on Cable.

"The Message"

In 1982 "The Message" by Grandmaster Flash and his Furious Five was released on Sugar Hill Records and it addressed drugs, poverty and inner city violence. It was a grim narrative that caught on quickly with African-Americans living in inner cities. The year before, his seminal album, *The Adventures of Grandmaster Flash on the Wheels of Steel* was released which showed his turntable skills. He had studied earlier DJs such as Pete Jones, Kool Herc and Grandmaster Flowers and first experimented with DJ gear in his bedroom at home. That was how he developed and honed his skills to become one of the most influential DJs in early rap.

There were three innovations popularized the Grandmaster Flash. First was the "backspin technique" or "quick-mix theory" where he isolated short drum breaks and extended them for longer periods. He used duplicate copies of the same record so he could have one record playing with the other cued up in the same place. When one break finished, he played the same break on a different turntable, then returned to the first record and, listening on headphones and "backspinning" (qued) up the first record to the same spot so he extended that section of the record.

Another technique was "punch phrasing" or "clock theory" where he isolated a short segment—often horns—from a record and punched them in over one of his extended drum selections.

The final innovation was "scratching," which is credited to Grand Wizzard Theodore but popularized by Flash. "Scratching" meant leaving the needle on a record while moving the record back and forth, with the distorted sound bleeding into the overall sound.

Grandmaster Flash

Grandmaster Flash was born Joseph Saddler in Barbado on January 1, 1958. His family immigrated to the Bronx in New York city and he grew up there and attended a vocational school which taught him how to repair electronic equipment. His father had a large record collection that mesmerized Flash, who developed a record collection of his own.

After high school, Flash played parties and worked with rappers Kurtis Blow and Lovebug Starski. He formed his own group comprised of Keith Wiggins ("Cowboy"), Melvin Glover ("Melle Mel") and Nathaniel Glover ("Kidd Creole"). "Cowboy" claimed to create the term "hip hop" while joking with a friend who had joined the Army. "Cowboy" mimicked a soldier marching, scat singing "hip hop, hip hop" and then worked that phrase into his stage appearances.

Two other rappers joined the group briefly before Guy Todd Williams ("Rahiem") and Eddie Morris ("Scorpio") joined and the group was named "Grandmaster Flash and His Furious Five." The group were pioneers in DJing and landed a regular gig at the Disco Fever club in the Bronx.

The group signed with Enjoy Records, owned by Bobby Robinson and released their first single, "Superrapin'" in 1979. In 1980 they signed with Sugar Hill Records and began releasing singles and touring. In 1981, the group released a seven minute single that featured the first scratching on record. Flash used records by other artists to create his own unique presentations. On that seven minute single he used "Rapture" by Blondie, "Apache" by Michael Viner's Incredible Bongo Band, "Another One Bites the Dust" by Queen; "Good Times" by Chic and an original, "Freedom."

That was the first album made entirely out of other records.

"The Message' was produced by Clifton "Jiggs" Chase, the in-house producer at Sugar Hill, and featured Duke Bootee, a session musician. Grandmaster Flash was not on "The Message" and neither were any members of the Furious Five except Melle Mel, who did the rapping. Grandmaster Flash was the leader and the originator of the sound of the records, which was essential when they performed live. His knowledge of electronics was a key to the group's sound and success.

The success of the song led to the group breaking up and Flash, Kidd Creole and Rahiem joined Elektra Records as "Grandmaster Flash."

Afrika Bambaataa released "Planet Rock" during the same period as "The Message." It became the only 12 inch single that was certified "Gold."

Age to Age

In 1982, Amy Grant released her album *Age to Age*, one of the most significant records in the history of contemporary Christian music. The album contained three singles, "Sing Your Praise to the Lord" (written by Rich Mullins), "El Shaddai" (written by Michael Card and John Thompson) and "In a Little While." Age to Age was the first Christian album to be certified "gold" by a solo artist and the first to reach platinum status. That was the first of nine consecutive albums by Amy Grant that were certified platinum, making her the most commercially successful Christian artist.

Bluebird Café

Amy Kurland established the Bluebird Café in June, 1982. The acoustic listening room only seated 90 but became a launching pad for a number of singer/songwriters, including Kathy Mattea, Garth Brooks and numerous others. The listening club is located at 4104 Hillsboro Pike in a strip mall in the Green Hills section of Nashville.

Chet Atkins leaves RCA

Chet Atkins had been connected to RCA since 1947, when he first signed a recording contract with the label. He rose to become Vice President in charge of Nashville operations but during the 1970s began scaling back his administrative duties. Concerned that RCA no longer appreciated his artistry, Atkins decided to leave RCA in 1982 and signed a recording contract with Columbia Records the following year.

"Crying My Heart Out Over You"

During the 1980s, led by the *Urban Cowboy* soundtrack, country music had gone "too far pop," according to its critics, and lost its core audience. Ricky Skaggs played a major role in bringing country music back to its traditional sound. A product of bluegrass, Skaggs reached back for old songs as well as new songs with an "old" sound. In December, 1981, he released "Crying My Heart Out Over You," written by Lester Flatt, Earl Scruggs, Carl Butler and Earl Sherry that was originally recorded by Flatt and Scruggs. The release, his third for Epic after "Don't Get Above Your Raising" and "You May See Me Walkin'," entered the Billboard country chart on January 23, 1982 and was his first number one; it remained on the country chart for 23 weeks. Skagg's reached number one on nine of his next twelve releases.

"I Will Always Love You"

Dolly Parton's "I Will Always Love You" reached number one for the second time in 1982 (the first was in 1974) when she performed it in the film,

Best Little Whorehouse in Texas. The song entered *Billboard's* country chart on July 31, 1982; it reached number 53 on the Hot 100 chart.

1983
Michael Jackson

The biggest pop star during the 1980s was Michael Jackson, who started as a child star with his family group, The Jackson 5 on Motown. The Jackson brothers, from Gary, Indiana, were comprised of Jermaine, Marlon, Jackie, Tito and Michael, who sang lead. They first recorded for Steeltown, a local independent label in 1968, and then signed with Motown, where their first hit was "I Want You Back" in late 1969. That was followed by "ABC," "The Love You Save," and "I'll Be There," all in 1970, followed by a string of hits, including "Dancing Machine in 1974. Michael's solo career began with "Got to Be There" in 1971, then "Rockin' Robin" and "Ben," both huge hits.

In 1976, the group left Motown, except for Jermaine, who had married Motown founder Berry Gordy Jr.'s daughter, Hazel. The group moved to Epic and Randy joined the group to replace Jermaine.

The group, who had to change their name from "Jackson 5" to "The Jacksons" with the label switch, were initially produced by Kenneth Gamble and Leon Huff. Their first two albums for Epic, *The Jacksons* in 1976 and *Goin' Places* in 1977 yielded only one top ten hit.

The Jackson's hosted a TV variety show in the summer of 1976 and Michael starred in the movie *The Wiz* in 1977; that soundtrack was produced by Quincy Jones. The Jacksons third release from Epic, which was self-produced, was *Destiny* and yielded the hit singles "Blame It on the Boogie" and "Shake Your Body (Down to the Ground)."

In 1979, Michael Jackson released his first solo album for Epic, *Off the Wall*, which sold seven million records. The Jacksons then released the album *Triumph*, followed by a tour; after the tour, Michael and producer Quincy Jones went into the studio and produced *Thriller*, which was released in 1982. The first single was "Billie Jean."

On May 16, 1983, the TV special "Motown 25" was shown on NBC. Celebrating the 25th anniversary of Motown Records, the show consisted mainly of Motown's past; however, after a performance by the Jacksons, Michael took the stage alone and performed "Billie Jean" wearing a white sequined glove on his right hand and a black fedora. Jackson's dancing, and introduction of the "moon walk," captivated the audience and that performance became the pivotal moment in his solo career.

That performance put a spotlight on a major change in pop music. Before Michael Jackson, a singer either played a guitar or piano; after Jackson, a pop singer had to dance.

On February 26, Jackson's *Thriller* album reached the number one position on the *Billboard* album chart and remained there for 37 weeks. On December 2, the 14-minute video "Thriller" was broadcast on MTV for the first time.

Sales for the *Thriller* album spiked, and the label continued releasing singles from the album. In all, there were six hit singles: "Billie Jean," "Beat It," "Wanna Be Starting Something," "P.Y.T. (Pretty Young thing)," "Human Nature," and "Thriller." The *Thriller* album spent 37 weeks in the number one slot on the pop charts and eventually sold over 30 million copies worldwide.

In the summer and fall of 1984, the Jacksons were on their "Victory Tour," a tour plagued by logistic problems from the concert promoters. After the tour, Michael became a solo artist.

Jackson created videos for the *Thriller* album for the singles "Billie Jean," "Beat It" and "Thriller." At first, MTV refused to air them; Robert Pittman, executive vice president and Chief Operating Officer of the parent company, Amex Satellite Entertainment Company, insisted the songs were not rock and roll but rather rhythm and blues--and MTV was only airing rock and roll videos. A public outcry, as well as Columbia's threat to pull all of its artist's videos off MTV, led the cable channel to change its mind. The result was that Michael Jackson's videos gave validity to MTV's claim as a ground-breaking medium for video and did much to advance the channel and music videos as a major part of rock promotion.

Bob Dylan

Dylan followed *Slow Train Coming* with albums that embraced his Christian faith, *Saved* (1980), *Shot of Love* (1981) and *Infidels* (1983), although by the time Infidels was released, Dylan material sounded more secular although his Christian faith, which had matured, weaved its way through the tracks.

Dylan's conversion caused more celebration in the gospel world than it did in the rock world, which regarded it primarily as an aberration and viewed it with alarm. Those who followed wherever Dylan led found they could not bring themselves to follow him into Christianity and the gospel world came face to face with a reality: the growth of gospel music in the future would not come from acceptance by the secular, or non-gospel, music world, or the public conversion of a secular star, but from better marketing within its own ranks.

Contemporary Christian Music in the 1980s

During the 1980s, a shift occurred in the gospel music industry as pop-oriented contemporary Christian music began to dominate a field that had been dominated by middle-of-the-road singers or Southern Gospel acts. Aimed at young people coming of age during the 1980s, contemporary Christian music developed along the lines of pop and rock music, copying the sounds from pop radio and fitting Christian lyrics to them. While rock fed on the rebellion inherent in the teenage years, contemporary Christian music led a generation towards being fans of Christianity. The commercial success of contemporary Christian artists, and the growth in contemporary Christian music, depended on reaching young Christians who were enthused about their faith.

For contemporary Christian music there were two links to the past: the Jesus Revolution and Bill Gaither. In 1980 Gaither and his group began performing concerts "in the round" because audiences of up to 15,000 wanted to see them. Bill Gaither showed gospel acts how to have major success on tour within the Christian world.

The single most important album released in contemporary Christian music during the 1980s was Amy Grant's *Age to Age*. Beginning with her debut album in late 1976, Grant had established herself firmly with the Christian audiences, giving herself a strong base from which to attempt such a revolutionary work.

Age to Age, released in 1982, dominated the Christian music industry that year and achieved "Gold" status within a year after its release--which no other Christian album had ever done. (*Alleluia* by the Gaithers and *Music Machine* by Candle both took several years to reach the "Gold" plateau in sales).

When Amy Grant, her producer Brown Bannister, and the management team of Mike Blanton and Dan Harrell, began planning the *Age to Age* album they decided to attempt a landmark album for the Christian market, akin to *Tapestry* by Carole King in the early 70s. They wanted to define contemporary Christian music and set a standard for Christian albums. Their marketing strategy was to saturate the Christian culture with Amy Grant--something they had been doing in progressive steps with the albums that came before *Age to Age*. They convinced youth directors and music ministers to become involved by bringing kids to concerts and hosting listening parties. They wanted the entire church world to know about Amy Grant and the success they achieved with *Age to Age* was a direct result of their penetration into the Christian market. (Almost 90 percent of the sales on *Age to Age* came through Christian bookstores.) Ironically, by creating an album that was such a landmark in Christian music, it had an appeal in the pop market from consumers who wanted one contemporary Christian album for their collection, or the curious who wanted to know what all the fuss was about.

In the long run, this penetration and saturation of the Christian market helped a new artist who emerged that same year. Sandi Patti became a major artist within the Christian world while Amy Grant increasingly headed in the direction of pop music. The church openly embraced Sandi Patti during the 1980s when she became the artist most honored within the gospel world. Her concerts (often at large churches) were more like a worship service as she stood on stage, leading the service, accepting that each member of the audience believed what she believed. Sandi Patti did nothing to challenge the faith of her audience; she accepted and encouraged it.

Michael W. Smith became a teen idol and one-man boy band for many young Christians through his recordings and concerts during the 1980s. It was Gospop--high energy music with a moral message--played by a musician with a mission. It reflected the musical preferences of the kids of the '80s who wanted to hear the timeless message dressed up in the fashion of "now." It was the Old Testament in Teen Beat, new wine in new wineskins, played fast but not loose and it had a whole lot more in common with the Beatles than it did with George Beverly Shea.

In addition to Amy Grant and Sandi Patti, the rock band Petra was dedicated to evangelizing their faith. Believing that their competition was the reigning royalty of rock--REO Speedwagon, Rush, Styx--Petra went after a comparable sound. Their early albums were rejected by Christian bookstores, who found it difficult to believe that hard rock could be performed by Christians.

Petra blazed the trail for gospel rock for a number of other acts. Although the group was not the first Christian rock act, they were the first truly successful act to sell large numbers of records and have large, successful tours which attracted thousands of kids to gospel concerts. It was often an uneasy alliance between rock and gospel, ministry and entertainment, but the 1980s saw an increasing number of acts who provided entertainment in a Christian concert setting.

Music became an increasingly dominant part of the Christian culture. Songs expressed the theology and views of that culture while singers and musicians openly proclaimed allegiance to those Christian-based cultural and social views.

By 1985, the Christian Bookseller's Association had 3,400 member stores out of a total of 5,200-5,500 that sold Christian products. The CBA stores generated $1.269 billion in sales in 1985, which meant the average store generated $235,000 in business, higher than their secular counterparts in the American Bookseller's Association.

The Christian bookstores were mostly family-owned, with about 56 percent in shopping or strip malls and about five percent in regional malls in 1985. The average owner was 37 years old (compared to a 59-year-old average owner in 1965) and often came armed with a degree in business. They saw themselves as retailers and businessmen, although they still acknowledged the ministry aspect of their business. That contrasted sharply with the Christian bookstores of the late-60s, which saw themselves as primarily a ministry which offered some religious books for sale to support that ministry.

Black gospel, in the latter part of the 20th century, split into two different camps, "traditional" and "contemporary." The traditional artists had their roots in the church choir and, musically, in blues and older R & B. Contemporary artists were influenced by the contemporary R & B sound, the Motown influences, jazz and disco--or dance--music heard on the radio. The contemporary sound generally appealed to younger audiences, whose ties to the church were not as strong, while the traditional sound appealed to older audiences and those who grew up with strong ties to the church.

Although those two paths existed in black gospel, they were not two totally separate roads but rather intertwining paths that lay close together. Often played on the same gospel radio programs, often back to back, the two types of black gospel were sold together in record bins at retail outlets. The difference was mostly a matter of attitude, on the part of artists as well as the audiences, which manifested itself in music that either scorned pop (traditional) or embraced it (contemporary).

Within black gospel during the mid-1980s was a move towards a smoother sound that appealed to the white audience. That smoother sound permeated the white gospel market and provided the initial impetus for traditionally white gospel labels to embrace that music and sell it through Christian bookstores. Many music marketing executives had picked up the cue from Sam Phillips and his Sun Records of the 50s and Motown of the 60s and sought to market black music to white audiences. It was a tried and proven formula for success and enabled several black gospel acts to enjoy large followings from white audiences during the 1990s.

The term "crossover" generally means a music that appeals to several different audiences and can appear on several different charts--country and pop, R & B and pop, jazz and R&B, rock and easy listening--and therefore can sell in much greater numbers. Within black gospel, the term "crossover" had a two-fold meaning. First, there was the crossover into the pop market and, second, the crossover into the white gospel market. The crossover into the pop market had generally come from artists who went from being black gospel artists to pop artists. Those artists had to abandon gospel to cross over. Once those artists switched, they were not considered gospel anymore. The key factor in the success of a gospel artist was commitment to the gospel and the Christian life, which shunned the trappings of the world. Dedicated fans and audiences wanted to hear gospel, not pop music. When an artist forsakes gospel music, the gospel audience generally forsakes that artist.

The crossover into the white gospel market became a much more lucrative and viable alternative for black gospel artists because it allowed them to expand their market while staying faithful to their Christian commitment. Too, the white audience was generally receptive to African American artists whose music was smoother and pop-influenced.

The success of Christian and gospel artists during the 1980s set the stage for their emergence on the *Billboard* pop charts during the 1990s, when the bar code technology of Soundscan led to unbiased reporting of sales. To the surprise of many within the non-Christian world, a number of Christian albums sold in Gold and Platinum numbers and achieved high rankings on the *Billboard* album charts.

The Second British Invasion

A second "British Invasion" came with the introduction of MTV in 1982. British acts made videos before American acts did; it was part of marketing them to television. American acts did not go heavily into video until MTV arrived. The first video played on MTV when it launched on August 1, 1981, was "Video Killed the Radio Star" by a British act, The Buggles.

Musically, the new groups were defined as "new wave" and "synthpop." During the 1980s a number of "hair metal" bands from Britain were popular. Acts in the "punk/new wave" trend were Dire Straits ("Sultans of Swing"),

The Police ("Roxanne" and "Every Breath You Take"), Elvis Costello and The Pretenders. British acts were also on the *Billboard* Disco charts with 12-inch singles.

British acts who benefitted from MTV were The Human League ("Don't You Want Me"), A Flock of Seagulls, Duran Duran and Billy Idol. The term "new music" was given to Culture Club ("Karma Chameleon")

In 1983, 30 percent of records sold in the United States were by British acts. The best selling single that year was "Every Breath You Take" by The Police; Annie Lennox and Boy George were also popular. In April, 1984, forty of the top 100 singles were by British acts.

Popular British acts during the 1980s and 1990s were Simple Minds, Tears for Fears, Dire Straits, Wham!, Eurythmics, Culture Club, Paul Young, Genesis, Yes, Simply Red, The Alan Parsons Project, Queen, David Bowie, Paul McCartney, Phil Collins and Elton John and The Smiths.

Digital Technology for Music

Not since the LP and 45 rpm record had been introduced in 1948 and 1949, respectively, had the industry had a major change in recording; the 8 track and then the cassette were really extensions of the 45 and LP in that they used the same analogue recording process to record the music. That began to change when the Compact Disc (CD) was introduced to American consumers in 1983.

The idea of "laser technology" had been introduced in 1960 but the only use for early lasers was as "pointers" for those who gave talks. However, in 1967 digital recording was first demonstrated and during 1977 the Philips Company, based in the Netherlands, began research on optical discs. Two years later Philips Industries demonstrated the compact disc, which could hold pictures and sound digitally. Laser discs—about the size of an LP--were introduced which held a movie but they did not catch on with consumers, who preferred the video cassette technology. In 1979, the Japanese electronics firm, Sony, agreed to join forces with Philips to develop a musical CD.

On October 1, 1982, the first music CDs were introduced in Japan; the price for initial players was $700-1,000 and discs were priced between $15 and $20. On February 23, 1983, the CD was introduced in Europe and in June of that year the CD was introduced in the United States. The price for an American CD player was around $1,000 and discs were $16.98; at the end of 1983 there were approximately 30,000 CD players in the United States and 800,000 discs had been sold.

The compact disc and player was a completely different system; the new CDs would not play on old turntables; consumers had to purchase a new player. It was incredibly expensive; the first CD players sold for over a thousand dollars and there were few discs to play; during the first month that the CD was marketed, there were only 16 titles available.

At the time the music CD was introduced to the world, there were only two CD manufacturing plants; one was in Hanover, West Germany, and the other was in Japan. The first CD manufacturing plant did not open in the United States until September, 1984 when one opened in Terre Haute, Indiana.

In November, 1984, the portable CD player was introduced in the United States and the following year was a turning point for the acceptance of the CD when 22 million were sold to American consumers. In 1985 the first album to sell a million CDs—*Brothers in Arms* by Dire Straits—was released and that same year the first CD-ROM (for Read Only Memory) was introduced for computers.

When the CD was introduced, the recording industry thought their problem of piracy—which was a concern with cassette tapes—had finally been solved. The digital technology was so new and so complex that a consumer could only create a digital copy if they built a CD manufacturing plant at a cost of millions. The early days of the CD were like the days of the record when the requirement of a manufacturing plant to make vinyl records barred people from making illegal copies.

At the end of 1987, there were nine million CD players and over 100 million discs had been sold; in 1988 production of CDs surpassed the production of vinyl records. Tape cassettes were still popular but tape copies, with their accompanying "hiss," were less desirable than the clean, clear sound of a digital recording.

The CD came on the market during the same year that cassettes caught up with LP sales. Large collections of albums that were not mobile became a burden; the cassette was smaller and portable.

Technology

On January 1, the beginning of the true Internet began when the ARPANET completed its migration to TCP/IP. Later that month, Lotus 1-2-3 was released for IBM PC compatible computers. In March, IBM released the IBM PC XT. Also in March, Chuck Hull invented the 3D printer and Nintendo's Family Computer, known as the Famicom, went on sale in Japan.

Rock and Roll Hall of Fame

By the mid-1980s, rock'n'roll had evolved from a rebellious music rejected by the mainstream to the core of mainstream American music and artists had gone from being outcasts and threats to the American middle class and their way of life to icons of American popular culture. In the early days of rock'n'roll, many people felt it would never last; by the mid-1980s, it was enshrined as a legacy of American popular culture.

A step in the transformation was the formation of the Rock and Roll Hall of Fame Foundation, which was established on April 20, 1983, following discussions about a Hall of Fame amongst record industry executives and musicians. The first step for the Foundation was to raise money to build a home for the Hall of Fame building and Museum. Several sites were considered: Memphis, Cincinnati, and New York City. The historical basis for considering Cleveland was that Alan Freed pioneered his rock'n'roll radio show there in the early 1950s, but the real reason that Cleveland was chosen was because civic leaders led an all out push to obtain the tourist attraction and the city pledged $65 million to fund building construction. Groundbreaking was held on June 7, 1993 and the museum opened on September 2, 1995.

The first induction ceremony was held at the Waldorf-Astoria Hotel in New York on January 23, 1986; the first inductees into the Rock and Roll Hall of Fame were James Brown, Little Richard, Elvis Presley, Fats Domino, Ray Charles, Chuck Berry, Sam Cooke, The Everly Brothers, Buddy Holly and Jerry Lee Lewis. Although Cleveland was chosen as the home of the Hall of Fame, record executives and artists preferred to have the ceremony in New York for a number of years.

Inductees into the Rock and Roll Hall of Fame include performers, "Early Influences," Sidemen and Non-performers (The Ahmet Ertegun Award). Since the original induction ceremony in 1986, the Rock and Roll Hall of Fame has inducted new Hall of Famers annually.

Teen Pop: 1990s

In 1950, there were approximately 3.1 million births in the United States. From that point the birth rate increased until 1961, when approximately 4.3 million were born. A decline in birth rates from 1961-1974 followed, but another increase in the rate began in 1975, when approximately 3.2 million were born.

Translating this into the youth record buying public, this meant that during the period 1958-1978, the population age 15-25 grew from 22 million to 43 million; that can explain the explosion in the number of albums sold during the 1960s and early 1970s. Between 1979 and 1995, the 15-24 demographics declined from 43 million to 37 million. However, during the 1996-2004 period, the 15-24 demographic grew from 37 million to 43 million.

Another trend emerged during that period as well: The record buying public's age dropped to the point that the 9-14 age group accounted for the creation of young stars who had significant album sales. The first beneficiary was the boy band, New Kids on the Block. Their creation went back to another boy group, the First Edition.

First Edition

During the early 1970s Larry Curtis Johnson (b. 1953) moved to Boston, Massachusetts from Deland, Florida; he had been with The Johnson Brothers and the Jonzun Crew. In 1980, Johnson changed his name to Maurice Starr and recorded two R&B albums, *Flaming Starr* and *Spacey Lady*; those albums did not sell and Starr's solo career floundered. Starr decided to form a group who would perform songs he wrote and produced; he started a record label, Streetwise, and built a studio.

A group of childhood friends who lived in the housing projects of Roxbury, Boston, formed a vocal group in 1978. Bobby Brown, Michael Bivins, Ricky Bell, Travis Pettus and Corey Rackley began singing together and met Brooke Payne, a local manager and choreographer, at a talent show in Roxbury. Payne saw the group as a new version of the Jackson 5 so he named the group "New Edition." During those early years, Rackley and Pettus left the group and were replaced by Ralph Tresvant and Ronnie DeVoe.

Maurice Starr held a "Hollywood Talent Night" in Boston, offering a first prize of $500 and a recording contract. In 1982, New Edition performed and, although they finished second in the talent contest, impressed Starr, who brought them into his recording studio and recorded what became their debut album, *Candy Girl*. The single, "Candy Girl" was released and entered the *Billboard* R&B chart in April, 1983 and reached number one; it reached number 46 on *Billboard's* Hot 100 chart. Their second single, "Is This the End," entered the R&B chart in July and rose to number eight; it reached number 85 on the *Billboard* Hot 100. Both sides of their third single, "Popcorn Love" b/w "Jealous Girl," entered the R&B chart in November and reached number 25; "Popcorn Love" reached number 101 on the Hot 100. All of those songs were co-written and co-produced by Starr.

CMT

On March 5, 1983, Country Music Television (CMTV) went on the air; it was founded by Glenn Daniels who served as its first president. It began as a video channel, airing country music videos 24 hours a day. It changed its name from CMTV to CMT and was launched from the facilities of Video World International in Hendersonville, a suburb about 20 miles north of downtown Nashville. CMT was acquired by Opryland in 1991.

The Nashville Network (TNN)

The Nashville Network (TNN) premiered on March 7, 1983 with a huge extravaganza of a show. Ralph Emery hosted the flagship musical talk/ variety show, "Nashville Now." Other shows broadcast on TNN included "Music City Tonight" hosted by Lorianne Crook and Charlie Chase, the Statler Brothers variety show, The Grand Ole Opry, dance shows such as "Club Dance" and "Dancin' at the Hot Spots," a game show, "Fandango," hosted by Bill Anderson, "Country Sportsman," "TNN Outdoors" and "TNN Motorsports" (which broadcast NASCAR races for several years). The TNN Viewers' Choice Awards was introduced in 1988. The network broadcast re-runs of "Hee Haw." In 1991, it acquired CMT (Country Music television) which was launched in 1983 but was a small, struggling station when TNN bought it. TNN and CMT were sold in 1997 by their Nashville based owners to Westinghouse Broadcasting Company, which merged with CBS. In 1999 CBS started cancelling country music shows and pushed towards a "country lifestyle" network for TNN featuring old movies and old TV series with a "country" tint. The guitar logo was dropped. In January, 2000, they premiered their first original dramatic series, "18 Wheels of Justice." In April, Viacom, which owned MTV, acquired CBS and announced TNN would become a "The National Network" and would be a general entertainment network to compete with USA and TNT. A number of original reality shows were introduced but the only shows drawing viewers were WWF/WWE wrestling and reruns of series such as "Star Trek: The Next Generation," "Baywatch," CSI" and MadTV." In early 2003, the owners announced they were dropping TNN and renaming the network Spike TV and show male oriented movies and TV shows. In May 1989, TNN reached over half of all U.S. television homes.

CMA Awards: 1983

The 17th Annual Country Music Association Awards were held at the Grand Ole Opry House in Nashville and hosted by Anne Murray and

Willie Nelson on October 10, 1983. Entertainer of the Year was Alabama, Song of the Year was "Always on My Mind" by Johnny Christopher, Wayne Carson Thompson and Mark James, Single of the year was "Swingin'" by John Anderson, Album of the Year was *The Closer You Get* by Alabama, Male Vocalist was Lee Greenwood, Female Vocalist was Janie Fricke, Vocal Duo was Merle Haggard and Willie Nelson, Vocal Group was Alabama, Instrumentalist was Chet Atkins, the Horizon Award was won by John Anderson and Instrumental Group was Ricky Skaggs Band; Little Jimmy Dickens was inducted into the Country Music Hall of Fame.

In the News

During the summer of 1983, a severe drought in the Midwest led to water shortages.

It was a dangerous world in 1983. The United States Embassy in Beirut was bombed, killing 63 people and on October 23 the military barracks in Beirut, Lebanon was bombed, killing 241 U.S. servicemen, 58 French paratroopers and six Lebanese civilians. In October 25, American military forces invaded Grenada.

In September, the Soviet Union shot down a commercial airliner, Korean Airlines Flight 007 after it entered Soviet airspace.

The Global Positioning System (GPS) was made available for civilian use.

"Martin Luther King Day" (the third Monday in December) was declared a federal holiday by President Ronald Reagan; it was first observed in 1986.

The biggest movies of the year were *Return of the Jedi* and *Flashdance*.

1984
Super Bowl Ad

The Super Bowl on January 22, 1985, saw the Los Angeles Raiders defeat the Washington Redskins 38-9. During the broadcast, Apple Computer ran an ad for its Macintosh personal computer; two days later consumers could buy it. Unfortunately, the computer did not meet sales expectations, which led to the exit of Steve Jobs from Apple.

On September 27, Michael Jackson's scalp was burned during the filming of a Pepsi commercial and he was admitted to a hospital to recover.

The Grammys

On February 28, 1985, the 26th Annual Grammys were held at the Shrine Auditorium in Los Angeles. The show was hosted by John Denver and 5.67 million viewers watched the show, broadcast on CBS. The big winner was

Michael Jackson, who took home eight awards, a record that eclipsed Roger Miller's seven Grammys in 1966.

The show began with Donna Summer performing "She Works Hard for the Money" and featured performances by Bonnie Tyler ("Total Eclipse of the Heart"), Chuck Berry with George Thorogood and Stevie Ray Vaughan ("Maybellene" and "Roll Over Beethoven"), the Eurythmics ("Sweet Dreams Are Made of This)," Linda Ronstadt ("What's New?"), Herbie Hancock ("Rockit"), The Oak Ridge Boys ("Love Song"), "Sheena Easton ("Telefone—Long Distance Love Affair"), Irene Cara ("Flashdance") and gospel numbers by Phil Driscoll and Albertina Walker ("Amazing Grace" and "Spread the Word"). Wynton Marsalis performed "A Finale" with an orchestra.

The winners:

Record of the Year: "Beat It" by Michael Jackson (Quincy Jones and Jackson producers;

Album of the Year: *Thriller* by Michael Jackson (produced by Quincy Jones and Jackson);

Song of the Year: "Every Breath You Take" (written by Sting for the Police);

Best New Artist: Culture Club;

Best Country Vocal, Female: "A Little Good News" by Anne Murray;

Best Country Vocal, Male: "I.O.U." by Lee Greenwood;

Best Country Performance by Duo or Group: "The Closer You Get" by Alabama;

Best Country Instrumental: "Fireball" by New South;

Best Country Song: "Stranger in My House," written by Mike Reid for Ronnie Milsap;

Best Jazz Vocal, Female: *The Best Is Yet to Come* by Ella Fitzgerald;

Best Jazz Vocal, Male: *Top Drawer* by Mel Torme;

Best Jazz Vocal, Duo or Group: "Why Not!" by Manhattan Transfer;

Best Jazz Instrumental, Soloist: *Think of One* by Wynton Marsalis;

Best Instrumental Jazz, Group: *At the Vanguard* by Phil Woods;

Best Instrumental Jazz, Big Band: *All in Good Time* by Rob McConnell;

Best Jazz Fusion, Vocal or Instrumental: *Travels* by the Pat Metheny Group'

Best Cast Show Album: *Cats (Original Broadway Cast Recording)*;

Best Video, Short Form: "Girls on Film/Hungry Like the Wolf by Duran Duran

Vest Video Album: *Duran Duran* by Duran Duran;

Best Pop Vocal, Female: "Flashdance..What a Feeling" by Irene Cara;

Best Pop Vocal, Male: "Thriller" by Michael Jackson;

Best Pop by Duo or Group: "Every Breath You Take" by the Police;

Best Pop Instrumental: "Being With You" by George Benson;

Best R&B Vocal, Female: *Chaka Khan* by Chaka Khan;

Best R&B Vocal, Male: "Billie Jean" by Michael Jackson;

Best R&B by a Duo or Group: "Ain't Nobody" by Chaka Khan and Rufus;

Best R&B Instrumental: "Rockit" by Herbie Hancock;

Best R&B Song: "Billie Jean" by Michael Jackson (Jackson songwriter);

Best Rock Vocal, Female: "Love Is a Battlefield" by Pat Benatar;

Best Rock Vocal, Male: "Beat It": Michael Jackson;

Best Rock by a Duo or Group: "Synchronicity" by The Police;

Best Rock Instrumental: "Brimstone and Treacle" by Sting;

Best Gospel, Female: "Ageless Medley" by Amy Grant;

Best Gospel, Male: *Walls of Glass* by Russ Taff;

Best Gospel by a Duo or Group: "More Than Wonderful" by Larnelle Harris and Sandi Patti;

Best Soul Gospel, Female: *We Sing Praises* by Sandra Crouch;

Bet Soul Gospel, Male: *I'll Rise Again* by Al Green;

Best Soul Gospel by Duo or Group: "I'm So Glad I'm Standing Here Today" by Barbara Mandrell and Bobby Jones;

Best Inspirational Performance: "He's a Rebel" by Donna Summer;

Best Ethnic or Tradition Folk: *I'm Here* by Clifton Chenier & His Red Hot Louisiana Band;

Best Traditional Blues: *Blues 'n Jazz* by B.B. King.

Bruce Springsteen

Bruce Springsteen was a throw-back, a man who was dedicated to the music, not the music business. His statement about his music, "This is the reason to live. It ain't a job and it ain't a business," was honest and heartfelt. Springsteen's music was made for the working class and he stressed his working class roots; his insightful lyrics defined the struggles of the working class during the 1980s when layoffs were occurring as companies merged and power brokers received huge windfalls while workers got laid off.

An important reason for Springsteen's enormous success must also be attributed to his label, Columbia. By the time *Born in the U.S.A.* was released in 1984, major labels had learned the art of marketing records, how to coordinate radio airplay, tours, advertising and publicity campaigns to create a huge impact on American culture.

In 1980, Springsteen released the album *The River*, with the hit single "Hungry Heart," then recorded an acoustic album, *Nebraska* in 1981. At that point, Springsteen was selling out arena but the album that solidified his status as superstar was *Born In the U.S.A.* released in 1984. Aided by a massive marketing campaign from Columbia, the album sold 20 million units.

The big challenge for an artist in the music industry is how to sell without selling out; Bruce Springsteen met that challenge by providing the music that the CBS organization could market to the masses. His reputation stayed high with fans because he was the real deal; his story resonated with his audience who saw part of themselves in the rock and roll of Bruce Springsteen. And because CBS was able to make his records available to fans in huge numbers, Bruce Springsteen reaped the rewards of a working class hero.

Cyndi Lauper

"Girls Just Want to Have Fun" by Cyndi Lauper became an anthem for young ladies when it was released to radio and on video at the end of 1983. It quickly became a favorite on MTV and at the first MTV Video Music Awards in 1984, won the Best Female Vocal Award.

The year 1984 was a breakthrough year for Cyndi Lauper; After "Girls Just Want to Have Fun," which reached number two on the Hot 100 and stayed there for two weeks (it remained on the Hot 100 for a total of 25 weeks), she followed with "Time After Time," which hit number one on the Hot 100, then "All Through the Night," which reached number five and "Money Changes Everything, which entered the Hot 100 just before Christmas and peaked at number 27 in 1985.

In 1985, Lauper sang "The Goonies 'R' Good Enough" for the film, *Goonies*, and in 1986 had a number one hit with "True Colors."

Cyndi Lauper was born in the Queens section of New York City on June 22, 1953. Her early influences were The Beatles, Ella Fitzgerald, Judy Garland and Billie Holiday. She began writing songs and playing the guitar when she was 12. From her early years, she was "different," dying her hair a variety of colors and wearing quirky, eccentric clothing. She stood out with her quirky sense of style.

She was expelled from high school and, at 17, spent time in the Canadian woods before she moved to Vermont and took classes in art at Johnson State

College. She worked at odd jobs to pay the rent and sang in various bands during the 1970s, doing cover songs.

In 1977, she had to stop singing for a year because of damaged vocal cords. The following year she met John Turi, a saxophone player, through her then-manager, Ted Rosenblatt. They formed a band, Blue Angel. Steve Massarksy, manager of the Allman Brothers Band, heard them and bought the Blue Angels contract from Turi and became their manager. They recorded a demo and were signed to Polydor.

Their album, *Blue Angel*, was released in 1980 but did not sell; the band broke up and Massarsky filed an $80,000 law suit against them, causing Lauper to go bankrupt. She worked in retail stores and as a waitress at IHOP and continued to sing in local clubs. In 1981, while singing in a bar, she met David Wolff, who became her manager. He arranged a contract with Portrait Records, a subsidiary of Epic in the CBS Records family.

Lauper had a quirky, punk-type look, crafted by stylist Patrick Lucas, that gave her visual appeal so it was not unusual that the title of her first album was *She's So Unusual*. It was released on October 14, 1983 and, led by the single, "Girls Just Want to Have Fun," became a hit, rising to number four on the Billboard album chart and then became an international hit, eventually selling over 16 million copies.

Cyndi Lauper benefitted from MTV; she was made for the visual medium and her catchy songs and eclectic style made her an instant star.

Payola: 1980s

On February 24, 1986, NBC Nightly News broadcast a story, "The New Payola." One of those who spoke on camera, DJ Don Cox, with WINZ in Miami, was beaten three days after the broadcast.

The record companies expressed shock and dismay publicly; privately, there was relief. The independent promotion people had been bleeding the labels financially and the labels, up to that point, had no recourse but to continue paying them in order to get their records on the radio. Now, there seemed to be a way out of those exorbitant payments and also a way to get rid of independent promotion men who were more than a touch on the shady side.

Three days after the broadcast, Capitol and MCA publicly announced they would no longer use independent promotion people, effective immediately. The next week, the Warner labels, RCA and Arista made the same announcement. At that point the holdouts were PolyGram, Chrysalis,

A&M and CBS. However, on March 5, those four labels announced they were also dropping all indie promotion people.

The way radio promotion worked through the 1960s and early 1970s was that a promotion person from a record label sent a single to a radio station and then called the program or music director--or both, depending on who made called the shots on which records were added to the playlist at a particular radio station--and talked about why the station should program the record. It was the art of persuasion backed by facts: how the record was doing in another city, the commitment the label had for the act, whether or not the artist was on tour in the area, initial sales of the record and the track record of the act producing hits.

There was certainly hype involved; promotion people have long been characterized by their enthusiasm and willingness to say or do anything to get a record played. There were perks--the promotion person paid for dinner if he went out with a PD, MD or DJ, some Christmas presents, free records and that sort of thing. Promotion had a cost, but it was not prohibitive and when you realize that people didn't buy a song they hadn't heard, the cost of getting radio airplay was well worth it. If a single record got on the radio and caught the fancy of the public, then the public might buy a million copies of the album.

Independent promotion people had long been part of the music business. They might be hired by managers, artists or publishing companies to give a little extra "push" to a record. Then record companies started hiring indies during the recession because the label staff was working so many other records and it was a good business decision: outsource some promotion and the manager, artist and publisher were happy plus the label received the advantage of some extra help.

A radio promotion person is like a lobbyist for a record company's product. He or she (it was mostly he) kept in constant contact with a radio station, served as a liaison between the label, the radio station and the artist, and let everyone know the cares and concerns of those involved. Because an independent promotion person did not have to represent an entire label's roster, he could concentrate more fully on a particular single and, to the radio programmer, was more believable than the staff promotion person who had to promote whatever was handed to him.

Along the way, several promotion men formed an alliance called The Network. The key people in that informal consortium were Joseph Isgro of Los Angeles; Fred DiSipio of Cherry Hill, New Jersey; Gary Bird of

Cleveland; Dennis Lavinthal of L.A.; Jerry Brenner of Boston; and Jerry Meyers of Buffalo. DiSpipio and Isgro were the leading figures in The Network where each member had a territory he was responsible for. The indie kept in constant contact with the radio stations in his territory and, in general, developed a closer personal relationship with the station personnel than the label did. In a short while, those indie promotion people became essential in order to get a single on a radio station. Labels had to hire them in order to assure airplay; during the 1980s, the record industry was spending approximately $40 million a year on independent promotion people. Since the record labels had grown so much, and were part of large corporations, those figures were written off as part of the cost of doing business.

There are numerous advantages of being "big"--mainly having the deep pockets to support distribution, promotion and marketing efforts--but there are also disadvantages. As the major labels learned during the late 1940s and throughout the 1950s, it is the small labels who are closer to "the street" and can spot trends--and capitalize on them--quicker. Small labels don't have the large overheads of a major label, so they don't have to feed a big machine daily in order to keep it running.

A record company operates best if it can combine the best of those two worlds--large enough to sell large quantities of a hit album but small enough to be able to recognize and capture new trends in the music industry. On one hand, a label must have a close personal relationship with each artist--like a small label--but, on the other hand, it must be a huge, effective machine when it comes to getting that artist's music spread throughout the entire country--in the media and in retail--and then collect that income.

After World War II, all record labels operated with independent distribution, which got the recordings to jukeboxes, who purchased a sizeable percentage of the singles released. As more stores stocked records, the independent distributors took care of those accounts. However, by the late 1950s, there were problems with independent distribution--at least by the standards of the major labels. First, any label, no matter how small, could get distribution. That created the problem of the singles charts being dominated by independent labels in the mid-1950s. Further, a label could not really "control" its recordings to make sure it received priority handling--it was just thrown into the hopper with all the other releases.

The major labels solved some of those problems by creating their own in-house or branch distribution systems. That meant that a major label controlled all of the records it released and made sure they went to retail for sales. However, there was a huge cost involved in setting up a distribution system that covered the entire United States and labels discovered they had to generate a lot of income in order to turn a profit. That led majors to either strike distribution agreements with small labels or purchase a number of smaller labels in order to feed the machine.

There are two basic truths about the music business: A record label has to have hits and has to have stars, but you cannot buy a hit and you cannot create a star because, ultimately, the market decides what is a hit and who is a star. No customer walks into a record store, looks at an album and says "Gee, the label spent so much money marketing this act that I'm obligated to buy it." Nor does a consumer see an advertisement for a concert and say, "Gee, there's so much money behind this act, I'm obligated to purchase a ticket to the show." People buy recordings and go to shows because they have a connection with that recording or that act and that connection is emotional and beyond rational explanation.

Having said that, a consumer learns about a recording or an act through exposure through the media; for the record industry, that has traditionally meant radio, so a label needs to spend money to give that record and artist an opportunity to be heard. After the record is heard, consumers can either accept or reject it, but without it being heard, the record and artist have little or no chance. That is why the major labels spent so much money on radio promotion.

By the 1970s, the major labels were well aware of lessons from the payola scandals of the 1950s. They were also aware that the Racketeer Influence and Corrupt Organizations statute (RICO) was empowered to levy large penalties on companies who engaged in bribery. Although the record industry can--and does--argue forcefully that "gifts" to radio station personnel are akin to gifts from lobbyists to politicians, it is an argument that has not been particularly effective when politicians have looked at the relationship between record companies and radio stations.

To protect themselves from RICO, major labels have hired independent promotion people to deal with radio stations as a way to construct a "wall" that isolated them from criminal liability. That was a major reason for the rapid growth of the use of independent promotion people; it also explained how indies obtained so much power over major labels so they could demand larger and larger sums of money for their services.

A by-product of that independent promotion network was the demise of small, independent labels. Because the price of promoting a record to radio was so steep, small labels could not afford it; thus, the major labels came to dominate the industry in terms or radio airplay and record sales. Further, independent distribution began to disappear because small labels could not afford to compete for airplay against big labels, and therefore had no leverage to get into retail outlets.

The basic truth about a record label not being unable to buy a hit or create a star remained true; however, another truth emerged: It was possible to stop a record from becoming a hit or an artist from becoming a star because of the huge amounts of money required to gain access to radio airplay and retailers.

At first, major labels bid against small labels, driving them out of business. Then major labels found themselves bidding against each other-- six major corporations driving up costs that continued to spiral upward. By 1985, it was estimated that a label spent $300,000 in order to promote a single record, with the total cost of the labels to get records promoted to radio ranging anywhere from $60 to $80 million each year. Those charges were built up station by station; an independent promotion person might charge $2,000 each time a single radio station started programming a single record. That was multiplied by the number of radio stations and the number of singles released. Further, there were usually "bonus" payments if a record got into the top ten or reached number one on the charts. It amounted to a lot of money being spent in order to get records heard on the radio.

That same year (1985), the record industry grossed approximately $4.5 billion with pre-tax profits of about $200 million (or less). In other words, independent promotion was increasingly cutting into profits and pulling significant money away from the bottom line. Still, major labels felt obligated to pay whatever the indies demanded because they were trapped in a situation they had created.

When the disastrous year of 1979 occurred, profits fell precipitously for the record business; labels dropped employees and cut back expenses--but kept independent promotion.

The recession in the record industry lasted through 1982. Profits were down and pressure was on to cut costs. In early 1981, the Warner Brothers group (Warners, Elektra, Atlantic, and Asylum) led a boycott of independent promotion; the belief was that this would lead to a weakening of the independent promoters power over the labels. However, Walter Yetnikoff, then-president of CBS Records, decided to undercut the boycott. The reason was simple competition: If others would not pay for indies, CBS could step in with payments and dominate radio airplay and sales. In a harsh corporate business climate, it was suicidal to lose a competitive edge. It was also possibly suicidal to continue subsidizing escalating costs. CBS decided that other labels could commit suicide while it reaped rewards. The other labels had no choice but to cave in and follow suit. Thus The Network became even more powerful in the record industry.

In 1982, CBS had its worst year since 1971; income was over $1 billion but profits were less than $22 million. The label was spending an estimated $10 million each year on independent promotion. What saved the label was the release of *Thriller* by Michael Jackson at the end of 1982; in 1983, the label recorded its highest profits ever.

The problem of the rising costs of independent promotion continued to plague the majors. In 1985, CBS spent about $12.8 million, MCA spent almost $9 million and Warner Brothers spent about $6 million on the indies.

By that time, the majors were completely trapped. If all the majors agreed to drop the indies, the labels would be subject to an anti-trust suit. The labels could not accuse the indies of payola because the labels were not supposed to be aware of that. A boycott by a single label would just give a competitive advantage to the other labels. A government probe was possible--but who wants the government to investigate the record business when who knew what might turn up?

There was a suggestion that the RIAA, the trade organization that represents the record labels, conduct an investigation into the indies; if evidence was discovered of misconduct, the labels could fire the indies with righteous indignation.

That problem was solved, at least temporarily, when NBC ran their news story in early 1986. That gave the labels the excuse they needed to drop the hot potato of independent promotion--at least for a while.

Investigations uncovered links to the Mafia; in February, 1988, the first indictments were handed down. Ralph Tashjian, Joe Isgro's chief liaison at key stations, was charged with bribery, distributing cocaine to radio personnel, tax evasion and obstruction of justice. Tashjian's wife, Valerie, was charged with abetting tax fraud. William Craig, who worked for Isgro was charged with bribery and tax evasion; George Wilson Crowell, with KIQQ in Los Angeles, was charged with failure to file tax returns.

At the end of November, 1989, Joe Isgro was charged with payola, drug trafficking, racketeering, obstruction of justice and tax fraud. Ray Anderson, former head of Epic Records, was accused of taking kickbacks from Isgro.

The 57 counts against Isgro were eventually thrown out; Isgro went on to become executive producer of the movie *Hoffa* in 1992.

Isgro, an alleged member of the Gambino crime family in New York, and two associates later served time in prison for running a loan sharking and extortion operation.

"God Bless the U.S.A."

Lee Greenwood's iconic song, "God Bless the U.S.A." was inspired by the Korean Air tragedy when a Soviet plane shot down Korean flight 007 on September 1, 1983. The plane was going from Anchorage to Seoul and strayed into Soviet airspace; all 269 on board were killed. Green recorded the song in November, 1983, and it was released on May 21, 1984; it entered the *Billboard* country chart on May 26 and reached number seven. During the 1984 Republican Convention, when Ronald Reagan was nominated for a second term, Greenwood performed the song. Greenwood has since performed the song numerous times for numerous events. The song became popular again after the 9/11 attack and during the war with Iraq in 1990 and 1991. In 2001 the single was re-released when the United States invaded Iraq. The 1984 version was CMA's "Song of the Year" for 1984.

Ronald Reagan re-elected

The Presidential election on November 6, 1984 saw Ronald Reagan defeat Walter Mondale. Reagan received 59 percent of the popular vote and carried 49 states in the Electoral College; the only states Mondale won was his home state of Minnesota and Washington, D.C.

"Do They Know It's Christmas?"

On October 23, the BBC News broadcast a special about the famine in Ethiopia. The report, presented by Michael Buerk, told of the starvation of thousands of people in Ethiopia, where ten million lives were at risk. The famine was caused by a lack of rainfall, which created a drought while the government put most of their money into the military. Bob Geldof, lead singer for The Boomtown Rats, an Irish rock band, watched that broadcast and was determined to do something.

Geldof, with Midge Ure from the group Ultrvox, formed Band Aid, a charity supergroup to raise money for the Ethiopian famine relief. They wrote a song, "Do They Know It's Christmas," called friends from other groups and on November 25, 1984, went into SARM studios in Notting Hill, London, and recorded the song with a group of participants that included

Phil Collins, Bono and Adam Clayton from U2, Steve Norman, John Keeble, Gary Kemp and Tony Hadley from Spandau ballet, John Taylor, Roger Taylor, Andy Taylor and Simon La Bon frm Duran Duran, Keren Woodward, Sara Dalin and Siobhan Fahey from Bananarama, J.T. Taylor, Robert "Kool" Bell and Dennis Thomas from Kool and the Gang, George Michael from Wham!, Sting, Boy George form Culture Club and Geldof's group, the Boomtown Rats.

Paul McCartney and David Bowie were not at the session but contributed a track that was dubbed onto the single.

The session was filmed and footage sent to news outlets, who aired it. The next morning, Geldof was a guest of Mike Read on the Radio 1 breakfast show. Geldof was scheduled on the show to promote the Boomtown Rats new album but, instead, promoted the "Do They Know It's Christmas" single and announced that every penny raised would go to the cause of Ethiopian famine relief. The British government objected, insisting they must collect their sales tax on the record, but Geldof used the media to draw attention to the issue and the British government backed down.

"Do They Know It's Christmas was released in the U.K. on November 29 and sold a million copies in the first week. It remained number one on the U.K. singles chart for five weeks and sold over three million copies.

Label News

Polygram Records was in financial trouble. They intended to merge with Warners but that merger was thwarted. They sold their publishing company for $100 million to a consortium of buyers led by Freddy Bienstock which bailed the label out of trouble. There were two giant publishing firms: Warner Music was the biggest in the U.S. while Chappell was the biggest in the world.

As the recording industry shifted from LPs to cassettes and then from cassettes (which had 53 percent of the business) to CDs (which were only about one percent of the business), labels faced the problem of which format to release their product. In December, Warner Bros Records became the first label to release a title in all three formats: LPs were priced at $8.98, cassettes also at $8.98 and CDs at $15.98 (they price was dropped from $18.98). CDs were catching on but the only active plant manufacturing CDs was CBS's in Terre Haute, Indiana, which had opened in September.

The biggest album that Christmas was Madonna's *Like a Virgin*.

1985
We Are the World

American artists, inspired by the efforts of British artists in famine relief, organized a supergroup, USA (United Support of Artists) for Africa and recorded "We Are the World," a song written by Michael Jackson and Lionel Richie. The idea came from Harry Belafonte with logistical help from manager Ken Kragen. A demo of the song was recorded on January 22, 1985, by Jackson, Richie and Stevie Wonder with Quincy Jones at Kenny Rogers' Lion Share Recording Studio. The demo was sent to the musicians the group hoped to enlist in the project, to be recorded on January 28, after "The American Music Awards" TV show.

A number of artists were scheduled to be in Los Angeles for the American Music Awards ceremony, held that same night, so they were available. Artists on the session included Ray Charles, Billy Joel, Diana Ross, Cyndi Lauper, Bruce Springsteen, Smokey Robinson, Bob Dylan, Paul Simon, Kenny Rogers, Tina Turner, James Ingram, Diana Ross, Willie Nelson, Dionne Warwick, Al Jarreau, Kenny Loggins, Huey Lewis, Kim Carnes, Steve Perry, Daryl Hall, Bette Midler, John Oates, the Pointers Sisters, Smokey Robinson, La Toya Jackson, Bob Geldof, Sheila E., Lindsey Buckingham, Dan Aykroyd, Harry Belafonte and Michael Jackson's brothers, Marlon, Randy and Tito.

The session was produced by Quincy Jones and Michael Omartian and recorded at the A&M Recording Studio in Hollywood. When they entered the studio, the artists saw a sign posted by Quincy Jones which said, "Please check your egos at the door."

Michael Jackson was the first to arrive and recorded his solo as well as the chorus by himself. During the session, the chorus was sung first and then the solo parts so artists would not leave after their solo.

"We Are the World" was released on March 7, 1985, and became the first single to be certified multi-platinum; it was number one on charts all over the world and the single, album, merchandise and volunteer contributions eventually raised over $63 million for humanitarian aid in Africa. The first cargo jet with food, medicine and clothing left for Ethiopia and the Sudan in June, 1985. About ninety percent of the money was sent for African relief—both short and long-term, with ten percent for the hungry and homeless in the United States.

Live Aid

The success of the singles "Do They Know It's Christmas" and "We Are the World" led to a concert, Live Aid, held July 13, 1985 simultaneously in London at Wembley Stadium, at John F. Kennedy Stadium in Philadelphia, and at venues in Australia and Germany. An estimated two billion viewers in 60 countries watched the TV broadcast. The concert, which began in the U.K. and continued at JFK Stadium in Philadelphia, lasted for 16 hours and raised approximately $285 million. Among those who performed at the concert were Paul McCartney, Mick Jagger, David Bowie, Tina Turner, Bob Dylan, Queen, the Boomtown Rats, Elvis Costello, U2, The Who, Tom Petty, Madonna, Joan Baez, Ronnie Wood, Crosby, Stills, Nash & Young, the original Black Sabbath with Ozzy Osbourne, Phil Collins, Teddy Pendergrass, Ashford and Simson, Duran Duran, and members of Led Zeppelin.

During Bob Dylan's performance, which closed the show, the singer suggested that perhaps some of the money should be sent to American farmers and that comment led to the creation of Farm Aid.

When Bob Dylan speaks, people listen.

Farm Aid

The first "Farm Aid" concert was held on September 22, 1985, in Campaign, Illinois and proceeds went to family farmers in the United States. Willie Nelson, John Mellencamp and Neil Young, inspired by Bob Dylan's comments during the Live Aid concert, organized the event. The event had far reaching rsults. Congress passed the Agricultural Credit Act of 1987 to help save family farms from foreclosure after Willie Nelson and John Mellencamp brought family farmers to testify to Congress about family farms in America.

Performers at the initial Farm Aid concert included both pop/rock and country performers. Those who performed were Willie Nelson, Alabama, Hoyt Axton, The Beach Boys, Jon Bon Jovi, Glen Campbell, Johnny Cash, the Charlie Daniels Band, John Denver, Bob Dylan, John Fogerty, Foreigners, Vince Gill, Arlo Guthrie, Merle Haggard, Emmylou Harris, Don Henley, Waylon Jennings, Billy Joel, George Jones, B.B. King, Carole King, Kris Kristofferson, Huey Lewis, Loretta Lynn, John Mellencamp, Roger Miller, Joni Mitchell, Nitty Gritty Dirt Band, Roy Orbison, Tom Petty, Charley Pride, Lou Reed, Kenny Rogers, Sissy Spacek, Brian Setzer, Tanya Tucker, Eddie Van Halen, Debra Winger and Neil Young.

Farm Aid is the only music fundraising event that continued after the original event. Every year since that event there has been a Farm Aid concert to raise money for farmers.

Madonna

Madonna's first chart records came in 1984. "Borderline" entered the Hot 100 on March 10 and rose to number ten, "Lucky Star" entered the Hot 100 and reached number four, and then "Like a Virgin," which entered the *Billboard* Hot 100 on November 17, reached number one just before Christmas and remained in that position in January for five more weeks. It was a controversial song by a controversial artist.

Her next single, "Material Girl," entered the Hot 100 on February 9, 1985, and reached number two; it was an anthem for the 1980s, which were defined by greed and materialism.

Madonna Louise Ciccone was born in Bay City, Michigan on August 16, 1958. She grew up in the Detroit suburbs; her father was an engineer designer for Chrysler and General Motors. Her mother, also named Madonna, died from breast cancer in December, 1963. Her father remarried in 1966 and Madonna held the marriage against him, which resulted in her early rebellion and a strained relationship with her father.

Madonna attended Catholic schools and received top grades; she was a straight A student but also an exhibitionist. She was on the cheerleading squad at her high school and received a dance scholarship to the University of Michigan. In 1978, she dropped out of college and moved to New York City where she worked as a waitress and took classes at the Alvin Alley American Dance Theater. She began working as a backup dancer and toured with French disco artist Patrick Hernandez on his 1979 world tour; Madonna sang backup and danced on the tour.

Madonna met musician Dan Gilroy and they moved in together and she formed her first band, the Breakfast Club, where she played guitar, drums, and sang. In the early 1980s, she had a new boyfriend, Stephen Bray, and they formed the band, Emmy. The two wrote songs together but Madonna, always ambitious, decided to embark on a solo career.

She impressed DJ and record producer Mark Kamins, who arranged a meeting for her with Seymour Stein, founder and head of Sire Records. Stein signed her to the label and released her first single, "Everybody" in October, 1982. That was followed by "Burning Up," released in March, 1983. She began working on her debut album with producer Reggie Lucas but was dissatisfied with the tracks so she asked her then-boyfriend, John

"Jellybean" Benitz, to help finish the production. Benitez provided new mixes and produced "Holiday," her third single and first international hit. The album was heavily influenced by disco and used the Linn drum machine, the Moog bass and a synthesizer. It was released in July, 1983, and included two top ten singles, "Borderline" and "Lucky Star."

Madonna was more than a singer; she was a leader in fashion and her outfits influenced young girls and women. Stylist Maripol helped create her "look," which featured bleached hair, fishnet stockings, a crucifix and lacy tops.

Madonna's second studio album, *Like a Virgin*, was released in November, 1984, and was an international hit; it reached number one in Germany, Italy, the Netherlands, New Zealand, Spain, and the U.K. as well as the U.S.

During the first MTV Video Awards in 1984, Madonna wore a wedding dress and rolled around suggestively on the top of a stage wedding cake. The performance brought her a lot of attention. For her next single, "Material Girl," Madonna recreated the performance of "Diamonds Are a Girl's Best Friend," by Marilyn Monroe in the 1953 film, *Gentlemen Prefer Blondes*.

Madonna began dating actor Sean Penn and married him in August, 1985. She began her career as an actress in 1985; she appeared in *Vision Quest* and sang on the soundtrack (her singles "Crazy For You" and "Gambler" came from the soundtrack) and then appeared in *Desperately Seeking Susan*, where she sang the song, "Into the Groove."

The "Virgin Tour" was her first American tour; it began in April, 1985 with the Beastie Boys as opening act. She started in clubs but soon played major arenas. The tour inspired a following of wannabes, young girls who dressed like Madonna. She had two more hits, "Angel" and "Dress You Up," but a near scandal erupted when *Penthouse* and *Playboy* magazines published nude photos of her that were taken in 1978 when she was desperate for money. Madonna refused to be a victim; she was unapologetic and defiant in defending herself.

The suggestive performances and nude photos made her a sex symbol and solidified Madonna's image as someone who was provocative, controversial and not afraid to follow her own arrow.

MTV: 1985

By 1985, MTV had tremendous clout. It had 25 million subscribers and pop acts had to release a video with each single. MTV made acts "cool"; without a video, an act could not compete with other popular acts.

Labels treated MTV like radio; they paid for the creation of a video, then sent it free to MTV and hoped they would be played so the album would sell. Videos became more and more expensive and the labels continued to pay; they hoped they would sell enough albums to pay for the costs of videos. There was no turning back; MTV did not pay for video production, only aired videos, while the labels allotted bigger and bigger budgets for videos. Fortunately, it was a good time for selling records and labels raked in the profits, although label executives knew they could not continue to make expensive videos on every artist, even though every artist wanted them. Unfortunately, videos sold poorly so labels could not recoup their costs there.

Videos became so popular that a new video channel, VH-1, was introduced at the beginning of 1985 and featured videos for an older demographic. The first video played was Marvin Gaye's performance of "The Star-Spangled Banner."

Videos and VCRS

Video cassettes and Video Cassette Recorders (VCRs) came of age during the 1980s.

The first commercially successful videotape recorder was introduced by Ampex in 1956; its price was $50,000 and it was primarily used in TV production as a way to hold down the costs of film, which delivered a higher quality but necessitated processing costs after the film was shot. With video, the playback was immediate. Besides, the notion of TV shows having the long term importance of film was dismissed; the prevailing idea was that television was a disposable media; only movies lasted for years.

In 1970, Philips developed the videocassette format, or VCR, and their system debuted in the United Kingdom. In 1975, Philips introduced the digital timer version where a clock could be set to tape a show. In 1975 the Betamax was introduced by Sony; the machine could record for up to an hour. A little less than a year later, the VHS format was introduced in the United States and that format could record for two to four hours. Although the Beta technology was a higher quality, American consumers preferred the convenience of the longer recording time of the VHS, which was manufactured in Japan by Matsushita, a rival of Sony. In 1977, the long playing video cassette was introduced which could record for up to six hours.

In 1984, Universal City Studio sued the Sony Corporation of America in an attempt to stop Sony from manufacturing machines that could videotape a television show or movie. Universal argued that it was a violation of copyright law for someone to tape a television show without authorization or payment to the copyright holder. Universal—and other Hollywood studios—felt the video cassette recorder was a threat to their business model because consumers watching a video could fast forward through commercials. Further, the companies felt that they—not consumers—should control how and when a show was broadcast.

The Supreme Court ruled against the Hollywood studio, saying that someone recording a show for their own private use in their home was not a violation of copyright law. Further, it was shown that most consumers preferred to "time shift" their shows; they were not making copies to sell but, instead, were watching a show when it was convenient for them.

The Hollywood studios had thought they could solve the problem of video by outlawing the manufacture of the machines that made video recorders. They were upset that instead of consumers going to a theater and paying to watch a movie, they rented a movie from a rental store. The attempt to solve the problem by eliminating the manufacture of recording technology failed and in 1986 there were 36.1 million VCRs in American homes.

That set a precedent so when the copying of music CDs became a problem, there were no lawsuits filed to stop the manufacturing of CD copying hardware.

Rap and Hip Hop in the 1980s

Rap music can be traced back to African-American preachers or the early black radio disc jockeys in the 1940s. Musically, there were acts like Barry White and Isaac Hayes in the early 1970s who "rapped" or talked in a low, sexy tone over music. But in terms of the contemporary music industry, rap is traced back to 1979 and the release of "Rapper's Delight" by the Sugar Hill Gang on the Sugar Hill label.

Hip Hop came from the streets of New York in the post-Civil Rights era in neighborhoods where African-Americans, Caribbean-Americans and Latin American youth lived. Musically, it was a descendent of soul and funk music, especially the music of James Brown and George Clinton. Also influential were the "Soul Train" TV show hosted by Don Cornelius, the dancing of the Jackson 5, particularly Michael Jackson, and disco music. Hip hop was a grass roots movement that was a product of technology as well as inner city life and was the first music trend where blacks embraced the music of their past.

One hundred years before, many African-Americans rejected slave songs and spirituals because they represented a past they wanted to forget; the blues that came from the Delta was a music to be forgotten once blacks arrived in cities and the raw rhythm and blues that came from the clubs of Chicago, Memphis and other cities was dismissed by many blacks during the Civil Rights era because it represented a music linked to memories of segregation they would rather forget. Until hip hop, African-Americans saw the music of their past as representing a time they wanted to put behind them and forget; blacks felt they could not progress if they embraced a music tied to a past that reminded them of an era that pushed them back rather than pulled them forward.

During the 1970s, in sections of upper Manhattan and the Bronx, youth often gathered in public parks or on their block for music that came from a disc jockey with a portable sound system. Disc jockeys, better known as DJs, like Kool Herc, Afrika Bambaataa and Grandmaster Flash began to "toast" or celebrate their triumphs as lovers.

On the streets were Puerto Rican youth who were "break dancing," doing acrobatic moves while boom boxes blared out a heavy beat, dominated by bass and drum. Break dancing became a test of athletic skills, a contest between individuals and groups to see who could outperform the other.

The mid-1970s was the era of disco clubs, who used "mixers" which allowed CJs (Club Jockeys) to move the sound between two turntables. In 1975, there were approximately 200-300 discos in New York City, and those CJs became stars as they mixed records, dubbed sound and toasted. The CJs in discos influenced the DJs on the street with their "wheels of steel" or dual turntables.

For black teenagers, inner city life centered around basketball and drugs. Although the post-Civil Rights era provided opportunities for many African-Americans, those who grew up in the inner city often saw a world where there was little or no hope. Many were raised in one parent homes, attended ineffective schools that were battle grounds, heard gunfire erupt at any time during the day or night, and watched friends, relatives and strangers dealing drugs.

How do you simply survive in such a culture? And, beyond that, how do you gain a sense of dignity, a self-respect as well as the respect of others? How can you afford to buy the things you crave?

Hip Hop, Basketball and the Hood

There are two ways to go from being a "nobody" to being a "somebody" in America: sports and entertainment. For the black culture that generally meant basketball and rap or hip hop. Those two fields were a way to rise above your social and economic background without denying it.

Basketball was the sport of inner city youth. There were basketball courts in inner cities and it is a game that can be played one on one or with full teams, five on five. If you were good enough, you got the respect and admiration of those in your 'hood, and if you were really good, there might be college and the NBA where you could make big money and travel first class.

Another way to make money was dealing drugs and African-American youths living in the inner city saw that drug dealers often had money, sharp clothes and fancy cars. Money, clothes and cars got respect and admiration as well. For the inner city youth, there were few, if any, jobs available and those that were open to inner city blacks were minimum wage. One good drug deal could net you more than a week at a minimum wage job.

The result was a culture within a culture; the culture of the 'hood, or local neighborhood, inside the American culture. This American culture seemed off limits and out of touch with life inside the 'hood. The American culture that had a direct bearing on inner city life for African-Americans was increasingly hostile to their plight during the late 1970s and early 1980s. That was especially true in the views African-Americans held towards government.

In his book, *Hip Hop America*, Nelson George states, "African-American belief in government duplicity toward them is deep-seated and even sometimes overly paranoid, yet there is an evil history that gives these conspiracies real credibility. From the Tuskegee syphilis experiments that poisoned the bodies of poor Alabama men with a venereal disease for over forty years at U.S. expense to the FBI putting microphones under Dr. Martin Luther King's bed to record his sex life and...subversion of black racial organizing, elements of this country's law enforcement branches have been performing nefarious deeds on its African-American citizens for decades."

During the early 1970s there was a crime wave perpetuated by drugs-- primarily theft to support a drug habit or violent crimes committed while on drugs--that concerned white Americans. The result was a crackdown on the drug trade. That led to courts aggressively sentencing people for low-level drug offenses like possession with the result that most African-Americans knew someone in the justice system, either as victim or perpetrator. For young black men, jail no longer meant a punishment but a rite of passage that defined their entry into manhood.

Living in the inner city, in the projects, violence was part of everyday life; it was part of day-to-day happenings. Living in that environment was accepted as part of a "rap" or performance, giving the performer an authenticity and legitimacy for that audience.

Blacks began adapting flamboyant new names, called "tags," to create an identity for themselves. That was a way to hide their real names from authorities as well as a way to label who they wanted to be. Those tags announced to the world that this young black man wasn't just another "Joe" but a unique individual. "Tags" became an important way to announce one's existence in a crowded, indifferent world.

In prisons and on the streets, African-American men learned to bond with other black men as protection and to gain power and respect. Women could not be trusted--they would leave one man for another to get more jewelry or a ride in a nicer car--so it was essential that men remain loyal to their crew. In confronting the world, African-American men disguised their hatred of authority with a stone face. Here is where gangsta rap was born.

Gangsta Rap

The drug culture in the inner city changed during the 1980s. Cocaine was an expensive drug and few could afford it; heroin declined because of the difficulty in obtaining a reliable, regular supply but angel dust, also known as PCP, was available and provided a creative stimulant to the hip hop culture. During the early 1980s, crack cocaine became an affordable drug and dealers developed a brisk trade because the intense high of that drug fades quickly. Drug dealers dealt with repeat customers as crack became a fast food drug and the crack trade led directly to gangsta rap.

Gangsta rap set the tone for much of the earliest rap recorded. Although middle class Americans--both black and white--were appalled by the violence in the lyrics, that violence was part of everyday life of inner city black youth who saw friends shot over a jacket or another friend stabbed to death after being hit with an errant basketball pass. Gangs fought each other, exacting revenge and became empowered by violence.

Respect was demanded and "dissing" someone was the ultimate insult; in a world that did not respect young black men, pride and self-respect gave those young men a dignity they craved. Pride and arrogance became part of their personality, a weapon against the outside world, a source of self-respect and a system of survival. Gangsta rap gave those living in that world a sense of empowerment; to those outside that world, it created fear and revulsion.

Hip Hop: The Growing Years

The period 1981-1985 was the developmental era for hip hop. Recordings came mostly from small, independent black-owned record companies who could not get radio airplay or the support from African-American record executives with major labels.

"The Message" by Grandmaster Flash came in 1982; in 1983, Herbie Hancock released "Rockit" and his video was shown on MTV. "I Feel For You" by Chaka Khan with Melle Mel was the first time an established star collaborated with a rapper; the album went platinum and the single went Gold.

Run-D.M.C. released "Rock Box" in 1984 and their album went Gold; in 1986 that group recorded "Walk This Way" with Aerosmith. The album *Raising Hell* by Run-D.M.C. sold three million units. *Licensed to Ill* by the Beastie Boys was also released in 1986 and that album sold four million units.

Although hip hop originated within the black culture, it was white entrepreneurial involvement that allowed this movement and music to survive and thrive. After the initial rap records from black-owned labels Sugar Hill, Enjoy and Winley, the next stage required the input of white, mostly Jewish, entrepreneurs. Those whites included Tommy Boy founder Tom Silverman and president Monica Lynch; manager and producer Dave (Funken) Klein; publicist Bill Adler; Jive Record's Barry Weiss and Ann Carli; Select's Fred Munao; Tuff City's Aaron Fuchs; Priority's Brian Turner; Fat Boys's Charles Stettler; Lyor Cohen, who was Russell Simmons's partner in Rush Management and Def Jam; Def Jam co-founder Rick Rubin; and booking agent Cara Lewis.

As hip hop progressed, it found a growing audience of young white boys.

Rap Hits

L.L. Cool J's "I Need Love," a rap ballad released in 1987, reached number one on the black singles chart and his album *Bigger and Deffer* sold two million units; that same year, "Push It" by Salt-N-Pepa became the first hit single by female rappers. In 1988, Will Smith launched his career when Jazzy Jeff & Fresh Prince and released "Parents Just Don't Understand." Tone Loc hit with "Wild Thing" in 1989,

Although hip hop started in New York, it was soon picked up by African-Americans in California who presented their own brand of this music to the world. In 1988, the landmark album *Straight Outta Compton* by NWA (the original line-up was Ice Cube, Dr. Dre, Arabian Prince with Eazy-E and MC Ren joining later and Arabian Prince dropping out) was released and became a major break-through album. That same year Public Enemy released "It Takes a Nation of Millions to Hold Us Back."

Rap reached the large, general public in September, 1988, when "Yo, MTV Raps!" premiered. The show racked up high rating, which led to a daily version in 1989 hosted by Dr. Dre, Ed Lover and T-Money. Black Entertainment Television had begun in 1981 but ignored rap until MTV's success. In 1989, BET debuted "Rap City." "The Box," which began in Miami at the end of 1985, broadcast a call-in request line for music videos that furthered hip hop music and fashion. Not only was hip hop now audible for the masses, it was also visible and the "look" of hip hop spread nationally and young whites began to adapt the fashions of inner city blacks.

Hip hop is unique in the history of the recording industry because most of the early musicians could not play a musical instrument; their "instruments" were a large record collection, turntables and a sampler. Since the E-mu Emulator was released in the American market in 1981, hip hop producers learned to use this digital technology to store, manipulate and play back any sound. To those musicians who came before rap, or those outside the field, the idea that someone using digital technology to sample music and then add percussion or other effects was not really creating music. To those in the world of hip hop there was no question: This was the very essence of creativity and making music.

Rap Crossovers

During the mid-1980s, Rap, which had initially appealed to the black culture, began crossing over into the white mainstream market, led by Run-DMC's hip hop version of Aerosmith's "Walk This Way." White as well as black engineers and producers began using the techniques of scratching and break beats pioneered by the early club DJs. Samplers, drum machines and synthesizes defined the sound of 1980s pop music. The early hits were recorded in expensive studios but with the development of computers with software that could sample and price decreases in synthesizers and computers, many engineers and producers discovered they did not need an expensive studio to make a records. They could do a lot at home.

Technology

During the early 1980s drum machines made it possible to provide a drum track by tapping fingers on keypads, also known as beat boxes, and the first programmable drum machine, the Roland TR-808, was popular with rappers and club DJs. There were Roland and Prophet synthesizers, the Linn Drum Machine and Fairlight and Synclavier samplers as well as the MIDI interface, created in 1983, which interfaced between a keyboard and a computer. Those technologies made it possible for producers who could not play a musical instrument to create songs.

In Sweden, producer Denniz PoP (Dennis Dagge) became a pioneer in using electronically programmed sound, tracks and beats with samples of existing music to create a new way of making music. In his book, *The Song Machine*, author John Seabrook stated that "Denniz PoP wasn't a musician in the usual sense of the word. He didn't play an instrument, he couldn't sing, and he didn't write music" but "By the early '90s he was making tracks exclusively on the computer, using an early version of Logic Pro, the music-production software that is native to the Mac."

In other technology news, the Internet's Domain Name System was created and the Commodore launched its Amiga personal Computers.

On September 13, Steve Jobs resigned from Apple Computer and began NeXT.

The first Nintendo home video game console in the U.S., was released as the Nintendo Entertainment System in October. In November, Microsoft released Windows 1.0.

Michael Jackson purchases Beatles publishing

On September 6, Michael Jackson purchased the publishing rights for most of the Beatles songs for $47 million. Bidding against Jackson was Paul McCartney.

Country Music in Decline?

An article in the *New York Times* in 1985, "Nashville Sound: Country Music in Decline" stated that "Stars who were selling a half a million to more than a million copies per album in the late 1970s are lucky to be selling half that today. Having a No. 1 country single used to mean around 350,000 records; now a country No. 1 sells an average of 100,000."

Nashville responded with the "New Traditionalist Movement" as artists Ricky Skaggs, George Strait, Randy Travis. Dwight Yoakam, Ricky Van

Shelton, Holly Dunn, Kathy Mattea, Keith Whitley, Reba McEntire, Alan Jackson, Travis Tritt. Clint Black, Mary Chapin Carpenter, Lorrie Morgan, and the Judds

Randy Travis

In 1985, Randy Travis exploded into a country music superstar, beginning with "On The Other Hand," which became CMA's "Song of the Year." During the 1980s he had a string of number one records, including "Diggin' Up Bones," "Forever and Ever, Amen," "I Told You So," "Deeper Than the Holler" and "Hard Rock Bottom of Your Heart." He had million selling albums and became the face and voice for the "New Traditionalists."

1986

Space Shuttle explodes

On January 28, 1986, the Space Shuttle Challenger lifted off from Cape Canaveral with teacher Christa McAuliffe and six astronauts aboard; 73 seconds after the launch, the Challenger exploded, killing all seven astronauts.

Metallica

Heavy Metal was well established as a genre by the spring of 1981 when Lars Ulrich, a Danish-born drummer, recruited guitarists James Hetfield and Hugh Tanner through an ad in *The Recycler*, a Los Angeles newspaper, for a jam session. Ulrich then convinced Brian Slagel, head of Metal Blade Records, to allow his group to record a track for a compilation album, *Metal Massacre*. The band was officially formed in October and was comprised of Lars Ulrich on drums; James Hetfield, lead vocalist and rhythm guitar; Dave Mustaine on lead guitar; and Ron McGovney on bass. Ulrich named the band Metallica and their first original song, "Hit the Lights" was on the compilation album *Metal Massacre I*, which was released in June, 1982.

Metallica's first live performance was in March, 1982, in Anaheim, California, then they opened for Saxon, a British heavy metal band. There were personnel changes with the group; bassist McGovney left and was replaced by Cliff Burton and the band moved to the San Francisco Bay area.

Concert promoter Johny "Z" Zazula financed Metallica's first album, *Kill 'Em All* (the label rejected the band's choice of *Metal Up Your Ass*) on his own label, Megaforce Records. The album was recorded in May,1983, in

Rochester, New York; just prior to the session the band fired Dave Mustaine because of drug and alcohol abuse in addition to violent behavior and replaced him with Kirk Hammett. Mustaine them formed the heavy metal group Megadeath.

Kill 'Em All only reached number 155 on the *Billboard* album chart but the band developed a growing fan base through touring. The band's second album, *Ride the Lightning* was recorded in Copenhagen and released in August, 1984; it reached number 100 on the *Billboard* album chart.

Metallica took a big step forward at the end of 1984 when they signed with Elektra Records; they also signed with Q-Prime Management. Their British label, Music for Nations, released a single, "Am I Evil" b/w "Blitzkrieg" which sold 40,000 copies in the U.K. The band did a European tour and then one in America, often playing festivals or on the bill with other heavy metal acts.

Metallica's third album, *Master of Puppets*, was recorded in Copenhagen and released in March, 1986; they opened for Ozzy Osbourne on a U.S. tour. The album was a commercial breakthrough, reaching number 29 on the *Billboard* chart, remaining on that chart for almost a year and a half and achieved "Gold" status (later six times platinum). In September, during a European tour, Metallica's bus overturned in Sweden and bassist Cliff Burton was killed. After some down time, Metallica hired Jason Newsted to replace Burton; they finished their tour in early 1987.

In 1988 Metallica released *And Justice For All*; it reached number six on the *Billboard* album chart and was certified platinum as the group toured to support the album, which was nominated for a Grammy in the Best Hard Rock/Metal Performance Vocal or Instrument category.

Heavy Metal

Heavy metal was linked to mid-1950s rock and roll because both appalled parents; indeed, this was one of the appeals of heavy metal. Heavy metal was a working class music that combined the hippie attitude of "do your own thing" to create a music that was despised by outsiders but strongly embraced by those inside their world. This was not "nice" music, but that was the point--the term "heavy metal" itself indicated something hard, durable, and cold-hearted. It was an apt description of a music intended to be offensive in everything from its decibel level to its lyrics and succeeded by adhering to a sound that shattered the sensibilities of the fans of soft rock.

Technology

On January 19, the computer virus "Brain" began to spread. In February, Pixar Animation Studios opened in California and the next month the Microsoft Corporation held its initial public offering of stock shares.

In May, "Dragon Quest," credited for establishing the template for role playing video games, was released in Japan.

In November, Sperry Rand and Burroughs merged to form Unisys, the second largest computer company. During the year, the first commercially available 3D printer was sold.

News

On October 9, the News Corporation completed its acquisition of the Metromedia group of companies and launched the Fox Broadcasting Company.

1987

U2

During the 1980s, U2 emerged as a group who not only had hit singles and best-selling albums, but also a social conscience. The group, comprised of Paul "Bono" Hewson (vocals), Adam Clayton (bass), Dave Evans (known as "The Edge; guitar), and Larry Mullen (drums), was formed in 1976 when they were students at Mount Temple High School in Dublin, Ireland. They were originally named "Feedback" and played cover songs from rock acts such as the Rolling Stones and Beach Boys. They changed their name to "Hype" before settling on "U2" in 1978. That year they won a talent contest in Limerick, Ireland, and signed with manager Paul McGuiness, who negotiated a recording contract with CBS Records in Ireland. They released their debut EP, *Out of Control* in 1979, which reached number one on the Irish pop chart.

The group was turned down by the U.K. office of CBS for worldwide distribution so they signed with Island Records for distribution in the United States. The group was a critical success from their first album, *Boy*, released in 1980, although several previous singles had failed to chart. They toured the United States and then returned to Great Britain.

Their second album, *October* (1981) was not only sold in regular retail outlets but also in Christian bookstores and reviewed in Christian periodicals. By their third album, *War* (1983), the Christian audience claimed them as their own, although they were signed to a secular label and pursued pop success. That album featured the hit single "Sunday, Bloody Sunday" about the Catholic-Protestant conflict in Northern Ireland. During their "War Tour," Bono waved a white flag when the band performed "Sunday, Bloody Sunday" and that became an iconic image. During that tour, the group recorded a live album, *Under a Blood Red Sky*, as well as a concert film, *Live at Red Rocks*.

In 1984, the group released *The Unforgettable Fire* album and in July, the following year, performed at the Live Aid concert.

The *Joshua Tree* album (1987), produced by Brian Eno and Daniel Lanois, contained their two biggest pop hits, "With or Without You" and "I Still Haven't Found What I'm Looking For." This was a breakthrough album, selling over 15 million copies. It was also the beginning of Bono's public activism as he and his wife, Ali, went to Ethiopia where they became involved in famine relief efforts.

Lyrically, the songs of U2 emphasized the struggle between the forces of good and evil or light and dark. For *The Joshua Tree* album they embarked on a world tour and became one of the most popular acts in the world. Their double-live album, *Rattle and Hum*, reflected their crowd-pleasing live shows.

Whitney Houston

By the end of 1987, Whitney Houston had racked up six number onee that held the top position for eleven weeks. In 1987, she had "I Wanna Dance With Somebody (Who Loves Me)," which was number two for two weeks, "Didn't We Almost Have It all," number two for two weeks, and "So Emotional," which entered the *Billboard* Hot 100 in October and peaked at number one in 1986.

Whitney Houston (born August 9, 1963, in Newark, New Jersey) came from a musical family; her mother was gospel singer "Cissy" (Drinkard) Houston and her older brother, Michael was a singer. Her first cousins were Dionne Warwick and Dee Dee Warwick, her godmother was Darlene Love and her honorary aunt was Aretha Franklin, who she met at age eight or nine when her mother took her to a recording studio.

Cissy Houston was a gospel singer and Whitney was grounded in gospel music; her first public performances came with the New Hope Baptist Church choir. Guided by her mother, Whitney continued to sing and met acts Chaka Khan, Gladys Knight and Roberta Flack. During her teen years, Whitney toured nightclubs where her mother performed; at 14 she was a backup singer on "Life's a Party," a single for the Michael Zager band and, at 15, sang background vocals for Chaka Khan and Lou Rawls. During the early 1980s, Whitney Houston became a model and appeared in *Seventeen*, *Glamour*, *Cosmopolitan*, and *Young Miss* magazines and in a TV commercial for the soft drink Canada Dry.

Houston worked with producers Michael Beinhorn, Bill Laswell and Martin Bisi on an album, One Down, credited to the group Matrial; Houston sang a ballad, "Memories," on that album She also sang on an album by Paul Jabara. Whitney's mother would not let her pursue a full time singing career until she finished school. By 1983, she had finished school and was singing in a nightclub in New York City when Arista A&R exec Gerry Griffith heard her and brought label head Clive Davis to see her. Davis was impressed and signed her to a world-wide contract with Arista.

Clive Davis did not want to rush a release from Houston; he wanted to find the right producer and the right song. She sang a duet, "Hold Me," with Teddy Pendergrass on his Love Language album and that single reached top five on the R&B chart. Houston then worked with producers Michael Masser, Kashif, Jermaine Jackson and Narada Michael Waldon on her self-titled debut album, which was released in February, 1985.

Houston's first single, "Someone for Me," was released in the U.K. but did not chart. For her debut single in the U.S., Davis and Arista wanted to establish her in the black marketplace first. Arista released the ballad "You Give Good Love," which reached number one on the R&B chart and number three on the Hot 100. Her album began selling and she appeared on a number of late-night TV talk shows. Her second U.S. single, "Saving All My Love for You," was her first number one on the *Billboard* Hot 100. Her next single, "How Will I Know," was number one for two weeks on the Hot 100, peaking in 1986. From that point forward, Whitney Houston's singles were in heavy rotation on MTV. A year after its release, her debut album was number one on the *Billboard* album chart and remained in that position for 14 weeks.

The final single from her first album, "The Greatest Love of All," was a cover of George Benson's 1977 release; it was number one for three weeks on the Hot 100. Houston followed this with a world tour and became an international star.

At the Grammy Awards, Whitney Houston won her first Grammy for Best Pop Vocal, Female for "Saving All My Love for You," which she performed during the Grammy telecast. She followed that with American Music Awards and an MTV Video Music Award. During the 1987 Grammys, "The Greatest Love of All" was nominated for Record of the Year.

In June, 1987, Whitney Houston' second album, Whitney, was released and debuted at number one on the *Billboard* album chart and the U.K. chart. Her single, "I Wanna Dance With Somebody (Who Loves Me)," was an international hit, topping the singles charts in Australia, Germany and the U.K. Her next singles, "Didn't We Almost Have It All," "So Emotional," and "Where Do Broken Hearts Go" all reached number one, giving her seven consecutive number one hits. Her album, *Whitney*, was certified platinum.

Bon Jovi

In 1987, Bon Jovi's "Livin' On a Prayer" was number one for four straight weeks and was a breakthrough single for him. His previous single, "You Give Love a Bad Name," was his first number one.

John Francis Bongiovi was born in Sayreville, New Jersey, on March 2, 1962. His joined his first band, Raze, playing piano and guitar. His next band, Atlantic City Expressway, was formed with David Bryan then, still a teenager, he formed John Bongiovi and the Wild Ones and played local clubs. In 1980, his next band, The Rest, released a single, "Runaway," that was played on local radio stations.

Bon Jovi's cousin, Tony Bongiovi, co-owned the Power Station, a popular studio in New York and he gave Bon Jovi a job there. At the studio, Bon Jovi recorded demos that were sent to record companies, but nothing clicked, although his first professional recording where he sang lead was "R2-D2 We Wish You a Merry Christmas," that was produced by his cousin.

Bon Jovi went to local radio station WAPP in 1983 to write and sing jingles for the station. Promotion director John Lassman suggested using "Runaway" on a compilation album of local homegrown talent; Bon Jovi had re-recorded it in 1982 with studio musicians. The song became popular and was played on other stations, which led Bon Jovi and David Bryan to form another band with bassist Alec John Such, drummer Tico Torres, lead guitarist Dave Sabo and guitarist Richie Sambora, a local musician. Sambora had a good track record; he had toured with Joe Cocker, was called to audition for Kiss and played in a group, Mercy.

The band played showcases and opened for local acts and were signed to Mercury Records by Derek Shulman. Jon Bon Jovi searched for a group name and came up with Johnny Electric, but Pamela Maher, an employee of their manager Doc McGhee, suggested "Bon Jovi," a two word name like Van Halen. Their debut album, *Bon Jovi,* was released in January, 1984, and contained the single, "Runaway," which reached number 30 on the *Billboard* Hot 100 while the album reached number 43.

Bon Jovi's second album, *7800 Degrees Fahrenheit* was released in 1985 and had three singles, "Only Lonely," "In an Out of Love" and "Silent Night." All three singles charted and the album reached number 37. The success of those singles and album led to tours in Japan and Europe and then a six month tour in the U.S, opening for Ratt. Jon Bon Jovi was developing a name; he played on the first Farm Aid concert in 1985.

Jon Bon Jovi was under pressure to come up with hit singles and a hit album. They hired professional songwriter Desmond Child to collaborate with Bon Jovi and Richie Sambora and they came up with "You Give Love a Bad Name" and "Livin' on a Prayer." The album, *Slippery When Wet*, was recorded in Vancouver with producer Bruce Fairbairn; the name "slippery when wet" came after they visited a strip club in Vancouver. The album was released in August, 1986, and hit number one on the Billboard album chart and stayed there for two weeks.

The success of the singles and album led to an MTV Video Music Award for "Livin' On a Prayer" and an award from the American Music Awards for "Favorite Pop/Rock Band" as well as a "Favorite Rock Group" trophy at the People's Choice Awards.

That made Bon Jovi a headline act and in the U.S.; they also headlined the Monsters of Rock festival in England. Their follow-up album, *New Jersey*, released in 1988, also reached number one and produced five hit singles. "Bad Medicine" and "I'll Be There for You" both reached number one on the Hot 100; "Born to Be My Baby," "Lay Your Hands on Me" and "Living in Sin" were all top ten singles.

Industry News

The record industry was in good shape in 1986; there were 350 million cassettes sold, 110 million LPs and 50 million CDs. However, 1987 was the tiping point for the acceptance of the CD by American music buyers. In February, 1987, LPs accounted for only 8 to 11 percent of sales while CDs accounted for 70 percent of sales; selling at $16.98 per CD, the new format generated windfall profits.

In May, Warner Music purchased 100 percent of Chappell publishing. Freddie Bienstock's consortium had bought the publishing for $100 million in 1985; two years later the company was sold to Warners for $285 million or $712.50 per song. Warners earned $50 million with their 300,000 copyrights; Chappell earned about $100 million annually with its 400,000 copyrights. Creating the Warner Chappell publishing company meant that the new company was four times the size of six of America's next largest music publishing companies.

On January 3, the Rock and Roll Hall of Fame inducted its first woman, Aretha Franklin, in addition to the Coasters, Eddie Cochran, Bo Diddley, Marvin Gaye, Bill Haley, Clyde McPhatter, Rick Nelson, Roy Orbison, Carl Perkins, Smokey Robinson and Jackie Wilson.

The Beatles had been reluctant to allow their albums to be released on CDs but in February, the first four Beatles albums, *Please Please Me*, *With the Beatles*, *A Hard Day's Night* and *Beatles for Sale* were released by Capitol in their original U.K. line-up in mono.

In July, Guns N'Roses released their debut album, *Appetite for Destruction* which, after a slow start, became the bestselling debut album of all time with 18 million copies sold in the U.S.

On August 31, Michael Jackson released *Bad*, his first studio album since Thriller; Bad contained five singles that reached number one and in September, Jackson began the Bad World Tour to promote the album.

On November 24, a TV special, "Rolling Stone Magazine's 20 Years of Rock'n'Roll, on ABC chronicled the 20th anniversary of *Rolling Stone*. The special featured new interviews as well as vintage footage of Jimi Hendrix, The Doors, the Rolling Stones, David Bowie, Sex Pistols, Bruce Springsteen and other rock legends.

The musical *Les Miserable* opened on Broadway during 1987; it would run for 6,680 performances, second only to the run of *Cats*.

BMG/RCA

In 1987 RCA Records was purchased by the Bertelsmann Music Group (BMG), which was headquartered in Germany.

The Bertelsmann organization began in 1824 when Carl Bertelsmann opened a print shop in Gutersloh, Germany; in 1835 he began a religious publishing house with his first major seller a hymnal for children titled *The Little Mission Harp*. The company began publishing novels in 1851 and grew steadily through the years. Carl's son, Henrich, had a daughter who married Johannes Mohn and Mohn eventually took over the publishing business because there were no male heirs. During World War II, Bertelsmann was the largest producer of Nazi propaganda; both Heinrich Mohn, who owned the company, and his son Reinhard, were members of the SS.

After World War II, the company was closed for several years before Reinhard Mohn re-founded the company in 1947. During the 1950s, the company created a book club and in 1958 entered the music industry when they formed Ariola Records. In 1964 Bertelsmann began a movie company.

In 1979 Bertelsmann purchased Arista, an American label, and in 1980 purchased Bantam Books. In 1986 Bertelsman purchased Doubleday Publishing and RCA Victor Records.

In 1987 Bertlesman organized the BMG Music Group with RCA Records and Arista. RCA had first been acquired by General Electric when they acquired NBC, but the company was uncomfortable with the music business, so they sold RCA to Bertelsmann for $333 million in December, 1986; the label earned back its entire purchase price in three years.

Sony

Sony was begun in Tokyo after World War II by Akio Morita and Masaru Ibuka, who met while serving in the Navy. Morita came from a wealthy samurai family; as the eldest son, he was expected to take over the family's brewery but, from an early age, Morita was fascinated by electronics; as a child he assembled a radio receiver and crude phonograph. At Osaka University, he was influenced by a professor of physics. Masaru Ibuka was an electrical engineer, 13 years older than Morita, and the two formed the Tokyo Telecommunications Research Laboratories with $500 in capital; it was incorporated on May 7, 1946.

In 1950 Sony began making tape recorders and sold them to schools and courts. In 1952, the American occupation of Japan ended and Sony learned that AT&T owned rights to the transistor, which they had invented at their Bell Laboratories in 1947, and were willing to license it. AT&T thought the only use for the transistor was in hearing aids. Morita and Ibuka saw the possibilities of using transistors for electronic equipment and purchased the license for $25,000. In 1953, Morita came to New York to conclude the deal and decided his company name (Tokyo Tsushin Kogyo Kabushiki Kasha) needed to be changed; he chose "Sony" from the Latin word for sound, sonus, even though sony itself meant nothing in any language.

In 1955 Sony brought the first transistor radio to the market. The idea of a small radio appealed to Japanese customers and Morita pioneered the philosophy of leading the public with new products rather than asking what kind of products the public wanted. The transistor radio was enormously successful and Sony continued to pioneer new uses for the transistor, eventually creating the Walkman, a tiny tape player.

Akio Morita spent months in the United States during the mid-1950s, learning the market and the culture, and in 1960 moved to New York, where he headed Sony's first United States subsidiary. Sony became the first Japanese company to offer its stock for sale in the United States.

Morita stayed in the United States for a little over a year but was bothered by a number of things in American culture, which included schools that were "too permissive," "too many lawyers" with "too much to say about how business should operate" and Americans who were "too individualistic" and American companies who were "too obsessed with quick profits."

During the 1970s, Sony established production facilities outside Japan, first in the United States (San Diego) and then in Europe. They developed the first Video Cassette Recorder (VCR), the Beta, and in 1975 had the entire market to itself; however, Sony would not license its technology and their Japanese rival, Matsushita, developed the VHS and eventually dominated the VCR market; by 1983 Sony's share of VCRs had shrunk to 12 percent.

Sony Buys CBS Records

Sony and Philips united to develop and market the Compact Disc and that's when Sony realized they needed an entertainment catalog for their hardware company. In 1986, Akio Morita began courting CBS Records. The initial offer from Sony was $1.25 billion, which CBS turned down, although CBS CEO and president Lawrence Tisch wanted to sell it. Board Chairman William Paley demurred; he felt that CBS Records was an integral part of the CBS organization.

In addition to his roles as president and CEO, Tisch amassed a nearly 25 percent stake in CBS, which gave him leverage. Tisch was a money guy; he had no appreciation for the cultural impact on America that CBS Records had with its deep catalog of recordings. Tisch was also wary of CBS Records president Walter Yetnikoff, who was a loose cannon.

In October, 1987, Ted Turner tried to acquire CBS with a hostile takeover but was thwarted. Tisch wanted to keep the CBS TV network but strip the other assets away for cash. CBS Songs, their publishing company, was sold to a group headed by investor Stephen Swid and music executives Charles Koppleman and Marty Bandier for $125 million. The investors quickly sold the publishing company to Thorn-EMI for $295 million.

Paley had been reluctant to sell and the Board had nixed an agreement to sell, engineered by Tisch, but the stock market crash on October 19, 1987, gave Tisch more leverage. He offered CBS Records to Sony for $2 billion towards the end of 1987 and Sony accepted.

News

"The Simpsons" first appeared as a series of short cartoons on "The Tracy Ulman Show" on April 19.

In August, the Federal Communications Commission rescinded the Fairness Doctrine, which required radio and television stations to present alternative views on controversial issues. From that point forward, radio and TV could focus on one political view during their broadcast; they no longer had to present the opposite view as well.

In December, Fluxetine, marketed as Prozac, was approved for use as an anti-depression pill by the Food and Drug Administration.

Technology

In March, the "Woodstock of physics" occurred during the annual meeting of the American Physical Society when 51 presentations addressed the science of high temperature superconductors.

In July, Konami released the video game, Metal Gear in Japan. The video games Five Nights at Freddy's and Team Fortress were also introduced in 1987.

In December, Microsoft released Windows 2.0 and during the year Thomas Knoll and John Knoll developed the first version of Photoshop.

1988
News: 1988

In 1988, for the first time, compact discs outsold LPs. In the ten years from 1978 to 1988, LP sales dropped 80 percent while the industry, as a whole grew. Sales of singles was nearly non-existent; singles only survived because they were needed to send to radio stations for airplay and for jukeboxes.

In April, Tommy Mottola was named to head CBS Records. In 1989, CBS purchased Tree Publishing in Nashville. It was one of the few independent publishing companies with a significant catalog. CBS needed music publishing; three years earlier CBS sold their publishing to a consortium headed by Stephen Swid, Martin Bandier and Charles Koppelman, who renamed the publishing company SBK.

The album Straight Outta Compton by NWA pulled the West Coast rap scene together and resulted in a number of gangsta rap artists and albums/ Nineteen eighty-eight was an election year. The Democrats nominated Massachusetts governor Michael Dukakis and the Republicans nominated Vice President George H.W. Bush, who won the election in November.

On January 26, *The Phantom of the Opera* debuted on Broadway; it became one of the most successful Broadway show, running for over 10,000 performances.

In Senate testimony, NASA scientist stated that man-made global warming had begun.

In 1988, the terrorist organization, Al-Qaeda, was formed by Osama bin Laden.

Technology

In March, Microsoft released Windows 2.1. The first computer worm distributed by the Internet, the "Morris worm," was written by Robert Tappan Morris and launched from the Massachusetts Institute of Technology.

TAT-8, the first transatlantic telephone cable to use optical filters, was completed, which led to more robust connections between the U.S. and European internet.

Tim Berners-Lee began to openly discuss his plans to for what became known as the World Wide Web.

1989
Year 1989

The year 1989 was tumultuous year, a year of upheavals that had far ranging impact. The end of the 1980s was the beginning of the end for the Soviet Union that had existed since World War II and the end of communism in a number of countries. It was a year that shook the world.

On January 7, Japanese Emperor Hirohito died; he was the Emperor who signed off on the Japanese military's bombing of Pearl Harbor in 1941 that led that nation into war against the United States and brought America into World War II. Since the end of World War II, Hirohito had been the Emperor of a peaceful Japan and he emerged during the 44 years after World War II as the symbol of a peaceful Japanese nation whose economy, at the time of his death, was the second largest in the world. The funeral of Hirohito on February 24 was attended by representatives from 160 nations.

The Supreme Leader of Iran, Ayatollah Ruhollah Khomeini, had established an Islamic state in Iran and on February 14 declared a fatwa, calling for the death of author Salman Rushdie and his publisher for releasing the novel, *The Satanic Verses*.

On March 24, the Exxon Valdez tanker ran aground in Prince William Sound in Alaska, resulting in 240,000 barrels of oil spilled into the water. It was the worst oil spill disaster in history.

On April, 14, the Federal government seized the Lincoln Savings and Loan Association in Irvine, California. Charles Keating, head of Lincoln, was sent to prison during the savings and loan crisis which saw lax oversight and highly speculative investments, as well as fraud, the closing of 1,043 of the 3,234 savings and loan banks, which were designed to collect deposits and issue home mortgages, car and other types of personal loans. The crisis cost American taxpayers over $200 billion for bank bailouts.

On April 27, there was a major demonstration in Beijing as part of the Tiananmen Square student protests, which continued. Zhao Zyang, who had replaced Hu Yaobang as General Secretary of the Communist Party, was sympathetic to the demonstrators but a group of Party leaders, led by Li Peng, wanted to crush the demonstrations. Zhao met resistance for his economic and political reforms.

Zhao refused to order the military to crush the rebellion but martial law was declared in China by the Politburo. On May 19, after he resigned as General Secretary, Zhao went to Tiananmen Square and gave a speech to the students. Shortly after, he was arrested and placed under house arrest for the rest of his life.

On June 4, live coverage on television saw the Chinese army march into Tiananmen Square with tanks and guns and crush the demonstrations.

In Iran, the Ayatollah Khomeini died on June 6; a large crowd rushed to obtain a last glimpse of his body, forcing the funeral to be postponed for a day.

Tom Petty

On Tom Petty's ninth album, *Full Moon Fever*, he recorded his anthem, "I Won't Back Down." The song, according to Petty, reflected the creed he lived by. The single, his seventh chart single, featured former Beatle George Harrison on guitar and backing vocals and reached number 12 on the Hot 100. His next single was "Runnin' Down a Dream" and the third single from that album, "Free Fallin'," reached number seven on the chart.

By the time Petty recorded his *Full Moon Fever* album, he had established a solid track record and earned a rock pedigree. He was born October 20, 1950, in Gainesville, Florida and first became interested in a career in music when he met Elvis Presley on the set of the movie *Follow That Dream*, which was filmed in Ocala. He was ten years old when he met Elvis through his uncle, who worked on the set. When Petty returned home after that encounter, he traded his Wham-O Slingshot to a friend for a collection of Elvis 45s.

Petty's next musical inspiration was the Beatles when they appeared on "The Ed Sullivan Show" in February, 1964. Petty was enthralled.

There were a lot of young men who formed bands after the Beatles appeared on the Sullivan show and Petty was no exception. He formed the Epics which evolved into Mudcatch, and included Mike Campbell and Benmont Tench, who became future Heartbreakers . The group was popular in Gainesville and recorded one single, "Depot Street," that didn't chart.

Tom Petty dropped out of high school when he was 17 to pursue music. That caused a conflict with his father, who verbally and physically abused him because he couldn't understand why his son wanted to chase the music dream instead of being a real man with a real job. In his personal life, Petty had an uneasy relationship with his father.

When Mudcatch broke up, Petty decided to embark on a solo career; Benmont Tench had formed a group and Petty, with Mike Campbell, joined. The other musicians were Ron Blair on bass and Stan Lynch on drums; this was the original Heartbreakers. The group recorded an album for Shelter Records and released a single, "Breakdown." The album reached number 55 on the Billboard chart and remained on the chart for almost a year. It was more popular in the U.K. than the U.S.A. so Petty toured there.

Their second album, *You're Gonna Get It* reached the number 22 spot on the album chart and had two chart singles, "I Need to Know" (#41) and "Listen to Her Heart" (#59).

Petty's third album, *Damn the Torpedoes*, released in 1979, was his breakthrough album. It reached number two on the *Billboard* album chart and stayed in that positon for seven weeks and a total of 66 weeks on the chart. The album sold almost two million copies and contained three singles, "Don't Do Me Like That" reached number ten and "Refugee" reached number 15. The third single, "Here Comes My Girl," only got to number 59.

That put him in the rock star category and he appeared with a number of other rockers on the Musicians United for Safe Energy concert at Madison Square Garden in September, 1979. His song, "Cry to Me," was released on the album, *No Nukes*.

Petty's next album, *Hard Promises*, was released in 1981 and reached number five on the album chart and sold platinum. On that album, he recorded a single with Stevie Nicks, "Stop Draggin' My Heart Around," which reached number three on the Hot 100 and stayed in that position for six weeks.

The album *Long After Dark*, released in 1982, reached number nine on the album chart. At the Live Aid concert in 1985, Petty and the Heartbreakers performed four songs from the Philadelphia stage. His *Southern Accents* album, released in 1985, reached number seven on the chart and contained the single, "Don't Come Around Here No More." Artista had to have a video for MTV so Petty starred in one dressed as the Mad Hatter, chasing Alice and the rabbit.

Tom Petty's live album, *Pack Up The Plantation,* released in late 1985, reached number 22 on the chart and led to an invitation from Bob Dylan to join his "True Confessions" tour. That led to Petty and Dylan (with Mike Campbell) writing "Jammin' Me," that made it to number 18. After his album, *Let Me Up (I've Had Enough)*, Petty joined Bob Dylan, Jeff Lynne, Roy Orbison and George Harrison in the Traveling Wilburys.

The first song they recorded, "Handle With Care," was originally planned as a "B" side for a George Harrison single, but the group believed it was too good for a "B" side and decided to record an entire album, titled *Traveling Wilburys, Vol. 1.* "Handle With Care" was the first single and "End of the Line" was their second. Their second album, done after Roy Orbison died, was titled *Traveling Wilburys, Vol 3* because a number of bootlegs from their sessions had been leaked that they considered that collection of songs as Traveling *Wilburys Vol. 2.*

All of that led to Petty's *Full Moon Fever* album, his first "solo" album, although some of the Heartbreakers played on it.

Class of '89

New talent emerged in 1989 in country music with the first chart records by Garth Brooks ("Much Too Young To Feel This Damn Old" and "If Tomorrow Never Comes"), Clint Black ("A Better Man," "Killin' Time" and "Nobody's Home"), Alan Jackson ("Blue Blooded Woman"), Mary Chapin Carpenter ("How Do" and "Never Had It So Good), Travis Tritt ("Country Club") and Dwight Yoakam ("I Sang Dixie") all debuted that year. During 1989 there were number one records by Rodney Crowell, The Judds, Alabama, Ricky Van Shelton, Keith Whitley, Reba McEntire, Shenadoah, Kathy Mattea, Steve Wariner and Rosanne Cash. During the next five years, the sound of country returned to a sound closer to its roots.

CMA Awards: 1989

The 23rd Annual Country Music Association Awards were held on October 9, 1989, and hosted by Anne Murray and Kenny Rogers at the Grand

Ole Opry House. Entertainer of the Year was George Strait, Song of the Year was "Chiseled in Stone" by Max D. Barnes and Vern Gosdin, Single of the Year was "I'm No Stranger to the Rain" by Keith Whitley, Album of the Year was *Will the Circle Be Unbroken: Volume Two* by the Nitty Gritty Dirt Band, Male Vocalist was Ricky Van Shelton, Female Vocalist was Kathy Mattea, Vocal Duo was The Judds, Vocal Group was Highway 101, Musician was Johnny Gimble, Horizon winner was Clint Black, Vocal Event and Music Video of the Year was "There's a Tear in My Beer" by Hank Williams Sr. and Hank Williams Jr.; Jack Stapp, Cliffie Stone and Hank Thompson were inducted into the Country Music Hall of Fame.

Record Industry News

Cassette sales peaked in 1989; from that point on, the CD was on a rapid ascent as consumers bought CDs to replace favorite LPs and cassettes as well as new releases. During the first six months of 1989, 96.8 million CDs were sold vs. 17.5 million LPs and consumers purchased 1.2 million CD players vs. 180,000 turntables. Labels compiled special boxed sets of past recordings and profits soared. Music consumers were in love with the Compact Disc.

Sony and Philips joined forces to develop a rewritable CD. Pre-recorded CD-ROM discs had featured elaborate video displays and audio for home computers but the audio could only be played, it could not be recorded.

Geffen Records was doing well with Guns N'Roses album, *Appetite for Destruction*, which sold 13 million copies. At the end of 1989, Geffen had notched up sales of $225 million with a catalog of 50 gold, 22 platinum and nine multi-platinum albums.

Wall Street had never paid much attention to the music industry; it was volatile, unpredictable and they didn't understand it but the 1980s was an era of mergers and the record industry caught Wall Street's attention. By the end of 1989, BMG owned RCA Records, Sony owned CBS Records and Warner Brothers was contemplating a merger with Time-AOL. Early in the 1990s, MCA Records was sold to Matsushita. Executives and shareholders at record labels focused on making money rather than making records.

Inducted into the Rock and Roll Hall of Fame were Dion, Otis Redding, the Rolling Stones, The Temptations and Stevie Wonder.

New Kids on the Block

New Edition, formed by Maurice Starr, embarked on their first major concert tour but when they returned to their homes in the projects, each member of the group received a check for $1.87; Starr explained that tour expenses were the reason they did not receive more. That led New Edition to leave Starr in 1984 and his label, Streetwise, after litigation; they then joined MCA Records. That led to Starr's decision to form an all white group of young boys with his business partner, Mary Alford; the group was patterned after First Edition and would record R&B songs written and produced by Starr.

Starr and Alford auditioned boys and began forming a group, first with 15-year old Donnie Wahlberg, then his brother Mark, Danny Wood, Jordan Knight and his brother, Jonathan. Mark Wahlberg dropped out and was replaced by 12-year old Joey McIntyre. Starr named the group Nynuk and rehearsed them after school and on weekends. He secured a contract with Columbia Records, who insisted the name of the group be changed; they became New Kids on the Block, which was the name of a rap song Donnie Wahlberg had written for their first album.

Columbia released their first album, *New Kids on the Block*, in April, 1986, which was, for the most part, written and produced by Starr. Their first single, "Be My Girl," reached number 90 on *Billboard's* R&B chart; their second single, "Stop It Girl," did not chart as the group toured clubs, bars and school dances in New England.

Starr convinced Columbia to release a second album and during most of 1987 and early 1988 the group was in the studio with Starr. The group was dissatisfied with their "bubblegum" sound and wanted more input into the songs and recording; as a result, Wahlberg, Wood and Jordan Knight were credited as "Associate Producer" on their second album, *Hangin' Tough*. Their first single from that album, "Please Don't Go Girl," did not immediately catch on at radio so Columbia decided to drop the group, but a station in Florida began playing it and received numerous requests. Columbia then decided employ a full promotion effort behind the single and group; they re-shot the video of the song and sent it to radio stations, who saw the visual appeal of the group. "Please Don't Go Girl" entered *Billboard's* R&B chart in April, 1988, and reached number 55; in June, it entered the *Billboard* Hot 100 chart and rose to number ten, remaining on that chart for 28 weeks.

Their album, *Hangin' Tough*, was released in September and the group appeared on several TV shows and was the opening act for a Tiffany tour in the U.S. That set up their fourth single, "You've Got It (The Right Stuff)," which entered *Billboard's* Hot 100 in November and reached number three, remaining on that chart for 26 weeks; it also entered the R&B charts and reached number 28. The single was helped by MTV, which put the video in regular rotation. Their next single, "I'll Be Loving You (Forever)" debuted on the Hot 100 in April, 1989 and was their first number one (it reached number 12 on the R&B chart).

New Kids on the Block had a string of hit singles in 1989, "Hangin' Tough," "Didn't I (Blow Your Mind)," "Cover Girl" and "This One's For the Children." By the end of that year their album, *Hangin' Tough*, was number one on the *Billboard* album chart, platinum eight times over and spent a total of 132 weeks on the chart. "This One's For the Children" was from their album *Merry, Merry Christmas*. Columbia released a video documentary of the band that included four videos of their hits and a live concert during their 1989 tour.

New Kids on the Block was one of the hottest musical acts in America by 1990 and their fourth album, *Step by Step* was released in May; the single, "Step By Step," entered the Hot 100 that month and reached number one, where it remained for three weeks; the album was triple platinum. Over half the songs on their fourth album were co-written and produced by the group's members. Their follow-up single, "Tonight" was a top ten but "Let's Try It Again" only reached number 53 and "Games" only reached number 58 in 1991.

During 1990 New Kids on the Block performed 200 concerts and had a successful pay-per-view TV special. They merchandised T-shirts, dolls, lunch boxes, buttons and trading cards; there were over 200,000 members in their fan clubs and a Saturday morning cartoon starred the group. That year, New Kids on the Block had over $800 million in merchandising sales and over $200 million in ticket sales; in 1991 they were the highest paid entertainers in the United States (beating Michael Jackson and Madonna) and performed at the Super Bowl's halftime show.

The rap against New Kids on the Block was that they could not sing and that Maurice Starr actually sang on their records. The group denied it but fans were skeptical after it was revealed at the end of 1989 that Milli Vanilli did not actually sing on their records. The New Kids on the Block admitted they performed with backing tracks during live performances and that Starr sang harmony on some background vocals; however, the group denied that Starr sang lead on their vocals.

By 1992, New Kids on the Block faced a backlash from critics, who dismissed their claim to be an urban act. Grunge and Gangsta Rap had become popular in the music industry, so a group with a clean cut, wholesome appeal was not appealing.

In 1993 they split with Maurice Starr and changed their name to NKOTB; their fourth studio album, *Face the Music*, was released in 1994 but did not have the commercial appeal of their previous albums. Almost all of the songs on that album were written and/or co-produced by members of the group; their final single, "Dirty Dawg," only reached number 66 on the *Billboard* Hot 100, lasting only six weeks on the chart.

Fall: 1989

On November 9, East Germans flooded through the checkpoints at the Berlin Wall after an announcement was made during a live broadcast that new rules for traveling from East to West Germany would be put in effect immediately. That was Europe's 9/11 (Europeans place the day first, then the month.)

During 1989, the first Al Qaeda cell in the United States began in New York City.

1990
CDs become the dominant format

During 1990 and 1991, CDs replaced records in store bins; vinyl became a staple in the cutout bins and retail chains either stopped stocking vinyl or severely cut back on availability. There were 90 million turntables in homes—but most were not being used. The emergence of CDs was an opportunity for record labels to make big profits; LPs sold for $8 or $9 while CDs sold for $16 or $18. Rap had grown and now accounted for about nine percent of all sales, or $70 million. Rap received little or no airplay but albums dominated the charts. Labels had to cut deals with people they'd rather not deal with in order to get into the rap market. Atlantic put up $10 million to bankroll Death Row Records, which was founded by rap producers Dr. Dre and Suge Knight, who both had criminal records.

During the 1990s, labels inserted new clauses in artists contracts which held back more money for recoupables. The new contracts continued to hold recording costs as recoupables but added "promotion" costs, which grew to where it included money for tour support, videos, marketing (posters, advertising, parties) and independent promotion fees. There was also a "new technology" deduction, which began when the cost of manufacturing was high for CDs because it was a start up cost.

Gonzo journalist Hunter Thompson summed it up when he wrote "The music business is a cruel and shallow money trench, a long plastic hallway where thieves and pimps run free, and good men die like dogs. There's also a negative side."

Time-Warner

In 1958 Warner Brothers expanded from the movie business to the music business, urged by new Board members and by the fact that the music industry was accounting for big profits while the movie industry felt threatened by television. They hired James Conkling, formerly head of Capitol and Columbia Records but Conkling's taste were more middle-of-the-road and not in tune with rock'n'roll and the tastes of a young audience. The label opened for business on March 19, 1958, and early releases came from actors signed to Warner Brothers: Tab Hunter, Edd "Cookie" Byrnes, Connie Stevens, Jack Webb and William Holden. They had a hit single, "Kookie, Kookie (Lend Me Your Comb)" by Ed Byrnes, who played "Kookie" Kookson on the TV detective series "77 Sunset Strip." They signed the Everly Brothers, who hit with "Cathy's Clown" and then signed comedian Bob Newhart, whose debut album, *The Button Down Mind*, reached number one on the pop album charts and went "Gold."

The growth of Warner Brothers came from purchasing several companies: Reprise from Frank Sinatra, Elektra from Jac Holzman and Atlantic from Ahmed Ertegun and Jerry Wexler.

In 1989, Warners merged with Time/Life, the publishing empire begun by Henry Luce in 1937. After that merger they became the largest entertainment/media company in the United States; their music division by 1995 accounted for 25 percent of their revenues.

The Time-Warner merge was an outrage to Time Inc.'s stockholders because it wasn't really a merger; Time had to buy Warners and that meant borrowing over $10.7 billion in order to pay off everyone. Time's stockholders saw that as an enrichment of Warner's top executives. Finally, it was agreed that 500 Warner executives received, in cash, $680 million and stock options at $38 a share. Steve Ross, Chair of Warners, received $193 million while Bob Daly and Terry Semel with the film division received $50 million each. The thirty law firms handling the buyout made $76 million. Over $60 million was received by four investment-advisory firms.

David Geffen was mad; Steven Ross had not informed him about the deal. Geffen's label was hot with Guns n'Roses, Whitesnake, Aerosmith, Cher and Don Henley. His distribution deal with Warners would soon expire and Ross wanted to keep Geffen but he had no leverage; Ross had given Geffen 100 percent of his record company. Geffen wanted to leave

Warners so he approached MCA about selling his company; they bought it for $550 million in stock.

MCA

The record label roots for MCA went back to Decca Records, formed in England in 1929 with the U.S. label founded in 1934. Music Corporation of America (MCA) began as a booking agency in Chicago in 1924 by bandleader Jules Stein. His company grew quickly and by the early 1940s controlled half the top named stars in American entertainment. Stein hired Lew Wasserman in 1936; in 1946 Wasserman became president of the Agency. During the next 15 years MCA became the largest producer of TV shows and films. In 1962, MCA merged as an equal with Decca Records with MCA as the surviving company. Decca owned 89 percent of Universal Pictures but, after the merger, MCA owned all of Universal. The Department of Justice ruled that MCA could not own both a talent agency and a movie company so MCA divested itself of the talent agency. That move was completed in 1966. The year before, 1965, MCA entered the music publishing business when it purchased Leeds Music and Duchess Music, headed by Lou Levy.

On March 1, 1973, all the recording divisions of MCA were united under the MCA label. The company continued to grow and in 1988 MCA purchased Motown, the label founded in 1960 in Detroit by Berry Gordy. In 1985, MCA bought Chess Records and in 1990 bought GRP Records and Geffen Records.

Matsushita was anxious to buy MCA but, during the negotiations, Thorn-EMI put in a bid of $750 million, which raised the price for MCA. In 1990, MCA was purchased by the Matsushita Electrical Industrial Company in Japan for $5.7 billion. Matsushita, who operated in the U.S under brand names that included Panasonic, had begun looking for a record company to buy after Sony bought CBS. They had won the video duel with Sony with their VHS model replacing Sony's Betamax in 1975.

Matsushita hired Michael Ovitz, head of Creative Artists Agency, to advise them in their search. Ovitz had advised Sony on its purchase of the film studio, Columbia Pictures. Prior to the sale of Geffen to MCA, Ovitz met with Masahiko Hirata, the second in command at the Japanese company, and recommended they pursue MCA five months after MCA purchased Geffen. Matsushita began serious negotiations with MCA. MCA's price per share was $34.50 but news of the negotiations leaked and the price per share increased to $54.25. Lew Wasserman, Chairman of the Board at MCA, set a purchase price of $71 per share.

That meant that David Geffen got $710 million. When the deal was completed, Eddie Rosenblatt continued to run the day-to-day activities of Geffen Records while David Geffen had a four year contract that gave him an annual salary or $660,000. When 1980 began, David Geffen was worth $30 million; when 1990 ended, Geffen was worth $1 billion.

The Japanese company did not mesh well with the Hollywood movie and music industries and in 1995 sold 80 percent to Seagram, a Canadian beverage empire headed by Edgar Bronfman, Jr. The music division of that corporate entity accounted for a little over 10 percent of total revenues by 1995--an important but relatively small part of their entertainment conglomerate. In 1998 MCA purchased Polygram Records and changed their name to the Universal Music Group.

MC Hammer & Rap

Rap exploded in 1990; MC Hammer's single, "U Can't Touch This" was number one on *Billboard's* R&B chart, reached the top ten on *Billboard's* Hot 100 chart and his album, *Please, Hammer, Don't Hurt 'em* was number one on the *Billboard* album chart for 21 weeks.

Stanley Kirk Burrell, born March 30, 1962 in Oakland, California, was one of eight children. Outside the Oakland Coliseum, where the Oakland A's played, 11-year-old Burrell chased stray baseballs to sell and danced accompanied by a beatboxer. Charles O. Finley, owner of the A's, saw the young boy and, impressed with his energy and flair, hired him as a clubhouse assistant and batboy. (Burrell served as batboy for the A's 1973-1980). He acquired the nickname "Hammer" because of his resemblance to Henry Aaron, who was known as "The Hammer." The "MC" came because he was "Master of Ceremonies" when he performed at various clubs when the A's played on the road.

After high school, Burrell attended college briefly, then served in the Navy for three years. Burrell and Jon Gibson, formed a Christian rap group, the Holy Ghost Boys, and recorded songs that were released on Gibson's album *Change of Heart*. That became contemporary Christian music's first authentic rap hit.

During the mid-1980s, Hammer borrowed $20,000 from Oakland A's players Mike Davis and Dwayne Murphy each to start a music business, Bust It Productions, that evolved into an independent label, Bustin' Records. Burrell recorded singles, sold records out of the trunk of his car and relentlessly marketed himself. His debut album as MC Hammer, *Feel My Power*, was released in 1987 on his Oaktown Records label. It was produced by Felton Pilate of Con Funk Shun and sold over 60,000 copies. Disc Jockey Tony Valera with KSOL played the track "Let's Get It Started," which became popular in clubs.

Hammer's single, "Ring 'Em" was promoted through street marketing by Hammer and his wife as well as on mix tapes on radio. It also became popular in dance clubs in the San Francisco Bay area. Hammer organized a troupe of dancers, musicians and backup vocalists for his shows and, at a show in an Oakland club, impressed a Capitol Records executive in the audience. Hammer had been offered recording contracts by major labels previously but turned them down because he was successful as an independent. The Capitol offer wasn't turned down; they gave him a $1,750,000 advance and a multi-album contract.

After signing with Capitol, Hammer re-issued his first album, *Let's Get It Started*, a revised version of Feel My Power with added tracks, that sold over two million copies. His album contained the singles "Pump It Up," "Turn This Mutha Out," "Let's Get It Started" and "They Put Me in the Mix," which all charted.

Hammer decided that he wanted his next album to be more musical. He recorded "U Can't Touch This," which he premiered on the Arsenio Hall Show in 1989. Hammer had developed a reputation for dissing other rappers so he named his next album *Please Hammer, Don't Hurt 'Em*. It was released in February, 1990, and included the single "U Can't Touch This," which samplbed Rick Hames' "Super Freak." The album was produced, recorded and mixed by Felton Pilate and James Earley in a studio installed by Hammer in the back of his tour bus; he recorded while touring.

The single "U Can't Touch This" debuted at number 27 on the *Billboard* Hot 100 and received extensive airplay; however, it was only released as a 12-inch single. Hammer followed "U Can't Touch This" with "Have You Seen Her" (a cover of the Chi-Lites record) and "Pray" (which was his biggest single, reaching number two on the Hot 100.

Please Hammer, Don't Hurt 'Em was the first rap album to achieve Diamond status (sales of over ten million) and led to a European tour and a movie. The success of MC Hammer spawned jealousy and backlash from the rap community, which criticized his clean-cut image, the repetitive lyrics and his reliance on extensive sampling of other artists. Those criticism were often heard in the rap records of other artists who, in the rap tradition, named names and settle scores with their lyrics.

MC Hammer became the first household name in rap and his success raised the awareness and popularity of rap in the mainstream.

Rap: 1990

The first rap song to reach number one on the *Billboard* Hot 100 was "Ice Ice Baby" by Vanilla Ice in 1990. That song, and Hammer's "U Can't Touch This," led the way in making rap more commercial and better known with the mainstream audience. In 1990, rap fully arrived as an accepted genre in middle America.

Public Enemy released *Fear of a Black Planet* in 1990, which followed their single, "Fight the Power," in 1989. The biggest selling single in 1989 was Ton Loc's "Wild Thing" and music journalists noted that almost a third of the songs on the *Billboard* Hot 100 during 1989 were hip hop songs.

The term, "Six Elements of the Hip Hop Movement" was credited to Ronald "Bee-Stinger" Savage, formerly with Zulu Nation, and inspired by Public Enemy's records. The "Six Elements" are Consciousness Awareness, Civil Rights Awareness, Activism Awareness, Justice, Political Awareness and Community Awareness in music.

There was a dark side to rap; the East Coast-West Coast that resulted in violence and the deaths of two major rappers, Notorious B.I.G. and Tupac Shakur.

Music News: 1990

MTV's "Unplugged" series, where artists performed a set with acoustic guitars, was broadcast for the first time on January 21

On April 16, a huge tribute concert for Nelson Mandela at Wembley Stadium in London celebrated Mandela's release from prison. Mandela appeared in a pre-taped 45 minute speech at the event. Artists who performed included Anita Baker, Tracy Chapman, Peter Gabriel, The Neville Brothers and Neil Young. The event was broadcast to 61 countries around the globe. Mandela was released on February 11 from Victor Verster Prison, near Cape Town, after spending 27 years behind bars.

Madonna continued to be controversial. On May 29, police threatened to arrest her in Toronto is she simulated masturbation while she sang "Like a Virgin." Madonna performed her set without changes and the police chose not to press charges; later the police denied they had threatened to arrest her but the threats were caught on film.

Tragedy struck the rock world on August 27 when Stevie Ray Vaughan and promoter Bill Graham were killed in a helicopter crash after a concert in East Troy, Wisconsin.

On September 4, Walter Yetnikoff stepped down as President of CBS Records after 15 years at the helm.

Rap act 2 Live Crew challenged authorities with sexually explicit lyrics in their songs. However, a Florida jury acquitted them of obscenity in October for a concert in June.

Milli Vanilli admitted to lip synching their hits, such as "Girl You Know It's True." They later had their Grammys revoked.

Technology

PSInet and EUnet, the first internet companies catered to commercial users, began selling Internet access to commercial customers in the U.S. and the Netherland.

The Nintendo World Championships were held on March 8, which began a year of gaming competitions in 29 American cities.

The TAT-8 fiber cable provided the first high speed transatlantic internet connection on March 15. The cable ran between CERN (European Organization for Nuclear Research) and Cornell University and allowed faster internet connection between the United States and Europe. On October 30, the cable failed, forcing a slow down in internet traffic between the United States and Europe.

Microsoft released Windows 3.0.

World News: 1990

The twentieth anniversary of Earth Day was celebrated on April 22.

In June, Joanne Rowling was riding on a train from Manchester to Euston Station in London when she got the idea for Harry Potter. She began writing the story, which she finished in 1995; it was published in 1997.

On June 13, the destruction of the Berlin War began; it had opened in November, seven months earlier.

British Prime Minister Margaret Thatcher, the first female Prime Minister of the U.K., resigned her office on November 22; she had been in power for 11 years.

Iraq Invades Kuwait: The start of the first Iraq War

On August 2, 1990, Iraq, led by Saddam Hussein, invaded Kuwait. Four days later the United Nations Security Council ordered a trade embargo against Iraq. On August 7, President Bush ordered U.S. combat planes and troops to Saudi Arabia in order to stop a possible attack by Iraq. The next day, Iraq announced that it had annexed Kuwait.

Egypt, Syria and ten other Arab states agreed to send forces to Saudi Arabia to protect it against a possible invasion. On August 22, President Bush called up U.S. military reservists to serve in the Persian Gulf crisis.

On September 11, President George H.W. Bush delivered a nationally televised speech where he threatened to use force to remove Iraq from Kuwait. The United Nations Security Council passed a resolution on November 29 authorizing military action in Iraq if the Iraqis did not withdraw their forces from Kuwait and free all foreign hostages by Tuesday, January 15, 1991.

On December 6, Saddam Hussein released a group of foreign hostages.

The Beginnings of the World Wide Web

In October, Tim Berners-Lee began his work on the World Wide Web; he had outlined his ideas for what became the World Wide Web 19 months earlier, in 1989. On November 12, he published a more detailed version. On December 20, Berners-Lee completed a test for the first webpage at CERN.

1991
CD-R (CD Recordable Disc) introduced

In 1990, the CD-Recordable disc (CD-R) was introduced and in January, 1991, Commodore marketed the first computer with a CD-ROM (Read Only Memory) player, followed by Macintosh in 1992.

In his book, *Appetite for Self-Destruction*, author Steve Knopper states that the music industry was not enthused with the development of the Compact Disc. To switch to the CD, the record labels "would have to shut down multimillion-dollar LP plants that had been operating for decades, which meant layoffs. They would have to reissue their entire catalogs in digital form. (Cassettes, for the time being, would survive; label executives believed two 'carriers,' an expensive one and a cheaper one, were the most the public could possibly handle without feeling swamped or confused.) They would have to persuade retailers to replace every LP rack in every store with smaller racks that accommodated compact discs. And they would have to change the artwork"

However, Knopper notes that the recording industry also felt that "The CD was an opportunity to change consumers' expectations about what music should cost" because the opening price for the CD was $16.95 while the price of LPs was "stuck at $8.98."

When the Compact Disc was introduced in the United States in June, 1983, there wasn't a single CD manufacturing plant in America; the following year, CBS converted their Terre Haute, Indiana, plant to CD production at a cost of $20 million, half of which came from Sony.

In 1983, there were 17.3 million CDs bought but, as the CD became the preferred carrier of music, that figure rose to 286.5 million in 1999, which meant the recording industry was flooded with cash.

Some music industry executives were concerned that there were some hidden dangers into creating a "perfect" digital carrier; they were right.

Sound Scan

The information on sales of recordings is collected each week by *Billboard* magazine, which compiles charts of the top songs and albums in the country in all music fields based on sales and airplay. SoundScan technology has been in place since 1991 and gives a quick, accurate reading of what sells and what doesn't. This differs greatly in the way charts used to be compiled.

Before SoundScan, *Billboard* and other trades regularly called a pre-selected group of record stores and distributors (called "reporters") around the country and asked a manager or assistant manager (or whoever was in charge of giving the report) to tell them the top sellers in the various categories (country, rock, rhythm and blues, etc.). Sales figures were not collected; the stores only gave a relative ranking. In other words, the top seller was such and such, the second was such and such, on down the line.

Since country music consumers generally did not shop in traditional record stores--either those in the mall or at free standing locations--those stores did not sell many country albums. Further, those stores generally employed young people who favored rock'n'roll or the popular music of the day and had an antipathy for country music at best and at worst a hatred. So they generally didn't report country sales along with pop sales.

Further, there was a psychological factor involved. Country music had its own section, generally at the back of the store, while pop music was at the front of the store so country music was not even considered in "pop" sales unless an album sold so well that it was moved to the front of the store. That happened to artists during the early 1970s such and Charlie Rich and during the late 1970s with Kenny Rogers. The key to big sales for country music was in "Crossovers," or records that "crossed over" from the country to the pop music charts. Not only did that mean the album was on both charts, it also meant it was moved to the front of the stores and reporters thought about it differently and reported it with the pop music releases. Although much has been made about the success of country music on the pop charts during the 1990s, in truth the sales of country artists Waylon Jennings and Willie Nelson during the "outlaw movement" in the mid-1970s, the success of Kenny Rogers, Alabama and Willie Nelson in the early 1980s after the "Urban Cowboy" phenomena, and the success of Randy Travis in the mid-1980s compared favorably with country sales during the 1990s. SoundScan was not in place before 1991, so there was a distorted picture of the popularity of country music. Simply put, it was generally assumed that rock ruled and country really could not compete in terms of sales.

With the advent of SoundScan, all those problems were eliminated; instead, the raw data of unbiased sales figures were reported and it was discovered that country music competed with pop sellers; in fact, it outsold a number of pop music sellers. That had been an open secret within the music industry for a number of years, at least among those in the accounting departments at the major labels, but the pop music world in general refused to believe that country music (or contemporary Christian music) could sell in such huge numbers. While Fleetwood Mac's albums were setting the pop music world on fire in the mid-70s, Slim Whitman was outselling them with his "Greatest Hits" package. That was different; Fleetwood Mac sold in retailers while Whitman sold over TV. Still, it was a harbinger of things to come.

The demographic, or age group, of country music buyers had generally been 35-50 but during the 1990s that figure dropped down into the teens--and that was important because young people who set the musical trends. Record companies regularly market to youth and the reason is fairly simple. The American culture is obsessed with youth and youth (ages 10-24) were the most active record buyers. Actually, the demographics of the record buying public had been divided into roughly three equal categories: 10-18, 18-25 and 25-50 with the 18-34 demographic the most desired group. Each of those groups bought about one third of the total recordings sold, but the older group (25-50) tended to mirror what younger people bought or they bought catalog ("oldies"). That was because, essentially, older people still wanted to remain young or keep their connection to "youth."

For country music to reach the youth--who tend to be more prone to fads--the music had to become "hip." That happened in two ways. First, the rise of CMT (Country Music Television) with its emphasis on videos broadcast directly into homes broke down old stereotypes of country music. Next, record companies signed attractive young artists who appealed to a young audience. Finally, the term "country" changed its meaning. That came from a shift in the American population.

Before World War II, rural areas in the United States had about two thirds of the population while the urban areas had about a third. In 1940, about 23 percent of the population lived on farms, a figure which had been declining throughout the twentieth century (in 1900 the figure was 39 percent). During that war, as war-related manufacturing plants opened in cities and there was an exodus into urban areas. With the wiring of cities and the profusion of electricity came the beckoning of bright lights in the big cities. No longer were people tied to daylight hours like they were on the farm. (Rural areas did not begin to receive electricity until after the Rural Electrification Bill was passed in 1936 and it was not until after World War II that rural America was fully wired for electricity.) By 1950 only 15 percent of the population lived on farms and a decade later that figure dropped to eight percent. It has continued to drop since and now hovers at less than two percent.

In cities, the image of the rural person was that of a country bumpkin, a hayseed and a rube. The image of the city dweller was that of someone cultured, sophisticated, wise to the ways of the world. So the term "country" was something most people fled; they wanted to be "citified." Thus the terms "country" and "country music" had a negative image with many in the nation.

The 1990 census showed the United States to be an urban nation. Actually, more people lived in the suburbs which surround a city than anywhere else, which meant that about 80 percent live in metropolitan areas. Only about 20 percent of the nation lived in rural areas and only 4.6 million (or less than 2 percent) lived on farms. However, by this time the cities suffered a negative image; it was viewed as an area of widespread violence, rampant crime, crowded living conditions, and--for inner city dwellers--hopelessness. Country living, on the other hand, had gained a lot of appeal. To live in the "country" meant to have freedom, fresh air and be free from the inner city worries. A home in the country became a status symbol and "country" clothing, furniture and music became increasingly desirable.

Leading the way for this change of image was the media, especially television and The Nashville Network (TNN), which went on the air in 1983 and Country Music Television (CMT), which debuted at about the same time. Originally, they were two separate companies, but in 1991 The Nashville Network, owned by the Gaylord Broadcasting Company, purchased CMT.

There's an old adage that says if you want to find the answer, follow the money. The answer to why country music became popular during the decade 1984-1994 lies, to a large extent, in the money. Country music had always been profitable, but the money came in different ways. Since World War II, the big money in country music came from publishing; a strong publishing industry was essentially the reason Nashville emerged as the capitol of country music. Sales of recordings of country music were always limited by a variety of factors: (1) lack of marketing from major labels (Nashville labels generally didn't have marketing departments until the 1980s), (2) lack of retail outlets where country music customers felt comfortable; (3) lack of accurate reporting of sales, which distorted the picture of country music sales and tended to perpetuate the stereotype of weak sales for country product; and (4) a negative image for the term "country" with a significant part of the population.

During the 1980s and 1990s that changed to the point where it was country music that was a profit center. Because country music generated money (profits from country music carried the pop divisions of several major labels during the 1980s) and because New York and Los Angeles executives did not want to deal with country music (preferring to remain in pop with the greater prestige and bigger superstars), then country executives, whose divisions generated profits for the labels, wielded an increasing amount of power and Nashville emerged as a power center in the musical corporate world.

To illustrate the growth in income from country music, let's look at the growth in radio. In 1961, the first year the Country Music Association compiled data for radio stations and probably the low point for country music (numerous stations had switched from country to rock'n'roll programming between 1956 and 1961) there were only 81 stations programming country music full time. By the last year of that decade there were 606 and during the 1970s that figure grew to 1,434. In 1980 there were 1,534 but by the end of that decade there were 2,108. Those numbers continued to expand into the 1990s so that in 1994 there were, according to the Country Music Association, 2,427 radio stations programming country music full time. That meant more people could hear country music and since radio airplay was, essentially, an advertisement for a recording, country music reached a lot of potential buyers.

Within the country music business community, the primary beneficiaries were the publishers. That was because income from terrestrial radio station airplay went to publishers and songwriters--not record companies or artists. Record companies only received income from the sales of recordings and artists received their primary income from personal appearances, although they also received royalties from the sales of recordings. Since the Nashville music industry's financial backbone was in publishing, that strengthened Nashville as a center for country music.

Death Row Records

In 1991, Suge Knight and Dr. Dre, a former member of NWA, formed Death Row Records. Dr. Dre had been signed to Ruthless Records, owned by fellow NWA member Eric "Eazy-E" Wright. A split with manager Jerry Heller over money led Suge Knight to obtain the recording contracts of Dr. Dre and The D.O.C.

Suge Knight, a leader in the West Coast Hip Hop scene, was known for his strong armed tactics in doing business. Death Row distributed the soundtrack for the film *Deep Cover* in 1992 and released Dr. Dre's debut album, *The Chronic*, and Snoop Dogg's debut release, *Doggystyle*, although there was considerable controversy over the lyric content on both albums. "Gangsta rap" was denounced for being antithetical to American values, for the degradation of black women, and for encouraging violence towards police officers.

Suge Knight signed Tupac Shakur, after bailing him out of jail, and 2Pac recorded his debut album. Knight courted controversy and soon there was an East Coast vs. West Coast "war" going on between rappers, with rappers trading insults and accusations on their recordings.

On September 10, 1996, Tupac was shot in Las Vegas; he died three days later. 2Pac's album, *Makaveli 7 Day Theory* was released in November and went Platinum. Snopp Doggy Dogg's *The Doggfather* was also released and went Platinum but Interscope dropped its distribution deal with the label after Suge Knight was convicted of parole violation and sentenced to prison for nine years.

In 2002, Suge Knight was released from prison. During his time in prison, Death Row Records released albums by 2Pac, Dr. Dre and Snoop Dogg but artists began to leave the label. In 2006, Suge Knight declared bankruptcy as he faced a number of lawsuits from former artists and employees. He was also investigated for incidents involving assault, shooting and robbery.

In January, 2009, WIDEawake Entertainment Group purchased Death Row Records for $18 million at an auction.

Mariah Carey

By the end of 1991, Mariah Carey had released five straight singles that reached number one on the *Billboard* Hot 100, holding that spot for 14 weeks.

Mariah Carey, born March 27, 1969 in Huntington, New York, was the daughter of a mother who was a sometime opera singer and vocal coach before her marriage and a father who was an aeronautical engineer. When Carey was three, her parents divorced and she and her brother moved in with their mother while her older sister lived with their father.

Mariah began writing poems and songs in high school and connected with Gavin Christopher and Ben Margulies to write songs. She worked as a waitress and worked with Margulies on a four song demo, which she tried to interest music labels with no success.

Carey became friends with pop singer Brenda K. Starr, who brought Carey to a gala party that was attended by Tommy Mottola, president of Columbia Records. She handed Mottola a tape and he listened to it on his way home. Mottolo was impressed and searched for her for two weeks; when he found her he signed her and began planning her commercial debut.

Columbia needed a female pop singer to compete with Arista, who had Whitney Houston, and Sire, who had Madonna. Carey wanted to continue working with Margulies but Mottola connected her with producers Ric Wake, Narada Michael Walden and Rhett Lawrence. Columbia then spent $1 million promoting her debut album, *Maria Carey*. The album entered the *Billboard* album chart on June 30, 1990, and rose to number one, where it remained for eleven weeks. The first single, "Vision of Love," written by Carey and Ben Margulies entered the Hot 100 chart on June 2 and reached number one, where it remained for four weeks and remained on the chart for 22 weeks. That single gave Mariah Carey her first Grammys for "Pop Female Vocalist" and "Best New Artist." Her second single, "Love Takes Time," also written by Carey and Margulies, reached the number one spot and stayed there for three weeks and on the charts for 26 weeks.

Carey's third single from the album, "Someday," again written with Margulies, spent two weeks at number one and "I Don't Wanna Cry," her fourth single from the album, written by Carey and Narada Michael Walden, hit number one and stayed for two weeks.

Mariah Carey and her five octave voice had arrived.

Carey's second album, *Emotions*, was heavily influenced by the Motown records she heard growing up. It was produced by Robert Civilles, David Cole and Walter Afanasieff and entered the *Billboard* album chart in October,

1991, after the single, "Emotions" entered the Hot 100 at the end of August. That single remained in the number one position for three weeks.

Ben Margulies did not write any more songs with Mariah Carey after that first album because of a legal dispute. Carey had signed a contract with Margulies before she signed with Columbia that guaranteed Margulies not only money from song writing but also half of her total earnings as well. Sony made it clear that he would only be paid as a songwriter so he filed suit, which led to Carey and him to part.

Carey had not toured to promote her first album and there was criticism from music journalists and industry outsiders that she couldn't pull off her studio sound in a live setting. Carey countered that she had stage fright and the production on the songs made it difficult to reproduce live. Still, the criticism continued so Carey and Walter Afanaisieff booked an appearance on "MTV Unplugged." Carey, with Afanasieff, sang her hits and added a cover of the Jackson 5 hit, "I'll Be There" from 1970. The "MTV Unplugged" appearance was successful and Sony released an EP of the songs she sang.

Amy Grant and "Baby, Baby"

Contemporary Christian act Amy Grant had a number one hit on the *Billboard* Hot 100 in 1991 with "Baby, Baby." It was the first single from her album *Heart in Motion*. The singles from that album, "Every Heartbeat," "That's What Love Is For" and "Good For Me" were also hit singles on the *Billboard* Hot 100. "Baby, Baby" was written by Grant and Keith Thomas, who produced the album. Inspired by her six-week-old daughter, Millie, Grant wrote the song in about ten minutes in her kitchen. "Baby, Baby" entered the *Billboard* Hot 100 on February 23, 1991, and was number one for two weeks; it was also number one on Billboard's Adult Contemporary chart. In addition to the U.S., "Baby, Baby" was a hit in the U.K., Switzerland, Australia, Austria, Canada, Germany, Ireland, Netherlands, New Zealand, Norway and Sweden. It was nominated for Grammys for Best Female Pop Vocal, Record of the Year and Song of the Year.

Music News: 1991

Music artists responded to the Gulf War by recording a rendition of "Give Peace a Chance." Performing on the song were Yoko Ono, Lenny Kravitz, Peter Gabriel, Alamah Myles, Tom Petty, Bonnie Raitt and others who were billed as "The Peace Choir." The single was rush released to radio.

The documentary, *Truth or Dare*, chronicled Madonna's Blond Ambition Tour in 1990; it was released to theaters.

Soundscan had an impact on the album chart. On May 25, *Billboard* began incorporating electronically monitored sales date to give a more accurate reading of what actually sold.

The first Lollapalooza tour was started by Perry Farrell as a farewell to his band, Jane's Addiction, which had just dissolved. On the tour were Siouxsie and the Banshees, Nine Inch Nails, the Rollins Band, Fishbone and Rage Against the Machine.

Freddie Mercury, lead singer of Queen, died on November 25 from AIDs.

On November 30, *Billboard* began using sales and airplay from SoundScan and Broadcast Data Services (BDS) respectively. The digital technology made the charts more accurate and less free of bias.

Cold War Ends

In 1991, the Cold War came to an end. During that year, the Union of Soviet Socialist Republics (USSR) fell apart when 15 sovereign republics emerged from the old Soviet Union.

On Christmas Day, Russian president Mikhail Gorbachev resigned. By that time, most republics had already seceded from the Soviet Union, ending the 74 year old state, which renamed itself the Russian Federation.

The Iraq War

Things were tense in the Middle East. A meeting between the American Secretary of State and the Iraqui Foreign Minister failed to reach an agreement for the withdrawal of Iraqui troops from Kuwait. On January 12, Congress passed a resolution that authorized the use of military force to expel Iraqui troops and on January 15, the United Nations deadline for the expulsion arrived. On January 16, the Gulf War, known as "Operation Desert Storm," began with air strikes by American planes.

During the first days of the war, Iraq fired Scud missiles into Israel. On February 7, ground forces moved across the Saudi Arabian border into Kuwait. A "smart bomb" fired by American forces struck an underground bunker in Baghdad, killing hundreds of Iraquis. Iraq continued firing Scud missiles but on February 26, Iraqui leader Saddam Hussein came on Baghdad radio and announced the withdrawal of troops from Kuwait. Those troops set fire to oil fields in Kuwait as they left. The next day, President Bush declared victory over Iraq and declared a cease fire.

On March 10, 540,000 American troops began leaving the Persian Gulf.

In April, the United Nations Security Council passed the "Cease Fire Agreement," demanding the destruction or removal of all chemical and biological weapons in Iraq. The agreement also demanded the end of research, development, support and manufacturing facilities for ballistic missiles with a range of over 150 km and the end of Iraq's support of international terrorism. Iraq agreed on April 6 and twelve days later declared some of its chemic weapons and materials but claimed it did not have a biological weapons program.

Creation of the World Wide Web

On August 6, 1991, Tim Berners-Lee announced the World Wide Web project and software in a newsgroup and set up the first website.

Other News: 1991

Los Angeles policemen beating motorist Rodney King were caught on film on March 3. Twelve day later, four L.A. police officers were indicted for the videotaped beating.

On April 1, Comedy Central began on cable TV.

The Super Nintendo Entertainment System was released in the United States on August 13.

On October 11-13, the United States Senate Judiciary Committee held interviews with Supreme Court nominee Clarence Thomas and his former aid, Anita Hill. Hill alleged that Thomas had sexually harassed her during the time she worked for him; he denied it and her testimony as a "high tech lynching." On October 15, the United States Senate voted to confirm Clarence Thomas to the Supreme Court by a vote of 52-48.

1992
CDs

In 1992, for the first time, CDs outsold cassettes; the recording industry was now a CD business.

There was a change in packaging that year that made them easier to handle. When CDs were introduced, they were packaged in a long box, approximately, 12 inches long. That was done so retailers could use the same bins for CDs as they used for LPs; two rows of CDs could be stocked where only a single row of LPs were held. There could be two CDs in a long box—one on top of the other—and retailers were concerned about theft; the long boxes were difficult to shoplift.

Record labels began to object to the long boxes; they were expensive and environmentally wasteful, so a decision was phased in to eliminate the long boxes release the CD in a jewel case.

The prices of CDs had come down but then went back up to $16.98, first with a Garth Brooks album on Capitol and then other albums. It was difficult for consumers to understand the price increase; there were now plenty of manufacturing plants making CDs and the CD already cost $3 more than the cassette. Actually, there was a simple answer: "The 16.98 price was all based on how much profit record labels (and their royalty cohorts, the artists) could squeeze out of one sale."

In 1992, Congress imposed a royalty on blank digital tapes and new technologies were introduced. The MiniDisc, half the size of the CD was introduced and so were the DAT (Digital Audio Tape) and CDD (Digital Compact Cassette) but none caught on. All of the new technologies needed new equipment that was incompatible with current equipment and many consumers had already purchased a Compact Disc player and a Video Cassette Recorder.

The Power and Demand of Artists

Artists became powerful and wanted more money and more control. Hit artists wanted extended contracts that reflected their success in the midst of a current contract and labels had to placate their hit acts so labels began to offer Joint Ventures with artists.

When Led Zeppelin founded their label, Swan Song, or Prince founded Paisley Park, the artists actually received little equity in the new label because the major label paid start up and on-going costs. The deal where Madonna established Maverick Records was something new for the music industry.

Madonna's contract had her earning an 18 percent royalty rate. In her new deal with Warner Brothers, Madonna received an advance of $5 million against a royalty rate of 20 percent. Her existing contract had her owing the label four more albums; that was increased to seven. HBO gave her over $2 million for two HBO concert specials and Madonna kept all of her merchandising rights. She had compiled a book of erotic photos of herself and poems titled Sex. As part of her new deal, Warner Books published her book but the "company was embarrassed by it—considered a 'low point' in publishing" and her companion album, *Erotica* "became the most returned in WEA memory."

Grunge

Grunge, often known as "the Seattle Sound," was commercially successful during the first half of the 1990s, led by Nirvana, whose single,

"Smells Like Teen Spirit" from their album *Nevermind* was a top ten single in 1992; Pearl Jam, who had a string of chart singles 1991-1998 (their single "I Got Id" b/w "Long Road" was a top ten single in 1998); Soundgarden, had a string of chart singles 1994-1996); Stone Temple Pilots had chart singles 1993-2000; and Alice in Chains had chart 1994-1995. Their albums sold well with the sound of distorted guitars under the influence to punk and heavy metal. Grunge groups played loud and their vocals generally screamed. The lyrics emphasized apathy, confinement, angst and social alienation. It was the opposite of a clean cut, slickly produced sound with smooth harmonies.

The themes of grunge were generally a dislike of society, alienation, self-loathing and depression. There was a pride in being authentic and not selling out; some of their clothes came from thrift stores with torn jeans, flannel shirts, oversized sweaters and hiking boots. The top grunge label was Sub Pop, based in Seattle, Washington.

Sub Pop

The Sub Pop label was founded in Seattle by Bruce Pavitt in 1986; in 1988 he was joined by Jonathan Poneman. The roots of the label go back to a fanzine, *Subterranean Pop*, formed by Bruce Pavitt in the early 1980s that focused on independent record labels. The project was developed by Pavitt to earn course credit at Evergreen State College in Olympia, Washington.

The name of the fanzine was shorted to *Sub Pop* and Pavitt began releasing compilation tapes of underground rock bands. Pavitt moved to Seattle in 1983 and issued his ninth and final issue to *Sub Pop*. He wrote a column, "Sub Pop U.S.A." for *The Rocket*, a local newspaper.

The first Sub Pop LP was released by Pavitt in 1986; the album was a compilation of material from artists such as Sonic Youth, Naked Raygun, Wipers and Scratch Acid. Sub Pop released an EP for Seattle-based Green River, *Dry As a Bone*, in 1987. In 1987, Jonathan Poneman provided $20,000 for the debut Soundgarden single, "Hunted Down" b/w "Nothing to Say" and their follow-up EP *Screaming Life*.

Jonathan Poneman became a full partner in Sub Pop, handling business and legal issues while Bruce Pavitt handled Artists and Repertoire. Both quit their jobs in 1988 to focus fully on Sub Pop. They raised $43,000, incorporated the label and released the first single by Mudhoney, a group comprised of former members of Green River. The single, "Touch Me I'm Sick" had a limited first pressing of 800, a strategy used to create demand. That strategy was later adopted by other indie labels.

Pavitt and Poneman dived deeply into the history of independent labels and concluded that every successful movement on rock had a regional basis. The wanted to create a band identity for Sub Pop and promoted the label more than the music. They wanted to market the "Seattle Sound," which was created by producer Jack Endino, who produced 75 singles, albums and EPs between 1987 and 1989. The recordings were done quickly and cheaply by standardizing certain studio techniques.

The first single by Nirvana, a band based in Aberdeen, Washington, was "Love Buzz," released in November, 1988. It was the first release from the Sub Pop Singles Club, a subscription service that sent subscribers singles by the label each month by mail. By 1990, the club had two thousand subscribers. Sub Pop became a powerful force in Seattle, the source of the "Seattle Sound" which became synonymous with the music scene in Seattle.

It was difficult for a small, independent label to gain attention from the mainstream American music press, so Davitt and Poneman decided to court the British press and flew Everett True, a journalist with *Melody Maker*, over to write an article on the local music scene. It worked; the British press embraced Sub Pop, grunge and the "Seattle sound."

Nirvana, formed by Kurt Cobain and Kristi Novoselic with a succession of drummers until Dave Grohl joined in 1990, released their first album, *Bleach*, on Sub Pop in 1989. The group then signed with Geffen Records, which acquired the *Bleach* album but paid royalties to Sub Pop, which kept the indie label afloat for years. Future Nirvana LPs *Nevermind* (1991) and *In Utero* (1993) were required to print the Sub Pop logo with Geffen's. Because of Nirvana's success, a number of Sub Pop bands signed with major labels, which led to a joint venture with Warner Bros Records. The end of that agreement came when Geffen, which owned 49 percent, was sold to MCA.

Curb Records

In 1986, Mike Curb left politics (he had been Lieutenant Governor of California and then Finance Chairman of the Republican Party under Ronald Reagan) and returned to the music industry full time. During the 1980s he created joint ventures with RCA, MCA and Capitol which resulted in hits by the Judds, Wynonna, Sawyer Brown, Lyle Lovett, the Bellamy Brothers, Hank Williams, Jr. and T.G. Sheppard. During the 1990s, Curb Records acquired distribution from EMI/Capitol, then Warner Brothers and the independent label signed Tim McGraw, LeAnn Rimes, Wynonna and Sawyer Brown, who all had multi-platinum albums.

By the end of the 1990s, Curb Records was the most successful independent record label in country music, although he continued to release pop records and soundtracks.

Gospel Labels

In 1992, Word Records was sold to Thomas Nelson for $72 million and EMI purchased Sparrow. In 1994, the Music Entertainment Group bought the Benson Music Group, along with Tribute/Diadem. At the end of 1996, Thomas Nelson kept Word's book division and sold the recording label to Gaylord Entertainment, which also owned the Grand Ole Opry and The Nashville Network. Gaylord then purchased Blanton/Harrell Entertainment, which managed Amy Grant and Michael W. Smith.

In 1996, Warner Brothers created Warner Alliance, which marketed Christian artists to the Christian Booksellers market, then created Warner Resound, which marketed gospel to the secular market.

In 1997, EMI bought ForeFront, adding to Sparrow and Star Song to create EMI Christian, headed by Bill Hearn. In June, 1997, the Zomba Music Group announced the formation of Provident Music Group by combining Brentwood Music, and Reunion--the label begun by Blanton and Harrell which had been sold to BMG before Zomba purchased it. Provident then purchased the Benson Music Group from the Music Entertainment Group.

Britpop

During the early 1990s "Britpop" emerged, which was influenced by the British music of the 1960s and 1970s as well as the indie rock scene that centered on London. The Smiths were a successful indie rock band and their emergence during the 1980s led to bands such as Suede, Blur, Oasis, Pulp and The Verve emerging during the 1990s. That, in turn, led to Cool Britannia, a cultural movement. The most successful British bands in England during the 1990s were Oasis, Blur and the female group The Spice Girls.

Bands were emphasized during Britpop with a basic line-up of guitar/bass/drums/vocals with keyboards sometimes part of the lineup. The groups wrote their own songs, played on the records, and aimed their material at British audiences; some acts, like Oasis, became huge in England but never broke as big in the United States. Britpop had catchy hooks but was aimed at the working class youth, with the British flag serving as nationalistic pride.

The area of Camden Town in north London was the center of the music and social scene during Britpop. In 1992, "Popscene," a single by Blur and

"The Downers," a single by Suede, are often considered the beginning of Britpop. Britpop was pro-British and, while not totally anti-American, was certainly anti-grunge, which was popular in the United States at that time.

Blur toured the United States in 1992 and the following year released the album *Modern Life is Rubbish*. There was a resentment of the influence American culture had on Britain and Britpop answered that with a celebration of "Britishness." In 1994, Blur released *Parklife*, an album that made them the most popular band in Britain. Oasis released their debut album, *Definitely Maybe* that same year and it quickly became a best-seller.

"The Battle of Britpop" was the competition between Oasis and Blur to have best sellers on the British charts. "Roll With It," a single from Oasis and "Country House," a single from Blur were released on the same day; Blur represented the south of England while Oasis represented the North. This "battle" became popular in the British press. Blur managed to sell more singles but Oasis managed to have hits in the United States with "Wonderwall" and "Champagne Supernova." Their second album, *(What's the Story) Morning Glory* was released in 1995 and became their third best selling album in British pop music history. Oasis was led by the Gallagher brothers, Noel and Liam. Unfortunately, the brothers could not get along and the band broke up.

The Spice Girls became globally popular with their single "Wannabe," which was number one for four weeks in 1997 in the United States. They continued to have hit singles, starred in a movie, and finally broke up in 2007.

Acts that emerged during that period include Radiohead, The Verve, Coldplay, Travis and Stereophonics.

As the twenty-first century began, there was a decline in British acts on American charts. In April, 2002, for the first time in over 40 years, there were no British acts on *Billboard's* Hot 100 chart.

History of the Internet

During the late 1980s and early 1990s, the basic platform for the global information revolution was in place using personal computers, FAX machines, the Windows operating system and dial-up modems connected to the global telephone network. The groundwork for all of this was laid much earlier, dating back to the 1960s and 1970s.

In 1962, J.C.R. Licklider at the Massachusetts Institute of Technology (MIT) began work for the Advanced Research Projects Agency (ARPA) at the Department of Defense. Licklider worked with colleagues at MIT,

UCLA and IBM on the concept of an "intergalactic network," which he had developed at MIT. In 1965, the first area network connection were created through ARPA and in 1967 the idea for the ARPANET, forerunner to the Internet, was created. The first host-to-host connection came on October 29, 1969 between the Stanford Research Institute and UCLA after the first attempt resulted in the computers crashing.

The formation of the internet paralled the development of the first mini-computer, introduced in 1965. That computer, priced $18,000, fit on a desk; IBM, the leading manufacturer of computers at that time, was locked into mainframes for businesses; the lowest IBM mainframe cost $90,000.

In 1971, Intel developed the computer chip, which allowed computers to be much smaller and less expensive. It also increased the speed of computers as they evolved from using vacuum tubes to transistors to an integrated circuits.

In 1972, Electronic mail, or "e-mail," was developed by Ray Tomlinson, who developed the user@host format. By the end of the next year, there were 30 institutions connected to ARPANET and in 1974 the daily traffic on ARPANET was over three million packets.

In 1977, Steve Jobs and Steve Wozniak introduced the Apple II computer; also introduced that year were the Commodore Pet and the Tandy TRS-80, which made computers available to consumers with off-the-shelf machines. Those personal computers were key to the development of computers for personal use as well for small businesses.

In 1979, the idea to link Universities to ARPANET was put in place. Also that year, software was introduced which allowed users to distribute news and bulletin-board like messages, which in turn created discussion groups and newsgroups connected on a variety of topics. At that point, no advertising was allowed on the ARPANET, and that dictum was rigorously enforced by its users.

In 1981, a number of Universities were connected to ARPANET. That same year, the first portable computer—about the size of a suitcase and weighing 24 lbs—was introduced and IBM marketed its first Personal Computer (PC). The next year, *Time* Magazine named the computer their Man of the Year and IBM clones entered the market.

The first video game was developed in 1982 as a way to demonstrate software for personal computers. Two years later, in January, 1984, the Macintosh Computer was put on the market. That year the domain names of .gov, .mil, .org, .edu. .net and .com were developed.

In 1985, the first version of the Windows operating system, developed by Microsoft entered the market. By the end of that year, the number of hosts on the Internet reached 2,000 and during the next two years the number of networks grew from to almost 30,000.

In 1988, the first "worm" infected computers and the following year the number of hosts grew from 80,000 in January to 130,000 in July to 160,000 in November.

The breakthrough operating system for personal computers was the Windows 3.0 system, which was introduced on May 22, 1990. That was the first user-friendly system for computers. In 1991, the World Wide Web (WWW) was developed by Tim Berners-Lee, a British engineer who used hypertext to facilitate sharing and updating information. Berners-Lee released his creation to the public for free, with no patents or royalties due in order for future developments and idea to be developed freely. Another system, "Gopher," had been developed by the University of Minnesota, but they saw it as a business opportunity and charged for access; the World Wide Web quickly caught on.

There were restrictions against the commercial use of the Internet in 1991 when Congress passed the Gore Bill, which created the National Research and Education Network, which paved the way for future developments on the National Information Infrastructure or what became known as "the information highway." By the end of 1991, there were over one trillion bytes or ten billion packets per month transported over the internet, which then had over 600,000 hosts and 5,000 separate networks.

Technology

By the end of 1992, the only people who had email were faculties at Universities and scientists at research facilities. That year, the number of computers passed the one million mark and the MBONE software was launched, which allowed audio and video to be on the internet.

The first text message was sent by a test engineer for Sema Group, using his personal computer. The text was sent via the Vodafone network to the phone of a colleague.

The next major development that made the Internet user-friendly came in 1992 when MOSAIC, a network browser, was created at the University of Illinois. In 1993, the Mosaic browser had 12 users and there were about 50 web sites—most of them just single pages. Marc Andreesen at the University of Illinois developed the "point-and-click" system around this time.

In mid-1994, MOSAIC Communications changed the name of their browser to Netscape and on August 9, 1995, Netscape went public. The Netscape browser was the key to igniting the internet boom. That browser made the internet available to everyone—not just scientists, engineers and techno-geeks who dominated the early development of computers and the internet—and allowed consumers to "surf the net."

The Netscape Browser came on the market at the same time as Windows 95 shipped, and that became the computer operating system used by most users worldwide. At that point—the mid-1990s—the computer and software industries moved from a platform tied to personal computers to an internet-based platform. Transforming applications that were the drivers of this revolution were e-mail and internet browsing. From those developments came a number of internet companies—Yahoo in 1995, Altavista in 1995 and Google in 1998—as well as web sites such as eBay and Amazon.

Nuclear Weapons and Climate Change

The threat of nuclear proliferation and climate change hung over Earth during 1992.

In January, Russian president Boris Yeltsin announced that Russia would no longer target American cities with nuclear weapons; they would also stop targeting American allies. President George H.W. Bush then announced that the United States would no longer target Russia and its allies with nuclear weapons.

That same month, North Korea signed an agreement with the International Atomic Energy Agency to allow international inspections of its nuclear power plants. In February, Iraq refused to abide by the United Nations Security Council's disarmament resolutions and in March the International Atomic Energy Agency ordered Iraq to destroy an industrial complex that was used to manufacture nuclear weapons.

In July, Iraq refused an inspection team from the United Nations access to their Ministry of Agriculture after the U.N. official obtained information that the site contained archives related to illegal weapons activities. The U.N. inspectors held a 17-day "sit-in" outside the building but left after they were threatened by Iraqi soldiers. Finally, Iraq agreed that U.N. weapons inspectors could search the Iraqi Agricultural Ministry building in Baghdad, but during the inspections at the end of July, nothing was found. The inspectors believed the records had been removed.

Climate Change was a concern as well and in May, the United National Framework Convention on Climate Change was adopted. In November, a report by the World Meteorological Organization reported an unprecedented level of ozone depletion in both the Arctic and Antarctic.

World News: 1992

In February, the Maastricht Treaty was signed, which founded the European Union.

A Freddie Mercury Tribute Concert, honoring the former lead singer of Queen, was held at Wembley Stadium in London on April 20. The televised concert reached over a billion people and raised millions of dollars for AIDs research

On April 29, 1992, the four police officers who beat Rodney King and were caught on videotape, were acquitted in a criminal trial, which led to massive rioting for the next six days in Los Angeles. By the end of the rioting, there were 53 dead and over $1 billion in damages.

During the Democratic National Convention in July, Arkansas Governor Bill Clinton was selected to represent the Democratic Party for the election in November. The Republican nominee was the incumbent, George H.W. Bush. On November 3, Clinton defeated Bush to become the forty-second president of the United States.

The North American Free Trade Agreement between the United States, Canada and Mexico was approved on August 12; the deal was formally signed in December, 1992.

The Turner Broadcasting System premiered their Cartoon Network, the first all animation TV channel, on October 1.

Just before Christmas, the "Archives of Terror" were discovered, which detailed the fate of thousands of Latin Americans who had been secretly kidnapped, tortured and killed by the military in Argentina, Bolivia, Brazil, Chile, Paraguay and Uruguay.

1993
Elvis Postage Stamp

The U.S. Postal Service decided to create an Elvis Presley postage stamp and solicited the public to choose between a young, 1950s Elvis and an older, 1970s Elvis; the younger Elvis won out. It was issued in January, 1993.

The Bodyguard **and "I Will Always Love You"**

The most famous Dolly Parton song is also the most famous Whitney Houston song.

Whitney Houston had been approached with film offers but had turned them down until the offer for *The Bodyguard* came. The film starred Kevin

Costner as Frank Farmer, the bodyguard and Houston as Rachel Marrson, a singing star stalked by a crazed fan. The film was released on November 25, 1992, and the soundtrack was released two days later.

Clive Davis and Whitney Houston were the executive producers for the soundtrack album and had control of the songs. "What Becomes of the Broken Hearted," which was a hit for Jimmy Ruffin in 1966, was scheduled to be the theme song for the film but it was discovered that it was set to be used in the film *Fried Green Tomatoes* so they needed another song. Kevin Costner suggested the Dolly Parton song, "I Will Always Love You," which had been a hit for her in 1974.

Whitney Houston's version of "I Will Always Love You" entered the *Billboard* Hot 100 on November 14, 1992, and rose to number one, where it remained for 14 weeks. *The Bodyguard* soundtrack entered the *Billboard* album chart on December 5 and reached number one, where it stayed for 20 weeks and on the chart for 141 weeks. During the Christmas season, the album sold over a million units in one week.

"I Will Always Love You" was a worldwide hit, reaching the number one spot on the charts in New Zealand, the U.K., Australia, Norway, France, Sweden, the Netherlands and Switzerland.

The follow up singles, "I'm Every Woman" and "I Have Nothing" both reached number four during 1993, giving Whitney Houston three songs in the top 20 at the same time.

Interscope Records

Interscope Records was founded by Ted Field in 1989 as a division of his film company, Interscope Communications. Engineer and Producer Jimmy Iovine wanted to start a record company and was introduced to Field by U2's manager, Paul McGuinness. Field and Iovine agreed to join forces and founded a joint venture with Atlantic Records. The label was headquartered in Westwood, California, and reversed the trend of attorneys and accountants heading record labels by putting music men in charge of the label.

The first release was "Rico Suave" by Gerardo, a rapper from Ecuador; it was released in December, 1990, and entered the *Billboard* Hot 100 chart on February 2, 1991 and rose to number seven. In May, 1991, *Sailing the Seas of Cheese* by Primus was released, followed by Marky Mark and the Funky Bunch's album, *Music for the People* in July. The single from that album, "Good Vibrations" (not the Beach Boys song) entered the *Billboard* Hot 100 on July 20 and reached number one.

A&R executive Tom Whalley signed Tupac Shakur and the label released *2Pacalypse Now* in November, 1991; that was Shakur's studio debut album and it reached number 64 on the *Billboard* chart.

In 1992, Interscope released the second album by Primus and the debut album from No Doubt. They also released *Meantime* by Helmet, *Bigger, Better, Faster, More!* by 4 Non Blondes and acquired *Circa: Now!* by Rocket from the Crypt. The label formed a joint venture with TVT/Nothing Records and released the EP *Broken* by Nine Inch Nails.

Interscope negotiated a deal with Dr. Dre and Suge Knight for $10 million to finance and distribute their label, Death Row Records. Dr. Dre had recorded his debut solo album, *The Chronic*, which was originally set to be released by Sony but that label declined, citing problems at Death Row and Dr. Dre's contract status. Jimmy Iovine agreed to release the album, although it had to be distributed with Priority Records, which was the label of N.W.A. when Dre was a member of that group. *The Chronic* was released in December, 1992 and introduced G-funk to the rap lexicon. The term came from Dr. Dre's single, "Nuthin But A 'G' Thang," which reached number two on the *Billboard* Hot 100 in 1993.

Interscope became a controversial label in 1992 when Vice President Dan Quale stated that Interscope should withdraw Tupac's album, *2Pacalypse Now*, claiming it was responsible for the death of a Texas state trooper, who stopped a motorist who was listening to the album on the tape deck of a stolen truck. The family of the state trooper filed a civil suit against Shakur and Interscope, stating that the lyrics, which were full of violence, created lawless action.

The audience for Interscope artists was white teens—80% of Interscope sales—who were also intrigued by the albums from Death Row and bought them as well.

Michael Jackson

The first time the National Football League's Super Bowl featured a major performer at halftime came at Super Bowl XXVII on January 31, 1993, when Michael Jackson performed. The show was a great ratings success and the Super Bowl began to regularly feature top performers and halftime spectaculars.

On February 10, Michael Jackson was interviewed by Oprah Winfrey—his first interview in 14 years—on a prime time special. It was one of the most watched interviews in the history of television. On August 10, it was announced that Jackson was being investigated for child molestation.

A civil lawsuit was filed against Jackson by 13-year-old Jordan Chandler and his parents on September 14, accusing Jackson of sexually abusing the boy during their friendship.

Jackson ended his Dangerous World Tour on November 11 in Mexico City and on December 22 released his first public statement about the child molestation charges leveled against him. In his videotaped statement, Jackson said the accusations were "totally false" and asked the public to "wait and hear the truth before you label or condemn me."

Rock and Roll Hall of Fame

At the Rock and Roll Hall of Fame induction, held January 12, 1993, in Los Angeles, Creedence Clearwater Revival, Ruth Brown, The Doors, Van Morrison, Sly & The Family Stone and Cream were all inducted; Cream reunited and performed for their induction. Groundbreaking for the building, to be constructed in Cleveland, occurred on June 7 with Chuck Berry, Pete Townshend and Billy Joel in attendance.

The Era of Garth

Garth Brooks dominated country music like no other artist ever had. beginning with his first number one single in 1989, "If Tomorrow Never Comes," and going through a string of top singles throughout the 1990s.

In 1990 Brooks' album *No Fences* was released and he had three number one songs that held those position for nine weeks. Brooks began 1990 with a song that reached number two, "No Counting You," then had number ones with "The Dance," "Friends in Low Places" and "Unanswered Prayers." Each of those songs stayed on the *Billboard* country chart for 20 weeks or more, a release pattern for Brook's records. Brooks' album was number one for 41 weeks and remained on the country album chart for 240 weeks—or almost five years.

The following year his *Ropin' the Wind* album was released; it reached number one and stayed in that position for 33 weeks and on the chart for 174 weeks. His hits that year were "Two of a Kind, Workin' On a Full House," "The Thunder Rolls," "Rodeo," "and "Shameless." By the end of 1991, Garth had sold 30 million copies of his first three albums. His releases were not without controversy; in 1991, TV networks would not air Brooks' video of "The Thunder Rolls" because of risqué content on domestic violence.

In 1992, Brooks released a Christmas album and then *The Chase*, which also went to number one and remained there for 16 weeks. Hit singles that year were "What She's Doing Now," "Papa Loved Mama," "The River," "We Shall Be Free" and "Somewhere Other Than the Night."

Garth Brook's album, In Pieces, was released in 1993 and it, too, reached number one. Hit singles included "Learning to Live Again," "That Summer," "Ain't Going Down (Til the Sun Comes Up,)," "American Honky-Tonk Bar Association," "Callin' Baton Rouge" "Standing Outside the Fire" and "One Night a Day."

By the end of 1993, Brooks had released 13 number one singles on the country chart.

Country music enjoyed explosive growth in the early 1990s and Garth Brooks led the way. In 1992, the top selling album was *Some Gave All* by Billy Ray Cyrus (4.7 million) while Garth Brooks had three in the top ten: *Ropin the Wind* (4 million), *No Fences* (3.1 million) and *The Chase* (3.1 million). The next year Garth made the top ten with *In Pieces*, which sold 2.8 million. In 1994 Tim MGraw was in the top ten sellers with *Not A Minute Too Soon* (3.2 million). In 1993, Garth Brooks sold 3.8 million with *The Hits* while Shania Twain sold 2.8 million. Brooks continued to sell in large numbers throughout the 1990s.

The explosion in country sales—and recognition by the music industry of the sales of country music—would not have happened without Soundscan. For the first time, there was unbiased reporting of album sales and country music proved to have some of the top selling albums across all genres.

Country Music during the 1990s

During the 1990s, country music's growth in album sales was attributed to country consumers buying CDs (often to replace old vinyl albums but also in special "packages" and "boxed sets"), an increase in the number of radio stations playing country music full time, and the introduction of the Sound Scan technology which reported accurate sales. The fact that country music sold well led retailers to stock more country music. Other factors in the sales of country music were the exposure country music had on TV with TNN and CMT, the growth of Wal-Mart, which offered a friendly atmosphere to country consumers, and the rise of rap music, which many young people did not like, leading them to country.

In addition to the sales of albums by Garth Brooks, Arista Records, which had Alan Jackson and Brooks and Dunn, sold 40 million albums by 1994. By 1995, Alabama had sold 57 million albums worldwide and had 41 of their singles reach the number one position on Billboard's country chart. Shania

Twain's album, *The Woman in Me*, sold over eight million copies after its release in 1995.

Ralph Emery and "Nashville Now"

Ralph Emery was the voice of country music for years because he hosted a late-night show on WSM where a who's who of country artists visited him and chatted. Emery also hosted an early morning TV show on WSM that featured a studio band-the last radio studio band in the nation. That local show became the most popular early morning TV show in Nashville for years. Emery ended his late night radio show in 1972 and, beginning in 1971, hosted the weekly syndicated radio show, "The Ralph Emery Show." From 1974 to 1980 Emery hosted the popular TV show "Pop! Goes the Country." Ralph Emery became the face and voice of country when he hosted "Nashville Now," a nightly entertainment show where he interviewed artists, did skits (including popular banter with Minnie Pearl where they shared jokes). Ralph Emery was the host of "Nashville Now" from the debut of TNN in March, 1983, until 1993. He was inducted into the Country Music Hall of Fame in 2007 and the National Radio Hall of Fame in 2010.

Steven Curtis Chapman.

Steve Curtis Chapman won more Gospel Music Association Dove Awards-a total of 58—than anyone else. He won the Grammy for Best Pop/ Contemporary Gospel Album 1992-1994 for *For the Sake of the Call, The Great Adventure* and the *Live Adventure*. In 1993 he won the GMA's "Song of the Year" for "The Great Adventure" and was the GMA's Songwriter of the Year 1989-1995; the GMA's Male Vocal of the Year 1990-1991 and the GMA's Artist of the Year 1990, 1991, 1993 and 1995. His success continued as he became the dominant Christian artist during the 1990s.

Trisha Yearwood

In 1993, Trisha Yearwood, known for her hits "She's In Love With The Boy," "The Woman Before Me" and "Wrong Side of Memphis," made her movie debut in *The Thing Called Love* (directed by Peter Bogdanovich), was the subject of an hour-long Disney special, "The Song Remembers When" and was the subject of a book, *Get Hot or Go Home* by Lisa Gubernick. Yearwood was a graduate of the Music Business program at Belmont University.

The Ryman

On April 30, 1991, Emmylou Harris recorded an album, At the Ryman, at the famous venue. That was a major factor in Gaylord's decision to renovate the Ryman and over Labor Day weekend in 1993 the Ryman was closed and a $8.5 million renovation began; the new Ryman featured statues of Roy Acuff and Minnie Pearl in the lobby.

The Revival of Johnny Cash

By 1993, Johnny Cash was almost a forgotten figure. He still recorded occasionally, but there wasn't much interest because Cash's albums weren't selling and there was little demand from the public to see Johnny Cash perform. In May of that year, Johnny Cash met rock and rap producer Rick Rubin. Cash and Rubin sat in Rubin's living room and recorded songs with Cash singing alone with his guitar. The album, *American Recordings*, was released a year later—in May, 1994—and received an enthusiastic review from *Rolling Stone*. Other glowing reviews followed as Cash and Rubin recorded a number of songs that were released on Rubin's label. Those recordings bought Johnny Cash back to legendary status and he became "hip" to a new audience of young rock fans.

Music news: 1993

Earth Day in 1993 was celebrated on April 16 with a big concert, headlined by Paul McCartney, at the Hollywood Bowl. Other performers included Ringo Starr, Steve Miller and Don Henley.

On April 22, the Who's "Tommy" opened on Broadway.

The biggest star on Sony, Mariah Carey, married the label's president, Tommy Mottola, on June 5.

On Prince's 35th birthday, June 7, 1993, he announced that he was changing his name to an unpronounceable symbol, which led to him being called "The artist formerly known as Prince."

World News: 1993

On January 20, 1993, Bill Clinton was sworn in as the 42nd President of the United States.

On February 26, 1993, the World Trade Center bombing occurred in New York City. A bomb was in a van that was parked below the North Tower; six people were killed and over a thousand were injured. That was the first attempt by the terrorist group Al Qaida, to blow up the World Trade Center.

In March, North Korea announced plans to withdraw from the Nuclear Non-proliferation Treaty and refused to allow inspectors access to nuclear sites.

In June, Iraq refused to allow UNSCOM weapons inspectors to install remote-controlled monitoring cameras at two missile engine test stands. In July, UN inspection teams left Iraq, then returned after Iraq agreed to the UNSCOM demands. Later that month, President Bill Clinton ordered the launch of a cruise missile, aimed at the Iraqi intelligence headquarters in Baghdad in response to an attempt to assassinate former President George H.W. Bush during his visit to Kuwait in April. In the Balkans, there were huge protests against the brutal reign of Slobodan Milosevic.

In September the "Oslo I Accord" was signed in Washington, D.C., proclaiming peace between PLO leader Yasser Arafat and Israeli Prime Minister Ytzhak Rabin.

The Maastricht Treaty took effect on November 1, formally establishing the European Union. In December, President Clinton signed the North American Free Trade Agreement (NAFTA) into law.

In technology, Windows NT 3.1, the first version of Microsoft's line of Windows NT operating systems, and Windows for Workgroups 3.1 were released.

The Branch Davidians

On February 28, 1993, agents from ATF (Alcohol, Tobacco and Firearms) and the Texas Army National Guard attempted to serve warrants at a compound where members of the Branch Davidians lived. The Branch Davidians were a religious group who believe we lived in end times, just before the second coming of Christ. Their history dated back to the 1950s but during the 1980s the group split into two factions. The faction led by David Koresh lived in a compound in Waco, Texas, where sexual abuse and weapon violations had occurred, prompting the ATF serve warrants.

A firefight broke out as attempts were made for the warrants to be served, resulting in the death of four ATF agents and 16 wounded.

The FBI then took over the mission and on April 19, after a 51 day siege, attempted to raid the heavily armed Branch Davidians in the compound and capture those inside by spraying tear gas into the facilities. During the raid several fires began which spread throughout the compound, killing Koresh and 82 of his followers.

1994

Denniz PoP

Denniz PoP lived in Stockholm, Sweden, a country of 9.5 million people with the highest percentage of English-speakers than any other non-English speaking country. Swedish acts, such as ABBA, had traditionally sung in English in order to reach a wide audience.

Denniz PoP had a hit in 1990 with Dr. Alban, a Nigerian dental student; Dr. Alban was a club disc jockey and Denniz PoP invited him to his studio, SweMix, to record "Hello Afrika" and "No Coke." He also produced "Another Mother" by Swedish singer Kayo.

In Gothenburg, about a five hour drive away from Stockholm, a four person techno group, Ulf Ekberg and Jonas Berggren, with two sisters, Jenny and Malin Berggren, had a primitive studio in the basement of an auto repair shop; they recorded with synthesizers and drum machine. After they heard "Another Mother," they wanted to meet Denniz PoP and drove to Stockholm but when they arrived, he was not available so they went back home, recorded "Mr. Ace" and sent him a cassette. Dennis played the cassette but wasn't impressed; however, the cassette became stuck in his car's tape player so he had to listen to it every day when he drove to and from work.

Finally, Dennis decided he heard something in the track and wanted to work on it further. Ulf Ekberg and Jonas Berggren had not heard from Dennis so they called him and he invited them to the studio, where he changed the title of the song to "All That She Wants."

Denniz PoP had his own criteria for pop songs. "A great pop song should be interesting in some way," he stated. "That means that certain people will hate it immediately and certain people will love it, but only as long as it isn't boring and meaningless. Then it's not a pop song any longer; then it's something else. It's just music."

"Absolutely every note, word, and beat had to have purpose to be fun," he continued.

"Though it's rare to have a pop hit without lyrics, the lyrics don't need to mean anything much; the disco era had shown that," stated Denniz. "Lyrics that command too much attention are likely to kill the dancing....song lyrics don't need to be poetry; they need only to tell you what you are supposed to feel when you hear the music they accompany."

"In addition to working rhythmically, the sound of the words had to fit with the melody," stated Denniz, an approach to songwriting later known as "melodie math," which meant that the lyrics had to meter out perfectly.

The Swedish group ABBA, who won the Eurovision Song Contest in 1974 with "Waterloo, "set a high bar when it comes to excellence in the studio," stated John Seabrook. "Virtually every moment in an ABBA song is exquisitely crafted, packed with studio-made ear candy—harmonies, countermelodies, and a variety of synthetic sounds—all of which became standard in pop music thirty years later." Virtually every producer in Sweden was influenced by ABBA.

Ace of Base

In the fall of 1992, "All She Wants" by Ace of Base was released in Denmark on Mega Records and became a number one hit in that country; in 1993 it hit in Europe, reaching number one for three weeks on the U.K. charts but no American record label wanted it; the common response was "The band will never work in the States."

Clive Davis, who was head of Arista Records at the time, was vacationing on a yacht in Europe when he heard "All That She Wants" and had the boat head to land so he could place phone calls to make a deal for the record. After he was back in his office in New York, Davis flew the group to New York where they went straight from the airport his office in a limo he sent for them. As they waited to see Davis, they were shown a forty-minute film about Davis's career in the music industry to prepare them meeting the legendary executive.

Clive Davis built his career on an obsession with hits on the radio. He wanted to release an album by Ace of Base but felt it needed at least two more hits. He suggested they record "Don't Turn Around," a song written by Albert Hammond and Diane Warren and, although the group initially objected, they recorded it and it became their next single. Davis prodded the group for more material and Jonas Berggren said he had been working on a song for their next album; Davis insisted on hearing it and on a subsequent trip to New York Berggren played him a demo of "The Sign." Davis sent the song to Denniz PoP to produce.

In September, 1992, Arista released the single, "All That She Wants" by Ace of Base; it was a huge hit, reaching number two on the *Billboard* Hot 100 ("Dreamlover" by Mariah Carey was lodged at number one). In December, 1993, Arista released "The Sign." It spent six weeks at number one on the Hot 100 and the album *The Sign* was number one for two weeks on the *Billboard* album chart and sold 23 million copies. Ace of Base had never toured the United States and had no following but had two hit singles in the Grunge era.

The following two albums by Ace of Base, *The Bridge* and *Cruel Summer* reached numbers 29 and 101, respectively on *Billboard's* album chart. Problems surfaced with the group; it was revealed that Ulf Ekberg had once belonged to a neo-Nazi party and the Berggren sisters hated flying so they didn't want to tour.

Cheiron

In 1992 Denniz PoP quit the SweMix studio and it was sold to BMG; Denniz and Tom Talomaa then built a new studio complex that Denniz named "Cheiron." There were three studios underground, all connected to the same vocal booth. Denniz had the vision of a "hit factory" and needed an American act because that market was the biggest; however, there was no hope of attracting any urban acts. Babyface was the producer behind Boyz II Men and Teddy Riley, creator of New Jack Swing, had Bobby Brown.

Ryman re-opens

The Ryman Auditorium re-opened on June 4, 1994, with a radio broadcast of "A Prairie Home Companion" hosted by Garrison Keillor. During that summer, Martha White sponsored a series of bluegrass shows at the Ryman.

Technology

In 1994, Microsoft announced it would no longer sell or support the MS-DOS operating system separately from Microsoft Windows and the first Internet radio broadcast was aired November 7 on WXYC, the student run radio station at the University of North Carolina, Chapel Hill.

For the first time, a gateway to the World Wide Web was offered by America Online. That opened up the World Wild Web to average Americans and meant that many early email addressed end with @AOL.

Music News: 1995

On February 11, 1994, the three surviving Beatles went into Abbey Road studio with a cassette tape of some songs John Lennon had written, but not finished, given to them by Yoko Ono. They began working on the songs with producer Jeff Lynne. The recording was part of the Beatles Anthology project where the Beatles told their story in video and in print. The first track, "Free As a Bird" was released in late 1995 and reached number six on the Hot 100 in 1996.

In September, an audio tape was discovered of John Lennon performing with the Quarrymen in 1957—the same night he met Paul McCartney. The tape was auctioned at Sotheby's in London for 78,500. GBP.

The rap group 2 Live Crew did a parody of Roy Orbison's "Pretty Woman" and were taken to court because they had not obtained permission from Acuff-Rose Music, who owned the publishing and controlled the copyright. The song had explicit sexual lyrics and Acuff-Rose deemed it offensive. The case went all the way to the Supreme Court, which ruled that a parody can be considered "fair use" and therefore legal.

Kurt Cobain's wife, Courtney Love, called the police in March, fearing that her husband was suicidal. Police came and confiscated four guns and twenty-five boxes of ammunition from Cobain's home. On April 8, Kurt Cobain's body was found; he had died three days before from a self-inflicted gunshot.

In June, Aerosmith became the first major band to premier a new song on the Internet when they provided "Head First" as a free download to 10,000 CompuServ subscribers during the first eight days of the song's release.

There was an attempt to recreate the magic of the Woodstock Festival in 1994 when Woodstock '94 was held August 12-14. Like the original Woodstock, there were a large number of gate crashers and there were heavy rains, turning the grounds into a giant sea of mud. Performing at the event were Bob Dylan, Crosby, Stills & Nash, Nine Inch Nails, Metallica, Aerosmith, Red Hot Chili Peppers, Green Day and Peter Gabriel.

In 1994, the film *The Lion King*, with songs by Elton John and Tim Rice made its debut.

Inducted into the Rock and Roll Hall of Fame were Elton John, John Lennon, the Grateful Dead, The Animals, Rod Stewart, Duane Eddy, Bob Marley and The Band.

World News: 1994

President Bill Clinton delivered his first State of the Union address on January 25; he called for health care reform, a ban on assault weapons and welfare reform.

The Winter Olympics began in Lillehammer in February

In March, China obtained its first connection to the Internet and Apple released the first Macintosh computers that used the new PowerPC Microprocessors.

Nelson Mandela was elected president of South Africa in April when that country held its first fully multi-racial elections. He was inaugurated on May 10. That marked the official end of apartheid in South Africa.

The "Chunnel," a train that ran from London to Paris in a tunnel under the English Channel, opened on May 6.

On June 12, 1994, O.J. Simpson's wife, Nicole Brown Simpson and Ron Goldman were stabbed to death in Simpson's home. The couple had married in 1985 but divorced in 1993. O.J. Simpson was considered a "person of interest" in the case and police requested he turn himself in on June 17; however, Simpson got in a white Ford Bronco driven by Al Cowlings who drove at a slow speed on the Los Angeles freeways while a TV audience of approximately 95 million watched. Finally, Cowlings drove the Bronco back to Simpson's mansion, where he was arrested. At a trial later, Simpson was declared "not guilty" of the murders.

During 1994, *The Lion King* became the highest grossing hand-drawn animated film released by Walt Disney Pictures.

During September and October, Iraq threatened to stop cooperating with UNSCOM inspectors and began to deploy troops to the Kuwait border again; the United States answered with troops deployed to Kuwait. In October, the President of the United Nations Security Council announced that Iraq must withdraw troops from the Kuwait border and immediately cooperate with weapons inspectors; Iraq then withdrew its troops.

During off-year elections in 1994, Georgia representative Newt Gingrich led a campaign that saw Republicans take control of the House of Representatives and the Senate for the first time in 40 years. In Texas, George W. Bush was elected Governor.

1995
Music Industry Revenue Streams

By the mid-1990s, there were three well-established revenue streams in the music industry. First, there were personal appearances. Booking agents and concert promoters worked together to place artists in a variety of venues, from small clubs to giant arenas. Income was generated by consumers who purchased tickets; the artist received either a set fee or a percentage of the gate with the booking agent received a percentage of the artist's money, usually 10 percent. The sale of merchandise--t-shirts, caps, pictures, etc.--generally came from personal appearances as fans purchased souvenirs of the artist. Merchandising can be a lucrative business and artists sometimes made as much or more from merchandising than from an actual appearance. Obviously, this varied from artist to artist; major acts make a great deal from personal appearances while lesser known acts must settle for less. The great majority of sales of merchandise occurs at a show or concert.

The second income stream was generated from airplay--on radio and TV--of recordings. Each radio and TV station paid an amount of money (based on a formula compiled from the size of their market, advertising revenues, and size of audience) to the performing rights organizations, BMI, ASCAP and SESAC. The performing rights organizations collected that money and paid songwriters and publishers for airplay. Record companies and artists received no money from radio or television airplay (or terrestrial airplay, as it was later called). Consumers paid indirectly for this when they bought products which were advertised. Each advertised product costs more at the store in order to absorb the advertising costs; the radio TV stations generated income from advertisers on their stations.

The final revenue stream came from the purchase of recordings by consumers. When someone walked into a store and bought a recording, the money went to the retailer, the wholesaler and recording company who paid a royalty to the artist and a pre-established amount per song to the publisher, who paid the songwriter . The only way a recording company made money was from the sales of recordings—not radio or TV airplay or an artist's appearances and merchandise. An artist earned made money from personal appearances(which generated most of the income for most artists) and royalties from sales of recordings but not from radio and TV airplay unless they were a songwriters.

All income generated by the music industry came from those sources.

Lou Pearlman

Lou Perlman was born in Queens and played guitar in a band, Flyer, but soon realized his dreams of stardom would not come to fruition. He owned a helicopter taxi business in New York then created Airships International in 1980. Perlman had the idea of advertising on the side of blimps and convinced the Jordache brothers (of Jordache jeans) to advertise on one. With money from the Jordaches, Perlman purchased the blimp he claimed he already owned.

The gold leaf paint on the blimp that advertised Jordache jeans on the side made the craft too heavy and it crashed shortly after takeoff, giving the Jordache brothers the media attention he had promised.

In 1991, Perlman re-located his business to Orlando and founded Trans Continental Airlines, which chartered jets that flew rock and pop acts, as well as other clients. One of his pop clients was New Kids on the Block; he arranged to see one of their shows and was captured by the fact that the young group made so much money in 1990 and 1991. He quickly saw that the group was marketed to young teenage girls who had access to money from their parents and grandparents. He also saw that the group was organized musically into bass, baritone, second tenor, first tenor and lead, but also had individual as well as group appeal. There was a mix of personalities, the "bad boy," the "cutting edgers," the "mainstreamers," a "jock," a "poetic" type for individualists and a "hunk" who appealed to the moms as well as the girls. (**Seabrook 50**)

Orlando was rich in singing talent because of Disneyworld and "The Mickey Mouse Club" TV show on the Disney channel. In 1992, Perlman placed an advertisement in the *Orlando Sentinel*, PRODUCER SEEKS MALE SINGERS THAT MOVE WELL, BETWEEN 16-19 YEARS OF AGE. WANTED FOR NEW KIDS-TYPE SINGING/DANCE GROUP. SEND PHOTO OR BIO OF ANY KIND.

With talent scouts Gloria Sicoli and Jeanne Tanzy he held the first auditions; he then found resumes of kids who had auditioned for shows and auditioned them and finally held a third round of auditions. Finally, he settled on the line-up of A.J. McLean, Howie Dorough, Nick Carter, Kevin Richardson and Brian Littrell and named them The Backstreet Boys.

The group had four months of vocal and dance training before their debut at SeaWorld in May, 1993. Perlman videotaped their performance and sent it to record labels but none were interested. The group continued to perform in and around Orlando and in the fall of 1993 did a national tour of high schools.

Perlman brought in Johnny Wright, tour manager for New Kids on the Block, to oversee their training and manage the group; Wright's wife, Donna also helped.

At the end of the year, during a performance in Cleveland, a friend of Donna Wright's, saw the group and called Bobby Duckett, a friend who worked at Mercury Records. Duckett, Senior Director of Artist Development and Touring, told David McPherson in the A&R department about the group. McPherson was interested and Lou Pearlman flew McPherson and Duckett first class to Hickory, North Carolina, to meet the group. The two men saw the group perform and were impressed with the audience reaction as well as the group's clothes and choreography.

McPherson recommended Mercury sign the group and they did, but because the group members were all minors they had to wait for a court-approved process before they could enter the studio. Pearlman did not want to wait and agreed to finance the recording sessions. From the end of 1994 into early 1995, Perlman paid for recording sessions but Mercury executives were not impressed; "they were afraid it would get laughed at because it was too corny" remembered McPherson.

David McPherson was being recruited by Jive Records to join the label in A&R. After McPherson joined Jive, he presented the idea of signing the Backstreet Boys to Clive Calder, owner of Jive. Caulder told McPherson, "Man, if I could have a group like that, it would be huge. Because even if America wasn't into a group like that right away, Europe is into boy bands right now, and that would help me with some business endeavors I have over there."

Jive Records

Clive Calder was born in Johannesburg, South Africa, where apartheid created two segregated countries—one for blacks and one for whites. Whites could only listen to music from whites and blacks could only listen to music made by blacks but everyone could listen to Motown Records. Calder grew up playing bass in Motown cover bands In Crowd and Calder's Collection. During the day he played sessions and in the evenings he played in clubs. In 1969, he obtained a job in A&R at EMI South Africa and spent 18 months with the label before he quit and formed his own label, Clive Calder Productions (CCP).

Calder has been described as "pathologically private," "shockingly fugal," "fanatically self-disciplined, socially remote, charming when he had to be, ruthless when he didn't." Calder neither drank nor danced and "Tax manuals made up his bedside reading." His business partner was Ralph Simon.

Calder loved the idea of the Motown hit factory and, like Berry Gordy with Motown, "insisted on controlling every aspect of the process of making a record: the artists, the songwriters, the producers, the production facilities, the session musicians—even the instrument rentals."

Calder, with white Rhodesian session musician Robert "Mutt" Lange, made cover versions of U.S. and U.K. hits, releasing them on CCP before the originals arrived in South Africa. Lange played on the tracks and sang on the tracks; records by female acts were sung by his wife at the time. The experience of "taking hit songs apart, figuring out how they worked, and putting them back together again gave both men a keen appreciation for what went into making a hit, knowledge that served them both very well later on," stated John Seabrook.

Lange became a hit maker for artists ranging from AC/DC to the Cars to Shania Twain, whom he married."

Calder, Lange and Simon moved to London in 1974 and became British citizens; there they formed a publishing company, Zomba, in 1977 and signed songwriters and producers. Lange produced the Boomtown Rats, Graham Parker and then the 1979 classic *Highway to Hell* by AC/DC.

In 1979 Zomba established an office in New York and formed a partnership with Clive Davis at Arista Records, suppling songs for Arista artists. In 1981 Calder and Simon formed Jive Records, which had A Flock of Seagulls, Billy Ocean and dance-pop singer Samantha Fox. Calder's experiences in London led to an awareness of Europop in addition to his R&B background.

Jive opened an office in New York in 1981 and negotiated a distribution agreement with Arista. Calder hired Barry Weiss to head the label after Weiss took him on an all night tour of New York clubs where Calder was exposed to hip hop, which led to a new direction for Calder and Jive.

During the 1980s, Jive's roster had rap artists Schooly D, DJ Jazzy Jeff & The Fresh Prince, KRS-One and A Tribe Called Quest in addition to R. Kelly and Aaliyah. Calder and Clive Davis split over rap; Davis never liked hip hop, preferring pure pop or rock bands where the groups usually wrote their own songs, which was not Calder's vision of a Motown-like hit factory.

The Bertelsman Music Group (BMG) wanted to buy Jive but Calder wasn't interested; however, he needed BMG's distribution and sales network so he agreed to sell 25 percent of Zomba to BMG in exchange for worldwide distribution by BMG. The contract gave Calder an option to sell Zomba to BMG for three times the company's most recent earnings any time before the end of 2002. BMG executives could not image Calder ever wanting to sell his "baby."

The agreement between Jive and BMG was not working well; BMG could not break Jive's R&B acts in Europe and pressured him for pop product. Calder eventually broke with BMG over European distribution by forming alliances with smaller distributers like Pinnacle, Southgate, and Rough Trade. Calder eventually purchased the smaller distributors so he could control Jive's European distribution.

Clive Calder was frugal and Lou "Big Pappa" Perlman was a high roller; Pearlman had invested over $1 million in the Backstreet Boys and Calder saw that as an opportunity to take the band to the next level. (Pearlman insisted the band members call him "Big Pappa.")

In May, 1995, Pearlman and Denise McLean, band member AJ's mom, went to New York to sign a recording contract with Jive for the Backstreet Boys. The contract stipulated that Pearlman was the band's manager (actually, Johnny Wright was) and that Pearlman was the sixth member of the Backstreet Boys, which allowed him to receive a cut from record sales, merchandising and touring income. When McLean objected to the contract, Pearlman responded it was a "take it or leave it" one time offer. McLean reluctantly accepted.

After the contract was signed, Jive began looking for songs, seeing the act as "pop" while the group members saw themselves as R&B, a white version of Boyz II Men. None of the songs found sounded like a hit to Calder, but the band had spent about half a million dollars in studio costs by then, much of it provided by Lou Pearlman.

Manager Johnny Wright knew concert promoters in Germany and arranged for the group to do shows there; the Germans loved them.

Martin Dodd, who had brought Ace of Base to Mega Records, was now head of A&R for Jive in Europe; he knew that few R&B or hip hop records broke in Europe but young Europeans had adapted the fashion and style of hip hop. Dodd suggested that Calder contact Denniz PoP to write song for the Backstreet Boys.

Denniz had established a hit making team at Cheiron by 1995. On the Cheiron team were Kristian "Krille" Lundon, Andreas Carlsson, Herbie Crichlow, Jake Schultz, David Kruger, Per Magnusson, Jorgen Elofsson, John Amatiello, and Martin Sandberg.

"Denniz's vision for the studio was that songwriting should be a collaborative effort," stated John Seabrook in his book, *The Song Machine.* "No one was supposed to be proprietary about his work. Songwriters would be assigned different parts of a song to work on; choruses would be taken from one song and tried in another; a bridge might be swapped out, or a hook. Songs were written more like television shows, by teams of writers who willingly shared credit with one another." Denniz "sought out proteges with different skill sets," continued Seabrook. "Andreas Carlsson was a gifted lyricist; Lundin had excellent technical skills; Jorgen Elofsson was adept at flowing melodies, while Rami Yacoub, a later Cheiron recruit, made slick beats." However, "no one could match the genius for crafting melodies that fit both dance tracks and ballads possessed by the baby faced, long-haired metal head named Karl Martin Sandberg.

Max Martin

Martin Sandburg (b. 1971 in Stenhamra, Sweden) was the son of a policeman with an older brother who loved KISS and glam rock bands. Martin had "learned music through Sweden's excellent state-sponsored music-education programs, receiving free private lessons in the French horn." He played brass in the school orchestra, then learned drums and keyboards.

Sandberg became front man and songwriter in the glam rock band It's Alive, which was signed to Cheiron's short lived label and released an album, *Earthquake Vision*, in 1994. Denniz PoP had produced the album. Sandberg had dropped out of high school and used the stage name Martin White. Martin loved pop music—his favorite bands included The Bangles and Depeche Mode—but other musicians he knew hated pop, which they considered shallow and uncool.

Denniz liked Martin's songwriting and allowed him to hang around the studio where, for two years, Martin absorbed lessons from Cheiron. Martin, unlike Denniz, was musically literate; he could read and write music and do musical arrangements. In 1995, Denniz and Sandberg wrote and produced the album *Fingers* by Herbie Crishlow. On the first single, "Right Type of Mood," the credits read "Produced by Denniz PoP and Max Martin." Sandburg asked, "Who's that?" and Denniz replied "It's You." And that's how Max Martin got his name.

The first success in the U.S. for Denniz PoP and Max Martin came in 1994 when they wrote and produced three songs for the R&B group 3T, comprised of the three sons of Tito Jackson of The Jacksons. Michael Jackson heard the songs and asked Denniz and Max to fly from Stockholm to Los Angeles to work with him on a song in his studio. Denniz and Max first declined but then accepted; the idea of meeting the King of Pop was too tempting. When they arrived in Los Angeles they were surprised to see Jackson's studio, which has been described as "a little shack." Denniz and Max were used to the state of the art studio at Cheiron. However, their reluctance to work with Michael Jackson was overcome when Jackson went into the vocal booth to sing; Max was "overcome."

That's why Denniz and Max were in Los Angeles when they received the call from Martin Dodd to write a song for the Backstreet Boys. McPherson was in Los Angeles and he met with them and played them the recording made at SeaWorld. Denniz and Martin were working on a song, "We've Got It Goin'" and agreed to send a demo; Clive Calder loved it and hired Denniz to produce the song.

The Backstreet Boys in Sweden

Denniz and Martin wanted to work at Cheiron in Stockholm so Calder asked Pearlman to pay for the group to travel to Sweden; he agreed.

The original plan was for the Backstreet Boys to spend a week recording "We've Got It Goin'" at Cheiron in the summer of 1995; it was produced by Denniz with lyrics contributed by Herbie Crichlow. Max Martin, an excellent singer with the voice of an artist, did the demo, including the harmonies. One of the secrets of Max Martin is that his demo vocals sound like a finished record. The Backstreet Boys finished the vocals in two days so the group recorded two more songs that Denniz and Martin wrote, "Quit Playing Games (With My Heart)" and another. The Backstreet Boys then left for concerts in Germany.

"We've Got It Goin' On" was released in the U.S. in September, 1995, but only reached number 69 on the *Billboard* Hot 100; radio stations were reluctant to play it because it sounded "too European." However, it was a major hit in Germany, Austria and Switzerland so Jive sent the band on a six month European tour, paid for partly by Pearlman. The group sang the song in French and Spanish for those markets and it was a hit there was well as in the French-speaking Quebec, Canada.

Jive began flying radio program directors, journalists and tastemakers to see the group in Canada; in cities like Rochester and Chicago, near the Canadian border, radio began to play the record but MTV refused; Americans were into grunge and rap and Europop was uncool.

During most of 1995, The Backstreet Boys toured Europe and then Asia—Japan and South Korea—where fans loved them.

Hanson

Hanson was three brothers, Isaac, Taylor and Zac who all played guitar and piano (Isaac also played bass and Taylor played drums) from Tulsa, Oklahoma. They first performed as The Hanson Brothers in 1992 but shorted their name to Hanson the next year. Their first album, *Boomerang*, was released in 1995 and their second album, *MMMBop*, was released in 1996 on an independent label. After performing at South By Southwest, they were signed to management by Christopher Sabec and then signed by Steve Greenberg to Mercury where they released their debut album, *Middle of Nowhere* in May, 1997.

Their first single, "MMMBop" entered the *Billboard* Hot 100 in May and reached number one, where it remained for three weeks and stayed on the chart for 22 weeks. The album sold ten million copies and Mercury released a documentary, *Tulsa, Tokyo and the Middle of Everywhere* and an authorized biography by Jarrod Gollihare reached number nine on the *New York Times* Best Seller list in February, 1998.

Hanson's second single, "Where's The Love" and their third single, "I Will Come to You" were both released in 1997 and they played arenas and stadiums during their tours. Mercury executives had initially dismissed the band as too "light" but their success with young, teenage audiences proved that there was a market for a boy band that appealed to teenage girls.

Unfortunately, their label, Mercury, which was purchased by Polygram in 1972, was purchased by Seagrams in 1998; in a corporate re-structuring, Mercury's roster was absorbed into the Universal Music Group, which placed Hanson with Island Def Jam. The merger and re-structuring meant that the new label turned down numerous songs by Hanson so, after three years of creative struggle, the group left the label. By the time they left, the band had sold over 16 million records.

Backstreet Boys in America

In 1997, Clive Calder felt the time was right to bring the Backstreet Boys into the American market. Their second single, "Quit Playing Games (With My Heart)," which had been recorded two years earlier at Cheiron, was released in May, 1997. On June 28 it entered the *Billboard* Hot 100 and soared to number two, remaining on the charts for 43 weeks. In November, their next record, "As Long As You Love Me" entered the *Billboard* Hot 100 and rose to number four, remaining on that chart for over a year—56 weeks.

The Backstreet Boys were back in Sweden at the end of 1997, where they were mobbed; however, none of the group had seen much money. Pearlman argued that the $3 million he had put into the group had to be recouped, that he had invested that much into creating, feeding, housing, training and transporting the group and so he needed to be paid back before he could pay the group.

In 1998, they had two top five singles, "Everybody (Backstreet's Back)" and "I'll Never Break Your Heart." In 1999 they had three chart singles, "All I Have To Give," "I Want It That Way" and "Larger Than Life." In 2000 they charted with "Show Me the Meaning of Being Lonely," "The One" and "Shape of My Heart."

Recording Acts

The Audio Home Recording Act was passed in 1992 which charged pennies for sales of digital audio tapes. That money was paid into a fund which was split between record companies, artists, publisher and songwriters become of income lost due to home taping. In 1995, the Digital Performance Rights in Sound Recordings Act was signed to fight subscription services on the Internet.

Warner Brothers splits from Interscope

By 1995, Warner Brothers owned 50 percent of Interscope Records "but the label had become to Time Warner an utter embarrassment." Their artists were in the headlines for the wrong reasons; Snoop Doggy Dogg was accused of murder, 2Pac was convicted o sexual abuse, Dr. Dre had been arrested for drunk driving and middle America did not like the explicit sexual and violent lyrics by gangsta rap artists or album. The label was making millions of dollars, but Warner Brothers felt they had to unload Interscope. By the end of September, an agreement to separate Interscope from Warners had been reached. Interscope owners Ted Field and Jimmy Iovine agreed to pay Warners around $115 million for Warners share of the label. The parties agreed that Warner Brothers would distribute Interscope product on an album-by-album basis until the end of March, 1996.

Interscope quickly sold the half of the label that had been owned by Warner Brothers to MCA for $200 million. Gangsta rap was repulsive and embarrassing but extremely profitable.

SoundScan for Christian Music

In 1995, Billboard began using the SoundScan technology to compile *Billboard's* religious music charts; the next year, sales of recordings reached $538 or a 30 percent increase in one year, placing it sixth in popularity of all music genres, behind rock, country, urban contemporary, pop and rap but ahead of classical, jazz, oldies and new age. The use of computerized compilations of record sales eliminated the bias against gospel and Christian music and during the following years it was not unusual to see Christian artists and albums top the *Billboard* 200 album chart.

Great American Country

A country music network, Great American Country (GAC) premiered on December 31, 1995. The full time country network featured videos as well as re-runs of old shows and movies and newly created shows.

Music News: 1995

Mo Ostin, long-time Chairman and CEO of the Warner Music Group, stepped down from that position on January 1.

Rapper Tupac Shakur was sentenced to from one and a half to four and a half years in prison on a sexual abuse charge on February 7. While in prison, Shakur's album, *Me Against the World* was released and Shakur became the first artist to have a number one album on the *Billboard* album chart while in prison.

On April 29, Shakur married Keisha Morris inside the Clinton Correctional Facility in New York. He was released on October 11 on $1.4 million bail posted by Suge Knight with Death Row Records; in return, Shakur signed a three album deal with Death Row.

On March 31, Tejano singer Selena was shot and killed by Yolanda Saldivar, her former personal assistant and former fan club president. Saldivar had been recently fired for embezzling money from the fan club. For Hispanics worldwide, this event was known as "Black Friday."

On July 18, Selena's album debuted at number one on the Billboard album chart.

Michael Jackson released a double album, *HIStory*, which became a best-selling multiple album with 35 million copies sold worldwide.

On July 9, Jerry Garcia performed his final show with the Grateful Dead at Solider Field in Chicago. On August 9, Garcia died from a year attack; he was 53. Deadheads all over the United States gathered to mourn his death.

The Rock and Roll Hall of Fame opened in Cleveland on September 1, Inducted into the Rock and Roll Hall of Fame in 1995 were The Allman Brothers Band, Al Green, Janis Joplin, Led Zeppelin, Martha and the Vandellas, Neil Young and Frank Zappa.

World News: 1995

On April 19, a truck bomb exploded outside the Alfred P. Murrah Federal Building in Oklahoma City; it killed 168 people, including eight Federal marshals and 19 children and injured 680. It destroyed about a third of the Murrah building and destroyed or damaged 324 buildings nearby, causing $652 million in damages.

Within 90 minutes after the explosion, Timothy McVeigh was stopped driving without a license plate and arrested for possession of illegal weapons. He and his accomplice, Terry Nichols, were soon arrested and charged in the worst case of domestic terrorism the United States had ever seen.

In July, Iraq threatened to end all cooperation with UNSCOM weapons inspectors if sanctions against the country were not lifted by August 31. Iraqi leader Saddam Hussein's son-in-law defected and Hussein revealed new information about Iraq's biological and nuclear weapons programs. Iraq then turned over its biological weapons and a large number of new documents about its WMD (Weapons of Mass Destruction) program.

In Burma, Nobel Peace Prize winner Aung San Suu Kyi was freed from house arrest.

In September, NATO airstrikes against Bosnian Serb forces continued after numerous attempts to end the Bosnian war failed. In November, negotiations began at the Wright-Patterson Air Force Base in Dayton, Ohio to end the Bosnia War. On November 21, the "Dayton Agreement" was reached to end the war; the document was signed on December 14 in Paris.

On November 16, the United Nations tribunal charged Radovan Karadzic and Ratko Mladic with genocide during the Bosnian War.

On October 3, O.J. Simpson was declared "not guilty" of the double murder of his former wife, Nicole Simple and Ron Goldman.

Toy Story, the first full length computer animated film, was released on November 22 by Pixar and Walt Disney Pictures.

1996
Ozzfest

On October 25, 1996, the first Ozzfest was held in Phoenix, Arizona. Osbourne's wife and manager, Sharon (daughter of former manager Don Arden) created Ozzfest and managed it with help from their son, Jack. The next day the second Ozzfest was held in Devore, California. It was an immediate hit with Heavy Metal fans and in 1997 a reunited Black Sabbath joined the Ozzfest tour. Ozzfest was a huge success; Ozzie's merchandise sales were over $50 million and the fests grossed over $100 million.

N'SYNC

Lou Perlman believed that wherever there was a McDonald's there was also a Burger King and where there was Coke there was also Pepsi so it was logical to create another group with the same target market: young teenage girls.

"The Mickey Mouse Club" on Disney's channel had been canceled in 1996 after seven years. Perlman sent out word that he was forming another group and a member of The Mickey Mouse Club, 16-year old Justin Timberlake let it be known he was interested. Joining Timberlake were

JC Chavez, Chris Kirkpatrick, Joey Fatone and Lance Bass; the group was managed by Backstreet Boys manager Johnny Wright. Perlman was hot and the new group was signed to Areola, a subsidiary label under BMG. The group went to Cheiron in Stockholm and recorded their first two singles, "I Want You Back" and "Tearin' Up My Heart."

"I Want You Back debuted on the *Billboard* Hot 100 in March, 1998, and rose to number 13; "Tearin' Up My Heart" debuted in July and reached number 15.

The Spice Girls

The popularity of U.K. boy bands Take That and East 17 led Heart Management (Bob and Chris Herbert) to create a girl group. An ad was placed in the trade magazine *The Stage* for girls 18-23 who could sing and dance; approximately 400 auditioned and a line-up of Victoria Adams, Melanie Brown, Melanie Chisholm, Emma Bunton and Ginger Halliwell were eventually chosen. Originally named "Touch," the group was given the name "Spice" from a song they recorded, "Sugar and Spice."

The group left Heart Management in March, 1995, over creative differences. They were brought to the attention of Simon Fuller of 19 Entertainment by producer Eliot Kennedy and the production team of Absolute. Fuller auditioned them for record labels and they were signed by Virgin Records in September, 1995. They changed their name to "The Spice Girls" because there was a rapper named "Spice." The group toured while they wrote and recorded.

Their debut single, "Wannabe," was released in July, 1996, in the U.K after the release of a video, which was an instant hit; the single debuted at number three and the following week reached number one in the U.K., remaining in that position for seven weeks. It eventually became a number one single in 37 countries. After releasing two more number one singles in the U.K., "Say You'll Be There" and "2 Become 1," which were hits in 53 countries; in December, they released their debut album *Spice* in Europe. The album sold 1.8 million copies and was number one for 15 consecutive weeks in the U.K. eventually selling over ten million copies.

During an appearance on the U.K. TV show "Top of the Pops," Peter Lorain and his colleagues gave the group members names based on their identities: Sporty, Scary, Posh, Baby and Ginger Spice.

The group was the biggest pop act in the world when they released "Wannabe" in the United States in January, 1997; it debuted at number three reached number one on the Billboard Hot 100 and remained there for four straight weeks. During 1997 "Say You'll Be There" and "2 Become 1" also became top five singles in the U.S. Their album, Spice, was released in February and became the best selling album in the U.S. in 1997 and eventually sold over 28 million copies worldwide. Their book, Girl Power! sold 200,000 copies in its first week in the U.K.

Telecommunications Act of 1996

The growth of cell phone users led to the Telecommunications Act of 1996. When AT&T was broken up in 1984, the FCC ruled that phone carriers could either provide local or long-distance services, but not both. That led to the awkward and inconvenient situation where phone users had to deal with two different services.

The Telecommunications Act allowed local phone companies to also carry long distance service and vice versa. That allowed local phone service providers to complete head-to-head with AT&T and the Baby Bells for local service.

That was part of the reason for the "dot com bubble" as companies sought to capitalize on the internet and the new telecom landscape to create new companies and services. The telecom companies invested about $1 trillion wiring the world, laying, in effect, too much fiber optic cable. Long distance phone rates went from $2 a minute to 10 cents and the transmission of data was virtually free.

On March 10, 2000, the dot-com bubble burst; NASDAQ composite index had peaked at 5048.62 (over double its value the year before) and then stocks plummeted. It was a major disaster for investors and companies but a huge benefit for consumers. Because of local broadband installed in office buildings, it pushed prices down for business as the capacity of the fiber optic cables kept growing. That made it cheaper and easier to transmit voices and data to any part of the world.

An unforeseen side effect of this bill came from a provision that allowed companies to own a lot of radio stations, which led a handful of companies, Clear Channel, Cox, Infiniti and Cumulus, to expand so that a company could own six to eight stations in a market and control the programming of these stations. No longer would local radio stations cater to a local market; stations fired local disc jockeys and programmers and centralized their power over what music was played on the radio.

The Telecommunications Bill led four conglomerates to own the stations with the largest listening audiences; previously, an individual or company could own up to 40 stations. Stations used to decide what to play or not play but after the Telecommunications act, the decision making was centralized and a handful of programmers decided what thousands of radio stations played. "Voice tracking" became a way to take a popular disc jockey and have him or her appear on a number of stations in smaller markets. They were fed local references, news and weather during the breaks and listeners were not aware that the local disc jockey they thought they were listening to was actually a voice coming to them from hundreds or thousands of miles away.

Industry News: 1996

By the middle of 1996, there was concern about a lack of growth in the music industry; the industry seemed to have stalled at around $12 billion in retail sales. Retailers made their profits by charging labels for posters on their walls, placement in the front of the store and subsidies for advertisements. Discount stores like Best Buy and Circuit City took sales away from retail chains such as Tower and Wherehouse who had, in turn, taken sales away from locally owned "Mom and Pop" stores. Best Buy bought the top 100 CD titles for around $10 and sold them for $9.98, gambling that the cheap CDs would attract buyers of microwaves and refrigerators into their stores.

Garth and Country Music during the 1990s

By the end of 1996 Garth Brooks had sold over 60 million albums and his 1996 tour sold out 115 show dates to gross $33 million. On August 7, 1997, Garth Brooks performed before a live audience of 250,00 that was broadcast on HBO. Later that year he released his *Sevens* album. During the 1990s Garth became, not only the top selling country artist of the 1990s but the top selling country artist of all time.

In addition to the sales of albums by Garth Brooks, Arista Records, which had Alan Jackson and Brooks and Dunn, had sold 40 million albums by 1994. By 1995 Alabama had sold 57 million albums worldwide and had 41 of their singles reach the number one position on Billboard's country chart. Shania Twain's album, The Woman in Me, sold over eight million copies after its release in 1995.

LeAnn Rimes and "Blue"

Disc jockey Bill Mack wrote "Blue" in 15 minutes at his home in Wichita Falls, Texas and recorded it at a recording studio in that town; he released it as a single in 1958 but it did not chart. Mack hired a female singer to do a demo of "Blue" in 1962; Roy Drusky suggested he pitch the song to Patsy

Cline and Mack gave a tape of the song to Charlie Dick, Patsy's husband, but Patsy died before she could record it. The song was recorded by Kenny Roberts in 1966, Roy Drusky during the 1960s, Polly Stepehns Exley in the late 1980s and Kathryn Pitt in 1993 before 11-year old LeAnn Rimes recorded it for her 1994 independent album, All That. Rimes' father, Wilbur, and her manager, Marty Rendleman, received the Exley version of the song when Bill Mack sent it to them. Mike Curb heard the recording and signed Rimes to Curb Records and re-recorded the song; it entered the *Billboard* country chart on May 25, 1996, and reached number ten; it reached number 26 on the *Billboard* Hot 100.

After the song was a hit, Polly Stephens Exley claimed she had written the second verse to "Blue" and a settlement was made.

"Change the World"

Eric Clapton's record of "Change the World" entered *the Billboard* Hot 100 on July 20, 1996, and reached number five, remaining on that chart for 43 week. The recording was on the soundtrack to the film *Phenomenon* starring John Travolta.

"Change the World" was written by three Nashville songwriters—Gordon Kennedy, Tommy Sims and Wayne Kirkpatrick—but none of them worked on it together in the same room. The idea came during a demo session at Quad Studios when Kennedy and Kirkpatrick recorded four songs, three of which were on Garth Brooks' *Chris Gains* album several years later. During the session, bass player Tommy Sims suggested the title "Change the World" and a chord progression with a bit of a melody. Several months later, Kirkpatrick asked Sims for a tape of his idea and wrote the chorus and the second verse except for one line. Sometime later, Kennedy asked Kirkpatrick about the song and received a tape copy of what he had done; Kennedy finished writing the music and he and Sims put down a demo in Columbus, Ohio, where Sims was working on an album by a church choir.. On the drive back to Nashville, Kennedy wrote the first verse and the missing line from the second verse by singing the lines into a small cassette recorder. At his home in Nashville, Kennedy recorded a demo of the song, playing the guitar parts and vocals by himself; this was the demo that Eric Clapton received.

"Change the World" was first recorded by Wynonna Judd on her album, *Revelations*, released in February, 1996.

"Change the World" by Eric Clapton was produced by Babyface (Kenneth Edmonds) and was a worldwide hit, reaching the top 40 in 20 countries. It won a Grammy for "Record of the Year," "Song of the Year" and "Pop Mae Vocal."

Music News: 1996

Tupac Shakur released the first rap double album, *All Eyez on Me*, on February 13; it sold over a million units in just four hours and enter the *Billboard* album chart at number one. It became one of the most important albums in the history of rap.

The Beatles released "Real Love," a song that John Lennon recorded on a tape but never finished as part of their Anthology project. The song reached number 11 on the Hot 100.

M.C. Hammer filed for bankruptcy on April 3.

Jay-Z's debut album, *Reasonable Doubt*, was released on June 25.

On August 1, MTV2 is launched with "Where It's At" by Beck the first video broadcast.

Tupac Shakur is shot several times on September 7 while riding in a car along the Sunset Strip in Las Vegas. Shakur had just been to the Mike Tyson-Bruce Seldon heavy weight fight. Six days later he died.

Wal-Mart announced on September 10 that it would not carry Sheryl Crow's self-titled album because of the lyrics, "Watch out, sister, watch out, brother/watch our children while they kill each other with a gun they bought at Wal-Mart Discount Stores."

John Anthony Gillis married Meg White on September 21 and changed his name to Jack White; a year later they formed the White Stripes.

Faith Hill and Tim McGraw were married on October 6.

Eminem's debut studio album, *Infinite*, was released on November 12.

Inducted into the Rock and Roll Hall of Fame were David Bowie, Gladys Knight and the Pips, Jefferson Airplane, Little Willie John, Pink Floyd, the Shirelles and the Velvet Underground.

World News: 1996

On January 3, Motorola introduced th world's smallest and lightest mobile phone o date, the Motorola TAC wearable cellular telephone.

In the African country of Burundi, two tribes, the Hutus and Tutsis fought; the Tutsis massacred over 450 in a few days in April.

There were continual problems with Iraq; the country refused UNSCOM inspections for biological weapons and weapons of mass destruction. The United States wanted to take military action but could not build support in the United Nations Security Council.

To climb to the summit of Mount Everest has been the goal of most mountain climbers. As the years passed, more inexperienced climbers attempted the trek so base camps were established higher up the mountain. On May 10, there were several teams high on Mount Everest when a sudden storm hit high and eight people died. By the end of May, at least four other climbers had died in the worst season of fatalities on the mountain to date.

The first mammal to be cloned successful from an adult cell was Dolly the sheep. She was born in Scotland on July 5.

The 1996 summer Olympics began in Atlanta, Georgia on July 19; on July 27 in Centennial Olympic Park there was a bombing that killed one person and injured 111.

On August 28, the Prince and Princess of Wales were divorced at the High Court of Justice in London. Her Royal Highness The Princess of Wales was restyled, Diana, Princess of Wales.

The Iraqi army attacked and captured Arbil, which led the United States to launch "Operation Desert Strike." In November, UNSCOM inspectors uncovered prohibited missile parts buried; Iraq refused to allow the UNSCOM teams to remove the missile engines for analysis.

On November 5, President Bill Clinton was re-elected, defeating Republican nominee Bob Dole.

1997
Britney Spears

The success of the Spice Girls, as well as the Backstreet Boys and N'Sync, led Lou Pearlman to plan an all girls pop band; he named the would-be group Innosense and, with the help of Lynn Harless, mother of Justin Timberlake, began recruiting members; 15-year old Britney Spears was one of the first to audition. She had joined "The Mickey Mouse Club" when she was eight but was released after the Disney organization felt she was too young. She moved to New York where she attended the Professional Performing Arts School and became an understudy for the Broadway musical *Ruthless*. In 1993, she returned to the Mickey Mouse Club where she joined members Timberlake, Ryan Gosling, and Christina Aguilera. She and her mother, Lynne, moved to Orlando in the summer of 1993.

In 1996, when she was 13, she contacted New York attorney Larry Rudolph, who represented Lou Pearlman, the Backstreet Boys and Toni Braxton. Britney passed the audition with Innosense but backed out at the last minute because she wanted a solo career. The connection with Rudolph led him to send her a tape of a song written by Toni Braxton that Braxton decided against putting on her album. Rudolph told Britney to make a demo of the song, singing it like Braxton, and send it to him. She did and had auditions with three labels, Mercury, Epic and Jive. The first two passed, which left Jive.

Jeff Fenster, senior vice president of A&R for Jive liked it but, aside from A&R executive Steve Lunt, none of the other Jive executives liked it. Britney sang the song in a low voice and that was not her best key.

At the audition with Jive, she sang "I Will Always Love You" and "I Have Nothing." When asked if she had anything else, she sang the National Anthem.

Clive Calder disliked female singers; the frugal Calder thought single females were too expensive and too risky and likely to create diva-like demands. However, Calder thought that Britney "who was inexpensive to sign, and so evidently eager to please" would not create problems.

Britney was offered a contract with a clause that allowed Jive to cancel within ninety days if the A&R department decided an album would not work.

Eric Foster White was the only pop producer at Jive; their in-house songwriters wrote urban music. White took her into his studio for some demos but Calder did not feel any were a hit.

Jive executives agreed that they wanted her to work with Max Martin so Max flew to New York to meet her. Max and Britney spent several hours in the studio and Max was impressed; "She's 15 years old; I can make the record I really want to make, and use her qualities appropriately, without her telling me what to do," said Max. "Which is kind of what happened."

Max and Rami Yacoub had co-written a song "Hit Me Baby (One More Time) which was intended for TLC, a three woman R&B group; they turned it down.

Max continued to work on the song with Britney in mind and sent a demo to Jive. "As was Max's method of demo making, all the hooks in the song were worked up to their finished state, but most of the verses were unfinished, often mere vowel sounds," said John Seabrook. Jive loved it.

"It's hard to imagine that anyone for whom English is a first language would write the phrase 'hit me baby' without intending it as an allusion to domestic violence or S&M," stated Seabrook in his book, *The Song Machine*. "That was the furthest thing from the minds of the gentle Swedes, who were only trying to use up-to-the-minute lingo for 'Call me.' Jive, concerned that Americans might get the wrong idea, changed the title to '…Baby One More Time.'"

Denniz PoP had not been feeling well throughout 1996; he had difficulty swallowing. Afraid of doctors, he put off going for an examination until December when it was discovered that he had a cancerous tumor in his esophagus. An operation removed the tumor but the cancer had spread to his brain. A second operation in January did not achieve positive results. Meanwhile, the Cheiron team continued working on the project for Britney.

Britney Spears flew to Stockholm in April, 1997, and on May 2 and 3 recorded "…Baby One More Time" and "Sometimes," which became her second single. By this time, the label "had the template for Britney's whole career—the innocent girl on the one side, and the sex Lolita on the other," said Lund.

Before she left Stockholm, the Cheiron team of Max Martin, Rami Yacoub, Kristian Lundin, Per Magnusson, David Krueger, Jorgen Elofsson and Andreas Carlsson had recorded six songs during a ten period on Britney that included all four singles which would be on her debut album.

During the summer of 1998 Britney Spears did a promotional tour of 26 shopping malls and some performing venues where she performed a four song set. She did not like the ideas presented for her first video; she wanted it "light" and suggested a girl looking for "hot" guys, dressed in Catholic school girl uniforms.

That summer was a painful one for Dennis Dagge—"Denniz PoP"— who lost weight and his hair and died on August 30.

Teen Pop and MTV

Radio had Top 40 programming, putting a few hit songs in high rotation, but MTV, which saw itself as the arbiter of "cool" shunned pop; instead they featured "MTV Jams" for rap and "Alternative Nation" for grunge. At their headquarters at 1515 Broadway in New York, they only added five new videos a week. They had never featured New Kids on the Block or the early Backstreet Boys videos but by 1998 they could no longer ignore the success of the Backstreet Boys and N'Sync; it was now "hip to be square."

They needed to acknowledge the market but did not want to lose their "cool" image; they solved that quandary in September, 1998 when they debuted "Total Request Live" where they played the ten most requested videos. That allowed MTV an escape; it was the audience, not the programmers, who picked the video. That was the breakthrough that put pure pop on MTV.

"...Baby, One More Time" was released on November 3, 1998, and went "Gold" that same day. It moved into heavy rotation with "1999" by Prince and dominated MTV viewing. (In 2008 "...Baby OneMore Time was voted most popular video of all time on MTV.)

The record soared to number one on the *Billboard* Hot 100 and remained in that position for two weeks and on the chart for 32 weeks. The album sold 30 million worldwide. That was Max Martin's first number one in *Billboard*.

Britney's second single, "Sometimes," only reached number 21 but her third single, "(You Drive Me) Crazy" was a top ten, giving her three hits in 1999.

The Backstreet Boys released their album *Millennium* in May, 1999, and their first single from that album, "I Want It That Way," a Max Martin song, was a worldwide hit that reached number six on the *Billboard* Hot 100. (The Backstreet Boys never had a single reach number one on the *Billboard* chart.) Their second single, "Larger Than Life" only reached number 25 but their third single, "Show Me the Meaning of Being Lonely," another Max Martin tune, also reached number six. Their album sold 1.1 million copies in its first week and was the best-selling album of 1999.

Britney's second album was released in March, 2000, and the single, "Oops!...I Did It Again," written by Max Martin and Rami, was a top ten single. In 2000, Britney Spears had four chart singles, "From the Bottom Of My Broken Heart," ""Oops!...I Did It Again," "Lucky" and "Stronger," which peaked in 2001.

The Cheiron group had become the go-to writing and production team in pop music; they received a royalty rate of 8 percent when other songwriting-production groups received 3-4 percent.

Steve Jobs and Apple

Steve Jobs and Steve Wozniak formed Apple Computer on April 1, 1976 in the Bay Area of California. The name "apple" came from Jobs.

Jobs and Wozniak met through a shared love of computers and technology and the young company did reasonably well its first year and even better when Wozniak, who was heavily into creating new products, created the Apple II computer in his kitchen. Jobs strength was his vision for new products that appealed to the users of personal computers.

Apple sold $7.2 million worth of stock in 1979, which made Steve Jobs a millionaire at 24; in 1980, the company went public. Wozniak left the company within four years.

The beginning of the downfall of the first stage of Apple came on January 24, 1984, when Apple introduced the Macintosh. The Mac appealed to artists, designers and college students but it was ahead of its time; sales fell far short of projections and the Apple Board of Directors voted Jobs out of the company.

During the next 15 years Jobs created NeXT and promoted a computer called "The Cube." It failed. He purchased "The Graphics Group," a special effects company created by George Lucas, the director of *Star Wars*. Jobs invested his own money in the company, which became Pixar, a computer animated firm which gave movie-goers *Toy Story, Finding Nemo* and *Cars*.

Meanwhile, Microsoft designed a Windows operating system like the operating system in the Macintosh and became the world's largest software company by the early 1990s. Apple was falling further and further behind Microsoft; in the fourth quarter of 1995, the company lost $68 million. That led the Apple Board of Directors to bring Steve Jobs back into the company during the summer of 1997. Jobs was given the job of "Interim CEO" at a salary of $1 a year.

Job's turned Apple around; by the end of his first year back as CEO, Apple showed a profit. Now, Jobs wanted to create new products to make Apple a major competitor to Microsoft again. His vision was the "Digital Hub Strategy" which aimed to make the Mac the center of a lifestyle. Ideas included iMovie and iPhoto and other entertainment oriented devices. A portable music player was not part of Jobs' initial vision.

Cellular Telephones

Before 1984, there was only one telephone company—American Telephone and Telegraph (AT&T) and no one could own a phone; instead, telephones were rented via a monthly charge for home phones.

The development of the cell phone initially used the idea of radio technology, which was installed in police cars and taxies as mobile radios which communicated with a home base.

Bell Labs, the research arm of AT&T, developed the concept of the cell phone in 1947; that same year the Federal Communications Commission (FCC) approved the development of Citizens' Band (CB) radios. In 1956, the first fully automatic mobile system was introduced in Sweden; each phone weighed 88 pounds. During the 1960s, AT&T developed a mobile telephone service for Amtrak and in 1970 the "call handoff" system was developed, which allowed mobile phones to move through several cell areas. Prior to this development, a cell phone had to remain within a service area of one base station in order to make and receive calls.

In December, 1971, AT&T sent the FCC a proposal for cellular service; during the 1970s, the FCC authorized AT&T to test the cellular concept and set aside frequencies for land mobile communication. The FCC also granted licenses to experiment with cell phones and authorized the construction of two developmental systems.

In 1982, AT&T's request for cellular phones was approved by the FCC, who adopted rules for commercial cellular telephone service. In October, 1983, the pilot commercial cellular system was instituted in Chicago and in December of that year, another system began in the Washington/Baltimore area.

In January, 1984, the anti-trust suit against the Bell System by the Department of Justice resulted in the breakup of AT&T. That year, Motorola shipped its first commercial portable cellular phone with a price tag of $3,000-4,000. By the end of 1988, commercial cellular systems proliferated and in 1990 the first digital cell phone was made in the United States.

During the 1990s, the cell phone became ubiquitous. In 1992 there were 10 million cell phone subscribers; in 1995 it was over 25 million as a second generation of mobile phone systems was introduced and users moved from carrying "brick" phones to smaller hand held devices.

By the end of 1997, there were over 50 million cell phone subscribers in the United States.

1998

Polygram

The roots of Polygram go back to Deutsche Grammophon, established as a subsidiary of the British Gramophone Company (which was a subsidiary of the Emile Berliner's United States Gramophone Company, the forerunner to Victor) in 1898. In 1917, during the first World War, Germany sealed its borders and Deutsch Grammophon became an independent company; in 1924 they began using the name "Polydor" outside Germany. In 1941 the German electronics firm, Siemens purchased the company.

In 1950, the Dutch electronics firm Philips began a record label, Phonogram. In 1962 Philips and Siemens merged and the label formed by Philips, Phonogram, was combined with the German label Polydor to form Polygram in 1972. Polygram purchased the American label Mercury, begun in Chicago in 1947, for their entry into the American market. In

1975, Polygram bought RSO, the label owned by Robert Stigwood, and in 1978 purchased France's largest record company, Barclay. In 1980, it purchased British Decca and the American firm, Casablanca, headed by Neil Bogart. In 1989, it purchased A&M Records, the label begun by Herb Alpert and Jerry Moss to market Alpert's Tijuana Brass recordings. In 1990 Polygram purchased Island, the label begun by Chris Blackwell in London in 1962 in order to distribute the Jamaican label in the United Kingdom. In 1993 they purchased Motown from MCA. In 1998 they were sold to MCA.

Portable Digital Music Players

A South Korean company, Saehan, created the first portable digital music player, the MP3Man. Diamond Multimedia marketed the Rio PMP300 beginning in September, 1998. RIAA sued Diamond Multimedia.

The Recording Industry Association of America (RIAA) attempted to block the release of the new Rio PMP300, an MP3 digital audio player on October 8. The RIAA argued that the player was a music piracy device. The claim by the RIAA was denied on October 27, which allowed the PMP300 to became the first commercially successful MP3 player.

Two former Apple employees, Bill Kincaid and Jeff Robin, created "Soundjam," which provided consumers with a way to organize their MP3s and play music over their computer speakers. That became the MP3 player that Mac users used. "Soundjam" evolved into "iTunes." The problem was there was no portable "player."

Technology

On June 25, Microsoft released Windows 98.

On September 4, Google, Inc. was founded by Stanford University graduate students Larry Page and Sergey Brin in Menlo Park, California. Page and Brin were working towards the PhD degrees at the time of the formation of Google.

Titanic

The biggest grossing movie for the year was Titanic, which premiered in December, 1997. The film grossed over $1 billion, the largest grossing film at that time. The theme song for the film, "My Heart Will Go On," was recorded by Celine Dion and entered the *Billboard* singles chart n February 28 and rose to number two, where it remained for two weeks. The song was written by James Homer and Will Jennings. The song won Grammys for

Record and Song of the Year and Pop Female Vocal as well as an Oscar for Best Song in a film.

Dixie Chicks

The third chart single for the Dixie Chicks was "Wide Open Spaces," which entered *Billboard's* country chart on August 22, 1998, and rose to number one where it remained for four weeks; it reached number 41 on the Hot 100. The song was written by Susan Gibson, who recorded the song when she was lead singer for The Groobees, whose album was produced by Lloyd Maines, father of Dixie Chicks lead singer Natalie Maines. "Wide Open Spaces" followed two hit singles, "I Can Love You Better" and "There's Your Trouble" on their debut album *Wide Open Spaces*. The Dixie Chicks—sisters Emily Erwin and Martie Seidel with Natalie Maines—won Grammys for Country Vocal Group for "There's Your Trouble" and CMA's Single of the Year award for "Wide Open Spaces."

Opryland Closes

The Opryland Theme Park was closed in 1998. The theme park had been a training ground for numerous young performers and musicians during the 25 years it had been an important part of the Nashville community. The park was an integral part of the success of Opryland Hotel; convention goers often brought their families and stayed extra days. The loss of the Opryland Theme Park had a negative effect on the hotel's convention business and the loss of the music park was a great loss to Nashville's music industry because it had been a source for new performers, songwriters, musicians and executives. It also hurt the tourism industry in Nashville, which suffered a decline for several years after Opryland closed.

On Music Row

By 1998, Warner Brothers Music (Reprise and Warner-Alliance labels) Mercury, BMG (RCA, Arista and BNA labels) MCA (Decca) and Sony (Columbia, Epic, Monument, Lucky Dog) all had offices on Music Row, an area that included Music Square East and West, Sixteenth, Seventeenth, Eighteenth, and Nineteenth Avenues South; the cross streets McGavock, Roy Acuff Place, Chet Atkins Place, Horton, Edgehill, Hawkins, South Street and sections of Division and Demonbreun. Bounded on South by Wedgewood and Belmont University, north by McGavock, east by Music Square East and west by Twentieth Avenue South. That area of less than two miles square was just over one mile long and less than half a mile wide.

World News: 1998

The United States and Great Britain threatened military action against Iraq, which then agreed to allow U.N. weapons inspectors to return to Baghdad. However, problems continued to exist and in December, President Bill Clinton ordered air strikes against Iraq after the United Nations withdrew all weapons inspectors.

During August, American embassies in Dar es Salaam, Tanzania and Nairobi, were bombed, killing 224 and injuring over 4,500. The bombings were linked to terrorist Osama bin Laden.

On December 19, the Republican-led House of Representative forwarded articles of impeachment against President Bill Clinton to the Senate. He became the second president in the history of the United States to be impeached.

Music News: 1998

Interscope Records paid $5,000 to a radio station in Portland, Oregon play "Counterfeit," a single by Limp Bizkit, fifty times. This was widely criticized as payola but the band received a great deal of publicity for the controversy.

On February 24, Elton John became "Sir John Elton" when he was knighted by Queen Elizabeth II at Buckingham Palace. However, the mistake was corrected and he was renamed Sir Elton John.

The first VH1 Divas Live concert was broadcast on April 14 on VH1. The concert starred Aretha Franklin, Gloria Estefan, Celine Dion, Shania Twain and Mariah Carey.

The first broadcast of "Total Request Live" on MTV came on September 14.

The Copyright Term Extension Act was signed into law on October 27, which gave the entertainment industry twenty more years of exclusive rights for works created since 1923.

Billboard changed its compilation of the Hot 100 chart to allow airplay-only singles or album cuts to be eligible for the chart.

The Broadway production of *Footloose* opened and the film *Blues Brothers 2000* was released in 1998.

Inducted into the Rock and Roll Hall of Fame in 1998 were The Eagles, Fleetwood Mac, The Mamas & the Papas, Lloyd Price, Santana and Gene Vincent.

1999
Country Music in the 1990s

In 1979, Wal-Mart sold $1 billion worth of merchandise in its 230 stores; in 1989 there were 1,402 stores which sold $8.1 billion worth of merchandise. Those simple facts are a primary explanation in the growth of sales in country music during the decade of the 1980s. The other factor that was key in attracting young people to country music was the growth of rap and hip hop music on pop radio. Many young people disliked rap and hip hop so, looking for an alternative, they found a pop-oriented sound in country music and, beginning in 1989, a number of new, attractive young country acts. Those acts included Garth Brooks, Clint Black, Alan Jackson, Brooks and Dunn, Vince Gill, Tim McGraw and Reba McEntire.

The story of retailing during the 1980s and 1990s is, in large part, the story of the phenomenal growth of Wal-Mart and other mass merchandisers during that period. Another mass merchandiser, K-Mart, overtook Sears as the nation's largest retailer during the 1980s while Wal-Mart moved up to number three. During the 1990s Wal-Mart overtook Sears and K-Mart and became the number one retailer in the United States.

Around 75 percent of country music was sold in mass merchandisers and nobody sold more country music than Wal-Mart. The explosion in country music in the 1980s and 1990s owes a much to Sam Walton as to Garth Brooks, Randy Travis, George Strait or any other country singer. Ironically, the spread of Wal-Mart and other merchandisers helped country music on one hand by exposing more consumers who buy country music to the product from its artists while, at the same time, it undermined the very values and traditions expressed in the music. The arrival of a Wal-Mart in a suburban community or small town usually meant the death of the town square, the independently owned store (called "Mom and Pops") which represented the small town view of America. They were replaced by a large store outside town where consumers went instead of the town square.

The mass merchandisers, as well as other retailers, had electronic scanners at their check-out counters which scanned bar codes and automatically recorded the item purchased, subtracted it from the store inventory, tallied up the price and showed the consumer how much to pay. In addition to having an impact on consumers who shopped, those scanners had a tremendous impact on country music because they gave an unbiased and accurate report of country music sales. .

Digital

By 1999, the Internet was a part of everyday life for many Americans, especially young Americans who spent countless hours surfing the web, sending emails and playing games.

The record industry was certainly aware of the internet; in 1998, the Secure Digital Music Initiative was created "to figure out a standard way to encrypt digital music files so they wouldn't go traipsing around the internet for anybody to download for free." That group was comprised of record label executives as well as representatives from Microsoft, Intel, Texas Instruments, Sony and Panasonic. The sticking point was that the report issued stated that a "compliant device" (perhaps like a Walkman or boom box) "would have the power to determine whether an online music file was copy-protected. If not, the music simply wouldn't play." That was a clash of cultures; the record industry loved the idea but "Electronics firms hated the idea of making music players designed not to play music." Both sides--the record labels and the electronic industry--stuck to their guns and the initiative eventually died.

That left a situation where the only way to obtain music on the internet was to obey the rules of copyright and deal with the major labels—who were perfectly happy raking in huge profits from CD sales—or ignore copyright laws and do it illegally.

From the major labels perspective, they had a nearly ideal situation; they controlled the content of their industry and felt no need to share it with others. The labels decided which artists to sign, what to release and when to release it, what catalogue items should remain in print and what songs to promote to radio. Artists saw the album as a single work and spent hours deciding on the sequence of songs. For the artist, the idea that a hit single could lead consumers to purchase an album which included less commercial—but, to the artist, more artistically valuable—songs was an advantage for the album. For the label, the fact that every time someone purchased an album they made approximately $10 was a huge windfall, which allowed them to sign more artists and develop them. It also meant that major record label executives could have huge salaries and expense accounts, live in mansions and drive expensive cars.

There was no one hired at a record label to do "strategic planning" with digital files or the internet. Those in the music industry were busy every day recording songs, getting them pressed, on the radio, in retail outlets, getting artists publicity, setting up personal appearances and tours, signing new acts, promoting established acts—in other words, doing the jobs that the music industry needed doing. There was no reason for anyone at a record label to be aware of a German Professor, Dieter Seitzer, and his work with digital files beginning in the late 1970s.

Seitzer was involved with transmitting speech quicker and more efficiently over phone lines. Along the way, Seitzer thought it might be a good idea to develop a way to send music files over phone lines as well. Seitzer was denied a patent; he was ahead of his time and the patent office did not understand what he was doing. Seitzer then assigned a graduate student, Karlheinz Brandenburg, the task of "shrinking" the music. Brandenburg developed the idea of "audio compression" and a number of scientists worked on that problem for over a decade. A number of companies—including Bell Laboratories and Philips Electronics—worked both together and separately and developed a compressed audio file.

None of those involved in that research were quite sure what would come out of it; a number of research projects sit on shelves or the ideas are buried in papers published in obscure journals. By 1991, the MP3 had been perfected but the majority of those involved saw the new development as a way to improve telephone communication.

The Moving Picture Experts Group (MPEG), a subgroup of the International Organization for Standardization (IOS) which creates standards for digital multimedia formats, merged several proposals and came up with a compression technology they labeled "ISO-MPEG-1 Audio Layer 3," or "MP3" for short. That file contained no copyright protection, but no one outside the research scientists was even aware of the MP3 file, much less the lack of copyright protection.

Two music fans, Rob Lord and Jeff Patterson at the University of California—Santa Cruz, discovered the MP3 technology and used it to promote their band, the Ugly Mugs, by encoding their songs in the MP3 format and sending them out via internet newsgroups. Surprised at the positive reaction—and the fact that they received requests for more music from all over the world—Patterson and Lord set up a web site, The Internet Underground Music Archive, which gave away free MP3s from unknown and unsigned bands.

There were some attempts to engage the music industry in the internet; Liquid Audio was formed by Gerry Kearby and that format, which had encrypted locks on digital music files, was turned down by the industry when the founder attempted to license music from the major labels.

Lou Pearlman's Fraud

The Backstreet Boys were surprised to discover that Big Poppa and the Cheiron group were behind N'Synch. Meanwhile, Pearlman had set up several fraudulent businesses—an insurance company and what he claimed was a fleet of 47 charter planes (there was actually only one plane). Pearlman was taking money earned by the Backstreet Boys and N' Sync to pay off his investors; he had set up a Ponzi scheme.

The Backstreet Boys sued Pearlman for fraud and breach of fiduciary duty in 1998; they claimed he kept $10 million of their revenues while giving them only $300,000 total. The lawsuit was settled by Jive, who gave Pearlman $30 million and a sixth of future earnings by the Backstreet Boys, which allowed Pearlman to continue his Ponzi scheme for eight more years.

N Sync had sold 15 million albums by 1998 but only received a per diem of $35; confronted about the finances, their label, Areola Munich and Pearlman gave each member a check for $25,000, which Lance Bass tore in shreds. Pearlman was receiving half of the merchandising income and royalties from sales of CDs and 20 percent of their touring income but refused to amend their contract. N'Sync took Big Poppa to court.

Rock and Roll Hall of Fame

Artists inducted into the Rock and Roll Hall of Fame in 1999 were Billy Joel, Curtis Mayfield, Paul McCartney, Del Shannon, Dusty Springfield, Bruce Springsteen and The Staple Singes.

Facts and Figures

Surveys showed that in 1999 the average American listened to over two hours on the radio each day.

There were approximately 30,000 albums released in a year but less than one percent of CD or cassette titles sold over 10,000 copies, according to Soundscan. The average Wal-Mart, which was a major retailer for CDs and cassettes, stocked about 4,000 titles. Consumers over 35 accounted for 35 percent of sales.

The backbone of both LP and CD formats was the rock album.

A problem had emerged with CDs—there were too many songs. The LP held about 20 minutes of music on each side while the CD held 76 minutes and 42 seconds. Because artists could put more on a CD, they did, which undermined the listening experience. A conclusion was that the CD was better for symphonies than for a collection of pop songs.

The LP encouraged more "active" listening because it is easier for a person to concentrate for 20 minutes than for 75 minutes. Also, after 20 minutes, the listener had to get up and turn over the LP, which kept the listener engaged. If they chose to open the arm that held the LP before it dropped to play, the phonograph played the LP over and over, which meant the listener absorbed the music more. Unlike the cassette or CD, the LP was not portable, so someone had to sit and listen.

What that meant was that those who listened to LPs in the 1960s and 1970s had a different listening experience than those who listened to CDs in the 1990s. Listeners to CDs in the 1990s heard more music while those who listened to LPs in the 1960s and 1970s heard less music but heard it "deeper."

Columbine

On April 20, 1999, two students at Columbine High School, Eric Harris and Dylan Klebold, walked into their school in Littleton, Colorado, a suburb of Denver, just after 11 a.m. They had a number of weapons, including sawed off shotguns, 9 mm pistols and homemade bombs. Apparently inspired by the Oklahoma City bombing, they entered the cafeteria where students were eating lunch and, at 11:19 a.m., began firing, killing 12 students, one teacher, and wounding 21 other students (3 students were injured while fleeing).

After exchanging gunfire with police, Harris and Klebold committed suicide.

During the shooting there was panic inside the school; after the shooting there was a panic in America that attempted to discover the reasons why two students engaged in a well-planned massacre.

Blame was placed on violent media, including music that was connected to the goth culture. American singer Marilyn Manson received blame, although neither of the two killers were fans. The German metal acts Rammstein and KMFDM were also blamed; the students were fans of those acts.

Contemporary Christian music artists believed that atheism was to blame, perpetuated by the story of Cassie Bernall, who reportedly answered "yes" when Eric Harris asked her if she believed in God. He then shot her in the head. A song, "This is Your Time" by contemporary Christian artist Michael W. Smith was a direct response to the shooting.

Nashville 1999

According to a survey, at the end of 1999, Nashville had around 90 record companies, almost 300 music publishers, 174 recording studios, 5,500 union musicians and 17 staffed professional organizations which, with tourism, accounted for a $2 billion industry. The Chamber of Commerce announced that it had adopted the Music City logo for promotional campaigns.

Faith Hill

Faith Hill had two huge hits in 1999, "Breathe" and "The Way You Love Me." "Breathe," written by Stephanie Bentley and Holly Lamar, entered the Billboard country chart on October 9, 1999, and rose to number one, where it remained for six weeks; it was number two on the Hot 100 for five weeks. "Breathe" was number one on the Adult Contemporary chart for 17 weeks and the Adult Top 40 chart. It was nominated for a Grammy for Best Female Country Vocal, Best Country Song and Song of the Year.

"The Way You Love Me," written by Keith Follese and Michael Dulaney, entered the Billboard country chart on November 27 and during 2000 reached number one, where it remained for four weeks and remained on the chart for 39 weeks; it reached number six on the Hot 100. Both of the records were produced by Byron Gallimore; "The Way You Love Me" was a hit in Australia, Belgium, Canada, Switzerland and the U.K.

World News: 1999

The Euro was established on January 1 in Europe; on that date, all local currency became "Euros." The transition came off smoothly.

In January, China announced new government restrictions on Internet use, especially in Internet cafes.

President Bill Clinton was acquitted in impeachment proceedings in the United States Senate on February 12.

Because of the increased value in Microsoft stock, Bill Gates became the wealthiest individual in the world in April.

There was a war in Kosovo; in April, Yugoslav forces closed Kosovo's main border crossing to keep Kosovo Albanians from leaving. In a tragic mistake, ethnic Albanian refugee convoys were repeatedly bombed by NATO warplanes for two hours; at least 73 refugees were killed. Another tragic mistake occurred in May when NATO dropped bombs on the Chinese Embassy in Yugoslavia; three workers were killed and 20 were wounded.

In June, Yugoslavia and NATO signed a peace agreement and NATO suspended air strikes after Slobodam Milosevic agreed to withdraw Yugoslav forces from Kosovo.

Napster debuted on June 1.

A plane piloted by John F. Kennedy Jr. crashed off the coast of Martha's Vineyard on July 16, killing Kennedy, his wife Carolyn Bessette-Kennedy and her sister, Lauren Bessette.

In November, the merger of Exxon and Mobil was completed, making ExxonMobile the largest corporation on the planet.

On December 31, the United States turned administration of the Panama Canel over to the Panamanian government. In Russia, Boris Yeltsin resigned as president, leaving Prime Minister Vladimir Putin as acting president.

Music News: 1999

In January, A&M Records was merged into the Universal Music Group to create Interscope Geffen A&M

The Artist Formerly Known as Prince filed lawsuits against nine Web sites for copyright and trademark infringement. The suit claimed that the web sites sold bootlegged recordings and made available unauthorized song downloads.

The "Diamond" award was introduced by the RIAA for albums or singles selling ten million units.

Billy Joel announced in April that he was giving up his pop career—performing no more pop concerts—in order to concentrate on classical music.

Eminem was sued by his mother who claimed $10 million should be paid to her because comments he made about her in public were slanderous and caused her emotional stress and financial harm. (She collected $1,600 two years later.)

The first complete album by a major artist available to download on the Internet was Hours by David Bowie. The Internet release came two weeks before the physical release.

Jeffrey Levy, a student at the University of Oregon, became the first person who was convicted of copyright infringement for downloading MB3s without permission. He was sentenced to two years of probation and limited Internet access.

Songs with the most airplay

In December, BMI announced the songs that had received the most airplay on radio and television during the twentieth century. At the top of the list, with over eight million plays, was "You've Lost That Lovin' Feeling," written by Barry Mann, Cynthia Weil and Phil Spector; the most famous version was by the Righteous Brothers. Next, with over seven million plays, were "Never My Love" written by Donald and Richard Addrisi and recorded by the Association, "Yesterday" by Lennon and McCartney and "Stand By Me, written by Jerry Leiber, Mike Stoller and Ben E.King with King's version the most popular followed.

Songs that received over six million airplays were "Can't Take My Eyes Off of You" written by Bob Crewe and Bob Gaudio for Frankie Valli; "Sittin' on the Dock of the Bay" written by Otis Redding and Steve Cropper and recorded by Redding; "Mrs. Robisnon" by Paul Simon, "Baby I Need Your Loving" by the Four Tops, written by Lamont Dozier, Brian Holland and Eddie Holland; "Rhythm of the Rain" written by John Gummoe and "Georgia On My Mind," written by Hoagy Carmichael and Stuart Gorrell.

Top Selling Albums in 1999

1. *Millennium* by the Backstreet Boys
2. *...Baby One More Time* by Britney Spears
3. *Come on Over* by Shania Twain
4. *NSYNC* by 'N Sync
5. *Ricky Martin* by Ricky Martin
6. *Christina Aguilera* by Christina Aguilera
7. *Supernatural* by Santana
8. *FanMail* by TLC
9. *Devil Without a Cause* by Kid Rock
10. *The Slim Shady LP* by Eminem

Albums that reached number one on the Billboard chart in 1999

(Albums with multiple weeks at number one are in parenthesis)
Flesh Blood of My Blood by DMX (3 weeks)
...Baby One More Time by Britney Spears (6 weeks)
Made Man by Silkk The Shocker
Chyna Doll by Foxy Brown
Fanmail by TLC (5 weeks)

I Am… by Nas (2 weeks)
Ruff Ryders—Ryde Or Die, Vol, I by Ruff Ryders
A Place in the Sun by Tim McGraw
Ricky Martin by Ricky Martin
Millennium by the Backstreet Boys (10 weeks)
Significant Other by Limp Bizkit (4 weeks)
Christina Aguilera by Christina Aguillera
Fly by the Dixie Chicks (2 weeks)
Ruff Ryders First Lady by Eve
The Fragile by Nine Inch Nails
Human Clay by Creed
Supernatural by Santana (12 weeks)
The Battle of Los Angeles by Rage Against the Machine
Breathe by Faith Hill
Issues by Korn
All the Way…A Decade of Song by Celine Dion (3 weeks)
Born Again by The Notorious B.I.G.

The End of the 20th Century

New Year's Eve 1999 marked the end of the twentieth century and there were major concerts heard around the world. At the MGM Grand in Las Vegas, Barbra Streisand headlined; The Eagles performed at the Staples Center in L.A., Billy Joel was at Madison Square Garden and Metallica, with Kid Rock and Ted Nugent performed at the Pontiac Silverdome in front of 54,000.

The biggest concert was at the Big Cypress Indian Reservation in Florida where Phish performed before 75,000 people.

Y2K

The Y2K fears proved to be unfounded. Those fears were based on a concern that computers, which used four digits for a date (e.g. April 9, 1999 was 040999) would create havoc when they rolled over to 2000. The problem was fixed and the worldwide disaster predicted by some did not occur.

2000
World News: 2000

At the stroke of midnight, Prince celebrated the new millennium by performing "1999" in New York City. In May, he announced that he had changed his name back to "Prince" because his publishing contract with

Warner/Chappell had expired. He had been known as an unpronounceable symbol since 1993.

On January 10, America Online (AOL) announced an agreement to purchase Time Warner for $162 billion, the largest corporate merger to that time.

On January 14, the Dow Jones Industrial Average closed at 11,722.98; on March 10, the NASDAW Composite Index reached an all time high and two weeks later, the S&P 500, the NASDAW-100 and the Wilshire 5000 all reached their peaks. It was the height of the dot.com bubble, a bull market that lasted over 17 years. After these peaks, dot.com stocks values dropped precipitously.

Technology

The PlayStation 2 was released in Japan in March; several months later it became the best-selling game console of all time. In August, the Nintendo GameCub was revealed.

In April, a court case, United States v. Microsoft Corp, ruled that Microsoft had violated U.S. antitrust law by keeping an "oppressive thumb" on its competitors.

The ILOVEYOU computer virus, that originated in the Philippines, spread quickly throughout the world in May, infecting tens of millions of Windows personal computers.

Shawn Fanning and Napster

Shawn Fanning wanted to enroll at Carnegie Mellon University in Pittsburgh, but the admissions office turned him down; instead, he enrolled at Northeastern University in Boston, although he didn't attend many classes. Fanning, born in 1980, grew up in the Boston area in a troubled family; his Mom and Dad divorced before he was born and he did not see much of his Dad, Joe Rando. Shawn's Mom married again, had four children and when they split, the kids ended up briefly in a foster home.

Shawn's uncle, John Fanning, took him in and in 1996 bought him an Apple Macintosh. Shawn immediately began surfing the internet and soon became a hacker.

In the mid-1990s, college students began swapping MP3s on line, then, in 1997, Michael Robertson created MP3.com, where computer users found free music. Fanning looked for a way to swap MP3s online that did not involve web search engines. One day, in his dorm room, Fanning conceived the idea for Napster, which created a central server for file sharing. Fanning's Internet Relay Channel (IRC) nickname was "Napster."

At the beginning of Fanning's second semester in college—January, 1999—he was working on Napster code. His uncle John Fanning, incorporated Napster, Inc. and took 70 percent of the business; Shawn owned the remaining 30 percent. In June, Shawn alerted about 30 friends—mostly other hackers he'd met on-line—about Napster. It wasn't long before 15,000 people had downloaded Napster.

During the summer of 1999, Frank Creighton, head of the anti-piracy division of RIAA, discovered Napster.com. Creighton sent an email to the Fannings, who were on the verge of receiving financing from venture capitalists. The Fannings answered his email, then stalled.

The Fannings wanted to create a huge base of users and by early October, 1999, Napster had 150,000 registered users; 3.5 million files were traded. On December 6, the RIAA filed a copyright-infringement lawsuit in San Francisco. By July, 2000, there were 20 million users on Napster.

Major label executives wee united in their opposition to Napster and "perceived online music sharing as theft, plain and simple, and had no interest whatsoever in jumping into bed with their sworn enemy." There was no question that Napster users were engaging in theft. But their stick-it-to-the-man righteousness drew much of the public to their side, and major labels were taking the biggest public relations hits they'd ever absorbed"

A meeting was set up between executives of Napster and major label executives—Edgar Bronfman, CEO of Seagram, which owned Universal, Thomas Middlehoff, head of Bertelsmann, which owned BMG, Nobuyuki Idei, head of Sony and Howard Stringer, head of Sony USA were all involved. The issue for the labels was copyright infringement.

On Napster's side was the Sony Corp. of America vs. Universal City Studios case in 1984 where the Supreme Court ruled that Sony could manufacture VCRs and people could record copyrighted TV shows for their own use, the Audio Home Recording Act of 1992, which allowed taped copes of albums as long as they weren't sold, and the Digital Millennium Copyright Act of 1998, which said that internet service providers were "safe" as long as they "didn't actively encourage illegal behavior."

Bronfman, Middlehoff and Idei all realized that Napster could give them 22 million on-line consumers and that computer technology would allow the record industry to discover the buying habits of individual consumers. At a meeting in Sun Valley, Idaho, on July 15, 2000, between the label executives and two men who represented Napster, Hank Barry, a corporate attorney and venture capitalist John Hummer, who had given Napster $65 million for a 20 percent share in the company, Barry offered a 50-50 split of Napster's future equity; the recording industry wanted over 90 percent. Middlehoff observed later that "the Napster people and the label people didn't really like each other. Bronfman did all the talking" No one was willing to negotiate or compromise; the meeting ended in ten minutes.

Meanwhile, the RIAA brought a case against Napster in San Francisco before United States District Judge Marilyn Hall Patel, who ruled on July 26, 2000, in favor of the record labels. After the Court case, Hank Barry offered the labels a 50 percent ownership split with Napster. The labels considered the dispute with Napster "dead" and, according to author Steve Knopper, "that was the last chance for the record industry as we know it to stave off certain ruin."

Knopper observed that "the opposition from executives at the major labels was understandable. Napster was enabling and encouraging, theft... file-sharing services trading in illegal music were engaged in copyright infringement. But the label chiefs were so bogged down in the file-sharing battleground that they refused to act on the digital future of the business. Many figured they would simply win in the courts and the CD-selling business would go back to normal. As a result, they wasted almost three critical years before agreeing to a functional, legal song-download service."

There was also the problem of the major labels dealing with a myriad of contracts and agreements with artists, music publishers and retailers. New contracts with artists would have to be negotiated because old contracts did not cover digital music. Those old contracts contained clauses about packaging and new technology deductions that managers and attorneys wanted to excise.

Knopper observed that the label heads "simply failed to recognize that the new way of doing business was worth the effort. Had the labels made a deal with Napster, they would have found several immediate advantages: a built-in user base of 26.4 million people, as of February 2001, most of whom were loyal and passionate about both music and the service itself; an efficient way of communicating with their customers, discerning their musical tastes, and aiming pitches for new albums and singles, and the flexibility to set prices at a number of levels, with models ranging from pay-by-the-song to monthly subscriptions."

However, Knopper added, "In fairness to the labels, the people who ran Napster weren't exactly open-minded, either. They were rebels by nature." John Fanning was quoted as saying "We will take down the music industry! And give away free stuff!" and in July 2000, Shawn Fanning was quoted in *Fortune* magazine saying, "I am the record companies' worst nightmare" which "alienated potentially receptive music business partners like Bronfman and Idei and it pushed less receptive partners even further into fight mode."

After court appeals, Napster was officially dead in February, 2001, and declared bankruptcy on May 14, 2002. Napster was gone but the file sharing problem was growing; services like Kazaa, Limewire, Gnutella and others took up where Napster left off but the new file sharers did not have a centralized system.

Teen Pop: 1998-2001

During the period 1998-2001, Teen Pop made the music industry an incredible amount of money. Led by acts Nsync, Backstreet Boys, Britney Spears and Christine Aguilera, those acts sold well over 100 million CDs worldwide and three acts—Backstreet Boys, Nsync and Britney Spears, sold over 96 million CDs.

N'Sync to Jive

Problems with BMG led Calder to obtain N'Sych for Jive, which handled production for their next album, *No Strings Attached*. Their first single, "Bye Bye Bye," was written and produced by Cheiron's Kristian Lundin, Jake Schulze, and Andreas Carlsson; it reached number four on the *Billboard* Hot 100 in 2000; their next single, "It's Gonna Be Me," written and produced by Cheiron's Max Martin with Andreas Carlsson and Rami Yacoub was a number one single that year. In March their album was released and sold 2.4 million in its first week. That would be the last album on the Billboard chart to sell more than two million copies in the first week of its release.

(In 2008 the United States government charged Lou Pearlman with defrauding a thousand investors of $300 million. Pearlman fled the country but was captured in Bali and entered the United States in chains; in May, 2008, Pearlman was sentenced to 25 years in prison; however, the judge offered to reduce his sentence a one month for every million dollars he paid back to investors.)

Independent Labels

During the 1970s, as major labels consolidated their control of record distribution through in-house distribution networks, it became increasingly difficult for independent labels to operate. The independent distribution network, which had handled major as well as independent labels, began to dry up as the majors took their business in-house. Also, the economic recession at the end of the 1970s made it difficult to stay in business with interest rates soaring to over 20 percent. A number of independent labels were purchased by majors during this period as the major label increasingly dominated the record business. It was the majors who had the distribution network to get records into retail outlets and could afford the high cost of doing business, which including making videos as the 1980s progressed, hiring independent promotion people to work records at radio, and providing tour support to artists on the road.

Major Labels

During the 1980s, most of the major labels were sold or merged with other companies. At the beginning of the 1980s four of the six major labels--RCA, CBS, Warner Brothers, and MCA--were American firms, headquartered in the United States. EMI/Capitol was a British firm while Polygram was a Dutch-owned firm. However, by the end of the 1980s, only Warner Brothers was still American owned with CBS and MCA owned by Japanese firms and RCA owned by a German firm.

By that point, all of the companies were multi-national firms, seeking to extend their reach into the world-wide market through mergers.

There's a difference between a global company and one that is multi-national. A global company markets a product world-wide. Consumer products like Coca-Cola are marketed by a global company and can be consumed anywhere in the world; a single advertisement can sell those products in a number of countries. A multinational company is one which has offices in a number of countries but whose products differ from country to country. The music industry is a mixture of both. A rock star may be a global commodity whose recordings are purchased and heard all over the world; however, the recording companies are really international firms whose various artists must appeal first to their home market. Many artists are never marketed outside their home market and, even if they are, there may be no consumer interest in other countries. The major recording firms are primarily multi-national companies who sometimes market a global product rather than global companies whose product(s) remain basically the same throughout the world.

Eminem

In May, 2000, *The Marshall Mathers LP* by Eminem was released; it sold almost two million copies during its first week. Previously, the top selling rap album was *Doggystyle* by Snoop Dogg and the top selling solo album was *...Baby One More Time* by Britney Spears. The first single from the album, "The Real Slim Shady," entered the *Billboard* Hot 100 in May, 2000, and rose to number four; it won a Grammy for Rap Solo. The next single, "The Way I Am," entered the Hot 100 in August and only reached number 58. On the third single, "Stan," Eminem confronted his new fame by taking the persona of a deranged fan who kills himself and his pregnant girlfriend. Many consider "Stan" to be one of the greatest rap songs ever written.

Eminem did not have an easy life growing up. He was born Marshall Bruce Mathers III on October 17, 1972, in St. Joseph, Missouri, the only child of Bruce and Debbie Mathers. His parents were in a band, Daddy Warbucks, that played along the border between the Dakotas and Montana before they separated and Bruce left the family and moved to California, where he had two more children. Mathers was bullied and beaten during his early school days and, as a teenager, wrote letters to his father that always came back "return to sender."

Debbie Mather re-married and had a son. Marshall and his mother often fought as they lived in a number of unstable homes in Michigan and Missouri. For most of his childhood, Mathers lived in a Detroit neighborhood that was primarily black; there were only three white households in that community.

As a child, Mathers was interested in storytelling, but not in school. Before he heard rap, he had ambitions to be a comic book artist.

Mathers first heard rap when Ronnie Polkinghorn, his mother's half brother, gave him the soundtrack to *Breakin'*, otherwise known as *Breakdancing: The Movie*. The film was released in 1984 and the last song on the album, "Reckless," was by Chris "The Glove" Taylor and David Storrs that featured a rap by Ice-T. Polkinghorn was a musical mentor of sorts with Mathers and when he committed suicide in 1991, Mathers was distraught and did not speak for days.

Debbie Mathers let a runaway, Kimberly Ann "Kim" Scott stay at their home; several years later Mathers and Kim began an off and on relationship.

Marshall Mathers spent three years in the ninth grade; he could not pass on time because of truancy and bad grades. When he was 17, he dropped out of Lincoln High. During his time in school, he preferred comic books to literature and disliked math and social studies. He was not a model student.

When he was 14, Mathers began rapping with Mike Ruby, a school friend; they adopted the names Manix and M&M, which evolved to Eminem. During lunch time, Eminem would sneak into Osborn High where he and fellow rapper Proof held freestyle rap battles. On Saturdays, he was a regular at open mic contests at the Hip Hop Shop on West 7 Mile Road, which was considered "Ground Zero" for the rap scene in Detroit.

Eminem worked on his raps, developing his rhymes. He wrote down long words and phrases and worked on rhymes for each syllable, even if the words did not make sense.

Eminem's reputation as a rapper in Detroit grew. He joined several rap groups, The New Jacks and then Soul Intent. He had a single on Soul Intent's 1995 album featuring Proof. Eminem and Proof teamed with four other rappers to form The Dirty Dozen (D12), who released their first album, *Devil's Night*, in 2001.

Eminem was arrested when he was 20 for his involvement in a drive-by shooting with a paintball gun. When the victim didn't appear in court, the case was dismissed.

Eminem was signed to FBT Productions, owned by Jeff and Mark Bass, and recorded his debut album, *Infinite*, for their independent Web Entertainment label. It was released in 1996 but didn't sell. One of the themes on that first album was his struggle to raise his newborn daughter, Hallie Jade Scott Mathers, with little money.

Eminem was an angry young man. When Detroit disc jockeys ignored his *Infinite* album and asked, "Why don't you go into rock'n'roll," Eminem channeled his anger into moody tracks. At home, living with Kim in a crime ridden neighborhood where his house was robbed three times, Eminem struggled to support his daughter. He obtained jobs cooking and washing dishes for minimum wage at a family style restaurant and became a model employee, working 60 hour weeks for six months after his daughter's birth.

Five days before Christmas, he was fired; with only $40 in his pocket he needed to buy her a gift. The frustration of poverty, of lack of success for his *Infinite* album and substance abuse led to a suicide attempt. He moved into his mother's mobile home with Kim and Hallie.

As he continued to rap, Eminem developed an alter ego, Slim Shady, who was violent and sadistic. He wrote angry raps about drugs, rape and murder.

In the spring of 1997, Eminem recorded his *Slim Shady EP*, which was released by Web Entertainment that winter. *The Source*, a hip hop magazine, featured Eminem in their "Unsigned Hype" column.

After Eminem was evicted from his home in 1997, he went to Los Angeles to compete in the Rap Olympics, an annual national rap battle competition; he finished second. A staffer for Interscope was in the audience and sent a copy of the *Slim Shady EP* to Jimmy Iovine, the head of Interscope. Iovine played it for Dr. Dre, who claimed that he'd never heard anything on a demo or unsolicited tape that was worth hearing, but when he heard Eminem rapping, he wanted to sign him immediately. Eminem was overwhelmed; Dr. Dre was one of his heroes.

Dr. Dre received criticism for signing a white rapper but he stuck to his guns; he knew Eminem was something special and wanted to work with him.

Dr. Dre signed him to his label, Aftermath Records, and recorded more material and released *The Slim Shady LP* in February, 1999. By the end of the year it was triple platinum.

The first single from the album, "My Name Is.." entered the *Billboard* Hot 100 in February and rose to number 36. He won the Grammy for Rap Solo. In January, 2000, "Forget About Dre," a duet with Eminem and Dr. Dre was released and reached number 25 on the Hot 100. That won a Grammy the following year for Rap Duo.

There was criticism leveled against Eminem by the Gay & Lesbian Alliance Against Defamation (GLAAD) because they considered Eminem's lyrics homophobic; however, Elton John performed with Eminem at the 43rd Grammy Awards ceremony in 2001 that honored recordings released in 2002. Elton John was criticized by GLAAD for the performance. Elton John and Eminem performed Eminem's song, "Stan."

Their performances was called "the hug heard round the world."

Music City U.S.A. in the 2000s

By the new century, Nashville was well established as "Music City U.S.A." but Music Row was in danger of being bulldozed by developers. Belmont and Vanderbilt Universities were in the area and their campuses were growing. Nearby 12th Avenue South was being developed and The Gulch, a blighted area where the trains used to roll into Nashville, was developed as well, putting Music Row in the middle of an area that was appealing to developers. Historic building were demolished—or came close to being demolished—and high rise condos were built.

O Brother, Where Art Thou?

In 2000, the film, *O Brother, Where Art Thou?* Was not a Nashville film, but it brought attention to traditional country and "old time" music. The film featured a number of Nashville acts singing, including John Hartford, Alison Krauss, Emmylou Harris, Gillian Welch, Chris Sharp and others. The soundtrack, produced by T Bone Burnett, won a Grammy for Album of the Year in 2001.

Americana Music Association

In September, 2000, the Americana Music Association (AMA) held its first convention in Nashville at the Hilton Suites. The roots of the AMA went back to 1999 when a group of about 30 from radio, record labels and media met informally at the South by Southwest conference in Austin, Texas, to discuss the possibility of forming a trade association. At a retreat in October, 1999, the Americana Music Association was born.

The Founding Council of the American Music Association was comprised of Grant Alden, Marie Arsenault, Jim Caligiuri, Dan Einstein, Jack Emerson, Sue Fawyer, Stephen Bond Garvan, Renee Grace, Jon Grimson, Michael Hays, Dan Herrington, Greg Hills, Brad Hunt, Dennis Lord, Chris Marino, JD May, Al Moss, Bev Paul, Brad Paul, Scott Robinson, Leslie Rouffe, Paul Schatzkin, Jessie Scott, Rod Seagram, Tiffany Suiters, Traci Thomas, Van Tucker, Jeff Weiss and Steve Wilkison

In 2003, the first Americana Honors and Awards became part of the convention with three individuals—Emmylou Harris, Billy Joe Shaver and T Bone Burnett—given lifetime achievement awards for performing, songwriting and executive achievement. A surprise performance by Johnny and June Carter Cash followed and Johnny Cash accepted the American Music Association's first "Spirit of Americana Free Speech Award," then recited his song-poem, "Ragged Old Flag." Because of ill health, that was the last public performance by Johnny and June Cash.

In 2008, the Americana Music Awards was moved to the Ryman Auditorium, where it has remained since. The Conference attracts about a thousand professionals and a total of more than 12,000 attend the nightly showcases. Those who have been honored at the American Music Awards include Mavis Staples, Gregg Allman, Judy Collins, John Prine, Joan Baez, Emmylou Harris, Steve earl, Rodney Crowell, Solomon Burke, Lyle Lovett, Allen Toussaint and Buddy Miller.

It is difficult to define Americana music; it's roots are in country, blues and other "roots" music with the "branches" being contemporary performers and performances that are rooted in the past and yet contemporary in presentation.

Presidential Election

The presidential election was held on Tuesday, November 7, 2000, with incumbent Vice President Al Gore and his Vice Presidential nominee, Joseph Lieberman running against George W. Bush, Governor of Texas and his Vice Presidential nominee, Dick Cheney.

On Tuesday night the winner was not announced because the vote in Florida was too close to call. After the November date, there was litigation and a series of legal battles for a month to determine the winner. State law in Florida required a recount, which was contentious and controversial. The vote counters in Florida reported that Bush won the election by 537 votes or .009 percent of the vote count, although there were questions about the accuracy of the recount.

Finally, the Supreme Court, in a 5 to 4 ruling, awarded the election to George W. Bush. Gore had won the popular vote, receiving 48.4 percent of the vote against Bush's 47.9 percent but in the electoral college, Bush had 271 votes, one more that necessary to be elected to the presidency.

2001
World News: 2001

George W. Bush was sworn in as the 41st President of the United States on January 20, 2001. On June 7, he signed the Economic Growth and Tax Relief Reconciliation Act of 2001, which provided large tax cuts. Bush had inherited a budget surplus and balanced budget from the Clinton administration and the Republican Congress felt that American tax payers should have the excess funds returned to them.

In August, Alabama Supreme Court Chief Justice Roy Moore ordered a monument with the Ten Commandments installed in the judiciary building, which led to lawsuits to have the monument as well as Moore removed.

Napster and Copy Protection

In 2001, at the height of its popularity, there were 13.6 million Napster users in the United States and sales of blank CDs outnumbered recorded CDs.

In July, Napster shut down their entire network to comply with a court injunction to halt trading of copyright files.

The music industry tried to combat digital piracy; in May, an album by Charley Pride, *A Tribute to Jim Reeves*, was the first compact disc to have copy protection in the U.S. and in November, BMG in the U.K. released *White Lilies Island* by Natalie Imbruglia. BMG was the first label to release discs with copy protection but soon re-issued the disc without copy protection because consumes were unable to play the CDs on their personal computers.

Blockbuster Music Contracts

There were blockbuster recording contracts signed in 2001. Mariah Carey signed a four album contract with Virgin worth a reported $80 million and Whitney Houston signed a six album deal with Arista worth over $100 million; it was the largest contract in the history of the music industry.

Other news

In September, the Justice Department of the United States announced it would no longer try to break up Microsoft but would, instead, seek a lesser antitrust penalty

On September 10, Secretary of Defense Donald Runsfeld gave a speech about the $2.3 billion in spending by the Pentagon that could not be accounted for. He stated that the Pentagon bureaucracy was the biggest threat to America.

Terrorists Attack the United States

On Tuesday morning, September 11, 2001, four commercial airplanes, filled with commercial passengers headed to California from northeastern airports,,were hijacked in mid-air by terrorists in a coordinated attack by Al Qaeda, led by Osama bin Laden. American Airlines Flight 11 and United Airlines Flight 175 flew into the World Trade Center's Twin Towers, leading to the collapse of both towers in an hour and 42 minutes. The 47 story tower at 7 World Trade Center also collapsed and there was damage to ten other large surrounding structures. American Airlines Flight 77 crashed into the Pentagon and United Airlines Flight 93 crashed into a field near Shanksville, Pennsylvania after passengers overtook the hijackers.

There were 2,996 killed and 6,000 injured from the attacks, including 343 firefighters and 72 law enforcement personnel.

Flights into and out of the United States as well as domestic flights were cancelled until September 13.

On September 14, a Historic National Prayer Service was held at the National Cathedral in Washington for victims of the attack; a similar service was held in Canada on September 17.

The attacks caused the shutdown of Wall Street and the New York Stock Exchange until September 17.

On September 18, letters containing deadly anthrax spores were mailed from Princeton, New Jersey to ABC News, CBS News, NBC News, the New York Post and the *National Enquirer*; 22 people were exposed and five died.

President George W. Bush addressed a joint session of Congress, televised to the American public on September 20 and declared a "War on Terror."

The September 11 attacks caused the cancellation or postponement of a number of musical events because of the cancellation of flights. MTV and VH1 suspended their regular programming to carry a newsfeed from CBS and the networks devoted round the clock coverage to the attacks and their aftermath. The broadcast of the Latin Grammy Awards was cancelled and the MuchMusic Video Awards, scheduled for September 23, was also cancelled.

Dangerous Songs

On September 14, Clear Channel Communications, which owned and programmed approximately 1,200 radio stations, issued a controversial memo to its radio stations that listed 165 songs it considered "lyrically questionable." Here is a partial list of those songs:

"A Day in the Life," "Lucy in the Sky with Diamonds" and "Ob-la-di, Ob-la-a" by the Beatles

"Imagine" by John Lennon

"(You're the) Devil in Disguise" by Elvis Presley

"Ruby Tuesday" by the Rolling Stones

"Knockin' on Heaven's Door" by both Bob Dylan and Guns 'n' Roses

"War," "I'm on Fire" and "I'm Goin' Down" by Bruce Springsteen

"Dancing in the Street" and "Nowhere to Run" by Martha and the Vandellas

"Blowin' in the Wind" and "Leaving on a Jet Plane" by Peter, Paul and Mary

"We Gotta Get Out of This Place" by the Animals

"Hit Me With Your Best Shot" by Pat Benatar

"And When I Die" by Blood, Sweat and Tears
"Rock the Casbah" by the Clash
"Wonderful World" by Sam Cook and Herman's Hermits
"New York, New York" by Frank Sinatra
"Travelin Band" by Creedence Clearwater Revival
"Mack the Knife" by Bobby Darin
"Bits and Pieces" by the Dave Clark Five
"The End of the World" by Skeeter Davis
"America" by Neil Diamond
"Learn to Fly" by the Foo Fighters
"Brain Stew" by Green Day
"Spirit in the Sky" by Norman Greenbaum
"See You in September" by The Happening
"Hey Joe" by the Jimi Hendrix Experience
"Dead Man's Curve" by Jan and Dean
"Only the Good Die Young" by Billy Joel
"Bernie and the Jets," "Daniel" and "Rocket Man" by Elton John
"I Feel the Earth Move" by Carole King
"Stairway to Heaven" by Led Zeppelin
"American Pie" by Don McLean
"Great Balls of Fire" by Jerry Lee Lewis
"Eve of Destruction" by Barry McGuire
"Another One Bites the Dust" by Queen
"Under the Bridge" by the Red Hot Chili Peppers
"Na Na Hey Hey Kiss Him Goodbye" by Steam
"Peace Train" and "Morning Has Broken" by Cat Stevens
"Wipe Out' by the Safaris
"Fire and Rain" by James Taylor
"Sunday, Bloody Sunday" by U2
"Jump" and "Dancin' in the Street" by Van Halen
"Get Together" by the Youngbloods
"Crash Into Me" by the Dave Matthews Band
Seven songs by AC/DC
All songs by Rage Against the Machine

The Music Industry Answers the Call for 9/11

The music industry came together on September 21 for a concert, "America: A Tribute to Heroes" that was televised, uninterrupted on 35 major and cable networks. Performers included Bruce Springsteen, Tom

Petty, Celine Dion, Neil Young, Stevie Wonder, Alicia Keys, Dave Matthews Band, Faith Hill, Mariah Carey and others. The concert raised over $200 million for victims of the September 11 attacks.

On October 20, "The Concert for New York City," broadcast on VH-1, featured performances by Paul McCartney, the Rolling Stones, Bon Jovi, The Who, Billy Joel and others. A "Volunteers for America" benefit concert was held in Atlanta with performances by the Edgar Winter Group, Mark Farner, The Knack, Eddie Money, Peter Frampton, Survivor, Kansas, Journey, Styx, REO Speedwagon, Bad Company, Lynyrd Skynyrd and others.

The next day, there was a benefit concert at RFK Stadium in Washington D.C. with performances by Michael Jackson, Aerosmith, Mariah Carey, James Brown, Backstreet Boys, 'N Sync and others.

A second "Volunteers For America" benefit concert was held in Dallas, Texas on October 21 that featured the same line-up as the "Volunteers for America" concert in Atlanta.

"Where Were You When the World Stopped Turning?"

The acts of terrorism on September 11, 2001 that destroyed the two towers of the World Trade Center were devastating to Americans. Alan Jackson had been walking outside his home when the planes hit the New York buildings and wasn't aware of what had happened until he went inside his home. Jackson wanted to write a song about the event and his feelings on that day but it was difficult—he didn't want to just write another patriotic song. A lot of those were being written. One Sunday morning at 4 a.m., Jackson woke up with the melody and opening lines to a song; he got out of bed, recorded his ideas into a digital recorder, and went back to bed. Later that morning, after his wife and daughters left for Sunday school, Jackson went into his home office and finished the song.

Jackson soon recorded "Where Were You When the World Stopped Turning" with producer Keith Steagall. Jackson was scheduled to perform "Where I Come From," which was his hit at the time, on the CMA Awards Show; however, his manager, Nancy Russell, played the song for CMA executives who were so moved that they decided to let Jackson premier the song on the show.

At the CMA Awards show, host Vince Gill welcomed the audience and then introduced Alan Jackson, who sat on a stool with an orchestra and backing singers behind him, and sang the song. When he finished he received a standing ovation. That video became the video for the song and the next day disc jockeys—who taped the broadcast—began playing it on their stations. The song debuted at number 25 on the chart and a week later it was at number 12; by that time, the record label had serviced the radio stations so on the December 29, 2001, country chart in *Billboard* it was number one, where it remained for five weeks. The song won a Grammy (Jackson's first) for Best Country Song and the following year received the CMA's Best Single and Song of the Year awards. The song was on the album, *Drive* (For Daddy Gene), whose release had been scheduled for May but was moved up to January. It was Jackson's tenth studio album and reached number one on Billboard's country album chart.

More terror legislation enacted

The Office of Homeland Security was established by President George W. Bush on October 8; the next day there was a second mailing of letters with anthrax from Trenton, New Jersey.

A wave of fear struck citizens of the United States after the September attacks and on October 26, President Bush signed "The Patriot Act" into law. The law allowed indefinite detention of immigrants; permission for law enforcement to search homes and businesses without the owner or occupant's permission; allowed the FBI to search telephone, email and financial records without a court order; and expanded access of law enforcement agencies to business records, including library and financial records.

A number of court cases were brought, challenging the Patriot Act, and Federal courts ruled a number of the provisions in the law were unconstitutional.

End of 2001

President George Bush signed an executive order on November 13 allowing military tribunals against any foreigners suspected of having connection to terrorist acts or planned acts against the United States

On December 2, one of the world's largest corporations, Enron, filed for Chapter 11 bankruptcy, five days after Dynergy canceled a buyout bid of $8.4 billion. It was the largest bankruptcy in the United States at that point.

Top Albums in 2001

The top five albums, according the Billboard 200 album chart in 2001 were:

1. *Hybrid Theory* by Linkin Park
2. *One* by the Beatles
3. *Invincible* by Michael Jackson

4. *All That You Can't Leave Behind* by U2
5. *Aaliyah* by Aaliayah

The top albums by sales, according to SoundScan were:

1. *Invincible* by Michael Jackson (6.5 million)
2. *Hybrid Theory* by Linkin Park (5 million)
3. *Hot Shot* by Shaggy (4.5 million)
4. *Celebrity* by N'Sync (4.4 million)
5. *A Day Without Rain* by Enya (4.4 million

2002
Super Bowl

On Sunday, February 3, 2002, the Super Bowl in New Orleans saw the New England Patriots and the St. Louis Rams tied 17-17 with one minute and thirty seconds left. Patriots quarterback Tom Brady led his team down the field with no timeouts and Adam Vinatieri kicked a field goal to lead the Patriots to their first Super Bowl win.

During the halftime show, U2 performed three songs. "Beautiful Day," "MLK" and "Where the Streets Have No Name" while the names of those lost in the 9/11 attacks were projected on a screen behind the stage. Janet Jackson had originally been scheduled to perform but allowed U2 to perform and give a tribute to victims of the 9/11 attack.

Euro notes and coins were issued on January 1, 2002; the change-over to a Euro currently had been done in 1999.

On February 6, Queen Elizabeth II of the U.K. celebrated her Golden Jubilee for 50 years onn the throne. On March 30, the Queen Mum—mother of Queen Elizabeth—died and her funeral was held at Westminster Abbey in London; she was laid to rest in Windsor Castle.

In February, the 2002 Winter Olympics were held in Salt Lake City, Utah.

Sales Decline

In 2002, it was announced that the music industry suffered a decline in sales for the first time since SoundScan began tabulating sales of recordings. The industry faced a barrage of digital piracy; after Napster was shut down, peer-to-peer sites such as KaZah, which had 8.3 million American consumers, Grokster and Morpheus popped up. The Wall Street Journal stated that "world-wide music sales totaled $39.8 billion in 1996 but were down to $33.6 billion in 2001." No album sold five million units during the past year.

American Idol

There is a "black swan" theory that says sometimes something totally unexpected—an unknown unknown—comes along and changes the game. For the music industry that was "American Idol" and the singing contest shows that followed.

No one in the music industry imagined the development of a TV program that featured singers competing for a record label contract would lead to a young singer becoming nationally famous over a ten week period and then their debut album sell millions.

Network television emerged during the 2000s as a way to discover and market new talent. Reality television provided "stars" from contestants who, before the show, were total unknowns. The music industry benefited the most from those reality shows, although there is criticism that the singers who emerge may not be prepared for a long-term career because they have not "paid their dues" in the traditional way.

"American Idol" was a spin-off of the British show "Pop Idol," created by Simon Fuller and originally broadcast in 2001. "American Idol" debuted on June 11, 2002, on the Fox network and became a top-rated show on television for six consecutive seasons.

A series of auditions were held nationally for contestants aged 16-28 (it was 24 during the first few seasons). Contestants are weeded out by the show's producers as auditions progressed, then a group of contestants were narrowed after performing for the "American Idol" judges.

The show employed a panel of judges—the original judges were producer and manager Randy Jackson, singer Paula Abdul, and music executive and manager Simon Cowell. Host for the show was Ryan Seacrest, who was joined by Brian Dunkleman during the first season. It made an impact on the music industry because, with the decline of radio listenership amongst young people, and the limited amount of airplay for new artists, TV shows like "American Idol" gave a national platform to ten singers each season. By the end of the season, the top three contestants—and sometimes more than those--had received enough national exposure to launch a career in the music industry that resulted in significant record sales.

Top winners during the first seasons included Kelly Clarkson, Ruben Studdard, Fantasia Barrino, Carrie Underwood, Taylor Hicks, Jordin Sparks, David Cook, Kris Allen and Lee DeWyze. Part of the agreement between contestants and the show's creator was that 19 Entertainment had the option to manage and/or record the contestants at the end of the show.

Kelly Clarkson

Kelly Clarkson won the first "American Idol" contest on September 4, 2001. She was born in Fort Worth, Texas and received music scholarships to the University of Texas, the University of North Texas and the Berklee School of Music but turned them all down to pursue a career in music. She moved to Los Angeles and recorded demos with songwriter Gerry Goffin but was turned down by every label. After her apartment burned, she moved back to Texas and took odd jobs (she worked as a waitress and a telemarketer) before she landed on "American Idol," where she appeared on the second broadcast.

After winning "American Idol," she released her first single, "A Moment Like This," which reached number one on the *Billboard* Hot 100 and became the best selling single of 2002.

19 Entertainment

19 Entertainment was founded in London by Simon Fuller in April, 1985, The company, originally an artist management firm, created and produced entertainment shows in the areas of TV/Film, Sports and Fashion and Music. The company created and produced "Pop Idol" in the U.K. and "American Idol" in the United States. American and Pop Idol contestants Adam Lambert, Carrie Underwood, Daughtry, Kelly Clarkson, Clay Aiken, Ruben Studdard, David Cook, Kris Allen, Crystal Bowersox and Lee Dewyze all had management and recording contracts with 19 Entertainment.

Simon Fuller sold 19 Entertainment to Robert Sillerman's CKX, Inc. in March, 2005 for $192 million but remained CEO of the firm until January, 2010, when he stared a new firm, XIX Entertainment.

Music News: 2002

Virgin Records bought out their contract with Mariah Carey for $28 million, basically paying her not to record any more for the label.

In March, Liverpool Airport was renamed the Liverpool John Lennon Airport.

In a deal reportedly worth $3 billion, BMG Music acquired the rest of the Zomba music group headed by Clive Calder.

BMG attempted to buy the assets of Napster but in September the file sharing company was ordered closed for good by a judge.

In the U.K., Robbie Williams signed a six album deal with EMI for 80 million GBP, the biggest deal for a U.K. artist.

On October 2, Jam Master Jay of Run-D.M.C. was shot and killed at a studio in Queens.

An episode of "The Simpson" broadcast on November 10 featured Mick Jagger, Keith Richards, Elvis Costello, Lenny Kravitz, Tom Petty and Brian Setzer in an episode set in a "Rock'n'Roll Fantasy Camp.

The "Concert for George" was held on November 29, 2002, at the Royal Albert Hall in London in honor of former Beatle George Harrison on the anniversary of his death exactly a year before. Performers who sang Harrison's songs on the tribute included Paul McCartney, Ringo Starr, Eric Clapton, Jeff Lynne and Billy Preston with special guest Ravi Shankar. The event was a benefit for the Material World Charitable Foundation.

Elected to the Rock and Roll Hall of Fame were Isaac Hayes, Brenda Lee, Tom Petty and the Heartbreakers, Gene Pitney, the Ramones and the Talking Heads.

Michael Jackson

Michael Jackson was in the news in July when he staged a public protest against Sony Music Chairman Tommy Mottola, accusing him of participation in a racist conspiracy to exploit black recording artists. Sony issued a statement saying the accusation was "ludicrous, spiteful and hurtful."

In November, during a concert tour, Jackson dangled his nine-month old son over the balcony of his hotel room in Berlin; later that day he released a statement saying it was a "terrible mistake.

Best Selling Albums: 2002

The ten best selling albums of 2002 were:
1. *The Eminem Show* by Eminem
2. *Nellyville* by Nelly
3. *Let Go* by Avril Lavigne
4. *Britney* by Britney Spears
5. *Laundry Service* by Shakira
6. *Silver Side Up* by Nickelback
7. *A New Day Has Come* by Celine Dion
8. *8701* by Usher
9. *Home* by the Dixie Chicks
10. *Missundaztood* by Pink

Music in Film

During 2002 the films 8 Mile, starring Eminem, Biggie & Tupac, Chicago (starring Renee Zellweger, Catherine Zeta-Jones and Richard Jones), and Standing the Shadows of Motown were released.

2003
Space Shuttle Disintegrates

The Space Shuttle Columbia had completed its mission in space and was returning to earth on February 1 when it disintegrated over Texas, killing all seven astronauts on board.

The Iraq War

In August, 1998, President Saddam Hussein of Iraq refused to cooperate further with weapons inspectors from the United Nations, claiming that inspectors were spying for the United States (this was later proven true). A coalition of countries had instituted economic sanctions against Iraq but when President Bush took office in 2001, his administration took a more aggressive stand towards Iraq, declaring it a rogue nation. There was a belief by key members of his administration that the Persian Gulf War in 1991, which ended when Iraq left Kuwait, had not been finished and the military should have continued on to Baghdad to overthrow Hussein.

On February 4, 2002, Secretary of State Colin Powell testified that Iraq had weapons of mass destruction (WMD) and that Hussein was harboring and supporting al-Qaeda. Both of those allegations later proved false. The Bush administration claimed that Saddam Hussein and Iraq posed an immediate threat to the United States and its allies.

In July, 2002, the CIA and an elite military group entered Iraq to prepare for an invasion. There were weapons inspectors in Iraq from the United Nations Special Commission (UNSCOM) and the International Atomic Energy Agency, but they had not completed their inspections and, so far, had not found any WMDs. The United States pushed for a United Nation Resolution to use force in Iraq and one was passed, although a number of countries, including Canada, France, Germany and Russia pushed for continued diplomatic negotiations. The push for war in Iraq continued from the Bush Administration, arguing that Iraq should be turned into a democratic state. In the end, only the U.K., Australia and Poland supported the United States

Beginning in January, there were protests throughout the world against a war with Iraq and on February 15, millions of people all over the world participated in an anti-war protest over the United States decision to invade Iraq. In October, 2002, Congress passed a Resolution that said the U.S. should use "any means necessary" against Iraq although, at that time, most Americans favored continued diplomacy. The push for war continued with a public relations campaign by the administration that war was necessary; a majority of Americans were persuaded.

On March 17, President Bush demanded that Saddam Hussein and his two sons, Uday and Qusay, surrender within 48 hours. At the end of those 48 hours, at 5:34 a.m. Baghdad time on March 20 (9:34 p.m. EST), the United States began aerial bombing, called "Shock and Awe" of Iraq and the invasion began. There were 248,000 U.S. forces, 45,000 from the U.K., 2,000 from Australia and 194 Polish troop. The Iraqi forces were quickly defeated and on April 9, Baghdad fell. On May 1, President George W. Bush announced "Mission accomplished."

The defeat of Saddam Husseim created a power vacuum in Iraq and mismanagement of the occupation led to Iraqi resistance and disputes between Shia and Sunni factions.

On December 13, Saddam Hussein was captured and no WMDs had been found. By that time, President Bush's approval ratings made him one of the most unpopular Presidents.

The iPod

In order to have a portable digital music player, the "tiniest hard drive ever made" was needed. Jobs signed an exclusive deal with Toshiba, which had developed a tiny drive that could hold 1,000 songs.

Engineer Tony Fadell was hired by Apple to work on this project and developed a "box the size of a pack of Marlboros with a cell-phone-sized screen at the top and push buttons at the bottom." (168) Apple executive Phil Schiller "showed a scroll wheel at the center which would control the gadget in lieu of a keyboard." A small firm, PortalPlayer, supplied the physical operating system and the external casing. Former Apple employee Paul Mererto had founded a software company, Pixo; Apple executive Jonathan Rubinstein's team hired them to write programs for the PortalPlayer.

The Apple teams worked fast; Jobs was a demanding taskmaster and Apple employees were used to working nights and days on projects to meet dealines. Their goal was to have a digital music player in stores by Christmas, 2001.

At that point there was no name for the device, so a team of writers submitted 60 or 70 names to Jobs, who narrowed it down to three; one of those was "Pod." After mulling it over, Steve Jobs decided to name the new device "iPod" and it was in stores on October 23, 2001, in time for the Christmas season. It looked cool.

The problem now facing Apple was that there was no legal digital music store for consumers to purchase songs for their new device.

The iTunes Store

After the demise of Napster, the music industry wanted to create their own online music store. Sony and Universal teamed to introduce PressPlay, which allowed 50 songs a month to be downloaded for $14.95. EMI, Warner and BMG created MusicNet, but that online store never got off the ground. The Warner label set out to create copy-protected songs for purchase on the internet; however, all the CDs they sold the previous 20 years or so did not have any copyright protection. Warners enlisted the help of Apple, and the teams liked a new digital format, Advanced Audio Coding (AAC) which allowed for copyright protection.

Jobs met with several Warner executives and warned them that labels were "trying to suck out all the money from digital music for themselves" and that Apple's customers "deserved better."Meanwhile, the iPod was available for purchase at Apple Stores but the $399 price tag stopped most customers from purchasing. (Critics said iPod stood for "Idiots Price Our Devices"). Also, the iTunes software was available for Mac computers, but there was no rush from consumers to buy it.

Steve Jobs began showing the iTunes Music Store to top record label executives; the first was Roger Ames, Chairman and CEO of Warner Music. A deal was worked out where a song could be downloaded for 99 cents. Ames went back to New York and told other top executives about the iTunes Store; soon, Doug Morris, head of Universal made an agreement with Apple.

Jobs opposed the idea of digital rights management, which prevented users from making unlimited copies of digital music files downloaded, but knew he had to concede that point in order to win over the record industry, particularly Sony, a rival electronics firm in addition to having a record company. EMI/Capitol and BMG also agreed to sell to the iTunes store, but Sony continued to hold out. Finally, Jobs called Sony Music's CEO Andrew Lack directly and told him the iTunes store would launch in two months "with or without Sony." Lack and several Sony executives then went to the Apple offices in Cupertino, California where Jobs demonstrated the iTunes

Store. After that demonstration, Sony agreed to join the other labels and made their recordings available on iTunes.

There were several reasons, according to author Steve Knopper, that record executives agreed to work with Apple. First was "Jobs's confidence and charm. At NeXT and Pixar he'd dealt with Hollywood executives all the time, so he didn't find powerful record people...particularly intimidating. Another was Apple's tiny market share at the time—just four or five percent of computer users owned Macintoshes, and the iPod-iTunes system was initially incompatible with Windows."

Further, Jobs told music executives "that Apple's marketing budget was $15 million to $30 million every quarter. This was free artist-publicity on par with MTV. Finally, many executives at record labels believed Microsoft was on the brink of releasing a digital music service that would compete fiercely with iTunes. Surely labels could play the two services off each other."

That last reason didn't pan out; Microsoft did not unveil its Zune digital music player until November, 2006.

Knooper also observed that "Executives from major labels had told pre-iTunes digital music services—including Napster and Real—that they couldn't license content because their hands were tied with artist contracts and publisher agreements" but Apple managed to surmount those problems because (1) The previous models that labels had discussed were subscriptions, which were more complicated, and iTunes's pay by-the-song approach was easier to work out; (2) failed early services such as MusicNet (which never went online) and Pressplay had already done much of the heavy lifting as far as haggling with artists, publishers, and attorneys; and (3) label execs were stubborn until they found something they liked, the iTunes Store."

On April 28, 2003, the iTunes Music Store opened with a catalog of 200,000 songs available for 99 cents each. Still, not everyone was on board; the Beatles, Led Zeppelin and Radiohead were holdouts.

Labels received 67 cents for every 99 cent song sold; artist, publisher and songwriting royalties in addition to marketing costs and business overhead had to come out of that 67 cents. The iPod quickly caught on with young people, who thought it was "cool" and the iTunes Store "pushed music fans to buy more and more iPods, for $300 to $500 apiece. In the fourth quarter of 2003, iPods generated about seven percent for Apple's $1.7 billion in revenue--$121 million overall."

During the 1990s, the record industry stopped making vinyl singles. The reasons were economic; there was no profit in singles because "The single cost too much to produce and didn't make up enough in sales. For years, major labels used singles as cheap or free promotional tools. They'd give them away to radio stations...they'd gussy them up and give them out at concerts" but, all the while, "the industry was looking for excuses to get out of it."The problem was that when the industry stopped making singles "and offered nothing to replace them, the industry stopped a whole generation from picking up the record-buying habit." Napster, and the iPod, marked the return of the single.

Jay-Z

Going from a nobody to a somebody can happen in sports and entertainment in America. That was the story of Jay-Z, who was born Shawn Corey Cater on December 4, 1969, in Brooklyn and raised in a housing project in the Bedford-Stuyvesant neighborhood. His father, Adis, abandoned the family when Shawn was young; his mother raised him and his three siblings.

Rap was born in the Bronx and during the late 1970s gained popularity; young dudes faced off with each other rapping or break dancing. It was easy to hear rapping and easy to meet rappers. Shawn met AZ when they both attended Eli Whitney High School. He met The Notorious B.I.G. and Busta Rhymes at the George Westinghouse Career and Technical Education high school. Shawn Carter never finished high school.

Black teenage boys faced a lot of closed doors; crack cocaine ran rampant in inner cities during the 1980s and Shawn, needing to make money, reportedly sold crack. He was reportedly shot three times during those years. It wasn't pretty but you rap what you know.

Shawn's mother bought him a boom box, also known as a "ghetto blaster," one Christmas, and that ignited an interest in music with Shawn. The boom box blasted the sounds of the inner city, which was heavy with beats. Strong, heavy, throbbing beats. Shawn Carter loved beats; they made his body move.

Hip hop is a way of life and "free styling," or making up raps on the spot, is a cornerstone of rap and a sorting out process where those with rapper talent emerge and those who don't have that talent, fall by the wayside.

Nicknames or "tags" are part of hip hop. Shawn was known as "Jazzy" in the neighborhood and he shortened that to "Jay-Z," in homage to his mentor, Jaz-O. During the late 1980s and early 90s, Jay-Z was heard on Jaz-O's "The Originators" and "Hawaiian Sophie." He gained widespread attention in the rap community when he was on Big Daddy Kane's album,

Daddy's Home on the posse cut "Show and Prove" in 1994. Jay-Z rapped on Kane's shows when Kane took a break; Jay-Z and Positive K would take the stage and freestyle until Kane returned.

Jay-Z was on Big L's "Da Graveyard" and Mic Geronimo's "Time to Build." His first solo single was "In My Lifetime"; he released a music video with that. No label was interested in Jay-Z so he created his own label, Roc-A-Fella, with Damon Dash and Kareem Biggs in 1995. His first single to reach the *Billboard* Hot 100 was "Ain't No Nigga," featuring Foxy Brown, that entered the chart on April 6, 1996, and peaked at 50. The "B" side was "Dead Presidents." His debut album, *Reasonable Doubt*, entered the *Billboard* album chart on July 13, 1996, and peaked at 23.

Jay-Z continued to release singles; "Can't Knock the Hustle" peaked at number 73 in 1996; Mary J. Blige sang back-up on that record. "Feelin' It" peaked at 79 and "Who You Wit" peaked at number 84. "Who You Wit" was in the film, *Sprung* starring Tisha Campbell.

In 1997, Jay-Z had a chart entry with "Sunshine," featuring Babyface and Foxy Brown and the next year he had "The City is Mine," featuring BLACKstreet, that peaked at 52.

On November 22, 1997, Jay-Z's album, *In My Lifetime*, entered the *Billboard* chart and rose to number three.

Jay-Z's album, *Vol. 2...Hard Knock Life* entered the album chart on October 17, 1998, and hit number one, where it remained for five weeks. It won a Grammy for Rap Album.

His next three albums all reached number one: *Vol 3...Life and Times of S. Carter* in 2000, *The Dynasty Roc La Familia* in 2000 and *The Blueprint* in 2001.

In 2003, his single "03 Bonnie & Clyde" featured Beyonce and was his first top five single.

Fan Fair moved

Fan Fair moved from the Nashville Fairgrounds to downtown Nashville and was renamed the CMA Music Fest in 2003.

International Bluegrass Music Association (IBMA)

The International Bluegrass Music Association (IBMA) was formed in 1985 and its first headquarters was in Owensboro, Kentucky; in 2003, the organization relocated its offices to Nashville, Tennessee. The IBMA hosted an annual convention and awards show from 2005 through 2012 the event was in Nashville before they moved the event to Raleigh, North Carolina. The offices of the IBMA remained in Nashville.

"It's Five O'Clock Somewhere"

Jimmy Buffett began his career in Nashville; his early hits, like "Come Monday" and "Margaritaville," were recorded in Nashville. Buffett left Nashville for Key West and those sand and sun songs soon became part of a pop star's life, but Buffett remained connected to the Nashville scene. On June 21, 2003, a song he recorded with Alan Jackson, "It's Five O'Clock Somewhere" entered the *Billboard* country chart and landed at number one, where it remained for eight straight weeks; it reached number 17 on the *Billboard* Hot 100. The recording won a Grammy for Best Country Song and a CMA Awards for Vocal Event. "It's Five O'Clock Somewhere" was written by Jim "Moose" Brown and Don Rollins and produced by Keith Stegall; it was included on Jackson's *Greatest Hits Volume II* album and became Buffett's first top 40 pop hit since the 1970s.

Buffett continued to record with country artists; in 2004 he joined Clint Black, Kenny Chesney, Alan Jackson, Toby Keith and George Strait on the Hank Williams song, "Hey Good Lookin.'" That same year he recorded with Martina McBride on "Trip Around the Sun" and in 2011 he recorded "Knee Deep" with the Zac Brown Band.

The Dixie Chicks

On March 10, 2003, less than two weeks before the invasion of Iraq began, the Dixie Chicks were on tour in England when lead singer Natalie Maines announced from the stage, "We don't want this war, this violence and we're ashamed that the President of the United States (George W. Bush) is from Texas." The statement received positive reaction from the British audience but there was a major backlash from country radio stations, who immediately pulled their records from the station's playlists and a boycott began of their concerts. Many fans still loved them—but country radio programmers were adamant in their refusal to not play any songs by the Dixie Chicks.

"Live Like You Were Dying"

It is not often that a song has a life-changing impact on listeners—or an artist—but "Live Like You Were Dying" with it's message of living life with no regrets did have a life-changing impact on listeners. The song was written by Tim Nichols and Craig Wiseman and was based on stories from families and friends who found a new perspective of life after being diagnosed with cancer. That perspective applied to Tim McGraw, who's father, former baseball star Tug McGraw, was dying as the song was being recorded. On March 12, 2003, Tug McGraw was hospitalized with a brain tumor; he died on January 5, 2004; the song entered the *Billboard* country chart four months later, on April 5. The video of the song showed McGraw pitching the final strike for the 1980 World Series champions Philadelphia Phillies. "Live Like You Were Dying" was number one for seven consecutive weeks; it reached number 29 on the *Billboard* Hot 100.

Music News: 2003

On January 10, Andrew Lack, former chief of NBC News, replaced Tommy Mottola as head of Sony's music division. Sony had suffered huge losses in their music division due to digital piracy.

On February 3, police responded to a 911 call from one of Phil Spector's neighbords and discovered the body of actress Lana Clarkson in Spector's home. Spector, a legendary producer and creator of the "Wall of Sound" was arrested for her murder.

On April 1, a number of people walked out of a Pearl Jam concert when lead singer Eddie Vedder criticized the Iraq War and made insulting comments about President Bush. Audience members shouted "shut up." In an attempt to calm the crowed, Vedder added, "Just to clarify...we support the troops."

In May, Ruben Studdard won the second season of "American Idol," edging out Clay Aiken.

On May 24, Paul McCartney performed a concert on Red Square in Moscow.

On July 5, after a six year absence, the Lollapalooza festival returned with a line-up that included Jane's Addiction, Audioslave, Incubus and Queens of the Stone Age.

At the MTV Music Awards in August, Madonna kissed Britney Spears and Christina Aguilera, sparking a controversy.

Johnny Cash died on September 12; in May, his wife, June Carter had died.

A legal version of Napster was launched on October 29, providing song downloads for 99 cents each or $9.99 a month for unlimited listening.

Michael Jackson was arrested on November 20 on charges of child molestation. A similar charge in 1993 was dropped after an out-of-court financial settlement with the family of a boy. After the arrest, CBS dropped a one hour TV special, scheduled for November 26, to promote his greatest hits album, Number Ones.

Mick Jagger was knighted in Buckingham Palace on December 12 for his services to the Prince of Wales.

Top Albums: 2003

The top five albums in 2003, according to the *Billboard* charts, were:

1. *Get Rich or Die Tryin'* by 50 Cent
2. *Come Away With Me* by Norah Jones
3. *Dangerously in Love* by Beyonce
4. *Number Ones* by Michael Jackson
5. *Home* by the Dixie Chicks

The top ten selling albums, based on SoundScan

1. *Get Rich or Die Tryin'* by 50 Cent
2. *Come Away With Me* by Norah Jones
3. *Stripped* by Christina Aguilera
4. *Number Ones* by Michael Jackson
5. *Meteora* by Linkin Park
6. *Dangerously in Love* by Beyonce
7. *A Rush of Blood to the Head* by Coldplay
8. *Fallen* by Evanescence
9. *In the Zone* by Britney Spears
10. *Let Go* by Avril Lavigne

2004
Super Bowl XXXVIII

The Super Bowl game on Sunday, February 1, between the New England Patriots and the Carolina Panthers--playing in their first Super Bowl-- was one of the most exciting Super Bowl games ever, with Patriots kicker Adam Vinatieri hitting a 41 yard field goal with four seconds remaining to give the Patriots a 32-29 win over the Panthers. But that's not why most people remember the game. Actually, they remember the halftime show.

Janet Jackson performed "All For You," then P. Diddy, Nelly and Kid Rock performed a mixture of their hits before Jackson performed "Rhythm Nation." Justin Timberlake came out and sang a duet with Jackson on "Rock Your Body," filled with suggestive moves. The last line of the song was "I'll have you naked by the end of this song" and as he sang it, Timberlake grabbed Jackson's costume sleeve and tore it off, exposing her right breast, adorned with a large sun shaped nipple shield.

CBS quickly cut to an aerial view of the stadium but it was two late; callers were already phoning the network, complaining about "indecent exposure."

Confronted with it later, Timberlake said it was a "wardrobe malfunction." That phrase lasted longer than the memory of the game itself. The incident became the most watched moment in TiVo history.

To add to the excitement, at the beginning of the second half, British streaker, Mark Roberts, came on the field disguised as a referee, stripped down to a thong, and proceeded to dance; he was tackled by a Patriots linebacker.

Keith Urban

In 2004, Keith Urban hit his stride as a country music superstar with "Days Go By," which was number one on the country chart for four weeks (and 31 on the Hot 100), and "You're My Better Half," which held at the number two spot for five weeks (number 33 on the Hot 100). It was his fourth consecutive year of having number one records.

Keith Lionel Urban was born in Whangarei, New Zealand, on October 26, 1967. The family moved to Queensland, Australia, where his father owned a convenience store. Keith Urban took guitar lessons and was first influenced by two rock guitarists, Mark Knopfler of Dire Straits and Lindsey Buckingham of Fleetwood Mac.

At 16, he was on the Australian TV talent show "New Faces" and then began making his name in the country music scene in Australia, appearing on the Reg Lindsay Country Homestead TV Program, Mike McClellan's Music Program and other TV shows. Urban and Jenny Wilson performed duets and won a "Golden Guitar" award at the Tamworth Country Music Festival. He performed regularly at the Northern Suburbs Country Music Club in Caboolture.

Urban signed with EMI in Australia and released his self titled debut album in 1990. He was on the compilation album, *Breaking Ground-New Directions in Country Music* (1990) and was nominated for Best Country Album by the Australian Recording Industry Association (ARIA) in 1991. Between 1993 and 1994 he toured with Slim Dusty, the Johnny Cash of Australia; Dusty and Urban recorded a duet of Dusty's "Lights on the Hill." The first time Keith Urban played on the Grand Old Opry he backed Slim Dusty.

In 1992, Urban moved to Nashville. He appeared in the music video of "Mercury Blues" by Alan Jackson and gained songwriting success, co-writing (with Vernon Rust) "Jesus Gets Jealous of Santa Claus" for the 1995 album *Christmas to Christmas* by Toby Keith, "That Was Him (This Is Now)" for 4 Runner and "Tangled Up in Love" for the Raybon Brothers 1997 album.

Keith Urban formed a band, The Ranch with drummer Peter Clarke and bassist Jerry Flowers in 1997. The Ranch released one album on Capitol and had two singles, "Walkin' the Country" and "Just Some Love" which reached the country singles chart in *Billboard*. He became known for his guitar playing and played on albums by Paul Jefferson, Tim Wilson and Charlie Daniels.

Urban released his self-titled debut album, produced by Matt Rollins, in 1999. The first single, "It's a Love Thing" entered the *Billboard* country chart in August, 1999, and peaked at 18. His next single, "Your Everything," entered the chart on February 26, 2000, and reached number four and his third single, "But For the Grace of God," reached number one on the country chart and remained on the chart for 30 weeks. His fourth single from that album, "Where the Blacktop Ends," reached number three and held that position for three weeks in 2001.

That debut album and hit singles led to him being awarded Top New Male Vocalist by the Academy of Country Music and the Horizon Award from the Country Music Association.

Keith Urban's second album, *Golden Road*, was released in 2002; he produced seven of the tracks and co-produced the other six with Dann Huff. The first single, "Somebody Like You," hit number one and remained there for six weeks and stayed on the chart for 41 weeks; it reached number 23 on the Hot 100. His next single, "Raining on Sunday," peaked at number three but his following two singles, "Who Wouldn't Wanna Be Me" and "You'll Think of Me" both hit number one and "You'll Think of Me" won a Grammy for Country Male Vocal and the *Golden Road* album sold three million copies.

Those hits in 2003 set up Keith Urban for his *Be Here* album that sold three million copies and carried the hit singles, "Days Go By," "You're My Better Half," "Making Memories of Us," "Better Life" and "Tonight I Wanna Cry."

Kanye West

Controversy is no stranger to Kanye West; he seems to court it. His actions and comments have angered and upset a number of people, but his track record producing hits for other artists as well as hit singles and albums for himself seems to cover him with a protective shield.

Kanye Omari West was born in Atlanta, Georgia, on June 8, 1977; his parents divorced when he was three and he moved to Chicago with his mother, Dr. Donda Williams West, who became Chair of the English Departmnet at Chicago State University. His father, Ray West, was a former Black Panther and the first black photojournalist at *The Atlanta Journal-Constitution*. When Kanye was 10, he lived in Nanjing, China, where his mother taught at Nanjing University as part of an exchange program.

Kanye grew up in a solid, middle-class home and did well in school. He began writing poetry when he was five and started rapping in the third grade and writing songs in the seventh grade. He wrote a rap song, "Green Eggs and Ham" at 13 and persuaded his mother to pay $25 an hour for him to record it in a studio. He received his first sampler when he was 15 and learned how to sample and program beats from his mentor, DJ No I.D.

West received a scholarship to Chicago's American Academy of Art but dropped out when he was 20 to pursue a dream of musical stardom.

During the mid-1990s, Kanye created beats for local artists; at 19 he produced eight tracks for the debut album of Chicago rapper Grav. He became a member and producer of the Go-Getters, comprised of him, GLC, Timmy G., Really Doe and Arrowstar. In 1999, they released their only album, *World Record Holders*. The album also featured Chicago-based rappers Rhymefest, Mikkey Halstad, Miss Criss and Shayla G.; the album was produced by West, Arrowstar, Boogz, and Brian "All Day" Miller.

Kanye West became well known as a producer; he produced a track on Foxy Brown's *Chyna Doll* album, and three tracks on Harlem World's album, *The Movement*. He produced six songs for *Tell 'Em Why U Madd* by Derie "D-Dot" Angelettie, who served as his manager.

In 2000, West began producing artists on Jay-Z's Roc-A-Fella Records and contributed to Jay-Z's album *Blueprint*. Kanye served as an in-house producer for Roc-A-Fella Records, producing Beanie Siegel, Freeway and Cam'ron; he served as a writer for songs by Ludacris, Alicia Keys and Janet Jackson.

Kanye West was known in the rap community as a producer, but he wanted to be known as a rapper. It was a frustrating time for him; no record label would give him an opportunity, although Capitol expressed interest.

The problem was that gangsta rap was popular at that time and rappers needed "street cred," which generally meant being part of the gangtsa community with an intimate knowledge of the gangsta lifestyle. Only ganstas could wrap. Kanye West had a solidly middle-class background and had been to college, not jail.

Damon Dash, head of Roc-A-Fella, finally agreed for Kanye to record a rap album because he was afraid of losing his services as a producer.

In October, 2002, Kanye West fell asleep at the wheel while driving home from a California studio and was involved in a head-on crash with another car; he suffered a broken jaw that had to be wired shut. Inspired by the accident, he wrote and recorded "Through The Wire" at the Record Plant Studio with his jaw wired shut. That song was on Kanye's mixtape, "Get Well Soon," released in December, 2002.

That song became the beginning of Kanye working on his debut album, *The College Dropout*, which he recorded in Los Angeles. The album leaked before its release, which led Kanye to remix, remaster and revise the album before its release. He made significant changes in the album, causing it to be postponed three times before it was finally released in February, 2004. The album was well received critically, peaked at number two on the *Billboard* 200 album chart and his debut single, "Through the Wire," debuted on the Hot 100 on November 29, 2003 and peaked at number 15 in 2004. His second single, "Slow Jamz" with Twista and Jamie Fox was number one. His fourth single, "Jesus Walks," was an expression of his faith and totally opposite the gangsta image projected by most rap artists but it reached number 11 on the Hot 100 and won a Grammy for Rap Song, opening new markets for him.

Kanye formed a label GOOD Records and a management company and affiliated with No I.D., John Legend and other artists. He continued producing; he produced singles for Brandy, Common, Slum Village and John Legend.

Kanye West spent more than a year and over $2 million on his second album, *Late Registration*. He hired string orchestras and collaborated with film score composer Jon Brion; the album sold over two million copies but it came with controversy.

In 2004, at the American Music Awards, Kanya stormed out of the awards after he did not win the Best New Artist award. During a benefit for Hurricane Katrina, West ignored the script and said, "George Bush doesn't care about black people." The outbursts continued but so did the hits.

Music news: 2004

Luciano Pavarotti gives his last performance in an opera, in *Tosca* at the New York Metropolitan Opera on March 13.

Ray Charles died on June 10 from acute liver disease.

Brian Wilson released *Brian Wilson Presents Smile*, an interpretation of the *Smile* sessions which were shelved in 1967.

The top selling albums in the U.S. in 2004 were:

1. *Confessions* by <u>Usher</u> (7.9 million)
2. *Feels like Home* by Norah Jones (3.8 million)
3. *Encore* by <u>Eminem</u> (3.5 million)
4. *When the Sun Goes Down* by <u>Kenny Chesney</u> (3 million)
5. *Under My Skin* by <u>Avril Lavigne</u> (2,9 million)
6. *Live Like You Were Dying* by <u>Tim McGraw</u> (2,7 million)
7. *Songs About Jane* by <u>Maroon 5</u> (2,7 million)
8. *Fallen –* <u>Evanescence</u> by (2,6 million)
9. *Autobiography* by <u>Ashlee Simpson</u> by (2,5 million)
10. *Now That's What I Call Music! 16* by Various artists (2.5 million)

Top selling albums globally in 2004 were:

1. *Confessions* by <u>Usher</u>
2. *Feels Like Home* by <u>Norah Jones</u>
3. *Encore* by <u>Eminem</u>
4. *How to Dismantle an Atomic Bomb* by <u>U2</u>
5. *Under My Skin* by <u>Avril Lavigne</u>
6. *Love. Angel. Music. Baby* by Gwen Stephani
7. *Greatest Hits* by <u>Robbie Williams</u>
8. *Greatest Hits* by <u>Shania Twain</u>
9. *Destiny Fulfilled* by <u>Destiny's Child</u>
10. *Greatest Hits* by <u>Guns N' Roses</u>
11. *Songs About Jane* by <u>Maroon 5</u>
12. *American Idiot* by <u>Green Day</u>
13. *Elephunk* by <u>The Black Eyed Peas</u>
14. *Greatest Hits: My Prerogative* by <u>Britney Spears</u>
15. *Anastacia* by <u>Anastacia</u>

Musical films

Beyond the Sea, starring <u>Kevin Spacey</u> as <u>Bobby Darin;</u> *De-Lovely* starring <u>Kevin Kline</u> as <u>Cole Porter</u> and Ashley Judd; *Ray*, starring <u>Jamie Foxx</u> as <u>Ray Charles</u> and *The Phantom of the Opera*, starring <u>Emmy Rossum</u> as Christine and <u>Gerard Butler</u> as the Phantom were released in 2004.

2005

World News: 2005

President George W. Bush was inaugurated for his second term on January 20.

In February, North Korea announced that it possessed nuclear weapons, which they believed they needed for protection against the United States. In September, they announced that they would stop building nuclear weapons in exchange for aid and cooperation.

Pope John Paul II died on April 2; over four million people traveled to the Vatican to mourn his passing. He was succeeded by Pope Benedict XVI on April 19, the 265th pope.

Charles, Prince of Wales, married Camilla Parker Bowles on April 9 in a civil ceremony at the Guildhall in Windsor's Castle. Upon her marriage, Camilla became Duchess of Cornwall.

The very first YouTube video was uploaded on April 23, 2005; it was titled "Me at the zoo."

On August 29, Hurricane Katrina reached landfall on the coast of the Gulf of Mexico and devastated New Orleans. Over a thousand people died and damage was estimated to be $108 billion.

The trial of Saddam Hussein began on October 19 and scientists announced in December that a 25-year-old Scottish man, Andrew Stimpson, was the first person cured of AIDs.

MySpace

MySpace began in August, 2003 by several employees with eUniverse and used the 20 million users and e-mail subscribers to launch it and it soon become the most popular social networking website. This was the main site where users could post recordings. In July, 2005, it was purchased by Rupert Murdoch's News Corporation for $580 million. MySpace's strategy was to build an audience around music and entertainment and they partnered with Google for advertising, and created tools like instant messaging, a video player, a music player, a virtual karaoke machine and a classifieds program but that made the site slow. MySpace was an important site for music fans but was overtaken by Facebook in April, 2008; they had attempted to buy Facebook in 2005.

Carrie Underwood wins American Idol and goes country

Carrie Underwood won the "American Idol" award on May 25, 2005. Winners of the "American Idol" award were required to sign a management contract with 19 Management and major label BMG/Sony to record (the companies had a "right of first refusal" with all contestants). It was expected that all winners would be marketed to the pop/rock market but Carrie Underwood, winner of the fourth "American Idol" contest, wanted to record for the country music audience. The result was a compromise on her first album with half the songs intended for the pop market and half for the country market. The pop release came first and "Inside Your Heaven" entered the *Billboard* Hot 100 on July 2, 2005 and reached number one. Her first country single, "Jesus Take the Wheel" made its debut at the Country Music Association Awards in 2005. The song was written by Hillary Lindsey, Gordie Sampson and Brett James and produced by Mark Bright. It entered *Billboard's* country chart on November 5 and reached number one, where it remained for six consecutive weeks; it reached number 20 on the pop chart. "Jesus Take The Wheel" won numerous awards—including the Academy of Country Music's Single of the Year," CMT's Breakthrough Video and Female Video of the Year, the Canadian Country Music's SOCAN Song of the Year, the Gospel Music Association's Country Song of the Year and Grammys for Best Country Song and Best Country Female Vocal.

From that point forward, Carrie Underwood was a country music star; her follow-up was "Before He Cheats," which became number one on the country chart for five consecutive weeks and number eight on the *Billboard* Hot 100.

Big Machine Records formed

Big Machine Records was founded in September, 2005 by Scott Borchetta, a veteran Nashville record industry executive. The label was initially a joint venture with Show Dog Records, headed by Toby Keith but that partnership ended in March, 2006. Big Machine's first artist was Taylor Swift, whose first album was released in 2006 and who became the top-selling musical artist of 2009 with her crossover hits. The label worked out joint arrangements with Garth Brooks, Martina McBride, Reba McEntire, Rascal Flatts and Trisha Yearwood in addition to signing and developing new acts. Their headquarters is on 16th Avenue S.

Concerts for Causes

There were a number of concerts held in 2005 to help those hit with disasters.

The tsunami that struck in the South Pacific the day after Christmas, 2004, inspired music artists to hold a benefit concert on January 22 at the Millennium Stadium in Cardiff, Wales, The Tsunami Relief Concert was the largest live music event held in the U.K. since the Live Aid concert in 1985. Performers on the concert included Madonna, Eric Clapton, Jools Holland, Manic Street Preachers, Lulu, Alex Jones, Charlotte Church, Kathering Jenkins, Feeder, Snow Patrol and Liberty X.

One week later in Vancouver, British Columbia, another concert staged for tsunami relief was held. Performers at the concert included Canadian artists Avril Lavigne, Chantal Kreviazuk, the Barenaked Ladies, Raine Maida and Sarah McLachlan.

On July 2, there were ten simultaneous Live 8 concerts throughout the world in the campaign to Make Poverty History.

The G7 Summit began in 1976 to bring the heads of the richest industrial countries together to discuss major international issues. The group included France, Germany, Italy, Japan, the U.K., Canada and the United States; in 2005, for the first time, Russia was included, making it a G8 Summit. The major issues discussed were climate change and the lack of development in African countries. During the conference, which was preceded by a meeting of the finance ministers of those countries, the United States agreed to write off $40 billion in debt owed by 18 African countries to the World Bank, the International Monetary Fund and the African Development Fund.

The concerts were organized by Bob Geldof and Midge Ure, who had organized the first African relief fund raiser in 1984 with the creation and sale of the single, "Do They Know It's Christmas." American artists contributed to African relief through their song, "We Are the World" and Geldof was involved in the creation of the Live Aid Concert in 1985.

The Live 8 concerts began with combined audience finger snap led by Will Smith to bring awareness to the fact that a child in Africa died every three seconds. Concerts were held in Japan, Philadelphia, London, Berlin, Rome, Paris and Johannesburg, South Africa.

In London's Hyde Park, performers included Paul McCartney and U2, who began the concert with "Sgt. Pepper's Lonely Hearts Club Band." Other performers included Pink Floyd (their final appearance with their "classic" lineup), Elton John, Bob Geldof, Madonna, Pete Doherty, Coldplay, Robbie

Williams Stevie Wonder, Rob Thomas (lead singer of Matchbox 20), Adam Lavine (lead singer of Maroon 5), The Who, Mariah Carey and Snoop Dogg.

In Canada, performers included Neil Young, Deep Purple and The Tragically Hip; Brian Wilson performed in Berlin.

United Nations Secretary General Kofi Annan and Microsoft co-founder Bill Gates spoke to the crowd at Hyde Park. South African President Nelson Mandela spoke to the crowd assembled in Johannesburg.

The event was broadcast on BBC One, MTV and VH-1.

After New Orleans was devastated by Hurricane Katrina, a "Concert for Hurricane Relief" was broadcast on NBC on September 2 and Shelter from the Storm: A Concert for the Gulf Coast and ReAct Now: Music & Relief was held the following week. There were also benefit concerts at Madison Square Garden and Radio City Music Hall held on September 20. During the "Concert for Hurricane Relief, rapper Kanye West made his controversial statement, "George Bush doesn't care about black people."

On December 10, International Human Rights Day, Amnesty International introduced the Make Some Noise campaign where artists recorded new versions of John Lennon songs for an album to raise money for the organization. Artists on the album included U2, Christina Aguilera, Aerosmith, Jackson Browne, Big & Rich, Green Day, The Black Eyed Peas, Jack Johnson, Ben Harper, The Flaming Lips and Duran Duran.

Music News: 2005

Mariah Carey made music history with her single, "We Belong Together," which became her sixteenth number one record and retained that position for fourteen non-consecutive weeks. "We Belong Together" became the first single to occupy the number one position on nine *Billboard* charts at the same time: the Hot 100, Hot 100 Airplay, Hot R&B/Hip Hop Songs, Hot R&B Hip-Hop Airplay, Pop 100 Airplay, Top 40 Mainstream, Rhythmic Airplay, Hot Dance Club Songs and Hot Ringtone.

On June 13, Michael Jackson was found not guilty of child molestation. In July, Lil' Kim was sentenced to a year and a day in prison for lying to a federal grand jury about her knowledge of suspects in a shooting outside a New York radio station in 2001. In August, Eminem entered rehab for dependency on sleep medication and Death Row Records CEO Suge Knight was shot in the leg during a pre-party at the MTV Video Music Awards in Miami.

The PlayStation 2 video game, "Guitar Hero" was released on November 8. The video game increased the sales of artists who had their songs included in the games and led to a trend in rhythm games, which became one of the most popular video game genres for several years.

The copy protection rootkit scandal broke on November 15. Sony BMG announced it would recall all of the estimated 15 million CDs containing copy protection because they posed serious security risks if played on PC disc drives.

On December 21, Elton John married David Furnish in London after new laws in Britain gave the same legal protections for gay and straight marriages.

2006
Desinty's Child and Beyonce

By the time Beyonce had her first solo number one's in 2003—"Crazy in Love" and "Baby Boy"—she had a strong track record as a record seller. By the end of 2006, Beyonce was established as a multi-Grammy winning best selling artist whose career spanned pop, rap and films.

Beyonce Giselle Knowles was born September 4, 1981, in Houston, Texas and began performing early in school choir, church choir and talent shows. When she was eight, Beyonce and her childhood friend Kelly Rowland met La Tavia Roberson during auditions for an all girl group; the three were placed with three other girls in Girls' Tyme, that rapped and danced in talent shows. R&B producer Arne Frager saw the group and brought them to his Northern California studio and placed them on the popular TV show "Star Search."

The group did not win but led to Beyonce's father, Mathew Knowles, quitting his job as sales manager at Xerox to manage the group. Knowles reduced the six member group to four and they opened for established R&B girl groups. They auditioned for record labels and were briefly signed to Elektra before they signed with Dwayne Wiggins's Grass Roots Entertainment in October, 1995.

They signed with Sony Music and recorded their first album for the Columbia label. Before their album was released, they changed their name to Destiny's Child (from the Book of Isiah). Their first single, "Killing Time," was on the soundtrack to the film, *Men in Black*.

The first single from their self-titled debut album, "No, No, No Part 2" entered the *Billboard* Hot 100 on November 29, 1997, and reached number three. The album debuted on *Billboard's* album chart on March 7, 1998, but only reached number 67.

Their second album, *The Writing's On the Wall*, was released in 1999 and entered the *Billboard* chart on August 4; it rose to number five. There were three hit singles on that album which all reached number one on the Hot 100. "Bills, Bills, Bill" entered the chart in June, "Say My Name" entered the Hot 100 on Christmas but peaked in 2000 at number one, where it remained for three weeks, and "Jumpin' Jumpin'" which entered the chart in May and reached number three, where it stayed for five weeks.

In addition to her releases with Destiny's Child, Beyonce recorded "After All Is Said and Done" with Marc Nelson, an original member of Boyz II Men for the soundtrack to the film *The Best Man*.

There was trouble brewing within Destiny's Child. Group members LeToya Luckett and LeTavia Roberson were unhappy with Mathew Knowles management; they were replaced by Farrah Franklin and Michelle Williams. Franklin was then dismissed from the group and the lineup for Destiny's Child became Beyonce, Kelly Roland and Michelle Williams.

Beyonce had personal problems during that period. Her long-time boyfriend left and she suffered from depression from being publicly blamed by the media for the breakup of Destiny's Child.

The remaining group members recorded the biggest single for Destiny's Child, "Independent Women Part 2," which was on the soundtrack to the film *Charlie's Angels,* starring Drew Barrymore. That single entered the *Billboard* Hot 100 on September 23, 2000, and rose to number one, where it remained for eleven weeks.

Their third album, *Survivor* entered the *Billboard* album chart in May, 2001 and reached number one, where it stayed for two weeks. Hit singles from that album included "Survivor," which reached number two and remained there for seven weeks, and "Bootylicious," which entered the Hot 100 in June and was number one for two weeks. The third single, "Emotion," reached number ten.

In October, 2001, they released the album *8 Days of Christmas* and the single by the same title, which landed at 102 on the *Billboard* Hot 100.

Beyonce began her career as an actress in the made for TV film, "Carmen: A Hip Hopera" with actor Mekhi Phifer; the movie was a modern day interpretation of the opera classic, "Carmen." In 2002, she played "Foxxy Cleopatra" in the comedy *Austin Powers in Goldmember*, starring Mike Myers, and released the single, "Work Out" from the soundtrack. In 2003 she starred with Cuba Gooding, Jr. in the comedy, *The Fighting Temptations*, and released the single from the soundtrack, "Fighting Temptation," with Missy Elliott, MC Lyte and Free.

Beyonce first worked with Jay-Z on "'03 Bonnie & Clyde," which entered the *Billboard* Hot 100 in October, 2002, and reached number four. Jay-Z was then featured on Beyonce's "Crazy In Love," which entered the Hot 100 in May, 2003, and reached number one and held that position for eight weeks. It was her first single and first number one as a solo artist. That song won Grammys for R&B Song and Rap-Sung Collaboration.

Beyonce's album, *Dangerously in Love*, was released on June 24 and debuted at number one and remained on the chart for 100 weeks. Her following single, "Baby Boy" featured Sean Paul; it entered the Hot 100 in August and hit number one, staying in that position for nine weeks.

The third single from the album, "Me, Myself and I" reached number four in 2004 and "Naughty Girl" reached number three.

Beyonce returned to Destiny's Child for their final album together, *Destiny Fulfilled*. The album was released in November, 2004, reached number two on the album chart and contained the hit singles, "Lose My Breath" and "Soldier," both which peaked at number three. They supported the album with a world tour and, at the end of the North American dates, split to pursue individual careers. Their greatest hits album was released at the end of 2005 and reached number one on the album chart.

Beyonce's second solo album, *B'day*, was released to coincide with her twenty-fifth birthday, September 4, 2004. The album debuted at number one and the first single, "Déjà Vu," featured Jay-Z; it reached number four on the Hot 100. Her next single, "Irreplaceable," released at the end of 2006, reached number one and remained there for ten weeks.

During 2006 she was in the comedy *The Pink Panther* with Steve Martin and sang "Check on It," the single from the soundtrack, which reached number one and held that position for five weeks. She also starred in *Dreamgirls*, a fictional account of the Supemes, based on the 1981 Broadway musical; Beyonce played the role based on Diana Ross and released the single, "Listen," from the film.

Fan Fair renamed CMA Music Festival

Fan Fair was renamed CMA Music Festival in 2004. Performances during the Festival were taped and broadcast on CBS on July 14 as "CMA Music Festival: Country Music's Biggest Party." Performers on the two hour TV show included Brooks & Dunn, Martina McBride, LeAnn Rimes, Brad Paisley, Gretchen Wilson, Uncle Kracker, Montgomery Gentry, Terri Clark, Pat Green, Rascal Flatts, Willie Nelson and Hank Williams Jr.

In 2006—six years after shifting from the Nashville Fairgrounds to downtown Nashville-- the CMA Festival set attendance records with 161,590 attending the event June 8-11, although the actual number of individuals was 25,000. It was held at the Nashville Convention Center, the city's Riverfront Park and the Titans football stadium, where the biggest concerts were held. Single day tickets to the event were $14 with the evening concert tickets costing $30. There were 33 acts who performed at the stadium with another 86 performed on duel stages at Riverfront Park. In all, there 326 artists and celebrities appeared at the Nashville Convention Center for autograph and photo sessions.

Music News: 2004

On February 22, Apple announced that "Speed of Sound" by Coldplay was the one billionth song downloaded on iTuens.

Taylor Hicks won season five of "American Idol"

On July 30, the last weekly edition of the legendary British TV show, "Top of the Pops" was broadcast; it had been on the air for 42 years.

The liquidation of Tower Records began on October 7, the bankrupt chain of record retailers closed its last store on December 22. The assets were purchased by the Great American Group.

CBGB, the legendary punk rock club in New York City, was closed on October 15 after a protracted dispute over rent; the final show was performed that night by Patti Smith.

On November 14, Microsoft released the first Zune media player, which competed unsuccessfully with the well established iPod and iTunes store.

Top 10 best-selling albums: 2006

High School Musical (cast soundtrack) (8.5 million)
FutureSix/LoveSounds by Justin Timberlake (8.3 million)
Loose by Nelly Furtado (8.2 million)
From Under the Cork Tree by Fall Out Boy (7.9 million)
Some Hearts by Carrie Underwood (6.9 million)
I'm Not Dead by Pink (6.5 million)
B'Day by Beyonce (5.7 million)
Love by The Beatles (5.6 million)
Daughtry by Daughtry (4.9 million)
Taylor Swift by Taylor Swift (4.5 million

Music Films

Music films released in 2006 included *American Hardcore* (a documentary of early hardcore punk rock);, *Dixie Chicks: Shut Up and Sing; Dreamgirls* starring Jamie Foxx, Beyoncé Knowles, Eddie Murphy, Danny Glover and Jennifer Hudson;, *Hannah Montana*, (a Disney Channel original series); *High School Musical*, (Disney Channel Original Movie); and *Neil Young: Heart of Gold,*.

2007

News: 2007

On January 9, 2007, classical violinist Joshua Bell performed before a sold out concert in Washington, D.C. Three days later, wearing a baseball cap, Bell performed in the Metro subway station at L'Enfant Plaza as an incognito busker. Bell played for almost 45 minutes, performing the same repertoire he had performed in his concert. A hidden camera recorded 1,097 people passing by with only seven stopping to listen—and only one who recognized him. His busking led 27 people to contribute $32.17 to his performance, not counting the $20 contributed by the lone passerby who recognized him. The performance, instigated by Gene Weingarten, columnist for the Washington Post, was shown on YouTube and a full-length documentary, *Find Your Way: A Busker's Documentary*, was released.

Nancy Pelosi was elected the first female Speaker of the House by Congress on January 4.

The original iPhone was introduced by Steve Jobs at the Macworld Keynote in San Francisco on January 9; on June 29 it was available to purchase in the United States. The first modern smart phone was later released in the U.K., France, Germany, Portugal, Ireland and Austria in November.

In February, the Intergovernmental Panel on Climate Change (IPCC) issued an assessment report concluding that global climate change is "very likely" to have a predominately human cause. On July 7, Live Earth, a worldwide series of concerts were held to initiate action against global warming. Concerts were held in New Jersey (Giants Stadium), London (Wembley), the Mall in Washington, Japan, South Africa, Germany, Australia, Brazil, China and Rome.

Artists who performed on those concerts included Sarah Brightman, Linkin Park, Kelly Clarkson, Alicia Keys, Kanye West, Bon Jovi, Fall Out Boy, Shakira, John Mayer, Rihanna, Beastie Boys, Duran Duran, Madonna, Foo Fighters, Red Hot Chili Peppers, The Black Eyed

Peas, Spinal Tap, Jack Johnson, Lenny Kravitz, Metallica as well as the reunited bands The Police, Genesis, The Smashing Pumpkins and Crowded House. The TV ratings for those concerts were "dismal" and "disappointing."

In February, North Korea, which had announced the test of a nuclear bomb the year before, agreed to shut down its facilities as a first step toward complete denuclearization in exchange for energy aid equivalent to 50,000 tons of heavy fuel oil.

Inducted into the Rock and Roll Hall of Fame in 2007 were Grandmaster Flash and the Furious Five, R.E.M., The Ronettes, Patti Smith and Van Halen.

Radiohead announced on October 1 that their new album, In Rainbows, scheduled to be released in ten days, would be offered to the public for whatever price they wanted to pay.

On December 10, Led Zeppelin reunited in London for their first show in 25 years and in Las Vegas, Celine Dion made her final performance in her five year engagement at Caesars Palace.

The film, *Across the Universe*, was released

Record Labels and iTunes

From the record labels perspective, there were several problems with iTunes. First, their business paradigm had changed from receiving approximately $10 per sale when consumers bought a CD to 67 cents when a consumer downloaded a song. When the iPod arrived, the single was back and consumers overwhelming preferred buying singles to albums.

Songwriters and publishers were hurt by this. When an album was sold, there were eight or nine songs that earned money even though they were not a single. Artists received less money because their royalties were based on a 67 cent sale rather than a $10 sale. And, of course, record labels grossed much less money.

Privately, a number of record executives began comparing Apple to MTV. Major labels agreed to give videos to MTV in the early 1980s as a promotional device; however, once the video channel was rolling, the labels realized they were losing a lot of revenue.

The major problem, from the label's perspective, was that "Apple had basically taken over the entire music business. Steve Jobs's agenda was not to make money off 99-cent digital songs...He used the songs to profit from expensive iPods. Labels made exactly zero dollars for every iPod sale. Not only that, record execs noted ruefully, there was no chance music fans were filling their 80-gigabyte iPods with 20,000 songs they'd bought for 99 cents a piece or ripped from their CD collections. Surely pirated music had something to do with the booming iPod sales as well."

In February, 2006, iTunes sold its 1 billionth download and digital single sales went from 19.2 million in 2003 to 844.2 million in 2007. Because of services like Kazaa and LimeWire, 4.3 million people around the world were illegally sharing files at any given time and approximately 95 percent of the songs on an average iPod were illegally downloaded.

Taylor Swift

On July 1, 2006, Taylor Swift's single, "Tim McGraw," entered the *Billboard* Country Chart; it peaked at number six and remained on the singles chart for 32 weeks. Her next song, "Teardrops On My Guitar" entered the chart on February 24, 2007, and peaked at number two. Her third single for Big Machine Records, "Our Song," reached the number one spot and remained there for six weeks. Taylor Swift had arrived as a country star.

Born on December 13, 1989, in Reading, Pennsylvania, Taylor Alison Swift is the daughter of Scott Swift, a financial advisor and a mother, Andrea, who had worked as a mutual fund marketing executive. During her early years, the family lived on a Christmas tree farm.

When she was nine, Swift became interested in musical theater and traveled regularly to New York City for vocal and acting lessons. Inspired by the songs of Shania Twain, Swift became interested in country music and began performing on weekends at local events. Her interest in country music grew when she saw a documentary on Faith Hill. Convinced that she should be in Nashville, 11-year old Swift and her mother went to Nashville with demo tapes of Swift singing Dolly Parton and Dixie Chicks hits to karaoke tracks. No label was interested.

The next year, when Swift was 12, she met a computer repairman and local musician, Ronald Cremer, who taught her how to play guitar and helped her write songs. Swift and her family began working with Dan Dymtrow, a New York-based music manager who helped her obtain modeling gigs with Abercrombie & Fitch in their "Rising Stars" campaign. She had a song on a compilation CD and performed on a RCA Showcase, which led to an artist development deal with that label and frequent trips to Nashville with her mother.

When Swift was 14, her father, wanting to help his daughter pursue a career in country music, transferred to the Nashville office of Merrill Lynch and her family bought a home in Hendersonville, a suburb about 20 miles north of Nashville. She graduated from a home schooling academy a year early.

Swift wrote songs with established Nashville songwriters; she began to write regularly with Liz Rose, honing her craft in two hour sessions on Tuesdays, after school. She was signed as a songwriter to Sony/ATV/Tree publishing, one of the leading publishers, but parted ways with RCA when she was 14.

Scott Borchetta, an executive with Dreamworks Records, was planning to start an independent label, Big Machine, when he saw her perform at the Bluebird Café in 2005. Her father purchased a three percent stake in the new company for about $120,000 and Swift became one of the first artists signed to the label. She began working on her debut album and convinced the label to hire Nathan Chapman as her producer; Chapman had produced her demos.

The self-titled album had three songs that Swift wrote alone and eight with established Nashville songwriters; it was released on October 24, 2006. It entered the country chart on November 11 and rose to number one, where it remained for eight weeks and on the chart for 60 weeks. It peaked at number six on the *Billboard* 200 album chart; her single, "Tim McGraw," peaked at 40.

Taylor Swift taught the Nashville music community about social media. She was young and actively engaged on the Internet and built a strong foundation for her career on social media. At 16, she could relate to an audience of teenage girls who liked country music, and they could relate to her. She had a string of hit singles in 2007 and 2008, with "Should've Said No" and "Love Story" reaching number one.

In 2008 she also had a string of chart singles on the Hot 100 with "You Belong With Me" reaching number two.

Taylor Swift's rise was, well, swift, and she was soon collecting awards from the Country Music Association, the Academy of Country Music and the Grammys.

Coachella

Coachella emerged in the twenty-first century as one of the premier music festivals in the United States. It is held each spring in Indio, California, at the Empire Polo Club. It was founded by Paul Tollett and Rick Van Santen, co-presidents of Goldenvoice, a concert promotion company.

The roots of the Coachella Valley Music and Arts Festival, as it is officially named, go back to Pearl Jam's frustration with Ticketmaster, which controlled the majority of ticketing for concerts and consistently added service charges to each ticket. Pearl Jam refused to play in Los Angeles because of that practice so that led them to perform in Indio, about 125 miles east of L.A. and about 25 miles east of Palm Springs in the Colorado Desert on November 5, 1993. They attracted a crowd of 25,000 at the Empire Polo Club, which validated that site as a place where a large concert could be held.

Paul Tollett owned Goldenvoice and the idea of staging a music festival came out of frustration. His small company could not compete with larger companies that offered larger advances to artists so he decided to hold a music festival in October, 1999, in Indio. The event came two months after Woodstock '99 and the problems at that event—looting, arson, violence and rapes—raised Tollet's insurance costs by 40 percent.

The first Coachella was held over two days, October 9 and 10, 1999, with headline acts Beck, the Chemical Brothers, Tool, Morrissey and Rage Against the Machine; Jurassic 5 and Underworld also played. Tickets were $50 each day; on Friday, 17,000 tickets were sold and on Saturday there were 20,000 tickets sold. Parking was free and each person admitted received a bottle of water. The event ran smoothly, although temperatures could soar to over 100 degrees Fahrenheit but the festival lost $850,000.

Because of the financial hole, there was no Coachella in 2000. For 2001, Tollett and co-president Rick Van Santen, decided to move the event to April to avoid the heat, and limit it to one day. They struggled to find acts until Jane's Addiction agreed to play, They had decided to book "trendy" acts instead of those with chart and sales success, hoping a line-up of "trendy" acts would attract a crowd; that gave Coachella the image as the "Anti-Woodstock."

In March, 2001, a month before the second Coachella, Tollett sold Goldenvoice to the Anschutz Entertainment Group (AEG) for $7 million. AEG wanted Tollett to continue booking the festival and Tollett retained complete control of the festival.

The festival became an annual event, gaining a worldwide reputation, and in 2004 had their first sell-out, drawing 110,000 over two days with headline acts the Pixies, Radiohead, Kraftwerk, The Cure, Belle and Sebastian and The Flaming Lips. Attendees came from all 50 states in the U.S. That year, AEG purchased half of Coachella from Tollett.

In 2005, headliners at Coachella included Coldplay, Arcade Fire, Weezer, M.I.A., The Prodigy, the Chemical Brothers, Nine Inch Nails, Bright Eyes, and Wilco. In 2006, Madonna and Daft Punk gave memorable performances; other headliners that year included James Blunt, Gnarls Barkley and Massive Attack; about 120,000 attended the festial, which grossed $9 million.

In 2007, the Coachella festival was extended to three days and headliners included the Red Hot Chili Peppers, Rage Against the Machine, Bjork, Arcade Fire, Scarlett Johansson and the Jesus and Mary Chain. That year Goldenvoice inaugurated the Stagecoach Festival, a country music festival held the weekend after Coachella. The attendance that year was 186,636 and the festival grossed $16.3 million.

By that time the Coachella Festival was established as a must attend music festival for music fans with a line-up of trendy as well as top name acts. It was also profitable. In 2017 the festival had an attendance of 250,000 and grossed $114.6 million.

Best selling albums: U.S. 2007

Daughtry by Daughtry
Konvicted by Akon
The Dutchess by Fergie
Hannah Montana by Various Artists
Some Hearts by Carrie Underwood
All the Right Reasons by Nickelback
FutureSex/LoveSounds by Justin Timberlake
High School Musical 2 by Various Artists
Minutes to Midnight by Linkin Park
B'Day by Beyonce
Graduation by Kanye West
Me and My Gang by Rascal Flatts
Love by The Beatles
The Sweet Escape by Gwen Stefani
Hannah Montana 2 by Various Artists
Awake by Josh Groban
Not Too Late by Norah Jones
Taylor Swift by Taylor Swift
Kingdom Come by Jay-Z

Best Selling Albums Globally: 2007

The Best Damn Thing by Avril Lavigne
Carnival Ride by Carrie Underwood

Back to Black by Amy Winehouse
Noel by Josh Groban
Long Road Out of Eden by The Eagles
Minutes to Midnight by Linkin Park
As I Am by Alicia Keys
Call Me Irresponsible by Michael Buble
Life in Cartoon Motion by Mika
Not Too Late by Norah Jones

2008

News: 2008

In January, stock markets around the world plunged from fears of a recession in the United States, fueled by the subprime mortgage crisis in 2007. In March and April, rising food and fuel prices caused riots and unrest in Third World nations.

In February, it was announced that *Thriller* by Michael Jackson was the biggest selling album of all time. To celebrate, Sony re-issued *Thriller 25* on its twenty-fifth anniversary.

The release of the *Guitar Hero: Aerosmith* video game in late June was the first time the *Guitar Hero* series was based around a single artist.

In August, eleven mountaineers died on K2, the second highest peak in the world, in the worst single accident in the history of that mountain.

The 2008 Summer Olympics were held in China on August 8-24.

In Sweden, the on-demand streaming service, Spotify, was launched on October 7.

In December, the human remains of Tsar Nichols II of Russia were found and identified using DNA analysis on December 5.

Live Nation announced on December 22 that the Sticky & Sweet Tour by Madonna was the highest-grossing tour for a solo artist. Over 2.3 million fans attended the 58 shows in Europe and the Americas and the tour grossed $280 million.

On November 4, Barack Obama was elected the first African-American President of the United States.

Musical films released during the year included *Cadillac Records*, a fictional portrayal of the legendary Chess Records in Chicago, *High School Musical 3: Senior Year* and *Hannah Montana & Miley Cyrus: Best of Both Worlds Concert*.

The iPod Problem

The major problem with the iPod was a lack of sound quality but the overwhelming number of fans "didn't care about sound quality" as "iTunes emerged as the biggest online retailer, taking more than 70 percent of the market and dwarfing later competitors like Napster...and stores from Microsoft, MTV, Sony Corp and Wal-Mart. By April, 2008, the Itunes Music Store had sold more than 4 billion songs around the world. It ranked No. 1, above Best Buy and Wal-Mart as the top overall music retailers in the United States."

Sales for the iPod peaked during the 2008-2009 Christmas season. Consumers were moving away from ownership to access and streaming provided that.

Clear Channel

Clear Channel Communication was founded in 1972 in San Antonio, Texas, by Lowry Mays and Red McCombs; it purchased its first FM station in San Antonio, then purchased its second, an AM station, in 1975 and purchased its first stations outside the San Antonio market in 1986. Congress relaxed rules for radio ownership somewhat in 1992 and by 1995 Clear Channel owned 43 radio and 16 television stations. After the Telecommunications Act of 1996, Clear Channel began buying stations until it owned over 1,200 stations.

The company expanded into billboard advertising by purchasing Eller Media in 1997 and created Live Nation for concerts and live events in 2005. In November, 2006, Clear Channel announced it would go private and divest itself of all its television stations and the 448 radio stations it owned outside the top 100 markets.

Clear Channel was criticized after 9/11 for banning songs, such as "Imagine" by John Lennon, because executives thought they were "inappropriate" for airplay. Clean Channel was also criticized for its close ties to the George W. Bush administration and for its role in March, 2003 when Dixie Chicks records were taken off a number of radio stations after lead singer Natalie Maines of the Texas-based group told a London audience that "we're ashamed the President of the United States is from Texas." Clear Channel was criticized for censoring opinions critical of President George W. Bush and other Republicans, including rejection of a billboard ad from a Democratic political advocacy group in 2004 that stated "Democracy is best taught by example, not by war."

Because of its buying spree in the late 1990s, Clear Channel was heavily leveraged and the interest payments on its debt became overwhelming. In 2008, they launched iHeart Radio, which streamed from their 750 stations online. Although it sold a number of its TV and radio stations, the interest on their debt held them down. In 2014, Clear Channel Communications was re-branded iHeart Communications.

Bonaroo

In 2008, *Rolling Stone* magazine named Bonaroo the "Best Festival" in the U.S. and one of "50 moments" that changed rock and roll.

The first Bonaroo Festival (a Creole slang term meaning a really good time) was in 2002. It was held on a 700 acre farm in Manchester, Tennessee, about halfway between Nashville and Chattanooga. The festival was founded by Superfly Productions and AC Entertainment; the individuals involved were Ashley Capps with AC Entertainment and Kerry Black (graphic design), Rick Farman (festival operations), Richard Goodstone (marketing) and Jonathan Myers (programming) of Superfly.

The founders of Bonaroo were all music fans and the event was inspired by their attendance at Phish concerts as well as Glastonbury, Coachela and Woodstock. The festival began with an emphasis on jam bands and folk rock but soon extended to cover a wide variety of performers and music; artists who have performed at the festival include U2, Eminem, Nine Inch Nails, Radiohead, Paul McCartney, Billy Joel, The Beach Boys, Kanye West, The White Stripes, Neil Young, Tom Petty, James Brown, Willie Nelson, Mumford and Sons, Bob Dylan, Jay Z, The Police, Bruce Springsteen, ZZ Top, Kings of Leon and the Beastie Boys.

Bonaroo begins on the second Thursday in June and lasts four days with many attendees camping out. In addition to multiple stages with live music, the festival also includes craftsmen and artisans, food and drink vendors, a comedy tent and a Ferris wheel.

The event is held just off I-24 near Manchester in Coffee County. The population of Manchester is a little over 10,000 but during Bonaroo there are over 100,000 there. According to a study, Bonaroo brings in over $14 million in business revenue and $4 million in personal income to Coffee Country.

The festival is known for being "green"; food and drink are sold in organic, recyclable containers and organizers contribute to environmental organizations as well as other charities.

Bonaroo began on a 700 acre farm that was leased but, in January, 2007, the organizers purchased 530 acres of the site and leased another 250 acres for camping and parking.

In 2016, one of the founders of Bonaroo, AC Entertainment, was purchased by Live Nation Entertainment.

Katy Perry

Katy Perry began her music career as a Christian artist, but that did not fit her. Her first album, recorded as Katy Hudson, was a Christian album that did not sell and she abandoned Christian music to concentrate on pop; from that Christian album to "I Kissed a Girl" was a long road, but along the way Katy Perry found her calling in pop music.

Catheryn Elizabeth Hudson was born October 25, 1984, in Santa Barbara, California; her parents, were Pentecostal pastors; during her childhood she moved around the country with her parents who founded churches, before returning to Santa Barbara. She had a strict, religious upbringing, attending Christian schools and listening primarily to Christian music; her parents discouraged secular music in their home and she only heard pop music surreptitiously when she sneaked CDs from her friends.

She began taking voice lessons at nine and became part of her parents ministry, singing in churches between the ages of 9 and 17. She received a guitar for her 13th birthday; at 15 she left school, after completing the requirements for a General Education Development (GED) degree to pursue a music career.

She was brought to Nashville by Steve Thomas and Jennifer Knapp to work on her songwriting; she began writing songs and recording demos and signed with Red Hill, who released her debut album, a Christian album titled *Katy Hudson*, on March 6, 2001. The album received positive reviews but few sales and the label went out of business in December.

Perry moved from Christian to secular music while writing songs with producer Glen Ballard; she moved to Los Angeles at 17. She also moved from being Katy Hudson to Katy Perry, using her mother's maiden name to avoid confusion with actress Kate Hudson.

Perry signed with the Java label, part of the The Island Def Jam Music Group, but Island Def Jam severed ties with Java. Perry was then signed as a solo artist to Columbia by A&R executive Tim Devine. During the next two years, she wrote and recorded songs for her debut album, working with songwriters Desmond Child, Greg Wells, Butch

Walker, Scott Cutler, Anne Preven, The Matrix, Kara DioGuardi, Max Martin and Dr. Luke. In 2006, before her album was completed, she was dropped from Columbia.

By that time, she had gained attention as a singer. One of the songs she recorded for Java, "Simple," was on the soundtrack to *The Sisterhood of the Traveling Pants* (2005) and she sang backing vocals on "Old Habits Die Hard" by Mick Jagger, which was on the soundtrack to Alfie (2004). She sang background vocals on "Goodbye for Now" by P.O.D., and appeared in several videos.

A publicity executive at Columbia, Angelica Cob-Baehler, took Perry's demos to Jason Flom, chairman of Virgin Records, who arranged for her to sign with Capitol Records. She worked with Dr. Luke and the two wrote "I Kissed a Girl" and "Hot N Cold" for her album *One of the Boys*. In November, 2007, Capitol began a campaign to promote her, releasing the video "Ur So Gay" in November, 2007, and a digital EP *Ur So Gay*. In an interview, Madonna said it was her favorite song at the time.

Her first single for Capitol, "I Kissed a Girl" created immediate response from radio airplay and entered the *Billboard* Hot 100 on May 24, 2008; it was controversial, drawing fire from both religious and LGBT groups. Religious groups criticized the homosexual themes while the LGBT groups criticized her for using bi-curiosity to sell records. The song hit number one on the Hot 100 and held that position for seven weeks. Her album, *One of the Boys*, was released on June 17 to mixed reviews; it peaked at number nine on the album chart and sold seven million copies.

Her second single, "Hot N Cold," entered the Hot 100 in July and peaked at number three.

In 2008, Perry went on her "Warped Tour" and hosted the 2008 MTV Europe Music Awards in November.

Katy Perry had found her calling.

Kings of Leon

The Kings of Leon (brothers Caleb, Nathan and Jared Followill with cousin Matthew Followill, moved to Nashville during the 1990s and formed their band, named after their grandfather, Leon Followill. Nathan and Caleb Followell signed with RCA in 2002 and decided to form a band with their younger brother, Jared. and cousin, Matthew; their first album, *Holy Roller Novocaine* was released in February, 2003. In July, 2003 their album Youth and Young Manhood was released in the U.K. and received critical and commercial success; it had no impact in the USA. The Kings of Leon continued to have hit singles and albums in the U.K. but no success in the U.S. until their song, "Use Somebody" was released in 2008. "Use Somebody entered the *Billboard* Hot 100 on October 11, 2008, and rose to number four, remaining on the singles chart for 57 weeks. "Use Somebody" won Grammys for Record of the Year, Rock Song and Rock Group Vocal.

The Great Recession

During the early 1980s, under the Reagan Administration, a 30 year period of financial deregulation began. The financial sector expanded from investment banks going public (bringing vast sums of stockholder capital and financial fraud, often tied to real estate investments. Large investment banks merged and developed financial conglomerates, which led to the creation of giant investment banks like Goldman Sachs.

During the period 2004-2006, the number of household properties subject to foreclosure in the U.S. grew.

In March, 2008, several prominent economists and members of the financial establishment warned that a recession was imminent while others stated that the United States was in a recession in March, 2008.

By mid-2008, there were widespread failures in financial regulation and breakdowns in corporate governance that resulted in too many financial firms acting recklessly and taking on too much risk. Excessive borrowing and risk by households and Wall Street were leading to a crisis. Home buyers were victims of predatory lenders, specifically the adjustable rate mortgages that mortgage lenders sold directly or indirectly via mortgage brokers.

By 2007, the top five investment banks (Bear Stearns, Lehman Brothers, Merrill Lynch, Goldman Sachs and Morgan Stanley) had accumulated approximately $4 trillion in debt.

During the weekend of September 13-14, 2008, Lehman Brothers declared bankruptcy, which came after a series of crisis beginning in late 2007. In the summer of 2007, Countrywide Financial secured a $12 billion bailout. In mid-December, 2007, Washington Mutual cut over 3,000 jobs and closed its sub-prime mortgage business. In mid-March, 2008, Bear Stearns received a $29 billion bailout from the Federal government. A run on the IndyMac Bank in Los Angles occurred in July, 2008, when depositors line up in the street to withdraw their money; on July 11, IndyBank was seized by federal regulars and called for a $32 billion bailout. That day financial markets plunged and mortgage lenders Fannie Mae and Freddie Mac were placed in conservatorship on September 7.

After Lehman Brothers declared bankruptcy, they failed to find a buyer. The Bank of America agreed to purchase Merrill Lynch and the giant AIG sought a loan from the Federal Reserve.

On September 15, stocks on Wall Street tumbled. The next day, the federal government agreed to give AIG an $85 billion rescue package with the Federal Reserve receiving 80 percent public stake in the firm.

On September 25, the biggest bank failure in history occurred when JP Morgan Chase agreed to purchase the banking assets of Washington Mutual.

By September 17, 81 public corporations had filed for bankruptcy in the United States.

By September 19, the Bush Administration estimated a range of $700 billion to one trillion would be required for a bailout to purchase troubled mortgage assets. Congress refused to approve and the Dow Jones dropped 777 points and stocks continued to drop.

A housing bubble caused home prices to increase greatly; when the economy collapsed, housing values fell, causing many home owners to owe more on their house than it was worth, and a sharp rise in unemployment led to foreclosures.

On October 3, President Bush signed a revised Emergency Economic Stabilization Act into law, creating a $700 billion Treasury fund to purchase failing band assets.

In January, shortly after taking office, President Obama signed the American Recovery and Reinvestment Act, known as "The Stimulus" to pump money into the economy to recover from the economic crisis. Under the Obama Administration, laws were passed to monitor, curtail and control bank lending and investment practices, which resulted in a more stable financial industry.

The Great Recession cost millions of jobs; from November 2008 to April 2009, an average of 747,000 jobs were lost each month. Despite the financial shenanigans on Wall Street that almost sent the United States into a second Great Depression, not a single leader involved stood trial or was sent to prison.

The Great Recession officially lasted until June, 2009, but recovery was slow and full recovery was not achieved until 2012.

2009
President Obama's Inauguration

On January 20, 2009, President Barack Obama was sworn in as the forty-fourth president of the United States. During an pre-inaugural concert held on January 18 at the Lincoln Memoria, titled "We Are One," the concert featured performances by <u>Mary J. Blige</u>, <u>Garth Brooks</u>, <u>Renée Fleming</u>, <u>Caleb Green</u>, <u>Josh Groban</u>, <u>Herbie Hancock</u>, <u>Heather Headley</u>, <u>Beyoncé Knowles</u>, <u>Bettye Lavette</u>, <u>Pete Seeger</u>, <u>Shakira</u>, <u>Bruce Springsteen</u>, <u>James Taylor</u>, <u>U2</u> and <u>Stevie Wonder</u>. Several of the songs performed had been used by <u>Obama's presidential campaign</u>.

At the Inaugural Ball, artists <u>Mariah Carey</u>, <u>Jay-Z</u>, <u>Alicia Keys</u>, <u>Shakira</u>, <u>Sting</u>, <u>Faith Hill</u>, <u>Mary J. Blige</u>, <u>Maroon 5</u>, <u>Stevie Wonder</u> and <u>Will.I.Am</u> performed.

Lady Gaga 2009

In 2009, Lady Gaga had seven chart singles on the *Billboard* Hot 100, beginning with "Poker Face," which reached number one, remained on the chart for 40 weeks and won a Grammy for Dance Single. Other top ten songs on the Hot 100 in 2009 were "LoveGame," "Paparazzi," "Bad Romance" and "Telephone", which entered the chart in 2009 and peaked at number three in 2010. It was a remarkable run for someone who had first entered the *Billboard* Hot 100 a year before. Her hit in 2008, "Just Dance," was a number one record that opened the door for her success in 2009.

Lady Gaga was born Stefani Joanne Angelina Germanotta on March 28, 1986, in New York City. Her father was an Internet entrepreneur and she grew up in affluent surroundings in Manhattan. She began piano lessons at four because her mother aspired for her to become a cultured young lady. She learned to play by ear and her parents enrolled her in Creative Arts Camp and encouraged her to pursue a career in music. In high school she performed in school plays and at open mic nights. She studied method acting at the Lee Strasberg Theatre and Film Institute for ten years and auditioned for shows in New York without much success.

When she was 17, Gaga was admitted to the Collaborative Arts Project,a music school at New York University where she studied music and worked on her songwriting by writing essays on a variety of topics, During her sophomore year, she dropped out to concentrate on her music career.

Gaga recorded two songs with hip hop singer Grandmaster Melle Mel in 2014 for an audio book to accompany *The Portal in the Park,* a Cricket

Casey children's novel. She formed the SGBand with friends from NYU and became a regular in the downtown Lower East Side club world. She was recommended to music producer Rob Fusari, who collaborated with Gaga to develop her songs and compose new material. Gaga and Fusari began dating and he began calling her "Lady Gaga, from Queen's song, "Radio Ga Ga."

Gaga and Fusari founded Team Lovechild to promote her career. They concentrated on dance music and sent demos to music industry executives. She was signed to Def Jam Records in September, 2006, but was dropped three months later. While performing in neo-burlesque shows, Gaga met Lady Starlight, who helped with her onstage persona. The duo began performing in downtown clubs and their live performances became known as "Lady Gaga and the Starlight Revue," billed as "The Ultimate Pop Burlesque Rockshow." In 2007, they performed at the Lollapalooza music festival.

In 2007, Lady Gaga was signed to Streamline Records, an imprint of Interscope by Vincent Herbert, and to Sony/ATV publishing where he was hired to write songs for Britney Spears, Fergie and the Pussycat Dolls. The next year she moved to Los Angeles to compete her debut album, *The Fame*, which was released on August 19, 2008. Her first two singles, "Just Dance" and "Poker Face" both reached number one. Her album, *The Fame* won a Grammy for Best Dance/Electronica Album and "Poker Face" won a Grammy for Best Dance Recording.

Michael Jackson

On March 5, Michael Jackson announced that his last concert series, "This Is It," would be held at the O2 Arena in London. Ten shows were originally scheduled but demand for tickets extended the shows to 50 and all of the tickets were sold in less than four hours.

Jackson went into rehearsals in Los Angeles for his shows but on June 25, a news bulletin announced that Jackson had been taken to a hospital.

Jackson was under the care of Dr. Conrad Murry, a cardiologist, who had given him a lethal dose of the drugs lorazepam, midazolam and propofol to help him sleep. During his sleep, Jackson stopped breathing and attempts at resuscitation were unsuccessful. Emergency medics arrived at 12:25 p.m. and Jackson was taken to the Ronald Reagan UCLA Medical Center where resuscitation efforts continued but at 1:13 p.m., Pacific time, Michael Jackson was pronounced dead.

The news spread quickly on-line, with several sites struggling to handle the traffic. MTV stopped its regular programming and showed Michael Jackson's videos.

On July 7, a public memorial was held at the Staples Center where artists Stevie Wonder, Usher, Mariah Carey, Jennifer Hudson, John Mayer, Lionel Richie and his brother, Jermain, performed and Queen Latifah read a poem, "We Had Him" by Maya Angelou. Preceding the memorial service, the family held a private service at Forest Lawn Memorial Park.

On September 3, Michael Jackson was entombed at Forest Law Memorial Park in Glendale, Caliofornia.

During the six month after Jackson's death, 8.5 million copies of his albums were sold, making him the top selling artist of 2009.

On October 28, the documentary Michael Jackson's *This Is It* was released, featuring him performing during rehearsals with behind the scenes footage. It became a best selling documentary, raising over $250 million.

Susan Boyle

When the TV show "Britain's Got Talent" was aired on April 11, 2009, TV viewers saw the panel of judges look in resigned amusement as a slightly frumpy 47-year-old woman stood on stage. Judge Simon Cowell looked resigned to an embarrassing disappointment as he asked the singer why she was there. The live audience for the TV taping seemed to wonder why she was there as well. Susan Boyle answered Cowell that she wanted a musical career. The look on Cowell's face said "Fat chance" but she was told to begin.

And then she began singing "I Dreamed a Dream" from *Les Miserable* and her strong, emotional voice overpowered the judge, the live audience and TV viewers at home. Everyone was gobsmacked. The audience began clapping and cheering.

When she finished, the panel of judges had learned a lesson; never take for granted that someone has no talent. Never assume a negative outcome before you've heard the talent. Don't judge a book by its cover.

Susan Boyle's performances spread over the internet and millions watched her performance on YouTube. Susan Boyle had talent!

Susan Boyle (born April 1, 1961 in Scotland) was the daughter of a miner and World War II veteran who sang at Bishop's Blaze. She took voice lessons from vocal coach Fred O'Neil and attended the Edinburgh Acting School.

Boyle used her life savings to record three songs, in 1998, "Cry Me a River," "Killing Me Softly" and "Don't Cry For Me, Argentina" and "Cry

Me a River" was included on a CD to commemorate the Millennium. She won several local singing contests and, encouraged by her mother and O'Neil, entered the "Britain's Got Talent" contest. She passed the auditions and then performed on the show before an astounded panel of judges. Amanda Holden, one of the judges, called it "the biggest wake-up call ever" when Boyle finished her song.

Susan Boyle recorded an album, *I Dreamed a Dream*, that was released in November, 2009, which became the fastest selling debut album in U.K. history. The album reached the top of the Billboard chart and remained there for six weeks and sold over three million copies.

Susan Boyle dreamed a dream that came true.

Music News: 2009

The inductees to the Rock and Roll Hall of Fame in 2009 were Little Anthony and the Imperials, Bobby Womack, Jeff Beck (as a solo artist), Run-D.M.C. and Metalica.

On May 3, Pete Seeger's 90th birthday was celebrated with a concert at Madison Square Garden. Performing on the concert were Bruce Springsteen, Joan Baez, Roger McGuin, Dave Matthews, Eddie Vedder and Pete Seeger.

The Beatles, who had resisted digital releases of their albums, saw their entire catalogue re-released as digital remasters with rare pictures, short documentaries, original and newly written liner notes with replicated U.K. artwork on September 9.

Garth Brooks came out of retirement to perform a solo acoustic show at the Encore Theater at Wynn, Los Vegas.

Best-selling albums in the U.S.: 2009

1. *Fearless* by Taylor Swift
2. *I Dreamed a Dream* by Susan Boyle
3. *Number Ones* by Michael Jackson
4. *The Fame* by Lady Gaga
5. *My Christmas* by Andrea Bocelli
6. *Hannah Montana: The Movie (Soundtrack)* by Hanna Montana
7. *The E.N.D.* by the Black Eyed Peas
8. *Relapse* by Eminem
9. *The Blueprint 3* by Jay-Z
10. *Only by the Night* by Kings of Leon

Best Selling Albums Globally: 2009

1. *I Dreamed a Dream* by Susan Boyle
2. *The E.N.D.* by The Blackeyed Peas
3. *This Is It* by Michael Jackson
4. *Fearless* by Taylor Swift
5. *The Fame* by Lady Gaga
6. *Crazy Love* by Michael Buble
7. *No Line on the Horizon* by U2
8. *Thriller* by Michale Jackson
9. *Number Ones* by Michael Jackson
10. *My Christmas* by Andrea Bocelli

2010
Haiti Earthquake

On January 12, a 7.0 magnitude earthquake struck Haiti, devastating the capital, Port-au-Prince; the death toll was over 315,000. Ten days later, a telethon, "Home for Haiti Now", was broadcast. Performers participating in the telethon were Wyclef Jean, Christina Aguilera, Beyoncé, Madonna, Bruce Springsteen, Jennifer Hudson, Mary J. Blige, Shakira, Sting, Alicia Keys, Dave Matthews, Neil Young, John Legend, Justin Timberlake, Stevie Wonder, Justin Bieber, Taylor Swift, Emeline Michel, Keith Urban, Kid Rock, Sheryl Crow, Coldplay, Bono, The Edge, Jay-Z, and Rihanna.

An album, *Hope for Haiti Now,* was recorded and on January 27 became the first digital-only album to reach number one on the *Billboard* 200 album chart.

A number of artists re-recorded "We Are the World" for Haitian victims of the earthquake and the song debuted during the opening ceremonies for the 2010 Winter Olympics in Vancouver, Canada. The single debuted at number two on the *Billboard* Hot 100 and number one on the *Billboard* Hot Digital Songs chart.

2010 Grammy Awards

The diversity of American popular music was seen at the 52nd annual Grammy Awards on January 31, 2010, honoring the releases of 2009. The show was regularly scheduled for February but was moved up so it would not conflict with the Olympics; the winter Olympics were in Vancouver that year. The Grammys were held in Los Angeles at the Staples Center. There were 109 awards in 30 categories but only ten were broadcast.

The show was centered on performances and there were usually several performers doing a medley. Performers included Lady Gaga, Elton John, Green Day, Beyonce, Pink, The Black Eyed Peas, Lady Antebellum, Jamie Foxx, T-Pain, Slash, Doug E. Fresh, Zac Brown Band, Leon Russell, Taylor Swift, Stevie Nicks, Dion Celine, Usher, Carrie Underwood, Smokey Robinson, Bon Jovi, Jennifer Nettles, Andrea Bocelli, Mary J. Blige, David Foster, Dave Matthews Band, Roberta Flack, Maxwell, Jeff Beck, Drake, Lil Wayne and Eminem. Presenters included Justin Bieber, the Jonas Brothers, Alice Cooper, Sheryl Crow, Miley Cyrus, Placido Domingo, Wyclef Jean, Norah Jones, Ke$ha, Miranda Lambert, John Legend, LL Cool J, Jenifer Lopez, Ricky Martin, Katy Perry, Lionel Richie, Carlos Santana, Seal, Ringo Starr, Keith Urban and several Hollywood actors and actresses. It was a mixture intended to appeal to a wide demographic with a wide taste of music.

Beyonce was nominated for ten awards—the most of any artist—and she won eight. Taylor Swift won four award while The Black Eyed Peas, Jay-Z and Kings of Leon each won three.

To give a sample of award winners:

Album of the Year: *Fearless* by Taylor Swift

Record of the Year: "Use Somebody" by Kings of Leon

Song of the Year: "Single Ladies (Put a Ring On It)" by Beyonce

Best New Artist: Zac Brown Band

Best Female Pop Vocal: "Halo" by Beyonce

Best Male Pop Vocal: "Make It Mine" by Jason Mraz

Best Pop Performance by Duo or Group: "I Gotta Feeling" by the Black Eyed Peas

Best Pop Collaboration: "Lucky" by Jason Mraz & Colbie Caillat

Best Pop Instrumental: "Throw Down Your Heart" by Bela Fleck

Best Pop Instrumental Album: *Potato Hole* by Booker T. Jones

Best Pop Vocal Album: *The E.N.D.* by The Black Eyed Peas

Best Traditional Pop Vocal: *Michael Buble Meets Madison Square Garden* by Michael Buble

Best Solo Rock Vocal: "Working on a Dream" by Bruce Springsteen

Best Rock Performance by a Duo or Group: "Use Somebody" by Kings of Leon

Best Hard Rock Performance: "War Machine" by AC/DC

Best Metal Performance: "Dissident Aggressor (live)" by Judas Priest

Best Rock Instrumental: "A Day in the Life" by Jeff Beck

Best Rock Song: "Use Somebody" by Kings of Leon

Best Rock Album: *21st Century Breakdown* by Green Day

Best Female R&B Vocal: "Single Ladies (Put a Ring on It)" by Beyonce

Best Male R&B Vocal: "Pretty Wings" by Maxwell

Best R&B Performance by Duo or Group: "Blame It" by Jamie Foxx & T-Pain

Best Traditional R&B Vocal Performance: "At Last" by Beyonce

Best R&B Song: "Single Ladies (Put a Ring on It)" by Beyonce

Best R&B Album: *BLACKsummers'night* by Maxwell

Best Contemporary R&B Album: *I am....Sasha Fierce* by Beyonce

Best Rap Solo: "D.O.A. (Death of Auto-Tuner)" by Jay-Z

Best Rap Performance by Duo or Group: "Crack a Bottle" by Eminem, Dr. Dre & 50 Cent

Best Rap/Sung Collaboration: "Run This Town" by Jay-Z, Rihanna & Kanye West

Best Rap Album: *Relapse* by Eminem

Best Female Country Vocal: "White Horse" by Taylor Swift

Best Male Country Vocal: "Sweet Thing" by Keith Urban

Best Country Performance by Duo or Group: "I Run to You" by Lady Antebellum

Best Country Collaboration: "I Told You So" by Carrie Underwood & Randy Travis

Best Country Instrumental: "Producer's Medley" by Steve Wariner

Best Country Song: "White Horse" by Taylor Swift

Best Country Album: *Fearless* by Taylor Swift

American popular music covers a wide spectrum, demonstrated best by the Grammy nominations and awards. In addition to those awards and award winners listed, there were also Grammys for Classical, Jazz, Gospel, Latin, American roots, Reggae, World Music, Children's Music, Spoken Word recordings, Comedy and Musical show as well as awards for production, video, album notes, engineers and film and TV.

Rock and Roll Hall of Fame

The inductions to the Rock and Roll Hall of Fame were held on March 15 at the Waldorf Astoria Hotel in New York City. Inducted were ABBA, Genesis, Jimmy Cliff, The Hollies and The Stooges.

Ringo at 70

Baby boomers were aging. Earlier in the year—on January 8—Elvis would have turned 75. On July 7, 2010, Ringo Starr turned 70. To celebrate his birthday, Ringo and his eleventh All-Starr Band performed a concert at Radio City Music Hall. Ringo and special guests Steven Van Zandt, Nils Lofgren, Billy Squier, Colin Hall (from Men at Work), Dr. John and Ray Davies performed with Ringo's son, Zak Starkey, who was drummer for The Who. Ringo's grandsons presented him with a Ludwig Drum set birthday cake. The closing song was "With a Little Help From My Friends," which segued into "Give Peace a Chance," with Yoko Ono in attendance. Everyone thought the show was over, but then Paul McCartney made a surprise appearance and sang the Beatles classic, "Birthday."

In November, the music from the Beatles was finally available on iTunes, after years of legal disputes.

World News: 2010

On April 20, the fortieth anniversary of Earth Day was celebrated. That same day, the Deepwater Horizon oil drilling platform in the Gulf of Mexico exploded, killing eleven workers and created an oil spill that damaged the waters along the southern United States coastline. The oil spill was one of the largest in history and prompted a debate about practices and procedures of offshore drilling.

In May, the International Monetary Fund and the Eurozone agreed to provide a 100 billion GBP (approximately $165 billion) bailout package for Greece and demanded that Greece adopt austerity measures.

The 2010 Flash Crash occurred on Wall Street when the stock market crashed for over 36 minutes because of a series of automated trading programs in a feedback loop.

WikiLeaks, an online publisher of anonymous, covert and classified material released to the public over 90,000 classified internal reports on July 25. The reports gave detailed accounts of American involvement in the War in Afghanistan from 2004 to 2010.

Burmese opposition leader Aung San Suu Kyi was released from house arrest on November 13; she had been incarcerated since 1989.

A street vendor in Tunisia, Mohamed Bouazizi, attempted suicide on December 17, which triggered the Tunisian Revolution and led to the Arab Spring in 2011, which led to unrest and revolution in the Middle East.

Jason Aldean and Kelly Clarkson

On November 20, 2010, the duet "Don't You Wanna Stay" by Jason Aldean and Kelly Clarkson entered the *Billboard* country chart and rose to number one, where it remained for three weeks; it reached number 31 on the Hot 100. Aldean was signed to Broken Bow Records, an independent label whose first chart success came in 2005 with Aldean's song, "Hicktown." Aldean had four number one singles on *Billboard's* country chart before he recorded "Don't You Wanna Stay," written by Andy Gibson, Paul Jenkins and Jason Seller; it was produced by Michael Knox and on his album *My Kinda Party*. Kelly Clarkson had won the first "American Idol" contest and had number one pop hits with "A Moment Like This" and "My Life Would Suck Without You." She was managed by Narvel Blackstock, who also managed Reba, and was married to Blackstock's son.

"Don't You Wanna Stay" made its debut on the 2010 CMA Awards Show and was then released as a single. It was nominated for a Grammy for Best Country Duo/Group. The song was also included on Clarkson's album, *Stronger*, released in 2011.

CMA Awards: 2010

The 44th Annual Country Music Association Awards was broadcast over ABC from the Bridgestone Arena on November 10, 2010, with hosts Brad Paisley and Carrie Underwood. Entertainer of the Year was Brad Paisley, Song of the Year was "The House That Built Me" written by Tom Douglas and Allen Shambline (recorded by Miranda Lambert), Single of the Year was "Need You Now" by Lady Antebellum, Album of the Year was *Revolution* by Miranda Lambert, Male Vocalist was Blake Shelton, Female Vocalist was Miranda Lambert, Vocal Duo was Sugarland, Vocal Group was Lady Antebellum, Musician was Mac McAnally, New Artist was the Zac Brown Band, Musical Event was "Hillbilly Bone" by Blake Shelton and Trace Adkins and Music Video was "The House That Built Me" by Miranda Lambert; inducted into the Country Music Hall of Fame were Jimmy Dean, Ferlin Husky, Bily Sherill and Don Williams.

Music City U.S.A. in the 2000s

By the new century, Nashville was well established as "Music City U.S.A." but Music Row was in danger of being bulldozed by developers. Belmont and Vanderbilt Universities were in the area and their campuses were growing. Nearby, 12th Avenue South was being developed and The

Gulch, a blighted area where the trains used to roll into Nashville, was developed as well, putting Music Row in the middle of an area that was appealing to developers. Historic building were demolished—or they came close to being demolished—and high rise condos were built.

Between 2010 and 2015 over 30 building in the Music Row area were demolished for redevelopment projects, mostly condominiums. Among the buildings demolished were Studio 19, where Ringo Starr had recorded, the Sound Shop, where Paul McCartney had recorded, Fireside Recording Studios where Porter Wagoner and Dolly Parton had recorded, Pete Drake's Studio, the advertising jingles firm Hummingbird Productions, and the building that formerly housed April/Blackwood Publishing, the building that formerly housed Kelso Herston Enterprises and 16th Edge Studios, and the Pilcher-Hamilton House, built during the 1870s and the former home of Councilman Jim Hamilton, who had represented the Music Row area while serving on the Metro Council.

Ticketmaster

During the 1970s, colleges and universities booked about half the concerts in the United States. Those colleges and universities had the facilities—usually a basketball arena—for a large concert, a student body who wanted to see live entertainment, and a large budget from student activity fees.

The committee to book acts on college campuses was comprised of students, who played a major role in picking the acts, and university staffers, who oversaw the day-to-day business of concert scheduling and promotion.

At Arizona State University in Phoenix, Arizona, two staffers, Albert Leffler and Peter Gadwa, with businessman Gordon Gunn started a company in 1976 which sold tickets to events. Their first event, a concert by the Electric Light Orchestra held at the University of New Mexico in 1977, was successful and the company quickly grew by making it easy for fans to obtain tickets to concerts without having to camp out all night before a box office opened.

In 1982, Fred Rosen became CEO of Ticketmaster and instituted an aggressive approach to business. By the end of the 1980s, Ticketmaster was the dominant seller of tickets in the country. They took over their major competitor, Ticketron, and during the 1990s expanded from selling tickets over the phone and at retail outlets to selling tickets over the internet.

Ticketmaster sold over 140 million tickets in 2007, but fans were increasingly frustrated with the extra fees that had to be paid to Ticketmaster in order to purchase a ticket to a concert or event. At the time it merged with Live Nation, it controlled 70 percent of the tickets sold for major concerts.

Live Nation

Clear Channel Communications, which owned radio stations, began a concert promotion company, Clear Channel Entertainment but, after criticism of conflict of interest, spun off their concert division as Live Nation. However, two members of the Board of Directors, L. Lowry Mays and Randall T. Mays, were sons of Mark Mays, a founder of Clean Channel and member of their Board.

Live Nation pioneered a new relationship with artists whereby they signed an artist to their concert promotion company and their record label, and promoted that artist through concerts and sales of merchandise.

Live Nation owned or operated 117 venues (75 in the United States) and promotes or produces over 22,000 events a year before over 50 million people. In 2007, they grossed $4.184 billion in revenue; they had 4,700 full time employees and 15,900 part-time.

Madonna's contract with Live Nation was announced in October, 2007. The contract had Madonna as their first recording artist for their label, Live Nation Artists. Other artists, because of on-going contracts with their labels, had signed with Live Nation for touring and concert promotion.

In addition to Madonna, U2, Jay-Z, Shakira and Nickelback all signed agreements with Live Nation, which offered them a large amount of money for long-term exclusive representation. Those deals could include the acts' merchandise sales, web site and recordings.

Social Marketing

During the second half of the 20th century, the standard way to market an act was to get their record on radio in high rotation and have their records in retail outlets so that consumers, who wanted to buy the record after hearing it on the radio, could purchase it. Radio airplay was supported and enhanced by print media—articles in newspapers and magazines—and appearances on television via shows and videos. Personal appearances allowed fans to see an act live; a hit record on the radio created demand for that act.

A successful recording act could earn enough from record sales to live comfortably. If the act wrote their own songs, the additional songwriting (and possibly publishing) income added more money.

In the first decade of the 21st century, that old model did not disappeared but it was certainly diminished. Although radio airplay was still important, it was much less important for pop/rock acts than in the past because young people listen to radio less than the preceding generations. Distribution used to be trucks and warehouses; recordings were shipped to various warehouse locations and then sent to stores via trucks or mail. The internet allowed a recording to be distributed all over the world in digital form with no trucks or warehouses.

For pop/rock/urban music, videos on MTV were a crucial form of exposure that attracted fans to purchase recordings. However, by the late 1990s, MTV executives realized that self-produced reality shows ("The Real World" and "Road Rule") received higher ratings, which produced more income than videos. Labels, which formerly spent up to $1 million for a video, lowered their budgets to $100,000—or less.

In the second half of the 20th century there were barriers for an act to enter the music industry. The cost of producing a recording involved renting expensive studios and manufacturing a record was costly as well. An individual could not get their recordings on radio or into retail outlets without major label promotion and distribution. Gatekeepers at record labels determined who would be signed and what would be released, gatekeepers at radio determined what records would be played, gatekeepers in the mainstream media determined who would be covered and exposed and gatekeepers at retail determined who would be stocked.

In the 21st century, an individual or group could record an album in their bedroom ("Bedroom Bands") with relatively inexpensive digital recording equipment. CD burners on computers allowed someone to manufacture a CD inexpensively and distribution was gained by making the recording available on the internet. An artist needed a web site—which many can create and build—a video on YouTube (which can easily be made by relatively cheap digital video cameras), and a web presence via Facebook, blogs, email, snapchat, twitter and various other digital media which are virtually free.

YouTube

YouTube became a major means for an artist or musician to present their work to the world. YouTube meant that, not only did an artist or musician have to make a recording, they also had to make a video of a performance. Popular videos were viewed millions of times as artists and songs received widespread recognition. YouTube became, for some artists, what pop radio and MTV used to be.

YouTube, was formed in February, 2005 by former PayPal employees Steve Chen, Chad Hurley and Jawed Karim. The idea for YouTube came when Hurley and Chen had difficulty sharing videos that were shot at a dinner party. (The "wardrobe malfunction" and Pacific tsunami were also inspirations because video of those events could not be easily found.) Sequoia Capitol gave the three young men $11.5 million in venture capital to fund the company in San Mateo, California and YouTube was officially launched in December. By that time, the site received eight million views a day; in July, 2006, over 65,000 new videos were uploaded each day and the site received 100 million video views each day.

In November, 2006, YouTube was purchased by Google for $1.65 billion. It was ranked as the third most visited site, after Google and Facebook. By the end of 2010, 48 hours of new videos were uploaded every minutes (soon to increase to 60 hours each minute and then 400 hours each minute by March, 2017) with 100 million video views each day.

The music industry's problem with YouTube is that it doesn't pay; YouTube doesn't pay for content and doesn't pay when content is show, arguing that it is a delivery medium. Another problem is how to sort through millions of videos to discover new music. For many singers, YouTube's content is simply too overwhelming to break through. The hope of many artists is that their video will go virile but, like winning the lottery, that is an almost impossible long shot.

Apple and iTunes

By 2007, Apple controlled 70 percent of the digital music market through iTunes and just about anyone could get their recording on iTunes, available for purchase. Other sites, such as CD Baby, were also available to sell digital as well as physical product. Web sites could take purchases from credit cards to sell recordings and merchandise while Twitter kept an artist and his or her fans in constant touch.

However, the purchase of downloads peaked during the 2008-2009 Christmas season and streaming became the primary way listeners access and consume music.

The one thing that remained essential was personal appearances. Without an artist doing live shows, it is doubtful they could build an audience. No matter how great a presence on the internet, the key to an artist earning money remains in the live arena.

Justin Bieber

Justin Bieber became more than a star; he was a model for millennials and a new era of marketing music in a time when all the old rules seemed to be breaking and new rules were being formed. He represented a new way for an artist to be discovered and promoted through social media. On the other hand, his career path was not so different from those who had come before him.

Justin Bieber was discovered on YouTube and much of his initial following came through social media such as YouTube and Twitter. His career was reminiscent of the careers of Frank Sinatra, Elvis Presley and the Beatles who went "virile" in another time. Sometimes an artist comes along and is captured by a time that thrusts him into the spotlight; that was the case for the artists just mentioned as well as Bieber.

The traditional method of breaking an act was to somehow find an act that gatekeepers, such as music industry executives, believed had potential for album sales and stardom and release a single to radio and then work hard to promote it. It involved building an artist over time through radio, TV, print and concert appearances. That still works, although it doesn't work as well. In the music business during the first decade of the 2000s, the "new" had not yet fully arrived and the "old" had not totally left. The "new" was the digital world, especially streaming, and the "old" was physical product as well as the traditional way of doing business.

Justin Bieber is a Canadian, born in London, Ontario, on March 1, 1994. He was an only child to parents who never married; his mother, Pattie Mallette, was underage when she gave birth. She raised Justin as a single Mom in low-income housing with the help of her parents, mother Diane, and stepfather, Bruce.

Bieber learned to play guitar, piano, drums and trumpet and, in 2007 at the age of ten, entered a talent contest. He did not win the talent contest, but his mother videoed the performance of Bieber singing Ne-Yo's "So Sick" and posted it on YouTube. Bieber continued to sing covers of R&B songs and his Mom continued to video those performances and post them on YouTube for family and friends.

A music business executive, Scooter Braun, ran across one of those videos on YouTube "by accident." He was impressed and tracked down Bieber and wanted to work with him. Pattie was reluctant because Braun was Jewish, but church elders convinced her to allow Justin this opportunity.

Baum took 13-year old Justin Bieber to Atlanta to record demos; a week later he was singing for Usher. Braun signed Bieber to the Raymond Braun Media Group, a joint venture between Braun and Usher. Justin Timberlake was also interested in signing Bieber but lost in a bidding war with Usher.

Bieber auditioned for L.A. Reid of The Island Def Jam Music Group; Reid signed him and appointed Chris Hicks, Vice President of Def Jam, to oversee Bieber's career at the label. In 2008, Justin Bieber and his mother moved to Atlanta and Braun became Bieber's manager.

Bieber's first single, "One Time," was released in 2009. It was a classic case of a white guy singing R&B songs and a young performer that the millennial generation could connect with and relate to. The YouTube video quickly caught on and Bieber's album cuts, "One Less Lonely Girl," "Love Me," "Favorite Girl," "Down to Earth," "Bigger" and "First Dance" became popular. Previously, a label spaced out singles but when an act goes "virile," like the Beatles did in 1964, they had songs from their previous as well as current albums receiving extensive airplay on the radio. The Beatles had 30 songs on the *Billboard* Hot 100 in 1964; Justin Bieber had seven songs on the chart in 2009 and eight in 2010. Those eight songs in 2010 were "Baby" (featuring Ludacris), "Never Let You Go," "U Smile," "Ennie Meenie," "That Should Be Me," "Struck in the Moment," "Somebody to Love" and "Never Say Never."

Because Justin Bieber was a Canadian, he had the benefit of the Canadian Content rule (Can-Con) which required Canadian radio to play a percentage of songs with Canadian content; those songs on the Canadian border could be heard in the United States. That led to Bieber's first album selling platinum in the United States and Canada and gold in Australia and New Zealand. The internet made being an international artist easy.

Justin Bieber became a phenomena, which led to TV appearances on top rated shows as well as live performances and downloads from the iTunes store at a time when the iPod was popular. Bieber sang "Someday at Christmas" for President Barack Obama and First Lady Michelle Obama which was televised on December 20, 2009. On New Year's Eve, he was on "Dick Clark's New Year's Rockin' Eve" with Ryan Seacrest.

Bieber's debut album, *My World 2.0*, released on April 1, 2010, debuted at number one on the *Billboard* 200 album chart; the album had seven hit singles in it.

Justin Bieber, in a one year period, became a superstar.

Major Labels

At the beginning of 2010 there were four major labels. In 2003, Time Warner decided to sell its music division in order to pay down debt incurred through the AOL merger. Warner Brothers had purchased Word Records in 2001; in 2002, Curb Records joined Warners as a partner with Word Records. In March, 2004, Edgar Bronfman, former head of MCA, led a group of investors that included private equity groups to purchase Warner Music for $2.6 billion.

In August, 2007, EMI was acquired by Terra Firma Capitol Partners for $.2 billion. Several major artists-including Radiohead and Paul McCartney—left the label while Coldplay threatened to leave.

In August, 2004, Sony and the Bertelsmann Music Group (BMG) entered into a 50-50 venture to form Sony BMG Music Entertainer, combining two of the oldest historic labels, Columbia and RCA Victor, into one firm. Four years later, in August, 2008, Sony agreed to acquire BMG's take in the company; in October, that agreement was completed with BMG out of the music business and Sony Music Entertainment now the sole owner of the recordings of labels that include Victor, RCA, Arista, Columbia, Epic, Bluebird, Okeh, and CBS Records.

Universal Music Group acquired BMG's music publishing division in May, 2007. UMG is still owned by Vivendi, a French media conglomerate headquartered in Paris. The Universal labels include recordings from Decca, MCA, PolyGram, Mercury, Motown, Interscope, A&M and Geffen.

Best Selling Albums: 2010: U.S.

1. *Recovery* by Eminem
2. *Michael* by Michael Jackson
3. *Speak Now* by Taylor Swift
4. *My World 2.0* by Justin Bieber
5. *The Gift* by Susan Boyle
6. *The Fame* by Lady Gaga
7. *Solider of Love* by Sade
8. *Thank Me Later* by Drake
9. *Raymond v. Raymond* by Usher
10. *Animal* by Ke$sha

Billboard Hot 100: Number One Hits: 2010

"Tik Tok" by Ke$sha

"Imma Be" by The Black Eyed Peas

"Break Your Heart" by Taio Cruz featuring Ludacris

"Rude Boy" by Rihanna

"Nothin' on You" by B.o.B featuring Bruno Mars

"OMG" by Usher featuring will.i.am

"Not Afraid" by Eminem

"California Gurls" by Katy Perry featuring Snoop Dogg

"Love the Way You Lie" by Eminem featuring Rihanna

"Teenage Dream" by Katy Perry

"Just the Way You Are" by Bruno Mars

"Like a G6" by Far East Movement featuring The Cataracs and Dev

"What's My Name" by Rihanna featuring Drake

"Raise Your Glass" by Pink

"Fireworks" by Katy Perry

CONCLUSION

In 1995, CDs were the dominate format for recorded music; they replaced cassettes that had replaced vinyl records. Some artists were selling millions of CDs and the CD was a favorite "gift" for music fans. Ten years later, the sales of CDs were in free fall and people were getting singles and albums free by illegally downloading. It was the music industry's worst nightmare. Digital had arrived.

The music industry first shifted to downloads; Apple had created the iPod in 2001 and then the iTunes store, which helped—but revenue from sales of recordings continued to sink. After 2005, there was a turnaround led by digital technology. Within a period of a few years, the music industry—and life itself—was transformed. Most of those transformational events occurred within a five year period.

February, 2005: YouTube was formed

2006: the Internet crossed one billion users.

July 2006: Google bought YouTube.

September, 2006: Facebook became open to everyone with an email address (formerly only students could belong).

January 9, 2007: Apple introduced the iPhone

2007: Amazon introduced the Kindle

2007: AirBnB was conceived

2007: Watson was launched—the first cognitive computer

2007: Intel introduced non-silicon materials into microchips

2007: Beginning of clean power revolution. There was an exponential rise in solar, wind, bio fuels, LED lighting and energy efficient buildings.

2007: DNA sequencing costs begin to fall drastically

October, 2008: Spotify was formed

2001: Wikipedia formed; in 2014 there were over 18 billion page views.

2009: Uber was formed

2008-2009: the app store came on stream and demand for data exploded

2000 Baidu was formed; in 2010 they had over four billion queries

1994: Amazon was formed; in 2015 it passed Wal-Mart as the leading American retailer

1999 Alibaba was formed; in 2016 it was the world's leading retailer

There was tremendous growth of four companies, Facebook, Google, Amazon and Apple that dominate the digital business world. All of the elements of computing power, processing chips, software, storage chips, networking and sensors tend to move forward roughly as a group. Moore's Law states that "The power of microchips will double every two years," and that has certainly been affirmed.

All of this transformed the music industry. In 1995, each country or territory had their own music industry that was more or less isolated from every other country. There were a number of British, Australian and Canadian acts who had success in America and a few American acts who were successful global acts, but below the superstar level, acts were limited by their access to other markets. During the 2000s, an act could be heard internationally via streaming and YouTube; no act was locked into their country except those in China and a few other countries

By 2015, digital piracy had been tamed, but not eliminated; beginning in 2015, the revenues for record companies began to increase annually, primarily through streaming. In 1995, there were Gatekeepers in the music industry: the record labels decided which artists to sign and what songs to release; publishing companies decided which songwriters to sign and radio station determined which artists received airplay and which did not. A distribution system, consisting of warehouses, trucks, trains and retail outlets determined what was available for purchase and how it got there. As the digital world grew, anyone could record a song or video on a laptop or smartphone, and upload it to YouTube or a streaming service for instant distribution.

As a society, we have been moving from ownership to access—personally owning your own CD vs. accessing numerous songs for listening—and from purchase to consumption, or purchasing a CD to hearing and seeing the act online.

The creative aspect of writing and recording songs has been changed through digital technology; today, many songs are written on a computer and recorded "in the box" with no live musicians performing. There are drums but no drummer, guitars but no guitar players and strings but no violins. Pop songs are not "written" but are built, adding pieces to the production until a full recording emerges.

There are no gatekeepers keeping out creative works; the audience is an active participant and there is a proliferation of recording artists, filmmakers and writers releasing their work through digital distribution. It is estimated that every 12 months there are eight million songs, two million books, 16,000 films, 30 million blog posts, 182 billion tweets and 400,000 new products presented to the world. However, distribution is not marketing so many of these offerings go unheard, unseen and unnoticed.

We have become "screen agers," using the screens on our cellphones, notebooks and computers to receive information. Outside our homes, there are screens at concerts, screens at airports and screens on highways that give us information or provide a better view. Even billboards now are often "screens."

We live in a "flowing" world; songs, films, TV shows and information flows to us and we can share it with our family and friends by directing it to flow to them. The culture of sharing allows each of us to benefit and benefit others by sending and receiving interesting new songs, films, clips or articles.

The major drawback of the digital world is the loss of privacy; major companies compile profiles on each of us using information from Facebook, Google, Amazon and Apple as well as cell phones, email, texting, tweets and retail purchases. For the most part, we have found it comfortable to reveal ourselves digitally, and marketing companies have gained a huge advantage in marketing their products to us based on digital profiles, but there is a dark side as well.

In the national and international worlds, we have knocked down barriers with technology and connected across the globe, but governments have had to deal with the fact that the computer is the new Atomic Bomb. An Atomic Bomb can wipe out hundreds of thousands of people but the computer can take down whole companies, infrastructures and nations. Hackers have already shown us how they can influence elections, undermine democracy, disrupt economies and wreak havoc on a variety of levels.

No one can imagine the future; no one traveling in a covered wagon pulled by horses or oxen on the Oregon trail during the 1800s imagined driving across the country in an air-conditioned car while listening to the radio, or music streaming from satellites into a car's stereo speaker. They could not imagine digital maps, weather forecasts, a GPS to guide them or calling or texting back home on cell phones to friends and family to let them know how things were going as they crossed the country.

This book cannot tell you what the future recording industry will be but, hopefully, it will tell you how it began, developed and arrived at where it is today.

ACKNOWLEDGMENTS

I am indebted to Mike Curb and the Mike Curb Family Foundation for supporting this, and other projects, I do.

BIBLIOGRAPHY

"4,500 Are Pouring Into WSM's Giant Spread." Billboard, Pctpber 22. 1966.

Abbott, Lynn and Doug Seroff. *Out of Sight: The Rise of African American Popular Music 1889-1895*. Jackson: University Press of Mississippi, 2002.

Abbott, Lynn and Doug Seroff. *Ragged But Right: Black Traveling Shows, "Coon Songs," and the Dark Pathway to Blues and Jazz*. Jackson: University Press of Mississippi, 2007

Adams, Frank. Wurlitzer Jukeboxes and Other Nice Things. Seattle, Wash: ARM Pub. Co, 1983.

Albertson, Chris. *Bessie*. New York: Stein & Day, 1972.

Ambrose, Stephen E. *Eisenhower: Soldier and President.* New York: Touchstone, 1990.

Amburn, Ellis. *Buddy Holly: A Biography*. New York: St. Martin's Press, 1995.

Amburn, Ellis. *Dark Star: The Roy Orbison Story*. New York: A Lyle Stuart Book published by Carol Publishing Group, 1990.

"America's Jukebox Craze: Coin Phonographs Reap Harvest of Hot Tunes and Nickels," Newsweek XV 23, June 3, 1940.

"America's Jukebox Craze: Coin Phonographs Reap Harvest of Hot Tunes and Nickels," Newsweek XV 23 (June 3, 1940)

Anderson, Bill. *I Hope You're Living As High On the Hog as the Pig You Turned Out To Be*. Hermitage, TN: TWI, Inc, 1994

Anderson, Bill. Whisperin' Bill: *An Autobiography: A Life of Music, Love, Tragedy and Triumph*. Atlanta: Longstreet Press, 1989.

Anderson, Omer. "Army Drops Bomb on 'Protests'" Billboard, January 15, 1966.

Antrim, Doron K. "Whoop-And-Holler Opera." Collier's, January 26, 1946. Vol 117, No. 4.

Appalachia on Our Mind: *The Southern Mountains and Mountaineers in the American Consciousness, 1870-1920*. Chapel Hill: University of North Carolina Press, 1978.

Arnold, Eddy. *It's a Long Way From Chester County*. Old Tappan, N.J.: Hewitt House, 1969.

Atkins, Chet with Bill Neely. *Country Gentleman*. Chicago: Henry Regnery Company, 1974.

Atkins, Chet. *Me and My Guitars*. Milwaukee: Hal Leonard, 2001, 2004.

Autry, Gene with Mickey Herskowitz. *Back in the Saddle Again*. Garden City, N.Y.: Doubleday, 1976.

Ayers, Edward L. *The Promise of the New South: Life After Reconstruction*. New York: Oxford University Press, 1993.

Babiuk, Andy. *Beatles Gear*. Milwaukee: Backbeat Books, 2001, 2002.

Babiuk, Andy. *The Story of Paul Bigsby: Father of the Modern Electric Solidbody Guitar*. Savannah, GA: FG Publishing, 2008.

Bacon, Tony. *50 Years of Gretsch Electrics*. New York: Backbeat Books, 2005.

Bacon, Tony. *The Fender Electric Guitar Book: A Complete History of Fender Instruments*. New York: Backbeat, 1992, 1998, 2007.

Bacon, Tony. *The History of the American Guitar: From 1833 to the Present Day*. New York: Outline Press, Ltd, 2001.

Badger, Reid. *A Life in Ragtime: A Biography of James Reese Europe*. New York: Oxford University Press, 1995,

Baker, Houston. "Hybridity, the Rap Race, and Pedagogy for the 1990s." *Black Music Research Journal* 11, Fall 1991.

Baker, Missy. "RCA's Studio B: Memories of Little Victor." *Mix*, March 1990.

Baldwin, Neil. *Edison: Inventing the Century*. New York: Hyperion, 1995.

Barfield, Ray. *Listening to Radio 1920-1950*. Westport, Conn.: Praeger, 1996.

Barlow, William. *Looking Up at Down: The Emergence of Blues Culture*. Philadelphia: Temple University Press, 1989.

Barnouw, Eric. *The Golden Web: A History of Broadcasting in the United States, Volume II: 1933-1953* New York: Oxford University Press, 1968.

Barnouw, Erik. *A Tower of Babel: A History of Broadcasting in the United States: Volume I: to 1933*. New York: Oxford University Press, 1966.

Barnouw, Erik. *The Image Empire: A History of Broadcasting in the United States: Vol. III: from 1953*. New York: Oxford University Press, 1970.

Barrios, Richard. *A Song in the Dark: The Birth of the Musical Film*. New York: Oxford University Press, 1995

Bart, Peter. *Fade Out: The Calamitous Final Days of MGM*. New York: William Morrow and Company, 1990.

Barth, Gunther. *City People: The Rise of Modern City Culture in Nineteenth-Century America*. New York: Oxford University Press, 1980.

Basie, Count as told to Albert Murray. *Good Morning Blues: The Autobiography of Count Basie*. New York: Random House, 1985.

Bastin, Bruce. *Red River Blues: The Blues Tradition in the Southeast*. Urbana: University of Illinois Press, 1986.

Bauer, Marion and Ethel Peyser. *How Music Grew: From the Prehistoric Times to the Present Day*. New York: G.P. Putnam's Sons, 1928.

Beatles, The. *Anthology*. San Francisco: Chronicle Books, 2000.

Bentinck, Henry. The Nation's Barn Dance. *Radio Guide*, Vol IV, Number 2. November 11, 1934.

Bergreen, Laurence. *As Thousands Cheer: The Life of Irving Berlin*. New York: Viking, 1990.

Bergreen, Laurence. *Capone: The Man and the Era*. New York: Touchstone/Simon & Schuster, 1994.

Bergreen, Laurence. *Louis Armstrong: An Extravagant Life*. New York: Broadway Books, 1997.

Berliner, Paul F. *Thinking in Jazz: The Infinite Art of Improvisation*. Chicago: University of Chicago Press, 1994.

Berry, Chad, ed. *The Hayloft Gang: The Story of the National Barn Dance*. Urbana: University of Illinois Press, 2008.

Berry, Chuck. The Autobiography. New York: Harmony, 1997.

Bertrand, Michael T. *Race, Rock, and Elvis*. Urbana and Chicago: University of Illinois Press, 2005.

Bloom, Allen. *The Closing of the American Mind*. New York: Simon & Schuster, 1987.

Blydstone, Richard. "About That Rug On Your Neck, Pal," A.P. *Nashville Banner*, July 5, 1970.

Bond, Johnny. *Reflections: The Autobiography of Johnny Bond*. Los Angeles, CA: The John Edwards Memorial Foundation, 1976.

Boorstin, Daniel. The Americans: The Democratic Experience (New York: Vintage Books, 1974.

Bowen, Jimmy with Jim Jerome. *Rough Mix: An Unapologetic Look at the Music Business and How It Got That Way--A Lifetime in the World of Rock, Pop, and Country as Told by One of the Industry's Most Powerful Players*. New York: Simon and Schuster, 1997.

Boyer, Horace Clarence (text) and Lloyd Yearwood (photography) *How Sweet the Sound: The Golden Age of Gospel*. Washington, D.C.: Elliott & Clark Publishing, 1995.

Bradford, Perry. *Born with the Blues: Perry Bradford's Own Story*. (New York: Oak Publications, 1965).

Branch, Taylor. *Parting the Waters: American in the King Years 1954-1963*. New York: Simon and Schuster, 1988.

Breighaupt, Don and Jeff Breithaupt. *Precious and Few: Pop Music in the Early '70s*. New York: St. Martin's Press, 1996.

Bronson, Fred. *The Billboard Book of Number One Hits: The Inside Story Behind the Top of the Charts*. New York: Billboard Publications, 1985.

Brooks, Tim and Earle Marsh. *The Complete Directory to Prime Time Network and Cable TV Shows 1946-Present*. New York: Ballantine Books, 1978, 1981, 1985, 1988, 1992, 1995, 2003.

Brooks, Tim. "Columbia Records in the 1890s: Founding the Record Industry" in *Association for Recorded Sound Collectors Journal* 10, 1978

Brooks, Tim. *Lost Sounds: Blacks and the Birth of the Recording Industry, 1890-1919*. Urbana and Chicago: University of Illinois Press, 2004

Broonzy, William and Yannick Bruynoghe. *Big Bill Blues: William Broonzy's Story*. London: Cassell & Co. 1955.

Broven, John. *Record Makers and Breakers: Voices of the Independent Rock'n'Roll Pioneers*. Urbana: University of Illinois Press, 2009.

Browne, David. *Fire and Rain: The Beatles, Simon & Garfunkel, James Taylor, CSNY and the Lost Story of 1970*. New York: Da Cappo Press, 2011.

Buckley, William. "Long Hair: A Symbol of the Exhibitionist," *Nashville Banner*, July 1, 1970.

"Bull Market in Corn." Time October 4, 1943. Vol 42, No. 14.

Burke, Ken and Dan Griffin. *The Blue Moon Boys: The Story of Elvis Presley's Band*. Chicago: Chicago Review Press, 2006.

Burt, Jesse C. *Nashville: Its Life and Times*. Nashville: Tennessee Book Co., 1959.

Burton, David. H. *Theodore Roosevelt*. New York: Twayne Publishers, Inc. 1972.

Burton, Thomas G. *Folksongs*. New York: Holt, Rinehart and Winston, 1984.

Buscombe, Richard. *The BFI Companion to the Western*. New York: Atheneum, 1988.

Bush, William J. *Greenback Dollar: The Incredible Rise of the Kingston Trio*. Lanham, Maryland: The Scarecrow Press, Inc., 2013.

Byworth, Tony. *The History of Country & Western Music*. New York: Exeter Books, 1984.

Campbell, Glen with Tom Carter. *Rhinestone Cowboy: An Autobiography*. New York: Villard Books, 1994.

Cantor, Louis. *Dewey and Elvis: The Life and Times of a Rock'n'Roll DeeJay*. Urbana and Chicago: University of Illinois Press, 2005.

Carman, Bob and Dan Scapperotti. *Roy Rogers: King of the Cowboys: A Film Guide*. Privately published, 1970 and 2000.

Carr, Patrick, ed. *The Illustrated History of Country Music*. New York: Dolphin, 1980.

Carter, Walter. *Gibson Guitars: 100 Years of an American Icon*. Nashville: Gibson Publishing, 1994.

Carter, Walter. *The Gibson Electric Guitar Book: Seventy Years of Classic Guitars*. New York: Backbeat Books, 2007.

"CARTridge Takes Play At Biggest NARM Parley." *Billboard*, March 19, 1966.

Casdorph, Paul D. *Let the Good Times Roll: Life at Home in America During WWII*. New York: Paragon House, 1989.

Cash, Johnny with Patrick Carr. *Cash: The Autobiography*. New York: HarperCollins, 1997.

Cash, Johnny. *Man in Black*. Grand Rapids, Michigan: Zondervan, 1975.

Castleman, Harry and Walter J. Podrazik. *All Together Now: The First Complete Beatles Discography 1961-1975*. New York: Ballantine, 1975.

Chanan, Michael. *Repeated takes: A Short History of Recording and Its Effects on Music.* London: Verso, 1995.

Chapman, Richard. *Guitar: Music, History, Players.* New York: Dorling Kindersley, 2000.

Charters, Samuel B. *The Country Blues.* New York: Rinehart & Co., 1959.

Churchill, Allen. "Tin Pan Alley's Git-Tar Blues." New York Times Magazine, July 15, 1951. Sec. 6.

Clark, Roy with Marc Eliot. *My Life: In Spite of Myself!* New York: Simon and Schuster, 1994

Clayson, Alan. *George Harrison.* London: MPG Books, 1996, 2003

Clayson, Alan. *John Lennon.* London: MPG Books, 2003

Clayson, Alan. *Paul McCartney.* London: MPG Books, 2003

Clayson, Alan. *Ringo Starr.* London: MPG Books, 1996, 2003.

Clayson, Alan. *The Quiet One: A Life of George Harrison.* Sanctuary, 1999 paper

Coffey, Frank. *Always Home: 50 Years of The USO.* Washington: Brassey's, a division of Maxwell Macmillan, Inc., 1991.

Cohadas, Nadine. *Spinning Blues Into Gold: The Chess Brothers and the Legendary Chess Records.* New York: St. Martin's Press, 2000.

Cohen, Norm. "I'm a Record Man: Uncle Art Reminisces" John Edwards Memorial Foundation Quarterly (1972)

Cohen, Norm. "The Skilet Lickers: A Study of a Hillbilly String Band and Its Repertoire" Journal of American Folklore 78 1965 229-44.

Cohen, Ronald and Rachel Clare Donaldson. *Roots of the Revival: American & British Folk Music in the 1950s.* Urbana: University of Illinois Press, 2014.

Cohn, Lawrence. *Nothing But the Blues: The Music and the Musicians.* New York: Abbeville Press, 1993.

Coleman, Mark. *Playback: From the Victrola to MP3, 100 Years of Music, Machines, and Money.* New York: Da Capo Press, 2003.

Collar, Douglas E. "Hello Posterity: The Life and Times of G. Robert Vincent, Founder of the National Voice Library" Ph.D. dissertation Michigan State U 1988.

Collier, James Lincoln. *Benny Goodman and the Swing Era.* New York: Oxford University Press, 1989.

Collier, James Lincoln. *Duke Ellington.* New York: Oxford University Press, 1987.

Conot, Robert. *A Streak of Luck.* New York: Seaview Books, 1979.

Coontz, Stephanie. *The Way We Never Were: American Families and the Nostalgia Trap.* New York: Basic, 1992.

Coontz, Stephanie. *The Way We Really Are.* New York: Basic, 1997.

Cooper, Peter. "How a happy accident revolutionized guitar sound." *Nashville Tennessean,* August 4, 2013

Cooper, Peter. "Music erases all differences for Daniels: Legend embraces past with Bob Dylan in new album. *The Nashville Tennessean,* March 30, 2014, 7E, 8E.

"Corn of Plenty." *Newsweek.* June 13, 1949. Vol 33, No. 24.

Cornyn, Stan with Paul Scanlon. *Exploding: The Highs, Hits, Hype, Heroes, and Hustlers of the Warner Music Group.* New York: HarperEntertainment, a Rolling Stone Press book. 2002.

"Country Music Goes to Town," Mademoiselle, April, 1948.

"Country Music is Big Business, and Nashville is its Detroit." Newsweek, August 11, 1952. Vol 40, No. 6.

"Country Music Snaps Its Regional Bounds." Business Week. March 19, 1966. No. 1907.

"Country Music: The Nashville Sound." *Time,* November 17, 1964. Vol 84, No. 22.

"Country Musicians Fiddle Up Roaring Business." *Life,* November 19, 1956. Vol 41, No. 21

Crafton, Donald. *The Talkies: American Cinema's Transition to Sound, 1926-1931*. New York: Scribner's, 1996.

Cray, Ed. *Ramblin' Man: the Life and Times of Woody Guthrie*. New York: W.W. Norton & Company, 2004.

Crosby, Bing as told to Pete Martin. Call Me Lucky. New York: SImon & Schuster, 1953.

Crowell, Thomas Y. *Stephen Foster, America's Troubadour*. New York: Thomas Y. Crowell Co., 1934, 1953.

Crumbaker, Marge and Gabe Tucker. *Up and Down With Elvis Presley*. New York: G.P. Putnam's Sons, 1981.

Curb, Mike with Don Cusic. *Living the Business*. Nashville: Brackish Publishing, 2017.

Cusic, Don. "Ray Whitley" in *The Cowboy in Country Music*, ed Don Cusic, p. 51-52.

Cusic, Don. "The Beatles and Country Music" in *International Journal of Country Music*, New York: Brackish, 2014.

Cusic, Don. *Discovering Country Music*. Westport, CT: Praeger, 2008.

Cusic, Don. *Eddy Arnold: I'll Hold You In My Heart*. Nashville: Rutledge Hill, 1997.

Cusic, Don. *Elvis in Nashville*. Nashville: Brackish, 2012.

Cusic, Don. *Gene Autry: His Life and Career*. Jefferson, N.C.: McFarland, 2007.

Cusic, Don. *It's the Cowboy Way!: The Amazing True Adventures of Riders In The Sky*. Lexington: University Press of Kentucky, 2003.

Cusic, Don. *Roger Miller: Dang Him!* Nashville: Brackish, 2012.

Cusic. Don. "Guitars, Cowboys and Country Music" in *The Cowboy In Country Music: An Historical Survey with Artist Profiles*. Jefferson, N.C.: McFarland and Company, 2011.

Cusic. Don. *The Cowboy In Country Music: An Historical Survey with Artist Profiles*. Jefferson, N.C.: McFarland and Company, 2011.

Czitrom, Daniel J. *Media and the American Mind from Morse to McLuhan*. Chapel Hill: University of North Carolina Press, 1982.

"D.J. Parley Ends Tonight At Opry." *Nashville Banner*, November 10, 1956.

D'Ambrosio, Antonino. *A Heartbeat and a Guitar: Johnny Cash and the Making of Bitter Tears*. New York: Nation Books, 2009.

Daniel, Wayne W. *Pickin' on Peachtree: A History of Country Music in Atlanta, Georgia*. Urbana: University of Illinois Press, 1990.

Dannen, Frederic. *Hit Men: Power Brokers and Fast Money Inside the Music Business*. New York: Random House/Times Books, 1990.

Daughtrey, Larry. "King of Grammys Says Wit Not All." Nashville *Tennessean*, April 15, 1965.

Davies, Hunter, ed. *The Beatles Lyrics*. New York: Little, Brown & Co. 2014.

Davies, Hunter. *The Beatles: The Authorized Biography Updated*. New York: W.W. Norton and Company, 1968, 1978, 1985, 2002, 2009.

Davis, Clive with Anthony DeCurtis. *The Soundtrack of My Life*. New York: Simon and Schuster, 2012

Davis, Francis. *The History of the Blues: The Roots, the Music, The People From Charley Patton to Robert Cray*. New York: Hyperion, 1995.

Davis, Louise Littleton. *Nashville Tales*. Gretna, GA: Pelica, 1982.

Davis, Ronald. L. Duke: The Life and Image of John Wayne. Norman: University of Oklahoma Press, 1998.

Day, Donald. *Will Rogers: A Biography*. New York: David McKay Company, 1962.

Dean, Jimmy and Donna Meade Dean. *Thirty Years of Sausage, Fifty Years of Ham: Jimmy Dean's Own Story*. New York: Berkley Books, 2004

Dearling, Robert and Celia with Brian Rust. *The Guiness Book of Recorded Sound*. Middlesex: Guiness Books, 1984.

Dellar, Fred and Roy Thompson. *The Illustrated Encyclopedia of Country Music*. New York: Harmony 1977.

DeLong, Thomas A. *Pops: Paul Whiteman: King of Jazz*. Piscataway, N.J.: New Century, 1983.

Demain, Bill. "When We Was Fab: Nashvillians remember Paul McCartney and Wings' working vacation here in 1974." *Nashville Scene*, April 18, 2002.

Denisoff, R. Serge. *Inside MTV*. New Brunswick, Transaction Publishers 1988, 1991.

Denisoff, Serge. "Massification and Popular Music," Journal of Popular Culture 9 (Spring, 1976) 881-88.

Dennison, Sam. *Scandalize My Name: Black Imagery in American Popular Music*. New York: Garland, 1982.

Deveaux, Scott. *The Birth of Bebop: A Social and Musical History*. Berkeley: University of California Press, 1997

Dick, Bernard F. *The Merchant Prince of Poverty Row: Harry Cohn of Columbia Pictures*. Lexington: University Press of Kentucky, 1993.

Diekman, Diane. *Live Fast Love Hard: The Faron Young Story*. Urbana: University of Illinois Press, 2007.

Dixon, Robert M. W. and John Goodrich. *Recording the Blues*. New York: Stein & Day, 1970.

Dixon, Willie and Don Snowden. *I Am the Blues: The Willie Dixon Story*. New York: Da Capo, 1989.

Doherty, Thomas. *Pre-Code Hollywood: Sex, Immorality, and Insurrection in American Cinema 1930-1934*. New York: Columbia University Press, 1999.

Douglas, Susan. *Inventing American Broadcasting, 1899-1922*. Baltimore: Johns Hopkins University Press, 1987.

Doyle, Don C. *New Men, New Cities, New South: Atlanta, Nashville, Charleston, Mobile, 1860-1910*.Chapel Hill: University of North Carolina Press, 1990.

Doyle, Don H. *Nashville Since the 1920s*. Knoxville: The University of Tennessee Press, 1985.

Duff, Morris. "Make Way for the Country Sound." Toronto Daily Star March 21, 1964. Section 2: pp 23-24.

Dumenil, Lynn. *Modern Temper: American Culture and Society in the 1920s*. New York: Hill and Wang, 1995.

Dunning, John. *On the Air: The Encyclopedia of Old-Time Radio*. New York: Oxford University Press, 1998.

Dunson, John and Ethel Raim Seeger, eds. *Anthology of American Folk Music*. New York: Oak Publications 1973.

Dylan, Bob. *Chronicles, Volume One*. New York: Simon & Schuster, 2004.

Dyson, Michael Eric. *Between God and Gangsta Rap: Bearing Witness to Black Culture*. New York: Oxford U.P., 1996 e, 1976.

Eberly, Philip K. *Music in the Air: America's Changing Tastes in Popular Music, 1920-1980*. New York: Hastings House, 1982.

Eddy, Don. "Hillbilly Heaven." *American Magazine*, March, 1952. Vol 153, No. 3.

Edwards, Leigh H. *Johnny Cash and the Paradox of American Identity*. Bloomington: Indiana University Press, 2009.

Eipper, Laura and Alice Alexander. "Rock'n'Roll King's Death Touches Music Community." Sub- head "Poor Health Rumors Seemingly Founded." *Nashville Tennessean*, August 17, 1977, p. 1, 6

Eipper, Laura. "Fans Create Tumultuous Elvis Scene." Nashville, *Tennessean*, Thursday, August 18, 1977. p 1, 10

Eisenberg, Evan. *The Recording Angel: Explorations in Phonography*. (New York: McGraw Hill, 1987).

"Elvis' Death at 42 Called Heart Attack; No Drugs Found." from Wire Reports. Nashville *Tennessean*, August 17, 1977.

"Elvis Signs Out, Draws Pay Today. Nashville *Tennessean*. March 5, 1960.

Ely, Melvin Patrick. *The Adventures of Amos'N'Andy: A Social History of an American Phenomenon*. New York: The Free Press, 1991.

Emerick, Geoff with Howard Massey. *Here, There and Everywhere: My Life Recording the Music of the Beatles*. New York: Gotham Books, 2006.

Emerson From: *Always Magic in the Air: The Bomp and Brilliance of the Brill Building Era* by Ken Emerson. New York: Viking, 2005.

Ennis, Philip H. *The Seventh Stream: The Emergence of Rock'n'roll in American Popular Music* Hanover, N.H.: Wesleyan U P 1992.

Erenberg, Lewis A. and Susan E. Hirsch, eds *The War in American Culture: Society & Consciousness During World War II*. Chicago: University of Chicago Press, 1996.

Erenberg, Lewis A. *Steppin' Out: New York Nightlife and the Transformation of American Culture, 1890-1930*. Chicago: University of Chicago Press, 1981.

Erenberg, Lewis A. *Swingin' the Dream: Big Band Jazz and the Rebirth of American Culture*. University. of Chicago Press.

Escott, Colin with George Merritt and William MacEwen. *Hank Williams: The Biography*. Boston: Little, Brown, 1994.

Escott, Colin with Martin Hawkins. *Good Rockin' Tonight: Sun Records and the Birth of Rock'n'Roll*. New York: St. Martin's Press, 1991.

Escott, Colin. "Inside Starday Records: A Conversation with Don Pierce." *Journal of Country Music*, Vol 17, No. 1. 1994.

Evans, James. *Prairie Farmer and W.L.S.: The Burridge D. Butler Years*. Urbana: University of Illinois Press, 1969.

Evans, Steve and Ron Middlebrook. *Cowboy Guitars*. Jacksonville, Arkansas: Centerstream, Publishing, 2009.

Farr, Jory. *Moguls and Madmen: The Pursuit of Power in Popular Music*. New York: Simon & Schuster, 1994.

Feather, Leonard. *The Jazz Years: Earwitness to an Era*. New York: Da Capo, 1987.

Fife, Austin E. and Alton S. *Cowboy and Western Songs: A Comprehensive Anthology*. New York: Clarkson N. Potter, 1969.

Fife, Austin E. and Alton S. *Heaven on Horseback: Revivalist Songs and Verse in the Cowboy Idiom*. Logan: Utah State University Press, 1970.

Finler, Joel W. *The Hollywood Story*. New York: Crown, 1988.

Fischer, Claude S. *America Calling: A Social History of the Telephone to 1940*. Berkeley: U of California P 1992.

Flink, James. *The Car Culture*. Cambridge, MIT Press, 1975.

Floyd, Samuel A. Jr. *The Power of Black Music: Interpreting Its History From Africa to the United States*. New York: Oxford University Press, 1995.

Fong-Torres, Ben. *The Hits Just Keep On Coming: The History of Top 40 Radio*. San Francisco: Miller Freeman Books, 1998,

"For Americans It's Music, Music And More Music, Says BMI Report." Billboard, December 24,1966.

Forbes, Camille F. *Introducing Bert Williams: Burnt Cork, Broadway, and the Story of America's First Black Star*. New York: Basic Books, 2008.

Forman, Murray. "Represent': race, space and place in rap music." Popular Music 19:1 (2000)

"Fort Knox No Longer Has Exclusive On Pot of Gold; WSM, Nashville, Talent Corners a Good CHunk of It," Variety, Oct 26, 1949:

"Frank B. Walker: Disk Biz Pioneer, Dies in L.I at 73" (Variety (Oct. 23, 1963).

Freidel, Frank. *Franklin D. Roosevelt: A Rendezvous with Destiny*. Boston: Little, Brown, 1990.

Friedlander, Paul. *Rock and Roll: A Social History*. Boulder, COL: Westview Press, Inc 1996.

Friskics-Warren, Bill. "Kris Kristofferson: To Beat the Devil: Intimation of Immortality." *No Depression*. March-April.

Fritchey, Clayton. "Number 1 Problem' Doesn't Make Sense, *Nashville Banner,* June 26, 1970.

Frith, Simon and Andrew Goodwin eds. *On Record: Rock, Pop, and the Written Word.* New York: Pantheon Books, 1990.

Gaisberg, F. W. *The Music Goes Round.* New York: Macmillan, 1942.

Gallup, George. "War Disillusionment Is High," *Nashville Banner,* June 28, 1970.

Gans, Herbert. *Popular Culture and High Culture.* New York: Basic Books, 1974.

Gelatt, Roland. *The Fabulous Phonograph: From Tin Foil to High Fidelity.* Philadelphia: J.B. Lippincott Co. 1954, 1955.

Gentry, Linnell. *A History and Encyclopedia of Country, Western, and Gospel Music.* Nashville: Clairmont, 1969.

George, Nelson. *The Death of Rhythm and Blues.* New York: Pantheon, 1988.

George-Warren, Holly. *Public Cowboy No. 1: The Life and Times of Gene Autry.* New York: Oxford University Press, 2007.

"Georgia Pop Festival Blares 'Disgrace' Note. Nashville Banner, July 6, 1970.

Ghianni, Tim. "Me and Kris: time-traveling with a legend on Music Row." The *Nashville Tennessean.* December 12, 2003

Ghianni, Tim. Nashville Starr: When Ringo Came to Town. *Nashville Scene,* July 3, 2008.

Giddens, Gary. *A Pocketful of Dreams: Bing Crosby: The Early Years 1903-1940.* Boston: Little, Brown, 2001.

Giulano, Geoffrey. *Dark Horse: The Life and Art of George Harrison.* New York: DaCapo Press, 1997.

Glatt, John. *Rage & Roll: Bill Graham and the Selling of Rock.* New York: Birch Lane, 1993.

Gleason, Ralph. "Eddy's the Man Who Helped Bring The Country Song to the Big Town." *San Francisco Chronicle.* July 15, 1951.

"Gold Guitars, The." Newsweek. April 4, 1966. Vol 67, No. 4.

Goldman, Herbert G. *Jolson: The Legend Comes to Life* (New York: Oxford, 1988). XXXX

Goldstein, Norm. *The History of Television.* New York: Portland House, 1991.

Goodman, Benny and Irving Kolodin. *The Kingdom of Swing.* New York: Frederick Ungar, 1939.

Goodman, Fred. *The Mansion on the Hill: Dylan, Young, Geffen, Springsteen, and the Head-on Collison of Rock and Commerce.* New York: Times Books, 1997.

Goodwin, Doris Kearns. *No Ordinary Time: Franklin and Eleanor Roosevelt: The Home Front in World War II.* New York: Touchstone, 1994.

Gordon, Roxy. "Partly Truth and Partly Fiction: A pilgrim's perspective on Kris Kristofferson." *No Depression,* November-December, 1999.

Gordy, Berry. *To Be Loved: The Music, the Magic, the Memories of Motown: An Autobiography.* New York: Warner Books, 1994.

Gould, Jonathan. *Can't Buy Me Love: The Beatles, Britain, and America.* New York: Harmony Books, 2007.

Graebner, William S. *The Age of Doubt: American Thought and Culture in the 1940s.* Boston: Twyane, 1991.

Graham, Bill with Robert Greenfield. *Bill Graham Presents: My Life Inside Rock and Out.* New York: Doubleday, 1992.

Green, Archie. "Hillbillky Music: SOurce and Symbol" *Journal of American Folklore.* 1965

Green, Douglas B. "Gene Autry" in *Stars of Country Music,* Bill C. Malone and Judith McCulloh, eds. Urbana: University of Illinois Press, 1975.

Green, Douglas B. *Country Roots: The Origins of Country Music.* New York: Hawthorn, 1976

Green, Douglas B. *Singing Cowboys.* Salt Lake City: Gibbs-Smith, 2006

Green, Douglas B. *Singing in the Saddle: The History of the Singing Cowboy*. Nashville: The Country Music Foundation Press and Vanderbilt University Press, 2002.

Greene, Joshua. *Here Comes the Sun: The Spiritual and Musical Journey of George Harrison*. Hoboken, N.J.: John Wiley & Sons, 2006.

Greenfeld, Howard. *Caruso*. New York: G.P. Putnam's Sons, 1983.

Griffis, Ken. *Hear My Song: The Story of the Celebrated Sons of the Pioneers*, Northglenn, Colorado: Norken, 2001.

Grossman, Gary H. *Saturday Morning TV: Thirty Years of the Shows You Waited All Week to Watch*. New Rochelle, N.Y.: Arlington House, 1981.

Grossman, James R. *Land of Hope: Chicago, Black Southerners, and the Great Migration*. Chicago: University of Chicago Press, 1989).

Gruhn, George and Walter Carter. "Gibson Super 400." *Vintage Guitar* magazine, September 16, 2009.

Guralnick, Peter and Ernst Jorgensen. *Elvis: Day By Day: The Definitive Record of His Life and Music*. New York: Ballantine, 1999.

Guralnick, Peter. *Careless Love: The Unmaking of Elvis Presley*. Boston and New York: Back Bay Books, 1999.

Guralnick, Peter. *Feel Like Going Home: Portraits in Blues and Rockn'n'Roll*. New York: Vintage, 1981.

Guralnick, Peter. *Last Train to Memphis: The Rise of Elvis Presley*. Boston: Back Bay Books, 1994.

Guralnick, Peter. *Lost Highway: Journeys & Arrivals of American Musicians*. Boston: David R. Godine, Publisher, 1979.

Guralnick, Peter. *Sam Phillips: The Man Who Invented Rock'n'Roll*. New York: Little, Brown and Company, 2015.

Guralnick, Peter. *Sweet Soul Music: Rhythm and Blues and the Southern Dream of Freedom*. New York: Harper & Row, 1986.

Haden, Walter Darrell. "Early Pioneers" in *Stars of Country Music*, Bill C. Malone and Judith McCulloh, eds. Urbana: University of Illinois Press, 1975.

Hagen, Chet. *Grand Ole Opry: The Complete Story of a Great American Institution and Its Stars*. New York: Owl, 1989

Hajdu, David. *Positively 4th Street: The Lives and Times of Joan Baez, Bob Dylan, Mimi Baez Farina, and Richard Farina*. New York: Farrar, Straus & Giroux 328 pp $25

Halberstadt, Alex. *Lonely Avenue: The Unlikely Life & Times of Doc Pomus*. New York: Da Capo Press, 2007.

Halberstam, David. *The Fifties*. (New York: Villard, 1993).

Hall, Claude. "Country Television Programs Enjoying Coast-to-Coast Hayride." *Billboard*, November 13, 1965.

Hall, Wade. *Hell Bent For Music: Pee Wee King*. Lexington: University of Kentucky Press, 1996.

Hamm, Charles. *Yesterdays: Popular Song in America*. New York: W. W. Norton, 1979.

Hammond, John with Irving Townsend. *John Hammond On Record*. New York: Sumit Books, 1977.

Handy, W. C. *Father of the Blues: AN Autobiography*. New York: Macmillan, 1941.

Harbaugh, William H. *The Life and Times of Theodore Roosevelt*. New York: Oxford University Press, 1975.

Hardy, Phil and Dave Laing, eds. *The Faber Companion to 20th Century Popular Music*. London: Faber and Faber, 1990.

Haring, Bruce. *Off the Charts: Ruthless Days and Reckless Nights Inside the Music Industry*. New York: Birch Lane, 1996.

Harries, Meirion and Susie. *The Last Days of Innocence: America at War, 1917-1918*. New York: Random House, 1997.

Harris, Michael. *The Rise of Gospel Blues: The Music of Thomas Andrew Dorsey in the Urban Church*, New York: Oxford University Press.

Harris, Roy. "Folk Songs." *House & Garden,* December, 1954. Vol 106, No. 6.

Harrison, George. *I, Me, Mine.* San Francisco: Chronicle Books, 1980, 2002.

Harrison, Nigel. *Songwriters: A Biographical Dictionary with Discographies.* Jefferson, N.C.: McFarland & Company, Inc. 1998.

Harrison, Olivia. *Living in the Material World.* New York: Abrams, 2011.

Hartman, Kent. *The Wrecking Crew: The Inside Story of Rock and Roll's Best-Kept Secret.* New York: St. Martin's Press, 2012.

Harvith, John and Susan Edwards Harvith. *Edison, Musicians, and the Phonograph.* New York: Greenwood Press, 1987.

Haslam, Gerald W. *Workin' Man Blues: Country Music in California.* Berkeley and Los Angeles: University of California Press, 1999.

Hemming, Roy. *The Melody Lingers On: The Great Songwriters and Their Movie Musicals.* New York: Newmarket Press, 1986.

Hemphill, Paul. "Kris Kristofferson is the New Nashville Sound." *New York Times,* December 6, 1970.

Hemphill, Paul. *The Nashville Sound: Bright Lights and Country Music.* New York: Simon and Schuster, 1970.

Hertsgaard, Mark. *A Day in the Life: The Music and Artistry of the Beatles.* New York: Delacorte Press.

Hilburn, Robert. *Johnny Cash: The Life.* Boston: Little, Brown and Company, 2013.

Hilmes, Michele. *Radio Voices: American Broadcasting, 1922-1952.* University of Minnesota Press.

Hitchcock, H. Wiley and Stanley Sadie, eds. *New Grove Dictionary of American Music.* London: Macmillan, 1986.

"Hoedown on a Harpsichord." *Time.* November 14, 1960. Vol 76, No. 20

Horstman, Dorothy. *Sing Your Heart Out, Country Boy.* New York: E.P. Dutton & Co., Inc., 1975.

Hoskyns, Barney. *Hotel California: The true-life adventures of Crosby, Still, Nash, Young, Mitchell, Taylor, Browne, Ronstadt, Geffen, the Eagles and their many friends.* Hoboken, N.J.: John Wiley & Sons, 2006.

Howlett, Kevin. *The Beatles: The BBC Archives: 1962-1970.* New York: Harper Design, 2013.

Huggins, Nathan Irvin. *Harlem Renaissance.* New York: Oxford University Press, 1971.

Hurst, Richard Maurice. *Republic Studios: Between Poverty Row and the Majors.* Metuchen, N.J.: Scarecrow Press, 1979.

Hyams, Jay. *The Life and Times of the Western Movie.* New York: Gallery, 1983

Hyland, William G. *The Song is Ended: Songwriters and American Music, 1900-1950.* New York: Oxford University Press.

"It Is Time For Us Americans To Check our Stitches,' Graham Says." *Nashville Banner,* July 6, 1970.

Ivey, Bill "The Bottom Line: Business Practices That Shaped Country Music." in *Country: The Music and the Musicians.* New York: Abbeville Press, 1988.

"Jack Kapp, Headed Decca Records, 47" *New York Times* Mar 26, 1949.

"Jack Kapp, Reasons for Popularity of Certain Selections and Their Effect on Sales" TMW XIX 3 (Mar 1923)

"Jack Kapp, Symbol of Americanism, Plugged in Congressional Record" *Variety.* Mar 30, 1949.

Jackson, John A. *American Bandstand: Dick Clark and the Making of a Rock'n'Roll Empire.* New York: Oxford University Press, 1997

Jackson, John A. *Big Beat Heat: Alan Freed and the Early Years of Rock & Roll.* New York: Schirmer, 1991.

Jarman, Rufus. "Country Music Goes to Town." *Nation's Business,* February, 1953. Vol 41, No. 2.

Jasen, David A. and Gene Jones. *Spreadin' Rhythm Around: Black Popular Songwriters, 1880-1930*. New York: Schirmer Books, 1998.

Johnson, E.R. Fenimore. *His Master's Voice was Eldridge R. Johnson: A Biography*. 2nd ed. Milford, Del: E.R. Fenimore Johnson, 1975.

Johnson, James Weldon and J. Rosamond Johnson. *The Books of American Negro Spirituals* (Two Volumes in One) New York: Da Capo Press, 1925, 1926 by Viking Press.

Johnson, James Weldon. *Along This Way: The Autobiography of James Weldon Johnson*. New York, Penguin, 1933; copyright renewed, 1961.

Johnson, James Weldon. *Black Manhattan*. New York: Atheneum, 1968. (From Studies in American Negro Life, August Meier, General Editor)

Johnston, Richard and Dick Boak. *Martin Guitars: A History*. New York: Hal Leonard, 1988, 1994, 2008.

Jones, George with Tom Carter. *I Lived To Tell It All*. New York: Villard, 1996.

Jones, Loyal. *Country Music Humorists and Comedians*. Urbana and Chicago: University of Illinois Press, 2008.

Jorgensen, Ernst. *Elvis Presley: A Life in Music: The Complete Recording Sessions*. New York: St. Martin's Press, 1998.

Kammen, Michael. *American Culture, American Tastes: Social Change and the 20th Century*. New York: Alfred A. Knopf 320 pp $30

Kazanjian, Howard and Chris Enns. *The Cowboy and the Senorita: A Biography of Roy Rogers and Dale Evans* by Howard Kazanjian and Chris Enss. Guilford, CT: Twodot, 2005.

Keil, Charles and Steven Feld. *Music Grooves: Essays and Dialogues*. Chicago: University of Chicago Press, 1994).

Kelley, Robin D.G. "Kickin' Reality: Kickin' Ballistics: Gangsta Rap and Postindustrial Los Angeles." In *Droppin' Science: Critical Essays on Rap Music and Hip Hop Culture*. Ed. William Eric Perkins. Philadelphia: Temple UP, 1996

Kenney, William H. *Recorded Music in American Life*. New York: Oxford University Press, 1999.

Keogh, Pamela Clarke. *Elvis Presley: The Man. The Life. The Legend*. New York: Atria books, 2004.

Ketchum, Richard M. *Will Rogers: The Man and His Times*. New York: Touchstone, 1973.

Killen, Buddy with Tom Carter. *By the Seat of My Pants: My Life in Country Music*. New York: Simon and Schuster, 1993.

Kiner, Larry F. and Philip R. Evans. *Al Jolson: A Bio-Discography*. Metuchen, N.J.: Scarecrow Press, 1992.

King, Nelson. "Hillbilly Music Leaves the Hills." *Good Housekeeping*, June, 1954. Vol 138, No. 6.

King, Tom. *The Operator: David Geffen*. New York: Random House, 2000.

Kingsbury, Paul and Alan Axelrod, eds. *Country: The Music and the Musicians*. New York: Abbeville Press, 1988.

Kingsbury, Paul. *The Grand Ole Opry History of Country Music: 70 Years of the Songs, the Stars, and the Stories*. New York: Villard Books, 1995.

Kirkpatrick, Jim. *Before He Was Fab: George Harrison's First American Visit*. Vienna, ILL: Cache River Press, 2000.

Knoedelseder, William. *Stiffed: The True Story of MCA, The Music Business and the Mafia*. New York: Harper Perennial, 1993.

Knopper, Steve. *Appetite for Self-Destruction: The Spectacular Crash of the Record Industry in the Digital Age*. New York: Free Press, 2009

Koenigsberg, Allen ed. *The Phonograph and the Patent System, 1877-1912*. Brooklyn, N.Y.: APM Press, 190.

Kraft, James P. *Stage to Studio: Musicians and the Sound Revolution, 1890-1950*. (Baltimore: Johns Hopkins University Press, 1996.

La Chapelle, Peter. *Proud to Be an Okie: Cultural Politics, Country Music, and Migration to Southern California.* Berkeley: University of California Press, 2007.

Lackmann, Ron. *Same Time...Same Station: An A-Z Guide to Radio from Jack Benny to Howard Stern.* New York: Facts On File, 1996.

Laforse Martin W. and James A. Drake. *Popular Culture and American Life: Selected Topics on the Study of American Popular Culture.* Chicago: Nelson-Hall, 1981.

Lanza, Joseph. *Elevator Music: A Surreal History of Muzak, Easy-Listening, and Other Moodsong.* New York: St. Martin's Press, 1994.

Larkin, Colin ed. *The Guinness Encyclopedia of Popular Music.* Middlesex, England: Guinness Publishing Ltd., 1995).

Lawrence, A.H. *Duke Ellington And His World: A Biography.* New York: Routledge.

Lawrence, Alistair. *Abbey Road Studios: The Best Studio in the World.* London: Bloomsbury, 2012.

Lee, Brenda with Robert K. Oermann and Julie Clay. *Little Miss Dynamite: The Life and Times of Brenda Lee.* New York: Hyperion, 2002.

Lee, Katie. *Ten Thousand Goddam Cattle: A History of the American Cowboy in Song, Story, and Verse.* Flagstaff, Ariz.: Northland Press, 1977.

Lemann, Nicholas. *The Promised Land: The Great Black Migration and How It Changed America.* New York: Vintage Books, 1991.

Leng, Simon. *While My Guitar Gently Weeps: The Music of George Harrison.* Milwaukee: Hal Leonard, 2006.

Leonard, Neil. *Jazz and the White Americans: The Acceptance of a New Art Form.* (Chicago: University of Chicago Press, 1972.

Leonard, Neil. *Jazz, Myth and Religion.* (New York: Oxford University Press, 1987.

Lerma, Dominique-Rene de ed. *Black Music in Our Culture.* Kent, Ohio: Kent State University Press, 1970.

Levine, Lawrence W. *Black Culture and Black Consciousness: Afro-American Folk Thought from Slavery to Freedom.* New York: Oxford University Press, 1978.

Levine, Lawrence, ed. *The Unpredictable Past: Explorations in American Cultural History.* (New York: Oxford University Press, 1993).

Levine, Lawrence. *High Brow/Low Brow: The Emergence of Cultural Hierarchy in America.* Cambridge: Harvard University Press, 1988.

Levy, Eugene. *James Weldon Johnson: Black Leader, Black Voice.* Chicago: The University of Chicago Press, 1973.

Lewis, David Levering. *W.E.B. DuBois: Biography of a Race: 1868-1919.* New York: Henry Holt and Company, 1993.

Lewis, David Levering. *When Harlem Was in Vogue.* New York: Penguin Books, 1979, 1981, 1997.

Lewis, Lisa A. ed. *The Adoring Audience: Fan Culture and Popular Media.* New York: Routledge, 1992.

Lewis, Tom. *Empire of the Air: The Men Who Made Radio New York:* Edward Burlingame Books/ an imprint of HarperCollins, 1991.

Lewisohn, Mark. *The Complete Beatles Chronicle.* New York: Harmony Books, 1992.

Lewisohn, Mark. *Tune In: The Beatles: All These Years.* New York: Crown Archetype, 2013.

Lieberson, Goddard. "'Country Sweeps the Country." *New York Times* Magazine. July 28, 1957.

Lightfoot, William E. "Belle of the Barn Dance: Reminiscing with Lulu Belle Wiseman Stamey." *The Journal of Country Music,* Volume XII, Number 1. pp 2-15.

Lightfoot, William E. "From Radio Queen to Raleigh: Conversations with Lulu Belle: Part I." Old Time Country, Vol VI No. II, Summer 1989.

Lipsitz, George. *Class and Culture in Cold War America: "A Rainbow at Midnight."* New York: Praeger, 1981.

Locke, Alain, editor. *The New Negro: Voices of the Harlem Renaissance*. New York: Atheneum, 1992.

Logsdon, Guy, William Jacobson and Mary Rogers. *Saddle Serenaders*. Salt Lake City: Gibbs Smith, 1995.

Logsdon, Guy. *"The Whorehouse Bells Were Ringing" and Other Songs Cowboys Sing*. Urbana: University of Illinois Press, 1989.

Lomax, John A. *Adventures of a Ballad Hunter*. New York: Macmillan, 1947.

Lombardo, Guy with Jack Altshul. *Auld Acquaintance*. Garden City, N.Y.: DOubleday& Co., 1975).

Lott, Eric. *Love and Theft: Blackface Minstrelsy and the American Working Class*. New York: Oxford University Press, 1993).

Love, Robert and Editors of Rolling Stone. *Harrison* (with Forward by Olivia Harrison). New York: Simon and Schuster, 2002.

Lynch, Vincent and Bill Hankin. *Jukebox: The Golden Age*. New York: Perigee Books, 1981.

MacDonald, Ian. *Revolution in the Head: The Beatles' Records and the Sixties*. Third Edition. Chicago: Chicago Review Press, 2005.

MacDonald, J. Fred. *Don't Touch That Dial! Radio Programming in American Life, 1920-1960*. Chicago: Nelson-Hall, 1979.

Magers, Boyd. *Gene Autry Westerns: America's Favorite Cowboy*. Madison, N.C.: Empire Publishing, 2007.

Mahar, William J. *Behind the Burnt Cork Mask: Early Blackface Minstrelsy and Antebellum American Popular Culture*. Urbana and Chicago: University of Illinois Press, 1999.

Malone, Bill and Judith McCullough eds. *Stars of Country Music*. Urbana: University of Illinois Press, 1975.

Malone, Bill C. Country Music U.S.A.: A Fifty-Year History (Austin: University of Texas Press, 1968).

Malone, Bill C. *Don't Get Above Your Raisin': Country Music and the Southern Working Class*. Urbana: University of Illinois Press, 2002.

Malone, Bill C. *Singing Cowboys and Musical Mountaineers: Southern Culture and the Roots of Country Music*. Athens, GA: The University of Georgia Press, 1993.

Malone, Bill. *Country Music U.S.A.* Austin, TX: University of Texas Press, 1968.

Maltin, Leonard. *The Great American Broadcast*. New York: Dutton, 1997.

Mansfield, Ken with Brent Stoker. *The White Book: the Beatles, the Bands, The Biz: An Insider's Look at an Era*. Nashville: Thomas Nelson, 2007

Mansfield, Ken. *The Beatles, The Bible and Bodega Bay: My Long and Winding Road*. Nashville, TN: Broadman & Holman, 2000.

Marchand, Roland. *Advertising the American Dream: Making Way for Modernity, 1920-1940*. Berkeley: University of California Press, 1985.

Marco, Guy A. ed. *Encyclopedia of Recorded Sound in the United States*. (New York: Garland Publishing, 1993.

Marcus, Greil. *Bob Dylan: Writings 1968-2010*. New York: PublicAffairs, 2010.

Marcus, Greil. *Like a Rolling Stone: Bob Dylan at the Crossroads*. New York: PublicAffairs, 2005.

Marek, Richard. "Country Music, Nashville Style." *McCall's* April, 1961. Vol 88, No. 7.

Marmorstein, Gary. *The Label: The Story of Columbia Records*. New York: Thunder's Mouth Press, 2007.

Martin, George with Jeremy Hornsby. *All You Need Is Ears*. New York: St. Martin's Press, 1979.

Martin, George with William Pearson. *With a Little Help From My Friends: The Making of Sgt. Pepper*. Boston: Little, Brown & Company, 1994.

Martland, Peter. *Since Records Began: EMI: The First 100 Years* Portland, Ore: Amadeus Press, 1997.

Mason, Bobbie Ann. *Elvis Presley: A Penguin Life*. New York: Viking, 2003.

McCall, Michael. "Freedom's Not Just Another Word," *Nashville Scene*, September 18, 2003.

McCloud, Barry, ed. *Definitive Country: The Ultimate Encyclopedia of Country Music and Its Performers*. New York: Perigree, 1995.

McCusker, Kristine M. *Lonesome Cowgirls and Honky-Tonk Angels: The Women of Barn Dance Radio*. Urbana: University of Illinois Press, 2008.

McDougal, Dennis. *The Last Mogul: Lew Wasserman, MCA, and the Hidden History of Hollywood*. New York: Crown, 1998

McElvaine, Robert S. *The Great Depression: America, 1929-1941*. New York: Times Books, 1984.

McKinney, Devin. *The Beatles In Dreams and History*. Cambridge, MA: Harvard University Press, 2003.

Mellers, Wilfrid. *A Darker Shade of Pale: A Backdrop to Bob Dylan*. New York: Oxford University Press, 1985

Mercer, Charles. "Elvis The Pelvis Belongs In Jungle, New York Writer Tells Steve Allen." AP Story datelined New York. Nashville *Banner*, June 22, 1956

Meyrowitz, Joshua. *No Sense of Place: The Impact of Electronic Media on Social Behavior*. New York: Oxford University Press, 1985.

Miles, Barry. *Paul McCartney: Many Years From Now*. New York: Henry Holt and Company, 1997.

Millard, Andre. *America on Record: A History of Recorded Sound*. Second Edition. Cambridge: Cambridge University Press, 2005.

Miller, James. *Flowers in the Dustbin: The Rise of Rock and Roll, 1947-1977*. New York: Simon & Schuster

Miller, Nathan. *Theodore Roosevelt: A Life*. New York: Morrow, 1992.

Miller, Stephen. *Johnny Cash: The Life of an American Icon*. London: Omnibus Press, 2003.

Montana, Patsy with Jane Frost. *Patsy Montana: The Cowboy's Sweetheart*. Jefferson, N.C.: McFarland & Company, Inc. 2002.

Moore, Jerrold Northrop. *Sound Revolutions: A Biography of Fred Gaisberg, Founding Father of Commercial Sound Recording*. Trowbridge, Wiltshire, England: Redwood Books, 1999.

Moore, Scotty as told to James Dickerson. *That's Alright, Elvis: The Untold Story of Elvis's First Guitarist and Manager, Scotty Moore*. New York: Schirmer Books, 1997.

Morris, Edmund. *The Rise of Teddy Roosevelt*. New York: Ballantine, 1979.

Morris, Edward. "New, Improved, Homogenized: Country Radio Since 1950." In *Country: The Music and the Musicians*. New York: Abbeville Press, 1988.

Moscheo, Joe. *The Gospel Side of Elvis*. New York: Center Street, 2007.

Mukerji, Chandra and Michael Schudson, eds. *Rethinking Popular Culture: Contemporary Perspectives in Cultural Studies*. Berkeley: U of California P, 1991).

Mussulman, Joseph A. *Music in the Cultured Generation: A Social History of Music in America, 1870-1900*. Evanston, Ill: Northwestern University Press, 1971).

Myrus, Donald. *Ballads, Blues and the Big Beat* New York: The Macmillan Co. 1966

Nachman, Gerald. *Raised on Radio*. New York Pantheon, 1998.

"NARAS' Nashville Unit Gets 200 New Members." *Billboard*, September 21, 1966.

"NARAS Puts Grammy Wheels in Motion With 'Eligibility' Forms." September 17, 1966.

"NARAS Revamps Grammy Awards Format; Fewer Prizes, Wider Scope." Variety. September 21, 1966.

Nash, Alanna with Billy Smith, Marty Lacker and Lamar Fike. *Elvis and the Memphis Mafia*. New York: Harper Collins, 1995.

Nash, Alanna. *Baby, Let's Play House: Elvis Presley and the Women Who Loved Him*. New York: itbooks, 2010.

Nash, Alanna. *Behind Closed Doors: Talking With the Legends of Country Music*. New York: Alfred A. Knopf, 1988.

Nash, Alanna. *The Colonel: The Extraordinary Story of Colonel Tom Parker and Elvis Presley*. New York: Simon and Schuster, 2003.

Nelson, Ken. My First 90 Years Plus 3. Pittsburgh, PA: Dorrance Publishing CO., 2007.

Newsom, Iris, ed. *Wonderful Inventions: Motion Pictures, Broadcasting, and Recorded Sound at the Library of Congress*. Washington, D.C.: Library of Congress, 1985.

Newsom, Jon ed. *Perspectives on John Philip Sousa*. Washington, D.C.: Library of Congress, 1983.

Nocera, Joseph. *A Piece of the Action: How the Middle Class Joined the Money Class*. New York: Simon & Schuster, 1994.

Norman, Philip. *John Lennon: The Life*. New York: Ecco, 2008.

Norman, Philip. *Shout! The Beatles in Their Generation*. New York: MJF Books, 1981.

Norrell, Robert J. *Up From History: The Life of Booker T. Washington*. Cambridge, MA: The Belknap Press of Harvard University Press, 2009.

Nye, David E. *Electrifying America: Social Meanings of a New Technology, 1880-1940* Cambridge, Mass and London, England: The MIT Press, 1991.

Oliver, Paul, Max Harrison and William Bolcom. *The New Grove Gospel, Blues and Jazz*. (New York: W. W. Norton, 1986.

Oliver, Paul. *Bessie Smith*. New York: Barnes, 1961

Oliver, Paul. *Blues Off the Record*. New York: Hippocrene Books, 1984.

Oliver, Paul. *Songsters and Saints: Vocal Traditions on Race Records*. Cambridge: Cambridge University Press, 1984.

O'Neal, Bill and Fred Goodwin. *The Sons of the Pioneers*. Austin: Eakin Press, 2001.

O'Neal, Bill. *Tex Ritter: America's Most Beloved Cowboy*. Austin, Texas: Eakin Press, 1998.

O'Neil, Thomas. *The Grammys: For the Record*. New York: Penguin, 1993.

Orr, Jay, editor. *Dylan, Cash and the Nashville Cats: A New Music City*. Nashville: Country Music Foundation Press, 2015.

Ottley, Roi and William J. Weatherby. *The Negro in New York: An Informal Social History, 1626-1940*. New York: Praeger, 1967.

Owens, Buck with Randy Poe. *Buck 'Em!: The Autobiography of Buck Owens*. Milwaukee: Backbeat Books (Hal Leonard), 2013

Paper, Lewis J. *Empire: William S. Paley and the Making of CBS*. New York: St. Martin's Press, 1987).

Paris, Mike and Chris Comber. *Jimmie the Kid: The Life of Jimmie Rodgers*. New York: Da Capo, 1977.

Passman, Arnold. *The Deejays*: New York: The Macmillan Company, 1971.

Pearce, Christopher. *Vintage Jukeboxes: The Hall of Fame*. Secaucus, N.J.: Chartwell, 1988.

Pecknold, Diane. *The Selling Sound: The Rise of the Country Music Industry*. Durham, N.C.: Duke University Press, 2007.

Peer, Ralph. "Discovery of the First Hillbilly Great," *Billboard* LXV 1953.

Perkins, Carl and David McGee. *Go, Cat Go!: The Life and Times of Carl Perkins*. New York: Hyperion, 1996.

Perkins, William Eric. "The Rap Attak: An Introduction." In *Droppin' Science: Critical Essays on Rap Music and Hip Hop Culture*. Ed. William Eric Perkins. Philadelphia: Temple UP, 1996 re: rap music

Peterson, Richard A. *Creating Country Music: Fabricating Authenticity*. Chicago: University of Chicago Press, 1997.

Phillips, Robert W. *Roy Rogers: A Biography, Radio History, Television Career Chronicle, Discography, Filmography, Comicography, Merchandsing and Advertising History, Collectibles Description, Bibliography and Index*. Jefferson, N.C.: McFarland & Co., 1995.

Phillips, Robert W. *Singing Cowboy Stars*. Salt Lake City: Gibbs Smith, 1994.

Picardie, Justine and Dorothy Wade. *Atlantic and the Godfathers of Rock and Roll*. London: Fourth Estates, 1990.

Pierce, Patricia Jobe. *The Ultimate Elvis: Elvis Presley Day by Day*. New York: Simon & Schuster, 1994.

"Pistol Packin' Mama." Life, October 11, 1943. Vol 15, No. 11.

Pleasants, Henry. *The Great American Popular Singers*. New York: Simon & Schuster, 1974.

Podolsky, Rich. *Don Kirshner: The Man with the Golden Ear*. Milwaukee: Hal Leonard Books, 2012

Ponce De Leon, Charles L. *Fortunate Son: The Life of Elvis Presley*. New York: Hill and Wang, 2006.

Porterfield, Nolan. *Jimmie Rodgers: The Life and Times of America's Blue Yodeler*. Urbana: University of Illinois Press, 1979.

Porterfield, Nolan. *Last Cavalier: The Life and Times of John A. Lomax*. Urbana: University of Illinois Press, 1996.

Portis, Charles, "That New Sound From Nashville," *The Saturday Evening Post*, February 12, 1965

Presley, Priscilla Beaulieu with Sandra Harmon. *Elvis and Me*. New York: G.P. Putnam's Sons, 1985.

"Presley's All Ready For Rock'n'Roll Go" Nashville *Tennessean*, March 4, 1960.

Prial, Dunstan. *The Producer: John Hammond and the Soul of American Music*. New York: Picador, 2006.

Pringle, Henry F. *Theodore Roosevelt, a Biography*. New York: Harcourt, Brace & World, 1956.

Pritchard, David and Alan Lysaght. *The Beatles: An Oral History*. New York: Hyperion, 1998.

Pritcher, Mark. "Chet Atkins and the Beatles" in *Mister Guitar*, Issue 34, Winter 1995.

Proceedings of the 1890 Convention of Local Phonograph Companies Nashville, TN: Country Music Foundation Press, 1974.

Pugh, Ronnie. *Ernest Tubb: Texas Troubadour*. Durham, N.C.: Duke University Press, 1996.

Quarles, Benjamin. *The Negro in the Making of America*, Third Edition. New York: Touchstone, 1964, 1969, 1987.

"Ralph Peer Dies at 67; Pioneered Global Music Publishing Concept" Variety Jan 27, 1960.

Read, Oliver and Walter L. Welch. *From Tin Foil to Stereo: The Evolution of the Phonograph*. Indianapolis: Howard Sams, 1977.

Redshaw, David. "Roger Miller" in *New Music Express*, June 16, 1973, p. 30

Reynolds, David. *Rich Relations: The American Occupation of Britain, 1942-1945*. New York: Random House, 1995.

Ribowsky, Mark. *He's a Rebel: The Truth About Phil Spector—Rock and Roll's Legendary Madman*. New York: E.P. Dutton, 1989.

Ritchie, Michael. *Please Stand By: A Prehistory of Television*. Woodstock N.Y.: The Overlook Press 1994

Ritz, David, editor. *Elvis By the Presleys*. New York: Crown Publishers, 2006.

Robert Shelton, Robert. "Nashville's Modern Folk," *New York Times*, March 21, 1965.

Roberts, David, editor. *British Hit Singles: Guinness World Records, 15th Edition*, edited by David Roberts. Great Britain: Guinness World Records Ltd, 2001.

Robertson, David. *W.C. Handy: The Life and Times of the Man Who Made the Blues*. New York: Alfred A. Knopf, 2009.

Robinson, Ray. *American Original: A Life of Will Rogers*. New York: Oxford University Press, 1996.

Roell, Craig H. *The Piano in America, 1890-1940*. Chapel Hill: University of North Carolina Press, 1989.

"Roger Miller Nominated For 9 Grammy Awards. Nashville *Tennesssean*, February 15, 1966.

Rogers, Dale Evans with Norman B. Rohrer. *Rainbow on a Hard Trail: Her Story of Life and Love*. Grand Rapids, MI: Fleming H. Revell, 1999.

Rogers, Roy and Dale Evans with Carlton Stowers. *Happy Trails: The Story of Roy Rogers and Dale Evans*. Waco, Texas: Word Books, 1979.

Rogers, Roy and Dale Evans with Jane and Michael Stern. *Happy Trails: Our Life Story*. New York: Simon & Schuster, 1994.

Romanowski, Patricia and Holly George-Warren, eds. *The New Rolling Stone Encyclopedia of Rock & Roll*. Simon & Schuster

Rose, Frank. *The Agency: William Morris and the Hidden History of Show Business*. New York: HarperBusiness, 1995.

Rose, Tricia. *Black Noise: rap Music and Black Culture in Contemporary America*. Hanover, CT: Wesleyan UP, 1994.

Rosenberg, Neil V. *Bluegrass: A History*. Urbana, ILL: University of Illinois Press, 1985.

Rosenberg, Neil. *Bluegrass Breakdown: The Making of the Old Southern Sound*. Urbana: University of Illinois Press, 1984.

Rumble, John Woodruff. "Fred Rose and the Development of the Nashville Music Industry, 1942-1954." Ph.D. dissertation, Vanderbilt University, 1980.

Rumble, John. "Behind the Board with Bill Porter: Part One." *The Journal Of Country Music*, Vol. 18, No. 1, 1996.

Rumble, John. "Behind the Board with Bill Porter: Part Three." The Journal Of Country Music, Vol. 19, No. 1, 1997.

Rumble, John. "Behind the Board with Bill Porter: Part Two." *The Journal Of Country Music*, Vol. 18, No. 2, 1996.

Russell, Tony. *Blacks, Whites and Blues*. New York: Stein & Day, 1970.

Russell, Tony. *Country Music Originals: The Legends and the Lost*. New York: Oxford University Press, 2007.

Russell, Tony. *Country Music Records: A Discography, 1921-1942*. New York: Oxford University Press, 2004.

Rust, Brian. *The American Record Label Book*. New Rochelle, NY: Arlington House, 1978.

Ryan, John. "Organizaitons, Environment and Cultural Change: The ASCAP-BMI Controversy" PhD dissertation. Vanderbilt University, 1982

Sadie, Stanley ed. *New Grove Dictionary of Music and Musicians*. London: Macmillan, 1980.

Salaam, Mtume ya. "The Aesthetics of Rap." *African American Review* 29:2 (1995 Summer)

Samuels, David. "The Rap on Rap," *The New Republic*, November 11, 1991.

Samuelson, Robert J. *The Good Life and Its Discontents: The American Dream in the Age of Entitlement: 1945-1995*. (New York: Times Books, 1995).

Sanjek, Russell. *American Popular Music and Its Business: The First Four Hundred Years: Vol. II From 1790 to 1909*. New York: Oxford, 1988.

Sanjek, Russell. *American Popular Music and Its Business: Volume III: From 1900 to 1984*. New York: Oxford University Press, 1988.

Sarris, Andrew. *"You Ain't Heart Nothin' Yet": The American Talking Film: History & Memory, 1927-1949*. New York: Oxford University Press.

Savage, William W. Jr. *Singing Cowboys and All That Jazz: A Short History of Popular Music in Oklahoma*. Norman: University of Oklahoma Press, 1983.

Scaduto, Anthony. *Bob Dylan*. New York: Castle Books, 1971.

Schilling, Jerry with Chuck Crisafulli. *Me and a Guy Named Elvis: My Lifelong Friendship with Elvis Presley*. New York: Gotham Books, 2006.

Schipper, Henry. *Broken Record: The Inside Story of the Grammy Awards.* New York: Birch Lane, 1992

Schlappi, Elizabeth. *Roy Acuff: The Smoky Mountain Boy.* Gretna, GA: Pelican Publishing Company, 1978, 1993.

Schulman, Bruce J. *The Seventies: The Great Shift in American Culture, Society and Politics.* New York: The Free Press.

Schwartz, Stephen. *From West to East: California and the Making of the American Mind.* New York: The Free Press.

Schwartzman, Arnold. *Phono-Graphics: The Visual Paraphernalia of the Talking Machine.* San Francisco: Chronicle Books, 1993.

Schyuller, Gunther. *The Swing Era: The Development of Jazz, 1930-1945.* New York: Oxford University Press, 1989.

Seabrook, John. *The Song Machine: Inside the Hit Factory.* New York: W.W. Norton & Company, 2015.

Sears, Richard S. *V Discs: A History and Discography* by Richard S. Sears Greenwood Press, 1980 Westport, CT.

Seeger, Mike. "Who Chose These Records? A Look Into the Life, Tastes, and Procedures of Frank Walker " in *Anthology of American Folk Music,* ed. John Dunson and Ethel Raim. New York: Oak Publications, 1973

Seemann, Charlie. "Gene Autry." *The Journal of the American Academy for the Preservation of Old-Time Country Music.* Issue No. 22; August, 1994.

Segrave, Kerry. *Payola in the Music Industry: A History, 1880-1991.* Jefferson, N.C.: McFarland & Company, Inc., 1994

Selvin, Joel. *Here Comes the Night: The Dark Soul of Bert Berns and the Dirty Business of Rhythm and Blues.* Berkeley: Counterpoint, 2014.

Sennett, Ted. *Hollywood Musicals.* New York: Harry N. Abrams, Inc. 1981.

Sforza, John. *Swing It!: The Andrews Sisters Story.* (University of Kentucky Press, 1999.

Shapiro, Marc. *Behind Sad Eyes: George Harrison.* New York: St. Martin's Press, 2002.

Sharp, Cecil. *English Folk Songs from the Southern Appalachians.* New York: Oxford University Press, 1932, 1952, 1960, 1966.

Shaughnessy, Mary Alice. *Les Paul: An American Original.* New York: William Morrow and Company, 1993

Shaw, Arnold. *Honkers and Shouters: The Golden Years of Rhythm & Blues* New York: Macmillan, 1978.

Shaw, Arnold. *The Jazz Age: Popular Music in the 1920s.* New York: Oxford, 1987.

Shaw, Arnold. *The Street That Never Slept: New York's Fabled 52nd Street.* (New York: Coward, McCann, & Geoghegan, 1971.

Sheehan, Neil. *A Bright Shining Lie: John Paul Vann and America in Vietnam.* New York: Random House, 1988.

Sheehy, Colleen J. and Thomas Swiss, editors. *Highway 61 Revisited: Bob Dylan's Road From Minnesota To the World.* Minneapolis: University of Minnesota Press, 2009.

Shelton, Robert and Burt Goldblatt. *The Country Music Story: A Picture History of Country & Western Music.* New York: Bobbs-Merrill, 1966.

Shelton, Robert. "Nashville's Modern Folk," *New York Times,* March 21, 1965.

Shelton, Robert. *No Direction Home: The Life and Music of Bob Dylan.* Beech Tree/ William Morrow, 1986.

Shepherd, John. *Tin Pan Alley.* London: Routledge & Kegan Paul, 1982.

Shilkret, Nathaniel. Edited by Niel Shell and Barbara Shilkret. *Sixty Years in the Music Business.* Lanham, Maryland: The Scarecrow Press, Inc., 2005.

Silber, Irwin. *Songs America Voted By.* Harrisburg, PA: Stackpole Books, 1971.

Simmons, Russell with Nelson George. *Life and Def: Sex, Drugs, Money and God.* New York: Crown, 2001

Singular, Stephen. *The Rise and Rise of David Geffen.* New York: Birch Lane, 1997.

Sisk, Eileen. *Buck Owens: The Biography*. Chicago: Chicago Review Press, 2010.

Smith, Gibbs. *Joe Hill*. Salt Lake City: Gibbs M. Smith, Inc. and Peregrine Smith Books, 1969 and 1984.

Smith, Joe. *Off the Record: An Oral History of Popular Music*. New York: Warner Books, 1988.

Smith, Richard Norton. *The Colonel: The Life and Legend of Robert R. McCormick 1880-1955*. Evanston, Ill: Northwestern University Press, 1997.

Smith, Wes. *The Pied Pipers of Rock'n"Roll: Radio Deejays of the 50s and 60s*. Marietta, GA: Longstreet Press, 1989.

Smulyan, Susan. *Selling Radio: The Commercilazation of American Broadcasting 1920-1934*. Washington, D.C.: Smithsonian

Snow, Hank with Jack Ownbey and Bob Burris. *The Hank Snow Story*. Urbana and Chicago: University of Illinois Press, 1994.

Snyder, Robert W. *The Voice of the City: Vaudeville and Popular Culture in New York*. New York: Oxford University Press, 1989.

Sounes, Howard. *Down the Highway: The Life of Bob Dylan*. New York: Grove Press, 2001.

Sounes, Howard. *Fab: An Intimate Life of Paul McCartney*. New York: Da Capo Press, 2010.

Southall, Brian, Peter Vince, Allan Rouse. *Abbey Road*. London: Omnibus Press, 1982, 1997, 2002.

Spitz, Bob. *The Beatles: The Biography*. New York: Little, Brown and Company, 2005.

Stambler, Irwin and Grelun Landon. *Country Music: The Encyclopedia*. New York: St. Martin's Press, 1997.

Starr, Larry and Christopher Waterman. *American Popular Music: From Minstrelsy to MTV*. New York: Oxford, 2003.

Sternfield, Aaron. "The Vietnam Conflict Spawning Heavy Barrage of Disk Tunes." *Billboard*, June 4, 1966

Sternfield, Aaron. "Nation's Colleges Offer Music Industry Lush Market of 5,900,000" Billboard Music on Campus," March 19, 1966.

Sternfield, Aaron. "The Vietnam Conflict Spawning Heavy Barrage of Disk Tunes." Billboard, June 4, 1966.

Sternfield, Aaron. "There's more money on college campuses than there is in Las Vegas." Billboard Music on Campus. March 27, 1965.

Sternfield, Aaron. "Record Marketplace, Talent Proving Ground Billboard Music on Campus, March 27, 1965.

Stewart-Baxter, Derrick. *Ma Rainey and the Classic Blues Singers*. New York: Stein and Day, 1970.

Stone, Jack. "Millions in Music--Hillbillies in Clover" The American Weekly Feb. 6, 1949

Stowe, David W. *Swing Changes: Big-Band Jazz in New Deal America*. Cambridge, Mass: Harvard University Press, 1994).

Streissguth, Michael, editor. *Ring of Fire: The Johnny Cash Reader*. New York: Da Capo Press, 2002.

Streissguth, Michael. *Like a Moth to the Flame: The Jim Reeves Story*. Nashville: Rutledge Hill Press, 1998.

Style, Lyle. *Ain't Got No Cigarettes: Memories of Music Legend Roger Miller*. Winnipeg, MB: Great Plains Publications, 2005.

Sudhalter, Richard M. and Philip R. Evens with William Dean-Myatt. *Bix: Man & Legend*. New Rochelle, N.Y.: Arlington House, 1974.

Sudhalter, Richard M. *Lost Chords: White Musicians and Their Contribution to Jazz, 1915-1945*. New York: Oxford University Press.

Susman, Warren L. *Culture as History: The Transformation of American Society in the Twentieth Century*. New York: Pantheon Books, 1984.

Swenson, John. *Bill Haley: The Daddy of Rock and Roll*. New York: Stein and Day, 1983.

Taraborreli, Randy. *Sinatra: A Complete Life*. New York: A Birch Lane, 1997.

Tawa, Nicholas E. *A Music for the Millions: Antebellum Democratic Attitudes and the Birth of American Popular Music*. New York: Pendragon, 1984.

Taylor, Derek. *It Was Twenty Years Ago Today*. New York: Simon & Schuster, 1987.

Taylor, Frank C. and Gerald Cook. *Alberta Hunter: A Celebration in Blues*. (New York: McGraw Hill, 1987.

Teeter, H.B. "Nashville, Broadway of Country Music." *Coronet*, August, 1952. Vol 43, No. 4.

Terkel, Studs. *The Spectator: Talk About Movies and Plays With the People Who Make Them*. New York: The New Press

Terrace, Vincent. *Radio's Golden Years: The Encyclopedia of Radio Programs, 1930-1960*. San Diego: A.S. Barnes, 1981.

"The Brakeman Auditions for Ralph Peer; A Milestone in Country Music," Billboard's World of Country Music Nov 2, 1963.

Thiele, Bob. *What a Wonderful World: A Lifetime of Recording*. New York: Oxford University Press, 1995.

Thomson, Elizabeth and David Gutman, editors. *The Dylan Companion: A Collection of Essential Writing About Bob Dylan*. New York: Delta/Doubleday, 1990.

Thomson, Graeme. *Behind the Locked Door: George Harrison*. London: Overlook and Omnibus Press, 2015.

Thygesen, Helge, Mark Berresford and Russ Shor. *Black Swan: The Record Label of the Harlem Renaissance*. Nottingham, Eng: VJM Pub 1996.

Tichi, Cecelia. *High Lonesome: The American Culture of Country Music*. Chapel Hill: University of North Carolina Press, 1994.

Tillery, Gary. *Working Class Mystic: A Spiritual Biography of George Harrison*. Wheaton, IL and Chennai, India: Theosophical Publishing House, 2011.

Tilley, Nannie M. *The R.J. Reynolds Tobacco Company*. Chapel. Hill: University of North Carolina Press, 1985.

Titon, Jeff Todd. *Early Downhome Blues: A Musical and Cultural Analysis*. Urbana: University of Illinois Press, 1977.

Tompkins, Jane. *West of Everything: The Inner Life of Westerns*. New York: Oxford University Press, 1992.

Tosches, Nick. *Country: The Biggest Music in America*. New York: Delta, 1977.

Townsend, Charles R. *San Antonio Rose: The Life and Music of Bob Wills*. Urbana: University of Illinois Press, 1976.

"Trades' Reaction to Petrillo's Disc Plan is Surprise at Elimination of Radio" Variety Feb 17, 1943.

Tribe, Ivan. *Mountaineer Jamboree: Country Music in West Virginia*. Lexington: University Press of Kentucky, 1984.

Troutman, John W. "Steelin' the Slide: Hawaii and the Birth of the Blues Guitar." *Southern Cultures*, Spring 2013. Global Southern Music, North Carolina Press.

Trynka, Paul, editor. *The Electric Guitar: An Illustrated History*. San Francisco: Chronicle Books, 1993.

Turner, Steve. *A Hard Day's Write: The Stories Behind Every Beatles Song*. London: Carlton, 1994, 1999.

Turner, Steve. *The Man Called Cash: The Life, Love, and faith of an American Legend*. Nashville: W Publishing Group, 2004.

Tuska, Jon. *The Vanishing Legion: A History of Mascot Pictures, 1927-1935*. Jefferson, N.C.: McFarland, 1982.

"U.S. Troops have 12-Satation Web" Variety Sept 8, 1943.

Vasey, Ruth. *The World According To Hollywood 1918-1939*. Madison: University of Wisconsin Press, 1997.

"V-Discs Spin Out to G.I. Audiences At Rate of 2,000,000 Annually" Variety May 10, 1944.

Vellenga, Dirk and Mick Farren. *Elvis and the Colonel: The True and Shocking Story of the Man Behind 'The King.'* London: Grafton Books, 1990.

Wald, Elijah. *How the Beatles Destroyed Rock'N'roll: A Alternative History of American Popular Music*. New York: Oxford University Press, 2009.

Waldron, Eli. "Country Music: The Squaya Dansu From Nashville." The Reporter, June 2, 1955. Vol 12, No. 11.

Walton, Sam and John Huey. *Made in America*. New York: Doubleday, 1992.

Warner, Jay. *Just Walkin' in the Rain: the true story of a convict quintet, a liberal governor, and how they changed southern history through rhythm and blues*. Los Angeles: Renaissance Books, 2001.

Weintraub, Jerry with Rich Cohen. *When I Stop Talking, You'll Know I'm Dead: Useful Stories From a Persuasive Man*. New York: Twelve, 2010.

Welding, Pete and Tony Byron, eds. *Bluesland: Portraits of Twelve Major American Blues Masters*. New York: Dutton, 1991.

West, Morris. "An Old Man and Long Hair," *Nashville Banner*, July 4, 1970.

Wexler, Jerry and D. Ritz. *Rhythm and Blues: A Life in American Music*. New York: Knopf.

Wheeler, Tom. *American Guitars: An Illustrated History: Revised and Updated*. New York: HarperCollins, 1992.

Whistenhunt, Elton. "Nashville NARAS Starts Campaign." Billboard, October 9, 1965.

Whitburn, Joel. *Billboard Top Pop Singles 1955-2015*. Menomonee Falls, Wisconsin: Record Research, 2016.

Whitburn, Joel. *Hot Country Songs: 1944-2008*. Menomonee Falls, Wisconsin: Record Research Inc., 2008.

Whitburn, Joel. *Pop Memories: 1890-1954: The History of American Popular Music*. Menomonee Falls, Wisconsin: Record Research, 1986.

Whitburn, Joel. *The Billboard Albums*, 6th Edition. Menomonee Falls, Wisconsin: Record Research, Inc. 2006.

Whitburn, Joel. Top 40 Country Hits: 1944-Present. New York: Billboard Books, 1996.

Whitburn, Joel. Top Country Albums 1964-1997. Menomonee Falls, Wisconsin: Record Research Inc., 1997.

Whitburn, Joel. *Top Pop Singles, 12th Edition*. Menomonee Falls, Wisconsin: Record Research Inc., 2009.

White, Forrest. *The Fender Inside Story*. San Francisco: GPI Books, 1994.

White, John I. *Git Along Little Dogies: Songs and Songmakers of the American West*. Urbana: University of Illinois Press, 1975.

White, Raymond E. *King of the Cowboys, Queen of the West: Roy Rogers and Dale Evans*. Madison: University of Wisconsin Press/Popular Press, 2005.

White, Timothy. *The Nearest Faraway Place: Brian, Wilson, the Beach boys, and the Southern California Experience*. New York: Henry Holt and Company, 1994

Whiteside, Jonny. Ramblin' Rose: The Life and Career of Rose Maddox. Nashville: Vanderbilt/Country Music Foundation, 1997.

Whitford, Eldon and David Vinopal. "Gibson SJ-200: On the Trail to the Original." *Vintage Guitar* magazine, August 10, 2004.

Wiener, Allen J. *The Beatles: The Ultimate Recording Guide*. New York: Facts On File, 1986, 1992.

Wiggins, Gene *Fiddlin' Georgia Crazy: Fiddlin' John Carson, His Real World, and the World of His Songs*. Urbana: University of Illinois Press, 1987.

Wikipedia

Wilder, Alec. *American Popular Song: The Great Innovators, 1900-1950*. New York: Oxford University Press, 1972.

Wile, Frederic William. *Emile Berliner: Maker of the Microphone*. Indianapolis: The Bobbs-Merrill Company, 1926.

Wilentz, Sean. *Bob Dylan in America*. New York: Doubleday, 2010.

Wilgus, D.K. "Country-Western Music and the Urban Hillbilly" in *Journal of American Folklore*, 1970

Williams Martin T. ed. *The Art of Jazz: Essays on the Nature and Development of Jazz*. New York: Oxford University Press, 1959.

Williams, Andy. *Moon River and Me: A Memoir*. New York: Viking, 2009.

Williams, Roger. Sing a Sad Song: The Life of Hank Williams. New York: Ballantine, 1973.

Wills, Garry. *John Wayne's America: The Politics of Celebrity*. New York: Simon & Schuster, 1997.

Wisenhunt, Elton. "NARAS Starts Campaign." Billboard, October 8, 1965.

WLS Family Album: 1933. Published by WLS, The Prairie Farmer Station, 1230 West Washington Boulevard, Chicago Illinois.

Wolf, Michael J. *The Entertainment Economy: How Mega-Media Forces Are Transforming Our Lives*. New York: Times Books, 1999.

Wolfe, Charles K. "Ralph Peer at Work: The Victor 1927 Bristol Sessions" in *Old Time Music*, No. 5 ed. Tony Russell (London: 1972).

Wolfe, Charles K. "The Triumph of the Hills: Country Radio, 1920-1950." In *Country: The Music and the Musicians*. New York: Abbeville Press, 1988.

Wolfe, Charles K. *Classic Country: Legends of Country Music*. New York: Routledge, 2001.

Wolfe, Charles K. *Tennessee Strings: The Story of Country Music in Tennessee*. Knoxville: University of Tennessee Press, 1977.

Wolfe, Charles. "Columbia Records and Old-Time Music" *John Edwards Memorial Foundation Quarterly* Fall, 1978

Wolfman Jack with Byron Laursen. Have Mercy! Confessions of the Original Rock'n'Roll Animal Warner, 1995.

Woodward, C. Vann. *Origins of the New South, 1877-1913*. (Baton Rouge: Louisiana State University Press, 1951.

Work, John W., Lewis Wade Jones, and Samuel C. Adams, Jr. *Lost Delta Found: Rediscovering the Fisk University-Library of Congress Coahoma County Study, 1941-1942*. Robert Gordon and Bruce Nemerov, Editors. Nashville: Vanderbilt University Press, 2005.

Wright, Gavin. *Old South, New South: Revolutions in the Southern Economy Since the Civil War*. New York: Basic Books, 1986.

Wright, Michael. "1,000 Years of the Guitar: A Contextual Reflection." *Vintage Guitar* magazine, July 5, 2001.

Wright, Michael. "Bradley Kincaid Houn' Dog Guitar," *Vintage Guitar* magazine, July 7, 2006. XXXX

Wright, Michael. "Harmony: The Parlor Years (1892-1914)." *Vintage Guitar* magazine, January 7, 2002.

Wright, Michael. "Supertone Gene Autry Roundup 1938." Vintage Guitar magazine, January 27, 2005.

Wynn, Neil A. Editor. *Cross the Water Blues: African American Music in Europe*. Jackson: University Press of Mississippi, 2007.

Yagoda, Ben. *The B Side: The Death of Tin Pan Alley and the Rebirth of the Great American Song*. New York: Riverhead Books, 2015.

Yetnikoff, Walter with David Ritz. *Howling At the Moon: The Odyssey of a Monstrous Music Mogul in an Age of Excess*. New York: Roadway Books, 2004.

Younger, Richard. *Get a Shot of Rhythm & Blues: The Arthur Alexander Story*. Tuscaloosa: University of Alabama Press, 2000.

Ziegler, Philip. *London At War: 1939-1945*. New York: Alfred A. Knopf, 1995.

Zolotow, Maurice. "Hayride." Theater Arts November, 1954. Vol 38, No. 11.

Zolotow, Maurice. "Hillbilly Boom. Saturday Evening Post, February 12, 1944. Vol 216, No. 33.

Zwonitzer, Mark with Charles Hirshberg. *Will You Miss Me When I'm Gone?: The Carter Family & Their Legacy in American Music*. New York: Simon & Schuster, 2002.